introduction to
SOCIOLOGY

 CANADIAN VERSION

introduction to SOCIOLOGY

 CANADIAN VERSION

GEORGE RITZER

University of Maryland

NEIL GUPPY

The University of British Columbia

 **SAGE**

Los Angeles | London | New Delhi
Singapore | Washington DC

Los Angeles | London | New Delhi
Singapore | Washington DC

FOR INFORMATION:

SAGE Publications, Inc.
2455 Teller Road
Thousand Oaks, California 91320
E-mail: order@sagepub.com

SAGE Publications Ltd.
1 Oliver's Yard
55 City Road
London EC1Y 1SP
United Kingdom

SAGE Publications India Pvt. Ltd.
B 1/I 1 Mohan Cooperative Industrial Area
Mathura Road, New Delhi 110 044
India

SAGE Publications Asia-Pacific Pte. Ltd.
3 Church Street
#10 -04 Samsung Hub
Singapore 049483

Printed in Canada

Library of Congress Cataloging-in-Publication Data

Ritzer, George.

Introduction to sociology / George Ritzer, University of Maryland, Neil Guppy, University of British Columbia. — Canadian version.

pages cm
Includes bibliographical references and index.

ISBN 978-1-4522-8207-7 (pbk.: alk. paper) — ISBN (invalid) 978-1-4833-0160-0 (web pdf) — ISBN 978-1-4833-2449-4 (epub)

1. Sociology. I. Guppy, Neil. II. Title.

HM585.R5682 2013
301—dc23   2013019950

Acquisitions Editor: Jeff Lasser
Associate Editor: Nathan Davidson
Editorial Assistant: Lauren Johnson
Production Editor: Brittany Bauhaus
Copy Editor: Melinda Masson
Typesetter: C&M Digitals (P) Ltd.
Proofreader: Caryne Brown
Indexer: Sylvia Coates
Cover Designer: Gail Buschman
Marketing Manager: Erica DeLuca

This book is printed on acid-free paper.

13 14 15 16 17 10 9 8 7 6 5 4 3 2 1

ABOUT THE AUTHORS

George Ritzer is Distinguished University Professor at the University of Maryland. Among his awards are Honorary Doctorate from La Trobe University, Melbourne, Australia; Honorary Patron, University Philosophical Society, Trinity College, Dublin; American Sociological Association's Distinguished Contribution to Teaching Award; and 2013 Eastern Sociological Society's Robin Williams Lecturer. He has chaired four sections of the American Sociological Association: Theoretical Sociology, Organizations and Occupations, Global and Transnational Sociology, and the History of Sociology. In the application of social theory to the social world, his books include *The McDonaldization of Society* (7th ed., 2013), *Enchanting a Disenchanted World* (3rd ed., 2010), and *The Globalization of Nothing* (2nd ed., 2007).

He is the author of *Globalization: A Basic Text* (Blackwell, 2010). He edited *The Wiley-Blackwell Companion to Sociology* (2012) and *The Blackwell Companion to Globalization* (2008) and coedited *The Wiley-Blackwell Companion to Major Social Theorists* (Vols. 1 and 2, 2012) and the *Handbook of Social Theory* (2001). He was founding editor of the *Journal of Consumer Culture*. He also edited the eleven-volume *Blackwell Encyclopedia of Sociology* (2007), the two-volume *Encyclopedia of Social Theory* (2005), and the five-volume *Wiley-Blackwell Encyclopedia of Globalization* (2012). He coedited a special double issue (2012) of the *American Behavioral Scientist* on prosumption. His books have been translated into over 20 languages, with more than a dozen translations of *The McDonaldization of Society* alone.

Neil Guppy is Professor and Head of Sociology at the University of British Columbia. He was Associate Dean (Students) from 1996 to 1999 and Associate Vice President (Academic Programs) from 1999 to 2004. Having taught at UBC since 1979, he has received both a University Killam Teaching Prize and a University Killam Research Prize. He is a graduate of Queen's University (BA/BPHE) and the University of Waterloo (MSc/PhD, 1981). He has published several books, including *Education in Canada* and *The Schooled Society* (both with Scott Davies), *Social Inequality in Canada* (with Edward Grabb), and *Successful Surveys* (with George Gray). His published work has also been in *Canadian Public Policy*, *Canadian Review of Sociology and Anthropology*, *Canadian Journal of Sociology*, *American Sociological Review*, and *International Migration Review*. His research interests include social inequality (especially class, ethnicity, and gender), work and occupations, and education.

BRIEF CONTENTS

DETAILED CONTENTS

1 AN INTRODUCTION TO SOCIOLOGY IN THE GLOBAL AGE 1

2 THINKING SOCIOLOGICALLY 34

3 RESEARCHING THE SOCIAL WORLD 72

4 CULTURE 112

5 SOCIALISATION AND INTERACTION 154

6 ORGANISATIONS, SOCIETIES, AND THE GLOBAL   194

7 DEVIANCE AND CRIME   230

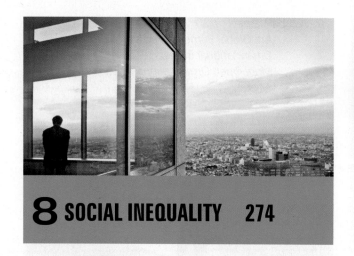

8 SOCIAL INEQUALITY 274

9 RACE, ETHNICITY, AND ANCESTRY 318

10 SEX AND GENDER 360

11 THE FAMILY 398

12 POLITICS AND THE ECONOMY   442

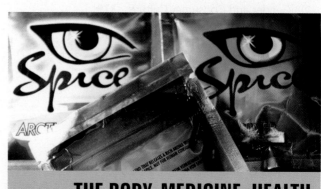

13 THE BODY, MEDICINE, HEALTH, AND HEALTH CARE   496

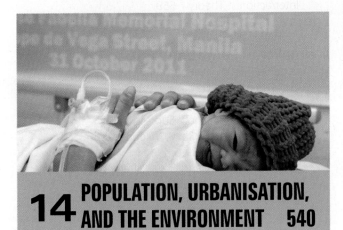

14 POPULATION, URBANISATION, AND THE ENVIRONMENT   540

15 SOCIAL CHANGE, SOCIAL MOVEMENTS, AND COLLECTIVE BEHAVIOUR   590

16 RELIGION AND EDUCATION   630

LIST OF FEATURES

PUBLIC SOCIOLOGY

McDONALDIZATION *Today*

BIOGRAPHICAL bits

VISUAL SOCIOLOGY PHOTO ESSAYS

GLOBAL FLOW MAPS

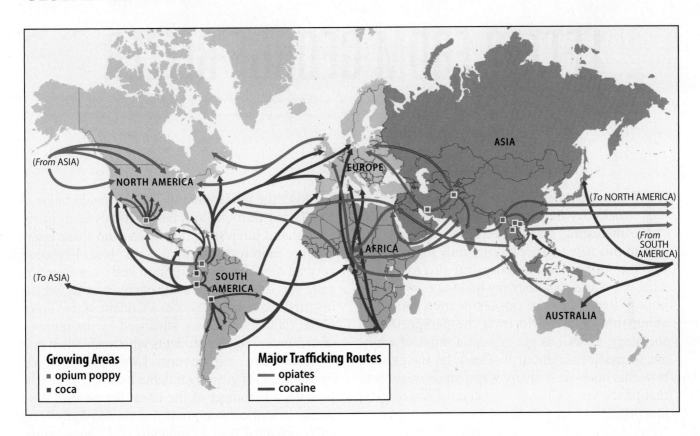

Growing Areas
- opium poppy
- coca

Major Trafficking Routes
— opiates
— cocaine

LETTER FROM GEORGE RITZER

To me, the social world, as well as the field of sociology that studies that world, is always interesting, exciting, and ever-changing. My goal in this new textbook is not only to introduce *you*, the student, to sociology, but also to discuss what has made sociology my lifelong passion. My hope is that readers of this text learn a good deal about the social world from the perspective of sociology, as well as get at least a sense of why I am so passionate about it. Please let me explain how this book is, in many ways, an expression of that passion as well as of my personal sociological journey.

My initial interests in the field were the sociology of work and of organisations, but I was quickly drawn to sociological theory and how even the most classical theories were relevant to, and at play in, my everyday life . . . and yours. This interest came to fruition in the publication of *The McDonaldization of Society* in 1993. In this book I apply and expand upon the famous classic theoretical ideas of Max Weber on rationality. I saw those ideas at work in my local fast-food restaurant, as well as in many other settings. The major themes addressed in *The McDonaldization of Society* are prominent in this textbook, especially in boxes scattered throughout its pages.

Journalists often interview me on the ideas behind "McDonaldization," and these experiences have allowed me to appreciate "public sociology," the impact of sociologists' work on the larger public. Public sociology is of increasing importance, and in this text I have highlighted not only the writings of sociologists whose work has had a significant public impact but also the work of journalists that is implicitly, and sometimes explicitly, sociological in nature.

After the publication of *The McDonaldization of Society*, my thinking and research moved in many related and interesting directions, and these interests are manifest throughout this text. I became very interested in consumption and, more specifically, was drawn to the study of credit cards, which inspired *Expressing America: A Critique of the Global Credit Card Society*. I was surprised by the number of my undergraduate students who maintained one or more credit card accounts. I was also distressed by their fears of growing indebtedness (in hindsight perhaps a harbinger of the Great Recession). Also in the area of consumption, I authored *Enchanting a Disenchanted World: Continuity and Change in the Cathedrals of Consumption*. Shopping malls, theme parks such as Disney World, Las Vegas–style casinos, and cruise ships are "cathedrals of consumption," which lure consumers and lead them to overspend and to go deeply into debt.

Later, as I reflected on my research on fast-food restaurants, credit cards, and cathedrals of consumption, I was drawn to a fascinating, newly emerging area of sociology—globalisation—in *The Globalization of Nothing* and *Globalization: A Basic Text*. I realised that all of the phenomena of interest to me had been invented in the United States but had rapidly spread throughout much of the world. Accordingly, this book includes a strong emphasis on globalisation with the hope that students will better understand that process and better appreciate their roles within our globalised world.

Most recently, my sociological journey has led me to the Internet, especially social networking sites such as Facebook, Twitter, and Pinterest. These sites are highly rationalised (or McDonaldized), are often sites of consumption (e.g., eBay), and are all globalised (Facebook alone has almost 1 billion users throughout the world). Throughout this book—in boxes (titled *Digital Living*) and in the narrative—the sociological implications of the Internet are discussed and explained; there is much in this topic for students to contemplate.

The above describes much of my personal sociological journey. I hope that this book will provide *you* with a starting point to begin your own personal sociological journey, to examine your social world critically, and to develop your own sociological ideas and opinions. It is my hope that this book better equips you to see the social world in a different way and, more important, use the ideas discussed here to help to create a better world.

George Ritzer
University of Maryland

LETTER FROM NEIL GUPPY

When SAGE Publications approached me with the idea of working on a Canadian version of George Ritzer's *Introduction to Sociology*, I was a touch sceptical, as I have not always been impressed by introductory sociology texts. Certainly, I was familiar with George Ritzer's stellar work in sociological theory and his excellent book, *The McDonaldization of Society*. From his work and research interests, I knew that our approaches to sociology were largely compatible. Immediately upon opening *Introduction to Sociology* I was hooked. It was much more global in scope than any of the other U.S. introductory sociology texts on the market. It also applied strong sociological reasoning to an array of topical issues, including consumption, social media, and the spread of McDonaldization. In short, it was a great starting point for our Canadian version.

I quickly realized that there were a number of things that I could do to help tailor and refine the material for the distinct needs of Canadian instructors and students alike. Overall, there were very simple things such as using the Queen's English throughout the text. Also, I went through the whole of the book and adjusted the narrative, the examples, and the photo program to give it a decidedly Canadian feel. More substantive changes came in providing Canadian sociology examples and research findings in every chapter. Some of the data in this Canadian edition—for example, the revenue differences of female and male physicians—have never been published previously. I was also able to integrate my own research interests in social inequality, work and occupations, education, and multiculturalism.

SOME MAJOR HIGHLIGHTS OF THE CANADIAN VERSION

- Addresses cross-national sociological differences between Canada and the United States.
- Includes many references to reflect the research of Canadian sociologists, popular-culture examples, and beyond.
- Integrates across most chapters topics of central Canadian relevance, including discussions of First Nations issues (Aboriginal land title, self-government), as well as more discussion of Quebec as a distinct society.
- Adds a wealth of Canadian data throughout, including some never previously published material.

The book that we have collaborated on here builds upon the solid foundation created by George Ritzer, and it is my hope that Canadian instructors and students will find this an enjoyable and relevant read, one that encourages informed and committed involvement with the key social issues of our time.

Neil Guppy
University of British Columbia

☑ *GEORGE RITZER*

Welcome to George Ritzer and Neil Guppy's **Introduction to Sociology: Canadian Version.** While providing a rock-solid foundation on the basic topics and concepts in sociology, Ritzer and Guppy focus on today's most compelling sociological phenomena: globalisation, the Internet, and consumption, including Ritzer's signature interest—the McDonaldization of society.

THEMES

GLOBALIZATION

Globalisation continues to attract increasing attention in the field of sociology as indicated in the recent founding and dramatic growth of the American Sociological Association's Section on Global and Transnational Sociology. As products of the "global age," students, like sociologists, are deeply immersed in innumerable aspects of globalisation.

THE INTERNET

The Internet's sociological significance grows by the day. Facebook has reached almost a billion members worldwide, and in early 2013 news and photos of the revolutions sweeping the Middle East and North Africa were flashed around the world instantly via various social networking sites. As the Internet grows, so does its impact on the sociological lives of students.

CONSUMPTION

Consumption continues to drive the cultures of developed and even developing countries. In North America and Europe the topic has been studied extensively, and now it has become a compelling sociological issue in places like China, where production has historically been the prevailing socioeconomic issue.

McDONALDIZATION

With restaurants in 120 countries worldwide, McDonald's is a global business enterprise. Ritzer, recognised for having established the theory of *McDonaldization*, uses this theory to introduce students to the worldwide impact of this business and cultural model.

PRESENTATION OF THEORY

In this text, theory is presented through a three-category system that is similar to the approach in most introductory sociology texts but is broader, encompassing both classical and important contemporary theories. Each category in this system (structural/functional, conflict/critical, and inter/actionist) encompasses two or more theories, including some of the newest and most important theories developed since the 1960s:

- *Structural/functional* theory includes structural functionalism and structuralism.

- *Conflict/critical* theory includes conflict theory, critical theory, feminist theory, queer theory, critical theories of race and racism, and postmodern theory.

- *Inter/actionist* theory includes symbolic interactionism, ethnomethodology, exchange theory, and rational choice theory.

Through this deft approach, Ritzer and Guppy are able to provide a traditional theoretical framework while exposing students to the innovative new theories that drive sociological discussion today.

FEATURES

- Timely and engaging *chapter-opening vignettes*, written in a vivid and distinctive storytelling voice, draw the reader into the chapter and spark meaningful classroom discussions.

- *Globalisation* boxes reinforce one of the central themes of the text by exposing students to compelling examples and case studies taken from cultures and communities from around the globe.

- *Digital Living* boxes highlight another major thematic thread of the text, allowing students to take an objective look at the Internet and the media in general and their profound effect on individuals and society.

- The quintessentially Ritzer *McDonaldization Today* boxes weave his theory of McDonaldization throughout the book and further help students to understand the theory and the increasingly rationalised society and world.

- *Global Flow Maps* provide geographical context and data on the global issue at hand.

- *Public Sociology* boxes explain how sociology is more than an academic discipline, and in several cases, like that of Andrew Cherlin, the content has been written by the public sociologists themselves.

- *Biographical Bits* introduce students to influential classical and contemporary sociologists who have had a major impact on the field.

- Evocative and visually stimulating *photo essays* at several places in the text present a visual representation of topics, such as work in a global world, cathedrals of consumption, and protests and revolutions worldwide.

- End-of-chapter features, such as chapter summaries, *Thinking about Sociology* discussion questions, *Applying the Sociological Imagination*, and *Active Sociology,* allow readers the opportunity to think critically about the concepts that they've learned in the chapter and take their learning beyond the classroom and the book.

OPEN-ACCESS STUDENT STUDY SITE

Found at www.sagepub.com/ritzercanadian

This open-access Student Study Site is intended to enhance students' understanding of the concepts in *Introduction to Sociology: Canadian Version*. On this site, students have access to flexible self-quizzes that are mobile compatible for students to test their knowledge!

INSTRUCTOR ANCILLARIES

Found at www.sagepub.com/ritzercanadian

This password-protected site provides instructors with everything that they need to prepare and teach their introductory course. Included on the site are:

- *Test Bank (Word®):* This Word test bank offers a diverse set of test questions and answers for each chapter of the book. Multiple-choice, true/false, short-answer, and essay questions for every chapter help instructors assess students' progress and understanding.

- *Respondus Test Bank:* A Respondus electronic test bank is available and can be used on PCs. The test bank contains multiple choice, true/false, and essay questions for each chapter and provides you with a diverse range of pre-written options as well as the opportunity for editing any question and/or inserting your own personalized questions to effectively assess students' progress and understanding. Respondus is also compatible with many popular learning management systems so you can easily get your test questions into your online course.

- *PowerPoint:* Chapter-specific slide presentations offer assistance with lecture and review preparation by highlighting essential content, features, and artwork from the book.

ACKNOWLEDGMENTS

I need to begin with my friends for decades, and coauthors of a previous introductory textbook, Kenneth C. W. Kammeyer and Norman R. Yetman. That book went through seven editions, the last of which was published in 1997. It was most useful to me in this text in helping to define various sociological concepts that have changed little over the years. I have also been able to build on discussions of many issues covered in that text. However, because of the passage of a decade and a half in sociology and in the social world (an eternity in both), as well as the innumerable changes in them, this text has comparatively little in common with the earlier one. Nonetheless, my perspective on sociology was strongly shaped by that book and the many insights and ideas provided by my friends and coauthors both before and during, and in the many years after, writing that book.

I had worked with Becky Smith as a developmental editor on previous projects. She had done a great job with those books, and she continued her good work on the first 10 chapters of this book. As time grew short, the work of developmental editor was picked up by Colin Grover, who finished the job in a timely and excellent fashion. Melinda Masson did an excellent job as copyeditor.

Several undergraduate and graduate students at the University of Maryland made important contributions to this project. I would especially like to thank Chih-Chin Chen who worked long, hard, and good-naturedly on various aspects of the book, especially the numerous figures to be found throughout the text. Another undergraduate, Michelle McDonough, also made important contributions to the book. Paul Dean, at the time a graduate student but now Assistant Professor at Ohio Wesleyan, made innumerable contributions to the text, especially those aspects of it dealing with globalisation. Nathan Jurgenson contributed his great expertise and experience to the parts of the text dealing with the Internet.

I would like to thank Professors Jack Levin, Andrew Cherlin, and Robert J. Brulle for writing boxes dealing with their own experiences in doing public sociology. Thanks also to contributions from PJ Rey, William Yagatich, Jillet Sam, Zeynep Tufekci, and Margaret Austin Smith. Also to be thanked for writing first drafts of parts of chapters are Professors William Carbonaro (Education), Deric Shannon (Politics), and Lester Kurtz (Religion).

At SAGE Publications, I am especially grateful for Vice President and Editorial Director Michele Sordi's confidence in, and support for, the project. She agreed from the beginning to spend and do whatever was necessary to make this a first-class introductory sociology text. As you can see from the finished project, she was true to her word. Michele also worked closely with me in an editorial capacity to help get the project through some of its most difficult periods. Michele was a positive force and upbeat presence throughout the writing of this book, and I am deeply grateful for who she is and what she has done.

I also need to thank Nathan Davidson at SAGE. The production of this book really took off when he took over its day-to-day management. We worked together closely for about a year on virtually every aspect of the final project. Before Nathan came on board, I was in danger of being overwhelmed by the demands of finishing this book, but he provided the hard work, great organisational abilities, and good sense that helped me complete it and finish it on time.

I am particularly grateful to the following reviewers, advisory board members, and class testers who provided enormously helpful feedback during various stages of manuscript development:

REVIEWERS

Sophia Krzys Acord, *University of Florida*

Kristian Alexander, *University of Utah*

Lori J. Anderson, *Tarleton State University*

Lester Andrist, *University of Maryland*

Margaret Austin Smith, *University of Maryland*

Libby Barland, *Lynn University*

Cari Beecham-Bautista, *Columbia College, Chicago*

Denise Bielby, *University of California, Santa Barbara*

Donna Bird, *University of Southern Maine*

David Daniel Bogumil, *California State University, Northridge*

Craig Boylstein, *Coastal Carolina University*

Yvonne Braun, *University of Oregon*

Robert Brenneman, *Saint Michael's College*

Rebecca Brooks, *Ohio Northern University*

Bradley Campbell, *California State University, Los Angeles*

Brenda Chaney, *Ohio State University, Marion*

Susan Claxton, *Georgia Highlands College*

Langdon Clough, *Community College of Rhode Island, Flan*

Jessica Collett, *University of Notre Dame*

Julie Cowgill, *Oklahoma City University*

Keri Diggins, *Scottsdale Community College*

Scott Dolan, *University at Albany, State University of New York*

Brenda Donelan, *Northern State University*

Gili Drori, *Stanford University*

Kathy Edwards, *Ashland Community and Technical College*

David G. Embrick, *Loyola University, Chicago*

Heather Feldhaus, *Bloomsburg University of Pennsylvania*

Pam Folk, *North Hennepin Community College*

Tammie Foltz, *Des Moines Area Community College*

Douglas Forbes, *University of Wisconsin, Stevens Point*

Sarah Michele Ford, *Buffalo State College*

S. Michael Gaddis, *University of North Carolina, Chapel Hill*

Deborah Gambs, *Borough of Manhattan Community College, City University of New York*

Joshua Gamson, *University of San Francisco*

Robert Garot, *John Jay College of Criminal Justice*

Gilbert Geis, *University of California, Irvine*

Bethany Gizzi, *Monroe Community College*

Barry Goetz, *Western Michigan University*

Roberta Goldberg, *Trinity Washington University*

Elizabeth Grant, *Chabot College*

Matthew Green, *College of DuPage*

Thao Ha, *MiraCosta College*

Kristi Hagen, *Chippewa Valley Technical College*

James Harris, *Mountain View College*

Gary Heidinger, *Roane State Community College*

Marta Henriksen, *Central New Mexico Community College*

Cedric Herring, *University of Illinois, Chicago*

Anthony Hickey, *Western Carolina University*

Joy Honea, *Montana State University, Billings*

John C. Horgan, *Concordia University Wisconsin*

Jeanne Humble, *Bluegrass Community & Technical College*

Gabe Ignatow, *University of North Texas*

Mike Itashiki, *Collin County Community College & University of North Texas*

Wesley Jennings, *University of South Florida*

Mike F. Jessup, *Taylor University*

James R. Johnson, *Southwestern Indian Polytechnic Institute*

Faye Jones, *Mississippi Community College*

Carolyn Kapinus, *Ball State University*

Mary Karpos, *Vanderbilt University*

Barry Kass, *Orange County Community College, State University of New York*

Zeynep Kilic, *University of Alaska, Anchorage*

Jeanne Kimpel, *Fordham University*

Chuck Kusselow, *River Valley Community College*

Richard Lachmann, *University at Albany, State University of New York*

Barbara LaPilusa, *Montgomery College*

Erin Leahey, *University of Arizona*

Maria Licuanan, *Kent State University*

John Lie, *University of California, Berkeley*

Cameron D. Lippard, *Appalachian State University*

Dongxiao Liu, *Texas A&M University*

David Lopez, *California State University, Northridge*

Jeanne M. Lorentzen, *Northern Michigan University*

Garvey Lundy, *Montgomery County Community College*

Aaron Major, *University at Albany, State University of New York*

Vanessa Martinez, *Holyoke Community College*

Suzanne L. Maughan, *University of Nebraska, Kearney*

Patrick McGrady, *Florida State University*

Paul McLean, *Rutgers University*

Rohald Meneses, *University of North Carolina, Pembroke*

Eric Mielants, *Fairfield University*

Jeff Mullis, *Emory University*

Megan Nielsen, *Midland University*

Charles Norman, *Indiana State University*

Michael J. O'Connor, *Hawkeye Community College*

Johanna Pabst, *Boston College*

Donna Phillips, *Bluegrass Community & Technical College*

Alex Piquero, *University of Texas, Dallas*

Dwaine Plaza, *Oregon State University*

Winnie Poster, *Washington University in St. Louis*

Malcolm Potter, *Los Angeles Pierce College*

Ekaterina Ralston, *Concordia University, St. Paul*

Rashawn Ray, *University of California, Berkeley*

PJ Rey, *University of Maryland*

Adrienne Riegle, *Iowa State University*

David N. Sanders, *Angelo State University*

Mary Satian, *Northern Virginia Community College*

Dave Schall, *Milwaukee Area Technical College*

Elizabeth D. Scheel, *St. Cloud State University*

Jerald Schrimsher, *Southern Illinois University, Carbondale*

Sandra Schroer, *Muskingum University*

Howard Schuman, *University of Michigan*

Frank Scruggs, *National Louis University*

Megan Seely, *Sierra College*

Vincent Serravallo, *Rochester Institute of Technology*

Mark Sherry, *The University of Toledo*

Amber Shimel, *Liberty University*

Kristen Shorette, *University of California, Irvine*

Julia Spence, *Johnson County Community College*

Steven Stack, *Wayne State University*

Donna Sullivan, *Marshall University, Huntington*

Richard Sweeney, *Modesto Junior College*

Joyce Tang, *Queens College, City University of New York*

Rae Taylor, *Loyola University, New Orleans*

Richard Tewksbury, *University of Louisville*

Santos Torres, *California State University, Sacramento*

Mark Vermillion, *Wichita State University*

PJ Verrecchia, *York College of Pennsylvania*

Russell Ward, *Maysville Community and Technical College*

Debra Welkley, *California State University, Sacramento*

Beau Weston, *Centre College*

Jeff Wilhelms, *Rutgers University*

Elizabeth Wissinger, *Borough of Manhattan Community College, City University of New York*

Rowan Wolf, *Portland Community College*

Susan Wortmann, *Nebraska Wesleyan University*

Kassia Wosick-Correa, *New Mexico State University*

James Wright, *Chattanooga State Technical Community College*

Yuping Zhang, *Lehigh University*

ADVISORY BOARD MEMBERS

Grace Auyang, *University of Cincinnati, Raymond Walters College*

Libby Barland, *Lynn University*

John Batsie, *Parkland College*

Cari Beecham, *Columbia College, Chicago*

Berch Berberoglu, *University of Nevada, Reno*

Miriam Boeri, *Kennesaw State University*

Ann Bullis, *College of Southern Nevada*

Josh Carreiro, *University of Massachusetts*

Susan Claxton, *Georgia Highlands College*

Evan Cooper, *Farmingdale State College*

Julie Cowgill, *Oklahoma City University*

David Embrick, *Loyola University, Chicago*

Heather Feldhaus, *Bloomsburg University of Pennsylvania*

Rosalind Fisher, *University of West Florida*

Kerie Francis, *University of Nevada, Las Vegas*

Joshua Gamson, *University of San Francisco*

Robert Garot, *John Jay College of Criminal Justice*

Matthew Green, *College of DuPage*

Gary Heidinger, *Roane State Community College*

Marta Henriksen, *Central New Mexico Community College*

Anthony Hickey, *Western Carolina University*

Jeanne Humble, *Bluegrass Community & Technical College*

Dai Ito, *Georgia State University*

Mike F. Jessup, *Taylor University*

Ellis Jones, *College of the Holy Cross*

Lloyd Klein, *York College, City University of New York*

Steve Lang, *LaGuardia Community College*

Dongxiao Liu, *Texas A&M University*

Tara McKay, *University of California, Los Angeles*

Rohald Meneses, *University of North Carolina, Pembroke*

Eric Mielants, *Fairfield University*

Ami Moore, *University of Northern Texas*

Amanda Moras, *Sacred Heart University*

Brigitte Neary, *University of South Carolina, Spartanburg*

Michael O'Connor, *Hawkeye Community College*

Aurea Osgood, *Winona State University*

Johanna Pabst, *Boston College*

Frank Roberts, *Mount San Antonio College*

Lauren Ross, *Temple University*

Janet Ruane, *Montclair State University*

Matthew Sargent, *Madison Area Technical College*

Lynn Schlesinger, *State University of New York, Plattsburgh*

Sarah Scruggs, *Oklahoma City University*

Meena Sharma, *Henry Ford Community College*

Nicole Shortt, *Florida Atlantic University, Boca Raton*

Chris Solario, *Chemeketa Community College*

William Staudenmeier, *Eureka College*

Donna Sullivan, *Marshall University*

Kevin Sullivan, *Bergen Community College*

Jaita Talukdar, *Loyola University, New Orleans*

Linda Treiber, *Kennesaw State University*

PJ Verrecchia, *York College of Pennsylvania*

Debra Welkley, *California State University, Sacramento*

Beau Weston, *Centre College*

George Wilson, *University of Miami*

Julie Withers, *Butte College*

Kassia Wosick-Correa, *New Mexico State University*

James Wright, *Chattanooga State Technical Community College*

CLASS TESTERS

Paul Calarco, *Hudson Valley Community College*

Joyce Clapp, *University of North Carolina, Greensboro*

Tina Granger, *Nicholls State University*

Dan Gurash, *Fairmont State University*

Lee Hamilton, *New Mexico State University*

AJ Jacobs, *East Carolina University*

Barry Kass, *Orange County Community College, State University of New York*

Stacy Keogh, *University of Montana*

Crystal Lupo, *Auburn University*

Tiffany Parsons, *University of West Georgia*

Lindsey Prowell Myers, *The Ohio State University*

Matthew Sargent, *Madison Area Technical College*

Michael Steinhour, *Purdue University*

Sheryl Switaj, *Schoolcraft College*

Ruth Thompson-Miller, *University of Dayton*

Deanna Trella, *Northern Michigan University*

Kristie Vise, *Northern Kentucky University*

Wendy Wiedenhoft Murphy, *John Carroll University*

Jane Young, *Luzerne County Community College*

AN INTRODUCTION TO SOCIOLOGY IN THE GLOBAL AGE

By drawing on modern sociology's 200-year history while looking to the future, today's sociologists have the tools and resources to understand better where we have been, where we are, and, perhaps most importantly, where we are going.

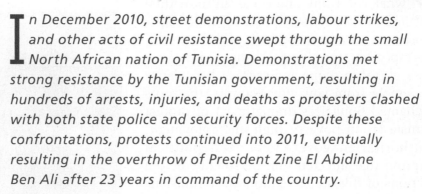

I n December 2010, street demonstrations, labour strikes, and other acts of civil resistance swept through the small North African nation of Tunisia. Demonstrations met strong resistance by the Tunisian government, resulting in hundreds of arrests, injuries, and deaths as protesters clashed with both state police and security forces. Despite these confrontations, protests continued into 2011, eventually resulting in the overthrow of President Zine El Abidine Ben Ali after 23 years in command of the country.

What event could have led to such a momentous social and political revolution after so many years of relative quiet? The Tunisian protests were triggered primarily by the self-immolation of Mohamed Bouazizi, a Tunisian street vendor. However, the sources underlying both the Tunisian revolution and the "Arab Spring," the wave of social unrest it inspired throughout the region, involve far more than a single act of protest. Without considering the social, political, and economic conditions of prerevolution Tunisia, it would be impossible to understand why Bouazizi set himself alight, and why thousands of Tunisians and others throughout the Arab world saw that act as an appropriate—and necessary—call for change.

As an academic discipline, sociology has traditionally endeavoured to understand the individual's place, even that of a Tunisian street vendor, within society and society's effect on the individual. In today's global age, however, transnational social structures and rapidly changing communication technologies have forever altered the ways in which humans interact with each other, as well as the societies that shape them. As the world has become increasingly globalised, sociology has developed an increasingly global perspective.

By drawing on modern sociology's 200-year history while looking to the future, today's sociologists have the tools and resources to understand better where we have been, where we are, and, perhaps most importantly, where we are going. However, some sociologists believe that helping people enact meaningful social change is the true end of sociology. The Tunisian protesters would certainly agree with them.

One of the most important lessons that you will learn in your study of sociology is that what you think and do as an individual is affected by what is happening in groups, organisations, cultures, societies, and the world. This is especially true of social changes, even those that are global in scope and seem at first glance to be remote from you. For example, the roots of Mohamed Bouazizi's dramatic act of protest in Tunisia lay in poverty, high unemployment, an authoritarian government, and political corruption that affected him personally. Before the actions of this street vendor, most Tunisians would never have risked their lives to protest their country's repressive regime. Yet he and tens of thousands of others in other countries in the region did just that. It's likely that your impression of the Arab countries and the majority Muslim population was much different before the Arab Spring than after. You may find yourself feeling a surge of appreciation for democracy or feeling more open than before to learning about Islam or studying the Arabic language. You may even be inspired to take actions yourself in support of ongoing changes in Tunisia and elsewhere. In those senses, you and many others have felt the impact of Bouazizi's actions.

A second important lesson in sociology is not only that you are affected by events but also that you are capable to some degree of having an impact on large-scale structures and processes. This can be seen as an example of the *butterfly effect*, a term popularised by the mathematician Edward Lorenz (1995). While generally applied to physical phenomena, the **butterfly effect** is also applicable to social phenomena (Mackenzie 2005). The idea is that a relatively small change in a specific location can have far-ranging, even global, effects, over both time and distance. For example, the actions of Bouazizi helped lead to the Tunisian revolution, which, in turn, led to street demonstrations and civil war elsewhere in the Arab world, including Yemen, Egypt, Libya, and Syria. The consequences of this series of events are still unfolding, but they certainly include the major changes that took place in those societies as well as the possibility of major international political realignments. They could also make for greater or diminished opportunities for business and personal relationships between people in the Arab world and those in the West.

The Arab Spring changed how people around the world perceived Arab peoples and cultures. Here, tens of thousands of Egyptian demonstrators rally in Cairo's Tahrir Square on July 29, 2011.

The 2011 earthquake—the fourth most powerful since worldwide record keeping began—devastated dozens of towns and villages along Japan's eastern coast and created islands of floating debris. The quake and its resulting tsunami left more than 15,000 dead, 5,000 injured, and 9,000 missing.

(Berton 2007). The debris will present persistent problems for shipping, fishing, and tourism industries—not to mention coastal dwellers and beachgoers. Disruptions to Japanese manufacturers had an impact on the already fragile recovery of the global economy after a deep recession. That may explain difficulties you might have had in 2011 in buying that Toyota you wanted or the latest iPhone.

These examples of the relationship between people and larger social realities and changes set the stage for the definition of the discipline to be introduced in this book: **Sociology** is the systematic study of the ways in which people are affected by, and affect, the social structures and social processes that are associated with the groups, organisations, cultures, societies, and world in which they exist.

Perhaps the arc of your life and career will be affected by the upheavals of the Arab Spring. More important, it is very possible that actions you take in your lifetime will have wide-ranging, perhaps global, effects.

A very different sociological example of the butterfly effect involves the magnitude-9.0 earthquake that shook Japan for more than six minutes in 2011. While this was a huge event as far as Japan was concerned, it was from a global perspective relatively minor, at least initially. The earthquake caused a massive tsunami, which reached as high as 124 feet (about 38 metres). Amid the devastation, damage to the Fukushima Daiichi nuclear power plant on Japan's Pacific coast came to occupy the world's attention and renewed the debate over the safety of nuclear power compared with other sources of energy. Some floating islands of debris and human remains washed to sea by the tsunami have begun to hit North American shores (National Oceanic and Atmospheric Administration 2013) and are expected to wash onto Hawaii's beaches and reefs for years to come (International Pacific Research Center 2011); other debris will continue to collect in the Great Pacific Garbage Patch, a locale in the Pacific Ocean that is twice the size of Texas

In 2005, Hurricane Katrina had devastating effects on the people of New Orleans. Many were forced to evacuate their homes—some never to return.

THE CHANGING NATURE OF THE SOCIAL WORLD— AND SOCIOLOGY

Sociology deals with contemporary phenomena, as you have seen, but it also has many longer-term interests because of its deep historical roots. In the fourteenth century, for instance, the Muslim scholar Abdel Rahman Ibn-Khaldun studied various social relationships, including those between politics and economics. Of special importance to the founding of sociology was the eighteenth- and nineteenth-century Industrial Revolution. During this "industrial age," many early sociologists concentrated on factories, the production that took place in those settings, and those who worked there, especially blue-collar, manual workers. Sociologists also came to focus on the relationship between industry and the rest of society, including, for example, the state and the family.

By the mid-twentieth century, manufacturing in the United States was in the early stages of a long decline that continues to this day—although manufacturing in other parts of the world, most notably China, is booming. Countries including Canada and the United States moved toward a "postindustrial age" (Bell 1973; Leicht and Fitzgerald 2006). In Canada, as well as the western world more generally, the centre of the economy, and the attention of many sociologists, shifted from the factory to the office—from blue-collar manual work to white-collar office work (Mills 1951)—as well as to the bureaucracies in which many people worked (Clegg and Lounsbury 2009; Weber [1921] 1968). Also involved was the growth of the service sector of the economy, ranging all the way from high-status service providers such as physicians and lawyers to lower-status house cleaners and those who work behind the counters of fast-food restaurants (Krahn, Lowe, and Hughes 2011).

More recently, the rise of the "information age" (Castells 2010) can be seen as a part, or an extension, of the postindustrial age. Knowledge and information are critical in this contemporary epoch as are the technologies—computers, smartphones—that have greatly increased the productivity of individual workers and altered the nature of their work. Just one of many examples is the current use of computer-assisted technologies to create designs for everything from electric power grids to patterned fabrics rather than drawing them by hand. In fact, it is not just work that has been affected by these new technologies; virtually everyone and everything has been affected by them. One aspect of this new technological world, Google, is so powerful that a cultural historian has already written a book titled *The Googlization of Everything* (Vaidhyanathan 2011). Thus much sociological attention has shifted to the computer and the Internet and to those who work with them (Baym 2010; Raine and Wellman 2012).

Canada has always had a significant resource extraction economy, although now more and more Canadians are employed in service sector jobs in large corporate offices in urban centres. This affects not only individuals but the types and sizes of the communities in which they live.

Computer-assisted design has vastly improved the efficiency and accuracy of architects, engineers, and professional artists around the world.

The rise of the information age has important personal implications. Had you been a man who lived in the industrial age, you would have worked for money (pay), and you would have done so in order to be able to buy what you needed and wanted; women's work in the private sphere was then, as it is still, largely uncompensated or compensated at a lower rate. In the postindustrial age, it is increasingly likely that men and women are willing, or forced, to work for free (C. Anderson 2009; Ritzer 2013; Ritzer and Jurgenson 2010) as, for example, bloggers or contributors to YouTube or Wikipedia. They may hope that such work will eventually have an economic payoff and perhaps even lead to a full-time job. In fact, there are many examples of individuals succeeding after starting out by "giving away" their labour. For example, Winnipeg's Sean Quigley is trying to use his snow-infused YouTube video version of "Little Drummer Boy" to launch a musical career.

You may also be willing to perform this free labour because you enjoy it and because much of what is important in your life is, in any case, available free on the Internet. There is no need for you to buy newspapers when blogs are free or to buy CDs or DVDs when music and movies can be streamed or downloaded at no cost or inexpensively from the Internet. A whole range of software is also downloadable at no cost. While all of this, and much else, is available free of charge, the problem is that the essentials of life—food, shelter, clothing—still cost money, lots of money.

This is but one of many social changes to be discussed in this introductory chapter, as well as the book as a whole, but the essential point is that the social world (people, groups, organisations, etc.)—*your* social world—is continually changing, and sociology is a field that is, and must be, constantly attuned to and involved in studying those changes.

CENTRAL CONCERNS FOR A TWENTY-FIRST-CENTURY SOCIOLOGY

While the social world has been changing dramatically over the last two centuries or so and sociology has adapted to those changes, sociology has also adhered to many of its traditional concerns. We have already mentioned industry, production, and work as long-term sociological interests; others include deviance and crime (see Chapter 7), the family (see Chapter 11), and the city (see Chapter 14). Of particular concern to many sociologists has been, and is, the issue of inequality as it affects the poor, racial and ethnic groups, women, and gays and lesbians (see Chapter 8). The bulk of this book will be devoted to these basic sociological topics and concerns. But there will also be a focus on the nontraditional and very contemporary issues of consumption, the digital world, and especially and most importantly globalisation.

GLOBALISATION

No social change is as important today as globalisation since it is affecting all aspects of the social world everywhere on the globe. While a date marking the beginning of globalisation cannot be given with any precision and in fact is in great dispute (Ritzer 2010c; Ritzer and Atalay 2010), the concept first began to appear in the popular and academic literature around 1990. Today, globalisation is a central issue in the social world as a whole as well as in sociology; globalisation and talk about it are all around us. In fact, we can be said to be living in the "global age" (Albrow 1996).

A major component of any past or present definition of sociology is "society." There are about 200 societies in the world, including Canada, China, and South Africa. **Society**—a complex pattern

DIGITAL LIVING

Sociologists as Bloggers

Traditionally, sociologists have communicated their ideas about the social world through books and journal articles. In recent years, however, many sociologists who want to speak directly to a broad audience have turned to blogging, which greatly democratizes the ability to publish what one is thinking. For example, danah boyd, a leading social media researcher, regularly posts about her research on a blog she calls Zephoria.

Many academic blogs feature posts by professional sociologists. For example, a set of sociology blogs (a "blog ring") called the Society Pages (http://thesocietypages.org) includes blogs on topics such as race, ethnicity, and immigration (the colour line); teaching sociology (Teaching TSP); visual sociology (Sociological Images); and technology and society (Cyborgology).

One recent blog on Cyborgology took on the issue of surveillance, focusing on how those in power in society watch the rest of us and record their observations. However, with the proliferation of smartphones, it has become possible for virtually everyone to observe everyone else and to record such observations. This gives rise to the phenomenon of *sousveillance*, or the ability of the powerless to watch and document the behaviour of those in power. In one case, a bicyclist pulled out his camera and recorded his interaction with a police officer. He was given a $50 ticket for not riding in the bike lane. But the blogger shows how various impediments in bike lanes make it impossible to always remain in those lanes.

Other blogs, while not written solely by sociologists, address issues that are covered in sociology textbooks. For example, the Feministing and Jezebel blogs tackle issues of sexuality and gender (see Chapter 10).

Blogging is not just a way for sociologists to make their ideas more public and more accessible; it also is an opportunity to build dialogue. Readers, whether sociologists or not, can comment directly on most blogs. Sociologists and members of the public can also share thoughts via Twitter, Facebook, and other social media. The rapid flow of sociological perspectives and information can bring a wider range of voices into the conversation, thus producing more diverse content than found in traditional academic sources. It is important to remember, however, that blogs are usually published without review by other sociologists. As a result, professional sociologists are concerned about blogs' legitimacy and encourage all of those involved to scrutinize carefully ideas found on those blogs.

SOURCE: Printed with the permission of Nathan Jurgenson and P. J. Rey.

---

of social relationships that is bounded in space and persists over time—has traditionally been the largest unit of analysis in sociology. However, in the global age, societies are seen as of declining importance (Holton 2011; Meyer, Boli, and Ramirez 1997). This is the case, in part, because there are larger transnational and global social structures—including the United Nations (UN), the European Union (EU), the Organization of the Petroleum Exporting Countries (OPEC), multinational corporations (MNCs) such as Google and ExxonMobil, and multinational nongovernmental organisations (NGOs) such as Amnesty International—that are growing in importance. In at least some cases, these transnational structures are becoming more important than individual societies. OPEC, for example, is more important to the rest of the world's well-being than are key member societies such as Abu Dhabi or even Saudi Arabia.

Social processes, like social structures, exist not only at the societal level but also at the global level, and these global processes are of increasing importance. Consider migration (see Chapter 14). People move about, or migrate, within and between societies. For example, many people have moved from eastern Canada to the Canadian West, and to the oil sands of northern Alberta in particular. However, in the global age people increasingly move between societies (see Global Flow Map 1.1), some halfway around the world. Major examples involve people migrating from and through Mexico to the United

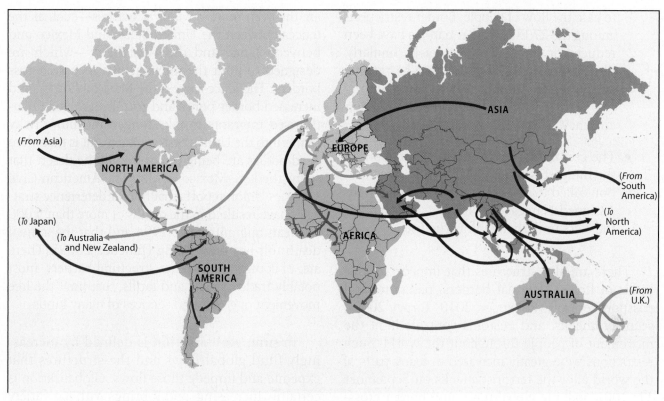

GLOBAL FLOW MAP 1.1 Major Contemporary Global Migration Flows

SOURCE: Adapted from *Stalker's Guide to International Migration*, Peter Stalker.

States (Massey 2003) and Canada (Massey and Brown 2010) and from a number of Islamic societies to Western Europe (Caldwell 2009).

There have always been population movements such as these, but in the global age people generally move around the world far more freely and travel much greater distances than ever before. Another way of saying this is that people—and much else—are more "fluid." That is, they move farther, more easily, and more quickly than ever before. The movement of products of all types is also more fluid as a result of the existence of massive container ships, jet cargo planes, and package delivery services such as FedEx and Purolator. Even more fluid is the digital "stuff" you buy on the Internet when you download music, movies, and so on. And in the realm of the family, tasks once confined to the home, such as caregiving and housework, have become increasingly fluid as those who can afford to do so often outsource such domestic labour (Yeates 2009). More generally, that greater fluidity is manifest in the information that flows throughout the world in the blink of an eye

as a result of the Internet, e-mail, and social networking sites such as Facebook and Twitter.

These flows can be expedited by structures of various types—social and otherwise. For example:

- Air cargo delivery will increasingly be facilitated by the development of the "aerotropolis" (Kasarda and Lindsay 2011). This is a preplanned city that is developed because of proximity and access to a large, modern airport. For example, New Songdo, South Korea, is being built because such an airport (Incheon) is nearby and easily reached by a 12-mile-long bridge. This is in contrast to the usual situation where the traditional airport (Pearson International in Toronto; LAX in Los Angeles; Heathrow in London) is built within or very close to a city centre. Traditional airports are typically too small and too difficult to reach, create too much noise for city residents, and cannot expand much beyond their current confines.

- The European Union (EU), founded in 1993, is an example of a social structure that serves to ease the flow of people. Border restrictions among the 27 EU member nations have been reduced or eliminated completely. Similarly, the creation in 1975 of the euro has greatly simplified economic transactions among the 17 EU countries that accept it as their currency.

- The continuing free flow of information on the Internet is made possible by an organisation called ICANN (Internet Corporation for Assigned Names and Numbers). It handles the Net's underlying infrastructure.

There are also structures that impede various kinds of flows. National borders, passports and passport controls (Robertson 2010; Torpey 2000), security checks, and customs controls limit the movement of people throughout the world. Such restrictions were greatly increased in many parts of the world after the terrorist attacks on September 11, 2001, making global travel and border crossing more difficult and time-consuming. Then there

are the even more obvious structures—such as the fences between the United States and Mexico and between Israel and the West Bank—which are designed to limit the movement of people across borders. The fences across the Mexican border, and increased border police and patrols, have led unauthorised migrants to take longer and more risky routes into the United States. One result is that more dead bodies are being discovered in the desert that spans the U.S.-Mexico border. The American Civil Liberties Union reports that border deterrence strategies have resulted in the deaths of more than 5,000 Mexican migrants since 1994 and that the annual death toll has been rising (Jimenez 2009). There are, of course, many other structural barriers, most notably trade barriers and tariffs, that limit the free movement of goods and services of many kinds.

In sum, **globalisation** is defined by increasingly fluid global flows and the structures that expedite and impede those flows. Globalisation is certainly increasing, and it brings with it a variety of both positive and negative developments (Ritzer

Barriers to global migratory flows can take a wide variety of forms. Checkpoints and bottlenecks, natural and manmade borders, physical walls and fences, and legal restrictions and security measures are all barriers to the flow of human movement.

In 2005, secretive British artist Banksy painted nine satirical images on the 26-foot-high (about 8-metre-high) concrete barrier that divides Palestine from Israel. Several of the paintings, located on the Palestinian side of the wall, portray Israel as a lush natural landscape.

2010c). On one side, most people throughout the world now have far greater access to goods, services, and information from around the globe than during the industrial age. On the other side, a variety of highly undesirable things also flow more easily around the world, including diseases such as HIV/AIDS and the adverse effects of global warming. Also on the negative side are such forms of "deviant globalisation" as terrorism, sex trafficking, the black market in human organs, and the black market in drugs (Gilman, Goldhammer, and Weber 2011).

CONSUMPTION

Beginning in the 1950s, another major social change took place in Canada and other developed countries. The central feature of many capitalist economies began to shift from production and work to **consumption**, or the process by which people obtain and utilize goods and services. During that period, the centre of the economy in industrialised nations such as Canada shifted from factories, mines, and offices to the shopping mall (Baudrillard [1970] 1998; Lipovetsky

2005). For many people, work and production became less important than consumption. It is impossible to ignore something that is such a large aspect of people's lives.

The dramatic increase in consumption was made possible by, among other things, increasingly available credit cards. They have become ubiquitous at shopping malls, on the Internet, and in many other settings. Thus one indicator of the increase in consumption in Canada is the increase in consumer debt. As you can see in Figure 1.1, consumer debt per household has grown dramatically since 1980. Total household debt is, as of 2011, 152 percent of disposable income (Crawford and Faruqui 2011–12). Part of this debt is backed by home ownership, but a sizeable amount of debt is credit card related and thus unsecured. Further, should interest rates climb sharply or house prices fall dramatically, the Canadian economy could be in serious trouble.

Consumption is certainly significant economically but is significant in other ways as well. For example, culture is very much shaped by consumption, and various aspects of consumption become cultural phenomena. A good example is the iPhone, which has revolutionised culture in

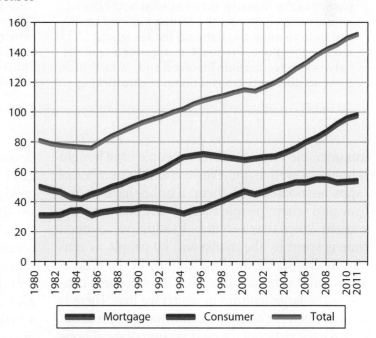

FIGURE 1.1 Growth of Canadian Household Debt Relative to Disposable Income (as %), 1980–2011

SOURCE: Adapted by authors from Crawford and Faruqui (2011–12).

GL⊕BALISATION

Sex Trafficking

One dimension of the increased flow of people due to globalisation is human trafficking (see B. Perrin 2010 for a Canadian focus). Human trafficking is the use of coercion or deception to force human beings into providing such services as slave labour, commercial sex, and organ donation. The trafficker and the buyer of the services conduct the financial transaction; the victims of trafficking participate against their will. Sex trafficking is a particular variety of trafficking whose victims are traded for the purpose of commercial sex, including prostitution, stripping, or pornography (Hodge 2008). Not all commercial sex involves human trafficking, so buyers of commercial sexual services and performances are often not aware that the sex workers have been trafficked. Lepp (2013) examines the linkages between sex trafficking and large sporting events, with a focus on the Vancouver Winter Olympics.

The number of trafficked victims is on the rise. One researcher estimates that currently 1.4 million women and girls are trafficked each year (Lee 2012b). Although sexual victimisation has always existed, globalisation creates greater opportunities and thus greater profits for traffickers (Farr 2005). Bars, dance clubs, massage parlours, the pornography industry, international hotel chains, airline companies, and the tourist industry create and help to meet the demand for sex labour around the globe. Predictably, organised criminal networks have become involved and, in fact, have come to dominate transnational sex trafficking.

Human trafficking has become illegal worldwide in large part because of this development.

Over the last few decades, many of the countries of the Global South (especially Thailand and the Philippines) and of the ex-Soviet Union and Eastern Europe have become major sources of sex workers, especially prostitutes. These sex workers may either work in these locales or be relocated, either voluntarily (although often under false pretences) or by force, to work in the sex trade in other parts of the world.

The multimillion-dollar "mail-order-bride" business, despite a veneer of respectability, is sometimes a form of sex trafficking as well. Women who are offered through mail-order-bride agencies are mostly from the Philippines, Laos, Burma, Vietnam, Thailand, and the former Soviet Union. This is a segmented market much like any other, however. For example, Thai women are often promoted as sex workers, while Filipina women are advertised as helpers and wives.

The flow of people in the global sex industry moves not only from less to more developed countries but also in reverse (S. Flynn 2011). In the sex tourism industry, buyers travel to less developed locales, such as Thailand, to avail themselves of the often cheaper and more exotic sexual services at their destination. While in the past the high cost of airfares has limited the number of sex tourists, increasingly inexpensive

---

innumerable ways. Millions of people have bought iPhones as well as the ever-increasing number of "apps" associated with them. iPhones have altered how and where people meet to socialize and the ways in which they socialize. In addition, so much time is spent by the media and by people in general in discussing the implications of the iPhone and similar products that they have become central to the larger culture in which we live. There is always much excitement when rumours start about the characteristics of the next version of the iPhone and its release date.

Consumption and globalisation are also deeply intertwined. Much of what we consume in the

developed world comes from other countries. In 2011 alone, Canada imported $48 billion worth of goods from China, while exporting only $16 billion worth of product to China (Asia Pacific Foundation 2012). Furthermore, the convenience of Internet commerce tends to make global realities and distances irrelevant to consumers. Finally, travel to other parts of the world—a form of consumption itself—is increasingly affordable and common, and a major objective of tourists is often the purchase of souvenirs from foreign lands (Chambers 2010; Gmelch 2010).

Sociologists are understandably interested in these developments. Early sociologists did travel opportunities have permitted more sex tourists to circle the globe in search of sex (D. Brennan 2004). The increasing demand for sex workers will undoubtedly lead to a further increase in women and children trafficked for sex in less developed parts of the world.

Sex trafficking has far more deleterious consequences for women than other forms of trafficking, such as for domestic work. Not only is sex work far more demeaning, but it also exposes victims to sexually transmitted diseases, HIV/AIDS, drug addiction, and a wide variety of other health risks. Trafficked individuals are frequently beaten, raped, stabbed, and strangled, and sometimes murdered, by traffickers, who are essentially their pimps. Pimps threaten victims' family members and hold their children hostage to prevent the women from escaping.

The great expansion of communication technologies in the global age has opened up new avenues for sex trafficking. Using the Internet, "customers" can find a sex worker almost anywhere in the world instantly, read reviews about the individual sex workers, exchange information on where to find prostitutes and the prices for sex workers, and so on. Websites for commercial prostitution tours from North America and Europe to Southeast Asia and the Caribbean offer package tours, quote prices, and advertise the sex workers and their services to the men of the developed world. In Cambodia, a U.S. resident started a "rape camp" that offered "Asian sex slaves" who were gagged, bound, and forced against their will into performing a variety of sex acts (D. Hughes 2000). Internet viewers could request and pay for specific rape acts over the Internet, while traffickers could avoid prosecution by using encryption technologies. This "rape camp" was ultimately shut down, but other creative methods of exploiting women and children continue to exist on the Internet.

Globalisation has led to a variety of negative developments, such as an increase in international sex trafficking. Here, Cambodian sex workers sit on the sidewalk along a street in Phnom Penh.

many studies of work, production, factories, and factory workers, and today's sociologists continue to study work-related issues. However, contemporary sociologists are devoting increasing attention to consumption in general (Sassatelli 2007) and more specifically to such phenomena as online shopping (Horrigan 2008), the behaviour of shoppers in more material locales such as department stores (D. Miller 1998; Zukin 2005), and the development of more recent consumption sites, such as fast-food restaurants (Ritzer 2013) and shopping malls (Ritzer 2010b).

Shoppers in Kyoto, Japan

McDONALDIZATION *Today*

The McDonaldization of Society

McDonaldization is the process by which the rational principles of the fast-food restaurant are coming to dominate more and more sectors of society and more societies throughout the world (Ritzer 2013). It leads to the creation of rational systems—like fast-food restaurants—that are characterised by the most direct and efficient means to their ends. McDonaldized systems have four defining characteristics:

- *Efficiency*. The emphasis is on the use of the quickest and least costly means to whatever end is desired. It is clear that employees of fast-food restaurants work efficiently: Burgers are cooked and assembled as if on an assembly line, with no wasted movements or ingredients, and digital ordering systems are used in conjunction with a limited menu to expedite the accurate placement of customer orders with the kitchen (Kelso 2011). Similarly, customers are expected to spend as little time as possible in the fast-food restaurant. Many of the chairs are designed to be somewhat uncomfortable, impelling customers to leave after about only 20 minutes so new customers can be seated. Perhaps the best example of efficiency is the drive-through window, a highly organised means for employees to dole out meals in a matter of seconds (Horovitz 2002). Overall, the fast-food restaurant seeks to ensure that both employees and customers act efficiently. The efficiency of one helps the other to behave in a similarly efficient manner.

- *Calculability*. You hear a lot at McDonald's about quantities: how large the food portions are—the

Big Mac, for example—and how low the prices are—the dollar breakfast, for example. You don't hear as much, however, about the quality of the restaurant's ingredients or its products. Similarly, you may hear about how many burgers are served per hour or how quickly they are served, but you don't hear much about other measures of employees' skill. A focus on quantity also means that tasks are often done under great pressure, which can mean that they are done in a slipshod manner.

- *Predictability*. McDonaldization ensures that the entire experience of patronizing a fast-food chain is nearly identical from one geographic setting to another—even globally—and from one time to another. For example, when customers enter a McDonald's restaurant, employees ask what they wish to order, following scripts created by the corporation. For their part, customers can expect to find most of the same menu items, especially at chain restaurants within their own country. Employees, following another script, can be counted on to thank customers for their order. Thus, a highly predictable ritual is played out in the fast-food restaurant.

- *Control*. In McDonaldized systems, a good deal of control is maintained through technology. French fry machines buzz when the fries are done and even automatically lift them out of the hot oil. The automatic fry machine may save time and prevent accidents, but it makes it impossible to meet a special customer request for brown, crispy fries. Similarly, the drive-through window

The sociological study of consumption sites involves, among many other things, a critical look at the ways in which they are structured in order to lead people to consume certain things and not others, to consume more than they might have intended, and to go into debt (R. Manning 2001; Marron 2009; Ritzer 1995). Take, for example, the website Ruelala.com, an "invitation-only" site that was established to sell expensive clothing to members at what are supposed to be huge discounts. The rationale behind the site is that because of its seeming exclusivity, people will be lured into buying more items, and spending more money on each item, than they would elsewhere. In

fact, however, the site is not as exclusive as it seems since members are urged to recruit their friends, and they get a $10 credit after the first purchase of every new member they bring to Ruelala.com.

Sociologists are also interested in how consumers use shopping malls and e-tailers in ways that were not anticipated by their designers. For example, people often wander through shopping malls and their many shops, which have been designed to spur consumption, without buying anything. Defunct malls are serving as impromptu skate parks. Students are using Amazon.ca as a source for term-paper bibliographies rather than buying the books. Travellers are

China is one of the largest and fastest growing markets for McDonald's. Between 2011 and 2013, McDonald's plans to open 7,000 new restaurants in China—nearly one every day.

can be seen as a technology that ensures that customers dispose of their garbage, if only by dumping it in the back seats of their cars. Control of customer behaviour can only go so far, however. All too often, McDonald's customers toss the familiar burger and fry packaging out their car windows and, in the process, litter the road and countryside. A 2009 report by Keep Britain Tidy revealed that just under a third (29 percent) of the fast-food litter in 10 British cities was composed of McDonald's wrappers and cups (Gray 2009).

Paradoxically, rationality often seems to lead to its exact opposite—irrationality. Just consider the problems of roadside litter due to drive-through services at fast-food restaurants. Or consider the inefficiencies associated with crowds of people clamouring at the counters and a long line of cars snaking its way—oh so slowly—past the drive-through window. Or the societal inefficiencies of dealing with childhood obesity that has been blamed, in part, on the ubiquity of fast food. Another of the irrationalities of rationality is dehumanisation. Fast-food employees are forced to work in dehumanizing jobs, which can lead to job dissatisfaction, alienation, and high turnover rates. Fast-food customers are forced to eat in dehumanizing settings, such as in the cold and impersonal atmosphere of the fast-food restaurant, in their cars, or on the move as they walk down the street. As more of the world succumbs to McDonaldization, dehumanisation becomes more the norm.

using Internet sites such as Expedia.com to compare prices but then buying airplane tickets from traditional travel agents or on an airline's website.

Social change continues, and the most recent economic recession has altered many things, including the degree to which society is dominated by consumption. Shoppers have cut back dramatically, and many consumption sites have experienced great difficulties. Many outdoor strip malls have emptied, and indoor malls have numerous vacant stores, including large department stores. Las Vegas, which has become a capital for the consumption of entertainment and high-end goods and services, is hurting. Dubai, aspiring to be the consumption capital of the East, hit a financial rough spot in 2009 and had to restructure $100 billion in debt. It seems possible, although unlikely, that even though we entered the consumption age only about a half-century ago, we now may be on the verge of what could be called the "postconsumption age." While excessive consumption and the related high level of debt were key factors in causing the recent recession, a postconsumption age would bring with it fewer jobs and a declining standard of living for many.

GL🌐BALISATION

The Shopping Malls of Dubai

The first modern, fully enclosed indoor shopping mall, Southdale Center, opened in Edina, Minnesota, in 1956 (Ritzer 2010b). Today, shopping malls are common throughout the western world. Though the modern shopping mall was an American invention, the mall concept has been globalised, and now malls are common in other parts of the world as well. For example, more than half of the largest malls in the world are currently located in China. At 9.6 million square feet and accommodating 1,500 retail outlets, the New South China Mall, located in Dongguan, is the largest mall in the world by a large margin (Pocock 2011). Many such international malls outshine those located in Canada. Suffice it to say that North America is no longer the leader in the most innovative, glitziest, and fanciest malls.

One locale notable for its malls is Dubai in the United Arab Emirates (UAE). Dubai covers more than 1,600 square miles (more than 4,000 square kilometers), mostly desert, and is on the coast of the Persian Gulf. The emirate boomed in the last few decades and now has a population of more than 2 million people, most of them expatriates who have found work there (C. Davidson 2008). Because of its dwindling oil reserves, Dubai is notable for having shifted from an economy dependent on oil to a diverse, "postoil" economy (Arnold 2011). Among other things, the emirate has become a regional, if not global, centre of consumption and has developed a thriving tourist industry. Visitors are drawn by the tallest building in the world—the Burj Khalifa—three artificial islands, and Dubai's over-the-top shopping malls.

While a model of economic development, Dubai has received its share of criticisms. Some of Dubai's residents work in highly paid professional and technical occupations, but many others work in the poorly paid service industry and in construction. The lavish lifestyles of the locals (the "Emirati"), the abysmal living conditions of construction workers, and the pervasive culture of what Thorstein Veblen ([1899] 1994) called "conspicuous consumption" have received notable scrutiny by critics (M. Davis 2006). For example, Arab sheikhs and rock stars pay upwards of $27,000 per night for rooms at the Burj Al Arab, a self-styled seven-star hotel that sits alone on a man-made island off the coast of Dubai ("Luxury—Cheaper Suites and Empty Beds" 2009).

At 3.7 million square feet in area and accommodating more than 1,200 retail outlets, the newest, largest, and most elegant of Dubai's malls is the Dubai Mall, which opened in 2008

Dubai, United Arab Emirates, is known for its large, lavish shopping malls—among other extravagant attractions.

("Dubai Mall Set for August 28 Opening" 2008). Among its most notable elements is a sophisticated shopping area for expensive jewellery—the largest gold souk, or ancient Arab bazaar, in the world. It also has a 10 million–liter aquarium behind the world's largest acrylic viewing panels (Stefania Bianchi 2010). Perhaps the most striking feature of the Dubai Mall is that, in the middle of one of the world's hottest and most arid deserts, it has an indoor ice rink, which can accommodate up to 2,000 skaters.

The Mall of the Emirates is much smaller than the Dubai Mall with only 520 shops, although it has a five-star Kempinski hotel and a 14-screen cinema complex (Mall of the Emirates 2010). The Mall of the Emirates has gone further than even the Dubai Mall in thumbing its nose at the heat of the desert—the mall houses Ski Dubai, a 400-meter indoor ski slope. Interestingly, the $2 billion American Dream mall, located just outside of New York City in New Jersey, has copied the Mall of the Emirates and built its own indoor ski slope (D'Elia 2011). However, the American Dream has been badly affected by the recent recession—as Dubai has—and has yet to open even though exterior construction is completed. In 2011 it was taken over (with economic help from the state of New Jersey) by the developers of the Mall of America in Minneapolis, and there is now progress on finishing and eventually opening the mall (R. Sullivan 2011).

The Ibn Battuta Mall in Dubai is modeled after Disney World in that it is "themed" (Gottdiener 2001). It encompasses six distinct areas—India, Persia, Egypt, China, Tunisia, and Andalusia. Each is characterised by architecture, motifs, and decorations characteristic of that area of the world. It also includes a 21-screen cinema and the only IMAX theatre in the United Arab Emirates. Mercato, another themed Dubai mall, features a design based on the Italian, Spanish, and French Renaissances ("Another Addition to Dubai's Malls" 2002). It is characterised by Tuscan and

Younis Al Mulla, general manager of Mall of the Emirates and Ski Dubai, walks past a polar bear mascot on the snow-covered slope at the Ski Dubai complex.

Venetian architecture and features cobbled streets and open piazzas.

Finally, Wafi is a Dubai mall that prominently features a building shaped like a pyramid. It could be modeled after the pyramids of Egypt—or maybe the Luxor casino hotel in Las Vegas. Within the mall can be found, among other things, a Planet Hollywood and Khan Murjan—a copy of a fourteenth-century souk (Wafi 2009). It also encompasses a small theme park.

The malls of Dubai are obviously involved in consumption, but they are also involved in the process of globalisation in numerous ways. Copying, and being copied by, American malls, attracting visitors from many parts of the world, and being affected by global economic processes such as the Great Recession are all indicators of global exchange and interconnectivity.

THE DIGITAL WORLD

Sociology has always concerned itself with the social aspects and implications of **technology**, or the interplay of machines, tools, skills, and procedures for the accomplishment of tasks. One example is the assembly line, a defining feature of early twentieth-century factories. Later, sociologists became interested in the automated technologies that came to define factories. However, technologies have continued to evolve considerably since then, and sociologists are now devoting an increasing amount of attention to the digital world that has emerged as a result of new technologies already mentioned in this chapter, such as computers, smartphones, and the Internet (Baym 2010; Cavanagh 2007).

It is important to note that while we will discuss the digital world throughout this book, living digitally is not separate from life in the social world. In fact, the two forms of living increasingly intersect and in the process create an augmented world for all involved. For example, the wide-scale use of smartphones allows people to text many others to let them know they are going to be at a local club. This can lead to a spontaneous social gathering at the club that would not have occurred were it not for this new technology.

The networking sites on the Internet that involve social interaction are the most obviously sociological in character (Aleman and Wartman 2008; Patchin and Hinduja 2010). These sites are important especially in the West, although Internet use is dramatically higher elsewhere in the world (see Figure 1.2). However, their importance is increasing in the Middle East and North Africa, as reflected in the role they played in recent social revolutions. Protesters used cell phones and the Internet to inform each other, and the world, about the evolving scene. Cell

phones and social networking also played a role in involving people in the riots that took place in London and elsewhere in England in mid-2011. To take another example, Facebook.com/yalaYL has become a key site where Israelis, Palestinians, and other Arabs communicate with each other about both everyday concerns and big issues such as the prospect for peace in the Middle East. This social networking takes place online while physical interaction between such people, and between their leaders, is difficult or nonexistent (Bronner 2011b).

One sociological issue is the ways in which social networking sites come between you and others and how this affects the nature of interaction. For example, Twitter limits you to 140 characters, but face-to-face communication has no such limits. On the other hand, face-to-face communication is limited to a shared physical space, whereas communication via Twitter travels anywhere there is a device connected to the Internet. Sociologists want to get a better handle on the nature of the differences, as well as the similarities, between mediated and nonmediated (for example, face-to-face) interaction. In technologically **mediated interaction**, technology such as the Internet and your cell phone come between you and others, while there

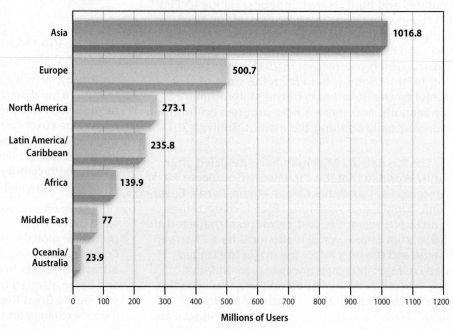

FIGURE 1.2 Estimated Internet Users by Geographic Region, 2011

Sociologists endeavour to understand how new technologies affect individuals, interactions, societies, and cultures. As technology changes, so too do the social world and field of sociology.

is no such interference in nonmediated interaction. People who are shy and insecure when it comes to dating or sex, for example, may be much more comfortable relating to others on mediated websites such as Match.com or OkCupid.com.

Another sociological interest related to the Internet is the impact on our lives of spending so much time interacting on social networking sites. For example, are you more likely to write term papers for your classes using shorter sentences and more abbreviations because of your experience with texting? Consider also the impact of the 7.5 hours per day—up by a full hour in only five years—that young people between the ages of 8 and 18 spend on electronic devices of all types (Lewin 2010). In some cases, little time for other activities (school work, face-to-face interaction) remains.

We may also multitask among several online and offline interactions simultaneously, as in class or while doing homework. You may think you do a great job of multitasking, but it can actually reduce your ability to comprehend and remember and thus lower your performance on tests and other assignments (PBS 2010).

Internet technology also affects the nature of consumption. More of it is taking place on such sites as eBay.ca and Amazon.ca, and that trend is expected to continue to grow. In 2010, a Pew study found that, on an average day, 21 percent of Internet users in the United States look for information about a service or product they are thinking about buying (Jansen 2010). It also is easier for people to spend money on consumption on Internet sites than in the material world. It is worth noting that these sites, as well as the Internet in general, are global in their scope. The ease with which global interactions and transactions occur on the Internet is a powerful spur to the process of globalisation.

GLOBALISATION, CONSUMPTION, THE DIGITAL WORLD, AND YOU

The three main concerns discussed above, taken singly and collectively, are of great concern not only to society in general and to sociologists but also to you as a student. You live a good part of your life in these three interrelated domains.

DIGITAL LIVING

The Internet in China

In the last three decades, no country has played, or will play, a larger role in changing the global economic and political landscape than China (Jacques 2009). Its economy has achieved unprecedented growth, and it became the second largest economy in the world in 2010; it is estimated it will surpass the United States as the world's largest economy as early as 2030 (Barboza 2010). However, the rising economic tide in China has not benefited everyone. Income inequality is extremely high. There are a number of recently minted billionaires and a rapidly growing middle class, but per capita income is still only approximately $3,600, which is similar to that in impoverished countries such as Algeria and El Salvador. Much of China's rural population and its factory workers remain very poor.

This divide extends to Internet use. Only about a third of China's population uses it currently. But that's still a lot of people. In 2010, about 420 million people in China used the Internet (China Internet Network Information Center 2010)—there are more Internet "citizens" in China than there are people in the United States. Since even now only a minority of China's population uses

the Internet, China's claim as the world leader in Internet use is slated to increase by an increasingly wide margin in the coming years. Furthermore, Chinese Internet users are young: 70 percent are under 30 (Ye 2008). This augurs well for future Chinese involvement in the Internet.

Among the major types of content that flow through the Internet in China are pirated films, music, and TV shows that can be watched free of charge; mobile Internet content such as ringtones; online multiplayer games; online communities with social networking and instant messaging; and celebrity gossip, photos, and videos of American and European sports ("Top Sites

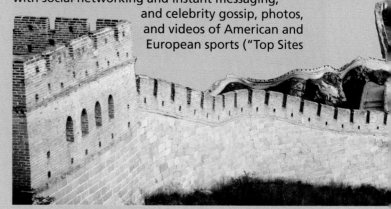

As a student, you live a truly global existence in a college or university where a significant number of your classmates come from elsewhere in the world and where your classes are increasingly taught by teaching assistants and professors from other parts of the globe. The ideas you are learning are the most global of all, flowing freely from virtually everywhere in the world to become part of lectures and textbooks.

As consumers, you and your classmates are likely well acquainted with the campus bookstore and the nearby shopping mall. In addition, on the Internet you are apt to find a nearly infinite variety of goods and services, the majority of

which are likely to come from the far reaches of the world.

Finally, an increasing portion of your education is obtained through the inherently global Internet—through such examples of e-learning as web-based courses and online degree programmes. In 2009, more than 4.6 million students were taking at least one online course (Allen and Seaman 2010). This constituted a growth rate in enrolment of 17 percent compared to a 1.2 percent growth rate for traditional courses.

The point is that not only are globalisation, consumption, and the Internet of great importance on their own, but they are of perhaps in China" 2011). On the surface, the types of content that are available on the Internet in China are not much different from those elsewhere in the world. However, the Chinese government has made an active effort to erect a barrier—a "Great Firewall"—to these flows (Segan 2011). This is part of a larger effort by the Chinese government to block all flows of information in a variety of ways, including censorship of news, control over television, and limits on bookshops and movie theatres (I. Bennett 2011). Barriers on the Internet include restricted access to a large number of foreign websites such as Wikipedia.org, Flickr.com, YouTube.com, and sometimes Myspace.com (BBC News 2010). There are also controversial filters on Google designed to keep material regarded by the Chinese government as politically sensitive from appearing in responses to searches. An awkward payment system controlled by the government restricts online shopping. New rules have come into effect limiting online video.

From the perspective of this chapter, the thing that is most interesting about these restrictions is how well they illustrate the relationship between global flows and structural barriers to those flows. China's efforts to censor the Internet have resulted in a unique Internet world in China. For example, many popular online communities consist entirely of Chinese citizens. In an increasingly global world, however, how long can China maintain barriers that few—if any—other countries in the world erect (Lacharite 2002)?

Although the majority of Chinese Internet users are completely oblivious of the existence of the Great Firewall (French 2008), there are signs of rebellion. Some Chinese Internet users have filed lawsuits against government-owned service providers, and a growing network of software writers have begun to develop code aimed at overcoming government restrictions (J. Kennedy 2007). Bloggers and webpage owners post articles to spread awareness of the Great Firewall and share links to programmes that will help Internet users evade it (French 2008). These are interesting signs of resistance to the Chinese government, although they could be extinguished at any moment through a massive show of power. It is instructive to remember how quickly the Chinese government quashed the Tiananmen Square revolt of 1989, which was undertaken to promote political and economic reform.

greater importance in the ways in which they interact with one another and interpenetrate with your life as a student—and the lives of virtually everyone else.

SOCIOLOGY: CONTINUITY AND CHANGE

Up to this point, this chapter has emphasised recent social changes and their impact on society and on sociology, but there is also much continuity in society, as well as in the field of sociology. This section deals with a number of traditional approaches and concerns in sociology that are of continuing relevance to even the most topical of sociological issues.

THE SOCIOLOGICAL IMAGINATION

The systematic study of the social world has always required imagination on the part of sociologists. There are various ways to look at the social world. For example, instead of looking at that world from the point of view of an insider, one can, at least psychologically, place oneself outside that world. America's "War on Terror" might look defensible from the perspective of an American, especially one who lived through 9/11, but it would look quite different if you imagined yourself in the place of an innocent Iraqi or Afghan who is caught in the middle in that war.

The phenomenon of being able to look at the social world from different perspectives caught the attention of the famous sociologist C. Wright Mills, who in 1959 wrote a very important book titled *The Sociological Imagination*. He argued that sociologists had a unique perspective—the **sociological imagination**—that gave them a distinctive way of looking at data or reflecting on the world around them.

A 1956 book by Mills, *The Power Elite*, demonstrates the application of the sociological

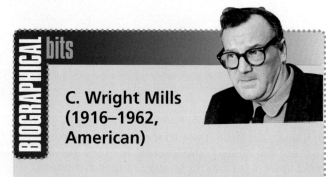

In 2011, the North Atlantic Treaty Organization (NATO) instituted a no-fly zone and bombing campaign against Libyan forces loyal to Colonel Muammar Gaddafi. Gaddafi lost power and his life—that's his hand sticking out of the bag—as a result of the revolt in his country.

imagination to the political world of his day. It was dominated by the "Cold War"—the nonshooting "war" that existed between the United States and the Soviet Union between the end of World War II in 1945 and the fall of the Soviet Union in 1991—and by the likelihood of nuclear war between the United States and the Soviet Union. Mills argued that a "military-industrial complex" consisting of the military and many defense industries had come into existence in the United States. They both favoured war, or at least preparedness for war, and therefore the expenditure of huge sums of taxpayer money on armaments of all types. In 1960, a few years after *The Power Elite* was published, President and former five-star general Dwight D. Eisenhower warned the nation, in his farewell address, of the threats to liberty and democracy posed by the military-industrial complex, to say nothing of their role in elevating the risk of war:

In the councils of government, we must guard against the acquisition of unwarranted influence, whether sought or unsought, by the military industrial complex. The potential for the disastrous rise of misplaced power exists and will persist.

We must never let the weight of this combination endanger our liberties or democratic processes. We should take nothing for granted. Only an alert and knowledgeable citizenry can compel the proper meshing of the huge industrial and military machinery of defense with our peaceful methods and goals, so that security and liberty may prosper together.

Sociology requires at least as much imagination today as it did in Mills's day, and probably more, to deal with new and emerging realities. For example, the risk of global warfare, especially nuclear war, has declined with the end of the Cold War and the demise of the Soviet Union. But a military-industrial complex not only remains in place in the United States but may be more powerful than ever. Consider the simultaneous wars in Iraq and Afghanistan, to say nothing of the seemingly open-ended and perhaps never-ending "War on Terror." Some sociologists would point out that the military and defense industries want, indeed need, hundreds of billions of dollars to be spent each year on armaments of all types. The new threats that arise regularly, real or imagined, lead to ever-greater expenditures and further expansion of the military-industrial complex. In Figure 1.3, for example, you can see that U.S. military expenditures more than doubled after the terrorist attacks of September 11, 2001—reflecting overlapping wars with Iraq and Afghanistan. Given the economic problems facing the United States, there is talk of cutting the defense budget in future years. Whatever happens, we can be sure that a military-industrial complex will survive and fight hard against any reductions.

Of recent concern, and relevant to our interest in the Internet, is "information war" (Tumber and Webster 2006). Instead of relying on armaments, an information war may involve barrages of propaganda by the warring parties—for example, Israel and the Palestinians and the United States and al-Qaeda. An information war can also involve "cyber-attacks," in which hackers engage in stealthy attacks on an enemy nation's computer systems. For example, computers in Estonia belonging to the government, newspapers, banks, and other large institutions were attacked in 2007; Estonian officials blamed the cyber-attacks on Russia. In 2010 the Stuxnet worm attacked a number of computers around the world, but it was especially aimed at Iranian nuclear facilities, which were apparently badly hurt by the attack. Most observers speculate that the attack was a joint U.S.-Israeli operation. It is likely that the American military-industrial complex will claim, not without some justification, that large sums of money now need to be spent and expensive new technologies developed in order to ward off, or engage in, cyber-attacks.

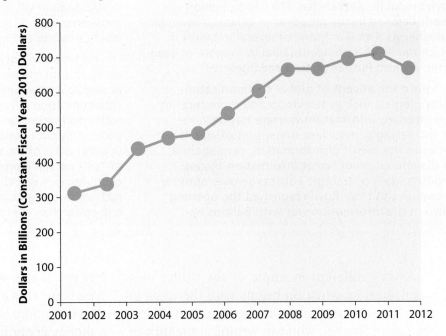

FIGURE 1.3 U.S. Defense Budget, 2001–2012

SOURCE: From Michael I. Norton and Dan Ariely, "Building a Better America—One Wealth Quintile at a Time." *Perspectives on Psychological Science*, January 2011: 9–12.

NOTE: Figures include base defense budget and Iraq- and Afghanistan-related operations but not nuclear weapons activities of the Department of Energy.

GL🌐BALISATION

The Russia–Belarus Information War

In 1991, following the prolonged Cold War between the Soviet Union (and its allies) and the United States (and its allies), the Soviet Union dissolved. The former superpower was split up into 15 independent nation-states. Two of the new states included Russia (by far the largest and most powerful of the post-Soviet states) and Belarus (a small country between Russia and Europe). For many years, Russia has sought to develop strong political and economic ties to Belarus for strategic purposes. From Russia's perspective, Belarus offers economic access to European clients, political access needed to increase its influence in Europe, and a "'natural shield' against military expansion from the West" (Golani 2011). Reciprocally, Belarus is in a position to develop its economy and infrastructure with stronger ties to Russia. However, the relationship between these two countries has become increasingly tense in recent years.

The growing tension was reflected in an information war between the two countries that began in 2010 (Schwirtz 2010). They quarrelled over natural gas prices and over one of Russian Premier Vladimir Putin's pet projects, a customs union between Russia and Belarus as well as another former Soviet republic, Kazakhstan. The customs union was nearly derailed by the president of Belarus, Alexander Lukashenko. This is only one of several instances in which the Belarus president failed to support, or even acted against, Russian policies and interests.

Since the advent of global communication technologies, such as television and more recently the Internet, information warfare has become an increasingly important dimension of war. It includes the use of disinformation, propaganda, or dissemination of secret information by one group to gain a strategic advantage over another group. In this case, Russia launched the opening salvo in the information war with Belarus by airing a television documentary in 2010 titled *Godfather*. The Godfather of the title was President Lukashenko, who was portrayed as a "bumbling tyrant enamored of Hitler and Stalin. He has political opponents killed, journalists silenced and elections rigged . . . while keeping his faltering country in a Soviet time warp." The documentary, Russia claimed, "covers the disappearances and killings of Mr. Lukashenko's political opponents over the years and shows video of armored police officers beating antigovernment protestors" (Schwirtz 2010:10). Only a few in Belarus could see the documentary, but it became available anywhere in the world on YouTube.

Shortly after the video was shown, Belarus fired back with an article in a government newspaper by Russian opposition leaders who were highly critical of Mr. Putin. More generally, they said: "Savagery has become the norm in Russian society" (Schwirtz 2010:10). The Belarus government's TV channel broadcast an interview with the president of Georgia (another former Soviet Republic), Mikheil Saakashvili, in which he called the attack on Lukashenko hypocritical since political killings were common in Russia. Saakashvili, who was hated by the Russian leadership, said, "This has the smell of a propaganda war" (Schwirtz 2010:10).

Information flows much more quickly and easily around the world than physical objects such as people and weapons, in part because of global communication networks. But the strategic use of such information can have dramatic impacts on state policies, public opinion, and collective action—even in other parts of the world. This kind of exercise of "soft power" appears increasingly likely in the contemporary world, where exercises of "hard power" such as shooting wars have become more dangerous and costly than ever.

A very different example of the utility of a sociological imagination begins with the ideas of one of the classic thinkers in the history of sociology, Georg Simmel, who was writing at the turn of the twentieth century. Among many other things, Simmel argued that money is crucial to a modern economy. For example, cash money allows people to be paid easily for their work and just as easily to buy goods and services. However, money not only speeds up consumption but also allows people to consume more than they otherwise would. While a money economy creates its own problems, it is the credit economy that nearly wrecked much of the global economy during the last few years. The availability of "money" had dramatically increased with the expansion of credit for individuals, in the form of mortgage loans, auto loans, and credit cards. People not only tended to spend all of the cash (including savings) they had on hand, but they increasingly went into debt because loans were easy to obtain. Simmel's imaginative thinking on money allows us to better understand the problems that easy credit can create.

Private Troubles and Public Issues

The sociological imagination may be most useful in helping sociologists see the linkage between private troubles and public issues. For example, prior to the onset of the recent recession, the sociological imagination would have been useful in alerting society to the fact that the increasing levels of individual consumption and debt, seen at the time as private issues, would soon morph into the near-collapse of the global economy, which is a public issue. Credit cards can create both private troubles and public issues. A person going so deeply into debt that there is no way out other than declaring bankruptcy is experiencing a private trouble. However, private troubles become public issues when high levels of personal debt and bankruptcy lead to such things as bank failures and even default on debts by various nations. Today, the sociological imagination could also be used to reflect on, for example, the fleeting nature of private social relationships on Facebook and Twitter and whether they will lead all types of social relationships in the future in the same direction.

Many other examples of the link between private troubles and public issues relate to young people and students. For example, ADHD—attention deficit/hyperactivity disorder—can easily be seen as a private trouble. For years, there was little public awareness of ADHD, and those who had it were likely to suffer alone. But since the 1980s, it has become clear that ADHD is also a public issue, and it is becoming a more important public issue. The prevalence of ADHD is controversial, with rates of diagnosis higher in some countries, such as the United States, than in Canada. Similarly, children born later in the year (e.g., December) are more likely to be diagnosed with ADHD than children born earlier (Morrow et al. 2012). Nevertheless, many children suffer from ADHD (a private trouble) even as the controversy around diagnosis is a

public issue about which more and better information is imperative.

In another example, a 2010 House of Commons presentation details the fact that women are more likely to select family medicine as opposed to specialty training (e.g., surgeons) (Federation of Medical Women of Canada, 2010). Women are more likely to be general practitioners or practical nurses than to be highly paid surgeons. Being limited occupationally causes many women personal troubles such as inadequate income and job dissatisfaction. It is also a public issue because it is unfair to women as a whole and because society is not the beneficiary of the many contributions of which women are capable.

The decision to pursue one major or career path over another could become a private trouble if a poor choice is made or is forced upon a student. Sociologists have also shown that such choices are very much related to larger public issues. If many people make such choices, or are forced into them—as women and other minorities often are—that would lead to public issues such as wide-scale job dissatisfaction and poor performance on the job. Culturally based ideas about gender often shape personal preferences in college or university major (Charles and Bradley 2009; Davies and Guppy 2013), and gendered beliefs about career competence steer women and men toward different types of jobs and away from others (S. L. Correll 2004; Creese and Beagan 2009). Being in a poorly paid and unsatisfying job is a personal trouble for an individual woman, but it is a public issue when large numbers of women find themselves in this situation.

The Micro-Macro Relationship

The interest in personal troubles and public issues is a specific example of a larger and more basic sociological concern with the relationship between microscopic (**micro**, or small-scale) social phenomena, such as individuals and their thoughts and actions, and macroscopic (**macro**, or large-scale) social phenomena, such as groups, organisations, cultures, society, and the world, as well as the relationship between them (J. Turner 2005). For example, Karl Marx, often considered one of the earliest and most important sociologists, was interested in the relationship between what workers did and thought (micro issues) and the capitalist economic system (a macro issue) under which the workers toiled. To take a more contemporary example, Randall Collins (2009) has sought to develop a theory of violence that deals with everything from individuals skilled in violent interactions, such as attacking those who are weak, to the material resources needed by violent organisations to cause other violent organisations to fall apart. An example of the latter is the well-equipped U.S. Navy SEALs team that killed Osama bin Laden in 2011 and through that act sought to help hasten the dissolution of al-Qaeda.

In fact, there is a continuum that runs from the most microscopic to the most macroscopic of social realities, with phenomena at roughly the midpoint of this continuum best thought of as meso realities (middle or intermediate). The definition of sociology presented at the beginning of this chapter fits this continuum quite well. Individual actions and thoughts lie on the micro end of the continuum; groups, organisations, cultures, and societies fall more toward the macro end; and worldwide structures and processes are at the most macro end of the continuum (see Figure 1.4). Although in their own work the vast majority of individual sociologists focus on only very limited segments of this continuum, the field as a whole is concerned with the continuum in its entirety as well as the interrelationships among its various components.

The Agency-Structure Relationship

American sociologists tend to think in terms of the micro-macro relationship. In other parts of the world, especially in Europe and in much of Canada, sociologists are more oriented to the agency-structure relationship (see Figure 1.5). The agency-structure continuum is complex, but for our purposes we can think of agency as resembling the micro level and structure as resembling the macro level.

The utility of the agency-structure terminology is that it highlights several important social realities and aspects of the field of sociology. Of greatest significance is the fact that the term *agency* gives great importance to the individual—the "agent"—as having power and a capacity for creativity (Giddens 1984). In sociological work on agency, great emphasis is placed on the individual's mental abilities and the ways in which these abilities are used to create important, if not decisive, actions.

However, these agents are seen as enmeshed in macro-level social and cultural structures that agents create and by which they are constrained. For example, as a student you help create the universities you attend, and you are constrained by them and the power they have over you; they can require you to do certain things (such as take specific courses in order to earn your degree) and prevent you from doing other things (such as taking courses that might be of greater interest, or even taking no courses at all). On the other hand, you as a student can act to change or overthrow those structures. You might organize student-run groups on topics of interest, such as religious rights or manga cartoons; attract many participants to the groups; and eventually prompt the university to add courses on those

Micro ⟵——————————————————⟶ Macro

FIGURE 1.4 The Micro-Macro Continuum

topics. Or perhaps you might organize students to stop enrolling in an elective course that seems irrelevant to their lives, which causes that elective to be dropped from the course catalogue.

Agents (you as a student, in this case) have great power. In the words of another important sociologist, Erving Goffman (1961b:81), individuals are **dangerous giants**; that is, they have **agency**, or the potential to disrupt and destroy the structures in which they find themselves (e.g., Mohamed Bouazizi, the Tunisian street vendor discussed in the opening section of this chapter). Yet often, agents do not realize the power they possess. As a result, social structures such as the university and the class you are currently taking function over long periods of time with little or no disruption by individual agents.

However, there are times, such as during the anti–Vietnam War protests of the late 1960s and early 1970s, when students have come to realize they are dangerous giants and act to change not only the university but also the larger society (Gitlin 1993). After a six-day student campout that completely trashed the office of Grayson Kirk, then president of Columbia University, he asked, "My god, how could human beings do a thing like this?"

There are far more minor, everyday actions that reflect the fact that people can be dangerous giants. Examples might include questioning a professor's argument or going to the dean to protest the excessive absences of an instructor. However, most people most of the time do not realize that they are dangerous giants—that they have the capacity to alter greatly the social structures that surround them and in which they are enmeshed.

One more distinctive thing about the agency-structure perspective is the idea that social structures are both constraining and enabling. As we will see in Chapter 2, there is a long tradition in sociology of seeing structures such as the university as mainly constraining people, if not being totally oppressive. While the agency-structure perspective acknowledges and deals with these constraints, it also makes the very important point that structures enable agents to do things they otherwise would not be able to do. For example, it is the global structure of the Internet that allows you to communicate easily and quickly with people throughout the world. It also permits you to consume many goods and services from the comfort of your home or dorm room rather than travelling, perhaps great distances, to obtain them. Similarly, while the university constrains you in many ways, it does offer you the knowledge and skills you need to succeed, or perhaps simply to survive, in the modern world. In thinking about and critiquing the constraining power of structures, it is important to remember that those structures also enable you in many different ways.

THE SOCIAL CONSTRUCTION OF REALITY

The discussion of agency and structure leads to another basic concept in sociology: the **social construction of reality** (P. Berger and Luckmann 1967). This approach argues that people at the

Agency ← → **Structure**

FIGURE 1.5 The Agency-Structure Relationship

micro end of the perspective—agents—create social reality, basically meso- and macro-level phenomena, through their thoughts and actions. That reality then comes to have a life of its own; that is, it becomes a structure that is partly or wholly separate from the people who created it and exist in it. Once meso and macro phenomena have lives of their own, they constrain and even control what people do. Of course, people can refuse to accept these constraints and controls and create new social realities. This process of individual creation of structural realities, constraint, and coercion then begins anew, in a continuing loop. It is this continuous loop that is the heart of the micro-macro relationship, the social world, and the field of sociology.

For example, in the realm of consumption, it is people—as designers, manufacturers, and consumers—who create the world of fashion (Entwhistle 2009). However, once the fashion world in general comes into existence, that world comes to have a great deal of influence over individuals who are part of that world. Famous fashion houses such as Dior and Givenchy come to dominate the industry and perpetuate their existence by continual fashion changes. These companies control people's tastes in fashion and thereby the nature of the clothing people wear. Changing fashions are highly profitable for the fashion houses. Consumers seem eager to buy the designs created by the leading fashion houses, although most often in the form of the relatively inexpensive knockoffs derived from them.

The power of the fashion industry, and the nature of its products, has been analysed by a number of sociologists (Lipovetsky [1987] 2002; Simmel [1904] 1971), most notably another of the early giants in the field, Thorstein Veblen. In a classic work, *The Theory of the Leisure Class*, Veblen ([1899] 1994) critiqued the high heel, and especially the skirt. He argued that women persist in wearing a skirt even though "it is expensive and hampers the wearer at every turn and incapacitates her for all useful exertion" (p. 171). Feminist theorists have extended this critique, arguing that beauty devices such as high heels help to maintain gender inequality by serving to limit women physically (Dworkin 1974; Jeffreys 2005). More subtly, these devices encourage women to engage in a

never-ending project of bodily discipline aimed at attaining what is, in fact, an unreachable beauty ideal created by society (Bartky 1990; N. Wolf [1991] 2002). Were it not for the fashion industry, would as many women wear tight skirts and spike heels?

Of course, many people do not go along with the constraints of the fashion industry; they do not wear what the industry wants them to wear, and they do not change their dress because of changes in fashion induced by the fashion industry. Many people have their own sense of fashion and create their own way of dressing. Others ignore fashion altogether. Of greatest importance from this perspective is the fact that the source of what is in fashion often does not come from the fashion industry but rather comes from the modes of dress put together by people themselves. The latter have, in a real sense, constructed their own social reality. In fact, there is a process known as "cool hunting" (Gloor and Cooper 2007) in which scouts for the fashion industry seek out new and interesting ways of dressing, often focusing on what young people in the suburbs, and in the inner city, are wearing. They bring those innovative ideas back to the fashion industry, and some of them are turned into next year's fashions.

Once this happens, however, we are back to a situation where the fashion industry is controlling, or is at least attempting to control, what people wear. Many will accept the new fashion, but others, especially the "cool" kids who are sought out by the cool hunters, will not. They may well have moved on to some entirely new sense of what they want to wear. They will again attract the attention of cool hunters, and the process will begin anew.

SOCIAL STRUCTURES AND PROCESSES

Another nineteenth-century sociologist, Auguste Comte, was important not only for inventing the term *sociology* in 1839 but also for being the originator of sociology as a field. Crucial for our purposes here is his early distinction between what he called "social statics" and "social dynamics." In his social *statics*, Comte looked at the various "parts" (structures) of society, such as the manufacturers and retailers of clothing fashions, and the ways in which they relate to one another, as well as to the whole of society. In looking at such relationships, Comte was concerned with social processes among and between parts of society, as well as in society as a whole. However, under the heading of social *dynamics* his main focus was on a specific social process—social change—and on how the various parts of society changed.

It is important to emphasize here that **social structures** are enduring and regular social arrangements, such as the family and the state. While social structures do change, they are generally not very dynamic; they change very slowly. **Social processes** are the dynamic and ever-changing aspects of the social world.

Globalisation can be divided into structures (such as the United Nations) and a variety of more specific social processes (such as the migration of people across national borders). In terms of consumption, we can think of the shopping mall (or Amazon.ca) as a structure and the shopping (or consumption) that takes place in it as a process. Finally, the Internet as a whole and social networking sites in particular are structures, while the communication and the social interaction that take place in them can be viewed as processes.

Needless to say, neither the shopping mall nor the Internet existed in Comte's day. Once again we see that the social world is constantly changing and that sociologists, as well as students of sociology, must be continually sensitive to those changes. However, some of sociology's earliest concepts continue to be applicable, and usefully applied, to the social world.

SOCIOLOGY'S PURPOSE: SCIENCE OR SOCIAL REFORM?

Comte was famous not only for examining the relationship between structure and process but also for arguing that such study ought to be scientific. He believed that the social world was dominated by laws and sociology's task was to uncover those laws. As those laws were uncovered, the science

of sociology would develop. But Comte was also concerned with the problems of his day and interested in solving them through social reform. In fact, to Comte, science and reform should not be separated from one another. A number of classic sociologists—Karl Marx, Émile Durkheim, Jane Addams, and others—shared this view. Marx and Engels's *Communist Manifesto* (1848) was not only a commentary on the social ills of the capitalist economy but a rallying cry to workers to organize and abolish capitalism.

Many of today's sociologists study social problems of all sorts such as poverty and crime, and they seek to use what they know in order to deal with these problems by suggesting ways of reforming society. They believe that these two activities are not necessarily distinct, and they can and should be mutually enriching. While many contemporary sociologists accept this position, a division has developed over time, with some sociologists focusing more on scientific research and others more engaged in activities designed to reform society and address social problems.

The sociologists who engage in "pure science" operate with the conviction that we need to better understand how the social world operates before we can change it, if that's what we want to do. That knowledge may ultimately be used by those who want to change society, or to keep it as it is, but that is not the immediate concern of the social researcher. For example, sociologists known as "ethnomethodologists" argue that the task of the sociologist is to better understand common forms of social behaviour (Rawls 2011). They research the details of everyday life, such as how we know when a laugh is expected in a conversation or when to applaud or boo during a speech. For them, the goal is purely knowledge and understanding. Such sociologists argue that using that knowledge to reform society might adversely affect or distort social behaviours.

Other sociologists take the opposite position. C. Wright Mills, for example, was little interested in doing scientific research; he was mostly interested in such social reforms as limiting or eliminating the unwholesome and worrisome ties between the military and industry in the United States. He was also critical of many of the most prominent sociologists of his day for their orientation toward being pure scientists, their lack of concern for the pressing problems of the day, and their unwillingness to do anything about them. Feminist sociologists have extended the argument, pointing out that the topics and methods of objective, scientific sociology themselves sometimes reflect, and ultimately reinforce, social inequality along the lines of race, gender, and class because they are based on the assumptions of society's elite.

For example, feminist scholar Cynthia Fuchs Epstein (1988) has argued that supposedly scientific distinctions between males and females have often been based on social biases. She states that these social biases can be explained by the "prejudices against women and cultural notions emphasizing differences between the sexes" (Epstein 1988:17). Until recently, scientific researchers have almost always been men. The questions about what problems were worthy of study reflected male interests, rather than female interests. For example, issues more relevant to women, such as rape and housework, were deemed trivial and overshadowed by other issues, such as achievement and power (Riger 1992). The assumptions about and interpretations of the people they studied represented a male perspective. They tended to use males as their research subjects and treated male behaviours and attitudes as universal. They did not consider how societies treat men and women differently and socialize them to feel and act in distinct ways. As a result, these seemingly "scientific" views of women reinforced false assumptions about male-female differences, held both men and women to supposedly universal male norms, and reproduced gender inequality (Rutherford, Vaughn-Blount, and Ball 2010).

The view that sociology has a social purpose has created renewed interest in what is now called public sociology. In contrast to professional sociology in which work is done for other sociologists, **public sociology** addresses a wide range of audiences, most of which are outside the academy. These publics include a wide variety of local, national, and global groups. Public sociologists write for these groups, and they can become involved in collaborative projects with them (Burawoy 2005; Clawson et al. 2007; Nyden, Hossfeld, and Nyden 2011). There have

been public sociologists from the beginning of the discipline, and they have existed throughout the field's history. However, in recent decades the field has been dominated by technically oriented sociologists working out of universities and think tanks who have done highly sophisticated work aimed, primarily, at other sociologists and sociology students with a similar orientation. This has been important work, and it has benefited the larger public by enhancing our understanding of society. Still, many Canadian sociologists are searching for better ways of reaching a larger public beyond the university. Interestingly, this is a lesser issue in Europe, where many of the leading sociologists have always been public sociologists.

In addressing the larger public, sociologists are urged to be driven more by their personal values, as well as by the values (for example, democracy) of the larger society, than by technical considerations. However, there is not one public to be addressed, but rather a number of diverse publics—for example, young people, parents, the aged—that have different issues and need to be addressed in different ways. Public sociology should not consist of sociologists' pronouncements on important issues but rather encourage a dialogue with these diverse publics. Nonetheless, most public sociologists believe that their work should be addressed to, and done on behalf of, the underdogs in society.

Public sociologists engage with the public in a variety of ways: writing blogs, books and articles for a popular audience, and op-ed pieces in newspapers; teaching as well as presenting public lectures and making TV appearances; and working directly with groups to help them achieve their goals. In addition, sociology sometimes becomes public through the work of nonsociologists (such as Eric Schlosser; see the next *Public Sociology* box) whose thinking is shaped explicitly or implicitly by sociological knowledge and a sociological perspective. Such work is often produced by journalists in the form of newspaper articles, books released by popular presses, or postings to a website capable of reaching a huge public audience. The type of work discussed throughout this section will be dealt with in a series of boxes headed *Public Sociology* to be found throughout this book.

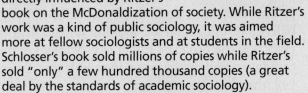

PUBLIC SOCIOLOGY

Eric Schlosser and *Fast Food Nation*

Usually public sociology is conducted by sociologists, and many of the examples of public sociology offered throughout this book will feature the work of sociologists. But journalists who become knowledgeable about a specific social issue may write articles, books, and blogs for a general audience that are based on sociological studies or that take a sociological approach. One of the best known and most influential pop sociology books by a journalist is Eric Schlosser's (2002) *Fast Food Nation*, which became a movie in 2006. Schlosser focuses on the nature of the food at fast-food restaurants. His work was directly influenced by Ritzer's

Eric Schlosser

book on the McDonaldization of society. While Ritzer's work was a kind of public sociology, it was aimed more at fellow sociologists and at students in the field. Schlosser's book sold millions of copies while Ritzer's sold "only" a few hundred thousand copies (a great deal by the standards of academic sociology).

For Schlosser, a nation is what it eats, and Americans (like the citizens of many other countries, including Canada) eat a great deal of fast food. What they eat is generally mediocre (although Schlosser likes McDonald's French fries, as do millions of others) and is likely to be a health risk, linked to high rates of diabetes, heart disease, and so on (Reinberg 2011). Obesity, which has been on the rise in Canada, has been linked to the proliferation of fast-food restaurants (I. Janssen et al. 2005).

Perhaps Schlosser's most important sociological argument is that the fast-food industry has a significant influence on the industries that grow and produce the food that it sells. Schlosser goes into great detail in his book about how the companies that grow potatoes, process frozen French fries, raise poultry and cattle, and pack meat have had to expand and rationalize (McDonaldize) their procedures in order to meet the growing needs of the fast-food industry. While these changes have led to dramatic increases in production in all of these industries, that growth has not come without costs. Meat and poultry are more likely to be disease-ridden, small producers and ranchers have been driven out of business, and millions of people have been forced to work in low-paying, demeaning, demanding, and sometimes outright dangerous

jobs. For example, in the meatpacking industry, safe, unionised, secure, manageable, and relatively high-paying jobs such as butchers in firms with once well-known corporate names such as Swift and Armour have been replaced by unsafe, nonunionised, insecure, unmanageable, and relatively low-paying positions within largely anonymous corporations (Novek 1992).

Schlosser advocates a number of social changes to deal with the problems created by fast food and the fast-food industry:

- Reform the industries that supply the fast-food restaurants, such as the meatpacking industry. Reforms would include not only better treatment of workers and a higher minimum wage but also more humane slaughter of animals. Schlosser believes that this change could be implemented quickly if it was demanded by the major players in the fast-food industry, especially McDonald's.

- Require that the fast-food industry assume more of its real costs to society. Thus, it should be required to pay at least part of the medical costs associated with the various health problems linked to its food, which is high in calories, cholesterol, and salt.

- Ban the advertising of fast food to children. While adults can assess the health dangers associated with a bacon double cheeseburger with a shake and large fries, children cannot. Just as we've banned cigarette ads in the interest of public health, we can ban ads for fast food targeted at children for many of the same reasons.

- Completely overhaul the federal food safety system. Instead of a number of widely dispersed and separate agencies, Schlosser suggests one agency with the power to improve food safety in the fast-food industry as well as among its suppliers.

Like many classic and contemporary sociologists, Schlosser is not only an observer and analyst of society but also a critic and social reformer. Although he is not a sociologist, he is doing public sociology.

SOCIOLOGY, THE OTHER SOCIAL SCIENCES, AND COMMON SENSE

Sociology is one of the social sciences—that is, it is one of the fields that study various aspects of the social world. Among the others are anthropology, communication, economics, geography, political science, and psychology. Generally speaking, sociology is the broadest of these fields; other social scientists are more likely to delve into specific aspects of the social world in much greater depth. Sociological study touches on the culture of concern to anthropologists, the nation-state of interest to political scientists, and the mental processes that are the focus of psychologists. However, that does not mean that sociology is in any sense "better" than, or conversely not as good as, the other social sciences.

Rather than compare and contrast these fields in general terms, the focus in this concluding section will be on the different ways in which these fields approach one of this book's signature concerns—globalisation:

- Anthropology: cultural aspects of societies around the world, such as the food people eat and how they eat it, as well as the differences among cultures around the globe (Inda and Rosaldo 2008).

- Communication studies: mediated and non-mediated communication across the globe, with the Internet obviously of focal concern in the contemporary world.

- Economics: production, distribution, and consumption of resources through markets and other structures that span much of the globe, especially those based on and involving money.

- Geography: spatial relationships on a global scale and mapping of those spaces (Herod 2009).

- Political science: nation-states, especially the ways in which they relate to one another around the world, as well as the way they have grown increasingly unable to control global flows of migrants, viruses, recreational drugs, Internet scams, and the like.

- Psychology: ways in which individual identities are shaped by increased awareness of the rest of the world and tensions associated with globalisation (such as job loss due to "offshoring"), which may lead to psychological problems such as depression (Lemert and Elliott 2006).

Sociology encompasses all of these concerns, and many others, in its approach to globalisation: globe-straddling cultures (such as consumer, or fast-food, culture), relationships between political systems (the European Union and its member nations, for example), communication networks (such as CTV and Al Jazeera, Twitter and Facebook), markets (for labour or stocks and bonds, for example) that cover vast expanses of the globe, the mapping of all of these, and even their impact, both good and bad, on individuals. You might want to study the other fields to get a sense of the depth of what they have to offer on specific aspects of globalisation, but if you are looking for the field that gives you the broadest possible view of all of these things, as well as the ways in which they interrelate, that field is sociology.

While sociology and the other social sciences have important differences, they are all quite different from commonsense understandings of the social world. While everyone today participates in globalisation in one way or another, few, if any, people study these phenomena in the way and to the degree that they are studied by social scientists. For example, you probably have a sense that globalisation has changed society—perhaps even an impression that it is changing your life. What you aren't likely to know without more detailed study are globalisation's causes, effects, and unknown linkages to other phenomena or the pros and cons of globalisation on a personal, societal, and global level. That more detailed knowledge is what could help you, and others, more successfully navigate the accompanying changes in social processes and structures.

One example of the gap between common sense and social scientific evidence pertains to the diagnosis of attention deficit/hyperactivity disorder discussed earlier in this chapter. Most people believe that ADHD diagnoses are not affected by the month in which a child is born. For example, for a 12-year-old child, whether he or she was born in January or December ought not to affect his or her likelihood of being diagnosed with ADHD. However, evidence shows that doctors overdiagnose ADHD in children born later in the year. Girls born in December are 70 percent more likely to be diagnosed with ADHD than girls born in January (for boys it is 30 percent higher). You might think there is a seasonal effect, but the analysis of Morrow and his colleagues (2012) suggests that the result is due to social processes involved in organizing the school year. December babies are the youngest, and therefore most immature, in their school classes, and this relative immaturity is being misinterpreted as ADHD, with the consequent medication that attends such a diagnosis.

While common sense is important, even to sociologists, there is no substitute for the systematic study of the social world in both its minutest detail and its broadest manifestations.

SUMMARY

Sociology is the systematic examination of the ways in which people are affected by, and affect, the social structures and social processes that are associated with groups, organisations, cultures, societies, and the world in which they exist. We and our actions are dramatically affected by the social world and, in turn, also impact the social world. As signature themes, this introduction to sociology focuses on three large structural forces in the social world that have drawn the attention of contemporary sociologists, namely globalisation, consumption, and digital technology.

As the world has become more globalised, individual societies have lost some of their significance, and larger, transnational organisations have become more prominent. Also, global society has become more fluid. People move more quickly and easily, as do packages, messages, and music, to name a few. It is this fluidity, as well as the structures that expedite and impede its flows, that define globalisation.

Another force in modern society is consumption, the process by which people obtain and utilize various goods and services. While consumption might seem like a good, and even fun, thing, sociologists have also identified some negative aspects of it, including issues with overconsumption, excessive and rising debt, and the increasing likelihood of defining ourselves in relation to what we own rather than to what we do or to our social relationships.

Technology has always been of interest to sociologists. Today, life in the digital world and its linkage to life in the "real world," as well as their associated technologies, have become major topics of study for sociologists. Technology also plays an important role in consumption, particularly with the shift from a highly social shopping experience, such as in a mall with other people, to the more isolated shopping that one does online.

All of these changes are easier to understand if you use what the prominent sociologist C. Wright Mills called the "sociological imagination," which means looking at phenomena not just from a personal perspective but also from a distinctively sociological perspective. Canadian sociologists, in particular, use the sociological imagination to understand the linkages between micro, small-scale phenomena and macro, large-scale social realities. These linkages can also usefully be approached in terms of a continuum from individual agency to structural control over individuals.

In both perspectives, the concept of the "social construction of reality" underscores the interaction between individuals and larger social structures. At the micro level, people create social realities through their thoughts and actions. As these realities spread and become habits that are widely followed, they eventually become much larger, macro phenomena that develop lives of their own. These realities then constrain and encourage individuals' thought and action.

Although many of the topics discussed in this book are things you are familiar with in daily life, that does not mean we should not take a systematic sociological approach to understanding them. Keep in mind that sociological phenomena are all around you, and you should have your own sociological imagination honed and ready as you explore the social world.

KEY TERMS ···

- Agency 25
- Butterfly effect 2
- Consumption 9
- Dangerous giant 25
- Globalisation 8
- Macro 23
- McDonaldization 12
- Mediated interaction 16
- Micro 23

- Public sociology 28
- Social construction of reality 25
- Social processes 27
- Social structure 27
- Society 5
- Sociological imagination 20
- Sociology 3
- Technology 16

THINKING ABOUT SOCIOLOGY ·····································

1. How is the Fukushima Daiichi nuclear disaster in 2011 an example of the butterfly effect? Use your sociological imagination to think of ways that your individual choices and actions influenced and have been influenced by this event.

2. Your social world is continually changing. What are some examples of new technologies that have been developed during your lifetime? How have they changed the way you interact with and relate to others?

3. How do the shopping malls being built in the United Arab Emirates (UAE) reflect increasing globalisation? Do you think these shopping malls lead to a sameness of culture around the world, or do they allow local areas to retain their differences?

4. What items are you most likely to buy using the Internet? How do social networking sites (Facebook.com, Twitter.com, Myspace.com) influence what you consume?

5. Beginning in 2010, WikiLeaks released thousands of confidential documents obtained from government, military, and corporate sources. Is this an example of an information war? Why or why not? What social structures have impeded the flow of this kind of information in the past?

How have the Internet and social networking sites made it easier to get around these structural barriers?

6. According to C. Wright Mills, how are private troubles different from public issues? How can we use the micro-macro distinction to show how private troubles are related to public issues?

7. What is the difference between structure and agency? Within your classroom, could you be a "dangerous giant"? In what ways does your classroom enable you to do things you would not be able to do otherwise?

8. What do sociologists mean by the social construction of reality? How can you apply this perspective to better understand trends in the music industry?

9. How is Eric Schlosser's *Fast Food Nation* an example of public sociology? Can you think of ways in which we can use "pure science" to better understand the fast-food industry? In your opinion, what should be the goal of research?

10. How does sociology approach globalisation differently than other social sciences? In your opinion, what are the advantages of using a sociological approach to understand globalisation?

APPLYING THE SOCIOLOGICAL IMAGINATION

Twitter has emerged as a way to instantaneously share information and keep up to date with what is currently happening. But how can we use Twitter to make sense of the interrelated processes of globalisation and consumption?

For this activity, go to Twitter.com and find the day's top trending topics worldwide. Explore these top trends by clicking on them and looking at the specific tweets. Do research on the Internet for topics mentioned in the tweets that are unfamiliar to you.

In what ways are these topics and tweets reflective of a globalised world? How are these topics and tweets related to goods and services that you consume? In what ways does Twitter facilitate the flow of information and goods globally? How does this influence the decisions and choices that individuals make at the micro level? How do these trends affect your own choices?

ACTIVE SOCIOLOGY

Globalisation is everywhere, from the clothes we wear to the portable electronic devices that shape our everyday existence. In order to recognize the power of globalisation, make a list of the countries represented in the clothes you are wearing, and in the contents of your pockets, backpack, purse, tote, satchel, or any item that transports your personal belongings. For example, you may find your footwear made in Cambodia, your coat made in Honduras, your T-shirt made in Vietnam, and your cell phone batteries made in South Korea. You may even find an item made in Canada! Most people have at least 10 products produced in different countries. While many companies produce products respecting human rights and ethical labour practises, many have a human cost. Clothing, for example, is often made using child or forced labour.

Select one item and track where your global product was produced, and assess whether your product used forced/child labour and ethical labour practises. There are numerous tools to help you be a just consumer.

- Free2Work (http://free2work.org) has a cell phone application that helps consumers grade companies on their labour prastices, reduce their "slavery footprint," and provide information on how to resist all forms of human trafficking as they shop. Swipe a bar code; reduce human trafficking!

- If you discover a "slavery footprint," Change.org (www.change.org) is dedicated to helping people develop and circulate online petitions on a variety of social issues.

STUDENT STUDY SITE

Visit the student study site at **www.sagepub.com/ritzercanadian** for additional web quizzes for further review.

THINKING SOCIOLOGICALLY

2

A sociologist's perspective on any given phenomenon is framed by the particular sociological theories to which he or she ascribes.

C anada is relatively young, as nations go. Perhaps because of this, debate about Canadian identity and our national future remains intense. In 1867 the four provinces of New Brunswick, Nova Scotia, Ontario, and Quebec launched the nation. In rapid succession Manitoba, British Columbia, and Prince Edward Island became partners as well, and in 1905 both Alberta and Saskatchewan joined. Newfoundland and Labrador joined most recently, in 1949. Yet from the outset, the distinctive nature of Quebec has stood out, where language, European ties, and religion help define a relatively unique cultural milieu. Political parties have formed to lead Quebeckers to an independent nation. Simultaneously, federal parties have sought to provide Quebec the latitude, within Canada, to have its own separate identity. At other times Anglophones from across Canada have rallied to support Quebec's distinctive and important contribution to Canada.

How would a sociologist explain such intense, and sustained, political tension? The answer to this question depends entirely on which sociologist you ask.

Like other scientists, sociologists use theories to make sense of the phenomena they study. A sociologist's perspective on any given phenomenon is framed by the particular sociological theories to which he or she ascribes.

Some sociologists might propose that political jockeying is a function of a stable government. Impassioned debate is necessary to the eventual resolution and implementation of a clear path forward. Others might suggest that Quebec sovereignty marked a struggle for power between the leading political factions. Conflict is a systemic product of inequality, and each *faction fights to promote its own interests. Still others might explain the tension as a symbol of the population's growing anxiety and ideological polarisation in a globalising, increasingly Anglicised North America. As the politicians represent their constituents, the politicians' interactions (or lack thereof) represent the dominant ideas, beliefs, and feelings of the Canadian people.*

In this chapter, you will come to identify the particular sociological theories that frame these perspectives—and many more. Each the product of decades (sometimes centuries) of development, these theories have undergone testing, modification, and critique by some of sociology's greatest minds. As you learn about the notable sociological thinkers (both classical and contemporary) and the theories they developed, consider the sociopolitical events that shaped them during their lives. Consider too the events that have shaped you and your own perspectives.

This chapter is devoted to the ways in which sociologists think, or theorise. All sociologists theorise, and while some stay very close to their data, others feel free to depart from the data and offer very broad and general theories—"grand theories"—of the social world (Skinner 1985). Most of this chapter will be devoted to grand theories and to the people who produced them.

Theories are sets of interrelated ideas that have a wide range of application, deal with centrally important issues, and have stood the test of time (Ritzer 2013). Sociological theories are necessary to make sense of the innumerable social phenomena and the many highly detailed findings of sociological research. Without such theories we would have little more than knowledge of isolated bits of the social world. However, once those theories have been created, they can be applied broadly to such areas as the economy, organisations, and religion, as well as society as a whole and even the globe. The theories to be discussed in this chapter deal

with very important social issues that have affected society over decades and will likely continue to affect it, including suicide, alienation, and exploitation in the work world, and revolution.

Consider the theory of violence mentioned briefly in Chapter 1 and being developed by Randall Collins (2009). In line with the definition of theory offered above, violence is clearly an *important social issue*. Collins seeks to develop a *broad theory* of violence that encompasses everything from a slap in the face to war; a quarrel to mass murder in gas chambers; drunken carousing to serial killing; and rape to the public stoning of people to death by the Taliban. Beyond being a very broad social phenomenon, violence usually generates powerful reactions among those who commit it, its victims, and those who witness it or read about it. As Collins (2009) puts it, violence is "horrible and heroic, disgusting and exciting, the most condemned and glorified of human acts" (p. 1). But the details of Collins's theory are not the concern here. Rather, it is the fact that he is seeking to develop a perspective that meets our definition of theory. We will need to see whether Collins's specific theory *stands the test of time*. However, it is clear that violence is an important social phenomenon worth theorising about (and studying), and Collins has taken an important step in developing such a theory.

Theorising about the social world is not restricted to sociologists such as Randall Collins; everyone theorises. What, then, distinguishes the theorising of sociologists from your own? One difference is that while you might theorise very casually, sociologists go about their theorising very systematically. For example, you might notice two people together, and by drawing upon your observations of how those people are interacting (what they are wearing and their nonverbal communication) and your ideas of romantic relationships and behaviours, you may conclude that they're dating. You have a (perhaps unconscious) theory about dating, and you draw upon it to interpret their actions and predict how they might interact next. In contrast, a sociologist might study behaviours among many pairs of people, carefully analyse the similarities and differences among them, compare those behaviours to people in other societies, and then theorise that a particular style of interaction characterises dating couples. At some level, we are all theorists, but professional sociologists draw systematically on scientific data to create and test their theories.

Another difference between you and trained sociologists is that you are pretty much on your own in your theorising, although the material in this book will help. In contrast, not only do sociologists work directly with, and read the work of, other contemporary sociologists, but they also base their theories on the work of many important thinkers in the field who have come before them. As the great physicist Sir Isaac Newton ([1687] 2005) put it: "If I have seen further it is only by standing on the shoulders of giants." Many of today's sociologists theorise because they are able to build on the thoughts of the classical "grand theorists" to be discussed in this chapter. To put it another way, many sociologists have, or can easily acquire, the "intellectual capital" of the discipline, the knowledge of past theories, that would be much more difficult for you as a student to acquire. However, all of today's sociologists were once students like you. This book will begin to give you the intellectual capital you need to start thinking like a sociologist.

CLASSICAL SOCIOLOGICAL THEORY

The roots of sociology lie primarily in early nineteenth-century Europe, although there were much earlier thinkers—Plato and Aristotle in the third and fourth centuries BCE, for example—whose ideas are relevant to sociology. Centuries later, Ibn Khaldun (1332–1406) developed sociological theories that dealt with such issues as the scientific study of society, the interrelationship between politics and the economy, and the relationship between primitive societies and the medieval societies of his time (Alatas 2011). Such topics were also of interest to nineteenth-century theorists and continue to be of interest today.

The emergence of sociological theory was closely related to intellectual and social developments throughout the nineteenth century in Europe. It is important to recognise that sociological theory did not develop in isolation or come of age in a social vacuum. In Chapter 1 we briefly mentioned the impact of the Industrial Revolution.

BIOGRAPHICAL bits

Auguste Comte (1798–1857, French)

- Comte never received a university-level degree, and he had a very marginal position in French academia.

- Nevertheless, his work achieved great notoriety.

- He scheduled what was to be a series of 72 lectures in his apartment, but the lecture series was halted suddenly when he had a nervous breakdown.

- Comte's mental problems led to an unsuccessful attempt at committing suicide by throwing himself into the Seine River.

- Modeling his thinking after Catholicism, Comte believed that his theories would become the new religion of humanity.

- He saw himself as becoming the high priest, the "pope," of that religion and as standing at the pinnacle of a world led by sociologist-priests.

Other changes that profoundly affected sociological theorising were the political revolutions that wracked European society (especially the French Revolution, 1789–1799), the rise of socialism, the women's rights movement, the urbanisation occurring throughout Europe, ferment in the religious realm, and the growth of science.

These are among the most important early sociological theorists:

- *Auguste Comte* is noted, as pointed out in Chapter 1, for invention of the term *sociology*, development of a general theory of the social world, and interest in developing a science of sociology (Pickering 2011).

- *Harriet Martineau*, like Comte, developed a scientific and general theory, although she is best known today for her feminist, women-centered sociology (Hoecker-Drysdale 2011).

BIOGRAPHICAL bits

Harriet Martineau (1802–1876, English)

- As a child, Martineau had to overcome both shyness and deafness, but she, unlike most other women of her day, was well educated.

- She began publishing on women's inequality by the time she was 18 years of age.

- Her family's business failed in 1829, and she decided to earn a living for herself, and her mother, by writing for the general public.

- She wrote poetry, history, and social and political analyses, as well as 1,500 newspaper columns.

- Martineau was also a novelist, and at their height her novels in the series *Illustrations of Political Economy* outsold those written by Charles Dickens.

- In 1853, Martineau undertook the task of translating and condensing Auguste Comte's work, making it accessible to a much broader audience. Comte himself was so impressed with her translation that he recommended it over his own.

- Martineau also traveled widely, and spoke publicly, on issues such as the abolition of slavery and women's rights.

BIOGRAPHICAL bits

Herbert Spencer (1820–1903, English)

- Spencer never earned an academic degree or held an academic position.

- An inheritance in his early thirties allowed him to live the rest of his life as a gentleman scholar.

- By the last third of the nineteenth century, his work made him world famous in many different fields.

- Spencer suffered from many different physical and psychological problems during the course of his life, including insomnia and a series of nervous breakdowns.

- Spencer, like Comte, practised "cerebral hygiene"; that is, he was unwilling to read the work of others and to clutter his mind with ideas other than those that emerged, seemingly magically, from his mind.

- Intellectual isolation hurt his work and reputation. Charles Darwin noted that Spencer's work would have been better if he had trained himself better and read more widely.

- *Herbert Spencer* also developed a general scientific theory of society, but his overriding theoretical interest was in social change, specifically evolution in not only the physical domain but also the intellectual and social domains (Francis 2011).

THE GIANTS OF CLASSICAL SOCIOLOGICAL THEORY

Although Comte, Martineau, and Spencer were important predecessors, the three theorists to be discussed in this section—Karl Marx, Max Weber, and Émile Durkheim—are the most significant of the classical era's social theorists and of the greatest continuing contemporary relevance to sociology (and other fields).

Karl Marx

Marx is often dismissed as an ideologue and, more recently, disparaged because of the failure of a social system—communism—that is generally considered to be his brainchild. In fact, the communism that came to be practised in the Soviet Union and other countries had little relationship to Marx's abstract sense of communism; he would have been as critical of it as he was of capitalism. However, there is an important sociological theory

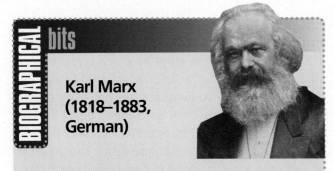

Karl Marx (1818–1883, German)

- Marx received a doctorate in philosophy from the University of Berlin in 1841.

- His early work was for a newspaper, and his articles expressed many of the views that would define his later work—democracy, humanism, and great idealism.

- Over the years, he published more articles and books, and his ideas grew more radical.

- He became involved with the Communist League and published, with Friedrich Engels (1820–1895), *The Communist Manifesto* (1848), which urged the workingmen of the world to unite to overthrow the "chains" imposed on them by capitalism.

- As a result of his radical ideas, Marx was expelled from Germany and France and ended up in London, England, in 1849.

- In 1852, he began his famous studies of working conditions that led to the writing of his major work, *Capital*.

- Although he was the great critic of capitalism, Marx received financial help from a capitalist, specifically, his frequent collaborator Engels, whose income came from a textile factory partially owned by his father.

in Marx's work (Antonio 2011). Its importance is reflected in the fact that many theorists have built on it and that many others have created theories in opposition to Marx's perspective (Sitton 2010).

Marx is mainly a macro theorist who focused most of his attention on the structure of capitalist society, a relatively new phenomenon in his day. Marx defined **capitalism** as an economic system based on the fact that one group of people—the **capitalists**—owns what is needed for production, including factories, machines, and tools. A second

group—the **proletariat**, or workers—owns little or nothing, except for its members' capacity for work and labour. In order to work and survive, the workers must sell their labour time, primarily their working hours, to the capitalists in exchange for wages.

In Marx's view, the capitalist system is marked by **exploitation**. The proletariat produces virtually everything but gets only a small portion of the income derived from the sale of the products. The capitalists, who do little productive work, reap the vast majority of the rewards. In other words, the capitalists exploit the workers. Furthermore, driven by the need to compete in the marketplace, the capitalists are forced to keep costs, including wages, as low as possible. Then, as competition with other capitalists intensifies, the pressure is on to reduce wages further. As a result, the proletariat barely subsists, living a miserable, animal-like existence.

In addition, the workers experience **alienation** on the job and in the workplace (Meszaros 2006). They are alienated because

- the work that they do—for example, repetitively and mechanically inserting wicks into candles or hubcaps on cars—is not a natural expression of human skills, abilities, and creativity;

- they have little or no connection to the finished product; and

- instead of working harmoniously with their fellow workers, they may have little or no contact with them. In fact, they are likely to be in competition or outright conflict with them over, for example, who keeps and who loses their jobs.

Thus, what defines people as human beings—their ability to think, to act on the basis of that thought, to be creative, to interact with other human beings—is denied to the workers in capitalism. As capitalists adopt new technologies to make them more competitive, alienation among the workers increases. For example, faster, more mechanised assembly lines make it even more difficult for coworkers to relate to one another.

From the perspective of Karl Marx, capitalism exploits—even enslaves—the proletariat. Here, Chinese construction workers (whom Marx might call proletariat) push carts under the scorching sun in Chongqing, China.

Over time, Marx believed, the workers' situation would grow much worse as the capitalists ratcheted up the level of exploitation and restructured the work so that the proletariat was even more alienated. The gap between these two social classes would grow wider and increasingly visible in terms of both the two groups' economic position and the nature of their work. Once workers understood how capitalism "really" worked, especially the ways in which it worked to their detriment, they would rise up and overthrow that system in what Marx called a proletarian revolution.

According to Marx, the outcome of the proletarian revolution would be the creation of a communist society. Interestingly, Marx had very little to say explicitly about what a communist society would look like. In fact, he was highly critical of utopian thinkers who wasted their time drawing beautiful portraits of an imaginary future state. Marx was too much the sociologist and concentrated instead on trying to better understand the structures of capitalist society and the ways in which they worked, especially to the advantage of the capitalists and to the disadvantage of the proletariat.

Marx believed that his work was needed because the capitalist class tried hard to make sure that the proletariat did not truly understand the nature of capitalism. One of the ways in which the capitalists did this was to produce a set of ideas, an **ideology**, that distorted the reality of capitalism and concealed the ways in which it really operated. As a result, the proletariat suffered from **false consciousness**—the workers did not truly understand capitalism and may have even believed, erroneously, that the system operated to their benefit. Marx's work was devoted to providing the proletariat with the knowledge that it needed to overcome these false ideas and to achieve a truer understanding of the workings of capitalism.

When the workers truly understood capitalism, Marx hypothesised, they could develop **class consciousness**, meaning that they would truly understand not only capitalism but also their collective role in it and their relationship to one another as well as to the capitalists. Class consciousness was a prerequisite of the revolutionary actions to be undertaken by the proletariat. The capitalists could never achieve class consciousness because, in Marx's view, they were too deeply involved in capitalism ever to see it clearly.

Marx's theories about capitalism are relevant to contemporary society. For example, in Canada, a capitalist country, the gap he predicted between those at the top of the economic system and the rest of the population is huge and growing. In 2013, the richest 20 percent of the population in terms of income had almost as much income as the rest of the population combined. Furthermore, as you can see in Figure 2.1, since 1980 those at the top have secured more of the income for themselves (Fortin et al. 2012; see also Organisation for Economic Co-operation and Development [OECD] 2011). Marx also theorised that capitalism would force the capitalists to find the cheapest sources of labour and resources wherever they exist in the world (Panitch 2009). As Marx predicted, corporations today search the globe for workers willing to work for lower wages, driving down wages closer to home and reaping as much profit as possible from lower labour costs.

However, history has failed to bear out much of Marx's thinking about the demise of capitalism. For example, there has been no proletarian revolution, and one seems less likely than ever. This is the case, if for no other reason, because the kind

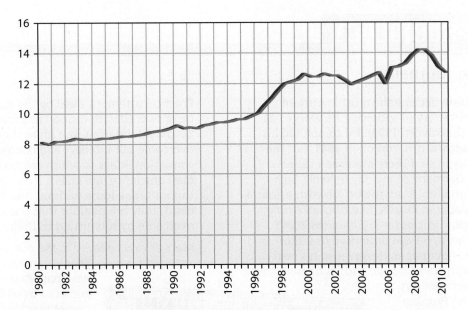

FIGURE 2.1 The Growing Share of Income (in %) Collected by the Richest 1 Percent of Canadians

SOURCE: Adapted from Fortin et al. (2012) and OECD (2011).

of proletariat of greatest interest to Marx—manufacturing workers—is rapidly declining in number and importance, at least in developed countries such as Canada and the United States (Rifkin 1995). Despite these threats to the proletariat, capitalism continues to exist, and Marx's ways of thinking about it, and the concepts he developed for that analysis, continue to be useful.

Max Weber

Although Karl Marx was a very important social theorist, he developed his ideas outside of the academic world, and it took time for those radical ideas to gain recognition from scholars. In contrast, Max Weber (pronounced VAY-ber) was a leading academician of his day (Kalberg 2011). Weber, like Marx, devoted great attention to the economy. Many of Marx's ideas informed Weber's thinking, if for no other reason than because Marx's ideas were finding a wide public audience at the time that Weber was active. Furthermore, Weber understood the dramatic changes, inspired at least in part by Marx's ideas, taking place in Europe and elsewhere. After all, Weber lived during, and analysed, the Russian Revolution in 1917 and the rise of communism there. Nevertheless, Weber rarely discussed Marx's theories explicitly. Thus, observers have characterised much of Weber's work as a debate with Marx's "ghost."

Weber's best known work is *The Protestant Ethic and the Spirit of Capitalism* ([1904–1905] 1958), which is a part of his historical-comparative study of religion in various societies throughout the world (see Chapter 3). One of the main objectives in this work was to analyse the relationship between the economy and religion. This is a good example of Weber's debate with Marx. Like Marx, Weber accepted the central importance of the economy in general, and of capitalism in particular, but he wanted to demonstrate the importance of other sociological variables. Marx had argued that religion was a relatively minor force that serves to distract the masses from the problems caused by capitalism. In Marx's ([1843] 1970) famous words, religion "is the opium of the people." In contrast, Weber focused on the central role that religion had played in the western world's economic development.

According to Weber, it was Protestantism in general, and especially Calvinism beginning in the seventeenth century, that led to the rise of capitalism in the West and not in other areas of the world. Calvinists believed that they were predestined to go to heaven or hell; that is, they would end up in heaven or hell no matter what they did or did not do. While they could not affect their destiny, they could uncover "signs" that indicated

PUBLIC SOCIOLOGY

Karl Marx, Journalist

Before Karl Marx became the most important theorist in the history of sociology, he worked as a journalist (Chakravorti 1993). He completed his rather dull doctoral dissertation in 1841, but the critical ideas expressed there made an academic career in the Germany of the day unlikely. So he turned to journalism. Marx took a job with a liberal-radical newspaper in Prussia, *Rheinische Zeitung*, and wrote many articles for it (Callinicos 2004). Within 10 months, he was promoted to editor-in-chief of the newspaper. However, in his own articles, Marx criticised Russia, and, as a result, the Russian government put pressure on the Prussian government to have him fired. Marx resigned before the newspaper closed its doors. Marx continued to work part-time in a number of journalistic positions, although he was expelled from several countries, such as France, for his radical ideas (P. Singer 1996).

Marx's early newspaper articles reflected a number of positions that he would try to disseminate to the public throughout his life. Among other things, Marx expressed his belief in democracy, humanism, and idealism (Blumenberg 2008). He was opposed to purely abstract thinking; ideas had to relate to the real world and its problems. He was also opposed to naïve speculation about a utopian future that was highly unlikely to ever come into being. Instead he focused on the here and now and on bringing about the overthrow of the capitalist system that had come to prominence throughout Russia and much of the western world. Finally, Marx rejected the views of activists who believed that the time was not right for revolution. In fact, he wanted to get on with the business of overthrowing the capitalist system. In one article, Marx ([1842] 1977) outlined the basis for his life's work:

Practical attempts, even by the masses, can be answered with cannon as soon as they become dangerous, but ideas that have overcome our intellect and conquered our conviction, ideas to which reason has riveted our conscience, are chains from which one cannot break loose without breaking one's heart; they are demons that one can only overcome by submitting to them. (p. 20)

Marx always believed in the power of ideas, and he expressed his own ideas in various ways. Writing newspaper articles was soon replaced by writing books, sometimes long and dense tracts. Although his works were often highly complex and theoretically rich, Marx never lost sight of the fact that he was in the business of creating ideas that would help the workers see and understand and rebel against the nature of the capitalist system that was oppressing them.

Marx served as the London correspondent for the *New York Tribune* from 1851 to 1862 (Elster 1999). He was a regular contributor to the newspaper and published close to 500 articles in it (although many of them may have been written with, or by, others, especially his longtime collaborator, Friedrich Engels). The meagre income earned from this work helped Marx survive during the period in which he researched and published much of his life's work on capitalism. However, he lost the *Tribune* job, in part because the founder, Horace Greeley, had come to dislike his work and in part because the American Civil War had come to dominate space in the newspaper. The loss of the *Tribune* job was a severe economic blow to Marx, and it marked the end of his career as a journalist—but not his desire to spread his social theories to a public audience.

Karl Marx served as the London correspondent for the *New York Tribune* newspaper from 1851 to 1862.

Max Weber (1864–1920, German)

- As a child, Weber was torn between the lifestyle and ideas of his father—a rational, practical, earthy bureaucrat—and those of his ascetic and highly religious mother. These topics—rational organisations and religion—became central concerns in his life's work.

- He received a PhD from the University of Berlin, and while his initial focus was the law, he later turned to other concerns— economics, history, and sociology.

- He was enormously productive, earning a professorship at the University of Heidelberg in 1896, at the age of 32.

- In 1897, Weber suffered a nervous breakdown precipitated by a fight with his father and his father's death soon after; Weber produced no work between 1897 and 1903.

- Weber produced most of his best known work after he emerged from his nervous breakdown. *The Protestant Ethic and the Spirit of Capitalism,* for example, was published in 1904–1905.

As the title of his book makes clear, Weber was interested not solely in the Protestant ethic but also in what it helped spawn—the "spirit of capitalism." The Protestant ethic was a system of ideas closely associated with religion, while the spirit of capitalism involved a transformation of those ideas into a perspective linked directly to the economy rather than religion. As the economy came to be infused with the spirit of capitalism, it became a capitalist economic system. Eventually, however, the spirit of capitalism, and later capitalism itself, grew apart from its roots in Calvinism and the Protestant ethic. Capitalist thinking eventually could not accommodate such irrational forms of thought as ethics and religion.

Despite his analyses of capitalism, Weber was not interested in capitalism per se. He was more interested in the broader phenomenon of **rationalisation**, or the process by which social structures are increasingly characterised by the most direct and efficient means to their ends. To Weber, this process was becoming more and more common in many sectors of society, including in the economy, especially in the most rational of economic systems—capitalism. Capitalism is rational because, for example, of its continuous efforts to

John Calvin, the theologian for whom Calvinism is named, played an influential role in the Protestant Reformation. First published in 1536, Calvin's seminal *Institutes of the Christian Religion* is still read today.

whether or not they were "saved" and going to heaven. A particularly important sign was economic success; achieving economic success was an indication that one was going to heaven. Single successful economic acts were not sufficient; Calvinists had to devote their lives to economic success and to other "good works." At the same time, the Calvinists believed in hard work and were quite frugal. This was the distinctive ethical system of the Calvinists, and more generally Protestants, that Weber referred to as the **Protestant ethic**.

find ways to produce efficiently more profitable products with fewer inputs and simpler processes. A specific and early example of rationalisation in capitalism is the assembly line, in which raw materials entered the line and emerged as finished products. Fewer workers performed very simple tasks in order to allow the assembly line to function efficiently. More recently, manufacturers turned to the just-in-time inventory system. Instead of storing components just in case they are needed, the just-in-time system relies on the delivery of materials when they are needed in the production process and makes highly efficient use of storage space and the funds needed to purchase materials.

Weber's work gives a clear sense of his opinion of rationalisation; he referred to it as creating an "iron cage." Consider his language regarding the cage-like character of capitalism:

> Capitalism is today an immense cosmos into which the individual is born, and which presents itself to him, at least as an individual, as an unalterable order of things in which he must live. It forces the individual, in so far as he is involved in the system of market relationships, to conform to capitalist rules of action. (Weber [1904–1905] 1958:54)

This negative view of rationalisation and its socially harmful effects has persisted and is frequently portrayed in popular entertainments, including *1984* (a book by George Orwell and a 1956 movie) and the movies *Brazil* (1985) and *V for Vendetta* (2006).

In sum, while for Marx the key problems in the modern world are the exploitation and alienation that are part of the capitalist economy, for Weber the central problem is the control that rationalised structures such as capitalism exercise over us in virtually all aspects of our lives. Furthermore, while Marx was optimistic and had great hope for socialism and communism, Weber was a pessimist about most things. Socialism and communism, he felt, would not eliminate or prevent the iron cage from enveloping us: "Not summer's bloom lies ahead of us, but rather a polar night of icy darkness and hardness, no matter which group may triumph externally now" (cited in Gerth and Mills 1958:128).

The character V, portrayed by Hugo Weaving in the 2006 film *V for Vendetta*, espoused a negative view of rationalisation.

Émile Durkheim

Émile Durkheim was a contemporary of Weber, and his lifetime overlapped to some degree with that of Marx, but he developed a very different theoretical orientation (Milibrandt and Pearce 2011). While Marx, Weber, and Durkheim can all be said to have focused on the macro end of the social continuum, Marx and Weber were both critical of the macro structures of prime concern to them—capitalism for Marx and rationalised structures for Weber. In contrast, Durkheim generally had a positive view of such structures.

In Durkheim's view, the major concern of the science of sociology is **social facts**, or macro-level phenomena, such as social structures and cultural norms and values, that stand apart from people and, more importantly, impose themselves

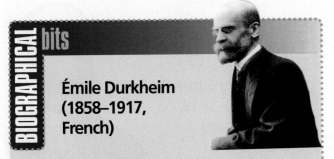

Émile Durkheim (1858–1917, French)

- Durkheim came from a family of rabbis and had studied to be a rabbi.

- He later disavowed his heritage, although the study of religion from a sociological perspective became a lifelong interest.

- He wanted sociology to be a science, and after he obtained a position at the University of Bordeaux in 1897, he taught the first course in social science.

- He also taught courses to schoolteachers and was interested throughout his life in teaching them the sociology of morality so that they could pass a moral system on to young people.

- Durkheim saw suicide as a moral sickness, and his concern for it helped lead in 1897 to his most famous book, *Suicide*.

- Although he was not a practising Jew, Durkheim was a leading public figure in defense of Alfred Dreyfus, the Jewish army captain who was a victim of anti-Semitism, which Durkheim saw, like suicide, as a moral sickness.

on people. Examples of social facts that impose themselves on you include the structure of your university and the Canadian government. They are Durkheimian social facts since they have an independent existence and are able to force people to do things. Durkheim felt that such structures and their constraints were not only necessary but highly desirable.

The differences among Marx, Weber, and Durkheim can be traced to the theorists' sense of the essential character of human beings. Both Marx and Weber had a generally positive sense of people as thoughtful, creative, and naturally social. They criticised social structures for stifling and distorting people's innate characteristics. In contrast, Durkheim had a largely negative view of people as being slaves

to their passions, such as lust, gluttony, and other deadly sins. Left to their own devices, he believed, people would seek to satisfy those passions. However, the satisfaction of one passion would simply lead to the need to satisfy other passions, and this endless succession of passions could never be satisfied. In Durkheim's view, these passions should be limited, but people are unable to exercise this control themselves. They need social facts that are capable of limiting and controlling their passions.

The most important of these social facts is the **collective consciousness**, or the set of beliefs shared by people throughout society. In Durkheim's view, the collective consciousness is a good thing; it is highly desirable not only for society but also for individuals. For example, it is good for us that we share the belief that we are not supposed to kill one another. Without a collective consciousness, murderous passions would be left to run wild. Individuals would be destroyed, of course, and so would society.

This leads us to one of the most famous research studies in the history of sociology, which Durkheim reported in *Suicide* ([1897] 1951). As a sociologist, Durkheim focused not on why any given individual committed suicide but rather on a more collective issue—suicide rates—and why one group of people had a higher rate of suicide than another. It was in many ways an ideal example of the power of sociological research. Using publicly available data, Durkheim found, for example, that suicide rates were not related to psychological and biological factors such as alcoholism or race and heredity. The cause of differences in suicide rates was not to be found within individuals. Rather, suicide rates were related to social factors that exert pressure on the individual, such as collective feelings of rootlessness and normlessness. Suicide literally destroys individuals but also constitutes a threat to society, since those who commit suicide are rejecting a key aspect of the collective consciousness—one should not kill oneself.

Suicide has at least two important characteristics. First, it was designed, like much sociological research today, to contribute to the public understanding of an important sociological problem or issue. Second, and more importantly for the purposes of this introduction to sociology, it demonstrated the power of sociology to explain one of the most private and personal of acts. Durkheim believed that if sociology could be shown to deal with suicide—which had previously been seen as the province of the field of psychology and placed responsibility most often on the individual—it could be shown to deal with any and all social phenomena.

Durkheim differentiated among four different types of suicide. The most important one for our purposes is *anomic suicide*. This relates to one of Durkheim's most famous ideas—**anomie**, or people's feeling that they do not know what is expected of them in society, the feeling of being adrift in society without any clear or secure moorings. The risk of anomic suicide increases when people do not know what is expected of them, when society's regulation over them is low, when their passions are allowed to run wild.

More generally, Durkheim believed that anomie was the defining problem of the modern world. In contrast to Marx and Weber, who worried about too much external control over people, Durkheim, at least in his thinking on anomie, worried about too little control. This broad view appeared in another famous Durkheim work, *The Division of Labor in Society* ([1893] 1964). He begins with an early form of society with little division of labour, in which people are held together by a type of solidarity—**mechanical solidarity**—stemming from the fact that they all do pretty much the same kinds of work, including hunting, gathering, and cooking. More importantly, people in this type of society have a strong collective consciousness.

However, Durkheim depicted a change over time in the direction of an increasing division of labour. Instead of everyone doing the same sorts of things, people tended to start specialising—some were hunters, others farmers, still others cooks—and what held them together was not their similarities but their differences. That is, they had become more dependent on one another; people needed what others did and produced in order to survive. Durkheim called this more recent form of social organisation **organic solidarity**. This can be a powerful form of solidarity, but it is accompanied by a decline in the power of the collective conscience. Since people were doing such different things, they no longer necessarily believed as strongly in the same set of ideas. This weakened collective conscience was a problem, Durkheim

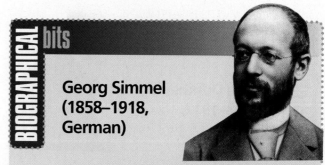

BIOGRAPHICAL bits

Georg Simmel (1858–1918, German)

- Simmel was born in the center of Berlin, received a PhD from the University of Berlin, and lived most of his life in that city.

- His urban roots led to a lifelong interest in the sociological study of the city and its effects on people.

- Simmel did not hold a regular academic post until near the end of his life, in part because he was a Jew in the highly anti-Semitic Germany of the day.

- He was always a marginal figure in German academia, but he succeeded as an unpaid lecturer (earning money only at the whim of students) because he was a fascinating lecturer.

- Simmel's skill as a lecturer carried over to his many interesting sociological essays and public lectures.

- He finally succeeded in obtaining an academic position at a minor university in 1914, but World War I intervened, his students went off to war, and the lecture halls were turned into military hospitals.

argued, because it progressively lost the power to control people's passions. Further, because of the weakened collective consciousness, people were more likely to feel anomic and, among other things, were more likely to commit anomic suicide.

OTHER IMPORTANT EARLY THEORISTS

Although Marx, Weber, and Durkheim are the classical sociologists whose theories have most shaped contemporary sociology, several others made important contributions as well. Georg Simmel, W. E. B. Du Bois, and Thorstein Veblen all had grand theories of society, and you will see references to their ideas throughout the book.

Georg Simmel

Georg Simmel, whose economic theories were mentioned in Chapter 1, offered an important grand theory that parallels those of the thinkers discussed above, but his major importance in contemporary sociology lies in his contributions to micro theory. Simmel believed that sociologists should focus on the way conscious individuals interact and associate with one another (Scaff 2011).

Simmel was interested in the *forms* taken by social interaction. One such form involves the interaction between superiors and subordinates. An example would be the interaction between the manager at Whole Foods or No Frills and those who stock the shelves at that supermarket. Simmel was also interested in the *types* of people who engage in interaction. For example, one type is the poor person, and another is the rich person. To Simmel, it is the nature of the interaction between these two types and not the nature of each that is of greatest importance. Therefore, poverty is not about the nature of the poor person but about the kind of interaction between poor and rich. A poor person is defined, then, not as someone who lacks money but rather as someone who gets aid from a rich person.

There is great detail in Simmel's analyses of forms of interaction and types of interactants, as there is in his larger macro theory. But for our purposes here, the main point is that Simmel was important to the micro-interactionist theories to be discussed in this chapter and at other points in this book.

W. E. B. Du Bois

Just as Harriet Martineau was a pioneer in bringing gender to the forefront in sociology, W. E. B. Du Bois was crucial to the later focus of sociology on race. While Du Bois lived long into the modern era, his most important theoretical work was completed in the early twentieth century (P. Taylor 2011).

Du Bois is best known in sociology for his theoretical ideas but was, like Durkheim and Weber, a pioneer researcher. In his 1899 book, *The Philadelphia Negro*, Du Bois reported on his studies of the residents of the seventh ward in Philadelphia, using a variety of social scientific methods, including field research, observation, and interviews.

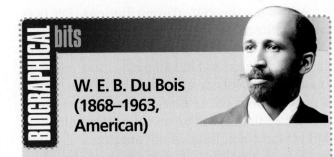

BIOGRAPHICAL bits

W. E. B. Du Bois (1868–1963, American)

- Du Bois had a comparatively advantaged upbringing, especially for a black man at the time.

- He went to Fisk University, studied at the University of Berlin, and got a PhD from Harvard.

- In 1896, he held only a temporary appointment as Assistant Instructor at the University of Pennsylvania, but he nevertheless was able to do the research there that led to an early (1899) classic study, *The Philadelphia Negro*.

- Du Bois taught sociology at Atlanta University from 1897 to 1910 and published many important research reports and books on Negro life in America.

- He was involved in the formation of the National Association for the Advancement of Colored People (NAACP), became its Director of Publications and Research, and founded its magazine, *Crisis*.

- Toward the end of his life, Du Bois developed more radical ideas. He eventually joined the Communist Party, gave up hope for racial equality in the United States, and moved to the African nation of Ghana. He died in Ghana on the day before the famous August 28, 1963, March on Washington highlighted by Martin Luther King Jr.'s "I Have a Dream" speech.

He dealt with such topics as the demographic characteristics of the residents and their situation in relation to such basic topics in sociology as marriage and the family, education, work, the church, housing, and politics. In addition, he dealt with such social problems as illiteracy and crime. Du Bois placed most of the blame for the problems experienced by black Philadelphians on whites, racism, and discrimination. However, he did not ignore the role played by African Americans in these problems. One example was their tendency to visit white physicians, thereby adversely affecting the livelihood of black physicians.

As for his theoretical contributions, Du Bois saw what he called the *race idea* as central. He saw a "color line" existing between whites and blacks in the United States, and he ultimately came to recognise that such a divide existed globally. This barrier was physical in the sense that African Americans could be distinguished visually, through their darker skin color, from white Americans. The barrier was also political in that much of the white population did not see African Americans as "true" Americans and thus denied them many political rights, such as the right to vote. And the barrier was psychological because, among other things, African Americans found it difficult to see themselves except as white society saw them.

One of Du Bois's goals, especially in *The Souls of Black Folk* (1903), was to lift the veil of race and give whites a glimpse of "Negroes" in America. He also wanted to show blacks that they could see themselves in a different way, especially outside the view that white society had prescribed for them. Politically, he hoped for the day when the veil would be lifted forever, thereby freeing blacks. However, he did understand that destroying the veil of race would require a great deal of time and effort.

Another of Du Bois's important ideas is **double-consciousness**. By this he means that black Americans have a sense of "two-ness," of being American and being African American. Black Americans want to tear down the barriers that confront them but do not want to give up their identity, traditions, knowledge, and experience. That is, black Americans are both inside and outside of dominant, white American society. Double-consciousness results in a sense among black Americans that they are characterised by "two souls, two thoughts, two unreconciled strivings; two warring ideals" (Du Bois [1903] 1966:5). Shelley Stigter (2005) has explored this among First Nations peoples.

Double-consciousness obviously produces great tension for black Americans, much greater than the tensions felt by white Americans in regard to their race. However, it also gives black Americans unusual insights into themselves, white Americans, and American society in general. Du Bois urged black Americans to reach full maturity as a social group by reconciling and integrating these two conflicting aspects of their selves.

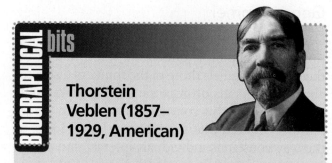

BIOGRAPHICAL bits

Thorstein Veblen (1857–1929, American)

- Veblen was raised poor on a farm in Wisconsin but eventually earned a PhD from Yale, in 1884.

- His poor background, lack of polish, and agnosticism regarding religion inhibited his academic career.

- As a Fellow at the University of Chicago, he began to publish scholarly work, most notably *The Theory of the Leisure Class,* in 1899.

- Veblen managed to obtain an assistant professorship at Chicago, but his career there was doomed, in part because he was a horrendous teacher who spoke in a monotone and had little of interest to say to his students; they dropped his courses in droves.

- Womanising helped cost him his position at the University of Chicago and a later position at Stanford University.

- Veblen died alone and impoverished (one of his former students sent him money each year) in a shack in Northern California.

Thorstein Veblen

Like many of the other figures discussed here, Thorstein Veblen had a broader theory (McCormick 2011), but given our focus in this book on consumption, we will discuss only the ideas associated with his most famous book, *The Theory of the Leisure Class* (Veblen [1899] 1994). One of Veblen's main concerns was the ways in which the upper classes show off their wealth.

One way to show off wealth is through *conspicuous leisure*, or doing things that demonstrate quite publicly that one does not need to do what most people consider to be work. Veblen believed that the wealthy want to demonstrate to all that they can afford to waste time, often a great deal of time. Sitting on one's porch sipping margaritas, perhaps in "Margaritaville," having workers tend to one's lawn, or frequently playing golf at expensive golf clubs would be examples of conspicuous leisure. However, the problem with conspicuous leisure is that it is often difficult for very many others to see these displays.

Thus, over time, the focus shifts for the wealthy from publicly demonstrating a waste of time to publicly demonstrating a waste of money; compare this set of values to the frugality of the Calvinists studied by Weber. The waste of money is central to Veblen's most famous idea, **conspicuous consumption**. It is much easier for others to see conspicuous consumption than to see conspicuous leisure. Examples include owning a 10,000-square-foot McMansion, driving around one's neighbourhood in a Porsche, and wearing expensive Dolce & Gabbana clothing with the D&G logo visible to all. The well-to-do, Veblen's *leisure class*, stand at the top of a society's social class system. Many in the social classes below the wealthy, the middle and lower classes, copy the *leisure class*. For example, people in lower social classes might buy cheap knockoffs of D&G clothing.

Veblen is important for focusing on consumption at a time when it was largely ignored by other social theorists. Furthermore, his specific ideas, especially conspicuous consumption, continue to be applied to the social world today. You can surely picture in your mind many examples of conspicuous consumption. Consider the brand names on your clothing, cell phone, and laptop, for instance. Are they the expensive brands with visible logos and high status, or are they the less expensive, no-name brands that bring with them little or no status?

CONTEMPORARY SOCIOLOGICAL THEORY

As sociology has developed and grown as a discipline, the grand theories of earlier sociologists have evolved and branched out into at least a dozen newer theories. The work of the classical theorists has influenced each of these theories. For example, Marx's thinking on the relationship between capitalists and the proletariat strongly affected conflict/critical theory, and Simmel's micro-sociological ideas on forms and types of interaction helped shape inter/actionist theories. As Figure 2.2 shows, these contemporary theories and the others reviewed in the rest of this chapter can be categorised under

Luxury boutiques, stretch limousines, and other accoutrements of conspicuous consumption have become common among China's moneyed class. Here, shoppers make purchases at a Shanghai Burberry store.

three broad headings: structural/functional, conflict/critical, and inter/actionist theories.

STRUCTURAL/FUNCTIONAL THEORIES

Structural/functional theories have evolved out of the observation and analysis of large-scale social phenomena. These phenomena include, for example, the state and the culture, the latter encompassing the ideas and objects that allow people to carry out their collective lives (see Chapter 4 for more on culture). The two major theories under the broad heading of structural/functional theories are *structural-functionalism*, which looks at both social structures and their functions, and *structuralism*, which concerns itself solely with social structures, without concern for their functions. Note that while they sound the same, structural-functionalism is one theory under the broader heading of structural/functional theories.

Structural-Functionalism

As the name suggests, **structural-functionalism** focuses on social structures as well as the

Structural/Functional Theories	Conflict/Critical Theories	Inter/actionist Theories
Structural-functionalism	Conflict theory	Symbolic interactionism
Structuralism	Critical theory	Ethnomethodology
	Feminist theory	Exchange theory
	Queer theory	Rational choice theory
	Critical theories of race and racism	
	Postmodern theory	

FIGURE 2.2 Major Sociological Theories

functions that such structures perform. Structural-functionalists were influenced by the work of Émile Durkheim, who discussed, for example, the functions of and structural limits placed on deviance. Structural-functional theorists start out with a positive view of social structures—in the case of deviance (see Chapter 7), those structures might include the military, the police, and the Canadian Security Intelligence Service—asserting that they are desirable, necessary, and even impossible to do without. However, as you will see later, not all sociologists view social structures as completely positive.

Structural-functionalism tends to be a "conservative" theory. The dominant view is that if certain structures exist and are functional—and it is often assumed that if they exist, they are functional—they ought to be retained and conserved.

A series of well-known and useful concepts was developed by structural-functionalists, especially Robert Merton ([1949] 1968). These concepts are easily explained in the context of one of this book's signature concerns, globalisation—specifically the issue of border controls such as passports (Torpey 2012), customs charges such as tariffs, and even the physical barriers, such as the wall between the United States and Mexico.

One central concept in Merton's version of structural-functionalism is **functions**, or the observable, positive consequences of a structure that help

it survive, adapt, and adjust. National borders are functional in various ways. For example, the passport controls at borders allow a country to monitor who is entering the country and to refuse entry to those it considers undesirable or dangerous. This function has become increasingly important in the era of global terrorism. Some of the individuals who perpetrated the 9/11 attacks on the United States entered the country by passing without notice through passport controls. Obviously, those controls were deficient. Now, however, more stringent passport and border controls serve the function of keeping out other potential foreign terrorists.

Structural-functionalism is greatly enriched when we add the concept of **dysfunctions**, which are observable consequences that negatively affect the ability of a given system to survive, adapt, or adjust. While border and passport controls clearly have functions, they also have dysfunctions. For example, after 9/11, the U.S. Congress passed at least 19 immigration-related acts (as compared to 5 new comprehensive acts in the preceding 15 years), and as a result it has become much more difficult for everyone to enter the United States (Kurzban 2006). This is true not only for potential terrorists but also for legitimate workers and businesspeople.

Television series *NCIS*—like *Law & Order*, *Criminal Minds*, and others—assumes a structural-functionalist perspective on society, as it depicts social structures such as the police and judiciary as positive elements of society.

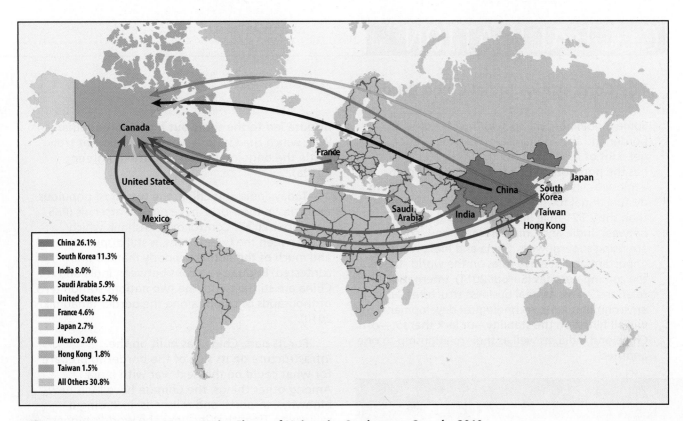

GLOBAL FLOW MAP 2.1 Major Flows of University Students to Canada, 2010

SOURCE: Adapted from Project Atlas, Atlas of Student Mobility. Institute of International Education, Inc.

Before September 11, 2001, 195,000 H-1B visas were being granted each year (*Vermont Bar Journal* 2005. These visas allow foreigners with special job skills to take jobs in the United States. In 2004, however, the quota dropped to 65,000. As a result, many talented people from other countries have decided to take their skills and their business elsewhere in the world, where there are fewer restrictions on their ability to come and go.

Students interested in enrolling at Canadian universities are another group experiencing the dysfunctions of border and passport controls. Students from abroad require a study permit to enter Canada, but, increasingly, Canadian Foreign Affairs have been closing embassies and consulates. One consequence of this has been to make it harder for international students to obtain the entrance paperwork they need to study in Canada. Many international students have decided therefore to study at universities in more welcoming countries, taking their talent, their valuable perspectives, and their tuition money with them. Global Flow Map 2.1 shows current flows of international students to Canada.

The fact that there are both functions and dysfunctions associated with structures raises the issue of the relative weight of the functions and the dysfunctions. How can we determine whether a given structure is predominantly functional or dysfunctional? In terms of the tightening of border controls, we would need to weigh the benefits of keeping out potential terrorists against the losses in international business transactions and university enrolment by overseas students. Such weightings are never easy.

Merton further elaborated on his basic theory by differentiating between two types of functions. The first is **manifest functions**, or positive consequences that are brought about consciously and purposefully. For example, taxes (tariffs) are imposed on goods imported into Canada from elsewhere in the world in order to make their prices higher compared with Canadian-made goods and to protect Canadian-based producers. That is a manifest function of tariffs. However, such actions often have **latent functions**, or unintended positive consequences. For example, when foreign products become more expensive and therefore

GL🌐BALISATION

The Contentious India–China Border

Some global borders, such as the Mexico–U.S. border and the Afghanistan–Pakistan border, get a lot of media attention. But no border has the potential to be more unstable or more explosive—in structural-functionalist terms, more dysfunctional for the global political structure—than the 2,521-mile (4,057-kilometre) border between India and China. Because both countries are rising superpowers, China and India will play important and decisive roles on the world stage in the coming decades (Suroor 2011). International relations, transnational business structures, and environmental and technological development will all hinge on the stability—or lack thereof—of China and India, as well as their relationship to one another.

A delegation of the Indian army (right) marches to meet a delegation of the Chinese army on the Chinese side of the India-China border to discuss peace and tranquillity along the border. A heap of stones signifies the border between the two countries.

Antagonism over the land between China and India stretches back to the 1841 Sino-Sikh War, in which premodern Indian forces invaded western Tibet (Lal 2008). Though the Chinese and Sikhs signed a treaty, the stage was set for further conflict. When in 1959 the Dalai Lama and thousands of his followers sought refuge from the Chinese government in India, China accused India of imperialism and seized almost 65,000 square miles (almost 105,000 square kilometers) of Indian land. Three years later, a major border

dispute led to the short but bloody Sino-Indian War, which the Chinese won, but it did not truly settle the ongoing border dispute (Polgreen 2010a).

Today, India and China, the two most populous countries in the world, have nuclear arsenals (PBS NewsHour 2006). Control over Kashmir, which lies between the two nations, is still disputed, and much of the border is poorly marked and contested. Because relations between India and China are still so tense, the two nations station tens of thousands of troops along the border (Bhaumik 2010).

For its part, China has built up the infrastructure on its side of the border to prepare for what could be the next war with India. Among other things, the Chinese have built new highways, airports, and railroads, including a railway to Tibet that includes the world's highest tunnel, at 16,000 feet (4,877 kilometres), so the road can be used throughout the year (Polgreen 2010a).

India has not developed its own infrastructure to a degree that even remotely rivals that of China's (Malik 2011). Part of the reason for the disparity is that China has a much stronger economy and is able to afford the high costs involved. China also has a larger middle class than India and already functions as a market for exports from other parts of the world (Nayyer 2010). In 2010, China's gross domestic product (GDP) ranked second in the world; by contrast, India's ranked tenth (International Monetary Fund 2011). China has also invested more than India in improving living standards (A. Sen 2011). See Figure 2.3 comparing the two countries on several economic and social measures.

Beyond feeling constrained by its economy, India fears that an invading Chinese army could use India's own infrastructure to penetrate deeply into the Indian subcontinent. India has traditionally relied on the rugged mountainous area between the two countries to protect itself. Nevertheless, India has recently begun bolstering its border infrastructure (Bhaumik 2010). A major step in this direction was the construction of a 5-mile (8-kilometre) tunnel through the Pir Panjal

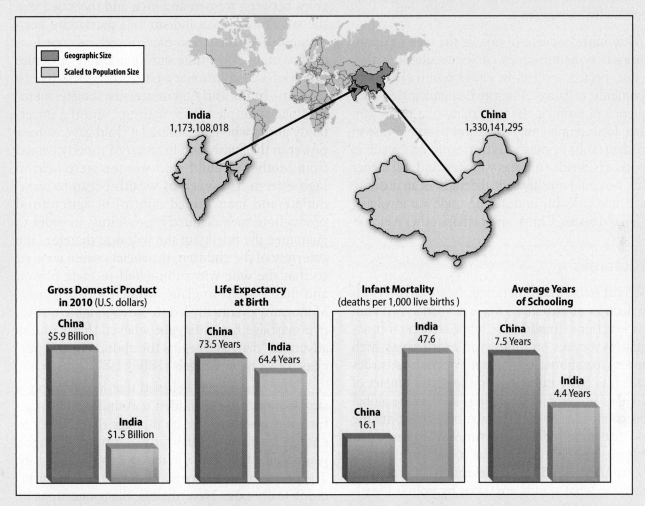

Geographic Size

Scaled to Population Size

India
1,173,108,018

China
1,330,141,295

Gross Domestic Product in 2010 (U.S. dollars)

China
$5.9 Billion

India
$1.5 Billion

Life Expectancy at Birth

China
73.5 Years

India
64.4 Years

Infant Mortality
(deaths per 1,000 live births)

India
47.6

China
16.1

Average Years of Schooling

China
7.5 Years

India
4.4 Years

FIGURE 2.3 An Economic and Social Comparison of China and India

SOURCE: Based on Geographic and population sizes from U.S. Census Bureau; Infant mortality estimates from World Factbook; GDP data from International Monetary Fund, "WEO Data: April 2011 Edition"; and other data from Amartya Sen, "Quality of Life: India vs. China," *New York Review of Books*, May 12, 2011.

mountain range, part of the Himalayas (Munford 2010). In the past, India has had to rely on the highly dangerous Rohtang Pass to move troops and supplies into contested areas. The name of this pass translates to "pile of corpses" because of the many people who have died attempting to make their way across it (Polgreen 2010a). Making matters worse for the Indian troops stationed on the other side of the pass—in the disputed territories—is the fact that the Rohtang Pass is snow-covered for six months of the year.

Construction began on the new tunnel in 2010 and is scheduled to take five years to complete. When it is complete, it will greatly improve the ability to resupply Indian troops in the disputed territories. However, in the case of war, the unintended consequence could be that hundreds of thousands of invading Chinese troops could march right through the pass and into India. India might then be tempted to use its nuclear weapons, which could lead to nuclear retaliation by China and an all-out nuclear war.

less desirable, Canadian manufacturers may produce more and perhaps better goods in Canada, as well as more jobs for Canadians. Note that in these examples, both manifest and latent functions are positive, like all functions within the structural-functionalist perspective.

One more concept of note is the idea of **unanticipated consequences**, or consequences that are unexpected and can be either positive or, more importantly, negative. A negative unanticipated consequence of tariffs is the possibility of a trade war. China, for example, might respond to an increase in Canadian tariffs by raising its own tariffs on Canadian imports. If Canada retaliates with new and still higher tariffs, we could quickly be in the midst of an unanticipated, and probably undesirable, trade war involving the United States, China, and perhaps other nations.

Structuralism

A second structural/functional theory, **structuralism**, focuses on structures but is not concerned with their functions. In addition, while structural-functionalism focuses on quite visible structures such as fences, passports, and customs operations, structuralism is more interested in the social impact of hidden or underlying structures, such as the global economic order or gender relations. It adopts the view that these hidden structures determine what transpires on the surface of the social world. Thus, for example, behind-the-scenes actions of capitalists determine what stands are taken by political leaders. This perspective comes from the field of linguistics, which has largely adopted the view that the surface, the way we speak and express ourselves, is determined by an underlying grammatical system (Saussure [1916] 1966).

Marx can be seen as a structuralist because he was interested in the hidden structures that really determine how capitalism works. So, for example, on the surface capitalism seems to operate to the benefit of all, but in fact hidden below the surface is a structure that operates mostly for the benefit of the capitalists, who exploit the workers and pay them subsistence wages. The capitalists argue that the value of products is determined by supply and demand in the market, but Marx argued that hidden beneath the surface is the fact that value comes

from the labour that goes into the products and this labour comes entirely from the workers.

Similarly, Marx's frequent collaborator, Friedrich Engels ([1884] 1970), looked at relationships between women and men and theorised that the structures of capitalism and patriarchy keep women subordinated to men. Engels assumed, as most writers of his time did, that family structure followed an evolutionary path from primitive to modern. In the early communistic society, members had multiple sexual pairings, and the uncertainty about who had fathered a child gave women power in the family and in society. Property passed from mother to child, and women were held in high esteem. However, as wealth began to accumulate and men gained control of agricultural production, men claimed more status. In order to guarantee the fidelity of the wife and therefore the paternity of the children, the social system evolved so that the wife was subjugated to male power, and men sought to claim women for their own. Monogamy eventually led to the even more restrictive marriage bond. Engels believed that with the advent of "marriage begins the abduction and purchase of women" (Engels [1884] 1970:735).

Given that Engels believed that female oppression is rooted in the hidden and underlying structure of property rights, he thought that the key to ending it was to abolish private property. Engels was mistaken, however, in his conception of history. The period he describes as "primitive communism" didn't really exist. Nevertheless, the connections he drew between gender inequality and the underlying structure of society have proved to be enduring, and many contemporary feminist theorists have built more sophisticated analyses upon them.

A structuralist approach is useful because it leads sociologists to look beyond the surface for underlying structures and realities, which determine what transpires on the surface. Thus, for example, military threats made by North Korea and its testing of missiles may not really be about military matters at all but instead be about its failing economic system. North Korea may hope that the symbolic expression of military power will strengthen its global prestige, frighten others, and perhaps coerce other countries, especially the United States, into providing economic aid.

A very useful sociological idea in the context of structuralism is *debunking*, created by mainstream sociologist Peter Berger (1963). **Debunking** plays off the idea that visible social structures such as the state are mere "facades." It is the task of the sociologist to debunk, or to look beneath and beyond, such facades. This is very similar to the approach taken by many structuralists, although there is an important difference. While the goal of many structuralists is merely to understand the underlying structure of, for example, the state, language, or family systems, debunking not only seeks such understanding but also critically analyses the underlying reality and its impact on visible social structures. Sociologists accomplish debunking by questioning societally accepted goals and the accounts provided by those in positions of authority. For example, while Canada seems to emphasise multiculturalism and ethnic tolerance, sociologists have pointed out that First Nations peoples struggle in Canada because their cultural ways are not respected and there is little tolerance for their traditions (Frideres and Gadacz 2011). Many sociologists see debunking as going to the very heart of the field of sociology.

CONFLICT/CRITICAL THEORIES

The idea of debunking is clearly critical in nature and is, therefore, a perfect lead-in to a discussion of conflict/critical theories. Several different theories are discussed under this heading: conflict theory, critical theory, feminist theory, queer theory, critical theories of race and racism, and postmodern theory. They all tend to emphasise stresses, strains, and conflicts in society. They are critical of society in a variety of different ways, especially of the power that is exercised over less powerful members of society.

Conflict Theory

The best known of these theories, at least in Canadian sociology, is conflict theory. It has roots in Marx's theory and can best be seen as an inversion of structural-functionalism, which **conflict theory** was designed to compete with and to counteract. While structural-functionalism emphasises what is positive about society, conflict theory focuses on its negative aspects. To the structural-functionalist, society is held together by consensus; virtually everyone accepts the social structure, its legitimacy, and its benefits. But to the conflict theorist, society is held together by coercion. Those who are adversely affected by society, especially economically, would rebel were it not for coercive forces like the police, the courts, and the military.

A good example of conflict theory is to be found in the work of Ralf Dahrendorf (1959). Although he was strongly influenced by Marx, he was more strongly motivated by a desire to develop a viable alternative to structural-functionalism. For example, while structural-functionalists tend to see society as static, conflict theorists including Dahrendorf emphasise the ever-present possibility of change. Where structural-functionalists see the orderliness of society, conflict theorists see dissension and conflict everywhere. Finally, structural-functionalists focus on the sources of cohesion internal to society, but conflict theorists see the coercion and power that holds together an otherwise fractious society.

Overall, conflict theorists such as Dahrendorf see two basic sides to society—consensus and conflict—and believe that both are needed. Sociology therefore needs, at least in this view, two different theories: conflict theory and "consensus" (or structural-functional) theory.

Dahrendorf offers a very sociological view of authority, arguing that it resides not in individuals—Barack Obama, for example—but in positions (e.g., the presidency of the United States) and in various associations of people. In his view, those associations are controlled by a hierarchy of authority positions and the people who occupy them. However, there are many such associations in any society. Thus a person may be in authority in one type of association but be subordinate in many others.

What most interests Dahrendorf is the potential for conflict between those in positions of authority and those who are subordinate. They usually have very different interests. Like authority, those interests are not characteristics of individuals but rather are linked to the positions they hold. Thus, the top management of a corporation such as Walmart has very different interests—for example, making the corporation more profitable by cutting wages—than those who hold such low-level jobs as greeter and who are interested in increasing their wages to meet basic needs. Because of this inherent tension and conflict, authority within associations is always tenuous.

In general, the interests of those involved in associations are unconscious, but at times they become conscious and therefore more likely to lead to overt conflict. *Conflict groups* may form, as when a group of greeters goes out on strike against Walmart. The coalitions formed out of resistance efforts often increase cohesion among group members, further uniting them and bolstering the strength of the movement (Coser 1956). The actions of conflict groups very often change society, as well as elements of society like the Walmart corporation, sometimes quite radically.

Critical Theory

While Marx's work was critical of the capitalist economy, **critical theory** shifted the focus to culture. While Marx believed that culture was shaped by the economic system, the critical school argued that by the early twentieth century, and at an ever-accelerating rate to this day, culture not only has succeeded in becoming important on its own but in many ways has come to be more important than the economic system. Instead of being controlled by the capitalist economy, the argument went, more of us are controlled, and controlled more often, by culture in general, specifically by the culture industry.

The **culture industry** is, in Weber's sense, the rationalised and bureaucratised structures that control modern culture. In their early years, the 1920s and 1930s, the critical theorists focused on radio, magazines, and movies; today the movies remain important, but the focus has shifted to television and various aspects of the Internet. These are critiqued for producing, or serving as an outlet for, **mass culture**, or cultural elements that are administered by organisations, lack spontaneity, and are phony. Two features of mass culture and its dissemination by the culture industry are of concern to critical theorists:

- *Falseness.* True culture should emanate from the people, but mass culture involves prepackaged sets of ideas that falsify reality. The reality shows that dominate television today are a contemporary example of mass culture. These programmes are also highly formulaic. They are presented as if they are authentic, but in fact they are scripted, highly controlled, and selectively edited—although in a different way than fictional dramas, comedies, and soap operas. They are also false in the sense that they give consumers of mass culture the sense that there is a quick and easy route to fame and fortune.

- *Repressiveness.* Like Marx, the critical theorists feel that the masses need to be informed about such things as the falseness of culture so that they can develop a clear sense of society's failings and the need to rebel against them. However, the effect of mass culture is to pacify, stupefy, and repress the masses so that they are far less likely to demand social change. Those who rush home nightly to catch up on their favourite reality TV shows are unlikely to have much interest in, or time for, revolutionary activities, or even civic activities and reforms. Additionally, according to some theorists, the "culture industry" has succeeded in creating a class of corporate brands that are globally recognised and sought after as cultural symbols (Arvidsson 2012; Lash and Lury 2007). Instead of engaging in revolutionary activities, many people are striving to keep up with, and acquire, the latest and hottest brands.

Critical theory can be applied to some of the newest media forms, such as YouTube and Facebook. Despite plenty of false and stupefying content on these sites, and much edifying material as well, they are not controlled by large, rationalised bureaucracies—at least not yet. Almost all of the content that appears on sites like YouTube and Facebook is provided by those who also consume material on the sites. The sites exercise little control over original content; they are arguably spontaneous and authentic. It's tempting to conclude that these new aspects of the culture industry are not assailable from a traditional critical theory perspective.

Yet it could be argued that while the content is not produced by the culture industry, the content is disseminated by it. So although many websites have yet to become profitable, they have come to be worth many billions of dollars each. More importantly, the masses are pacified, repressed, and stupefied by spending endless hours watching YouTube videos or updating their Facebook pages and following day-to-day, even minute-by-minute,

DIGITAL LIVING

Chatroulette

Chatroulette is a social networking website that was not created by a large, rationalised, and bureaucratised corporation—it was created in 2009 by a then 17-year-old Moscow high school dropout named Andrey Ternovskiy (Ioffe 2010). Ternovskiy started Chatroulette with a $10,000 loan from his father, and within months, it had about 2 million unique daily users.

When you log on to Chatroulette, two video windows appear. In one, if you have a webcam, is your own live image; in the other is the live stream of a randomly chosen chat partner (S. Anderson 2010). You can interact with this partner using voice, text, and video, or you can click "Next" to be reconnected instantaneously with a new partner. You may encounter practically anyone and anything while surfing partners in Chatroulette. In addition to bored teenagers, performing musicians, celebrities, and people in outlandish costumes, chat partners may include "copulating couples, masturbators, [or] a man who has hanged himself (it's fake)" (Ioffe 2010:55). Researchers from the Web Ecology Project found that 1 in 20 users encounter nudity while on Chatroulette (A. Leavitt and Hwang 2010).

Chatroulette experienced hard times in 2010, and the number of unique daily visitors dropped to 500,000 (Wortham 2010). A major problem with user retention seemed to be the "misbehaviour"

of some chat partners. In fact, *New York Times* correspondent Brad Stone (2010) advised, "Parents, keep your children far, far away."

While its popularity may be fading, Chatroulette ushered in a genre of Internet "roulette" sites that rely on serendipitous interaction as their main attraction (O'Dell 2010). Newer sites like Tinychat, TextSlide, vChatter, and Chatfe are also based on randomness and serendipity; however, their developers are trying in various ways to avoid the problems that plagued Chatroulette. Some of the newer sites rely on texting (eliminating the possibility of nudity and sex acts on the screen), a form of identification (as anonymity encourages bad behaviour), or connections based on similar interests (such as backpacking or running marathons) (Rao 2010).

The development of these new sites indicates that Ternovskiy was on to something when he created Chatroulette. Newer sites (for example, Airtime) may be tweaking the original model, but the impressive initial success of Chatroulette seems to indicate that systems that allow people to meet and interact authentically on the Internet will continue to expand and proliferate. Assuming they do, people will have even less time to critically analyse society, let alone rebel against it.

developments in the lives of others. The same could be said of Twitter's tweets, which inform us instantaneously that, among other things, one of our friends has gotten a haircut or a manicure. While people do find friends, learn useful things, and may even foment revolutions on Twitter (as in the case of the "Arab Spring" uprisings in 2011), they also may spend, and likely waste, endless amounts of time on it. Not infrequently, they also find that one or more corporations are trying to act like their "friends" in order to get them to consume certain products.

Feminist Theory

Historically, male social theorists have received the most attention (one exception, mentioned above, is Harriett Martineau), and to a large extent that is still the case today. Not surprisingly, then, social theories

in the main have ignored women and the distinctive problems they face (one exception is the work of Engels discussed above). Feminist theorists point up this masculine bias. There are many feminist theories, and they deal with many different issues, but a central aspect of **feminist theory** is to be critical of the social situation confronting women. Feminist theory also offers ideas on how women's situation can be bettered, if not revolutionised.

Feminist theory embraces a variety of theoretical positions (Lengermann and Niebrugge 2008; Tong 2009). One fundamental debate within feminist theory is whether or not gender inequality causes, or results from, gender differences. A few feminist theorists (Rossi 1983) believe that there are *essential* (or biologically determined) differences between men's and women's behaviour, and that gender inequality is a result of the social

Most scholars, especially feminists, argue that differences between men's and women's behaviors are determined not biologically but rather socially.

devaluing of female characteristics (such as nurturing). But the majority of feminist scholars argue that gender differences are *socially constructed*. In other words, the differences we see between men's and women's behaviour are not biologically determined but rather are created socially.

Even feminist theorists who agree that gender differences are socially constructed disagree on the underlying causes. One view is that men, as the dominant group in society, have defined gender in such a way as to purposely restrain and subordinate women. Another view holds that social structures such as capitalist organisations and patriarchal families have evolved to favour men and traditionally male roles. Both structures benefit from the uncompensated labour of women, and so there is little incentive for men as a dominant group to change the status quo. Clearly these perspectives all involve a critical orientation.

There is also a broad consensus among feminist theorists that women face extraordinary problems related directly to gender inequality and thus equally extraordinary solutions are needed. However, feminist theorists vary in the degree to which they are willing to support dramatic, even revolutionary, changes in women's situation. Some feminist theorists suggest that the solution to gender inequality is to change social structures and institutions so they are more inclusive of women. Others argue that because those very structures and institutions create gender difference and inequality,

we must first deconstruct and then rebuild them in a wholly different way (D. Smith 2000).

Women of color have sometimes been dissatisfied with feminist theory for not representing their interests very well. Several scholars argue that feminist theory generally reflects the perspective of white women while ignoring the unique experiences and viewpoints of women of color (P. Collins 2000; hooks 2000; Nakano-Glenn 2000). Similarly, studies related to race tend to focus largely (or wholly) on the position of men. Thus many contemporary feminists have advocated scholarship that takes into account not just gender but also how it intersects with race and ethnicity, social class, and sexuality. The upcoming discussion of critical theories of race and racism in this chapter provides more detail on this view.

Queer Theory

The word *queer* is conventionally used as an umbrella term for gays, lesbians, bisexuals, and transgendered, transsexual, and intersexed persons. However, queer theory is not a theory of queers. In fact, it stands in contrast to the field of gay and lesbian studies, which focuses on homosexuality. Rather, **queer theory** is based on the idea that there are no fixed and stable identities that determine who we are (Plummer 2012). It is therefore impossible to talk about any group of people, including those who are either gay or straight, on the basis of a single shared characteristic. Being homosexual does not mean that you have sexual relations only with those of the same sex, just as being heterosexual does not preclude other kinds of sexual relationships. Advocates of queer theory point out that modern western culture cannot be understood without critiquing modern definitions of homosexuality and heterosexuality (Sedgwick 1991).

Queer theory does not focus on homosexuality itself but does study the dynamics of the relationship between heterosexuals and homosexuals, especially the historic exercise of power by heterosexuals over homosexuals. In this respect, queer theory is clearly a form of conflict/critical theory. In recent decades, however, homosexuals have consistently and successfully contested the blatant power of heterosexuals to control gay men's and lesbians' lives. Although some of the most serious

GL⦿BALISATION

Female Genital Mutilation Around the Globe

Female genital mutilation (FGM; also called female circumcision or female genital cutting) involves the removal of a portion of a girl's exterior genitals (S. Lee 2007, 2012a). It is performed somewhere between a girl's infancy and puberty. It is mainly a Muslim practise centered in North Africa, although it is also practised in some Arabian countries, especially those close to North Africa, as well as in scattered other areas in the world (Indonesia, for example). Within North Africa, nearly all women have been circumcised in Somalia, Egypt, and Djibouti, and 90 percent of women in Sudan have undergone the procedure. As a result of globalisation, FGM is now performed in the United States and Europe by migrants from these areas. It is estimated that about 140 million women, or 5 percent of the global population, have been circumcised; about 6,000 female circumcisions are performed every day (S. Lee 2007).

Many Muslims consider it a religious duty to perform, and to have girls undergo, the operation, although it (as well as male circumcision) is not discussed in the Qur'an. It is, however, mentioned in the sayings of Mohammed, and the practise is supported by many Muslim leaders (although a few have condemned it).

There are four basic forms of FGM. In the first, sometimes called the Sunnah (in accordance with Muslim law) circumcision, the hood covering the clitoris, and perhaps part, or all, of the clitoris, is removed. The second, or clitorectomy, is the most common form (80 percent of the cases) involving the complete removal of the clitoris and parts of the labia minor. In the third, and most extreme, type, infibulations, all of the external genitalia are removed, and the remaining tissue is stitched together, leaving only a small opening for the passage of urine and menstrual blood. This form, practised in about 15 percent of cases, is most valued because the small opening is believed to ensure the girl's virginity as well as increasing a male's sexual pleasure upon intercourse with an infibulated woman; infibulation therefore tends to increase the marital value of a girl who has undergone it.

The fourth type is defined by the World Health Organization as "all other harmful procedures to the female genitalia for non-medical purposes, e.g. pricking, piercing, incising, scraping and cauterising the genital area."

Of course, all of these procedures are painful and carry with them the risk of infection—since they tend to be carried out in nonsterile environments—as well as long-term complications such as urinary and vaginal infections, cysts, infertility, impaired childbirth, and the need for repeated surgeries to open and resuture the opening.

Culturally, FGM is valued, especially in patriarchal societies, because it is more likely to ensure that a bride is a virgin. In some cases, it is considered an honour for a husband to open his stitched wife's vagina on the wedding night through penile penetration (and to suffer dishonour if he fails). In other cases, the males may cut open the stitching with a razor, a piece of glass, or even a dagger. FGM is supposed to reduce female sexual desire and is based on the cultural belief that females are sexually wanton, so that without the operation they would likely be promiscuous both before and after marriage.

There have been various efforts to eliminate or reduce the practise or, failing that, to make it safer or to find alternatives to it. Pressure from women's organisations has led to the banning of FGM in 14 African countries. The most successful efforts have been those undertaken at the grassroots level. Outside of North Africa, the procedure may be greatly modified, whereby there is no actual cutting but a drop of blood is drawn from, say, the clitoris. In effort to eliminate the procedure, Kenya has a "Circumcision through Words" programme. Girls are taught such things as self-esteem and at the conclusion have a coming-of-age ceremony with certificates, gifts, and a feast. However, it is clear from the statistics cited above that FGM remains preeminent in some parts of North Africa, is common in other countries in the region, and has spread throughout the world.

GL⊕BALISATION

The Hijras of India

India boasts one of the richest religious histories in the world. Four of the world's major religions originated there. For example, Hinduism is considered the oldest religion and philosophical system in the world; it has the fourth most adherents of any of the world's religions. Over 80 percent of Indians are Hindus. Buddhism (which was the dominant India religion until the ninth century), Jainism, and Sikhism also originated in India. Along with these ancient and more common religions, many other religions are represented in much smaller numbers.

The hijras are one of India's smaller religious communities. It is estimated that there are about 50,000 hijras in India, mostly in the cities in the northern part of the country. Hijras tend to work and live together in communal households of five to fifteen people, operating like one large family. They share their incomes and chores. Since they are supposed to embody the power of a mother goddess, Bahuchara Mata, the main role of hijras in Indian society is a religious one. They engage in religious rituals and perform at various rites of passage (a source of their income) such as the birth of a child, weddings, and festivals in the temple. Other income is derived from begging or prostitution.

What makes hijras relevant in a discussion of queer theory is that hijras are considered neither men nor women; they represent a third gender, "one of the very few alternative gender roles currently functioning in any society" (Nanda 1999:xi). Their existence underscores gender possibilities beyond the male and female in the real world. Similar gender categories include berdaches, xaniths, and "manly hearted women" in African and American Indian societies (Lorber 1994). The hijras call into question our belief that there are only two natural, biologically based genders.

Such third gender roles, as well as gender transformations, are important as mythological themes. However, many have fallen into disuse or been eliminated by the cultural imperialism associated with modernisation, westernisation, or colonialism. As India has modernised, the rituals and cultural traditions of many subcultural groups (like the hijras) have been undermined by the spread of rationalised organisations and western education.

Most hijras cannot reproduce; they have neither male nor female sex organs. A few are born that way, or with both male and female sex organs (they are intersexed), but most are born males. In order to become a hijra, a person who is born with male sex organs has traditionally been emasculated, that is, undergone surgery that removes both the penis and the testicles.

---

abuses of heterosexuals' social power have waned, power continues to be exercised over homosexuals in other, more subtle ways. For example, homosexuals often govern their behaviour so that heterosexuals feel comfortable, as when they avoid even mild shows of affection in public.

Queer theory is in the early phases of development. It promises to play a central role in the development of general theories about those who stand on the margins of society, to deepen our understanding of the full spectrum of sexuality, and to dispel a variety of myths. In addition, it could disrupt hierarchies of power. At the least, it promises to broaden acceptance of sexual and other minorities and to promote greater inclusion for all.

Critical Theories of Race and Racism

As we saw earlier, W. E. B. Du Bois was a pioneer in the study of race and racism. In recent years this perspective has blossomed in sociology under the heading of **critical theories of race and racism** (Slatton and Feagin 2012). Theorists with this perspective argue that race continues to matter globally and that racism continues to adversely affect people of colour. Given its history of slavery and racism, the United States has often been singled out for such analysis.

That tradition is slowly changing, however, and some hijras do not undergo the surgery. In contrast to a sex change operation, no vagina is created to replace the male sex organs.

Hijras are neither men nor women, but they normally adopt the mannerisms of, and dress like, women. They insist that those outside the hijra community refer to them as women. Some hijras, especially those who are older, claim to have no sexual desire. However, younger hijras are quite clear about having such desire and that their desire is targeted toward males. Hijras who become prostitutes service a male clientele. Others become mistresses to men or marry men and refer to these men as their husbands. Marriage may occur in conjunction with, or perhaps after, a life as a prostitute.

Most hijras perform two important social roles within Indian society, one religious and the other sexual, through their activities as prostitutes. Although they are stigmatised and often abused by the larger society, hijras have nevertheless been able to create a viable subculture, one that is able to give their lives considerable meaning.

Most hijras live in the cities in the northern part of India. Here, two hijras dance during a protest march of sex workers at the World Social Forum in Bombay, India.

Some commentators have argued that racism today is of little more than historical interest because whites have become "colour-blind." People promoting a policy of colour-blindness argue that we should ignore skin colour when discussing social groups and that skin colour should also not be used in hiring or admissions policies. However, critical theorists of race and racism disagree. They argue that while skin colour has nothing to do with a person's physical or intellectual abilities, colour-blindness ignores the unique experiences of racial minorities, including the social consequences of years of racial discrimination. As a result, critics of colour-blindness argue that it is little more than a "new racism," a smoke screen that allows whites to practise and perpetuate racial discrimination (Bonilla-Silva 2009).

The idea that racism continues has been very much in the news since the election of the first African American president in the United States, Barack Obama, in 2008. Some—including former President Jimmy Carter—charge that criticisms of President Obama's qualifications for office and of some of his policies are a sign of thinly veiled racism. For example, until the public release of Obama's birth certificate in 2011, sceptics (including then–presidential candidate Donald Trump) at least implied that the president was not born in the United States. The so-called birther argument might not have come up if President Obama's mother and father had both been white and if his name had been Barry O'Brien. Racism also reveals itself in the heated debates over racial profiling or "authentic" refugees.

Of particular importance to recent work in this area is the idea of **intersectionality**, which points to the fact that people are affected not only by their race but also by their gender, sexual orientation, class, age, and global location. The confluence, or intersection, of these various statuses and the inequality and oppression associated with combinations of them are what matter most. Not only can we not deal with race, gender, class, and so on separately, but we also cannot gain an understanding of oppression by simply adding them together. For example, a poor black female lesbian faces a complex of problems different from the problems faced by a poor person or a black person or a woman or a lesbian.

Majority-minority relations are contentious in many parts of the world, not just in Canada. Europe, for example, has a long history of racism that includes centuries of colonialism, the African slave trade, anti-Semitism, and the Holocaust. Racial turmoil abated after World War II, but it is again on the rise—at least in part because of the large influx of immigrants in the early twenty-first century. Racist propaganda, hate speech, and incitement to violence have become much more common in recent years, notably in France, Austria, Germany, Sweden, and the United Kingdom. The main victims have been Muslims, Jews, people of North African/Arab origin, and Roma people from Central and Eastern Europe, who are among the largest immigrant groups in these countries. They are largely powerless because Europe has not experienced anything like the U.S. civil rights movement, which served to mobilise and organise black Americans.

Postmodern Theory

Postmodern theory has many elements that fit well under the heading of critical theory, although there is more to it than critique (Lipovetsky 2005). The term *postmodern* is used in various ways in relation to social theory:

Postmodernity is the state of society beyond the "modern era," which was the era analysed by the classic social theorists. Among the characteristics of the modern world is rationality, as discussed in Weber's work. The postmodern world is less rational, is nonrational, or is even irrational. For example, while in the modern world groups such as the proletariat can plan in a rational manner to overthrow capitalism, in the postmodern world such changes come about accidentally or are simply fated to occur (Baudrillard [1983] 1990). Although modernity is characterised by a highly consistent lifestyle, postmodernity is characterised by eclecticism in what we eat, how we dress, and what sort of music we listen to (Lyotard [1979] 1984).

Postmodernism refers to the emergence of new and different cultural forms in music, movies, art, architecture, and the like. One characteristic of these new cultural forms is pastiche. "Modern" movies, for example, are told in a linear fashion, and "modern" art is made up of internally consistent elements. But postmodern cultural forms are pastiches that combine very different elements that, from a modern perspective, often seem incompatible with one another. Thus postmodern buildings might combine classic and modern styles. Postmodern movies might deal with historical realities but also include very

Cowboys & Aliens, released in 2011, is a pastiche of two dissimilar genres of film—western and science fiction. This unlikely combination exemplifies postmodernism.

modern elements such as songs from the present day. For example, the 2001 movie *Moulin Rouge!* is set in the year 1900, yet it features contemporary pop music. Another postmodern movie, *Blade Runner* (1982), takes place in twenty-first-century Los Angeles where futuristic police cars fly over traditional areas such as Chinatown and a seemingly traditional detective hunts dangerous artificial humans, or "replicants." Even the detective seems to be a pastiche of human and nonhuman elements.

Postmodern theory is a theoretical orientation that is a reaction against modern theory. Postmodern theory tends to be expressed in nonrational ways—for example, as a series of terse, often unrelated statements rather than a logical, well-argued volume or series of volumes as in the work of modern thinkers such as Marx and Weber. Postmodernists are opposed to the grand narratives—the broad depictions of history and society—offered by modern theorists, such as the increasing rationalisation of the world and the rise of the "iron cage" constraining our thoughts and activities. Instead, they offer more limited, often unrelated snapshots of the social world. In fact, postmodernists often deconstruct, or take apart, modern grand narratives. Postmodernists are also opposed to the scientific pretensions of much modern social theory, adopting instead a nonscientific or even antiscientific approach to the social world. Feminist postmodernists reject the very language used by modern feminist scholars, because words such as *lesbian* have been constructed out of modern, male-centered thought (Tong 2009). To some observers, the sociological study of deviance has all but disappeared due to postmodern conclusions that deviance is a purely relative phenomenon, dependent strictly on the definitions of those who have the power to define what is deviant (Sumner 1994).

In spite of, or perhaps because of, these differences, postmodern theory offers a new and important way of theorising. Postmodern social theorists look at familiar social phenomena in different ways or adopt a very different focus for their work. For example, in his study of the history of prisons, Michel Foucault ([1975] 1979) was critical of the modernist view that criminal justice had grown progressively liberal. He contended that prisons had, in fact, grown increasingly oppressive through the use of techniques such as constant, enhanced surveillance of prisoners. Similarly, he argued against the traditional view that in the Victorian era people were sexually repressed; he found instead an explosion of sexuality in the Victorian era (Foucault 1978).

The most important postmodernist, Jean Baudrillard (1929–2007), argued that we are now living in a consumer society where much of our lives is defined not by our productive work but by what we consume and how we consume it. The postmodern world is in fact characterised by **hyperconsumption**, which involves consuming more than we need, more than we really want, and more than we can afford. The generally rising level of debt in Canada in the past decade is a sign of the hyperconsumption pointed to by Baudrillard (see Chapter 1).

Another of Baudrillard's critical ideas that demonstrates the nature of postmodern social theory is simulation. A **simulation** is an inauthentic or fake version of something, and Baudrillard saw the world as increasingly dominated by

Hyperconsumption and simulation go hand in hand at fast-food restaurants like McDonald's. Here, hundreds of people line up around the first McDonald's restaurant to open in the Soviet Union on January 31, 1990.

McDONALDIZATION *Today*

Islands of the Living Dead

Max Weber saw the rationalisation process as leading to more and more rationalised structures such as bureaucracies. These are what he called "iron cages," or, by some translations, "shells as hard as steel," from which there is increasingly less chance of escape (Baehr 2001). When Ritzer (2013) updated and expanded Weber's rationalisation thesis in *The McDonaldization of Society*, he argued that the fast-food restaurant, rather than the bureaucracy, has become the model for the rationalisation process. But is it accurate to think of a fast-food restaurant, or even the entire system of McDonaldized restaurants and other businesses, as an "iron cage"?

Clearly, a single fast-food restaurant is not a cage, let alone one whose bars are made of iron: You are free to leave any fast-food restaurant you enter. The analogy does not hold for the entire system of McDonaldized restaurants and other businesses either: There are still plenty of non-McDonaldized alternatives from which to choose. In fact, it could be argued that the spread of McDonaldized businesses encourages the development of non-McDonaldized alternatives for those who do not like such businesses—or at least do not want to spend all of their time in them. A recent proliferation of independent farmers' markets (up

16 percent in 2010) exemplifies this trend (Pegg 2010).

So, instead of viewing McDonaldized businesses as creating an iron cage, Ritzer casts them as "islands of the living dead." One source for this image is the work of Michel Foucault ([1975] 1979), who argues that we have created a "carceral archipelago" of "islands" (prisons, but also schools and workplaces), each of which serves to incarcerate, or imprison, us. Ritzer sees each McDonaldized setting as an island. (As you may have noticed, one thing that all of these metaphors have in common is that they are highly critical of the phenomena they are describing; they are examples of critical sociology.)

The idea of the "living dead" populating McDonaldized businesses comes from the movies of George Romero, especially *Night of the Living Dead* (1968). One of Romero's later living-dead movies, *Dawn of the Dead* (1978), takes place in a shopping mall, a highly McDonaldized setting. Similarly, a portion of Robert Kirkman's *Walking Dead* comic book series takes place in a prison, and the 2011 zombie video game *Dead Island* is actually set on a commercial resort island (Orkin 2011). For Romero, the living dead are zombies, but for Ritzer, they are the individuals who consume and work on and within the islands of McDonaldization. They

---

simulations. For example, when we eat at McDonald's we consume Chicken McNuggets, or simulated chicken. It is fake in the sense that it is often not meat from one chicken, but bits of meat that come from many different chickens. When we go to Disney World, we enter via Main Street, a simulation of early America that is really a shopping mall, and we go on simulated submarine rides in order to see simulated sea life rather than going to a nearby aquarium to see "real" sea life. When we go to Las Vegas, we stay in casino hotels that are simulations of New York of the early to mid-twentieth century (New York, New York), Venice (The Venetian), and ancient Egypt (Luxor). The idea that we increasingly consume simulations, and live a simulated life, is a powerful critique not

only of consumer society but more generally of the contemporary world.

INTER/ACTIONIST THEORIES

The slash between *inter* and *action(ist)* in the heading to this section is meant to communicate the fact that we will deal with two closely related sets of theories here—those that deal mainly with the interaction of two or more people (symbolic interactionism, ethnomethodology, and exchange theory) and those that focus more on the actions of individuals (rational choice theory). A common factor among them, though, is that, in contrast to the theories above that focus on the macro are "dead" in the sense that they are highly controlled by the structures of McDonaldized businesses. If you were to watch both sides of a drive-through window at a fast-food restaurant during a lunch or supper rush, you would observe a great deal of rote, scripted behaviour. The "zombies" who order are not required to think very hard about what they are ordering, and the "zombies" who serve them use the same few phrases and repeat the same few motions over and over again.

Of course, this depiction is a simplification; a lot of "life" takes place on McDonaldized islands as well. Most customers seem not only to enjoy the food but also to have a lot of fun while they consume it. Furthermore, like any island, each McDonaldized island is surrounded by the sea—in this case the sea of alternative, non-McDonaldized settings. While the islands are getting bigger, and there are more and more of them, there are still strongholds that remain zombie-free and non-McDonaldized.

At zombie walks, individuals dress up as zombies and stumble along designated routes, forming a sort of campy parade. Here, individuals dressed as zombies exit a McDonald's restaurant before attempting to set a zombie walk world record during a 2007 screening of *The Zombie Diaries* in London, England.

structures of society, these theories focus on the micro level of individuals and groups.

Symbolic Interactionism

As the name suggests, **symbolic interactionism** is concerned with the interaction of two or more people through the use of symbols. Interaction is clear enough—we all engage in mutual action with many others on a daily basis, whether it be face-to-face or more indirectly via cell phone, e-mail, or social media. But interaction could not take place without symbols: words, gestures, and even objects that stand in for things. Symbols allow the communication of meaning among a group of people.

Although we can interact with one another without words, such as through physical gestures like the shrug of a shoulder, in the vast majority of cases we need and use words to interact. And words make many other symbols possible. For example, the Harley-Davidson brand has meaning because it symbolises a particular type of motorcycle, and both the brand name and the motorcycle are further symbolised by nicknames such as *Harley* and *hog* (Holt 2004).

Symbolic interactionism has several basic principles:

- Human beings have a great capacity for thought, which differentiates them from lower animals. That innate capacity for thought is greatly shaped by social interaction, however. It is during social interaction that people acquire the symbolic meanings that allow them to exercise their distinctive ability to think. Those symbolic meanings in turn allow people to act and interact in ways that lower animals cannot.

- Symbolic meanings are not set in stone. People are able to modify them based on a given situation and their interpretation of it. The Christian cross, for example, is a symbol that can vary in meaning. Christians throughout the world define it in positive religious ways, but many in the Islamic world view it as a negative symbol recalling the twelfth- and thirteenth-century Crusades waged against their world by the Christian West.

- People are able to modify symbolic meanings because of their unique ability to think, which symbolic interactionists frame as people's ability to interact with themselves. In that interaction with themselves, people are able not only to alter symbolic meanings but also to examine various courses of action open to them in a given situation, to assess the relative advantages and disadvantages of each, and then to choose one of them.

- It is the pattern of those choices of individual action and interaction that is the basis of groups, larger structures such as bureaucracies, and society as a whole. Most generally, in this theoretical perspective, symbolic interaction is the basis of everything else in the social world.

Symbolic interactionists are interested in how various aspects of identity are created and sustained in social interaction. For example, symbolic interactionists argue that gender (like ethnicity or career identity) is something that we "do" or perform (West and Zimmerman 1987). Gender is a means of identifying ourselves with a particular sex category. Thus a male may take pains to act in a masculine way so that he will be seen as male by both himself and others. In some respects, his behaviour (which is socially determined) can be considered symbolic of the male sex (which is largely biologically determined). People who see his behaviour can then simply relate to him as male, according to the meaning of the symbolic behaviour that has developed over time through innumerable interactions. Gender (i.e., masculinity and femininity) is thus both a result and a cause of social interaction.

Ethnomethodology

While symbolic interactionism primarily deals with people's interactions, it is also concerned with the mental processes, such as mind and self, that are deeply implicated in these interactions. **Ethnomethodology** is another inter/actionist theory, but it focuses on what people *do* rather than what they think. The term *ethnomethodology* comes from a Greek root that refers to people (*ethno*) and the everyday methods through which they accomplish their daily lives. In other words, ethnomethodologists study the way people organise everyday life.

Ethnomethodologists regard people's lives and social worlds as practical accomplishments that are really quite extraordinary. For example, one ethnomethodological study of coffee drinkers attempts to understand their participation in a subculture of coffee connoisseurship (Manzo 2010). Learning to enjoy coffee itself is something of an accomplishment; taking that enjoyment to the next level and becoming a connoisseur requires even more doing.

Ethnomethodologists take a different view of large-scale social structures than do structural-functionalists, who tend to see people and their actions as being highly constrained by those structures. Ethnomethodologists argue that this view tells us very little about what really goes on within structures such as courtrooms, hospitals, and police departments. Rather than being constrained, people act within these structures and go about much of their business using common sense rather than official procedures. They may even adapt those structures and rules to accomplish their goals. For example, an employee at the Bay might violate the rules about handling returns in order to please customers and to make the process easier or less stressful. Police departments have rules about categorising a death as homicide or manslaughter. However, police officers often apply their own commonsense rules rather than organisational rules in order to interpret the evidence.

Many ethnomethodologists study conversations. In that study, they focus on three basic issues (Zimmerman 1988):

- *Vocal cues as an element of conversation.* Conversation involves not only words but also vocal cues such as pauses, throat-clearings, and silences. These nonverbal vocal behaviours could well be important methods in making conversation. For example, one may sit silently in order to force the other to speak. Or, clearing one's throat may be meant to express disapproval of what the other person is saying.

- *Stable and orderly properties of conversations.* For example, the people in conversation generally take turns speaking and know when it is their turn to talk. Ethnomethodologists might examine how those properties change when two strangers converse rather than two friends. One of their findings has been that a higher-status person is more likely to interrupt a lower-status person.

- *Actions necessary to maintain conversations.* The properties of conversation are not carved in stone. Those involved in the conversation can observe them, enforce them, or upset them. For example, turn taking is a stable and orderly property of a conversation, but in an actual conversation you would need to act in order to get your turn to speak. Turn taking does not occur automatically.

The best known example of an ethnomethodological approach relates to gender (Stokoe 2006). Ethnomethodologists point out that people often erroneously think of gender as being biologically based. It is generally assumed that one does not have to do or say anything in order to be considered masculine or feminine; we are born that way. But, in fact, there are things we all do (for example, the way we walk) and say (for example, the tone of our voice) that allow us to accomplish being masculine or feminine. That is, being masculine and feminine is based on what people do on a regular basis. This is clearest in the case of those who are defined as being male or female at birth (based on biological characteristics) but then later do and say things that lead others to see them as belonging to the other gender (based on social characteristics). For example, Dorothy Lucille Tipton successfully passed as Billy Lee Tipton in the mid-1900s because it was impossible for a woman to succeed as a jazz musician in those days. She had relationships with women and lived with one long

enough to adopt three sons. While such cases are extreme, we all say and do things that allow us to accomplish our gender (and, in certain ways, the opposite gender). If this is the case for gender, a great many other facts of our everyday lives can be analysed as accomplishments.

Exchange Theory

Like ethnomethodologists, **exchange theorists** are not concerned with what goes on in people's minds and how that affects behaviour; they are interested in the behaviour itself and the rewards and costs associated with it. The key figure in exchange theory, George Homans (1910–1989), argued that instead of studying large-scale structures, sociologists should study the "elementary forms of social life" (Homans 1961:13).

Exchange theorists are particularly interested in social behaviour that usually involves two or more people and that involves a variety of tangible and intangible exchanges. For example, you can reward someone who does you a favour with a tangible gift or with more intangible words of praise. Those exchanges are not always rewarding; they also can be punitive. You could, for example, punish someone who wrongs you by slapping him or complaining about him to mutual acquaintances.

In their actions and interactions, people are seen as rational profit seekers. Basically, people will continue on courses of action, or in interactions, in which the rewards are greater than the costs. Conversely, they will discontinue those in which the costs exceed the rewards.

While exchange theory retains an interest in the elementary forms of social behaviour, over the years it has grown more concerned with how those forms lead to more complex social situations. That is, individual exchanges can become stable over time and develop into persistent **exchange relationships**. For example, because you and another person find your initial interactions rewarding you may develop a friendship, which is one particular type of exchange relationship.

Exchange relationships rarely develop in isolation from other exchange relationships. For example, your new friend probably has other friends who are engaged in exchange relationships with one another, and you may well become involved in some of them. All of these exchange relationships may become so highly interconnected that they become a single network structure (K. Cook et al. 1983).

Key issues in such network structures, and in exchange relationships more generally, are the power that some members have over others, as well as the dependency of some members (Molm 2007; Molm and Cook 1995). Exchange theorists are interested in studying the causes and effects of these status differences within exchange relationships and networks. For example, variations in the wealth, status, and power of individuals and their families affect the position they come to occupy in a social network and influence their ability to succeed educationally, financially, and occupationally (N. Lin 1999).

Rational Choice Theory

As in exchange theory, in rational choice theory people are regarded as rational, but the focus is not exchange, rewards, and costs. Rather, the basic principle in **rational choice theory** is that people act intentionally in order to achieve goals. People are seen as having purposes, as intending to do certain things. In order to achieve their goals, people have a variety of means available to them and choose among the available means on a rational basis. They choose the means that are likely to best satisfy their needs and wants; in other words, they choose on the basis of "utility."

There are two important constraints on the ability to act rationally (D. Friedman and Hechter 1988):

- *Access to scarce resources.* It is relatively easy for those with access to lots of resources to act rationally and reach their goals. Those who lack access to such resources are less likely to be able to act rationally in order to achieve their goals. A simple example is that, if you have access to money, you can rationally pursue the goal of purchasing food for dinner. However, without access to money, you will have a much harder time taking rational actions that will lead to the acquisition of food needed for dinner. Those with lots of resources may be able to pursue two or more goals simultaneously (obtaining the money needed for dinner and for club hopping afterward with friends), but those with few resources may have to forgo one (socialising with friends) in order to be able to attain the other goal (getting enough money to eat).

- *Requirements of social structures.* The structures in which people find themselves—businesses, schools, hospitals—often have rules that restrict the actions available to those within the structures. For example, the need to work overtime or on weekends may restrict a person's ability to socialise. Similarly, being a full-time student may limit one's ability to earn enough money to always be able to obtain the kind of food one prefers to eat.

Rational choice theorists understand that people do not always act rationally. They argue, however, that their predictions will generally hold despite these occasional deviations (J. Coleman 1990).

SUMMARY ·······

Sociologists use theories to make sense of social phenomena. These theories help sociologists interpret, explain, categorise, and predict social phenomena—sometimes even using theory to change the world. The most important early sociologists were Auguste Comte, the inventor of the term *sociology*; Harriet Martineau; and Herbert Spencer. However, the main theorists of classical sociology are Karl Marx, Max Weber, and Émile Durkheim.

Marx focused the majority of his attention on macro issues, particularly the structure of capitalist society. Unlike Marx, Weber did not focus exclusively on the economy but considered the importance of other sociological variables, particularly religion. Durkheim believed that the control that social structures and cultural norms and values have over individuals is not only necessary but also desirable.

Three other early sociological theorists are important. Instead of examining macro structures, Georg Simmel focused on the micro-level issues, or interactions among individuals. W. E. B. Du Bois was a pioneering researcher of race in America at the turn of the twentieth century. Thorstein Veblen focused on consumption and particularly the ways the rich show off their wealth. One way they do this is through conspicuous consumption.

There have been major developments in contemporary sociological theory. One structural/functional theory is structural-functionalism with its focus on large-scale social phenomena. Structural-functionalists such as Robert Merton are concerned with both social structures and the functions—and dysfunctions—that such structures perform. In contrast, the second structural/functional theory, structuralism, is not concerned with functions. It focuses on the social impact of hidden or underlying structures.

Conflict/critical theories tend to emphasise societal stresses, strains, and conflicts. Conflict theorists emphasise that society is held together by power and coercion. Feminist theory critiques the social situation confronting women and offers ideas on how their situation can be bettered, if not revolutionised. Queer theory addresses the relationship between heterosexuals and homosexuals but stresses the broader idea that there are no fixed and stable identities that

determine who we are. Critical theories of race and racism argue that race continues to matter. They also raise the issue of oppression involving the intersection of gender, race, sexual orientation, and other social statuses. Postmodern theory is similarly critical of society. Inter/actionist theories deal with micro-level interactions among people and, to a degree, individual action. Symbolic interactionism, for instance, is concerned with the effect of symbols, including words, on the interaction of two or more people. Ethnomethodology focuses on what people do rather than what they think and often analyses conversations. Exchange theory, similar to ethnomethodology, is concerned not with what people think but with their behaviour itself. Rational choice theory considers behaviour to be based on rational evaluations of goals and the means to achieve those goals.

Sociological thought on a range of important issues is based on these theories, both classic and contemporary. In the next chapter, we will investigate the various tools sociologists use to analyse data and develop theories.

KEY TERMS

- Alienation   39
- Anomie   46
- Capitalism   39
- Capitalists   39
- Class consciousness   40
- Collective consciousness   45
- Conflict theory   55
- Conspicuous consumption   49
- Critical theories of race and racism   60
- Critical theory   56
- Culture industry   56
- Debunking   55
- Double-consciousness   48
- Dysfunction   50
- Ethnomethodology   66
- Exchange relationship   67
- Exchange theory   67
- Exploitation   39

- False consciousness   40
- Female genital mutilation (FGM)   59
- Feminist theory   57
- Function   50
- Hyperconsumption   63
- Ideology   40
- Intersectionality   62
- Latent functions   51
- Manifest functions   51
- Mass culture   56
- Mechanical solidarity   46
- Organic solidarity   46
- Postmodern theory   63
- Postmodernism   62
- Postmodernity   62
- Proletariat   39
- Protestant ethic   43
- Queer theory   58

THINKING ABOUT SOCIOLOGY

1. What are theories, and how do sociologists use theories to make sense of the social world? In what ways are theories developed by sociologists better than your own theorising?

2. According to Karl Marx, what are the differences between capitalists and the proletariat? How are workers alienated on the job and in the workplace? Do you think workers in Canada are alienated today? Why or why not?

3. Max Weber said the world is becoming increasingly rationalised. What are the benefits and disadvantages of rationality? In what ways is McDonaldization the same as, or different from, rationalisation?

4. Why has our collective consciousness weakened over time, according to Émile Durkheim? Do you think that globalisation continues to weaken our collective consciousness? Why or why not?

5. You live in a world that is increasingly dominated by consumption. How are the items that you consume reflective of Thorstein Veblen's concept of "conspicuous consumption"?

6. What are the functions and dysfunctions of using the Internet to consume goods and services? On balance, do you think that consumption through the Internet is positive or negative?

7. What is mass culture, and why are critical theorists concerned about the dissemination of mass culture? Do you think the Internet and social networking sites are elements of mass culture and part of the traditional "culture industry"?

8. Why is feminist theory considered a critical theory?

9. Some have said that Barack Obama's election in 2008 signalled a change in race relations. How would the critical theories of race and racism outlined in the chapter respond to such a statement?

10. According to symbolic interactionist theory, why are symbols so important to our interactions? In what ways has language changed because of the development of the Internet?

APPLYING THE SOCIOLOGICAL IMAGINATION

How can we use ethnomethodology to understand social interactions on the Internet? First, select a website that allows people to interact with one another (e.g., Facebook, Twitter, your favourite interactive blog, an online discussion forum, the comments section of an article on your local newspaper's website).

Now apply an ethnomethodological approach by observing the actions and interactions on the site. In what ways do conversations and interactions on the site you chose have stable and orderly properties? What rules and conventions keep the interactions orderly and stable? How do people know what is expected of them? Do people violate the rules? How do others respond when the rules are broken? Are the rules that govern online interactions different from the rules that govern face-to-face interactions?

ACTIVE SOCIOLOGY ···

How do people use and discuss sociological concepts and theories in everyday life? Go to Twitter and search trending sociological concepts from this chapter. Some examples include *alienation, conspicuous consumption,* and *intersectionality.* How do uses that you found on Twitter add to your understanding of these concepts from Chapter 2? Choose a concept from this chapter that interests you. Create a tweet, using the concept in a hashtag. How does your tweet add to the discussion about the topic?

STUDENT STUDY SITE ···

Visit the student study site at **www.sagepub.com/ritzercanadian** for additional web quizzes for further review.

RESEARCHING THE SOCIAL WORLD

Geology and oceanography may understand and explain physical phenomena such as climate change, but to understand and explain the motivations, beliefs, and actions that affect climate change we need sociologists and their research methods.

Humankind has made amazing advances throughout its short existence on Earth. From the development of agriculture to the Industrial Revolution to the modern era of globalisation, each generation has pushed humankind further into an unknown future. While technological development has improved life expectancies, standards of living, manufacturing, communication, and transportation throughout the world, our advancement as a species has come at a significant ecological price.

Climate change, marked by long-term fluctuations in Earth's intricate and interwoven weather patterns, has occurred since the formation of the planet. Some fluctuations affect only specific regions, while others affect the entire world. Some span decades, whereas others span millions of years. Though gradual climate change is a natural process, a growing body of research suggests that the significant recent changes in Earth's climate are directly attributable to human activities (such as fossil fuel combustion and deforestation).

While careful research and analysis have led to a scientific consensus among leading geophysicists, geologists, and climatologists (among others), humankind's impact on climate change remains a hotly debated issue. If the available evidence is comprehensive enough to convince the scientific community of humankind's impact on climate change, why do some people remain fiercely unconvinced? Moreover, who precisely is opposed to the notion that human actions are a major cause of climate change, and how have institutional forces influenced their personal beliefs over time?

The answers to these questions lie in a wholly different—yet remarkably similar—kind of research. Geology and oceanography may understand and explain physical phenomena such as climate change, but to understand the motivations, beliefs, and actions that *affect climate change we need sociologists and their research methods. There are many types of social research, but each can be used to uncover heretofore unknown truths about climate change, as well as many other social issues. Thus, sociology is a science like (and also unlike) any other.*

Like all scientists, passionate sociologists may unintentionally let their personal feelings or their drive to succeed interfere with their research. Though we all make occasional mistakes, research methods must be ethical, reliable, and valid for the results to be widely accepted. This is especially important to keep in mind since contemporary sociological research often deals with heated issues such as the role of people and society in climate change.

As you learn about the major types and purposes of sociological research, consider the issues and phenomena that you yourself might like to research. You might someday have an opportunity to do so.

Sociology is a science of the social world, so research is absolutely central to sociology. All sociologists study the research of others, and most do research of their own. While they may theorise, speculate, and even rely totally on their imagination for answers to questions about society, they almost always do so on the basis of data or information derived from research. Put another way, sociologists practise **empiricism**, which means that they gather information and evidence using their senses, especially their eyes and ears. Of course, we all use our senses to experience the world, but in addition sociologists adopt the scientific method, or a similarly systematic approach, in search of a thorough understanding of sociological topics. They have a variety of methods at their disposal—and experience a few significant constraints—in researching and analysing society.

THE SCIENTIFIC METHOD

You have undoubtedly learned about the **scientific method** in your science classes (Carey 2011). It is a structured way to find answers to questions about the world. The scientific method employed by sociologists is much the same as in other sciences. Figure 3.1 diagrams the following list of steps:

1. A sociologist uncovers *questions in need of answers.* These questions can come from issues in the larger society, personal experiences, or topics of concern within the field of sociology. The best and most durable research often stems from issues that are important to the sociologist doing the research. Karl Marx, for example, detested the exploitation of workers that characterised capitalism, and Max Weber feared the impact of bureaucracies (see Chapter 2). These powerful feelings spurred their important research on, and key insights into, these monumentally important social realities.

2. Recognising that others have likely done similar or related research in the past, sociologists review the *relevant literature.* After more than a century of doing research, sociologists have learned a great deal about many things. It would make no sense to start over from the beginning as if those in the field knew nothing about the topic being studied. For example, Ritzer's work on McDonaldization is based on a review of work on rationalisation by Max Weber ([1921] 1968), his successors (such as Kalberg 1980), and contemporary researchers (Ram 2007). Ritzer concluded that the fast-food restaurant is an apt, current example of the rationalisation process. Similarly, others have reviewed Ritzer's work and the work of other scholars on McDonaldization (for a collection of this work, see Ritzer 2010d). They have amplified on the concept, and they have applied it to, among many other domains, religion (Drane 2001, 2008), higher education (Hayes and Wynyard 2002), social work (Dustin 2007), and Disney World (Bryman 2004).

3. Researchers often develop *hypotheses,* or educated guesses, about how social phenomena can be expected to relate to one another. For example, Uri Ram (2007) hypothesised that Israeli society would grow increasingly McDonaldized,

Steps in the Research Process

```
Researcher          Researcher          Researcher
uncovers    →       reviews the    →    develops
question in         relevant            hypotheses
need of             literature          about how
answer                                  phenomena
                                        relate to one
                                        another

Researcher          Researcher          Researcher
identifies a   →    collects data  →    analyzes data
method that will
enable him or her
to answer the
research
question
```

FIGURE 3.1 The Scientific Method

and he found evidence to support that idea. As another example, Marx hypothesised that the conflict between capitalists and workers would ultimately lead to the collapse of capitalism. Over the years, conflict between capitalists and workers has increased in some areas of the world, but it has decreased in others. Capitalism has not collapsed—although it came close in 1929 at the beginning of the Great Depression and maybe in 2008 at the onset of the latest recession. This makes clear that hypotheses are, simply, hypotheses. They may not be confirmed by research or borne out by social developments.

4. Researchers must choose a *research method* that will help them answer the research question. Sociology offers diverse methodological tools, and some are better than others for answering certain kinds of questions. For example, some sociologists are interested in how people's social class shape their opinions about social issues. They may use surveys and quantitative methods to evaluate the relationship between class position and attitudes. Other sociologists are interested in how people interpret social phenomena and how this meaning-making shapes social action. They may use qualitative methodologies such as observation to study these issues. Specifically, they might observe how two individuals interact in a romantic context and how they interpret certain gestures, adornment, and other nonverbal cues to assess the

interest of the other person. Sociologists select from among these and other methods to best answer their research question.

5. Researchers use their chosen method to *collect data* that can confirm, or fail to confirm, their hypotheses. Many classical sociologists conducted their research in libraries, and some contemporary sociologists do as well. But most contemporary

Protesters in Greece and around the world reacted negatively to austerity measures imposed in response to the global financial crisis of the late 2000s. In the North America, many went jobless while some corporations and financial institutions received large bailouts.

sociologists venture out into the field to collect data through observations, interviews, questionnaires, and other means.

6. Researchers conduct an *analysis of the data* collected and their meaning in light of the hypothesis that guided the research. For example, as you learned in Chapter 2, Émile Durkheim hypothesised that those who were involved with other people would be less likely to commit suicide than those who lived more isolated existences and were experiencing what he called anomie. That is, being integrated with other people would, in a way, "protect" an individual from suicide. Analysing data from several nineteenth-century European countries, Durkheim ([1897] 1951) found that the suicide rates were, in fact, higher for widowed or divorced people (see Figure 3.2). Those who are married are presumably more socially integrated than people in these other categories.

The research process begins all over again if a researcher comes up with additional questions when analysing the existing data. This occurrence is very familiar to social researchers in the contemporary world. For example, Robert Putnam (2001), in his famous book *Bowling Alone,* addresses the applicability of Durkheim's concept of anomie in the contemporary world. As the title of his book suggests, he found that people are less likely now to bowl in leagues and more likely to bowl alone. More generally, people have increasingly been doing many things alone that in the past they did with other people. Further analysis of Durkheim's work might lead to the hypothesis that people who "bowl alone" might well be more likely to commit suicide.

Here's an even more current example. Imagine how relying on social networks such as Facebook might affect a person's susceptibility to suicide. You already know something about Durkheim's work

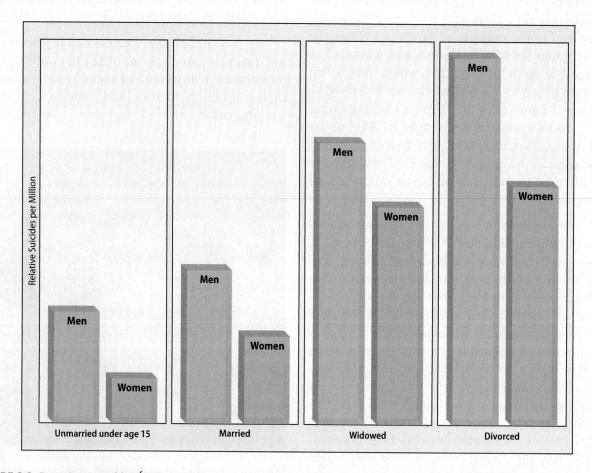

FIGURE 3.2 Data Reported by Émile Durkheim in *Suicide*

SOURCE: Durkheim, Émile. *Suicide*. New York: Free Press, 1951. p. 262.

NOTE: These consolidated data come from Prussia, Baden, Saxony, and Wurttemburg between 1846 and 1893. Numbers in some categories are extrapolations.

on suicide having read this far in the book, but as a real sociologist, of course, you would conduct a much more thorough review of the relevant theory and research on this issue. You would find some work that argues that social networking can prevent suicide (Luxton, June, and Kinn 2011). From this, and from what you now know about Durkheim's thinking, you might hypothesise that those who have many Facebook friends are more socially integrated and therefore less likely to commit suicide than those who have few Facebook friends, or are not on Facebook at all. An alternative hypothesis would be that no matter how many friends one has on Facebook, those who have few, if any, friends in the "real world" are more likely to commit suicide. How would you collect data to test your hypotheses? You'd probably need to get some data about a group's Facebook friends, friends in the real world, and suicide rates. You would then analyse the patterns in these data. And then, if all goes well, you could determine whether either of these hypotheses is supported by the evidence. That is a scientific approach to answering your questions.

THE DEVELOPMENT OF SCIENTIFIC KNOWLEDGE

The scientific method implies that a science develops gradually and cumulatively as one set of findings builds on another. Some studies fail to confirm earlier findings, and those come to be seen as dead ends; other findings are confirmed. Confidence in those findings grows as they are confirmed by additional research, and eventually some of them begin to be treated as scientific facts. All sciences are built on such facts. Over time and with additional research, however, some widely accepted facts may be found to be mistaken. For example, early scientists who studied the brain believed that women's relatively smaller brain size in comparison to men's was evidence of mental inferiority. Later research demonstrated that brain size does not determine intelligence, so those earlier ideas are no longer accepted (S. Gould 1981; Van Valen 1974). But some facts do survive empirical tests, and those are the ones that come to be the basis of what we think of as a science. For example, as you learned in this chapter's opening vignette, an accumulation of

data from research on climate patterns is what leads most scientists to treat the idea of climate change as a scientific fact. The Intergovernmental Panel on Climate Change (IPCC) is the most authoritative group of scientists from around the world that evaluates evidence of climate change. The IPCC (2007) built on past findings to confirm that global warming is a scientific fact and that human activity is the main force behind it. This gradual and orderly pattern of scientific development is what we would expect from the systematic use of the scientific method and the evolution of a science.

Thomas Kuhn ([1962] 1970), a philosopher of science, proposed a different model of scientific development that focuses on the role of scientific breakthroughs. To Kuhn, what defines a science is the existence of a **paradigm**, a general model of the world that is accepted by most practitioners in the field. Examples include the idea in astronomy that Earth and the other planets revolve around the Sun and the idea in biology that "germs" cause most infectious diseases. With a generally agreed-upon paradigm, scientists need not squabble among themselves over their general orientation and their most basic premises; they are free to do research within the confines and safety of that paradigm. As research expands on the paradigm, it is "fleshed out" in a series of tiny steps. Its fundamentals remain unaltered, at least for a time.

But some research does not support the dominant paradigm, and serious questions begin to be raised. If those questions are not answered and new ones continue to be raised, the old paradigm eventually collapses and is replaced by a new paradigm. In other words, a scientific revolution occurs. Kuhn argues that it is in those revolutions, the death of an old paradigm and the birth of a new one, that science takes great leaps forward. For example, for centuries scientists believed that Earth was at the centre of the universe, with the Sun orbiting around it (a geocentric model). It was not until the sixteenth century, when better research methods became available, that the geocentric paradigm began to be supplanted by a paradigm that saw Earth orbiting around the Sun (a heliocentric model). This was a revolution in astronomical thought. In the centuries that followed, other astronomers built on that knowledge and came to the consensus that Earth and the Sun are in fact parts of one solar system within one galaxy of many in the universe. Heliocentrism remains the dominant paradigm for explaining the relationship between Earth and the Sun, but new paradigms are developing to explain the role of both bodies in the universe as astronomers currently understand it.

Kuhn's single-paradigm approach fits very well with the history of the hard sciences such as astronomy and physics, but sociology and the other social sciences can perhaps better be seen as examples of "multiple paradigm science" (R. Friedrichs 1970; Ritzer 1975). No single paradigm in sociology is powerful enough to unify the discipline. The result is that research tends to occur within each paradigm within the discipline, expanding all of them over time but not contributing to a consensus within sociology as a whole. Furthermore, some of the research stemming from one paradigm may be in conflict with research stemming from other paradigms. Because of these differences and conflicts, the development of sociology as whole tends to be slower and more sporadic than that of the hard sciences. Additionally, because there has never been a single dominant paradigm, there have never been any paradigm revolutions in sociology. Rather, the fortunes of various paradigms rise and fall over time.

One key aspect of a multiple-paradigm science is that it is more difficult to accumulate knowledge that is accepted by practically everyone in the field. Sociologists do not operate in the safety of the confines offered by a science with a single dominant, and broadly agreed-upon, paradigm. The most basic assumptions of a given sociologist, or group of sociologists, are constantly open to question and attack by those who operate on the basis of other paradigms. The result is that sociologists often spend a good deal of time defending the specific assumptions behind a given piece of research.

There is a much less settled, universally agreed-upon knowledge base in sociology than in, say, biology or astronomy. Nonetheless, there is a substantial body of knowledge in sociology, some of which is summarised throughout this book. Because it lacks a dominant paradigm, there are also many more controversies in sociology than in some other fields. Thus, you will find in sociology many facts, as well as many interesting, stimulating, and exciting debates.

BIOGRAPHICAL bits

Dorothy Smith (1926–, British/Canadian)

- Smith was born in Yorkshire, England, receiving her PhD from Berkeley in 1963.

- Deeply moved by the emerging women's movement, Smith organized a session for Berkeley graduate students to "tell their stories" about gender inequities in academia.

- By 1967 she had moved to the University of British Columbia, where she helped to establish a women's studies program and taught some of the first women's studies courses in Canada.

- Smith advocates a "sociology for people" that begins in the particularities of an actual, everyday world. She calls her particular approach *institutional ethnography*.

- Institutional ethnography is a method that uses everyday experience as a lens to examine social relations and social institutions. Her book *Institutional Ethnography: A Sociology for People* (2005) has become a foundational text for classes in sociology, ethnography, and women's studies.

- In 1994, Smith became an adjunct professor at the University of Victoria, where she continues her work in institutional ethnography.

SOCIOLOGICAL RESEARCH

Sociological knowledge is derived from research using a number of different methods. In most cases, the method chosen is driven by the nature of the research question. Imagine that you are a sociologist and want to study the beliefs and behaviours of casino gamblers. You might start by using the research method of observation. Observation can take a variety of forms, ranging from participating at the roulette table as a fellow gambler to watching and listening at a distance.

A more direct and focused approach would be to interview those who have come to a casino to gamble. You might ask them questions about their expectations before they arrived and how those expectations related to their own previous experiences as well as to what they heard from others about their gambling experiences. This would be a more efficient use of your time because it would not entail waiting around for gamblers to do or say something relevant to your research question. However, in interviews people might not be willing to talk to you about their gambling experiences, especially if they have been losing money. Furthermore, even if they are willing to talk to you, they might not give you totally honest answers. Or you might have trouble getting permission to access a casino to interview patrons.

Another technique would be to conduct a survey. However, questions for a survey are not easy to formulate in just the right way. You would also need to figure out a good way of distributing the questionnaires to your respondents. You could hand them out to people leaving the casino, but many may not be willing to take them at that point especially if, as is likely, they have stayed up late gambling or have lost money. Even if they did take a questionnaire, they

What sorts of research might be conducted among these gamblers in Tokyo? What public policies and efforts to curb social problems might benefit from new knowledge regarding gambling?

might not answer the questions or mail the questionnaire back to you. Instead of handing out the questionnaires randomly to people leaving the casino, you could be more systematic and scientific by obtaining a list of guests at a given casino hotel, but it is highly unlikely that you would be given such private information. You could just get a sample of people from the phone book in your hometown and mail them questionnaires, but it is unlikely that many of them have visited a casino recently. Among the relatively few who have, only a very small number are likely to return the completed questionnaires to you.

You could also create an experiment. For example, in a social science laboratory at your university, you could set up a casino-style poker table. You could recruit students as participants in the experiment and tell them that the typical player loses 90 percent of the time and that previous research has shown that most players lose most of the time. You could then ask them whether, in spite of that information, they still want to gamble at your poker table. Of greatest interest would be those who say yes. You would want to interview them before they start "gambling" at your table, observe them as they gamble, and interview them again after they have finished. Did they start out believing, despite all the evidence to the contrary, that they would win? How could they have retained such a belief in spite of all the counterevidence? What are their feelings after gambling at your table, and did those feelings seem to be related to whether they won or lost? How likely are they to gamble again?

Observation, interviews, surveys, experiments, and other research methods are all useful and important to sociologists. All have strengths but also limitations. Before examining those strengths and limitations in more detail, you need to examine one important distinction among research methods.

QUALITATIVE AND QUANTITATIVE RESEARCH

One common way in which sociologists think about different research methods is by classifying them according to the kinds of data they seek to collect and analyse. Is the method essentially qualitative or quantitative?

GL🌐BALISATION

Port Security

Sociologists know that good theories are grounded in empirical observations. While in some cases our data are close at hand—often sociologists speak to basic aspects of our own everyday lives—sometimes our research questions require us to leave our everyday lives behind for a time, to travel great distances, and, occasionally, to face danger. When Carolyn Nordstrom embarked on her three-year journey to gather qualitative data on globalised crime, she had to do all three of these things.

During one leg of her journey, she investigated port security by strolling through the ships and shipyards across Africa, Europe, and America. She posed a simple question: "How far, as an undefined person—possibly a shipping agent or a terrorist—could I get across the so-called protected zones of the USA borders?" (Nordstrom 2007:195). Then, she proceeded to test this question by engaging in a real-world experiment. She found that she

> often made it to the water and to ships, and back, without being stopped. Even those berths with wire fences and closed gates guarded by security personnel asking for identification were surprisingly easy to enter. (Nordstrom 2007:195)

Though U.S. officials report that 6 percent of all shipments entering the country are checked, Nordstrom determined through her interviews with various dockworkers that even this small number is overly optimistic. During many of the days she spent at the Los Angeles dock, she observed for herself that the large X-ray machine that was supposed to be used to scan for contraband was never operated.

These findings forced Nordstrom to probe further: Given heightened security concerns after the 9/11 terrorist attacks, what could explain such an obvious lack of security regarding what entered and exited the country? Was it poor organisation or malfeasance? Were dockworkers corrupt or lazy? Any of these

explanations might account for lax security at a single port, but not for the trend of lax security in ports throughout the world. Sociologists are interested in structural explanations that are generalisable across many situations.

Nordstrom's work can be characterised as sociological because she offers us a broad explanation as to why security amounts to little more than an "illusion" in international shipping circuits: Global trade markets depend on rapidly flowing distribution networks in order to be economically viable. Such enormous amounts of material move across the border each day that it would literally require an army of inspectors and a vast array of scanning equipment to check every crate that came through. The cost is almost inconceivable.

Cape Town, South Africa, for example, received 3,010 vessels in 2002 (a little more than 8 each day). A large ship holds about 6,000 huge containers. It takes roughly five hours to inspect one container. This amounts to 30,000 hours to inspect the entire ship or 1,250 days of around-the-clock work. Thus, to inspect an entire ship, it would take an astounding 3.42 years. Ships are even bigger today than they were in 2002 (and there are a lot more of them), with the result that it might take even longer to inspect one of them. Due to these basic logistical and economic realities, Nordstrom concluded that comprehensive security is simply impossible given available resources. For Los Angeles to even achieve the supposed inspection rate of 6 percent, for example, the port would have to process 1,973 containers each day.

In addition to pointing up a fundamental problem with security in the international shipping industry, Nordstrom's research shows how multiple methods, both qualitative and quantitative, can be used together to produce a generalisable finding that works across the many manifestations of a complex system.

Qualitative research is any method that does not require statistical methods for collecting and reporting data (C. Marshall and Rossman 2010). Observation and open-ended interviews are two of the qualitative methods used by sociologists. These methods are used to capture descriptive information about an incredibly wide range of social phenomena—from social movements to cultural practises to people's lived experiences and feelings to the way in which organisations function to interactions between nations. By gathering information from a small number of groups and individuals, they often produce rich data about the social world and in-depth understanding of particular social processes. Sometimes they help provide insights about new areas where little research has been done. However, because qualitative methods usually rely on small sample sizes, the findings cannot be generalised to the broader population; for this, we use quantitative methods.

Quantitative research involves the analysis of numerical data derived usually from surveys and experiments (Creswell 2008). The analysis of quantitative data on groups of people can help us describe and better understand important observable social realities. For example, in her analysis of employment among full-time postsecondary students in Canada, Katherine Marshall (2010), a sociologist working for Statistics Canada, discovered

that almost one in two students now work for pay during the academic year, whereas in the late 1970s only about one in four did. Using survey data from many years she discovered several reasons for this upward trend. First, schooling has become more expensive recently, and employment earnings help meet these costs. Second, the worry about sizeable student debt upon graduation has likely spurred more students to seek employment during the school year. Third, although about 70 percent of students still find summer employment, this level is related both to the health of the economy and to summer jobs programmes implemented by governments. Marshall's work also helps to spotlight the growing demand for cooperative education opportunities in the Canadian postsecondary system.

The mathematical method used to analyse numerical data is **statistics**. It is a powerful tool, and most sociological researchers learn at least some statistical methods. Statistics can aid researchers in two ways:

- When researchers want to see trends over time or compare differences between groups, they use **descriptive statistics**. Their purpose is to describe some particular body of data that is based on a phenomenon in the real world (Salkind 2004:8–10). For example, researchers have used survey data to track trends in edu-

Qualitative Research

Quantitative Research

Qualitative research, such as conducting an interview, does not require statistics for collecting or reporting data. Conversely, quantitative research entails the analysis of numerical data derived from, for example, group surveys.

cational attainment over time and then used statistical analysis to describe how educational attainment varies by race, gender, and age (S. Davies and Guppy 2013).

- To test hypotheses, researchers use **inferential statistics**, which allow researchers to use data from a relatively small group to speculate with some level of certainty about a larger group. For example, through a field experiment on labour market discrimination, Oreopolus (2009) found that when people with comparable résumés applied for the same job, those with white-sounding names (such as Emily and Greg) were 40 percent more likely to be granted a job interview than applicants with Chinese, Indian, or Pakistani names (such as Tai, Ananya, and Haniya). Over 6,500 résumés were sent to employers, and the responses were used to draw broader inferences about the population of job applicants.

Sociologists do debate the relative merits of quantitative versus qualitative methods, but they generally recognise that each method has value. Each method has its own set of strengths and limitations in terms of what it can do to help a researcher to answer a specific question. Furthermore, there is a broad consensus that quantitative and qualitative research methods can complement one another (Ragin 1987; Rueschemeyer, Stephens, and Stephens 1992). In practise, sociologists may combine both quantitative and qualitative research methods in a single study.

OBSERVATIONAL RESEARCH

As mentioned earlier, one of the primary qualitative methods is **observation**, which involves systematic watching, listening to, and recording what takes place in a natural social setting over some period of time (Hammersley 2007). The observational techniques of sociologists are similar to the work of investigative journalists, who also learn a great deal about their topic by keeping their eyes and ears open. The most common observational methods among sociologists are participant and nonparticipant observation.

There are several key dimensions to any type of observation in sociology:

- *Degree to which those being observed are aware that they are being observed.* This

dimension can vary from everyone involved being fully informed about the research to being observed from afar or through hidden cameras, one-way mirrors, and the like. The reality TV series *Undercover Boss* involves a kind of covert observational research. Top-level executives work at lower levels in their own firms in order to learn more about the work and the workers. Of course, the boss might have ulterior motives such as uncovering and firing incompetent workers, but sociologists who do such research are not supposed to have such motives; they are simply interested in learning more about the work world.

- *Degree to which the presence of the observer affects what those being observed do.* Especially when they are aware that they are being observed, people often present themselves the way they think the observer expects or will accept. An example would be gang members who do not engage in illegal activities in the presence of a researcher.

- *Degree to which the process is structured.* Highly structured observational research might use preset categories or a checklist to guide observations. At the other end of the spectrum, some observations seek the widest possible range of data and are totally open and unstructured.

Journalists such as the ones accosting actor Russell Crowe seek to collect data, although they generally do so less systematically than sociologists.

PUBLIC SOCIOLOGY

Robert Park and "Scientific Reporting"

Robert Park (1864–1944), who coauthored the first real textbook on sociology, felt a strong need to work outside the academic world and thus started his career as a journalist. He said: "I made up my mind to go in for experience for its own sake, to gather into my soul . . . all the joys and sorrows of the world" (Park [1927] 1973:253). He particularly liked to wander around and explore the social world. For example, he wrote of "hunting down gambling houses and opium dens" (Park [1927] 1973:254).

In his reporting, Park wrote about city life in vivid detail. He would go into the field, observe carefully, and then write up his observations. He called his method *scientific reporting,* which was essentially the kind of social research that later came to be called *participant observation.*

In 1898, at the age of 34, Park left the newspaper business and returned to school, eventually completing his doctoral dissertation in 1904 at the University of Heidelberg in Germany. Instead of taking an academic position, Park went to work for the Congo Reform Association, an organisation dedicated to exposing the abuses and exploitation of the Congo by the Belgians. He then became secretary to Booker T. Washington at Tuskegee Institute.

Park joined the Department of Sociology at the University of Chicago in 1914 and played a central role during its heyday. His use of the city as a kind of laboratory for his observational studies helped move the Chicago department into a leadership position in sociology. Park had an important indirect effect on Canadian sociology, serving as an important mentor for Everett Hughes, one of the early giants of Canadian sociology (see Helmes-Hayes 1998; E. Hughes 1943).

Park's case demonstrates the close association between journalism and at least some forms of sociology. Throughout his life Park retained an interest in, and a passion for, the accurate description of social life. However, he grew dissatisfied with journalism because it did not fulfill his intellectual needs. In contrast to journalism, sociology draws upon theory and uses more systematic methods of data collection and analysis. Park's ability to use sociological methods to pursue his deep interest in reforming society and overcoming its ills, especially with regard to race relations, is an important reason to consider him a public sociologist.

Some of the most famous research in the history of sociology has been done using the observational method. Examples include studies that produced such books as *The Philadelphia Negro* (Du Bois [1899] 1996), *Street Corner Society* (Whyte 1943), and *The Barbershop Singer* (Stebbins 1996).

Participant and Nonparticipant Observation

There are two major types of observational methods. One is **participant observation**, in which the researcher actually plays a role, usually a minor one, in the group or setting being observed. A participant observer might work as a salesperson for different vendors to learn about culture and consumption (Hanser 2008) or become a (quasi-)member of a gang (S. Venkatesh 2008). Robert Stebbins, who taught at the University of Calgary for many years, is perhaps the most prolific participant observer in Canadian sociology. He has provided insider accounts of magicians (1984), musicians (1996), kayakers, snowboarders, and mountain/ice climbers (2005), among others. In another example of a classic study, a sociologist researched gender segregation in the corporate world of the 1970s by, among other things, participating in group discussions and meetings at a major U.S. company (Kanter 1993). More recently, Kevin Haggerty (2004) has reported his sociological observations on what he calls "ethics creep." Haggerty was a member of a research ethics board at the University of Alberta, and as a participant in many decisions about what did and did not constitute ethical conduct among researchers, he came to the conclusion that there was a growing rupture between following the rules and acting ethically. In important ways the bureaucratic rules had become red tape that made ethical actions difficult and disingenuous.

The Discovery Channel's TV show *Dirty Jobs* is essentially an informal exercise in participant observation. The show's star, Mike Rowe, is not a trained sociologist, and he is not trying to uncover the sociological aspects of the jobs he is studying, but he is a participant observer. In each episode, he actually does the job that is being examined—he is a participant—and he observes the workers as well as their dirty jobs. Among the jobs Rowe has performed and observed since 2005 (the first year of the show) are "turd burner," owl vomit collector, baby chicken sexer, sheep castrator, rat exterminator, maggot farmer, diaper cleaner, and high-rise building window washer.

The second observational method is **nonparticipant observation**, where the sociologist plays little or no role in what is being observed. For example, Nathan Young and Ralph Matthews (2010), two sociologists, examine the controversy over the industrialisation of the salmon fishing industry. At one time salmon were solely caught in the wild, but now increasingly around the world, and on both the east and west coasts of Canada, salmon are farmed, much as wheat or potatoes are farmed. This industrial process has created enormous controversy, including the effects on wild stocks, the role of science, and the value of the jobs created. Young and

Matthews observed the ongoing disputes between different groups, the farm owners, the environmentalists, the fish and food scientists, and so forth. They attended workshops and conferences, protest events and promotional activities, all to get a better appreciation of how and why the controversy was played out. They did not participate as salmon farmers, but they observed multiple venues in which the controversies around salmon farming occurred.

The *Real World* reality show, which began on MTV in 1992, can be seen as another example of nonparticipant observation. Of course, sociologists are not involved in this show, and the observation is not as systematic as it would be if it were a sociological study. The show is based on selecting a group of young people who have never met to live together in a house. The show takes place in a different city every year; in 2010, it was set in New Orleans. Although a camera operator is there to record at least some of the group's activities, no outsider is present in the house to participate in those activities. The "observers" are the viewing audience. They can be seen as amateur nonparticipant observers in the sense that they "study" interaction patterns and other sociological aspects of what goes on among the residents.

In reality, there are no firm dividing lines between participant and nonparticipant observation, and at times they blend imperceptibly into one another. The participant often becomes simply an observer. An example is the sociologist who begins with

Mike Rowe has observed and performed a wide gamut of unconventional occupations on the Discovery Channel's *Dirty Jobs*. Though this program's episodes are not framed as sociological research, Rowe is essentially playing the part of a participant observer.

participant observation of a gang, hanging out with members in casual settings, but becomes a nonparticipant when illegal activities such as drug deals take place. And the nonparticipant observer sometimes becomes a participant. An example is the sociologist who is unable to avoid being asked to take sides or share opinions in squabbles among members of a Little League team or, more likely, among their parents.

Ethnography

At times sociologists are interested in an observational method traditionally associated with anthropology. **Ethnography** is the creation of an account of what a group of people do and the way they live (Hammersley 2007), usually entailing much more intensive and lengthy periods of observation than traditional sociological observation. Researchers may live for years with the groups, tribes, or subcultures (such as gamblers) being studied.

Sociologists interested in a variety of topics advocate the use of ethnographic methods. Brian Wilson (2002) studied the rave subculture in Southern Ontario. He attended rave parties, interviewed rave partiers, hung out with ravers, and attended rave radio station sessions. His intent was to provide an authentic insider's account of the lifestyle of ravers, a subculture many knew nothing about because their views and activities were often distorted by the popular press. Like Wilson, feminist researchers are especially concerned that study participants not be exploited by the research process.

Normally ethnographies are by their nature small in scale, microscopic, and local. Researchers actually observe people, talk to them, and conduct interviews with them over an extended period of time. Nevertheless, the ethnographic method has now been extended to the global level. For instance, Michael Burawoy (2000) argues that a **global ethnography**—a type of ethnography that is grounded in various parts of the world and that seeks to understand globalisation as it exists in people's social lives—is the best way to understand globalisation. He and his colleagues "set out from real experiences . . . of welfare clients, homeless recyclers, mobilized feminists, migrant nurses, union organizers, software engineers, poisoned villagers, redundant boilermakers, and breast cancer activists in order to explore *their* global contexts" (Burawoy 2000:34).

Three interconnected phenomena are central to the global ethnographies undertaken by Burawoy and others:

- Do people experience globalisation as an external force? If so, is it a force to be combated or accepted?
- In what ways, if at all, do people participate in creating and furthering global connections?
- Do people work for or against those things that are global in scope?

Burawoy and his colleagues sought to answer these questions wherever in the world they undertook their studies.

One example of a global ethnography is a study of how marginalised groups are able to resist being pushed around even though they appear to have little economic power. Jennifer Chun (2009), a colleague of Burawoy's but now at the University of Toronto, examines how low-wage service workers (e.g., golf caddies, university cleaning staff) in South Korea and the United States are able to organise for both monetary benefit and moral advantage.

Dorothy Smith (2005) has pioneered the method of **institutional ethnography**. One way to understand this is to realise that all institutions have formal and informal rules. There are the official rules of the firm or the school, and there are the ways in which things actually happen in the firm or school. Normal institution-speak comes from the top down and provides the public relations spin of the ruling interests. Smith opts to highlight the standpoint of the underlings, the working people at the lower echelons of an institution, showing how their experiential viewpoints of institutional processes and power relations differ from the official institutional discourse. Griffith and Smith (2005) use this method of inquiry in their examination of how governments have reduced their school financing budgets by downloading more and more responsibilities on families, a process that intensifies the academic advantages of students from better-off families.

INTERVIEWS

While observers often interview those they are studying, they usually do so very informally and

DIGITAL LIVING

Netnography

The Internet is a social world. Communications, relationships, and groups—which are among the most basic concerns of sociologists—are key elements of the Internet. The most obvious aspects of the Internet of interest to sociologists are online discussion forums, as well as social networking sites such as Facebook, Myspace, and Twitter. Because of them, access to discussions, social relationships, and social groups has expanded. However, fundamental concepts (such as norms), theories (such as symbolic interactionism; see Chapter 2), and methods (especially observation) are much the same both online and offline. Not surprisingly, netnography, or an account of what transpires online, has become a highly relevant method for sociological research (Turkle 1997, 2011).

Netnographers are observing thousands of phenomena online. For example, a netnographer might join the online fan club of a world-famous rock star in order to learn something about the relationship between a star and her fans. The researcher might be able to interact directly with the fans and the star through a Twitter feed. Netnographers can also intently study the use of Facebook by activists such as took place in Egypt while they were engaged in the ultimately successful effort to overthrow longtime dictator Hosni Mubarak in 2011. Membership in this emerging online community gave researchers real-time access to ongoing global communication. When the success in Egypt spawned popular social uprisings in other countries, researchers had the opportunity to study how newly emerging popular movements in one country can shape others.

Another example of netnography is illustrated in the map shown here, which uses Crowdmap software to plot the location of occurrences reported via user-generated videos, images, blogs, and tweets. This crowdmap was published by Voice of America in the Middle East in a project called *Behind the Wall*, which collects social media reports on street demonstrations, such as those described in Chapter 1, in Syria, Yemen, and Bahrain (Samnani and Nur 2011). Figure 3.3 plots street demonstrations in Syria in 2011. The maps are a new way to document oppression and record history in the making. These new social media reports also provide many other new opportunities for understanding social dynamics.

Globalisation, introduced in Chapter 1, is one subject that is far easier to study on the Internet than it is anywhere else (Kozinets 2002). Instead of needing to be in several places around the world, netnographers who study globalisation can do most, if not all, of the research from their computers. Many online communities are global in their scope, engaged in global communications, and generating global actions of various kinds (for example, efforts to deal with the causes of climate change). A great attraction of these

An art student from Helwan University paints the Facebook logo on a mural commemorating the 2011 revolution that overthrew Egyptian President Hosni Mubarak. As the Egyptian protests escalated, activists painted icons of the protests, including Facebook, which they used to organise protests.

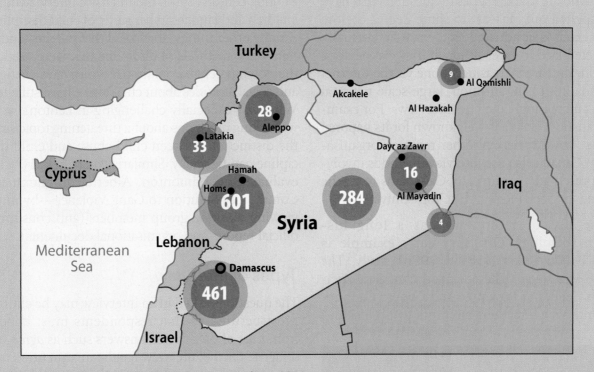

FIGURE 3.3 Number of Syrian Street Demonstrations, 2011

SOURCE: From VOA Middle East Voices: Behind the Wall-Syria crowdmap, in Hina Samnani and Lolla Mohammed Nur, "Crowdmapping Arab Spring—Next Social Media Breakthrough?" June 28, 2011.

communities to the researcher is that they can be tapped into instantly, with little effort, and at no cost. However, language barriers can be a problem. It is also important to remember that people in some parts of the world are unable to access the Internet very often, or even at all, so their interests are not going to be well represented online.

Netnography, like all social research, raises ethical questions. For example, researchers who join an Internet community to observe its ongoing communications might not inform other members of the community that they have joined with the objective of studying it. Their motives are reasonable—not tainting the evidence—but their means may raise eyebrows. Such nonparticipant observers have been called "lurkers." This type of deception is more difficult in face-to-face groups where the researchers see those they are deceiving on a regular basis and must conceal this deception from them, perhaps while looking them straight in the eye.

One way of avoiding this ethical problem, at least to some degree, is to study the group's archived material rather than its ongoing communication. (Another advantage of studying archived material is that it avoids the problem that knowledge of the presence of a researcher could affect the nature of communication among the participants.) However, studying the archives does not avoid all ethical problems. It is akin to researchers not revealing that they are surreptitiously examining the personal letters, photo albums, or diaries of the people they are studying. The netnographer would need to get consent from all members of an online community to be allowed access to the group's archives. So although netnography is a new tool in the researcher's kit, it has its ethical issues and drawbacks—like every other research method.

on the spur of the moment. Other sociologists rely mainly, or exclusively, on **interviews** in which information is sought from participants (respondents) who are asked a series of questions that have been spelled out, at least to some degree, before the research is conducted. Interviews are usually conducted face-to-face, although they can be done by phone and are increasingly done via the Internet (Fontana 2007). In addition, large-scale national surveys increasingly include interviews. For example, Statistics Canada is well known for its national surveys, but a variety of other research organisations in Canada also use interview methods involving representative samples of Canadians (e.g., the Institute for Social Research at York University).

The use of interviews has a long history in sociology. One very early example is W. E. B. Du Bois's ([1899] 1996) study, *The Philadelphia Negro*. The so-called chocolate sociologists Seebohm Rowntree and George Cadbury used interviews in their attempts to understand poverty in England, a method that was followed in Montreal in the late 1890s by Sir Herbert Brown Ames (Guppy and Gray 2008). More recently, Rhonda Lenton (1990) did intensive interviewing of children and families in her study of child discipline. Among other things, she found that parents tend to mimic the methods of discipline that were used by their own parents, even though times have changed and social attitudes about child abuse have stiffened. What was especially challenging in Lenton's work was asking questions about a threatening topic since the distinction between child abuse and child discipline can be tricky. Similarly, Jana Grekul (2011) evaluated an Edmonton, Alberta, programme—Community Solution to Gang Violence—by interviewing working group members (and consulting official reports and organisational documents).

Types of Interview

The questions asked in an interview may be entirely prestructured so that respondents must choose from a set of preselected answers such as *agree* and *disagree*. Or the interview can be unstructured and completely open-ended, as is the case with questions asked by observers. An unstructured interview offers no preset answers; respondents are free to say anything they want to say.

Prestructured interviews are attractive when the researcher wants to avoid any unanticipated reactions or responses from those being studied. In a prestructured interview, the interviewer attempts to

- behave in the same way in each interview;
- ask the same questions using the same exact words and in the same sequence;
- ask closed-ended questions where the participant must choose from a set of preselected responses;
- offer the same explanations when they are requested by respondents; and
- not show any kind of reaction to the answers no matter what they might be.

Interviews conducted in this way often yield information that can be coded numerically and then analysed statistically, as is the case with data obtained from questionnaires.

A global ethnographer seeks to understand the effect of globalisation on people's lives, such as the impact of foreign-born nurses on the nursing profession.

BIOGRAPHICAL bits

Michael Burawoy (late 1940s–, British)

- Burawoy is a professor and teacher of sociology at the University of California–Berkeley.

- He has used participant observation to research workplaces in four different countries: the United States, Hungary, Zambia, and Russia. He was quoted in *The Village Voice* in 2001 as saying, "The dream of my life was to get a job in a steel mill in a socialist country."

- He is an avowed Marxist whose most famous work, *Manufacturing Consent: Changes in the Labor Process Under Monopoly Capitalism* (1979), explores why workers consent to conditions of exploitation.

- He has been a strong advocate of *public sociology*—sociology that seeks to reach public audiences outside the academy—as a way of linking research and the public, thereby broadening dialogue about pressing social issues.

- Burawoy served as president of the American Sociological Association in 2003–2004 and used the occasion of his presidential address to promote the idea of public sociology.

SOURCE: Byles (2003).

There are problems associated with prestructured interviews. First, interviewers often find it difficult to live up to the guidelines for such interviews. They are frequently unable to avoid reacting to answers (especially outrageous ones), they may use a different intonation from one interview to another, and they may change the wording, and even the order, of the questions asked. Second, respondents may not respond accurately or truthfully. For example, they may give answers that they believe the interviewer may want to hear. Third, and most important, closed-ended questions limit the responses, possibly cutting off important, unanticipated information that might be provided by a more free-flowing interview.

The latter problem is solved by the use of open-ended or *unstructured interviews*. The interviewer begins with only a general idea of the topics to be covered and the direction to be taken in the interview. The answers in unstructured interviews offer a good understanding of the respondents and what the issues under study mean to them. Such understandings and meanings are generally not obtained from structured interviews. However, unstructured interviews create problems of their own, such as yielding so much diverse information that it is hard to offer a coherent summary and interpretation of the results.

The Interview Process

Conducting interviews, especially those that are prestructured, usually involves several steps. The researcher does not simply make a list of questions and start asking them.

1. The interviewer must *gain access* to the setting being studied. This is relatively easy in some cases, such as interviewing one's friends in the student union or a local bar. However, access would likely be much more difficult if one wanted to interview one's friends in a sorority house or on the job. They might be less eager to talk to a researcher—to any outsider—in such settings. Some groups, such as the top executives of major corporations or the extremely wealthy, have the resources to insulate themselves; they can be quite difficult for researchers to gain access to and thus may be underrepresented in sociological research.

2. The interviewer must often seek to *locate a key informant* (Rieger 2007), or someone who has intimate knowledge of the group being studied and who is willing to talk openly to the researcher about the group. Key informants can help the researcher gain access to the larger group of respondents and verify information being provided by them. The latter is useful because interviewees may well provide erroneous, perhaps purposely erroneous, information. For example, in William F. Whyte's (1943) famous study of street corner society, a leader of the group,

Unstructured interviews, often referred to as oral histories, are conducted to capture unique perspectives about personal experiences and events. Such interviews are employed to give voice to the disenfranchised (whose accounts might otherwise go unheard). Oral histories of immigrants to Canada are now recorded for many different ethnic groups.

"Doc," served as Whyte's key informant. In Sudhir Venkatesh's (2008) study of a Chicago housing project and its gangs, his key informant was the gang leader "J.T." Of this relationship, Venkatesh (1994) says, "In the course of my fieldwork I became dependent on the continual support of J.T." (p. 322). J. T. not only corrected Venkatesh's misinformation and misinterpretations but also retained the right to delete information that might disclose his identity or that of his gang.

3. The interviewer must seek to *understand the language and culture* of the people being interviewed. In some cases this is very easy. For example, it is not a great problem for an academic interviewer to understand the world of university students. However, it is more difficult if the people to be interviewed by academicians are members of motorcycle gangs or prostitutes in a brothel with their own very different language and culture. In these kinds of cases, it becomes all too easy for the researcher

to misunderstand or to impose incorrect meanings on the words of respondents.

4. The researcher must *gain the trust of the respondents and develop a rapport* with them. Establishing trust and rapport can be easy or difficult, depending on who you are. Feminist scholars would point out that researchers' social position—well educated, relatively powerful—may intimidate the less privileged people they study. Older researchers may have trouble interviewing students; former gang members may have trouble getting information from current members of a gang. In a few cases, trust and rapport need only be earned once, but in many cases, they need to be earned over and over. And trust can easily be lost. Venkatesh had to work constantly on his rapport with J.T., gang members, and many others who lived in the projects. In fact, J.T. at first thought Venkatesh might be a cop and later on confessed that he was never 100 percent sure that Venkatesh was not a policeman. Venkatesh was also in constant danger of losing the very tenuous trust his participants had in him and what he was doing. There was ever-present fear on the part of his participants that he was in league with a rival gang or would inform on them to the police.

SURVEY RESEARCH

Survey research involves the collection of information from a population, or more usually a representative portion of a population, through the use of interviews and, most importantly, questionnaires. While some sociologists do their own surveys, most rely on data derived from surveys done by others such as Statistics Canada or the Institute for Social Research at York University, which conducts various opinion polls and other studies.

Interviews, as we know, involve questions being asked by the researcher in person or on the telephone. The Labour Force Survey, undertaken monthly by Statistics Canada, uses face-to-face interviews involving a large sample of Canadians (the information is used for, among other things, calculating the unemployment rate). In contrast, **questionnaires** are self-administered, written sets of questions. While the questions can be presented to respondents on a face-to-face basis, they are more often delivered to them by mail, asked over the telephone, or presented in web-based formats. Questionnaires are now increasingly filled out on one's personal computer and over the phone (Guppy and Gray 2008).

Types of Survey

There are two broad types of survey. The first is the **descriptive survey** designed to gather accurate information about, for example, those in a group, people in a given geographic area, and those in organisations. A descriptive survey might gather data on the level of sexual activity of university students, the employment status of Canadians, or the way former Blockbuster employees are coping with job loss. The best known descriptive surveys are those conducted by organisations such as Environics, which describe preferences, beliefs, and attitudes of a given sample of people.

In one example of descriptive survey research using the Internet, a survey was placed on a website designed to allow married people to find extramarital sexual partners. Based on a sample of more than 5,000 respondents, the data showed that females were more likely than males to engage in "sexting" (see Chapter 10) and that males and females involved in serious real-life relationships were about equally likely to engage in cheating both online and in real life (Wysocki and Childers 2011).

The Canadian General Social Survey has been conducted regularly since 1985 by Statistics Canada. Martin Turcotte (2011) combined information from 12 different years to chart access to university by students from different social class backgrounds. He wanted to see if there was greater equality of educational opportunity more recently. First he described the growing trend of more people obtaining university degrees more recently, rising from about 15 percent of 25- to 39-year-olds in 1986 to just over 30 percent in 2009. But his question was whether, relative to other classes, students from working-class backgrounds were increasing their presence.

To get at this he had to uncover potential causes for university access, and in particular explain whether or not the effect of parental background was still a strong predictor of university attendance.

If parental background still mattered a lot, this might mean more working-class students might be at university, but their relative chances of attending university might not have increased. That would mean that equality of educational opportunity had not changed. Figure 3.4 shows what he found. The two lines in the upper half of the graph represent students whose parents had some university experience, whereas the lower two lines are for students from families where no parent went to university. The two sets of lines are not converging as greater equality of educational opportunity would imply (but notice that relative to men's, women's university attainment has increased noticeably).

Sampling

It is almost never possible to survey an entire population, such as all Canadians or all students at your college or university. Thus survey researchers usually need to construct a **sample**, or a representative portion of the overall population. The more careful the researcher is in avoiding biases in selecting the sample, the more representative of the whole group the findings are likely to be.

The most common way to avoid bias is to create a **random sample**, a sample in which every member of the group has an equal chance of being included. Random samples can be obtained by using a list of, for example, names of all the professors at your university. A coin is tossed for each name on the list. Those professors for whom the toss results in heads are included in the sample. More typical and efficient is the use of random number tables, found in most statistics textbooks, to select those in the sample (Guppy and Gray 2008). In our example, each professor is assigned a number, and those whose number comes up in the random number table are included in the sample. More recently, use is being made of computer-generated random numbers. Other sampling techniques are used in survey research as well. For example, the researcher might create a **stratified sample** in which a larger group is divided into a series of subgroups and then random samples are taken within each of these groups. This ensures representation from each group in the final sample, something that might not occur if one simply did a random sample of the larger group. Thus random and stratified sampling are the safest ways of

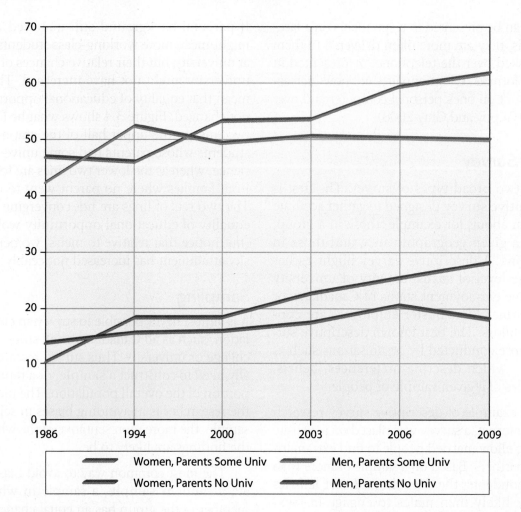

FIGURE 3.4 University Degree Attainment (%) of Canadian-born People 25–39 by Sex and Parents' Educational Background

SOURCE: Authors' calculations from Turcotte (2011); based on Statistics Canada, General Social Survey.

NOTE: Note that the dates on the x-axis are uneven, so interpreting the annual rate of change is deceiving.

drawing accurate conclusions about a population as a whole. However, there is an element of chance in all sampling, especially random sampling, with the result that findings can vary from one sample to another. Even though sampling is the safest way of reaching conclusions about a population, errors are possible. Random and stratified sampling are depicted in Figure 3.5.

Sometimes researchers use **convenience samples**, which avoid systematic sampling and simply include those who are conveniently available to participate in a research project. For example, Bob Brym and Rhonda Lenton (2001) wanted to explore online dating, so they used both a random sample of Canadians, contacted by telephone using

random-digit dialing, and a self-selected sample of people who accessed one of Canada's leading online dating sites. By comparing the two samples they were able to provide some description of the demographic differences between the two groups. Those using the online dating site were, as you might expect, younger, better educated, and more likely to be employed than members of the general public. Online users were busier and reported using the online site as a more efficient way to meet other singles. Online respondents also noted that workplace romance was declining because of worries about sexual harassment. However, as Brym and Lenton caution, they cannot tell how representative their online respondents are because these respondents all self-selected (but getting a random sample of

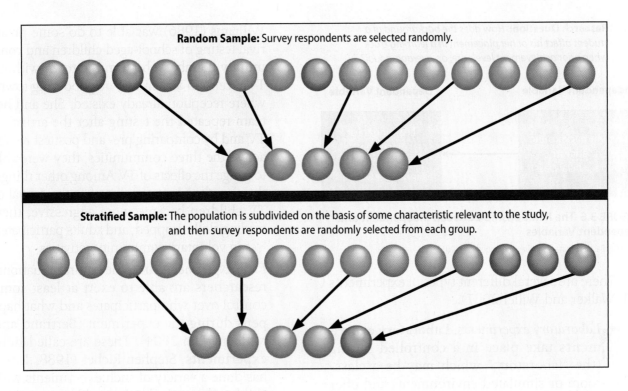

FIGURE 3.5 Random Samples and Stratified Samples

online dating site users would have been extremely difficult). Research based on convenience samples is usually only exploratory, as it is almost impossible to draw any definitive conclusions from such research. There are, however, some cases in which convenience sampling is not only justified but can be useful. For researchers trying to study elite social networks (such as political leaders or the wealthy), simply gaining access to the group can be a task in itself. Convenience sampling—surveying anyone to whom one is introduced—may be the only way to proceed (Tansey 2006). Convenience sampling also sometimes leads to larger, more scientific projects that might rely on random or stratified samples.

EXPERIMENTS

Sociologists do not do nearly as many experiments as researchers in hard sciences such as chemistry or even in other social sciences such as psychology. However, some sociologists do perform experiments, and experimentation is one of the fundamental methods in the field. An **experiment** involves the manipulation of one or more characteristics in order to examine the effect of that manipulation (Guppy and Gray 2008).

A sociological study by Riley and Ungerleider (2012) provides a good example of a sociological experiment. They wanted to know if a student's background (e.g., the student's ancestry, gender, or social class) was instrumental in how teachers decided on the future learning trajectories of the student. That is, was scholastic achievement or student background most influential in determining whether someone was placed in a remedial, standard, or advanced learning track? To do this the researchers created student files where achievement level was held constant, on average, but where student background varied. The major finding of this experiment was that student background had an effect on decisions about learning placement, above and beyond the influence that prior achievement levels had.

In this experiment, we can clearly see the relationship between two important elements of an experiment: independent and dependent variables. As Figure 3.6 shows, in Riley/Ungerleider experiment, the **independent variable**, the condition that was manipulated by the researcher, was the student's family background. The **dependent variable**, the characteristic or measurement that resulted from the manipulation, was the learning track in which the student was placed.

Research Question: *How does the background of a student affect his or her placement in a learning track when prior achievement levels are, on average, equal?*

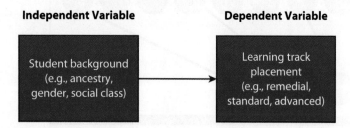

FIGURE 3.6 The Relationship between Independent and Dependent Variables

SOURCE: Based on data from Riley and Ungerleider (2012).

There are several different types of experiments (H. Walker and Willer 2007):

- *Laboratory experiments.* **Laboratory experiments** take place in a controlled setting (the "laboratory," which may be a classroom or simulated environment) and offer the researcher great control over the selection of the participants and the independent variables—the conditions to which they are exposed (Lucas, Graif, and Lovaglia 2008). The famous experiments by Solomon Asch on conformity (see Chapter 5) were laboratory experiments. This type of experiment can be difficult to organise and sometimes yields artificial results, but it allows for more accurate tests of research hypotheses. Some important results regarding the undervaluation of women's work have come from such studies, often because it is only under experimental conditions that we can control other influences and thus gain confidence in the finding that it is solely the differential evaluation of gender that is at work (Foschi 2000).

- *Natural experiments.* Experiments in which researchers take advantage of a naturally occurring event to study its effect on one or more dependent variables, called **natural experiments**, offer the least experimenter control over independent variables (De Silva et al. 2010). A classic Canadian example involves the introduction of television to a remote community in British Columbia. Because the community was in a secluded valley, television reception was not available until 1973. Prior to TV coming to the community, Tanis

Williams (1986) was able to do some prearrival testing of school-aged children and community members, both in the town without TV reception and in two neighbouring towns where reception already existed. She and her team repeated the testing after the arrival of TV, and by comparing pre- and posttest results across the three communities, they were able to gauge the effects of TV. Among other things, their results suggested that after the arrival of TV children became more aggressive, their reading skills dropped, and adults participated less in voluntary community activities.

- *Field experiments.* In some natural situations, researchers are able to exert at least some control over who participates and what happens during the experiment (Bertrand and Mullainathan 2004). These are called **field experiments**. Stephen Richer (1988, 1990) has done a variety of such experiments with children where he has been able to intervene in school settings to see how children react to different gendered arrangements. By analysing the drawings and paintings of children, he has examined how the production of gender segregation unfolds.

Some observers see a bright future for experimentation in sociology, in part because of its growth in neighbouring fields such as psychology and especially in fields such as economics and political science that in the past did not do much experimentation. Another reason is the potential to use the Internet as a site for sociological experiments (Hanson and Hawley 2011; Lauster and Easterbrook 2011).

SECONDARY DATA ANALYSIS

All of the methods discussed thus far involve the collection of new and original data, but many sociologists engage in **secondary data analysis** in which they reanalyse data collected by others. Secondary analysis can involve a wide variety of different types of data, from censuses and surveys to historical records and old transcripts of interviews and focus groups. Until recently, obtaining and using some of these secondary data sets was labourious and time-consuming. Today, however, thousands of data sets are available on the web, and they can be accessed with a few keystrokes. A number of websites provide both the data sets and statistical software to look at them in different ways (Schutt 2007).

Secondary analysis very often involves statistical analysis of government surveys and census data. The technique has a long history in sociology, extending back to Karl Marx analysing government statistics at the British Library. The Canadian census data that are collected every 10 years—they were last collected for 2010—are a gold mine for sociologists both here and abroad. For example, Lautard and Guppy (2011) used census data to track the changing representation of ethnic minorities in the Canadian labour force from 1931 to 2006. A persistent finding in Canada has been the existence of a vertical mosaic with Anglophone Canadians as a group earning the highest average incomes, holding many of the best jobs, and predominating as members of the corporate elite (Clement 1975; Porter 1965). Other ethnic groups have gradually made gains, but the verticality of the mosaic has not collapsed. It is not unusual for one body of data to lead to hundreds of secondary analyses. For example, the *World Values Survey* (WVS n.d.; see also the next *Globalisation* box) has

been used to produce over 400 research publications in more than 20 different languages. Some of this research has used the WVS to examine what social, cultural, and economic factors contribute to an individual's happiness. Figure 3.7 shows a "happiness map" among the citizens of various countries included in the surveys from 1999 to 2001. Another study examined data from 1981 to 2007 and found that perceptions of freedom of choice are more likely to lead to higher levels of happiness (Inglehart et al. 2008). However, subsequent research may look differently at the data and describe new parts of the puzzle. Using similar data from the WVS, another study looking at individual cases within countries demonstrated that inequalities in health quality, among other factors, also shape happiness (Ovaska and Takashima 2010).

While secondary analysis is far easier and far less expensive than collecting one's own data, especially large amounts of data, it has distinctive problems. For one thing, secondary researchers cannot refine their methods on the basis of preliminary research. For another, since others have chosen the methods of data collection, the data may not be ideal for the secondary researcher's needs. It is possible

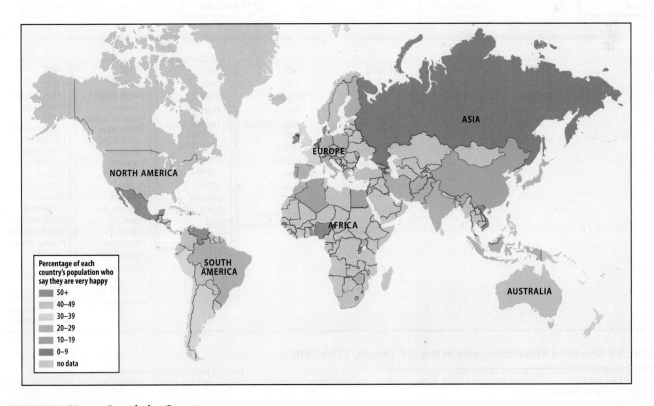

FIGURE 3.7 Happy People by Country

SOURCES: From World Values Survey. Reprinted with permission.

that the research may have to be abandoned until an appropriate data set is available or created. In some cases, researchers who find the data set inadequate for a study of their original interest may find that other relevant issues are covered better by the data. Another type of problem with using government data sets is political: Certain types of sensitive data might not be collected. Or social or political changes may end the collection of certain types of data or change the way the data are reported or categorised. For instance, Canadian census data on ethnicity have changed over the years to accommodate changing demographics and sensitivities

(see Figure 3.8). The resulting inconsistencies in the data set over time can pose great difficulties for the secondary researcher (Lautard and Guppy 2011).

HISTORICAL-COMPARATIVE METHOD

The goal of **historical-comparative research** is to contrast how different historical events and conditions in various societies led to different societal outcomes. The hyphenation of *historical-comparative*

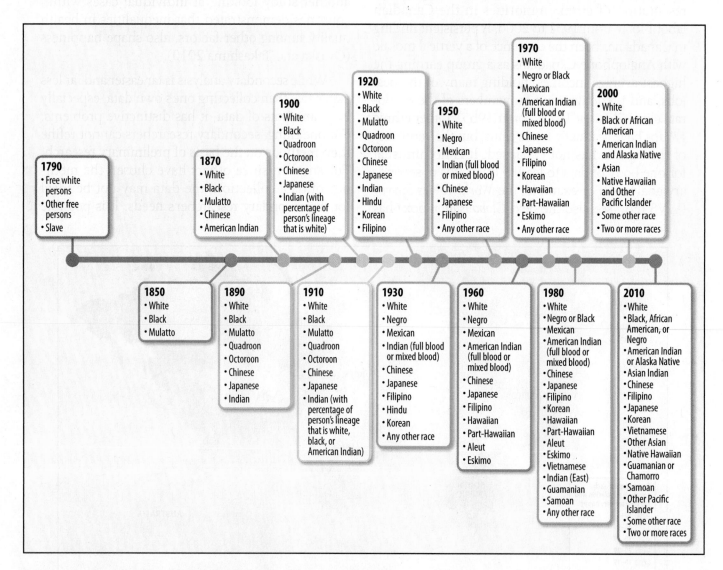

FIGURE 3.8 Changing Racial Categories in the U.S. Census, 1790–2010

SOURCES: Adapted from "Through the Decades." U.S. Census Bureau; "2000 Census of Population, Public Law 94–171 Redistricting Data File: Race". U.S. Census Bureau; "2010 Census Questionnaire Reference Book," U.S. Census Bureau; and Karen R. Humes, Nicholas A. Jones, and Roberto R. Ramirez, "Overview of Race and Hispanic Origin: 2010," 2010 Census Briefs, Issued March 2011, U.S. Census Bureau.

NOTE: The U.S. Census is conducted every 10 years. The censuses mentioned here are the ones in which significant changes were made in racial categories.

makes it clear that two separable methods are being combined. The historical component involves the study of the history of societies, as well as of the major components of society such as the state, religious system, and economy. The addition of the comparative element, comparing the histories of two or more societies, or of components of societies, makes it more distinctively sociological.

One of the things that differentiate history and historical-comparative sociology is the level of historical detail. Historians go into much more detail, and collect much more original historical data, than do sociologists. In contrast, sociologists are much more interested in generalising about society than are historians. Perhaps the best way to exemplify the difference between a historical-comparative sociologist and a historian is in the concept of the ideal type (Clegg 2007; Weber [1921] 1968). An **ideal type**, to Max Weber, is a distorted or exaggerated image of reality that is not meant to be an accurate depiction of reality, as would be the goal for historians, but rather is designed to help us better understand social reality. It is a sort of measuring rod. Thus, for example, Weber developed an ideal type of bureaucracy, which exaggerated its rational elements. He then used that ideal type to compare organisations in different societies and time periods in terms of their degree of rationality. Not surprisingly, he concluded that organisations of the modern West are the most rational and thus best approximate the ideal type of the bureaucracy.

Weber is the preeminent historical-comparative sociologist in the history of sociology (Mahoney and Rueschmeyer 2003; Tyrell 2010; Varcoe 2007). Consider his comparison of the world's major religions and their impact on the economy. Through comparative analysis of the histories of Protestantism in the West, Confucianism in China, and Hinduism in India, Weber sought to determine which religions fostered the development of capitalism and which served to impede its development. Of course, Weber knew that capitalism had developed in the West and not in China and India. The issue, then, was what about these religions (and many other social factors) did or did not foster the emergence of capitalism. A key factor was the fact that in contrast to Protestantism, the other religions did not foster rationality and efficiency and a striving for material success. Sometimes, they even served to inhibit rationality and efficiency, thus preventing the development of capitalism.

More recent instances of historical-comparative research have covered a wide range of issues. One researcher used a historical-comparative approach to elucidate critical differences in the timing and character of modern pension systems that developed in Britain, Canada, and the United States (Orloff 1993). This analysis highlights the role played by states and political institutions. Another researcher used historical-comparative research to elaborate four distinct kinds of states that developed in early modern Europe (Ertman 1997). Careful examination of the evidence from a number of earlier cases suggested that theories about state development based on war needed to be further refined. Although war remained an influence on the shape and character of European states, the long-standing structure of local government and the timing of geopolitical competition played even more important roles in explaining differences (see Kestnbaum [2012] for a current review of work on the relationship between the state and war).

Some scholars have combined the use of other methods with historical-comparative analysis in order to generate important theoretical insights about more contemporary issues. Although we typically imagine the field of economics to be a uniform science throughout the world, Marion Fourcade (2009) shows us otherwise in her study of how the economics profession differs in France, Britain, and the United States. Fourcade used in-depth interviews with economists to supplement existing historical evidence in order to show how the profession has taken on distinctly different shapes in the three countries. Overall, she has found that economics in France is more closely aligned with the state, in Britain it is more moral and oriented to the welfare of all, and in the United States it is more oriented to science.

CONTENT ANALYSIS

Another type of secondary analysis, called **content analysis**, involves the systematic and

GL◍BALISATION

World Values Survey

The World Values Survey (WVS) is one of the main sources of survey data for research on globalisation. It is a source of cross-cultural data on the impact of globalisation on people's worldviews, values, and basic motivations. The WVS collects demographic data and asks people in each surveyed country roughly 250 questions about personal values and beliefs. For example, respondents are asked to prioritize various aspects of their lives, including family, politics, work, religion, and service to others. Respondents are queried about their responsibility for raising children, as well as protecting the environment. They are also asked whether they would be comfortable having some of the following live near them—criminals, people of a different race, Muslims, Jews, immigrants or foreign workers, those with AIDS, homosexuals, and drug addicts.

The WVS emerged out of the European Values Study, which, in its first wave in 1981, was limited to 20 highly developed European countries. Since then, the survey has expanded to 97 countries, covering nearly 90 percent of the population of the world (WVS 2007:2, 5). Since changes in values and preferences appear to be linked to level of economic and technological development, it was important to include societies across the entire range of development, from less developed (or industrial) to highly developed societies. This expansion also enabled the WVS to hire native social scientists from many different countries. The result was a more culturally conscious research design, analysis of data, and interpretation

of results. The expansion of the project has also permitted the dissemination of advanced methods of social analysis to developing societies in which such research is just emerging.

Sociologists have used data collected through the World Values Survey for a wide variety of studies related to globalisation. For instance, one study based on over 20 years of WVS data found that people in almost all industrial societies have generally shifted from being religious and traditional toward being more secular and

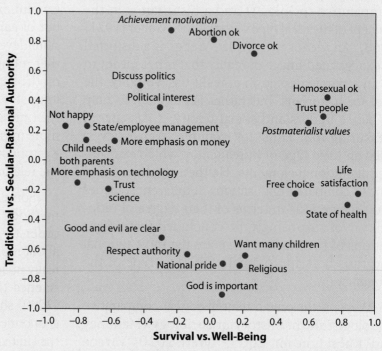

FIGURE 3.9 Scattergram of Global Values Measured in World Values Survey

SOURCE: From Inglehart, Ronald, *Modernization and Postmodernization.* © 1997 Princeton University Press. Reprinted by permission of Princeton University Press.

objective analysis of the content of cultural artefacts in print, visual, audio, and digital media, including photographs, movies, advertisements, speeches, and newspaper articles (Wolff 2007). The goal is to use qualitative and especially quantitative methods to understand the content of a message. In one well-known study, Herbert Gans (1979) did a

quantitative and qualitative content analysis of news on television and in news magazines to identify patterns in the reporting of the news. For example, he found that well-known people were dealt with much more frequently than unknowns; among non–war-related stories, government conflicts and disagreements were more likely to be rational (Inglehart and Baker 2000). Respondents who identify with religion emphasize family values and tend to be more conservative on such issues as gender roles, childbearing and child rearing, divorce, abortion, sexual norms, euthanasia, and suicide. They also have high levels of national pride; they tend to be nationalistic. Respondents with secular values exhibit contrary preferences on each of these topics. They are also often more tolerant and accepting of nontraditional social roles.

The other major dimension of global variation is the distinction between survival and self-expression values. For respondents in industrialised and developed countries, who tend to have fewer worries about survival or about meeting their basic needs for food and shelter, priorities have shifted from the emphasis on economic and physical security (that is, survival) to an interest in well-being and personal happiness. With this greater self-expressiveness comes a greater tolerance of minorities—including foreigners, gays, and various ethnic groups—who might otherwise be found threatening. This increase in trust and tolerance creates the type of social environment that is most conducive to the development of democracy.

The scattergram shown in Figure 3.9 plots a variety of values along these two dimensions. For example, people who accept divorce rank toward the secular-rational end of the spectrum (toward the top of the vertical axis); those who respect authority stand toward the traditional end (toward the bottom). Those who believe that a child needs both parents score toward the survival

end of the horizontal dimension (toward the left side); those who express life satisfaction rank very high on self-expression (toward the right side).

The WVS has also been used to define *cultural zones* based on this spectrum of values. As you can see in Figure 3.10, the English-speaking world generally embraces values that fall between traditional and secular-rational. But it ranks high on self-expression values, reflecting the relative well-being of its populace.

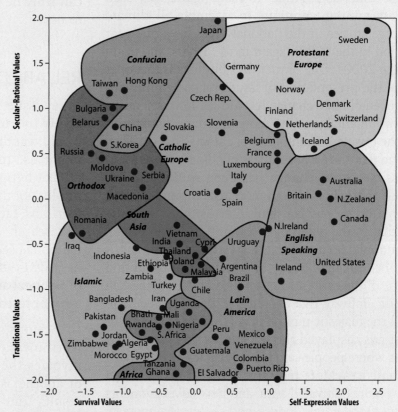

FIGURE 3.10 World Values Survey Cultural Map

SOURCE: From Ronald Inglehart and Christian Welzel, "Changing Mass Priorities: The Link Between Modernization and Democracy." *Perspectives on Politics* June 2010, Vol 8, No. 2, p. 554. Reprinted with the permission of Cambridge University Press.

dealt with than government decisions. Gans supplemented the powerful insights that derived from his content analysis with additional participant observation research among journalists working at NBC and CBS news and *Time* and *Newsweek* magazines. This additional work enabled him to produce an incredibly rich and detailed account of the

various political, commercial, and other forces that produce the values and informal rules that guide journalism. Wilkes, Corrigall-Brown, and Myers (2010) used content analysis in examining indigenous people's protests in Canada in an attempt to understand what factors were associated with how the press chose to frame or package protest activity. Related to this, Corrigall-Brown and Wilkes (2012) have examined differences between how textual accounts frame protests and how such protests are contextualised in pictures. It turns out that images reflect fewer power differences whereas textual accounts are more prone to marginalising the less powerful.

Historical trends in how climate change is depicted in the Canadian print media were the focus of a content analysis conducted by Nathan Young and Eric Dugas (2011). They wanted to know how, if at all, press coverage of climate change might differ across time. To examine this they used a data mining technique to assemble all climate change stories in the national press for a one-year period in the 1980s, again in the 1990s, and again in the 2000s. One of their key findings is that over time the presentation of issues related to human-induced climate change has moved from scientific, environmental issues to more mundane discussions of the business and politics of climate change. They argue that the early edginess of climate change and possible social change has been routinised and made more mundane in more recent press reports. Content analysis is useful in areas other than the media. In the realm of consumption, for example, you could do a content analysis of ad campaigns for the Canadian Rocky Mountains. You could find some of the earliest ads, produced by the Canadian Pacific Railway, that encouraged people to come to visit the majestic mountains of the West. These earliest ads displayed the Rockies as pristine wilderness where people came to enjoy authentic outdoor experiences. More recently the Rockies have taken on a more cultivated aura, and now advertisements point to the hotels, lodges, and ski lifts that increasingly proliferate around Banff and Jasper. Of course, there were many different ads during each of these periods, and a thorough content analysis of the ads, or a sample of them, would be necessary to reveal the degree to which ads in those periods stuck with the central theme. You might also contrast these themes with other possible themes. For instance, you might want to compare the way gendered bodies are depicted in advertisements during these eras. In any of these cases, you would systematically mine the existing artefacts and carefully and systematically analyse their content.

ISSUES IN SOCIAL RESEARCH

The research conducted by sociologists raises a number of issues of great importance. Some are about how we should interpret the data that sociologists collect. Some are about the obligations that sociologists have to research participants and society as a whole. Other issues are raised by sociologists themselves. As mentioned earlier, sociology is a multiple-paradigm science—with a full range of debates not only on various sociological perspectives but also on whether sociology can truly be as objective as a science is presumed to be.

RELIABILITY AND VALIDITY

A key issue with sociological data relates to the ability to trust the findings. As a sociologist, you would want to be reassured that the data that you might use to further your own research, to formulate hypotheses, or to tell colleagues and the public about your research represent the social world as accurately as possible. As a consumer of research, you would do well to evaluate the methods used in order to assess their trustworthiness. This issue is frequently raised about reports of political and social surveys, but it affects every form of research.

Scientists talk about two dimensions of trustworthiness: reliability and validity. **Reliability** involves the degree to which a given question, or another kind of measure, produces the same results time after time. In other words, would the same question asked one day get the same response from the participants or the same measurement on the scale on the following day, or week, or month? For instance, do those involved in your hypothetical study of Las Vegas gamblers give the same answers at various points in time to questions about whether or not they routinely lose money when gambling?

The other dimension of trustworthiness is **validity**, or the degree to which a question, or another kind of measure, gets an accurate response. In other words, does the question measure what it is supposed to measure? For example, suppose you asked gamblers, "When you leave the casino, do you consider yourself a 'winner'?" You may be asking this question to find out whether they left the casino with more money than they had upon arrival. However, they may interpret the question more broadly as asking about the total experience of being at a casino. Thus, even though they have lost money, they might answer yes to the question because they had a great time and consider their losses as part of the price for having such an experience. A more valid question might be "On balance, do you win more money than you lose while gambling in casinos?"

RESEARCH ETHICS

Ethics is concerned with issues of right and wrong, the choices that people make, and how they justify them (Zeni 2007). World War II and the behaviour of the Nazis catalysed events that made ethics a central issue in research. The Nazis engaged in horrendous medical experiments on inmates in concentration camps (V. Spitz 2005). This is the most outrageous example of a violation of the ethical code in the conduct of research, but it is certainly not the only one. A well-known Canadian case involves a student at the University of Saskatchewan who in 1965 volunteered to participate in what he was told was a "safe test" involving a new drug. The student suffered a heart attack as a result of the experiment, was in a coma for several days, and was never able to return to his studies. In arriving at a decision in *Halushka v. University of Saskatchewan*, the Court of Appeal held

Rap music videos that focus on sex and materialism feature women who are overwhelmingly thin. In the 2006 music video for "Everytime tha Beat Drop," slender R&B artist Monica and hip-hop group Dem Franchize Boyz perform amid an array of material possessions.

that informed consent had not been given because the procedure and its associated risks and benefits had not been properly explained. This is a landmark decision in Canada because it was precedent setting as to what constitutes "informed consent." Between 1932 and 1972, at the Tuskegee Institute in Alabama, poor black men suffering from syphilis were studied to learn about the progression of the disease. They were not treated for the disease and eventually suffered painful deaths (Reverby 2009).

A more recent issue of research ethics is the case of Henrietta Lacks (Skloot 2011). Lacks was a poor black woman who died of cervical cancer in 1951. Without her knowledge or consent, some of her tumour was removed. Cancer cells from that tumour live on today and have spawned much research and even highly successful industries. While those cells have led to a variety of medical advances, a number of ethical issues are raised by what happened to Lacks and subsequently to her family. For example, should the tumour have been removed and cancer cells reproduced without Lacks and her family knowing about, and approving of, what was intended? Would the procedures have been the same if Lacks had been a well-to-do white woman? Finally, should Lacks's descendants get a portion of the earnings of the industries that have developed on the basis of her cancer cells?

No research undertaken by sociologists has caused the kind of suffering and death experienced by the people being studied in Nazi Germany or in the Saskatchewan operating theatre, or even the ethical firestorm raging around the Lacks case. Nonetheless, this research is the context and background for ethical concerns about the harmful or negative effects of research on the participants in sociological

BIOGRAPHICAL bits

Herbert Gans (1927–, American)

- Gans was born in Cologne, Germany, and in 1940 left Nazi Germany for England and then the United States, where he became a citizen in 1945.

- He studied sociology at the University of Chicago and social planning at the University of Pennsylvania, where he earned a PhD.

- In the early 1950s, he worked as a social researcher and planner, first for an architectural firm designing two new towns and then for the predecessor to the U.S. Department of Housing and Urban Development. He has been a prominent consultant to government and public policy agencies throughout his career.

- He worked in academia starting in 1953 and was a professor of sociology at Columbia University from 1971 to 2007. Upon retiring, he continued to write and to participate in public discussions of social policy.

- Gans used participant observation to research a number of his works, including *The Urban Villagers* (1962; about a close-knit Italian American community and the effects of urban renewal), *The Levittowners* (1967; about the social development of a lower-middle-class suburb), and *Deciding What's News* (1979; about how four mainstream news outlets culled and disseminated information to the public).

- He is also known for other important books on culture and media, such as *Popular Culture and High Culture* (1999) and *Democracy and the News* (2003), and for sociologically oriented reviews of movies, including *All the President's Men* and *Jaws*.

- Gans is thought to have been the first to introduce the term *public sociologist,* in his presidential address at the 1988 American Sociological Association annual meeting.

research. There are three main areas of concern: physical and psychological harm to participants, illegal acts by researchers, and deception and violation of participants' trust. A final issue discussed here is the structure established to safeguard participants from these kinds of negative actions.

Physical and Psychological Harm

The first issue, following from the Nazi experiments, is concern over whether the research can actually cause participants physical harm. Most sociological research is not likely to cause such harm. However, physical harm may be an unintended consequence. In field experiments where children are involved there is always the risk of unintended injury.

A much greater issue in sociological research is the possibility of psychological harm to those being studied. Even questionnaire or interview studies can cause psychological harm merely by asking people about sensitive issues such as sexual orientation, drug use, and experience with abortion. This risk is greatly increased when, unbeknownst to the researcher, a participant is hypersensitive to these issues because of a difficult or traumatic personal experience.

Some of the more extreme risks of psychological harm have occurred in experiments. The most famous example is Stanley Milgram's (1974) laboratory study of how far people will go when they are given orders by those in authority. This study was inspired by the discovery after World War II that Nazi subordinates went so far as to torture and kill innocent citizens if ordered to do so by their superiors. In the Milgram experiment, the members of one group, the "learners," were secretly paid to pretend that painful shocks were being applied to them by the other group of participants, the "teachers," who were led to believe that the shocks they thought they were applying were very real. The researcher, dressed officially in a white coat and projecting an aura of scientific respectability, would order the "teachers" to apply shocks that appeared to be potentially lethal. The "teachers" did so even though the "learners," who were in another room and not visible, were screaming with increasing intensity. The research clearly showed that if they were ordered to do so by authority figures, people would violate the social norms against inflicting pain on, and even possibly endangering the lives of, others.

The results of the Milgram experiment are important in many senses, but here we are concerned with what the study did to the psyches of the people involved in the study. For one thing, the "teachers" came to know that they were very responsive to the dictates of authority figures, even if they were ordered to commit immoral acts. Some of them certainly realised that their behaviour indicated that they were perfectly capable in such circumstances of harming, if not killing, other human beings. Such realisations had the possibility of adversely affecting the way participants viewed, and felt about, themselves. But the research has had several benefits as well, for both participants and others who have read about the Milgram studies. For example, those in powerful positions can better understand, and therefore limit, the potential impact of orders to subordinates and how far they might be willing to go in carrying them out.

Another famous study that raises similar ethical issues was conducted by Philip Zimbardo (1973). Zimbardo set up a prison-like structure called "Stanford County Prison" as a setting in which to conduct his experiment. Participants were recruited to serve as either prisoners or guards. The conditions in the "prison" were very realistic, with windowless cells, minimal toilet facilities, and strict regulations imposed on the inmates. The guards had uniforms, badges, keys, and clubs; they were also trained in the methods of managing prisoners.

The experiment was supposed to have lasted six weeks, but it was ended after only six days. The researchers feared for the health and the sanity of those acting as prisoners. Some of the guards insulted, degraded, and dehumanised the prisoners; only a few were helpful and supportive. However, even the helpful guards refused to intervene when prisoners were being abused. The prisoners could have left, but they tended to

The Tuskegee syphilis experiment, conducted between 1932 and 1972, is one of the most egregious violations of research ethics in the modern era. Today, codes of ethics and review boards ensure that such breaches of ethics do not occur.

go along with this situation, accepting both the authority of the guards and their own lowly and abused position. The ethical issues are similar to those raised by the Milgram research. Some of the guards experienced psychological distress, but it was worse for the prisoners when they realised how much they had contributed to their own difficulties. Social researchers learned that a real or perceived imbalance of power between researcher and participant may lead a participant to comply with a researcher's demands even though they cause distress. However, as in the case of Milgram's research, the Zimbardo research yielded positive by-products, such as a greater understanding of how those put in guard positions may lose their humanity and how submissive prisoners can become.

Illegal Acts

In the course of fieldwork, a researcher might witness or even become entangled in illegal acts. This problem often confronted Sudhir Venkatesh (2008) in his research on gangs in and around a Chicago housing project. A famous Canadian case involves Russel Ogden, studying at Simon Fraser University, who investigated assisted suicides among people dying from HIV/AIDS. Ogden was subpoenaed to present evidence in court related to these suicides, but he refused to testify on the grounds that he had provided the people involved in his study with a guarantee of anonymity. Ogden was, in the end, not compelled to testify, but he endured a lengthy struggle. It remains possible that not informing the police, or refusing to turn over research notes, could lead to fines or imprisonment for researchers (Emerson 2001; Van Maanen 1983).

Violation of Trust

There are several ways that researchers can betray participants' trust in the research enterprise. For instance, the researcher might inadvertently divulge the identity of respondents even though they were promised anonymity. There is also the possibility of exploitative relationships, especially with key informants. Exploitation is of special concern in cases where there is a real or perceived imbalance of power—often related to race, class, or gender—between researcher and participant. In the Tuskegee case, for example, African American men suffered the adverse effects of the research even though syphilis is distributed throughout the larger population. Although this research should not have occurred under any circumstances, a more equitable research design would have meant that most of the participants would have been white males.

It is also a betrayal of trust for the researcher to develop inappropriate relationships with participants. One noteworthy example of this latter point is a study conducted by Erich Goode (2002) in order to better understand the stigma of obesity. He has publicly acknowledged that he had sexual relations with some of his female informants

In 2002, British artist Rod Dickinson conducted *The Milgram Re-enactment*, a replication of Milgram's experiment, in front of a live audience. The audience observed the performance from behind one-way mirrors.

and argues that he was able to obtain information that may not have been obtainable by any other means. However, one must ask at what cost to his participants this knowledge was obtained. One can only imagine how his participants felt when some of them discovered that Goode had an ulterior motive in having an intimate relationship with them. Many of his participants were already very sensitive about their body image and their relationships with men. Because Goode's participants did not have full knowledge of his motives, they were unable to make informed choices about engaging in sexual relations with him. In this case, the power imbalance between researcher and participant led to exploitation.

The best known example of research involving deception and intrusion into people's lives is Laud Humphreys's (1970) study of the homosexual activities of men in public restrooms (*tearooms*). Humphreys acted as a lookout outside tearooms and signalled men involved in anonymous acts of fellatio when members of the public or the police were approaching. He interviewed some of the men involved with full disclosure but also noted the license numbers of some of those he observed, tracked down their addresses, and appeared at their homes a year or so later, in disguise, to interview them under false pretences. There he uncovered one of the most important findings of his study: Over half of the men were married, with wives and families. They were involved in the tearoom trade not because they were homosexual but because sexual relations in their marriage were problematic.

Humphreys deceived these men by not telling them from the outset that he was doing research on them or, with those he interviewed under false pretences, the true nature of the research. His research had at least the potential of revealing something that most of the participants wanted to conceal. He later admitted that if he had the chance to do the research over again, he would tell the participants about his true role and goal. But the research itself is not without merit. It helped to distinguish between homosexual acts and homosexual identity. Also, homosexuals had very difficult lives in the early 1970s. Nearly half of his participants were covertly bisexual or homosexual and faced numerous difficulties, if not danger, if they "came out." Thus, there were very strong reasons for them to keep their homosexual activity hidden. Many of these men also experienced considerable stress trying to live as married men while simultaneously engaging in impersonal homosexual activity with strangers. Humphreys's research provided some much needed insight into their lives.

Informed Consent and Ethical Review Boards

Various ethical codes have been devised to protect people from overzealous or malicious researchers. The Hippocratic Oath taken by medical doctors offers helpful guidelines for dealing with human participants. The Nuremberg Code was developed in 1947 to protect biomedical research subjects after revelations of the Nazi experiments on concentration camp inmates. Codes such as these were later broadened to a concern for all research involving human participants. Such ethical codes have helped to protect research participants, but it is important to realise that they are only codes of conduct and not enforceable laws and regulations.

Following the judgment in *Halushka v. University of Saskatchewan,* issues of informed consent and research ethics more broadly have become major concerns of institutions engaged in basic research, principally hospitals and universities. Now all Canadian research funded by government is required to have ethical oversight. For example, the *Tri-Council Policy Statement: Ethical Conduct for Research Involving Humans* (see www.pre.ethics.gc.ca/eng/index) is the definitive document on research ethics for university

BIOGRAPHICAL bits

Margrit Eichler (1942 -, German/ Canadian)

- Eichler grew up in Germany, studied in Germany and the United States (Duke University), and immigrated to Canada in 1970.

- She taught at both the University of Waterloo and the University of Toronto.

- Her book *Nonsexist Research Methods: A Practical Guide* (1991) was a landmark text in raising issues of research ethics in Canadian social science, as well as, of course, in flagging bias in a variety of disciplines.

- She teaches with a feminist and sustainability perspective front and centre.

- She developed, together with Mary Anne Burke, the BIAS FREE Framework, a tool for identifying and avoiding biases in health research that derive from any social hierarchy. This framework grew out of her work on nonsexist and feminist methodology.

researchers. As well, all hospitals and universities have formed their own ethical research boards (ERBs).

ERBs are designed to deal with the issue of deception in social research and the harm that social research can do to the participants. Members of ERBs are typically faculty researchers from a wide variety of disciplines, along with members of the community. ERBs generally protect three broad ethical principles:

- *Respect for persons.* Participants—especially those with diminished capacities such as physical or mental disabilities—are to be treated with dignity and respect.

- *Beneficence.* As little harm as possible is to be done to participants, and every effort is to be made to be of benefit to them. However, there are exceptions where the benefits of the research are overwhelming and the harm to be done is unavoidable.

- *Justice.* Research should operate on the principle of justice so that burdens and rewards are distributed in an equitable manner.

Of particular importance is that most ERBs require evidence of written **informed consent** of those being studied. Typically, researchers present a statement for participants to sign that ensures informed consent and includes such items as what the study entails and why it's being conducted, how and why the research participants have been recruited to participate, what participation involves, the risks and benefits associated with participation, the degree to which their privacy and confidentiality will be protected, how the study safeguards vulnerable populations (such as children, prisoners, and the impaired), and whom the participants can contact at the university if they have further questions. Participants have a right not only to be aware that they are being studied but also to know about the potential harms and benefits that they might experience in the course of the research. Research that does not have such consent, and more importantly poses dangers to participants, is likely to be turned down by ERBs unless it is justified by extraordinary reasons.

In addition to the statement for participants, researchers submit a research protocol that provides an overview of the way in which the research will be conducted. For example, if the research is interview-based, the protocol might specify that the interviewer will first provide the participant with an introduction to the research and a review of the participant's role in the research, show the informed consent form that will be signed by participants, and provide a basic script of the questions that will be asked during the interview. ERB committees then review these materials and decide whether the proposed research plan should be approved, modified, or disapproved. Finally, as noted earlier, these ERBs are themselves the subject of sociological research as regulatory or surveillance organisations enacted to influence social processes (Haggerty 2004).

OBJECTIVITY, OR "VALUE-FREE" SOCIOLOGY

Another issue relating to sociological research is whether researchers have been, or can be, objective. That is, do they allow personal preferences and judgments to bias their research? Many argue that value-laden research jeopardizes the entire field of sociology. The publication of such research and public revelations about those biases erode and could destroy the credibility of the field as a whole. In the history of sociology, this discussion is traceable, once again, to the work of Max Weber. Taken to its extreme, *value-free sociology* means preventing all personal values from affecting any phase of the research process. However, this is not what Weber intended in his work on values, and it is instructive to take a brief look at what he actually meant.

Weber was most concerned with the need for teachers, especially professors, to be value free in their lectures. This issue arose in Weber's day in Germany, at least in part because of the growing number of Marxist-oriented teachers, many of whom wished to use the classroom to express Marxist ideology and to raise the consciousness of students about the evils of capitalism—perhaps even to foment revolution against the capitalist system. Weber was opposed to Marxism, but he was also more generally opposed to using the classroom to express any values. He took this position because he felt that young students were neither mature nor sophisticated enough to see through such arguments. He believed they were also likely to be too intimidated by the position of their professors, especially in the authoritarian Germany of his day, to be able to evaluate their ideas critically. The idea of, and the need for, value freedom in the classroom seems clear and uncontestable. However, we must realise that all professors, like all other human beings, have values. Therefore, the best we can hope for is for them to strive to be as objective as possible in the classroom.

Weber did *not* take the same position with reference to research. In fact, he saw at least two roles for values in social research. The first is in the selection of a question to be researched. In that case, it is perfectly appropriate for researchers to be guided by their personal values, or the values that predominate in the society of the day. The second is in the analysis of the results of a research study. In that analysis, sociologists can, and should, use personal and social values to help them make sense of, to interpret, their findings. These values are an aid in interpretation and understanding, but they are not to be used to purposely distort the findings or mislead the reader of a report on the study.

In Weber's opinion, the only place in research to be value-free is in the collection of the research data. This is a rather unexceptional argument meaning that researchers should do everything they can to prevent bias in the data-collection process. Few, if any, observers would accept the opposing position that it is perfectly acceptable to engage in such distortions. Such a position would undermine all research and the scientific status and aspirations of sociology.

Some sociologists, especially feminist and critical scholars (Reid 2004), question whether even this limited attempt to conduct value-free research is possible, or even desirable (D. Smith 2005). In a famous essay, Alvin Gouldner (1962) argued that value-free sociology is a myth. Even when researchers strive to be completely objective, they still carry with them their own experiences, assumptions about the world, and personal biases that inevitably shape the ways in which they approach their research and collect their

data. The fact that women and people of colour were largely overlooked by social researchers until relatively recently is an example of how an unquestioned assumption—the belief that the experiences of men and women or of people of colour and whites are all the same—can be problematic. For this reason, many scholars (such as Bourdieu 1992) argue that the researchers should be extremely reflective and explicit about their own social position and how that might influence the research process.

In contemporary terms, what Weber argued for was an attitude of objectivity during the research process. But there is another kind of objectivity, *procedural objectivity,* which entails reporting the research in such a way that any reader will understand how the research was conducted. As many details as possible should be reported to allow for outside assessment of the research. Among other things, details about sampling, the questions asked in interviews or on questionnaires, statistical procedures employed, known limitations about the research, and so on should be made available in research reports. Then other researchers can, if they choose, repeat, or replicate, the study in order to see if they get the same results. The ability to replicate research is a hallmark of any science.

An Iraqi Shiite scholar lectures his students at a school for clerics in the holy city of Najaf. While philosophical instruction may be spiritually enlightening, it is not value-free.

SUMMARY

Most sociologists practise empiricism, which means they gather information and evidence using their senses to explore the social world. They do this systematically using the scientific method. First, a sociologist finds a question that needs to be answered. Next, the researcher reviews the literature to see what has already been found about the specific question. The sociologist then develops a hypothesis, an educated guess about how social phenomena of various types can be expected to relate to one another. Data are then collected that can confirm, or fail to confirm, the hypothesis. Finally, the researcher analyses the data in relation to the initial hypothesis.

What defines a science is a paradigm, a general model that is accepted by most practitioners in a field. Sociology is a multiple-paradigm science, which means that no one paradigm unifies all sociologists and therefore sociologists tend to work in different paradigms. As a result, the discipline experiences many lively debates—as well as possessing a rich store of knowledge.

Sociologists use different research methods depending on the research question they are studying. Quantitative methods yield data in the form of numbers, and qualitative methods yield verbal descriptions. Observation involves systematic and purposive watching, listening to, and recording what takes place in a natural social setting over some period of time. Another method of data collection is interviews, in which information is sought from respondents who are asked a series of questions, usually on a face-to-face basis. Survey research, which permits the study of a broader population, involves the collection of data through interviews and questionnaires. A less common method of data collection in sociological research is experimentation, which involves the manipulation of one or more independent variables in order to examine the effect of that manipulation on dependent variable(s).

Sociologists often also engage in secondary data analysis, in which they reanalyse data collected by others. Secondary data may consist of statistical information, historical documents and analyses, or the content of cultural artefacts and messages.

Sociological research raises a number of important issues. One relates to questions of reliability, the degree to which a given measure produces the same results time after time, and validity, the degree to which a measure gets an accurate response. On a broader level, social researchers are concerned with ethics—for example, whether research can cause physical or psychological harm to participants. Problems with questionable research ethics led to the development of ethical review boards, which vet proposed projects before they are allowed to proceed. A key requirement is that researchers obtain informed consent from their respondents. Participants must be told about the true nature and purpose of the study and of any sensitive or dangerous aspects of the research.

Also addressed in this chapter is the degree to which we can consider social research value-free. It is generally recognised that bias is difficult to avoid altogether. However, clear and objective descriptions of research procedures will enable other researchers to evaluate and perhaps replicate them.

KEY TERMS

- Content analysis 97
- Convenience sample 92
- Dependent variable 93
- Descriptive statistics 81
- Descriptive survey 91
- Empiricism 74
- Ethics 101
- Ethnography 85
- Experiment 93

- Field experiment 94
- Global ethnography 85
- Historical-comparative research 96
- Ideal type 97
- Independent variable 93
- Inferential statistics 82
- Informed consent 106
- Institutional ethnography 85
- Interview 88

THINKING ABOUT SOCIOLOGY

1. What steps do researchers take when applying the scientific method? How would you apply the scientific method to get answers to a question you have about the social world?

2. What does it mean to say that sociology is a multiple-paradigm science? What are the benefits and disadvantages of being a multiple-paradigm science?

3. What are the differences between participant and nonparticipant observational methods? How do sociologists ensure that their observations are systematic using both approaches?

4. What is the key value of conducting ethnographic research? How would a global ethnography help you to make sense of your own place in the world?

5. Researchers use interviews to gather data by asking individuals a series of questions. How do researchers choose between pre- and unstructured interviews? What are the advantages and disadvantages of each type of interview?

6. Why do sociologists who conduct surveys rely on samples? What techniques do researchers use to avoid biases in their samples?

7. A researcher uses the World Values Survey to examine the relationship between people's religious beliefs and their level of happiness. In this study, what is the independent variable, and what is the dependent variable? What reliability and validity issues could arise conducting this survey across countries?

8. Some experiments allow researchers to take advantage of a naturally occurring event to study its effect on one or more dependent variables. Can you think of any recent events that might have been conducive to natural experiments? What would be the dependent variable or variables in your example?

9. What are some ethical concerns raised by sociological research? Use specific examples from research discussed in the chapter to describe these ethical concerns. How do IRBs help keep research ethical?

10. What role do values play in the research process? According to Weber, when is objectivity most important?

APPLYING THE SOCIOLOGICAL IMAGINATION

How can we use surveys to describe the attitudes of all students at your university toward globalisation? Construct a survey consisting of 10 questions to determine how much students know about globalisation and the extent to which they think that globalisation is positive or negative. Check the Internet for surveys conducted by other researchers and organisations to see what types of questions are commonly asked to get at these sorts of questions. For

your own survey, be sure to consider whether it will be structured or unstructured and whether it will be administered face-to-face, by mail, or over the web. How would you go about sampling students at your school? Why?

Once you have considered all of the above, take a convenience sample of five of your friends and administer the survey to them. What are your findings?

ACTIVE SOCIOLOGY ....

Have you ever responded to an online poll or survey? Perhaps you've called in to vote for your favourite performer on a show such as *American Idol*. How is this kind of survey similar to and different from scientific research? Facebook contains a feature called "Facebook Questions," where you can poll your friends about a specific topic. Go to Facebook and create a question about a current issue. Construct four or five preselected responses, and post your question. Collect the data in a few days. How many people responded? What trends do you see in their responses? For example, do *variables* such as age or geographic location appear to influence how people answered the question?

How is the research that you completed like the scientific research you read about in this chapter? What are some of the problems with collecting data in this way—particularly concerning issues of *reliability, validity, objectivity,* and *ethics*?

STUDENT STUDY SITE ....

Visit the student study site at **www.sagepub.com/ritzercanadian** for additional web quizzes for further review.

CULTURE

Through globalisation, as American culture spreads around the world, American coolness and America's cool icons are not far behind. Coolness is, of course, just a small aspect of culture. Still, it speaks to large cultural issues. Who and what do you and your peers consider cool?

*I*n 1957, Miles Davis released Birth of the Cool, *a seminal and genre-defining cool jazz album. The term cool can be traced to fifteenth-century Africa, where the Yoruba word* Itutu *(literally translating to "cool") was used to denote a person who was calm and steady as cool water. Centuries later, Miles Davis's hallmark album gave new life to the term. In the late 1950s and early 1960s, cool was used to describe beat poetry, film noir, abstract expressionist art, and—of course—jazz.*

Certain aesthetics and attitudes that define coolness have remained constant for the past 50 years. Acting with self-assurance and awareness, even in the face of adversity or reprimand, is cool. Expressions, postures, and vocal patterns that connote nonchalance and composure are cool. Dressing fashionably and using contemporary slang is cool. Cutting-edge technology is cool. Being young and hip is cool. However, the specific characteristics of cool in any situation rely entirely on a person's contemporary culture and the cultural regulations that allow people to live in harmony with those around them.

Today, the specific people and things considered cool differ remarkably from the cool icons of the mid-twentieth century. Lady Gaga, Panda Bear, K'NAAN, or Nicki Minaj might be considered cool, at least for the moment. It's important to realise that different cultures have different norms, values, and symbols and thus consider different traits and mannerisms to be cool (or uncool). A person might work for years to be cool in the eyes of her peers, but if thrust into a new subculture (such as university), she may have to start from scratch. Her iPhone 4S might have been cool a few years ago, but it isn't anymore.

Coolness takes on many forms. What is cool in Vancouver or Toronto is not necessarily cool in Montreal. And what is cool in Canada or the United States is not necessarily cool in Bangalore or Jakarta. For example, though a moustachioed, middle-aged man might be considered uncool in Canada, he might be considered an ultracool Bollywood heartthrob in parts of India. A cool attitude in China might be considered conservative and materialistic in Italy. But though coolness is culturally relative, globalisation and Americanisation have altered some countries' values and norms. As American culture spreads around the world, American coolness and America's cool icons are not far behind.

Coolness is, of course, just a small aspect of culture. Still, it speaks to many larger cultural issues. Who and what do you and your peers consider cool? What does that say about you and your culture?

A s you read this chapter, keep in mind that you are actually immersed in many different cultures. For example, you are likely to be involved to some degree or another in Canadian culture, consumer culture, digital culture, and the culture of university life. In addition, you are continually learning the rules of these and other cultures. Much of that learning happens almost effortlessly, as you live your daily life. But cultures that are new to you, such as university culture, or that are evolving rapidly, such as digital culture, are likely to require much, and continuing, effort, alertness, and flexibility on your part.

A DEFINITION OF CULTURE

Culture encompasses the ideas, values, practises, and material objects that allow a group of people, even an entire society, to carry out their collective lives in relative order and harmony. There are so many ideas, values, practises, and material objects associated with most cultures that no one individual can possibly know them all or what they all mean. But individual members must know at least the most basic and important elements of the culture. Knowledge of a common culture leads people to behave in similar ways and to adopt a similar way of looking at the world.

Consider the cultures of the Hells Angels, the Bandidos, and the Rock Machine, three rival motorcycle clubs (Caine 2008). The clubs have been bitter rivals with several gang-related deaths over the past decade. Members of the gangs distinguish themselves from each other in a variety of ways, including their bikes, their colours, their insignia, and their jackets. These colours, insignia, and other symbols are very meaningful to gang members, helping them mark territories, easily identify friends and foes, and signify their values. The meaning of these symbols was created by the group itself, and the symbols have been passed down from one gang member to another. Symbols like these may also be passed along from a gang in one locale to those situated elsewhere (the Hells Angels is now a global organisation). Although the Rock Machine and the Bandidos have been bitter rivals, they have also tried a merger but with very mixed success. Allegiances to these gangs are passionate,

Members of the Bandidos distinguish themselves from members of other gangs with specific colors, hand signs, phrases, and other cultural symbols.

and the shooting wars between the gangs reflect the intensity of these cultural identities.

In contrast, for those who are not members of the in-group, an idea, a value, a practise, or an object may have little meaning, may mean something completely different, or may even have no meaning at all. For example, most people understand 81 as a number, and not a particularly meaningful number, but for members of the Hells Angels this number has cultural significance (with *H* and *A* being the eighth and first numbers of the alphabet, respectively). The Hells Angels also use patches, somewhat akin to military medals, but the exact significance of each patch is known only to members of the gang (see www.hells-angels .com/?HA=faq).

The existence of a culture and common knowledge of it are so important that newcomers to the group, especially children, are taught its basic elements early. They then expand on that knowledge as they mature and become more integral members of the group.

At the same time, culture is constantly being affected by changes both internal and external to the group. Among the *internal changes* are the average age of the population within that group, with the result that the culture increasingly reflects the needs and interests of younger or older people. For example, in Canada and other aging societies, television programmes and the advertisements associated with them are more oriented to older people than is the case in societies with a large proportion of younger people (Carter and Vega 2011). Technological innovations, among other things, are *external changes* that are likely to alter a group's culture significantly. For example, with the growth in use of smartphones, text messages have become increasingly popular, especially among young people, as a communication method, and phone conversations have become proportionally less common. Thus not only newcomers to the group, but also those who have participated for years, must constantly learn new aspects of culture and perhaps unlearn others that are no longer relevant.

The rise of the smartphone has created a whole new set of realities for which clear and firm cultural rules are not yet in place. One such rule involves what should and should not be discussed on a smartphone when others, especially strangers, are close enough that they can overhear what is being said. For example, one of the authors recently took an Amtrak train from Washington, DC, to New York City. A woman sitting behind him was talking on the phone with her mother about her difficulties in getting pregnant. In another conversation with a nurse, she discussed the status of her eggs. We're not sure the woman would have wanted to share these experiences with a stranger if they were talking face-to-face. And we're not at all sure a stranger would want or need to know about this part of her life. The personal nature of smartphones, and of many of the conversations that take place on them, is often in conflict with the public setting in which the phones are used and in which the conversations occur.

Then there is the issue of smartphone use intruding on others' consciousness. Long, loud, and frequent smartphone conversations are not a problem in the privacy of one's home, but they are a problem in public areas where there is an expectation of quietude, as at a nice restaurant. The same author found out for himself how rude a smartphone conversation may be perceived, and the consequences, on his return trip from New York. Amtrak now has "quiet cars" for those who do not want to be plagued by the cell phone conversations of strangers. The author found himself in one, but he didn't know what it meant to be in such a car. Soon after the trip began, his wife called, and they began a conversation. Almost immediately, a man sitting a few

Province/Territory	Prohibitions on handheld devices	Prohibitions on hands-free devices	Restrictions on other distractions
British Columbia	All handheld electronic equipment is banned.	Novice drivers are not allowed to use hands-free electronic equipment.	Careless driving legislation; television sets cannot be visible to the driver.
Alberta	Holding, viewing, or manipulating a communications device or a handheld or wireless electronic device is banned.	None.	With exceptions (for example, GPS systems fixed to the car), electronic screens cannot be visible to the driver; reading, writing, hygiene or any other activity that distracts a driver.
Saskatchewan	All handheld communication equipment is banned.	Novice drivers are not allowed to use hands–free communication equipment.	Careless driving legislation; electronic screens visible to the driver must be attached to the car and can only be used to aid the driver with the task of driving.
Manitoba	All handheld electronic devices are banned.	None.	Imprudent driving legislation.
Ontario	All handheld wireless communication devices are banned.	None.	Careless driving legislation; with exceptions (for example, GPS systems), electronic screens cannot be visible to the driver.
Quebec	All handheld devices that include a telephone function are banned.	Hands-free devices that include a telephone function are permitted.	Careless driving legislation.
New Brunswick	All handheld electronic devices are banned.	None.	Also banned: manual programming & adjusting of any GPS navigation system while driving. Television screens, monitors, DVD players, and computer screens not permitted within the visual range of the operator of a motor vehicle.
Nova Scotia	All handheld cellular phones are banned; text messaging is banned on any communications device.	None.	Careless driving legislation; screens cannot be visible to the driver.
Prince Edward Island	All handheld wireless communication devices are banned.	None.	Careless driving legislation; operational televisions cannot be in any position within a vehicle.
Newfoundland & Labrador	All handheld cellular phones are banned; text messaging is banned on any communications device.	None.	Programming GPS when car is in motion is banned; careless driving legislation.
Yukon Territory	Handheld devices used for talking, texting, or e-mailing are prohibited.	Graduated Driver's license holders are not allowed to use handheld electronic devices for talking, texting or e-mailing or any hands-free devices.	Exceptions: Citizen's band (CB) and other simple push-to-talk two-way radios may be used.
Northwest Territories	All handheld electronic devices are banned.	None.	Careless driving legislation.
Nunavut	None.	None.	Careless driving legislation.

Current as of January 5, 2012.

FIGURE 4.1 Laws Enacted to Ban the Use of Cell Phones while Driving, by Province/Territory

SOURCE: http://www.tc.gc.ca/eng/roadsafety/safedrivers-distractions-current-legislation-1074.htm (retrieved September 20, 2012).

rows in front of him jumped up and glared at him angrily, while another passenger gently tugged on his sleeve and pointed to the "quiet car" sign. The author now understood its meaning and said good-bye to his wife. This illustrates the power of culture and also how we learn about new cultural elements and developments, sometimes the hard way.

A more formal set of rules regarding cell phones is being developed to control their use while driving. It has become apparent—both from insurance company statistics and from experimental research—that using a handheld cell phone while driving increases the risk of accidents (Horrey and Wickens 2006). A very active media campaign was developed—promoted by Oprah Winfrey, among others—to discourage people from using handheld cell phones while driving. As shown in Figure 4.1, all Canadian provinces have enacted laws against the practise, and some safety advocates are pressing for even broader laws targeting "distracted" driving. As with wearing seat belts, cultural habits are hard to change, but eventually the practise of phoning while driving will be stigmatised enough that it will be a rare occurrence (as it is now rare for people not to use seat belts).

Although we generally accept and learn the various components of culture, sometimes we refuse to comply with, or even accept, them. For example, the traditional culture of Canada disapproves of pre-marital and extramarital sexual relationships, but many people have come to reject these prohibitions. Indeed, it could be argued that both of these forms of sexual behaviour have come to be widely accepted and have, in fact, become part of the culture.

THE BASIC ELEMENTS OF CULTURE

All groups have a culture. Furthermore, cultures relate to such things as athletics, cooking, funeral ceremonies, courtship, medicine, marriage, sexual restrictions, bodily adornment, calendars, dancing, games, greetings, sexual taboos, hairstyles, personal names, religion, and myths. However, the specific content of each of these elements, and many more, varies from culture to culture. Cultures differ from one another mainly because each involves a unique mix of values, norms, objects, and language

inherited from the past, derived from other groups, and created anew by each group.

VALUES

The broadest elements of culture are **values**, the general and abstract standards defining what a group or society as a whole considers good, desirable, right, or important. Values express the ideals of everything from a group to an entire society.

In his classic work, *Democracy in America* ([1835–1840] 1969), the French writer Alexis de Tocqueville detailed what he perceived as America's values. Among the things that Americans valued in the early nineteenth century were democracy, equality, individualism, "taste for physical comfort," spirituality, and economic prosperity. Although Tocqueville wrote about his impressions of the United States almost 200 years ago, the vast majority of Americans today would accept most, if not all, of the values he described (L. Crothers 2010).

Canadians, of course, share many of these identical values, yet many Canadians would see themselves as culturally different from Americans, whether French Canadians, English Canadians, or new (immigrant) Canadians (Grabb and Curtis 2010). Americans, of course, find their core values so natural and incontrovertible that they expect them to be accepted in other cultures around the world. However, such a belief has had some disappointing, even disastrous, consequences for the United States. For example, when the United States undertook invasions of Iraq and Afghanistan, one of the objectives was the creation of democratic regimes in those societies. The assumption was that Iraqis and Afghans wanted the same kind of democracy as the one that exists in the United States. It is extremely difficult, if not impossible, to impose a value, such as the value of democracy, on a society where it does not already exist, or where it exists in a very different form.

Researchers using data collected through the World Values Survey have found that to be the case (Welzel and Inglehart 2009). As you may recall from Chapter 3, the World Values Survey has gathered data from a variety of countries around the world on individual views on gender equality; tolerance for abortion, homosexuality, and divorce;

Alexis de Tocqueville (1805–1859, French)

- Tocqueville came from a family of aristocrats who suffered during the French Revolution of the late 1700s.

- While many former political rulers were sentenced to death, Tocqueville's family escaped the guillotine.

- With a friend, Tocqueville spent time travelling throughout the United States to study political issues such as democracy, equality, and freedom.

- After his return to France, he wrote the still famous *Democracy in America*, based on his experiences, which was published in 1835.

- A second volume published in 1840 was much more of a sociological than a political analysis of the United States.

- Tocqueville admired the United States and the freedom it produced but had reservations about equality in the United States because he believed it favoured mediocrity and did not give enough of a role to aristocrats (such as himself).

- He later became a critic of French despotism.

desire for autonomy over authority (for example, obedience and faith); and democratic participation over security. Respondents in countries where personal freedom is not valued highly—such as Pakistan, Jordan, and Nigeria—tend to think of antidemocratic authoritarian regimes as being democratic. The surveys also showed that citizens within these countries have little knowledge of the meaning of liberal democracy. There is little chance that Canadian-style democracy would succeed in these countries.

NORMS

Norms are the informal rules, based on values, that guide what people do and how they live. Norms tell us what we should and should not do in a given situation (Dandaneau 2007). Many norms are informal—that is, not formally codified, not written down in any one place. The norms that have been codified—that are written down and formally enforced through institutions such as the state—are **laws**. Rules regarding speaking and texting on handheld smartphones while driving are examples of how informal norms may be codified into laws.

You are expected to follow the norms and obey the laws, but the consequences for failing to do so are usually very different in the two cases. If you violate the law against homicide, then you can expect to be arrested and incarcerated. But if you

A law may be repealed if its regulations are no longer normative. In the United States, the 1896 case *Plessy v. Ferguson,* which permitted racial segregation in public schools and private businesses, reflected widespread norms of the era. When norms began to shift, the 1954 Supreme Court case *Brown v. Board of Education of Topeka* overturned the earlier ruling. However, though segregation was officially abolished, racial tension and subjugation persisted in many parts of the country.

fail to follow the norm of using utensils to eat your dinner and you eat instead with your fingers, all that might be expected are a few raised eyebrows and a "tsk tsk" or two from your dinner companions. However, such relatively mild reactions are not always the case. For example, violations by a gang member of a norm against fleeing a fight with another gang may lead to physical violence, death, and other not-so-subtle outcomes.

Norms are reinforced through **sanctions**. As is clear in the preceding examples, punishments (negative sanctions) can be used, but rewards (positive sanctions) can also be employed. For example, dinner companions might grin slightly when you use the right utensil, and gang members would be likely to approve of those who stay and fight. In other words, sanctions may be applied when norms are observed as well as when they are violated. For example, children who bring home report cards with lots of As and Bs may be praised, which is a positive sanction, while those whose report cards show lower grades may get a stern lecture from a parent, a negative sanction. Sometimes either positive or negative sanctions are enough to enforce norms, but in general enforcement is more effective when positive and negative sanctions are used in tandem—applying both "the carrot and the stick." Most people follow norms primarily because sanctions are associated with them.

Not all norms are the same, are equally important, or carry with them the same penalties if they are violated. A distinction made over a century ago by William Graham Sumner ([1906] 1940) remains useful today. On the one hand, there are **folkways**, or norms that are relatively unimportant. Whether they are observed or violated, they carry with them few if any sanctions. For example, many university classes have norms against texting during a lecture, but the norm is frequently violated. When violations are detected by alert instructors, the negative sanctions, such as asking the student to stop or to leave the room for the rest of class, are generally mild. In contrast, **mores** (pronounced MOR-ays) are more important norms whose violation is likely to be met with severe negative sanctions. Students

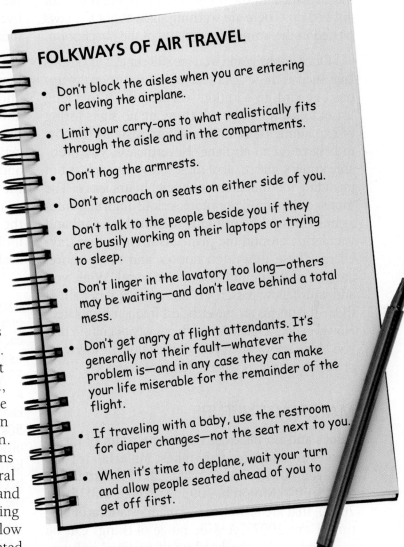

FOLKWAYS OF AIR TRAVEL

- Don't block the aisles when you are entering or leaving the airplane.
- Limit your carry-ons to what realistically fits through the aisle and in the compartments.
- Don't hog the armrests.
- Don't encroach on seats on either side of you.
- Don't talk to the people beside you if they are busily working on their laptops or trying to sleep.
- Don't linger in the lavatory too long—others may be waiting—and don't leave behind a total mess.
- Don't get angry at flight attendants. It's generally not their fault—whatever the problem is—and in any case they can make your life miserable for the remainder of the flight.
- If traveling with a baby, use the restroom for diaper changes—not the seat next to you.
- When it's time to deplane, wait your turn and allow people seated ahead of you to get off first.

who use their smartphones to cheat on exams are violating mores (as well as campus rules). If their actions are witnessed or discovered, they may be subjected to severe negative sanctions, such as failing a class and even being expelled from school. While Sumner makes a clear distinction between folkways and mores, in fact they exist along a continuum so that it is often hard to distinguish with certainty where a folkway ends and a more begins.

For a good example of the differences between laws and the various types of norms, consider the situations you may encounter if you travel by airplane. First, if you want to get through airport security with a minimum of hassle, you need to observe laws regarding the belongings you can carry onto the airplane and the things you must and must not say and do. There are warning signs about the laws posted in the immediate vicinity of the checkpoint.

Once on the plane, you are still subject to various laws such as those against smoking or carrying weapons onboard. In addition you are subject to a long list of folkways, although there are no signs listing or explaining them or orientation sessions on how to behave on an airplane. Nevertheless, you probably know some or all of these folkways, such as not intruding too much on your neighbour's space. The mores of air travel are more serious informal rules against things like drinking too much alcohol and wandering around the plane disturbing other travellers. These unwritten norms, and many more, are part of the culture of airplane travel. While you and your fellow passengers know most, if not all, of them, the norms are nevertheless frequently violated. However, it is a reflection of the power of culture that you likely know when you are violating the folkways or mores as well as when others are doing so.

MATERIAL CULTURE

Values and norms exist within the realm of ideas. However, culture also takes material forms. **Material culture** encompasses all of the artefacts, the "stuff" (Molotch 2003; Steketee and Frost 2011), that are reflections or manifestations of culture (Dant 2007). A wide range of things can be included under the heading of material culture, including the clothes we wear, the homes we live in, our computers and iPhones, the toys our children play with, and even the types of money that we use, such as the Toonie.

Culture shapes these objects. For instance, the value Canadians place on economic prosperity is reflected in such material objects as games like Monopoly. This game was first patented in the mid-1930s, and its icon is a well-dressed, economically successful tycoon with a monocle, named Rich Uncle Pennybags. There are now online and CD-ROM versions of Monopoly, as well as countless editions of the game specially designed around various cities, sports teams, television programmes, and hobbies (including a version for fashion-minded girls). Similarly, one of the objectives in the online virtual world Second Life is the accumulation of as many Linden Dollars—ultimately convertible to real dollars—as

possible. However, unlike Monopoly, the real objective in Second Life is not really to "win" by having the most money, but to "hang out" and socialise.

Material culture also shapes the larger culture in various ways. For example, in playing Monopoly, children are learning about, helping to support, and furthering a culture that values wealth and material success. To take a different example, the centuries-old Canadian value of individual freedom and individualism has been greatly enhanced by the widespread adoption of such material objects as the automobile, the single-family home, and the smartphone. The last named, gives us highly individualised and mobile access to the vast world available on the phone and the Internet.

Material culture exists not only in these individual objects but also in the relationships among various objects (Baudrillard [1968] 1996). For example, each brand of beer has meaning in part because of its place in the larger system of beer brands. Labatt 50 is an especially popular beer in Northern Ontario and Quebec, but Labatt Blue is an overwhelming favourite in the rest of Canada (where, if you bring 50s to a party, they are less likely to be drunk by others; Bigge 2003). Labatt Blue was initially marketed as Labatt Pilsner, but among the culture of beer drinkers it was referred to as "Blue" because of the colour of the label, so Labatt changed the name.

SYMBOLIC CULTURE AND LANGUAGE

On the other side of the coin is **symbolic culture**, which includes those aspects of culture that exist in nonmaterial forms. In fact, we have already discussed two key forms of symbolic culture—values and norms. Symbolic culture is in many ways more important than material culture. However, there is no clear line between material and nonmaterial culture. Most, if not all, material phenomena have symbolic aspects, and various aspects of symbolic culture come to be manifest in material objects. Examples include buying American rather than Japanese or Korean automobiles as a symbol of one's patriotism, purchasing an iPad as an example of one's technological sophistication, and using cloth diapers versus disposables as a symbol of one's commitment to "green" parenting.

GL🌐BALISATION

Queuing in Hong Kong and India

We are accustomed to forming spontaneously straight, orderly lines—for example, to board an airplane, order food, buy a beer at an athletic event, or attend a popular concert (Helweg-Larsen and LoMonaco 2008). This form of queuing is something that we usually associate with the modern world, especially a McDonaldized world. It is more efficient to form a queue than to mill about in a crowd. In other words, forming a straight and orderly line is a norm within modern society.

But standing in straight lines is less normative in other societies, particularly less developed, less modern, and less McDonaldized societies. For example, when forming a line in India, people might begin to form a queue. However, when the line begins to get too long, new arrivals will begin standing next to someone in line and when joined by still others will form what looks like a new limb on a tree. Eventually, a number of such limbs will be formed, creating what in effect looks like a human evergreen tree (Giridharadas 2010). A further complication is that few people have problems with cutting into line: "They hover near the line's middle, holding papers, looking lost in a practised way, then slip in somewhere close to the front. When confronted, their refrain is predictable: 'Oh, I didn't see the line'" (Giridharadas 2010). To prevent others from cutting in line, people (mostly men) end up standing very close to the people in front of them. One consequence is that the body parts of the people in line tend to touch.

There is a long history of queues in many other cultures, most notably British culture. However, although Hong Kong was a British colony (as was India) for well over a century, queuing arrived when McDonald's first opened there in 1975. At first, milling crowds were shouting out orders and waving money at the counter people. McDonald's subsequently introduced queue monitors, who were responsible for getting customers to form orderly lines. This practise not only succeeded at McDonald's, but has become characteristic of middle-class culture in general in Hong Kong. In

fact, older residents often credit McDonald's with bringing the queue to Hong Kong.

More recently in India and elsewhere, the queue is being challenged by the "market mentality." That is, it is increasingly believed, especially by the affluent, that they should be able to use their money to get to the head of the queue or to avoid the queue altogether. For example, while there are lines at Hindu temples, those who can pay get in much shorter VIP lines or avoid lines entirely. Indian clubs have "rope-lines" for the majority of visitors, but those who can afford to purchase premium memberships get in faster. This is also the case at most Canadian airports where people purchasing more expensive tickets get an exclusive, and faster, line for the security check.

Such market-driven arrangements are more efficient for those who can afford them. Of course, they complicate life for those who cannot. Letting the well-to-do enter more quickly makes the wait even longer for everyone else. Furthermore, these market-driven systems, like all such systems, create a much more stratified world. This was not the case in either milling crowds or first-come, first-served queues, where being the loudest or the first to arrive—not the wealthiest—got one to the head of the line.

The language we use reflects how we think and see the world. Do you recognize any of the brand names visible in this photograph taken at the 30th Annual IGA Food Store Convention in 1956? This photo also highlights the confluence of Canadian and American material culture (i.e., Ajax, Quaker Oats, Kellogg's).

One important aspect of symbolic culture is **language**, a set of meaningful symbols that enable communication. Language, especially in its written form, allows for the storage and development of culture. Cultures with largely oral traditions do manage to accumulate culture and transmit it from one generation or group to another, but written language is a far more effective way of retaining and expanding upon a culture.

Perhaps more importantly, language facilitates communication within a culture. The words reflect how we think and see the world. They also shape and influence culture. Suppose a time traveller from the 1950s arrived at a modern-day supermarket to buy something to eat for breakfast. This visitor would be bewildered by brand-name breakfast cereals like Bamm-Bamm Berry Pebbles, Bear Naked, Count Chocula, Franken Berry, Kix, Lucky Charms, and so on. Kellogg's Frosted Flakes, with a sprinkling of sugar, was a noteworthy innovation in the 1950s. The exotic and varied flavours we have now would be a marvel. The point, however, is that having names for a large number of cereal brands allows

the consumer to make much finer distinctions and judgments about breakfast and much else.

The contemporary world has given us a wealth of new words. For example, in the digital era, e-mail and advertisers gave us the word *spam* for the avalanche of unwanted messages. In the world of social networking, Twitter has given us the word *tweet* to describe the brief messages on that system. The consumption-oriented nature of our society has also led to the creation of many new words, a large number of them brand names. For example, the *iPod* is the leading portable music device; it led to the development of the sales of *iTunes*. The *iPhone* is a leading *smartphone* (another new word), and it has led to a booming industry in *apps* (applications) of all sorts. Similarly, globalisation has led to new words, including *globalisation* itself, which was virtually unused prior to 1990. The boom in sending work to be performed in another country or countries has given us the term *outsourcing* (Ritzer and Lair 2007).

Words like these are shared by people all over the world and allow them to communicate with one another. Communication among people of different cultures is also easier if they share a mother tongue. As you can see in Global Flow Map 4.1, which is a simplified map of world languages, African cultures use a variety of official and national languages. People in countries where French is the official language, such as Burkina Faso and Niger, can transact their business more easily with one another (assuming relations are tranquil) than when they are dealing with the African nations where Arabic or Portuguese is the primary language, such as Mauritania and Cape Verde.

Communication between cultures is never as easy or as clear as communication within a given culture. For example, the 2003 movie *Lost in Translation* deals with communication difficulties experienced by Americans in Japan. The lead, played by Bill Murray, is a famous American actor visiting Japan to do commercials. Among

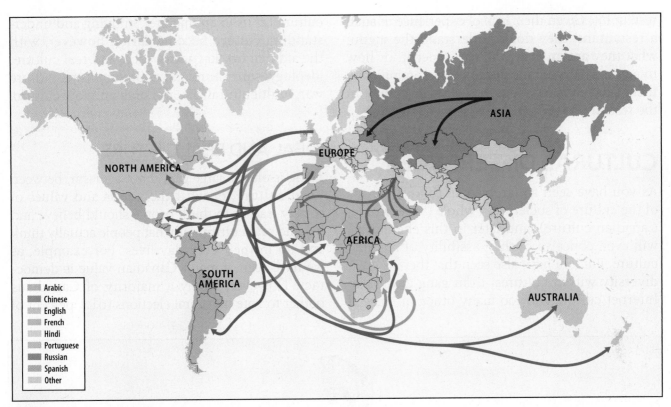

GLOBAL FLOW MAP 4.1 Distribution of Major Languages

other things, he is unable to understand how a large number of words spoken in Japanese become, when translated for him, a very small number of English words. He seems to suspect that the translator is purposely not telling him things. He also finds himself unable to understand what the director of the commercial he is filming wants him to do, even when the directions are translated into English.

In a world dominated by consumption, communication between cultures also takes place through the viewing of common brands. However, brand names well known in some cultures may not translate well in other cultures. As a result, brands are often renamed to better reflect other cultures. Take the following list of well-known brands in Canada and elsewhere and the way they are translated into Chinese:

Brand	Chinese Translation
Nike	Enduring and Persevering
BMW	Precious Horse
Heineken	Happiness Power
Coca-Cola	Tasty Fun
Marriott	10,000 Wealthy Elites

While such name changes are common, some Chinese brands are simply phonetic translations of global brands. For example, Cadillac is translated as "Ka di la ke." Although this means nothing to the Chinese, the fact that it is foreign gives it an aura of status and respectability. However, if Microsoft had used a phonetic translation of its search engine Bing, it would have been in big trouble. In Chinese, *Bing* translates into "disease" or "virus." Rather than be seen as disease-ridden or a carrier of a virus, Microsoft changed its Chinese name to *Bi ying*. This has the far more appealing meaning of "responding without fail." Peugeot did go ahead with the name *Biao zhi*, although it turned out that name sounds much like the Chinese slang word for "prostitute." As a result, Peugeot has become the butt of a number of dirty jokes (Wines 2011).

Even when people share a language, communication may be difficult if their backgrounds and values are too different. In the popular and influential HBO (2002–2008) series *The Wire*, a police major takes some inner-city youths from Baltimore (the site of the series) to a fancy restaurant. Given their lack of experience in such a restaurant, they don't understand the menu, what they are ordering, how to order it, or how to eat it. The symbolic culture that is familiar to them is far different from the symbolic culture of the restaurant.

CULTURAL DIFFERENCES

As you have seen so far, we can think in terms of the culture of society as a whole (for example, Canadian culture), and later in this chapter we will even conceive of the possibility of a global culture. But you have also seen that there is great diversity within cultures, from gang culture to Internet culture and too many other variants of culture for us to enumerate. Studying and understanding culture become easier, however, with the aid of a few key ideas: ideal and real culture, ideology, subculture and counterculture, culture war, multiculturalism, and high and low culture.

IDEAL AND REAL CULTURE

There is often a large gap, if not a chasm, between **ideal culture**, or what the norms and values of society lead us to think people should believe and do, and **real culture**, or what people actually think and do in their everyday lives. For example, as we have seen, a major Canadian value is democracy. However, barely a majority of Canadians bother to vote in federal elections (61.1 percent of

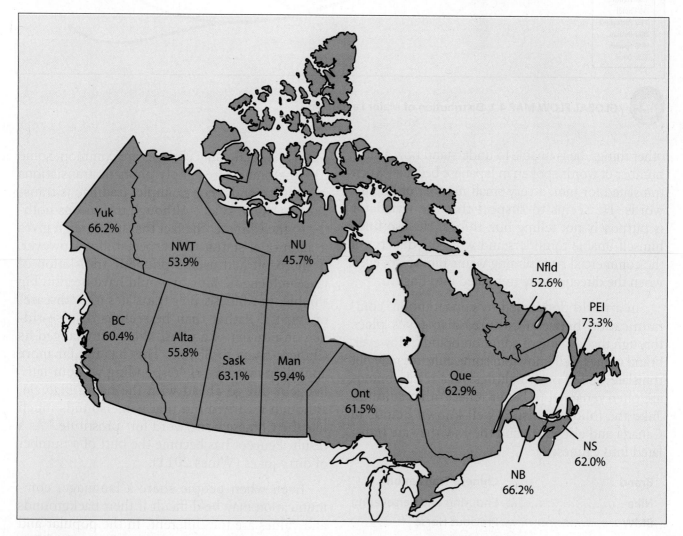

FIGURE 4.2 Federal Election Voter Turnout Among Eligible Voters by Province and Territory, 2011

SOURCE: http://www.sfu.ca/~aheard/elections/results.html (retrieved September 20, 2012).

eligible voters voted in the 2011 election) (Elections Canada 2013). (See Chapter 12.) A far smaller percentage of those who are eligible vote in provincial and municipal elections (see Figure 4.2). Worse, very few Canadians are active in politics in other ways, such as canvassing on behalf of a political party or working to get people out to vote.

In another example, the cultural ideal that mothers should be completely devoted to their children (Blair-Loy 2003; B. Fox 2009) often comes into conflict with the lived reality of the many women who work outside the home and must balance their time between work and family. One area where this contradiction becomes apparent is with breast-feeding, which at least for some women is becoming a norm, once again, of motherhood (Avishai 2007; Stearns 2009, 2011). But the labour- and time-intensive nature of breast-feeding, along with the fact that most women have jobs or other constraints in their lives, makes breast-feeding difficult or impossible. The result for an individual mother can be great ambivalence toward breast-feeding and, at times, the feeling that she has failed to live up to the standards of being a "good mom" (L. Blum 2000; P. Taylor, Funk, and Clark 2007).

IDEOLOGY

An *ideology* is a set of shared beliefs that explains the social world and guides people's actions. There are many ideologies in any society, and some of them become dominant. For example, in Canada, meritocracy is a dominant ideology involving the widely shared belief that all people have an equal chance of succeeding economically based on their hard work and skills. Many people act on the basis of that belief and, among other things, seek the education and training that seem to be needed to succeed.

However, even with dedication and adequate education and training, not everyone succeeds, and this reflects the key fact that not all ideologies are true. For one thing, they may come from, and be true for, some groups of people (such as those in the upper classes) and not for others (those in the lower classes) (Mannheim [1931] 1936). For another, they may be outright distortions used by one group to hide reality from another group (Marx [1857–1858] 1964). In this sense, it could

BIOGRAPHICAL bits

Patricia Marchak (1936–2010, Canadian)

- Marchak, born in Lethbridge, Alberta, was an exceptional high school swimmer in the Vancouver neighbourhood of Kitsilano, winning scores of competitive trophies.

- As a student, she was both the editor of her high school newspaper, *Kitsilano Life,* and the editor-in-chief of *The Ubyssey.*

- In 1997 you could have found her interviewing members of the Asociación Madres de Plaza de Mayo (mothers of "disappeared children") in front of the Presidential Palace in Buenos Aires.

- In 2000, still pursuing a project on social justice and crimes against humanity, she could be found interviewing survivors of the Pol Pot/Khmer Rouge regime that left nearly a million dead in Cambodia.

- *No Easy Fix: Global Responses to Internal Wars and Crimes against Humanity* (2008) relied on those interviews, and much additional evidence, to document some of the major human rights violations of recent decades and address the limitations of international attempts to deal with them.

- Her best-selling book *Ideological Perspectives on Canada* (1981) detailed the ways in which systems of ideas acted as filters to distort the ways in which people understood society and their places within it.

be argued that meritocracy is an ideology created by the upper classes to hide the fact that those in the lower classes have little or no chance of succeeding. This fact is hidden from them in order to prevent them from becoming dissatisfied and rebellious. If the lower classes accept the ideology of meritocracy, they may be more likely to blame themselves for failing rather than the upper classes or the economic system as a whole.

SUBCULTURES

Within any culture there are **subcultures** that involve groups of people who accept much of the dominant culture but are set apart from it by one or more culturally significant characteristics. In Canada, major subcultures include the LGBT community (lesbians, gays, bisexuals, and transgendered persons), Caribbean migrants, Hasidic Jews, hip-hop fans, cross-country skiers, and youth subcultures. Muslims are becoming an increasingly important subculture in Canada (especially in larger cities like Montreal), and they already constitute a major subculture in many European countries, most notably Great Britain.

There are subcultures in the realm of consumption as well: "Brand communities" developed around a particular brand-name product (Muniz and O'Guinn 2001). Harley-Davidson motorcycle riders are one such subculture, with distinctive clothing, events, and norms (the only bike of the Hells Angels). Brand communities have formed around Apple products, such as the Macintosh computer (the "Mac") or around the BlackBerry. The members of these communities share a number of cultural elements, including norms. In the case of the Mac, for example, some community members positively sanction *jailbreaking,* a method for hacking into Apple's software in order to get around its restrictions and limitations.

Any society includes many subcultures, such as golfers or those devoted to fishing, that develop around particular styles of entertainment and fashion and share a special vocabulary. A great deal of attention has been devoted to "deviant" subcultures, such as those that involve punks, goths, and the like (Berard 2007). In Great Britain, "football hooligans," those who often engage in violence at, or surrounding, soccer matches, constitute a deviant subculture largely specific to that society (Dunning, Murphy, and Williams 1986). However, there are also many "straight" youth subcultures such as straight-edge music fans who eschew alcohol and drugs (www.straightedge.com).

Another example of a subculture can be found in the world of skateboarders. The majority of skateboarders accept most of society's culture, norms, values, and language. But they also differ in some ways. For instance, many of them are more willing to take risks than others are. They also have their own vocabulary. It happens that a family member is a skateboarder, so one of the authors is (vaguely) familiar with these terms. However, it took him a long time to understand them. When he did, he was able to get a better sense of skateboarding and its intricacies. Of course, his understanding pales in comparison to the understanding of those immersed in the skateboarding subculture and its distinctive language. Deirdre Kelly, Shauna Pomerantz, and Dawn Currie (2005) have explored the subculture of girl skateboarders, picking up on some of the themes in Avril Lavigne's music.

COUNTERCULTURES

Groups that not only differ from the dominant culture, but whose norms and values may be incompatible with those of the dominant culture, are called **countercultures** (Binkley 2007; Zellner 1995). They may, in fact, consciously and overtly act in opposition to the dominant culture. The term *counterculture* was introduced by Theodore Roszak ([1968] 1995, 1969) in the late 1960s, in reference to hippies, antiwar activists, and radical students. An even earlier example of a counterculture was the Ku Klux Klan. Klan members rejected the Canadian value of equal treatment for all by mistreating members of various minority groups, especially blacks. The Canadian branch of the KKK was much smaller than in the United States, and was concentrated mainly in the West, and in particular in Saskatchewan (Robin 1992).

Computer hackers are a contemporary example of a counterculture (S. Levy 2010). Many hackers simply seek to show their technical mastery of computers through relatively benign actions such as writing free computer software. But a minority are devoted to subverting authority and negatively affecting the Internet. They write malicious code in order to disrupt or even shut down the normal operations of computers. In one famous case, Robert Tappan Morris unleashed a worm that slowed down thousands of computers, making many of them unusable. There are many other cases of break-ins to government and corporate computer systems in order to steal secret information.

In the realm of consumption, an important contemporary counterculture is formed by those who are associated with, or sympathetic to, the "voluntary simplicity movement" (Elgin 2010; Grigsby 2004). Sociologist Juliet Schor (1993, 1998) has critiqued the dominant American culture's emphasis on what she calls "work and spend." That is, we are willing to work long hours in order to be able to spend a great deal on consumption. In addition, she points out the ways in which our consumer culture has led to the commercialisation of childhood, with advertising pervading all aspects of children's lives (Schor 2005). As a countercultural alternative, she suggests that we both work less and spend less and instead devote ourselves to more meaningful activities. Living a simpler life means avoiding overconsumption, minimising the work needed to pay for consumption, and doing less harm to the environment.

Globalisation, especially economic globalisation, has also spawned a number of very active countercultural groups. They are not necessarily antiglobalisation, but they favour alternative forms of globalisation (R. Kahn and Kellner 2007; Pleyers 2010). In fact, many of them are part of the process of globalisation. The World Social Forum (WSF) was created in 2001 after a series of antiglobalisation protests, especially in Seattle in 1999 and Quebec City in 2001. Its members come from all over the world. The WSF's slogan is "Another world is possible." That other world is less capitalistic and allows for more democratic decision making on matters that affect large portions of the world's population. Those who accept this kind of perspective are clearly part of a counterculture. They oppose the dominant capitalist culture, which is spreading around the world and prioritises maximising profits over democratic decision making.

CULTURE WARS

In the 1960s, the hippies, student radicals, and anti–Vietnam War activists vocally, visibly, and sometimes violently rejected traditional Canadian and American norms and values. Among other things, they rejected unthinking patriotism and taboos against recreational drugs and sexual freedom. The term **culture war** was used to describe the social upheaval that ensued—that is, a conflict pitting a subculture or

Ollie: A jump performed by tapping the tail of the board to the ground.

Nollie: A jump done by tapping the nose of the board instead of the tail.

Kickflip: A jump in which the skater kicks the board into a spin before landing back on it.

Kickturn: A turn performed by balancing on the rear wheels while quickly swinging the front of the board in a partial or a full turn.

Fakie: A backward move done while standing in a normal stance.

Alley-oop: A trick that is performed in the opposite direction to where the skater is moving.

Grind: The scraping of one or both axles along a railing, an edge, a curb, or another obstacle.

Nosegrind: A grind in which only the front set of wheels is used (Gallegos 2008).

GL🌐BALISATION

Moscow's "Roofers"

Moscow—and Russia more broadly—was globally isolated only two decades ago. But since the fall of the Soviet Union and Russia's recent economic development, it has become rapidly integrated into the global economy (Jeffries 2011). Russia is the world's largest producer of oil and a major producer of natural gas, and, with increased foreign investment, its capital city has changed dramatically. One indication of economic development and the integration of Russia and Moscow into the global economy is the great expansion of the country's fast-food industry. For example, McDonald's now has 279 restaurants in Russia. The leading franchisee for Papa John's in Russia said: "I could succeed in my sleep there is so much opportunity here" (Kramer 2011:B1). Russia's economic development is most visible in Moscow, an increasingly modern city of about 13 million people. It is there that we find a new subculture—Moscow's "roofers."

Unlike traditional roofers, the "roofers" of Moscow do *not* work on roofs of buildings. Rather, they simply sneak onto the rooftops and luxuriate in being there, enjoying the sights (other buildings) and sounds (birds, traffic). Because of the great changes occurring in Moscow, the vistas are constantly new and changing. The "roofers" have enjoyed the sight of the razing and renovation of old buildings, as well as of the erection of new buildings throughout the city.

It is not easy to gain access to Moscow's roofs. Buildings often have locks with electronic or manual keypads. "Roofers" crack the codes, sometimes by simply using various combinations of the buttons that show the most use by residents. They also bluff their way into buildings by pretending over intercoms to be deliverymen, letter carriers, or neighbours.

No one knows how many "roofers" there are in Moscow—the activity is illegal, and it is often practised in small groups of two to three people, usually in their late teens or early 20s. Much of the "roofer" subculture exists on the Internet. One online community of "roofers" has about 1,500 members. "Roofers" blog about their experiences and exchange stories and pictures through social networking sites. They have developed, as is the case among many subgroups on these websites, their own jargon. It is they who label themselves *roofers,* the concierges of buildings are called *konsa,* and *party buses* are the police vans that occasionally gather them up and take them to jail.

Those involved in the "roofer" subculture seem to do it for the unique experiences, to get away from the routine. Others see themselves as explorers, even pioneers. Still others are rejecting business and work and seeking something that they consider more important than money. Nevertheless, some "roofers" have created a business conducting tours of the "best roofs" of St. Petersburg—another major Russian city—costing between $13 and $80 per person. Others, with permission from the building owners, are using the rooftops for birthday and wedding celebrations.

Roofers relax atop a St. Petersburg high-rise.

In 2011, hacker group Lulz Security (or LulzSec) orchestrated high-profile attacks on PlayStation Network, an online video gaming service, as well as several security and governmental websites (such as those of InfraGard and the CIA). LulzSec also completed a hacking challenge issued by Black & Berg Cybersecurity Consulting, but publicly refused the challenge's prize money.

counterculture against the dominant culture, or conflicts between dominant groups within a society. Culture wars sometimes lead to the disruption of the social, economic, and political status quo.

In Canada today, the major culture war involves a series of battles between those who see themselves as on the conservative end of the sociopolitical spectrum and those who view themselves as on the liberal end. This war is largely viewed as a political battle over such things as government spending, taxes, social services, environmental measures, and so on. Conservatives generally favour less government spending, lower taxes for the wealthy, fewer entitlements for the poor, and minimal environmental regulations; liberals usually favour higher government spending on education, health care, and services for the poor; less military spending; and stricter environmental regulations.

There are also important differences in fundamental values between these groups. Consider, for example, the long-running battle over abortion. The political battle is over legal limits to abortion and contraception, but the underlying values have to do with one's definition of life and attitude toward women's role in society. Similarly, much heat is generated over "family values," with conservatives worrying about the decline in the traditional nuclear

family, the increasing prevalence of cohabitation and single parenthood, and homosexual marriages and child adoptions. They place more emphasis on strict moral codes and self-discipline. In contrast, liberals place more significance on empathy, openness, and fairness (McAdams et al. 2008) and tend to see these developments in the family as signs of greater acceptance of people's differences and circumstances. Within the field of sociology, in fact, there is intense debate among family scholars who argue that the family is in decline (Popenoe 1993, 2009) and those who feel the concept of the family needs to be broadened to embrace the multiplicity of ways in which people experience kin connections (M. Baker 2009) (see Chapter 11).

The conservative-liberal culture war is also fought out in the popular media, where these sorts of issues are debated endlessly. Although journalists seek to portray their work as professional, many readers would see the *National Post* as a more conservative newspaper as compared to the *Globe and Mail*. And of course all political parties love to hate the media, constantly carping about the political leanings of the press that undermine their particular political interests. More broadly, Marsha Barber and Ann Rauhala (2008) have interviewed Canadian newsmakers to examine issues of political leanings and professional codes. Examples of culture wars are also to be found in the digital world. For example, open-source advocates believe that the Internet, or at least large portions of it, should be protected from control by governments or corporations. They support free open-source software (Linux, Firefox, OpenOffice, GNU Image Manipulation programme), as well as free access to information. One of their models is Wikipedia, where anyone can create entries and modify them. They oppose the dominant players on the Internet, including Microsoft, Google, Apple, and Internet service providers. These large corporations are seen as carving up the digital world and controlling access in order to generate huge profits. There is a constant low-level conflict going on between members of these two cultures and the groups that support them.

MULTICULTURALISM AND ASSIMILATION

A great deal of attention has been paid in recent years to another aspect of cultural diversity—**multiculturalism**, or an environment in which

PUBLIC SOCIOLOGY

Todd Gitlin and the Culture Wars

Todd Gitlin is an American sociologist, journalist, novelist, and poet who was born in 1943. He has been actively involved in the culture wars since his early days as a college student. In 1963–1964, he was president of Students for a Democratic Society (SDS), one of the most famous radical student movement organisations of the day. He helped organise both the first national protest against the Vietnam War and the first American demonstrations against corporate involvement in apartheid South Africa. Gitlin's view of his activist role is reflected in his quote: "I am a realist as well as an idealist, and I think that it is incumbent upon those of us in opposition to try to work within what are always arduous circumstances to stretch the limits of the possible" (Monbiot and Gitlin 2011).

Gitlin has written extensively on media and communications. His work has had an impact both on sociology and on the larger public. One of his most famous books is *The Whole World Is Watching* (1980), an analysis of major news coverage of the early days of the anti–Vietnam War movement. In this book, Gitlin draws on interviews with movement activists, news coverage, and his own experiences to analyze how the media reported on the antiwar movement and other movements. He shows that the media tend first to ignore movements and, when they finally do cover them, selectively focus on only certain parts of the story. Despite their claims of neutrality and objectivity, they thereby distort the reality and treat these movements as abnormal social phenomena. In overemphasising the revolutionary rhetoric and distorting what social movements do, the media help to destabilise them. Gitlin demonstrates how, in supporting "moderate" societal reforms, the media further undermine more radical social movements.

Gitlin currently serves as a professor of journalism and sociology at Columbia University. His former academic positions include professor of sociology and director of the mass communications program at the University of California, Berkeley, and professor of culture, journalism, and sociology at New York University. In line with his early activism, Gitlin has sought to reach wider audiences with his sociological analyses. His social commentary has appeared in a variety of newspapers (*The New York Times, Los Angeles Times, The Washington Post, San Francisco Chronicle*), magazines (*The Nation, Mother Jones,* poetry in *The New York Review of Books),* and other outlets (National Public Radio). He also served as a member of the Board of Directors of Greenpeace USA from 2003 to 2006. Gitlin has sought to engage a variety of publics (including students, everyday citizens, and bystanders) by using sociological ideas to help them make better sense of the world and to imagine the range of human and social possibilities.

SOURCE: Printed with the permission of Paul Dean.

In 2007, actor Sean Penn joined co-founder of Code Pink Medea Benjamin in a Washington, DC, march against the war in Iraq. Todd Gitlin found that media outlets tend first to ignore, then to focus on only certain parts of such protests.

cultural differences are accepted and appreciated both by the state and by the majority group (Madood 2007). These cultural groups can be based on ancestry, race, ethnicity, nationality, or language. Canada is at one and the same time a country where

multiculturalism has been relatively successful. One could point to relatively high rates of immigrants becoming Canadian citizens or rates of ethnic intermarriage. However, Canada also houses difficult tensions around ancestral and ethnic issues as

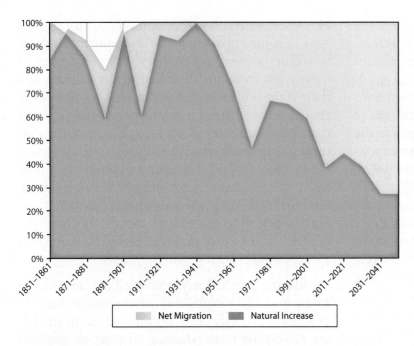

FIGURE 4.3a Contributions of Natural Increase and Net Migration to Population Growth, 1851–2041 (Projection From 2011 to 2041)

SOURCE: Author's calculations from Statistics Canada, CANSIM Table 051-0004 and Demography Division, Statistics Canada.

NOTE: Natural increase = births–deaths; Net migration = immigration–emigration; Net migration was negative in 1851 to 1911 due to people leaving Canada, mainly to the USA.

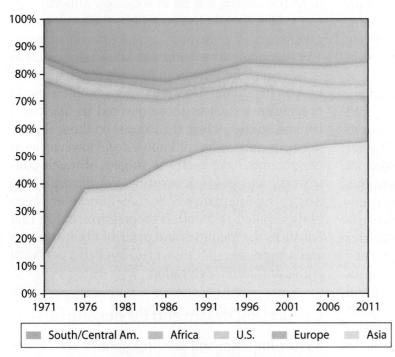

FIGURE 4.3b   Source Regions of Canada's Immigrant Population, 1971–2011

SOURCE: Author's estimates from Statistics Canada, Census of Population (www.statcan.ca).

judged by the aspirations of many Quebecois for separation or of First Nations peoples for recognition and self-government.

When it comes to ethnicity or national origin, therefore, multiculturalism has not always been celebrated in this country. The dominant culture, whether British or French, has been primarily interested in **assimilation**, or integrating the minority group into the mainstream. As a so-called nation of immigrants, the population of Canada has always had to resolve issues of cultural diversity. Until late in the twentieth century, most immigrants to Canada were from Europe (see Figure 4.3). Many of these groups did assimilate to a large degree, even if their assimilation occurred over a couple of generations. Today we do not think twice about whether or not German Canadians or Italian Canadians, for instance, are "regular" Canadians.

But immigrants from the next large wave, in the 1980s and beyond, have experienced more difficulty finding a comfortable home in Canada (Reitz 2012). If you refer again to Figure 4.3, you can see that the flow of immigrants is now mostly from Asia. These immigrants, from a variety of countries, such as China, India, and the Philippines (the top source countries in recent years), often live in largely separate enclaves in urban areas, speak their native languages, and retain their basic cultures, such as their tastes in dress and food. It remains to be seen whether, and to what degree, they will be assimilated into mainstream culture or their culture will be accepted as a valued element of Canadian culture. What Figure 4.3a shows is that over time the contribution of net migration (that is, immigrants minus emigrants) is growing as the main reason for annual population increases in Canada. The contribution of natural increase, births minus deaths, has been slowing. Figure 4.3b reveals a complementary change. Not only is net migration becoming the main factor in population growth, but the source of the migratory flow has shifted dramatically from Europe to Asia.

Unlike in Australia, Canada, or the United States, in European societies, particularly the Scandinavian countries and the Netherlands, multiculturalism is relatively recent. They have traditionally been almost monocultures and even now, during a period of widespread global migration, have a smaller proportion of foreign-born residents than Canada (where close to 20 percent of people are foreign born). However, beginning in the 1950s, many European countries began to experience a labour shortage (Fassman and Munz 1992; Fielding 1989). Large numbers of people from poorer Southern European countries such as Spain and Italy migrated to Northern European countries. Later, migration flowed from less developed countries outside of Europe, such as Turkestan, other largely Islamic countries, and many African countries. The fall of the Soviet Union in 1991 brought additional Eastern Europeans from places such as Albania. Many Northern European governments had intended for these immigrant workers to stay only a short time, but many of the immigrants built lives for themselves, brought their families, and chose to remain. The result is that European countries today are far more multicultural than they were several decades ago.

More recent immigrants to Europe bring with them very different cultures and a very different religion (Islam, for example) than that of the largely Christian Europe; they have also been relatively poor. The relatively small, monocultural country of the Netherlands has had trouble digesting its roughly 1 million Muslim immigrants. France has experienced riots in the suburbs of Paris that are heavily populated by poor immigrants from North Africa (see Chapter 2). In 2009, the Swiss voted to ban the building of new minarets associated with Islamic mosques. In a 2011 protest against Muslim immigration to his country, a Norwegian right-wing extremist bombed government buildings in Oslo, killing 8 people, and later killed another 69 people during a shooting spree at a summer camp related to the country's ruling party. In short, European countries today have more cultural diversity than ever, but the situation is fraught with tension, conflict, and danger as people from very different cultures, religions, and languages struggle to find a way to live side by side (Caldwell 2009).

Identity Politics

The goal of multiculturalism and coexistence among people of different cultures still exists.

However, in recent years some minority groups have become impatient with the dominant culture's unwillingness to accept them and have asserted their right to retain their distinctive culture and their right not to assimilate, at least totally. These groups have engaged in **identity politics**, or used their power to strengthen the position of the cultural group with which they identify (Nicholson 2008; Wasson 2007). Identity politics has a long history, more recently including the black power, feminist, and gay pride movements in many parts of the world. The goal of such movements has been the creation of a true multicultural society, one that accepts minorities for who they are.

Identity politics has played itself out not only on streets in public protests and demonstrations but also in schools and especially in universities. In the latter, the central issue has been whether all students should be required to learn the "canon"—a common set of texts, sometimes referred to as the "great books"—and a body of knowledge long regarded as of central importance. For example, the works of Marx, Weber, and Durkheim are often thought to be the canonical texts in sociology. Minority cultures claim that the canon reflects the interests and experiences of white middle- and upper-class males and that alternative bodies of knowledge, such as those created by women and people of colour, are at least as important. The result was a proliferation of programmes such as those devoted to black and feminist studies, where the focus is on those alternative texts and bodies of knowledge. However, such programmes have been the subject of much controversy and political scrutiny. For example, the Africentric Alternative School in Toronto has been hotly debated as a both a progressive change that enhances the identities and pride of black students and a regressive shift moving us back to a period of ethnic and racial segregation.

Cultural Relativism and Ethnocentrism

Multiculturalism and identity politics are closely related to **cultural relativism**. The idea is that aspects of culture such as norms and values need to be understood within the context of a person's own culture and that there are no cultural universals, or universally accepted norms and values. In this view, different cultures simply have different norms and values, and there is no way to say that one set of norms and values is better than another (Weiler 2007). Thus, for example, those in western countries should not judge Islamic women's use of head scarves. Conversely, those in the Islamic world should not judge western women's baring of their midriffs.

Cultural relativism runs counter to the tendency in many cultures toward **ethnocentrism**, or the belief that the norms, values, traditions, and material and symbolic aspects of one's own culture are better than those of other cultures (S. Brown 2007b). The tendency toward ethnocentrism both among subcultures within Canada and in cultures throughout the world represents a huge barrier to greater cultural understanding. However, to be fair, a belief in one's own culture can be of great value to a culture. It gives the people of that culture a sense of pride and identity. Problems arise when ethnocentrism serves as a barrier to understanding other cultures, a source of conflict among cultures, or an excuse for one culture to deny rights or privileges to another.

HIGH AND LOW CULTURE

A final aspect of cultural differences relates to the distinction between high culture and low culture.

High culture has tended to be associated with societal elites, seen as the product of artists or skilled professionals, and thought of as aesthetically rich. So, the music of Beethoven, the art of Rembrandt, and the literature of Marcel Proust would all be seen as high culture. These are all regarded as classics, as part of the canon. In contrast, **low culture** (sometimes referred to as popular culture) has been associated with the masses, seen as the homogenised and standardised product of massive corporations, and viewed as lacking in redeeming aesthetic qualities (Adorno and Horkheimer 1997). Here we might think of the hit tunes of Nickelback; the paintings of Thomas Kinkade, "Painter of Light"; and the fiction of Stephenie Meyer, the *Twilight* author. Not all low culture is corporate in nature; folk music culture and the culture of pubs in Great Britain and of skid row bars in Canada can also be seen as low culture. However, very often low culture becomes popular because it is supported and disseminated by large corporations (e.g., in fashion or music).

Many of the critical theorists discussed in Chapter 2 dismissed low culture and extolled the virtues of high culture. However, in recent years sociologists and other scholars have come to question, if not reject, this evaluation. A prominent French sociologist, Pierre Bourdieu (1984), argued

The juxtaposition of the Aria Resort and Casino and the Excalibur Hotel exemplifies the distinction between high and low culture, especially architecture, in Las Vegas, Nevada.

that there is a struggle for power within society between the elites and the masses, a struggle that is usually won by the elites. Thus the elites are allowed to define what is considered high and low culture. More importantly, the elites exclude the masses from learning about, and producing, high culture through the creation of expensive training schools and schools of higher education. In addition, the masses cannot afford to consume high culture (for example, they generally cannot afford to attend the opera) or the education through which they learn about high culture (prep schools and elite universities, for example). The conclusion is that, if what is regarded as high culture is the result of victory in a struggle for power, the claim that high culture is aesthetically superior to low culture must be called into question.

Some have in fact argued that high culture has much to learn from low culture. For example, the most sophisticated of architects have adopted elements of the architecture of Las Vegas casino hotels (Klingmann 2007; Venturi, Brown, and Izenour 1972). Indeed, some of these architects are now involved in designing and building structures in Las Vegas. For example, the famed architect César Pelli designed the Aria Resort and Casino, the centerpiece of the new CityCenter complex in Las Vegas.

Indeed, the lines between high and low culture are increasingly blurred (DiMaggio 1987). The masses can now see live performances of the Metropolitan Opera in their local movie theatres, and the elites spend far more time enjoying various forms of popular culture, such as going to the movies and watching TV and YouTube, than they do at the opera. The famous opera *Aida* by Giuseppe Verdi was transformed into a popular musical of the same name, produced by the Disney Corporation and with music by Elton John. Important aesthetic distinctions can still be made in the realm of culture. However, those distinctions have become more difficult to make, are not as clear-cut, and are not as important as they once were (Halle [1993] 2007, 2007).

EMERGING ISSUES IN CULTURE

Culture is continually in the process of change, just as it is continually in the process of being

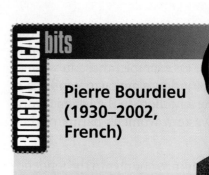

BIOGRAPHICAL bits

Pierre Bourdieu (1930–2002, French)

- Bourdieu came from a humble, rural background, but he was able to attend and eventually teach at the most prestigious universities in France.

- As a student, he came to reject the Marxist, especially Stalinist, ideas that were very powerful at the time in French academia.

- He was drafted in 1956 and spent two years in the French army in Algeria; he stayed on to write a book about his experiences.

- After returning to France, he became a major intellectual figure in Paris and eventually the world as a whole.

- While he had rejected Marxist ideas early in his career, some of those ideas—to focus on people's practises and do theory that relates to those practises—continued to be expressed in his work.

- His most famous book, *Distinction: A Social Critique of the Judgment of Taste* (1984), argued that our tastes (for food, music, and other types of culture) come from our social position, especially our social class, rather than supposedly inherently positive properties of those cultural objects.

transmitted from one generation to the next. Some of the ways in which today's culture is changing are worthy of further exploration in this book. In this section, we will focus on global culture, consumer culture, and cyberculture.

GLOBAL CULTURE

There are certainly major differences within Canadian culture—ideal versus real, subcultures, and so on—but few would dispute the idea that there is a notable gulf between French Canadian and English Canadian culture. This sets us apart from countries such as Australia, Sweden, or the United States, where the idea of one culture has more resonance. However, discussing anything like a global culture, a culture common to the world as a whole, is not as easy. Some elements of material culture, including Big Macs and sushi, cars, and communication technology, have spread widely around the world, but the globalisation of values, norms, and symbolic culture cannot be so easily pinpointed—and is not always appreciated.

Certain values, such as egalitarianism, have emerged and proliferated around the globe. While many societies have embraced gender equality, it is by no means a universal value.

The Globalisation of Values

We have already discussed how values differ, sometimes greatly, from one society to another. How, then, can we discuss global values—values that are shared throughout the world (Sekulic 2007c)? Some scholars argue that global values exist because all people share a biological structure, which produces universal tendencies, including common values. Others contend that while particular values vary from country to country, the underlying structure of values is much the same across societies. However, the most persuasive argument for the existence of global values is traceable to the process of globalisation. The global flow of all sorts of things—information, ideas, products, and people—produces realities in most parts of the world that are more similar than ever before in history (Lechner and Boli 2005). If these realities are increasingly similar, then it seems likely that what people value would come to be increasingly similar throughout the world.

In fact, the globalisation of values has been the subject of the World Values Survey discussed above and in Chapter 3. One of the major findings of this research is a wide-ranging global shift from valuing economic prosperity and material success to valuing more quality-of-life issues such as lifestyle (free time to enjoy the activities and company that one prefers) and self-expression (the opportunity to express one's artistic talents). Other emerging global values are egalitarianism, especially as it relates to men and women, and liberalisation of sexuality.

However, do these changes signify the emergence of truly global values? While they probably hold for the most developed societies in North America, Europe, and Asia, do they apply to most of the less developed world? Probably not! For example, there is little evidence that all societies are accepting greater equality between men and women and more liberal sexual values. There are also generational differences within many societies, even those that are highly developed, with younger people

Some elements of America's material culture have spread around the globe. Here, an Egyptian man selling clay pots can be seen wearing a Nike-branded hat.

more likely to accept these quality-of-life values than the older generations (Welzel and Inglehart 2009).

In short, we can accept the idea that globalisation has brought with it greater acceptance of some values in a larger part of the world, but that is a very long way from saying that we have a global value system. For example, although many societies have welcomed greater access to information from around the world through the Internet and other digital media, China has erected what is called the "Great Firewall" (see Chapter 1), seeking to restrict the ability of its people to view the entire range of Internet sites and therefore the global values on view in at least some of them.

Cultural Imperialism

Many have the strong view that what affects global culture most of all is **cultural imperialism**, or the imposition of one dominant culture on other cultures (Tomlinson 1999, 2012). Cultural imperialism tends to destroy local cultures. Let us look briefly at two examples of cultural imperialism in contemporary India:

- Saris are a key element of Indian material culture. Indian saris have traditionally been made of silk and woven by hand in a process that can take as much as two months for each sari. Elaborate designs are interspersed with strands of gold thread and green silk. However, India's roughly 1 million sari makers are now threatened by machine-made saris, especially from China (Wax 2007). A culture that emphasises inexpensive, machine-made products is imposing itself on a realm in another culture that has emphasised local products, practises, and indigenous skilled workers. In the process, the local sari-making culture is being destroyed, and the sari itself, a distinctive Indian product, is losing its unique character.

- There is also a long tradition in India of professional letter writers, or men who place themselves in prominent locations (for example, near a train station) and write letters for poor, illiterate migrants. Many are able to survive on the pittance they are paid for each letter. However, the spread from the West of the cell phone, and of text messaging, is rendering the professional letter writers, and the cultural traditions associated with them, obsolete.

There is certainly a great deal of cultural imperialism in the world today, with much of it associated with the United States (L. Crothers 2010; Kuisel 1993). The process of **Americanisation** involves the importation by other countries of a variety of cultural elements—products, images, technologies, practises, norms, values, and behaviours—that are closely associated with the United States. One example is the American movie industry. Its popularity around the world has decimated the movie industries of many countries, including Canada and France. (India is one exception with its thriving Bollywood productions, such as the 2009 Academy Award winner for best picture, *Slumdog Millionaire*; Rizvi 2012). Another successful American cultural export is its taste for food, especially fast food and the way in which it is eaten (quickly, with one's hands, standing up or in the car). McDonald's is a prime example, but another of note is Starbucks (B. Simon 2009), which has been surprisingly successful in exporting its model of large, slowly consumed cups of coffee. In contrast, in France and Italy and other countries, the historic preference has been for quickly consumed tiny cups of espresso, and Starbucks has met resistance in those places. Starbucks stores are now located in more than 50 countries (see Figure 4.4).

Cultural imperialism certainly exists, but it would be wrong to overestimate its power. Local cultures can be quite resilient—not all suffer the fate of French movie producers and Indian sari makers and letter writers. For example:

- The powerful process of Americanisation is often countered by **anti-Americanism**, which is an aversion to America in general, as well as to the influence of its culture abroad (Huntington 1996; O'Connor and Griffiths 2005).

- Many cultures—Chinese and Islamic cultures, for example—have long, even ancient, histories. Those cultures have resisted at least some impositions from other cultures for centuries, and they are likely to continue to resist changes that threaten their basic values and beliefs.

- Local cultures modify inputs and impositions from other cultures by integrating them with local realities and in the process produce **cultural hybrids** that combine elements of both (Nederveen Pieterse 2009). Examples of hybridisation include the British watching Asian rap performed by a South American in a London club owned by a Saudi Arabian; another example is the Dutch watching Moroccan women engage in Thai boxing. In the fast-food realm, McDonald's sells such hybrid foods as McChicken Korma Naan, which caters to those in Great Britain who have developed a taste for Indian food (including the many Indians who live there); McLaks, a grilled salmon sandwich in Norway; and McHuevos, hamburgers with poached egg in Uruguay.

Thus cultural imperialism needs to be examined in the context of the counterreactions to it, counterflows from elsewhere in the world, and the combination of the global and local to produce unique cultural elements.

CONSUMER CULTURE

Recall that in Chapter 2 we discussed Thorstein Veblen's ([1899] 1994) concept of *conspicuous consumption*. When the idea was introduced at the turn of the twentieth century, its focus was on the wealthy and their desire to demonstrate their wealth by flaunting mansions, yachts, designer clothes, and so on. While there is no shortage of conspicuous consumption today, it is also the case that not being so conspicuous about one's consumption, engaging in what we might call *inconspicuous* consumption, is valued in some circles. Examples include a well-to-do professor at a topflight university dressing in baggy khakis or tattered jeans, and hockey stars driving economy cars. Larry David, the creator of *Seinfeld* and the model for the "George" character on the show, conspicuously drives a Prius on his HBO programme, *Curb Your Enthusiasm*. However, it is worth noting that the Prius can be seen as representing another kind of conspicuous consumption—a conspicuous concern for the environment.

Whether it is conspicuous or inconspicuous, consumption clearly is highly valued in Canada. That makes Canadian culture a **consumer culture**, one in which the core ideas and material objects relate to consumption and in which consumption is a primary source of meaning in life (Belk 2007; Sassatelli 2007; Slater 1997). Meaning may be found in the goods and services that you buy, in the process of buying them (in shopping malls, cybermalls, etc.), in the social aspects of consumption (shopping with your friends or family), and even in the settings in which consumption takes place (the Toronto Eaton Centre or the West Edmonton Mall, eBay, etc.) (Ritzer, Goodman, and Wiedenhoft 2001).

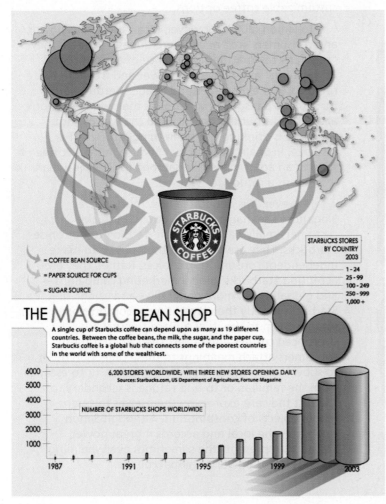

FIGURE 4.4 Starbucks' Global Reach, 2003

SOURCE: Reprinted by permission of Miguel Angel Centeno, Princeton Globalization Project.

GL🌐BALISATION

Starbucks in Singapore

Singapore is a small group of islands in Southeast Asia; it covers a space slightly smaller than metropolitan Toronto. In spite of its small size, it has grown increasingly wealthy (Yew 2000). With some of the busiest ports in the world, it has developed strong international trading links. Singapore has leveraged these links and its exports in consumer electronics and information technologies to develop a bustling economy. However, while its per capita gross domestic product is higher than that of many European countries, so is its economic inequality (Central Intelligence Agency 2013c).

On Singapore's famous Orchard Road, the city's largest commercial strip for well-to-do residents and tourists, you will find a Starbucks. You will also find, among other familiar names, McDonald's, Borders, Dunkin' Donuts, Guess jeans, an Armani boutique, Hard Rock Cafe, Toys "R"Us, California Pizza Kitchen, Hilton, and 7-Eleven.

Bryant Simon (2009) discovered that Starbucks customers in Singapore attribute a variety of meanings to their consumption of this American brand of coffee—meanings that were not necessarily those the company intended. For example, for upper-middle-class teens, patronising an American establishment signifies their independence from rigid family or community structures and demands. For other Singaporeans, to consume Starbucks coffee is to be cosmopolitan and stylish. One consumer felt that Starbucks had replaced McDonald's as the "in-place" in Singapore.

Simon also compares Starbucks to a more traditional Singapore chain, Kopitiam (which literally means "coffee shop"). He notes that Kopitiam produces only a few combinations of coffee, offers low prices, and provides very simple seating and décor. It is highly functional, unlike Starbucks, which offers fancy couches and chairs and a staggering array of customizable coffee options.

To Simon (2009), however, local culture has power, and consumers are "never mere dupes." Instead, they "regularly rework the significance of a product and its meaning" and "have the power and freedom to reinterpret the messages and images before them" (p. 320). As a result, Simon argues that, when you look at all the Starbucks stores around the world, "not everyone is drinking the same thing" (p. 327). For instance, in Spain, Starbucks is "not so much a coffee shop as an adult milkshake saloon" (p. 323); in Japan, it serves as a refuge for women.

However, it is debatable how much power Singapore's teenagers or any other Starbucks customers really have over their decision to patronise Starbucks. They are not using their power to make independent consumption choices. Rather, they are accepting Starbucks' global marketing campaigns—and globalisation more generally—and using Starbucks exactly the way this megacorporation intends them to use it: as a place to purchase overpriced coffees and lattes. The fact that these consumers attach meanings to these objects in order to subvert their parents or their community, to escape from the familiar, or to find refuge is secondary to the fact they are expressing themselves through global objects of consumption. Although Simon celebrates the local and accords it great power, Starbucks represents the sometimes overwhelming homogenising power of global culture.

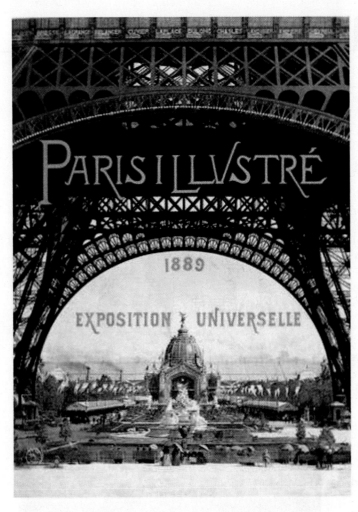

Poster for the 1889 World Exposition in Paris

There are norms about the consumption process as well—for example, customers should wait patiently in the queue at the cashier, casino gamblers should not flaunt their winnings in front of other gamblers and should tip dealers, and so on.

Consumer culture is rather unique in the history of the world. In the past, culture has generally focused on some other aspect of social life such as religion, warfare, citizenship, or work. In fact, in the not-too-distant past in Canada and other developed countries, the core ideas and material objects of culture related to work and production, and people were thought to derive their greatest meaning from their work. This was true from the Industrial Revolution until approximately 1970, when observers began to realise that developed societies, including Canada and especially the United States, were beginning to derive more meaning from consumption (Baudrillard [1970] 1998). Of course, work continues to be important, as do religion and

citizenship, but many people in the world now live in a culture dominated by consumption.

The roots of today's consumer culture can be traced further back in history, to when popular settings of consumption, such as large expositions, world's fairs, and department stores, began to arise (R. Williams [1982] 1991). France in the mid-nineteenth century was particularly important to this development, as home of the trend-setting Le Bon Marché department store and several world's fairs, including the first truly international exposition. In these settings, consumption became democratised. It was no longer restricted to the aristocracy and to men. It became popular with the middle class and, as their ability to afford consumption improved, with the working class as well.

It could be said that the rise of consumer culture was linked to the rise of the modern world in the West (Campbell 1987). Today, of course, consumer culture has arguably become *the* culture of the modern West and indeed of modernity in general. But consumer culture has also globalised to a great degree. It has become firmly entrenched in such nonwestern places as Singapore, Hong Kong, and Dubai. Japan has been called the premier consumer culture. Even in today's China, known for its production-oriented culture, 1 billion–plus citizens are becoming more and more consumption oriented (Hanser 2008).

Children in a Consumer Culture

The most controversial aspect of consumer culture may be the participation of children. In a consumer culture, it is important that children be socialised into, and become actively involved in, consuming (Albanese 2009; D. Cook 2007). Consumption by children has not always been valued, however. In fact, there were once strong norms against it. Children were not considered able to make informed choices about consumption and were therefore seen as even more susceptible than adults to exploitation by advertisers and marketers.

An important change began to take place in the mid-nineteenth century with the advent of department stores. Some stores offered supervised

GL🌐BALISATION

Japanese Consumer Culture

We tend to think of the United States as having the ultimate consumer culture. However, a pretty good argument can be made that Japan is the premier society in the world as far as consumption is concerned. Devastated by World War II, Japan was a latecomer to consumer society. The United States, Great Britain, and other countries were already far advanced before mass consumption began to emerge in Japan in the 1960s. But by the 1980s, spurred by a boom in the Japanese economy led by companies such as Toyota and Sony, the Japanese were consuming with a vengeance. In fact, by the middle of the 1980s, rampant consumption helped lead Japan into an economic "bubble," which burst with the crash of the Tokyo stock market in 1989. More recently, the Japanese economy has suffered the Great Recession in 2008, the massive recall of Toyota automobiles in 2010 because of faulty brakes, and the effects of the devastating earthquake, tsunami, and Fukushima nuclear accident in 2011.

Nevertheless, the Japanese have become avid, highly sophisticated, and well-informed mass consumers (Clammer 1997). Much the same could be said about mass consumers in the United States and elsewhere in the world. However, Japanese consumers are defined by a high degree of rationality; indeed, they may be more focused on convenience and efficiency than American consumers. Consider the central role of vending machines in Japan: Japan has the highest number of vending machines per capita in the world, and they provide everything from snacks and beverages to eggs, ice, beer, umbrellas, flowers, neckties, sneakers, fresh vegetables, batteries, hot French fries, board games, pornographic magazines, and even smart cars (or, to be more precise, smart car

An interesting aspect of consumer culture is the way in which it has spread beyond the economy to other aspects of society.

brochures and stickers) (14 Cool Vending Machines from Japan 2009).

Another example of this rationality is the eagerness with which the Japanese have embraced

play areas so that parents could shop more easily. A key development by the mid-twentieth century was children's sections in department stores; they were eventually subdivided into shops for babies, children, and teens. Also during this period, radio programmes, movies, and TV shows were increasingly directed at children. Disney was a leader in this trend. TV shows of the 1950s, including the Davy Crockett series (*King of the Wild Frontier*), prompted the sales of hundreds of millions of dollars' worth of simulated coonskin caps and other merchandise for

children. More recently, children have come to be targeted directly by advertisers on Saturday morning TV shows and cable channels such as Nickelodeon that specialise in children's programming.

In fact, marketing aimed at children is now pervasive. For example, the Disney Company has begun directly marketing baby products, and thus the Disney brand, to new mothers in maternity wards. In schools, branded products are sold at book fairs, and corporate sponsorships

American fast-food chains. For example, there are more than 3,300 McDonald's restaurants in Japan, to say nothing of other American chains. The only country with more McDonald's restaurants is the United States, with more than 14,000 restaurants; Canada is a distant third with fewer than 1,500. To give these numbers even broader context, there are about 32,000 McDonald's restaurants worldwide, so Japan has more than 10 percent of the total (McDonald's 2010).

Furthermore, Japan has many fast-food chains of its own. The preference for a rationalised way of eating is clear in the popularity of the "beef bowl," Japan's contribution to fast food. A beef bowl is an all-in-one meal including beef, rice, noodles, and various other ingredients. There are three big chains of beef bowl restaurants in Japan—Sukiya, Yoshinoya, and Matsuya (Tabuchi 2010).

Kura is a Japanese chain of 262 sushi restaurants. Most of the waiters in a Kura restaurant have been replaced by conveyor belts that carry sushi in its various forms to the diner (Tabuchi 2010). Similarly, sushi chefs have been largely replaced by sushi-making robots. This is particularly striking because the traditional sushi chef was, and is, highly skilled and greatly valued.

The use of conveyor belts to deliver sushi is not new. They were first used in Japan in the late 1950s; however, Kura has raised their use to new heights by using them in conjunction with advanced information technology and computers (Tabuchi 2010). Video cameras make it possible for the conveyor belts, and everything else in each restaurant, to be watched over by supervisors in three centralised control centers. All of this allows Kura to operate its restaurants with relatively few workers, with a high degree of efficiency, and at much lower cost and therefore greater profitability than traditional sushi restaurants.

Diners order their own food using touch screens. They are also required to put their finished plates into a tableside bay so that the bill can be calculated automatically. Not only do the consumers at Kura "work" to produce their own meals, but unlike many of those employed in fast-food restaurants throughout the world, they seem to like the work.

adorn everything from sports stadiums to classroom supplies. Brands and logos are woven into textbook problems and examples. Market researchers observe the way children use and respond to products and advertising messages not just in focus groups and in the lab, but also in natural settings such as school and the home. Additionally, marketers have discovered that the "pester power" of children—the ability for children to nag their parents into buying something—is effective not only for selling children's products but also for getting children to influence their parents' purchases. For example, a 2011 automobile ad on TV, meant for viewing by adults, features two boys talking about their parents' choice of automobile—bringing not only pester power but also peer pressure into the consumption mix.

Overall, children are much more immersed in consumer culture today than ever before. They learn at an early age to value it as well as the norms involved in participating in it. As adults, then, they will fit well into a culture with consumption at its core.

This commercial for the Toyota Highlander uses pester power and peer pressure to sell a sport utility vehicle. Toward the end of the video, the child exclaims, "Just because you're a parent doesn't mean you have to be lame."

Nontraditional Settings for Consumption

An interesting aspect of consumer culture is the way in which it has spread beyond the economy to other aspects of society. Higher education is another realm increasingly characterised by consumer culture. Students and their parents shop around for the best university and the most conspicuous degrees or for the best values in a university education. University rankings, such as those published by *Maclean's* and *The Globe and Mail,* are big business. For-profit universities have become a booming industry, with enterprises including the University of Phoenix and Quest University enrolling hundreds of thousands of students in the market for a degree on a more flexible schedule. Once enrolled in university, students shop for the best classes, or at least the best class times. Not long ago students were largely passive recipients of their education, but now they are more active consumers of it. For example, they regularly rate their professors and choose classes on the basis of the professors with the best ratings. They are also much more likely to make similar demands for up-to-date "products" and attentive service from their professors and universities

as they do from salespeople and shopping malls.

An important site of consumption is now the Internet (D. Miller and Slater 2000). A good portion of the time that people spend on the Internet is related to consumption, either directly (purchasing items on eBay .ca, Amazon.ca, or Zappos .com; Groupon's ads, its "deal of the day," and the purchase of its discount coupons; etc.) or more indirectly (buying things on Second Life with Linden Dollars or on FarmVille with real dollars). Although more Canadians than Americans use the Internet, 81.3 percent of Canadians versus 74.2 percent of Americans, our southern neighbours are more likely to use the Internet for shopping (39 percent of Canadians and 52 percent of Americans) (Statistics Canada 2011a). Still, online shopping has grown to over $15 billion in Canada in 2009, and the number of shoppers and the value of their purchases will continue to rise unless some security catastrophe were to undermine consumer confidence. It could be argued that people, especially children and teens, are becoming more immersed in consumer culture as they become more deeply enmeshed with the Internet; consumer culture is an increasingly inescapable part of their daily lives. Furthermore, consumption on the Internet is more and more wedded to the material world. For example, goods ordered on Amazon.ca are delivered to our doors by couriers. That level of integration is being ratcheted up even further. You can now pay for parking and rental cars using apps on smartphones. There is even an iPhone app that allows a renter to open the doors of her Zipcar, which can be rented by the hour or the day, and honk its horn.

A Postconsumer Culture

The recent recession technically lasted from the fall of 2008 to mid-2009, but the economic effects are still

Many people are building chicken coops at home to produce their own eggs, even though maintaining chickens often costs more than buying eggs at the grocery store. This discrepancy is outweighed by the pleasure of connecting more intimately with one's food source.

felt. In Canada, unemployment hovers around 7 percent, still above the roughly 5–6 percent rate through the early years of the last decade, and the stock market's Toronto Stock Exchange Composite Index has an average that is still below its high point, reached just before the onset of the recession (or a decline of about 15–20 percent in late 2012). The depth and persistence of these effects have caused observers to question many things about the economy, including the durability of consumer culture. The latter, after all, has a history of perhaps a half-century, although some elements such as the department store go further back. The world existed without a consumer culture before, and it could potentially do so again.

Thus the recession has caused us to think about the possibility of a *postconsumer* culture. Many consumers have lost their ability and desire to consume, at least for now. They have many reasons to spend

carefully: unemployment and an absence of income, a decline in the value of retirement funds and of homes, and most generally a fear, almost irrespective of one's economic situation, that the recession could heat up again, leading to what is called a "double dip" in the economy. But there's more to it than lack of money: Consumers, even those who are well off, are described as "more socially conscious and embarrassed by flashy shows of wealth" (Bannon and Davis 2009:A21, A24). As a result, consumption centers throughout the world—Las Vegas, Dubai, Macau— are hurting, and at least some consumption settings, and even entire locales, are facing bankruptcy.

A major concern around consumption relates to savings. Over time Canadians have been prudent financial managers, but this has changed recently as savings rates have fallen in the wake of rising consumerism. Figure 4.5 shows household savings as a percentage of disposable income. Although there has been a recent uptick in both countries, the rates are historically low. Recall too that consumer debt has been rising in both countries, making consumption growth all the more fragile.

These changes in the behaviour of consumers and their attitudes speak to a change in the larger value system. Consuming less is a sure indication of at least a temporary decline of consumer culture and may even be the beginning of a postconsumer culture. Among the characteristics of such a culture, beyond buying less and saving more, are renting consumer items, pride in buying less expensive or even recycled items, buying less showy brands (a Kia rather than a BMW), dining at home more often than eating at restaurants, and showing a greater concern for the environment in terms of what one buys and, more importantly, does not buy. It is not clear that we are in a postconsumer culture, and, if we are, it is uncertain how long it will last. However, just as we entered what is best described as a consumer culture in the last half of the twentieth century, it is at least possible that we are entering a postconsumer culture in the first half of the twenty-first century.

Culture Jamming

Another chink in consumer culture has been created by organised groups actively seeking to subvert

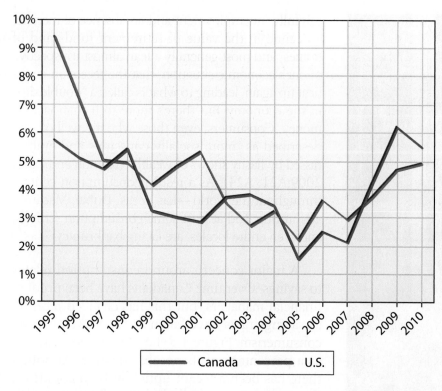

FIGURE 4.5   Household Savings Rate for Canada and the United States, 1995–2010

SOURCE: *OECD Factbook 2013: Economic, Environmental and Social Statistics.*

NOTE: The percentage of household savings related to the disposable income of households.

Shepard Fairey, the artist who designed the Barack Obama "Hope" poster, began his career as a culture jammer and street artist. Fairey's consumerism-critical work often entails the repetition of radical imagery and slogans such as "Obey" and "This is your God."

aspects of both consumer culture and the larger culture. For example, **culture jamming** involves radically transforming an intended message in popular culture, especially one associated with the mass media, if not turning it on its head completely. It is a form of social protest aimed at revealing underlying realities of which consumers may be unaware. The hope is that once people are made aware of these realities by culture jamming, they will change their behaviours or perhaps even band together to change those underlying realities.

The best examples of culture jamming are to be found in the Vancouver-based magazine *Adbusters* and in media campaigns it sponsors. *Adbusters'* main targets are in the realm of consumption, especially web and magazine advertisements and billboards. The idea is to transform a corporation's ads, which of course are aimed at increasing consumption of its products, into anticorporate, anticonsumption advertisements (Handelman and Kozinets 2007).

An interesting example can be found in a Dove commercial that was jammed by Greenpeace, a nonprofit environmental advocacy group (and another organisation begun in Vancouver). You may be familiar with the Dove commercial ("Onslaught") that shows a little girl's face, with musical lyrics (by Simian) saying, "Here it comes . . . here it comes . . . here it comes," and then the video rapidly shows a number of sexy female images that bombard the girl. The video shows how media messages encourage women to consume beauty products. The video ends with a very positive social message to "talk to your daughter before the beauty industry does." One aim of the commercial is to make Unilever, the company that owns the Dove brand, look like a socially responsible company. Greenpeace's play on this ad ("Onslaught[er]") drew upon the same music and form as the Dove commercial. The Greenpeace video starts by showing an Indonesian girl, Azizah, and the same lyrics, "Here it comes . . . here it comes . . . here it comes." It then rapidly shows images of rainforests, wild animals, and natural beauty, then images of chain saws and deforestation. It ends with Dove commercials promising to make your skin soft and silky, noting that "98% of Indonesia's lowland forest will be gone by the time Azizah is 25" and that "most is destroyed to make palm oil, which is used in Dove products." The Greenpeace video is meant to subvert the Dove brand by shedding light on the company's environmentally destructive practises, in hopes that consumers will then put pressure on Dove to end these practises.

The following are some additional examples of the ways in which culture jamming turns commercial messages inside out:

- "Joe Chemo"—rather than Joe Camel—shows an emaciated version of the Camel character (who, of course, smokes Camel cigarettes) in a hospital bed undergoing chemotherapy, presumably for lung cancer caused by smoking.

- "Tommy Sheep" is a spoof of a Tommy Hilfiger ad, with sheep (presumably representing the conformists who buy such clothing) pictured in front of a huge American flag.

- "Absolute on Ice," spoofing an Absolut vodka ad, depicts the foot of a corpse (presumably killed by excessive alcohol consumption) with a toe tag.

- "True Colors of Benetton" depicts a man wearing a Benetton shirt but with wads of money stuffed in his mouth. The ad is designed to underscore the true objective of Benetton—and of all corporations in capitalist society: money and profits.

In 2009, Dove's advertising campaign to promote media awareness was culture jammed by Greenpeace. The environmentalist organization altered a Dove commercial to criticize the company's rainforest-destroying harvesting of palm oil.

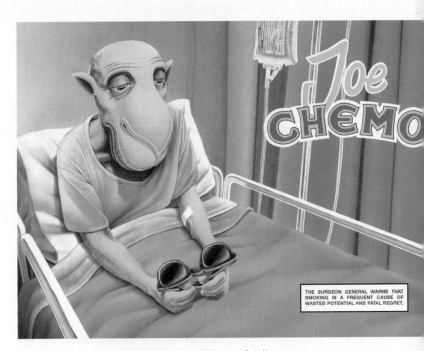

The first image of Joe Chemo ran in a 1996 issue of *Adbusters* magazine. Less than a year later, R. J. Reynolds retired Joe Camel as the mascot for its Camel brand of cigarettes.

All of the above show the hidden realities (sickness, death, and other miseries) and goals (conformist consumers, obscene profits) of corporations. A broader objective is to show viewers the folly of consumer culture, which encourages the consumption of numerous harmful (cigarettes, alcohol) and wasteful (expensive clothing) goods and services.

DIGITAL LIVING

Commercialization and Web 2.0

In its early years, the Internet was dominated by what has been called Web 1.0 (Ritzer and Jurgenson 2010). The early Yahoo! and AOL sites were, and still to a large extent are, two examples of Web 1.0. Basically, those who owned and controlled these sites decided on what was to be provided to those who accessed their sites; there was little or no choice, and few, if any options, were available to the user.

Web 1.0 sites continue to exist, but the Internet has come to be dominated by Web 2.0 sites. These sites are dominated by user-generated content. Those who access Web 2.0 sites are not simply consumers (as they were of Web 1.0 sites), but they are prosumers of those sites, both producing and consuming the content. This is true of all of the major sites (Facebook, Myspace, Wikipedia, Second Life, Flickr, eBay, Amazon), as well as blogs and many other aspects of the Internet. Instead of simply and passively reading news stories written by others on Yahoo! or the *Globe and Mail* website, more of us will be both creating blogs and reading, as well as commenting on, blogs written by others. Instead of merely watching videos created for the major TV networks, we will produce *and* watch the videos on YouTube. Rather than gazing at pictures produced by professional photographers, we will download our own photos on Flickr while examining those downloaded by others.

While some corporations associated with Web 2.0 (eBay, Amazon) have been hugely profitable, largely because the products they offer are not free, others have yet to generate a profit. However, many investors believe that many free sites have huge potential for profit and will be the new media giants in the coming years.

Take Facebook, for example. At the time of this writing, about 850 million people in 119 countries are on Facebook, a number that continues to grow (Cosenza 2011). (The lines shown in the photo on the facing page illustrate friendship connections on Facebook—the brighter the area is, the more connections there are.) It clearly costs a great deal of money to provide all of those users with the computer capacity needed to meet all their needs (for example, to write on people's walls, to play Scrabble online), and the users pay nothing for those services.

One interesting and instructive example of how Facebook will earn money, and allow other companies to do the same, is its Disney application, Disney Tickets Together. One could have bought a ticket for the 2010 release of *Toy Story 3* directly through this app. More importantly, the app automatically alerted one's

CYBERCULTURE

The Internet is, as mentioned before, one site for the proliferation of consumer culture and perhaps of postconsumer culture. It is also the site of an entirely new culture—cyberculture. That is, the Internet as a whole (as well as the individual websites that it comprises) has the characteristics of all culture, including distinctive values and norms.

Some of the distinctive values within cyberculture are openness, knowledge sharing, and access. These values have their roots in the open-source software that emerged before computing became an attractive commercial opportunity and in the knowledge sharing and continuous improvement that were the practise when early computer professionals survived through reciprocity (Bergquist 2003). These roots have been maintained through the open-source movement, through actions against censorship, and through organisations such as the Free Software Foundation and the "copyleft" movement. These "cyberlibertarians" favour user control of information and applications and free products (Himanen 2001), in line with the values of a postconsumer society. They are in conflict with the more dominant values of profit maximisation and control of the Internet by large corporations. This conflict of values, a culture war

Facebook friends that a ticket had been purchased, and it prompted the buyers to invite their friends to also buy tickets to the same show. In addition, users were given the option of inviting friends who were not members of the *Toy Story 3* site (which has about three quarters of a million members). People used this application to buy tickets as a group of as many as 80 people to see *Toy Story* 3. With this app, Disney is going beyond simply creating greater awareness for its movies; it is using the members of its site to acquire new customers directly. Those who use the site are prosumers, not only buying tickets themselves but also doing unpaid work for Disney by recruiting their

friends ("producing" additional moviegoers) to see the movie with them (Barnes 2010).

As with many of its applications, Facebook makes no money directly from these transactions. However, as this kind of thing develops and spreads, Facebook will demonstrate, once again, its enormous capacity to generate income for others. That, in turn, will lead an increasing number of companies to advertise on Facebook and to pay increasing fees for those advertisements. It is the revenue from the nearly infinite advertising possibilities that will make Facebook an even greater media giant in the future.

by the definition offered earlier in this chapter, goes a long way toward defining the Internet today.

Various norms have also come to be a part of cyberculture. Internet users are not supposed to hack into websites, create and disseminate spam, unleash destructive worms and viruses, maliciously and erroneously edit user-generated sites such as Wikipedia, and so on. Many norms relate to desirable behaviour on the Internet. For example, creating and editing entries on Wikipedia is supposed to be taken seriously and done to the best of one's ability. Once an entry exists, the many people who offer additions and deletions are expected

to do so in a similar spirit. Those who purposely add erroneous information on Wikipedia will suffer the stern disapproval of other contributors to, and users of, the site, and they may be banned from Wikipedia by those who are involved in its management.

There is, of course, much more to the culture of the Internet. But the point is that cyberculture, like all cultures, is emerging and evolving as other changes take place within and around it. The biggest difference from other cultures is that, because the Internet is so new and the changes in it are so rapid, cyberculture is far more fluid than culture in general.

SUMMARY

Culture encompasses the ideas, values, norms, practises, and objects that allow a group of people, or even an entire society, to carry out their collective lives with a minimum of friction. Values are the general, abstract standards defining what a group or society as a whole considers good, desirable, right, or important. Norms are the rules that guide what people do and how they live. Culture also has material and symbolic elements. Material culture encompasses all of the objects and technologies that are reflections or manifestations of a culture. Symbolic culture, the nonmaterial side of culture, is best represented by language.

You are immersed in a diversity of cultures. Within the dominant culture to which you belong are subcultures, which include people who may accept much of the dominant culture but are set apart from it by one or more culturally significant characteristics. A culture may also contain countercultures, which involve groups of people that not only differ in certain ways from the dominant culture but whose norms and values may be incompatible with those of the dominant culture. Given this diversity within a culture, it is not surprising that many times culture wars break out, pitting one subculture or counterculture against another or against the dominant culture.

Another aspect of the diversity in culture results when people from one culture become embedded in the culture of another state or majority group. Many cultures tend to be ethnocentric, in that they believe that their own culture's norms, values, traditions, and

the like are better than those of other cultures. Many times newcomers are expected to assimilate—that is, replace elements of their own culture with elements of the dominant culture. However, a society that values multiculturalism accepts, and even embraces, the cultures of many different groups and encourages the retention of cultural differences.

High culture has tended to be associated with societal elites, has been seen as the product of artists or skilled professionals, and has been thought of as aesthetically rich. Low culture, sometimes also referred to as popular culture, is associated with the masses, seen as homogenised and standardised products of massive corporations and viewed as lacking in virtually any redeeming aesthetic qualities. However, the lines between high and low culture have come to be increasingly questioned by sociologists, and they are increasingly unclear.

Culture is constantly changing, both influencing and influenced by changing social realities. Some scholars have argued that globalisation has increasingly led to social realities in most parts of the world being more similar than ever before, what they call a global culture; others attribute the change to cultural imperialism. Another example of our changing culture revolves around the dominance of consumer culture, in which the core ideas and material objects relate to consumption. A final example of our changing culture is related to digitalisation. Given the speed with which the Internet changes, cyberculture tends to be much more fluid than culture in general.

KEY TERMS

- Americanisation   136
- Anti-Americanism   136
- Assimilation   131
- Consumer culture   137
- Counterculture   126
- Cultural hybrid   137
- Cultural imperialism   136
- Cultural relativism   132
- Culture   114
- Culture jamming   144
- Culture war   127

- Cyberculture   146
- Ethnocentrism   133
- Folkways   119
- High culture   133
- Ideal culture   124
- Identity politics   132
- Language   122
- Law   118
- Low culture   133
- Material culture   120
- Mores   119

THINKING ABOUT SOCIOLOGY

1. Who and what do you and your peers consider cool? What does that say about you and your culture? How do you think the concept of coolness in Canada in the mid-twentieth century was different from today's concept?

2. How and why might the western value of democracy have created tensions in Iraq and Afghanistan?

3. As part of our material culture, what values do smartphones reflect? In what ways have "brand communities" or other subcultures formed around smartphones and the use of smartphones?

4. Consider the new terminology that has developed around the Internet. How does this language reflect changes in the world around us? In what ways does this new language shape the world around us?

5. Skateboarders compose a subculture because they have certain cultural differences (for example, language, dress, values) that set them apart from other groups in society. What is another example of a subculture in Canada, and what elements of this culture (both material and symbolic) make it unique?

6. How does a counterculture differ from a subculture? Is it reasonable to say that computer hackers are part of a counterculture? Can you think of other examples of countercultures?

7. What is the difference between assimilation and multiculturalism? Would you say that Canada is an assimilationist or a multiculturalist society? Would you say that multiculturalism is more a part of the ideal culture or the real culture of Canada? Why?

8. Identify and explain an example of high culture and low culture from the world of television or film. Do you agree that the line between high culture and low culture is disappearing? Why or why not?

9. What do we mean by a global culture? Do you think the evolution of popular social networking sites such as Facebook and Twitter is related more to the evolution of a global culture or more to Americanisation? In what ways are these sites reflective of cultural hybridisation?

10. To what extent are you and your friends embedded in a consumer culture? How has the development of technology (the Internet, smartphones, etc.) helped to create this consumer culture?

APPLYING THE SOCIOLOGICAL IMAGINATION

Multinational chains (including McDonald's and Starbucks) are important cultural actors in an increasingly globalised world. These multinational corporations have made great efforts to promote an image and a culture around their brands. For this exercise, spend some time outside of class at an outlet of one of your favourite global chains. Pay close attention to the ways in which informal and formal norms are created in the space through decor, language, layout, and so on.

How does the physical space govern behaviour within the location? How does the physical space relate to the kind of image the company is trying to create for its brand? In what ways are the norms that operate within the store reflective of the larger norms of society? Do any of the norms conflict with larger societal norms?

Do some research on the Internet to see the ways in which these stores operate differently in other countries. How do they compare and contrast? Given the similarities or differences across countries, would you say such global chains are signs of cultural imperialism or hybridisation?

ACTIVE SOCIOLOGY

The McDonaldization of society reflects values of efficiency, predictability, calculability, convenience, and rationality, and documents the replacement of humans with nonhuman technologies. In order to understand better the process of McDonaldization, students will join a Facebook group created by the professor/instructor of his or her course. Each student will post two photos that illustrate the power and pervasiveness of McDonaldization. Photos should be original, and the subjects of the photos can be natural and spontaneous, or creatively constructed. Students will provide a brief sociological commentary demonstrating how their photos reflect some aspect of McDonaldization. Students will also need to comment on three additional photos. The comments are designed to engage online discussions as they explain, extend, question, clarify, or challenge their own or classmates' ideas. Comments are designed to reflect sociological insight. Excellent commentary explains concepts or ideas, shares relationships between ideas, or displays keen sociological insight.

STUDENT STUDY SITE

Visit the student study site at **www.sagepub.com/ritzercanadian** for additional web quizzes for further review.

Fast-Food International

While McDonaldization is pervasive throughout most of the world's cultures and industries, it is perhaps nowhere as readily evident as in the industry that gave it birth —fast food. Following the lead of McDonald's Ray Kroc, mid-twentieth century restaurant owners embraced the franchise model, founding homogeneous restaurant chains that proliferated across America. Before long, the franchise model spread to and throughout the rest of the world. Not only did American franchisers open their chains on foreign grounds, but local entrepreneurs saw and utilized the model, tailoring it to their societies' unique populations, tastes, and cultures.

However, fast food long predates McDonald's and takes distinctive forms in almost every culture.

Young Chinese women are seen eating shaobing, a Chinese-style sesame pancake, in a campaign promoting the new offering at KFC restaurants in Chongqing.

A long-standing fast-food offering throughout the Middle East, doner kebab, a Turkish dish made of roasted meat cooked on a rotating vertical spit, has taken the western world by storm. Chef Cango, a recent immigrant to Germany from Turkey, cuts doner kebab in a Turkish restaurant in Berlin.

Restaurant workers prepare hamburgers at North Korea's first fast-food restaurant, the Samtaeseong, in the isolationist nation's capital city of Pyongyang.

Nepalese cuisine typically entails a colourful mix of starches (such as rice), curries, chutneys, and soups. While such dishes may not seem conducive to fast food, street vendors have begun selling precooked snacks and meals in some of Nepal's heavily trafficked areas.

A man sells fast food in Sonepur, India. Normally a small rural hamlet, the settlement comes alive every year with the arrival of tens of thousands of visitors for the Sonepur Mela fair, an annual event timed to begin on the full moon of the Hindu month of Kartik Purnima.

An indigenous Aymara family eats fried chicken and French fries at a local fast-food chain in La Paz, Bolivia. At fast-food restaurants such as this, prices rarely exceed $1 for a complete meal.

Entrepreneur Jasmine Lim gets ready to take orders at her Fukuburger food truck in downtown Las Vegas. The individuality and unique offerings of these modern food trucks mark an uncommon step away from McDonaldization within the fast-food industry.

SOCIALISATION AND INTERACTION

From the colour of the blanket you were first swaddled in to the outfit you picked out today, you have been socialised to look, think, act, and interact in a way that allows you to live harmoniously with those around you—at least most of the time.

5

On June 22, 2012, at Rideau Hall in Ottawa, Canadian Forces Corporal Brian Bélanger was awarded the Medal of Military Valour, one of this country's highest military honours. Bélanger was nominated for this prestigious award for risking his own life in the successful attempt to rescue a wounded Afghan colleague.

According to his official citation, Bélanger's Canadian-Afghan unit was ambushed by enemy troops, resulting in a comrade being wounded. "Exposing himself to enemy fire, Corporal Bélanger, the patrol's medical technician, resolutely made his way to the wounded soldier and dragged him to cover. As bullets continued to ricochet around them, he administered first aid. Because of his professionalism and dedication, Corporal Bélanger saved the life of a fellow soldier."

Why would a person put his life on the line to save the life of another? It's tempting to label Bélanger a born hero—an individual destined for greatness. The sociologist, however, might defer to an old cliché: Heroes aren't born—they're made. Bélanger was socialised by family, teachers, friends, and, later, the Canadian Forces.

All these agents of socialisation have an effect on individuals, but the Canadian Forces are particularly adept at socialising new recruits into thinking and acting like fellow soldiers (that is, putting the duty before the self). Strict organisational and behavioural regulations enable the individual to perform his or her duties and conduct himself or herself in a manner that conforms to expected procedure. As the citation notes, it was his professionalism that won the day, his adoption of the military creed of "doing a job."

Though most of us will never face enemy gunfire, we too are who we are because of the people, institutions, and social structures *that have surrounded us since birth (and even before). From the colour of the blanket you were first swaddled in to the outfit you picked out today, you have been socialised to look, think, act, and interact in a way that allows you to live harmoniously with those around you—at least most of the time. Perhaps that means making it through class without embarrassing yourself . . . or perhaps it means playing the role of a hero.*

In this chapter, you'll learn how socialisation and social interaction shape who we are, and, in turn, how who we are shapes how and with whom we interact. This is the most basic level of sociological analysis. But, in fact, sociologists are concerned with everything from the smallest social realities to the largest trends and developments in the social world—what is, as we saw in Chapter 1, the **micro-macro continuum** (Ritzer 1981, 2013; J. Turner 2010). That is, sociologists study everything

- from the individual and even more micro aspects such as the individual's mind and self;
- to interactions among individuals;
- to groups often formed by those interactions, as well as the interactions that serve to make up groups;
- to formally structured organisations;
- to societies; and,
- increasingly in our "global age" (Albrow 1996), to the world as a whole as well as a wide array of global relationships.

This idea of a micro-macro continuum has two implications. First, it demonstrates that sociologists are concerned with a very wide range of social phenomena. Second, the idea of a continuum means that rather than being clearly distinct, social phenomena tend to blend, often imperceptibly, into one another. For example, the interaction that takes place in a group is difficult to distinguish from the group itself, and the relationships between nation-states are difficult to distinguish from

regional and even global linkages. Everything in the social world, and on the micro-macro continuum, interpenetrates.

This chapter and the next will introduce you, at least briefly, to the full range of sociological concerns along the micro-macro continuum. We will start with the smallest-scale social phenomena and work our way to ever-larger social phenomena as these two chapters progress.

THE INDIVIDUAL AND THE SELF

Sociologists rarely, if ever, concern themselves with any particular individual. Rather, the concern is with individuals in general. A prime issue is what, if anything, distinguishes humans as individuals from other animals. While some would argue that it is characteristics such as a larger brain or opposable thumbs, most sociologists believe that the essential difference between humans and other animals is the distinctive interaction that humans are capable of having with other humans.

An important source of this view is data about individuals who grow up in social isolation and who do not experience normal human interaction during their development. For instance, we have information on cases in which children have been locked in a closet or in a single room for much, or all, of their childhood (Curtiss 1977; K. Davis 1940, 1947).

Of related interest is the existence of *feral*, or wild, *children*—that is, children who have been raised in the wilderness by animals (M. Newton 2002). The best known example of a feral child is the fictional Tarzan, subject of a series of stories and novels written in the early twentieth century by Edgar Rice Burroughs, as well as many movies based on the stories. The infant son of English aristocrats living in the African jungle, Tarzan was raised after his parents' death by great apes in the wilderness. The most famous real case of a feral child, or at least most researchers think it is real, involves a young boy who was discovered roving naked in the woods near Aveyron, France, in 1797 (Lane 1975; Shattuck 1980). Apparently, he had lived most or all of his life there among the wild animals. When found and adopted by a local doctor who named him Victor, he displayed few, if any, human characteristics. For

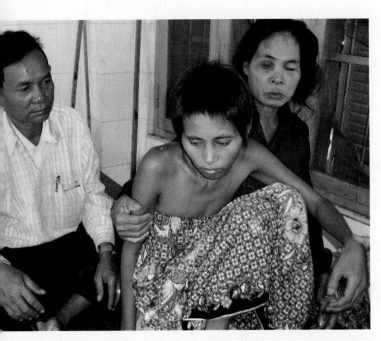

In 2007, news of Cambodian "jungle woman" Rochom P'ngieng's return to civilisation gripped the small South Asian country when P'ngieng was hospitalised after spending 18 years living in a forest. Here, P'ngieng sits with her parents at a hospital in Ratanak Kiri province.

example, he lacked language and was only able to learn a few words even after years of tutoring. Having lacked human contact and interaction in his early childhood, Victor was unable to become fully human. His story was the subject of a motion picture by the great French director François Truffaut titled *L'Enfant Sauvage* (1970).

While the Tarzan character is purely fanciful and there is considerable room for doubt in the details of the "wild boy of Aveyron" story, today's researchers have well-documented cases of children—victims of severe neglect and, usually, abuse—who spent their formative years deprived of human contact. Such children did not talk and showed little in the way of human emotion. Long after one little girl was discovered, efforts to socialise her were only minimally successful. She persisted in spitting and blowing her nose near and on other people, and she masturbated frequently (sometimes in public) and with whatever object was available (Curtiss 1977). The overall conclusion from the literature of feral children and those raised in isolation is that people do not become human, or at least fully human, unless they are able to interact with other people, especially at an early age.

The concept of "feral" children relates to the fundamental question of the relationship between "nature" and "nurture." The nature argument is that we are born to be the kinds of human beings that we ultimately become; it is built into our "human nature." The nurture argument is that we are human beings because of the way we are nurtured, the way we are raised by other human beings who teach us what it is to be human. Of course, both nature and nurture are important, but the cases of feral children indicate that nurture is in many ways more important than nature in determining the human beings we become.

SYMBOLIC INTERACTION AND DEVELOPMENT OF THE SELF

As the example of feral and isolated children suggests, development as a human presupposes the existence of other humans and interaction with and among them. This brings us into the domain of symbolic interactionism, which developed many ideas of great relevance to this view of humans. In general, the interaction that takes place between parents and children is loaded with symbols and symbolic meaning.

One early symbolic interactionist, Charles Horton Cooley (1864–1929), explained how parents help children develop the ability to interact with others in his famous concept of the **looking-glass self**, or the idea that we as humans develop a self-image that reflects how others respond to us. Since children's earliest interactions are typically with their parents, it is that parental interaction that is most important in the formation of a self-image. This point helps explain why feral children and others who spend their formative years in prolonged social isolation are unlikely to form a fully developed self-image: There are no others to respond to them. Normally, it is as we interact with others, especially when we are young, that we develop a sense of our selves.

The major thinker associated with symbolic interactionism is one of Cooley's contemporaries, George Herbert Mead. We have already encountered a few of Mead's ideas in Chapter 2. We now need to look further into his thinking in order to deal with the issue of human development. While Mead ([1934] 1962) was very concerned with the

Parents help their children develop self-images that reflect how others respond to them. Charles Horton Cooley called this external view of oneself the looking-glass self.

micro level (the individual, mind, self), he prioritised the social (including interaction). In fact, it is this prioritisation of the social that distinguishes sociologists from psychologists in their studies of individuals and interaction. Mead's ideas have withstood the test of time, and many of them continue to be at the core of sociological thinking on the more micro aspects of the social world.

Humans and Nonhumans

In order to make his arguments, Mead distinguished between humans and nonhumans. While both humans and nonhumans are capable of making gestures (such as by raising a limb), in Mead's view only humans are able to interact on the basis of significant symbols. By **gestures**, Mead means the movements of one individual that elicit an automatic and appropriate response from another individual.

Both animals and humans are capable of not only gestures but also *conversations of gestures* whereby they use a series of gestures to relate to one another. Thus, the snarl of one dog may lead a second dog to snarl in return, and that second snarl might lead the first dog to physically ready himself to attack or be attacked. In terms of humans, Mead gives the example of a boxing match where the cocking of one boxer's arm might cause the other boxer to raise an arm to block the anticipated blow. That raised arm might cause the first boxer to throw a different punch or even to hold back on the punch. All of this occurs, as in the case of animals, instantaneously and with few, if any, conscious thought processes.

In addition to physical gestures, animals and humans are both also capable of vocal gestures. The bark of a dog and the grunt of a human (boxer) are both vocal gestures. In both cases, a conversation of vocal gestures is possible as the bark of one dog (or the grunt of a boxer) elicits the bark (or grunt) of another. However, when humans (and animals) make a facial

Because people are increasingly so globally mobile, they are likely to feel as if their selves are dispersed and adrift in various places in the world.

BIOGRAPHICAL bits

George Herbert Mead (1863–1931, American)

- Although he never received any graduate degrees, Mead was a distinguished professor of philosophy at the University of Chicago from 1894 until his death.

- He began teaching a course in social psychology in 1900.

- Mead published little in his lifetime; his great fame came initially from his teaching.

- The sociology students who took his courses took notes that became the basis of Mead's most famous work, *Mind, Self, and Society* (1934).

- A course on social psychology, strongly influenced by Mead's thinking, began to be taught in the sociology department at Chicago in 1919.

- Mead's ideas strongly influenced the development of sociological theory, especially symbolic interactionism.

gesture, they cannot *see* that gesture (unless they happen to be looking in a mirror). In contrast, both animals and humans can *hear* their own vocal gestures.

It is the vocal gesture that truly begins to separate humans from animals. In humans, but not lower animals, the vocal gesture can affect the speaker as much and in the same way as the hearer. Thus, humans react to and interpret their own vocal gestures and, more importantly, their words. Furthermore, humans have a far greater ability to control their vocal gestures: We can stop ourselves from uttering sounds or saying various things, and we can alter what we say as we are saying it. Animals do not possess this capacity. In short, only humans are able to develop a language out of vocal gestures; animals remain restricted to isolated vocal gestures.

Symbolic Interaction

Of greatest importance in distinguishing humans from animals is a kind of gesture that can *only*

be made by humans. Mead calls such a gesture a **significant symbol**, a gesture that arouses in the individual the same kind of response as it is supposed to elicit from those to whom the gesture is addressed. It is only with significant symbols, especially those that are vocal, that we can have communication in the full sense of the term. In Mead's view, although more and more research on animals tends to contradict it (including Gerhardt and Huber 2002), ants, bees, and dogs are unable to communicate by means of such symbols.

Over time, humans develop a set of vocal significant symbols, or language. *Language* involves significant symbols that call out the same meaning in the person to whom an utterance is aimed as in the person making the utterance; they have meaning to all parties involved. In a conversation of gestures, only the gestures are communicated; with language both the (vocal) gestures and the meanings are communicated. One of the key functions of language is that it makes the mind and mental processes possible. To Mead, thinking (and the mind; see below) is nothing more than an internalised conversation that individual humans have with themselves. Thinking involves talking to oneself; it is little different from talking to other people.

Symbols also make possible what is obviously another pivotal idea to symbolic interactionism— **symbolic interaction**. Interaction on the basis of significant symbols allows for much more complex interaction patterns than would occur where interaction is based only on gestures. Because people can think about and interpret significant symbols, they can interact with large numbers of people and make complex plans for some future undertaking. They can interpret the symbolic meaning of what others say and do and can understand, for example, that some of them are acting in accord with their plans. Animals lack the ability to make complex plans and to understand that other animals are not acting in accord with such plans.

However, since Mead's day, a great deal of research on animals, especially primates, demonstrates that they are able to think, that is, to plan and to calculate, in at least a rudimentary way (Ristau 1983; Schmitt and Fischer 2009). For instance, scrub jays engage in planning behaviour to store away a diverse cache of food they will not eat until the following morning (Raby et al. 2007). Meerkats,

Exploring concepts such as self, personhood, and social identity, the 2011 science-fiction film *Rise of the Planet of the Apes* speculated what might happen if primates in captivity suddenly gained the ability to think, reason, and interact—even speak—as humans do.

which often prey upon poisonous animals, teach their young how to deal with these potentially dangerous food sources by disabling the prey they present to young meerkats (A. Thornton and McAuliffe 2006). Chimpanzees demonstrate deceptive behaviour when it helps them access a food they like (Woodruff and Premack 1979). Most of this research suggests that animals' thinking deals with something specific in their environment and focuses on responding to it, whereas human thought can be considerably more complex (Premack 2007).

Mind and Self

Central to Mead's ideas about the development of human beings, and the differences between humans and nonhumans, are the concepts of mind and self. As pointed out above, the **mind** is an internal conversation that arises, is related to, and is continuous with interactions, especially conversations that one has with others in the social world. Thus, the social world and its relationships and interactions precede the mind and not vice versa. This conceptualisation stands in contrast to the conventional view that prioritises the brain and argues that we think first and then engage in social relationships. It also differs from the view that the mind and the brain are one and the same thing. The brain is a physiological organ that exists within us, but the mind is a social phenomenon; it is part of, and would not exist without, the social world. While the brain is an intracranial phenomenon, the mind is not.

The **self** is the ability that develops over time to take oneself as an object. Key to the development of self is the ability to imagine being in the place of others and looking at oneself as they do. In other words, people need to take the role of others in order to get a sense of their own selves. There are two key stages in Mead's theory of how the self develops over time:

1. **Play stage.** Babies are not born with the ability to think of themselves as having a self. But as they develop, children learn to take on the attitudes of specific others toward themselves. Thus, young children play at being Mommy and Daddy, adopt Mommy's and Daddy's attitudes toward the child, and evaluate themselves as do Mommy and Daddy. However, the result is a very fragmented sense of the self, which varies depending on the specific other (for example, Mommy *or* Daddy) being taken into consideration; young children lack a more general and organised sense of themselves.

2. **Game stage.** The child begins to take on the role of a group of people simultaneously rather than the roles of discrete individuals, thereby developing a self in the full sense of the term. Furthermore, each of those different roles comes to be seen as having a definite relationship to all of the others. It is the ability to take on multiple roles, indeed the entirety of roles in a given group, that begins to give children an organised personality, one that does not vary depending on the individual role (Mommy, Daddy) that the child happens to be taking. This development allows children to function in organised groups and, most importantly, greatly affects what they will do within a specific group.

Mead offers the example of a baseball game (or what he calls "ball nine") to illustrate his point about the game stage of development. It is not enough in a baseball game for you to know what you are supposed to do in your position on the field. In order to play your position, you must know what those who play all other eight positions on the team are going to do. In other words, a player, every player, must take on the roles of all of the other players. A player need not have all of those roles in mind all of the time; three or four of them will suffice on most occasions. For example, a shortstop must know that the centre fielder is going to catch a particular fly ball; that he is going to be backed up by the left fielder; that because the runner on second is going to "tag up," the centre fielder is going to throw the ball to third base; and that it is his job as shortstop to back up the third baseman. This ability to take on multiple roles obviously applies in a baseball game, but it applies as well in a play-group, a work setting, and every other social setting.

To take a more contemporary example from the college classroom, students are often asked to work together on group projects to be presented to the class. Each student will not only have to prepare her part of the project and presentation but will also need to know, and coordinate with, what each of the other presenters, as well as the group as a whole, will do. One might have to know the content of each presentation and the sequence of presentations, along with the time allotted to each of them. Such group work resembles that of Mead's baseball team, where all members have to be familiar with and know the roles of all of the others involved in order to be successful as a group. This is, in essence, what children learn in the game stage, and they continue to implement and practise this ability throughout their lives.

The Generalised Other

Mead also developed the concept of the **generalised other**, or the attitude of the entire group or community. Individuals take the role of the generalised other; they look at themselves and what they do from the perspective of the group or community. The generalised other becomes central to the development of self during the game stage. In the baseball example, the generalised other is the attitude of all nine players on a baseball field at any given time—and perhaps the attitude of the team manager and coaches as well. In the classroom example, it is the attitude of the group working on the collaborative project. In the family, to take still another example, it is the attitude of all members of the family.

In taking on the perspectives of the generalised other, children begin developing more fully rounded and complete selves. They can view and evaluate themselves from the perspective of a group or community and not merely from the viewpoint of discrete others. To have a coherent self in the full sense of the term, as an adult one must become a member of a group or community and be sensitive to the attitudes common to the community.

Having members who can take the role of the generalised other is also essential to the development of the group, especially in its organised activities. The group can function more effectively and efficiently because it is highly likely that individual members will understand and do what is expected of them. In turn, individuals can operate more efficiently within the group because they can better anticipate what others will do.

This discussion might lead you to think that the demands of the generalised other produce conformists. However, Mead argues that, while selves within a group share some commonalities, each self is different because each has a unique biographical history and experience. Furthermore, there are many groups and communities in society and therefore many generalised others. Your generalised other in a baseball game is different from your generalised other in a classroom or in the family.

The "I" and the "Me"

Critical to understanding the difference between conformity and creative thinking and acting is Mead's distinction between two aspects, or phases, of the self—the "I" and the "me." Bear in mind that the "I" and the "me" are not things; they do not exist in a physical sense. We would not find the "I" or the "me" if we dissected the brain. Rather, the "I" and the "me" are subprocesses that are part of the larger process that is thinking. An individual sometimes displays more of the "I" aspect of the self and sometimes more of the "me" aspect.

The **"I"** is the immediate response of an individual to others. It is that part of the self that is unconscious, incalculable, unpredictable, and creative. Neither the person nor the members of the group know in advance what that response of the "I" is going to be. The shortstop on a baseball team does not know in advance—nor do his teammates—whether he will react brilliantly to a batted ball or react badly and make an error. Similarly, a daughter at a holiday dinner does not always know

GL🌐BALISATION

North American Professional Hockey and Japanese Baseball

There is a tendency to identify certain sports with certain nations. Hockey is Canada's sport, baseball is emblematic of the United States, close to motherhood and apple pie! But both ice hockey and baseball are increasingly global sports. Consider professional ice hockey. First, it is organized via the "National Hockey League" (NHL), although less and less of it is "national." Of the thirty plus teams, seven are in Canada and over twenty are in the United States. Second, while many players come from Canada and the United States, more and more players are from other countries. Third, although still rare, more NHL games are being played outside of North America.

Globalisation can be seen in the countries of origin from which players come. As Global Flow Map 5.1a shows, in the 1971–72 season, 94.7 percent of the players were Canadian. In contrast, in the 2011–12 season only 53.4 percent of players

were Canadian. The diversity of countries of origin is shown in Global Flow Map 5.1b. Numerical data paint a much more global picture of ice hockey as a professional sport than the name, the National Hockey League, implies.

Contrasting baseball in the United States and Japan provides a more culturally nuanced understanding of globalization and sport. The game of baseball originated in the United States, but baseball in the USA and Japan are very different creatures. Baseball spread beyond the confines of the United States by moving first to Cuba by 1860, China by 1863, and Japan and Korea by the early 1870s (W. Kelly 2007). However, after this early start, Japan did more to disseminate baseball than did the United States. Japan promoted baseball in its empire in countries including Korea, Taiwan, Southeast Asia, and Oceania in the Pacific. Baseball is not a common

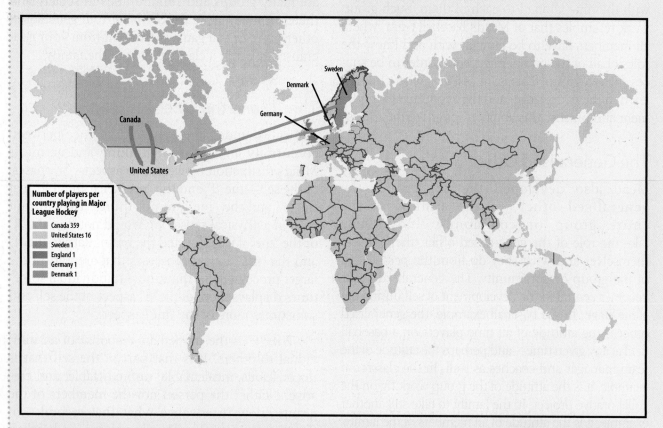

Number of players per country playing in Major League Hockey

- Canada 359
- United States 16
- Sweden 1
- England 1
- Germany 1
- Denmark 1

GLOBAL FLOW MAP 5.1A Global Home Countries of Players in the National Hockey League, 1971–1972

SOURCE: http://www.quanthockey.com/ (retrieved September 24, 2012).

sport in Mainland China, India, Europe, Russia, Africa, the Middle East, or much of South America.

Several factors limited the global spread of baseball. First, it became a big business in the United States monopolised by a small number of owners. They helped to stabilise and systematise the sport "into regular seasons, stadium fixtures, continuing player contracts and monopolistic associations of owner-operators" (W. Kelly 2007:84). Thus baseball solidified in an American context, which left little room for, or interest in, global expansion. Second, baseball was "promoted in highly nationalistic terms as embodying American values and inculcating an American character" (W. Kelly 2007:84).

While the most successful example of the spread of baseball is to be found in Japan, baseball there is quite different from the game played in the United States (although the rules are basically the same). It has been aggressively appropriated by the Japanese. As one former American baseball star put it after playing a year in Japan, "This isn't baseball—it only looks like it" (quoted in W. Kelly 2007:88). The following is a good comparison of the differences between baseball in the two countries: "Free-spirited, hard-hitting, fun-loving, independent-minded American baseball players are pitted symbolically against team-spirited, cautious, self-sacrificing, deeply deferential, intensely loyal [Japanese] samurai with bats" (W. Kelly 2007:86). In other words, there is a different generalised other in Japanese baseball than in American baseball. While American baseball players are led to think they are supposed to succeed largely on their own, Japanese players believe that their generalised other expects them to subordinate individual achievement to team success.

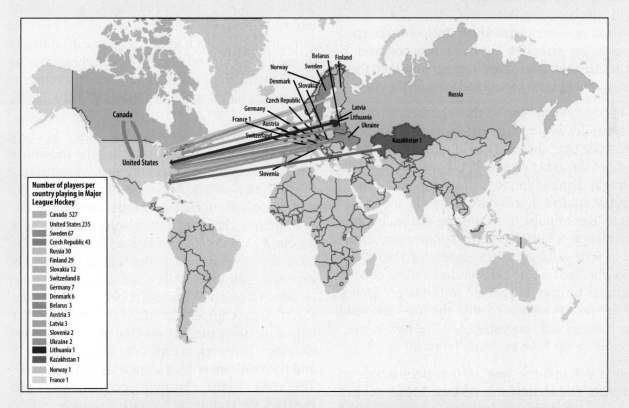

Number of players per country playing in Major League Hockey

Canada 527
United States 235
Sweden 67
Czech Republic 43
Russia 30
Finland 29
Slovakia 12
Switzerland 8
Germany 7
Denmark 6
Belarus 3
Austria 3
Latvia 3
Slovenia 2
Ukraine 2
Lithuania 1
Kazakhstan 1
Norway 1
France 1

GLOBAL FLOW MAP 5.1B Global Home Countries of Players in the National Hockey League, 2011–2012

SOURCE: http://www.quanthockey.com/ (retrieved September 24, 2012).

NOTE: Although hockey has not become popular with most sports fans around the world, it is global to the degree that it attracts professionals from other countries and is played in other countries. During the 2011–12 season, only 53.4 percent of players were Canadian in origin, in contrast to 1971–72 when the percentage was 94.7.

in advance what she is going to say or do, and the same is true of the other family members at the dinner table. That is what makes for frequent squabbles, if not outright battles, on such family occasions. As a result of the "I," people often surprise themselves, and certainly others, because of the unexpected things they say and do.

Mead greatly values the "I" for various reasons, including the fact that it is the source of new and original responses; in addition, it is the "I" that allows a person to realise the self fully and to develop a definite, unique personality. The "I" also gives us the capacity to have an impact on the groups and communities in which we live. Moreover, in Mead's view, some individuals, including the great figures in history, have a larger and more powerful "I" and are therefore able to have a greater impact on these entities, as well as on society and even on the globe.

While the "I" is unconscious, incalculable, and unpredictable, the "me" allows the individual to analyse and critique his own thoughts and actions from an external point of view.

In contrast, the "**me**" is the organised set of others' attitudes assumed by the individual. In other words, the "me" involves the adoption by the individual of the generalised other. For example, your "I" might dispose you to introduce yourself to an attractive student in this class, but your "me" might counter that impulse by suggesting that such a self-introduction is not considered appropriate behaviour in your social group (the generalised other). To Mead, the "me" is conscious understanding of what a person's responsibilities are to the larger group. The behaviours associated with the "me" also tend to be habitual and conventional. We all have a "me," but conformists have an overly powerful "me."

It is through the "me" that society is able to dominate the individual. In fact, Mead defines "social control" as the dominance of the "I" by the "me." Through the "me," individuals control themselves with little or no need for control by outside influences. In the "me" phase, however, individuals analyse and critique their own thoughts and actions from the point of view of the social group

and what its criticisms are likely to be. Thus, in most cases, the group need not criticise individuals; they do it themselves. In other words, self-criticism is often, in reality, criticism by the larger society.

Nevertheless, people and society as a whole need both the "I" and the "me." For the individual, the "me" allows for a comfortable existence within various social groupings, while the "I" lends some spice to what might otherwise be a boring existence. For society, the "me" provides the conformity needed for stable and orderly interaction, while the "I" is the source of changes in society as it develops and adapts to the shifting environment.

Others have demonstrated that members of a given culture internalise the social sentiments considered the norm in their culture, such as attitudes toward different types of cheating; refer to those sentiments during social interaction; and maintain those sentiments within the culture over time (Heise 1979, 2007).

The "I" and the "Me" in Consumer Society. While the "me" generally provides the individual with some comfort and security, that is less the case in consumer society. The reason is that consumer society is all about change, and as a result the "me" is constantly changing. For example, one might be expected to adopt a given fashion at one time, but soon after an entirely different fashion comes to be expected. Instead of stability, "consumers must never be allowed to rest" (Bauman 1999:38). Of course, the "I" always impels the individual in unpredictable directions such as making unusual fashion decisions. However, in consumer society *both* the "I" and the "me" are at least somewhat unpredictable. This serves to make many people uneasy because they lack the comfort of a strong and stable "me."

While this is generally the case, it is very much related to one's position in the stratification system. It is those in the middle class who are most likely to experience this unpredictability because as rapidly as they change, they are led to desire many more

changes than they can afford to make. The upper class is also confronted with a rapidly changing world of consumption, but those in it can afford to change whenever it seems necessary. The lower class can afford little, with the result that those in it are unable to change what they consume to any great degree. However, the lower class experiences the uneasiness associated with not being able to keep up with changing demands of the "me."

THE INDIVIDUAL AS PERFORMER

Another important symbolic interactionist who has contributed to sociologists' understanding of the self and how it develops is Erving Goffman. Goffman's work on the self is deeply influenced by Mead's thinking, especially the tension between the "I" and the "me." In Goffman's work this distinction takes the form of the tension between what we want to do spontaneously and what people expect us to do (Goffman 1959).

Goffman developed the notion of **dramaturgy**, which views an individual's social life as a series of dramatic performances akin to those that take place in a theatre and on a stage. To Goffman, the self is not a thing possessed by the individual but the dramatic product of the interaction between people and their audiences (P. Manning 2007). While most performances of the self are successful, there is always the possibility of disruption. Goffman focuses on this possibility and what people can do to prevent disruptions or to deal with them once they occur.

Impression Management

When people interact with others, they use a variety of techniques to control the image of themselves that they want to project during their social performances. They seek to maintain these impressions even when they encounter problems in their performances (P. Manning 2005). Goffman (1959) called these efforts to maintain a certain image **impression management**.

For example, in your sociology class you might typically project an image of a serious, well-prepared student. Then one night you stay up late partying and do not get the reading done before class. When the instructor asks a question in class, you try to maintain your image by pretending to be writing busily in your notebook rather than raising your hand. Called on nonetheless, you struggle, in vain, to give a well-thought-out, serious answer to the question. The smiles and snickers of fellow students who know that you were out partying late the night before might well disrupt the performance you are endeavouring to put on. To deflect attention from you to them, you might suggest that they try to answer the question.

Impression management directly relates to the plot of many movies. In some cases, characters who feel outside of the mainstream do a great deal of work to present a "normal" façade. This type of impression management is clear in the popular *Twilight* movie series. Kristen Stewart's character, Bella Swan, tries to give her father the impression that her boyfriend, Edward Cullen, is just a regular teenage boy—not a vampire. The Cullen "family," a group of vampires who have renounced drinking human blood, adopts the pretences of human behaviours, such as living in houses, eating, and sleeping. They seek to give the impression that they are normal so as not to draw suspicion to themselves and the fact that they are anything but normal.

While the idea of impression management is generally applied to face-to-face social interaction, it also applies to interaction on social networking sites. For example, many people constantly change the pictures on their Facebook page in order to alter the image of themselves that is conveyed to others.

Front and Back Stage

Carrying forward the theatrical analogy, Goffman (1959) argues that in every performance there is a **front stage**, where the social performance tends to be idealised and designed to define the situation for those who are observing it. In the example above, in class you are typically performing in your front stage. Your audience is the teacher and perhaps other students. As a rule, people feel they must present an idealised sense of themselves when they are in their front stage (presenting that seemingly well-thought-out answer). Because it is idealised, things that do not fit the image must be hidden. For example, you might hide the fact that you were partying the night before and are now ill prepared to answer questions intelligently.

Also of concern to Goffman is the back stage. In the **back stage** people feel free to express themselves in ways that are suppressed in the front. Thus, you might well confess to your friends in the cafeteria after class to partying and to faking answers to questions in class. If somehow your front-stage audience—the instructor in this case—sees your back-stage performance, your ability to maintain the impression you are trying to project in the classroom, in the front stage, is likely to become difficult or impossible in the future.

Differences in front- and back-stage performances can be stark—especially in the political arena. Though German Chancellor Angela Merkel, former French President Nicolas Sarkozy (right, with British Prime Minister David Cameron), and former Italian Prime Minister Silvio Berlusconi often appeared cordial and conciliatory when speaking together about the European debt crisis in 2011, their working relationship was described as contemptuous, poisonous, and outright dysfunctional.

The back stage plays a prominent role in our lives. For every one of our front-stage performances, there is one or more back stages where all sorts of things happen that we do not want to be seen in the front stage. For example, when summer camp is over, counsellors are often "friended" by campers on Facebook. In order to allow the campers to stay in contact with them through Facebook, counsellors might post limited, carefully edited profiles to special Facebook pages. This is, in effect, the counsellors' front stage for former campers. However, the counsellors might retain a back-stage version of their Facebook pages, with profiles that the ex-campers are unable to see.

The existence of two stages, front and back, causes us all sorts of tensions and problems. We are always afraid that those in the front stage will find out about our back stage, or that elements of the back stage will intrude into the front stage.

These ideas are central to Leslie Picca and Joe Feagin's *Two-Faced Racism: Whites in the Backstage and Frontstage* (2007). The central point of this study of white college students is that what they say and do differs depending on whether they are in their front stage or their back stage. When they are in their back stage with friends and family, as well as with other whites, they often feel free to talk and act in a blatantly racist manner. Examples include telling racist jokes and mocking minority group members. However, when they are in their front stage in a public setting, especially with visible minorities present, what they say and do is very different. They may act as if they are blind to a person's colour or even be gratuitously polite to nonwhites. Thus, while overt racism may have declined in the front stage of public settings, it persists in the back stage (Sallaz 2010).

While the distinction between front and back stage

GL🌐BALISATION

The Self in the Global Age

The self is not fixed. There are various ways in which it changes. For example, it changes over the course of our lives. On a day-to-day basis, changes in the self depend on the nature of the impression we want to make on others (Goffman 1959). The self also changes with large-scale transformations in the social world, and no change has been more dramatic, and had more powerful impacts on the self, than globalisation.

There are many things we can say about the self in an increasingly globalised world, but the focus here is on the impact on the self of the increasing mobility associated with globalisation. Among many other things, globalisation brings with it the increasingly easy movement of all kinds of objects, ideas, and knowledge, as well as people. People can now move physically with great ease throughout the world, and, perhaps more importantly, they can move even more easily on a digital basis via e-mail, Twitter, Facebook, Skype, and the like. This mobility is of great importance in itself (Urry 2007), as well as because of its impact on the self: "The globalization of mobility extends into the core of the self" (A. Elliott and Urry 2010:3).

Globalisation has a variety of positive and negative effects on the self. On the positive side, the self can become more open and flexible as a result of all of the new and different experiences associated with the global age. More descriptively, the large number of brief interactions in the global age through, for example, meetings at airports or on planes as well as digitally can lead to a different kind of self more oriented to the short-term and the episodic than to that which is long-term or even lifelong.

Of greatest concern are the negative effects of globalisation, especially the great mobility associated with it, on the self. At the extreme, Lemert and Elliott (2006) see globalisation as "toxic" for the individual, including the self. For example, because people are increasingly so globally mobile, they are likely to feel as if their selves are either dispersed and adrift in various places in the world or existing even more loosely in global cyberspace. Furthermore, while in the past the self was increasingly likely to be shaped by close personal relationships, it is now more likely to reflect the absence of such relationships and a sense of distance, even disconnection, from others. At the minimum, this can lead to a different kind of self than that which existed before the global age. At the maximum, it can lead to one that is weak because it is untethered to anything that is strong and long lasting.

A more familiar pathology associated with the global age is being preoccupied with, even obsessive about, all of the digital mobile technologies closely associated with both globalisation and heightened mobility. For one woman, the experiences of being so deeply enmeshed in these technologies "has left the self drained and lifeless" (A. Elliott and Urry 2010:41). While the selves of many people may not be affected as strongly and as adversely as this, it is clear that globalisation and the mobility associated with it have had a great effect on the self, and that impact is only likely to grow exponentially in the future.

---

is important, bear in mind that these are not "real" places, nor are they rigidly separated from one another. That is, what is the front stage at one point in time can become the back stage at another point in time. Nevertheless, in general, people are most likely to perform in an idealised manner in their front stage when they are most concerned about making positive impressions. They are likely to perform more freely in their back stage among those who are more accepting of less-than-ideal behaviour and attitudes.

SOCIALISATION

An individual learns and generally comes to accept the ways of a group or a society of which he or she is a part.

Socialisation is the name for this process. It is during the socialisation process that children develop a self as they learn the need, for example, to take on the role of the generalised other. Socialisation almost always involves a process of interaction as those with knowledge and experience teach those with a need to acquire that knowledge or to learn from others' experiences.

In addition to Mead and his work on the play and game stages, many important social thinkers have dealt with the issue of socialisation, including the psychoanalyst Sigmund Freud (1856–1939), the psychologist and philosopher Jean Piaget (1896–1980), and the psychologist Lawrence Kohlberg (1927–1987). None of these thinkers is a sociologist, but neither was Mead. However, Mead's teaching and ideas had a direct and profound influence on sociology, especially symbolic interactionism, while these other thinkers were, and continue to be, marginal to sociology. Nonetheless, they did have important and useful ideas about, and insights into, the socialisation process as well as the mind and mental processes.

Freud (2006), of course, is best known for a theory of the mind similar to Mead's. Rather than the "I" and the "me," Freud differentiates between the *id* (like the "I," unconscious and impulsive), the *superego* (like the "me," a reflection of societal expectations), and the *ego* (which mediates between the id and the superego and allows people to function in the social world). More important for our purposes here is Freud's thinking on socialisation, which focuses primarily on the early stages of life dominated by various forms of sexuality. Of greatest importance in his theory is the *Oedipal conflict* confronting 4- to 5-year-old children. For boys, this primarily revolves around a desire for their mothers and resulting jealousy and hostility to their fathers. Eventually, this conflict is resolved in the direction of the fathers, boys come to identify with their fathers, and the hostility abates. Girls also go through this stage, but they are less able to resolve it well, ending up with greater insecurity and jealousy, as well as hostile feelings to their mothers, and eventually themselves, because of their lack of a penis. Of course, many feminists (Chodorow 1978, 1988; Mitchell 1975) have attacked this and other aspects of Freud's theories on various grounds. Among other things, Freud is criticised for his emphasis on the penis, for the fact that boys fare better than girls in his theory of socialisation, and because he ignores the very important role of the mother in the socialisation process.

Piaget, like Mead, has a stage theory of development. Piaget has a much more elaborate theory of development than Mead that encompasses more stages that children go through from birth to adolescence. While Mead's stages are sociological in nature (especially the play and game stages), Piaget's are much more cognitive and relate to the processes by which children learn to think for themselves, to think more abstractly, and to deal with hypothetical situations (Piaget and Inhelder 1972).

Kohlberg is most concerned with gender role socialisation, or the process by which children acquire a sense of themselves as boys or girls. This is pretty well understood by the age of 3, and by about age 6 gender roles are pretty firmly fixed. These roles are learned through symbolic interaction with others, especially parents. What is most important about this is that the acquisition of gender identity strongly affects the child's attitudes, values, and activities (Kohlberg 1966).

There is much more to each of these theories, and there are, of course, many other theories of socialisation, but this gives you a sense of some of them and a context in which to think about and assess the more sociological approaches to socialisation discussed in this section.

From a sociological perspective, socialisation can generally be divided into two parts. Socialisation during childhood sets the course for a lifetime and has been a central focus for researchers. However, researchers have increasingly recognised that socialisation continues over a lifetime and have pointed up a variety of ways in which adults continue to learn how to function within their society.

CHILDHOOD SOCIALISATION

A central concern in the study of socialisation is those who do the socialising, or the **agents of socialisation** (Wunder 2007). The first and often most effective agent of socialisation is the child's parents and other family members, but throughout life a variety of individuals and institutions help the child learn society's norms and culture. They include the individuals with whom the developing person interacts—teachers and peers—as well as broader, less personal influences, such as the educational system, the media, and consumer culture. All play a part in creating an individual who can effectively operate within and shape culture.

Primary Socialisation and the Family

Newborns, infants, and young children acquire language, identities, cultural routines, norms, and values as they interact with parents and other family members, a process known as **primary socialisation**. This socialisation lays the foundation for later personality development (Rohlinger 2007). Early socialisation performs various functions for society as well, such as equipping the young to fit

McDONALDIZATION *Today*

McSchools

There is no question that schools in the United States are highly McDonaldized. For example, school curricula are standardised within school districts and states in an attempt to improve "educational outcomes" usually defined as higher graduation rates and improved scores on standardised tests. In recent years, many innovative and creative courses have been eliminated to allow more time for standardised courses.

The U.S. government also tries, with occasional success, to influence local educational systems by, for example, allocating funds to systems that do what is asked of them. For example, as part of its economic stimulus package to counter the effects of the Great Recession, the Obama administration allocated billions of dollars to public schools. But while the administration could seek to persuade the schools to do certain things with the money, it could not tell them what to do with it. At the most, schools that did not do what was expected of them would not get any additional stimulus money (Rotella 2010). On the one hand these programmes are appreciated by cash-strapped schools and those who believe that problems with the educational system can be solved by national policymakers, but on the other hand some people worry about the McDonaldization of the schools when a central authority is in control.

Interestingly, education, and much else, in Great Britain is far more McDonaldized than it is in the "home" of McDonaldization, the United States. In the United Kingdom the state exercises much more centralised control over education than in the United States, where local school systems have considerable independence. There is an even greater obsession in the United Kingdom than in the United States with quantifiable educational indicators such as student test scores and comparative rankings of schools. The official name for this British program is School and College Achievement and Attainment Tables. Schools are constantly audited and ranked on a variety of numerical measures, giving rise to what has come to be known as the "audit society." In focusing on such quantifiable variables in schools, one observer contends that the "government has come to believe . . . you do indeed fatten a pig by weighing it" (G. Wilkinson 2006:89), the point being that constant measurement does not, in itself, improve schools, or anything else.

Great predictability is demanded of schools in the United Kingdom as a result of the introduction in 1988 of a nationwide educational curriculum. Further, much of what takes place in the schools is tightly scripted, which reduces the schools' diversity and distinctive identity. Control is exercised over the schools by an elaborate bureaucratic system and by nonhuman technologies such as measurement and checking instruments. Ironically, while there are lots of these controlling mechanisms, none of the agencies involved in exercising control is a professional organisation of educators.

One solution to the problem of "McSchools" is to focus on the everyday activities of education, rather than outcomes, and make them the centre of concern (G. Wilkinson 2006). One example is to allow excellent teachers to create new and exciting ways to educate students. McDonaldizing education through some central authority tends to discourage this sort of creativity.

---

and violated. The next day saw a groundswell of people in the downtown core cleaning up the city centre. Others felt compelled to post pictures or to help identify rioters (C. Schneider and Trottier 2012). For this group, Mead's "me" was front and centre.

The Vancouver hockey riot is not an isolated event, even though such riots are not routine. In March 2012 there was a St. Patrick's Day riot, involving over 1,000 people, in London. Ontario and Quebec saw rioting associated with political protests of tuition fee increases through the spring and early summer of 2012. Political protests are a particular form of political socialisation, a venue where people form peer networks that can play intense roles in future political action (Stoddart and Tindall 2012).

Gender

Sociologists devote a great deal of attention to gender socialisation (Doucet 2009; Rohlinger 2007), or the

The Hell's Angels is the world's largest and most active motorcycle club. The Angels are often in conflict with other groups, be they other gangs or organizations of government.

transmission of norms and values about what boys and girls can and should do. You have already seen a couple of examples, and we briefly mentioned Kohlberg's psychological theory of gender socialisation.

Even before babies are born, their parents start to "gender" them—painting rooms blue for boys and pink for girls. Parents often dress baby girls in frilly dresses and affix bows to their bald heads to signal to others that the children are girls. These gender differences are reinforced by the toys children are likely to be given by parents—trucks and soldiers for boys, dolls and dollhouses for girls. As children grow up, they learn from their parents what behaviours are considered appropriate and inappropriate for their gender. For example, parents give girls a great deal of sympathy for crying, while boys are told to "be a man" and not cry after an injury. Boys also are expected to have an interest in sports, to play rough with each other, and to be unable to sit still. Girls, in contrast, are expected to express more "ladylike" behaviours, such as sitting quietly and sharing. Many children come to see these traditional gender expectations as natural expressions of being male or female. For South Asian immigrant girls there is additional stress because more stringent

rules for women often apply in these ethnic communities (Talbani and Hasanali 2000).

The feminist movement of the 1970s challenged the idea that girls could not be active or that boys could not be nurturing (Lorber 2000). Today, girls are more likely to aspire to high-level careers, such as law and medicine. Some parents pride themselves on raising girls who engage in stereotypically male activities, such as team sports. Yet many parents continue to strongly discourage boys from expressing an interest in activities that are stereotyped as "for girls" (Kane 2005). Illustrating this difference, *tomboy* can be a positive term applied to a girl who likes physical activity and plays with boys. *Sissy*, in contrast, is a derogatory term for boys who express an interest in quieter types of play or playing with girls (Thorne 1993). Traditional gender socialisation remains especially strong for boys (Kane 2006).

Historically, traditional socialisation for gender roles has been reinforced in various settings throughout society such as schools, sports, and the mass media. In school, teachers and curricula tended to support traditional gender norms, and peer groups in the school setting were likely to be segregated by gender (Thorne 1993). In sports, girls were channelled into different sports than boys; for example, girls tended toward figure skating while boys played hockey. When girls did play "male" sports, their efforts were often labelled differently, such as calling girls' football teams "powderpuff" football. Boys' sporting activity still tends to dominate; for example, in prime times for games and practises men's basketball still has preference over women's basketball at both the high school and the university level. The gap has narrowed appreciably, however. At the elite level of Olympic athletics the gender balance is far better, although only recently has women's ski jumping been added to the Winter Games (for 2014). Conversely, gender balance in activities long understood as feminine, such as ballet and modern dance, still is some distance from equity.

The media, especially movies, TV, and video games, have also tended to reinforce children's traditional gender role socialisation. However, that, too, is changing. More television programmes feature strong female characters (*Powerpuff Girls, Dora the Explorer, Buffy the Vampire Slayer, Dark Angel, Battlestar Galactica, Burn Notice, Charlie's*

Angels), especially numerous shows featuring female cops and police chiefs (*Dexter, The Wire, Flashpoint, Dark Blue*). Female action stars (Sigourney Weaver in the *Alien* movies, Angelina Jolie in most of her films and as the fictitious Lara Croft in the *Tomb Raider* video game series) are increasingly likely to play strong and aggressive characters. Young adult novels may also have strong female leading characters, such as the extremely smart Hermione Granger in the *Harry Potter* series and Katniss Everdeen from the *Hunger Games* series.

Change is less obvious in other settings. Malls tend to reinforce traditional gender roles by offering separate shops for boys and girls, men and women. The Disney amusement parks offer highly differentiated attractions for boys ("Pirates of the Caribbean") and girls ("It's a Small World"). Most video games are aimed at boys, while girls are offered computer games focused on facial makeovers and shopping. This media emphasis on girls' and women's appearance is not new. Movies, television

The feminist movement in the 1970s challenged the idea that girls cannot be active and successful. Here a Canadian basketball player drives to the paint during a Canada–USA women's basketball game at the 2012 London Olympics.

programming, and advertisements have been widely critiqued for decades for their unrealistic portrayal of women's bodies (Bordo 1993; E. Cole and Henderson 2005; Neuendorf et al. 2009). Many of the action heroines (for example, those in James Bond movies) continue to embody traditional male preferences for female bodies: young, attractive, and slender. Young women comparing themselves to these versions of adult Barbie dolls become anxious about their own bodies (Currie 1997). Media images of women may also reaffirm racial stereotypes, with young women of colour often sexualised or portrayed as poor and irresponsible (P. Collins 2004).

Mass Media and New Media

Until recently, much of the emphasis on the role of the mass media in socialisation has been on the role played by television and the enormous number of hours per week children spend in front of their TVs (Comstock and Scharrer 2007). While TV remains an important socialisation agent, especially for young children, it is clear that as children mature, especially in the middle and upper classes, more of their socialisation is taking place via the computer, smartphones, video games, and other new and emerging technologies (Rideout, Foehr, and Roberts 2010). As the range of media devices has expanded, so has the portion of time spent using them. As Figure 5.2 shows, in comparison to time spent using computers for leisure or playing video games, TV viewing is still hugely significant (at six times more minutes per day than computing). Notice, however, that the time devoted to TV and to reading for pleasure declined between 1998 and 2010, whereas both computing and video game playing increased, as we would expect.

The pattern in 2010 was different among the younger generation, as captured in Figure 5.3. TV viewing was still dominant, but only three times more prevalent than non–work-related computing. In comparison to the total population (Figure 5.2), young people spent much more time computing and playing video games, and less time reading for pleasure and watching TV. For younger generations, new media devices are becoming increasingly important as socialising media.

Of course, a world of wonderful information is available on the computer via Google and

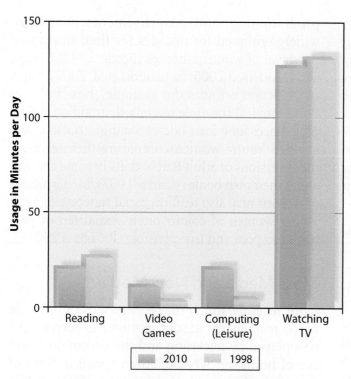

FIGURE 5.2 Time on Selected Activities for Total Population, 2010

SOURCE: Authors' calculations from Statistics Canada, *General Social Survey*, 2011b.

Consumer Culture

Consistent with the emphasis on consumption in this book, and in the contemporary world, it is important to understand that one needs to be socialised in order to consume, especially to devote a significant portion of one's life to consumption. As is the case with many other things, much of this socialisation takes place early on in the family, in schools, and in peer groups.

However, much more socialisation now takes place in consumption sites themselves rather than in the family or schools. For example, pre-teens and teens spend a large amount of time at the shopping mall either with their families or, as they mature, more on their own and in the company of peers. Although young people may be going to a movie in the mall's multiplex or just "hanging out" there, rather than shopping, the fact remains that those activities take place in a setting devoted to shopping and consumption (D. Cook 2004; C. Rose 2010). Children readily learn the nuts and bolts of how to consume. They also learn various norms and values of consumption, especially to value the processes of consumption and shopping, as well as the goods and services acquired through those processes. There is even a game, *Mall Madness,* which socialises children into the realities of shopping at a mall. In the game, the "mall" has 18 different stores where players can use credit cards to shop; children are thereby also socialsed into credit card use. The object of the game is to be the first player to buy all six items on one's shopping list and return to the game's starting point. In other words, the winner in the game, and in much of consumer culture, is the best consumer.

Online consumption and shopping sites (such as Amazon.ca and eBay.ca) are also socialising agents. Navigation and buying strategies are learned at the digital retailers, and those have an effect on consumption in the brick-and-mortar world. For instance, many younger people who have grown up with online shopping are adept comparison shoppers, comparing products online and looking for the best possible deal before making a purchase. Some storefront retailers have gone out of business as a result of online competition, further reinforcing the use of online retailers. Other storefront retailers have developed new

other forms of new media, but there are also lots of worrying things online, which children especially can easily find or stumble upon. In addition, access to the computer has changed the viewing experience considerably. Watching TV programmes or movies is a passive activity. Even when "adult themes" are presented, the child is an observer, not a participant. However, on computers and other new digital media, the child can play video games such as *Grand Theft Auto* and *Call of Duty: Modern Warfare.* These games engage children in simulations of anti-social activities including stealing cars and shooting people with AK-47s. Clearly, the nature of the socialisation implicit in such games is at odds with the lessons that parents and teachers wish to impart.

Smartphones and social networking sites play a role in socialisation as well, mostly through the influence of peers. A great deal of peer socialisation also takes place via sites such as Facebook and Twitter (Buckingham 2008; Watkins 2009). All of this is so new, and new forms of media are emerging so rapidly, that it is hard to know exactly what role the new media will play in socialisation in the future, but their role is likely to be increasingly powerful and pervasive.

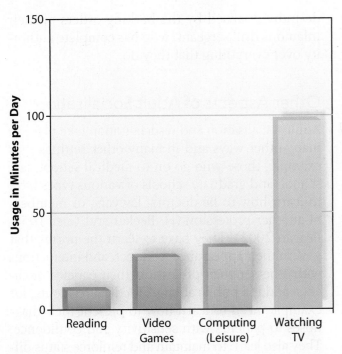

FIGURE 5.3 Time on Selected Activities for 15- to 24-Year-Olds, 2010

SOURCE: Authors' calculations from Statistics Canada, *General Social Survey*, 2011b.

hybrids of online and storefront retailing, offering consumers the ability to buy online and then pick up the item at a local outlet—where consumers may make unplanned purchases. These new forms of retailing are just new ways of socialising young people into our culture of consumption.

Socialisation into consumerism also reinforces lessons about race, class, and gender. As Christine Williams shows in her book, *Inside Toyland* (2006), consumer choices—where to shop, what brands to buy, what products are appropriate for whom—contribute to the maintenance of social inequalities. Girls face pressures to consume beauty products that encourage them to live up to an idealised and usually unattainable level of female beauty (Wiklund et al. 2010). For example, Barbie dolls are often presented as an ideal form of the female body that is physically impossible to attain in real life. Such toys socialise children not only into a consumer culture but into one that reproduces and reinforces harmful gender expectations as well.

ADULT SOCIALISATION

A great deal of socialisation takes place in later life as people enter the work world and become independent of their families, and adult socialisation is of increasing importance to researchers.

Workplaces

At one time socialisation into a workplace was a fairly simple and straightforward process: Many workers were hired to work for jobs in large corporations (General Motors, Hydro-Québec) and remained there until they reached retirement age. Especially for those who held jobs in the lower reaches of the corporate hierarchy, socialisation occurred for the most part in the early stages of a career. Today, however, relatively few workers can look forward to careers in a single position within a single company. Increasing numbers of workers change employers, jobs, and even careers with some frequency. Each time workers change jobs, they need **resocialisation** to unlearn old behaviours, norms, and values and learn new ones. One can no longer rely, assuming it was ever possible, on what one learned as a child, in school, or in early years on the job.

For a variety of reasons sociologists suspect that the workplace is becoming more dynamic, with fewer people securing a lifelong career with one employer. Changing jobs during a career or having a career entailing many jobs is the likely scenario for more and more young people. In a service economy where more and more jobs depend upon knowledge and where more and more people are availing themselves of lifelong learning, more job shifting is likely. Lifelong learning and knowledge acquisition are both fundamental components to resocialisation. The pressures of globalisation are also such that firms have to be more nimble, changing up how and what they do more rapidly than in the past when the pace of innovation was slower. Innovation too means resocialisation. Finally, more and more employers are seeking to reduce labour costs by introducing nonstandard (or flexible) work that is part-time, temporary, or contractual (Fuller 2009).

Total Institutions

Many adults find themselves at some point in their lives in some type of total institution (Goffman 1961a). A **total institution** is a closed, all-encompassing place of residence and work set off from the rest of society that meets all of the needs of those enclosed in it.

A major example of a total institution is the prison. Upwards of 40,000 Canadians are in prison (International Centre for Prison Studies 2012). On initial entry into prison, inmates undergo formal resocialisation in the form of being told the rules and procedures they must follow. But of far greater importance is the informal socialisation that occurs over time through their interactions with guards and especially with other inmates (Walters 2003). In fact, other inmates often socialise relatively inexperienced criminals into becoming more expert criminals; prisons are often "schools for crime" (Sykes [1958] 2007; Walters 2003).

Another total institution is the military. Members generally live in military housing, often eating together, sharing the same living quarters, and having access to all necessary services on a military base. They must follow strict rules of dress, conduct, physical appearance, and organisation of their time. This image of the military as a total institution is especially clear in Stanley Kubrick's film *Full Metal Jacket* (1987). For example, the film depicts military recruits getting their heads shaved, eliminating control over their own appearance; they are also harassed and de-individualised by the barking orders of their infamous drill sergeant, who has complete authority over everything that they do.

Other Aspects of Adult Socialisation

Adult socialisation and resocialisation take place in many other ways and in many other settings. For example, those who go on to medical school, law school, and graduate schools of various types have to learn how to be doctors, lawyers, or members of another profession (H. Becker and Geer 1958; Beagan 2003). They have to learn the norms that govern their appearance, conduct, and interactions with others in their profession, their patients or clients, and the public at large. Medical residents, for example, need to learn how to present their diagnoses to patients with sensitivity and confidence. They also learn to maintain and reinforce status differences between doctors and nurses.

Many consumption settings also offer formal socialisation aimed mostly at adults, at least on initial visits. Casino hotels helpfully offer newcomers lessons on the various forms of gambling and implicitly on how to lose their money. Cruise ships, especially the new megaships, offer first-time travellers orientations to, and tours of, the sometimes vast ships, including their onboard casinos and shops.

The recession that began in 2008 also necessitated resocialisation. Many lost their jobs and their homes. Some were reduced to an entirely different existence, doubled up with family or friends or, if truly unlucky, in their car or on the streets. Learning to live on one income instead of two requires considerable adult resocialisation, and becoming unemployed and homeless obviously requires even more.

Total institutions, including the Kingston Penitentiary, are spaces where competing socialisation processes occur, as authorities seek to rehabilitate prisoners while some inmates seek to resist authority and influence their peers.

There are a number of other situations that lead to the need for adult socialisation or resocialisation (Brim 1968; Lutfey and Mortimer 2006; S. Wilson 1984):

- Family changes. Separation, divorce, death of a spouse, and remarriage involve particularly important transitions for the adults who are involved, not just the children. They require considerable adult resocialisation into new relationships, new household organisation, and new public images.

- Geographic mobility. Job change, retirement, and migration are increasingly likely. People undergoing any of these transitions must be resocialised into not only new physical environments but also new subcultures.

- Changes associated with aging. As people age, they gradually become disengaged from work, which has implications for relationships and financial well-being. A retired person must become resocialised into this new status. People are also living much longer and therefore are likely to experience longer periods in which their health deteriorates (Connidis 2010; Wister 2011). It may be difficult for people who see themselves as competent adults to experience the significant impact of disability on the ways that they interact with the world.

Since we live in a global age, it is clear that adults also need to be resocialised, probably many different times as they age, into this new and ever-changing world. Some global socialisation occurs on the job: As employers increasingly seek a global market and establish global outposts, employees have more opportunities to experience other cultures. Global socialisation is also aided by the Internet, which, of course, is itself increasingly global. Interaction with global websites, news sources, and other people throughout the world by e-mail or on social networking sites plays an important role in global socialisation. We are all socialised globally to participate in consumer culture (Poff 2010), and students experience global socialisation through study-abroad programmes.

INTERACTION

So far in this chapter we have focused on the socialisation of individuals, but socialisation generally involves **interaction**—that is, social engagement involving two or more individuals who perceive, and orient their actions to, one another (vom Lehn 2007). Interaction has generally been seen as involving face-to-face relationships among people, but in the twenty-first century interaction is increasingly mediated by smartphones and social media. Interaction is an important topic of study in itself because of its ubiquity and its influence on individuals. It is also a key building block for more macroscopic social phenomena such as networks and groups, as well as the larger organisations, societies, and global domain that will be explored more deeply in the next chapter.

Interaction occurs throughout our lifetimes. Examples include interactions between parents, children and their siblings, teachers and students, coworkers, and medical personnel and patients.

FACTORS AFFECTING SOCIALIZATION:

- Parents and family
- School and teachers
- Racial expectations
- Mass media
- Consumer culture
- Total institutions
- Geographic mobility
- Age and aging
- Peers and friends
- Gender roles
- Social class
- New media
- Workplace norms
- Societal changes
- Family changes

Interaction early in the life cycle, especially in the family and schools, tends to be long-term and intense. Later in life interaction tends to be brief and more fleeting (a quick hello on the street or a brief conversation at a cocktail party), although the interactions with family members tend to remain intense.

Various sociological theories have been brought to bear on interaction. For example, as you learned earlier in this chapter, George Herbert Mead and later symbolic interactionists distinguished between a conversation of gestures and interaction that relies on symbols such as language. Georg Simmel believed that human interaction not only gave rise to society but also met a basic human need to be sociable. In the following discussion, you will see references to a variety of theories that deal with interaction.

SUPERORDINATE-SUBORDINATE INTERACTIONS

Simmel saw society as being defined by interaction; moreover, he differentiated between the forms that interaction takes and the types of people who engage in interaction. For example, one "form" of interaction is the relationship between a *superordinate* and a *subordinate* (Simmel [1908] 1971a). This type of relationship is found in many settings and includes

We tend to think that the relationship between a superordinate and a subordinate eliminates the subordinate's independence, but such a relationship does not meet the definition of interaction unless the subordinate has at least some freedom to be an active party to the interaction.

a teacher and a student in a classroom, a judge and a defendant in a courtroom, and a guard and a prisoner in a jail. While we tend to think of this relationship as eliminating the subordinate's independence, the fact is that a relationship between the two cannot exist unless subordinates have at least some freedom to be active parties to the interaction. The relationship between an employee and a supervisor is a good example. If the employee cannot react to the supervisor's direction, there is no interaction—only one-way communication from the supervisor to the employee. Furthermore, experimental research has demonstrated that the greater the equality in an employee-manager relationship, the greater the amount of two-way communication, and the less resentment, anger, and worry the subordinate feels when conflict arises with the manager (C. Johnson, Ford, and Kaufman 2000).

As discussed in Chapter 2, another type of superordinate-subordinate relationship that Simmel analysed is the one between a benefactor and a "poor" person (Simmel [1908] 1971b). Simmel, as is characteristic of his work, uniquely defined *poor* in terms of relationships and interactions. The conventional view is that a poor person is someone who lacks resources. For Simmel, in contrast, a poor person is one who is aided by others (that is, receives charity), or at least has the right to that aid. In this approach, students who can pay for school only through need-based financial aid and loans would be defined as poor. In receiving aid, the poor person and the benefactor are involved in a specific kind of interaction in which one party gives and the other receives. That is, they are involved in an exchange relationship, although it is a highly unequal relationship.

RECIPROCITY AND EXCHANGE

To those sociologists who theorise about exchange, interaction is a rational process in which those involved seek to maximise rewards and to minimise costs. Interaction is likely to persist as long as those involved find it rewarding, but it is likely to wind down or end when one or both no longer find it rewarding. An important idea in this context is the social norm of **reciprocity**, which means that those engaged in interaction expect to give and receive rewards of roughly equal value (Fehr,

Fischbacher, and Gächter 2002; Gouldner 1960). When one party feels that the other is no longer adhering to this norm, not giving about as much as she is receiving, the relationship is likely to end.

Studies of exchange relationships, like much else in sociology, are now being challenged to find ways of dealing with new forms of virtual interaction: e-mail, social networking sites, and interaction on Skype. One researcher who has explored the effects of virtual reality on interaction in the "real" world, and vice versa, concludes that "the constantly evolving avatar [or digital representation of oneself] influences the 'real' self, who now also orients toward virtual, yet all-too-real others" (Gottschalk, 2010). In other words, interactions in the digital realm and the physical realm both influence the self. Additional research questions come to mind quite readily. For example, are people compelled to cooperate to the same extent in the digital realm (such as when using e-mail communication) as they are in the material world (such as during in-person communication) (Naquin, Kurtzberg, and Belkin 2008)?

"DOING" INTERACTION

Another interactionist theory of great relevance here is ethnomethodology, which focuses on people's everyday practises, especially those that involve interaction. The basic idea is that interaction is something that people actively "do," something that they accomplish on a day-to-day basis. For example, the simple act of walking together can be considered a form of interaction; engaging in certain practises makes it clear that you are walking with a particular someone and not with someone else (Ryave and Schenkein 1974). You are likely to walk close to, or perhaps lean toward, a close friend. When you find yourself walking in step with a total stranger, you behave differently—separating yourself, leaning away, saying "excuse me"—in order to make it clear that you are not walking with that stranger and not engaged in interaction with her. More complex forms of interaction require much more sophisticated practises.

Ethnomethodology also spawned **conversation analysis**, which is concerned with how people do, or accomplish, conversations. For example, you must know and utilise certain practises in order to carry on a successful conversation: You must know when it is your turn to talk or when it is appropriate to laugh at a comment made by someone else (Jefferson 1979). Conversation analysts have taken the lead in studying conversations, and interaction more generally, in great detail and depth. They typically record a conversation using audio or video devices so they can study it in more detail; then they can transcribe those conversations to create a written record of a conversation.

INTERACTION ORDER

While every instance of interaction may seem isolated and independent of others, they are all part of what Erving Goffman (1983) called the **interaction order**, a social domain in its own right. It is organised and orderly, but the order is created informally and governed by those involved in the interaction rather than by some formal structure such as a bureaucracy and its constraints (M. Jacobs 2007). One example of an interaction order is a group of students who form a clique and develop their own norms governing their interaction. In this thinking, Goffman is following Simmel's view that society is based, in a real sense, on interaction; society is, in many ways, interaction.

The interaction order can be seen in many settings and contexts, but one particularly good one is the way people spontaneously form queues and wait for the doors to open at a rock concert or at Walmart on the "Black Friday" after Thanksgiving. (Of course, the 2008 incident in which a greeter at Walmart was crushed to death by a rampaging crowd once the doors opened indicates how quickly the interaction order can break down.) Some sociologists have suggested that human interaction with animals is another place to observe interaction order (Jerolmack 2009a). In fact, there is a relatively new sociological theory—actor-network theory—that seeks to include not only animals but inanimate objects in the interaction order (J. Law and Hassard 1999).

STATUS AND ROLE

Status and role are key elements in the interaction order, as well as the larger structures in which such interactions often exist. A **status** is a position within a social system that is occupied by people. Within the university, for example, key statuses are professor and student. A **role** is what is generally expected of a person who occupies a given status (Hindin 2007). Thus, a professor is expected to show up for class, to be well prepared, to teach in an engaging manner, to hold office hours, and so on. For their part, students are also expected to attend class, to listen and sometimes to participate, to avoid texting and checking their Facebook page during class, to complete the required assignments, and to take, and pass, examinations.

The concept of status can be broken down further. One form of status is an **ascribed status**, or a position in which individuals are placed, or to which they move, but where such placement or movement has nothing to do with what people do or the nature of their capacities or accomplishments. This can be seen clearly in the realm of gender, where in all but a few cases we are categorised as a male or a female irrespective of our actions or abilities. The same point applies to age and racial status. In contrast, an **achieved status** is a position acquired by people on the basis of what they accomplish or the nature of their capacities. For example, becoming a graduate of the college or university that you attend, becoming a spouse, becoming a parent, and becoming a successful entrepreneur are all achieved statuses.

Whether it is ascribed or achieved, a status can become a **master status**, or a position that is more important than any others both for the person in the position and for all others involved. For example, being the star on the swim team at the University of Calgary is likely to override all other statuses for the student-athlete.

Roles can be congruent; that is, the expectations attached to a given status can be consistent (for example, going to class and doing your homework). But they can also come into conflict (for example, going to class and keeping up with your social life). **Role conflict** can be defined as conflicting expectations associated with a given position or multiple positions (Merton 1957). A professor who is expected to excel at both teaching and research can be seen as having role conflict. Devoting a lot of time to research can mean that a professor is ill prepared to teach her classes. Or the professor may be torn between the expectations of being a teacher (prepare for class) and those of being a parent (play with his children). A student may need to deal with the role conflict between being a

student and studying and being a friend and going with buddies to see a crucial football game.

Much research has been done on the role conflicts experienced by workers with domestic obligations. Each role interferes with the ability to satisfactorily meet the expectations associated with the other role (D. Moore 1995). Research has supported this idea. For example, working women, who still tend to be responsible for the care of children and the home, experience higher levels of stress and poorer physical health than working men (Gove and Hughes 1979; G. Lowe 2003; Pearlin 1989). The heavy burden of the female caretaking role inhibits women's ability to fulfill their role as caretakers of themselves.

Another role-related problem is **role overload**, in which people are confronted with more expectations than they can possibly handle. Students during final exam week are often confronted with role overload in trying to satisfy the expectations of several professors and courses. One study on "time crunch" and mental health suggests that feeling under time pressure is likely the active ingredient in role overload, which in turn affects people's psychological well-being (Roxburgh 2004).

There is a tendency to see roles as fixed and unchanging and as constraining on people. However, people do demonstrate the ability to modify their roles, at least to some degree. Thus, the professor in the above example might take her child to the office so that she can perform parent and teacher roles simultaneously. Researchers have noted that parents adopt a variety of work-family strategies—such as reducing work hours, turning down promotions, or negotiating trade-offs with one's partner—to reduce work-family conflict (P. Becker and Moen 1999; Suzanne Bianchi and Milkie 2010).

MICRO-LEVEL SOCIAL STRUCTURES

Through an accumulation of persistent patterns of interaction and social relationships, individuals contribute to the creation of **social structures**, which are enduring and regular social arrangements (Hunt 2007). Social structures include everything from the

DIGITAL LIVING

Facebook Relationships

You're seeing someone. It's great! It's wonderful! You feel awkward and happy and nervous. But is it a "real" relationship? Is it "Facebook official"? Once both partners confirm the relationship publicly via Facebook, the status change appears on your friends' (and friends of friends') Facebook home pages, and they can publish comments on the relationship if they so choose. The status remains on your profile until you change it, at which point your friends will be alerted once again that your relationship status has changed.

Had he dealt with it, French sociologist Pierre Bourdieu might have described a Facebook relationship status as a kind of "symbolic capital"—a socially recognised symbol that offers status to individuals who hold it. For example, social titles such as the Duke of Nottingham or President of the Student Body, and symbols such as the Greek letters on the tote bag of a sorority member, confer prestige upon their bearer. This symbolic capital legitimates these individuals' social activities. Symbolic capital alone is not enough to completely validate your activities or your social functions, or to guarantee your competence. That is, you'll need more than just the symbolic capital of your degree and your teacher certification to be a good teacher. But symbolic capital can help individuals access resources associated with a social position.

In the case of the Facebook relationship status, it is symbolic because the status alone does not fully describe the complexity of your relationship. It merely represents—symbolises— that you and your significant other are involved in a mutually and publicly recognised relationship. As a symbol of that relationship, it is a simplification that makes that relationship easily and widely recognizable to others. Thus, knowledge of your relationship can "travel" easily—almost like cash, or capital. You can "exchange" that symbol for resources such as attention (appearing on your friends' home pages), for claims to legitimacy or exclusivity (you and your significant other are marked as "taken"), or for claims about wrongs or grievances (it becomes readily apparent to all those who see that your significant other is leaving messages for someone else that you are entitled to some comfort, encouragement, advice, or even retribution). In short, your Facebook relationship status is itself a kind of "capital" that can quickly and easily be converted into meanings that may further advantage you and shape a number of your social relationships.

SOURCE: Printed with the permission of Margaret Austin Smith.

The symbolic capital offered by Facebook legitimates a person's social activities, relationships, and interests. Here, Facebook cofounder and CEO Mark Zuckerberg explains how connections are made on the popular social networking site.

---

face-to-face interaction that is characteristic of the interaction order, to networks, groups, organisations, societies, and the globe. This chapter focuses on the micro-level social structures—interpersonal relationships, social networks, and groups. Chapter 6 covers larger-scale social structures.

INTERPERSONAL RELATIONSHIPS

A good place to start a discussion of social structure is with another famous set of concepts created by Georg Simmel (1950) to describe the structures common to interpersonal relationships: **Dyads** are two-person groups, and **triads** are three-person groups.

Dyads are the most basic of interpersonal relationships, but they often evolve into triads—as when a couple welcomes a new child. It would appear on the surface that the addition of one person to a dyad, creating a triad, would be of minimal importance sociologically. After all, how important can the addition of one person be? Simmel demonstrates that no further addition of members to a group, no matter how many that might be, is as important as the addition of a single person to a dyad. A good example is the dramatic change in the husband-wife relationship caused by the arrival of a first child. Another is the powerful impact of a new lover on an intimate dyadic relationship. In cases like these, social possibilities exist in the triad that do not exist in a dyad. For example, in a triad two of the parties (for example, the wife and the child) can form a coalition against the third (for example, the husband). Or one member of the triad, say, the child, can take on the role of mediator or arbitrator in disputes involving the other members.

The most important point to be made about Simmel's ideas on the triad is that it is the group structure that matters, *not* the people involved in the triad or the nature of their personalities. Different people with different personalities will make one triad different from another, but it is not the nature of the people or their personalities that make the triad itself possible (Webster and Sell 2012).

SOCIAL NETWORKS

Simmel's work, especially on social forms, also informs the study of social networks (Chriss 2007). The most basic social networks involve two or more individuals, but social networks also include groups, organisations, and societies; there can even be global networks.

Network analysts are interested in how networks are organised and the implications of that organisation for social life. They look at the nodes, or positions, occupied by individuals (and other entities) in a network, the linkages among nodes, and the importance of central nodes to other nodes in the network. Figure 5.4 demonstrates a network with low centrality and one with high centrality. In the low-centrality network, one node appears in the centre, but it is actually linked to only two other nodes. The central node in the high-centrality example is far more influential; every other node is connected to it, and there is only one link that is independent of the central node. Those who occupy positions that are central in any network have access to a great many resources and therefore have a considerable ability to gain and to exercise power in a network.

Opposite Degrees of Network Centrality

Low Network Centrality

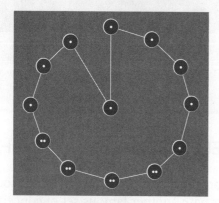

High Network Centrality

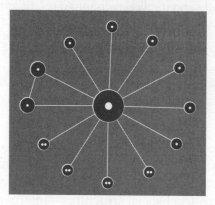

FIGURE 5.4 Social Network Centrality

SOURCE: Reprinted by permission of S. Joshua Mendelsohn.

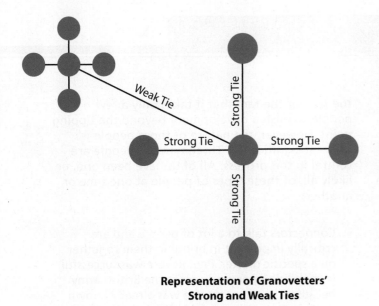

**Representation of Granovetters'
Strong and Weak Ties**

FIGURE 5.5 The Strength of Weak Ties

A key idea in network theory is the "strength of weak ties." We are all aware of the power of strong ties between, for example, family members or among those who belong to close-knit social groups such as gangs. However, Mark Granovetter (1973) demonstrated that those who have only weak ties with others (that is, they are just acquaintances) can have great power. While those with strong ties tend to remain within given groups, those with weak ties can more easily move between groups and thus provide important linkages among and between them (see Figure 5.5). Those with weak ties are the ones who hold together disparate groups that are themselves linked internally by strong ties.

Researchers generally find that at least half of all workers in the United States have obtained their jobs through informal means, meaning referrals, rather than formal job postings (Marsden and Gorman 2001; Pfeffer and Parra 2009). It makes sense, then, to understand the strength of weak ties. If you are looking for a job, you may want to seek out the help of friends and acquaintances who have weak ties to many groups, because they are likely to have many diverse and potentially useful contacts at a number of different employers. Those who are responsible for hiring need to keep in mind that access to network resources is largely dependent on one's own social

position. Social network research has shown that socioeconomically disadvantaged individuals suffer an additional deficit in both strong and weak network ties (Bian 1997; Granovetter 1973, 1974; N. Lin 1999; N. Lin and Bian 1991; N. Lin, Ensel, and Vaughn 1981; Wegener 1991). Thus they have an additional disadvantage in finding jobs. To overcome this barrier to finding talented workers, an employer may want to seek ties to networks that include the socioeconomically disadvantaged.

One point worth underscoring in any discussion of social networks is the importance of Internet networks, including Facebook, Skype, and Twitter. This is another domain where weak ties can be of great importance. On Facebook, for instance, you may have hundreds, even thousands, of "friends." However, it is clear that these "friendships" involve

OkCupid's OkTrends blog analyzes and interprets data collected from millions of member profiles and interactions that take place on the popular dating and social networking website. By comparing variables such as personality traits, beliefs, explicit sexual preferences, and interaction styles, the blog arrives at a variety of fascinating—sometimes startling—conclusions. The graph depicted here shows that the response rate for those who use netspeak in their first message fall below the average response rate.

PUBLIC SOCIOLOGY

Malcolm Gladwell's *Tipping Point*

Malcolm Gladwell (1963–) is a Canadian journalist who draws on many different fields, especially a wide range of social sciences, including sociology. He also ranges across an incredibly wide variety of social phenomena. In his best known book, *The Tipping Point* (2000), he deals with diverse topics such as *Sesame Street,* the beginning of the American Revolution, teenage suicide in Micronesia, and the dramatic drop in the crime rate in New York City in the mid-1990s. He is able to deal with so many different topics because, unlike an empirical sociologist, he does not collect any data of his own; indeed he relies on little data. He bases his generalisations on conversations and newspaper accounts. Indeed, he offers generalisations that few sociologists would feel comfortable making, but they are nevertheless intriguing and often quite insightful.

In *The Tipping Point* Gladwell deals with the kinds of phenomena mentioned above, and many others, arguing that they all operate like infectious diseases. They can start very small, simmer for a while, explode, and then die away. Of greatest interest to him is that "tipping point" when things suddenly, rather than gradually, either explode or die off. For example, he is interested in why an "epidemic" of teenage suicide suddenly arises, or in why a long-running crime wave seemingly peters out overnight. Much of his explanation relates to the power of word-of-mouth communication (what sociologists would call verbal interaction), especially in the beginning, but also at the end, of these social epidemics.

Like many early sociologists, Gladwell develops basic "laws" to explain what it takes to reach and go beyond the tipping point. The first is the *law of the few,* or the fact that it takes only a few people to push a development beyond the tipping point. However, the nature of those people is of great significance. Three types of people are central in this process. All of us have been one, or likely all, of these types of people at one time or another:

- *Connectors* talk to a lot of people and are critically important in bringing them together on a specific matter. Paul Revere was successful in mobilising people to resist the British army because as a connector he was already known to them before he took his fateful ride, and through that ride he was able to bring them together.

- *Mavens* are recognised experts. They may acquire their expertise formally or quite informally, but in either case, others come to regard them as mavens and pay attention to them because of their expertise. When such people come to believe that something important is happening, and tell others about it, a social epidemic becomes more likely to occur. In the 1990s, New York City Mayor Rudy Giuliani came to be seen as a maven on crime and how to control it. When he took action to help bring down the crime rate and said that crime was dropping, he helped push the city toward the tipping point, after which the crime rate did drop dramatically.

- *Salesmen* are those who sell the idea that an epidemic is imminent or under way; their sales pitch helps to fuel the epidemic. It could be

weak ties, in fact far weaker ties than analysts such as Granovetter had in mind. It is also important to note that because they leave objective traces—e-mail messages, writings on a Facebook wall—such networks are much easier to study than, for example, those that exist in face-to-face interaction, which usually leave few material traces.

GROUPS

We have already encountered the key sociological concept of groups at several points in this chapter, especially in Simmel's ideas on the dyad and beyond. A **group** is a relatively small number of people who over time develop a patterned relationship based on interaction with one another. However, just because we see a small number of people—say, in a queue waiting to board a plane—that does not mean that they necessarily constitute a group. Most people in a queue are not likely to interact with one another, to have the time or inclination to develop patterned relationships with one another, or, if they do interact, to do so beyond the time it takes to board the plane and find their seats.

argued that both Rudy Giuliani and Paul Revere sold ideas—the British are coming, the crime rate is dropping—that led to social epidemics.

The second of Gladwell's laws is the *law of stickiness* of the message. Stickiness relates to the likelihood that a message will stay with those who hear it; people hear many messages, but only a few are sticky. Sticky messages are more likely to take us beyond the tipping point. Paul Revere's message—"The British are coming, the British are coming!"—was such a message, and it stuck with many who heard it, galvanising them to resist the British and ultimately to begin the Revolutionary War.

Finally, there is the *law of the context;* the context in which the message is heard matters a great deal. In the case of Paul Revere, the fact that he rode in the middle of the night, waking many people, made a huge difference. If the context had been different, had he ridden during the day when people were busy with other things, the impact of his message may have been greatly reduced.

Gladwell's work is useful and intriguing "pop sociology," but it has its scholarly limitations. In a review of a more recent book by Gladwell, *What the Dog Saw,* a Harvard psychologist finds a number of problems, including Gladwell's use of the term *igon value* instead of the correct *eigenvalue.* This leads him to conclude, "Readers have much to learn from Gladwell the journalist and essayist. But when it comes to Gladwell the social scientist, they should watch out for those igon values" (Pinker 2009:12).

Malcolm Gladwell, a history graduate from the University of Toronto

Types of Groups

Several key concepts in sociology relate to groups. Consider the traditional distinction between the primary group and the secondary group (Cooley 1909). **Primary groups** are those that are small, are close-knit, and have intimate face-to-face interaction. Relationships in primary groups are personal, and people identify strongly with the groups. The family is the model of a primary group, although as we will see in Chapter 11, the family is often riddled with many conflicts, and at least some members leave the family or are driven from it. Primary groups can also take unlikely forms. A 2009 study of people in New York City who tend pigeons and fly them from the rooftop documents the formation of primary group ties among the members involved in this rare animal practise activity (Jerolmack 2009a). Such group ties can be stronger for these individuals than class and ethnic ties.

In contrast, **secondary groups** are generally large and impersonal, ties are relatively weak, members do not know one another very well, and the groups' impact on members is typically not very powerful. Members of a local parent-teacher association would be a good example of a secondary group.

Primary and secondary group ties can occur in the same social context. For example, the primary group for servicemen and servicewomen is usually the squad or platoon, where the secondary group is typically the company, battalion, brigade, or regiment (in descending order of closeness) (Siebold 2007). Another example of primary and secondary group ties, this one from a college student's point of view, appears in Figure 5.6.

Also worth mentioning are **reference groups**, or those groups that you take into consideration in evaluating yourself. Either your reference group can be one to which you belong, or it can be another group to which you do not belong but nevertheless often relate (Ajrouch 2007; Merton and Kitt 1950). People often have many reference groups, and those groups can and do change over time. Knowing people's reference groups, and how they change, tells us a great deal about their behaviour, attitudes, and values. While we often think of reference groups in positive terms (a group of people whose success you would like to emulate), they also can be negative if they represent values

or ways of life that we reject (say, neo-Nazis). The group to which one belongs is not necessarily the most powerful group in one's life.

Reference groups can be illustrated in the case of immigrants. Newly arrived immigrants are more likely to take those belonging to the immigrant culture, or even those in the country from which they came, as their reference group. In contrast, their children, second-generation immigrants, are much more likely to take as their reference group those associated with the new culture in the country to which they have immigrated (Kosic et al. 2004).

One final set of concepts that help us to understand the sociological importance of groups is the distinction between in-groups and out-groups (W. Sumner [1906] 1940). An **in-group** is a group to which people belong and with which they identify, perhaps strongly. An **out-group** is a group to which outsiders, at least from the perspective of the in-group, belong. Thus, the group you sit with at your regular table in the college dining hall or fast-food court would be the in-group, while other groups at other tables might be the out-groups. While the differences between these groups can be insignificant (whether they get their food in the food court from McDonald's or Pizza Hut), they can also come

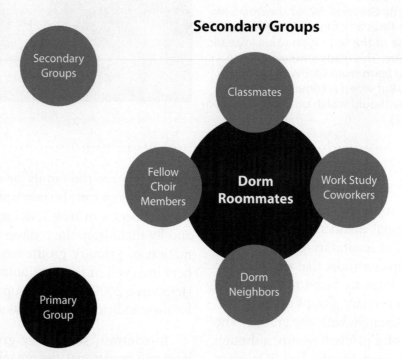

FIGURE 5.6 A University Student's Possible Primary and Secondary Groups

to be very important ("jocks" vs. "geeks"), so that each group not only accepts its ways but also rejects the ways of the others. In extreme cases this can lead to conflict between the in-group and the out-group. Research suggests that hostility often arises when in-groups perceive the out-group as constituting a threat to their self-interest (Rosenstein 2008). This is particularly evident in research on immigration (Schlueter and Scheepers 2010; S. Schneider 2008), where native-born individuals (representing the in-group) maintain discriminatory attitudes toward a growing population of foreign-born individuals (representing the out-group).

In-groups and out-groups play a prominent role in the television show *Glee*. The show centres on a group of high school students who perform in the campus glee club (a singing group). The club contains students with a wide variety of identities—there are cheerleaders, football players, goths, nerds, and rebels. Members of the glee club consider themselves an in-group. Yet, within the high school campus, the "glee kids" are considered the out-group, reviled by jocks and nerds alike for their focus on singing. Emphasising their out-group status, glee kids frequently are ridiculed and physically targeted by the jocks. Another example is to be found in the movie *Mean Girls* (2004). Those involved in the in-group are considered "fabulous but evil." Many students in the out-groups know who the "mean girls" are and at least some of the intimate details of their lives. This is because many students in the out-groups hope to become part of the in-group. Some of these aspirants are called "desperate wannabes." Members of the out-groups also model their behaviour after the ways in which those in the in-group behave.

Conformity to the Group

We have seen that group members generally conform to certain aspects of the group with which they prefer to identify. Some conformity is clearly necessary for a group to survive. If everyone "did his or her own thing," or went his or her own way, there would be no group. But too much conformity can have disastrous consequences. A central issue in the sociological study of groups has been the degree to which members conform to the expectations and demands of the group despite their own misgivings. The previously discussed experiments

Some conformity is necessary for a group to survive. What conformity is evident among this group? What conformity might not be so visible?

by Stanley Milgram (1974) generally demonstrated that people tended to conform to authority figures who were demanding the administration of painful shocks. Groups often develop informal authority structures that can induce the kind of conformity uncovered by Milgram.

Another series of experiments conducted by Solomon Asch (1952) showed that groups with no clear authority figure also promote conformity. He demonstrated that the power of the group is so great that it may override our own judgments and perceptions (Asch 1952; Kinney 2007). In one of the experiments, groups of seven to nine students were assembled. All but one (the subject) were confederates of the researcher. All but the subject knew the details of the experiment; only the subject believed that the experiment was investigating vision. Each group was shown two cards, one with one vertical line on it and a second with three such lines (see Figure 5.7). One of the lines on the second card was the same length as the line on the first card. The other two lines were clearly different. All the students were asked to choose the line on the comparison card that matched the single line on the reference card. As they had been instructed, the confederates chose, out loud, one of the wrong lines. When the subjects' turn came—the subject

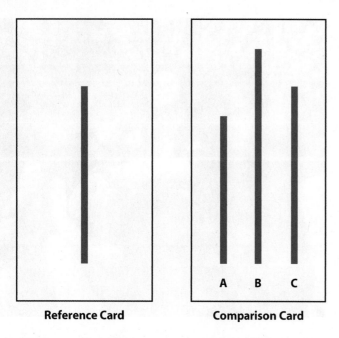

Reference Card   **Comparison Card**

FIGURE 5.7 Solomon Asch's Conformity Experiment Cards

SOURCE: Adapted from Solomon E. Asch, Opinions and Social Pressure, *Scientific American,* 193 (1955), pp. 31–35.

was always positioned last in the group—many of them, about a third, tended to conform to the group's erroneous choice and chose a wrong line. They made the wrong choice even though they apparently knew it was the wrong choice.

There is no question that some people conform to group demands, especially to demands presented by someone in authority in the group, at least some of the time. However, it is important to remember that about two thirds of the choices in the Asch conformity experiments indicated independence from the group. It is also important to note that these experiments are decades old, and many of them occurred in a period of American history more defined by conformity than is the case today.

Yet obedience to authority has not disappeared. In the mid-2000s, a prank phone caller targeting fast-food restaurants across the country demonstrated the relevance of Milgram's work outside of the laboratory (Wolfson 2005). Posing as a police officer on the phone, the caller informed managers that one of their employees was suspected of stealing. While some managers became suspicious of the caller's real identity, others followed his directions—even when they were asked to strip-search and, in one case, sexually assault, an employee. These incidents suggest that many people are still willing to obey authorities such as the police, even when they are asked to participate in actions at odds with their own perceptions and values.

SUMMARY

This chapter examined the aspects of the social world on the micro end of the continuum, namely individuals and groups. The sociological perspective on the individual and the self focuses on how these aspects affect the individual's ability to take part in society. Cooley's concept of the looking-glass self, the idea that humans develop a self-image that reflects how others respond to them, is fundamental to sociology. Symbolic interactionism has been a key theory in the sociological study of how individuals develop a sense of self. George Herbert Mead defined self as the ability to take oneself as an object and over time gain a sense of who one is.

As mind and self develop through interaction, growing children come to incorporate a sense of the generalised other, which allows them to take the role of the entire group or community in which they are embedded and thus operate more smoothly within

society. During the play stage children learn to take on the attitudes of specific others toward themselves; in the game stage they can begin to take on the role or attitude of the entire group, the generalised other.

Erving Goffman built on Mead's theories, particularly the tension between the "I" and the "me." Goffman believed that in every interaction, or performance, individuals have a front and a back stage. The front stage is where the individual operates in a comparatively fixed and idealised manner to define the situation for those who are observing the performance. In the back stage, people are better able to express freely things that are suppressed in the front stage.

Mead's ideas on the development of the self lead directly to the idea of socialisation, the process through which a person learns and generally comes to accept the ways of a group or of a society as a whole. Primary socialisation begins with newborns and infants, and as they develop, children experience secondary socialisation. Socialisation does not end with childhood—adults continue to be socialised throughout their lives. Gender socialisation is a running theme in all interactions.

Interaction is crucially important to socialisation and many other aspects of the social world. Simmel believed society was defined by interaction. Sociologists from a variety of theoretical perspectives have examined interaction. Interaction is deeply involved in people's statuses within social systems and their related roles. Conflicting expectations are often associated with a given status. In addition, those expectations associated with one status often conflict with those tied to others.

Patterns of interaction and social relationships that occur regularly and persist over time become social structures. The smallest social structure is a dyad, which may sometimes become a triad. A group is still a relatively small social structure, made up of a number of people who over time develop patterned relationships.

KEY TERMS

- Achieved status   182
- Agents of socialisation   168
- Anticipatory socialisation   169
- Ascribed status   182
- Back stage   166
- Conversation analysis   181
- Dramaturgy   165
- Dyad   183
- Front stage   166
- Game stage   160
- Generalised other   161
- Gesture   158
- Group   186
- "I"   161
- Impression management   165
- In-group   188
- Interaction   179
- Interaction order   181
- Looking-glass self   157
- Master status   182
- "Me"   164

- Micro-macro continuum   156
- Mind   160
- Out-group   188
- Play stage   160
- Primary groups   187
- Primary socialisation   168
- Reciprocity   180
- Reference groups   188
- Resocialisation   177
- Reverse socialisation   170
- Role   181
- Role conflict   182
- Role overload   182
- Secondary groups   187
- Self   160
- Significant symbol   159
- Social structures   182
- Socialisation   167
- Status   181
- Symbolic interaction   159
- Total institution   177
- Triad   184

THINKING ABOUT SOCIOLOGY

1. How can we use the literature on feral children to explain the importance of interaction to human development? In what ways does this relate to the "nature versus nurture" debate?

2. According to Mead, what distinguishes humans from nonhumans?

3. How does the socialisation process help individuals develop their sense of self? Why are games so important to the socialisation process?

4. What is the difference between the "I" and the "me"? Why do people and society as a whole need both the "I" and the "me"?

5. According to Goffman, in what ways do we use impression management within our front-stage regions? Why would a sociologist say that racism has increasingly been relegated to the back stage? What is problematic about this development?

6. Why are families important agents of socialisation? How do families from higher social classes socialise their children differently than families from lower social classes? What effects might these differences in socialisation have on children?

7. How are we socialised to be consumers? In what ways has the Internet resocialised us as consumers?

8. In what ways is being a fifth grader in Canada both an ascribed and an achieved status? What does this suggest about the differences between roles attached to ascribed statuses versus achieved statuses?

9. In the realm of social networks, why are "weak ties" helpful when looking for a job? What effect has the Internet had on the development of weak ties and strong ties?

10. In what ways do we use images in the mass media as reference groups? How do the mass media help to define in-groups and out-groups?

APPLYING THE SOCIOLOGICAL IMAGINATION

How can we understand gender socialisation through consumption? This chapter argues that malls tend to reinforce gender roles by offering separate shops for female and male consumers.

For this activity, go to your local mall and identify stores for men (and boys) and stores for women (and girls). In what ways are the stores different? Pay attention to the differences in items sold, the nature of those items, the way each store is set up, and even differences in music or lighting. What do the differences in these stores suggest about the differences between men and women and what is expected of them?

ACTIVE SOCIOLOGY

How do you use your own social media pages (e.g., Facebook, Twitter, Pinterest) to manage impressions in the minds of others? How do you present yourself? Do a content analysis (see Chapter 3) of the items (photographs, status updates, links, etc.) on one of your social media pages. What do the items say about you? Identify two or three general themes, based on the analysis of your content. Then consider the following:

- What status do you possess on the site, and what corresponding roles do you perform?

- Where/how did you learn these things (that is, who or what were important *agents of socialisation*)?

- How does this page represent the *front stage*? How is your *back stage* different from the way you've presented yourself on the website?

- How does your page identify your *in-groups* and *out-groups*?

STUDENT STUDY SITE

Visit the student study site at **www.sagepub.com/ritzercanadian** for additional web quizzes for further review.

ORGANISATIONS, SOCIETIES, AND THE GLOBAL

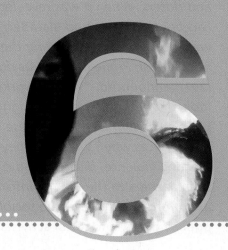

When groups of individuals begin to question the authority and rationality of the bureaucracies that govern and protect them, they may voice concern about, seek to change, or even rebel against those structures.

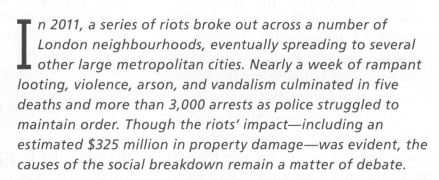

*I*n 2011, a series of riots broke out across a number of London neighbourhoods, eventually spreading to several other large metropolitan cities. Nearly a week of rampant looting, violence, arson, and vandalism culminated in five deaths and more than 3,000 arrests as police struggled to maintain order. Though the riots' impact—including an estimated $325 million in property damage—was evident, the causes of the social breakdown remain a matter of debate.

The riots initially escalated from peaceful protests held in Tottenham, London, after police shot and killed 29-year-old Mark Duggan during an attempted arrest. Although perceived police brutality may have sparked the riots, other institutional problems likely fuelled them. England's dampened economy, growing unemployment, cuts in public services, racial tension, and systemic mistreatment of the poor have all been cited as possible motivations for the riots.

Each of these factors speaks to the relationship between the individual and the organisations and institutions that frame his or her life. Just as universities cannot exist without willing students, social order cannot be maintained if citizens refuse to adhere to society's shared laws and norms. When groups of individuals begin to question the authority and rationality of the bureaucracies that govern and protect them, they may voice concern about, seek to change, or even rebel against those structures.

Technology and globalisation facilitate the global flow of information. This flow has only increased as more and broader networks have emerged, marking a fundamental shift in the way we communicate. The nearly instantaneous dissemination of ideas has become a bonanza for everyone, including revolutionaries and rioters. When it was revealed that Facebook, Twitter, and BlackBerry Messenger were used extensively during the London riots, British Prime Minister David Cameron (2011) announced, "We are working . . . to look at whether it would be right to stop people communicating via these websites and services when we know they are plotting violence, disorder and criminality." Such barriers to the flow of information are of profound interest to sociologists, public figures, and social activists alike.

As finance, media, ideology, and information flow more easily around the globe, so too do social problems that may have at one time been isolated to a particular region or society. England's weakened economy and the anxiety that it caused were both mirrored by and intrinsically linked to economic crises occurring throughout the western world. England's socioeconomic climate contributed to the riots, and the leaders of nation-states experiencing similar circumstances most assuredly took note.

This chapter picks up where the previous one left off—with groups—and moves on to the more macroscopic levels of interest to sociologists: organisations, societies, and the globe as a whole. While these social structures are discussed here as if they are clearly distinct from one another, the fact is that they tend to blend together in many almost imperceptible ways.

The individuals, interactions, and groups of focal concern in Chapter 5 all exist within, affect, and are affected by the various macroscopic phenomena of concern here. In fact, neither microscopic nor macroscopic social phenomena make

much sense without the other. Individuals, interactions, and groups do not exist in isolation from macro-level phenomena, and the latter make no sense at all without micro-level phenomena. That is, organisations, societies, and global social relationships cannot exist without individuals, interactions, and groups. What is new here is the emergence, largely because of the explosive growth of digitality, of an increasingly networked social world where both micro-level and macro-level phenomena are ever more closely intertwined (Raine and Wellman 2012). And this is related to the dramatic expansion of globalisation as a process and of the growth of global relationships at every point in the continuum that runs from the most microscopic to the most macroscopic social phenomena. You are, of course, deeply implicated in all of this. In fact, young people are the most likely to participate in, and be affected by, these recent developments, especially those involving digitized interrelationships.

ORGANISATIONS

The social world is loaded with **organisations**, which are collectives purposely constructed to achieve particular ends. Examples include your college or university, which has the objective of educating you as well as your fellow students; corporations, such as Apple, Google, and Walmart, whose objective is to earn profits; the International Monetary Fund (IMF), which seeks to stabilize currency exchanges throughout the world; and Greenpeace, which works to protect and conserve the global environment.

Organisations are collectives purposely constructed to achieve particular ends. Here, Greenpeace activists march along Rio de Janeiro's Copacabana beach in protest of a Forest Code bill approved by the National Congress on June 19, 2011. Some 2,000 members of the environmental activism organisation took part in the march against the controversial bill, which expanded permissible Amazon rainforest deforestation.

There is a particularly long and deep body of work in sociology that deals with organisations (Godwyn and Gittell 2011), much of it traceable to the thinking of Max Weber on a particular kind of organisation, the bureaucracy. As you may recall, a **bureaucracy** is a highly rational organisation, especially one that is very efficient. The bureaucracy is a key element of Weber's theory of the rationalisation of the western world. In fact, along with capitalism, the bureaucracy best exemplifies what Weber meant by rationalisation. For decades the concept of bureaucracy dominated sociological thinking about organisations, and it led to many important insights about the social world. However, as the social world has changed, so too has sociological thinking about organisations. New concepts are supplementing the concept of bureaucracy to enrich our understanding of these new realities.

BUREAUCRACIES

Throughout his work Weber created and used many "ideal types" as methodological tools to study the real world and with which to do historical-comparative analysis (see Chapter 3). An *ideal type* is a model in which reality is greatly exaggerated. One of Weber's most famous ideal types was the bureaucracy. While the ideal type of bureaucracy is primarily a methodological tool, it also gives us a good sense of the advantages of bureaucracies over other types of organisations.

The ideal-typical bureaucracy is a model of what most large-scale organisations throughout much of the twentieth century looked like, or at least tried to resemble. Figure 6.1 is an organisation chart for a typical bureaucracy. A bureaucracy has the following characteristics:

- There a continuous series of offices, or positions, within the organisation. Each office has official functions and is bound by a set of rules.

- Each office has a specified sphere of competence. Those who occupy the position are responsible for specific tasks and have the authority to handle them, and those in other relevant offices are obligated to help.

- The offices exist in a vertical hierarchy.

- The positions have technical requirements, and those who hold those offices must undergo the needed training.

- Those who occupy the positions do not own the things needed to do the job (computers, desks, etc.); the organisation provides officeholders with what they need to get the job done.

- Those who occupy a particular office—chief executive officers, for example—cannot take the office as their own; it remains part of the organisation.

- Everything of formal importance—administrative acts, decisions, rules—is in writing.

The development of the bureaucracy is one of the defining characteristics of western society. In Weber's view, it was a key source of the superiority of the West over other civilisations in the operation of society as a whole as well as of its major components such as the military. Weber felt that in meeting the needs of large societies for mass administration, there is no better organisational form than, and no alternative to, the bureaucracy.

Authority Structures and Bureaucracy

Weber's work on bureaucracy is related to his thinking on three types of authority structures. Before getting to those types, we need two preliminary definitions. **Domination** is the probability or likelihood that commands will be obeyed by subordinates (Weber [1921] 1968). There are degrees of domination. Strong domination involves a high probability that commands will be obeyed; domination is weak when those probabilities are low. **Authority** is a particular type of domination; it is legitimate domination. The key question, then, is what makes authority legitimate as far as subordinates are concerned.

Weber differentiates among three types of authority:

- **Rational-legal authority.** Domination is legitimated on the basis of legally enacted rules and the right of those with authority under those rules to issue commands. For example, the prime minister of Canada has

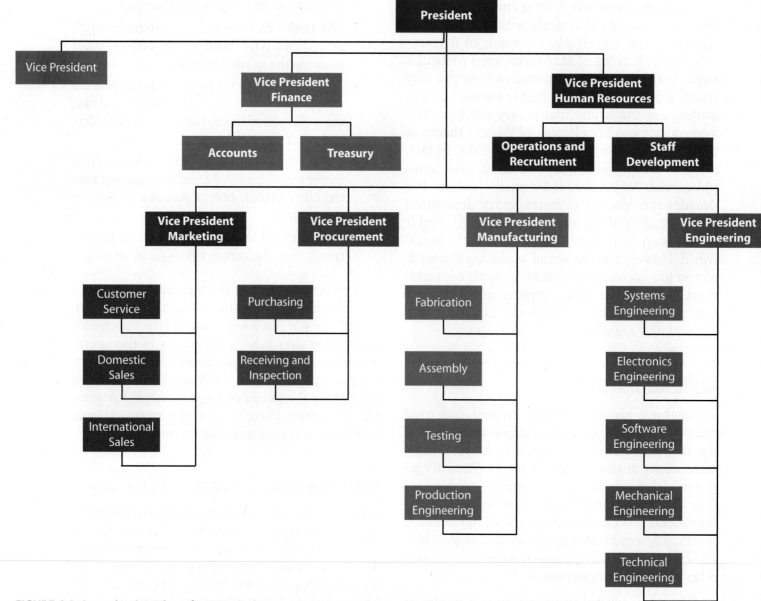

FIGURE 6.1 Organisation Chart for a Typical Bureaucracy

rational-legal authority because he is duly elected in accord with the country's laws. He therefore has the legitimate right to issue various commands, such as his decision to withdraw Canadian combat troops from Afghanistan by 2012. Many Canadians would like to have seen an even earlier withdrawal, and some no doubt would have liked troops to remain even longer to fulfill more successfully the initial objectives. Whatever one's personal position, the prime minister had the legitimate authority to make the decision he did. Similarly, your professors have rational-legal authority because of the nature of their positions in, and the rules of, the university. They can, for example, demand that you read this chapter, take an exam on it, and complete other course requirements.

- **Traditional authority.** Authority based on the belief in long-running traditions is traditional authority. For example, although the pope is elected by the College of Cardinals,

Rational-Legal Authority   **Traditional Authority**   **Charismatic Authority**

Bill Gates leads primarily by way of rational-legal authority, Queen Elizabeth of England by traditional authority, and Mahatma Gandhi by charismatic authority.

his authority within Catholicism is based primarily on the long traditions associated with his position. At the university, it is traditional for senior professors with many years of service, especially those who are well known on the campus or internationally, to acquire authority in their departments as well as in the university as a whole.

- **Charismatic authority.** The third type of authority is based on the devotion of followers to what they define as the exceptional characteristics of a leader. Large numbers of people believed that Martin Luther King Jr. and Mahatma Gandhi had such exceptional characteristics and, as a result, became their devoted followers. A professor who is considered to be a charismatic teacher by her students is likely to attract a large number of adoring students and to have, as a result, authority over them as well as other professors interested in learning how to improve their teaching techniques.

Each type of authority can spawn its own organisational form, but it is rational-legal authority that

is most associated with bureaucracy. In comparison to the bureaucracy, the organisations based on traditional and charismatic authority are less rational. They are, for example, less efficient than the highly efficient bureaucracy.

Rationality and Irrationality

Much sociological research on organisations in the twentieth century took Weber's highly rational model of a bureaucracy as a starting point for the analysis of the ways in which bureaucracies actually worked. However, much of that research found Weber's model to be unrealistic. For one thing, there is no single organisational model; the nature of the organisation and its degree of rationality is contingent on such factors as its size and the technologies that it employs (Orlikowski 2010; Pugh et al. 1968). For another, researchers found Weber's ideal-typical bureaucracy to be overly rational. They concluded that, at best, organisations exhibit a limited form of rationality, what is called **bounded rationality** (H. Simon [1945] 1976; O. Williamson 1975, 1985). That is, rationality is limited by the instabilities and conflicts that exist in most, if not all, organisations and the domains in which they operate (W. Scott 2008). It is also constrained by inherent limitations on humans' capacities to think and act in a rational manner. Some members of the organisation are capable of acting more rationally than others, but none are able to operate in anything approaching the fully rational manner associated with Weber's ideal-typical organisation (Cyert and March 1963).

The military is an example of an organisation with bounded rationality. One source of instability in the military is the personnel cycling in and out of it, especially combat zones. Conflicts exist between branches of the armed forces and between central command and those in the field. In addition, military actions are often so complex and far-reaching that military personnel cannot fully understand them or decide rationally what actions to take. This is sometimes referred to as the "fog of war" (Blight and Lang 2005).

A good deal of sociological research on bureaucracies has dealt with the "irrationalities of rationality," the irrationalities that often accompany the seemingly rational actions associated with the bureaucracy (Ritzer 2013). For example, Robert Merton ([1949] 1968) and other observers found that instead of operating efficiently, bureaucracies introduce great inefficiency due to, among other things, "red tape." *Red tape* is a colloquial term for rules that a bureaucracy's employees are needlessly required to follow. It also includes unnecessary online and off-line questions to be answered and forms to be filled out by the clients of a bureaucracy. Bureaucracies generally demand far more information than they need, often to protect themselves from complaints, bad publicity, and lawsuits. Red tape also includes the telephone time wasted by keeping clients on hold and forcing them to make their way through a maze of prerecorded "customer service" options. In the end, clients often discover that they have been holding for the wrong office or, as is increasingly the case today, that they can resolve their problem only by visiting the company's website.

Catch-22, a term derived from a 1970 movie and an earlier novel of the same name by Joseph Heller (1955), means that bureaucratic rules may be written in such a way that one rule makes it impossible to do what another rule demands or requires. Heller's story takes place during World War II and focuses on a burned-out pilot who wants to be excused from flying further combat missions. One of the military's rules is that he could be excused from such missions if he has a doctor declare him crazy. However, there is another rule—Rule 22—which states that anyone rational enough to want to get out of combat could not possibly be crazy; it is the ultimate in sanity to want to avoid life-threatening activities. If the pilot followed the first rule and did what was required to avoid flying combat missions, catch-22 would make it impossible for him to get out of those missions.

Another source of irrationality is the **bureaucratic personality**, who follows the rules of the organisation to such a great extent that the ability to achieve organisational goals is subverted (Merton [1949] 1968). For example, an admissions clerk in a hospital emergency department may require incoming patients to provide so much information and fill out so many forms that they do not get medical care as promptly as it may be needed. Similarly, a teacher might devote so much time and attention to discussing and enforcing classroom rules that little real learning takes place.

In these and in many other ways, the actual functioning of bureaucracies is at variance with Weber's ideal-typical characterisation. However, it is important to remember that Weber was well aware of at least some of these possibilities, and his ideal type was created as a methodological tool, *not* as an accurate description of reality.

The Informal Organisation

A great deal of research in the twentieth century focused on the **informal organisation**, on how the organisation actually works as opposed to the way it is supposed to work—as depicted, for example, in Weber's ideal-typical formal bureaucracy (Blau 1963). For example, those who occupy offices lower in the bureaucratic hierarchy often have greater knowledge and competence on specific issues than those who rank above them. Thus, fellow employees may seek the advice of the lower-level bureaucrat rather than the one who ranks higher in the authority structure. Similarly, a recent study found that those interested in land conservation are more likely to be influenced by informal contacts

BIOGRAPHICAL bits

Robert K. Merton (1910–2003, American)

- Meyer Robert Schkolnick was born on July 4 in Philadelphia to Jewish immigrants from Russia.

- At the age of 14 he adopted the Americanized name Robert Merton to better promote himself as a magician.

- In Philadelphia he took advantage of many opportunities to learn about and observe the social world, including the teeming streets of his neighbourhood.

- He won a scholarship to Temple University, where he found sociology to his liking, and went on to receive his PhD from Harvard University.

- He taught sociology and social research for more than 50 years at Columbia University.

- Merton was interested in the subtle patterns in society and developed several famous concepts that have become commonplace, including *bureaucratic personality, unintended consequences, role model,* and *self-fulfilling prophecy.*

- His work, mostly in the structural-functional tradition, influenced public policy; for example, his research on successfully integrated communities was a key element in the Supreme Court's decision to desegregate public schools.

- He is considered the founder of the sociology of science and became the first sociologist ever to win the National Medal of Science (1994).

- A former student said, "If there were a Nobel Prize in sociology, there would be no question he would have gotten it."

- Ironically, his son, Robert C. Merton, did win a Nobel Prize in economics in 1997.

SOURCES: C. Crothers 2011; M. Kaufman 2003; Sica 2008.

outside a conservationist organisation than by those in the organisation (Prell et al. 2010). To take another example, employees sometimes do things that exceed their job description, but they more often do less, perhaps far less, than they are expected to do. Finally, contrary to the dictates of the formal organisation, the most important things that take place in an organisation may never be put in writing. They are deliberately handled orally so that if anything goes wrong, there is no damning evidence that could jeopardise careers and even the organisation as a whole.

The danger of putting things in writing in organisations has only become worse in the age of digitalisation. Posts to the Internet, in particular, can exist forever and be circulated widely and endlessly. This danger was pointed up in 2010 and 2011 when a global organisation, WikiLeaks, released many previously unpublished official government documents, including some relating to the Afghanistan war (see the next *Globalisation* box). These documents revealed, among other things, secret ties between the Pakistan security forces and the Taliban. The public release of this information jeopardized the lives of people in Afghanistan working undercover for the allied forces and disrupted the already troubled Pakistan–U.S. relations. However, there are those, including those involved with WikiLeaks, who feel that secrets and secret agreements pose the greatest dangers to the lives of people. For example, it is widely believed that Pakistan's security forces are secretly helping the Taliban kill NATO (North Atlantic Treaty Organization) soldiers.

While power is supposed to be dispersed throughout the offices in some bureaucracies, it often turns out that the organisation becomes an **oligarchy** with a small group of people at the top illegitimately obtaining and exercising far more power than they are supposed to have. This can occur in any organisation, although this undemocratic process was first described by Robert Michels ([1915] 1962) in the most unlikely of organisations—labour unions and socialist parties that supposedly prized democracy. Michels called this "the iron law of oligarchy" (Guillen 2010). Those in power manipulate the organisation (by, for example, structuring elections to work to their advantage) so that they and their supporters can stay in power indefinitely. At the same time, they make it difficult for others to get or to keep power. While oligarchy certainly develops in such organisations, its occurrence is, in reality, neither iron nor a law. That is, most such organisations do not become oligarchical. Nevertheless, the tendency toward oligarchy is an important organisational process not anticipated by Weber's ideal-typical bureaucracy.

Weber's model also makes no provision for infighting within organisations. However, internal squabbles, and outright battles, are everyday phenomena within organisations. This is particularly evident in the government and other very large organisations, where one branch or office often engages in pitched turf battles with others. For example, in his book *Obama's Wars,* investigative journalist Bob Woodward (2010) revealed numerous conflicts within the Obama administration over the direction of the war in Afghanistan. Obama's own advisors clashed; for example, Vice President Joe Biden called the now-deceased Richard Holbrooke, then special representative to Afghanistan, "the most egotistical bastard I ever met" (P. Baker 2010:A12). There were also conflicts between Obama's advisors and others. For example, Afghanistan commander General David Petraeus disliked Obama advisor David Axelrod because he was "a complete spin doctor" (P. Baker 2010:A12). This kind of conflict is also apparent in universities, where those in charge of closely related academic departments such as psychology, anthropology, and sociology often battle over increasingly scarce resources, or even the direction of the university as a whole and what it should emphasize.

Gendered Organisations

Weber's model also does not account for discrimination within organisations. In the ideal bureaucracy, any worker with the necessary training can fill any job. However, as "gendered organisation" theorists, such as Joan Acker (1990, 2009), have shown, bureaucracies do not treat all workers the same (Pager, Western, and Bonikowski 2009). Jobs often are designed for an idealized worker—one who has no other obligations except to the organisation. Women, and sometimes men, who carry a larger responsibility for child rearing can have difficulty fitting this model. Women may face "a double ghetto" (P. Armstrong and Armstrong 2010)

or have to balance the "competing devotions" of motherhood and work (Blair-Loy 2003; Wharton and Blair-Loy 2006). Organisations may also discriminate (consciously or unconsciously) in hiring and promotions, with white men (who tend to populate the higher levels of bureaucracies) being promoted over women and minorities (Alvesson and Billing 2009; Kay and Gorman 2008). Some women in male-dominated organisations find they hit a "glass ceiling"—a certain level of authority in a company from which they can rise no higher (J. Acker 2009; M. Young and Wallace 2009). They can see the top—hence the "glass"—but cannot reach it. Within other organisations, particularly female-dominated ones, men can find themselves riding the "glass escalator" (C. Williams 1995)—an invisible force that propels them past equally competent, or even more competent, women to positions of leadership and authority, as happens for school principals, for example.

Relatively few women are corporate leaders. For example, in no country in the world do women occupy a majority of the seats on the boards of directors of corporations. As shown in Figure 6.2, Norway has the most equitable balance, with just over 40 percent of board seats occupied by women. In Canada, which ranks only 14th in the world, barely 1 in 10 board seats is occupied by women. It is the very rare corporate board, anywhere in the world, that actually has a woman as its chair. Many countries, including Canada, the United States, and member states in the European Union, have set up advisory groups to try to promote greater representation on corporate boards in an effort to expand the talent pool.

In an interesting analysis of the glass ceiling in a global context, it was found that women executives face a "double-paned" glass ceiling. There is the pane associated with the glass ceiling that exists in the employing company in the home country, and there is a second pane that is encountered when women executives seek work experience in a foreign locale of the corporation. This is a growing problem since experience overseas is an increasing requirement for top-level management positions in multinational corporations. However, corporations have typically "masculinized" these expatriate positions and thereby disadvantaged females. Among the problems experienced by women who succeed in getting these positions are sexual harassment, a lack of availability of programmes (e.g., career

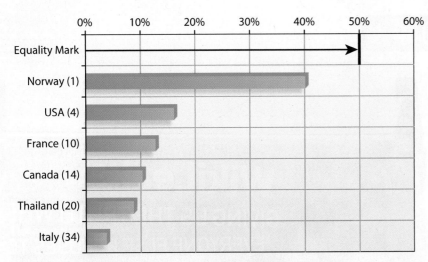

FIGURE 6.2 Women on Corporate Boards, Selected Countries

SOURCE: Catalyst. Retrieved September 28, 2012 (http://www.catalyst.org/publication/433/women-on-boards).

Note: Figures in parentheses refer to country rank order (i.e., Norway has the most women on boards).

counselling) routinely available to men, a lack of adequate mentoring, and male managers who are more likely to promote male rather than female expatriates. Much of the blame for this problem lies in the structure of the multinational corporations, and with the men who occupy high-level management positions within them. However, female managers bear at least some of the responsibility for their problems because, for example, of their greater passivity and their lesser willingness to promote themselves for such expatriate management positions (Insch, McIntyre, and Napier 2008).

The idea of a glass ceiling relates to vertical mobility—and its absence—for women in organisations. A related concept is the "glass cage," which deals with the horizontal segregation of women (and other minorities) (Kalev 2009). The idea here is that men and women doing the same or similar jobs operate in separate and segregated parts of the organisation. As in the case of the glass ceiling, it is difficult, especially for women, to move between the cages. In spite of the fact that the cage is made of glass, the skills and abilities of women tend to be less visible, and, as a result, stereotypes about them abound. In addition, women have less communication with those outside their particular cage, are less likely to learn about jobs available elsewhere, are not as likely to get high-profile assignments, and are less likely to get needed training. The situation confronting women would improve if there were more collaboration across the boundaries of the glass cage. Of

course, the ultimate solution involves the elimination of both the glass cage and the glass ceiling.

A third interesting idea here is that of the "glass cliff" (M. Ryan and Haslam 2005). While the glass ceiling and the glass cage deal with barriers to the mobility of women within organisations, the glass cliff describes what can happen to women who experience upward mobility when the organisation is going through hard times. The implication is that women who rise to high levels at such times end up in highly precarious positions. Of course, the same would be true of men, but M. Ryan and S. Haslam (2005) find that women are more likely than men to move into positions on boards of directors when the organisation has been performing badly. This means they are more likely than males to find themselves at the edge of that organisational cliff.

Problems in Organisations

The ideal-type bureaucracy also makes no provision for an array of problems in the organisation or for problematic organisations (D. Friedrichs 2007), but in the real world there is no shortage of either. The most heinous example of a problematic (to put it mildly) organisation is the Nazi bureaucracy responsible for the murder of 6 million Jews, and others, during the Holocaust (Bauman 1989). Al-Qaeda, the Mafia, and Mexican drug cartels, among many others, would also be considered by most people to be problematic organisations. In addition, many less developed countries in the world regard global organisations such as the International Monetary Fund and the World Bank as problematic organisations because of the damaging austerity programmes and other forms of "structural adjustment" they impose on recipient countries in exchange for monetary assistance and other help (Babb 2005).

An organisational scandal broke in mid-2011 when it was revealed that the British newspaper *News of the World,* part of Rupert Murdoch's global media conglomerate, News Corporation, had hacked

GLOBALISATION

WikiLeaks

Because it is online, WikiLeaks exists everywhere; it is a global phenomenon, and it has had an impact throughout the world. Indeed, it has become emblematic of both digitality and globalisation, as well as the inherent relationship between them. Started through dialogues between dissidents and hackers in several countries around the world, WikiLeaks seeks to release information that exposes the actions of governments and others.

WikiLeaks achieved worldwide notoriety in 2010 when it began publishing messages, some classified, related to the Iraq and Afghanistan wars, as well as a variety of American diplomatic cables. The U.S. attorney general said, "The national security of the United States has been put at risk . . . by these actions that I believe are arrogant, misguided and ultimately not helpful in any way" (M. Johnson and Hall 2010:6A). A U.S. senator said that he believed WikiLeaks violated the Espionage Act, which prohibits people from releasing classified information (Savage 2010).

What caused this uproar? WikiLeaks is a website launched in 2006 by Australian activist

WikiLeaks, and its founder, Julian Assange, have drawn both ardent support and fervent disdain. Here, a billboard along Santa Monica Boulevard depicts Assange and advertises support for his organisation's distribution of confidential information.

Julian Assange, who, as a young man, was a hacker. The hacker culture that had emerged in the early years of the Internet involved the innovative, sometimes destructive, modification of computer software and hardware. Some hackers became highly political as part of a movement that came to be known as *cyberlibertarianism* (see also Chapter 4). They took on the task of applying such

into the phones of a murdered schoolgirl, victims of a 2007 terrorist attack in London, and families of British soldiers killed in Iraq and Afghanistan (see Chapter 12). Thus, the newspaper scooped its rivals not by operating more rationally but because it engaged in such illegal behaviours as phone hacking. The public outcry grew so loud that News Corp. had to close down *News of the World* even though it was highly successful, sold millions of copies per week, and was the leading English-language newspaper in the world in terms of sales (Lyall 2011).

Sexual harassment is one of many organisational problems (Lopez, Hodson, and Roscigno

2009) that are less spectacular than those discussed above, but are much more common. Cases of sexual harassment rarely get the publicity accorded to *News of the World*. One exception is the suspected 2011 rape of a hotel worker by then–International Monetary Fund head Dominique Strauss-Kahn and the revelation that this was far from the only case of such harassment by Strauss-Kahn. Nonetheless, sexual harassment is widely practised, and a great many women are harmed by it. Usually it takes the form of high-ranking men demanding sexual favours from those, usually women, in positions lower than theirs in the hierarchy. For example, there have been many allegations of libertarian principles as complete and full civil liberties to the Internet.

WikiLeaks itself is devoted to the belief that information should be free. The WikiLeaks website states that "publishing improves transparency, and this transparency creates a better society for all people. Better scrutiny leads to reduced corruption and stronger democracies in all society's institutions, including government, corporations and other organisations. A healthy, vibrant and inquisitive journalistic media plays a vital role in achieving these goals" (WikiLeaks 2010). WikiLeaks depends upon individual users throughout the world to submit information, documents, and various files to a drop box on its website. The use of a digital drop box allows users to submit information anonymously. It also keeps WikiLeaks itself from being directly involved in obtaining the information.

So far, WikiLeaks has been most interested in publishing the confidential and sensitive information of governments, most notably the U.S. government. In fact, WikiLeaks' slogan is, "We open governments." Assange has made it clear, however, that in the future WikiLeaks will also publish documents that expose corporate corruption and deceitful business practises (A. Greenberg 2010).

Despite the leaks, it is unclear if WikiLeaks has made, or will make, the U.S. government (or other governments) more transparent or more likely to discontinue the classification of sensitive information. The Obama administration has responded to WikiLeaks' activities by seeking to better control such information and to limit the amount of information available to lower-ranking members of the military and the Department of Defense (Shane 2010). Thus, rather than achieving the goal of freeing information, WikiLeaks may have contributed to making such information less accessible and more secure. It has also exposed the names of confidential sources. This has put the lives of informants at risk—and may discourage future informants (J. Burns and Somaiya 2010a, 2010b). But Assange understood from the beginning that the government response to WikiLeaks would be for it to become more secretive. He and his fellow hackers are likely to keep trying ever more sophisticated ways to access and reveal secret information. Regardless of the outcome, WikiLeaks has sparked a global debate over its role in releasing sensitive information, and in the global political affairs (such as the wars in Iraq and Afghanistan) for which it has released documents.

As of this writing, Assange is under house arrest in Great Britain. He is being detained because of a charge of sexual assault in Sweden. Furthermore, WikiLeaks is in danger of being shut down because of a "financial blockade" that prevents most people from making needed financial contributions to the site (J. Burns 2011).

SOURCE: Printed with the permission of William Yagatich and Nathan Jurgenson.

---

sexual harassment or abuse of female service members in the armed services and the Royal Canadian Mounted Police (RCMP). There have been mounting criticisms of the RCMP for failing to react adequately to these forms of deviant behaviour (D. Moore 2012). Then there is the sexual harassment of young boys by priests and other church officials that has caused great problems for one of the largest organisations in the world, the Catholic Church. This has been a huge problem not only because of the behaviour of priests but also because church officials have not done nearly enough to dismiss those responsible and make it more difficult for this kind of harassment to occur in the future (Doyle 2003).

Disasters (and other unplanned outcomes) are deeply problematic for organisations and often occur as the result of rational organisational processes (Vaughan 1996). For example, in the 1980s the National Aeronautics and Space Administration (NASA) operated on the basis of what it considered a highly reliable and rational plan. As a result, it focused, among many other things, on a variety of quantifiable factors in order to keep the Space Shuttle *Challenger* on schedule for its launch. In doing so, it cut a number of corners and engaged in various economies. While these made sense from the perspective of NASA as a rationalised organisation, it contributed to the disaster on January 28,

In April 2010, an explosion at the Deepwater Horizon offshore oil drilling rig killed 11 people and caused a massive oil leak that flowed unabated for nearly three months. One hundred and seventy-one million imperial gallons (779 million litres) of crude oil spilled into the Gulf of Mexico (National Response Team 2011), causing immeasurable ecological, economic, political, and health-related damage. This disaster affected not only the responsible corporations but also local businesses, governmental agencies, volunteer groups, and other organisations.

1986, in which *Challenger's* fuel tank broke apart, causing the in-flight destruction of the shuttle and the death of seven crew members.

Contemporary Changes in Bureaucracy

In the last several decades bureaucratic organisations have undergone a number of important changes that do not fit well with Weber's view of organisations. For one thing, contrary to Weber's thinking on the likelihood of their growth and spread, many of the largest organisations, especially industrial organisations and labour unions, have been forced to downsize dramatically; the idea that "bigger is better" is no longer the rule in most organisations. Instead of constantly adding new functions, and more employees, organisations are now likely to focus on their "core competencies." For example, the Ford Motor Company is focusing on manufacturing automobiles and not, as it once did, on making, among many other things, the steel for the frame and the rubber for the tires. Ford

also sold off the Volvo and Jaguar lines in order to focus on the Ford brand. In a now-popular phrase, organisations have come to concentrate on becoming "lean and mean" (B. Harrison 1994).

In order to adapt to a rapidly changing environment, contemporary organisations have also been forced to become more flexible and more agile than is suggested by the ideal-type bureaucracy. For example, it appears that Ford has become flexible enough to compete with rising automobile manufacturers such as Hyundai. However, when organisations lack such flexibility today, there is a strong likelihood that they will decline or disappear. For example, Blockbuster and its large chain of video stores failed to adapt sufficiently and fast enough to competition from Netflix and its movies-by-mail and later streaming of movies, as well as to Redbox and its video-dispensing kiosks. As a result, Blockbuster went bankrupt in 2010, but some stores remain in business, and it also rents movies online and through its own video kiosks. However, it lags far behind Netflix and Redbox in those domains.

Former IMF leader Dominique Strauss-Kahn, left, was accused of sexually assaulting Nafissatou Diallo, a 32-year-old maid, on July 28, 2011, in New York. After a lengthy investigation, charges were dropped against Strauss-Kahn, who described his encounter with Diallo as "a moral fault" and "inappropriate." Since then, fresh charges of sexual impropriety have been levelled against Strauss-Kahn in his home country of France.

Yet another important organisational development is the increasing trend toward **outsourcing**, or the transfer of activities once performed by one organisation to another organisation in exchange for money (Ritzer and Lair 2007). Since the early 2000s, outsourcing has increased dramatically. Hospitals outsource the operation of their cleaning services and laundry. Governments, including the federal government, also outsource work to other organisations, especially private businesses, to do their payroll or special projects. An example that has gotten a lot of negative publicity has been the outsourcing by the U.S. government of many military and para-military activities in Iraq to a company known as Blackwater. When news media raised alarms over the company's involvement in unwarranted killings and use of unnecessary force, the company changed its name to Xe Services and later Academi.

Another recent trend in organisations not anticipated by Weber's ideal-type bureaucracy is to turn work formerly performed by officeholders over to the clients. For example, we are increasingly filling out census forms on our own, thereby doing work that used to be done by census takers. We are scanning checks into a cell phone instead of handing them to a teller, reviewing a restaurant or movie online rather than reading a review by a professional critic, talking about our experiences with products or brands on social networking sites instead of passively accepting advertising messages from the producers, and scanning our own groceries in self-checkout lanes (see Figure 6.3). In taking on these tasks, clients and consumers are turned into producers, at least for a time. In other words, consumers have been transformed into *prosumers*, combining the acts of consumption and production (Ritzer, Dean, and Jurgenson 2012) (see Chapter 4). This is yet another wide-ranging and pervasive change that is dramatically transforming the nature of organisations and organisational life.

Globalisation and Bureaucracy

Most organisations of any significant size have become increasingly global. They are affected by numerous global realities and changes and in many cases have, themselves, become global forces and players. The global reach of McDonald's is well known. It has restaurants in about 120 countries throughout the world. However, in the fast-food industry, Yum! Brands (Pizza Hut, KFC, etc.) is in almost as many countries—110—and has more restaurants than McDonald's. Walmart is another global powerhouse with 3,600 stores in 15 countries. There are other organisations with a presence in Canada that have roots elsewhere in the world. Examples include IKEA, based in Sweden, with 303 stores in 37 countries; H&M, an apparel retailer, from Sweden; T-Mobile, a telecommunications company originating in Germany; HSBC, a financial services provider from Hong Kong and Shanghai; and Zara International, a fashion retailer, whose home base is in Spain (Ritzer 2013).

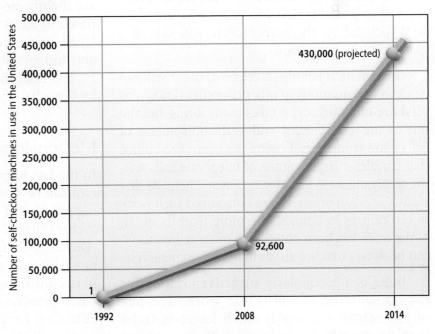

FIGURE 6.3 The Use of Supermarket Self-Checkout Machines in the United States, 1992–2014

SOURCE: http://web.mit.edu/2.744/www/Project/Assignments/humanUse/lynette/2-About%20the%20machine.html

Consumers have been transformed into prosumers, meaning that they play the roles of both consumer and producer. Here, a woman acts as both bank customer and bank teller as she navigates an ATM's prompts.

Spanning much of the globe is a challenge to any organisation and forces it to adapt to global realities in innumerable ways. Ford Motor Company, for example, recognized some years ago that producing a different model car for every country or global region was very inefficient. And so it focused on the manufacture and sale of a global car, the Ford Focus.

Globalisation has also accelerated the transfer of work to organisations in other countries, known as **offshore outsourcing**. It takes many forms, but the one we are most familiar with is the outsourcing of call centre work. A call centre is a centralized office that handles a large volume of telephone calls asking an organisation for information and help. At first many Canadian organisations outsourced such work to call centres in Canada, but more recently much of the work has been outsourced offshore because it can be done outside Canada much less expensively.

India is a particularly attractive location for the outsourcing of call centre work. The pay of call centre workers is much lower in India than in North America, and many Indians speak excellent English. In fact, many call centre workers are expected to "pose as Canadians" as part of their employment—adopting Canadian names and hometowns, among other things—a strategy referred to as "national identity management" (Poster 2007). For Indian women, working at call centres can provide financial autonomy. Yet, the number of women working in these jobs—particularly in the night shift—has raised cultural anxieties about changing gender norms within India (Patel 2010). Women working at night—rather than being at home—is unusual. Additionally, unmarried women who work at call centres are more able to support themselves financially, and thus be less beholden to family demands.

In recent years the Philippines has caught up with, and passed, India as the dominant locale for call centre work. There are now about 400,000 Filipino call centre workers compared to the roughly 350,000 such workers in India. The main reason for the change is that the residents of this former American colony are very familiar with western culture, and their English is not as accented as the British English spoken by most Indians. Filipinos are likely to watch American TV shows, follow American sports teams, and eat hamburgers. North American companies are making this choice even though Filipino workers are slightly more expensive—$300 a month compared to $250 per month—than Indian workers. By the way, the great attraction of both Filipino and Indian call centre workers is that they earn far less than the roughly $1,700 a month earned by Canadian call centre workers.

McDonaldization and Bureaucracy

In the late twentieth century the fast-food restaurant can be seen as the best example of the ongoing process of rationalisation first described by Weber (Ritzer 2013). While the chain of franchised (Dicke 1992) fast-food restaurants is a relatively new and important organisational development, it is continuous with the bureaucracy and its basic principles: efficiency, predictability, calculability, control, and the seemingly inevitable irrationalities of rationality. What, then, distinguishes McDonaldized fast-food restaurants from bureaucracies?

McDonaldization is applicable to both large organisations and relatively small organisations. The principles of bureaucracy tended to be applied only to state governments and giant corporations like Ford and Walmart. Such bureaucracies still exist, although in many cases they are much smaller than they once were. The principles of McDonaldization can be applied not only to large corporations such as Starbucks but also to small restaurants and all sorts of small enterprises. In short, the model of the McDonaldized fast-food restaurant has much wider applicability than the bureaucratic model. There is an infinitely greater number of small enterprises throughout Canada and the world than there are state governments and large corporations.

McDonaldization is applicable to both consumption-oriented organisations and production-oriented organisations. The bureaucratic model was most applicable, outside of the government, to large production-oriented corporations. However, Canada has moved away from a society dominated by work and production to one dominated by consumption. As a result, the large corporation involved in goods production has declined in importance, at least in western countries such as Canada (where it was never very dominant). In its place we have seen the rise of similarly large corporations, such as Tim Hortons, Rogers, and the Royal Bank, devoted to consumption. While the corporate structures of these organisations remain highly bureaucratised, their real heart lies in the numerous smaller outlets that constitute the source of income and profit for the organisation. Thus, of greatest importance now is the McDonaldization of those outlets and not the bureaucratisation of the larger organisation in which they exist.

The key point is that bureaucratisation involves a kind of rationality that is highly centralised and largely invisible to those who consume the goods and services produced by these organisations. Few people have much person-to-person contact with the Canada Revenue Agency or with the bureaucracy that runs Honda. However, McDonaldization is both very local and highly visible to those who consume in settings such as fast-food restaurants. People have a lot of direct, person-to-person contact with those who work in McDonaldized settings. This means, among other things, that the fast-food

As Canada has moved away from production and toward consumption, leading corporations have followed suit. Of greatest importance now is the McDonaldization of consumption-oriented outlets (such as Tim Hortons franchise locations) and not the bureaucratisation of the larger organisation in which they exist (such as the Tim Hortons company as a whole).

restaurant, indeed almost all McDonaldized systems in the realm of consumption, need to be much more "customer friendly" than does the traditional bureaucracy. Counter people are trained to smile and wish you a "nice day" (Leidner 1993). At Walmart there is even an employee—the greeter—whose sole task is to be warm and friendly to customers when they enter the store. Then there are those "smiley faces" that customers see throughout Walmart. Similarly, Apple maintains its physical presence through aesthetically pleasing stores, which frequently include "genius bars"—staffed by friendly and knowledgeable staff who can answer questions in person and fix your laptop. In contrast, Canada Revenue has no full-time greeters or smiley faces.

Despite the spread of McDonaldization, some are speculating that it, like bureaucratisation, has

DIGITAL LIVING

eBayisation

Taking the eBay online auction site as its model, eBayisation implies that the digitalised world in which it exists is in the process of displacing in importance the material world that is the domain of McDonald's (Ahuvia and Izberk-Bilgin 2011). In an emerging era of global, Internet-based, and information-based enterprises, the concept of McDonaldization may be of declining utility.

The basic dimensions of eBayisation are very different from those of McDonaldization:

- *Variety.* eBay offers millions of products; McDonald's only a few dozen.

- *Unpredictability.* The predictable products of McDonald's are quite unlike the highly unpredictable products on eBay—for example, a Hero Chinese Symbol Engraved Stone Ocean Pebble Rock.

- *Highly specific and limited control.* Whereas eBay sellers interact directly with buyers of their products, with little involvement of the eBay organisation, McDonaldized systems exercise more widespread control.

McDonald's may be fast, but eBay is vast; McDonald's offers some things most of the time, but eBay offers almost everything all of the time. As our world continues to move in the direction of digitisation, eBayisation may prove to be a more useful concept than McDonaldization.

passed its peak. The above *Digital Living* box discusses an important online organisation—eBay—as well as the issue of whether it is important and different enough to be a new model of organisational development in the contemporary world.

NETWORK ORGANISATIONS

While the bureaucracy and the fast-food restaurant both continue to be important in the early twenty-first century, organisations continue to change and to evolve, and entirely new organisational forms are coming into existence. One such new form is the network organisation. As we will discuss in more detail below, the **network organisation** is defined by its networks and is characterized by a horizontal structure, fuzzy boundaries, dispersed decision making, and flexible production. It came about in the wake of the revolution in informational technology in the United States in the 1970s, including the infusion of television into North American life and the introduction of home computers, PDAs, and the Internet (S. Allan 2007). The network model is also inextricably entwined with globalisation. Most of the important functions and processes in the information age are increasingly dominated by these networks, and many of them are global in scope. This revolution led, in turn, to a fundamental restructuring of the global capitalist system beginning in the 1980s. For example, multinational corporations grew in importance, and those that were narrowly nation-based experienced serious declines or were, themselves, transformed into multinationals.

Characteristics of the Network Organisation

This new organisational form has several notable characteristics. Of greatest importance is the idea that an organisation is composed of several **networks**, or "interconnected nodes." A network organisation has the following characteristics:

- *Horizontal structure.* Instead of the vertical and hierarchical structures that characterize classic bureaucracies, network organisations are flatter, meaning that there are fewer positions between the top of the organisation and the bottom.

- *Fuzzy boundaries.* Network organisations are not seen as distinct entities with clear and definite boundaries, as would be the case with a bureaucracy. Rather, organisations intertwine with one another in many ways. Most obviously, they form strategic alliances with other organisations that have similar or complementary goals.

- *Dispersed decision making.* Many of the differences between network organisations and bureaucracies stem from a number of highly successful Japanese innovations, such as more collective decision making and involving many more people in the organisation in the decision-making process.

- *Flexible production.* Manufacturing organisations with a network model have moved away from mass production and toward more flexible production methods, such as variable and limited production runs.

An organisation with these characteristics is, in comparison with a bureaucracy, more open, more capable of expansion, more dynamic, and better able to innovate without disrupting the system.

In the global information economy, at least in developed nations, the nature of work is being transformed. Workers, including manufacturing employees, are dealing more with information and less with material processes (A. Bernard 2009; Caprile and Pascual 2011). In manufacturing this has reduced the total number of employees needed,

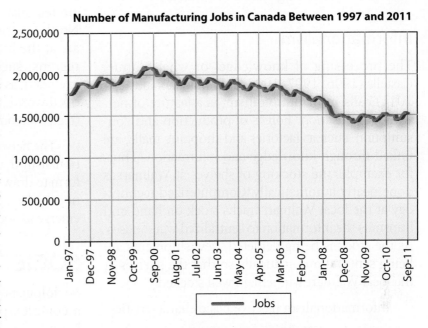

FIGURE 6.4 Canadian Manufacturing: Output versus Jobs, 1997–2011

SOURCE: From Statistics Canada, CANSIM Tables 377-0008 (manufacturing output in constant dollars) and 281-0023 (manufacturing employment); calculations by authors.

even as output increases (see Figure 6.4). In addition, network organisation allows for new kinds of work arrangements because information can flow anywhere, especially anywhere there is a computer. Thus, for example, more people can work from the comfort of their homes, in transit on airplanes, and in hotels anyplace in the world (B. Alexander, Ettema, and Dijst 2010; Kaufman-Scarbrough 2006). This change is reflected in the 2009 movie *Up in the Air,* which depicts efforts to move away from firing people in person and toward doing it via videoconferencing on the computer.

Informationalism

The processing of knowledge, or what Manuel Castells (1996, 1997, 1998; Subramanian and Katz 2011) calls **informationalism**, is a feature of network organisation. Forces of production and consumption, such as factories and shopping malls, are linked through knowledge and information. Thus, for example, the stocking of shelves at Walmart is done nearly automatically. Computerized technology at the local Walmart tracks stock on hand and transmits the information to centralized warehouses. As the stock is being depleted, new shipments are being sent out automatically so that the shelves at the local Walmart will remain well stocked.

Informationalism has five basic characteristics:

- Technologies act on information, such as the depletion of stock at Walmart.
- These technologies have a pervasive effect, as information transmitted to personal computers, PDAs, and smartphones increasingly becomes a part of all human activity.
- All organisations, and other systems using information technologies, are defined by a "networking logic" that allows them to affect a wide variety of processes and organisations to which they are linked. For example, Walmart has linkages to its many suppliers throughout the world.
- The new technologies are highly flexible, allowing them to adapt and to change constantly.
- The specific technologies associated with information are already merging into a highly integrated system that cuts across many different organisations and areas of

the world. Thus, for example, the Internet, e-mail, and text messaging link innumerable global organisations.

As a result of informationalism, a new, increasingly profitable global informational economy has emerged. The productivity of firms and nations depends on their ability to generate, process, and apply knowledge-based information efficiently. Global communication systems allow those involved in this economy to operate as a unit on a worldwide scale. While it is a global system, there are regional differences, even among those areas—North America, European Union, Asia Pacific—that are at the heart of the new global economy. Other regions, such as sub-Saharan Africa, are largely excluded, as are pockets of deprivation in the developed world, including poor areas in Canadian cities (e.g., Vancouver's downtown eastside).

The network organisation, as well as the informationalism that defines it, is the latest organisational form to draw sociologists' attention, but it is certainly not the last. New organisational forms are likely to emerge as society and the world continue to change.

SOCIETIES

Sociologists have traditionally defined society as a complex pattern of social relationships that is bounded in space and persists over time (Ray 2007). This definition has two key characteristics. First, it is very abstract. Second, this abstractness allows it to encompass the gamut of social relationships. Thus, in these terms, a triad (a three-person group) and any larger group would be a kind of society, as would Canada and other countries, as well as global organisations such as the United Nations and the International Monetary Fund.

There is a long tradition in sociology of thinking about, and studying, such highly diverse societal forms. A classic analysis of this type was created by Ferdinand Toennies ([1887] 1957), who differentiated between two broad types of societies—*gemeinschaft* and *gesellschaft*. He labelled traditional societies **gemeinschaft societies** and defined them as being characterized by face-to-face relations. Toennies considered families, rural villages, and small towns to be *gemeinschaft* societies. Such societies tend to be quite small because they are

based on such intimate interaction. Relationships between people were valued for their intrinsic qualities, such as familiarity and closeness and not, or at least not merely, for their utility. *Gemeinschaft* societies continue to exist in many parts of the world, including Canada.

More modern societies are **gesellschaft societies** characterized by impersonal, distant, and limited social relationships. In such societies those relationships tend to be entered into for what people can gain—relationships are often means to ends—rather than for their intrinsic qualities.

Gesellschaft societies can be small in scale; social groups and communities can have the characteristics, such as impersonality, of a *gesellschaft* society. For instance, employees within an office may work together 40 hours or more a week, but only interact with one another in a highly businesslike way. Furthermore, after they go home to their "real life," and intimate relationships, they are likely to rarely, if ever, interact with coworkers outside of the workplace. However, *gesellschaft* societies are much more likely to be large-scale societies, or to exist within them.

Of course, *gemeinschaft* and *gesellschaft* are ideal types. In the real world, including today's world, aspects of both exist in all societies. The abstract and broad-ranging definition of society mentioned above encompasses both *gemeinschaft* and *gesellschaft* societies, and everything in between. Furthermore, both concepts can be applied to every social relationship, from the smallest societies such as dyads and triads to the largest societies such as China.

Although the earlier general definition of society has its utility, *society* can be more narrowly and specifically—and usefully—defined as a relatively large population that lives in a given territory, has a social structure, and shares a culture. Canada, China, and Chile would be societies in this macro-level sense of the term; a triad or a group or an organisation would not be a society. This definition also fits the thrust of this chapter, which ends with a discussion of the most macroscopic global level of social organisation.

One of the best known theories of society in this sense was created by the leading structural-functionalist, Talcott Parsons. In fact, he wrote a book titled *Societies* (Parsons 1966). As a structural-functionalist, Parsons had a very positive view of macro-level societies. He was concerned with the major structures of societies, including the economy, the political system, systems responsible for transmitting culture and its norms and values (e.g., schools), and the legal system, which is responsible for the integration of society. Clearly, these are key components of society in the macro sense of the term.

Social theorists who analyze societies do not stop at their borders, but also examine the relationships among and between societies. In fact, there is an entire field—international relations—that deals

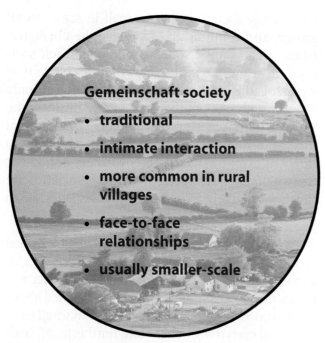

Gemeinschaft society

- traditional
- intimate interaction
- more common in rural villages
- face-to-face relationships
- usually smaller-scale

Gesellschaft society

- modern
- means-to-end interaction
- more common in towns and cities
- distant, limited relationships
- usually larger-scale

Comparison of *gemeinschaft* and *gesellschaft* societies

with these relationships. However, in recent years the focus of such scholarship has shifted beyond societies and even their interrelationships to the even more macroscopic global level.

THE GLOBAL

Most work on the global level of social organisation does not start with the concept of a society, but rather works with a different set of basic concepts. All of these concepts are consistent with the macroscopic sense of society:

- **Nation:** a large group of people linked through common descent, culture, language, or territory. Nations can exist in contiguous geographic areas regardless of country borders, as is the case with Kurds living in what is called Kurdistan, a region naively overlapping Iraq, Iran, and Turkey (see Figure 6.5). Nations can also be spread throughout much of the world, such as the Roma people, or gypsies, who live throughout Europe and increasingly in the United States and Canada.

- **State:** a political organisational structure with relatively autonomous officeholders (e.g., in Canada the prime minister functions largely independently of the senate and the Bank of Canada) and with its own rules and resources

coming largely from taxes. The Canadian government would be an example of a state.

- **Nation-state:** an entity that encompasses both the populations that define themselves as a nation and the organisational structure of the state. Israel is a nation-state since it has a state government and encompasses a nation of Jews (although there are large numbers of Muslims in Israel and in the occupied territories as well).

Of greater importance in the global age is the idea that these entities, especially the nation-state, are losing influence due to globalisation and broad global processes.

Controlling Global Flows

The nation-state is under siege largely because it has lost or is losing control over a number of global flows (Cerny 2007). In many ways, it is informationalism that threatens the nation-state. E-mail and tweets, to take two examples, flow around the world readily and quickly. There is little or nothing the nation-state can do to stop or limit those flows, although China, among others, keeps trying. One example is China's Internet "Great Firewall," which is described in the next *Digital Living* box (see also Chapter 1). During the 2011 uprisings in Egypt, the government attempted to locate an "off

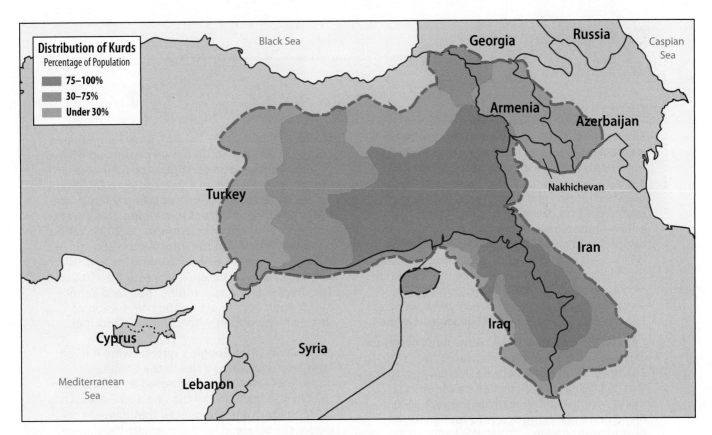

FIGURE 6.5 The Kurdish Nation and the Countries in Which It Lies

SOURCE: From *The Kurdish Nation and the Countries in Which It Lies,* GlobalSecurity.org.

switch" for the Internet to prevent the flow of news and images about the protests but were unable to block them completely (Richtel 2011b). There are many economic, financial, and technological flows around the world that involve information of various kinds. Global information flows have the potential to subvert the authority of nation-states because they cover a much larger geographic area than the nation-state. This is especially true of information that would cast a negative light on the nation-state (for example, distribution of information throughout China about the great inequality that exists there or its human rights abuses).

A more specific example of the decreasing ability of nation-states to isolate themselves from global processes is the economic crisis that began in the United States in late 2007 and cascaded rapidly around the world. For example, dramatic drops in the American stock market (see the 2011 movie *Margin Call* for a fictionalized treatment of the origins of that economic crisis) were followed by declines in many other stock markets in the world. Similarly, bank failures in the United States

were quickly followed by even more ruinous bank failures in other countries, most notably Iceland and Ireland. This series of events illustrates the importance and power of global flows, and demonstrates the inability of the nation-state to do much, if anything, to limit their impact within its borders on its economy and the lives of its citizens. "In a global financial system, national borders are porous" (Landler 2008a:C1). Global economic flows move more quickly than ever, if not instantaneously, and are so fluid that they are difficult, if not impossible, to stop with the barriers available to nation-states.

Information and economic flows are just two of the many global flows that nation-states cannot control. Among the others are flows of undocumented immigrants, new social movements, expertise in various domains, terrorists, criminals, drugs, money (including laundered money and other financial instruments), sex trafficking (as shown in Global Flow Map 6.1), and much else. Then there are global problems, such as HIV/AIDS, H1N1 flu, tuberculosis (TB), and the effects of global warming, which flow

DIGITAL LIVING

China's Great Firewall

The Internet is often talked about as a place where people from around the world come together to freely exchange ideas. But, to lift a phrase from George Orwell, some Internet users are more equal than others. In fact, many countries—Iran, North Korea, and China, to name a few—impose restrictions on what information can pass in and out of their computer networks. When users in these countries attempt to access sites that we might consider to be mundane parts of our everyday lives, such as Facebook, Google, Twitter, or one of the mainstream news services, they receive a screen saying that access is denied.

China's "Great Firewall" is the most notorious example of censorship on the web (P. Norris 2010; Zhang 2006), perhaps because it extends to more than 1.3 billion people or 19.6 percent of the world's population. As early as the year 2000, China began blocking access to foreign news sites such as *Le Monde,* CNN, the BBC, and *The New York Times.* Named after one of the man-made wonders of the world (the Great Wall of China), the Great Firewall is the world's largest form of online censorship. According to one report (Watts 2006), "An internet police force—reportedly numbering 30,000—trawls websites and chatrooms, erasing anti-Communist comments and posting pro-government messages." A website called greatfirewallofchina.org allows you to search the Internet through a server on the Chinese mainland and see which sites are currently blocked.

Of greater concern to many in the West is the fact that many leading tech companies (including BlackBerry, Microsoft, Yahoo!, and Google) have agreed to engage in their own censorship of Chinese content as a condition for their access to Chinese markets (Dann and Haddow 2008). Many accuse these companies of violating the human rights of Chinese citizens by helping China crack down on dissidents. For example, in 2005, Yahoo! provided China with the information about the accounts of a Chinese dissident, who is still serving a 10-year sentence as a result (Helft 2007). The dissident, Wang Xiaoning, has sued Yahoo! in U.S. court for "abetting the commission of torture" by working with Chinese authorities.

In 2010, after Google's systems were hacked by agents with alleged ties to the Chinese government, the company moved its servers from the Chinese mainland to the semiautonomous city of Hong Kong and announced that it would no longer cooperate in blocking results for Chinese users (R. Stone and Xin 2010). However, within a matter of days, the Chinese government was able to use its own infrastructure to reinstate the censorship and reassert its power and control over global flows of ideas and information.

While Google is the most popular search engine in the world, it has roughly half of the market share (33 percent) held by China's leading search engine, Baidu, which controls 63 percent of the market. Baidu, which is based in China, cannot leverage the same resources against the Chinese government that the American Google can, so it is likely that censorship will continue in China for the foreseeable future.

---

around the world readily and cannot be handled very well by a nation-state operating on its own.

A great deal of evidence today indicates that the nation-state has become increasingly porous, but the fact is that no nation-state has ever been able to exercise complete control over its borders (Bauman 1992). For example, people's ability to travel from one European country to another was largely unimpeded until the World War I era, when passports were introduced on a large scale for the first time. It is not the porosity of the nation-state that is new, but rather the dramatic increase in that porosity.

Thus, the largest unit of analysis in sociology has now become the globe and especially the global flows that best define globalisation today. The concept of globalisation appears throughout this book in an informal sense, but it is now time for the formal definition of *globalisation*: "a transplanetary *process* or set of *processes* involving increasing *liquidity* and the growing multidirectional *flows* of people, objects, places and information as well as the *structures* they

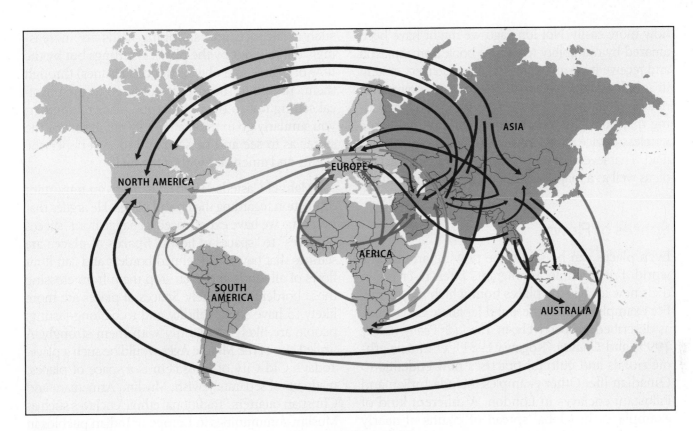

GLOBAL FLOW MAP 6.1 Major Routes of Sex Trafficking, 2006

SOURCE: United Nations Office on Drugs and Crime. 2006. *Trafficking in Persons: Global Patterns.*

encounter and create that are *barriers* to, or *expedite,* those flows" (Ritzer 2010c:2; see also Chapter 15). Clearly, this is a view that goes beyond the nation-state and sees it enmeshed in, and subordinated to, a global set of flows and structures.

OTHER GLOBAL FLOWS

Globalisation is increasingly characterized by great flows of not just information, ideas, and images but also objects and people. For example, food now flows more quickly and to more people around the world. Examples of food being sold in locales far from their source include fresh fruit from Chile (Goldfrank 2005), fresh sushi from Japan, and live lobsters from Prince Edward Island. Looking at a very different kind of flow, migration within countries and from one country to another has become more common as well.

In addition, other kinds of physical objects are becoming increasingly more liquid and thus able to

Globalisation entails increasing liquidity and the multidirectional flows of people, places, objects, structures, and information around the world. As globalisation increases, the world becomes a vastly more interconnected place.

flow more easily. Not long ago we might have been amazed by our ability to order a book from Amazon and receive it via an express package delivery system in as little as a day. That method, however, now seems notably sluggish compared to the speed of downloading that book, in perhaps less than a minute, on a wireless device such as Amazon's Kindle or Apple's iPad. That level of liquidity and flow is a major aspect of, as well as a major contributor to, globalisation.

Spaces of Flows

Even places can be said to be flowing around the world. For example, immigrants often re-create in their new locales the places from which they came. For example, both Chinese and Japanese Canadians, as described, respectively, in *The Jade Peony* (Choy 1995) and *Obasan* (Kogawa 1981), chronicle ethnic rituals and cultural practises now endemic to Canadian life. Other examples include Indian and Pakistani enclaves in London. A different kind of example is the global spread of chains of nearly identical fast-food restaurants. Furthermore, places such as airports and shopping malls are increasingly defined not by the physical settings but by the flow of people and objects (food, airplanes) through them. You go to the airport not to go to the physical setting but to travel from one place to another; you similarly go to the mall not so much to visit the stores as to see and be seen and to experience the events and amenities within the mall.

Manuel Castells (1996) has made an important distinction regarding the flow of places. He argues that over time we have experienced a change from "spaces of places" to "spaces of flows." **Spaces of places** are settings that have well-defined borders and can limit flows of all kinds and even stop them from crossing those borders completely. Spaces of places are more likely to have some solidity and to be long-lasting; people are likely to identify with them strongly. A walled city of the Middle Ages would be such a place. Today's Old City of Jerusalem is a space of places, made up of separate Jewish, Muslim, Armenian, and Christian quarters. Traditional ethnic enclaves such as Muslim communities in Europe or Indian pueblos in the United States also have many of the characteristics of a space of place.

Today, in contrast, we are witnessing the emergence of an increasing number of **spaces of flows**, which are unlikely to have clear and defensible borders; they are likely to be quite fluid and more likely than spaces of places to be temporary in nature. People are less likely to identify strongly with the more evanescent spaces of flows. An airport is an excellent example of a space of flows and indeed is a telling example of spaces in the global age. The Tom Hanks movie *The Terminal* (2004) further illustrates the nature of an airport when his character is forced to remain there for months because he lacks the papers necessary to enter the United States. The discomforts associated with the fact that he is unable to move, that for him the airport has become a space of place, only serve to make still clearer that an airport is fundamentally a space of flows. Drive-through windows at fast-food restaurants are another good example of a space of flows; virtually all there is to this space are the flows. Yet another good example is

The Old City of Jerusalem is a space of places, made up of separate Jewish, Muslim, Armenian, and Christian quarters. The Temple Mount has been one of the world's most important—and most contested—religious sites for thousands of years.

the shopping mall. The movie *Paul Blart: Mall Cop* (2009) demonstrates the fluid and temporary nature of relationships in the mall: Because of this, no one there takes things very seriously, including the work of the mall cop.

Landscapes

Although global flows and globalisation contribute to some degree of homogenisation of the social experience around the world, they also contribute to greater global cultural diversity and heterogeneity. A very important contribution to thinking on the latter aspects of global flows is Arjun Appadurai's (1996) work on what he calls **landscapes**—*scapes* for short—or fluid, irregular, and variable global flows that produce different results throughout the world. As we will see below, these scapes can involve the flow of many different things, including people and ideas. At the heart of Appadurai's thinking are five types of landscapes that operate independently of one another to some degree, and may even conflict with one another:

- **Ethnoscapes** involve the movement, or fantasies about movement, of various individuals and groups such as tourists and refugees. The ethnoscape of undocumented immigrants is of particular concern these days. They are often poor people who have in the main been forced to move because of poverty and poor job prospects in their home country. They also move because of the belief, sometimes the fantasy, that economic conditions will be better for them elsewhere in the world, especially in the more developed countries of Canada, the United States, and western Europe.

- **Technoscapes** involve mechanical technologies such as the containerized ships now used to transport freight, informational technologies such as the Internet, and the material such as refrigerators and e-mail that moves so quickly and freely throughout the world via those technologies.

- **Financescapes** involve the use of various financial instruments in order to allow huge sums of money and other things of economic value (e.g., stocks, bonds, precious metals [especially gold]) to move through nations and around the world at great speed, almost instantaneously. The great global economic meltdown beginning in 2007 demonstrated quite clearly the importance and the power of financescapes in the contemporary world.

- **Mediascapes** involve both the electronic capability to produce and transmit information around the world and the images of the world that these media create and disseminate. Those who write blogs and download photos (e.g., Flickr) and videos (YouTube), global filmmakers and film distributors, global TV networks (CNN, Al Jazeera), and even old-fashioned newspapers and magazines create a variety of mediascapes.

- **Ideoscapes** are, like mediascapes, involved with images, although they are largely restricted to political images that are in line

The 2004 film *Control Room* documented Qatar-based Al Jazeera's coverage of the United States' 2003 invasion of Iraq. Addressing such issues as media bias, freedom of the press, and Al Jazeera's prominence and portrayal around the world, *Control Room* provides a unique look into the controversial and widely popular television network, as well as its supporters and detractors.

Arjun Appadurai (1949–, Indian)

- Appadurai was born and educated in Bombay (now Mumbai), India, and graduated from Elphinstone College with an intermediate arts degree before coming to the United States.

- He gained his BA at Brandeis University in 1970 and his MA in 1973 and PhD in 1976 from the University of Chicago.

- Appadurai's doctoral research was a study of a car festival held in the Parthasarathy Temple in Madras, India.

- Currently, Appadurai is the Goddard Professor of Media, Culture, and Communication at New York University.

- He is the founder (and now president) of PUKAR—Partners for Urban Knowledge, Action and Research—a nonprofit organisation in Mumbai.

- He has served as a consultant or advisor for many public and private organisations, including UNESCO and the World Bank.

- His current research focuses on ethnic violence in the context of globalisation, especially in Mumbai, and grassroots globalisation.

- His diverse interests are reflected in the title of his website www.arjunappadurai.org: "Writings & Reflections on Globalization, Food, Cinema, Design, & Cities."

with the ideologies of nation-states. Also included here are images and counterideologies produced by social movements that are oriented toward supplanting those in power or at least gaining a portion of that power. Thus, for example, the United States has one ideoscape that disseminates negative images and information about al-Qaeda; in turn, al-Qaeda has an ideoscape that responds with similarly negative images and information about the United States. News conferences by U.S. presidents attacking al-Qaeda's terrorism are met by videotapes by al-Qaeda leaders critiquing American imperialism. Ideoscapes may be disseminated through mediascapes and technoscapes (for example, shipping propaganda-laden books by containerized shipping throughout the world).

Further increasing the global heterogeneity that results from the interaction of these landscapes is the fact that the impact of one can be at variance, even in conflict, with another. In addition, these landscapes are interpreted differently by people and groups in different parts of the world, depending on both the culture in which they exist and their own subjective interpretations of the scapes. Despite the fact that powerful forces create at least some of these scapes, those who merely live in them or pass through them have the power not only to redefine them in idiosyncratic ways but also ultimately to subvert them in many different ways. For example, those on guided tours of various parts of the world designed to show a given locale in a particularly positive light can break off from the tour and see and hear things that lead to a very different impression of the locale. When they return home, they can portray that locale in a way that contradicts the image presented by the tour creators and guides.

GLOBAL BARRIERS

The globe, and the flows that increasingly pervade it, are of central concern to sociology. However, there is another aspect of globalisation that is of increasing concern to sociology, and that is the various global barriers to these flows. The world is made up of not just a series of flows but also many structure such as trade agreements, regulatory agencies, borders, customs barriers, standards, and so on (Inda and Rosaldo 2008). Any thoroughgoing account of globalisation needs to look at the ways in which structures both produce and enhance flows as well as alter and even block them. In other words, there is interplay between flows and structures, especially between flows and the structures that are created in an attempt to inhibit or to stop them (Shamir 2005).

GL🌐BALISATION

Cricket in India

The sport of cricket has attracted a lot of attention from those interested in globalisation in general and sport in particular (Appadurai 1996; J. Kaufman and Patterson 2005). Cricket was brought to India by the British colonialists, with the first recorded cricket match being played by British sailors in western India in 1721. For some time, Indians were only spectators as they watched games between army soldiers and officers. But Indians eventually began playing cricket themselves. In 1932 India played its first professional match against the British (BBC News 2004). That game took on an international feel and gave many Indians a sense of nationhood 15 years before winning their independence from Great Britain in 1947.

Arjun Appadurai (1996) argues that over the years, cricket has become decolonized, indigenized in India so that it is "no longer English-mediated" (p. 104). He recognizes that imperial England needed to create cricket teams in its colonies that it could play against and presumably defeat easily. India and the other colonies were perfect for this role. However, the Indians have transformed cricket and made it their own.

Of particular importance in the transformation of cricket in India has been the role played by the media and language. Mass Indian publications—books, magazines, and pamphlets—liberated cricket from its "Englishness" and dealt with cricket matches in native terms; they "vernacularized" cricket. The game came to be played widely in the streets, playgrounds, and villages of India, the second most populous country in the world. Indians also read about their favourite teams and stars and heard about them on the radio and saw them on TV. This served to make cricket an important part of the fantasy lives of many Indians. Top Indian cricket players are among the highest-paid celebrities in one of the world's fastest-growing economies.

In India, and elsewhere in former English colonies, cricket has come to be dominated by the locals and not by England; the Indians have "hijacked" the game from the English. In the process, they have transformed cricket, making it a much more aggressive game, one that is less "sportsmanlike" and, perhaps most important, much more spectacular. To Appadurai (1996), cricket "now belongs to a different moral and aesthetic world" (p. 107). It has become an "instrument for mobilizing national sentiment in the service of transnational spectacles" (Appadurai 1996:109). Thus, to take one example, matches

between rivals India and Pakistan resemble a war. When the two countries faced off in the semifinals of the 2011 Cricket World Cup, the game held the nation's (and undoubtedly Pakistan's) attention, with many Indians skipping work to watch the game (Betegeri 2011). In such matches, as well as in many other international cricket matches, "England . . . is no longer part of the equation" (Appadurai 1996:109).

While there is much merit in Appadurai's analysis, it is important to remember that cricket was brought to India by the British. It is out of the interaction between the cricket brought by the British and the cricket produced by the Indians that the distinctive form of Indian cricket emerged. In today's world, many cultural forms involve such combinations and unique outcomes.

Cricketers play an informal game in Varanasi, India, along the banks of the Ganges River.

PUBLIC SOCIOLOGY

The "Flat World" of Thomas Friedman

Thomas Friedman (1953–), winner of several Pulitzer Prizes, is one of the most influential journalists in the world. In part, his influence comes via his regular columns in *The New York Times,* but more important for our purposes are his books, especially those on globalisation.

In *The Lexus and the Olive Tree* (1999) Friedman sought to capture the essence of globalisation, especially its tensions, in his distinction between the modern automobile (the Lexus) and the ancient realities (the olive tree) that continue to dominate much of the world. Friedman sees the Lexus as a threat to the olive tree. That is, "all the anonymous, transnational, homogenizing, standardizing market forces and technologies" constitute a threat to local culture and identity (T. Friedman 1999:29). While Friedman sees movement toward the Lexus model in the global world of today, he argues that there is a need for a "healthy balance" between it and the model of the olive tree.

Friedman has a highly positive view of globalisation, seeing it as a democratising force in the realms of technology, finance, and information. Above all else, to Friedman globalisation marks the triumph of free market capitalism. When a country recognizes the rules of the free market and agrees to abide by them, it dons what he calls the "Golden Straitjacket." As far as he is concerned, if nations around the world want to be successful, they have no choice but to don that jacket. In doing so, they experience the advantages of globalisation, but also the negative effects associated with this one-size-fits-all model. For example, many Canadian jobs have been lost to other areas of the world where wages are lower.

The World Is Flat: A Brief History of the Twenty-first Century (T. Friedman 2005) is even better known and more influential than Friedman's earlier book on

Thomas Friedman

globalisation. The central point of this book is that the barriers and hurdles to competing successfully on a global scale have declined, if not completely disappeared. In other words, the global playing field has been increasingly levelled, making it possible for more and more people to play, to compete, and to win. Small companies and even individuals anywhere in the world have an unprecedented ability to compete successfully on a global basis. Friedman (2005) is not just describing a trend but praising it as well, and this is clear when he says that the "world is flattening and rising at the same time" (p. 231). In his view, everyone is benefiting from the flat world.

The flat world thesis implies an elimination of all barriers to free trade—and virtually everything else, for that matter. That is, in a flat world, trade is free to roam everywhere and to get there without impediments. Indeed, the opposite of a flat world is one with lots of barriers—some high, some low—that serve to impede free trade. Those barriers include tariffs, quotas, restrictions, regulations, and so on.

Many sociologists disagree (Antonio 2007) with Friedman about the desirability of all global flows, especially those associated with free trade, and the need to eliminate all barriers to them. Not all global flows are desirable, and at least some barriers are worth retaining in order to protect some individuals and structures from the ravages of free-floating global flows. Further, most sociologists and other social scientists disagree with Friedman on the existence, or even the possibility, of a flat world (an entire 2008 issue of *Cambridge Journal of Regions, Economy and Society* is devoted to the topic: "The World Is Not Flat: Putting Globalization in Its Place"). Much of sociology is premised on the idea that those with power will erect barriers of all sorts that enhance their interests and that, in the process, adversely affect others and create great inequalities.

As has already been mentioned, the most important and most obvious barriers to global flows are those constructed by nation-states. There are borders, gates, guards, passport controls, customs agents, health inspectors, trade regulations, and so on, in most countries in the world. Although undocumented immigrants, contraband goods, and digitized messages do get through those barriers, some other phenomena that nation-states deem to be not in their national interest are successfully blocked or impeded. For example, in 2006 the U.S. government blocked a deal in which a Dubai company was to purchase an American company involved in the business of running America's ports (*The Economist* 2006). The government felt that such ownership would be a threat to national security since foreign nationals, perhaps enemies, could acquire information that would allow terrorists easy access to U.S. ports. As another example, in 2008 the Canadian government blocked the $1.3 billion sale of the space technology division of Vancouver-based MacDonald, Dettwiler and Associates Ltd. to Alliant Techsystems Inc. of the United States, arguing that the sale was not in the best interests of Canada. In 2010 the U.S. government blocked the sale by an American firm

of its fibre optics business to a Chinese investment corporation on the grounds that it would constitute a threat to America's national security (Bushell-Embling 2010). Some have noted that as nations focus more on "nationalism and militarism," their openness to international trade and other formalized "flows" across borders decreases (Acemoglu and Yared 2010).

Are Global Barriers Effective?

However, many of the barriers created by nation-states are not effective. For instance, it is highly doubtful that the very expensive fence under construction between Mexico and the United States will be able, assuming it is ever fully completed, to reduce significantly the flow of undocumented immigrants to the United States. Similarly, it is not clear whether the wall between Israel and the West Bank will stop the flow of terrorists into Israel the next time hostilities in the Middle East flare up. The wall is certainly not stopping Palestinians and Israelis from communicating person-to-person via digital media, as the next *Digital Living* box demonstrates.

In the European Union (EU), barriers to movement between member countries have been greatly reduced, if not eliminated. In creating a structure that allows people and products to move much more freely and much more quickly, the EU has attempted to make Europe much more a space of flows than a space of places. However, at least one country—Denmark—has sought to reestablish border controls (BBC News 2011). After more than 10 years with no border controls, the Danish government claimed that it has experienced an increase in transborder crime and that new customs inspections would help curb organized crime. The move, however, has been sharply criticized by some other EU countries, such as Germany, which see the open borders as essential to European unity.

Organisational Barriers

There are many different kinds of organisations that, though they may expedite flows for some, create all sorts of barriers for others.

Palestinians climb over the controversial Israeli-built concrete barrier as clashes break out in 2011 between Israeli security forces and Palestinian activists on the 44th anniversary of the 1967 Six-Day War. While some barriers to the flows of globalisation are intangible, some of the most important and obvious barriers are the physical obstacles constructed by nation-states.

DIGITAL LIVING

A Virtual Bridge Between Palestinians and Israelis

While processes of globalisation have made it easier for people and resources to move around the world, some borders continue to be rigorously defended and policed (Naples 2009). One such border exists between Palestine and Israel, with physical contact between the people in the two nations being highly limited. Leaders from the two sides rarely meet on a face-to-face basis and, in fact, have not met since 2009. Interaction between the people themselves is greatly limited because heavily guarded, gated, and walled borders stand between them, and residents face constant surveillance (Zureik 2011). Concern in Israel about terrorism makes the crossing difficult for Palestinians who have jobs or relatives in Israel and impossible for suspected Palestinian terrorists.

While it is difficult to move people physically across these borders, Palestinians and Israelis can communicate virtually via the Internet. The site Facebook.com/yalaYL (*yala* is Arabic for "let's go"; YL stands for *young leaders*) was created in 2011 by an Israeli, the president of the Peres Center for Peace, who said, "All communication today is on the Internet—sex, war, business—why not peace? . . . Today we have no brave leaders on either side, so I am turning to a new generation, the Tahrir Square [the main site of the Egyptian protests that brought down the regime of Hosni Mubarak] and Facebook generation." Even though the site is Israeli in origin, it is supported by Palestinians, including a Palestinian National Authority official, who said, "Believe me, they don't know each other at all. . . . Since Israelis and Palestinians don't meet face to face anymore, this is a virtual place to meet" (Bronner 2011b). More than half the active visitors to the site have been Arabs, and most of those have been Palestinians.

While lots of postings deal with common everyday interests such as music and sports, of greatest importance are those that are concerned with peace between Israelis and Palestinians.

Said a Palestinian graduate student, "I joined immediately because right now, without a peace process and with Israelis and Palestinians physically separated, it is really important for us to be interacting without barriers" (Bronner 2011b). The hope of the founder of the site is that the joint projects that develop between Israelis and Palestinians on the site will lead the leaders of both sides in the direction of seeking peace.

The site also enhances the level of mutual understanding between Palestinians and Israelis. An 18-year-old Palestinian college student said, "This is my first contact with Israelis. . . . A friend of mine told me about it, and I think it's cool. I joined a few days ago. It helps me understand the difference between Israel and the occupation" (Bronner 2011b). These Israelis and Palestinians are breaking through the physical borders and reconnecting in a more fluid, globally connected online world. Inspired by the model of yalaYL, groups around the world (including the Italian government, a Barcelona soccer team, and MTV) have sought to become involved in the processes of globalisation.

For example, nation-states create protectionist tariff systems (Reuveny and Thompson 2001) that help their own farms send agricultural products (wheat) and manufacturers send goods (automobiles) across the borders of other nation-states while inhibiting the inflow of goods from their foreign competition. Another example is found in the two-tier system of passport control at international airports, where citizens usually pass through quickly and easily while foreigners often wait in long lines.

Multinational corporations use market competition rather than trade policies to achieve similar results. Toyota, for instance, is devoted to optimising the flow of its automobiles to all possible markets throughout the world. It also seeks to compete with and outperform other multinational corporations in the automobile business. If it is successful, the flow of automobiles from competing corporations will be greatly reduced, further advantaging Toyota.

Labour unions are also organisations devoted to promoting the flow of some things while working against the flow of others (Bronfenbrenner 2007). Unions often oppose, for example, the flow of undocumented immigrants because they are likely to work for lower pay and fewer, if any, benefits such as health insurance than indigenous, unionized workers. Similarly, labour unions oppose the flow of goods produced in nonunion shops, in other countries as well as their own. They do so because the success of nonunion shops would put downward pressure on wages and benefits, adversely affecting unionized shops and, in turn, hurt the union and its members. On the other hand, many employers are eager to look the other way when hiring undocumented immigrant labour. Because these labourers lack documentation, they are easy to exploit and take advantage of; employers can threaten to deport them if workers demand higher wages and better working conditions, or threaten to organize.

More Open Organisations

Organisations of many types that seek to control global flows are facing increasing competition from organisations that are becoming more fluid and open. The best known computer operating systems are produced by Microsoft (Vista and Windows 7). They cost a great deal and are closed: Only those who work for the company can, at least legally, work on and modify them. In contrast, a traditional closed organisation—IBM—has embraced the Linux system, a free computer operating system that welcomes changes contributed by anyone in the world with the needed skills. IBM has also opened up more and more of its own operations to outside inputs. Another example is Apple, whose Macintosh operating system has traditionally been closed but which is allowing outsiders to produce applications for its iPhone and iPad. Many other manufacturers of smartphones have followed suit. The free online encyclopaedia Wikipedia, or wikis more generally, encourage virtually anyone, anywhere in the world, to contribute. In contrast, traditional and very costly dictionaries such as *Merriam-Webster's Collegiate Dictionary* (2008) and encyclopaedias like *Encyclopaedia Britannica* (2010) and *The Blackwell Encyclopedia of Sociology* (Ritzer 2007) are closed to contributions from anyone other than selected and invited experts.

In October 2011, the U.S. Senate passed a bill that would impose tariffs on Chinese goods imported into the United States. Proponents argued that drastic measures were necessary to counter unfavourable Chinese currency manipulation, while detractors warned that if the bill became law, it might initiate a trade war between China and the United States.

Even with the new open systems, structural realities help some and hinder others. For example, to contribute to Linux or Wikipedia one must have a computer, computer expertise, and access, especially high-speed access to the Internet. Clearly, those without economic advantages—people in the lower classes in developed countries or people who live in the less developed countries of the Global South—are on the other side of the "digital divide" and do not have access to the required tools. As a result, they are unable to contribute to, or to gain from, open systems to the same degree as those in more privileged positions. Recently released findings that women are less likely than men to contribute to Wikipedia suggest that there are additional social factors to be considered as well (N. Cohen 2011). This further suggests that women in the Global South are doubly disadvantaged when it comes to access to these open systems—and much else.

Unions have been prominent in the push to stop the flight of manufacturing jobs offshore. Here workers in London, Ontario, protest the closing of Electro-Motive Diesel in a move that saw over 500 manufacturing jobs leave Canada.

Though unions often oppose the flow of undocumented immigrants into America, many individuals and families persist, entering the United States at any cost.

Thus, despite the new openness, most organisations and systems remain closed to various flows. These barriers usually benefit some (elites, males) and disadvantage others (the poor, females).

SUMMARY

In this chapter, we focus on the macro end of the micro-macro continuum with a sociological examination of organisations, societies, and the globe. The classical sociologist Max Weber was particularly interested in organisations, specifically the bureaucracy. Much sociological work on organisations is based on Weber's model of bureaucracy. However, this work often found his model to be unrealistic.

One critique of Weber's model is that bureaucracies are not as highly rational as Weber believed and that their rationality is limited by the instabilities and conflicts that exist in organisations. Other research dealt with the irrationalities that often accompany the seemingly rational actions associated with bureaucracy. Although power is supposed to be held by many individuals in a bureaucratic organisation, most often people in a small group at the top obtain and exercise far more power than they are supposed to have.

There have been several changes to bureaucratic organisations over the last several decades. One major change is that franchising, especially of McDonaldized fast-food restaurants, has become an increasingly important model for organisations seeking to operate more rationally. This model is applicable to both large corporations and relatively small outlets that are crucial parts of these organisations. Another difference between McDonaldization and bureaucratisation is the greater applicability of the former to organisations devoted to consumption, rather than production.

Another new organisational form is network organisations. Compared with classic bureaucracies, networks are less hierarchical, more open and flexible, and more capable of expansion and innovation.

The next level of social organisation on the micro-macro continuum is the society, a relatively large population that lives in a given territory, has a social structure, and shares a culture. Talcott Parsons identified several structures that are particularly important to modern societies, including the economy, the political system, the systems responsible for transmitting culture and its norms and values, and the legal system.

Sociological research on the global, the most macro of social structures, has its own set of basic concepts. A key structure in global analysis is the nation-state, which combines the organisational structure of the state and a population that defines itself as a nation of people with shared characteristics. However, the nation-state as a form of social organisation is under siege because of global flows over which it has little control—for example, flows of

information, economic phenomena, and new social movements.

Consequently, sociologists are coming to focus more attention on the global, the process of globalisation, and in particular the global flows that best define globalisation. Manuel Castells, for instance, argues that globalisation has brought a change from spaces of place to spaces of flows. Arjun Appadurai focuses on five different types of landscapes or scapes. Each global setting has a unique combination of these scapes. The result is global cultural diversity and heterogeneity. There are also limits to global flows, mainly created by macro-level entities like nation-states and labour unions.

KEY TERMS

- Authority   197
- Bureaucracy   197
- Bureaucratic personality   200
- Bounded rationality   199
- Charismatic authority   199
- Domination   197
- Ethnoscapes   219
- Financescapes   219
- *Gemeinschaft* societies   212
- *Gesellschaft* societies   213
- Ideoscapes   219
- Informal organisation   200
- Informationalism   212
- Landscapes (scapes)   219
- Mediascapes   219

- Nation   214
- Nation-state   214
- Network organisation   210
- Networks   211
- Offshore outsourcing   208
- Oligarchy   201
- Organisation   196
- Outsourcing   207
- Rational-legal authority   197
- Spaces of flows   218
- Spaces of places   218
- State   214
- Technoscapes   219
- Traditional authority   198

THINKING ABOUT SOCIOLOGY

1. What are the characteristics of the ideal-typical bureaucracy? What are some of the ways the ideal-typical bureaucracy is unrealistic?

2. It is often the case that those who occupy offices lower in the bureaucratic hierarchy have greater knowledge and competence than those who rank above them. What does this suggest about

the ideal-typical bureaucracy? Can you think of examples from your own experiences where this is the case?

3. According to Weber, what are the three types of legitimate authority? How is rational-legal authority related to his concept of bureaucracy?

4. Over the last several decades, what changes have bureaucratic organisations undergone?

How are these changes reflective of increasing globalisation?

5. What is informationalism, and how has informationalism affected the global economy? How is the emergence of informationalism related to the development of new communication technologies such as the Internet, social networking sites, and smartphones?

6. How has the process of globalisation threatened the nation-state? What sorts of barriers have nation-states developed to limit global flows? What sorts of flows have nation-states been unable to limit?

7. In what ways has globalisation created a shift from spaces of places to spaces of flows? What have been the benefits and disadvantages of this shift?

8. Discuss each of Appadurai's landscapes, with special focus on the disjunctures (with examples) among and between them. What are the implications of these disjunctures for the process of globalisation?

9. How are network organisations different from classic bureaucracies? In what ways are network organisations reflective of what Thomas Friedman would call the "flat world"?

10. How are open-source technologies reflective of a more fluid and open world? What structural barriers have transnational corporations created to limit these open-source technologies? What do you think is going to be the direction of the future? Why?

APPLYING THE SOCIOLOGICAL IMAGINATION

You are at the centre of two of the key issues discussed in this chapter—globalisation and networks. Try to list the many ways in which your life on any given day is affected by globalisation. Now enumerate the many networks in which you are involved. How many of those networks are global in scope? Which ones? How has your involvement in each of them affected your sense and understanding of other parts of the world as well as the globe as a whole?

ACTIVE SOCIOLOGY

In this chapter, we discuss the concept of *prosumer* and describe how society is increasingly organized around people being both consumers and producers. One part of society that prosumerism has almost completely inundated is the travel industry. Traditionally, professionals guided your planning—from making reservations and how to get the best deals to where to find the most romantic restaurants. Today, whether planning a summer vacation or a Friday night date, you are the planner, and the ideas are at your fingertips. Sites such as Expedia (www .expedia.ca) allow you to purchase all of your leisure and travel needs at one site—airline tickets, hotels, restaurants, and rental cars. You can choose from premade packages or create your own. When you are ready to check out, you are even offered add-ons: tours and special events. Not sure where to go? Expedia will provide you with reviews and images from other amateur travellers. You can even take it on the go with a smartphone app or connection to your Facebook account. Browse Expedia or a comparable site and make a comprehensive list of everything that one can do there. How much of what you can do and see is provided by a professional, and how much is provided by various "prosumers"? How do you think this has changed the leisure and travel industry? What other travel and leisure sites or apps do you know of that turn the customer into the prosumer?

STUDENT STUDY SITE

Visit the student study site at **www.sagepub.com/ritzercanadian** for additional web quizzes for further review.

DEVIANCE AND CRIME

As a culture shifts, so too does its definition of deviance. And as global cultures change, groups invariably struggle to revise or reaffirm prevailing norms and laws—those regarding sexual deviance are no different.

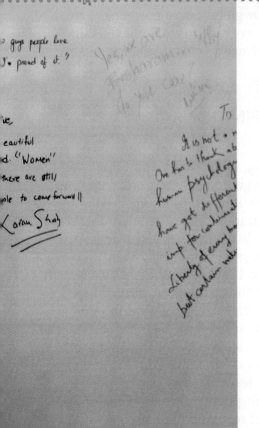

In 2011, more than 3,000 women, men, and transgendered individuals walked the streets of Toronto in the inaugural SlutWalk, a march in protest of the perception that provocative clothing choices encourage—and even excuse—rape and other forms of sexual abuse. SlutWalk marches, often accompanied by speeches and workshops, have since been held in Australia, England, India, Brazil, South Africa, and several U.S. cities.

The Toronto SlutWalk was organised in response to an address by Police Constable Michael Sanguinetti to a group of law school students. During the address, the constable said, "I've been told I'm not supposed to say this; however, women should avoid dressing like sluts in order not to be victimized" (Rush 2011).

Sanguinetti's comments speak volumes about western perceptions of sexual deviance. The pejorative label slut *is applied to a woman who deviates (or is believed to deviate) from expected norms and engages in sexual activity outside of a committed relationship. No matter her actual sexual conduct, any woman who dresses in a way that deviates from a normalised (thus, acceptable) presentation of sexuality may be assumed to be a slut. Because such women are (or present themselves as) sexually deviant, Sanguinetti's reasoning follows, they should expect—possibly deserve—to be punished.*

However, a 2003 study found that victims' attire is not a significant factor in sexual assault. Instead, rapists look for signs of passivity and submissiveness—traits that are actually more likely to be associated with wearing concealing clothing. As illustrated by this disconnect between perception and reality, normalised ideas of sexual deviance (and the stigmas it carries) can be slow to change. Inevitably, however, as a culture shifts, so too does its definition of deviance. And as global cultures change, groups invariably struggle to revise or reaffirm prevailing norms and laws—those regarding sexual deviance are no different. The SlutWalks that occurred around the world in 2011 may be a marker of that struggle.

This chapter deals with two closely related social phenomena: deviance and crime (Downes and Rock 2011; E. Goode and Thio 2007). Most forms of deviance—for example, being an alcoholic—are not crimes. However, all crimes—theft, murder, rape—are forms of deviance. In order to become a crime, a form of deviance needs to be negatively sanctioned by the legal system, a process known as **criminalisation** (Hillyard 2007; Jenness 2004). However, criminalisation does not occur of its own accord; some interest group must seek to have a type of deviance criminalised. This is a political decision, and it is linked to the desire on the part of one powerful group to exert social control over the actions of another group. As you will see, the determination that something is deviant is also the result of a similar social process.

DEVIANCE

What exactly is deviance, and where is the line between deviance and nondeviance? Without giving it much thought, many people would likely express the absolutist view that certain things are deviant in all places, for all groups and at all times (Little 2007). However, from a sociological perspective, no act, belief, or human characteristic is inherently deviant (R. Perrin 2007). Rather, to the sociologist, deviance is socially defined. Thus, **deviance** is any action, belief, or human characteristic that members of a society or a social group consider a violation of group norms for which the violator is likely to be censured or punished (Ben-Yehuda 2012; E. Goode 2007a).

If a powerful group wants to have a form of behaviour defined as deviant in order to have social control exercised over those who engage in it, it is

likely to be so defined. At the same time, powerful groups are likely to use their power to resist the efforts of others to define the powerful group's behaviours as deviant. For example, in the wake of the collapse of the financial market, bankers fought, largely successfully, against being seen as deviant for their predatory policies (Braithwaite 2010). Finance gurus began to package together loans with various risk levels and sell these as "asset-backed commercial paper." However, few people appreciated the various levels of associated risk (Chant n.d.), and subsequently a financial crisis enveloped not just Canada and the United States but the entire globe. Social power has a great deal of influence over who gets defined as deviant and suffers the negative consequences of such a definition.

SHIFTING DEFINITIONS OF DEVIANCE

In addition to being influenced by power relationships, what is thought to be deviant will vary from one time period to another, from one geographic location to another, and from one group to another. Consider obesity. Two centuries ago being obese was generally considered normal, even a good thing (H. Schwartz 1986). It was seen as a sign of affluence and the ability to afford plentiful food. Obesity was also seen as a sign of good health. But in Canada today, in spite of the fact that obesity is extremely common, many people consider it a form of deviance (E. Goode and Vail 2007; K. Roberts et al. 2012). It is recognised as having powerful negative effects on people's health (Schafer and Ferraro 2011). The realisation has also grown that the illnesses associated with obesity affect everyone in the form of higher health care costs and insurance premiums.

However, some observers are highly critical of this increasing tendency to see obesity as a form of deviance, or as a "discredited bodily state" (Monaghan 2007:68). They argue that there is nothing inherently wrong with, or deviant about, being obese. Many obese people argue that that's just the way they are; it's a tendency in their body that they are unable to alter. It is also argued that some people choose to be obese and prefer it as a bodily state. If being muscular or thin is not considered a form of deviance, why should we think of obesity in that way? Still, many people in Canada today, at least among the declining number of people who are not overweight, do view it as deviant.

Just as obesity has over time gone from being defined as normal to being considered deviant, other conditions have moved from deviance to normality (Dombrink and Hillyard 2007). Until a couple of decades ago, most people in Canada would have considered tattoos (and body art more generally, including body piercing [Koch et al. 2010]) as "discredited bodily states"; a tattoo was seen as deviant in and of itself, or it was assumed to signify membership in some deviant group, such as a biker gang. Today, a much greater proportion of Canadians consider tattoos normal, and indeed many more young people have gotten tattoos themselves. Once associated with working-class individuals who never attended college, tattoos have become much more common today among college students. Once restricted largely to men, tattoos are more and more popular today with women.

According to reports released at the Centers for Disease Control and Prevention's 2009 Weight of the Nation conference, two in three adults and one in five children are overweight or obese in the United States. Canadian obesity rates are not as high as in the United States, although the rates are more similar when comparing non-Hispanic whites in the United States and the equivalent population segment in Canada (Shields, Carroll, and Ogden 2011).

Some women, such as Kat Von D, have also gained fame as tattoo artists, a historically male-dominated occupation that has become so accepted that many in it aspire to be, or consider themselves, professionals (Maroto 2011). And tattoo parlours, once limited to the marginal areas of town, are now found on Main Street, as well as in the shopping mall, perhaps next to the maternity shop or the toy store. Tattoos have become just another product of our consumer society (M. Atkinson 2003; Patterson and Schroeder 2010).

As another example of the movement from deviance to normality, consider Canadian attitudes toward premarital sex (L. Roberts, Clifton, and Ferguson 2005). Today, premarital sex is so common and widely accepted that it is considered normal in most groups (Wellings et al. 2009). Furthermore, "hooking up," or having sexual relationships outside of committed romantic relations, common among youth today, was considered deviant behaviour in earlier generations (Bogle 2008; M. Lewis et al. 2011; Wentland and Reissing 2011). Much the same can be said about cohabitation before marriage (see Chapter 11); it once was defined as "living in sin." Today the pendulum has swung entirely in the other direction, to the point where couples who do not live together before marriage may be considered deviant. In other words, cohabitation has become normative (Popenoe 2009; Sassler 2007). Homosexuality is another form of sexual behaviour that has moved away from being considered a form of deviance (see Chapter 15). Its normalisation is reflected in a host of social changes such as the inclusion of same-sex partners in family benefits offered by employers and the growth of same-sex marriages. Popular musicians such as k. d. lang and Ashley MacIsaac, and athletes such as Brian Orser and Mark Tewksbury, publicly identify as gay and maintain successful careers. Gay and lesbian characters also are featured prominently on television shows such as *Being Erica* and *Saving Hope*.

Of course, some members of Canadian society cringe at the idea that premarital sex, cohabitation before marriage, and homosexuality are becoming normative. Religious fundamentalists, for example, may believe in an absolute moral standard by which these behaviours are deviant, no matter how many other people consider them normal. Fundamentalists believe that only married heterosexuals should live together and have sexual intercourse with one another (Hendershott 2002; B. Powell et al. 2010).

There are great differences from one geographic area to another in the way some behaviours are defined. At one time, smoking cigarettes was an accepted, even admired, form of behaviour in Canada and the United States. For example, the characters in the TV show *Mad Men,* which deals with the advertising industry in New York City about a half-century ago, are often seen smoking—and drinking alcohol—heavily, with great pleasure, and in their offices. Now, of course, smoking is widely considered to be deviant in Canada. However, smoking is certainly not viewed as deviant in most parts of Europe. It is considered quite normal in China (Kohrmann 2008), which consumes more tobacco than any other country in the world. In 2010 there were just over 301 million smokers in China; over half of all Chinese men were smokers (Yang et al. 2011). Smoking marijuana in public is another behaviour defined differently according to geographic location. It is considered deviant by most groups in Canada, but in the Netherlands marijuana smoking, while technically illegal, is quite normal. As you will see in the next *Globalisation* box, however, some changes are taking place in the Dutch attitude toward marijuana.

Even within the same society, groups differ on what is and is not considered deviant. For example, the residents of a typical retirement community would likely consider marijuana smoking deviant, but it is normal on nearby university campuses, as well as on virtually every other campus in the country. To take another example, many Canadians would consider eating certain body parts of animals as odd, if not deviant, including testicles, hearts, and eyes, whereas among different groups these are considered delicacies (e.g., prairie oysters, served as "crown jewels" during the royal visit of William and Kate to the Calgary Stampede).

While there are great differences in what is considered to be deviant, it is important to remember that deviance has existed for all groups, in all parts of the world, and for all times.

GLOBAL FLOWS AND DEVIANCE

Deviance can be seen as a global flow. Obviously, people who are defined as being deviant can move around the world quickly and easily. In addition, definitions of deviance flow even more easily from society to society. For example, through its "war on drugs," the United States has made a strong effort to have drug use throughout the world defined as a form of deviance and to make drug use illegal wherever possible. While there have been successes, many societies and cultures have resisted this effort and persist in viewing at least some drug use as normal. For example, use of the stimulant drug *khat* is normal in Yemen. The flip side of that phenomenon is that alcohol use in Yemen is considered deviant but thought to be quite normal in Canada.

Global trends toward normalising what was defined at one time and in some places as deviant are even clearer and more pronounced. This is particularly the case with changes in the acceptability of various forms of sexuality. Ever-greater portions of the world accept premarital sex, cohabitation

Smoking marijuana—and, increasingly, tobacco—is defined differently according to geographic location. Here, an older man smokes by the Ganges River in Varanasi, India. While smoking in public is prevalent across Asia and some parts of Europe, it has been banned in most public spaces in Canada.

Rethinking the Dutch Approach to Marijuana Use

The Netherlands has long been the model of an open and tolerant society. It was the first nation in the world to allow same-sex marriage and euthanasia. It is also one of the most secular nations in the world. However, recent changes related to globalisation seem to be threatening at least some of this openness. The threats can be seen in many areas of Dutch life, especially in the growing hostility to mass immigration (Lechner 2008). Globalisation is also threatening one of the things the Netherlands is most famous for: its openness to drug use in general, and especially to the sale and use of marijuana and hashish. Although marijuana is technically illegal in the Netherlands, smoking marijuana in public is not unusual, and there are "coffee shops" throughout the country where marijuana is sold openly. Many cafes have marquees, resembling those in fast-food restaurants, which offer the customer the choice of many varieties of the drug; "Amnesia," "Big Bud," and "Gold Palm" are just a few examples.

Tourists have been drawn to these shops for decades. But in recent years Dutch citizens have begun to see "drug tourism" (Uriely and Belhassen 2005) as a social problem. This is especially the case in border cities such as Maastricht, which lie just a few miles from Germany, France, and Belgium. Selling marijuana is illegal in these neighbouring countries, but the European Union's open borders have made it easy to drive to the Netherlands to get marijuana. As a result, Maastricht and other Dutch border cities are plagued with traffic jams, noise, and, more importantly, crime. The large numbers of visitors in search of marijuana have attracted criminals who want to sell them other, harder drugs, which are definitely illegal. What is worse, these criminals have been involved in shootouts and killings. The Dutch are shocked by this development because they saw their openness to marijuana as a way of keeping their young people safer, not endangering them in new and unforeseen ways.

As a result, some Dutch towns have closed their coffee shops. Overall, the number of such shops

declined dramatically from a high of about 1,500 to about 700 in 2010, and that number is likely to decline further. The city of Maastricht went further, introducing a law to ban drug sales to foreigners, making the sale of marijuana legal only to Dutch citizens. Although the law's opponents argued that it would violate the European Union's free trade rules by discriminating against some EU citizens (namely the non-Dutch) (Daley 2010a), the European Court of Justice approved the measure in 2010.

Efforts continue in the Netherlands to limit drug use in general and marijuana use in particular. For example, in late 2011 the Dutch government decided to reclassify high-potency marijuana as a hard drug and to put it in the same category as cocaine and ecstasy. As a result, Dutch cafés will be forced to sell milder forms of marijuana (Netherlands 2011).

before marriage, and, to a lesser degree, homosexuality. According to the International Lesbian, Gay, Bisexual, Trans and Intersex Association (ILGA), as of 2010 "deviant" sexuality was protected by anti-discrimination laws in 53 countries, and same-sex unions were recognised in 26 countries (see the ILGA map in Figure 7.1). However, the barriers to normalising such forms of sexual behaviour remain in place and quite powerful in large parts of the world. (The ILGA map indicates that deviant sexual behaviour was punishable by death or imprisonment in 76 countries.) This is especially the case in Islamic societies, which tend to be more absolutist on matters relating to sexual deviance and where deeply held religious beliefs serve as such a barrier. In spite of the barriers, these behaviours exist, often covertly, in these societies and may well be expanding in the wake of increasing global acceptance.

DEVIANCE AND CONSUMPTION

The most obvious relationship between deviance and consumption is the use of goods and services that are illegal or considered deviant. This form of consumption often involves committing deviant, or illegal, acts in order to be able to afford to consume. For example, many drug addicts are forced into committing criminal acts such as prostitution, shoplifting, mugging, and breaking and entering in order to pay for the high cost of their illegal drugs, among other things.

Poverty drives some to commit illegal and/or deviant acts in order to be able to afford to consume that which is necessary for survival (Edin and Lein 1997; Livermore et al. 2011). There are many reasons for engaging in prostitution, including the need to pay for illegal drugs, a history of abuse and rape, and being forced through human trafficking or other coercion, as well as simply a last-ditch effort to survive (M. Kennedy et al. 2007; Weitzer 2009). However, many women, and men, engage in prostitution in order to earn the money needed to be able to afford to consume various conventional goods and services.

A striking example of the relationship between deviance and consumption is the "mall girls" of Warsaw, Poland, the subject of a 2010

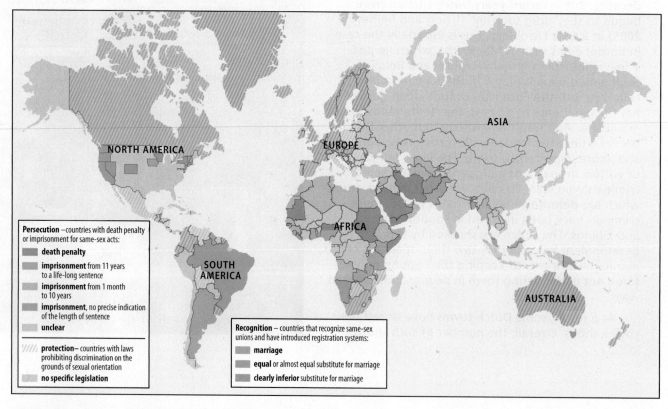

FIGURE 7.1 Lesbian and Gay Rights around the World, 2010

SOURCE: "ILGA Launches 2011 ILGA State-Sponsored Homophobia Report," 2011. Reprinted by permission of the International Lesbian, Gay, Bisexual, Trans and Intersex Association.

documentary film of the same name. These teenage girls (15 years of age or younger) are so drawn to the malls and the goods and services on offer there that they are willing to engage in sex in these settings (in the restrooms or outside in the parking lot), not for cash but for the goods and services themselves. Thus they exchange sex for pricey sushi dinners in the mall, as well as for Chanel scarves, "designer jeans, Nokia cell phones, even a pair of socks," especially those with brand names and expensive designer labels (Bilefsky 2010:A8). Because no money is exchanged, the girls do not see themselves as prostitutes, and they call their clients "boyfriends," "benefactors," or "sponsors." This phenomenon is linked by some to a postcommunist decline in values and the declining power of the Catholic Church in Poland. The maker of the documentary film argued that "the shopping mall has become the new cathedral in Poland" (Bilefsky 2010:A8).

Defining Deviant Consumption

As with all sorts of deviance, definitions of what is deviant consumer behaviour are frequently in dispute. For instance, deviant consumers often do not see a relationship between deviance and their consumption patterns. Using the services of prostitutes or smoking marijuana may well be seen by most Canadian "consumers" of prostitution or marijuana as completely justifiable and therefore not a form of deviance. Their actions are, in part, due to the fact that the laws prohibiting consumption of the services of prostitutes, and the use of marijuana, are rarely enforced. "Johns" and "Janes" are rarely arrested, and if they are, they ordinarily only get a legal slap on the wrist. Purchasing and smoking marijuana are treated in a similar fashion, at least for the white middle class.

However, those who consume the "wrong" drugs are more likely to be considered deviant than those who consume the "right" drugs. Thus, people who consume alcohol, even if they consume it excessively, are far less likely to be considered deviant than people who use marijuana. And the purchase and use of "harder drugs" that are associated with the have-nots in society, such as crack cocaine and heroin, are dealt with more harshly than the purchase and use of either alcohol or marijuana (Chriqui et al. 2002:ix; Jackson-Jacobs 2005:835).

"Dangerous Consumers"

Interestingly, in the era before the recent recession, the deviants in the realm of consumption were often considered to be the individuals who did not consume enough. They have been called "dangerous consumers" (Bauman 1997; Ritzer 2001a). They included the unemployed, the poor, "dropouts," those who voluntarily sought to simplify their lives, and those who saved rather than spent their money. Their insufficient consumption posed a threat to the success of consumer society and to an economy that had come to depend on high levels of consumption. Similarly, those who did not go into debt to the credit card companies and to banks for car and home loans were also considered to be dangers to the economy—despite the fact that lesser consumption may be better for the long-term sustainability of humanity, the environment, and even the economy.

The idea of dangerous, or deviant, consumers can be applied more broadly. Clearly, consuming illegal goods and services is considered deviant, but consuming merely the "wrong" products and services can also be seen as a threat. For example, buying secondhand goods, or worse, obtaining such goods free of charge from charities, threatens those with a vested interest in an ever-expanding economy. Such acquisitions do little or no good for the producers of various products, those whose jobs depend on those producers, the government collecting taxes from those producers and workers, and the consumption-based economy as a whole. Similarly, the use of public or welfare services can be viewed as a deviant form of consumption because, among other things, it constitutes a drain on government coffers and on the national economy.

Recent changes in the economy demonstrate, once again, the relative nature of deviance. After the onset of the recent recession, those who came to be defined as deviant or dangerous were those who consumed too much, and who went too deeply into debt. For example, those who bought homes even though there was no way they could afford the mortgage payments, at least after an initial period of uncommonly low interest rates and monthly payments, came to be seen as deviants who had jeopardised not only their own way of life but also the economy as a whole.

The police crack down on drugs in the Morro do Adeus slum in Rio de Janeiro, Brazil.

Similarly, while savings had been considered deviant during boom times, the view emerged that it was preferable—normal—to save, and, as a result, the savings rate in Canada rose, at least in the short run (see Chapter 11). Those who saved money came to be seen as normal, and those who went into debt, especially too deeply, were now viewed as the deviants.

THEORIES OF DEVIANCE

Deviance is a very good topic to study if you want to better understand the utility of, and contrasts between, the main types of sociological theories—structural/functional, conflict/critical, and inter/actionist. But before getting to these theories it is important to make a key distinction in theories of deviance:

- **Explanatory theories** are concerned with trying to explain why deviance does or does not occur (E. Goode 2007b). These theories are also thought of as being scientific, or "positivistic," because they view deviant behaviour as objectively real, and they suggest that these forms of real behaviour can be studied empirically. Explanatory theories assume that deviant behaviour is determined by a wide variety of factors,

such as the biological makeup of the deviant and the structure of the larger society. For example, the social class system ensures that large numbers of people will live in poverty, at the bottom of the hierarchy, and that some of them will commit deviant and criminal acts in order to survive (Meier 2007b). Some of the earliest theories of deviance were explanatory in nature. The Italian physician Cesare Lombroso (1835–1909), for example, focused initially on the role of biological factors—primitive, "ape-like" characteristics—in people who committed deviant acts, especially criminal acts such as theft, rape, and murder. Lombroso's biological approach was discredited, but recently some sociologists have returned to this question of biological roots of deviance. One team of researchers showed that juvenile delinquency could, in part, be explained by some genetic characteristics but that the social environment could reduce the effects of genetics (Guo, Roettger, and Cai 2008). In other words, genetics was not decisive but rather interacted with the social environment.

- **Constructionist theories** are concerned with achieving a greater understanding of the process by which people define and classify some behaviours as normal and others as deviant—in other words, how they construct deviance within their society (Henry 2007). Unlike explanatory theories, which focus mainly on deviants and what they do or are (poor, ape-like, prone to juvenile delinquency), constructionist theories focus on something that explanatory theories take for granted: those who are in power and the actions they take to create and define deviance in the first place. This means that research and theorising are directed at those who create and enforce the moral order and their definitions of deviance instead of focusing on those who commit deviant acts. Rather than seeing deviance as "real," this perspective sees it as a social construction. For example, midwives (virtually all of whom are women) and their practices were considered quite normal and went largely unnoticed in New Orleans (and elsewhere) until they were demonised by various powerful male-dominated groups in the city and came to be seen as deviants. Physicians through the city's coroner's office and the local medical society, newspapers, and the criminal justice system conspired against the midwives. By the 1940s and 1950s, they eventually succeeded in having midwives thought of as "evil" and as deviants engaged, among other things, in an "abortion racket" (Frailing and Harper 2010).

Of the three types of theories to be discussed below, the structural/functional and conflict/critical theories fall into the explanatory category, while the inter/actionist theories fit within the constructionist approach.

STRUCTURAL/FUNCTIONAL THEORIES

A good place to start is with the thinking of Émile Durkheim, one of the classic sociological theorists and creator of what later came to be known as structural-functionalism. While Durkheim focused on crime, it is possible to extend his thinking to deviance more generally. His basic argument was that because deviance and crime have existed in all societies at all times, and in that sense, they are "normal," they must have positive functions for the larger society and its structures. In other words, deviance would not have existed, exist, or continue to exist were it not for the fact that it was and is functional.

The most important function of deviance in Durkheim's view is that it allows societies, or groups, to define and clarify their collective beliefs—their norms and values. Were it not for deviance, norms and values would not come into existence. More importantly, the norms and values that limit or prohibit deviance would grow weak without the need to be exercised on a regular basis in response to deviant acts. The public as a whole, officials, and even potential deviants would grow progressively less aware of, and sensitive to, the existence of these prohibitions. Thus, in a sense society needs deviance. Without periodic violations of standards of conduct, those standards would become less clear to all concerned, less strongly held, and less powerful (Dentler and Erikson 1959; Jensen 1988).

Strain

A more contemporary structural/functional approach to deviance is known as **strain theory** (Patchin and Hinduja 2011). According to strain theory, a discrepancy exists between the larger structure of society, especially what is valued, and the structural means available to people to achieve what is valued. Strain exists when the culture values one thing, but the structure of society is such that not everyone can realise that value in a socially acceptable way. There are two major ways in which strain theory exemplifies a structural/functional approach. First, it is concerned with structures, especially the structures, such as the educational system, that provide the institutionalised means to cultural goals. Second, it deals with structural relationships (for example, between hard work and success) between those goals and institutionalised means.

The most obvious and important example in Canada, and in many other developed societies throughout the world, is the strain produced by the fact that although a high value is placed on material success, the structure of society does not give everyone an equal chance of attaining that success. Thus, contrary to the ideal of equal opportunity and a "level playing field," in reality most poor people in Canada have little or no chance of gaining the experience, training, education, and stable career that are the prerequisites for economic success. Nevertheless, they are still likely to value economic success, and at least some find alternative ways of achieving it (Bourgeois 2003; Duneier 1999).

For adults, unemployment is the kind of strain that one might think would generate criminal activity. Stephen Baron (2008) examined how the strain of unemployment affected the criminal behaviour of 400 homeless street youth in Vancouver. First he showed that young people who were unemployed were more likely to engage in property crime and the sale of drugs than were those who had even a temporary connection to the labour market. Second, and more importantly, he found that the effect of unemployment is mediated by a young person's sense of financial dissatisfaction and relative deprivation. That is, when being unemployed led people to being upset with their economic position, this triggered criminal activity. Some people who were unemployed but who were not angry or dissatisfied with their economic circumstances did not engage in crime. Simply being unemployed is insufficient to generate criminal behaviour. It is only under the strain of one's circumstances, triggered in this case by unemployment but experienced as disgruntlement, that criminal deviance occurs.

Ponzi Schemes

While we usually associate such deviant careers (Groenemeyer 2007) with those from the lower reaches of society such as sex workers (Sanders 2007), choices of deviant careers to achieve material success are also made at the upper levels of society. In 2010, most Canadians became aware of a financial executive and manager of other's people's wealth named Earl Jones. Jones grew rich, at least as near as one can tell, by convincing people that if they invested money with him, he could guarantee them annual financial returns of 8 percent or more. He deluded over 100 people, including his brother and sister-in-law, to invest with him. Jones used the money to create a Ponzi scheme (see Figure 7.2), a system whereby instead of investing people's money as promised, he used some of it to pay returns to other investors, leading them to believe he was remarkably successful. Meanwhile he used the fund as a "personal piggy bank" to finance his own lavish lifestyle, taking what investigators later estimated was tens of millions from investors over the years. In 2010 Jones was convicted of fraud and sentenced to 11 years in prison. The Royal Bank of Canada (RBC) settled a lawsuit brought against it by the victims of Jones's Ponzi scheme by paying them over $15 million. The suit alleged that RBC had not provided sufficient financial oversight.

It is often easier for people in the upper classes to make deviant career choices, and they may well prove far more lucrative than such career choices in the lower class. However, those who are well-off are usually led into deviant careers not because of strain, or because conventional means are closed off, but rather because they are easier, quicker, and perhaps even more lucrative means to financial success. Furthermore, it is far easier for such people to evade detection for quite some time, perhaps even for life. Despite the fact that Jones was convicted and imprisoned, those who are most likely to end up in prison are those in lower-status deviant careers such as sex workers or people who are "undereducated and ill-prepared for the labor market" (Wakefield and Uggen 2010:395). Thus strain theory is of far greater utility in helping us to understand deviance among those who are less well-off than among elite members of society.

Ponzi schemes, of course, are not restricted to Canada or the developed world—they exist everywhere in the world. Take the case of Benin, a small, impoverished nation on the west coast of Africa that was recently ravaged by an indigenous Ponzi scheme not unlike the one perpetrated by Earl Jones. But while Jones's victims were primarily wealthy Canadians, almost all of the victims in Benin were poor.

The fraud began when rumours spread that great riches were to be made by investing in a supposedly spectacularly successful company called Investment Consultancy and Computing Services (ICC). The company gained credibility when pictures were circulated of Benin's president posing with leaders of ICC and when other government leaders appeared on television with ICC officials. Many of these leaders—even the country's president—who were implicated in this scandal had, like Jones, chosen a deviant career. They offered official-looking contracts with the requisite legitimising stamps, seals, and even an image, for some reason, of the Statue of Liberty. Making the investment even more attractive was the fact that ICC participated in various "good works" such as being involved in supporting hospitals and orphanages, digging wells for needed water, and contributing to charities. More selfishly and materialistically, investors were promised that they would recoup almost half their investment within three months. Of course, since this was a Ponzi scheme, some early investors were handsomely rewarded, but in the end, most investors lost all the money they had put into the company.

Although many elderly Canadians were hurt by Jones's Ponzi scheme, they represented only a tiny proportion of the entire population. On the other hand, a much larger proportion of Benin's population

FIGURE 7.2 **Mechanics of a Ponzi Scheme**

was affected either directly, by lost investments, or indirectly because many extended family members suffered from a given individual's losses. One source estimates that more than 50,000 people—in a country of about 9 million—were defrauded out of close to $200 million. Overall, at least a quarter of Benin's citizens were affected, and some argue that most of the population was hurt in one way or another.

Adaptations to Strain

The most important strain theory was developed in the mid-1900s by one of the leading structural-functionalists, Robert K. Merton. The issue at the heart of Merton's theory is the way people relate to the institutionalised means (such as getting a college degree and working hard) that are needed to achieve such cultural goals as economic success. Of greatest interest in this context is the strain placed on some people by the relationship of means and ends. Merton identified five possible relationships between means and ends and associated them with five types of adaptations:

- **Conformists** are people who accept both cultural goals such as making lots of money and the traditional means of achieving those goals, including hard work. Conformists are the only one of Merton's types who would not be considered deviant.

- **Innovators** accept the same cultural goals the conformists do, but they reject the conventional means of achieving them. Innovators are deviants in that they choose nonconventional routes to success. Earl Jones would be one example, though an extreme one; other innovators choose legal routes to success. Snowboarder Sarah Burke who created, and then competed in, a new extreme—and dangerous—sport and chose it as a career path is an example of an innovator whose deviance was perfectly legal.

- **Ritualists** realise that they will not be able to achieve cultural goals, but they nonetheless continue to engage in the conventional behaviour associated with such success. Thus, a low-level employee might continue to work

Earl Jones, from Montreal, was sentenced to prison for 11 years after defrauding clients of millions of dollars in a financial Ponzi scheme.

diligently even after realising that such work is not going to lead to much economic success. Merton sees such diligent work with no realizable goal as a form of deviance.

• **Retreatists** reject both cultural goals and the traditional routes to their attainment. Retreatists have completely given up on attaining success within the system. One example is Theodore Kaczynski, who gained notoriety as the "Unabomber." At the time of his arrest in 1996, Kaczynski had been living for some 20 years in a cabin in a remote area of Montana without water or electricity, using a bicycle as his only means of transportation. To demonstrate his anger at modern society's "industrial-technological system," he had mailed off more than a dozen bombs, which

killed 3 people and injured 23 others. After a long and complicated trial, he was sentenced to life in prison. Kaczynski's case has many interesting aspects, including the fact that he used the U.S. mail, part of the system he despised, to deliver his bombs and thereby his antiestablishment message. Moreover, it can be argued that Kaczynski was a conformist before he became a retreatist. Prior to his withdrawal from society he had gotten a PhD from the University of Michigan in mathematics and had begun an academic career at the University of California, Berkeley.

• **Rebels** are like retreatists in that they reject both traditional means and goals. However, in their stead they substitute nontraditional goals and means to those goals. In a sense that makes them doubly deviant. Revolutionaries such as Ernesto "Che" Guevara can be seen as fitting into the rebel category. Guevara rejected success as it was defined in Cuba during the 1950s, and instead chose to assist Fidel Castro in his effort to overthrow the country's dictatorial system. Furthermore, he chose unconventional means—guerrilla warfare waged from the mountains of Cuba and, eventually, Bolivia—to attain his goals.

Adaptations of means to ends exemplifies a structural/functionalist approach because some of the adaptations are highly functional. Conformity certainly has positive consequences in the sense that it allows the social system to continue to exist without disturbance. Innovation is functional because society needs innovations in order to adapt to new external realities; no society can survive without innovation. Even rebellion can be seen as functional because there are times when society needs more than gradual innovation—it needs to change radically. Structural-functionalism is concerned not only with functions but also with dysfunctions. For example, ritualists and retreatists can be seen as largely dysfunctional for society, or at least as having more dysfunctions than functions. The unchanging behaviour of ritualists contributes little or nothing to the requirements of an ever-changing society, and retreatists contribute even less because they are uninvolved in, and have withdrawn from, the larger society.

Social Control

Another subtheory that can be discussed under the heading of structural/functional theory is Travis Hirschi's (1969) **social control theory**, which focuses on the reasons why people do *not* commit deviant acts. In brief, people are less likely to commit deviant acts if they have a variety of social bonds, and they are more likely to commit such acts if those bonds are weak. While Hirschi's theory has wide application to deviance in general, he was most interested in young people and juvenile delinquency.

Social control involves the structures of society and the people who act on behalf of those structures. In a sense, Hirschi sees those structures and the people who work on their behalf as functional for society. People who are involved in those structures and are responsive to those who act on their behalf are more likely to be conformists, and less likely to become deviants. However, those who are more likely to become deviants are not deeply involved in those structures and not responsive to their demands or to those of the people who act on their behalf. In terms of the latter, Hirschi (1969) contends: "If a person does not care about the wishes and expectations of other people . . . then he is to that extent not bound by the norms. He is free to deviate" (p. 18). One structure of great importance to Hirschi is the family. If a young person does not have deep bonds to his family and his parents, he will be more likely to engage in deviant behaviour. The school is another important structure. If a young person is not involved in school and with teachers, she is likely to be more inclined to deviant behaviour. More informal factors are also important. For example, those who do not have close personal relationships or who are not involved in extracurricular activities, such as sports, are also more inclined to deviance. The lack of a job and involvement in the work world has similar effects. Without such attachments and involvements, young people are less likely to accept conventional goals or internalise the norms of society. Lacking attachments to family and conventional norms and goals, there is little to prevent a person from becoming a deviant, a juvenile delinquent, or even a career criminal. The lack of other vested interests such as owning a house is also likely to contribute to deviant behaviour. People in such situations have little or nothing to lose in violating norms and laws.

In later work, Hirschi (2004) described these as "inhibitors," or "factors that one takes into account in deciding whether to commit a criminal act" (p. 545). If young people lack such inhibitors as ties to family and parents, or schools and teachers, they are more likely to become juvenile delinquents (Intravia, Jones, and Piquero 2011).

This view is consistent with structural-functionalism in that it focuses on larger structures (family, work, and the housing market), those who exist in those structures and act on behalf of them (parents, teachers), and the positions that people do or do not hold in those structures. Involvement in these structures is likely to inhibit nonconformist behaviour, while a lack of such involvement makes such behaviour more likely.

CONFLICT/CRITICAL THEORIES

Structural-functionalists trace the source of deviance to the larger structures of society and the

Aaron Evans, 21, was sentenced to seven months in prison after being captured on camera breaking into a car in Bristol, England. Reports described Evans as having no fixed address. Social control theorists would argue that the absence of this important social bond influenced Evans's likelihood to commit crime.

GL◍BALISATION

China's "Walk of Shame"

In the United States people have become accustomed to seeing televised "perp walks." These usually involve accused criminals, sometimes celebrities, walking to waiting police cars, to court, or to jail accompanied by scowling police officers. Most "perps" seem embarrassed and uncomfortable to be paraded in front of the community and the viewing audience in such a fashion. In a country that has the world's highest incarceration rates, shaming has frequently had an odd and tenuous place in the criminal justice system (Kohm 2009).

Such perp walks, however, pale in comparison to the "shame parades" common in China (A. Jacobs 2010). These have a long tradition there, but they became much more common during the highly oppressive communist regime of Mao Zedong, who ruled the country from 1949 to 1976. People accused of being "enemies" of communism and the state, as well as more common criminals, were subjected to such parades, sometimes ending in public executions. While public executions have ended in China, there are still "mass sentencing rallies, during which convicts wearing confessional placards are driven through the streets in open trucks" (A. Jacobs 2010:A3). Women accused of prostitution have also been forced to participate in shame parades, including being shackled and "roped together and paraded barefoot through crowded city streets" (A. Jacobs 2010:A1). Beyond that, in some areas of China the names and addresses of prostitutes have been published and, in the age of the Internet, posted online. Such forms of mass media allow shaming to be extended to a global level (Kohm 2009).

However, in 2010 the government sought an end to public shaming and called, instead, for "rational, calm, and civilized" law enforcement (A. Jacobs 2010:A1). This is not China's first effort to end public shaming, but similar attempts in the past have failed.

Public shaming has been part of Chinese culture for a long time, and once again it might prove difficult to eliminate the practice.

As a reflection of the power of culture, public shaming is also part of Chinese culture in other parts of the world. For example, in New York City, some Chinese immigrant owners of supermarkets have been posting photographs of shoplifters in their stores (Kilgannon and Singer 2010). It is not clear whether or not this practice is legal, but its existence in the Chinese community in New York and elsewhere reflects the global power of cultural norms.

Women accused of prostitution are sometimes shackled, roped together, and paraded through crowded city streets.

strains they produce or the fact that they do not exercise adequate social control over people. Conflict/critical theorists, especially conflict theorists, are also interested in those structures and their effect on people, but they adopt a different orientation to them. A major focus is the inequality that exists in those structures and the impact that it has on individuals. In conflict theorists' view, inequality

causes at least some of the less powerful individuals in society to engage in deviant—and criminal—acts because they have few, if any, other ways of succeeding in society (E. Goode 2007b). In this, they are similar to the innovators in Merton's taxonomy of adaptations to strain. Conversely, those in power commit crimes, especially corporate or white-collar crimes (S. Simpson 2002; S. Simpson and Weisburd

2009), because the nature of their high-level positions in various social structures (business, government) makes it not only possible but also relatively easy for them to do so. Further, conflict theorists argue, those in power in society create the laws and rules that define certain things as deviant, or illegal, while others are defined as normal. They do so in a self-serving way that advantages them and disadvantages those who lack power in society.

The conflict view of deviance has been extended to many other acts on the basis of racial, sexual, gender, age-related, and other social inequalities (R. Collins 1975). For example, questionable acts committed by racial minorities are more likely to be labelled as deviance or crime than are the same acts committed by majority group members. Before the repeal of state antisodomy laws by the U.S. Supreme Court in 2003, police in some states could arrest homosexuals for having sex with one another in the privacy of their own homes. Heterosexuals engaging in sodomy—that is, having oral or anal sex—in their own homes would almost never be arrested for such acts even though they were illegal in some locales. Some geographic areas have curfews for teenagers, meaning that a teenager who is out after a certain time can be labelled as deviant; curfews for adults are almost unheard of except during emergencies such as a natural disaster or a state of martial law. Again, this list can be extended greatly, but the point is that conflict theorists tend to see those who rank low in the system of social stratification, on any dimension, as being more likely to be labelled as deviant.

Deviance and the Poor

Conflict theories can be applied to social inequalities throughout the ages. For instance, they form the basis of research by William Chambliss (1964) on vagrancy laws in medieval England. These laws came into existence as feudalism was falling apart; the first vagrancy law was enacted in England after the Black Death, around 1348. In the feudal system, serfs were forced to provide labour for landowners, but with the end of feudalism, and therefore of serfdom, a new source of labour was needed. Not coincidentally, the former serfs now lacked a permanent home or source of income and

wandered about the countryside. Those in power saw them as a likely group to provide the needed labour at little cost and created vagrancy laws. Then it became illegal for those without work or a home to loiter in public places; some of those itinerants were arrested under the new laws. As a result, many people who otherwise might not have worked for the landowners were forced to work in order to avoid arrest and imprisonment.

Contemporary conflict theorists, heavily influenced by Marxian theory, have come to see deviance as something created by the capitalist economic system. Today's definitions of deviance serve the interests of the capitalists, especially by further enriching them, and they adversely affect the proletariat, especially the poor, who grow even poorer. This view is well summed up by Jeffrey Reiman and Paul Leighton's *The Rich Get Richer and the Poor Get Prison* (2009). As the title of this book implies, the best examples of this process lie in the realm of crime rather than deviance, although to be seen as a crime an act must be first defined as deviant. For example, as we saw above, at the close of the Middle Ages it was in the interest of elite members of society to define vagrancy as deviance and as a crime. Such a definition seems fair and even-handed until we realise that elite members of society are rarely, if ever, going to be without work and a home and are therefore unlikely to be defined as vagrants. It is only the poor who are going to find themselves in those situations, with the result that they are just about the only ones who are going to be affected by the laws against vagrancy. As the great novelist Anatole France ([1894] 2011) once commented sarcastically, "The law, in all its majestic equality, forbids the rich as well as the poor to sleep under bridges on rainy nights, to beg on the streets, and to steal bread."

Conflict theorists do not argue that have-nots never commit crimes or deviant acts. Rather, they argue that it is because of the laws (for example, not to sleep under bridges) created by societal elites that the actions of the have-nots are singled out for notice and for sanctions. Furthermore, the cost to society of elite deviance is much higher than the costs associated with crime and deviance among society's have-nots. Compare, for example, the millions of dollars Earl Jones cost his clients to the few dollars a con artist or a mugger wrests from his victims.

Deviance and the Elite

Great efforts are made to legitimise elite crimes and acts of elite deviance (D. Simon 2012) and, failing that, to pay little or no attention to them. Those who rank high in such hierarchies as business, government, and the military have a much greater ability to commit deviant acts (for example, to sexually harass a subordinate), to have them seen as being legitimate, and to get away with them.

However, as is clear in the Earl Jones case, there are limits to the ability of elites to get away with deviant and criminal behaviour. There are times when the acts are so extreme that they can no longer be hidden, and they come to light and become great public issues. Once this happens, even the most elite members of society have a difficult time escaping negative judgment and perhaps even punishment and imprisonment.

In fact, there is a long list of scandals involving elite public figures of various types who have been found to have committed deviant acts. In the main their acts have been so extreme, or the revelations about them became so public, that they could not be ignored. However, what has often caused difficulties for those involved has been their awkward efforts to lie about, or cover up, their offences once they first become public. In many cases, especially in this era of the Internet, evidence is uncovered or witnesses come forward that make clear that the public figure has been deceiving the public and the authorities. The following are a few notable examples in the Canadian context (there are innumerable others everywhere in the world):

- In perhaps the most famous example of all, the Liberal Party of Canada was found to have received kickback payments from organisations that received taxpayer money that was intended to showcase the contributions of the Government of Canada to the Province of Quebec. The so-called sponsorship money was doled out in ways that were hard to track and to groups that were mainly aligned with the Liberal Party. Exactly who was responsible for the misappropriation of funds remains elusive because of denials and apparent cover-ups by those powerful individuals most closely involved.

- Robert Dziekaiski, a Polish citizen, died on October 14, 2008, at Vancouver International Airport after having been Tasered five times by four Royal Canadian Mounted Police officers. The Honourable Thomas Braidwood investigated and concluded the officers were in error in using a Taser and that they subsequently acted in ways that misrepresented their true behaviour.

- In 2007 the foreign minister of the Canadian federal government, Conservative Member of Parliament Maxime Bernier, was forced to resign after leaving sensitive North Atlantic Treaty Organization documents in the home of his ex-girlfriend Julie Couillard. Bernier initially denied any wrongdoing.

- In 2005 Vincent Lacroix, who had founded the Norbourg Financial Group, was found to have bilked thousands of investors out of millions of dollars. Lacroix is still serving jail time for his crimes.

- In 1988 Ben Johnson won the Olympic 100-metre dash in a world record time of 9.59 seconds. Three days later he was stripped of his medal for having taken an illegal performance-enhancing drug.

- In 2011 Conrad Black, a former newspaper magnate, was convicted of mail fraud and obstruction of justice. Black, born in Montreal and also known as Lord Black of Crossharbour, is a member of the British House of Lords. He served his prison time for the two convictions in the United States.

- In 2009 former theatre impresario Garth Drabinsky was convicted of fraud and forgery charges, hailed at the time as one of the first major white-collar crimes ever successfully prosecuted in Canada.

However, the view of conflict theorists is that as lengthy as this list of elite deviants and criminals might be, it is merely the tip of the iceberg. Because elites have a wide variety of means at their disposal to conceal their actions, there are many, many more acts of deviance and criminality by elites that escape detection and punishment; they can persist for years, decades, or even a lifetime. It is often the case among elites that a scapegoat is put forward to be punished, while many others who committed similar acts escape negative sanctions. Earl Jones, like Bernie Madoff in the United States, may be seen as a scapegoat whose arrest and punishment satisfied at least some of the public's and media's thirst for someone to blame for the recent financial crisis. In Jones's case, one might argue that officials with the Royal Bank of Canada, who have paid out settlements to some of his victims, were aware, or at least should have been aware, of his fraudulent actions.

INTER/ACTIONIST THEORIES

The third major type of theory employed in this book, inter/actionism, can also be used to analyze deviance. For example, to the rational choice theorist, a person chooses deviance because it is a rational means to some desired goal. Gang members join gangs because of the camaraderie and perceived protection offered by the gang (Melde, Taylor, and Esbensen 2009), as well as access to a world in which the member can obtain money and achieve recognition and high status (K. Bell 2009; Decker and Curry 2000). Earl Jones went about creating, expanding, and concealing his Ponzi scheme in a highly rational manner, as did those involved in Benin's Ponzi scheme.

Ethnomethodologists are concerned with the ways in which people "do" deviance—that is, the everyday behaviours in which they engage that produce deviance. People need to adopt methods of speech and forms of behaviour that would make their deviance invisible to most others. In a classic ethnomethodological study, Harold Garfinkel ([1967] 2003) describes the painstaking steps taken by Agnes, a male-to-female transgendered person, to "pass" as a woman. She not only changed her manner of dress, posture, and demeanour but also underwent physical changes. However, there are times when those who are deviant will want to talk and act in ways that make clear that they are deviant. For example, gang members may use certain phrases, dress in certain ways, and display certain tattoos in order to make their allegiance clear to other members of the same gang—and to members of opposing gangs (see Chapter 5). However, when they interact with the public or the police, gang members may speak and dress in a way that conceals, or at least attempts to hide, their membership in the gang.

Labelling

Symbolic interactionism is of great utility in analysing deviance and fills in many of the gaps in understanding left by structural/functional and conflict/critical theories. One variety of symbolic interactionism—labelling theory—is particularly useful in thinking about deviance. From that perspective, at least two things are needed for deviance to occur:

- Symbol, or in this case a "label." In the realm of deviance, a number of labels are particularly powerful negative symbols: alcoholic, drug addict, pedophile, adulterer, and so on. The golfer Tiger Woods is a good example of the power of labels. He had become a well-known public symbol, even a brand. His name conjured up images of not only a great golfer, but someone who seemed "squeaky-clean." In 2009 he was

Lord Black of Crossharbour, a Montreal-born member of the British House of Lords and former owner of one of the world's largest newspaper empires, was convicted of mail fraud and obstruction of justice.

involved in a car crash that led to revelations of cheating on his wife with multiple women, and a painful separation that led to divorce. Now the labels adulterer and sex addict have been linked, perhaps inextricably, with his name, and his reputation and public image have been badly tarnished. Even though the accusations had nothing to do with golf, several of his corporate sponsors dropped him because they no longer wanted to be associated with a person who was labelled so negatively. They feared that his spoiled reputation would be extended to them and adversely affect their businesses and profits. It took years for Woods to regain his greatness as a golfer, but he did win a major championship in early 2012.

- Interaction between a person or a group doing the labelling (the labeller) and a person or group to whom the label is applied (the labellee). During this interaction one or more of these labels is applied to the deviant. Those who do the labelling are known as social control agents. Some of these agents (police, psychiatrists) are performing official functions, but far more often it is friends or family who label others as, for example, drunks or womanisers. When public figures are labelled as deviant, the media and their representatives are often the ones who do the labelling.

From the perspective of **labelling theory**, a deviant is someone to whom a deviant label has been successfully applied (H. Becker 1963). This stands in contrast to the view of the public and many sociologists who focus on what an individual does in order to be labelled a deviant. Also of interest in labelling theory is the way the person labelled as deviant is affected by the label (Dotter and Roebuck 1988; Gove 1980; Walsh 1990). Among other things, the label can be accepted to varying degrees, or efforts can be made to resist, reject, or shed the label. People will also vary greatly in how they react to, and feel about, being labelled a deviant. For example, some might be mortified by being labelled a sex addict, but others might take pride in it.

Labelling theory is also concerned with the actions and reactions of social control agents, as well as their interactions with those being labelled (Pontell 2007). From the labelling perspective "deviance is not a consequence of the act the person commits, but rather a consequence of the [creation and] application by others of rules and sanctions to an 'offender'" (H. Becker 1963:9). A focus on social control agents, rather than deviants, leads to the view that deviant labels are not necessarily applied uniformly; some people and some forms of deviance are more likely than others to be labelled as deviant. Thus, murderers and the act of murder are almost uniformly labelled as deviant (and criminal), but in many other cases the process is more selective and less clear-cut: "Some men who drink too much are called alcoholics and others are not; some men who act oddly are committed to hospitals and others are not; some men who have no visible means of support are hauled into court and others are not" (K. Erikson 1964: 11–12). Overall, people are more likely to be socially defined as deviant when they are poor, work in low-status occupations, or are in similarly devalued circumstances (Goffman 1959). A person in a more advantageous social situation often escapes being defined or labelled as deviant, despite manifesting the same forms of behaviour.

PRIMARY AND SECONDARY DEVIANCE

An important distinction that flows from labelling theory is that between primary and secondary deviance.

- **Primary deviance** involves early, random acts of deviance such as an occasional bout of drinking to excess or an act here or there that is considered to be strange or out of the ordinary. Virtually all of us commit such acts; we all have engaged in various forms of primary deviance (J. Wallerstein and Wyle 1947). Isolated acts of primary deviance rarely, if ever, lead to the successful application of a deviant label.

- Of far greater interest to labelling theorists is **secondary deviance** or deviant acts that persist, become more common, and eventually cause people to organise their lives and personal identities around their deviant status. Thus, if a person moves from isolated sexual encounters to being obsessed with such encounters and to seeking them out whenever and wherever possible, that person may be labelled a sex addict. It is possible, as in the case of Hank Moody (lead character on the HBO show *Californication*), and perhaps Tiger Woods, that the label of sex addict will be more important than all other definitions of the self. When that happens, sex addiction becomes a form of secondary deviance. In one recent study, body modifications such as tattoos and body piercings were shown to be acts of primary deviance that are related to forms of secondary deviance such as drug abuse and juvenile delinquency (Dukes and Stein 2011).

While labelling theory tends to focus on others labelling an individual as deviant, it is possible, even likely, that individuals label themselves in this way (Thoits 1985, 2011), that they may do so

before anyone else does (D. Norris 2011), and that they may act in accord with the self-imposed label (Lorber 1967). This is consistent with the view of the leading symbolic interactionist, George Herbert Mead, who saw the mind as an internal conversation with oneself. Such an internalised conversation may certainly lead to labelling oneself as deviant.

KEY IDEAS IN THE LABELLING PROCESS

Social control is the process by which a group or society enforces conformity to its demands and expectations. One way in which this is accomplished is through the creation and application of rules and labels. This leads to the distinction between rule creators and rule enforcers. **Rule creators** are usually elite members of society who devise its rules, norms, and laws (K. Ryan 1994). Without rule creators and their rules there would be no deviance. Rule creators are usually (but not always) distinct from **rule enforcers**, who threaten to, or actually enforce, the rules (Bryant and Higgins 2010). Another important idea here is that of **moral entrepreneurs**, or those

Primary Deviance   **Secondary Deviance**

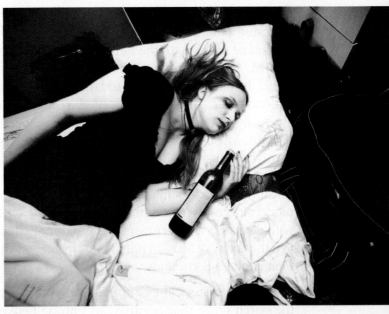

While primary deviance entails sporadic acts of deviance, secondary deviance involves acts that persist and eventually cause a person to organise her life around the deviant status.

individuals or groups of individuals who come to define an act as a moral outrage and who lead a campaign to have it defined as deviant and to have it made illegal and therefore subject to legal enforcement (H. Becker 1963; Lauderdale 2007). Drugs are a good example of this, especially globally, since moral entrepreneurs located especially in the United States have taken it upon themselves to have them defined as illegal and their use as deviant. They have done so even though the use of many of these drugs (such as marijuana) is common and accepted not only in many societies throughout the world but also among a large portion of the American population. Another example is obesity. A key role in obesity as a form of deviance is played by moral entrepreneurs, or what Monaghan, Hollands, and Pritchard (2010) call "obesity epidemic entrepreneurs." These are people such as owners of weight-loss centres who have a vested interest in obesity being defined as a problem that is capable of correction. One famous example of a moral entrepreneur was U.S. Senator Joe McCarthy, who in the 1950s created a public fervour over the existence of communists in the government and elsewhere (such as Hollywood). As a result, many were labelled communists (often falsely) and therefore came to be seen in a negative light, perhaps for the rest of their lives.

Moral Panics

Moral entrepreneurs can stir up such a fuss that they can cause a **moral panic**, or a widespread but disproportionate reaction, to the form of deviance in question (E. Goode and Ben-Yehuda 1994, 2009; Hier 2011). It could be argued that today we are witnessing a moral panic over the threat posed by immigrants, especially those who are undocumented. Especially recently, Muslims have been singled out as a group involved in a moral panic, in Canada, the United States, and Europe. Even though the vast majority of Muslim immigrants make good neighbours and are model citizens in their immigrant homes, the linkage with al-Qaeda and terrorism has profoundly unsettled the ability of Muslim immigrants to integrate into their adopted homelands.

A good historical example of a moral panic is the witch craze that occurred in Europe between the fourteenth and sixteenth centuries (Ben-Yehuda 1980, 1985). The idea of witches existed before this time, but it was seen as a more complex phenomenon involving both bad and good witches. In any case, no assumption was made about a conspiracy between women and Satan to corrupt the world. However, in this era Dominican friars took the lead in defining witchcraft as such a conspiracy and as a crime subject to corporal punishment—burning at the stake. The friars were the moral entrepreneurs in this case, and they played a key role in generating a moral panic that came to involve large numbers of people. That panic, in turn, led to the painful deaths of hundreds of thousands of people, mostly women.

Moral panics are, by definition, exaggerated. Thus, the threat posed by witches in the fifteenth century, the communists in the 1950s, and immigrants and even terrorists today is made out by many, especially moral entrepreneurs, to be greater than it really is. One of the ways to do this is to create a "folk devil" who stands for what is feared. In the case of communism it was Joseph Stalin or Mao Zedong; more recently terrorism made Osama bin Laden a folk devil.

Stigma

Erving Goffman's (1963) *Stigma* is a very important contribution of symbolic interactionism to our understanding of deviance. A **stigma** is a characteristic that others find, define, and often label as unusual, unpleasant, or deviant. Goffman begins his book with analyses of physically stigmatised individuals (one of Goffman's examples involved those missing a nose, for example) and then introduces a wide array of other stigmas, such as being on welfare. In the end, readers come to the realisation that they have been reading not only about people who are unlike them, with major physical deformities, but rather about themselves: "The most fortunate of normals is likely to have his half-hidden failing, and for every little failing there is a social occasion when it will loom large, creating a shameful gap" (Goffman 1963:127). Goffman's idea of a stigma has attracted many scholars and has been applied to many forms of deviance, such as working in the sex trade (Scambler and Paoli 2008; W. Wong, Holroyd, and Bingham 2011), mental illness (Payton and Thoits 2011), and advocacy by mothers of children suffering from Asperger's syndrome (Hill and Liamputtong 2011).

There are two types of stigmatised individuals. The individual with a **discredited stigma** "assumes his differentness is known about already or is evident on the spot" (Goffman 1963:4). In contrast, those with a **discreditable stigma** assume that their stigma "is neither known about by those present nor immediately perceivable about them" (Goffman 1963:4). An example of a discredited stigma might be a lost limb or being a member of a minority group viewed negatively by others, while discreditable stigmas include having done poorly in school or having a prison record. As is to be expected from the symbolic interactionist perspective, of great importance is the symbolic nature of the stigma and the interaction with others, especially those thought to be normal. Because the physical nature of a discreditable stigma is not visible to others, neither are its symbolic qualities. Nevertheless, the people with such a stigma want to make sure it remains secret and thus try to conceal the stigmatising information during most interactions. However, in the case of a discredited stigma (such as being morbidly obese), those with the stigma must deal with the tension associated with interacting with people who view them negatively because of the stigma.

One real-life example of the symbolic weight of a discreditable stigma is the story of Anatole Broyard, a literary critic, author, and black man who lived his adult life as a white man. After his death in 1990, it came to light that he was born into a mixed-race family in Louisiana who were classified as black. Growing up in the 1920s and 1930s, Broyard realised that being black carried a discredited stigma, a stigma that could limit his educational and employment opportunities. Being very light-skinned, he was able to enlist in the military as white during World War II, when the armed forces were racially segregated. In other words, he was able to transform being black from a discredited to a discreditable stigma. After the war, he entered college and began his literary career as a white man. This type of experience is what Goffman (1963) refers to as *passing*—deliberately hiding an identity or characteristic that could be discrediting. Broyard and his wife raised two children in the suburbs of Connecticut who were unaware of their ancestry. When they learned about their heritage soon before Broyard's death, they struggled with suddenly "becoming black" (Broyard 2007).

The idea of discreditable stigma has wide applicability to the contemporary world. For example, the court records of juvenile offenders are often hidden from the public or expunged to avoid stigmatising otherwise promising young people for a lifetime. People with mental illness or substance abuse problems often go to great lengths to hide the real reason for unscheduled absences from work. Parents of children who are mentally disabled, and those who are especially mildly impaired, "mainstream" their children in standard classrooms in part so their disability will be more likely to be discreditable than discredited. The theme of hiding stigmatising conditions is common in popular entertainment as well: In the movie *Philadelphia* (1993), actor Tom Hanks plays a high-powered lawyer in a prestigious law firm who is diagnosed with HIV during the early years of the epidemic. As the disease progresses, he tries but ultimately fails to conceal the signs that he has the disease, such as skin blemishes associated with Kaposi's sarcoma. When it becomes clear to the leaders of his firm that he has AIDS, he is fired. This movie, unlike some, realistically portrays the painful, destructive effects of revealing a discredited stigma.

In the 2010 film *Easy A*, loosely based on Nathaniel Hawthorne's *The Scarlet Letter*, high school student Olive Penderghast (Emma Stone) stiches a red *A* into her clothing after earning an unfounded reputation as sexually promiscuous. In this film—as in its source material—a discreditable stigma is transformed into a discredited one.

CRIME

While there are many ways to define it, **crime** is simply a violation of the criminal law (Whitehead 2007). As pointed out above, it is the fact that it violates the law that differentiates crime from other forms of deviance. **Criminology** is the field devoted to the study of crime (S. E. Brown 2007a; Rosenfield 2011). Many, but certainly not all, criminologists are sociologists. (The next *Public Sociology* box, for example, introduces Wendy Roth and Robert Gordon.) While many criminologists are now found in departments and schools devoted to the study of criminology, a large number work in sociology departments. There is a sociology of crime, but the field also includes those from many other disciplines, such as psychologists, economists, biologists, and anthropologists, as well as officials who once worked in the criminal justice system. In fact, the field today has become much more multidisciplinary, even interdisciplinary (Wellford 2012).

While there is growing interdisciplinarity in the study of crime, sociology plays an important role in it. Clearly a variety of sociological factors (including social class and race [Chilton and Triplett 2007a, 2007b) are involved in who commits crimes and which crimes they commit. The same sociological factors are involved in who gets caught, prosecuted, and incarcerated, as well as how much of the sentence they actually serve. And such factors are involved in what happens to people after they serve their sentences and whether they are likely to end up back in prison.

The "father of criminology" is Cesare Lombroso, who published *The Criminal Man* in 1876 (McShane and Williams 2007). The title of the book reflects the fact that the focus of early criminologists was on criminals and their innate physical or psychological characteristics. Criminals were seen as being defective in various ways, and the goal was to study scientifically the defects and those who had them in order to deter crime. While the major causes lay within the individual, they were seen as being beyond his or her control. In fact, Lombroso's main focus was on the "born criminal." Hence, the early criminologists adopted the view that such people needed the external control of the criminal justice system. Lombroso was also prone to gross and indefensible generalisations, such as contending that Gypsies "murder in cold blood in order to rob, and were formerly suspected of cannibalism. The women are very clever at stealing" (cited in F. Williams and McShane 2007:2663).

In more recent years criminology has shifted away from its focus on criminals and their defects and to a concern with the social context of criminal actions and the effect of those actions on the larger society. A key figure in bringing a sociological perspective to criminology was Edwin Sutherland. Sutherland studied a variety of issues in criminology, such as white-collar crime, the death penalty, and prisons, but his greatest influence was his textbook *Principles of Criminology* (Sutherland 1924). The book went through 10 editions and was used by students for nearly 70 years. Sutherland was a symbolic interactionist. This perspective helped shift the focus in criminology from the criminal and his misdeeds to society, especially the societal reaction to those actions, including the labels placed on criminals.

Off-duty police reservist Bobby Lawrence (left) takes aim at a thief who attempted to steal his cell phone from his car in the Johannesburg, South Africa, suburb of Hillbrow. Sociology has a long history of examining crime and criminals and one of the most important fields employed by criminologists.

Sutherland's most important contribution to the sociology of crime is **differential association** theory. The main point is that people learn criminal behaviour. Therefore, who a person associates with is crucial. One's family and friends—the primary group—are important sources of attitudes toward crime, knowledge about how to commit crimes, and rationalisations that help one live with being a criminal. Today, we would need to add the fact that criminal behaviour can also be learned through television, songs, and especially the Internet. Many criticisms were levelled at differential association theory; even Sutherland later came to criticise it on various grounds. For example, it didn't explain why some people became criminals while others exposed to the same situations did not. One of Sutherland's own criticisms was the fact the theory did not give enough attention to the role of opportunity in committing crimes.

While the above focuses on the causes of crime, especially those that are sociological in nature, criminology has long had a second focus on the criminal justice system (Wellford 2012). This interest is traceable to another early Italian scholar, Cesare Beccaria (1738–1794) (McShane and Williams 2007). Beccaria was a lawyer by training and received a doctorate in law. He is best known for his 1764 book, *On Crimes and Punishments,* and its concern with such issues as the origins of law and the criminal justice system. His work led not only to an interest in this system but also to whether its major components—law enforcement, courts, and corrections (Culver 2007)—were fair, effective, and just. In terms of the latter, much work has been done on the (un)fairness, especially as far as race is concerned, of arrest decisions by the police, length of sentences, and likelihood of receiving the death penalty.

CRIMINAL JUSTICE SYSTEM

The criminal justice system in Canada consists of various loosely connected government agencies and individuals who work in those agencies. Among other things it is involved in the apprehension, prosecution, and punishment of those who violate the law. It also seeks to prevent those violations before they occur. Finally, the criminal justice

BIOGRAPHICAL bits

Edwin H. Sutherland (1863–1950, American)

- Sutherland received his PhD from the University of Chicago.

- He founded and chaired the Department of Sociology at Indiana University and trained a number of the leading criminologists of the twentieth century.

- His theory of differential association, first developed in 1939 and refined over the years, was an important step in the development of a sociology of crime.

- He was the first to use the term *white-collar crime* and published a monograph with that title in 1949.

- This was important in moving the field's focus away from lower-status offenders and in the direction of including "elite" criminals.

- He was ahead of his time in terms of his critique of corporate criminals, as well as of the punitive nature of sexual psychopath laws.

system has much more general responsibilities, such as ensuring public safety and maintaining social order (Tepperman 2010). The major components of the criminal justice system are law enforcement, the courts, and the correctional system.

As a general rule, the criminal justice system is not supposed to operate on an automatic basis (but see the *McDonaldization Today* box later in the chapter). That is, the individuals who work in the system are expected to use their professional judgment and, more generally, individual discretion in their decisions. As a result, police officers do not give tickets to all speeders, prosecutors do not bring all cases to court, and judges do not give the same sentence to all who violate the laws against possession of marijuana. Such discretion at all levels is needed to allow the system to operate in a reasonably efficient fashion. For example, if all of those convicted of a minor crime such as marijuana possession were sentenced to long jail or prison terms, the jails and prisons would be even more overcrowded than they are now. By the way, the distinction between jails and prisons is that the former are locally controlled while the latter are controlled by the provinces or the federal government.

Even with much discretion in the American criminal justice system, an enormous number of people are in the jail and prison system. In 2009 there were 2,292,133 adults incarcerated in federal and state prisons and jails. The United States has the highest rate of incarceration (about 1 percent of the adult population) in the world. It has 750,000 more prisoners than China and 1.5 million more than Russia (see Figure 7.3). Although it has only 5 percent of the world's population, the United States has 25 percent of the world's prisoners (Cullen, Jonson, and Nagin 2011). Canada in contrast to the United States has a much lower rate of incarceration. Whereas in 2010 the U.S incarceration rate was the highest in the world at 730 per

100,000 people, Canada's rate was 117, ranking it 129th in the world. On any given day in 2010–11 there were just over 160,000 adult offenders in Canada's correctional system. However, less than one quarter of these people were in prison. Canada has about 40,000 prisoners at any one time, with about 14,000 in federal confinement, about 24,000 in provincial or territorial prisons, and a little over 1,500 in youth custody. For the other three quarters, most are on some form of probation (Dauvergne 2012).

Beyond those in prison, the criminal justice system also oversees others who are on parole or probation. **Parole** involves the supervised early release of a prisoner for such things as good behaviour while in prison. Parole officers work with those on parole to help them adjust to life outside prison and to be sure they are not violating the conditions of their release. If they do violate those conditions, they can have their parole revoked, and they can be sent back to prison. Those who are convicted of less serious crimes may be placed on **probation**,

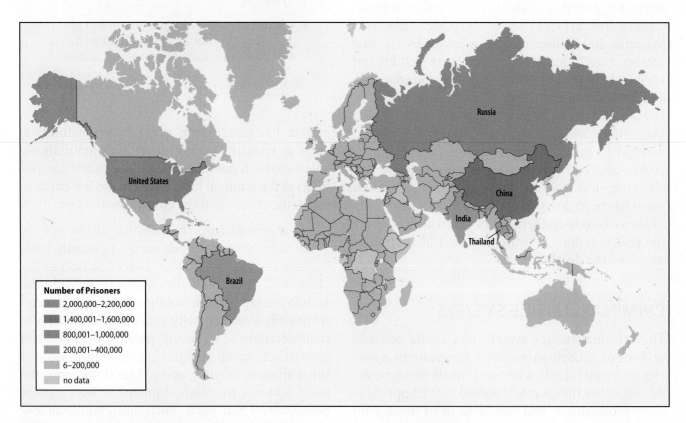

FIGURE 7.3 Inmate Populations by Country, 2004

SOURCE: Data: *Number of Prisoners: World Prison Population List,* 5th edition. Map: Peter Wagner, 2004, Prison Policy Initiative. Reprinted with permission.

PUBLIC SOCIOLOGY

Sociologists on Crime: Wendy Roth and Robert Gordon

Crime stories are media favourites. There is little better to increase ratings than to print or show sensational details of criminal activity—the nitty-gritty details of bad guys sell papers and boost audiences. Sociologists are often asked to comment on criminal activity or crime trends. Thus they play an important role in the public affairs of the nation by offering explanations of puzzling events. Typically sociologists don't comment on the psychopathology of particular criminals, but they might comment on patterns of crime or repeated criminal activity. The expertise of sociologists is also used in crafting legislation that deals with aspects of law enforcement.

So, for example, Wendy Roth, a sociologist at the University of British Columbia, has studied school shootings. The rampage killings that are exemplified in Canada at Dawson College in Montreal (2006) and Taber, Alberta (1999), have occurred around the world. Roth coauthored a book, *Rampage: The Social Roots of School Shootings* (Basic Books 2004), about such shootings, in which they sought patterns of communality among these dreadful incidents. In various media interviews she has explained that while there is no single cause of these horrific tragedies, factors, including social marginalisation, personal vulnerability, access to guns, and cultural scripts fusing violence with masculinity, are important elements of any adequate explanation.

Robert Gordon, also a sociologist, is the director of the School of Criminology at Simon Fraser University. Like Roth, he has been a frequent commentator in the media on a variety of issues, but his public contributions also highlight the role sociologists play in the policy domain. Gordon has been a frequent consultant with government in the drafting of legislation. For example, he has assisted the Ministry of the Attorney General in British Columbia in crafting law related to governing admissions to care facilities and the use of restraint in facilities (Bill 26; 2007). His expertise has played an important role in helping to shape the laws by which we all live.

---

whereby they are released into the community, but under supervision and under certain conditions, such as being involved in and completing a substance abuse programme. If the offender does not adhere to these conditions, is arrested, or is convicted, probation can be revoked. In that case, a new, more restrictive probation can be imposed, or the offender can be sent to prison. Both parole and probation require the involvement of a bureaucracy, especially the parole and probation officers involved in it. These systems, like the prison and jail system, are very costly.

It might be argued that this cost of prisons—as well as the parole and probation systems—is justifiable if they taught people that "crime does not pay." In other words, a case might be made for mass imprisonment if it rehabilitated prisoners so that they there were less likely to commit crimes after they were released. But does a prison term serve as deterrence to the commission of crimes after an inmate is released from prison? It is obvious that prisoners are deterred while imprisoned from further crime, although some seem to be able to engage in crimes while in prison. After a prisoner is released, those involved in the criminal justice system are interested in the issue of **specific deterrence**, or whether the experience of punishment in general, and incarceration in particular, makes it less likely that the ex-prisoner will commit crimes in the future. In other words, the issue is whether an individual will be "scared" straight by punishment, especially incarceration (Apel and Nagin 2011).

Recidivism, or the repetition of a criminal act by one who has been convicted for an offence, is a crucial issue in the criminal justice system (P. Smith 2007). However, most research in the field has shown that prisons do a poor job of rehabilitating prisoners and as a result do not reduce recidivism. Instead, there is evidence that prisons are "schools for crime" and that those in them learn new and better criminal techniques. In other words, prisons have a "criminogenic" effect leading to more rather than less crime (Cullen, Jonson, and Nagin 2011). Nonetheless, no experts would argue for the elimination of punishments, including imprisonment, for most crimes. However, there is a need for more focused forms of specific deterrence (Braga and Weisburd 2011). Furthermore, there are important individual and situational differences that have an impact on the effectiveness of such deterrence. For example, whether an individual is deterred is affected by such factors as the person's impulsivity and such situational factors as involvement in alcohol and drug abuse (Piquero, Paternoster, Pogarsky, and Loughran 2011). However, whatever the individual and situational factors and whatever forms of deterrence are employed, they are not likely to live up to the expectations of those who favour deterrence. What is needed is a focus on what forms of specific deterrence will be effective on what types of criminals and under what circumstances.

General deterrence deals with the population as a whole and whether individuals will be less likely to commit crimes because of fear that they might be punished or imprisoned for their crimes (Apel and Nagin 2011). Although it is not clear

how many people do not commit crimes because of fear of punishment, it is clear that it constitutes some level of deterrence to some who might otherwise become criminals.

The ultimate example of both forms of deterrence is capital punishment, or the death penalty (Paternoster, Brame, and Bacon 2007). Someone who is executed clearly cannot commit another crime. However, there is evidence that even capital punishment is not a strong general deterrent to crime (Cohen-Cole, Durlauf, Fagan, and Nagin 2009).

Canada is one of many countries that have abolished the death penalty. In 1976 the death penalty, legally known as capital punishment, was removed from the Canadian Criminal Code. It was much earlier, however, in 1962, that the last executions took place in Canada. On December 11 both Ronald Turpin and Arthur Lucas were hanged in the Don Jail in Toronto. Turpin had murdered a police officer, and Lucas had killed an informer and witness. Since both murders were judged to be premeditated, they involved the death penalty. These were the last of some 740 people who were lawfully executed in Canada (Leyton-Brown 2010).

Many other countries have abolished the death penalty, including the United Kingdom, France, and Germany. The United States continues to employ it. The five leading countries in the world in terms of the number of people executed are China, Iran, North Korea, Yemen, and the United States. The United States ranks fifth, with 46 executions in 2010 (Amnesty International 2011). The application of capital punishment continues to be highly controversial. In fact, many death sentences in the United States are accompanied by active campaigns against them and vigils protesting executions both before and as they occur. There are many who feel that it is morally wrong to kill anyone. Others are opposed to the death penalty because it is likely that at least some innocent people are killed in the process (Aronson and Cole 2009). Finally, there is strong evidence of bias, especially racial bias, in capital punishment. Many studies have shown that blacks, and nonwhites more generally, who are convicted of killing whites are more likely to get the death penalty than whites who kill other whites (Paternoster 2007).

Parole board hearings are conducted to ascertain whether someone should be conditionally released from prison early, have his or her records suspended, or be granted clemency

TYPES OF CRIMES

Crime statistics are collected by various agencies of the government, but they are organised via Statistics Canada. The numbers in Figure 7.4 provide a portrait of criminal activity in Canada, at least to the extent that crimes reported to the police and police arrest statistics accurately capture criminal activity. Two broad types of crime are reported. **Violent crime** involves the threat of injury or the threat or actual use of force. The violent crimes reported in the figure are murder, robbery, and aggravated assault. **Property crimes** do not involve injury or force, but rather are offences that involve gaining or destroying property. While there are others, such as shoplifting and forgery, the major property crimes include breaking and entering, auto theft, and arson. Another important way of distinguishing crimes is between **indictable offences**, or more serious crimes punishable by a year or more in prison, and **summary convictions**, or minor offences punishable by imprisonment of less than a year.

Beyond these broad types, a number of more specific types of crime are important to society and to criminologists:

- **White-collar crime** is a category proposed (as mentioned in the previous *Biographical Bits*) by Edwin Sutherland. White-collar crimes are those committed "by a person of responsibility and high social status in the course of his occupation" (Geis 2007b:850). Sutherland focused on the nature of the offenders (for example, their high status), while other definitions concentrate on the nature of the offence, with the result that white-collar crimes also include such crimes as passing checks with insufficient funds committed by people of lower social status. Sociologists sometimes distinguish between "suite crime" and "street crime" (Goff and Reasons 1978).

- **Corporate crime** is a related notion, involving legal organisations that violate the law and including such illegal acts as antitrust violations, stock market violations such as insider trading, Ponzi schemes (see above), and false advertisements (Geis 2007a).

- **Organised crime** can involve various types of organisations, but is most often associated with syndicated organised crime, especially the Mafia, which uses violence, or its threat, and the corruption of public officials to profit from illegal activities (Griffin 2007). Other examples of organised crime are Mexican drug cartels and the Russian Mafia.

- **Political crime** can be either an offence against the state to affect its policies, such as the assassination of one of its officials, especially its leader (as in the assassination of U.S. president John F. Kennedy), or an offence by the state, either domestically (for example, spying on citizens) or internationally (state-sponsored terrorism; bribery of a foreign official) (Tunnell 2007).

| | Number of Persons Charged | | | | | |
| | Under 18 years of age | | | 18 years of age and over | | |
Offense Changed	1998	2011	% Change	1998	2011	% Change
TOTAL	107,448	58,864	−82.5	383,583	413,756	7.3
Violent Crimes	**24,477**	**20,345**	**−20.3**	**129,337**	**149,606**	**13.5**
Homicide	56	45	−24.4	432	466	7.3
Armed Robbery	**3,576**	**3,542**	**−1.0**	**6,258**	**7,285**	**14.1**
Aggravated Assault	311	365	14.8	1,748	2,519	30.6
Property Crimes	**61,550**	**22,683**	**−171.3**	**155,596**	**120,481**	**−29.1**
Break and Enter	16,007	4,977	−221.6	25,534	15,109	−69.0

FIGURE 7.4 **Trends in Absolute Numbers of Criminal Charges, Canada, 1998–2011**

When he was 16, David Milgaard was convicted, and sentenced to life imprisonment, for the murder of Gail Miller, a nursing aide in Saskatoon. In 1992, 23 years after his conviction, the Supreme Court of Canada set aside Milgaard's sentence, and he was released from prison. Subsequently Larry Fisher was convicted of the rape and murder of Gail Miller.

- **Hate crimes** are crimes that stem, in whole or in part, from the fact that those who are being victimised are in various ways different from—by race, religion, sexual orientation, gender, national origin, and disability status—and held in contempt by, the perpetrators (Levin 2007).
- **Cybercrime** (see next *Digital Living* box) is a more recent and increasingly important type of crime. It targets computers (for example, by hacking), using them to commit traditional crimes (for example, theft from a bank account or of a credit card number) or to transmit illegal information and images (for example, child pornography, insider

trading, identity theft, plans for a terrorist act, or "cyberterrorism") (Nunn 2007).
- **Consumer crimes**, or crimes related to consumption, include shoplifting and using stolen credit cards or credit card numbers.

Although these are all classified as crimes, they are not all considered equally abhorrent. In line with the idea that deviance is defined by elites, so are crimes and criminal punishments. Thus white-collar and corporate crimes are often downplayed while the crimes usually associated with those in the lower social classes—for example, violent crimes, especially indictable offences, and property crimes—receive a great deal of attention from the police, the media, and the public.

CRIME STATISTICS

Crime statistics are notoriously difficult to collect and often quite inaccurate. While Canadian crime data are more accurate than most, there are still serious problems in data collection. One key source of data in Canada is the Uniform Crime Reporting Survey (UCR), compiled by Statistics Canada and relying on local police reports. However, there are errors in local police reports (see Farmer 2003; Leavitt 1998), and in all local jurisdictions some crimes (street crimes) are more likely to be reported than others (white-collar crimes). Indeed, the rate of reporting crimes to police varies not only by the type of crime but also by victim or witness characteristics, as well as by levels of trust or esteem of the police in the local neighbourhood or jurisdiction (Baumer and Lauritsen 2010). Moreover, as police procedures change, so too may crime statistics. Thus, if police in one area decide to focus on a particular type of crime, the rate of that crime will likely "rise" from one year to the next, whether or not there are in fact higher incidences of that crime. Finally, some crimes simply go unreported by victims for fear of humiliation, reprisal, or other negative outcomes. Kevin Haggerty (2001) provides an in-depth sociological account of how crime is counted. He makes the case that official statistics (or the counting processes of any bureaucracy)are subject to interpretation given that human judgements are involved in decisions about counts (as, for example, what constitutes a suicide or a valid ballot).

Errors and omissions that find their way into the UCR are overcome to some degree by another major source of data on crime, the *General Social Survey on Victimization (GSS-V)*, which is based on asking people whether or not they have been victims of a crime in the previous six months. The GSS-V is administered by Statistics Canada every five years. The big advantage of this survey is that it uncovers crimes not reported to the police, although it, too, has a variety of problems, such as relying on the respondents' self-definitions of what they consider a crime. Victimisation studies tend to show a much higher level of crime in Canada than does the UCR—for example, in 2009, the latest year from which data are available, it is estimated that two thirds of victims of criminal acts did not report the crimes to police (S. Brennan 2012; Perreault and Brennan 2010). To gather a true sense of crime in Canada, it is important to rely on more than one source of data.

While it is difficult to compare crime statistics cross-nationally and globally, it is intriguing to compare rates of crime in Canada and the United States. For example, studies done in the 1990s showed that the United States had about 2.5 times as many robberies as other advanced societies, and that it had a homicide rate 6.5 times the rate in other countries in the sample (Whitehead 2007). In comparison to Canada, the United States is a more violent society. Capital punishment still occurs in the United States, and the murder rate is about 3 times higher in the United States. Indeed, for most measures of violent crime the rates are higher in the United States (Gannon 2001). Conversely, for crimes against property, the rates are often similar or higher in Canada. For example, there were about a third more break-ins and auto thefts in Canada than in the United States in 2000 (Gannon 2001). For both countries the trends over time are largely similar, with homicide rates declining recently in both countries.

DEMOGRAPHICS AND CRIME

Of great interest to criminologists is the relationship between various demographic characteristics and crime. There are important differences among groups of people based on differences in age, gender, race, and social class.

Age

One important demographic issue is the relationship between crime and age, or stage in the life course (Piquero and Gomez-Smith 2007). Under that heading it is important to distinguish crime in general from **juvenile delinquency** (Maahs 2007), which, in Canada, involves crimes committed by those who are less than 18 years of age. Of particular importance is the fact that people are most likely to commit crimes in their late adolescence. Most teenage crime involves little more than dabbling in a few criminal activities (drug use, shoplifting, petty theft) and in most cases ends with the onset of adulthood and adult responsibilities. Of course, some teenage criminals commit serious crimes and continue into adulthood; they may become "life-course persistent" criminals. Nevertheless, the crime rate drops precipitously through the adult years and approaches zero in the later years of adulthood (Bosick 2009; Moffitt 1993; Piquero et al. 2012). See Figure 7.5.

Gender

The vast majority of crimes are committed by men, but there has been a long-term increase in the number of women arrested for committing crimes (Gartner, Webster, and Doob 2009; Mahony 2011), even violent crimes, and in being incarcerated for their crimes (see Figure 7.6). Sprott and Doob (2010) report girls being treated more paternalistically than boys in bail proceedings. However, among adults, Mahony (2011) reports that for those charged with a crime, women are less likely than men to be found guilty and, when they are found guilty, are less likely to receive a sentence involving custody. There are a variety of possible explanations for this, involving the types of crime, but also a possible consequence of women being less likely to be charged with multiple offences and of more women than men being first-time offenders, both factors that affect sentencing.

Women may be increasingly likely to commit and be convicted of crimes for a variety of reasons:

- Having greater opportunities than in the past to commit crimes (for example, they are more likely to be associated with gangs)
- Occupying more high-level positions than in the past where white-collar crime is more likely

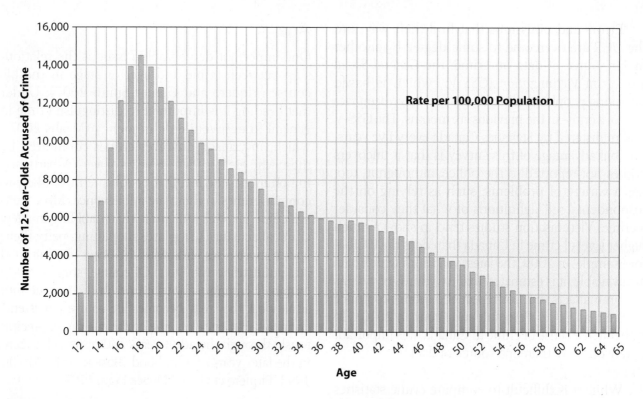

Rate per 100,000 Population

FIGURE 7.5 Persons Accused of Crime, Aged 12 to 65 Years, in Canada, 2011
SOURCE: S. Brennan (2012).

- Having more responsibility for supporting a household, as a single mother would be, but still being mired in low-paying, marginal occupations or, worse, being unemployed

- Being treated more like male offenders as general attitudes toward women's role in society change, especially among law enforcement officers and judges

- Becoming more involved with drugs and therefore with drug-related crime

Women are also more likely to be the victims of certain crimes, especially sexual assaults, harassment, and forcible confinement (see Mahony 2011). Conversely, men are more likely to be the victims of murder, robbery, and extortion.

Ancestry and Race

A disproportionate number of Aboriginal and African Canadians are caught up in the criminal justice system. For example, as Figure 7.7 shows, for Census Day in 2006, the respective incarceration rates of Aboriginal and non-Aboriginal Canadians in Saskatchewan (Census Day is chosen because this gives the most accurate count of the population). Overall, Aboriginal people

While the vast majority of crimes are committed by men, the number of women arrested and incarcerated for committing crimes—even violent crimes—has risen steadily in recent years.

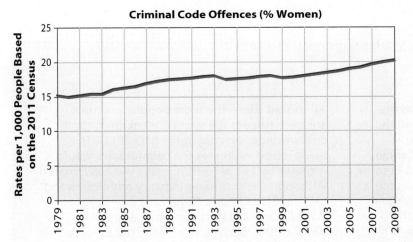

FIGURE 7.6 Women as Percentage of Adults Charged With Criminal Code Offences, 1979–2009 (Estimates)

SOURCE: Estimates by authors based on Mahony (2011, p. 23).

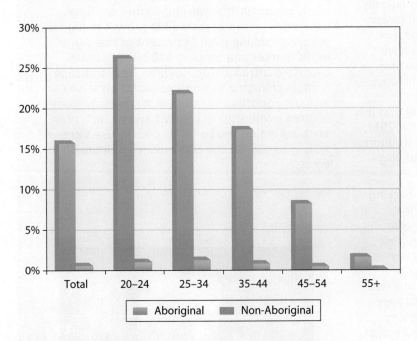

FIGURE 7.7 The Disproportionate Rate of Incarcerations Among Aboriginals, by Age Group, Saskatchewan, May 16, 2006

SOURCE: Authors' calculations based on data in Table 6 of Perreault 2009; rate per capita (1,000).

NOTE: The column labeled "Total" means that for every 1,000 aboriginal people, just over 15 were in custody on May 16, 2006. For every 1,000 non-aboriginals, fewer than one person was in custody that same day.

are 30 times more likely to be incarcerated (Perreault 2009). These findings are similar in other provinces, although the gap is not as wide elsewhere.

In Canada the visible minority population experiences about the same level of victimisation as non-visible minority members (Perreault 2004), although

members of visible minority groups have less confidence in the criminal justice system (Cao 2011). However, Aboriginal Canadians experience more crime than do non-Aboriginals. Scrim (2012) reports that Aboriginal people are three times more likely than non-Aboriginals to be the victims of violent crime.

While these statistical facts are indisputable and reflect major differences based especially on ancestry, it is also the case that biases exist at various points in the criminal justice system. For example, ancestry and race often play a role when the police are deciding whether or not to make an arrest and may in some cases (such as when the victim is white and the accused is nonwhite) be a factor in court decisions on guilt or innocence (Kochel, Wilson, and Mastrofski 2011; Weinrath 2007; Wortley and Tanner 2003). Race also plays a role in other aspects of the criminal justice system, such as whether a criminal gets probation or parole (see the January 2011 special issue of the *Canadian Journal of Criminology and Criminal Justice*).

Social Class

Finally, there is the issue of social class and crime (Chilton and Triplett 2007a). We have already touched on this matter in discussing the greater ability of elite members of society to get away with committing crimes. Those in the upper classes are more likely to commit crimes that evade police detection, while crimes more characteristic of the lower classes—street crimes—are more likely to be detected and handled by the police (Braithwaite 1997).

Social class is related to crime in a number of other ways. Those in the lower social classes are more likely to be driven to a life of crime because of economic need (Baron 2008; Wakefield and Uggen 2010). Furthermore, they are more likely to

DIGITAL LIVING

Cybercrime

Certain characteristics of the web, such as the infinite reproducibility of information and the ease of distributing that information across time and space, lend it to new modes of crime. Significantly, the Internet allows crime to become increasingly globalised. As a result, cybercrime is seldom restricted to national borders. However, it is important to remember that, while the infrastructures through which crimes are committed have changed, the social problems and individual incentives that motivate crime remain much the same. As with traditional crime, there is a wide range of crimes committed using the Internet. One of the most common and widespread Internet crimes is hacking, or illegally accessing data. Others are digital content piracy and government and industrial espionage. For example, American intelligence agencies have publicly condemned both China and Russia for using the Internet to steal valuable technology from the U.S. government and American corporations. The losses are so substantial that it is impossible to estimate their value (Shanker 2011). Then there are harassment and bullying through online social networks and distribution of illegal content (such as child pornography).

Identity theft through phishing and hacking databases is another common form of crime on the Internet. It is subject to intense media attention, and many businesses advertise their ability to prevent such theft. The most common form of identity theft is unauthorised use of a credit card account. It is estimated that, in a two-year period, 5 percent of American adults were the target of attempted or successful identity theft. Losses totalled $17.3 billion (U.S. Bureau of Justice Statistics 2008).

Music and video piracy is, undoubtedly, the most widespread form of criminal activity on the Internet. The Recording Industry Association of America (RIAA [2011]) estimates over 40 billion illegal downloads occurred between 2004 and 2009 (that is roughly six songs for every person on Earth!). The era of mass digital file sharing began in June 1999 with the meteoric rise of Napster, the notorious content-sharing hub. Though Napster was ordered to shut down in July 2001, other pirate sites have been adept at finding new ways to skirt the law. The IFPI (International Federation of the Phonographic Industry) reports that, in 2011, 89 percent of all torrent files—the most popular protocol for peer-to-peer file sharing—link to content that infringes on copyrights (IFPI 2011). The same report estimates that digital sales would increase by 131 percent if piracy were eliminated. Although the recording industry and Hollywood saw profits plummet 32 percent from 2003 to 2010 (Sisario 2011), critics often argue that much of the damage is self-inflicted because the industries have resisted modernisation. For years, consumers had few options other than piracy for obtaining digital content.

The launch of the iTunes store in January 2001 made the process of purchasing digital music easier for the average consumer. iTunes ushered in an era of incredible growth in digital sales, controlling over 70 percent of the digital music market and topping $10 billion in sales by 2010 (Luttrell 2010). However, the landscape is again changing as music subscription services including Spotify shift the paradigm away from content ownership to content access. Such sites are banking on the belief that many users are willing to pay for the convenience of immediate access

SOURCE: Printed with the permission of PJ Rey.

Identity theft is subject to intense media attention, and many businesses advertise their ability to prevent such theft. The most common form of identity theft is unauthorised use of a credit card account.

GL⦿BALISATION

Women and Crime in Taliban-Controlled Afghanistan

While gender inequality is falling throughout much of the world (Dorius and Firebaugh 2010) as a result of modernisation and the spread of global human rights norms, some countries remain intensely strong patriarchal societies. Afghanistan is one such country, ranking next-to-last out of 102 countries regarding gender inequality in social institutions (Branisa, Klasen, and Ziegler 2009). For example, in areas of Afghanistan where the Taliban are still in control, women are confined to their homes or strictly supervised in public, so they have little opportunity to commit most types of crime that Americans consider worthy of the name. However, women are subject to severe punishment for social offences such as adultery and elopement. Despite bans on such practices throughout much of the world, under Islamic sharia law it is permissible to this day to stone people to death, especially women, as well as to amputate parts of the body. The practice was described in gruesome detail in the 2008 movie, *The Stoning of Soraya M.*

Stoning achieved a great deal of notoriety when the Taliban were in power in Afghanistan and is still being employed in some areas of Afghanistan. The practice made the news in 2010 when a couple, who had been unable to persuade the woman's family to allow them to marry, was stoned to death for eloping. The man was married with two children, but that was not the problem. Afghan men can have as many as four wives. The problem was that the woman was engaged to a relative of the man, but refused to marry him. A religious court found the couple guilty and sentenced them to death by stoning.

The couple had run away, but they were tricked into returning by family members who said that they would be allowed to marry. Once they returned, the punishment was decided upon and carried out by a group of about 200 villagers (no women allowed). When the punishment commenced, members of the Taliban were the first to cast stones; others, including family members (the man's father and brother and the woman's brother), soon joined them. The woman died first from multiple wounds caused by the stones; the man died soon after. The crowd was reported to be joyful and festive during the stoning because the couple was perceived to have committed a crime (Nordland 2010).

Shortly before this, a pregnant woman, a widow, was convicted of "fornication" with a man she said had promised to marry her. For that crime, she received 200 lashes with a whip and then was shot to death. Such punishments can only contribute to the high death rates in Afghanistan, which is second to none in global death rate (Central Intelligence Agency 2013b).

---

be convicted and sent to prison, in part because of their inability to afford the expensive legal defense teams available to elite members of society. For example, exactly how much Conrad Black paid in legal fees to fight the charges against him will likely never be known, but there is little doubt the figure runs to the tens of millions of dollars.

The fact that a greater percentage of Aboriginal people (and other minorities) are arrested for, and convicted of, crimes may be traceable to their over-representation in the lower classes. For example, Aboriginal Canadians earn lower incomes than do their non-Aboriginal peers, and it may be this greater economic stress, their poverty, or straitened class position that accounts for the higher crime rates (D. Wilson and MacDonald 2010). Such a view is particularly characteristic of conflict/critical theorists, especially those associated with Marxian theory (Sims 2007).

GLOBALISATION AND CRIME

The amount of global, or cross-border (Andreas and Nadelmann 2006; Shelley, Picarelli, and Corpora 2011), crime has increased with globalisation; globalisation makes cross-border crime increasingly possible and more likely. International crime has existed for centuries in such forms as piracy on the oceans and the African slave trade. However, today there seems to be far more of it. This may be due to the fact that because of the increase in global criminal flows, much more public and government attention seems to be devoted to these crimes. Fortunately, action against crime does flow almost as easily as the crimes themselves.

The growth in global crime is largely traceable to increasing concern with drugs in the United States in the late 1960s and early 1970s, as well as Western European interest in terrorism during

McJustice

The criminal justice system may not always appear to function very rationally or efficiently. For example, the police often do not apprehend criminals, and they occasionally botch cases by failing to follow established legal procedures. The courts are overwhelmed by the number of cases that they are required to deal with, yet they often get bogged down with lengthy and costly trials and numerous appeals. Correctional institutions seem to be the most irrational. They are overflowing and have little or no time or resources to rehabilitate criminals. Even more irrational is the fact that criminals often leave prisons better criminals than when they entered (Sykes [1958] 2007). In spite of, or perhaps because of, these irrationalities, all facets of the criminal justice system have sought to McDonaldize their operations in various ways.

One of the ways in which the police force has sought to grow more efficient is to adopt a zero-tolerance approach to various offences, thereby eliminating the need to spend time deciding whether or not to enforce a law (Robinson 2010). Also increasing the efficiency of police operations is the use of new advanced technologies, as well as the shift from standard patrol cars to smaller, seemingly equally effective, one-person vehicles. In the courts, frequency of plea bargaining has increased dramatically. This means that cases are settled informally before they ever go to lengthy and expensive trials, which clog up court calendars and slow down legal proceedings.

In terms of calculability, in an economically distressed climate, public agencies such as the police are forced to focus on, and to adapt to, limited funding. As a result, they seek to maximise security with minimal resources. In the courts we find the guilty being given longer sentences and offenders serving a larger portion of their sentences in prison. In the prison system there is a focus, given the ever-growing number of inmates with mandatory sentencing, on building more prisons, and housing more prisoners in those institutions.

Greater predictability is exemplified by sentencing guidelines and mandatory sentences. Classification and segregation of prisoners on the basis of the risks they pose make for greater predictability in the management of given types and groups of prisoners. As for control, the police are able to exert greater control over serious crime because of a series of recent laws (such as Bill 36, the Canadian Anti-Terrorism Act) and the loosening of existing laws constraining the police. Courts have become much more oriented toward crime control. Finally, increasing control in the prison system is best exemplified by the use of new advanced technologies to manage prisons (Bulman 2009; S. Hart 2003; Mampaey and Renaud 2000).

However, in spite of, or perhaps because of, McDonaldization, Canadians are less sure of receiving justice from the justice system. The McDonaldization of the criminal justice system has come at the cost of reducing the likelihood that defendants will get the "due process" they are supposed to receive. This is a major irrationality associated with the McDonaldization of the criminal justice system.

Sergeant Neil Owen of the Strathclyde Police, headquartered in Glasgow, Scotland, holds a prototype Unmanned Airborne Vehicle (UAV). The Strathclyde Police, like a rising number of European and U.S. police forces, has begun to use such advanced technology.

roughly the same period. Drugs and terrorism now top the list of global concerns as far as crime is concerned, but others include "clandestine trade in sophisticated weaponry and technology, endangered species, pornographic materials, counterfeit products, guns, ivory, toxic waste, money, people [the trafficking in human beings; B. Perrin 2010], stolen property, and art and antiquities" (Andreas and Nadelmann 2006:5). All of these involve flows of all sorts—drugs, money, human victims (for example, those to be used as prostitutes), and human perpetrators (such as terrorists), as well as various illegal things that flow through the World Wide Web (for example, child pornography, laundered funds, the spread of computer viruses).

These illegal flows have been aided by the decline of the nation-state and its increasing inability to reduce, or halt, these flows. Furthermore, global criminal cartels have come into existence to expedite illegal flows and to increase the profits that can be derived from them. The book *McMafia* (Glenny 2008) attributes much of their success to increasingly sophisticated organisational methods (including economies of scale, global partnerships, and the opening of new markets) that are copied from leading legitimate businesses such as McDonald's. New technologies have also been employed to make at least some criminal flows more successful. For example, one cartel used a primitive submarine to transport drugs. The Internet has made a number of illegal flows (for example, child pornography and Internet scams) much easier and is largely impervious to efforts at control by individual nation-states.

"Criminalisation" of Global Activities

As pointed out earlier, crime (and deviance) is always a matter of social definition or social construction. So although the power of nation-states has generally declined in the global age, it continues to matter greatly in what comes to be *defined* as global forms of deviance and crime. In the era of globalisation, the nation-states of Western Europe and the United States have played the central role in criminalising certain activities; it is *their* sense of morality and *their* norms of behaviour that have come to be the rule in much of the world (Andreas and Nadelmann 2006). The global criminalisation of drug use is a good case in point.

However, while there have been a number of efforts to define drug use as deviant and illegal, they have not always been successful. The global drug trade has in fact expanded in spite of great efforts by Canada, the United States, and other nation-states to at least reduce it.

Much of the publicity about drugs, including the ways in which they are implicated in globalisation, involves cocaine and heroin. Great attention is devoted to, for example, the growing of poppies in Afghanistan and drug production in Guatemala and the ways in which drugs from those areas, and many others, make their way around the world. A relatively new global drug is methamphetamine (meth), made easily and cheaply in home-based "cooking facilities" from pseudoephedrine, the main ingredient in a number of cough, cold, and allergy medications. The AMC television show *Breaking Bad* deals with the "cooking" of meth by an ex–high school chemistry teacher in New Mexico and meth's often violent relationship to the drug trade in nearby Mexico. Once largely an American phenomenon, the production and use of

According to the United Nations' 2012 World Drug Report, methamphetamine use and production have recently proliferated throughout East and Southeast Asia. Commonly referred to as *shabu*, the methamphetamine produced in Asia tends to be remarkably pure—and potent.

GL⊕BALISATION

Crime on the Mexican American Border

The international drug trade has a long and complex history that is rooted, for example, in the disparity in wealth between North America and South America, as well as the fact that the United States places stricter prohibitions on drug use than most other countries. Though prohibitions in the United States on alcohol and drug use extend back into colonial times, President Richard Nixon intensified and centralised enforcement of drug restrictions, declaring a "war on drugs" in 1969. The policy has persisted for decades, notably expanding under the Ronald Reagan and Bill Clinton administrations. The U.S. Federal Bureau of Investigation reported that in 2009 the number of arrests for drug-related offences totalled 1,663,582, or 12.2 percent of all arrests in the United States (U.S. Department of Justice—Federal Bureau of Investigation 2010).

The United Nations Office on Drugs and Crime (2010) estimates that 155 million to 250 million people globally (3.5 to 5.7 percent of the world's population, aged 15–64) used illegal substances at least once in 2008, with the largest markets in North America and Europe. Because there is no way for affluent Americans who want these drugs to obtain them legally, a lucrative black market has emerged (see Global Flow Map 7.1). Drug cartels, taking advantage of lax regulation and weak enforcement mechanisms in South and Central America, have developed a complex infrastructure to produce drugs and smuggle them into the United States. Roughly 60 percent of all illicit drugs found in the United States enter through the Mexican border (Archibold 2009). The illegal drugs most trafficked across that border include marijuana, methamphetamine, and cocaine.

The cartels, each competing for a larger share of the multibillion-dollar industry, have ignited a series of turf wars. To secure or expand their hold on profitable drug routes, they are smuggling weapons from the United States, where guns are plentiful and laws regulating their purchase are lax, to Mexico. Possessing assault rifles, grenades, and bulletproof vests, gangs are now often better armed than local police forces. Moreover, because the drug trade is so much more profitable than other industries in Mexico, cartels are often able to buy off poorly paid local police officials. Violent crime on the Mexican side of the border has become commonplace. In 2009, about 3,400 people were killed in the border city of Tijuana alone (Thompson and Lacey 2010). The Mexican border city of Ciudad Juárez is one of the most dangerous and deadly cities in the entire world. In fact, the violence has gotten so bad that thousands of Mexicans are fleeing their homes—some even seeking political asylum in the United States (McKinley 2010). In an effort to combat this lawlessness, the Mexican government has made long-term deployments of federal police and soldiers to the border region.

Violence is also spilling over the American side of the border. In 2009, more than 200 home invasions were reported in Tucson, Arizona, and three quarters of them were directly linked to the drug trade (Archibold 2009). Police believe that in some cases, Americans have been murdered simply for crossing paths with drug traffickers in the process of sneaking across the border (Archibold 2010).

Violence stemming from the drug trade is now so significant that it has come to dominate U.S.-Mexican relations. In 2010, Secretary of State Hillary Clinton told the Mexican government, "We know that the demand for drugs drives much of this illicit trade, that guns purchased in the United States are used to facilitate violence here in Mexico. The United States must, and is doing its part to help you, and us, meet those challenges" (cited in Thompson and Lacey 2010).

methamphetamine is beginning to expand globally. For example, it is a growing problem in the Czech Republic and Slovakia, and the fear is that it will spread from there throughout the European Union and many other parts of the world as well (Kulish 2007). There are several aspects of crime, especially as it relates to drugs, which help account for why global, as well as national, efforts to counter it are largely unsuccessful. First, those who commit the crimes do not require a great many resources. Second, they do not need very much expertise to commit the crimes. Third, such crimes are easy to conceal. Fourth, in many cases the crimes are not apt to be reported to the police or other authorities. Finally, the crimes are those for which great consumer demand exists and there are no readily available alternative products (for example, drugs) or activities (for example, prostitution) (Andreas and Nadelmann 2006).

Another development hindering efforts to control global crime is the establishment of **free-trade zones**, or geographic areas that are controlled by corporations rather than the nation-state in which they exist. Most free-trade zones are in the Global South, and they include the maquiladoras in Mexico and the Cavite Export Processing Zone in the Philippines. These areas serve to expedite the flow of illegal products, and they are efficient transit points for all sorts of legal (and illegal) products moving throughout the world. Free-trade zones impose no tariffs, and there is minimal oversight over most of these zones since goods do not officially enter the country in which the zone exists. A raid on a free-trade zone in Dubai revealed the role Dubai plays in the global distribution of counterfeit medications (Bogdanich 2007). In this case, the fake drugs travelled from China, to Hong Kong, through Dubai, and then to Great Britain, the Bahamas, and ultimately to an Internet seller who marketed them to Americans as Canadian drugs. Such shipments are difficult to intercept, and it is even more difficult to find out where the products have been manufactured.

However, it would be wrong to judge global efforts to control drugs, as well as other illegal substances and activities, as complete failures. The fact is that while drugs continue to flow readily throughout the world for the reasons suggested above, the industrial west and principally the United States has had considerable success in internationalising its views, laws, procedures, and efforts at enforcement. As mentioned earlier, powerful societies are often able to get weaker societies to adopt their ways of doing things. Foreign governments have altered their laws and methods of law enforcement to more closely match western laws on drugs; acceded to demands by western nations to sign law enforcement treaties; adopted advanced investigative techniques; created specialised drug enforcement agencies; stationed law enforcement representatives in other countries; enacted various laws on

conspiracy, asset forfeiture, and money laundering relating to drugs; and provided greater assistance to western countries, and changed laws, on financial secrecy. In other words, we have seen a westernisation and, some would argue, an Americanisation of law enforcement throughout much of the world.

Global Crime Control

The growth in global crime has been met, of course, by the growth of international policing and of the role of the police in international relations (Andreas and Nadelmann 2006; Bowling and Sheptycki 2012). The United States has taken the lead in countering forms of global crime other than drugs and in influencing other nations to work against them. In the early twentieth century its focus was on "white slavery" (prostitution), during the Cold War it was the control of weapons and advanced technology, and in the mid-1980s the focus shifted to the regulation of securities markets, especially insider trading. Following the onset of the recent recession, the focus shifted again to abuses in the global financial system as well as illegal economic activities, such as opening secret bank accounts in other countries, especially Switzerland and the rate-rigging practices used in setting the daily LIBOR (London Inter-Bank Offered Rate), the most widely used interest rate in the world ("Interest Rates" 2012).

Since 9/11, there has been a dramatic erosion of distinctions in the world of criminal justice in an effort to forestall further terrorist attacks and to catch or kill people defined as terrorists. For example, the distinction between law enforcement and intelligence operations has eroded as law enforcement authorities seek to gain intelligence on potential terrorists. The distinction between law enforcement and security has also eroded. For example, the USA PATRIOT Act (Uniting and Strengthening America by Providing Appropriate Tools Required to Intercept and Obstruct Terrorism Act), signed into law on October 26, 2001, played a key role in this erosion by, for example, extending the concern of law enforcement agencies to domestic terrorism. In addition, surveillance of the border between the United States and Mexico, and in immigrant

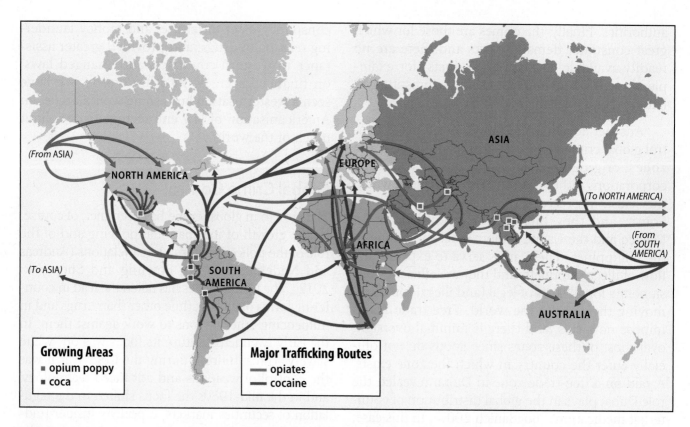

GLOBAL FLOW MAP 7.1 Major Trafficking Routes of Black-Market Drugs, 2007

SOURCE: From Gilman, Nils; Jesse Goldhammer; and Steven Weber. *Deviant Globalization: Black Market Economy in the 21st Century.* Copyright © 2011 Continuum Publishing Company. Reprinted with permission.

communities in the United States, has increased. In the process, many immigrants have been defined as criminals, apprehended, and then returned to Mexico. It is important to note that far less attention is devoted to surveillance on the much longer border with Canada, and those who do cross that border illegally are much less likely to be defined, or apprehended, as criminals.

Some European countries instituted a similar, though not as extreme, toughening of border controls and surveillance. However, within the European Union, border controls and surveillance were relaxed. Border law enforcement within the European Union became more homogeneous as criminal justice norms and procedures became more similar and law enforcement contacts and information exchange among member states became more regular. Of great importance was the formation of Europol, which allowed better and increased communication and cooperation among national police agencies.

While these efforts have improved global crime control, there are also a variety of downsides associated with these efforts. For one thing, democracy and civil rights may be threatened by these efforts. Crime control efforts are not always as transparent as they need to be, and the officials involved often need to be more accountable. For another, tougher border and immigration controls have led to more daring and dangerous efforts to cross borders, leading to more deaths in the process. In addition, the global antidrug campaign has generated high levels of crime, violence, corruption, disease, and so on. Efforts by the United States to deal with trafficking in women and children focus more on criminalising that traffic than on protecting the human rights of the women and children being trafficked. Finally, the attention and money devoted to international crime and its control have tended to distract attention, and to take money away, from efforts to deal with a wide range of fundamental issues within nation-states, including the welfare of large portions of society.

Between 2007 and 2011, approximately 40,000 people were killed in the drug war that continues to ravage Mexico to this day. Here, overcrowded forensic lockers in Ciudad Juárez, Mexico, are filled to the ceiling with the bodies of drug-related shooting victims.

Extreme, sometimes intrusive surveillance has become the norm in many hubs of inter- and intranational travel. Here, an array of video cameras is used to record activity at a Singaporean subway station.

Public efforts to control global crime have been far from totally successful. In at least one case—the killings in Mexico related to the drug wars between gangs—people have been trying to deal with the problem on their own. Between 2007 and 2011 approximately 40,000 people were killed in the drug war that continues to this day to ravage Mexico and is beginning to spread across the border into the United States. The police have failed to halt the carnage, and even the use of the military has not met with much success. The media, often intimidated by the gangs, have often failed to provide needed and accurate information about criminal activities.

Many Mexican citizens have given up hope of help from the state and the media. They have begun to try to help themselves, most notably through crowdsourcing information via social media such as Twitter (4 million Mexican users) and Facebook (almost 30 million Mexican profiles) (J. Sullivan 2010).

In late 2011, 35 bodies were dumped on a Veracruz highway at rush hour. Before police and the media had arrived on the scene, Twitter was alive with messages such as "Avoid Plaza Las Americas" and "There are gunmen . . . they're not soldiers or marines, their faces are masked" (Cave 2011:5). More generally, social media have been used to warn of shootouts involving drug gangs and of roadblocks set up by the drug cartels.

While social media were used elsewhere in the world (Tunisia, Egypt) to help bring about social revolution, in Mexico they have been employed to help people deal with crime. They provide people with not only needed information but also a sense of social support, as well as offering a bit of certainty in a highly uncertain world.

However, the drug gangs may be striking back. Two mangled bodies were found hanging from a bridge in a city bordering the United States with a nearby sign: "This will happen to all the Internet snitches" (Cave 2011:5). While the drug lords have been successful in intimidating centralised media, police, and the military, it may be much more difficult to control the decentralised masses that are anonymously crowdsourcing information about drug-related violence.

SUMMARY

For sociologists, a person or action is deviant when it is socially defined as such. Although different parts of the globe may differ in what they define as deviant, deviance exists in all parts of the world. Durkheim, whose work was crucial to the development of structural-functionalism, argued that since deviance and crime have always existed in all societies they are, in essence, normal and have positive functions for society.

Strain theory is a more contemporary version of structural-functionalism, which argues that deviance is more likely to occur when a culture values something, such as material success, but the societal structure does not allow everyone the ability to achieve this value in a socially accepted way. Merton developed the most useful strain theory for the contemporary world, examining the way people relate and react to the institutionalised means that are needed to achieve cultural goals. Travis Hirschi's social control theory has affinities with structural-functionalism, though it focuses on why people do not commit deviant acts.

Conflict theorists see inequality, in particular economic inequality, as the cause of much deviance. Conflict theorists argue that those who are in the lowest classes engage in deviant or criminal behaviour because they otherwise have few ways of achieving normative societal goals, whereas those in the upper classes commit crimes because the nature of their positions makes it relatively easy to do so.

Structural/functional and conflict/critical theories of deviance are examples of explanatory theories, theories that are concerned with trying to explain why deviance occurs. Inter/actionist theories of deviance are an example of constructionist theories, which are concerned with achieving a greater understanding of the process by which people create a moral order that serves to define and classify some behaviours as normal and others as deviant.

From an inter/actionist perspective, two things are necessary for deviance to occur. First, a symbol or label (such as *alcoholic*) is needed, and then an interaction must occur between a social control agent, the person or group doing the labelling, and the person or group to whom the label is applied. Labelling theory contends that a deviant is someone to whom a deviant label has been successfully applied. Another inter/actionist perspective comes from Goffman's writings on stigma, a characteristic that others find, define, and often label as unusual, unpleasant, or deviant.

Crime is a form of deviance that is a violation of the criminal law. The major components of the criminal justice system are law enforcement, the courts, and the correctional system. Criminologists often try to understand and explain the relationship between crime and demographic characteristics such as age, gender, race, and social class.

Increasing globalisation has been associated with increases in global or cross-border crime, particularly regarding the international drug trade. These illegal flows are aided by the decline of the ability of nation-states to halt these flows. The United States and Western Europe have played a central role in defining global criminal acts and the most appropriate ways to deal with them.

KEY TERMS

- Conformists 241
- Constructionist theories 238
- Consumer crime 258
- Corporate crime 257
- Crime 252
- Criminalisation 232
- Criminology 252
- Cybercrime 258
- Deviance 232
- Differential association 253
- Discreditable stigma 251

- Discredited stigma 251
- Explanatory theories 238
- Free-trade zones 267
- General deterrence 256
- Hate crimes 258
- Indictable offences 257
- Innovators 241
- Interaction 248
- Juvenile delinquency 259
- Labelling theory 248
- Moral entrepreneurs 249

THINKING ABOUT SOCIOLOGY

1. What do sociologists mean when they say that deviance is socially defined? Given a sociological approach, in what ways is obesity deviant, and in what ways is it not?

2. How can we understand deviance as a global flow? How do countries differ in terms of their interpretation of what is deviant? In an increasingly globalised world, what are the consequences of these differing interpretations?

3. How does consuming the "wrong" products and services make someone a deviant? What does this suggest about the relationships between power and deviance?

4. Adolescents and teenagers value a certain level of independence from their parents. Often, teenagers want more control over their own lives. They want to be able to do what they want to do without the need for permission from their parents. Apply Merton's strain theory to an understanding of how teenagers might behave given this desire for more independence.

5. In what ways is the public shaming of criminals in China related to labelling theory? What influence has globalisation had on this practice of global shaming?

6. Why do those who rank high in such hierarchies as business, government, and the military have a much greater ability to commit deviant acts, to have them be seen as being legitimate, and to get away with them? What does this suggest about the "fairness" of deviance?

7. What are the differences between a discredited stigma and a discreditable stigma? What is an example of each?

8. How is crime different from deviance? Why do some forms of deviance become criminalised and others do not?

9. How have Canada's police, courts, and corrections become increasingly McDonaldized? In what ways does the criminal justice system operate irrationally?

10. What sort of barriers do countries attempt to implement in order to limit the global flow of drugs? Why have these been relatively unsuccessful?

APPLYING THE SOCIOLOGICAL IMAGINATION

In this exercise you will use an ethnomethodological approach to understand the stable and orderly properties of interactions on the Internet. You will need to pay specific attention to the ways in which rules are broken on the Internet.

First select a website that allows for people to interact with one another (such as Facebook, Twitter, your favourite interactive blog, an online discussion forum, or the comments section of an article on your local newspaper's website). In what ways does the Internet help facilitate behaviour that might be deviant elsewhere? What norms are broken on the Internet that might not be broken in face-to-face interactions? What sorts of structural barriers exist on the Internet that might limit deviant behaviour? Overall, do you think deviant behaviour flows more easily because of the Internet?

ACTIVE SOCIOLOGY

Folkway violations—that is, mild forms of deviance—often provide good examples of humour. In today's society, a lot of this kind of deviance can be instantly shared via text messaging and online. Several websites are devoted to sharing (for the sake of humour) acts of deviance as witnessed in public. One of these is People of Walmart (www.peopleofwalmart.com).

How do the photos on the site demonstrate deviance? Are there any that cross the line from violations of folkways to violations of mores? Is there any evidence of potentially illegal activity? Have you ever posted to a site like this? How does the fact that deviant actions can be instantly and permanently seen influence what you do in public?

STUDENT STUDY SITE

Visit the student study site at www.sagepub.com/ritzercanadian for additional web quizzes for further review.

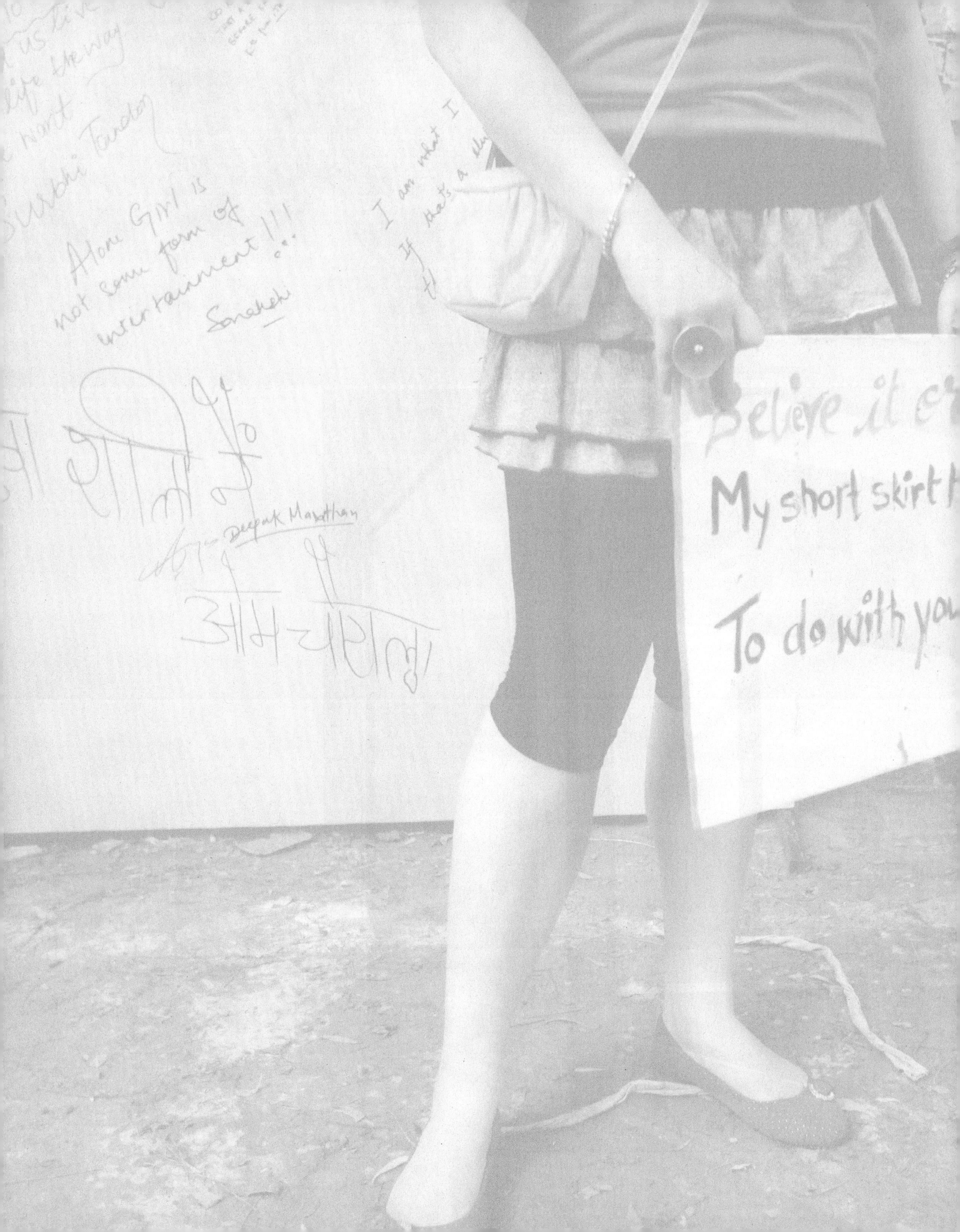
My short skirt
To do with

SOCIAL INEQUALITY

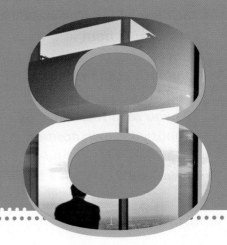

8

Increasing concentrations of wealth, power, and status have given an elite few the power to ascend to the very highest levels of the global system of social inequality. The norms, tastes, and beliefs they share have been shaped not by any given local culture, but by a global one.

According to journalist Chrystia Freeland, an unprecedented shift is taking place in the global socioeconomic structure. Deregulation of global trade and advances in information technology have led to the emergence of a small, ultrarich class of elite entrepreneurs and executives who think and operate much differently than their predecessors. "Our light-speed, globally connected economy has led to the rise of a new super-elite . . . a transglobal community of peers who have more in common with one another than with their countrymen back home," says Freeland (2011). Investment (both emotional and financial) in one's own country falls by the wayside given the overwhelming focus on business—no matter where that business takes place.

Some have suggested that the United States (and much of the northern hemisphere) is shifting toward a plutocracy, a governmental and social structure whereby "the rich display outsize political influence, narrowly self-interested motives, and a casual indifference to anyone outside their own rarefied economic bubble" (Freeland 2011). Indeed, eight months after Freeland's article was published, business magnate and third richest person in the world Warren Buffett wrote an opinion piece in The New York Times calling for higher taxes on the ultrarich. Fellow billionaire Charles G. Koch responded, "I believe my business and non-profit investments are much more beneficial to societal well-being than sending more money to Washington" (Foster 2011).

Increasing concentrations of wealth, power, and status have given an elite few the power to ascend to the very highest levels of the global system of social inequality. The norms, tastes, and beliefs they share have been shaped not by any given local *culture, but by a global one. Because many of these elites achieved their successes rather than being born into them, they are fiercely driven and, in some cases, ambivalent toward the socioeconomic strain felt by the middle and lower classes of their home countries. As you read the following chapter, think about your own position in your country's stratified society. And—just for fun—imagine what you'd do with a billion dollars.*

We often hear that the world is unfair, a statement generally meaning that a relatively small number of people have way too much, while most of the rest, especially us, have far too little. In Canada, this unfairness is made abundantly clear when we see or read news reports about the excesses of the super-rich, such as multimillion-dollar bonuses, private jets, and mansions worth tens of millions of dollars. At the other extreme, the gap is just as clear when we encounter homeless people begging on street corners or squeegee kids at traffic lights in big cities.

What is it that some people have, or are thought to have, and others lack? The most obvious answer is money and that which money buys. However, **social inequality** involves social differences that are consequential for the lives people lead, and especially the rewards and benefits they control. Beyond economic rewards social inequality involves other important areas such as status, or social honour, and power. Social inequality has a profound effect on how monetary and nonmonetary resources are distributed in Canadian society and around the globe.

DIMENSIONS OF SOCIAL INEQUALITY

Any sociological discussion of inequality (or stratification) draws on an important set of dimensions derived from the work of the great German social theorist Max Weber ([1921] 1968; see also Bendix and Lipset 1966; Ultee 2007a, 2007b). These three dimensions are social class, status, and power.

SOCIAL CLASS

One's economic position in the system of social inequality, especially one's occupation, defines a person's **social class**. One's social class position strongly determines and reflects one's income and wealth. Those who rank close to one another in wealth and income can be said to be members of the same social class. For example, Galen Weston (who owns Loblaw and Holt Renfrew) and Arthur Irving (who owns Irving Oil) belong to one social class; the janitor in your university building and the mechanic who fixes your family car belong to another. Terms often used to describe a person's social class are *upper class* (investors, for example); *middle class* (for example, semi-professionals such as nurses, veterinarians, air traffic controllers, travel agents, firefighters, and teachers); *working class* (clerical and sales workers); and *lower class* (part-time workers and the unemployed, for example). Figure 8.1 illustrates the relationships among occupation, income, and social class in Canada. Its teardrop-like shape approximates the percentage of Canadians in each class; there are substantially more people in the working and lower classes than there are in the upper class. As we will soon see, Canada is even more stratified than is suggested by Figure 8.1.

As discussed in Chapter 2, Karl Marx had a different conception of social class than did Weber. To Marx, social class was defined by ownership of the *means of production,* the resources necessary for production to take place such as factories, machines, tools, and raw materials. Those who owned the means of production were the *capitalists,* and they stood at the pinnacle of the stratification system. Members of the *proletariat* lacked the means of production and therefore had to sell their labour time to the capitalists in order to work and be productive. This created a hierarchal stratification system with the capitalists on top and the proletariat standing far lower in that hierarchy. This constituted a class system in the sense that the capitalists kept the vast majority of profits for themselves, had higher incomes, and accumulated

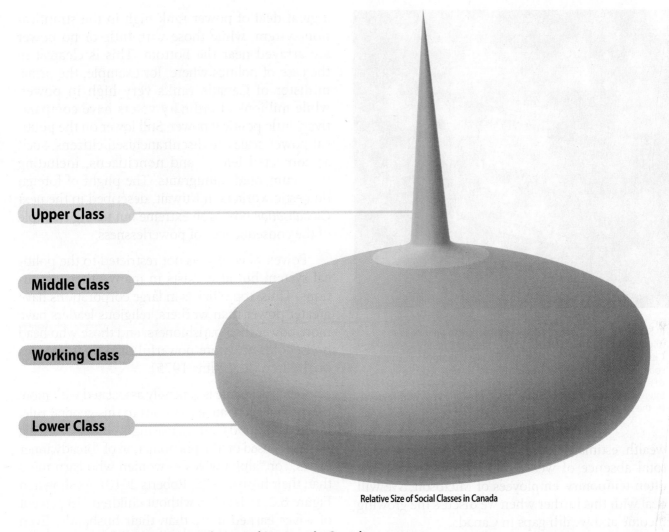

Upper Class

Middle Class

Working Class

Lower Class

Relative Size of Social Classes in Canada

FIGURE 8.1 Social Classes, Occupations, and Incomes in Canada

great wealth. In contrast, the capitalists barely paid the proletariat enough to survive. Thus the proletariat found it impossible to accumulate wealth.

While Marx's conception of social class is still useful, changes in the economic system have made it less relevant today. For example, it is now much harder to argue that capitalists are defined by, and gain their position in the system of inequality from, their ownership of the means of production. Such capitalists have come to be replaced by corporations, whose stocks and bonds are owned by thousands, hundreds of thousands, or even millions of share- and bondholders. The people who stand at the pinnacle of the stratification system today own a disproportionate number of these stocks and bonds; they do not own, at least not directly, the

means of production such as factories. They may also hold positions at or near the top of these corporations, but again, those positions do not give those who hold them ownership of the means of production.

Today, members of the proletariat still occupy lower-level positions in these corporations, they still must sell their labour time for access to the means of production, and they continue to be relatively poorly paid. However, they may be minor stockholders in these corporations, for example through their pension investments. Still, there is a vast economic difference today between those who occupy high-level positions in corporations and/or own large blocks of stocks and those at the bottom who own a few shares. Contrast Bill Gates's

In September 2011, social and political activists undertook an ongoing series of demonstrations, marches, and protests in New York City's financial district. The movement, called Occupy Wall Street, sought to bring attention to the struggles of the lower classes and to end governmental partiality toward corporate and upper-class interests. Occupy groups were active across Canada as well, inspired by the original Wall Street movement.

wealth, estimated at about $50 billion, to the near-total absence of wealth among the lower-level, often temporary, employees of Microsoft. We will deal with this further when we discuss the growing income and wealth gaps in Canada.

STATUS

The second dimension of the system of inequality, *status*, relates to the prestige attached to one's positions within society. The existence and the importance of this dimension demonstrate that factors other than those associated with money are considered valuable in society. For example, physicians are always awarded very high prestige when Canadians are asked to rank occupational prestige (Goyder 2009), and this prestige often translates into doctors being treated as authorities or experts on many matters, including nonmedical matters.

POWER

A third dimension of social inequality is **power**, the ability to get others to do what you want them to do, even if it is against their will. Those who have

a great deal of power rank high in the stratification system, while those with little or no power are arrayed near the bottom. This is clearest in the case of politics where, for example, the prime minister of Canada ranks very high in power, while millions of ordinary voters have comparatively little political power. Still lower on the political power scale are disenfranchised citizens, such as convicted felons, and noncitizens, including undocumented immigrants. The plight of foreign domestic workers in Kuwait, described in the next *Globalisation* box, is an extreme but telling example of the consequences of powerlessness.

Power, of course, is not restricted to the political system but also exists in many other institutions. Thus, top officials in large corporations have greater power than workers, religious leaders have more power than parishioners, and those who head households are more powerful than their spouses or children (R. Collins 1975).

Greater income is generally associated with more power, but there are exceptions to this general rule. In the late 2000s, an increasing number of media stories focused on the phenomenon of "breadwinner wives," or "alpha wives"—women who earn more than their husbands (S. Roberts 2010). As shown in Figure 8.2, in families without children, 28 percent of wives earned more than their husbands. Even in families with three or more children, 21 percent of women earned more than their husbands. And this occurs despite women generally earning lower wages than men, as we will see later in the chapter. Furthermore, in spite of their greater income, these women may not have greater power in the marital relationship and in many cases will need to be content sharing power with their husbands (Cherlin 2010). In fact, many high-earning women have great difficulty even finding a mate, and they face disapproval for breaking gender norms. Expectations regarding gender, and other types of minority status, can clearly complicate power relations.

CONSISTENCY/INCONSISTENCY ACROSS DIMENSIONS OF INEQUALITY

Some people rank similarly across all three dimensions of social inequality. For example, a supervisor

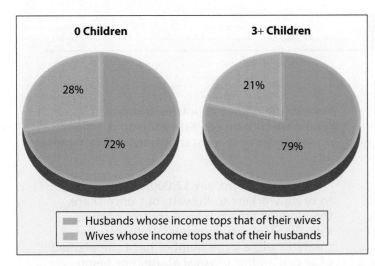

0 Children	3+ Children
28%	21%
72%	79%

■ Husbands whose income tops that of their wives
■ Wives whose income tops that of their husbands

FIGURE 8.2 Comparison of Wives' and Husbands' Earnings in Canada, by Family Size, 2006

SOURCE: Authors' calculations from data in Cool (2010, Table 6).

within a corporation is likely to earn a middle-class income, to enjoy middling prestige, and to have at least some power. This is known as **status consistency**, or *crystallisation* (Lenski 1954). However, it is far more likely that people will be characterised by **status inconsistency**—their position on one dimension of stratification will be different, perhaps very different, from their positions on the other dimensions of stratification (Stryker and Macke 1978). For example, famous movie stars, musicians, and athletes are likely to earn huge sums of money—they are high in social class—but they are not likely to have much power. While they often acquire great wealth, stars (such as Lindsay Lohan) with well-publicised legal and moral issues (such as drug addiction) are likely to have little status—even with their high incomes.

ECONOMIC INEQUALITY

A major concern in the sociological study of stratification is **economic inequality**, a condition whereby some positions in society yield a great deal of money, status, and power while others yield little, if any, of these. While other bases of stratification exist, the system of inequality in Canada, and much of the contemporary world, is based largely on money. Money is not inherently valuable and desirable; it has these characteristics only when it is so defined in a money economy (Simmel [1907] 1978). In such an economy, the occupational structure is characterised

by a payment system in which those in higher-level positions, and who perform well in these positions, are rewarded with larger paychecks. The use of money as a reward makes money seem valuable to people; they come to desire it for itself, as well as for what it will buy.

While today we rely on paper-fabric blends, metal coins, and, increasingly, digital tallies to represent wealth, other kinds of economies existed before the development of the money economy and continue to exist, at least to some degree, to this day in, for example, northern Ecuador (Ferraro 2011). One is a barter economy in which people exchange goods with one another without money mediating the exchange. In such economies, there is little or no need for money, and there are other ways of recognising people's relative contributions than the size of their bankrolls. It is worth noting that even within advanced money economies, we find a great deal of barter. Thus, it is not unusual for people to exchange services, or to do a service in exchange for some product. This is often done, illegally, to avoid the taxes that would more likely need to be paid if money did change hands. Of course, there are also transactions—such as illegal drug transactions or under-the-table labour—where money changes hands without any records that might attract the attention of the Canada Revenue Agency.

French social theorist Jean Baudrillard ([1976] 1993) criticised the money economy and the economic exchange that lies at its base. He argued instead for an economy and a society characterised by symbolic exchange. In **symbolic exchange**, people swap all sorts of things, but most importantly, the process of exchange is valued in itself and for the human relationships involved and *not* because of the economic gains—the money—that may be derived from it. A greater contribution to the group's well-being may be rewarded with higher ranking in the group rather than with more money. In such a system, you might acquire a high-level position by helping others more than they help you and by gaining recognition for your helpfulness.

Still, while other bases are possible, money remains at the root of the Canadian system of inequality. Money can take the form of income or wealth.

GL⊕BALISATION

Domestic Workers in Kuwait

Kuwait is a small Persian Gulf nation-state with vast oil reserves. Because oil commands a high price on the global market, Kuwait is exceptionally wealthy. In fact, according to the *CIA World Factbook* (2013a), Kuwait's oil enables the country to have the 18th highest gross domestic product (GDP) per capita in the world—greater than Canada, the United States, and nearly all of Europe. The country's wealth conveys many advantages to Kuwaiti citizens, who enjoy state-funded education, health care, and retirement income, as well as virtually guaranteed employment—generally in the oil industry or oil-related investment banking. Wealth allows Kuwaitis to hire domestic workers, mostly women, from many relatively poor countries, including the Philippines, Sri Lanka, Nepal, and Indonesia (Fahim 2010). Attracted to Kuwait by higher wages, these workers are able to send substantial remittances back to their home countries, but power relationships between Kuwaiti employers and domestic workers are starkly unequal (Fernandez 2010).

A family might pay $2,000 to an agency to bring workers to Kuwait, but once there, the workers are under the control of their Kuwaiti employer-sponsors. While some are treated well, a large number have complained of sexual and/or physical abuse, not being paid their wages, and restrictions on their movements by, for example, withholding their passports. During the feast of Ramadan, some domestics claimed that they were forced to work especially hard and for very long hours. In one case, a maid said that she was allowed to sleep only two hours a night; she finally left when her employer asked her to wash windows at 3 a.m. However, these problems are not restricted to Ramadan. In one case, a Sri Lankan maid escaped what she claimed was 13 years of imprisonment, without pay, by her Kuwaiti employer. In another, it was reported that a Filipino maid was tortured and killed, and her employers then took her body to the desert and ran over it with a car to make her death appear to be an accident. Finally, a Filipino domestic sought help from her agency because of an abusive family. When the family members found out, they threw her out of a third-floor window, breaking her back.

With few options, many domestics flee to their embassies for protection. They might sleep on the floor of the Nepalese embassy or be packed, 200 strong, in a hot room in the Philippines embassy where they sleep on their luggage. With the acceleration of globalisation, large numbers of poor people are travelling far from home in the hopes of finding work or, in many cases, being trafficked illegally. In many places in the world, including Canada, they have few, if any, rights and are subject to a wide range of abuses. Without rights, legal representation, or money, they are often powerless. They exist at the bottom of often very highly stratified societies.

Two bedraggled Filipino guest workers sit on the floor amid a pile of their belongings at the Philippine Embassy safe house after running away from the slave-like abuses of the Kuwaiti families that employed them.

Income is the amount of money a person earns from a job, a business, or returns on various types of assets (for example, real estate rents) and investments (for example, dividends on stocks and interest on bonds). Income is generally measured year by year—for example, you might have an income of $25,000 per year. Wealth, on the other hand, is the total amount of a person's financial assets and other property accumulated to date less the total of various kinds of debts, or liabilities. Assets include such things as savings, investments, homes, and automobiles, while examples of debts include home mortgages, student loans, car loans, and amounts owed to credit card companies. If all your assets totalled $100,000 but you owed $25,000, your wealth (or net worth) would amount to $75,000. Wealth can be inherited from others, so that a person can be very wealthy yet have a modest income; many elderly widows and widowers find themselves in this position. Conversely, people can earn substantial incomes and not be very wealthy because, for example, they squander their money on expensive vacations or hobbies, or on alcohol or drugs.

INCOME INEQUALITY

Sociologists are interested in inequality in status and power, but they tend to be most concerned with economic inequality. In many parts of the world, incomes became more equitable from the late 1920s until the 1970s. However, since the 1970s, there has been a substantial increase in income inequality in many countries, with a few individuals earning a great deal more and many earning little more. Even in Canada, which we often historically and erroneously regard as an egalitarian society, the top 1 percent of Canadians earned 14 percent of all income in the 2010s, up from 8 percent in the late 1970s (Fortin et al. 2012). The top 0.1 percent—yes, one tenth of a percent—earned 5.5 percent of the nation's total income in 2007; it was only 2 percent in the 1970s (Yalnizyan 2010).

Inequality became a hot political issue in 2011 with the release of government reports showing increasing inequality and poverty in the United States. This information was a major factor in the Occupy movement, which began near Wall Street in New York City. The main reason why the Occupy movement spread to Canada is clear in the accompanying figures.

BIOGRAPHICAL bits

Jean Baudrillard (1910–2007, French)

- Baudrillard is one of the most famous social theorists of the last century.

- He got his doctorate in sociology and taught that subject at the University of Paris–Nanterre.

- His 1970 book, *The Consumer Society*, was a pioneering work in the sociology of consumption.

- Later in his career, he moved away from sociology and refused to identify with any specific discipline.

- By the 1980s, he had become an international celebrity on the basis of a number of important books and a series of provocative, even outrageous, ideas (such as those in a 1991 book titled *The Gulf War Did Not Take Place*).

- While he was not focally interested in social stratification, his thinking on "symbolic exchange" laid the basis for thinking about an alternative to the system of stratification in capitalist society.

The simple fact is that the average inflation-adjusted, after-tax family income of the top 1 percent of earners in Canada increased dramatically between 1980 and 2010, as Figure 8.3 shows. Others in the top 20 percent (81st to 99th percentile) did well, but not nearly as well, with an increase of 65 percent in income. At the other end of the spectrum, the income for those in the bottom fifth increased by only 18 percent. The 60 percent in the middle, those between the top 20 percent and the bottom 20 percent, saw an increase of slightly less than 40 percent in income. Another way of looking at income inequality is the fact that the top 20 percent of the population had over 50 percent of all income—more than the bottom 80 percent. At the other end of the spectrum, the bottom 20 percent had only 5 percent of all income—down from 7 percent in 1979. The middle 60 percent had the rest of the income (over 40 percent), but their percentage of income had declined slightly from 1979. Between 2005 and 2007, the after-tax income of the top 20 percent was greater than the income for everyone else (the other 80 percent).

Explaining Income Inequality

Several broad reasons have been put forth to explain recent increases in income inequality:

- *Technological advances.* The highest-paying jobs in recent years have been created in high-tech, high-skill areas such as information technology (IT). Many Canadians did not receive the training necessary to find jobs in the high-tech workforce. In fact, there is an insufficient supply of people adequately trained to handle such highly skilled work. As a result, income inequality due to technological advances may be a short-term problem that will be rectified as more people are trained for such jobs. However, many older workers in other sectors may lack the education needed to acquire the necessary skills, may be too tied down by other obligations at this point in their lives to move to new job locations, or may be too tainted by their long-term unemployment even to be considered for the new

jobs. Furthermore, there may not be nearly enough of these high-tech jobs to make up for the lost jobs in other sectors.

- *Family change.* In recent years marriage patterns have changed such that people earning high wages are more likely now than in the past to marry one another. For example, if more physicians now marry other physicians, whereas previously physicians married nurses, this will increase family incomes for the most well-off. Evidence of this patterning of marriage homophily exists in Canada (Hou and Myles 2008).

- *Social power.* Another part of the increase for the top 1 percent of earners may be the higher wages that are now given to top-ranked executives in the financial sector especially, but also to those heading the largest commercial enterprises in the country. This, however, can be only part of the explanation, because the top 1 percent of Canadian earners include many people, including physicians and lawyers, who are not corporate executives (Fortin et al. 2012).

- *Political climate.* A variety of political decisions help explain the increase in income inequality. There is, for example, political opposition in Canada to raising the minimum wage, or to raising it very much. As a result, in real dollars, the minimum wage has actually stagnated in recent decades, and those who hold minimum-wage jobs have lost ground to those in higher-paying occupations. More generally, powerful conservative political forces work hard to maintain the current

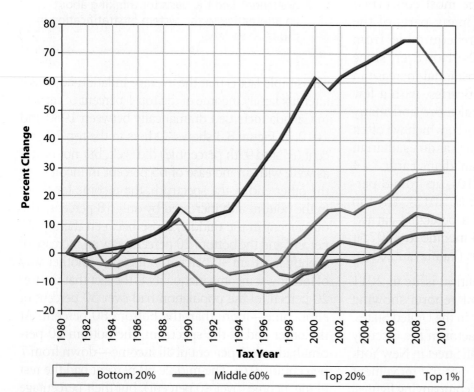

FIGURE 8.3 Growth of Average Incomes by Income Group, 1980–2010

SOURCE: Human Resources and Skill Development Canada (2012), and Fortin et al. (2012) (after-tax family income).

NOTE: Canadian families grouped by income in 2010 constant dollars.

system of inequality, which benefits them and therefore increases income.

A series of more recent and narrower changes has also contributed to the huge and growing income gap:

- Tax changes made in recent years have flattened the tax rate so that richer Canadians are now not taxed at as high a rate as they were historically and they can increasingly shelter more of their income from taxation. Taxes and government transfers were doing less to equalise income in 2010 than they had in 1980. That is, taxes had grown less progressive (M. Lee 2007).
- Incomes for executives and superstars in sports and entertainment have skyrocketed. This is part of what has been called a *winner-take-all* society (R. Frank and Cook 1995), a Darwinian economy in which the rich use their advantages to succeed wildly and the poor, with few if any advantages, grow increasingly worse off (R. Frank 2011).
- Tax policies have shifted to favour long-term capital gains, which involve income derived from investments in capital such as real estate, stocks, and bonds that are held over one year. At this point, long-term capital gains and dividend income from corporations are taxed at less than the rate for ordinary income. This is a huge advantage for the after-tax income of the rich, especially the super-rich, who own a disproportionate share of the capital and therefore reap almost all the benefits of the low capital gains tax.

WEALTH INEQUALITY

As unfair as income inequality may seem, the greatest disparities in society—the greatest differences between the haves and the have-nots—are found not in disparities in income but rather in the enormous differences in wealth in society. Inequality in wealth tends to be much greater than income inequality, as you can see in Figure 8.4. Like income inequality, wealth inequality has tended to increase in recent years in Canada and other western countries (J. Davies 2009; Mishel and Bivens 2011;

Wilterdink 2007). While those Canadians struggling the most saw their net worth eroded between 1999 and 2005 by over 70 percent, the richest Canadians saw their net worth rise by over 40 percent. See Figure 8.5.

Those with great wealth live a lifestyle beyond the wildest dreams of those who live on the lowest rungs of the economic ladder. Wealth brings with it a wide range of advantages:

- It can be invested anywhere around the world in stocks, bonds, real estate, and the like in order to yield greater income and to generate even greater wealth.
- It can be used to purchase material comforts of all sorts: large homes, vacation retreats, luxury cars, and custom-tailored clothes, as well as the services of housekeepers, gardeners, personal trainers, tax lawyers, and so forth.
- It can afford a high level of financial security, allowing the wealthy, if they wish, to retire at an early age with the means to live well for the rest of their lives.
- It purchases far greater freedom and autonomy than less wealthy individuals can acquire. An example would be the freedom to leave unsatisfactory employment without worrying about how the bills will be paid.

These are just some of the ways that wealth benefits individuals.

Status, Power, and Wealth

Perhaps of greatest importance is the fact that wealth not only accords a high-level position on one dimension of stratification—social class—but it is also an important factor in gaining similar positions on the other dimensions of inequality—status and power. Those who have great wealth tend to rank high in social class because class is, to a considerable degree, defined economically, and wealth is a key economic indicator of it. Those with great wealth are also generally able to buy or to otherwise acquire that which gives them high status and great power. There are exceptions, however, to the link between great wealth and high social class, such as those who retain a high social ranking even though they have lost much or most

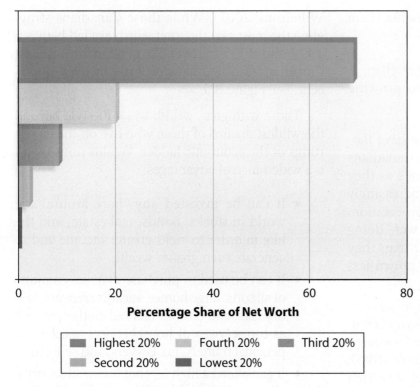

FIGURE 8.4 Percentage Share of Net Worth of Canadians by Quintile Group, 2005

SOURCE: Statistics Canada (2006).

recognition as philanthropists by, for example, attending $1,000-a-ticket charity balls or even donating the money needed to build a new wing of a hospital.

Power over employees is a fact of life for wealthy individuals who own businesses or run other organisations. Their needs for financial, household, and personal services give the wealthy another source of power. They have the ability to direct the activities of many charities and civic groups. And if that isn't enough, the wealthy can buy more power by bribing political officials or making generous campaign contributions to favoured politicians. Such contributions often give donors great behind-the-scenes power. In some cases, the wealthy choose to use their money to run for public office themselves; if successful, such families come to occupy positions that give them great power. These families can even become political dynasties with two or more generations obtaining high

of their wealth over time. Another exception is the nouveau riche, whose inelegant tastes and behaviours may lead others in the upper class to refuse to accept them as members of their class. However, in general, those with great wealth *are* members of the upper class.

In terms of status, the wealthy can afford more and better-quality education. They can, for example, send their children to very expensive and highly exclusive prep schools and Ivy League universities in the United States. In some elite universities, being a "legacy"—the son or daughter of an elite who attended the same school—can increase the chances of gaining admission. This practice is sometimes called "affirmative action for the rich" (R. Kahlenberg 2010). At Princeton in 2009, for example, 41.7 percent of legacy applicants were admitted compared to 9.2 percent of nonlegacies. The wealthy can also purchase more of the trappings of high culture, such as subscriptions to box seats at the opera or multimillion-dollar paintings by famous artists (which as investments can be very profitable). The wealthy can also achieve great

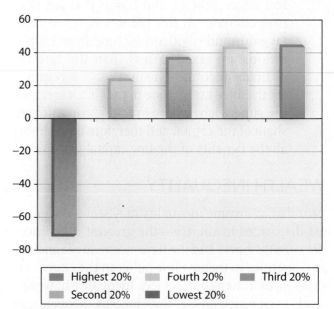

FIGURE 8.5 Share of Total Wealth Gain of Canadians by Quintile Rank, 1999–2005

SOURCE: Statistics Canada (2006).

NOTE: Wealth of Canadians grouped by quintile rank where 1 = lowest 20% and 5 = highest 20%.

PUBLIC SOCIOLOGY

Dalton Conley on Social Inequality

Dalton Conley is a true Renaissance man. Before he was 40 years of age, he had become a distinguished professor of sociology, chair of the sociology department at New York University, and dean of NYU's social sciences department. According to his website, in 2010 Conley was pursuing a doctorate in biology at the Center for Genomics and Systems Biology at NYU, studying transgenerational phenotypic plasticity and socially regulated genes. He published a well-known personal memoir, *Honky* (2001b), about the experience of growing up as a white child in New York City projects and the advantages he had over children of colour growing up in the same environment. He has also authored very important articles in the major sociology journals, as well as influential books aimed at an academic audience. As a public sociologist, he has published numerous pieces in newspapers and other nonacademic media outlets.

Dalton Conley

In his many pieces for academic and public media, Conley has dealt with a wide range of issues including urban poverty, the black-white wealth gap, the family as a social stratifier, and corporate crime. His main area of interest, however, is inequality within and across generations and the relationship between inequality and siblings, race, physical appearance, and health and biology. Let us look at a sampling of insights to be derived from some of his journalistic work:

- In a 2004 essay in *The Chronicle Review* titled "For Siblings, Inequality Starts at Home," Conley details the surprisingly large differences in the fates, especially the economic fates, of siblings. He sees three basic factors involved in such differences. The first is the broad social or economic changes at the societal level. For example, a child born during the boom years of the early twenty-first century had brighter prospects than did a sibling born after the start of the Great Recession. A second factor that can have a dramatic impact on siblings' futures is changes in the family, as when parents divorce or a parent dies. Finally, there are individual factors such as a serious illness affecting one of the siblings, or violence perpetrated on one rather than the other. For all of these reasons,

there are huge differences between siblings, and they often create great tensions for the siblings and the family as a whole. This is but another reason why the family is not the warm and fuzzy institution it was thought to be in, say, the 1950s.

- In a 2008 op-ed piece in *The New York Times* titled "Rich Man's Burden," Conley focuses on stratification among the most well-to-do members of society. He details how those near the top of the income hierarchy work more, more even than those on the bottom of the stratification hierarchy. The reason is that those in the top half of the stratification system are very conscious of those above them and the fact that the latter may be pulling further and further ahead of them. As a result, even though they are well-off, those near the top tend to work harder and longer hours in order to try to keep up, or at least to keep the gap from growing wider.

- In a 2001(a) essay in *The Nation* titled "The Black-White Wealth Gap," Conley shows that while black-white *income* differences are important, the difference between the races in their total *wealth* (net worth) is even greater. At the time he wrote this essay, among families with less than $15,000 in income, whites had an average net worth of $10,000, while blacks' net worth was zero. In middle-class families earning $40,000 a year, white families had a net worth of $80,000, while for black families the total was about half that. Among the super-rich, only two black Americans were on the *Forbes* list of the 400 richest Americans. Today, there is only one black American—Oprah Winfrey—on that list. Winfrey's estimated net worth of $2.7 billion places her only 130th on that list. Whites have had a number of advantages, such as long-term wealth, allowing assets to be passed down from one generation to the next. And blacks have had many disadvantages, including barriers to black property accumulation, especially of that most important, albeit now tarnished, component of net worth—home ownership.

This is but a brief sampling of Conley's journalistic work aimed at offering more accessible sociological insights into important problems associated with social inequality.

political office. Joseph P. Kennedy earned large sums of money during the Depression and used it to become a powerful political figure. He used his money and his political influence to help his sons get elected: John F. Kennedy as president, Ted Kennedy as senator, and Bobby Kennedy as senator before he was assassinated while running for the presidency. Prescott Bush made his money on Wall Street and became a U.S. senator. His son, George H. W. Bush, became president of the United States, as did his paternal grandson, George W. Bush. Former Prime Minister Paul Martin is likewise from a rich family, and is a major owner of Canada Steamship Lines, a world-class transportation company.

The lifestyles that large amounts of money can buy are a source of interest and fascination for many people. In the 1980s, Robin Leach hosted a popular TV show called *Lifestyles of the Rich and Famous*. This show took viewers "behind the scenes" to explore the mansions of the elite. On a modern version of this show, MTV's *Cribs,* celebrity musicians and athletes show off their homes, pools, cars, and other trappings of wealth. Reality TV shows, such as Bravo's *Real Housewives* series and E!'s *Keeping Up with the Kardashians,* feature the daily lives of an elite group of the extremely wealthy. The fictionalised trials and tribulations of the elite also are prominent on nighttime dramas, such as *Gossip Girl* and *Revenge*. These shows highlight the gap between the wealthy and everyone else. For example, many of the real-life elites do not know how to do things that seem commonplace to many, such as pumping their own gasoline or waiting in line at the Ministry of Transportation office for a driver's license. The prevalence of such entertainment suggests a deep curiosity about how people with a great deal of status, money, and power live.

The Perpetuation of Wealth

One of the great advantages of the wealthy is their ability to maintain their social class across generations. Their ability to keep their wealth, if not expand it,

often allows the members of the upper class to pass their wealth, and the upper-class position that goes with it, to their children. Financial mechanisms (for example, generation-skipping trusts) have been devised that allow the wealthy to pass their wealth on not only to the next generation, but to generations to come. Thus, wealth tends to be self-perpetuating over the long term.

The wealthy are able to perpetuate their wealth in large part because they have been able to use their money and influence to resist taxation systems designed to redistribute at least some of the wealth in society. For example, the wealthy have fought long and hard against the estate tax, which places a high tax on assets over a certain amount that are left behind when they die. Many of the wealthy prefer to call the estate tax, in more negative terms, a "death tax." Canada does not have an estate tax or inheritance tax.

Like having a great deal of wealth, a lack of wealth also tends to be self-perpetuating. Those who have little or no personal wealth can be fairly sure that their children, and generations beyond them, will also lack wealth. Of course there have been, and will be, many exceptions to this pattern, but in the main there is great consistency from generation to generation. This contradicts the Horatio Alger myth, which tells us that anyone can get ahead, or rise in the stratification system, through hard work and effort. The Horatio Alger myth is functional in that many people believe in it and continue to strive to get ahead (and some even do), often in the face of overwhelming barriers and odds. But it is also dysfunctional in that it tends to put all the burdens of achieving success on the shoulders of individuals. The vast majority of people are likely to fail and to blame themselves, rather

Though panned by critics, 2010's *Sex and the City 2* was a commercial success, grossing nearly $300 billion worldwide. In the film, successful author Carrie Bradshaw (Sarah Jessica Parker) and her friends take a lavish vacation to Abu Dhabi, where they stay in a luxury hotel, shop for expensive clothing, and drink cocktails. The resounding success of such films exemplifies the public's fascination with the upper-class elite.

GL🌐BALISATION

The Advantages of the Elite in Pakistan

As in any society, those at the top of the social hierarchy in Pakistan have great advantages. Pakistan, which has become increasingly integrated into the global economy in the last several decades, has experienced some growth but remains a highly unequal society (Shahbaz 2010). In fact, as its economy has grown, the country has experienced rising income inequality (Khan and Faridi 2008). According to the Pakistan Institute of Legislative Development and Transparency, some of the richest people in Pakistan are politicians. The average net worth of members of Parliament is nearly $1 million; the richest member is worth in excess of $37 million. Members of Parliament make the tax rules, and those rules tend to advantage them and to disadvantage others in society, especially the poor. Indeed, in Pakistan, as elsewhere, it is the poor and their taxes that subsidise the rich and go a long way toward supporting the government and its expenditures.

According to Pakistani rules, anyone earning above $3,488 per year must pay income tax. However, it is estimated that while about 10 million Pakistanis *should* be paying income tax, because of a lack of law enforcement only about a quarter of that number do; only 2 percent of Pakistan's 170 million people pay income tax. The result is that Pakistan ranks near the bottom of world societies in terms of revenue from taxes.

One successful businessman who is also a member of Parliament tried to pay his taxes but claimed his payment was refused by tax collectors who did not want to rock the boat as far as the tax situation was concerned. His payment was finally—reluctantly—accepted after he wrote a letter to a senior official (Tavernise 2010).

A major advantage to the wealthy in Pakistan is the fact that there is no federal tax on agriculture. Even though about half of the country's population works in that sector of the economy, it is the big landowners, including many government officials, who benefit the most from this tax law. Poor farmers and farmworkers earn too little to benefit much from this exclusion.

Another of the great advantages of Pakistan's wealthiest citizens is a law passed in the 1990s that forbids authorities from raising questions about money transferred into Pakistan from abroad. Of course, it is mainly, if not completely, the rich who are able to engage in such transfers, especially large transfers, which often involve illegally obtained funds. For example, Pakistan is a significant transit area for drug trafficking from Afghanistan to global drug markets.

The wealthy also profit from tax-free goods that enter the country en route to Afghanistan, but that never get there. For example, 50,000 tons of black tea were imported into Pakistan in 2009 to be sent on to Afghanistan, but "not a single cup of black tea was drunk in Afghanistan" (Tavernise 2010:A9). Furthermore, since more than half of Pakistan's economy is off the books—part of the "underground, or informal, economy" (Neuwirth 2011)—it is impossible to tax that part of the economy. Needless to say, much of the underground economy is dominated by the elites, and their profits from it are free of taxation.

As in many other locales, including Canada, much tax revenue in Pakistan comes not from income tax, but rather from sales tax. The problem is that a sales tax is a "regressive tax," meaning that it falls hardest on those least able to pay it. As a result of the tax system, the wealthy in Pakistan can afford apartments in London, large homes, servants, expensive cars, chauffeurs, and manicures at luxurious spas. The poor in Pakistan, like the poor everywhere, are, well, poor. They are able to glimpse the lifestyle of the rich, to lust after it, and perhaps to grow angry about the great disparities in wealth and lifestyle. Such anger fuels resentment and ultimately protests and even some of the terrorism that plagues Pakistan.

The poor in Pakistan not only live in the shadow of palaces and skyscrapers that demonstrate riches they will never attain, but many of the impoverished work on constructing these monuments to wealth and live in hastily erected slums near construction sites.

than the unfairness of the highly stratified system, for their failures.

POVERTY

Poverty and the many problems associated with it are of great concern both to sociologists and to society as a whole (Guppy and Hawkshaw 2009; Iceland 2007). Poverty is troubling for many reasons, most importantly for its negative effect on the lives of the poor themselves. Those suffering from poverty are likely to be in poor health and to have a lower life expectancy. More generally, poverty hurts the economy in various ways. The vibrancy of the working class is reduced because poverty adversely affects at least some employees and their ability to work; they may be less productive or lose more work time due to illness. Another example is that the level of consumption in society as a whole is reduced because of the inability of the poor to consume very much. Crime, social disorder, and revolution are more likely where poverty is widespread.

The great disparity between the rich and the poor is considered by many to be a moral problem, if not a moral crisis, for society as a whole. The poor are often seen as not doing what they should, or could, to raise themselves out of poverty. They are seen as disreputable, which makes them objects of moral censure by those who have succeeded in society (Matza 1966). They may be blamed for the degradation of society. However, some see poverty as an entirely different kind of moral problem. They argue that the poor should be seen as the "victims" of a system that impoverishes them (W. Ryan 1976). The existence of large numbers of poor people in otherwise affluent societies is a "moral stain" on that society (D. Harvey 2007). Something about a society that allows so much poverty must be amiss.

ANALYSING POVERTY

It may be tempting to blame the poor for the existence of poverty, but a sociological perspective notes the larger social forces that create and perpetuate poverty. To the sociologist, poverty persists for three basic reasons:

- Poverty is built into the capitalist system, and virtually all societies today—even China—have a capitalist economy. Capitalist businesses seek to maximise profits, and they do so by keeping wages as low as possible and by hiring as few workers as possible. When business slows, they are likely to lay people off, thrusting most of them into poverty. It is in the interest of the capitalist system to have a large number of unemployed, and therefore poor, people. This population serves as what Marx called the "reserve army of the unemployed," a readily available pool of people who can be drawn quickly into the labour force when business booms and more workers are needed. This reserve army also keeps existing workers in line and reluctant to demand much, if anything, from management.

- Competition among social classes encourages some elite groups of people to seek to enhance their economic position by limiting the ability of other groups even to maintain their economic positions. The elites do so by limiting the poor's access to opportunities and resources such as those afforded by various welfare systems.

- Government actions to reduce poverty, or ameliorate its negative effects on people and society, are generally limited by groups of people who believe that the poor should make it on their own and not be afforded the aid of the government. They also believe that government aid reduces the incentives needed for people to do on their own what is needed to rise above the poverty line. These beliefs are fairly common among political conservatives.

There are two broad types of poverty:

- *Absolute poverty* is a measure of what people need in order to survive; it focuses upon deprivation. In Canada Christopher Sarlo (2006), in conjunction with the Fraser Institute, developed a measure of poverty that captured the amount of money necessary to buy the basic necessities of life. It is important to note that while the poor in Canada may be poor by some absolute standard and in some absolute sense, they are often much better off than the poor in most other places in the world.

- *Relative poverty* is defined not by some objective standard but rather by the fact that some people, irrespective of income, are, or feel themselves to be, poor relative to others to whom they relate; it focuses on inequality. Townsend (2010) offers such a relative view when he argues that poverty occurs when "resources fall seriously short of the resources commanded by the average individual or family in the community in which they live" (p. 99). Adam Smith ([1776] 1991) argued for such a relative definition of poverty by noting that all communities had "established rules of decency" and only if people had the money to meet these basic levels would they escape poverty.

Poverty in Canada

Canada has no official definition of poverty and hence no formal measure of poverty. This is surprising given how frequently politicians debate issues of the poor or how often poverty is an item in the national media. Unlike the United States, where a poverty line is clearly defined, Statistics Canada offers Canadians a set of "low income" lines.

Poverty is about low income, but exactly what threshold an income needs to fall below for someone to be living in poverty is open to debate. First, what exact amount of money constitutes *low* income differs for a single person and a large family. It also differs depending on where you reside since the cost of living in northern Canada or in large cities can be higher than elsewhere. Further, the adequacy of income depends on your health and ability level since, for example, dealing with a disability is more costly. Second, whether or not income is low depends on what you think that income should buy—in the words of Adam Smith (see above), what constitutes "decency"? Most Canadians would agree that indoor toilets, running water, children's books, electricity, and safe, nutritious meals are mandatory. But where does the line of "decency" get drawn? What is essential or basic when it comes to food, clothing, and shelter?

This latter objection is what makes the idea of an absolute poverty line difficult (Sarlo 2006

defines an absolute poverty line by excluding children's books, for example). The bare essentials might be enough to keep you alive, but they would not allow you to participate freely and effectively in a democratic society. Also, as the standard of living rises in a country, should it rise for everyone, including the poor, or only for those who are not poor? If it should rise for everyone, then poverty has to be defined relatively. Most sociologists, and indeed most Canadians, adopt some form of a relative poverty line when they gauge what income is adequate to function in Canadian society. A **poverty line**, or income threshold, is an income below which an individual or a family would have great difficulty meeting the living expenses necessary for sustainability. A household whose income falls below the threshold is considered poor. Poverty lines vary from country to country. In Canada Statistics Canada annually produces a "low income cut-off" (LICO) line, an income threshold that is just sufficient to buy the basic essentials necessary to survive adequately in a democratic society like Canada. The LICO is a hybrid between an absolute poverty line because it targets the amount of money needed to meet the essentials of life and a relative poverty line because it calculates that amount in relation to the expenditures of a family with average income (Statistics Canada 2012f). For 2011 the LICO for a family of four in a large city was a pretax income of $43,292 ($36,504 after tax), and $23,298 for a single adult. In 2010, about 9 percent of the Canadian population (3.1 million people) lived at or below the LICO. Although there has been some historical movement in the percentage of families living in poverty in Canada, there have been no dramatic increases or decreases in the last few decades.

Figure 8.6 shows various incomes that some would consider as poverty lines. The first bar on the right is Statistics Canada's LICO (all bars are calculated for a family of four). Beside it is a more intuitive measure of poverty, an agreed-upon "low income measure" (LIM), used frequently in international comparisons. It is calculated as one half of the adjusted median household income in a nation, where "adjusted" means that household size is taken into account (10.3 percent of families fell below this line in 2010). The middle bar

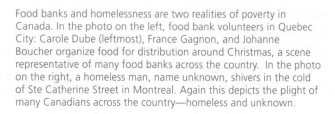

Food banks and homelessness are two realities of poverty in Canada. In the photo on the left, food bank volunteers in Quebec City: Carole Dube (leftmost), France Gagnon, and Johanne Boucher organize food for distribution around Christmas, a scene representative of many food banks across the country. In the photo on the right, a homeless man, name unknown, shivers in the cold of Ste Catherine Street in Montreal. Again this depicts the plight of many Canadians across the country—homeless and unknown.

is based on calculations from the Fraser Institute (Veldhuis, Karabegovic, and Palacios 2012) and is established with reference to the absolute income a Canadian family of four would need. The next two lines are the incomes that a family of four would receive in British Columbia and Ontario if they received social assistance (i.e., welfare). Even if one adopts an absolute definition of poverty, as does Sarlo, it is clear that Canadian families receiving welfare are living in "straightened circumstances." Furthermore, recall that these are poverty *lines* and that unfortunately some families must make do with incomes that fall below these lines. The **depth of poverty** refers to this phenomenon of families living below the poverty line. In the 2000s the depth of poverty in Canada was around 20 percent, or, in other words, on average poor families were subsisting on incomes that were 20 percent *below* the poverty line (Guppy and Hawkshaw 2009; UNICEF 2012). There is no question that poverty

is a huge problem in Canada, but it is almost certainly far greater than we ever imagined.

One frustrating aspect of poverty, and its amelioration or reduction, is that agreement on the definition and measurement is so difficult. Like a line in the desert sand, the poverty line, no matter how defined, has an arbitrariness to it. Decency or straitened circumstances are elusive concepts that are tied to community standards, and even some notion of absolute bare necessities is problematic because of a lack of agreement on what is essential. For international comparisons, more and more organisations such as the United Nations, UNICEF, and the World Bank are using the concept of LIM (see above), half of the median income of a country. This has the advantage of being easy to compute and compare country to country. Figure 8.7 takes advantage of this and places poverty in an international context by comparing rates of child poverty across a number of different countries. This allows us to answer the question of whether Canada is doing a comparatively good or bad job of addressing poverty. In comparison to a range of other rich, industrialised countries, the child poverty rate in Canada is in the worse half of the distribution. UNICEF estimates that about 13.3 percent of children in Canada, more than 1 of every 10 children, live in poverty. Canada has a lower rate than the United States but a higher rate than the United Kingdom, France, and the Scandinavian countries. Notice too that for Canada more children live in poverty than is the case for the population as a whole (13.3 versus 10.3 percent, respectively). This implies that we do not do as good a job as we might in protecting children from the ravages of poverty.

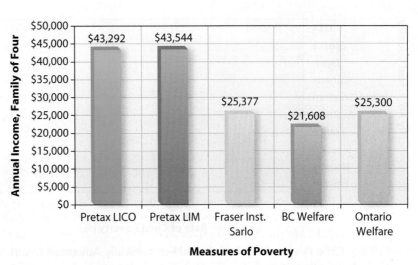

FIGURE 8.6 Five Examples of Poverty Measures and Welfare Rates for a Family of Four Living in a Large Canadian City, 2010

SOURCES: LICO and LIM — http://www.statcan.gc.ca/pub/75f0002m/2012002/lico-sfr-eng.htm
Sarlo — Fraser Forum, March/April 2012
BC Welfare — Fraser Forum, March/April 2012
Ontario Welfare — estimate from http://www.socialassistancereview.ca/income-assistance-and-other-benefits

Finally, we can also ask whether or not governments play an effective role in helping to lessen poverty. How much, if at all, do governments act like Robin Hood, taking from the rich and giving to the poor? The UNICEF report provides data showing that the Canadian system of government taxes and transfers does help to ameliorate child poverty, although whether it could be even more successful is a matter of concern. In Canada, before Robin Hood (the government) intervenes, about 25 percent of children live in poverty, and this is reduced to 13.3 percent after taxes and transfers (see Figure 8.8). By way of comparison, this is much better than what occurs in the United States, but roughly similar to what occurs in France. There clearly is a redistribution of income occurring in Canada. What remains contentious is whether this is too much or too little—too much in that conservatives would like to see less government intervention, and too little in that others would like to see fewer children living in poverty.

Who Are the Poor?

At one time far more women than men were poor, but recently these numbers have converged so that now while 9 percent of Canadians are living in poverty, 9.3 percent of women as compared to 8.7 percent of men live in poverty. Rather than thinking of the feminisation of poverty (implying that all women have greater likelihood than men to be poor), a more accurate picture comes from noticing those particular groups of people who are poor, and noting that more people in these groups tend to be women. So, for example, the following groups tend to live disproportionately below the poverty threshold (Statistics Canada 2012f):

Single parents: More women than men are single parents, and the poverty rate for female lone-parent families is 21.8 percent (well above the 9 percent for the general population; based on LICO).

Seniors who live alone: Women outlive men and are thus more likely to live alone in their final years. Especially because many elderly women do not have adequate pensions, more single elderly women than men live in poverty (15.6 percent versus 11.5 percent).

Two other groups whose chances of living in poverty are higher are First Nations peoples and recent visible minority immigrants. Based on the 2006 census, Noél and Larocque (2009) estimate that at least 20 percent of

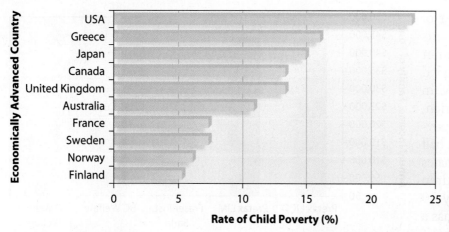

FIGURE 8.7 Child Poverty Rate in Selected Economically Advanced Countries

SOURCE: UNICEF (2012, Figure 1b, p. 3).

NOTE: The percentage of children living in households with adjusted (for family size) after-tax incomes lower than 50 percent of the national median.

K. Marshall (2006) documents the uneven division between women and men of household chores, and Kay and Hagan (1998) report that women earn less than men as lawyers.

Women earn less money than men from employment (see Figure 8.9). Although the gap has narrowed over time, there is a persistent discrepancy. Part of the gap occurs because women more often take on household responsibilities, and this limits their ability to earn wages equivalent to men. Although, as Katherine Marshall (2006) shows, these gendered roles in the home may be converging (i.e., shared), there is still a notable discrepancy, with women more likely, for example, to take time off to tend to children who are sick. The second major factor is that women's paid work continues to be segregated such that more women than men work in occupations that are relatively low paying (Drolet 2002). The work of women continues to be undervalued. A final way to examine this female-male pay gap is to ask how Canada compares internationally. Of the major industrialised countries, Canada has an above-average female-male wage gap

Aboriginal Canadians were living in poverty, as compared to about 10 percent of the non-Aboriginal population. Recently new immigrants to Canada have also been having more trouble settling in their new homeland, and an increasing number are falling below the poverty line (Reitz et al. 2009).

Complicating the issue of poverty among women are two other issues. First, women tend to take on much more of the domestic household duties than do men, including child care, meal preparation, and cleaning. This greater domestic involvement contributes to a second issue for women. Household responsibilities make it more difficult for women to earn the higher salaries that come with frequent job promotions. One of the persistent issues is that work, both household and labour market work, has been historically segregated by sex (pink jobs and blue jobs if you will), with the work women do in the home and in the workforce valued less. For example, Creese (1999) shows how women's work was undervalued in labour union struggles,

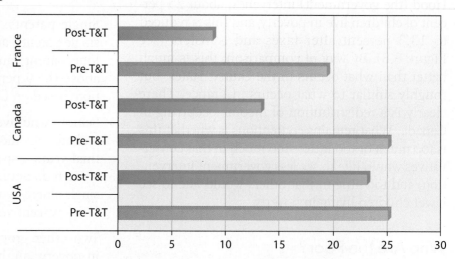

FIGURE 8.8 Child Poverty Rates (%) Before and After Taxes and Transfers, Selected Countries

SOURCE: UNICEF (2012, Figure 8a, p. 19).

NOTE: T&T refers to Taxes and Transfers.

(Cool 2010), perhaps in part because of the ability of young men to find high-paying work in Canada's resource industries (e.g., oil and gas, mining).

SOCIAL MOBILITY

Those who live in poverty are understandably eager to improve their lot. However, virtually everyone in a stratified system is concerned with **social mobility** (van Leeuwen and Maas 2010), the ability or inability to change one's position in the hierarchy. *Upward mobility,* the ability to move higher (Miles, Savage, and Bühlmann 2011), is obviously of great concern, especially for those who are poor; upward mobility is the route out of poverty. The middle class may have an even greater desire to be mobile than the poor, for they are likely to have experienced at least some of the possibilities associated with upward mobility. They have some class, status, and power, but they tend to want more. They often want to move into the upper class. Even those in the upper class are interested in and concerned about upward mobility. They often want to move to higher-level positions than their rivals within the upper class. They are also interested in keeping tabs on those below them who may be moving up the ladder, threatening to supplant them, and perhaps even reaching positions higher than their own.

People in all social classes are also concerned about *downward mobility.* That is, people worry about descending to lower levels within their social class or to lower classes (for example, dropping from the upper to the middle or even lower class). Downward mobility causes people real hardships, but even its mere possibility is a great cause of concern. Immigrants and refugees who move to a new country almost always experience downward mobility during the first generation in their new locale. This is especially true of those who held high-level occupations in their countries of origin (Gans 2009). More generally, it is likely that given the current economic problems in the world, many people will experience downward mobility relative to their parents' status as well during their lifetimes. As one columnist put it: "Young people today are staring at a future in which they will be less well off than their elders, a reversal of fortune that should send a shudder through everyone" (Herbert 2011).

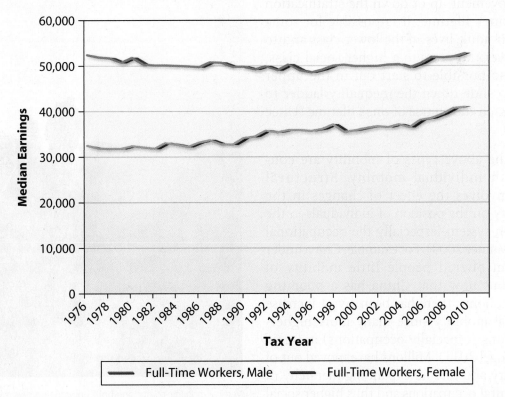

FIGURE 8.9 Median Earnings by Gender, 1976–2010, Canada

SOURCE: Calculations by authors from Statistics Canada, CANSIM 202-0407

TYPES OF SOCIAL MOBILITY

To this point, we have discussed upward and downward mobility, but there are a number of other types of social mobility as well. Upward and downward mobility are the key components of the general process of **vertical mobility**. Also of interest is **horizontal mobility**, or movement within one's social class. For example, a chief executive officer (CEO) may become CEO of a much larger corporation that brings with it much greater compensation. At the other end of the spectrum, the plumber who becomes a taxi driver also exhibits horizontal mobility (Ultee 2007a).

Sociologists are also concerned with two other types of mobility. One is **intergenerational mobility**, or the difference between the parents' social class position and the positions achieved by their children (Wanner 2009). Children who rise higher in the system of inequality than their parents have experienced upward intergenerational mobility, while those who descend to a lower position on the ladder have experienced downward intergenerational mobility. **Intragenerational mobility** involves movement up or down the stratification system in one's lifetime. It is possible for some to start their adult lives in the lower class and to move up over the years to a higher social class, but it is also possible to start out in the upper class and to slide down the inequality ladder to a lower class in the course of one's lifetime (Ultee 2007b).

All of the above types of mobility are concerned with individual mobility. **Structural mobility** involves the effect of changes in the larger society on the position of individuals in the stratification system, especially the occupational structure (Wanner 2009). For example, China under communism offered people little mobility of any type, but now that China has a booming capitalist economy, there has been a vast increase in structural mobility since many more higher-level positions (especially occupations) are now available (Vogel 2011). Millions have moved out of the peasantry and into an expanding hierarchy of nonagricultural occupations and thus higher social positions. For a more detailed description of structural mobility, see the next *Globalisation* box.

STRUCTURAL MOBILITY IN CANADA

There have been many changes in the occupational structure of Canada over the last century. These changes have profoundly affected **occupational mobility** and, ultimately, all of the other types of mobility. For example, in 1900, the largest single occupational category was farming. A male born in 1900 was likely to have a father who was a farmer, but over time, farmwork became a smaller part of the economy, and there were few opportunities for a son in farming. He might have ended up in a wide range of occupations, but wherever he ended up, he was likely to have experienced occupational mobility. He was also likely to experience upward intergenerational mobility since his occupation was apt to have been of higher status and offer higher pay than his father's. Even if the son had started in farming, he was unlikely to have ended up in farming. Thus, he would have experienced upward intragenerational mobility as well.

If we fast-forward to 1930, we find that the largest occupational category was no longer farming, but manual, or blue-collar, work. Fathers, and

Vertical mobility, comprising both upward and downward mobility, indicates immediate changes in the social position of an individual or family. Horizontal mobility indicates movement of an individual or family within a fixed social class.

John Porter (1921–1979, Canadian)

- Porter was Canada's most important sociologist from 1950 to the late 1970s. His work in social inequality continues to have influence.

- Born in Vancouver, he completed his education at the London School of Economics in the United Kingdom. Reflecting on his time at the LSE, Porter noted that he was most animated by "a concern for ethical principles in social life."

- On returning to Canada he joined the faculty of Carleton University. Porter was also a visiting professor at Harvard University and the University of Toronto.

- *The Vertical Mosaic: An Analysis of Social Class and Power in Canada*, Porter's most important work, was published in 1965. It was the study of equality of opportunity and the exercise of power by bureaucratic, economic, and political elites in Canada. Porter was concerned with challenging the image that Canada was a classless society with "no barriers to opportunity."

- The *Vertical Mosaic* imagery depicts the many groups, defined principally by class and ethnicity, that make up Canada, and shows them as vertically arrayed on dimensions of power and privilege.

perhaps their sons, were likely to do manual work, perhaps in a factory or in one of Canada's resource industries (i.e., fishing, logging, mining). However, since that time industrial work has also declined in Canada. A Canadian worker today is much more likely to be in a white-collar occupation (professional, managerial, clerical, or sales; the service sector of the economy) than in a manual occupation. In other words, she is likely to have experienced intergenerational mobility. Some contemporary workers who started out as factory workers and then moved into some sort of white-collar work have also experienced intragenerational mobility.

Inter- and intragenerational upward mobility was characteristic of Canada throughout the twentieth century as the country prospered and the number of high-level occupational positions expanded greatly. There were certainly those in the twentieth century who experienced downward mobility, but they were far outnumbered by those who experienced upward mobility. However, with the Canadian economy struggling in the early part of the twenty-first century and other global economies rising dramatically (especially the BRIC countries: Brazil, Russia, India, and China), it is likely that we will see a rise in downward mobility and a decline in upward mobility in Canada. Another way to think about mobility is to ask whether if you are poor it is likely that your children will be poor when they are your age (or if you are rich, whether or not your children are likely to be rich at the same age). Think about this as intergenerational income mobility. Do poor children become poor adults? It turns out that your family background (rich or poor) is a good, but not perfect, predictor of your adult income. In other words, there is some mobility such that the poor are able to escape poverty, although the likelihood of still being poor is still relatively high. In comparison to the United Kingdom, France, and the United States, there is more mobility in Canada. However, Canadians experience less mobility than do their peers in Norway, Australia, or Denmark (Conference Board of Canada 2009). A sharper focus on this type of mobility comes from seeing how many Canadians remain in poverty year upon year. After all, students typically fall below the poverty line if they are understood as unattached individuals (i.e., not supported by their family). It turns out that in Canada many of the people below the poverty line are only there for a short period. That is, poverty is relatively transitory for most, but not for all, poor people. One group that has higher rates of chronic poverty is lone parents although the picture here is improving (Murphy, Zhang, and Dionne 2012; Richards 2010).

The work of John Porter (1965) and Wallace Clement (1975) shows how through much of the last century power in Canada was controlled by a small group of wealthy Anglophone families. Their grip on corporate power made mobility extremely difficult, especially mobility into elite circles. More recently the makeup of the Canadian elite has

GL⊕BALISATION

Social Stratification in Once Socialist Israel

At its founding in 1947 as a homeland for Jews, especially the victims of the Holocaust, Israel was dominated by Zionists such as David Ben-Gurion, the country's first prime minister, and Golda Meir, a later prime minister. Zionism was a political movement aimed at finding a Jewish homeland. Zionists were steeped in socialist principles—opposed to capitalism and in favour of social equality (at least for Jews). Israeli socialism was best exemplified by the *kibbutz*, a collective community based on the principles of Zionism.

The early kibbutz was largely agricultural, although some later kibbutzim were more oriented toward manufacturing and tourism. The land was owned communally, as were all tools, machines, and even clothing. In the early decades of kibbutz life, the children were seen as belonging to the community; they were even breast-fed by mothers other than their own. Above all, there was a strong notion of equality. Kibbutz members were all to be rewarded according to Karl Marx's (1938) principle: "From each according to his ability, to each according to his need" (p. 10). Even gifts to kibbutz members were treated, as least theoretically, as communal property and were to be distributed equally among the members.

This system began to break down for various reasons, especially the declining economic importance of agriculture, the formation of capitalistic enterprises within the kibbutz, and the fact that more and more people who lived in the kibbutz began to take business and professional jobs outside of it. Much of this process was driven by Israel's integration, beginning in the 1980s, into the global economy (Fogiel-Bijaoui 2007, 2009). Kibbutz production systems faced competition in a market increasingly dominated by global financial arrangements that were inconsistent with the kibbutz's founding ideals. A free market model of economic development (D. Harvey 2005) led to privatisation of property and goods, which, of course, led to increasing stratification within the kibbutz. Those who remained in, and wedded to, its socialist ideals dropped to the bottom of the stratification system within the kibbutz. Many kibbutz members experienced great personal dissatisfaction, and their belief in the kibbutz system declined.

As Israel became more integrated into the world economy in the 1980s and 1990s, its right-wing government began selling off state-owned assets. Participation in collective decision making and direct democracy diminished as assets were sold off to capitalists who transformed many of them into highly profitable capitalist enterprises. Furthermore, some of the early capitalists began to expand into other businesses and came to control a complex web of highly profitable enterprises. Many of the owners of these webs—the "tycoons"—have become extraordinarily rich, as have those who hold high positions in them.

The high level of equality that once prevailed within Israeli society has given way to a highly stratified society in which a small number of families control the 10 largest businesses in Israel with about 30 percent of the economy. As a result, Israel now has one of the "largest gaps between rich and poor in the industrialized world" (Bronner 2011a). In fact, there is more wealth concentration in Israel than there is in Canada, Great Britain, and the United States.

Like other areas throughout the world, dissatisfaction with rising inequality, as well as high prices, led to massive protests throughout Israel in 2011. At the top of the protesters' list of objectives was "minimizing social inequalities" (Bronner 2011a). More concretely, the protesters wanted more affordable housing, food, and gasoline; lower taxes; and restoration of lost social services. Most generally, there was a feeling that the once just system (at least for Jews in Israel) had grown increasingly unjust.

begun to change with access becoming more open to people of other ethnic origins, although many Anglophone families still dominate (including the Westons and Irvings, mentioned earlier).

The good news for Canadian workers is that intragenerational mobility can be affected by access to human capital resources. For example, a university education is very helpful not only for obtaining initial employment but also when education is pursued throughout a career. Ongoing education can be a resource for maintaining employment and likely for becoming upwardly mobile (J. Berger, Motte, and Parkin 2009). Figure 8.10 shows that education pays off. With each increase in educational level, there is a significant increase in lifetime income.

ACHIEVEMENT AND ASCRIPTION

Thus far, we have been describing a system of social inequality defined by status, power, and class—especially economic class. This, however, is but one type of inequality system. A chief characteristic of this system is the idea that social positions are based on **achievement**, or the accomplishments, the merit, of the individual. For example, a person becomes a physician and thereby attains a high-level position in the occupational hierarchy, only after many years of education, hard work, and practical experience. Conversely, some people believe that a person at or near the bottom of the stratification system is there because he lacks achievement. These people might suggest that a homeless person is homeless because she has not worked hard enough to make a comfortable living. The idea that achievement determines social class is accurate to some extent, but the fact is that where a person ends up in the system of inequality may have little or nothing to do with achievement. Instead, it can be explained by external factors over which the individual has little control.

A person's status usually has a great deal to do with **ascription**, or being born with, or inheriting, certain characteristics such as race and gender, wealth, and high status (or, conversely, poverty and low status). Thus, a person's position in the social hierarchy may be due to nothing more than the accident of being born a man or a woman, black or white. At the extremes, ascribed status has little

One of the keys to bringing developing societies out of poverty is to ensure that girls and young women are allowed equal access to education. According to the International Monetary Fund, the social benefits of educating girls include higher incomes, lower infant mortality rates, and greater personal freedoms. Thus, upward mobility through education benefits not just the young woman but her entire society as well.

or nothing to do with a person's accomplishments, skills, or abilities.

CASTE AND SLAVERY

An extreme system of inequality associated with ascription is **caste**, which is usually thought of as one of the most rigid and closed stratification systems. The best known caste system is found in India, but it has occurred elsewhere, such as in fifteenth- to nineteenth-century Japan, as well as in the era of apartheid—1948 to 1994—in South Africa (Jalali 2007). Indeed, the caste system and the apartheid system of racial inequality are often seen as similar (Slate 2011).

A caste system is closed in several senses. For one, the possibility of individual mobility is severely restricted—it is almost impossible for a person to move out of the caste group into which he or she is born. There also exist limited possibilities for a change in status of the caste group as a whole. The caste system is reinforced by the fact that castes are usually *endogamous,* meaning that people marry within their own caste (see

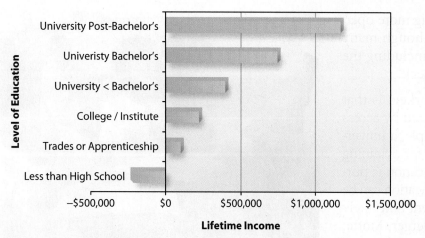

FIGURE 8.10 Earnings Premium Relative to a High School Graduate over 40 Years, 2006 Census Data

SOURCE: J. Berger and Parkin (2009, Table 1.II.2).

NOTE: The dollar figures refer to how much more or less one earns, over a lifetime, compared to a high school graduate.

Chapter 11). Further, contact with those from other castes, especially those with a higher rank, is prohibited or greatly limited, often by elaborate rituals and customs. For example, those from lower-ranked caste groups such as the *Dalits*, the "untouchables" who currently represent 16 percent of the Indian population, are often relegated to menial positions. There, they may not be permitted to eat with members of a higher-ranked caste, or even touch the food to be eaten by the latter. This poses great difficulties, especially in a modern society of fast-food restaurants, where the food eaten by persons of higher-ranking castes is likely to be prepared and served by persons of lower-ranking castes. Since membership in a caste is hereditary and various economic and social resources have been unevenly distributed among the castes, inequality is often reproduced across multiple generations. Marriages are still likely to be arranged within castes, and individual castes continue to survive as they compete for secular resources (Srinivas 2003). The poor in India are still disproportionately found among the lower-ranking castes. The caste system is also still important in rural areas, where the Dalits are, among other things, banned from temples and the use of village water wells. As a group, they continue to be desperately poor, powerless, landless, and largely illiterate.

Though caste survives in contemporary India, the caste system has been altered greatly by various social changes. After India gained independence in

1947, legal changes were instituted to address inequities among the castes. The constitution prohibited discrimination against those considered untouchables and others in public places. Affirmative action provided avenues of social mobility to the Dalits—now called the "scheduled castes" by the government. For example, positions are reserved for Dalits in universities and in the government bureaucracy.

An economic boom transforming much of India, urbanisation, a crisis in agriculture, affirmative action policies, and political changes have prompted some sociologists to argue that the caste system is fast breaking down. Take the case of Ashok Khade (Raman 2011). His family belonged to the Dalits. Battling great odds, such as living under staircases and working as a stevedore by day while going to night school for a degree in engineering, Khade invested in education. He now owns a business empire worth Rs 550 crore—approximately 5.5 billion rupees, or almost $110 million. He is part of a group of 31 entrepreneurs (including one woman) who are now referred to as the Dalit *crorepatis*, Dalits with at least 10 million rupees.

Still, for all their successes, Dalit entrepreneurs faced exclusion within the market, particularly in terms of the credit needed to build and expand their businesses (Raman 2011). Sociologist Surinder S. Jodhka (cited in Raman 2011) argues that achieving success is difficult for Dalit entrepreneurs who lack access to social networks and cultural and economic resources: "It is a tough struggle in a market where businesses are run on networks and caste lines, and being a Dalit often means no land and virtually no assets. The discrimination is not just on the lines of untouchability, a whole structure of stereotypes is built around them—that they lack the required skills or can't speak good English." Dalit entrepreneurs face a brutal market and an exploitative informal sector, as well as declining public investment and shrinking avenues of employment in the government sector. To better their odds, they have tried to create their own social capital through the formation of business networks such as the Dalit Indian Chamber of Commerce and Industry (DICCI). That some of them are succeeding is a sign that there are cracks in the caste system in India.

Another extreme stratification system associated with ascription is slavery. **Slavery** is a system in which people are defined as property, involuntarily placed in perpetual servitude, and not given the same rights as the rest of society. Slaves, of course, exist at or near the bottom of the inequality system, as was the case in the American South before the end of the Civil War. Some forms of slavery persist to this day, such as child slavery in Southeast Asia (Rafferty 2007), a phenomenon that is at least in part related to human trafficking (see Chapter 1) (B. Perrin 2010). Children, particularly female children, are being used not only for hard labour, but for the sexual gratification of adults. In each country where this sort of slavery occurs, existing structures shape the nature of slavery. In India, for instance, children who become sex slaves are most likely to be victims of the caste system as well (Hepburn and Simon 2010).

THEORIES OF SOCIAL INEQUALITY

Within the sociology of social inequality, the major theoretical approaches are structural/functional and conflict/critical theory (de Graaf 2007; Grabb 2007). Also to be discussed here are inter/actionist theories of stratification.

As in all areas of the social world, different theories focus on different aspects of social inequality. Instead of choosing one theory over another, it may make more sense to use all of them. Structural/functional and conflict/critical theories tell us much about the macro structures of stratification, while inter/actionist theories offer great detail about what goes on within those structures at the micro levels.

STRUCTURAL/FUNCTIONAL THEORY

Within structural/functional theory, it is structural-functionalism that offers the most important—and controversial—theory of inequality. It argues that all societies are, and have been, stratified and,

In India, the caste system works against Dalit members. Here, one woman cleans public lavatories. Many Dalits are impoverished, and even those who try to earn a better life struggle against stereotypes and limited resources.

further, that societies need a system of inequality in order to exist and to function properly (K. Davis and Moore 1945). It is needed first to ensure that people are motivated to occupy the less pleasant, more difficult, and more important positions in society. Second, inequality is needed to be sure that people with the right abilities and talents find their way into the appropriate positions. In other words, what is required is a good fit between people and the requirements of the positions they occupy.

The structural/functional theory of stratification assumes that higher-level occupations, such as physicians and lawyers, are more important to society than such lower-level occupations as labourers and janitors. The higher-level positions are also seen as being harder to fill because of the difficulties and unpleasantness associated with them. For example, both physicians and lawyers require many years of rigorous and expensive education. Physicians are required to deal with blood, human organs, and death; lawyers have to defend those who have committed heinous crimes. It is argued that in order to motivate enough people to occupy such positions, greater rewards, such as prestige, sufficient leisure, and especially large amounts of money, need to be associated with them. The implication is that without these high rewards,

DIGITAL LIVING

Caste on the Internet

The resource inequalities associated with caste in India have tended to influence Internet access. Individuals and groups belonging to higher-ranking castes are disproportionately represented on the Internet. Higher-ranking individuals are more likely to have the income and language skills, especially proficiency in English, to be able to access and communicate on the Internet. Yet even among these higher-caste individuals, caste manifests itself in many ways on the Internet.

The Internet is becoming a popular medium for matrimonial services and, in the process, encouraging people to marry within their castes. Information regarding eligible brides and bridegrooms supplements off-line caste-based matrimonial services and newspaper matrimonials. The Internet is also home to multiple matrimonial websites that perpetuate caste divisions by servicing multiple castes with separate sections (such as www.shaadi.com) or by servicing a single caste (for instance, www.agarwal2agarwal.org).

In addition, the Internet is increasingly being used to maintain castes. The Nair Service Society (NSS) has set up a website, www.nss.org.in, in order to disseminate information about, and encourage the welfare of, the Nair caste.

Members of castes also use the Internet to organise themselves into caste networks and communicate with caste members throughout the world. They may set up stand-alone websites such as www.hebbariyengar.net or use social networking websites such as Orkut or Facebook. For instance, members of the Mukkulathor caste have created a group called "Thevar Community" on Facebook (www.facebook.com/groups/bulletravi), which has more than 500 members. These websites and social networking sites also provide a forum for caste members to discuss the histories and practices of their particular castes, as well as contemporary economic, political, and social issues that they perceive as being relevant to their castes. Often, websites and groups provide safe spaces where members can raise issues that might attract censure if raised off-line in public spaces. Among such issues would be a questioning of the continuation of the caste system or contemplating the end of the

high-level positions would remain understaffed or unfilled. As a result, structural-functionalists see the system of inequality as functional for the larger society; in this case, it provides the physicians and lawyers needed by society.

CONFLICT/CRITICAL THEORY

Conflict/critical theories tend to take a jaundiced view of stratified social structures because they involve and promote inequality. They are especially critical of the structural/functional perspective and its view that inequality is functional for society. Conflict/critical theory takes a hard look at who benefits from the existing system and how those benefits are perpetuated.

Critical theorists focus on the control that those in the upper levels of the system of inequality exercise over culture (Kellner and Lewis 2007; Lash and Lury 2007). In contrast to Marx's emphasis on the economy, they see culture as of utmost importance in the contemporary world. Elites are seen as controlling such important aspects of culture as television and movies, and as seeking to exert increasing control over the Internet and such major social networking sites as Facebook and Twitter. Elites use the media to send the kinds of messages that further their control. Furthermore, the amount of time that those lower in the stratification system are led to devote to TV, video games, movies, and the Internet is so great that they have little time to mobilise and oppose, let alone overthrow, those in power.

Social Rewards and Status

While critical theorists focus more on culture, conflict theorists are mainly concerned with social structure (Huaco 1966; Tumin 1953). Conflict theorists ridicule the idea that higher-level positions in the social structure would go unfilled were it caste-based affirmative action policies.

Others use the Internet to attack the caste system. For instance, the group Dalit Freedom Network utilises the Internet to protest discrimination against Dalits, to coordinate its activities, and to organise members on its website, www.dalitnetwork.org. Some groups on social networking sites, such as the Facebook group "End Caste System, End Communal Hatred, and Be a Human!" (www.facebook.com/ groups/136066263161299), provide spaces for individuals who would like to end the caste system. The Internet also provides a space for intercaste matrimonial services focused on ending the caste

system, such as the Pratibimb Mishra Vivah Mandal (www.pratibimb.info).

SOURCE: Printed with the permission of Jillet Sam.

not for the greater rewards they offer. They ask, for example, whether higher-level positions in the stratification system are less pleasant than those at the lower end of the continuum. Is being a surgeon really less pleasant than being a garbage collector? The argument being made by structural-functionalists seems preposterous to conflict theorists and to many others.

Conflict theorists accept the idea that higher-level positions such as being a lawyer may be more difficult than lower-lev\l positions such as being a garbage collector. However, they wonder whether these positions are always more important. Is a lawyer who engages in shady deals or who defends mobsters more important than a garbage collector? In fact, the garbage collector is of great importance to society. Without garbage collectors, diseases that could seriously threaten society would develop and spread.

Conflict theorists also criticise the idea that those at the upper levels of the system of inequality require the large rewards offered to them. Many people would be motivated to occupy such positions as CEO of a multinational corporation or hedge fund manager without such extraordinary rewards. Fewer economic rewards for those at the top, and more for those on the bottom, would reduce the economic gap and make for a more equal society. Conflict theorists also argue that providing huge sums of money to motivate people is not the only way to get them to pursue an advanced education or whatever else is necessary to occupy high-ranking positions. For example, the status or prestige associated with those positions would be a strong motivator, as would the power that comes with them. It may even be that economic rewards motivate the wrong people to occupy these positions. That is, those interested in maximising their income rather than doing right by their patients and clients are being motivated to become surgeons. Focusing on the rewards associated with making positive contributions to society would likely improve the way medicine, law, business, finance, and other high-status occupations function.

Gender, Race, and Class

Operating from another variant of conflict/critical theory, feminist theorists tend to focus on the unequal positions of women and men in society. Because men owned the means of production in the development of capitalism, they gained positions of great power and prestige that yielded major economic rewards (Hartmann 1979). Women, by contrast, were relegated to subordinate positions. Over the years, women's position in the Canadian stratification system has improved with the entrance of more women in the workforce and greater legal protections against workplace gender discrimination. There are now many more women in such high-ranking positions as physician and lawyer. Yet compared to men overall, women still occupy a subordinate position in the system of inequality and can find it hard to rise very high in that system.

Women at the highest levels of the corporate world still face barriers unique to their gender. Recent research finds that women tend to give themselves lower self-ratings than do men. This internalised modesty about work performance contributes to lower upward mobility over and above external factors such as the glass ceiling (Hutson 2010) (see Chapter 6). Women also face a "motherhood penalty" (Correll, Benard, and Paik 2007) in the workplace that limits upward mobility among women with children. Mothers seeking jobs are less likely to be hired, are offered lower salaries, and are seen by others as less committed to the workplace. Illustrating how pervasive this penalty is, the wage gap between women without children and mothers is greater than the wage gap between men and women (Boushey 2008; Hausmann, Ganguli, and Viarengo 2009).

Yet another type of conflict/critical theory, **critical theories of race and racism**, argues that a similar white-controlled inequality system has put whites on top, and kept racial, ethnic, and ancestral minorities in subordinate positions. Minorities face huge, sometimes insurmountable, barriers to moving into, or even close to, high-level positions. As evidence of this, Pendakur and Pendakur (2012) show how minority status affects employment earnings.

Colonialism, Imperialism, and Postcolonialism

At the global level, several conflict/critical theories have implications for the study of inequality. **Theories of colonialism** deal with the various methods employed by one country to gain control, sometimes through territorial conquest, of another country or geographic area. **Colonialism** generally involves settlers as well as formal mechanisms of control over a country's colonies (P. Williams and Chrisman 1994a). The colonial power often creates an administrative apparatus to run a colony's internal affairs. Once the stronger country is in power, it then seeks to exercise political, economic, cultural, and territorial control over that area. Of course, the main point is to exploit the weaker areas for the stronger country's benefit. In some cases—most famously, in the case of the British Empire—many areas of the world are colonised by one country.

Imperialism involves control *without* the creation of colonies, the associated settlers, or the formal methods of control. Imperialism is more defined by economic control and exploitation, while colonialism is more about political control. Of course, the two are often combined. The British were both imperialists *and* colonialists.

Vladimir Lenin ([1917] 1939), the first leader of the Soviet Union, was an important early theorist of imperialism. As a Marxist, Lenin believed that the nature of capitalistic economies, and of the nation-states that are dominated by such economic systems, leads them to seek out and control other geographic areas. The implication for **social stratification** is that those associated with the imperial power come to grab and occupy the highest-level positions wherever they go in the world. While some locals may be elevated to important positions, they remain under the control of the representatives of the imperial power. There is also a sense of global stratification here, with imperial and colonial nations on top and those subjected to imperial control on the bottom. The implications of colonialism for social stratification are much the same as imperialism. Colonial settlers come to occupy top-level positions while the natives are generally relegated to subordinate positions.

Today, few, if any, colonies remain, the result being that we can now think in terms of **postcolonialism** (Bhambra 2007b). Clearly, the term implies the era in once-colonised areas *after* the colonising power has departed. However, postcolonial thinking and work are often already well under way before the colonising power departs. The most notable work on postcolonialism is Edward Said's *Orientalism* ([1979] 1994), which deals with this problem in the context of negative stereotypes developed in the West about those who live in the East, including both Asia and the Middle East. The issue raised is the difficulty experienced by "Orientals" in developing a positive identity in light of all of the negativity about them in the West, which dominated the East in various ways, including imperialism and colonialism, until very recently. The problem from the point of view of social stratification is that while "Orientals," and "natives" more generally, acquire high-level positions when the colonial powers leave, they may lack the positive sense of self needed to handle these positions adequately. Thus, colonialists and imperialists may continue to exercise economic and political control behind the scenes: While they may no longer actually occupy high-level positions in the stratification system, they may be able to control the locals who do hold these positions.

World system theory focuses on the current stratification system among nation-states. It envisions a world divided mainly between the *core* and the *periphery*. The nation-states associated with the periphery are dependent on, and exploited by, the core nation-states (Wallerstein 1974). There are also a number of states in the middle, the *semiperiphery*. Countries in the core, semiperiphery, and periphery shift over time. At one time, Great Britain was the core nation-state in the world, but it was replaced by the United States by the time of World War II. Today, the United States is slipping, and China, at one time a peripheral country, shows every sign of moving to the core. Canada is clearly a core country now, but there is no reason to presume it may not at some point slip into the semiperiphery or even the periphery.

The world system theory is a conflict/critical theory, strongly influenced by Marxian ideas, that offers a very different view of social inequality than is typical in most Marxist approaches. As you will recall, Marxists generally focus on stratification within societies, especially between the capitalists at the top of the system of inequality and the proletariat at or near the bottom. World system theorists focus not on a particular country, but on the world as a whole. Instead of a concern with the capitalists exploiting the proletariat, world system theory focuses on the exploitation of the periphery by the core.

INTER/ACTIONIST THEORY

From an inter/actionist theory perspective, social inequality is a function not so much of macro-level structures, but of micro-level individual actions and interactions. While both structural/functional and conflict/critical theorists see inequality as a

Vladimir Lenin

vertical structure, inter/actionists see it as much more of a process or a set of processes. As a process, stratification involves interactions among people in different positions. Those who occupy higher-level positions may try to exert power in their interactions with those below them, but the latter can, and usually do, contest such exertions of power.

Among the inter/actionist theories, symbolic interactionists see social inequality as much more fluid than do structural/functional and conflict/critical theorists. While the theories discussed above focus mainly on economic factors, symbolic interactionists are much more concerned with the struggle over things that are symbolically important to those at various positions in the stratification system. Those in positions of power define what they

On September 23, 2011, President of the Palestinian National Authority Mahmoud Abbas applied for his country to gain membership and legal recognition as a sovereign state in the United Nations. Currently, Palestine is only recognized as a permanent observer.

BIOGRAPHICAL bits

Immanuel Wallerstein (1930–, American)

- Wallerstein received all of his degrees from Columbia University, including a doctorate in 1959. He also taught there for a time.

- In 1976, he was named a Distinguished Professor at the State University of New York at Binghamton, where he served until retirement in 1999.

- He achieved fame early in his career for his work on Africa.

- However, Wallerstein's greatest contribution was his 1974 book *The Modern World System,* as well as two later volumes on that topic.

- His work is noted for its strong theoretical base and for dealing with a wide range of historical phenomena.

- His main contribution to the field of social stratification has been to shift the focus of Marxian theory from within the nation-state and the differences and exploitative relationships between capitalists and the proletariat to the world system and the differences and exploitative relationships between geographic areas he called the core, semiperiphery, and periphery.

have as of great importance, and those below them may accept that definition and work to gain those symbols. However, the latter can also reject those definitions and find or create other symbols that are of importance to them and that serve to elevate them and their positions. For example, those in lower-level positions may reject the long hours and high stress associated with higher-level positions and place a higher value on positions that involve less responsibility and offer more reasonable hours, and therefore more time to enjoy leisure activities. Paid work may be less central to their identities.

Ethnomethodologists note that people may exist within a stratified structure, but what really matters is what they *do* within such a structure. As in other aspects of the social world, people use common-sense procedures to operate and make their way in such structures. These procedures are used by elites and the downtrodden alike in order to "do" their position in the system. For example, elite members of society are likely to carry themselves with authority and self-importance, while those in the bottom rungs of the system of inequality are more likely to appear overburdened and to slouch through the day. In other words, one of the ways in which people do stratification is in their body language.

People can and do use the system of inequality to accomplish their goals. On the one hand, elites may get others to do their bidding merely by acting as elite members of society and sporting the trappings of that position, such as driving a Porsche. On the other hand, those at the bottom may use their position to extract handouts at street corners or from charitable agencies. Alternatively, they may use their position to obtain loans or scholarships that allow them to move up the stratification system. Clearly, sociological theory regarding inequality entails a vibrant, ongoing discussion offering a variety of insights and perspectives.

CONSUMPTION AND SOCIAL STRATIFICATION

Much of this chapter relates to issues of production and work, but social inequality is also related to consumption in various ways. For one thing, different positions in the stratification system involve differences in consumption. Most obviously, those in the upper classes are able to afford to consume products (such as yachts, Maserati automobiles, and Dom Pérignon champagne) and services (such as those provided by accountants, chefs, and chauffeurs) that those in the middle and especially the lower classes cannot even contemplate. For another, the nature of consumption itself forms a system of inequality; the consumption of certain sorts of things accords a higher position than does consumption of other kinds of things.

STRATIFIED CONSUMPTION

Fashion is a good example of a stratified form of consumption. Georg Simmel ([1904] 1971) argued that those in higher levels of the stratification system continually seek to distinguish their consumption from those below them. This is evident in the realm of fashion where the elites adopt new fashions, thereby displaying that they can afford the latest styles. However, elites soon find that those below them have copied their fashions with cheaper, if not cheap, imitations. Thus fashion, as well as other choices by elites, has a tendency to "trickle down" the social inequality structure to the middle and eventually the lower classes. To distinguish themselves from the masses, elites must continually move on to new and different fashions. This phenomenon most obviously applies to fashions in clothing, but there are fashions in many other things as well, such as cars, homes, vacations, and even ideas (Lipovetsky [1987] 2002, 2005).

Simmel's contemporary Thorstein Veblen ([1899] 1994) also theorised about stratification and consumption. In Veblen's view, the elite members of society want to be "conspicuous." In the past, they were conspicuous about their accomplishments in the work world, but over time, these feats became less and less visible as they came to be concealed by factory walls and office buildings. As a result, elites shifted more toward *conspicuous consumption,* wanting others to see what they are able to consume,

Activities such as wearing business dress, using a hands-free Bluetooth device to conduct business on the go, and having a steely gaze are all indicators of an executive class level. These visual cues are part of how people act within class structure.

especially those things that serve to differentiate them from those who are in lower social classes (see Chapter 2). Thus, their money came to be invested in mansions, ostentatious furnishings, fine riding horses, expensive automobiles, designer dresses, and exquisite jewellery because such things can be easily seen and admired by others.

This is a key difference between Simmel's and Veblen's theories: Simmel's concept of trickle-down fashion assumes that the middle and lower classes will, in a sense, copy the consumption patterns of the elite. On the other hand, Veblen believed that because the things that the elite consume are very expensive, their consumption patterns cannot be copied so easily by those who rank lower in the stratification system. Therefore, elite status is expressed and solidified through conspicuous consumption. What appears to involve unnecessary expense has a payoff in supporting and enhancing the status of elites. In fact, in Veblen's view, the factor that distinguishes elites from others is their ability to engage in wasteful consumption.

SOCIAL CLASS AND TASTE

A person's taste in consumption also helps in deciding the social class to which that person belongs. For example, if you read *The Globe and Mail* (whether online or in hard copy), you are likely to be classified as in the middle or upper class. However, if you read *24 Hours* or don't follow the news at all, you will be classified by most as standing lower in the stratification system. While taste can be demonstrated in the purchase and display of expensive consumer goods, it also can be shown much more subtly in the way one talks, the kind of music one listens to, and the books one reads. Good taste in these and other areas demonstrates and enhances the position of elite members of society. It supposedly shows that they have good breeding, have come from a good family, have a good education, and, especially, have the good taste to value things not simply because of how much they cost or for their monetary value. Those without such taste, who have taste for the necessary rather than the good taste of elites (Holt 2007), in music for example (Prior 2011), are likely to be relegated to the lower reaches of the stratification system.

Taste must be considered not only in terms of how others classify you but also by how you classify yourself through your demonstration of taste, lack of taste, or, more extremely, tastelessness. For example, at a formal business luncheon, a conservative suit would show good taste, while either a tuxedo or a sports jacket would show a lack of taste; being either over- or underdressed demonstrates lack of taste regarding appropriate attire. A T-shirt and jeans would be completely tasteless, and might result in your losing a business opportunity. Demonstrations of taste or tastelessness are not simply demonstrations of individuality but also linkages to the larger social world, especially the social class system.

The Quest for Distinction

Both Simmel and Veblen focus on the economic aspects of consumption, but a more contemporary French sociologist, Pierre Bourdieu (1984; T. Bennett et al. 2009), adds a cultural dimension to the analysis of consumption and stratification. What animates Bourdieu's work is the idea of **distinction**, the need to distinguish oneself from others. Both Simmel and Veblen deal with the desire of elites to distinguish their superior economic position through the wasteful things it enables them to buy. Although he too recognises the economic factors involved, Bourdieu adds the more cultural dimension of taste to the analysis of consumption and stratification (Gronow 2007). That is, elites seek to distinguish themselves from others by their good taste. With members of the lower classes constantly imitating the tastes of the upper classes, the latter are continually forced to find new ways to achieve distinction. In other words, in Bourdieu's view, in order to achieve distinction elites are forced to become evermore refined, sophisticated, and exclusive in their tastes.

Perhaps the most important aspect of this work on distinction and taste is that it is closely related to struggles for power and position within the system of inequality. On the one hand, elites use culture to obtain and maintain their position. They might do this by focusing on high culture, such as opera or art (see Chapter 4). Such taste helps elites gain high-level positions in the stratification system and to make those below them accept their lesser positions in that system. The focus of elites on high culture serves to exclude the lower classes from higher-level positions in the stratification system and even from thinking of trying to move into those positions. Even those from the lower classes who manage to acquire considerable wealth are not likely to have or to develop the level of cultural sophistication needed to appreciate something like ballet. Like Marxian theorists, Bourdieu and his followers see the system of inequality as an arena of ongoing struggle. However, while Marxists tend to see this as largely an economic struggle, Bourdieu, although he certainly recognises its economic aspects, sees it as a cultural struggle.

Elites as Cultural Omnivores

The idea of *cultural omnivores* (Katz-Gerro and Jaeger 2011; Peterson and Kern 1996) offers a very different view of the relationship between social class, consumption, and taste. From this perspective, elites are not seen as refined and exclusive in their tastes; elites are not viewed as "snobs." Rather, they are seen as having very diverse tastes ranging from those that are highly refined to those that are unrefined, even coarse. Furthermore, elites are not seen as having exclusive tastes, but rather tastes that are wide-ranging and inclusive. In other words, elites are omnivores who appreciate all sorts of things. Thus, elites might attend both the opera and kickboxing matches; might download highbrow books on their Kindle as well as pornography on their hard drives; and might buy both opera arias and country and western music from iTunes. In contrast, those in lower classes have more limited tastes, which might be more oriented toward kickboxing, pornography, and country and western music; in other words, those in the lower classes are less likely to be omnivores.

Another example of the amalgamation of high and low culture is to be found in what is called "fast fashion," a retailing strategy led by such Europe-based firms as H&M and Zara. Although they have become global firms, these brands are rooted in Europe because the fashion capitals of the world, the centres of expensive haute couture (high fashion), are there—especially Paris and Milan (Lipovetsky [1987] 2002). This is important because the styles of fast fashion firms are heavily influenced by the creations of the world's great fashion houses. As soon as they are shown, they are quickly copied (Steele 2011), produced (Menkes 2008), and shipped around the world by the fast fashion firms. The copies created by the fast fashion companies are helping erode the difference between stratified tastes.

As we have seen, there are several contrasting views on the social stratification of consumption—on why people at various levels of society consume what they do. The overriding point, however, is that many in the world, and especially in Canada and the United States, are enmeshed in such a consumer culture. Whether we buy tickets to the ballet or kickboxing, we are participating in a highly stratified consumer culture.

GLOBALISATION AND STRATIFICATION

It is clear that all societies are stratified on the basis of class, status, and power. However, as is clear in the theories of Immanuel Wallerstein, it is also the case that the nations of the world form a stratified system. The nations at the top are those that tend to be better off economically, to wield great power in many parts of the world, and to be looked up to around the globe. Conversely, the nations at the bottom of the global stratification system are likely to be very poor, to have little power outside (and perhaps even inside) their borders, and to be looked down upon by many throughout the world. Global stratification is a macro-level phenomenon that has profound effects at the micro level of individuals' relationships and opportunities.

THE GLOBAL NORTH AND SOUTH

Stratification on the global level is often seen as a divide between those nation-states located in the northern hemisphere (more specifically, the north temperate climate zone)—the Global North—and those located in the tropics and southern hemisphere—the Global South. For centuries, the North has dominated, controlled, exploited, and oppressed the South. Today the North encompasses the nations that are the wealthiest, most powerful, and highest status in the world, such as Canada,

The opera, once available only to the elites of society, has become more available to all classes.

China, Germany, Great Britain, France, and the United States. The South, on the other hand, has a disproportionate number of nations that rank at or near the bottom in terms of global wealth, power, and prestige. Most of the nations of Africa would be included here, but there are others, especially in Asia, such as Afghanistan and Yemen.

Position in the global stratification system greatly affects stratification within a given society. A nation, like the United States, that stands at or near the top of the global stratification system has a larger proportion of middle- and upper-class positions than does a low-ranking nation, like Somalia, that is dominated by lower-class positions and the poverty associated with them. This stratification has been recognised by institutions such as the International Monetary Fund, which distributes funds from countries in the Global North to those in the Global South (see Global Flow Map 8.1).

THE BOTTOM BILLION

There is certainly great inequality between the North and the South, but a focus on that relationship tends to obscure the full extent of global inequality. Consider what have been called the "bottom billion" of global residents (Collier 2007). The vast majority (70 percent) of the people in the bottom billion are in Africa, but countries such as Haiti, Bolivia, and Laos are also significant contributors.

Wherever they live, the bottom billion have incomes of only about a fifth of those in other developing countries. They also have many other serious problems, such as:

- A low life expectancy of about 50 years; the average is 67 in other developing nations.
- A high infant mortality rate; 14 percent of the bottom billion die before their fifth birthday, versus 4 percent in other developing countries.
- A higher likelihood of showing symptoms of malnutrition; 36 percent of the bottom billion are malnourished, as opposed to 20 percent in other developing countries (Collier 2007).

The nations that encompass most of the bottom billion rank near the bottom of the global system of inequality. These countries are extremely poor, exert little or no power on the global stage, and have little prestige. Furthermore, their situations have worsened in recent years as a result of the global recession (D. Alexander 2010). However, these nations still aspire to move up the global ladder. Some, such as India and especially China, have had great success in recent decades in improving their positions in the global stratification system. However, most nations at the bottom face huge, if not insurmountable, barriers to improving their positions, including frequent conflicts with neighbours, civil wars, and revolutions (Collier 2007). They are also likely to have experienced one bad government after another. Some, like Somalia, are "failed states" that have virtually no national government and, as a result, have lost control of much, or even all, of their own countries (Marchak 2008). Perhaps of greatest importance is that the situation in such countries has grown worse in recent years (D. Alexander 2010), and many have fallen further behind not only the developed countries but the other less developed countries as well.

RACE TO THE BOTTOM

Those nations that rank low in the global stratification system often have to engage in a so-called economic race to the bottom in order to have a chance of eventually moving up the global hierarchy. The basic method is to offer lower prices than the competition—usually other low-ranking countries.

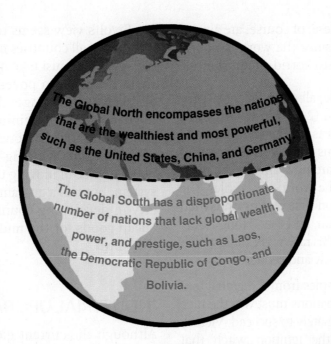

The Global North encompasses the nations that are the wealthiest and most powerful, such as the United States, China, and Germany.

The Global South has a disproportionate number of nations that lack global wealth, power, and prestige, such as Laos, the Democratic Republic of Congo, and Bolivia.

Such nations may lower prices by reducing costs, which they do by offering their citizens lower wages, poorer working conditions, longer hours, ever-escalating pressure and demands, and so on. An especially desperate nation will go further than the others to degrade wages and working conditions in order to reduce costs and attract the interest of multinational corporations, but the "winning" less developed nation remains a favourite only until it is undercut by another low-ranking country eager for jobs. In other words, the countries that get the work are those that "win"

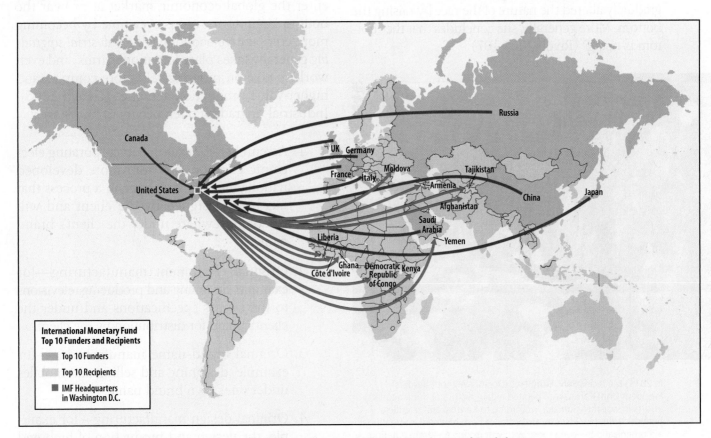

Legend:

International Monetary Fund Top 10 Funders and Recipients

- Top 10 Funders
- Top 10 Recipients
- ■ IMF Headquarters in Washington D.C.

GLOBAL FLOW MAP 8.1 International Monetary Fund: Top 10 Funders and Recipients

the race to the bottom. These, of course, are almost always pyrrhic victories, since the work is poorly paid and subjects workers to horrid circumstances.

A similar point is made, albeit in far more general terms, by Pietra Rivoli (2005) in her study of the global market for T-shirts. If one takes the long historical view, the nations that won the race to the bottom centuries ago are now among the most successful economies in the world. In textiles, the race to the bottom was won first by England, then the United States, then Japan, and then Hong Kong. The most recent winner of this race was China, which now is moving up industrially and economically.

Rivoli generalises examples from the global textile industry to argue that nations must win the race to the bottom in order ultimately to succeed. Victory in this race is, in her view, the "ignition switch" that turns the economy on and gets it rolling. Thus, she concludes, those who criticise globalisation are misguided in their efforts to end this race. However, Rivoli does recognise that globalisation activists have gradually altered the nature of the race by raising the bottom. More generally, she concludes that the "bottom is rising" (Rivoli 2005:107).

In 2011, Médecins Sans Frontières (Doctors Without Borders) President Unni Karunakara painted a grim picture of humanitarian efforts in war-torn Somalia. According to Karunakara, relentless political strife, lawlessness, and violence have hindered international aid organizations—even those with vast resources—from entering large swaths of Somalia affected by drought and famine. "We may have to live with the reality that we may never be able to reach the communities most in need of help," said Karunakara.

Rivoli's view seems to endorse the race to the bottom for all countries interested in development. However, we must take note of the fact that it leads them deeper into poverty, for at least a time. It also greatly advantages the wealthy North, which is guaranteed a continuing source of low-priced goods and services as one country replaces another at the bottom. Winning the race to the bottom is no guarantee of moving up the global stratification system, but it is a guarantee of low wages and poverty in developing countries in the South *and* of cheap goods for the middle and upper classes in the North.

INDUSTRIAL UPGRADING

Although the current global economic system is based, at least in part, on a race to the bottom, we must not ignore evidence of improvement in less developed countries and their industries (Bair and Gereffi 2003). At least some of the countries that enter the global economic market at or near the bottom begin to move up over time by becoming more competitive economically. *Industrial upgrading* generally takes place as nations, firms, and even workers take on progressively more complex and higher-value production activities (Gereffi 2005). Industrial upgrading often occurs in four stages:

1. Assembly—for example, incorporating electronic components from more developed nations into a smartphone in a process that has been designed by the client and will be sold elsewhere under the client's brand name.

2. Original equipment manufacturing—for example, designing and producing televisions to the client's specifications and under the client's brand for distribution by the client.

3. Original brand-name manufacturing—for example, designing and selling automobiles under one's own brand name.

4. Original design manufacturing—for example, the design and production of high-end audio equipment, which is simply purchased and resold by the client.

Some variations in this process occur, depending on the nation and industry in question; apparel, electronics, and fresh vegetables all have different processes. However, movement up this hierarchy tends to occur in those nations undergoing industrial upgrading. For example, the early success of Chinese industry was based on China's victory in the race to the bottom, but the Chinese are now moving away from low-end production (such as T-shirt manufacturing) and toward the production of higher-value products (such as original brand-name automobiles) with higher pay and better working conditions for many Chinese workers.

Another example of industrial upgrading is to be found in Mexico, especially its *maquiladora* manufacturing operations (Gereffi 2005, 2009). The first-generation maquiladoras were labour-intensive, employed limited technologies, and assembled finished products for export—apparel, for example—using components imported from the United States. Second-generation maquiladoras are more oriented toward manufacturing processes that use automated and semiautomated machines and robots rather than human labour. They are more likely now to be centred in the automobile, television, and electrical appliance industries. Third-generation maquiladoras, now supplanting second-generation operations, do more research, design, and development, and are more dependent on highly skilled labour, such as engineers and technicians. Maquiladoras have gone from relying on inexpensive labour to being competitive on the basis of their productivity and high quality, although wages are still far below those in the United States.

While the maquiladoras may have advanced, a lot of workers may not have kept pace with this development. Many of the maquiladoras employ women, as they are seen as more docile and agile than men. Such factory work has provided women with new economic opportunities. It has also, however, opened them up to new possibilities of exploitation and violence. In the 1990s and early 2000s, researchers and journalists began to draw attention to the "maquiladora murders" (Arriola 2006–2007) in Ciudad Juárez, a Mexican city directly across the border from El Paso, Texas. While the numbers are debated, conservative estimates propose that

Many products sold in Canada are made in China because of lower manufacturing costs. This may change if other countries can undercut China's low labour costs.

300 to 400 women working in maquiladoras have disappeared, many of their bodies turning up in the desert (Arriola 2006). The conditions within the maquiladoras themselves also present health hazards. Filmmakers Vicky Funari and Sergio de la Torre highlighted these conditions in their documentary film, *Maquilapolis* (2005). The film follows a group of women in Tijuana, Mexico, who organise and protest unsafe work conditions, such as exposure to toxic chemicals and the practice of toxic dumping in their poor neighbourhoods. Yet as they push for change in their lives, the globalisation of labour begins moving production outside of Mexico. In the end, workers are unsure if they will still have jobs or if the maquiladoras will cross the seas to China in search of cheaper labour. The process of industrial upgrading within a nation is always threatened to some extent by the race to the bottom, although skilfully moving up the

hierarchy to a more complex and highly valued form of manufacturing can reduce the sting.

THE GLOBAL DIGITAL DIVIDE

There are those who believe that globalisation, especially the globalisation of trade, will lead to a reduction of global poverty. For example, recall from Chapter 6 that Thomas Friedman (2005) argues that we are witnessing the emergence of a "flat world," meaning that the barriers to participation in the global economy are declining or even disappearing. Even the poor in the least developed countries in the world will be able to participate in the global economy and raise themselves and their country out of poverty. A flatter, more equitable global economy is perhaps possible, and it can be created through such measures as the elimination of tariffs and other trade barriers. Of particular importance is the Internet, which allows for participation, at least theoretically, by anyone, anywhere in the global, digital economy. However, although this is true in principle, in reality there is a daunting global digital divide (Drori 2006, 2010). Figure 8.11 shows the percentage of people in different regions of the world who have access to the Internet. For example, while almost 80 percent of those in North America are Internet users, only slightly more than 10 percent of those in Africa use the Internet.

The main barriers to global equality in Internet access and use are the lack of infrastructure within less developed countries and the low incomes in those areas that make complex digital technologies, and therefore access to the Internet, prohibitively

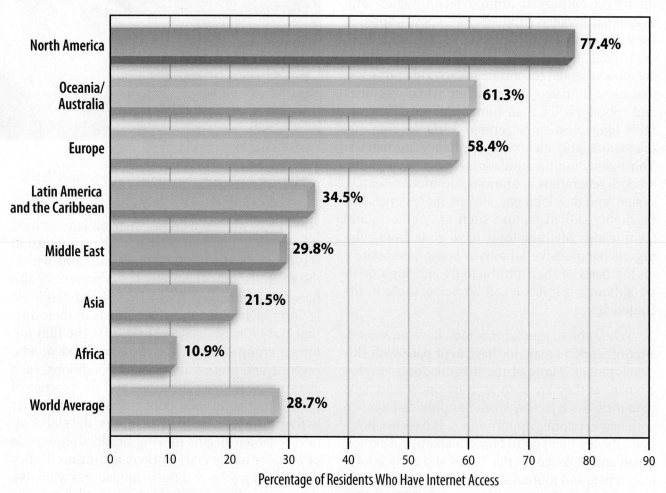

FIGURE 8.11 Internet Access by Geographic Region, 2010

SOURCE: Adapted from Internet World Stats. Copyright © Miniwatts Marketing Group.

NOTE: Percentages are based on a world population of 6,845,609,960 and 1,966,514,816 estimated Internet users on June 30, 2010.

expensive. Language represents another source of inequality on the Internet. Most web pages are in English, and very few are in languages other than English, German, Japanese, French, Spanish, or Swedish (Bowen 2001; EnglishEnglish.com n.d.). Clearly, those who do not speak any of these languages—the overwhelming majority of whom live in the Global South—are at a huge disadvantage on the Internet, and may even find the Internet completely inaccessible because of the language barrier.

However, there are signs that the digital divide is being reduced significantly. This was clear, for example, in the wide-scale use of social media in the 2010–2011 Arab Spring revolutions in Tunisia, Libya, and especially Egypt (see Chapter 15). The digital divide is beginning to be bridged by the rising accessibility of relatively simple and inexpensive PDAs, iPhones, other smartphones, iPads, and Internet tablets that are essentially mini-computers. More than 500 million new smartphones were projected to be sold worldwide in 2012. In 2013, it is estimated that smartphones will outsell personal computers for the first time ever (Wollman 2011). Industry analysts indicate that mobile Internet access is ramping up significantly faster than desktop Internet access ever did.

An important reason for the rapid expansion of mobile access is not only that mobile devices are relatively inexpensive, but that they do not require the expensive, hardwired infrastructure needed by traditional computers and computer systems. Cellular signal access provides Internet access at increasingly high speeds. Much of the less developed world will be able to leapfrog stages of technological development that were experienced by the developed world. Similarly, less developed nations have leapt straight to solar power rather than erecting huge power plants run by coal, oil, or nuclear energy. Some nations avoided having to build fixed phone line systems by moving straight to mobile phone technology. Leapfrogging traditional computer systems and adopting PDAs instead could greatly reduce the global digital divide in a relatively short period.

SUMMARY

Inequality involves social differences that are consequential to the lives people lead. In the Canadian money-based system of inequality, wealth and income are key determinants of social class. However, social stratification also, as Weber argued, involves status and power.

Since the late 1970s, Canada has experienced increasing income inequality. However, the greatest economic differences in Canadian society are due to differences in wealth. People with great wealth often have high class, status, and power as well, and they can usually pass along most of those advantages to future generations. Those with less or little wealth are not able to pass much on to future generations, who in turn have a difficult time amassing their own wealth.

At the very bottom of the spectrum are those who live in poverty. In Canada, there is no single measure of poverty, but several competing poverty lines, which demarcate the level of income that people are thought to need in order to survive in our society. Members of minority groups, women, and children are overrepresented among the poor. Many more Canadians feel themselves to be poor relative to others in this society. However, the Canadian poor, even when measured in absolute terms, are far better off than are the poor in some other parts of the world.

Social mobility is a concern for all people in a socially stratified system. While individuals in Canada throughout the 1900s generally experienced upward mobility intergenerationally and throughout their own lifetimes, it seems likely that individuals in the twenty-first century are more likely to experience downward mobility. Sociologists are also concerned with structural mobility. A main characteristic of the system of inequality in Canada is its emphasis on individual achievement. However, social positions can also be obtained through inherited characteristics, such as wealth or caste.

Structural-functional theories of stratification argue that all societies are, and have been, stratified and, further, that societies need a system of stratification in order to function properly. Conflict theorists challenge this assumption, particularly the idea that positions of power in the system of inequality are somehow more important. Several globally focused critical theories address colonialism, imperialism, and postcolonialism and their effect on the inequality of nation-states. Finally, symbolic interactionists view stratification as a process or set of processes involving interactions among people in different positions.

Social inequality is related to consumption in a number of ways. Those in the upper class can afford expensive items that those in the lower classes cannot, and the elite use their patterns of consumption to distinguish themselves, sometimes conspicuously, from those beneath them. Social inequality also occurs on a global level. Most often, analysts talk about a divide between the Global North and the Global South. However, we can further distinguish a very poor bottom billion. Many nations with these dire economic conditions engage in a "race to the bottom" to attract investment by multinational organisations and hope to eventually move up the global hierarchy.

KEY TERMS

- Absolute poverty 288
- Achievement 297
- Ascription 297
- Caste 297
- Colonialism 302
- Critical theories of race and racism 302
- Depth of poverty 290
- Distinction 306
- Economic inequality 279
- Horizontal mobility 294
- Imperialism 302
- Income 281
- Intergenerational mobility 294
- Intragenerational mobility 294
- Occupational mobility 294
- Postcolonialism 303

- Poverty line 289
- Power 278
- Relative poverty 289
- Slavery 299
- Social class 274
- Social inequality 276
- Social mobility 293
- Social stratification 302
- Status consistency (or crystallisation) 279
- Status inconsistency 279
- Structural mobility 294
- Symbolic exchange 279
- Theories of colonialism 302
- Vertical mobility 294
- Wealth 281
- World system theory 303

THINKING ABOUT SOCIOLOGY

1. According to Max Weber, what are the various dimensions of social stratification? What are some examples of people who rank highly on each of the dimensions? Other than the examples discussed in the chapter, can you identify individuals who are status inconsistent?

2. How does the system of social stratification in Canada differ from the symbolic exchange system of stratification discussed by Jean Baudrillard?

How are the two systems of social stratification related to values in society?

3. What is the difference between income and wealth? Which is more important to explaining the differences between the haves and the have-nots? Why?

4. How has inequality in Canada changed since the 1970s? In what ways are the explanations for these trends related to globalisation?

5. What are the differences between absolute and relative poverty? How can we use inter/actionist theories to understand relative poverty?

6. How best can we understand the gendered nature of poverty? What factors help explain the position of women in the system of social inequality?

7. How has the nature of individual social mobility in Canada changed since the 1900s, and in what ways are these changes related to structural mobility?

8. According to structural/functional theories, how is inequality beneficial to society? How can the income and wealth of celebrities and sports stars be used as a criticism of this model?

9. How does social inequality operate at the global level? In what ways are the bottom billion disadvantaged in the global stratification system?

10. How does access to the Internet and new technologies relate to the system of inequality? How can the Internet be used to alter social inequality?

APPLYING THE SOCIOLOGICAL IMAGINATION

According to Pierre Bourdieu, elites create a distinction between themselves and the masses of people by defining "good taste." For this exercise, examine how taste works in the social world by taking a look at items in an industry of your choice (such as fashion, food, art, clothing, cars, homes, music) that supposedly reflect "good taste."

If necessary, use the Internet to research tasteful items in the industry you choose (search words like *luxury, designer, gourmet,* and so on). Go to different websites and pay attention to how the items are marketed and the language used to describe them. In what ways are differences created around these products? How do lower-cost items mimic these items? Do you think that globalisation and the Internet are changing how taste differentiates people? Why or why not? In the industry you choose, is taste ever defined by people in more disadvantaged positions?

ACTIVE SOCIOLOGY

Social class is visible in all parts of society. Even when we don't realise it, we are "doing" social class through our language, desires, style, and leisure activities. As our lives become more visible on social media sites, we can easily take note of the way class is apparent in everyday life. Examine your own Facebook Timeline as well as those of three or four of your friends. How do your status updates, photos, and likes illustrate your social class position? What about those of your friends? Are issues of class or economic stratification blatantly, or more subtly, discussed? If yes, how so? If not, why not? What do you think your posts and others' say about the display of social class and economic inequality in Canada?

STUDENT STUDY SITE

Visit the student study site at **www.sagepub.com/ritzercanadian** for additional web quizzes for further review.

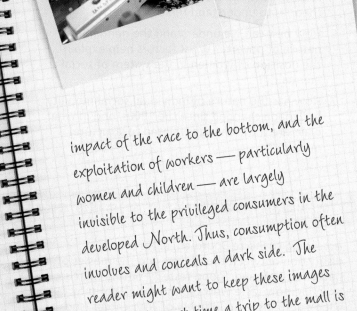

The Harsh Realities of Work in a Global World

While inexpensive clothing, jewellery, electronics, and other products may seem like a bargain to those living in the Global North, they often come at a heavy social price. The day-to-day realities of life and work, the impact of the race to the bottom, and the exploitation of workers — particularly women and children — are largely invisible to the privileged consumers in the developed North. Thus, consumption often involves and conceals a dark side. The reader might want to keep these images in mind the next time a trip to the mall is contemplated.

Bangladeshi women head to work in Dhaka. Female day labourers such as these are in high demand throughout Bangladesh because they work for less pay and are considered to be more diligent than male labourers.

Residents of the Cairo, Egypt, settlement Manshiet Nasser collect garbage in the streets of their neighbourahood. The settlement's 17,000 residents, called *zabbaleen* (literally "trash people"), collect, sort, and sell the trash and leftovers discarded by Cairo's residents.

Seven-year-old Shaheen Akram works with her family in a brick factory on the outskirts of Islamabad, Pakistan. Whole families, often trapped in bonded labour agreements, work long hours under direct sunlight to make and transport ceramic bricks for large Pakistani masonry companies.

South Korean watch manufacturer Romanson operates a factory at the expansive Kaesong industrial complex in Kaesong, North Korea. In North Korea, Romanson pays one half of what it pays Chinese workers, and just one thirtieth of what it pays South Korean workers.

A child harvests coffee beans in El Paraiso, Honduras. The country's agribusinesses and exporters take advantage of inexpensive child labour as Honduras strives to become the largest coffee exporter in Central America.

Migrant workers, many carrying their young children, leave for work in the industrial city of Gurgaon, India. While Gurgaon has India's third highest per capita income and is home to multinational corporations such as General Electric, Bank of America, and Coca-Cola, it is also home to a large population of workers who must face unforgiving temperatures as they walk—sometimes miles—to work.

Young boys from India's rural areas are purchased for 5,000 rupees—approximately $98—and forced to work up to 12 hours a day in factories such as this textile plant in Jaipur, India. It is illegal to hire children to work in sweatshops in India, but the practice remains common among both local and foreign enterprises.

RACE, ETHNICITY, AND ANCESTRY

Racism, xenophobia, ethnic conflict, and ethnocentrism are sensitive topics for most people. However, denying that these difficult problems persist, whether out of ignorance or out of arrogance, will only serve to perpetuate them.

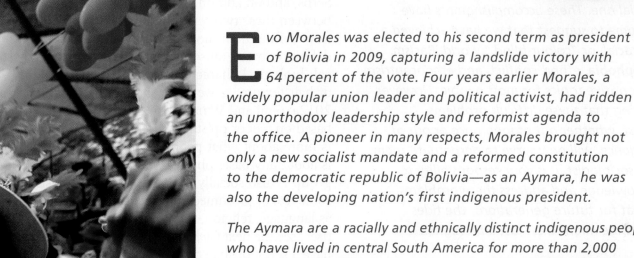

Evo Morales was elected to his second term as president of Bolivia in 2009, capturing a landslide victory with 64 percent of the vote. Four years earlier Morales, a widely popular union leader and political activist, had ridden an unorthodox leadership style and reformist agenda to the office. A pioneer in many respects, Morales brought not only a new socialist mandate and a reformed constitution to the democratic republic of Bolivia—as an Aymara, he was also the developing nation's first indigenous president.

The Aymara are a racially and ethnically distinct indigenous people who have lived in central South America for more than 2,000 years. Conquered first by the Incas, then by Spanish colonists, the Aymara lived as an indentured minority group until Bolivia won its independence in 1825. Despite achieving technical freedom, the Aymara continued to be stereotyped and discriminated against by the country's Spanish-descended majority.

After nearly two centuries of marginalisation, a number of Aymara movements were established to engender social equality and political power among Bolivia's indigenous populations. Organisations such as the militant Tupac Katari Guerrilla Army and Evo Morales's own Movimiento al Socialismo (MAS) challenged racist norms and championed sweeping reform. Running on a string of successful MAS actions (including the ousting of the previous president) and a populist platform of farmers' rights and antimilitarism, Morales transcended prevailing stereotypes and expectations, rising to his country's highest office.

Like Nelson Mandela before him and his contemporary, Barack Obama, Evo Morales is a living symbol of a particular culture's ongoing struggle with prejudice, racism, and institutional *discrimination. Morales's presidency marks an important step in Bolivia's social evolution, but it by no means signifies that the Aymara have achieved social equality. Racism and ethnic discrimination have permeated Bolivia for hundreds—if not thousands—of years. During that time, the country's majority groups have accumulated wealth, power, and prestige— assets they will likely be reluctant to share.*

*It took roughly eight generations for Bolivia to elect its first indigenous president—slightly longer for the United States to elect its first biracial one. These accomplishments have led some to suggest that we have achieved a postracial, or "colour-blind," world. Racism, **xenophobia**, ethnic conflict, and ethnocentrism are sensitive topics for most people. However, denying that these difficult problems persist, whether out of ignorance or out of arrogance, will only serve to perpetuate them. As a sociologist, it is your responsibility to acknowledge and address these problems, so that for future generations, the tides of change might crest just a bit higher.*

A discussion of race, ethnicity, and ancestry flows naturally from a discussion of social inequality. The problem is not so much that people are recognised as having certain physical features or are associated with certain cultural characteristics; after all, many people are proud of their features, ancestors, and heritage. The problem is rather that they receive less status, power, and wealth—or are even abused—because of these circumstances.

While many scholars and citizens have come to believe that racism is on the wane and the chances for racial integration and a postracial society have improved (Alba 2009; Wise 2010), there are others who contend that it not only continues to exist, but remains highly virulent. We will get to that discussion soon, but before we do we need to put the issues in a broader context and in the process define some concepts basic to a sociological understanding of race, ethnicity, ancestry, and multiculturalism.

THE CONCEPTS OF RACE, ETHNICITY, AND ANCESTRY

Globally, many groups of people have been singled out for differential treatment on the basis of their appearance. These include people who are white, black, brown, red, and yellow—or gypsies, Jews, Semites, Arabs, Crees, Tibetans, Finns, Serbs, and on and on. You may notice a difference between these two sets of groups. Social scientists now define them more carefully. **Race** is a social definition based on some real or presumed physical, biological characteristic, such as skin colour or hair texture, as well as a shared lineage (I. Law 2012a; Omi and Winant 1994). That is, while it is based on real or presumed bodily differences, race is more about what people define it to be than it is about any basic physical differences. An **ethnic group** is also socially defined, but on the basis of some real or presumed cultural characteristic, such as language, religion, traditions, and cultural practises (see the next *Globalisation* box). Ethnic groups have a sense of shared origins, they have relatively clear boundaries, and they tend to endure over time. They are recognised as distinct from others not only by those who see themselves as part of the ethnic group but also by outsiders. In contrast to race and ethnicity, **ancestry** highlights a specific group of Canadians, indigenous or **Aboriginal** peoples. Ancestry distinguishes those groups who have an enduring and legitimate claim to being the first inhabitants of a specific geographical space.

While they have been defined separately, the lines between races, ethnic groups, and ancestral peoples are not always clear. Races are often considered ethnic groups, and ethnic groups are often considered races. For instance, *white* is a racial category that is frequently subordinated to ethnic categories such as Italian Canadian, German Swiss, or White Russian. Similarly, *black* has become "ethnicised." For example, F. James Davis (1991) argues that blacks in the United States are now a self-conscious social group with an "ethnic identity." The creation of Kwanzaa in the

1960s, the maintenance of black English (or Ebonics) and soul food, the development of hip-hop, and the establishment of two Afrocentric schools in Toronto all speak to the significance of *African Canadian* as a cultural identity—not just a racial one. On the other side of the coin, Jews, most notoriously in Nazi Germany during the Holocaust, have frequently been thought of not simply as an ethnic group, but also as a race. However, Jews do not all come from the same genetic stock; some have Semitic features, and others have European features. They do tend to share some ethnic characteristics, most notably a religion and a cultural history. Thus, while we will at times discuss race and ethnic groups separately in this chapter, the reader should bear in mind the strong overlap between them. As we will also see, Aboriginal peoples object to being classified as either a racial or an ethnic group, claiming that their prior occupancy of North America means their **First Nations** status should be recognised separately.

HISTORICAL THINKING ABOUT RACE

The concept of race has an ancient history. It has taken many different forms over the centuries, but it always serves as a way of differentiating among groups of people and creating hierarchies that empower some and disempower, or disadvantage, others (Song 2007). Race has also played a key role in most imperial conquests, often with whites imposing their will on, and then exploiting, other races. During the peak of the British Empire, for example, the British controlled India, the West Indies, and West Africa, all of whose dark-skinned populations were subordinated to the British. The rationalisations for this pattern of dominance included both "scientific" and cultural explanations.

"Scientific" Explanations

Following the Enlightenment, and especially in the nineteenth and early twentieth centuries, folk ideas about race were supplemented with "rational," even "scientific," justifications for treating people of other races differently (Blatt 2007). While the Enlightenment thinkers believed in the unity of humankind, they also believed in classifying many different things, including people. One result was classification schemes based on race. These schemes ranged from as few as four races, such as Carolus Linnaeus's 1740 distinction among American, European, Asiatic, and African races, to schemes identifying as many as 30 or more races (Arthur and Lemonik 2007a).

A more ominous result was to use allegedly fixed biological characteristics not simply to differentiate among groups of people, but to justify "scientifically" the unequal distribution of wealth, power, prestige, access to resources, and life chances of subordinate racial groups. In 1795, a German naturalist invented the idea of the Caucasian race as the first and most perfect race. In 1800, a French scientist, Georges Cuvier, argued that race was involved in social hierarchies and that whites stood on top of those hierarchies.

Charles Darwin's *On the Origin of Species* ([1859] 2003) also spurred interest in racial categories, which were considered analogous to species in the animal kingdom. Later in the nineteenth century Darwin's work led to the idea of social Darwinism, associated with the sociologist Herbert Spencer. Among other things, social Darwinism was taken to mean that racial differences were the result of evolutionary differences among the races. One race was better off, and another was worse off, because of evolution. Further, society was not to try to tamper with, reduce, or eliminate these differences; it was not to interfere with the evolutionary process. With the creation of the IQ test in the early 1900s, IQ was used not only to differentiate among races but to demonstrate racial superiority and inferiority.

Also during the nineteenth century, Gregor Mendel's work on genetics and heredity led to the idea that the races could be distinguished from one another on the basis of their genetic makeup. This idea played a role in the development of the eugenics movement, which notoriously argued that the human population could be improved genetically through scientific manipulation. Especially in the first half of the twentieth century and during the Nazi era, eugenicists, among other things, defended racial segregation, opposed interracial marriage, and sought the restriction of immigration and the compulsory sterilisation of those considered "unfit." In Alberta the Sexual Sterilization Act was only repealed in 1972, after several thousand

GL🌐BALISATION

Threats to the Roma

Gypsies (or Roma, as they prefer to be called) long have been, and continue to be, singled out and discriminated against for various reasons. They include their dark skin, mysterious origins, and Romani language; the distinctive way in which they dress; and their cultural tradition of living an itinerant lifestyle, setting up camps in various places and refusing to become part of any society in which they find themselves. They tend to form tight-knit groups, marry other gypsies, and have a strong sense of family. They feel safer among other Roma and in the midst of a familiar Roma culture.

Gypsies may appear one day and live on the outskirts of a community, but they rarely, if ever, become an integral part of it. They are eventually likely to leave. When they do, they may not go very far and may well return again in the future. Thus the Roma are an excellent example of what Georg Simmel ([1908] 1971c) called the "stranger." They are never too close to or too far from the established community.

Roma form tight-knit groups, marry other Roma, and pass a strong sense of family from generation to generation. Here, a Roma family relaxes on the outskirts of a small European village.

The Roma live in many parts of the world today, including Canada and Brazil, but their population has long been concentrated in Europe. In 2011 it was estimated that there were between 7 million and 8 million gypsies in Europe (Lydaki 2012). The map shown in Figure 9.1 indicates where the European Roma are concentrated.

The Roma have traditionally been regarded with suspicion and prejudice, and they suffer all the negative social consequences of being a powerless minority group. To be "gypped," or swindled, is a derogatory expression linked to gypsies. During World War II, the Nazis were especially harsh on the gypsies, rounding them up and shipping them to concentration camps; between 200,000 and 600,000 gypsies died in the camps (Lydaki 2012). The Roma are no longer being annihilated en masse, but in the years since the European Union was formed officially in 1993, hostility against gypsies has again increased. The extremely negative reaction to them has been part of the general explosion in hostility to immigrants throughout the European Union.

What is new in the era of the open borders created by the European Union is that many more Roma than ever before have made their way from Eastern Europe to France and other wealthy Western European countries, seeking relief from poverty and limited prospects. Like other global flows of people, they have been able to cross borders more freely. However, because of their greater numbers and in the face of other globalising processes, many European countries have recently violated human rights that had been guaranteed to them by a 2009 European treaty (Phillips, Connolly, and Davies 2010). Some European countries have expelled gypsies to reinforce what they perceive to be their national

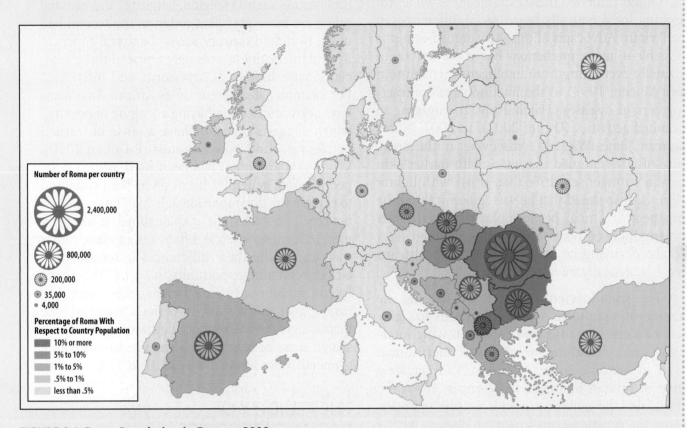

FIGURE 9.1 Roma Population in Europe, 2009

SOURCE: Dbachmann, Romani_population_average_estimate.png, Wikimedia Commons, 1/22/2009. Accessed 11/29/11 at http://en.wikipedia.org/wiki/File:Romani_population_average_estimate.png. Data from European Roma and Travellers Forum, Council of Europe.

identity (Bancroft 2005). In 2010 French President Nicolas Sarkozy, like some other European leaders, expelled Roma from his country and had their camps dismantled (Saltmarsh 2010). Sarkozy also offered them several hundred dollars each if they would leave France and return to Romania or Bulgaria (Simons 2010a, 2010b). This offer led to a storm of protest over trying to bribe a particular minority into leaving France (Erlanger 2010a, 2010b). Human rights groups threatened France with legal action for failing to protect the rights of the Roma, who are, after all, EU citizens (Castle 2010). It was even speculated that the result would be counterproductive: Many Roma would take the money, leave the country for a short period of time, and then return to France. France would have given them the equivalent of a paid vacation.

Ironically, Roma culture is threatened by the Roma's own activities. Many are now settling down in cities, which poses a threat to their itinerant way of life. Their traditional jobs (e.g., peddling) are being threatened by social and technological change. However, the high rate of illiteracy among gypsies continues, and children in the camps tend not to attend school. Their lack of education will almost undoubtedly lock them in to a marginal position in society for the foreseeable future. As a result, even after the current furor dies away, relations between gypsies as a minority group and the majority will likely continue to be problematic.

individuals who were judged to be mentally unfit had been sterilised to prevent their having children (McLaren 1990).

Others criticised these extreme ideas while still arguing for genetically based racial differences in behaviour. Advocates of this view argued that it is possible to make predictions based on race about virtually everything from intelligence (Herrnstein and Murray 1994) to the likelihood of contracting certain diseases (Hatch 2009) to engaging in criminal activities (Duster 2003). In 2007, Nobel laureate James Watson (codiscoverer of the structure of DNA) argued that races with darker skin have a stronger sex drive than those with lighter skin. He also stated that he was "gloomy about the prospect of Africa" because blacks scored lower on intelligence tests than whites. Watson later recanted, saying he did not believe that Africans were "genetically inferior" (I. Law 2012a).

The pseudoscientific focus on race as the source of significant social differences has gotten a recent boost because of the growing interest in genetics and the success of the international Human Genome Project, which seeks to create a map of human biological differences. However, the goal of the genome project is simply "to understand the genetic factors in human disease, paving the way for new strategies for their diagnosis, treatment and prevention" and to "accelerate the pace of medical discovery around the globe" (National Institutes of Health 2011). Relative intelligence, personality types, and behaviours are not a focus of study.

Contemporary sociologists typically reject "scientific" explanations of race, including the view that genetic differences create socially significant differences among racial groups. Sociological research focused on genetics tends to take the stance that genes matter, but so does environment (Guo, Roettger, and Cai 2008).

Cultural Explanations

Even though "scientific" explanations of race continue to exist, explanations based on social and cultural factors such as religion, language, and national origin are more prevalent today. In the second half of the twentieth century, ideas of cultural superiority and inferiority increasingly replaced those associated with biological superiority and inferiority. For example, at different times African Americans have been described as having a "culture of poverty," which suggests that they have a sense of learned helplessness and powerlessness (P. Cohen 2010). While this argument has been used against poor people more generally, it has often been racialised to explain the disproportionately high rates of black poverty. Like "scientific" explanations, it has been used to legitimate racial differences in class, rather than explaining these differences in terms of the lack of economic opportunity that some races have faced throughout history. Furthermore, such cultural explanations show how the concept of race increasingly resembles that of **ethnicity**, which is a shared sense of belonging to and identifying with a given ethnic group (Eriksen 2010, 2012).

THE FLUIDITY OF RACIAL CATEGORIES

One of the reasons that sociologists look upon the concept of race with skepticism is that there is nothing intrinsic about any racial group that makes it distinct from any other; race is a dynamic and fluid

Though U.S. President Barack Obama is the offspring of a white mother and a black African father, he is referred to—and refers to himself—as black or African American. This is a legacy of the hypodescent rule. Here, President Obama delivers the 2012 State of the Union address on January 24 in Washington, DC.

social concept. There are many examples of the fluidity and variability of the race concept. For example, U.S. President Barack Obama is the offspring of a white mother and a black African father—yet he is referred to as black or African American, not "half black" or "half African American." This is a legacy of the **hypodescent rule**, also known as the "one drop" rule or the "one Black ancestor rule" (F. James Davis 1991). In Virginia persons with as little as one-sixteenth African ancestry were considered by law to be black; in Florida it was one-eighth. In the early twentieth century, several states, including Tennessee and Alabama, adopted a so-called one drop rule, meaning that a person with the slightest traceable amount of African ancestry was considered black.

The fluidity and variability of the race concept is even clearer when we adopt a global perspective. In South Africa during apartheid (1948–1994), there were three racial categories: white, black, and coloured. Whites were descended from Europeans and blacks from Africans. The coloured category was more complex, including both those with mixed racial backgrounds (who might also have been labelled black) and those descended from Asians. In many Caribbean and Latin American countries, especially Brazil, race is a matter of gradations between black and white, with indigenous descent and social status factored in as well. In this case it is especially clear that the colour of one's skin does not determine whether a person is "black" or "white." It is also true that someone defined as black in Canada might be considered white in, say, Peru. Clearly, racial categories embrace far too much variation to claim a scientific basis.

Complicating racial, ethnic, and ancestral categories even more is the increasing rate of intermarriage across what have been traditional group boundaries. Now it is much more common than was the case even a few decades ago to have people of European descent marrying others of Asian origins or to have people who have lived in Canada for generations marrying recent migrants from Africa. In the First Nations communities there has been a long-standing pattern of intermarriage between Indian people and Europeans, resulting in a specially designated group, the Métis of Canada—although who exactly may claim Métis status remains disputed. Here we find a Canadian example of blood rule; in Alberta Métis must have at least one-quarter Indian blood (Frideres and Gadacz 2011). In Canada the 2006 census estimated that 289,400 couples were in mixed unions. That is, just under 4 percent of all Canadian marriages involved people crossing racial or ethnic boundaries in finding a marriage partner. This was a sharp increase from 1991, when only 2.6 percent of couples were in mixed unions (Milan, Maheux, and Chiu 2010). People of Japanese descent have the highest pairing of out-group coupling.

Although this complicates the picture of ethnic, racial, and ancestral composition of Canada, a rough estimate of population composition is

Ethnocultural Group	% of Canadian Population	Population Size
English	35	12,000,000
French	25	8,600,000
Other European	24	8,300,000
Asian	10	3,500,000
Aboriginal	3	1,040,000
African/Arab	3	1,030,000
South American	1	350,000
Total Canadian Population	100	34,500,000

FIGURE 9.2 Estimate of Ethnocultural Composition of Canada, 2008

SOURCE: Authors' calculations from Statistics Canada, General Social Survey, 2008.

provided in Figure 9.2. Although no longer the majority group in Canada, people who trace their roots of descent to the United Kingdom are numerically the largest group, followed by the French. Although the Aboriginal population is estimated at approximately 3 percent of the Canadian total, it is this group that is the fastest growing based on higher fertility rates than others (see Chapter 14).

What is now Canada, although initially occupied by First Nations people, was a colony both of England and of France. One of the first consequences of this colonisation was the decimation of First Nations peoples. While exact numbers remain in dispute and may never be settled, some authoritative estimates suggest that less than a tenth of the original indigenous population remained after European contact (Frideres and Gadacz 2011). What caused this horrific loss of life? Diseases such as cholera, smallpox, and tuberculosis, against which First Nations peoples had no immunity, wreaked total havoc on their numbers.

More recently a key driver in the composition of the population has been immigration, and in recent decades this has changed noticeably in Canada. While European migration to North America was the key population source as Canada expanded, now Canadian population growth is driven principally by migration from Asia (see Chapter 4, Figure 4.3). An alternative way to see how the flows of new migrants to Canada have changed is to consider the source countries from which most immigrants come in any one year. This is captured in Figure 9.3 by comparing the top 10 countries from which immigrants moved to Canada in 1966, 1981, and 2010. In 1966 the only non-European source countries were Australia, the United States, and China. Notice that in 2010 the listing of the top 10 countries is more geographically diverse, but the top 3 sources are Asian. What all of this has meant, from the indigenous population through colonisation to recent shifting patterns of immigration, is a very diverse population. We return to this below in an extended discussion of multiculturalism, but before that we turn to issues of personal identity.

1966		1981		2010	
Country of Origin	**Number**	**Country of Origin**	**Number**	**Country of Origin**	**Number**
United Kingdom	63,291	United Kingdom	21,154	Philippines	36,578
Italy	31,625	United States	10,559	India	30,252
United States	17,514	India	8,256	People's Republic of China	30,197
Germany	9,263	Vietnam	8,251	United Kingdom	9,499
Portugal	7,930	People's Republic of China	6,551	United States	9,243
France	7,872	Hong Kong	6,451	France	6,934
Greece	7,174	Phillipines	5,859	Iran	6,815
China	4,094	Poland	3,850	United Arab Emirates	6,796
The Netherlands	3,749	Jamaica	3,667	Morocco	5,946
Australia	3,329	Portugal	3,290	Republic of Korea	5,539
All Countries	194,743	All Countries	128,618	All Countries	280,681

FIGURE 9.3 Top 10 Source Countries of Immigrants to Canada, 1966, 1981, 2010

SOURCE: 1966 and 1981 figures from Library and Archives Canada, Immigration Statistics, retrieved October 15, 2012 (http://epe.lac-bac.gc.ca/100/202/301/immigration_statistics-ef/index.html). 2010 figures from Annual Report to Parliament, 2011, retrieved October 15, 2012 (http://www.cic.gc.ca/english/resources/publications/annual-report-2011/section2.asp).

RACIAL, ETHNIC, AND ANCESTRAL IDENTITIES

Many individuals from oppressed groups go to some lengths to identify with the dominant group. They might adopt the cultural values and practises of the dominant race. For instance, linguistic assimilation—adopting English or French and leaving the old language behind—is almost inevitable among almost all immigrant groups in Canada. In addition, it is common for individuals to change their names to have a more Canadian sound, whether that be first names or surnames.

Some individuals who find themselves among a minority have the advantage of physically resembling the dominant, or charter, group. Those who don't might go so far as to straighten, curl, or colour their hair or to lighten their skin. They might go even further and consider cosmetic surgery. For example, rhinoplasty is a popular cosmetic surgery procedure that is easily available in all of Canada's major cities. One website that specialises in cosmetic surgery promises to address surgically the fact that (quoted from the website) "Asian skin is normally heavy, thick and sebaceous. The nasal bridge on Oriental noses can often be low, wide, and flat. . . . As an Asian patient considering rhinoplasty, you may find you want to increase the amount of definition" (O. Smith 2012). On the other hand, however, many of those in a subordinate race or ethnic group have proudly embraced their racial or ethnic heritage.

Ethnicity is a sense of who one is and of the group to which one belongs. Identities, therefore, are at the heart of social bonds. Among the many groups in Canada that have developed strong ethnic or ancestral identities are First Nations peoples, Jamaican Canadians, Irish Canadians, Orthodox Jews, Newfoundlanders, Chinese Canadians, Muslims, and Polish immigrants. Because they are often so strongly felt, identities are also often at the heart of struggle among groups. Historically, for example, First Nations populations were distinct. While these distinctions still exist, pan-Indian movements since the 1960s have helped Native Canadians gain pride in their cultures, forging bonds between nations and creating a strong Aboriginal identity. This sense of panethnicity is also seen with Latinos and Asian Canadians, and can be witnessed in many residential neighbourhoods. Issues of identity are focal for individuals, and how people understand themselves in ancestral, ethnic, and racial terms is obviously important to them. This importance is heightened if they are not in a privileged position, as discussed further below. But beyond this individual interest, ancestry, ethnicity, and race have larger structural implications influencing how people from different origins make their way in Canadian society. It is to these larger issues that we now turn.

COLONIALISM AND MULTICULTURALISM

The understanding of ancestry, ethnicity, and race is tied up with the formation of Canada as a nation-state. Aboriginal peoples are believed to have arrived in North America at least 12,500 years ago, closely after the last ice age receded (Meltzer 2009). Christopher Columbus arrived at

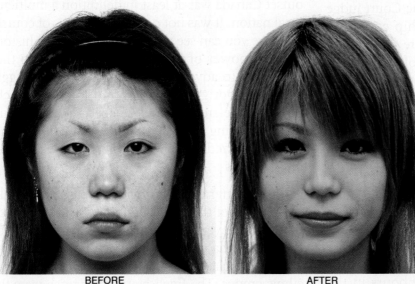

BEFORE　　**AFTER**

Reshaping the eyelids so that they fold into themselves can make the appearance of some Asians more closely resemble that of Caucasians. Risa Arato, a Japanese woman, is shown in these two photos both before (left) and after her reconstructive eyelid surgery. Facing less social stigma and encouraged by new no-scalpel procedures, more Japanese than ever are undergoing cosmetic surgery.

least 7,500 years later. Contrary to a long-standing myth, he did not discover North America. He was perhaps the first European to arrive, even though he himself thought he had landed in India (and hence the name "Indians" for the local inhabitants). A fairly rapid period of colonisation followed Columbus's arrival. Initially, for what is now Canada, this meant the establishment of European linkages with Aboriginal peoples in the development of the fur trade, fishing, and timber industries.

Throughout North America, as in other parts of the world, Aboriginal people were overwhelmed by the arrival of Europeans. A substantial part of that process was mentioned earlier, the monumental loss of life of Aboriginal peoples. That massive loss of life made it easier for Europeans to establish their own power structures whereby the laws of the land became English/French laws, the land itself became the property of settlers with Aboriginal peoples often sequestered on reserve lands, and the customs and culture of Aboriginal peoples were made illegal via such government proclamations as the Indian Act.

Here are two simple yet telling ways to understand the power of colonisation. If you read most of the early history books about Canada, you will understand that whenever Indians won a war they were savages who massacred people. When Europeans waged war on Indians, and won, this was victory (McDiarmid and Pratt 1971). Here is a second example. In a relatively recent court case involving an historical land claim of First Nations peoples, a British Columbia Supreme Court judge effectively ruled that such ownership could not have occurred because Indians were of a "lower primitive order" with "an absence of any written history, wheeled vehicles, or beasts of burden" (Cruikshank 1992). They could not have been thought to own the land, just as animals could not be thought to own the land. Both of these examples highlight a way of thinking, a mind-set, which portrays the colonised Indian people as lesser human beings. It illustrates a mentality of taken-for-granted power and privilege. And, of course, for Aboriginal peoples it leaves a horrible legacy, and a struggle that continues to this day.

The colonisers were both the British and the French. Unlike our southern neighbours in the United States, where the old colonisers were defeated in the American Revolution, the Canadian state was founded by two charter groups, the English and the French, both of whom continue as important bastions of ethnic power. Certainly the British defeated the French on the Plains of Abraham in 1759, and consequently much of Canadian law and history is replete with British authority. However, the French presence remains powerful as evidenced by a Canadian population that has at least one quarter of its roots in France, our two official languages, and the important leadership of a succession of French prime ministers from Wilfrid Laurier to Pierre Trudeau and beyond.

The Quebec Act of 1774, enacted by the British Parliament, was consequential for Canada's future. The act effectively created two official languages, recognised the power of the Catholic Church, and entrenched the civil laws of France for use in private disputes in Quebec. It is in this act that a bilingual, bicultural Canada was legally enshrined. Early legislation also set in place legal precedents for Aboriginal peoples. The British sought to have Aboriginal peoples as their allies in any possible battles with the French, and so the Royal Proclamation of 1763 established the right to Aboriginal self-government and the principle of negotiating land ownership (even though these provisions were for decades totally ignored). As you might surmise, if the French had certain rights, such as language rights, and if Aboriginal peoples had laws of self-government, then almost from the outset Canada was at least in definition a multicultural nation. It was not quite that simple, of course, but here you can see the long reach of legal history and the power of democratic rule. Turning that definition to advantage has been a long struggle both for Aboriginal peoples and for the French. Successive referenda about Quebec separation, and the rebranding of Indian people as First Nations, which occurred in the 1970s, signal those continuing struggles.

John Porter (1965) provided a particularly telling portrait of this societal fabric when he defined Canada as a vertical mosaic (see Chapter 8). For Porter, Canada was a nation fractured by ethnicity, with its population best conceived of as a mosaic of ethnic groups. The English and the French were the dominant "charter" groups, the two groups with the most wealth and power. Of these he argued that "economic power belong[ed] almost exclusively to [White Protestants] of British origin" (Porter 1965:286). Arrayed below the English and the French were groups tied to the north of Europe (e.g., the Finns and Germans), then those from southern Europe (e.g., the Italians and Greeks), followed by the Chinese and "Native Indians." The ethnic groups were the mosaic pieces, pieces that were vertically arrayed based on relative wealth, power, and advantage.

Raymond Breton (1964) introduced the concept of "institutional completeness" that nicely complemented Porter's work. Breton argued that when new migrants arrived in a country they could integrate with one of three groups: their own ethnic community, the larger receiving community (e.g., Canada), or the other ethnic communities; or they could remain unintegrated. For Breton the social organisation of the immigrant's own ethnic community was critical. To the extent this community had its own religious centres, town halls, newspapers, ethnic businesses, and so forth, it could be said to be institutionally complete. If all that a new immigrant might want could be found in the social organisation of her ethnic community, there would be institutional completeness. This would obviously help to sustain ethnic attachment and perpetuate the existence of mosaic boundaries.

What the work of Porter and Breton highlighted was the continuing endurance of ethnic group boundaries in Canada. Institutionally complete ethnic communities helped sustain the ethnic mosaic Porter identified. This was one feature of the process that led Canada to be described increasingly as a multicultural society. The earlier legislative provisions for the French and for First Nations peoples helped reinforce this multicultural fabric. In the early years of Canada, racial, ethnic, and ancestral diversity were largely understood as threats to British dominance. The Chinese head tax and residential schooling are two examples of Canadian practises highlighting the threat that non-British peoples, "others," posed.

A major change came with a set of events surrounding the Second World War. First, the gradual realisation of the horrors of the Holocaust, especially in the context of the Universal Declaration of Human Rights in 1948 by the United Nations, led people to begin rethinking diversity. Second, many groups of Canadians, including both the Chinese and Aboriginal peoples, had fought side by side with others in the war. A more nuanced understanding of racial, ethnic, and ancestral diversity began to slowly emerge. The U.S. civil rights movement of the 1960s helped in fostering this change, as did the increasing emphasis on human rights more broadly. This new way of thinking is critical to understanding **multiculturalism**, especially in light of the fact that about 20 percent of Canada's population is foreign born, higher than almost any other country in the world (New Zealand and Australia have similar rates).

Perhaps the most significant legal recognition of this came in Canada with the incorporation of a permanent antiracist multicultural framework in the Canadian Charter of Rights and Freedoms in 1982 (Dewing and Leman 2006; Ley 2010). Canadian courts were thereby required to make their decisions in the light of Canada's multicultural past and present. A further step occurred in 1988 when Prime Minister Brian Mulroney's Progressive Conservative government passed the Multiculturalism Act, the first national multiculturalism law in the world. The Employment Equity Act, first passed in 1986 and amended in 1995, also developed one of the strongest legal systems supporting minority rights. It is in this context that the concept of "visible minority" was introduced in Canada, a designation introduced to help in monitoring the degree to which racial, ethnic, and Aboriginal peoples were successful, or not, in the Canadian labour market. Statistics Canada (2012a) formally defines the term as follows: "persons who are non-Caucasian in race or non-white in colour and who do not report being Aboriginal."

However, while these processes helped create a multicultural society, you can argue that they did little to erode the vertical nature of that mosaic. The extent to which there remains inequality within multicultural Canada is a matter of debate, but as will be seen momentarily, inequality across racial, ethnic, and ancestral lines is an enduring feature of Canadian society. Before discussing inequality directly, the Canadian patterning of interaction among racial, ethnic, and ancestral groups needs to be placed in international context.

PATTERNS OF INTERACTION

On a larger scale, when racial, ethnic, and ancestral groups interact, the outcomes tend to follow one of four patterns: *pluralism, assimilation, segregation,* or *genocide.* **Pluralism** exists in societies where many groups are able to coexist without any of them losing their individual qualities. For example, in pluralistic societies there might be multiple religions worshipped and many languages spoken. Canadian multiculturalism tends, at least for the majority of people, toward this patterning of interaction. Importantly, however, to repeat Porter's characterisation, it is pluralism that retains a decidedly vertical arrangement, and especially for some groups, including First Nations peoples and blacks. **Assimilation** occurs when a minority group takes on the characteristics of the dominant group and leaves its old ways behind. In Canada, assimilation occurs when immigrant groups choose to give up their native language for English or French or when they adopt mainstream Canadian cultural values and customs. Sometimes, though, assimilation is forced upon groups. During the late nineteenth and early twentieth centuries, many Aboriginal peoples were forced into residential boarding schools where they were given new names, forced to speak English (and punished for speaking their native languages), and taught Christianity (J. Hare 2007). This was a largely failed attempt at assimilation.

Sometimes the result is **segregation**—the physical and social separation of different groups. Historically, segregation was mandated by law for many First Nations communities where formal treaties were signed and Indian tribes assigned to particular land. Further, the Quebec Act (see above) effectively created a separate space, with special customs and rules, for the descendants of the former French colony. While levels of segregation have changed, such history set into motion practises that continue to segregate groups. Segregation also comes about by residential choices, and in many Canadian cities and towns it is common to see neighbourhoods that are defined by their ethnic composition (i.e., Chinatowns in Montreal and Victoria, or Chinese communities in Richmond Hill in Greater Toronto or Richmond in Greater Vancouver).

Genocide—an active, systematic attempt at eliminating an entire group of people—is a final outcome of racial, ethnic, and ancestral group relations (a topic returned to at the close of the chapter). Frideres and Gadacz (2011) refer directly to the "genocidal depopulation of Aboriginal people by the actions of Europeans" (p. 2). Others point as well to the cultural genocide of First Nations communities, where policies and practises of the Canadian government, such as residential schooling, decimated indigenous culture (Cardinal 1969). The Nazi attempt to exterminate Jews, gypsies, homosexuals, and other minority groups during the Holocaust is another example, or the killings of millions by the Khmer Rouge in Cambodia (Marchak 2008).

Each of these four processes has played out in Canada, and to some extent which is more plausible depends upon your vantage point. If you are of Aboriginal ancestry, then genocide helps in understanding what colonisation has meant for you and your communities. If you are a white, Protestant male born in Rosemont or Rosedale, an upper-class neighbourhood in (respectively) Montreal or Toronto, then pluralism might seem the most illuminating. If you are black and living around Jane and Finch in Toronto, segregation corresponds most closely to your reality. For yet others, third- or fourth-generation Italians for example, the process of assimilation might resonate the best. The rhetoric of Canada as a multicultural society speaks most closely to pluralism, but in reality the practises that pluralism implies have not been evenly experienced by all groups.

THE SOCIAL CONSTRUCTION OF DIFFERENCE

Earlier in human history, white people earnestly discussed whether black persons had souls or whether they were more beast than human. Their descriptions said less about the observable characteristics of black people than about their own need to construct a clear and significant difference between black people and themselves. Today most whites are no longer so extreme in their denials that blacks and other racial, ethnic, and ancestral minorities are fully human. But the insistence on significant differences between racial, ethnic, and ancestral groups persists.

We tend to think of people's group affiliations as being objective in the sense that they are based on such externally observable characteristics as the colour of one's skin, sex, or age. However, the fact is that all racial, ethnic, and ancestral statuses are products of social definitions, including the social definition of seemingly objective traits. This is especially the case given the mixing of groups through intermarriage and offspring. The emphasis on social definitions is based on one of the classic arguments in sociology: "If men [sic] define situations as real, they are real in their consequences" (W. Thomas and Thomas 1928:572). No genetic or biological markers objectively separate us into different racial, ethnic, and ancestral groups; we do it to ourselves.

STEREOTYPES, PREJUDICE, AND DISCRIMINATION

A **stereotype** is a generalisation about an entire category of people. Stereotypes frequently appear in daily social interaction. Stereotypes about racial, ethnic, and ancestral minorities tend to work against them. In department stores security guards may, without apparent cause, follow black customers, sales personnel may view First Nations shoppers with suspicion, cashiers may avoid physical contact with Indo Canadian customers when giving change, or a white customer may exhibit nervousness when dealing with a Chinese grocer—all because of a stereotype about how "others" act.

As generalisations, stereotypes are the basis for prejudice and discrimination. **Prejudice** involves

negative attitudes, beliefs, and feelings toward others, and **discrimination** is the unfavourable treatment of others arising from the negative stereotypes of prejudice (I. Law 2007). Discrimination can take place either formally (for example, on the job) or informally (for example, in social situations). It can take place in realms ranging from education, to jobs, to housing, to health care, to the criminal justice system. However, it always involves overt behaviour. Members of the dominant or advantaged group unfairly deny members of other groups access to opportunities and rewards that are available to the advantaged, such as invitations to after-work gatherings or low-interest home loans.

Discrimination and prejudice do not necessarily occur in concert with one another. People can be prejudiced without discriminating; they need not act on their prejudices. However, stereotypes, prejudice, and discrimination often interact. For example, black women often face stereotypes that they are overly sexual and financially irresponsible (P. Collins 2004).

In Canada today, much overt discrimination has been outlawed. Members of First Nations, blacks, and other ethnic minorities are supposed to receive fair treatment in jobs, housing, and education.

People in advantaged positions do not experience discrimination or prejudice on a regular and

Racial profiling, whereby a police officer demonstrates heightened suspicion of crime among a minority population, is one form of racial prejudice. Being pulled over for one's race—for being in the wrong part of town, for example—is sometimes attributed to the satirical crime of "driving while black."

ongoing basis and thus may have trouble sympathising with others who do experience it. In fact, members of advantaged groups do not have to repeatedly consider whether their daily experiences reflect or do not reflect discrimination and prejudice. Peggy McIntosh (2010) sees this freedom from daily consideration of such issues as "white privilege." She identifies "white privilege" as obliviousness to the sorts of questions that minorities experience on a regular and ongoing basis. Being seen as a serious customer when shopping, being able to see others represented in a variety of roles on television, and not having to speak on behalf of all white people are just a few examples of white privilege.

In turn the idea of white privilege is an example of ethnocentrism, the idea that the norms, values, and customs of one's own group are superior (S. Brown 2007b; W. Sumner [1906] 1940). Quite literally ethnocentrism is the view that "my" culture (*ethno*) is central (*centrism*). This leads us then to look at other groups, and judge them, through the lens of our own preferences, our own ways of thinking and doing things.

If you ask any Canadian on the street whether he or she discriminates against others, you are almost certain to be told that the person is not prejudiced and considers all people to be equal. Yet racial, ethnic, and ancestral discriminatory attitudes and behaviours persist—just ask members of any racial, ethnic, or ancestral minority. They are likely to have experienced, or to know someone who has experienced, discrimination at the hands of others, mainly whites, or within the structure of an organisation or society as a whole. Examples abound. *Out in the Cold* is a documentary film about the alleged practise of Saskatoon police officers dumping Aboriginal men outside the city limits in the dead of winter, a practise implicated in the death of Neil Stonechild. The apparent disproportionate shooting of black men by police officers, as in the Michael Eligon case in Toronto, would be another example. In short, individuals see themselves as not discriminating, yet minorities constantly report being the victims of discrimination.

Erving Goffman's ideas on dramaturgy can be used to analyze this disparity (Slatton and Feagin 2012). Whites often quite unconsciously conceal or play down their discriminatory actions in their front stage. However, when they are in their back stage with those they are confident hold similar views, especially other whites, they are quite comfortable making inherently racist comments or telling discriminatory jokes. If they happen to be in a place where outsiders, especially minority group members, might intrude, they may use a code word or symbol instead of an overt slur. Ironically, although only those in the insiders' group are supposed to know what is actually being said and that what has been said is a slur, most minorities are sensitive to all the slurs expressed; it may be how they preserve their self-respect or even survive. Further, it is important to remember that such slurs and discriminatory practises are not just perpetuated by whites. Whites are more frequently in positions of authority and power, but other racial, ethnic, and ancestral groups are not free from their own prejudices and discriminatory practises.

FOUNDATIONS OF DISCRIMINATION

Social Structure and Discrimination

In Canada, whites disproportionately occupy higher-level positions, and Aboriginal people are more likely to be near or at the bottom of the occupational hierarchy. However, this is an overly simplistic picture of racial, ethnic, and ancestral stratification in Canada (Grabb and Guppy 2009). For one thing, there are people of First Nations ancestry scattered throughout every level in that hierarchy, even in its highest reaches as exemplified, most notably, by singer Shania Twain, actor Tom Jackson, and federal cabinet minister Leona Aglukkaq. For another, large numbers of whites exist at or near the bottom rungs in that hierarchy.

One of the main indications of racial, ethnic, and ancestral inequality is the extent to which poverty is linked to ancestry. Figure 9.4 shows the relationship between ancestry and poverty. It is a fact sheet assembled to illustrate the appalling conditions under which many First Nations people live. Several points are noteworthy. First, these conditions are in substantial part the legacy of colonisation. Second, the opportunities to be successful when starting in these conditions are exceedingly limited. Third, these conditions have existed for decades—they are conditions that are endemic to First Nations communities across the country. The historical influences of segregation and legal discrimination in generations past, coupled with the economic benefits of white privilege, help perpetuate economic disadvantages for First Nations.

Culture and Discrimination

Some sociologists argue that a part of the larger culture of Canada, and other countries, is a "**white racial frame**" through which whites, and to some degree other groups, view race (Feagin 2010; Slatton and Feagin 2012). In Canada this can be usefully thought of as "white framing," a particular slant or interpretation of life that favours the advantaged position of whites of European background. White framing includes an array of discriminatory ideas, stereotypes, stories and tales, images, powerful emotions, and various inclinations to discriminate against others. Essentially this is a framing that accentuates that which is valorised. "White" itself is loaded with positive affect from purity (white wedding) to cleanliness (white as light and bright in contrast to black as dark and dirty) to intending no harm (white lie). The good guys are "white knights," while the bad cowboys in the old western movies typically wore black hats. What is seen as successful or virtuous are things at which white people more typically excel, from graduating from university to gaining a professional job to living in the suburbs. In other disadvantaged groups these "successes" are sometimes seen as selling out or "acting white." These images are largely responsible for perpetuating stereotypes, as is seen throughout movies, music videos, and television shows.

This set of ideas is pervasive throughout Canadian culture and is found in and affects many, if not all, of Canada's structures and institutions. These ideas come to "operate as a taken-for-granted, almost unconscious common sense" (Winant 2001:293) in the minds of the individuals who accept them. Thus, for example, many, if not most, Canadians have come to believe that the Puritan work ethic that underlies white culture is more likely to lead to greater educational and occupational success than any other culture. Many members of Canadian racial, ethnic, and ancestral minorities have adopted this individualistic work ethic instead of valuing their traditional emphasis on family rather than career or a nonmaterialistic approach.

Discrimination based on race, ethnicity, and ancestry has often been, and can still be, a matter of physical domination of others by, for example, the state (as witnessed in Canada's Indian Act). However, discrimination is now more a matter of **hegemony**. That is, discriminatory practises, such as colonisation, subordinate others more on the basis of dominant ideas, especially about cultural differences, than through material constraints.

National Aboriginal Day, Friday, June 21, 2013

Too many Aboriginal people live in poverty in Canada. The statistics speak for themselves:

- One in four First Nations children live in poverty.
- Diabetes among First Nations people is at least 3 times the national average.
- First Nations people suffer from diseases such as tuberculosis at 8 to 10 times the rate of Canadians in general.
- More than half of First Nations people are not employed.
- Among First Nations children, 43 percent lack basic dental care.
- High school graduation rates for First Nations youth are half the overall Canadian rate.

FIGURE 9.4 Fact Sheet: Making Aboriginal Poverty History

NOTE: This is a sheet assembled by the authors from previous versions of a similar fact sheet distributed on National Aboriginal Day, always occurring on June 21. Sourced from http://www.psac-afpc.com/what/humanrights/june21factsheet1-e.shtml and http://www.afn.ca/index.php/en (retrieved October 19, 2012).

Discriminatory practises against job applicants exemplify discrimination's prevalence in Canada today.

INSTITUTIONAL DISCRIMINATION

While there is a general tendency to emphasise individual prejudice and discrimination in discussing discrimination, from a sociological perspective it is institutional discrimination that is the far bigger problem. **Institutional discrimination** results from the day-to-day operation of social institutions and social structures and their rules, policies, and practises (Arthur and Lemonik 2007b). Another way of putting this is to say that discrimination may be "systemic" within a society (Feagin 2006, 2010). It is certainly built into the fabric of Canadian society, especially its most important and powerful social structures.

Institutional discrimination is found in many settings:

- Educational systems—for example, the underfunding of schools where the student body is disproportionately First Nations.
- Labor markets, where equally qualified candidates from disadvantaged racial, ethnic, or ancestral backgrounds are less likely to obtain interviews and jobs than their white counterparts. For example, after sending out about 6,000 résumés for online job postings, Philip Oreopoulos (2009) found that applicants with English-sounding names were 40 percent more likely than applicants

with Chinese, Indian, or Pakistani names (all else being equal) to receive replies.

- The courts and prison system where drug laws and enforcement heavily penalise the selling and possession of the kinds of drugs, especially narcotics, that young black and First Nations men are more likely to use or sell, while laws against the use of the drugs of preference among affluent whites—especially cocaine—are less likely to be enforced by the system.

- The health care system where disadvantaged groups are likely to receive poorer-quality treatment in, for example, emergency rooms rather than in the private offices of physicians.

Most social institutions and structures in this country do not intend to discriminate on the basis of race, ethnicity, or ancestry; in fact, Canadian law generally prohibits such discrimination. Many policies and practises genuinely attempt to be fair. Nevertheless, they may have a de facto discriminatory effect. Take, for example, the employment policy that favours seniority in economic downturns. This is not an unreasonable idea, but minority members are overrepresented among the less senior personnel due to historically limited opportunities. Thus such "last hired, first fired" policies have the unintended discriminatory outcome of resulting in the disproportionate firing of members of disadvantaged groups. Here is a second example. First Nations students often struggle in university. One reason for this is the competing norms of the university and the First Nations community. When a community member is seriously ill or dies, it is common, and many Aboriginal people would say mandatory, that they come back to the community to support this person and their family. And they return not just for a few hours, but for a few days. Getting universities to honour this cultural practise has been a continuing struggle for First Nations people, and, of course, universities argue their rules for late assignments must be fair to all students.

The "Invisibility" of Institutional Discrimination

Individual acts based on discrimination are often out in the open and easy for all to see. However, institutional discrimination is far subtler—often

A Muslim woman walks by anti-Muslim graffiti on one of the walls of a grand mosque under construction in Saint-Étienne, France. Nazi and anti-Arab slogans were painted both at the construction site and at a building serving as a provisional mosque. What might have compelled a person or people to write this graffiti?

even invisible. Individual acts that are reflective of prejudice (e.g., shouting a racial epithet) or discrimination (a taxi driver refusing to pick up a First Nations passenger) are easy to discern. However, the mundane operations of a large organisation are generally difficult, if not impossible, to see.

In addition, large numbers of people benefit from the discrimination of larger structures. Among other things, more advantaged groups often benefit from higher-paying jobs, better working conditions, and power over others, especially over groups who are refugees, recent immigrants, or temporary workers in Canada. It is these latter groups that often take on the dirty and demanding low-paying jobs, such as working in a meatpacking plant, custodial or security jobs, or orderly work in hospitals. Many of those who benefit from this situation have a deep, if perhaps unacknowledged, interest in seeing institutions continue to operate to their benefit and to the detriment of others.

Because their day-to-day operations are largely invisible, institutions that operate in a discriminatory manner are much less likely to be seen as a public issue or problem than individual acts of prejudice or discrimination. This is the case in spite of the fact that institutional discrimination is a far greater problem for disadvantaged people than individual discrimination and prejudice. In addition, the comparative invisibility of institutional discrimination makes it far more difficult to find ways of dealing with, or even just reducing, it.

INTERSECTIONALITY

Some groups may be described as disadvantaged or minority groups, and individuals may belong to more than one such group—for instance, black homosexuals or disabled native Indians. Many experiences and problems they have as one type of minority overlap and intersect with others common to another type of minority. Thus, these experiences need to be examined under the broader heading of **intersectionality**, or the idea that members of any given minority group are affected by the

Institutional discrimination is found in many settings, including large corporations and organisations. Corporate cultures and hiring and promotion practises may be such that career advancement becomes difficult—if not impossible—for minorities in some organisations. In fact, relatively few of the senior executives or members of the boards of directors of Canada's major corporations come from disadvantaged racial, ethnic, or ancestral backgrounds.

GL⊕BALISATION

Qataris, Strangers in Their Own Land

Because of rapid economic growth, the citizens of Qatar are strangers, although very privileged ones, in their own country (Slackman 2010a). That is, they are a minority, even a subculture, in their country. Qatar is heavily dominated by immigrants. For example, one Qatari said that of 300 employees at an electric company in which he works, only 4 or 5 are Qataris. Overall, of a population of nearly 850,000 people, only about 15 percent are Qataris. Much the same is the case with the native Emiratis in Dubai and the other United Arab Emirates.

Through its oil and natural gas reserves, Qatar has attained the highest per-capita income in the world, and in 2010, it had the world's highest growth rate (it also has the world's highest per-capita emissions of carbon dioxide, nearly double that of the second highest nation). A staggering 96 percent of Qataris live in urban environments, and Qatar features the world's second lowest unemployment rate (0.5 percent).

In addition to helping Qatar become host of the 2022 World Cup, its tremendous wealth has allowed it to import enormous numbers of people to do most of the work. The immigrants have all types of jobs, but the vast majority are involved in low-status, poorly paid work in services and in the vast construction projects that have characterised the region. The immigrants have few rights, and they can never become citizens; they can never become Qataris. According to the CIA *World Factbook* (2013c), many of these immigrants also become victims of human trafficking, by being forced mostly into involuntary work but also into commercial sexual exploitation.

Education, health care, electricity, and water are free to Qatari citizens—which leads to high consumption levels and contributes to their role as one of the world's top per-capita contributors to global warming. Furthermore, when they marry, they are given loans to build houses and free land on which to build them. If they do not have a job, they are eligible for public assistance. They receive generous pensions, and they are likely to refuse any work they do not consider "suitable" to the status of a Qatari citizen. When they do work, they might have little to do other than read the newspaper and sip tea. As a result, Qataris live a lifestyle that is the envy of much of the rest of the world. It is not unusual to see Qataris driving Mercedes Benz automobiles and owning other trappings of wealth and the good life. Even unemployed Qataris often have servants (Slackman 2010b).

However, all is not well in Qatar and the United Arab Republic. For one thing, the economic and building boom has slowed as a result of the global recession that began in late 2007. Thus, many building projects have been halted or never started. Many immigrants no longer have work, but they do not have the money to return home. They are stuck in Qatar, living in abominable conditions, making them more susceptible to human trafficking. Many immigrants who are well paid and living an elegant lifestyle are resentful that they can never become citizens. Thus they cannot wait for their contracts to end so that they can return home. Many will happily

---

nature of their position in other arrangements of social inequality (P. Collins 1990, 2012). This concept was developed, at least initially, to deal with the situation confronting women of colour, who face discrimination on two dimensions, but it can be extended to all disadvantaged groups.

Minority group members are seen as being enmeshed in a "matrix of oppression" that involves not only their ethnicity but also their gender, their sexual orientation, their age, their social class, their religion, their ability status, and the part of the globe, North or South, in which they live. The problems associated with being a member of multiple oppressed groups are not simply additive, but the disadvantages multiply, as do their effects.

The converse is also true. That is, a person who holds a number of statuses that are highly valued by society is likely to be extremely advantaged. One of the most esteemed groups consists of people who are male, white, Anglo-Saxon, upper class, heterosexual, and adult. This could be seen as a "matrix of power and advantage" and is exemplified by John Porter's (1965) economic elite. Many, although not all, of Canada's prime ministers would qualify. Almost every corporate leader, or chief executive officer, would qualify.

Qatar is a nation of stark economic inequality. After a construction company abruptly closed, its 700 immigrant labourers were forced to live on charity, fight off rats, and sleep amid piles of trash in the company's ramshackle compound called Industrial Zone 18 (left). Meanwhile, wealthy Qatari women are served drinks in the Rolls-Royce showroom in Doha, Qatar (right).

do so even though they earn far more money in Qatar than they could at home.

The native Qataris are not happy with their situation either. They feel that foreigners are getting high-status jobs that should go to them. The Qataris believe, some think quite rightly, that many citizens still lack the education, skills, and qualifications to compete with foreigners. When they do get jobs, many Qataris complain that they are not paid as much as foreign workers.

They are not happy that English, not Arabic, is the preferred language in many employment settings.

Although Qatari culture remains predominant, wherever Qataris turn—on the street, in the market, in restaurants, and in hospitals—they confront elements of other cultures. Qataris are surrounded by foreigners. Still, they are a minority that retains most of the benefits of being the "majority."

Looking at the allocation of Canada Pension Plan (CPP) benefits for the elderly yields another good illustration of the concept of intersectionality. In calculating CPP payments, employment and income history matter. People who earn more and work more during their lifetime receive higher payments in retirement. Because women, and First Nations women in particular, face the double burden of greater domestic duties and lower wages in paid employment, and thus lower lifetime wages, their retirement income is lower. Whites, especially men who work for an employer without interruption for childbearing, also are more likely than others

to receive pensions from employers. Advantage and disadvantage are cumulative and thus have long-term consequences. Workplace experiences also reflect the concept of intersectionality. Women who work in male-dominated jobs—occupations ranging from high-level professional jobs, such as finance, to blue-collar jobs, such as construction—often face discrimination and limits to advancement. Men who work in female-dominated jobs, such as nursing and elementary school teaching, can find themselves, in contrast, quickly promoted to positions of authority. Christine Williams (1995) has labelled the latter the "glass escalator" effect. But not all men

BIOGRAPHICAL bits

Patricia Hill Collins
(1948– , American)

- Collins was born to a supportive and extended black family in Philadelphia.

- In the 1970s she worked as a curriculum specialist in various public schools.

- She returned to school and obtained her doctorate in sociology from Brandeis University in 1984.

- She spent much of her career at Cincinnati University and is now Distinguished University Professor at the University of Maryland.

- She has sought an alternative way of doing social theory focusing on black women and their voices rather than just the voices of theorists.

- This perspective is best expressed in her *Black Feminist Thought* (1990).

- This book won both the Jessie Bernard and C. Wright Mills awards from the American Sociological Association.

- Collins was president of the American Sociological Association in 2009.

have access to this glass escalator. Rather, men who are racial or ancestral minorities can find themselves facing both gender and race-based discrimination in traditionally female professions. In other words, they do not benefit in the same way as white men do because of the ways in which racialised stereotypes interact with gender expectations.

RACE, ETHNICITY, ANCESTRY, AND EDUCATION

Economic success is in large part predicted by educational opportunity and achievement. As you can see in Figure 9.5, which shows the relationship between race/ethnicity/ancestry and educational attainment, opportunity is more elusive for some than for others. At the bottom of

the graph is a bar showing that 23.7 percent of 25- to 35-year-old white (Caucasian) Canadians had a university degree in 2001. For Asians this percentage increased to 41 percent, suggesting that for people from Asian backgrounds multicultural Canada was pluralistic. However, at the other extreme, 6.2 percent of young First Nations people had a university degree. More recent data, unfortunately available for only two groups, show that for Aboriginal people their degree attainment has increased slightly, to 8 percent, but the gap "is somewhat larger than it was in 2001" when Aboriginal people are compared to non-Aboriginal Canadians (Statistics Canada 2012g).

Racial, ethnic, and ancestral inequality in learning outcomes is a critical dimension of social inequality. First Nations, black, and Hispanic students have lower academic success levels by the end of high school. The most obvious explanation for these differences is that these students are significantly more likely to come from poor families than white students. Since family background is the strongest predictor of how much a student learns, it is possible that racial, ethnic, and ancestral gaps in education are simply due to these differences.

Most students, from the full array of diverse backgrounds, begin schooling with a positive frame, eager to learn and do well. However, success in the school system varies by racial, ethnic, and ancestral group, and especially by the time students enter high school the early "eager to learn" approach may have diminished. Some scholars suggest that adolescents from disadvantaged groups are more likely to disengage in school because they are exposed to an "oppositional" peer culture. Black and First Nation students may equate doing well in school with "acting white." Consequently, to fit in with their peers and to affirm their racial and ancestral identity, these students may exert less effort and in turn attain lower grades. They identify less with school achievement and educational success and more with peer group culture and pride (Dei 2008, 2010).

Making schooling pay is also at issue here. The success of various groups at turning their education into earnings is critical. Pendakur and Pendakur (2012) show that the colour of one's skin still has important consequences for take-home pay. Taking into account a variety of other possible explanations, they show that individuals' race, ethnicity, and ancestry matter in terms of how much money they are likely to make. Furthermore, they show that relatively little has changed in this picture over the short window from 1995 to 2005. To return to the earlier themes of multiculturalism and the vertical mosaic, their evidence shows that Canada still has a colour-coded vertical mosaic, even if it is a mosaic that has become somewhat less rigid over time.

RACE, ETHNICITY, ANCESTRY, AND CONSUMPTION

White Consumption of Aboriginal Culture

Many whites are interested in consuming products associated with ethnic minorities. Consider the popularity of sushi restaurants and salsa as a condiment, among many other things. Whites have a strong, long-standing interest in consuming aspects of black culture (P. Collins 2009). There is, for example, a lengthy history of white interest in jazz, much of which comes from the black community. More recently, various aspects of black music (e.g., rap), and culture more generally (e.g., ways of dressing, talking, walking), have been of great interest to whites, especially young whites.

One of the clearest ways of understanding consumption patterns by race, ethnicity, and ancestry is to think about the artwork of First Nations and Inuit

Pier 21 was the landing place for many immigrants who made their way from Europe to Canada. The museum displays a host of material related to the many journeys immigrants to Canada endured as they made their way to these shores.

artists. A substantial portion of this art is expensively priced, affordable only by the most advantaged in society. Many members of Aboriginal communities cannot afford this art, whether in the form of jewellery, or carved masks, or paintings, or sculpture. However, the consumption of First Nations culture has been highly selective. It could be argued that whites are interested in consuming "everything but the burden" associated with First Nations culture (cited in P. Collins 2009:141). Whites tend to select out of First Nations culture only that which they think is desirable or valuable. Artwork is prized, and occasionally First Nations writers sell well in mainstream Canadian stores, but much of First Nations heritage, from recreational pursuits to hunting to tastes in food, are largely ignored. Items of interest are those that are marketable and from which a profit can be earned.

White interest in consuming "everything but the burden" could also be taken to mean that whites are unwilling to accept the burden of their responsibility for the problems that exist in First Nations communities and that can be traced to the legacy of discrimination. Acceptance and consumption of a few aspects of First Nations culture can be seen as helping to assuage white responsibility, at least collectively, for the difficulties that exist within that community.

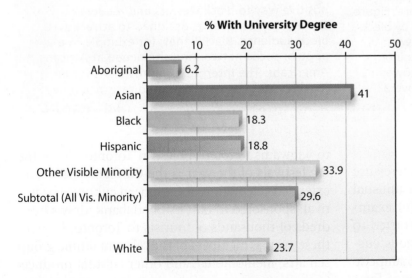

% With University Degree

Aboriginal	6.2
Asian	41
Black	18.3
Hispanic	18.8
Other Visible Minority	33.9
Subtotal (All Vis. Minority)	29.6
White	23.7

FIGURE 9.5 Percentage of Canadians Between 24 and 34 With a University Degree by Visible Minority Status, 2001

SOURCE: Frenette (2005).

DIGITAL LIVING

Race and Ethnicity on the Internet

The user cannot tell the race or ethnicity of the person on the other end when visiting a website, reading a blog post, or even carrying on a text conversation. So why would race and ethnicity matter in the context of the Internet?

One answer to that question involves the "digital divide," the disparity in Internet access between those who can afford a high-speed connection and those who cannot. In the United States and Canada, whites and Asians tend to have great access to high-speed Internet via broadband; large numbers of both blacks and Hispanics have little or no access to the Internet. This is another area where minority status and social class interact: Not having equal income or wealth, nonwhites generally have less access to the Internet than whites.

How one accesses the Internet also differs across race and ethnicity. For example, blacks and Hispanics are far more likely than whites to access the web via mobile phone (Horrigan 2009). Blacks are also highly overrepresented on Twitter, which can be accessed by mobile phones without expensive broadband service (Fox, Zickuhr, and Smith 2009).

As for social networking, whites prefer Facebook—a social network that had its origins in the elite, largely white context of Harvard University—and nonwhites prefer Myspace. Figure 9.6 shows the changing use of Facebook by blacks, Asian Pacific Islanders, and Hispanics between 2006 and 2009. In all cases, only a small minority were Facebook users, although blacks showed a strong upward trend. In line with the overall growth of Facebook, it is likely that there are many more users of Facebook today in all three groups. However, it is also likely that they lag far behind the number of white users of Facebook.

Social media researcher danah boyd (2010) uses a spatial image to discuss the movement of white youth away from Myspace to Facebook as a kind of "white flight" similar to the white exodus from the cities to the suburbs. In her view, the primarily white "suburbs of Facebook" are fenced in, walled, and gated, resembling the gated communities that dot our more affluent suburbs. As a result, Facebook profiles are typically more private than Myspace profiles. Unattended profiles on Myspace are often littered with spam—"digital graffiti"—turning it into a "digital ghetto." In his book, *The Young and the Digital*, S. Craig Watkins (2009) found a similar trend. Among the surveys and interviews he conducted with young people of different races, he saw coded, racialised language to describe the move from Myspace to Facebook. Myspace was referred to as "crowded, uneducated, and trashy," while Facebook was described as "clean, educated, and selective." He argues that such language exemplifies and reinforces class and racial distinctions in the online world.

However, just as Black Entertainment Television and *Ebony* magazine cater in a positive way to black viewers and readers, there are Internet sites designed to attract a black audience. BlackPlanet, for example, is a popular social networking site aimed at African Americans. The Internet also provides a forum for discussing race relations and racism in new

Commercialisation of Ethnicity

Minority groups sometimes seek to commercialise themselves—to sell themselves and their unusual or unique offerings to a larger public. For example, many tourists visiting Hawaii are attracted to the "luaus," marketed as unique indigenous customs. Similarly, tourists at the Calgary Stampede can buy a variety of knickknacks that have First Nations cultural connections, from headdresses to wigwams to totem poles. In Toronto one of the big festivals of the year is the Caribana festival, an extended celebration of Caribbean culture. The festival, sponsored in part by Scotiabank, draws hundreds of thousands of tourists to Toronto. In all of these events, members of the relevant ethnic group sell arts, memorabilia, and other cultural products to the "consumers" of the experience. In this way, they can be said to be commercialising themselves.

ways. Damali Ayo, a conceptual artist, started the website www .rent-a-negro.com to make a statement about the ways in which blacks often have to educate their white friends and acquaintances about how to recognise racism. As Ayo notes, she was feeling overburdened from all the invitations she received to talk to various groups and organisations to offer a "black" perspective. Her satirical website offers a fake price listing for whites who want to bring a black viewpoint to their offices, parties, or colleges. Her point is to draw attention to the burden racial minorities face to educate whites about how racial disparities are propagated. Other blogs including www .racialicious.com discuss current events relating to race relations in the United States and Canada and comment on issues of race and popular culture.

Of course, the Internet can also be used to propagate racism. Cyber-racism consisting of racial slurs and racist remarks can be posted on the Internet while the person posting the comment remains invisible and anonymous. Jessie Daniels

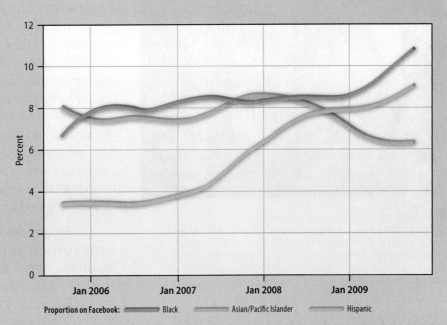

FIGURE 9.6 **PROPORTION OF MINORITIES ON FACEBOOK IN THE UNITED STATES, 2006–2009**

SOURCE: Based on "How Diverse Is Facebook?" Cameron Marlow, December 16, 2009.

(2009) has investigated the ways in which white supremacists move their message onto the Internet. She found numerous "cloaked websites" that, for example, seem to be about civil rights but are actually authored and written by white supremacist groups. Such sites demean the civil rights movement and its leaders, especially Martin Luther King Jr., and put forward the white supremacist agenda.

There is an international market for cultural and ethnic products, which people in some parts of the world seek to exploit. Some ethnic groups in southern Africa have become like business corporations in their attempt to capitalise on what they have to offer to the global market (Comaroff and Comaroff 2009). Some ethnic and racial minorities are going so far as to seek exclusive rights to their culture through legal means (Kasten 2004). If they control their "brand," either they can sell parts of it themselves (for example, through exclusive rights to tourism, or by sole rights to its distinctive products), or they can sell the rights to aspects of that culture to third parties (for example, majority group members taking "Zulu tours" to Africa). The reverse is also the case, as some transnational corporations seek to use ethnic brands to their advantage.

Minority groups sometimes seek to commercialise their cultures by selling themselves and their unique offerings to a larger public. Here, a tourist snaps a picture of colourfully dressed Zulu women at Shakaland, an "authentic" Zulu *kraal* (ranch) where tourists can sample native foods, view dance performances, and visit an *isangoma* (witch doctor).

Notice, for example, how Starbucks sells coffees from a range of exotic locales, including Ethiopia. Country locations are a prominent feature of some Starbucks coffees, from Sumatra to Colombia to Kenya. The Ethiopian government has tried to trademark certain of its coffees in an attempt to gain a higher price for its product, and it has been successful in some locations, including Canada, although not in the United States (Fellner 2008).

SOCIAL MOVEMENTS AND ETHNICITY AND ANCESTRY

Two of the most influential movements in Canadian history have revolved around race, ethnicity, and ancestry. Powerful groups have pressed the case both for French-speaking Canadians and for First Nations peoples. Although neither group has attained complete success as of yet, both groups have pressed their case consistently for the last few decades.

Quebec Separation

At Canada's inception as a nation, in 1867, various estimates place the percentage of French speakers at about 30 percent. Today, as shown in Figure 9.7, that percentage has declined to about 22 percent. If you were a Quebecker, where over 80 percent of people use French as their main language at home, you might worry about this gradual erosion of French-language speakers. If it is not checked, this will mean the slow extinction of French as a culture. You might think this especially so if you find all around you a sea of English language, in the rest of Canada and to your south in the United States. Also worrying might be the tendency for immigrants to Canada to opt for English as opposed to French as their official language of communication (Lachapelle and Lepage 2010).

Looking more closely at Figure 9.7 we can see a comparison of people who say French is their mother tongue, the language they first learned at birth, and people who report using French as the language currently spoken most often at home. First, from 1971 to 2006, both percentages are declining. Second, proportionately fewer people report using French regularly now, compared to learning French as their mother tongue

As Japanese people were expelled from the British Columbia coast their homes, property, and belonging were confiscated and sold. The fishing boats shown here were a major source of livelihood for Japanese families, many of who were forced to move even though they were Canadian citizens.

BIOGRAPHICAL bits

Raymond Breton (Canadian)

- Breton was born in Montmartre, Saskatchewan, a village that dubs itself "The Paris of the Prairies." Given this French locale in an Anglophone province, it is perhaps not surprising that Breton is a world authority on ethnocultural communities.

- He had a distinguished career in sociology at the University of Toronto. His research focused on immigration, ethnicity, language, and intergroup relations.

- His publications speak to this expertise, including *Ethnic Relations in Canada: Institutional Dynamics* (2005); *A Fragile Social Fabric? Fairness, Trust and Commitment in Canada* (2004, coauthored); and *The Illusion of Difference: Realities of Ethnicity in Canada and the United States* (1994, coauthored).

- His seminal idea of "institutional completeness" is a classic statement of how social structures make ethnic communities vibrant, sustainable entities in which individuals can thrive.

- In 2008, Breton became an officer of the Order of Canada.

(true for any year of comparison). Both of these trends signal an erosion of the French language. Third, the final column suggests that the erosion is slowing, but it is ongoing nevertheless. Another comparison, although one not in the figure, is that for English, 67 percent of Canadians reported this as the language they use most often in the home, both in 1971 and 2006. There is no parallel erosion of English as a language, as compared to French.

Language is at the heart of a person's culture. Our identity is intricately intertwined with our language, including the words with which we think, our accent, and our comfort zone. For Quebeckers it is this erosion of language that is understood as critical to the sustainability of a vibrant French culture. There have been a variety of policy initiatives to counteract this language erosion. One is the "revenge of the cradle." A way to increase the French language would be to have more children who speak French, thus helping to ensure through population numbers the sustainability of the language. In Quebec there have been policies, including financial incentives, to increase the birthrate. A second policy tool is through language laws. The use of French has been promoted by encouraging immigrants to Quebec to learn French and send their children to schools where French is the language of instruction. Coupled with this is the insistence that businesses use French as a means of communication and that English-only signage not occur. You could imagine a variety of other ways to promote retention of the French language.

Years	Population of French mother tongue		Population of French as the language spoken most often at home		Difference	
	number	percentage	number	percentage	number	percentage
1971	5,792,710	26.9	5,546,025	25.7	−246,685	−1.2
1981	6,177,795	25.7	5,923,010	24.6	−257,785	−1.1
1991	6,562,060	24.3	6,288,430	23.3	−273,630	−1.0
2001	6,782,320	22.9	6,531,375	22.0	−250,945	−0.9
2006	6,892,230	22.1	6,690,130	21.4	−202,100	−0.7

FIGURE 9.7 Population of French Mother Tongue and Population of French as the Language Spoken Most Often at Home, and Difference between the Two, Canada, 1971–2006

SOURCES: Statistics Canada, censuses of population, 1971–2006.

Retrieved May 1, 2013 (http://www12.statcan.ca/census-recensement/2006/as-sa/97-555/table/t7-eng.cfm).

GL⦿BALISATION

The Warao of Venezuela

The Warao are a small minority group indigenous to Venezuela. Historically, they have lived on or near the country's waterways in houses built on stilts. When Europeans landed in the area for the first time, the houses reminded the Europeans of Venice, and thus they named the area Venezuela ("Little Venice").

Their situation should have improved since they lived in a country headed by Hugo Chávez, who traced part of his own ancestry to another indigenous minority group, the Pumé people. As president, and prior to his death in 2012, Chávez committed himself to empowering minority groups

Despite the late Hugo Chávez's ministry of indigenous peoples, native university, and indigenous health care projects, the Warao continue to live in appalling squalor. Here, a Warao woman nurses a child in a trash-laden village on the shores of the Orinoco River in Venezuela. Most Warao women have a number of babies, but infant mortality is high, and female life expectancy is low.

and improving their living conditions (Romero 2010). Using its great oil wealth, Venezuela claims that it now has one of the most equitable income distributions in Latin America (rivaling that of Uruguay, the least stratified country in South America). Among other things, Chávez created a new ministry of indigenous peoples and funded a native university and indigenous health care projects. This was welcomed by the indigenous peoples of Venezuela (totalling about a half-million), including the Warao, who appreciated the programmes as well as Chávez's own indigenous background.

However, the Warao continue to live in appalling squalor. While some live in remote areas of Guayana, others scavenge in the garbage dumps of Ciudad Guayana and compete with vultures for scraps of food, including rotting chicken from Arturo's, a Venezuelan fast-food chain. One observer noted a 4-year-old girl nibbled on a rotting chicken wing competing with flies for the food. Her mother said, "This is how we live" (Romero 2010:10). Close by are elegant boutiques selling luxury goods to the well-to-do of Venezuela. While some Warao subsist (or not) in this way, others survive by prostituting themselves, by begging, or by selling trinkets at intersections. The prostitutes may fall prey to HIV infections and the scavengers to thieves, as well as to the huge compacting trucks in the trash dumps that can, and have, crushed scavengers to death.

The trash dump *Cambalache* was described by one anthropologist as "the worst place I have ever seen in my life" (Romero 2010:10). However, said a leader of the Warao, "We're never going to leave this place. . . . We've claimed this land and made our life in the dump, and this is where our future rests" (Romero 2010:10). The Warao have staked their claim to this piece of territory. Like native groups in colonised countries around the world (including Canada and the United States), they often suffer from discrimination and are highly marginalised.

An even more radical response, though, would be to separate from Canada. Creating a separate nation would be a way that could help to forestall the relentless march of English encroachment. And that of course is exactly what the Party Québécois, the separatist party in Quebec, has opted to do. In both 1980 and 1995 separate referenda were held in Quebec. The question was straightforward—would you be in favour of or against separation? Both times those against separation were in the majority, but in 1995 the vote was 50.6 percent against and 49.5 percent in favour (in 1980 only 40 percent had been in favour).

Language preservation, as a core aspect of the retention of a vibrant French culture, is only one of the important social forces promoting the press for separation. In terms of ethnic identity many in the province of Quebec came to see themselves not as French Canadians, but as Québécois. More recently the phrasing "distinct society" has been used to describe Quebec, and there is certainly sociological evidence to suggest such a designation. In a rigorous comparative analysis of Canada and the United States, Edward Grabb and James Curtis (2010) argue that Quebec represents one of four distinctive regions, with the other three being the U.S. South, the northern United States, and English Canada. Their analysis suggests that the latter two regions are relatively similar on core values and deep underlying principles that motivate action, similar in large part because of their common origins as British colonies. Quebec (and the U.S. South) differs because its underlying structures, especially with respect to religion, governance, and an agrarian economy, mark it off as different from other regions. The distinctiveness of Quebec, according to Grabb and Curtis (2010:248), stems from its "French and Catholic origins, which promoted an alternative set of core values in its population and its major social structures."

What has changed in Quebec is that the old system was, in comparison to other regions in Canada and the United States, more conservative, authoritarian, and hierarchal (somewhat like the U.S. South) but has transformed into "the most liberal, permissive, or tolerant population in North America" (Grabb and Curtis 2010:248). Quebec experienced a sharp break with the past in the 1960s, a period commonly referred to as the "Quiet Revolution" where an old hierarchical collectivism, dominated by the Catholic Church, was overthrown in favour of a more liberal, independent, nationalism. Hence was born not just separatist politics, but also a population more supportive than others in North America of interracial marriages, gay rights, and liberal approaches to criminal justice.

Aboriginal Self-government and Land Claims

The word *Indian* has all but vanished in Canada. Certainly in some parts of the country the term *Indian* is still used, but most mainstream media, most discussion in our urban centres, and almost all government discussion at the provincial and federal level is about First Nations peoples and, sometimes, Native Canadians. This change of wording is more than symbolic, even though it contains powerful symbolism. For people of Aboriginal origin it asserts their ancestral status as the first peoples on the land that is now Canada. It asserts, by naming, a claim to the land, an authoritative declaration about prior occupancy. This is power at work. Here is a strong claim to personal identity: "I am one of the founding peoples of this territory." *First Nations* also disputes the language of the charter groups, the idea of the two founding nations of the English and the French. First Nations not only asserts primacy but also recognises Aboriginal peoples as multiple nations, nations that ought to have nation-to-nation relationships with the federal government. A parallel naming process is also changing the spelling of many First Nations tribes from English spellings (e.g., Nishga and Micmac)

Shawn A-in-chut Atleo, National Chief of the Assembly of First Nations, represents thousands of First Nations peoples from a diverse group of Aboriginal tribes in Canada. One of his most pressing cultural concerns is the gradual extinction of many First Nations languages.

to spellings more congruent with native dialect (e.g., Nisga'a and Mi'kmaq). There is therefore, in the language of sociology, both the micro, or personal, sense of membership and identity, but there is as well the important macro or structural sense of First Nations as a legally recognizable entity with which other nations must deal.

According to the 2006 Canadian census, 1,172,790 individuals identified as Aboriginal. This included 698,025 First Nations people, including members of the Cree, Haida, Ojibway, and Mi'kmaq nations; 389,785 Métis people; and 50,485 Inuit people (the Inuit live mainly in the north of Canada). Between 1996 and 2006 the Aboriginal population increased by an estimated 45 percent, well above the 8 percent growth rate of the non-Aboriginal population. In international comparison, Canada has the second largest

Aboriginal population, at 4 percent (the Maori of New Zealand compose about 15 percent of that country's inhabitants). Notice, as Figure 9.8 displays for First Nations people, there is much diversity among these distinct groups.

Representing this diverse group are many different organisations. As a social movement the Assembly of First Nations (AFN) has risen to become an increasingly powerful force in Canadian politics. The election for the leadership of the AFN has become national news, the assembly can count on regularised meetings with senior government officials, and governments increasingly consult with the AFN over a host of matters related to Aboriginal people. Similar national organisations exist for both the Inuit (the Inuit Tapiriit Kanatami) and the Métis (National Council).

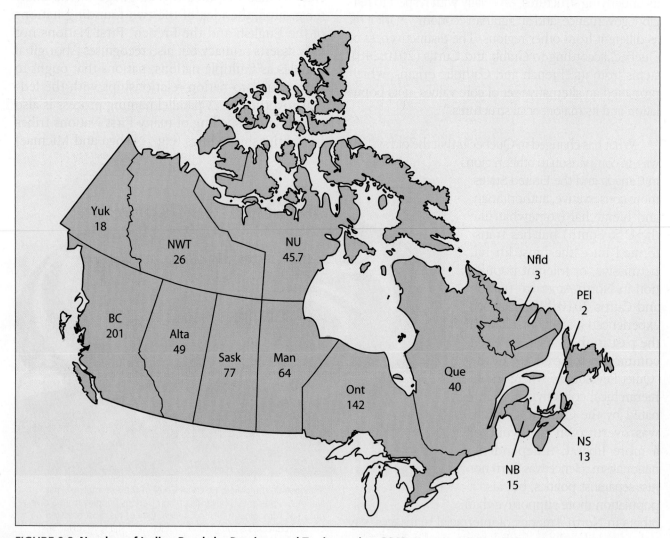

FIGURE 9.8 Number of Indian Bands by Province and Territory, circa 2010

SOURCE: Retrieved October 25, 2012 (http://www.aboriginalcanada.gc.ca/acp/community/site.nsf/eng/bc-all-b.html).

Perhaps the greatest success of Aboriginal peoples is the creation of Nunavut, carved out of the former Northwest Territories. This is self-government in action, a large tract of territory where the Inuit population now has democratic control of its land base. Other successes of this sort have also occurred, especially for the Nisga'a nation in northern British Columbia, but also for the Tsawwassen people in the very south of the same province. Increasingly the Canadian courts have recognised legal tenets, such as the Royal Proclamation of 1763, and urged provincial and federal governments to do more to resolve long-standing disputes about governance and land. Progress is slow and uneven, but continues to this day (Frideres and Gadacz 2011).

RACE AND ETHNICITY IN GLOBAL CONTEXT

For at least the last few hundred years, ethnic and ancestral identities have been closely tied to nation-states, as we have just seen for First Nations peoples and for the Québécois. Other comparative examples abound. Until the modern era, the population of Ireland almost exclusively embraced the Gaelic language and Irish culture; the population of Ceylon (now Sri Lanka) almost exclusively embraced a Ceylonese identity. Historically, one major factor has been **diaspora**, which is the dispersal, typically involuntary, of a racial or ethnic population from its traditional homeland and over a wide geographic area. However, in recent years, with the increase in globalisation and the corresponding decline in the nation-state, national identities have tended to be diluted. Ethnic identity, as well as other kinds of identity—class, race, and gender, as well as age, sexual orientation, and others—have simultaneously grown in importance.

The existence of so many identities on the global stage has increased the possibility of people having hybrid ethnic identities. That is, an increasing number of people identify not only with, say, the ethnic group into which they were born, but also with other ethnic groups in geographic areas to which they may have migrated. Thus, migrants from India to China might see themselves as both Indian and Chinese.

ETHNIC IDENTITY AND GLOBALISATION

Some see globalisation as a threat to ethnic identity; they see globalisation as leading us toward a world of homogeneous identities. However, others argue that globalisation is not a threat to ethnic identity. These are some of the reasons they cite:

- Ethnic identities are not nearly as fragile as is often believed. Ethnicity is inculcated from birth, within the family and then, often, in school and by the surrounding culture, and thus usually becomes part of a person's core identity.

- Globalisation can be a force, maybe the most significant force, in the creation and proliferation of ethnic identity (Tomlinson 2000). Ethnic groups and many aspects of their culture flow around the globe creating new pockets of ethnic identity and reinforcing that identity in particular locales. Global pressures toward a homogenised identity may also stiffen a person's resolve to maintain ties to an ethnic culture.

- Ethnic identity and globalisation are part of the same modern process. For example, through the development of advanced forms of communication, globalisation allows ethnic

Although the Klu Klux Klan are often associated solely with the southern USA, the KKK operated in Canada, especially on the prairies.

PUBLIC SOCIOLOGY

W. E. B. Du Bois and the Negro Press

Although W. E. B. Du Bois held a variety of academic positions and published a number of important books ranging from sociological research to sociological theory, he also spent a good portion of his life as a journalist. He became a correspondent for a black newspaper, *The New York Globe*, in 1882 when he was only 15 years old. After he graduated from Harvard in 1905, he wrote for various black and white newspapers and magazines. He eventually founded his own magazines, and in 1910 one of them became *The Crisis*, the official magazine of the National Association for the Advancement of Colored People (NAACP), which came into existence in the same year.

Du Bois was the NAACP's director of publications and research. He established *The Crisis* in large part because of his belief that other black newspapers devoted too little space and attention to the news. Through *The Crisis* Du Bois was able to disseminate his ideas widely largely because he was solely responsible for its editorial content. Among his many targets was Booker T. Washington, whom he regarded as far too conservative. He felt that Washington was much too willing to subordinate blacks to whites. More specifically, he objected to Washington's well-known and influential view that blacks should be trained for, and be satisfied with, manual work. Du Bois was in charge of *The*

Crisis until 1934, when a dispute with the director of the NAACP led him to resign because of the organisation's position in favour of "voluntary segregation" in order to further black advancement.

Du Bois continued his journalistic career writing for, among other publications, *The Amsterdam News* in New York City between 1939 and 1944. During World War II some black journalists were attacked, primarily by white journalists, for disloyalty because they criticised fascism both abroad and in the United States (at least in relationship to the treatment of black Americans). Du Bois responded to the critics by writing that "apparently the white world has suddenly become conscious of the Negro press. . . . What white commentators think they have discovered is that the Negro press is exciting the mass of Negroes to discontent and even to violence. As a matter of fact what they are really seeing is the intensity of feeling and resentment which is sweeping over the Negro people" (Franklin 1987:40–44).

Du Bois continued to function as a journalist for years, often with relatively small black newspapers, which he felt made an extremely important contribution to explaining the plight of black Americans and giving them an outlet to express both their grievances and their goals. Thus in addition to being a top-ranked sociologist, Du Bois was one of the great public sociologists of all time.

group members who have spread throughout the world to stay in touch with one another for the express purpose of maintaining familiar traditions. This more powerful sense of ethnic identity can be exported back to the home country through the same forms of global media. This is part of the broader process of transnationalism—in this case the separation of ethnic or national identity from any specific geographic territory.

GLOBAL PREJUDICE AND DISCRIMINATION

Racism is not exclusive to the West in general, or to Canada or the United States in particular, but exists in many societies throughout the world. For example, in Japan differences in skin colour, hair, and even body odour have been used to

distinguish among races such as the Ainu and Buraku. Japanese citizens whose genetic heritage is partly Caucasian or African are also subject to prejudice within their own country.

To this point, we have focused on racial, ethnic, and ancestral relations within specific nation-states, especially Canada. But we can also examine these relations in a global context. The North-South distinction is a key factor. The North is shorthand for the developed nations mostly in the northern hemisphere, while the South refers to those nations concentrated in the southern hemisphere, which are less developed or perhaps undeveloped. Most of the "bottom billion," or the poorest billion people in the world (Collier 2007, 2012), are minority group members in the Global South. Few from the bottom billion are in the North. In fact, the richest billion people in the world are largely in the Global North and are mainly members of dominant racial and ethnic groups.

The Black Power movement employed a number of distinct cultural symbols, such as the raised fist. Dating back to ancient Assyria, the raised fist symbolises solidarity, strength, and resistance. Here, South African politician Winnie Mandela gives a black power salute as Coretta Scott King speaks to the media during her visit to Mandela's home in Soweto, South Africa, in September 1986.

It has long been the case that the Global North and its majority groups have dominated, controlled, exploited, and oppressed the Global South and its minority groups. Historically, imperialism, colonialism, economic development, Westernisation, and Americanisation have worked in large part to Northerners' advantage and to the disadvantage of Southerners. More contemporaneously, the system that dominates globalisation today—especially free-market economics—helps those in the advantaged categories in the Global North and hurts, often badly, those in the disadvantaged categories in the Global South (D. Harvey 2005).

Interestingly, advantaged groups from the Global North often invented minority groups in the Global South. One example is the creation of "Indians" as an oppressed minority group after

the British colonised India. To that point, Indian society had its own highly developed system of majority and minority castes. Another example derives from Orientalism, a set of ideas and texts produced by the Global North that served as the basis of systems designed to dominate, control, and exploit the Orient (the East) and its many minority groups (Said [1979] 1994).

GLOBAL FLOWS BASED ON RACE AND ETHNICITY

Another way to think of majority-minority relations and their relationship to globalisation is to think in terms of global flows. Both race and ethnicity can

In largely homogeneous, collectivist cultures such as Japan, racial and ethnic minorities are regarded with attention and curiosity at best, and racism and discrimination at worst. According to the United Nations, the ethnic communities most affected by xenophobia and racism in Japan include the Bukaru, Ainu, indigenous Okinawans, Koreans, Chinese, and new immigrants. Here, Ainu elder Haruzo Urakawa looks on during the 2008 Indigenous Peoples Summit in Hokkaido, Japan.

be said to flow around the world. One manifestation is the migration of people of various races and ethnic groups who move around the world today with greater ease and rapidity than ever before. People in the most advantaged racial and ethnic groups, largely from the North, are more likely to be "tourists" who are able to move about freely. In contrast, those in minority categories are more likely to be "vagabonds" who either are immobile or move only because they are forced to (Bauman 1998). It is the vagabonds who are more likely to be migrating, when they can, from South to North. Tourists are highly unlikely to move permanently from the North to the South, although they might visit parts of the South on business or vacation.

Another form of global flow related to race and ethnicity includes the social and cultural aspects of race and ethnicity. As we have seen, neither race nor ethnicity is defined by objective characteristics such as "blood," genes, or skin colour. Rather, both are defined socially and culturally. As social constructions, as ideas, race and ethnicity flow across borders and around the world effortlessly. A good example is the global spread of anti-Muslim prejudice today. Globalised mass communication helps spread these ideas, but they are also carried by people—both tourists and vagabonds—who are

taking advantage of inexpensive means of travel, especially by air.

Paul Gilroy's (1993) *The Black Atlantic: Modernity and Double Consciousness* is an important work on majority-minority relations that stresses global flows. As the title makes clear, Gilroy is particularly interested in the flows that relate to blacks in the Atlantic region (Global Flow Map 9.1 shows that flow, as well as other flows of slaves from Africa to other parts of the world): "I have settled on an image of ships across the spaces between Europe, America, Africa and the Caribbean as a central organizing symbol. . . . The image of a ship . . . in motion" (Gilroy 1993:4). This image encompasses the flow of slaves from Africa to the eastern coast of the Americas and the later return of some blacks to Africa. It also encompasses the circulation of activists, ideas, books, works of art, and the like that relate to blacks and race relations. All are seen as involved in "displacements, migrations, and journeys" (Gilroy 1993:111). Gilroy argues that in trying to understand global flows based on race we should focus not on national boundaries but rather on the black Atlantic. Gilroy's sense of race emphasises flows instead of hard-and-fast definitions. Although not frequently acknowledged, slavery was part of Canadian history, for both the British and the French up until about 1830, and among First Nations groups across the country (Winks n.d.).

The Bedouin are a nomadic, mostly desert-dwelling Arab ethnic group that traverses vast swaths of the Middle East. Depending on available resources, Bedouin travel fluidly as families, *goum* (small groups), descent groups, and tribes. Similar to the Roma in Europe, Bedouin are fiercely loyal, and many adhere to traditional honour codes and strict justice systems.

Positive and Negative Flows

Those in the Global North, especially members of dominant racial and ethnic groups, are able to create structures that greatly enhance positive or protective flows. For example, in locales dominated by advantaged groups, the police and medical systems allow personnel to flow easily and quickly through well-established structures. In Canada, the 911 phone system quickly summons help, and even elderly people who cannot get to a telephone have medical alert buttons. Setting up the complex network to handle these emergencies is an expensive proposition. Minority groups, especially in the Global South, have little or no access to such structures and therefore to the positive flows expedited by them. Those in the minority categories are far less likely to participate in the globe's positive flows of money, commodities, food, health care, technologies,

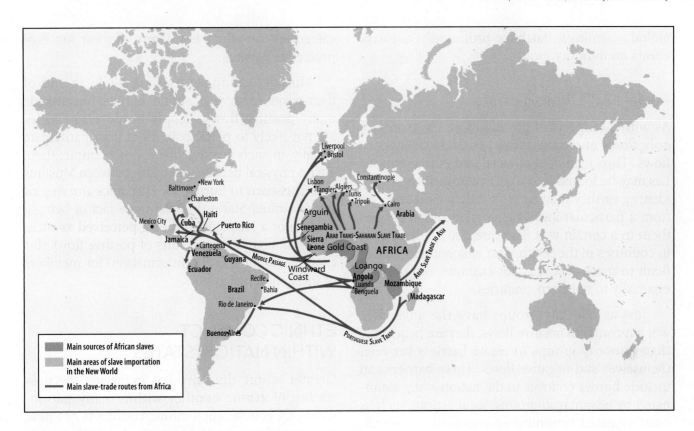

GLOBAL FLOW MAP 9.1 **Slave Trade Routes, 1518–1850**

and the like. Conversely, those in the advantaged categories are likely to be in the thick of these positive flows, both as creators and as beneficiaries.

On the other hand, the structures that expedite negative flows are more likely to dump into, and to be found in, areas dominated by disadvantaged racial, ethnic, and ancestral groups. For example, illegal structures allow the relatively free flow of weapons into and through many areas of the world, but especially those dominated by minority groups. Much stronger structures are in place to prevent their flow into advantaged areas dominated by majority groups. Another example is the tendency for people in the Global South to live in close proximity to disease vectors such as malaria-bearing mosquitoes and chickens carrying avian flu. The result is that they are at greater risk of contracting vector-borne diseases. In contrast, dominant group members in the Global North are far more likely to live at some distance from, or to be heavily protected from, disease-carrying mosquitoes or live chickens, to say nothing of the vectors for many other diseases.

Racism itself can be seen as having wide-ranging negative consequences for minority group members as the ideas and practises associated with it flow around the world (D. Goldberg 2009). In fact, this flow of racism around the world has been referred to as the "racialization of the globe" (Dikötter 2008). Nevertheless, racist ideas and practises are certainly not the same throughout the world, but rather are adapted and modified in each locale. They are affected by local ideas, as well as local economic, political, and military realities. As a result, racism as it involves blacks is not the same in Great Britain, Ghana, or Canada.

Those in minority groups throughout the world are more likely to be on the receiving end of such negative flows as borderless diseases, crime, corruption, war, and most environmental problems. Those in the dominant groups certainly cannot completely avoid these negative flows, but they are far better able to insulate and protect themselves from them. Furthermore, those in advantaged groups often initiate negative flows (armaments, global warming) that have profoundly negative effects on minority groups.

Racial and Ethnic Barriers

As with all aspects of globalisation, there are not only flows of various kinds, but also barriers to flows. Thus members of racial and ethnic minorities may be locked into a particular racial or ethnic identity, or they may be physically unable to move from a particular area (e.g., a ghetto) that defines them in a certain way. They are also likely to exist in countries in the South from which it may be difficult to move (because, for example, of poverty), especially to northern countries.

Just as majority groups have the advantage when it comes to positive flows, they are better able than minority groups to create barriers between themselves and negative flows. These barriers can include border controls in the nation-states dominated by advantaged groups, local actions such as creating gated communities patrolled by guards, and even individual actions such as having alarm systems installed in one's home. Those in minority

More than 2,000 firearms were knowingly sold and trafficked to criminal organisations in Mexico during the U.S. Bureau of Alcohol, Tobacco, Firearms and Explosives' 2009–2010 "Fast and Furious" sting operation. By June 2011, the weapons had been linked to nearly 180 crime scenes throughout Mexico. According to U.S. Attorney General Eric Holder, the operation was "flawed in its concept and flawed in its execution."

categories can afford few, if any, of these kinds of protective barriers.

Minority group statuses are likely, in and of themselves, to serve as "subtle" barriers that impede many positive flows. People in those categories are not likely to participate, or at least participate equally, in such positive flows. For example, there are no physical barriers, no walls, between Muslims and Christians in Europe, or Hispanics and Anglos in the United States, but the mere fact of being a Muslim or a Hispanic, or being perceived as such, serves as a barrier to all sorts of positive flows (for example, of jobs, useful information) for members of these minority groups.

ETHNIC CONFLICT WITHIN NATION-STATES

Greater ethnic diversity has increased the possibility of ethnic conflict within many nation-states. Of course, such ethnic conflict is not new. Among the most notable examples in the twentieth and twenty-first centuries have been conflicts between Turks and Armenians in Turkey; Germans, especially Nazis, and Jews in Germany; Tamils and Sinhalese in Sri Lanka; the Tutsi and Hutu in Burundi; and Arabs and ethnic Africans in Darfur, and the conflict between various ethnic groups—Slovenes, Croatians, Serbs, Bosnians, Montenegrins, Macedonians, and Albanians—after the breakup of Yugoslavia in 1991. However, today with more members of ethnic groups in more and more countries, there is the potential for a great increase in the number, if not the intensity, of ethnic conflicts (Marchak 2008).

One example occurred in Paris in 2008 (Erlanger 2008). The 19th arrondissement on the edge of Paris is very large, poor, and ethnically and racially diverse, and has high crime rates. The area is divided into three enclaves, dominated by Arabs largely from North Africa, blacks mainly from Mali and Congo, and Jews. Youth gangs in each area are major factors in the conflict. The youths not only live in separate enclaves, but they also go to separate schools. According to the deputy mayor in charge of youth affairs, this creates a situation in which "the kids don't know each other and that creates a logic of rivalry" (quoted in Erlanger 2008:A11). The conflict reached a peak with the beating of a 17-year-old Jewish youth who was attacked and put into a coma by a group of young blacks and Arabs because he was wearing a skullcap.

This episode is consistent with hate crime patterns in Canada and the United States, where whites are least likely to be victimised and where, when minority group members are aggressors, they tend to victimise members of other minority groups (Bodinger-deUriarte 1992). In fact, the most disturbing examples of ethnic conflict tend to involve the dominant group's efforts to "deal" with ethnic minorities by getting rid of them. Their methods include expulsion, ethnic cleansing, and genocide.

Expulsion

In the realm of majority group conflict with racial and ethnic minorities, expulsion may seem on the surface to be relatively benign, because minorities are not purposely injured or killed in order to get rid of them. **Expulsion**, or the removal of a group from a territory, can take two forms (G. Simpson and Yinger 1985). In *direct expulsion*, minority ethnic groups are forcibly ejected by the majority through military and other government action. In *voluntary expulsion*, a minority group can leave of its own volition because it is being harassed, discriminated against, and persecuted. Of course, in the real world these two forms of expulsion occur in concert with one another. And although physical harm may be relatively light, social and economic harm can be considerable. The people who are forced to leave typically lose much of their property, and their social networks are often irretrievably broken.

The forced resettlement of the Japanese during World War II is a clear example of expulsion. Although about 80 percent of the Japanese who had their property confiscated and were sent to internment camps were Canadian citizens, they nevertheless were expelled from the British Columbia coast although there was no evidence of their disloyalty to Canada (Adachi 1976; Sugiman 2009). The Canadian government eventually apologised to Japanese Canadians, and some institutions have

chosen to try to redress the wrongs of the past. For example, the University of British Columbia has granted honorary degrees to 76 students who were forced to leave the campus because of the federal law.

Many of those racial and ethnic groups involved in diasporas have experienced both forms of expulsion. This is particularly true of Jews and gypsies, who have often moved because they have been both forcibly ejected (e.g., Jews by the Romans from Jerusalem in the second century AD) and moved voluntarily (those German Jews who left before the Holocaust because of harassment or who left both Czarist Russia and the Stalinist Soviet Union for similar reasons).

Ethnic Cleansing

One of the processes of greatest concern in the context of ethnicity and globalisation is ethnic cleansing. **Ethnic cleansing** is defined as the establishment by the dominant group of policies that allow or require the forcible removal of people of another ethnic group (Oberschall 2012; Sekulic 2007a). Of course, Nazi actions against Jews and Roma fit the definition of ethnic cleansing.

Ethnic cleansing achieved more recent notoriety during the wars that were associated with the dissolution of Yugoslavia in 1991. Many of the ethnic groups that dominated various regions sought to create areas that were ethnically homogeneous, and they did this by expelling and even killing members of other ethnic groups. For example, Croatians were expelled from parts of Croatia inhabited by Serbs. Bosnia, which declared independence in 1992, was composed of three major ethnic groups—Slavic Muslims (the largest single group), Serbs, and Croats. Serbian armed forces created ethnically homogeneous enclaves by forcibly removing the other ethnic groups, especially Muslims.

In situations of ethnic cleansing, women and girls often have been targeted with physical violence and murder, as well as, in many cases, sexual violence. In Bosnia in the 1990s, Serbian men systematically raped an estimated 50,000 Muslim and Croatian women as part of their campaign of terror. Since the Serbian police were in positions of power,

GL🌐BALISATION

Ethnic Conflict in a French Planned Community

Villeneuve—whose name means "new town"—is a modern planned community located in Grenoble, France (a city with 160,000 residents). Villeneuve was conceived in the idealistic period of the late 1960s and constructed in the early 1970s, as part of the "new city" movement to create urban environments that avoided many of the problems that plagued traditional cities. Among the urban problems the planners tried to avoid was the segregation of groups of people by ethnicity and wealth in public and private housing. In addition, traditional cities had witnessed the separation of the places where people lived from where they shopped and from public services (schools, health care) and from public spaces (e.g., parks). Villeneuve was designed not only to avoid these problems, but also to benefit from Grenoble's beautiful location at the foot of the French Alps where two rivers and three mountain ranges converge.

Nearly 100 cars and several businesses were torched in the Villeneuve riots, while angry youths armed with baseball bats and iron bars attacked a tram car and forced its passengers out. Though police in riot gear were eventually able to disperse the crowds, it was only after a great deal of damage was already done.

Central to the planning of Villeneuve was the creation of subsidised low-income housing to ensure a mix of social classes in the community. Said one left-wing politician in 2010, "In the spirit of '68 [an idealistic year of student rebellion in France and elsewhere, including the United States and Canada], we made a bet, that with this social mixing we could help everyone advance. . . . Of course, that was 40 years ago" (Erlanger 2010c:A7). Over the years, a large immigrant community developed in Villeneuve, largely comprising people from the North African region known as the Maghreb (Arab North Africa including Algeria, Morocco, Mauritania, Tunisia, and Libya), as well as from sub-Saharan Africa. These global flows of people did, at first, bring more diversity, but as this African immigrant population grew, many white middle-class families who could afford to leave

departed. The result is that the population of Villeneuve dropped from 16,000 to 12,000 and became not only less heterogeneous, but also poorer. Unemployment increased. Quiet during the day, the area was increasingly taken over at night by "bands of unemployed youth . . . there are drugs and arms, and a sharp increase in cases of personal aggression and robbery" (Erlanger 2010c:A7).

This was the context for a riot that broke out in 2010 after a North African, who had robbed a casino, was killed in a shootout with police. The following night, a "mob set nearly 100 cars on fire, wrecked a tram car and burned an annex of city hall. The police, reinforced by the national riot police, responded in 'Robocop' gear . . . and made a number of arrests" (Erlanger 2010c:A7).

Seeking to bolster his declining political fortunes, French President Nicolas Sarkozy made a speech in Grenoble in which he placed the events in Villeneuve in the context of his campaign to get tough on immigration and crime. He condemned the violence and blamed it on "'insufficiently regulated immigration' that has 'led to a failure of integration.'" Sarkozy went on to declare that "when you open fire on an agent of the forces of order, you're no longer worthy of being French" (Erlanger 2010c:A7). Critics contend that Sarkozy was trying to mobilise nationalist sentiment to increase his political popularity. In a backlash against these immigrants, he threatened to revoke their French citizenship. Grenoble's socialist mayor responded: "'We're in one of the so-called great countries of human rights . . . going to war against criminals' really means 'going to war against an ethnic community, against a neighborhood . . . [it's] insane'" (Erlanger 2010c:A7).

it was difficult for the women who were victims of rape to get help or to prosecute their attackers. As of 2010, only 12 of the potential 50,000 cases had been prosecuted (Cerkez 2010).

Mass rape as a weapon of war has also occurred in the region of Darfur within Sudan, with the government-supported *janjaweed* militiamen raping Darfuri women and girls held in refugee camps. In 2008, Sudan's president, Omar Hassan Ahmed Bashir, was accused by the prosecutor of the International Criminal Court of the Hague of not only mass genocide but also propagating rape as a weapon of war and terror (Scheffer 2008). As of this writing, this case has not been tried (Simons 2010c).

Genocide

The most extreme cases of ethnic conflict involve an active, systematic attempt at eliminating an entire group of people, or genocide. *Genocide* was defined in 1948 by the United Nations Convention on the Prevention and Punishment of the Crime of Genocide as "acts committed with the intent to destroy, in whole or in part, a national, ethnic, racial, or religious group" (cited in Karstedt 2007:1909–10). Genocide is seen as the crime of the twentieth century, and it shows every sign of continuing to define the twenty-first century.

However, as Figure 9.9, dealing with the relationship between colonialism and genocide, shows, this phenomenon predates the twentieth century. The earliest genocide depicted here dates back to 1492, but it is undoubtedly the case that there were many other instances of genocide long before that. In Canada there is an argument that the Beothuk people, who once lived in what is now Newfoundland, were wiped out by colonialism, although the claim is disputed and is therefore not included on the map.

The UN convention on genocide was prompted by the Nazi Holocaust, which was a systematic effort to eliminate a variety of "undesirable" ethnic minority groups, including Jews, Roma, Poles, and other Slavic people. At first, the Holocaust occurred within the confines of Germany, but it later spread to the European countries allied with, or conquered by, Germany. It was in that sense

global, and it would have undoubtedly become far more global had the Nazis achieved their goal of world conquest. For example, had the Nazis succeeded in conquering North America, we would have undoubtedly seen the genocide of Jews on this continent.

A later example of large-scale genocide was the mass killings, during the era of the rule of Joseph Stalin, that took place throughout the then-vast Soviet Empire. In the main, though, genocide continues to be practised within nation-states. Examples include the murder of millions by the Khmer Rouge in Cambodia in the mid- to late 1970s, the Bosnian Serb murder of tens of thousands of Bosnians and Croats in the 1990s, and the killing of hundreds of thousands of ethnic Africans in Sudan since 2003 by the ethnic Arabs.

The global age has brought with it the globalisation of genocide as instances of it have flowed around the world (Karstedt 2012). That is, genocide has become another negative flow making its way from one part of the world to another. The last half of the twentieth century witnessed instances of genocide in Europe (Bosnia), Africa (Rwanda), Asia (Cambodia), and Latin America (Chile), while in the early years of the twenty-first century Africa (Darfur) and Asia

Several films, such as 2004's *Hotel Rwanda* and 2010's *Earth Made of Glass*, have documented or dramatised the 1994 ethnic cleansing of an estimated 800,000 Tutsi in Rwanda. In *Hotel Rwanda*, Don Cheadle portrays Paul Rusesabagina, a hotelier who rescued and defended more than 1,200 Tutsi citizens during the massacre.

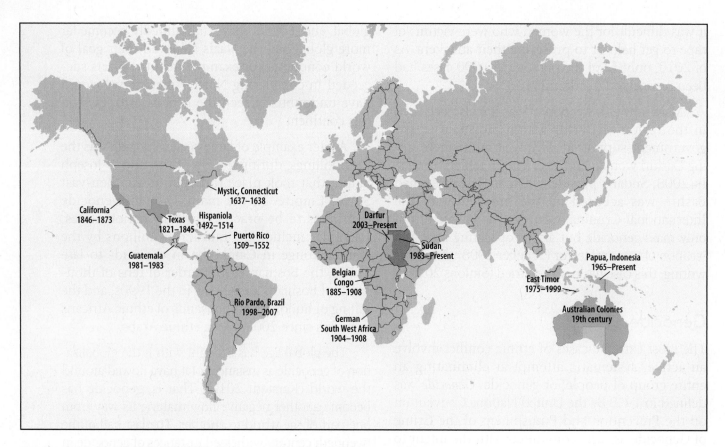

FIGURE 9.8 Selected Colonial and Indigenous Genocides, 1492–Present

SOURCE: Copyright © Genocide Studies programme, Yale University. Used with permission.

(Sri Lanka) have become centres of genocide. Genocide may become more likely in the future because of globalisation—of proliferating and accelerating global flows of ideas, agitators, and arms. Added to this is the increased inability of nation-states to block many of these flows.

SUMMARY

Race has historically been defined on the basis of some real or presumed physical or biological characteristic, as well as a shared lineage. In the second half of the twentieth century, race began to be defined less as a matter of biological difference and more as a cultural phenomenon, which makes it more akin to the concept of ethnicity. Ethnic groups are typically defined on the basis of some real or presumed cultural characteristic, such as language, religion, traditions, and cultural practises. Ancestral groups call attention to Aboriginal or indigenous peoples, people who in Canada have worked hard to keep their status separate from that of racial or ethnic groups.

Although definitions of race have taken many different forms over time, race, ethnicity, and ancestry have always served as a way of stratifying individuals into groups with more or less power. When we think of dominant and subordinate groups, we need to think beyond just the sheer number of people in a group. The dominant group, even if it has fewer members than the minority groups, comprises the individuals in society with more money, prestige, and power. Intersectionality, or belonging to more than one type of minority (for example, being black and female), often compounds the disparities. The dominant group is likely to exploit members of the minority groups, and thus there is always the potential for conflict between majority and minority groups.

All races and ethnic groups are involved in consumer culture, though their involvement often varies. Life in a consumer culture may be difficult for minorities, as they are surrounded by things they cannot afford and are subjected to aggressive marketing for certain products, some of which are harmful. In addition, members of the majority may appropriate elements of minority culture—as when whites purchase the artistic works of Aboriginal artisans.

Majority-minority relations devolve into racial, ethnic, or ancestral discrimination when the dominant group defines others and attributes to them negative characteristics. It is the combination of xenophobia and ethnocentrism that makes this type of discrimination so powerful. Current discrimination is more often a matter of hegemony, or the advantaged group foisting its culture on the minority, than of legal and material constraints on minority groups.

There are several forms of racism. There is some evidence that individual-level prejudice and discrimination against minority groups in Canada is on the decline. However, institutional discrimination persists; larger social structures are generally seen as still operating to the detriment of racial, ethnic, and ancestral minorities. Discrimination can also be seen in culture. The white cultural frame, which includes an array of discriminatory ideas, stereotypes, stories and tales, images, powerful emotions, and

various inclinations to act pejoratively, is pervasive throughout Canadian society and impacts many structures and institutions.

Majority-minority relations in a global context can often be best represented by the North-South divide, wherein the North, which has more advantaged group members, dominates and oppresses those in the South, who are more often minority group members. Dominant groups are generally better able to create barriers between themselves and others and various negative global flows. Advantaged groups are also better at creating structures that enhance positive or protective global flows. Generally, minority group status impedes many positive flows.

Accelerating globalisation has been accompanied by increases in the number and importance of ethnic identities. However, greater ethnic diversity within nation-states has opened up more possibilities for ethnic conflict within these borders. At the extreme, ethnic conflict leads to expulsion, ethnic cleansing, and genocide of minorities by the majority within a territory.

KEY TERMS

- Aboriginal 320
- Ancestry 320
- Assimilation 330
- Diaspora 347
- Discrimination 331
- Ethnic cleansing 353
- Ethnic group 320
- Ethnicity 324
- Expulsion 353
- First Nations 321
- Genocide 330
- Hegemony 333
- Hypodescent rule 325

- Institutional discrimination 334
- Intersectionality 335
- Multiculturalism 329
- Orientalism 349
- Pluralism 330
- Prejudice 331
- Race 320
- Racism 348
- Segregation 330
- Stereotype 331
- White racial frame 333
- Xenophobia 320

THINKING ABOUT SOCIOLOGY

1. What is the difference between race, ethnicity, and ancestry? What are the similarities? How have biological and cultural explanations helped to create these differences?

2. Barack Obama is the offspring of a white mother and a black African father, but more often than not he is referred to as black.

What does this suggest about the nature of race? What are the consequences of this perception?

3. What criteria do sociologists use to define a dominant racial, ethnic, or ancestral group? How do dominant groups maintain their positions of privilege?

4. Considering some of the examples provided in this chapter, how do your consumption patterns reflect racial, ethnic, and ancestral identity?

5. According to danah boyd, how can we use race to understand the differences between Myspace and Facebook? In what ways is Facebook like a high-end gated community? What are the potential consequences of these differences?

6. What do you understand the term *multiculturalism* to mean? How has multiculturalism been supported by various Canadian governments?

7. What is institutional discrimination, and what are some examples of institutional

discrimination? In what ways is institutional discrimination more problematic than individual discrimination?

8. How would you characterise majority-minority relations on a global level? What sort of advantages do majority groups have on the global level?

9. How is globalisation changing the nature of ethnicity on a global scale? In what ways have ethnic groups been able to use advances in communication and media to retain their ethnic identity? Do you agree that globalisation is creating a universal culture?

APPLYING THE SOCIOLOGICAL IMAGINATION

Many scholars and citizens have come to believe that racial, ethnic, and ancestral tensions are declining and the chances for integration have improved, but we also know that corporations pay attention to racial, ethnic, and ancestral differences when marketing their products.

For this activity, conduct a qualitative content analysis of advertisements in two different magazines: a mainstream magazine that is part of the dominant culture (e.g., *Vanity Fair, Cosmopolitan, Maclean's*)

and a traditionally racialised or minority magazine (e.g., *Essence, Ebony, MBE Magazine, Sway*). Compare and contrast the ads in the magazines. Can you identify any differences between the magazines in terms of the products or themes of their ads? What sorts of images are used in each of the magazines? In what ways are the advertisements reflective of larger majority-minority group relationships in Canada? How can we use this exercise to explain the relationship between stratification and consumption?

ACTIVE SOCIOLOGY

Racial, ethnic, and ancestral issues appear to be all around us, yet some people claim that these issues are a thing of the past. In what ways is race, ethnicity, or ancestry a salient part of your life? Use your Facebook and/or Twitter pages to examine this. How much, if at all, do you talk about race, ethnicity, or ancestry? Why? How racially, ethnically, or ancestrally diverse are your friends or the people who follow you on these pages? Explain. Consider

a current issue that in some way is related to race, ethnicity, or ancestry (e.g., at the time of this writing, the killing of Trayvon Martin is big). Post something related to that issue on your Twitter or Facebook page. Watch the replies/responses that you get. What are people saying about this issue? How does what people post (or don't post) on Facebook and Twitter influence your understanding of the issues discussed in this chapter?

STUDENT STUDY SITE

Visit the student study site at **www.sagepub.com/ritzercanadian** for additional web quizzes for further review.

SEX AND GENDER

While sex and gender are universally meaningful, different cultures' approaches to these cardinal topics vary enormously . . . attitudes toward sex and gender shift not only across space but also over time.

10

In 2011, several dozen Saudi Arabian women entered their family cars and drove to various locations throughout the country's sprawling metropolitan cities, performing mundane errands and meeting up for social dates. While this might sound like an ordinary day to most westerners, the undertaking made a bold and controversial statement about equality, civil rights, and gender relations in the conservative Middle Eastern kingdom. Throughout Saudi Arabia, women are prohibited from driving. A fundamentalist interpretation of Islamic law, enforced by the mutaween (morality police), subjects all women to strict norms and laws, among which is a ban on driving. Many women apprehended while participating in the protest were simply admonished and escorted home by the traffic police, but Shaima Jastaina was not so fortunate. For participating in the protest, Jastaina was convicted of driving without permission and sentenced to 10 lashes.

Those lashes were never administered, however. In an unprecedented move, Saudi Arabian King Abdullah bin Abdul-Aziz Al Saud overturned Jastaina's sentence shortly after it was handed down. The sentence had come two days after King Abdullah decreed that women would be admitted into the country's consultative assembly, and that all women would be granted the ability to vote in the country's next municipal election. Some observers saw Jastaina's sentence as an admonishment of the king by Saudi Arabia's ultraconservative court system.

For a person to be prohibited from driving simply because she was born a female may seem unreasonable to you, but your culture's sex and gender norms likely seem equally unreasonable to others around the world. For example, in Canada, female genital mutilation is unacceptable, while male genital mutilation (circumcision) is an accepted practise, although it is in decline. In Egypt, the opposite is true. While sex and gender are universally meaningful, different cultures' approaches to these cardinal topics vary enormously.

As recent events in Saudi Arabia have shown, attitudes toward sex and gender shift not only across space but also across time. Global flows, technological advancements, and a feminisation of labour (among other important factors) have changed how people around the globe perceive appropriate sexual behaviour and gender performance. As King Abdullah and the female drivers saw neighbouring nations shaken by Arab Spring demonstrations, they saw an opportunity for reform. The full extent of that reform, however, is yet to be seen. For the people of Saudi Arabia, the ongoing struggle between religious tradition and sexual revolution is exhilarating and terrifying, joyful and heartrending. For sociologists, it's a testament to the intricate beauty of a living, breathing culture.

S ex and gender are two of the most decisive—and divisive—factors in determining how we interact with those around us. Culture frames our thoughts and actions about sex and gender, as well as how we are perceived and treated by others. A person who challenges a cultural frame by expressing an uncommon sexual preference or protesting patriarchal rules may be labelled a deviant and may be subject to legal repercussions—or worse.

Sex and gender are terms that are often used interchangeably and confused with one another. However, it is important that they be distinguished clearly. **Sex** is principally a biological distinction between males and females based on fundamental differences in their reproductive organs and functions. **Gender** is based on what, given a person's sex, are considered appropriate physical, behavioural, and personality characteristics. The key difference is that sex is based *mainly* on biological differences, whereas gender is based on social distinctions (B. Ryan 2007). But they have important similarities from a sociological perspective. This chapter will describe how sociology approaches questions of sex and gender.

SEX AND SEXUALITY

Although we tend to think in terms of two—and *only* two—biological sexes, in fact there is a continuum between male and female anatomy (Fausto-Sterling 1999). In the middle of that continuum are individuals with some combination of the genitalia of both males and females. In the past, such people were called hermaphrodites, and doctors altered infants' genital structures to better match the typical male or female anatomy (Coventry 2006). But today people with ambiguous genitalia are more usually referred to as **intersexed**, and they are more often spared surgery, at least until they are old enough to be identified, or to identify themselves, with one sex or the other (Zeiler and Wickstrom 2009). Also in the middle are **transsexuals**, those who may have the genitalia of one sex or the other, but who believe that they are locked into the wrong body. While some remain, often uncomfortably, in those bodies, others take hormones to change their sexes, and some undergo genital reassignment surgery.

This idea of a sexual continuum extends to male and female hormones as well. For example, both males and females have the hormones oestrogen and testosterone, although the amounts vary greatly from individual to individual within and between sexes, as well as over time (Kimmel 2004). Both sexes have breasts, and although women typically have larger breasts than men do, the size of some men's breasts exceeds that of some women's. Breast cancer is largely a disease of women, but some men contract the disease. Facial hair is usually thought of as a male characteristic, but some women grow enough facial hair to require regular shaving. Biologically, there are no absolutely clear-cut differences between men and women.

Also pointing against the idea that there are simply two sexes is the fact that at a global level there are a number of cultures in which there exists a "third gender" (J. M. Ryan 2012). This is a truly distinct gender and neither man nor woman, nor a combination of the two. Examples include the hijras of India (see Chapter 2), the berdache of a number of Indian cultures, Thailand's kathoeys, and the fa'afafine of Samoa.

At the 2011 MTV *Video Music Awards*, pop music icon Lady Gaga (Stefani Germanotta) made waves by cross-dressing and performing as male alter ego Jo Calderone. A longtime advocate of sexual freedom, Lady Gaga's performance could be considered an example of transgenderism.

SEXUAL SELVES

Of central interest to sociologists is **sexuality**, or the ways in which people think about, and behave toward, themselves and others as sexual beings (Plummer 1975). Sex and sexuality are not always identical. A person who is biologically female (or who believes she should be in a female body) may engage in sexual behaviour with either men or women, or for that matter with both or neither. Given the multiple dimensions of both sex and sexuality, there is much variation among individuals.

There is now a huge and growing body of literature on the sociology of sexuality (Plummer 2012). While bodies and biology are deeply involved, the bulk of this work deals with the social, social-psychological, and cultural aspects of sexuality. Sociologists have become more interested in sexuality for a number of reasons:

- the growing number of sexually linked social problems, especially the HIV/AIDS epidemic;
- the greater visibility of sex-related social movements, especially those associated with gays and lesbians (Ross 2009);
- technological change, such as the arrival of erectile dysfunction drugs, including Viagra and Cialis, and the media's presentation of sex of infinite variety;
- the globalisation of sexuality, for example sex tourism and sex trafficking (Lepp 2013; B. Perrin 2010);
- more brazen expressions of sexuality in consumer culture—not only widespread commerce in sexual activity but also the use of sexuality to sell virtually everything; and
- the development of the Internet, where sexuality is readily available and a vibrant commercial sex culture has developed.

People express their sexualities for many different reasons; it is rarely simply a matter of sexual release. Culture gives us patterns, rules, and codes to manage our sexualities and their expression. Gender roles and power dynamics affect our sexualities, as do race and class (B. Scott and Schwartz 2008). What people do and do not do is symbolically important to them and to others in society. The stories that people tell and do not tell about their sexualities are of great significance to them. These stories are of great symbolic importance, telling us much not only about the storytellers and their listeners but also about the societies in which they live.

Sexuality is also a prime area for the sociological study of emotions (Stets and Turner 2007). To the individual, sexuality is emotionally "hot," but there are various social forces that seek to cool it off. This was a concern to Max Weber, who saw the process of rationalisation as an "iron cage," as described in Chapter 2, that served to limit many things, including sexual expression. The next

McDONALDIZATION *Today*

The McDonaldization of Sexuality

It is easy to think of many things being McDonaldized, but sexuality is not one that comes immediately to mind. While the McDonaldization of public aspects of our lives is worrisome enough, when it affects this most private, mysterious, and intimate of realms, it seems much more troubling. Nevertheless, we have witnessed the rationalisation and bureaucratisation of sexuality. Kathryn Hausbeck and Barbara Brents (2010) note that we are in danger of being entrapped "in Weber's fearsome iron cage: coldly colonising our imaginations and brushing up against our skins" (p. 117). This image of McDonaldized systems physically touching our bodies and even entering and controlling our consciousness brings concern about McDonaldization to a whole new level.

The McDonaldization of sexuality affects not only the act of sex itself but also the ease and efficiency with which one can consume sexual aids and other adult products. Here, condoms, sex toys, and performance-enhancing pills are sold alongside snacks and chewing gum in a public vending machine in China.

The rationalisation and bureaucratisation of sex seems particularly intrusive and injects sterility into something that is supposed to be anything but sterile. In fact, sexual relations and relationships seem to be unpredictable in terms of when they happen and what transpires when they do occur; they are best accomplished inefficiently; they have much more to do with the quality of the experiences than their quantitative aspects; and they do not appear to be subject to technological control, especially control by mechanical technologies.

Nevertheless, much about sexual relations has been McDonaldized. We have become

- more concerned about making the outcomes (orgasms and their depth) more predictable;

McDonaldization Today box explores a few of the ways in which the emotions associated with sexual expression have been cooled off.

Sexual Identities and Orientations

We all have sexual identities. One element of sexual identity is **sexual orientation**, which involves who you desire, with whom you want to have sexual relations, and with whom you have a sense of connectedness (B. Scott and Schwartz 2008). Sexual orientation is typically divided into four categories: **heterosexuality**, or sexual desire for the opposite sex; **homosexuality**, or desire to have

sexual relations with someone of the same sex (J. M. Ryan 2012); **bisexuality**, or a desire for sexual relations with both sexes; and **asexuality**, or a lack of sexual desire (Kim 2011). Expression of these orientations varies among individuals; for example, one heterosexual is not like all others in the degree of desire for members of the opposite sex. In addition, a person's sexual orientation and romantic tendencies may differ. For example, a bisexual may have sexual relations with people of both sexes but prefer romantic relationships with members of the opposite sex. Layered onto sexual orientation are a variety of other sexual identities, such as sex addict—like the main character in the

- more interested in improving the efficiency of performance through, for example, self-help manuals that offer advice on how to become a more effective and efficient partner;

- more focused on the quantitative aspects of sex, such as how many times we have sex each week or how many orgasms we have during a typical encounter; and

- more interested in using technologies such as date-rape drugs, Viagra, vibrators, and sex toys in sexual relationships.

Application of the dimensions of McDonaldization to personal sexual relations may make us squeamish, but it should come as no surprise that they do apply, and very systematically, to the sex industry. Hausbeck and Brents (2008) spent over 10 years observing the legal brothels in Nevada and found the following signs of McDonaldization:

- On entering one of the brothels, customers are presented with a lineup of available women. They are urged to choose quickly, and there is often a printed menu of sexual options. Time limits may be set and timers used to let the participants know when they must leave—whether or not they have accomplished their mission.

- Brothels tend to offer highly predictable heterosexual sexual relations. These encounters are dominated by traditional notions of sex roles as well as by dominant ideas about how prostitutes should look and behave.

- Sexuality is paid for by the minute.

- Not only are technologies such as timers employed, but so are surveillance technologies such as video cameras and microphones to make sure that customers adhere to the time limits and to protect the employees/sex workers in case sex acts get out of hand.

Today's consumer can select other forms of sexuality that are much more McDonaldized, including pornographic magazines, paid phone and virtual sexuality, adult videos, and sexually explicit content on numerous paid and unpaid websites. Perhaps the most obviously McDonaldized aspects of the sex industry are the "adult superstores," modeled after chains such as Bed Bath & Beyond, and "gentleman's clubs," some of which are part of chains. For example, Rick's Cabaret and its other chains—Onyx, XTC, and Tootsie's—operate in a number of large cities. The website for Rick's Cabaret looks much like that for the Hard Rock Cafe, with a tab offering T-shirts, caps, and "expandable" briefcases, all with the Rick's logo emblazoned on them.

While there is no shortage of McDonaldization in the world of sexual relations, there are also signs of resistance to it. For example, some of a brothel's customers demand at least the appearance of intimacy, closeness, and affection. If they can't get non-McDonaldized sexuality, they at least want it to appear as if it is non-McDonaldized.

TV series *Californication*—or sex worker or celibate. Sexual identity adds considerable complexity to the male-female sex continuum.

Sexual identities reflect changes in the larger society, and they have a profound effect on the individuals with those identities, as well as those to whom those individuals relate. These identities, and feelings about them, are not static. The best known example is the increasing openness about identifying as gay or lesbian. It is no longer necessary in many environments to hide those identities and is in fact possible to be very public, and to feel very good, about one's gay or lesbian identity (Plummer 2007a). This was

nowhere clearer than in Showtime's hit cable television program, *The L Word*, which ran from 2004 to 2009. The show followed the lives of several lesbian women who were friends, lovers, professionals, mothers, and mistresses. Many of the women in the show were not only friends—some dated one another. The show featured not only lesbians but also gay men, transgender people, transsexuals, bisexuals, and even straight men and women (although the latter were in the minority). There were interracial couples, lesbian couples with children, single mothers, lesbians in the army, and so on. There were a great deal of nudity and lots of explicit sex scenes. *The L Word* became so popular that it led to a reality show titled *The Real L Word*, which continues on Showtime. Male homosexuality has also become more visible in films and on television. Many gays and lesbians applaud this open portrayal of their lifestyles. In addition, the development of TV channels geared toward the LGBTQ (lesbian, gay, bisexual, transsexual, and queer) community such as LOGO reflects a wider acceptance of diverse forms of sexuality within mainstream media outlets.

Pedophilia, or sexual attraction to children, has received much negative publicity in recent years—especially when it leads to sexual abuse of children. Pedophilia has long existed in many realms, but it became more visible in the late 1990s, when scandals involving the sexual abuse of children within the Roman Catholic Church became common knowledge. This publicity has negatively affected the self-concepts and identities of not only the young men who were victimised by it, but also the priests involved in sexual relations with minors. The religious identities of many other Catholics were shaken by these revelations.

The negative, long-standing consequences of the sexual abuse of First Nations children in residential schools are next to impossible to exaggerate. The lives of many individuals, families, and communities were utterly devastated. As a token effort in compensation for the sexual, physical, and emotional abuse suffered, the Canadian federal government issued a formal apology and offered compensation payments to individuals (see Indian Residential Schools Adjudication Secretariat). As a second example, two former National Hockey League players, Sheldon Kennedy and Theo Fleury, claimed that they had been sexually abused by Graham James when James was their hockey coach. In January 1999 James pled guilty to over 300 charges of sexual assault. In March 2012 he was sentenced to another two years in prison as a result of additional changes levelled against him.

Sexual identities encompass a wide range, and growing number, of sexual subcultures. These subcultures include not only the LGBTQ community and pedophiles but also subcultures such as those associated with cross-dressing ("drag"), polyamory (multiple love relationships), and BDSM (bondage, domination, submission, and masochism). Furthermore, there are multiple subcultures within each that are constantly

The Canadian Boy Scouts have been negligent in handling sexual abuse cases. In 1995 Fred Miller, formerly a senior Scouts official, was convicted of sexually assaulting young children. Unfortunately, the Boy Scouts is not an exception when it comes to abuse, since similar abusive instances have occurred in sports, the church, schools, and families.

coming together and splitting apart (Bauer 2008; Gates 1999). Thus, for example, there are many gay subcultures, including drag kings and queens, gay Christians, and gay couples.

The increasing multiplicity of sexualities and sexual communities makes conflicts over the boundaries of sexualities increasingly likely. For example, where, exactly, is the line between heterosexuality and homosexuality? How many homosexual acts does it take to make one a homosexual? Young adults often experiment with sexuality and sexual behaviour in an effort to discover those boundaries for themselves.

Men's and Women's Sexual Scripts

The differences in sexuality between men and women are perhaps greater than in any other aspect of our intimate lives (Naples and Gurr 2012).

Although biological differences play a role in gender differences in sexuality, the sociological view is that social and cultural factors are of far greater importance. Socialisation plays a key role here, as men and women learn sexual behaviour by observing and learning from others. Of special importance is the learning of gender-appropriate **sexual scripts**, or the generally known ideas about what one ought to do and what one ought not to do as far as sexual behaviour is concerned.

The male script focuses on the penis as the basic "tool" to be used in sexual relations. Sexuality is defined, then, as coitus, because it involves the use of the penis and its insertion into the vagina. Therefore, the only real sexuality as far as most men are concerned is coitus; it's the only real way to use the penis appropriately and to achieve pleasure. Excluded are many nongenital forms of sexuality since the only "true" form of sexuality for males, like the penis itself, is outside one's self. Men are also supposed to approach sexuality like work: to be knowledgeable about it and good at it, to operate efficiently, and to be in control of both their own bodies and those of their partners. In contrast, for women sexuality is more like play, efficiency is devalued, and there is no strong need to be in control. Given the internal nature of the vagina, the sexual script for women is much more inwardly focused. It is also broader, involving many more acceptable ways of experiencing real sexuality and thinking of many more nongenital parts of the body as sexual in nature.

The social aspect of sexual behaviour is also gender-driven. Men are expected to be in charge of arousal; women are expected to be aroused. Men are expected to be driven by lust and desire while women are supposed to be aroused by that and not to arrive at a sexual encounter "in lust." Susan M. Shaw and Janet Lee (2009) argue that men engage in "instrumental sex (sex for its own sake) . . . and women engage in expressive sex (sex involving emotional attachments)" (p. 179).

These are, of course, gross generalisations, and there are great differences in these male and female scripts. Nonetheless, such scripts are widely shared. The learning of these scripts, and the scripts themselves, better account for gender differences in sexuality than do biological differences. The next *Public Sociology* box deals with one

sociologist's contribution to clarifying sexual scripts for those who did not learn as much as they would have liked early in life.

Sexual scripts detail what one ought and ought not to do as far as sexual behaviour is concerned. Men are expected to be knowledgeable about and good at sex, to operate efficiently, and to be in control of both their own bodies and those of their partners.

SOCIAL CONSTRAINTS ON SEXUALITY

There is an increasing sense, not without reason, that sexuality has grown increasingly free of social constraints. This is clear in many realms of the social world, but one example is the way the media treat sexuality. There is, for example, an MTV reality show titled *16 and Pregnant*, which deals with younger teens going through the trials and tribulations of pregnancy. Other broadcasts with similar themes are the TV movie *The Pregnancy Pact* and, on occasion, the popular network TV program *Glee*. These programmes demonstrate a relaxed attitude toward teenage sexuality: that it is OK for teenagers to have sexual relations, maybe even unprotected relations; to become pregnant; and perhaps even to have the babies that may result.

While there is much to support the idea of increasing sexual freedom, human sexuality is never totally free. There is, for example, the school in Mississippi that cancelled its senior prom because a homosexual student wanted to bring her lesbian friend as a date (Joyner 2010).

Society contains structures such as school, family, law, police, and religion, as well as customs, that constrain sexuality. In addition, constraints on sexuality are closely linked to larger social phenomena

PUBLIC SOCIOLOGY

Pepper Schwartz on Sexuality

Pepper Schwartz is a sociologist who focuses on sexuality and sexual relationships. She has published several scholarly books (most notably, in 1983, *American Couples: Money, Work, Sex* with Philip Blumstein), as well as more than 40 scholarly articles. However, Schwartz does not limit herself to dull academic tracts or dry scholarly topics. She is also well known to the general public through the articles and columns she has contributed to many magazines and newspapers, including the monthly columns "Sex and Health" for *Glamour* magazine (with Janet Lever) and "Talking About Sex" in *American Baby* magazine. She also blogs on MedHelp.org and PerfectMatch .com and has appeared regularly on KIRO-TV in Seattle.

For all they learn growing up and from the media about sexuality and sexual scripts, people still have a lot of questions. The following is a sampling of Schwartz's journalistic advice (often in collaboration with Janet Lever), offered in response to questions from readers:

Pepper Schwartz

> Orgasms are greatly affected by our thoughts and emotions. If you finally get an evening alone with your partner after a period of abstinence . . . It doesn't take much technique to get you over the top.

> At other times, as you know, technique matters. A woman's arousal is heightened when her partner stimulates erogenous zones in addition to her breasts and genitals. . . . Direct clitoral stimulation, instead of just vaginal intercourse, also results in more vaginal contractions, which is why some women claim their vibrator gives them the most intense orgasms. (*Glamour*)

> Children are so absorbing that it's easy to have them become the focus of your marriage, but you risk falling into the role of parents rather than lovers. Reinvesting in your relationship should be a priority. Taking care of your emotional intimacy isn't a luxury but a necessity. (*American Baby*)

> Painful intercourse (medically termed "dyspareunia") is the most common sexual complaint that women report to their gynecologists . . . pain is frequently experienced by those having sex for the first time. This is completely normal, as the vaginal channel is often so naturally tight at first intercourse that inserting even a finger might be painful. The vagina becomes more elastic over time and generally will adapt to penetration, though it may tighten in response to pain, anticipated pain, or a general fear of penetration. Therapists encourage using generous amounts of a commercial lubricant and penetrating very gradually, perhaps starting with a finger, then two, until entry is more comfortable. (*Sexual Health*)

Schwartz has recently discussed some of her own sexual adventures in *Prime: Adventures and Advice on Sex, Love, and the Sensual Years* (2007). This book is aimed at a popular audience. She is interested not only in revealing much about herself, but also in continuing to offer advice on sexuality and on relationships, sexual and otherwise.

Schwartz's focus on the topic of sexuality started in the early 1970s, while she was earning her PhD at Yale University. During that time she coauthored or coedited three books on sexuality, including *Sex and the Yale Student* and *The Student Guide to Sex on Campus*. Currently she is a professor of sociology at the University of Washington.

and hierarchies. One of the most important of these is minority status.

Generally speaking, the sexuality of oppressed minorities is more likely to be constrained than is the sexuality of the dominant group. For example, men have historically been freer to express their sexuality, while women have been subjected to a number of physical and social traditions that discourage them from the free exercise of their sexuality. More extremely, women are more likely to be abused and raped and to sell their sexuality while men are more likely to be sex offenders and sex addicts and to buy sexual relations.

Culture and Consent

Important to a discussion of social constraints on sexuality are the concepts of consensual sex, sexual assault, and rape. All involve issues of the relative power of the individuals involved in sexual activity. **Consensual sex** is defined as sexual intercourse that is agreed upon by the participants in an informed process. **Sexual assault** encompasses sexual acts of domination usually enacted by men against women. Such assaults can occur between strangers, but they usually occur between acquaintances. **Rape**, also a form of domination, is violent sexual intercourse (Rudrappa 2012).

Communities vary in the possibility of sexual violence and constraints on the kinds of behaviours that might lead to such violence. In many religious communities, strong expectations for modesty and sexuality only within marriage keep sexual violence to a minimum. In contrast, the nature of sexuality in colleges can promote a "rape culture" (Argiero et al. 2010; Boswell and Spade 1996), or an environment conducive to rape. Rape cultures tend to be prevalent in and around college campuses due to the overpowering presence of alcohol and drugs, the age of the population, and the ratio of men to women.

Sexual assaults have, to put it mildly, very serious consequences. According to the World Health Organization (WHO) and RAINN (Rape, Abuse, and Incest National Network), the largest anti–sexual violence network in the United States, survivors are 3 times more likely to suffer depression, 4 times more likely to contemplate suicide, 6 times more likely to suffer from post-traumatic stress disorder (PTSD), 26 times more likely to abuse drugs, and 13 times more likely to abuse alcohol as a coping mechanism (RAINN 2009b).

SEX AND CONSUMPTION

Regardless of the constraints on sexuality, everyday life has been sexualised to a large degree—the world has been "made sexy" (P. Rutherford 2007). In our consumer society, sex is used to encourage consumption of all sorts of things that are not inherently sexual. Advertisements use sexualised images to promote innumerable products, from cars to toothpaste, from clothing to soft drinks. The implication in many of these ads is that use of the product leads to sexual relationships. The well-known media adage that "sex sells" shows no signs of going out of fashion. However, researchers have found that women on average have a strong negative reaction to explicit sexual content in advertising and are less likely to buy the merchandise being promoted with these types of ads (Dahl, Sengupta, and Vohs 2009). In comparison, men tend to feel positively toward such ads.

More blatant than the use of sexual images to sell products and services is the way in which human sexualities themselves have been increasingly turned into commodities and marketed (Y. Taylor 2007). Of course, the consumption of sex is nothing new—after all, prostitution is often referred to as the "oldest profession." What is new since the mid-twentieth century is the rise of a huge sex industry, one whose tentacles span the globe. This sexual marketplace can be seen as a conglomeration of five interlocking markets (Plummer 2007b):

- *Bodies and sexual acts.* This market includes prostitution and other forms of sex work, such as stripping and table and lap dancing. "Real sex" involving "real bodies" is available for purchase by those with the ability to pay.

- *Pornography and erotica.* Sexual images and text are not generally thought to involve "real sexuality" or "real bodies." However, pornography and erotica can be associated with, or lead to, real sexual acts and relations, including masturbation and sexual intercourse. The production, distribution, sale, and consumption of pornography increasingly take place on the Internet. There is, in fact, no clear line between "real sexuality" and sexuality on the Internet.

- *Sexualised objects*. Sexualised objects include sex toys (for example, inflatable blow-up dolls), drugs that are thought to enhance sexual sensations ("poppers" or nitrate inhalers), costumes for sadomasochistic sex, dildos, vibrators, and lingerie (Coulmont and Hubbard 2010).

- *Sexualised technologies*. People around the world increasingly consume contraceptives as well as drugs such as Viagra and Cialis (Katsulis 2010). The latter are supposed to be used to treat erectile dysfunction (ED), although many men without ED use these drugs to enhance the sexual experience for themselves and their partners. Other sexualised technologies include surgeries for everything from making oneself more sexually attractive (breast-enhancement surgery, revirgination/vaginal rejuvenation, penile enlargement, genital reconstructive surgery) to changing one's sex (sex-reassignment surgery). Digital technologies, such as smartphones and the Internet, have been similarly sexualised. See the next *Digital Living* box for one such phenomenon.

- *Sexualised relationships*. One example of a sexualised relationship is the mail-order bride. In addition, bars and other consumption sites are often locales for beginning sexualised relationships. Help for improving a sexualised relationship can be purchased from highly paid sex therapists, from self-help books of all sorts, and now increasingly from websites across the Internet.

SEXUAL DEVIANCE

As is the case with deviance in general, what is considered sexual deviance varies greatly from place to place, from time to time, and among different individuals and groups. There is no universal definition of sexual deviance. (For an example of place-based definitions of deviance, see the next *Globalisation* box.) An example of historical

BIOGRAPHICAL bits

Ken Plummer (1946–, British)

- Plummer has his BA and PhD from the University of London.

- He has taught at the University of Essex in England, as well as the University of California, Santa Barbara.

- He sees himself as a humanist in search of less human suffering and a better social world.

- His main interests in sociology have been sexuality and intimacy.

- Plummer has edited the journal *Sexualities* for many years.

- He is best known for books such as *Sexual Stigma* (1975) and *Modern Homosexualities: Fragments of Lesbian and Gay Experience* (1992).

- Illness caused him to retire in 2006, but he continues to be very active in sociology.

- He still feels "young at heart."

- He looks forward to continuing engagement with students.

- Plummer feels he still has quite a few books in him to write.

- He is "still crazy" about sociology after all these years.

fluidity in definitions of sexual deviance is marital rape. There was no notion of marital rape for most of human history. Wives did not have the right to deny the advances, even the forcible advances, of their husbands. However, largely as a result of the women's movement, marital rape has come to be seen in many parts of the world as a deviant act and, in some cases, even illegal. Marital rape can be defined as "any unwanted intercourse or penetration (vaginal, anal, or oral) obtained by force, threat of force, or when the wife is unable to consent" (RAINN 2009a). It occurs when a spouse is

DIGITAL LIVING

Sexting

Sexuality has become increasingly mobile, thanks to sexting, or the ability to e-mail or text explicitly sexual photos primarily via smartphones. Sexting may be fun, but it is not harmless. In 2011, Anthony Weiner, for example, was forced to resign as a U.S. congressman when it was discovered that he had been tweeting close-up photos of his erect penis concealed by his undershorts to a young woman. There have also been a number of scandals involving high school students sexting and then living to regret it.

Sexting among young people has led social media networks to work toward limiting minors' access to adult-based content. Some mobile carriers limit the amount of adult content available on their network for fear of children accessing such content.

Nevertheless, a sizable number of teens are engaging in sexting. A survey by the Associated Press and MTV of 1,200 teenage respondents found that more than a quarter of them admitted to some form of sexting (Grier 2010). Some have discovered the disadvantages of sexting. Some girls perceive that, paradoxically, "the Internet is making boys more aggressive sexually—more accepting of graphic images or violence toward women, brasher, more demanding—but it is also making them less so, or at least less interested in the standard-issue, flesh-and-bone girls they encounter in real life who may not exactly have *Penthouse* proportions or porn-star inclinations" (Alex Morris 2011).

Another potential problem with sexting is the link to *cyberbullying*—Internet practises that are harmful to other individuals. Middle school girls have confessed that they send suggestive photos of themselves to boys to "mess with other girls' boyfriends." Furthermore, nearly one out of five teens who received sext messages said they passed them on to someone else; 50 percent of them admitted they forwarded the images to multiple recipients (Grier 2010). The forwarding of sext messages may expose those in the photos to ridicule, scorn, and even retaliation by aggrieved boyfriends and girlfriends.

Many organisations are working to teach teens about cyberbullying. For example, LG created a public service ad that counselled teens to think hard before sending a potentially harmful text of themselves or others. MTV created a website, www.athinline.org, to provide guidelines and information about sexting and online bullying. These are the basic tenets of its Digital Rights Project:

Online and on my cell, I have the right to

- live without pressure or abuse;
- step in and help if I see someone getting harassed;
- end unhealthy relationships;
- take control of my decisions; and
- disconnect whenever I want.

forced to take part in sexual acts without her (or his) consent. In Canada, as of 1983, marital rape, referred to as "sexual assault" in the Criminal Code, was deemed a criminal activity.

Marital rape is but one example of what has been described as "defining deviancy up" (Karmen 1994). This occurs over time as behaviours that were once overlooked or tolerated come to be increasingly discouraged, deterred, forbidden, and outlawed (B. Scott and Schwartz 2008). Another good example is **sexual harassment**, which involves unwanted sexual attention, such as sexually oriented remarks and jokes, advances, and requests that take place in the workplace or in other settings (Zippel 2007). This, too, was considered quite normal not too long ago, but the women's movement has also helped to redefine sexual harassment as a form of sexual deviance.

The whole idea of sexual deviance, as well as many specific behaviours that have in the past been considered deviant, is being contested with the increasing acceptance of a very wide range of sexual activities. However, there are still people, groups, and societies that regard at least some forms of sexual behaviour as deviant. Many people with conservative social values consider homosexuality to be deviant, although the evidence that it is often biologically based continues to accumulate. Strong responses to instances of pedophilia indicate that it is certainly considered a deviant practise by most Canadians.

Four criteria have been used to define a given form of sexual behaviour as deviant (Tewksbury 2007):

- *Degree of consent of those involved.* Sexual relations are more likely to be considered deviant when one of the parties does not agree to, and even resists, the acts involved. Rape is the most obvious form of nonconsensual sexual relations (Brownmiller 1975; L. Kelly 2007). Exhibitionism is another example. The person viewing the actions of an exhibitionist has not consented to the revelations; if he or she did consent, the actions would not be exhibitionism.

- *Nature of the person or the object involved in the sex act.* Sex with children is considered deviant because children are not usually associated with sexuality. To a far lesser extent, sex with objects, such as a slice of liver (as in Philip Roth's [1969] *Portnoy's Complaint*) or a zucchini, is also considered deviant for the same reason.

- *Nature of the action involved or the body part employed.* Violent sexual relations are considered deviant by most people (although not sadists and masochists). Some consider anal intercourse deviant. The use of body parts not usually thought of as sexual—feet, the nose, the ear—in the sexual act is also considered deviant, at least by most.

- *Place in which the sexual act takes place.* Even "normal" sex acts are considered deviant if they occur in, for example, a church, synagogue, or mosque.

GENDER

As explained at the beginning of this chapter, sex is largely biologically based (though it is also affected powerfully by social and cultural factors), whereas gender is a social distinction and social definition. However, gender can be enacted in many different

Members of Ukrainian activist organisation FEMEN stage a protest in front of Ukraine's Education Ministry to denounce the sexual harassment of students by university professors.

GL⊕BALISATION

"Crowd Licentiousness" in China

A reflection of global cultural differences in sexuality is the case of Ma Yaohai, a 53-year-old Chinese professor of computer science whose online name was "Roaring Virile Fire." Ma was sentenced to three-and-a-half years in prison in 2010 for what was called "crowd licentiousness" (E. Wong 2010). The "crime" involved the organisation of at least 18 orgies where an informal club of swingers engaged in group sex and partner swapping. The law under which the professor was prosecuted was a leftover from an old Chinese law against "hooliganism," or sex outside of marriage, which was abandoned in 1997. Before the old law was dropped, the leader of a swingers club was executed for his crimes under the "crowd licentiousness" law.

China is changing enormously with its involvement in capitalism, consumer culture, the Internet, and globalisation. The punishment of Ma Yaohai seems out of step with a China in which sexual content is readily available online, brothels are proliferating, and premarital sexual relations are common among young people. There is a website, Happy Village, with a chat room devoted to swinging.

Moreover, love and sex are discussed more openly on radio and television (B. Scott and Schwartz 2008).

Ma Yaohai was sentenced to prison. At his trial Ma exclaimed, "How can I disturb social order? What happens in my house is a private matter" (E. Wong 2010:A8). Nevertheless, he was sentenced to prison. Others in China protested this infringement on personal freedom, specifically the ability to engage in freely chosen sexual activity such as group sex.

This case is not only out of step with current realities in China, but it is even more distant from the realities of sexual life in many parts of the world. Like many other parts of the world, China has clearly grown increasingly "sexy," but its laws have certainly not kept pace. This is a case of "cultural lag" (Ogburn 1922). Chinese law is out of step with the behaviour of the Chinese people and with the norms and values in Chinese culture as they relate to sexual behaviour. Since many Chinese are going to resist efforts to make their lives less "sexy," it seems likely that the law will change or, at least, never be enforced again. It is also likely that Professor Ma will either avoid prison or, if he does go to prison, serve only a token sentence.

---

ways, and in recent years that range of behaviours has increased greatly. Thus gender is a social construction that is subject to change, sometimes quite dramatic change, over time.

While sex is more inborn, although we learn sexualities as well, gender is a largely learned behaviour; to a great degree, we *learn* to be men and women. For example, we learn the appropriate physical appearance, behaviour, and personality for a man or a woman. Learning, understanding, and viewing one another as male and female is a social process. Our parents hold certain ideas about gender-appropriate behaviour. Later we learn gender through socialisation in schools. Expected behaviour is further reinforced within same-sex social circles, during a period when boys tend to play only with boys and girls tend to play only with girls (Kimmel 2011). Of course, the media—print, television, and Internet—also have a great effect on our sense of gender-appropriate behaviour.

FEMININITY AND MASCULINITY

Useful in this context is the distinction between "femininity" and "masculinity." These are gender identities, the meaning of being a "woman" or a "man," acquired during the socialisation process (Laurie et al. 1999; Lind 2007). There is a tendency to develop stereotypes of the meaning of being a woman (mother, nurturant, emotional) and a man (father, tough, unemotional). However, these stereotypes are in reality not natural or biological but rather socially constructed. As Simone de Beauvoir (1973) famously put it, "One is not born, but rather becomes, a woman" (p. 301). The same is true, of course, for a man. Furthermore, these categories are fluid, have wide ranges, and differ greatly both historically and geographically.

Yet the distinction between masculine and feminine persists. Central to the attempt to explain why is the work of Raewynn (née Robert W.) Connell (1987, 1997), an Australian sociologist who coined

Children learn to perform expected behaviours within same-sex social groups. Young boys are often socialised on all-male sports teams to be competitive, assertive, unafraid, and tough. This expected behaviour is perpetuated both on and off the field.

a result of gender discrimination within the workplace (Kimmel 2011).

In Connell's view, hegemonic masculinity acts in concert with emphasised femininity to subordinate women. It also serves to subordinate men who do not live up to the stereotype of hegemonic masculinity, including men who are nonwhite, homosexual, and/or poor. In addition, just as many men are subordinated by hegemonic masculinity, many women—lesbians, bisexuals, career women, athletes—do not live up to the ideals associated with emphasised femininity and are adversely affected by the stereotypes (Butler 1990). Of note in this context are **transgender** individuals, whose gender identity does not conform to the sex to which they were assigned at birth and who move across the gender line in behaviour by, for example, cross-dressing. Thus transgendered individuals also challenge mainstream ideas of masculinity and femininity.

Interestingly, while men benefit greatly from hegemonic masculinity, it is largely invisible to them—and to scholars, at least until recently. Not having to think about masculinity is one of the dividends of gender inequality for men. In contrast, women think a great deal about masculinity since they are so oppressed by it in many different ways.

It is important to remember that masculinity and femininity need to be detached, at least to some degree, from sex and the body. That is, men can act in feminine ways, perhaps by nurturing others, and women can behave in a masculine manner, perhaps by competing aggressively. At the beginning of this chapter, the continuum between the male and female sexes was discussed. Similarly, we should not think in simple, dualistic terms about gender; there is a continuum between masculinity and femininity, which results in part from the variety of socialisation patterns that both women and men experience over the life course. Moreover, individuals can be high in both masculinity *and* femininity, or low in both. Therefore, we must think of gender performance as being fluid rather than static.

the terms *hegemonic masculinity* and *emphasised femininity* and analysed the roles that these ideas have played in global gender inequality. **Hegemonic masculinity**, linked to patriarchy, is a set of socially constructed ideas about masculinity that focuses on the interests and desires of men. Characteristics associated with hegemonic masculinity include, but are not limited to, being white, tall, athletic, Protestant, young, married, northern, heterosexual, a father, college-educated, fully employed, having a good complexion and weight, and being successful in sports. Emphasised femininity is a set of socially constructed ideas that accommodates to the interests of men and patriarchy and involves the compliance of females. **Emphasised femininity** focuses on social ability rather than intellect, ego-stroking, and acceptance of the roles of mother and wife as

GENDER, WORK, AND FAMILY

One of the most studied issues in the field of gender is the relationship among gender, work, and

BIOGRAPHICAL bits

Raewynn (née Robert William) Connell (1944–, Australian)

- Connell was educated in Australia and currently holds a university chair at Sydney University.

- She has made important contributions to the study of social stratification and to the study of gender.

- She is best known for contributions to the sociology of masculinities.

- Her best known work in this area is the book *Masculinities* (2005).

- Connell is a transgender woman who says she now *knows* she is a woman.

- However, she feels that there is still much work to be done on her gender transition.

- Her current work is on intellectuals.

- Her current thinking is also relevant to globalisation as she works toward the development of a "southern theory" to counter the bias toward work done in the Global North.

family (Siltanen and Doucet 2008). The main concern is the ways in which the intersection of work and family varies by gender. For example, it has been shown that married or cohabiting males do better at work and are more productive, at least in part, because their wives are handling more of the responsibilities in the home. Men's wages also tend to increase when they marry or cohabit (Ahituv and Lerman 2007; Korenman and Neumark 1991). As you can see in the historical look at household incomes in Figure 10.1, married men have always enjoyed incomes greater than male lone parents or single men. However, female lone parents and single women have historically had incomes significantly below those of married couples. Although not shown in the figure, men continue to contribute more money to household income (59 cents of every dollar). This earnings difference has been narrowing over the past few decades (K. Marshall 2009). Many of these inequities are based on traditional gender roles in the family.

Separate Spheres

Prior to the Industrial Revolution, women and men together occupied both the private sphere, or domestic life in and around the home, and the public sphere, or job sector/general public. More specifically, women and men shared the breadwinner and domestic roles.

Industrialisation brought forth social change, namely the separation of the public and private spheres. Men became the breadwinners, venturing forth into the public world of work; women were less likely to work outside the home and were relegated to the private sphere (Kerber 1988). The "cult of domesticity" that arose argued that women should display

- submissiveness to their husbands and other male authorities,
- piety as moral exemplars within the home,
- purity in being virgins at marriage and strict monogamy thereafter, and
- domesticity in being well-trained in the domestic arts and caretaking (Welter 1966).

Middle- and upper-class women were those most likely to be able to meet the demands of the cult of domesticity.

Since the mid-twentieth century, this once clear-cut, gender-based differentiation between the public and private spheres has been breaking down. Now women are more likely not only to be in the work world (England 2010; K. Marshall 2010) but, increasingly, to be the principal—or even the only—wage earner in the family. The family characterised by a division between male/breadwinner and female/homemaker has increasingly given way to more blended roles, and even to role reversals, especially in dual-earner families.

Dual-Earner Households

A key issue in the study of gender, work, and family is the difference in the way men and women use their

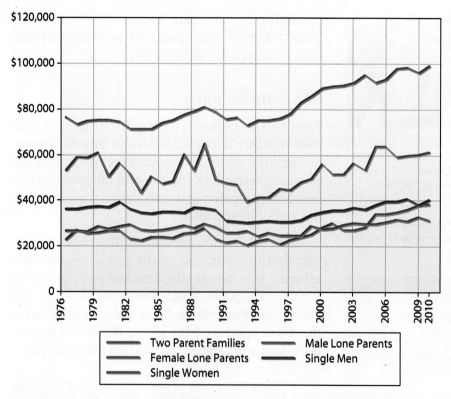

FIGURE 10.1 Average Canadian Household Income (2010 Dollars) by Marital Status and Gender, 1976–2010

SOURCE: Statistics Canada, CANSIM 2020702, calculations by authors.

time in the era of dual-earner families. Research work on this topic includes Meg Luxton's ([1980] 2009) *More Than a Labour of Love* and Arlie Hochschild's (2003) *The Second Shift*. These authors argue that in dual-earner families with children, wives who take jobs outside the home tend to be saddled with a second body of work—their traditional tasks of child care and housework—when they get home from their paid job. Such women can be said to be working a "second shift." Figure 10.2 presents data on gender differences in performing household responsibilities. The figure shows, of all the time a young couple (aged 20–29) devotes to paid work and housework, the percentage that is contributed by women. To show how this is changing, the left panel is for Generation X (born 1969–78), and the right panel is for Generation Y (born 1981–90). Since children significantly affect how couples spend their time, the figure also shows differences for families with and without kids. Men typically devote more time to paid work, although the differences are slim. Women typically devote more time to housework, and when families have kids, women devote quite a bit more time to household responsibilities. For example, among

Generation Y, women did 64 percent of the housework when kids were present.

Just as there is occupational segregation in the paid labour force, with more men as engineers and foresters and more women as nurses and elementary school teachers there is a division of labour in the household. Even though men are contributing more nowadays to domestic duties, men tend to more frequently barbeque the steaks while women buy the steaks (and look after much of the rest of the meal as well). Men tend to shovel the snow or look after car repairs, whereas women, even when they work full-time, are most often on call to look after sick children or clean the toilet. At least some of the earnings difference in wages and salaries that women experience in the paid labour force is a consequence of this uneven division of labour in the home. So despite recent changes with women working more hours in the paid labour force and with men contributing more to household duties, the second shift continues to exist, and it has consequences that reach beyond the household (Siltanen and Doucet 2008).

According to a 2010 United Nations (UN) report, women worldwide shoulder vastly more household responsibilities than men. As you can see in Figure 10.3, however, Canadian women have the

	Generation X (born 1969–78)		Generation Y (born 1981–90)	
	Paid Work	**Housework**	**Paid Work**	**Housework**
No kids	48%	57%	52%	48%
With kids	46%	61%	36%	64%

FIGURE 10.2 Wives' Percentage Contribution to Paid Labour and Household Labour in Canada by Gender, Family Type, and Generation

SOURCE: Authors' calculations from K. Marshall (2012).

lightest burden among women in all regions. Perhaps the major explanation for this is the greater affluence of Canadian families and their ability to afford more and more sophisticated household appliances, to afford more meals in restaurants, and to hire people to help with household tasks more often.

Supermoms

The media are an important contributor to social pressures on women to be "domestic goddesses." Prevailing images of happy moms (especially celebrity moms such as Sarah Jessica Parker and Angelina Jolie) tending to their children's every need subliminally manipulate many women into feeling that they must become supermoms. As a result, women are daily subjected to a heavy promotion of impossible ideals of mothering. "Mothers are subjected to an onslaught of beatific imagery, romantic fantasies, self-righteous sermons . . . and totally unrealistic advice about how to be the most perfect and revered mom in the neighborhood, maybe even in the whole country" (Douglas and Michaels 2006:228). This pressure to be the best mother is part of "the ultimate female Olympics" (Douglas and Michaels 2006:231). In order to become the best, mothers must always smile and be understanding, must never be tired, and must make their kids the centre of their universe.

GENDER AND EDUCATION

Gender inequality in access to, and experience in, educational systems is an important source of gender inequality throughout Canadian society and across the globe. Historically, families invested relatively little in the education of females because they were expected to stay at home as wives and mothers. Thus, there was a gender gap in education in many countries, including

Canada. Increasing awareness of this gap has led to significant efforts to overcome the problem and subsequently to great gains for women in education (S. Davies and Guppy 2013; Dorius and Firebaugh 2010).

This is not to say that all the traditional male advantages in education have disappeared. While gender differences in courses taken in Canadian high schools are declining, females are still less likely to take advanced computer classes and more likely to take courses in word processing and data entry. Such differences persist in university, where women are more likely to be in fields such as education, English, and nursing and less likely to be in areas such as science, technology, and engineering that are more likely to lead to higher pay. This kind of sex typing in education is a global phenomenon.

Educational Achievement and Attainment

When boys and girls begin school, there are few substantial differences in their levels of achievement

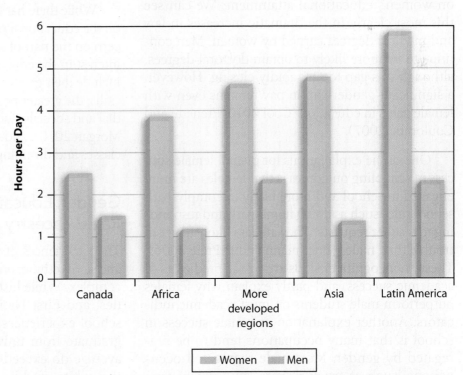

FIGURE 10.3 Average Hours per Day Spent on Housework by World Region and Gender, 2010

SOURCE: K. Marshall (2006).

NOTE: Data are latest available, from 1999 to 2010.

(Aud and Hannes 2011). However, from 4th through 12th grade, female students consistently score higher than male students on both reading and writing assessments. Recent data indicate that by the end of high school males hold a very small advantage over females in math and a larger advantage in science. Interestingly, international comparisons indicate that the male-female gap in math in Canada is relatively small compared to that in other industrialised nations (Aud and Hannes 2011).

Today gender differences in educational attainment generally favour females. Females are significantly more likely than males to graduate from high school and to attend college or university (S. Davies and Guppy 2013). In 1960 women earned less than 30 percent of undergraduate degrees in Canada; today, well over 50 percent of such degrees go to women (S. Davies and Guppy 2013). Today women are more likely than men to receive a bachelor's or master's degree (Association of Universities and Colleges of Canada 2011). Changing societal attitudes about gender roles and declining sexism have had dramatic effects on women's educational attainment. We can see this most clearly in the dramatic increases in law and medical degrees earned by women. Men continue to be more likely to obtain doctoral degrees, although this gap too is rapidly closing. However, a significant gender gap in pay remains even with female gains in education (Cool 2010; Frenette and Coulombe 2007).

One of the explanations for overall female success in schooling outcomes is that females are more engaged in school and more likely to comply with school rules such as doing homework and responding to teacher requests. They are less likely to get in trouble than males (Buchmann and DiPrete 2006). These "noncognitive" skills are strong predictors of academic success, and partly explain why females outperform male students on most academic indicators. Another explanation of female success in school is that many occupations tend to be segregated by gender. Most male-segregated occupations, such as truck drivers, auto mechanics, and firefighters, do not require postsecondary schooling, while most female segregated

occupations, for example preschool teacher, registered nurse, and dental hygienist, require schooling beyond high school. This occupational segregation is increasingly responsible for female advantages in educational attainment (J. Jacobs 1996).

Gender and the Hidden Curriculum

While females have experienced a number of formal gains in the educational realm, informal educational problems remain. The root cause is often the **hidden curriculum**, or a school's unofficial norms, routines, and structures through which students learn various behaviours, attitudes, and values (Giroux and Purpel 1983; L. Hamilton and Powell 2007). Most schools foster competitiveness, a push for achievement, and understanding of the social hierarchy within the school (B. Scott and Schwartz 2008). Because they are socialised from infancy to act on these preferred values, boys are likely to get more attention in class from teachers, to be asked more questions, to get more constructive criticism, and at least in the early years of school to monopolise class discussions (Sadker and Sadker 1994).

While there has been a great deal of focus recently on the educational problems of females, there is concern on the part of some that this has led to a lack of interest in the educational problems of males. These include their greater problems in language and verbal skills, the greater possibility that they will be in remedial and special education classes (Hibel, Farkas, and Morgan 2010), and their greater likelihood of failing classes and dropping out of school.

Gender, Education, and Race/Ancestry

The experiences of women and men from different ancestral, ethnic, and racial groups are increasingly complex. While historically women, visible minorities, and First Nations people have had difficult school experiences, now more women than men graduate from university, and Asian students on average do exceedingly well. We also know that that white, middle-class boys do better in school than boys from the working class and boys from First Nations, black, or Latino backgrounds

(S. Davies and Guppy 2013). Because of media images that have depicted black male youth as pathological and criminal, black youth are often viewed as insufficiently childlike by teachers and school administrators (Ferguson 2001). In other words, black male and female children are "adultified." Consequently, their mistakes in school are often considered intentional, and sometimes sinister, rather than merely youthfully inept. Moreover, African American girls are thought to be more sexually advanced than their white peers, a characteristic that needs to be controlled. At the same time, black boys are not allowed to be "naturally naughty." Physical expressions of masculinity that would be considered typical among their white peers are viewed as insubordinate. As a result, in school black boys learn that to act obedient is to survive and that disobedience will lead to disciplinary action.

Schools have a wide range of expectations for students from different demographic groups, "allocating girls to home economics and sewing courses, lower-class youngsters to slower tracks, and black children to compensatory programmes" (B. Hare 2001:97). Although women have average years of schooling that are higher than men, women are still concentrated in some fields of study, such as nursing and social work, while men still dominate in engineering and forestry. There also continues to be a bifurcation in Canada between college and university, with college students, both women and men, more likely to come from working-class backgrounds. These practises have long-term effects on educational and occupational attainment, including being relegated to low-skill and low-paying jobs.

GENDER AND CONSUMER CULTURE

In consumption, as with much else in the social world, there are gender differences and inequalities. Since the Industrial Revolution, production has been centred outside the household and the function primarily of men, while women, relegated to the home, were assigned the role of being consumers (C. Williams and Sauceda 2007). This is both different and unequal since

England's Kingsmead Primary School student population is diverse—a fact reflected in the 42 different languages spoken by children at the school. According to government data, Kingsmead children are some of the most economically deprived in the country. Despite these challenges, the school's academic achievement is above the national average—an impressive feat, considering that 85 percent of the school's pupils speak English as a second language.

historically production has been far more highly valued than consumption.

Consumption, Work, and Family

Not only have women been defined as the prime consumers, but their consumer practises are closely tied to their domestic practises and their roles in the home. Women consume to care for, and on behalf of, their families (DeVault 1991). More extremely, it has been argued that much of women's shopping relates to love, especially their love of family members (D. Miller 1998). In one way or another, women generally consume for their families and to help them fulfill their responsibilities to the home and to those who live there.

DIGITAL LIVING

Gender and the Internet

When the web first became available to the broader public, it was mostly a low-bandwidth environment that could be accessed only with hard-to-use technology. Computers were clunky and did not always work as they should. Plus, the main method of connectivity, dial-up modems, kept a phone line busy for the duration of the interaction.

There were not many interactive sites, and the ones that existed tended to be text-only environments. Some of the most prominent early sites were called multiuser dungeons, or MUDs, because they were descendants of sites where people played online versions of the popular board game *Dungeons and Dragons*. The culture on these sites was to use avatars—pseudonyms—rather than personal names.

Considering all these factors, it should not be surprising that the early Internet attracted mostly male users with an interest in technology. Another factor shaping the user base was the fact that the early Internet attracted many people who were looking for an alternative space where they could meet with like-minded people who were not necessarily present in their off-line lives. Hence, the early Internet included many communities and sites devoted to interests that might be considered at the margins of mainstream society.

Theorists of the early Internet observed all this activity, especially on MUDs, and wondered if the Internet allowed people to be free of ascribed statuses and identities such as gender and race. After all, users of MUDs freely chose their name, their gender, and even their species. In *Life on the Screen*, Sherry Turkle (1995) argued that identity in cyberspace may be "decentered, multiple and fragmented" and that cyberspace plays a prominent role in "eroding boundaries between the real and the virtual, the animate and inanimate, the unitary and multiple self"

(p. 10). Many theorists also thought "gender" would become one of these categories that would erode in cyberspace (R. Stone 1991).

In time, the Internet expanded and became more mainstream and easier to access. It started to include equal numbers of women and users not necessarily interested in technology but who simply wanted to use technology to socialise, to shop, and to interact. As a result, our understanding of how gender online interacts with gender off-line changed. The rise of sites such as Facebook, which require people to use their real names and make it easy to post many pictures of themselves, has made gender even more prominent—rather than making it less important as the early theorists had speculated.

Most current research finds that women and men tend to replicate certain off-line gender patterns online. Women who tend to do most of the work of kinship and socialising tend to do so online as well, and women are prominent users of social networking sites. Men can be found in large numbers among editors of Wikipedia—a high-conflict environment where people argue about the correct point of view. In my own research on gender and Facebook, for example, I found that women interacted more with their close friends and family, whereas men were more likely to be searching for other people. In the end, this reflects gender patterns we see in the off-line world.

Women and men portray themselves differently online, and women are rewarded for posting sexualised photographs of themselves. Female students are more likely than males to have private profiles (Lewis et al. 2011). So, it looks like cyberspace does not completely free us from gender, after all, and that life on the screen looks somewhat like life off the screen.

SOURCE: Printed with the permission of Zeynep Tufekci.

However, as more women have entered the work world in recent years, their consumption patterns have changed. For one thing they are now more likely to consume an array of subcontracted services such as cleaning and child care. Much of this work is done by other women; women are subcontracting work to other women (Bowman and Cole 2009). For another, they are more likely to consume for themselves rather than for others. For example, greater involvement in the work world requires the consumption of a wider variety of clothing.

Advertising and Gender

Much of advertising and marketing is targeted at either women or men. Advertising targeted at women in the first half of the twentieth century focused on household products, those that helped them with their responsibilities to home and family. As more women entered the labour force, at least some advertising came to focus on the needs of working women of, for example, labour-saving devices in the home.

Feminist critiques of advertising beginning in the 1970s attacked the emphasis in advertisements on weight, especially slimness, and beauty. The main argument was—and is—that these advertisements set up ideals that few women could approximate, thereby adversely affecting their self-esteem (Bordo 1993).

As mentioned previously, the media have a propensity to influence mothers—both working and at-home moms—to focus on maintaining domestic happiness (Douglas and Michaels 2006). More recently, in line with general trends in society, advertising has focused more on allowing women to purchase what they need in order to be unique individuals (Zukin 2005). Of course, there is a huge contradiction involved in offering generally available, brand-name products as a way of achieving uniqueness (Maguire and Stanway 2008).

Interrelated aspects of consumer culture, and the social world more generally, come together to control women's and men's consumption behaviour. For example, gender ideals in advertising are reinforced by the spatial segregation of women's and men's departments in department stores and shops in the malls; on television networks (Lifetime mainly for women, Spike mainly for men); in television shows (*Modern Family* versus *Hockey Night in Canada*); in movies ("chick flicks" versus action movies); and in lifestyle magazines (*Chatelaine* and *O, The Oprah Magazine* versus *GQ* and *Esquire*). However, as with consumption in general, adult women and men are not simply passive in the face of these pressures. They are able to resist, or even actively reconstruct, the messages being communicated to them (Zlatunich 2009).

Women and Girls as Consumers

As one sociologist put it, "For a large number of girls . . . , participating in the consumer realm is the defining feature of life as a girl" (Best 2007:724). In earlier periods girls' involvement in consumer culture had more to do with the roles they were playing, and were likely to play, as adults in the family. As girls have gained more freedom from those expectations and are spending more money of their own, they have been courted more aggressively and differently by advertisers and marketers (N. Deutsch and Theodorou 2010). This is particularly clear in the efforts made by the cosmetics and clothing industries to sell to young women by, among other things, advertising in magazines (*Seventeen, Teen Vogue*) aimed at them as well as through pop-up advertisements on the Internet. One of the unfortunate consequences of this for young girls is increased rates of eating disorders and body dysmorphia—an obsession with perceived flaws in one's body, as well as the hypersexualisation of their lives (Hesse-Biber 1996; Kimmel 2011).

Several historical events mark the development of greater interest in girls, and children more generally, as consumers (D. Cook 2007). One was the emergence of the department store in the middle and late 1800s and the celebration of Christmas, and its associated gifts, by department stores such as the Bay. Children's consumer culture gained great impetus when department stores began to have separate departments for toys and, more importantly, separate departments for boys' and girls' clothing. At about the same time, the media and entertainment began to focus more attention on children, again often divided along gender lines. Movies, television programmes, and more recently television networks—Nickelodeon, for example—are increasingly dedicated to children. Now, of course, children are being targeted on their computers, their iPhones, and myriad other new and yet-to-be created technologies that have a ready audience among teenagers and even younger children (S. Kahlenberg and Hein 2010; Sheldon 2004).

Intersectionality in Gender and Consumption

Being a woman intersects with race and class and other minority statuses to affect how and what women and men consume. Also affected is how they interpret, construct, and reconstruct images and ideas offered up in advertisements, consumption settings, and the media. According to leading marketing research analysts, 85 cents of every dollar spent by American blacks in 2009, a total of $565 billion or more, was spent as a result of the influence of black females. By comparison, in the general population females make 62 percent of brand-buying decisions.

GENDER AND SPORT

Historically, boys and men have been far more likely than girls and women to be encouraged to participate in sports. As a result, males participate more in organised competitive sports, and they dominate coaching and administrative positions in the sports world. Sport is seen as teaching, perpetuating, and celebrating hegemonic masculinity, including competitiveness, physical aggression, and dominance over one's opponent. Females have historically been defined as inferior in the world of sport (Mansfield 2007) because they did not generally live up to masculine ideals in terms of strength, speed, jumping ability, toughness, and so on. Thus, in general, females have not participated as much, or as ardently, in sport as males and have not risen as high as males in most administrative hierarchies in the sports world.

However, this began to change in the 1970s as a result, in large part, of protests by feminists. In addition, greater knowledge of the importance of sport and fitness to health led to the promotion of physical activity for women. As a result, female opportunities and participation rates in sport have increased. Greater awareness of human rights and feminist issues served to reduce discrimination against females in sport and to prevent or remove barriers to their participation.

The masculine ideal in sports is powerful throughout the social world. In detention facilities, for example, where incarcerated males need to project hegemonic masculinity to avoid being persecuted, physical prowess is viewed as largely the only way for men to demonstrate their masculinity.

Sports and fitness activities in prison allow male prisoners to "do masculinity" (Sabo 2005:110). Sports reports in the media are almost exclusively about men, and when university sport is reported in the national press it is almost, although not exclusively, about male teams (e.g., men's ice hockey, football).

Sports often serve to shape gender identity for men. However, the need to live up to the masculine ideal can limit men and prevent them from being all they can be in sports and in much else. Those males who do not excel, or who do not participate at all, in sports are likely to have their masculinity, even their heterosexuality, questioned. This overemphasis on hegemonic masculinity is rooted, sometimes to males' own detriment, in how males are socialised to participate in sport by their fathers (White, Young, and McTeer 1995). Participation in sport engenders an ideology that physical prowess is an exhibition of masculinity and that pain and injuries should be ignored, hidden, normalised, or disrespected. These coping mechanisms for dealing with pain are internalised by men to the detriment of their overall health.

And, for those men who participate in athletic programmes that are not considered sports, such as ballet, there are larger pressures to "do masculinity" when interacting with other males. For example, in a study of the ballet world, males reported that they constantly dealt with homophobic stereotypes (McEwen and Young 2011). These dancers see their participation in dance as "challenges [to] dominant notions of appropriate ways of doing gender and being a man" (McEwen and Young 2011:15). They cope by redefining dance as a masculine athletic endeavour that requires even more physical prowess than sports.

GENDER, HEALTH, AND MORTALITY

Women tend to have significantly longer life spans than men, especially in developed countries. There is great variation between the genders in life expectancy around the world; in 2000 the range was from 84.19 years in Japan—where women lived until age 87.71 while men lived until 80.85—to 52.78 years in Malawi—where women lived until age 53.62 and men until 51.95 (Central Intelligence

While female athletes are often forced to live up to hegemonic masculine ideals, men who participate in athletic programmes that are not considered sports (such as ballet) are pressured to "do masculinity" when interacting with other males.

Agency 2013c, 2013d). In Canada, women live until about 83.3 years of age and men until 78.8 (see Figure 10.4).

Figure 10.4 shows that the life span for both males and females increased in Canada between 1930 and 2010. However, it has increased more for females than for males. While in 1930 women lived, on average, two years longer than men, the gap widened to over seven years in the 1980s, although it has narrowed recently to less than five years. The major factor in the increase of the life span of women is the great reduction in the number of deaths in childbirth (World Health Organization 2009). Notice that although the masculine stereotype stresses physical prowess and strength, women typically outlive men and have done so for many decades in Canada (this is even true if you compare life expectancy for women and men who have lived to age 65; once reaching this transition women still outlive men by about three years).

However, women suffer from more illness and other health-related problems than men do. The greatest difference between the genders is in depression; females are almost twice as likely as men to suffer from this disease (Government of Canada 2006). The leading causes of death for men are lung cancer and heart attacks, whereas for women the leading causes of death are lung cancer and stroke (Statistics Canada 2012d).

Over the course of illness, women are more likely to be confined to bed, to take sick leave, to visit doctors and hospitals, and to report more symptoms than men. There is some doubt that women are actually more likely to be ill than men, but it is clear that women are more likely to admit that they are sick and to report that fact to others.

Researchers do not fully understand gender differences in life span and ill health, but the major

	Male	Female	Difference
2010	78.8	83.3	4.5
2000	76.3	81.7	5.4
1990	74.4	80.8	6.4
1980	71.7	78.9	7.2
1970	69.3	76.4	7.1
1960	68.4	74.2	5.8
1950	66.3	70.8	4.5
1940	63.0	66.3	3.3
1930	60.0	62.1	2.1

FIGURE 10.4 Canadian Life Expectancy by Gender, 1930–2010

SOURCE: Dominion Bureau of Statistics, Life Expectancy Trends, 1967; Statistics Canada, CANISM Table 102-0512.

factors involved are biological differences, behavioural differences, and psychosocial factors related to symptoms and behaviour when ill, including seeking health care. Socialisation patterns appear to push women into more behaviours that maintain health, such as monitoring of diseases and having physicals and checkups.

GENDER, CRIME, AND DEVIANCE

Crime is another area in which clear gender differences exist. Across cultures, gender is the strongest predictor of crime, and it is men and boys who are most likely to commit crimes (Messerschmidt 2007). Conversely, women and girls are involved in the criminal justice system most frequently as the victims of crime. Nevertheless, women have made up an increasing proportion of adults charged by the police with crimes over the last few decades. Figure 10.5 depicts the gender differences in arrests for property crimes in Canada, as an example of gender differences. While more males than females commit property crimes, the percentage of property crimes committed by Canadian females actually

increased between while the percentage of property crime by males decreased slightly.

Various ideas have been put forth to explain why males are overrepresented in crime and deviance:

- *Family socialisation:* Females are more controlled by their mothers during childhood than are males and are therefore less likely to engage in criminal behaviour when they are older (Hagan 1989).
- *Strain:* Males and females face different expectations, and the inability to meet those expectations leads to strain. For example, males are under greater pressure than females to succeed materially, and the strain that is created when they fail to achieve material success can lead to higher rates of property crime (Agnew 2001).
- *Response to adversity:* Men are more likely to blame others for their failures while women are more likely to blame themselves. As a result, males are likely to see their masculinity as being affirmed by being angry, and striking out, at others through property crimes and violent crimes.

There are several basic, sometimes contradictory, explanations for the differences between men and women in terms of deviance and crime, as well as the changing nature of those differences.

One of the factors that makes for *less* female crime and deviance is *male* "chivalry." Males in powerful positions may be too chivalrous to see females as deviants and may protect them from such a label (Gadsden 2007). In addition, males have simply not been socialised into seeing females as deviants, with the result that they are far less sensitive to deviant acts committed by females

	Total	Male	Female	Male Percentage	Female Percentage
Property Crime—1979	978,552	682,562	295,990	79%	21%
Property Crime—2009	1,050,590	656,186	394,404	73%	27%

FIGURE 10.5 Arrests for Property Crimes by Gender in Canada, 2000–2009

SOURCE: Mahony (2011:23).

than males. The result is an underestimation of actual female deviance and crime.

Male patriarchy has a similar effect. The patriarchal family, as well as other patriarchal institutions, is designed to prevent females from engaging in deviance and crime (Gadsden 2007). Girls are generally taught to avoid taking risks while males are socialised to seek out risky situations and to meet their challenges. Many forms of deviance and crime certainly carry with them a high degree of risk. The result may be less female deviance and crime.

One of the factors making for *more* female deviance and crime is women's liberation. As women have attained greater equality with men in other areas of social life, the gap between men and women in terms of deviance and crime has also narrowed (Gadsden 2007). In other words, an unintended consequence of women's liberation is, and will increasingly be, greater involvement of women in deviance and crime.

A second factor contributing to more female deviance and crime is female victimisation. Females are more likely than males to be abused as children. The women who have been victimised are more likely than other women to engage in deviance and crime and to find themselves in prison (Gadsden 2007). For example, young women who have been abused are more likely to be runaways, a form of deviance that is itself related to other forms of deviance such as truancy (Thrane and Chen 2010). Runaways, in turn, are more prone to engage in a variety of crimes, such as petty theft and prostitution, in order to support themselves.

Finally, economic marginalisation contributes to more female deviance and crime. Hard economic times, along with gender discrimination in the workplace and patriarchy, are thrusting more women, especially single mothers, below the poverty line. As they become increasingly desperate, they commit more property crimes (Pollock 2001).

SEX, GENDER, AND GLOBALISATION

It should not surprise you to learn that globalisation has affected sexuality, sexual behaviour, and gender-related expectations and behaviours, as it has affected every other aspect of social life.

SOCIAL CHANGE AND THE GLOBALISATION OF SEXUALITY

Globalisation is one of a number of forces that are changing sexuality in the twenty-first century (Plummer 2012). The globalisation of sexuality is linked to a variety of social changes that are altering not only sexuality but much of what transpires in the social world:

- *Globalisation of media:* Sexuality is a growing presence in the global media. The Internet and the social networks that it has engendered are most important. However, photos, movies, music, advertising, and television have also gone global. These media have been sexualised; they can even be said to have undergone a process of "pornographication" (McNair 2002).

- *Increasing urbanisation:* Urbanisation is a key trend across the globe, and it has contributed both to increasing sexuality and to the globalisation of sexuality (D. Bell 2007). Cities are at the centre of freedoms of all sorts (Simmel [1903] 1971), including sexual freedoms. Residents of global cities learn a great deal about what is possible and what is "cutting edge" from one another, including the latest developments in sexuality. Further, sex trafficking and sex tourism take place primarily in the world's cities. The world's major cities, including London, Hong Kong, and Shanghai, are the nodes in global "sexscapes" (Kong 2010).

- *Global network of "sexperts":* A group of experts in fields such as medicine, law, psychology, and education are considered "sexperts." They are part of a global network who share expertise and who travel among the world's cities, studying and speaking on the subject of sexuality. Some of these sexperts, such as Doctor Ruth, have become media stars, especially on TV, and their ideas are broadcast and shared widely around the world. They are also likely to publish books,

Tracey Cox is a British author, television personality, and contributor to a number of magazines and radio programmes. A self-professed "supersexpert," Cox has written more than a dozen books (including 2008's *Secrets of a Supersexpert*) and hosted several television shows (such as the ongoing series *The Sex Inspectors*) intended to help couples and individuals improve their sex lives.

some of which become global best sellers translated into many different languages, as well as widely read blogs.

- *Globalisation of social movements:* A wide range of social movements dealing with issues relating to sexualities has arisen. Among them are the women's and gay movements (see Chapter 15), as well as more specific movements focused on such issues as repressive sex laws. Many such movements are global in scope, and their personnel and ideas flow easily around the globe.

- *Increased mobility:* It is relatively easy now for people to travel to another locale far from home. Thus sexual intercourse itself has become a global phenomenon, with large numbers of people in various parts of the world increasingly having sex with one another (Altman 2001; D. Frank 2012).

GLOBAL FLOWS RELATED TO SEX AND SEXUALITY

Sexuality is flowing around the world in a multitude of other ways, such as via sex trafficking, sex tourism, gay global parties, and the sexual diaspora as members of various sexual subcultures move easily around the world and from one society to another. In addition, all sorts of sexual goods and services are being shipped and sold globally, especially via the Internet.

Sex has also become a global phenomenon politically. There are now a number of laws that operate globally, such as laws against the sexual exploitation of children. Global organisations such as UNICEF monitor these laws and seek to protect the vulnerable from sexual predation. Laws around the world dealing with various sexual crimes such as rape have grown increasingly similar (DiMaggio and Powell 1983).

At a cultural level, norms and values about sex have been changing, and those changes have tended to flow around the world. As a result, such norms and values have grown increasingly similar in many parts of the world. For example, there has been a general movement away from trying to control sexuality as a way to maintain the collective order and procreation. At the same time, there has been a movement toward viewing sexuality as a series of acts that are mainly about pleasure and self-expression. Nonmarital sex has also become increasingly normative in many (but certainly not all) parts of the world. Another example of global cultural change involves the global diffusion of such sexual identities as straight, gay, and bisexual. Almost anywhere you go in the world, you will find similar identities, norms, and values relating to sexuality.

Sexual Minorities in Global Context

A key issue for sexual minorities in the context of globalisation is the barriers that inhibit their movement around the world or encourage their flow from one place to another (Altman 2001; Binnie 2004; Carrara 2007). Those barriers may be erected within their home country, as well as between countries. Barriers at home that might push them to migrate include a lack of equal opportunity in the workplace and bans on same-sex marriages. A

Western women sometimes travel to Jamaica to enjoy the sand, sun, and glistening seas—and sometimes the company of local men. Sex tourism, like sex trafficking and the sexual diaspora of various sexual subcultures, is a flow that has increased as globalisation has become more pervasive.

variety of other problems, such as physical assaults, and even murders, of sexual minorities, can force them to seek a better life elsewhere in the world. They can also be pulled elsewhere in the world by better conditions, such as more opportunities to work and marry. Urban environments are attractive because large and visible groups of sexual minorities are often accepted by the majority group in cities.

Other aspects of globalisation, such as inexpensive air travel, the Internet, and sex tourism, have made it easier for sexual minorities to communicate and to be with those who share their orientation and lifestyle. Globalisation has also contributed to the rise of gay and lesbian global social movements and to the increasing acceptance in large parts of the world of same-sex sexual relationships (Frank and McEneaney 1999).

Yet, while globalisation has aided sexual minorities, globalisation has also assisted the spread of homophobia and other forms of prejudice and discrimination (Binnie 2004). Globalisation has not been an unmitigated good as far as sexual minorities are concerned.

Global Sex Industry

The sex industry has become increasingly important to global capitalism. Bars, dance clubs, massage parlours, the pornography industry, international hotel chains, airline companies, and the tourist industry create, and help to meet, the demand for sex labour around the globe. It is almost impossible to get accurate numbers on those involved in the global sex industry, and at least some of the data are likely fabricated (Steinfatt 2011). The most authoritative source is the annual report of the U.S. State Department, which, in 2010, estimated that 12.3 million people throughout the world, both adults and children, were in forced labour, bonded labour, and forced prostitution around the world. The UN Global Initiative to Fight Human Trafficking (2007) estimates that a far smaller number of people are involved, but even with that smaller number it estimates that sex trafficking yields annual profits of $31.6 billion. Over the last few decades, most of the countries of the Global South and Eastern Europe have experienced an unparalleled growth in at least one aspect—and undoubtedly others—of the global sex industry: prostitution. Many of these prostitutes find their way to the developed nations of the Global North.

The flow of people in the global sex industry not only moves from the South to the North but also in the other direction. Over the past 30 years, the global sex tourism industry has grown to be a multibillion-dollar enterprise (Wortman 2007). While there is some sex tourism that moves in the direction of the developed countries of the North (for example, to Amsterdam in the Netherlands), much of it involves the flow of customers from the North to the less developed countries of the South (Katsulis 2010). For example, Thailand receives millions of sex tourists every year from North America, Western Europe, Australia, and Japan, bringing in billions of dollars (Bales 1999). Several factors have contributed to the rise of sex tourism.

Poverty leads large numbers of women in sex-tourist destinations to participate in the industry. Low-cost travel has permitted more sex tourists to circle the globe in search of sexual relations (Brennan 2004). Finally, the Internet expedites sex tourism as well. Information about havens for those interested in sex tourism is readily available through websites, chat rooms, e-diaries, blogs, promotional videos, and guidebooks (Wortman 2007). Advice is accessible and readily obtainable on the best tourist sites to visit, the best sex workers at those sites, how to arrange a visit, and even how to negotiate with largely submissive sex workers in order to get the lowest price for various services (Katsulis 2010). It is even possible through the Internet to organise a customised package tour of the best locations in the world for sex tourism.

GLOBAL MIGRATION AND GENDER

The global economy has contributed to an unprecedented increase in female migration: "Women are on the move as never before in history" (Ehrenreich and Hochschild 2002:2). Some have referred to this trend as the "feminisation of migration." Much of this global flow involves women from the South moving, legally and illegally, to the North to handle work that was historically performed by northern women (Runyon 2012). Nine of the largest countries from which women are emigrating are China, India, Indonesia, Myanmar, Pakistan, the Philippines, Sri Lanka, Thailand, and Bangladesh. The migrants largely become nannies (Cheever 2002), maids (Ehrenreich 2002), and sex workers (D. Brennan 2002).

This migrant labour enriches the North and enhances the already elevated lifestyle there. Many female labour immigrants clean and care for largely affluent children and their families while also trying to send money to their families in their home country (Hondagneu-Sotelo 2000). Domestic work is now considered the largest labour market for women worldwide. See Global Flow Maps 10.1 and 10.2 for how the source countries for women emigrating to Canada have changed from 1971 to 2006.

BIOGRAPHICAL bits

Arlie Hochschild (1940–, American)

- Hochschild has all of her advanced degrees from the University of California, Berkeley.

- She served as a professor at Berkeley for most of her career.

- Hochschild is now an emeritus professor.

- Much of her work is concerned with the sociology of emotions.

- In *The Managed Heart* (1983) she deals with the "emotional labour" of, for example, flight attendants who must deal with passengers who are cranky or abusive, or who fear turbulence.

- Such emotional labour has now "gone global" as care workers from the Global South must perform such labour for the families that employ them in the Global North.

- In *The Second Shift* (1989) she analyzes how couples divide up not only the physical but also the emotional work in the home.

- In *The Time Bind* (1997) Hochschild deals with the time demands at work and the tensions that are produced because of an inadequate amount of time to devote to family activities.

- She has won a number of awards, including a lifetime achievement award from the American Sociological Association for public understanding of sociology.

- In other words, she has been a public sociologist whose work has been widely read outside of academia.

Undocumented and informal female migration, which is common for women migrating to the North for domestic work, exposes women to the worst forms of discrimination, exploitation, and abuse (UN 2006; Pratt 2012). They can be held as debt hostages by recruitment agencies until their transportation and placement fees are

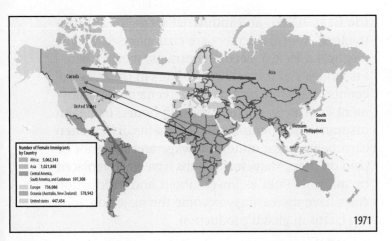

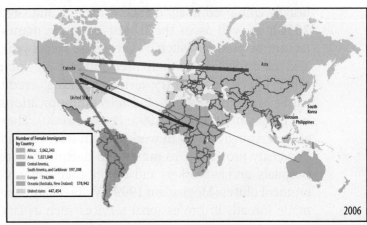

 GLOBAL FLOW MAPS 10.1 and 10.2 Changing Source Areas of Female Emigration to Canada, 1971 and 2006
SOURCE: Chui (2011, Chart 4).

paid, locked up in the houses of their employers, treated inhumanely, and sometimes even murdered. An increasing number of migrant women are victims of sexual abuse, sex trafficking, and prostitution.

FEMINISATION OF LABOUR

There has been a notable increase in women's labour force participation rates worldwide (see Figure 10.6), particularly in the Americas and Western Europe. Even though there are significant variations within and across regions, women's labour force participation has also risen substantially in sub-Saharan Africa, North Africa, Eastern Europe, Southeast Asia, and East Asia over this period (Cagatay and Ozler 1995; Heintz 2006; Moghadam 1999). While the progress in women's employment status is linked, at least in part, to gender equality movements, the key factor in this change is the better integration of an increasing number of areas into the world economy through trade and production.

The increasing participation of women in the labour force has been termed the **feminisation of labour** (Standing 1989). This refers to the rise of female labour participation in all sectors and the movement of women into jobs traditionally held by men. This global trend has occurred in both developing and developed countries.

In many developed countries, educated middle-class women have made inroads into professional and managerial employment. However, in the global paid-labour market, women are

While many women workers are migrating from the Global South to the Global North, some men are migrating in the opposite direction. Combined with the world's recessed economy, strict immigration laws instructing schools, hospitals, and police to check for proof of citizenship have caused many undocumented workers to flee the North. While there have been recruiting efforts to hire unemployed North Americans to fill vacated agricultural positions, the hard work, long hours, low pay, transportation costs, and experience needed have proven to be serious obstacles.

heavily employed in agriculture (Preibisch and Grez 2010), as well as in the labour-intensive manufacture of products such as garments, sportswear, and electronics. Women predominate in such office jobs as data entry, airline booking, credit cards, word processing, and telecommunications (C. Freeman 2001; Gaio 1995; Pearson 2000). They are increasingly likely to work as both teachers and university professors, as nurses and doctors in state hospitals, and as workers and administrators in government offices (Moghadam 1999). Women have also made inroads in professional services such as law, banking, accounting, computing, and architecture.

Women and Informal Employment

At the same time as some women are finding success in the paid work world, others are being limited by the nature of their arrangements with employers. Informal employment, which has increased in many countries, includes temporary work without fixed employers, paid employment from home, domestic work for households (de Regt 2009), and industrial work for subcontractors. Informal sectors are characterised by low pay and a lack of secure contracts, worker benefits, and social protection. Workers in the informal economy do not have wage agreements, employment contracts, regular working hours, or health insurance or unemployment benefits. They often earn below legal minimum wage and may not be paid on time. Many formal jobs have been replaced by informal ones as lower labour and production costs have increasingly become the major organising factor in global production.

While greater informal employment characterises both the male and female labour force globally, women and men are concentrated in different types of informal work. Men are concentrated mainly in informal wage and agricultural employment, while women are typically concentrated in nonagricultural employment, domestic work, and unpaid work in family enterprises. Compared to men's informal employment, women's employment is much more likely to have lower hourly wages and less stability. In order to reduce labour costs, most multinational corporations establish subcontracting networks with local manufacturers employing low-paid workers, mostly women, who can be terminated quickly and easily. In these production networks women are more likely to work in small workshops or from home. Many women accept the lower wages and less formal working arrangements of home-based work in order to be able to continue to carry out household responsibilities.

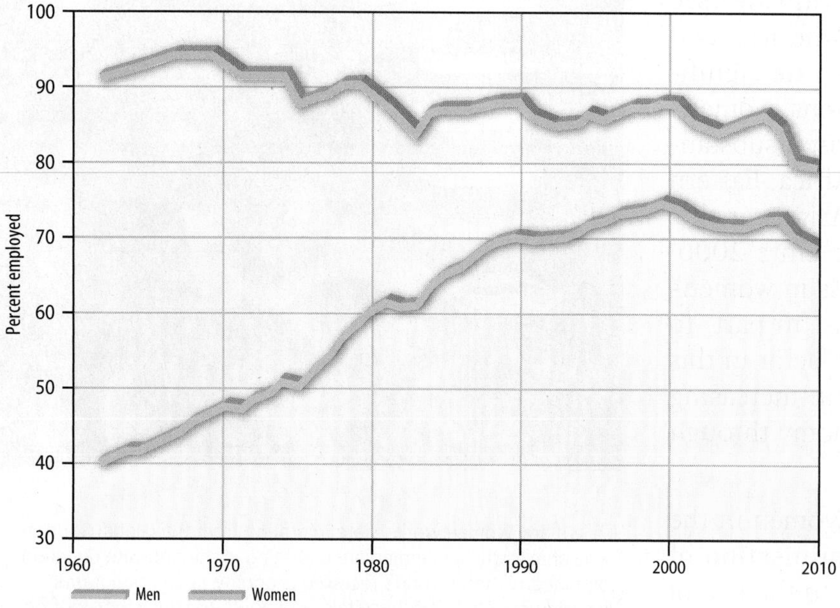

Female Proletarianisation

The feminisation of labour, especially in the developing economies, is often accompanied by **female proletarianisation**, as an increasing number of women are channelled into low-status, poorly paid manual work. Globally, more women are being drawn into

FIGURE 10.6 Global Employment by Gender, 1962–2010

SOURCE: Based on "End of the Gender Revolution," Reeve Vanneman, Department of Sociology, University of Maryland. Authors' calculations from Current Population Survey (CPS) data provided by the Integrated Public Use Microdata (IPUMS) files.

NOTE: Percentage employed ages 25–54.

labour-intensive and low-paying industries such as textiles, apparel, leather products, food processing, and electronics (Villareal and Yu 2007). Jobs in these industries are characterised by the flexible use of labour, high turnover rates, part-time and temporary employment, and a lack of security and benefits. Women are preferred in these industries because they will typically work for lower wages, and they are seen as easier for male employers and managers to supervise. They are considered not only to be more docile but also to have greater patience and more dexterity than men in performing standardised and repetitive work. Female employment is also characterised by poorer and more dangerous working conditions and more compulsory overtime with no extra pay. Although in Canada fewer women are now trapped in poverty than was historically the case, poverty is an increasingly feminised experience in many regions of the world.

A great deal of attention has been focused on the place of women in what has been called the "global assembly line" (J. Collins 2003). While high-status research and management are likely to be found in the North, assembly-line work is relegated to the less developed nations of the South (Ward 1990). Women are much more likely to be employed in the latter than in the higher-level positions in the developed countries.

In the corporate economic centres, especially global cities, large amounts of low-wage labour are required, and again women often fill the bill. They help to maintain the offices and lifestyles of entrepreneurs, managers, and professionals through clerical, cleaning, and repair work and labour for companies providing software, copying paper, office furniture, and even toilet paper (Sassen 2004). Furthermore, the vast majority of provisioning and cleaning of offices, child tending, and caring for the elderly and for homes is done by immigrants, primarily women (J. Acker 2004).

Women in Export Processing Zones

Export processing zones (EPZs) are special industrial areas, often in developing countries, designed to draw foreign companies and capital investment. EPZs offer multinational companies incentives including exemption from labour and

Assembly-line work is usually relegated to the less developed nations of the Global South. Here, workers assemble shirts at the Elite Garments Industries factory in Dhaka, Bangladesh.

environmental regulations, taxes, tariffs, and quotas. A wide range of products is produced in EPZs including tennis rackets in St. Vincent (Caribbean), furniture in Mauritius, and jewellery in Thailand. However, EPZs mainly focus on the production of textiles, clothing, and electronics for the mass market. EPZs are characteristically unstable, as companies are continually setting up new ones where labour is cheaper and regulators are more compliant.

It is often suggested that EPZs reduce poverty and unemployment and, as a result, facilitate the economic development of the host countries. Even if this does occur, it does not occur without serious costs. Working conditions are brutal in most EPZs, where violence and abuse are daily routines. A workday may consist of impossibly long shifts with unpaid overtime, nonpayment for workers on sick leave, insufficient health and safety measures, monitored access to bathrooms, sexual harassment, physical abuse, and in some cases forced consumption of amphetamines to ensure efficiency. Working conditions are particularly hard on women, especially those who are pregnant and with infants. In most EPZs mandatory pregnancy testing is a condition for employment and for maintaining a job. In some cases gender bias intersects with age discrimination. EPZs tend to hire mostly young and single women; women over 25 years of age are usually not hired since they are seen to be more likely to bear children (Pun 1995). Because of the harsh working conditions and low pay, female (and male) workers often burn out; the turnover rate in EPZs is very high (Sivalingam 1994).

GENDER, WAR, AND VIOLENCE

Men are certainly more likely to be killed or wounded in warfare than women. However, a 2004 Amnesty International report described women as "bearing the brunt of war." More specifically, women are more likely to be the noncombatant victims of organised collective violence, including multinational wars that involve empire building, bilateral wars among nations usually over territory, wars of liberation from colonialism and tyrannical governments, and civil wars (Gerami and Lehnerer 2007).

Several changes have made it more likely that women will be the victims of international violence. One is the change in the nature of warfare. For example, "asymmetric warfare" involving forces of unequal capabilities often takes the form of shoot-outs in the streets. Obviously, civilians—women, but also children and the elderly—are more likely to be victims than when conventional ground battles take place. Generally, the line between combatants and civilians has blurred, with the result that more civilians, including women, have become the victims of warfare. Finally, more women are in the armed forces in various countries, and this greatly increases their chances of being the victims of violence.

A consequence of war that also affects women is the use of rape and sexual assault as weapons (see the next *Globalisation* box). They have long been used to weaken and demoralise the nation-states and ethnic enclaves in which the victims live. One example occurred in the war in Bosnia (1992–1995) where Bosnian Serb soldiers and officers committed various war crimes, including systematically raping Bosnian Muslim women. The Serbs went so far as to set up camps where the goal was the impregnation of Bosnian women (Salzman 2000). This is one technique of ethnic cleansing. By giving birth to children with Serbian "blood," the children born to Bosnian women as a consequence of rape would have Serbian "blood" and thus no longer have "pure" Bosnian "blood."

Ultimately the number of the invader's descendants in the invaded country would rise. Rape as a tool of war is also used to traumatise the victims and to humiliate the enemy by "taking" their women. As is true with rape in general (Rudrappa 2012), rape in warfare is not a sexual act, but rather is an act of power (Brownmiller 1975). Beyond rape and sexual assault, forced prostitution and slavery are used against women in times of warfare.

Women who are fortunate enough not to experience such horrors may still find their lives, as well as the locales in which they live, disrupted by international violence. Women are likely to be impoverished by such violence, and their homes may be destroyed. Shortages of all sorts during times of war are likely to affect those at home, especially women. One organisation estimates that women make up 70 percent of those internally displaced by conflicts (International Organization for Migration 2005).

Women may be called upon to care for the wounded, and they may be injured not only physically but psychologically. The larger community in which they live is disrupted, as the women are no longer able to devote as much attention to their normal duties and responsibilities as mothers, for example.

Interestingly, women can also benefit from warfare and its disruption of business as usual. Among other things, they can gain greater economic independence, more freedom to act, and greater mobility. With the norms and values of society disrupted, women can do things they could not do before: acquire a more public role in the community and society, gain greater responsibility for decision making, and generally acquire more power.

THE GLOBAL WOMEN'S MOVEMENT

As you have seen, globalisation and the rise of a global economy have created or exacerbated a variety of inequities faced by women. One response has been expansion of the international women's movement (see Chapter 15). It has grown dramatically in recent years because of problems created for women by globalisation. It has also expanded because of the increased ability of those working

GL🌐BALISATION

Rape as a Weapon of War

The use of rape as a weapon of war has been so virulent in the African nation of the Democratic Republic of Congo that the UN special representative on sexual violence in conflict called it the "rape capital" of the world (Mawathe 2010). Since 1996, Congo has been characterised by more or less constant warfare and ongoing rebellions. Nine African nations and a couple of dozen armed groups have been involved in a shifting pattern of violence and exploitation (Adam Hochschild 2011; Marchak 2008). The conflict persists because of the existence of many different rebel groups, an army that is in disarray, a UN peacekeeping force (numbering about 18,000) that is ineffectual, the existence of and battle over valuable minerals (tin, gold, etc.), and the isolation of villages from one another. The warring groups often use women's bodies as a battleground, where rape is a sign of power of one group over another. Groups may also use rape in the hopes of gaining concessions from those in power, or they may rape out of simple frustration or boredom with life in the forest (Adam Hochschild 2011).

In one case in Congo, four armed rebels barged into a hut and repeatedly raped an 80-year-old grandmother in the presence of children. The rapists themselves were so much younger than the woman that she cried out: "Grandsons . . . Get off me!" (Gettleman 2010). They eventually did, but with about 300 other rebels from at least two different groups, they went from hut to hut gang-raping about 200 women. After the rapes, women said they heard hollering throughout the night. It sounded as if the rebels were celebrating. The grandmother lay bleeding on the floor listening to the celebration.

A few days later a UN peacekeeping force passed through the area and saw signs of violence and looting. However, when asked by UN soldiers the villagers did not say anything about the rapes. A UN officer said: "Sometimes . . . the women here are ashamed to tell a soldier, especially a male soldier, that they've been raped. And we don't have any female soldiers" (Gettleman 2010:A3).

The area is so dangerous that villagers are afraid to go to markets without a UN escort. When they do, they tend to walk behind trucks carrying a few peacekeepers. They constantly yell to the trucks to drive more slowly because they are afraid of a gap developing between the trucks and the line of villagers. If such a gap develops, it is not uncommon for armed rebels to leap out of the woods and grab a few villagers. Particularly vulnerable are women who, in the current environment in Congo, are highly likely to be raped, perhaps repeatedly.

The consequences for the women can be severe. Many of the women who were raped are rejected by their husbands, who call them "dirty" (Mawathe 2010). Other survivors are severely injured. The psychological trauma leaves some women entirely emotionless. The rape survivors may find expert medical care and the support of other survivors at specially established medical centres, but their despair is likely to persist for years, if not for a lifetime.

A Rwandan Hutu rebel gropes a local woman as he passes her on a crowded mountain path near the village of Kimua in eastern Congo. Congolese community leaders say they warned local United Nations officials and begged them to protect villagers. Just days later, rebels gang-raped scores of people in the village, from a month-old baby boy to a 110-year-old great-great-grandmother.

on behalf of the movement to travel globally and to communicate with one another. The international women's movement has a long history traceable back to the late 1800s (Rupp 1997). It has focused on issues such as reproductive rights, labour issues, and sexual harassment. Its greatest triumphs have related to women's right to vote in countries around the world (Ramirez, Soysal, and Shanahan 1997).

A key event was the UN International Women's Year in 1975 and four related world conferences—Mexico City (1975), Copenhagen (1980), Nairobi (1985), and Beijing (1995) (Alter Chen 1995). Given its dominance mainly by patriarchal males, the UN is an "unlikely godmother" of the women's movement (M. Snyder 2006). However, these meetings created interpersonal networks throughout the globe, and the expansion of the Internet has greatly increased the ability of women to interact and to mobilise on a global basis.

A variety of specific issues were the focus of the UN meetings as well as the larger global movement: human rights (Yuval-Davis 2006), economic concerns, health care issues, and violence against women. The movement has also come to focus on the adverse effects of global capitalism (for example, increased global trafficking in women),

the lack of women's voices in global civil society, the growth of antifeminist fundamentalist movements (the Taliban, for one), and the HIV/AIDS epidemic. More generally, the international women's movement has focused attention on issues of global justice for women and other minorities. It has had a strong impact on the UN and has helped create strong linkages between the UN, national governments, and nongovernmental organisations (K. George 2007).

Women throughout the world have not only been involved in the global women's movement, but they have also responded at local and regional levels to common problems caused by globalisation. They also localise global political activities undertaken by the international women's movement and global human rights groups. In addition, they organise against global activities such as militarism and conflict and use global organisations (such as the UN and international nongovernmental organisations) to help in local and regional activities (Naples and Desai 2002). However, even the activities that have been primarily or exclusively local in nature have had a profound effect globally. Even with all the local variations, feminism can be seen as "a truly global phenomenon" (Marx Ferree and Tripp 2006:viii).

SUMMARY

Sex and *gender* are terms that are often used interchangeably, but it is important to remember that sex is primarily a biological distinction between males and females; gender is based on what, given a person's biological category, are considered appropriate physical, behavioural, and personality characteristics.

Although sex is often thought of in terms of only two sexes, there is actually a continuum. Sexuality, or sexual behaviour, interacts with sex to create a wide variation in the expression of both sex and sexuality—people are not simply female or male, homosexual or heterosexual. However, everyone's behaviour is controlled to a great extent by sexual scripts, or ideas about appropriate sexual behaviour, which are quite different for men and women. These scripts account more clearly for gender differences in sexuality than do biological differences.

What is considered sexually deviant varies among different times and places. For example, sexual harassment, usually by men, was considered normal in the not-too-distant past but is now defined as a form of sexual deviance. Other sexual behaviours defined as deviant are generally judged on the basis of four criteria: the degree of consent, the nature of the person or object involved, the nature of the action or body part employed, and the place where the act takes place.

Gender is a social construction and can be enacted in a variety of ways. Hegemonic masculinity works in concert with emphasised femininity to subordinate women and create gender inequality. These constructs are the basis for gendered organisations and institutions, in which advantage and disadvantage are primarily based on gender differences. In these structures, men and women are placed in different domains, and gender inequality is built into these domains.

In Canada and other developed countries, many traditional gender inequalities are abating, creating a mixed picture. For example, the male breadwinner–female homemaker model is not as prevalent in families as it once was, although women still tend to do more housework and child care than men, even when both are employed outside the home. In schools, girls often excel academically, but boys get more attention. Although there are now more female than male college undergraduates, men, even men who are recent graduates, tend to earn more money than women. In the realm of consumption, although women have historically been defined as the prime consumer in a household, advertising and other consumption-related media are directed to both women and men. While historically boys and men have been more encouraged to participate in sports, girls and women now have more opportunities to participate. Women and men also experience differences in health and mortality. For example, men and women are prone to different diseases, and women tend to have longer life spans than men. Being male is the strongest predictor of crime, though arrest rates for crime among women are increasing.

Globalisation reinforces preexisting gender structures on a global scale. Further, norms and values about sex have flowed across the world and grown increasingly similar over time. The greater flow of people also creates more opportunity for traffickers to transport women and children for sexual exploitation.

Globalisation is linked to the increasing number of women working in the Global South. While this might seem to be a positive development, there are some negatives—for example, the increase in women drawn into low-status, poorly paid, and sometimes dangerous manual work. Women around the world tend to be employed in informal sectors of the economy, which often includes work that is temporary, low paying, and with limited benefits. On the global level, women are also suffering as rape has become a prominent weapon of war. That reality, combined with other sex- and gender-related global issues, has led to the development of the international women's movement, which has gained strength since the UN celebrated the International Women's Year in 1975.

KEY TERMS

- Asexuality   364
- Bisexuality   364
- Consensual sex   369
- Emphasised femininity   374
- Female proletarianisation   390
- Feminisation of labour   389
- Gender   362
- Hegemonic masculinity   374
- Heterosexuality   364
- Hidden curriculum   378
- Homosexuality   364

- Intersexed   362
- Pedophilia   366
- Rape   369
- Sex   362
- Sexual assault   369
- Sexual harassment   372
- Sexual orientation   364
- Sexual scripts   367
- Sexuality   363
- Transgender   374
- Transsexual   362

THINKING ABOUT SOCIOLOGY

1. What do sociologists mean when they say that there are no clear-cut biological differences between men and women?

2. What are the differences in the ways that men and women approach sexuality? How

are the differences in approaches related to the socialisation process? Do you think that increasing equality between men and women will affect these approaches?

3. How has sexuality been McDonaldized or become an element of consumption? What effect does the McDonaldization of sexuality have on our sexual selves and our sexual identities?

4. What is the difference between sex and gender? How does sex affect gender? How does gender affect sexuality?

5. What are the differences in the ways that men and women experience "hegemonic masculinity" and "emphasised femininity"? How do these constructs help create and reinforce gender stratification?

6. How do men and women differ in terms of their educational experiences? In what ways does the hidden curriculum of educational systems reinforce gender stratification?

7. Historically, why have women and men been treated differently as consumers? What events have changed the way women are thought of as consumers?

8. In what ways has the sex industry become increasingly important to global capitalism? How is the sex industry reflective of gender stratification? How is it reflective of inequalities between the Global North and Global South?

9. What do sociologists mean by the "feminisation of labour"? What are the benefits and disadvantages of the feminisation of labour? How has the feminisation of labour influenced female migration?

10. What changes have made it more likely that women around the world will be the victims of international conflict? What types of violence are women most likely to experience?

APPLYING THE SOCIOLOGICAL IMAGINATION

According to the chapter, the United Nations is the "unlikely godmother" of the global women's movement. Despite being led primarily by men, the UN has been a key ally in the global women's movement. In fact, it is responsible for the most complete international agreement on the basic human rights for women, the Convention on the Elimination of All Forms of Discrimination against Women, also known as CEDAW.

For this activity, do research on the history of CEDAW. How does CEDAW define discrimination against women? What are the basic principles of the articles of the convention? How do these relate to the issues discussed in this chapter? What countries have ratified CEDAW? What sort of success has CEDAW had in addressing issues of global gender stratification?

ACTIVE SOCIOLOGY

Pinterest (www.pinterest.com) is a website of virtual bulletin boards where you can "pin" items of interest to you. Like many forms of real life, bulletin boards on Pinterest tend to become a display of gender. How do the preconstructed categories reflect normative ideas about gender? Which categories are designed for whom? Explore boards and pins on this site. In what ways do they reflect contemporary constructions of masculinity and femininity? For example, type "motherhood" in the search bar and examine

the results. What types of pins (images, designs, photographs, etc.) come up? How is motherhood presented? If you don't already have an account, create one. (Note: You can log in through Facebook.) Once you have your account, create a board that illustrates your own gender socialisation. What things, people, ideas, and other influences taught you how to be a man or a woman? Find and display relevant images on your bulletin board to demonstrate gender socialisation.

STUDENT STUDY SITE

Visit the student study site at **www.sagepub.com/ritzercanadian** for additional web quizzes for further review.

THE FAMILY

Family-based reality shows paint a picture of domestic dynamics that is captivating and sociologically intriguing—but by no means complete. Where reality shows stop, sociology begins enhancing our understanding of family.

I n 1973, the U.S. Public Broadcasting Service (PBS) aired a 12-part documentary called An American Family. *The groundbreaking series, widely credited as the first reality television show, intended simply to chronicle the happy, mundane lives of husband and wife Bill and Pat Loud and their five children. Over the course of the series, however, cracks in the family's calm and collected façade became apparent, and the cement that joined the Loud family together eventually began to crumble. Viewers came to witness events theretofore unseen on American television, such as the real-life separation and subsequent divorce of Bill and Pat, and the coming out of eldest son Lance, making him the first openly gay person to appear on television.*

In the years since An American Family aired, family-based reality television shows have flourished—to say the least. To distinguish themselves from the avalanche of similar programmes, contemporary series tend to focus on exceptional families such as those of celebrities (Keeping Up with the Kardashians), with a large number of children (19 Kids and Counting), of the wealthy (My Super Sweet 16, the Real Housewives series), or with an uncommon lifestyle (Teen Mom, All-American Muslim).

It should come as no surprise that family-based reality shows are so enormously popular. Family is a universal social institution; it constitutes a person's first group and primary socialiser and, for many, a lifelong source of companionship and security. Because the institution of family is such a central part of life, it is natural for one to be fascinated by—and even feel connected to—the intimate relationships and conflicts forged within other people's families (especially if those people are already famous or otherwise socially exceptional).

As the wide variability in reality television families indicates, the structure of the "family" can take a great number of forms. Extended and nuclear family structures have proven popular over the last 100 years, but recent social changes have quickly led to a wide variety of alternative options. Some couples marry for love, others marry for purely economic reasons, and an increasing number choose not to marry. Some have children in the double digits, while others have none at all. Some maintain exclusive partnerships until death, while others remarry, and still others incorporate new members into existing relationships.

Family-based reality shows paint a picture of domestic dynamics that is captivating and sociologically intriguing—but by no means complete. There are just about as many definitions of family as there are cultures in the world. Among the several dozen family-based TV programmes currently in production, how many focus on homelessness, honour killings, or polyandrous Himalayan families? Reality shows have largely sidestepped critical social issues such as poverty, gender inequality, and the prevalence of domestic abuse. They have not adopted a global perspective, choosing instead to focus on traditional upper- and middle-class western family structures. Thankfully for our understanding of family, however, where reality shows stop, sociology begins.

FAMILY, MARRIAGE, AND INTIMATE RELATIONSHIPS

The family, defined as a group of people who are related by descent, marriage, or adoption, is especially important in socialising children so that they are better able to fit into the larger society. Sociologists view the family as a universal social institution that is central to social life (J. Powell and Branden 2007). Sociologists are interested in such issues as the relationship between family and marriage, the different forms taken by families, and how families are formed and maintained, expand and contract, and even dissolve.

SOME BASIC CONCEPTS

In this section, we will define such basic concepts and ideas as marriage, intimacy, and love and explore their roles in the family.

Marriage

Marriage is the legal union of two people allowing them to live together and to have children by birth or adoption. Families govern various issues that relate to marriage, such as the "meanings of marriage" as well as "the number of marriage partners" (Shaw and Lee 2009:378). In terms of the latter, monogamy is a marriage of one wife and one husband (although given changing laws relating to gay marriage, monogamy now also can include two women or two men), and polygamy involves multiple spouses. Polygyny, a family with multiple wives, is a more common form of polygamy than polyandry, which includes multiple husbands. Cenogamy involves group marriage.

Key to understanding the family is endogamy, or marrying one with similar characteristics in terms of race, ethnicity, religion, education level, social class, and so on. In contrast, exogamy involves marrying someone with characteristics that are dissimilar on these, and other, dimensions. Throughout history, families have been defined much more by endogamy than exogamy. In recent years, endogamy has declined in importance, and there is more exogamy. For example, there has been an increasing tendency of Canadians to marry those of another ancestry, ethnicity, or race (Milan, Maheux, and Chui 2010). However, as a general rule, families continue to be characterised more by endogamy than exogamy.

In the last several decades the nature of both family and marriage has undergone a series of rapid and dizzying changes. It is less and less clear exactly what constitutes marriage and a family. Furthermore, whatever they are today, one thing is clear—the close linkage between marriage and the family has been greatly reduced, if not broken. Nevertheless, most people in Canada are involved

While the traditional nuclear family (left) has proven a stable family structure, it is but one of many types of familial organisation. A polygamous family group comprising one husband, two wives, and their children (right) sits in a traditional reed community building on the banks of the Tigris and Euphrates Rivers in southern Iraq.

in a marriage, often more than one, during their lifetimes. And those who do marry will create families, although they may not stay together as long as did families in the past. Being married and in a family does not mean that the same people will remain in them for the duration of their lives. Marriage and the family will remain important intimate relationships, but they will not be the only, or even the dominant, forms of intimacy in the future (see page 403).

Intimate Relationships

The word *intimacy* is often associated with sexual relationships, with people being "intimate" with one another. More generally, however, **intimacy** can be defined as a close and personal relationship. Thus, an **intimate relationship** involves partners who have a close, personal, and domestic relationship with one another. This intimate relationship is a by-product of courtship rituals in which two people are attracted to each other, develop intimacy, enjoy each other's company, and identify as a couple after a period of dating.

The nature of intimacy is not static, but changes over time. Fifty or a hundred years ago, couples could be intimate without necessarily sharing very much about themselves with each other, especially their most private thoughts. However, in western culture today, intimacy increasingly involves disclosing

much, if not everything, about oneself to one's partner (L. Jamieson 2007). Levels of disclosure tend to be gendered (Kimmel 2011). Because females are socialised to engage in communication in which they express their emotions, whereas males are socialised to suppress their emotions and communicate little about them, women tend to function as emotional caretakers within heterosexual relationships. In other words, women tend to be the ones to share first and to help males share by drawing them out. The assumption made by most women is that such self-disclosure will strengthen a relationship because there are no secrets and therefore there will be no surprises, or at least fewer of them, as the relationship develops.

Love

Intimacy in domestic relationships is, of course, often associated with love. There are many different definitions, and a wide variety of types, of love. Of greatest utility here is the distinction between passionate love and companionate love (Frieze 2007). **Passionate love** has a sudden onset, has strong sexual feelings, and tends to involve idealisation of the one who is loved. Obviously, passionate love brings with it great intimacy, although it is an intimacy that is very likely to be short-lived. In contrast, **companionate love** develops more

gradually, is not necessarily tied to sexual passion, and is based on more rational assessments of the one who is loved. Companionate love is more likely than passionate love to lead to longer-lasting intimate relationships. However, these two types of love are not clearly distinguished from one another. This is clearest in the fact that long-term intimate relationships often start out with passionate love, but in those that succeed over time it tends to be combined with, or even supplanted by, companionate love.

Passionate love, also known as romantic love, has a long and interesting history. For example, some of our more recent senses of love are traceable to 1950s consumer culture (Shaw and Lee 2009). It was then that love became closely associated with consumption and travel. The movie, automobile, fashion, and makeup industries capitalised on, and disseminated ideas on, romantic love. Each of these industries, in its own way, glamourised romance and conveyed the message that romance

was associated with commodities that were available for a price:

- The movie industry associated romance with luxury products (diamond rings, mink coats) that served as markers of affection.
- The automobile industry portrayed outings by car—and the private intimacy afforded by those outings—as a way of cementing a relationship.
- The fashion and makeup industries encouraged women to buy certain products with the promise that they would help them find romance and love.

More recently, Zygmunt Bauman (2003) has sought to get at the essence of love in the contemporary world in his book *Liquid Love*. On the cover of that book is a heart drawn in the sand. However, the sea is nearby, and the implication is that love will soon be washed away by the waves. To Bauman, love, like everything else in today's liquid society, is fleeting. This clearly applies to passionate love, but in Bauman's theory, even companionate love is today forever at risk of erosion and disappearance. This represents a severe challenge to all intimate relationships, especially marriage, and to all of those involved in them. However, liquid love can also be seen as offering people freedom from lifelong, loveless relationships, as well as innumerable experiences with love during their lifetimes and the possibility of many different relationships built on that love. Clearly, this would be not only a much more liquid love life, but a more liquid life, than that experienced by most people in the past.

Extending Bauman's ideas on the liquidity of love, it can be argued that our main concerns in this chapter—the family and marriage—are also increasingly liquid. Because they are now so liquid, the borders of marriage and the family are increasingly difficult to define. More importantly, many traditional forms of marriage and the family seem in imminent danger of being washed away. As a result, many sociologists have moved away from a focus on the family and marriage and prefer to discuss, instead, more vague and more amorphous phenomena such as "relationships" or "personal life." This can be called the "new orthodoxy" in the sociology of marriage and the family.

Though most well known for the Narnia series of children's books, author C. S. Lewis also wrote extensively about religion and philosophy. In 1960's *The Four Loves*, Lewis details four distinct types of love: *storge* (fondness through familiarity, such as in a family), *phileo* (the love shared between good friends), *eros* (passionate, romantic yearning), and *agape* (pure, unconditional caring).

A broadened perspective is made necessary by the dramatic changes that have taken place, and continue to occur, in and around marriage and the family. Nevertheless, most people, including most sociologists, continue to think in terms of marriage and the family (B. Powell et al. 2010). We will do the same in this chapter, although it is in the context of an understanding that both are changing dramatically and refer to far more liquid phenomena than they did in the past.

BROAD CHANGES IN MARRIAGE AND THE FAMILY

We will discuss two broad changes in this section—the decline of marriage and changes in the family household.

DECLINE IN MARRIAGE

In 1971, married couples constituted 64 percent of all households (see Figure 11.1); by 2007:58 percent of all Canadian households were married couples. The traditional **nuclear family** involving two adults and one or more children has dropped to just under 40 percent of all families, and even then a rising percentage of those parents live common law (see Figure 11.2).

Another way of understanding this sea change in marriage and the family is to look from the vantage point of children. The nuclear family has declined as the typical family form in Canada such that children now experience a diversity of alternative family arrangements (see Figure 11.2). More and more children are raised in lone-parent households. Many gay and lesbian couples are raising children. The number of children living with stepparents is accelerating. Finally, more and more children are being raised by legal guardians other than their biological parents, although sometimes this is their grandparents.

Perspectives on the Decline of Marriage

The decline in marriage (and the family) has led to some fascinating new perspectives on the status of marriage today.

The Views of Andrew Cherlin. Andrew Cherlin (2004) focuses on what he calls the "deinstitutionalization of American marriage." By **deinstitutionalisation** he means that the social norms relating to marriage have weakened, and, as a result, people increasingly question their actions, or those of others, as they relate to marriage. While he focuses on this deinstitutionalisation in the United States, he recognises that a similar process is occurring in much of Europe, as well as in Canada. In the mid-twentieth century, especially in the United States, few questioned marriage and the creation of a nuclear family, with the result that most plunged into both, sometimes successfully, but more often with dubious or even disastrous results. Now, with marriage and, perhaps, the nuclear family and the family household deinstitutionalised, it is much easier for people *not* to plunge into such an arrangement and to experiment with many other arrangements.

Cherlin discusses five factors in the deinstitutionalization of marriage. First, as more women entered the labour force, the clear division of labour in the family between homemaker and breadwinner began to break down.

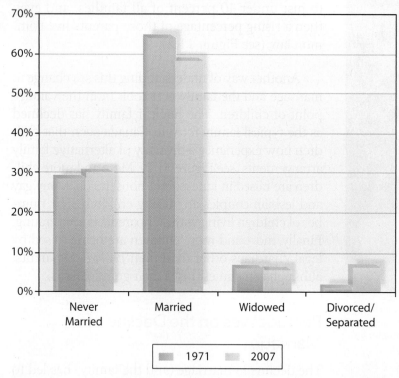

FIGURE 11.1 Marital Status of Canadians 15 Years and Older, 1971 and 2007

SOURCE: Calculations by authors, Statistics Canada, CANISM Table 051-0010.

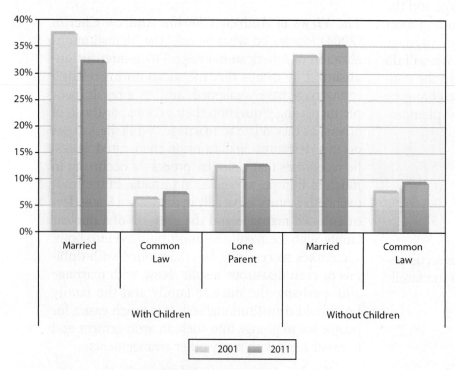

FIGURE 11.2 Family Types by Presence of Children, 2001 and 2011

SOURCE: Authors' calculations from Statistics Canada (2012f, Figure 1).

The once-clear norms about what men and women were to do in a marital relationship were eroding, and this contributed to a more general lack of clarity about marriage, as well as the family. Second, the norms about having children within the context of marriage and the family were also eroding. This was demonstrated in the dramatic increase in childbirth outside of marriage (see Figure 11.2). Third, the high and increasing divorce rate between 1970 and 1990 contributed to the deinstitutionalisation of marriage (see Figure 11.3). Although the divorce rate has stabilised recently, the high rate between 1970 and 1990 had a seemingly irreversible impact on attitudes toward marriage. Fourth is the growth in cohabitation, which began in the 1970s and accelerated as the twentieth century ended. Finally, there is the same-sex marriage that flowered in the 1990s and has grown further in the twenty-first century.

Cherlin embeds these ideas on deinstitutionalisation in a long-term model of change in the twentieth century. In the early twentieth century **institutional marriage** was the dominant form. The focus in such a marriage was on the maintenance of the institution of marriage itself. There was less concern that those involved would love or be good companions to one another. Today, many see the time of institutional marriage as past; but there are also those who see it as alive and well and with a future (Lauer and Yodanis 2010).

By the middle of the twentieth century, a model of **companionate marriage** (see above section on companionate love) had become dominant (Amato et al. 2007; Burgess and Locke 1945). The companionate marriage meshed well with the nuclear family and involved a clear division

McDONALDIZATION *Today*

McFamily

Although many social phenomena demonstrate a trend toward *increasing* McDonaldization, that is not necessarily the case with the Canadian family. There are contradictory developments and changes in the family from the perspective of McDonaldization (Raley 2010).

On the one hand, the structure of the family seems to be undergoing a process of *de-McDonaldization*. That is, the once highly predictable, cookie-cutter nuclear family (mom, dad, and 2.2 children) is in decline, and a whole range of very different family forms is on the rise.

The earlier structure of the family was McDonaldized in a number of ways. For example, it was generally expected that a man would partner with a woman for life and that the man would go to work, the woman would stay home, and children would arrive in due course and be raised jointly by the parents. Today there is much greater variability among men and women who marry, including the fact that women are more likely to be in the labour force and may earn as much as, or more than, men. There is also no longer an assumption that only a man and a woman can marry. Further, it is no longer assumed that marriage is for life; people may move into and out of several marriages, as well as other types of relationships. And, it is no longer expected that couples will necessarily have children or, if they do, that they will have children within the context of a marriage.

This change from a highly McDonaldized family structure to one far less McDonaldized

The McDonaldized family and appropriate familial roles have long been normalised in children's toys. With little variation, toy families often comprise an endogamous mother and father, their two to three children, and perhaps a family pet. If families move away from McDonaldization, will children's toys reflect the cultural shift?

is traceable to many factors, including the fact that although the early form was efficient, many found it, like a fast-food restaurant, predictable, unsatisfying, and even oppressive. The emphasis now is more on the quality of the relationship and on the lives of any children that may result, rather than such quantitative factors as the number of years a couple has maintained a marriage or the number of children they have.

On the other hand, when one looks at the lifestyle of today's family, one finds a strong trend in the direction of further McDonaldization. This is seen, for example, in

- the impatience of married or cohabiting partners to move into a relationship and to see quick—and highly positive—results;

- their reliance on the quick fixes offered by popular books and TV shows (*Dr. Phil*);

- their dependence on a variety of nonhuman technologies such as cell phone "family share" plans;

- the structuring and scripting of many family activities such as spousal "date nights"; and

- their utilisation of a wide range of McDonaldized settings for family activities, including birthday parties at chain restaurants.

In spite of these and other contemporary lifestyle changes that point in the direction of greater McDonaldization, the family may be uniquely suited to slowing its spread.

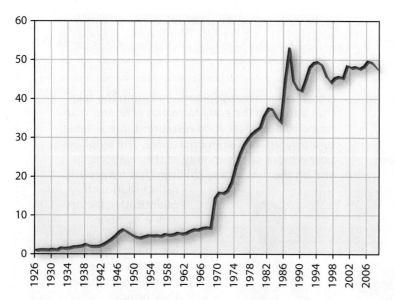

FIGURE 11.3 Divorces as a Percentage of Marriages, 1926–2008
SOURCE: Kelly (2012, Chart 1).

of labour between the single-earner breadwinner—almost always the male—and the female homemaker. In spite, or perhaps because, of the strict division of labour, husbands and wives were held together by bonds of sentiment, friendship, and sexuality. They were supposed to be each other's companions, including being each other's friends, confidants, and lovers; romantic love was an essential component of companionate marriage.

In the 1960s, a dramatic shift began to take place in the direction of the **individualised marriage** (Lauer and Yodanis 2011). The focus of the companionate marriage was collective in nature. The goal was the satisfaction of the couple, the family as a whole, and the roles the couple played in the family. However, that focus began to shift increasingly in the direction of the satisfaction of each individual involved, as well as to individuals' ability to develop and express their selves. In addition, instead of being as rigid in structure as the companionate marriage, individualised marriage became increasingly open and flexible. Furthermore, couples were becoming more open with each other in communicating about, and dealing with, problems. Many of those involved, as well as many observers, applauded the greater freedoms and sensitivities associated with individualised marriage.

A major factor in the rise of individualised marriage was the changing place of women in society. For example, as more women went to work, they were no longer restricted to the homemaker role and reliant on the male breadwinner. As more women obtained a higher education, their occupational prospects were enhanced, and this put them in a context where ideas associated with companionate marriage were increasingly open to question. The greater access of women to contraception and to abortion freed more women from the constraints of companionate marriage, in terms of producing and socialising children.

As a result of all of these changes, people feel freer to never marry, to marry later, to end unhappy marriages more readily, and especially to engage in many other types of intimate relationships. Yet, in spite of all of the change, the vast majority of people—perhaps as high as 90 percent—will eventually marry, although many of their marriages will end long before the "till death do us part" stage is reached. Thus, marriage has not deinstitutionalised to the degree anticipated by Cherlin.

In fact, in a more recent book, *The Marriage-Go-Round*, Cherlin (2009) adopts a somewhat different perspective defined by a "carousel of intimate partners." Some of those intimate partners are to be found in marriages, but those marriages are more likely to end; people are likely to remarry, perhaps more than once. Rounds of separation and divorce add to the merry-go-round and its increasingly dizzying speed. Then there may be a series of cohabitations into and out of which people move. Thus, many people have not given up on the idea, and even the practice, of marriage, but it exists side by side with the often conflicting notion of individualism. People want to be legally defined as couples and as families, but they also want to be free of constraints and to act as they wish as individuals. Current sociological research underscores this paradox. On the one hand, researchers are told that most people, including

Brides and grooms from underprivileged families take part in a mass-marriage ceremony in the eastern Indian city of Kolkata (Calcutta) on Valentine's Day 2012. While many Indians and Indian Americans see institutional marriages arranged by fiancés' families as an anachronistic custom, there are some who see it as an important tradition with a long future.

young adults, want an "exclusive, lifelong intimate partnership, most commonly a marriage" (Hull, Meier, and Ortyl 2010:37). On the other hand, people often indicate by their behaviour that they want to be free of such bonds. Canadians remain committed to the ideal of marriage, but in reality they spend fewer of their adult years married than previous generations.

Nevertheless, there are those who remain wedded to the traditional notion of marriage. They can be called "marriage naturalists" who view "marriage as the *natural* expected outcome of a relationship that has endured for a period of time" (Kefalas et al. 2011:847). In contrast, so-called marriage planners need to deal with a number of practical realities before they can consider marriage. These include finding a well-paying job and being able to create and support a separate household. *Marriage naturalists* "see marriage as being a prerequisite to being an adult," and *marriage planners* "want to establish themselves as adults *before* they wed" (Kefalas et al. 2011:870).

While they are going about creating those realities, marriage planners and marriage naturalists may have premarital sexual/romantic relationships, cohabit, and bear children out of marriage. All of the latter phenomena have been found by sociological researchers to have risen in recent years. Kefalas et al. (2011) found that the marriage naturalists were more likely to be rural, while the marriage planners had to arrange their intimate lives around the realities of urban life. In addition, the marriage naturalists were closer to the realities of marriage in mid-twentieth-century Canada, while the marriage planners better fit the realities of the postindustrial West and the wait-and-see attitude more characteristic of the early twenty-first century.

There is today a debate between those who see marriage in decline and those who emphasise its resilience (Amato 2004). Those who see marriage in decline focus on such things as the rising divorce rate and the increase in the number of children born out of wedlock. These are seen as problems in themselves and as indicators of larger problems, such as an excessive focus on the individual and an inadequate concern for the collective. Those who focus on the resilience of marriage argue, for example, that divorce allows people to escape from marriages from which people ought to escape, especially those marriages that are dysfunctional in various ways such as being abusive. Having children out of wedlock may have the positive effect that fewer children will be locked into families in which they are socialised poorly or even abused physically and psychologically.

Whether or not they are married or remain married, people will continue to form families. Much sociological research has dealt with such families, especially the problems associated with them.

The Views of Anthony Giddens. The British sociologist Anthony Giddens (1992) developed an ambivalent view on the new individualised forms of marriage and of relationships more generally. In his view, key to this new form of relationship was what he called "self-disclosing intimacy." Couples were disclosing much more to each other and, as a result, were able to achieve much more intimate relationships with one another. This was linked more to the honest relationships in individualised marriage than to those associated with companionate marriage, which were more likely to be based on all sorts of secrets or half-truths. Thus, companionate marriages in the past, and even the many that continue today, may survive for decades or a lifetime even though they may be based on deceptions that leave one or both partners in the dark. The partners often remain in such marriages for reasons other than their openness and honesty. They may stay together because of social norms against divorce or "for the sake of the children."

Giddens recognises the advantages of self-disclosing intimacy, but he also argues that intimate relationships based on full disclosure are made much more fragile by such disclosures, especially as the disclosures continue and proliferate over time. The more weaknesses one reveals to a partner, the more likely that partner is to become disappointed with the relationship. Despite this, Giddens, as well as many others today, seems to prefer relationships based on mutual disclosure because he believes they are likely to be more mutually satisfying, equal, and democratic. Further, he contends that almost anything is preferable to being locked into the kind of dishonest and unsatisfying relationship often associated with companionate marriage.

Since marriage of any kind can be confining and limiting, Giddens (1992) coined the term *pure relationships* to describe a new reality. A **pure relationship** is one that is entered into for its own sake, or for what each partner can get from it, and those involved remain in it only as long as each derives enough satisfaction from it. While they could exist within marriage, such relationships are more likely to exist outside of such a legal relationship. As a result of the increasing predominance of this idea, at least among young people, a relationship is likely to be ended when couples no longer find their relationship satisfying. It is also likely that another, different pure relationship (or several) will be formed in relatively short order, or perhaps even simultaneously with the existing one. This fits with the increasing individualisation of contemporary society as well as the closely related phenomenon of individuals wanting more choices and greater freedom of choice. It represents a greater degree of individualisation than even that found in individualised marriage. Less

constrained by marriage, or more likely not married at all, couples are free to individualise their lives to a much greater degree. Marriage is seen as just one of a wide range of lifestyle choices open to couples. In whatever type of intimate relationship people find themselves today, the possibility that it will dissolve is never very far from their consciousness.

The idea of the pure relationship had its origins in western society, although like many such ideas in the global age, it has flowed readily around the world to many locales.

The Views of Ulrich Beck and Elisabeth Beck-Gernsheim. A similar set of ideas was developed in Germany by Ulrich Beck and Elisabeth Beck-Gernsheim (1995, 2002) who argued that marriage of any form had become only one of many ways of living together or apart. These forms are not mutually exclusive, and people are not forced to choose any one of them and certainly not once and for all. This is related to various other ideas developed by Ulrich Beck (see Chapter 13). One is **reflexive modernity**, or a new stage in the modern world, especially in the West, where people are increasingly self-aware, including of the fact that they are free of structural constraints (such as marriage) (Beck 1992). This means that people are better able to create themselves reflexively, their relationships, and more generally the societies in which they live. Beck's (1992) general argument applies well to relationships between couples: "The newly formed social relationships and social networks now have to be individually chosen; social ties, too, are becoming *reflexive*, so that they have to be established, maintained, and constantly renewed by individuals" (p. 97). Clearly, changes in relationships are but a small part of a series of broader changes.

Another idea central to Beck's work and to the changes being discussed here is **cosmopolitanism**, or the ability to transcend local constraints on thought and action and to take into account many different points of view, being open to a variety of external and global influences. From the perspective of our concern here, couples no longer need to be locked into the view that the only alternative open to them is marriage. There is a world of different types of relationships available to them, and marriage is only one type. Adopting a cosmopolitan orientation toward marriage allows for better, more well-informed choices, even within marriage.

However, there are those who have questioned the range of new ideas, like those discussed above, about intimate relationships. For example, Lynn Jamieson (1998) has questioned the importance of self-disclosing intimacy. There are many forms of intimacy other than those based on self-disclosure, and good relationships are based on more than such disclosures. For example, negotiating an equitable division of labour in the home may do more for increasing intimacy than a wide range of self-disclosures.

Back to Georg Simmel. Interestingly, a major critique of these new ideas on marriage and the family is implicit in the work of one of sociology's classic social theorists, Georg Simmel (see Chapters 1, 2, and 5). In his famous essay on secrecy, Simmel ([1906] 1950) argues that while there is always a temptation to reveal all to a partner in an intimate relationship, especially marriage, such revelations would be a big mistake. In his view, all relationships require a certain proportion of both openness and secrecy, and marriage is no exception. Even if it were possible to disclose everything about oneself, and it almost certainly isn't, this would only serve to make marriage boring and matter-of-fact because all possibility of the unexpected would be eliminated. Finally, most of us have limited internal resources, and every revelation reduces the (secret) treasures that we have to offer to our mates. Only those few with great storehouses of personal assets and accomplishments can afford numerous revelations to a marriage partner. All others are left denuded—and perhaps less interesting—by excessive self-revelation. The contrast is striking between Simmel's ideas, written over a century ago, and the current thinking of many who emphasise the importance of revealing all to intimate partners.

NONFAMILY HOUSEHOLDS: "GOING SOLO"

Nonfamily households are those in which a person lives either alone or with nonrelatives. Of greatest interest is the growth of one-person households, or people living alone. As is clear in

According to Georg Simmel, relationships require a certain proportion of both openness and secrecy, and marriage is no exception. While there is a temptation to reveal all to a spouse, some revelations could do more harm than good.

Figure 11.4, we have witnessed an increase in such households from 9.3 percent in 1961 to over 27 percent of all households in 2011.

One-person households, or "singletons," are the subject of Eric Klinenberg's (2012) *Going Solo: The Extraordinary Rise and Surprising Appeal of Living Alone.* One of the things detailed in this work is the long-term increase in the number of people living alone in the United States (a similar process is occurring in Canada). The number grew from 9 percent of all households in 1950 to 3 times that many today. Overall, 31 million Americans now live alone. The fastest growing segment of the population going solo is young adults between 18 and 34. In 1950 only a half-million of those in this age group lived alone, while today the total of 5 million is 10 times the number in the mid-twentieth century. Fifteen million of those who are middle-aged (35–64) live alone, while 10 million of the elderly are singletons. More women (17 million) than men (14 million) live alone. Going solo is mainly an urban phenomenon; more than half of dwellings in Manhattan are one-person residences, while over 60 percent of Stockholm residents live alone.

There are several reasons for the increase in singletons. First, increasing economic affluence

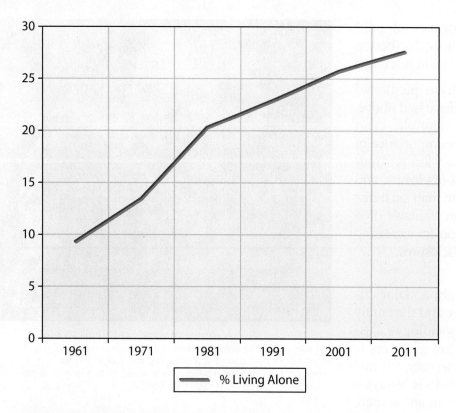

FIGURE 11.4 Percentage of Canadians Living Alone, 1961 to 2011

SOURCE: Statistics Canada. 2012c. "Fifty Years of Families in Canada, 1961 to 2011." Ottawa, ON: Statistics Canada,

2012:17–18). Interestingly, singletons may also be more socially active than those who live with others. It is certainly true that those who live alone have problems, but so do those who live with partners.

THE FAMILY HOUSEHOLD

The **family household** is a residential unit of one or more people occupying a given domicile who are related by blood, marriage, or adoption. It is distinguished by the fact that those involved are related but not necessarily married and by their occupation of a specific domicile. One member of the family household—the *householder*—owns or rents the property, as well as maintains it.

has made it possible for more people to afford the greater costs associated with living alone than sharing expenses with others. Second, it is consistent with the growth of individualism in Canada and much of the developed world. Third is the rising status of women and their higher levels of education and their higher-paying jobs. With greater independence, they are more likely to marry later, separate, or divorce. Fourth, the communications revolution has allowed people to communicate with other people, and be entertained, while they are home alone. Fifth, mass urbanisation has made the active social life of the city available to more people. Finally, there is the aging of the population and the fact that as people live longer they are more likely to find themselves alone.

While in the past living alone might well have been considered a problem, Klinenberg argues that increasing numbers of people are coming to prefer going solo. It allows people to pursue "individual freedom, personal control, and self-realization. . . . It allows us to do what we want, when we want, on our own terms" (Klinenberg

As a form of an intimate relationship, the family household, like the family itself, has been declining in Canada and in the Global North more generally. For example, in 1961, 91.6 percent of households were married couples, but that declined to 67 percent in 2011. This means, of course, a corresponding increase in alternative household formations, and this increase came largely from common law unions, especially in Quebec (Statistics Canada 2012c).

Beyond the decline of the married-couple household and the increase in the one-person household, a variety of other changes in the family household are worth mentioning:

- People are living longer. More are able to maintain their households and family structure for many more years than they were in the past.

- Women outlive men. This means that late in life many women live alone in nonfamily households (31.5 percent of women 65 years of age and older lived alone in 2011 as compared with only 16 percent of men in the same age group) (Statistics Canada 2012d).

- Families have been growing smaller. For example, between 1961 and 2011 there was a decrease in households including 5 or more people from 32.3 percent to 8.4 percent of all households, while households with only 1 person increased from 9.3 percent to 27.6 percent of all households. Overall, the number of people per family declined in that time span from 3.9 to 2.9.

- Declines in the family household are related to declines in the number of births to married women in two-parent families, increases in births to unmarried women (leading to more one-parent families), and increases in the proportion of divorced people.

ALTERNATIVE FORMS OF FAMILIES

Recent social changes have made it possible for people to choose a nontraditional family structure for themselves, including cohabitation, single-parent families, nonresident parents, stepfamilies and blended families, lesbian and gay families, and couples living apart together.

Cohabitation

Cohabitation as couples or living common law is understood as sharing a home and a bed without being legally married, and where the partner is either of the same or the opposite sex (Sassler 2007; A. Thornton, Axinn, and Xie 2007). Common law relationships are growing rapidly in Canada, especially in Quebec. Statistics Canada began collecting data on cohabitation only in 1981, when just over 5 percent of all families were living common law. By 2011, 16.7 percent of families were living common law (see Figure 11.5). In comparative perspective, Canada has a cohabitation rate similar to Argentina, France, South Africa, and Sweden (see Figure 11.6), and much higher than the United States (about 7 percent in 2010).

It is unclear exactly how many people are involved in such relationships because cohabitation is not a formally constituted relationship, and it leaves no legal records. Furthermore, it varies by province as to how many months or years a couple must be together to be categorised as cohabiting. It is clear, however, that more young men and women (especially between 25 and 35) are living together outside of marriage even if they are not considered, or do not consider themselves, a cohabiting couple. Living together in this way has come to be considered as a quite common tryout for, and pathway to, marriage, although few people plan to marry when they begin cohabiting. Then again, marriage may never occur or even be discussed, and cohabiting couples may break up and move on to other relationships. A declining number—less than 50 percent—of cohabiting couples end up getting married.

At one time cohabitation was associated with being poor, less educated, or in the lower classes—it was seen as the "poor man's marriage." More recently, cohabitation has become increasingly common among those with advanced education. Common law relationships are much more likely in Quebec than in other provinces. In 2012, 36.6 percent of couples in Quebec (same or opposite sex) were living common law, while in the rest of Canada the comparable percentage for couples was 16.2 percent (see also Ménard 2011).

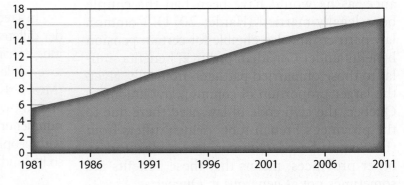

FIGURE 11.5 Percentage of Canadian Families that Live Common Law, 1981–2011

SOURCE: Calculations by authors from Statistics Canada (2012c, Figure 1).

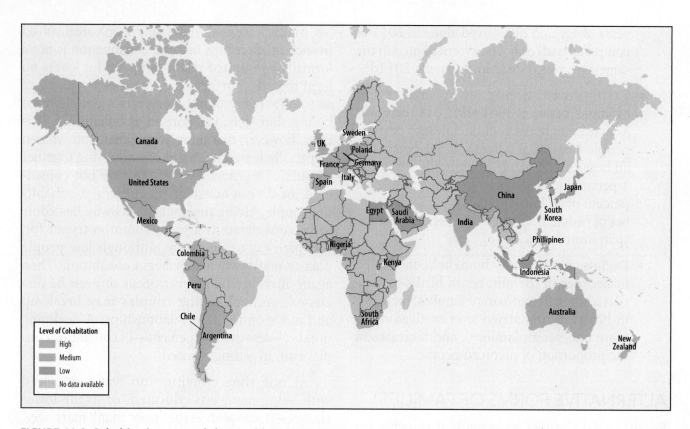

FIGURE 11.6 Cohabitation around the World, 2005–2009

SOURCE: *The Sustainable Demographic Dividend: What Do Marriage and Fertility Have to Do with the Economy?* National Marriage Project.

Increasingly, Canadian law treats common law relationships as analogous to marriage even though a cohabiting couple is not legally married. For example, in a 1995 legal case the courts ruled that a cohabiting adult should be treated as equivalent to a married partner. John Miron was uninsured but injured in a car accident. His common law partner had insurance that could cover his claim. The Supreme Court ruled that Miron should be covered by his partner's insurance, as he would have been had the couple been legally married (Harder 2011). Common law partners are also eligible for certain pension benefits under Canadian practice, benefits similar to those of married partners. Ironically, given the larger proportion of common law unions in Quebec, the civil code of law used there due to the province's French roots, which differs from the British-based common law code used in other provinces, means that these benefits are sometimes not as generous in Quebec.

There are various rationales that people offer for cohabiting. For some couples, common law

arrangements are an easy way to spend more time with each other. This is a way of enhancing a relationship because it deals with a variety of logistical problems, such as eliminating lengthy trips to see one's partner. A second rationale is the belief that partners can save money cohabiting because they share expenses rather than pay for everything on their own. For others they see cohabitation as a kind of "test drive" of a relationship to assess the compatibility of the partnership.

In a recent U.S. study, Penelope Huang found gender difference in terms of the ways in which cohabiting enhanced the relationship: Women focused on love while men focused on sex. As one man put it, "Most girls want to have the connection with the guy and know it's a relationship. 'Cause women, their number one thing in life is to have good relationships with people. . . . Guys, the thing they strive for is sex, so it's kind of a tradeoff" (Huang et al. 2011:887).

The biggest gender differences revolved around cohabitation's disadvantages. Women saw it as less legitimate and as entailing less commitment than

DIGITAL LIVING

Death and Funerals on the Web

As is true of much else, even death and the associated funerals have changed in the age of the Internet, especially Web 2.0. For example, there is the issue of what happens to our Facebook profiles after we die. With over 1 billion users worldwide, thousands of Facebook users die every day. At the moment, there is no system in place to systematically remove the pages of those who pass away. Perhaps we will begin to see digital wills that tell our heirs what should be done with our Facebook pages and, more generally, all of the content we produce online in the course of our lives.

It is not uncommon to commemorate important events on the Internet. For example, weddings, anniversaries, and birthdays are now celebrated on Facebook and Twitter. However, some things, most notably funerals, have been generally off limits—but no longer. Funerals for celebrities, as well as memorial services for those killed in tragic incidents, have become online events, sometimes drawing thousands of viewers. Now we are beginning to see more mundane funerals and memorials on the web. This has been made possible by the increasing availability to funeral homes of low-cost, easy-to-use software that can be used to stream funerals and memorials to loved ones, and those who are unable or unwilling to go to the actual event. In addition, such funerals are now, in effect, open to the general public throughout the world.

The technology that enables the streaming of funerals and memorials has been in existence for quite some time, though it has been slow to catch on. Some funeral directors are concerned about invading the privacy of a grieving family. They might fear that people will view the funeral and use its contents in ways that family and close

friends would not appreciate. Then, some funeral directors find it difficult to even discuss streaming the funeral with a family that is grief-stricken.

On the other hand, a generation comfortable with sharing personal experiences with their "friends" on Facebook and Twitter might well be comfortable with streaming a family member's funeral to other family members and friends.

A funeral for singer Whitney Houston was telecast publicly at Whigham Funeral Home in Newark, New Jersey. While the technology to stream funerals has been in existence for quite some time, it is beginning to catch on with funeral homes and grieving families.

---

marriage, while males were most concerned with the decline in freedom compared to being single. In terms of the latter, males focused on their loss of personal autonomy with regard to space, social activities, choice of friends, and sexual freedom. Overall, however, for both men and women the benefits of cohabitation outweighed the disadvantages.

Cohabitation varies greatly around the globe. Sweden has a long history of cohabitation, and the process is well institutionalised there. In excess of 90 percent of first partnerships are cohabitations, and roughly half of all first births are to cohabiting couples. The legal status, or the rights and privileges, of those who cohabit is virtually the same as that of married couples in terms of such things as social security and taxes (K. Wilk, Bernhardt, and Noack 2010). The high rate of cohabitation has led to a decline in the importance of marriage and of the customs, rituals, and ceremonies associated with it. Couples that cohabit and then marry might well give the date they met as their anniversary. Instead of constituting a decisive break, young people are likely to drift away from their families of orientation, perhaps in stages, and then settle down and cohabit with someone else (Popenoe 1987). However, since 1998 there is evidence of change in this pattern as more Swedes have been marrying. This reverses a long-term decline in marriage in Sweden between the 1960s and the 1990s (Ohlsson-Wijk 2011). Other, mainly Catholic European countries—Italy and Spain—have much lower rates of cohabitation, although this possible Catholic effect does not operate in Quebec (Ménard 2011). There is evidence of the spread of cohabitation throughout much of Europe, including Eastern Europe, and elsewhere.

Lone-Parent Families

Among the developed countries, Canada has a relatively high rate of lone-parent families (just under 25 percent of all households with children in the 2011 Canadian census), while Japan has the lowest (10.2 percent). In Europe the northern countries—for example, United Kingdom (25 percent), Ireland (22.6 percent), and Denmark and Germany (both 21.7 percent)—have the highest rates of lone-parent families. It is mainly the southern European countries—Greece and Spain (5 percent), Portugal (6 percent), and Italy (7 percent)—that have the lowest rates of such families (Rowlingson 2007). See Figure 11.7 for the percentage of single-parent households in selected countries.

Nonresident Parents

Nonresident parents involve families in which fathers or mothers live apart from their children (Smyth 2007). Nonresident parents are mainly fathers, although the number of mothers in this category is increasing. Historically, there have been many reasons for fathers to be absent from their families. They include the demands of work, war, and incarceration. Today, though those reasons continue to

exist, major reasons include nonmarital childbearing with the parents never having lived together, the breakdown of a cohabitating relationship, and marital dissolution. Historically, because of the resource-based nature of much of the Canadian economy, fathers are often away fishing or mining, for example.

In the popular media, nonresident parents have been viewed negatively, often being labelled "deadbeat dads" or "bad moms." In the case of absent fathers, the term *masculinisation of irresponsibility* has been used to describe "the refusal of fathers to provide economically for their children" (Kimmel 2011:173). However, recent evidence tends to indicate that such labels are unfair. Many nonresident parents want to be active in their children's lives, but they face major problems in their efforts to play such a role. There are various emotional issues involved, such as the heartache associated with brief and intermittent visits with children. The major difficulties are practical in nature, including a lack of adequate time to handle parental responsibilities. This has given rise to terms like *Disneyland Dads* because all such fathers have time for is brief

Although it is not clear how many months, or years, a couple must be together to be categorised as cohabiting, many cohabiting couples live and operate in a manner similar to married couples. Even if they are not legally recognised as a household, cohabiting adults may share household chores, responsibilities, finances, and impactful decisions.

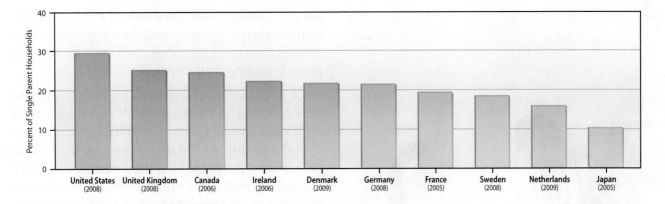

FIGURE 11.7 Single-Parent Households in Selected Countries

SOURCE: U.S. Census Bureau, Statistical Abstract of the United States: 2012.

visits or recreational trips. When nonresident fathers are able to spend time with their children, however, research shows that children have higher academic achievement (Kimmel 2011). Other difficulties confronting nonresident parents include a lack of financial resources due to the demands of child support, lack of adequate space in the new home for children, difficulty in maintaining sufficient contact with children, additional responsibilities associated with a new home and perhaps a new family, and the difficulty of meeting the children's needs as far as things like extracurricular activities are concerned. Many nonresident parents—somewhere between 20 percent and 50 percent—cannot deal with some or all of these difficulties, with the result that they have little, or even no, interaction with their children. This, in turn, can cause many problems for the children involved, including poor performance in school and even suicide.

Women typically have greater problems as nonresident parents than men. They generally have fewer financial resources, and this makes it more difficult for them to perform the role. They are therefore less likely than men to pay child support. Women may also believe that from a financial perspective, fathers are in a better position to raise the children involved. Or, in the case of transnational mothers (Hondagneu-Sotelo 2000; Hondagneu-Sotelo and Avila 2005), as mentioned in Chapter 10, providing financial resources for their children may serve as the only way in which mothers can engage with their children while also tending and nurturing their nonbiological children. Gender roles, such as being nurturant and

caretakers for children, put more pressure on females to be highly active as nonresident parents. Gender roles may also lead women to be labelled negatively because they are living apart from their children. In spite of these difficulties, nonresident mothers are more likely than are such fathers to see their children, to see them more frequently, to have richer and more open encounters with them, and to maintain contact with them through telephone calls, e-mail, or text messaging.

Stepfamilies and Blended Families

A **stepfamily** involves two adults who are married or cohabiting, at least one of whom has a child or children from a previous marriage or cohabitation living with them (M. Coleman and Ganong 2007a). A **blended family** includes some combination of children from the partners' previous marriages or relationships along with one or more children of the currently married or cohabiting couple. Stepfamilies and blended families have become more common in Canada because about half of all marriages include a partner who was previously married. Of all families with children, the 2011 Canadian census showed that 12.6 percent were stepfamilies.

Although the differences are not great, stepchildren tend to have more problems (behaviour problems, difficulties at school) than those who grow up living with their original parents. One explanation is that stepfamilies are "incomplete institutions" (Cherlin 1978). That is, in dealing with problems, stepfamilies do not have the

Though they may desire to be more than disneyland dads and moms, emotional anguish, logistical issues, and financial difficulties prevent many nonresident parents from playing active roles in their children's lives.

institutionalised guidelines and support that exist for first-marriage families.

There are a variety of differences between stepfamilies and first-marriage families. First, they are more complex because the children are likely to spend time with a stepparent as well as with the mother or father from their first-marriage family. Second, there is often insufficient time to develop the family routines and rituals that are likely to have existed in first families. Children may well have difficulty adapting to these new, nonroutinised ways of living. Third, the bonds between first-marriage parents and children are better established and closer, at least at first, than the new spousal bonds. This can make it difficult for the stepparent, at least early in the relationship, although this situation improves over time as the stepparent finds roles to play in

the new family. Fourth, the lack of a legal relationship between stepparents and their stepchildren can cause a variety of problems, such as a lack of any rights regarding their stepchildren after a divorce.

A stepfamily can be difficult for both stepfathers (R. Edwards and Hadfield 2007) and stepmothers (M. Coleman and Ganong 2007b). For stepfathers the relationship with stepchildren can be difficult because it is mediated by a third party, the mother. Stepfathers might, for example, resent all the time the mothers are spending with the children. If stepfathers have their own biological children, this can create conflicts over loyalties and the allocation of scarce money and time. Stepfathers might also have difficulties serving as father figures within the stepfamily. However, stepmothers might well have greater difficulties than stepfathers because they feel the expectations of them are ambiguous. For example, it may be unclear how they should act toward their stepchildren or whether they are impinging on the role of the biological mother. Stepmothers may also be frustrated by the lack of support from their partners. Having children with stepfathers can create problems as stepmothers are likely to feel closer to those children than to their stepchildren.

Lesbian and Gay Families

It is very difficult to get accurate numbers on the gay and lesbian population as a whole, let alone on those involved in long-term relationships, including those in which children are present. Gays and lesbians were largely invisible a half-century ago due to cultural and legal biases and sanctions. That began to change in the era of sexual liberation of the 1960s and 1970s.

A major factor in the gay and lesbian community in general, and in gay and lesbian family formation in particular, has been the HIV/AIDS epidemic that emerged in the 1980s (Heaphy 2007a). Among other things, the gay and lesbian community reacted by building institutions to better deal not only with HIV/AIDS but with many other things as well. One of the institutions that was buttressed in this period was the gay and lesbian family. Previously, gay and lesbian couples often came together because of the need for support and comfort in the face of a hostile environment. Today, such linkages have become more affirmative in nature, especially as the larger society has become more accepting of homosexuality and of gay and lesbian families as an institution. Lesbian and gay politics has devoted more attention to these individuals' right to marry, adopt children, and be parents.

Gay and lesbian couples have various similarities with, and differences from, straight families. One important difference is that gay and lesbian couples tend to be more reflexive and democratic in their family decisions and practices than straight couples. This is particularly the case over the contentious issue in contemporary dual-labour straight families—the way in which domestic duties are negotiated and organised. They are less constrained by gender roles, with the result that they are freer in their negotiations over couple and family practices. Another difference is over monogamy. Although the latter is assumed (but often violated) by straight couples, same-sex male couples are not as wedded to the idea or practice of sexual exclusivity; they negotiate over this issue and develop clear ground rules on nonmonogamous sexual relationships. Gay male relationships tend to be more fragile while lesbian relationships tend to be far more stable. Some of the reasons for these gender differences are related to the previous discussion in Chapter 10 about gender socialisation patterns and sexual scripts (Kimmel 2011).

Studies of children of same-sex couples have tended to indicate that growing up in those families does not have adverse effects on children, such as psychological or developmental problems, or at least any more or different adverse effects than growing up in straight families. However, most of this research has been done on children brought into a same-sex family, but conceived, and having spent at least some time, in a previous heterosexual family. Now, however, same-sex couples are more likely to become parents themselves in various ways, such as artificial insemination (Mamo 2007), adopting children, becoming foster parents, or becoming surrogate parents. While we do not yet know much about such children, there is no reason to assume they will be adversely affected by these methods of achieving same-sex parenthood. In fact, there is every reason to believe that they

In the 2008 film *Step Brothers*, Brennan Huff (Will Ferrell) and Dale Doback (John C. Reilly) are unemployed middle-aged men living in their parents' respective houses. When their parents meet and marry, Huff and Doback move in together as stepbrothers. Though an absurdist portrayal, this film addresses many of the common challenges and conflicts faced by families as they blend, such as disputes over power, property, and privacy.

will do at least as well as children raised in traditional heterosexual families.

Same-sex marriage is a major issue these days (Biblarz and Stacey 2010; Heaphy 2007b). As late as the 1990s, there was no legal recognition of such marriages *anywhere in the world*. Furthermore, such marriages face considerable hostility and intolerance. A key event occurred in September 2000 in the Netherlands when the right to marry was extended to same-sex couples. In the ensuing decade a number of other countries throughout the world (Canada, Belgium, Norway, Sweden, Spain, and South Africa, as well as Mexico City) came to permit same-sex marriages. In recent years a number of states in the United States have legalised same-sex marriages (Connecticut, Iowa, Maine, Maryland, Massachusetts, New Hampshire, New York, Rhode Island, Vermont, and Washington, as well as the District of Columbia). The polar views on same-sex marriage are that, on the one hand, it is seen as an expression of greater tolerance in the population as a whole, while on the other hand, it is viewed by some as yet another threat to religion, morality, and heterosexual marriage.

Same-sex couples are more likely today than ever before to become parents.

There is considerable ambivalence in the gay and lesbian community about legal marriage. Some welcome the validation it offers. They also appreciate gaining the same legal rights and benefits as those of straight married couples in terms of child support, medical decision making, and inheritance. Many gays and lesbians also welcome legal marriage because of the challenge it poses to the dominance of heterosexual norms and values. Others see marriage as surrender to *heteronormativity*, or the view that heterosexuality is the normal sexual orientation, and as a threat to the distinctive character of gay and lesbian culture and ways of life. Gays and lesbians are seen as submitting to outmoded notions of commitment and to rules that can stifle their uniqueness and creativity, especially as they affect relationships. As a result of this ambivalence, while many gays and lesbians feel that they ought to have the right to marry, only a few would actually marry if they had the opportunity (Considine 2012). They are likely to see their current relationships as offering greater possibilities for freedom, creativity, and equality than marital relationships.

Couples Living Apart Together

Couples living apart together (LAT) involve both heterosexuals and homosexuals, who define themselves as couples without the necessity of living together (Holmes 2007). They have separate residences within the same geographic area and are, in that sense, different from commuter marriages where there is a second home or one partner is frequently away on business trips. In both LATs and commuter marriages, however, the partners, especially the women, have at least some measure of independence that may not have been possible in the past. Because of their greater financial independence, men have long possessed the ability to live apart, but in recent years, more women have achieved the economic independence that permits them to live apart, if they wish.

Overall, LAT indicates that there is an increasing understanding that living together, or even being in close proximity, is not necessary to intimate relationships. Some have come to the view that such more distant relationships can be liberating and exhilarating, while it should be borne in mind that the travel involved, and the periodic isolation, can have a variety of negative effects. LAT is clearly related to increased individualisation, where more people realise that they can live alone, and successfully, rather than assuming that they must live with someone else. However, not everyone has equal access to LAT since it requires, for example, greater economic resources and more flexibility at work. These are advantages members of the majority group and those individuals of a higher social class are more likely to have than those in various minority groups (for example, ancestral, ethnic, and racial minorities) or in a lower social class. The future growth of LAT depends on various social changes, such as the expansion of national and even global labour markets and the development of better and cheaper means of transportation. The continuing growth of women's participation in LAT depends on the continuation of progress toward greater gender equality so that the remaining barriers to their involvement in such living arrangements are further reduced or eliminated.

THEORISING THE FAMILY

Whatever the family form, the main types of theory outlined in Chapter 2 and used throughout this book—the structural/functional, conflict/critical, and inter/actionist theories—can be utilised to think about, and shed light on, the family (Cheal 2007).

STRUCTURAL/FUNCTIONAL THEORY

Writing in the mid-twentieth century in the heyday of marriage, the nuclear family, and the family household, Talcott Parsons, the preeminent structural-functionalist, saw the family as a structure with very important functions for society as a whole. The nuclear family was especially important in the America of Parsons's day. Its structure freed family members from the obligations of an **extended family**—two or more generations of a family living in the same household or in close proximity to one another—and allowed them the mobility needed in the industrial society of the time. Parsons also argued that the family system of the day functioned efficiently and effectively because of the clear distinction between "expressive (female) and instrumental (male)" roles (Kimmel 2011:147).

Of greatest concern to Parsons, and to structural-functionalism, was the need for order in society. A very important source of that order is the socialisation of children into how they are supposed to act as well as the process by which they learn the norms, values, and morality of society. That which was communicated during childhood socialisation tends to be internalised by children and becomes part of what is generally called their "conscience" (Parsons 1951). The personality in general, and the conscience in particular, is shaped during childhood socialisation and remains relatively stable throughout the life course. The family, especially in the heyday of the nuclear family, played a crucial role in socialisation. Furthermore, such a family was more likely to communicate a more coherent sense of a society's culture and morality than any other family form.

However, the socialisation that occurs in childhood can become dated over time as the child matures into adulthood. In addition, people experience different situations as they mature, with the result that there is constant need for socialisation throughout the life cycle, including adult socialisation, socialisation for old age, and even socialisation in preparation for death. Nevertheless, the norms and values learned in childhood tend to remain in place and remain a potent force throughout the life span, usually requiring modest reinforcement. Parsons certainly did not see the family as devoid of problems or the process of socialisation as seamless, but he did not emphasise the problems associated with either. Rather, as the name of his theoretical approach suggests, he saw the family and socialisation as functional for society.

This kind of thinking has been picked up by those sociologists who emphasise the functions of the family:

- First, society must at least replace those who die. This is accomplished through childbearing, which has traditionally been preferred to occur within the family.
- Second, the family fulfills the need to provide physical and emotional care to children.
- Third, the family fulfills the socialisation function discussed above.
- Fourth, the family shares resources in order to meet its economic needs.
- Fifth, there is intergenerational support as parents continue to support their adult children economically, emotionally, and in many other ways.
- Sixth, the family has traditionally served to control sexual behaviour. That control varies greatly from one society to another; in Canadian society, whatever control the family had over sexuality seems to be in decline.
- Finally, the family is a mechanism for helping children find a place in society, especially in its stratification system.

There are many criticisms of the structural/functional theory of marriage and the family, not the least of which is that it is applied best to the realities of the 1950s but is increasingly out of touch with today's realities. It simply "doesn't take into account the diversity of family structures and roles found in . . . marriages and families" (B. Scott and Schwartz 2008:349). Moreover, structural/functional theory has a conservative bias that "tends to promote and rationalize the status quo," including of marriage and the nuclear family. Furthermore, it tends to "understate disharmony and conflict," and more generally the array of family-related problems to be discussed below (B. Scott and Schwartz 2008:349).

CONFLICT/CRITICAL THEORY

Unlike structural-functionalists, conflict theorists never saw the family as a coherent unit or as contributing in an unambiguously positive way to the larger society. For one thing—as pointed out above and as we will discuss later in this chapter—the family itself is riddled with stresses, strains, and conflicts that lead to all sorts of problems for the family, its members, and society as a whole. The family is an especially rich arena for conflicts based on gender and age (for example, sibling rivalries, or children versus parents). Such conflicts are closely related to the issue of power within the family and conflict over who has the most power, how it is used (and abused), how it is exercised, and so forth. Above all, conflict can arise when one or more family members seek to wrest power from those who possess it.

In contrast to Talcott Parsons's harmonious view of the family, Randall Collins (1975) looks at conflict within the broader system of social stratification, as well as within formal organisations and the family. Collins sees the family as an arena of gender conflict in which males have historically been the winners, leaving female family members in an inferior position. Similarly, when it comes to age-based conflict within the family, parents are generally victorious and children relatively powerless.

A key issue in looking at inequality and conflict within the family is the resources possessed by the various parties involved. In terms of the conflict between adults and children, parents have a variety of resources including greater size, strength, experience, and ability to satisfy the needs of the young, and as a result the young are likely to be dominated by the adults. Among the few resources possessed by the young are their physical attractiveness and physical prowess. As a result, "girls are taught to capitalize on good looks, cuteness, and coyness [and] boys discover that athletic ability and performance are what

count for males" (Kimmel 2011:157). However, as children mature, they acquire other resources and are better able to resist adults. The result is more conflict between the generations as children mature.

Feminist Theory

Feminist theory tends to adopt a conflict view of the relationship between genders in general and, more specifically, as that relationship exists within the family (Siltanen and Doucet 2008). Feminist theorists see the family as being internally stratified on the basis of gender. Men and women are seen as possessing different economic and social positions and interests, and they struggle over those differences. Males have been able to create and to impose a gendered division of labour within the family that benefits men and adversely affects women. The family is seen as a patriarchal structure in which males exercise power and oppress women. Male control is enhanced by an ideological mechanism whereby traditional family norms are upheld. For example, girls tend to learn to accept the idea that they should put family responsibilities ahead of everything else, including their personal development and satisfaction. This tends to engender and support masculine power and privilege. Some consequences of masculine privilege and power include "expecting or taking for granted personal and sexual services, making and/or vetoing important family decisions, controlling money and expenditures, and so forth" (Shaw and Lee 2009:387). According to the staunch feminist Emma Goldman, "the institution of marriage makes a parasite of woman, an absolute dependent" (Shaw and Lee 2009:298). By buying into the ideology of masculine power and privilege, women are, in effect, supporting and enabling their own oppression. This ideology is seen as a major impediment to the liberation of women in the family and elsewhere in society. Overall, it could be argued that from a feminist perspective, the family is a concept and a structure created and disseminated by males in order to serve their own interests and not those of females. Yet it is important to note that "the balance of power in marriage (or any domestic partnership) depends in part on how couples negotiate paid labour and family work in their relationships" (Shaw and Lee 2009:388).

Conflict theorists maintain that the family is an especially rich arena for conflict—such as that based on age. Conflicts between parents and their children are closely related to the issue of power within the family. Who has the most power, how it is used (and abused), and how it is exercised are common points of generational conflict.

INTER/ACTIONIST THEORY

The inter/actionist theory discussed in this section, exchange theory, looks at the family from a more microscopic perspective than either structural/functional or conflict/critical theories.

Exchange Theory

Exchange theorists look at the family from the perspective of choices made on the basis of rewards and costs. People enter marital relationships because they think the rewards associated with marriage will outweigh the costs. They also tend to think marriage will be more rewarding than the alternatives to it, remaining single or becoming involved in other kinds of intimate relationships. Heterosexual marriage benefits men and women; however, men generally benefit the most. "All psychological measures of indices of happiness and depression suggest that married men are much happier than unmarried men . . . husbands report being more satisfied than wives with their marriages; husbands live longer and enjoy better health benefits than unmarried men" (Kimmel 2011:153). However, both married men and women live longer with fewer health problems, have more sex, save more money, and have fewer psychological problems such as depression than unmarried men and women.

A marriage is likely to break down when the reward-cost calculation leads the partners involved to see the marriage as no longer profitable or to realise that other alternatives are more profitable. From this perspective, a marriage is likely to break down for two reasons. First, it will collapse if the individuals involved come to the conclusion that their marriage is not as profitable to one or both partners as other marriages with which they are familiar. In other words, they come to feel deprived relative to these other married couples. Second, a marriage is likely to break down if the partners come to believe that greater rewards or lower costs are to be found in alternatives, such as becoming single again, marrying someone else, or becoming involved in some other type of intimate relationship such as cohabitation. In the latter case, the rewards of a different partner might be offset by costs, such as the effect such a change will have on any children involved.

PROBLEMS IN THE FAMILY

There is a wide variety of family troubles, but we will focus on a few of the major ones in this section. The five basic models of family conflict (Kellerhals 2007) include the "deficit" model, the "overload" model, the "cultural tensions" model, the "conflict of interest" model, and the "anomie" model.

FAMILY CONFLICT

Conflict is endemic to family life, with numerous flash points between husband, wife, and children in a traditional nuclear family, and innumerable other possibilities for conflict in the wide array of other forms of intimate relationships. While divorce is usually seen as the major result of family conflict, conflict often exists long before a divorce, and it may not even lead to divorce. Much conflict simmers below the surface in many families, surfacing only now and then. Family conflicts may arise over such things as the family's objectives, resources, or the need to protect the interests of various family members.

Many feminist theorists believe that men have been able to create and impose a gendered division of labour within the family. This position seems to be supported by the inescapability of traditional gender roles in many parts of the world. Here, a Jordanian Bedouin woman is relegated to the role of caretaker in her house located in a small village near As Safi, Jordan.

The "Deficit" Model

The "deficit" model contends that deficits in the socialisation of family members contribute to family conflicts. Poor socialisation can be attributed to parents getting married at too young an age and therefore not having progressed through enough of the socialisation process themselves to do a good job of socialising their children. Other deficits in socialisation that contribute to family conflict are growing up in an unstable, conflict-laden, poverty-stricken, or economically insecure family where opportunities for proper socialisation and learning how to relate to others are limited. Inadequate education can adversely affect the ability to socialise children, as well as to communicate and negotiate within the family structure. Another deficit is a lack of ties with kin, or the larger social structure. Such linkages can help prevent conflict within the family.

The "Overload" Model

The "overload" model is traceable to the work of Philipe Aries (1978), in which it is argued that because the public sphere has declined, the private sphere, including the family, has had to take up

the slack, thereby overloading it with responsibilities. With the state and other aspects of the public sphere doing less, and likely to do even less in light of the Great Recession, the family has had to compensate by meeting more and more of the needs of family members, such as providing money to aged, retired family members. An overburdened family is likely to be subject to much more conflict stemming from so many expectations as well as from an inability to satisfy many of them.

The "Cultural Tensions" Model

The "cultural tensions" model focuses on strains traceable to the existence of family commitments and responsibilities on the one hand and the increasing emphasis in society on the self and individualisation on the other hand (Beck and Beck-Gernsheim 2002). Individuals are seen as torn between these two phenomena, and the inability to do both can lead to conflict in the family. This is especially the case when family members focus too much on themselves and downplay or ignore family responsibilities.

The "Conflict of Interest" Model

The "conflict of interest" model involves the tension between the increasing equality in the family and the structural inequalities that exist in society as a whole, especially in employment. Thus, while many now believe that there should be equality within the family, structural realities mean that women who work are likely, as we have seen, to continue to handle an inordinate amount of responsibility at home as well. The injustice felt by many can lead to heightened conflict in the family.

The "Anomie" Model

According to the "anomie" model, conflict stems from the fact that contemporary families are left to their own devices in negotiating and organising their relationship (see Chapter 2). This stands in contrast to the past, where extended families and larger social groups, as well as broader norms and values, were of much more help in organising family relationships. Among the difficult things that need to be worked out within the family are defining its priorities, the division of work and labour both inside and outside the family, defining what is private and what is not, sharing economic and material resources, and how much contact there is to be outside the family and how intensive those contacts are to be. All of these can, and often do, become areas over which family members conflict.

ABUSE AND VIOLENCE WITHIN THE FAMILY

Heightened conflict within the family can lead to abuse and violence. This can take various forms, but the most common are parental abuse of children, and husbands who use violence against their wives, considered "battered women" (Dunn 2005). Far less common is women abusing and behaving in a violent manner toward their children and even their husbands. Violence within the family can take emotional or psychological forms. It can also involve physical and sexual abuse (Carmody 2007). Although norms that relate to the acceptability of such behaviour have changed in recent years, such abuse and violence are still common and accepted in some groups and parts of the world. In such cases, parents feel justified in abusing children, and husbands think it is acceptable to batter their wives. While there are some exceptions, we should remember that the vast majority of those who engage in such behaviour are not considered deranged (Straus 1980).

Child Abuse

Hundreds of millions of children throughout the world are abused, as well as maltreated and exploited (S. Bell 2011). According to the World Health Organization, "child abuse or maltreatment constitutes all forms of physical and/or emotional ill-treatment, sexual abuse, neglect, or negligent treatment or commercial or other exploitation, resulting in actual or potential harm to the child's health, survival, development, or dignity in the context of a relationship of responsibility, trust, or power" (cited in Polonko 2007:448). In the United States alone, official reports indicate that several million children (15 percent) have been severely maltreated, but this number deals only with official reports, and the actual number is much higher. Furthermore, it includes only those who have been the victims of severe abuse and who clearly have been injured. The most common forms of child abuse are parents hitting their child with an object (20 percent); kicking, biting, or hitting their child with their fists (10 percent); and physically beating up the child (5 percent) (Kimmel 2011). Fathers or father surrogates are most likely to commit these offences. While the absolute numbers are lower in Canada, the patterns are similar (Public Health Agency of Canada 2010).

The impact of child abuse is great, especially for the children involved, but also for the parents (or adults) and the larger society. Physical and emotional abuse and violence toward children can lead to an increased likelihood of cognitive impairment (lower IQ and levels of educational attainment), impaired ability to reason morally (a weakly developed conscience), and a greater likelihood of engaging in violence and crime. Such children are themselves more likely to be violent toward other children, including siblings, and later in life to abuse their own children, their spouse, and even elderly parents.

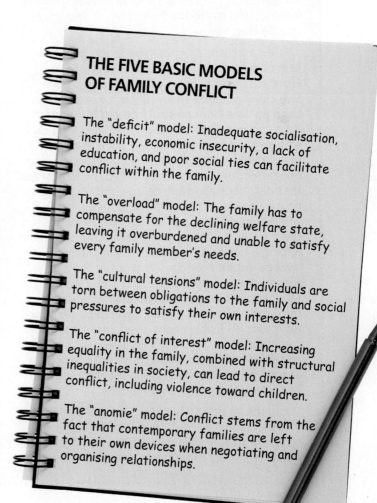

THE FIVE BASIC MODELS OF FAMILY CONFLICT

The "deficit" model: Inadequate socialisation, instability, economic insecurity, a lack of education, and poor social ties can facilitate conflict within the family.

The "overload" model: The family has to compensate for the declining welfare state, leaving it overburdened and unable to satisfy every family member's needs.

The "cultural tensions" model: Individuals are torn between obligations to the family and social pressures to satisfy their own interests.

The "conflict of interest" model: Increasing equality in the family, combined with structural inequalities in society, can lead to direct conflict, including violence toward children.

The "anomie" model: Conflict stems from the fact that contemporary families are left to their own devices when negotiating and organising relationships.

DIGITAL LIVING

The Family and the Internet

There is great concern that the Internet, as well as the technologies needed to access it, such as the computer, the iPhone, the iPad, and the like, has radically altered many things, including family life. This is far from the first time there have been worries about the impact of technology on the family. Previous alarms were sounded over the effect of the telephone, the automobile, and the television, among others. The impact of these technologies was great, although it was often the case that the concerns were overblown. Furthermore, the impact varied from family to family, and was especially affected by the social class of the family. However, the impact of the newer technologies seems greater and more pervasive. For example, today people consume 12 hours of media a day at home on average compared to 5 hours a day in 1960. In the remainder of this box we look at the impact of the Internet and related technologies on one upper-middle-class family.

Mr. and Mrs. Campbell live in a rented four-bedroom home in an affluent suburb of San Francisco (Richtel 2010a). The Campbells have two children, aged 16 and 8. Mr. Campbell has been involved in successful Internet businesses since the mid-1990s. He is currently working on a software venture—he recently completed a $1.3 million deal—and he is deeply enmeshed in, and dependent on, the Internet. In fact, he almost lost that deal because in the deluge of daily e-mails he overlooked a crucial message for almost two weeks. Operating from home, he works with three computer screens simultaneously (sometimes adding a laptop and an iPad). One screen has tweets, instant messages, and group chats; the second displays computer codes and is where Mr. Campbell Skypes with colleagues; and the third has a calendar, e-mail, a web browser, and his music. His involvement, even obsession, with computer technology (he falls asleep with either a laptop or an iPhone on his chest and goes online as soon as he opens his eyes in the morning) has had a negative effect on his family.

In the morning while Mrs. Campbell is making breakfast, she watches the news in the corner of a computer screen while her husband uses the rest of the screen to catch up on his e-mail. When things are tough emotionally for Mr. Campbell, he deals with it by escaping into video games. When the family goes on vacation, he has a difficult time putting his devices aside and staying away from e-mail and the Internet. Both mother and daughter complain that Mr. Campbell prefers technology to his family. The son's grades recently fell, and blame was placed on the amount of time he devoted to his technologies (he has two computer screens in his bedroom as well as his iPhone).

Although she spends a lot of time on the Internet texting, on Facebook, and checking her own e-mail 25 times a day, Mrs. Campbell would love to see her husband spend less time with his technologies and more time with his family. However, she knows that he gets "crotchety" if he does not get his technology "fix." She understands that technology is a big part of Mr. Campbell's and her son's lives and identities. In loving them, she feels she must accept the role that technology plays in their lives. Her understanding and acceptance, however, does not contradict the fact that these technologies and the Internet have contributed to the innumerable stresses and conflicts in the family life of the Campbells and in the lives of many other families.

The impact of smartphones, tablets, and other new technologies seems greater and more pervasive than that of technologies from eras past. Some concerned parents worry that an increasing reliance on Internet-enabled devices has led to a decline in meaningful communication, familial engagement, and educational proficiency.

There is often a cycle of violence and abuse toward children that stretches across several generations (S. Steinmetz 1987). Many of the parents who mistreat and abuse their children were themselves victims as children and, as a result, may have developed mental and substance abuse problems that can increase the likelihood of maltreatment (Public Health Agency of Canada 2010).

There is also a cost to society. These costs are traceable to such things as social services provided to families, the lesser contributions of victims to society, and related criminal justice and health care activities. While there are things that can be done to deal with adults involved in terms of intervention and prevention, the structure of society as a whole needs to be addressed in various ways. Of greatest importance is the need to change a culture where children are viewed as property that parents and other adults can treat, and abuse, in any way they want. Children also need to be seen as having human rights. In addition, children need to be better protected, helped, and treated by the various agencies involved. More generally, society and the government need to believe in and support a wide range of policies that are of benefit to children, such as more and better child care.

Domestic Violence

Domestic violence entails the exertion of power over a partner in an intimate relationship that involves behaviour that is intimidating, threatening, harassing, or harmful (Carmody 2007). The spouse can be harmed physically, as well as sexually, emotionally, and psychologically; the violence can occur multiple times (Goodlin and Dunn 2011). A debate in this area is whether the concept of domestic violence should be restricted to physical violence, or whether abuse in all of these areas qualifies as domestic violence.

A great deal of research has been done on family violence, and several general conclusions can be drawn from this work (U.S. Department of Justice 2012):

- The majority of spousal abuse victims are women, accounting for at least four of every five victims.
- When physically or sexually assaulted, children and adolescents are most often the victims of someone they know.

In December 2011, seven months after her arranged marriage to a 30-year-old man, 15-year-old Sahar Gul was admitted to a Kabul, Afghanistan, hospital malnourished and with severe injuries. According to Afghani officials, Gul's in-laws locked her in a basement bathroom, tortured her with cigarettes and hot irons, ripped out her hair and fingernails, and broke her fingers—all in an attempt to force her into prostitution. The impact of such abuse is great not just on the people involved but on the society at large; Gul's story galvanised a new call for women's rights in Afghanistan.

- One of the leading causes of injury to women is partner abuse.
- Aboriginal people are three times more likely than non-Aboriginal people to be spousal abuse victims.
- Among spousal abuse victims, about one third report that children saw or heard the violence.
- It is difficult to leave a violent relationship, and the risk of serious, even fatal, injury is greatest when one does try to leave such a relationship.
- Domestic violence is a major cause of homelessness.
- Women are more likely than men to die due to spousal homicide.

Because gender socialisation often leads men to see violence as an appropriate means of communication, it follows that most abusers tend to be male. In addition to imposing great costs on victims and their families, domestic violence is costly to society. Those abused are not likely to be able to function as well in the larger society as those who are not victimised. For example, the abused have higher levels

PUBLIC SOCIOLOGY

Andrew Cherlin on Public Sociology, in His Own Words

I have written for, and spoken to, the print and electronic media about family and demographic issues since I took a job as an assistant professor of sociology at Johns Hopkins University in the late 1970s. To do so I had to *unlearn* the lifeless writing style and jargon-filled speech that sociologists unfortunately learn in graduate school. (Not that sociology stands out in this regard. Just try to read the convoluted cultural criticism that your postmodernist English professor writes these days.) In their place, I had to learn new writing and speaking skills.

To write op-ed pieces for newspapers (so-called because they usually appear on a page that is opposite the editorial page), I had to learn how to (1) engage the reader's interest, (2) make a single point, and (3) present my interpretation, all in about 700 words. I also had to be willing to accept failure. During my career, I have submitted more than 20 op-ed pieces to the *New York Times*, and the editors have accepted 9 of them. That's actually a good batting average. If you can't tolerate being rejected more than you are accepted, you won't publish many op-eds.

My early newspaper and magazine pieces led to telephone calls from reporters who wanted a quote from an academic expert for a story they were writing. Here I had to develop another skill: how to say something that helps the reader understand the topic in 25 words or less. It's harder than you might think to get to the heart of an issue in a sentence or two.

I have found that print (and now online) reporters can usually be trusted to put my remarks in the proper context. Many reporters cover family and demographic issues day after day, and they become quite knowledgeable. Interviewers whose work is heard on National Public Radio are also quite good. Television, however, is another story. Typically, a harried producer who rarely covers the family will be given an assignment at 10:00 a.m., call me at 10:30, send a crew to film me by 2:00, and then splice five or ten seconds of my remarks into a piece that will run on the evening news at 6:30. Sometimes the producer will include nothing if the piece has to be shortened at the last minute. I often feel used and discarded by television, in contrast to my generally positive experiences with print, online, and radio media.

Overall, though, my work with the media has served me well. It has allowed me to place my ideas before a broad audience. It has also expanded the reach of my academic work because I have tried to apply the same principles of clear exposition and jargon-free (well, not quite free) prose to my scholarly books and articles.

If you would like to get your ideas to a general audience, how might you start? I would suggest submitting short pieces to your local newspaper, where competition is less keen, or to the many websites that now post social commentary. In an age of social media and search engines, an article in your hometown newspaper or in a specialised blog can get surprising visibility on the Internet and can lead to opportunities to further expand your audience. And if you are serious, get a copy of a good guide to nonfiction writing, such as William Zinsser's *On Writing Well* or William Strunk and E. B. White's *The Elements of Style*. Good writing is essential to becoming a public sociologist.

SOURCE: Printed with the permission of Andrew Cherlin.

of absenteeism from work. Furthermore, society often needs to pay the costs associated with medical treatment, police involvement, court expenses, and shelters for those who have been victimised.

Elder Abuse

The elderly do not escape abuse merely because of their advanced age. This is certainly an ancient problem, although it has come to wide-scale public attention only in the last half-century. In a recent year Canada police reported nearly 7,900 seniors were the victims of violent crimes (Statistics Canada 2011c). The elderly are abused in various ways, including physically, psychologically, financially, sexually, and through neglect. Among other things, we know that elderly men are more likely to be abused than women and adult children and spouses are most likely to perpetrate the abuse. Beyond the elder abuse committed by family members, there is the fact that such abuse takes place in residential care facilities for the elderly.

POVERTY AND THE FAMILY

There is a close relationship between family structure and poverty (Lichter 2007). For example, 10.6 percent of Canadian children living in married-couple families lived in poverty, but for female-headed families it was almost four times as much (37.9 percent) (see Figure 11.8). The likelihood of poverty for female-headed families is much less in Canada than in the United States largely because of more generous social support programmes. This concentration of poverty among female-headed households tends largely to reflect consequences of gender inequality.

The big debate here is not over the facts but over whether the family structure causes poverty or poverty causes problems within the family. On the one hand, the argument is made that a weak family structure, one for example where women are left alone to raise children, causes poverty. Such women are apt to be poor because they are unlikely to be able to work outside the home, and the children are poor because they are not adequately supported by these women or their absent fathers. On the other hand, it is contended that poverty causes families to crumble. Women are left alone to raise children as the men leave because they cannot support them or because the mothers are more likely to qualify for welfare if the father is absent. The emotional and economic stresses associated with being poor are likely to put intolerable strains on the family.

Being unmarried is likely to be associated with poverty for women with children. Divorce is also likely to drive women, especially those who are already in a marginal economic situation, into poverty. More generally, divorce is likely to affect almost all women adversely. The only debate in this area is how badly women will be affected and how much they will be hurt economically, as well as in other ways.

Former National Hockey League star, Theo Fleury, stands in front of the child abuse monument as he prepares to begin the "Victor Walk," a trek in May of 2013 from Toronto to Parliament Hill to raise awareness of child sexual abuse and encourage harsher sentences for convicted pedophiles.

THE FAMILY, CONSUMPTION, AND THE RECENT RECESSION

The recent recession caused many changes in Canadian society and throughout the world. The

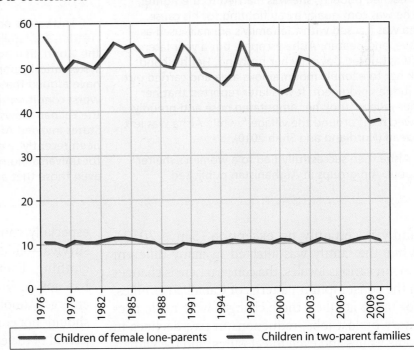

FIGURE 11.8 Percentage of Children Living Below Poverty Line by Family Type in Canada, 1976–2010

SOURCE: Authors' calculations, Statistics Canada, CANISM Table 202-0802.

NOTE: Poverty is measured as family incomes that are less than one half of the adjusted household median income (with adjustments for family size).

GL🌐BALISATION

"Losing One's Nose" Among the Taliban in Afghanistan

Among the Taliban of Afghanistan, the phrase "losing one's nose" has two different, but intimately related, meanings. For males, it means that they have been humiliated or embarrassed by their wives. In Taliban culture, men are said to have lost their nose; in Canada the males might be said to have lost some other, more intimate, body part. In other words, they have been emasculated by their wives. For a female in Taliban culture, losing one's nose has a much more dramatic meaning—a woman can literally have her nose and other body parts cut off for humiliating her husband. An instance of this attracted great public attention in 2010 because *Time* magazine put the picture of such a woman, 18-year-old Aisha, on its cover.

Aisha's crime? She had run away from home because, she claimed, her in-laws were beating and abusing her. For that a Taliban judge decreed that her nose and both ears be cut off.

At 12 years of age, in a custom known as *baad*, Aisha and her sister had been given to the family of a Taliban fighter as compensation for the fact that her uncle had killed a relative of that fighter. When she reached puberty, she was married to the fighter, but he was continually away fighting for his cause. Aisha was housed with the family's animals, used as a slave, and beaten. Aisha escaped, but a year later she was hunted down by her husband. Her husband took her to a lonely mountainous area and carried out the judge's judgment. It was later reported that her father-in-law "took her amputated nose and proudly showed it off around the village," while Aisha was left for dead (Nordland and Shah 2010).

Aisha then successfully fled to a women's shelter in Kabul. Aid groups in Afghanistan publicised the event when she was safe, and in this case, the international community quickly responded. The U.S. embassy in Kabul facilitated her transportation to the United States, and thanks to the charity of a hospital in southern California, Aisha received reconstructive surgery. Before surgery, Aisha was given a prosthetic nose while undergoing treatment for emotional problems that she experienced because of her mutilation.

Under normal circumstances, receiving medical treatment would be as much as Aisha could have hoped for—the Afghan government rarely intervenes in local legal affairs. But in this case, her father-in-law eventually appeared in an urban center, where he was arrested by police. Local authorities argued there is no provision in the law that requires a runaway child bride's nose be cut off. Instead, they contended, "this is against Afghan-ism . . . against every principle in the world, against humanity" (Nordland and Shah 2010). Because Aisha has chosen to remain in the United States where her safety can be guaranteed and she has opted not to return to Afghanistan to testify, punishment against the other offenders will be difficult.

This case is one example of how laws and customs for family practices vary significantly around the world. In many of these cases, women are systematically oppressed, but human rights groups have argued that Afghan women face some of the worst conditions in the world. And while many of the Taliban's laws were overturned when the United States invaded Afghanistan in 2001, some laws have been recently reinstated. Despite growing demands for universal human rights, local norms and customs—even those that are damaging—can remain strong.

family is certainly no exception (Sauvé 2012). While the family was affected in many different ways in various locales, the concern here is changes in the consumption patterns of Canadian families. For many families, these changes were made necessary by lost jobs, reductions in pay, declines in home values and even foreclosures, and the withering of investment accounts, retirement funds, and college savings plans.

Clearly, many families have had less, sometimes a lot less, to spend on consumption of all kinds, especially consumption of what is not needed for survival—items besides food, shelter, and (some) clothing. Even if the family's economic position has not declined markedly, a perception has still emerged among many that they could, or at least should, not consume the way they had in the boom period of the early twenty-first century. Many families have responded not only by consuming less but also by reducing their level of debt and by saving more—the savings rate in Canada has declined in the recent decade and now is near all-time lows (see Figure 11.9). At the same time, family debt has

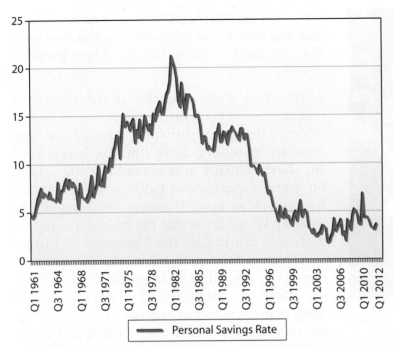

FIGURE 11.9 Personal Savings Rate (in %) in Canada, 1961–2012 (by Quarter)

SOURCE: Calculations by authors from Statistics Canada, CANISM Table 380-0004.

increased, as we saw in Chapter 1, so in 2012 for every dollar of after-tax disposable income a family had, the family owed on average about $1.65.

Prior to the recession in 2008–2009, those who could afford it often engaged in "conspicuous consumption" (Veblen [1899] 1994). When they could, they purchased showy and expensive houses, cars, clothes, and more. Such purchases often cost more than they could really afford. However, they felt good about such purchases and were interested in showing them off whenever possible. Now, however, even those who can still afford such things are less anxious to display them publicly. They are aware that many around them are going through hard times, and they do not want to make these people feel even worse than they do about their diminished economic position.

Some families are not only buying less but also concentrating more on engaging in family activities, especially those that cost little or nothing (Cave 2010). Activities such as watching television together (or alone), reading, socialising with friends or family, and going to museums are more in vogue in these more difficult economic times. In addition, family members are more willing to discuss their reduced circumstances and changed patterns of consumption among themselves as well as with those in other families. While such topics may have been a source of embarrassment at one time, the realisation that many families are in the same situation has made it easier to discuss them publicly. For example, it is easier for many to tell their children that the family needs to eat out far less often and to tell friends that they cannot afford to go out to dinner. Families are also willing to discuss more openly their financial straits and even to share stories about the bad economic decisions they might have made in the past (Tugend 2010).

Some families are even more willing to reevaluate the whole idea of the consumer culture in which they were so immersed before the recession. There is even a questioning of what Juliet Schor (1998) called the "work-and-spend" syndrome that many had embraced. That is, families are wondering whether one or both partners have to work as long and as hard as they did in the past just to be able to consume more—to buy more expensive goods, services, and experiences. Some families are even coming to accept the ideas of the "voluntary simplicity" movement (Elgin 2010) by

Fashion model, Nora Lokuruka, shops at a variety of thrift stores because she is unable to afford the fancy clothes she wears in her modeling career. Thrift stores play a vital role for people living in poverty.

Youth unemployment is high in most countries of the world as aging populations postpone retirement due to the recent world recession. Here a young job seeker speaks with representatives from the McMaster University Continuing Education program at an April 2013 Jobs Fair in Hamilton, Ontario.

downsising their homes, getting rid of all sorts of things they may have never needed in the first place, and in the end living a simpler, far less expensive lifestyle. Many are coming to realise that "the acquisition of material goods doesn't bring happiness" (S. Rosenbloom 2010).

Of course, there are great differences among and within families on this. Some may embrace this new attitude toward consumption, and others, especially children, may not. This could, of course, lead to tension within the family.

Reductions in family consumption can also lead to other problems. For example, were such reductions to continue and to grow, many corporations would be devastated and even go out of business. This would serve to worsen the economic prospects. For another, tax revenue would decline, and that would likely worsen the economic situation. On the other hand, reduced consumption can help mitigate the negative environmental effects associated with the production and consumption of those goods.

GENDER INEQUALITIES

Intimate relationships, especially marriages, are unequal as far as the men and women involved

are concerned. Marriages from the point of view of men and women can be so different that they seem like completely different systems. These inequalities take several forms (Shehan and Cody 2007).

The first is the inequality in the amount of time devoted to household tasks. Although there is evidence that gap is shrinking, especially because men are spending more time on housework (K. Marshall 2010), at least until recently women on average spent about twice as much time on housework as men. However, as discussed in Chapter 10, we know that the intersection of race and class can impact the likelihood of further involvement by men in housework. In addition, men spend more time on tasks that are discretionary, at least to some degree, while women are more likely to perform regular, repetitive labour. Mothers are more likely to look after feeding and clothing the children, while fathers are more likely to engage in recreational activities with the children. The disparity is even greater when it comes to the care of the ill and the elderly; this is almost always the near-total responsibility of females.

Then there are various gender inequalities in power and decision making. As in sociology in general, power here is defined as the ability to impose one's will on others despite their

In the wake of the recent world economic recession, families are turning away from activities that entail conspicuous consumption and toward activities that cost little or nothing. Here, a family has a picnic on the lawn near Bara Gumbad, a fifteenth-century tomb located in New Delhi, India.

At least a dozen women are admitted to the burn department of Afghanistan's Herat Hospital every week; a growing number of women are setting themselves alight to protest domestic violence in Afghanistan's tradition-bound, male-dominated culture. In the case of 25-year-old Shahima, violence was induced not by her husband, but by her stepfamily: "I was unhappy with my husband's family. There was nothing to make me happy in my life. He was nice to me, but his mother and sisters, with whom we live, punished me all the time."

BIOGRAPHICAL bits

Anne Martin-Matthews (Canadian)

- Martin-Matthews was born and raised in St. John's, Newfoundland.

- She has recently completed two terms (2004–2011) as the scientific director of the Canadian Institute of Aging.

- Under her leadership, the institute led the development of the Canadian Longitudinal Study on Aging (CLSA), a 20-year study of 50,000 Canadians aged 45–85.

- She was social sciences editor for the *Canadian Journal on Aging*, and its editor-in-chief from 1996 to 2000.

- Her publications include two books, *Aging and Caring at the Intersection of Work and Home Life: Blurring the Boundaries* (2008) and *Widowhood in Later Life* (1991).

- She holds a Distinguished Alumnus Award from McMaster University; a Commemorative Medal for the Golden Jubilee of Queen Elizabeth II, awarded by the Canadian Association on Gerontology; and an Honorary Degree in Civil Law from Newcastle University (UK).

- As Canadian society grows older—the average age of Canadians went from 26.2 to 39.9 between 1971 and 2012—sociological research like that undertaken by Martin-Matthews will become ever more significant.

opposition. This can involve forcing a spouse to do something or to define a situation in a particular way. In heterosexual marriages, men are favoured in terms of power within the marital relationship because of their greater size and strength, they are likely to earn more money, and they are likely to dominate conversations, thereby swinging decisions their way. In addition, male power tends to be institutionalised and supported by religions and their customs (especially by Evangelical Christians, Hasidic Jews, Amish, and Mormons) as well as by governments and their policies. The latter often assume that husbands are the household heads and are responsible for the support of wives and children, and that wives are supposed to take care of the household and the children.

Shaw and Lee (2009) would label the aforementioned model of a marriage or domestic partnership as the head-complement model. Women or wives in this model tend to complement the head's role "by being supportive and encouraging in emotional and material ways" (Shaw and Lee 2009:388–89). The "junior partner/senior partner" is another model of marriage or domestic partnership. Within this model, both partners work outside the home, yet one partner's work is considered secondary to that of the senior partner. In addition, this junior partner, typically female, is largely responsible for the home and child care/rearing. In addition, she may likely leave the labour force if the family requires her presence at home. Power is more equitably shared than in the head-complement model because the junior partner provides some financial resources and controls the household. Yet female junior partners experience dual stressors—household job responsibilities as well as their external job responsibilities. Lastly, there is the "equal partners" model. Individuals in this model do not follow the traditional marriage model. Instead, jobs are viewed equally, domestic duties are shared, and, if necessary, partners engage in negotiations concerning who is the primary breadwinner and who is primarily responsible for domestic needs. This last model, although it works to dismantle traditional notions of marriage, is infrequently seen in contemporary marriages.

As we saw above, women are more likely to be the victims of intimate violence than men even though men are more likely to be victimised by violence in general. Globally, in 1993 the United Nations adopted the Declaration on the Elimination of Violence against Women. Within the United Nations, UN Women (previously UNIFEM) is particularly concerned with the violence perpetrated globally against women and girls, especially in the family. There is a strong preference for male children throughout much of the world, with the result that female embryos are more likely to be aborted, female infants are more likely to be the victims of infanticide, and female children are more likely to be the victims of violence.

Globally, wife beating is the most common form of family violence. In some parts of the world, this is taken to extreme lengths, in which wives are beaten to death. Brides may be burned to death because of (supposed) infidelity, or even because the bride's family was unable to pay the dowry in full to the husband. In some parts of the world women are stoned to death for such offences. The movie *The Stoning of Soraya M.* (2008), based on a 1994 novel of the same name, tells the true story of an Iranian woman stoned to death by members of the community, including her father and sons, on the basis of a false accusation by her husband—who wanted another woman—that she had been unfaithful to him. Some cultures support honour killings, or the killing of females because they have engaged in such "dishonourable" behaviours as infidelity, same-sex sexual relations, wanting out of an arranged marriage, seeking a marriage on their own, and even refusing to adhere to the dress code. There has been a good deal of publicity about, and public uproar over, honour killings in places including Pakistan, Egypt, Turkey, and Iran.

DIVORCE

Divorce increased in western nations during the twentieth century. Canadian divorce rates are similar to those in many other western industrial nations, although lower than rates in the United States (see Figures 11.10 and 11.11).

Canadian divorce legislation was modernised in 1968, and that is the year that divorce rates began climbing in Canada. Comparing divorce rates across nations is tricky because these changes in legislation make for dramatic differences, but in many western countries divorce rates are becoming more similar. For example, "between 1971 and 2007, the crude divorce rate increased from 0.73 to 2.8 in Belgium, from 0.88 to 2.0 in the Netherlands, from 1.2 to 2.4 in the United Kingdom, from 0.42 to 1.2 in Greece, and from 0.32 to 0.80 in Italy" (Amato and James 2010:3).

Figure 11.11 shows that Canadian experience now is similar to that of many western European nations. For 2007, the crude divorce rate in Canada (divorces per 1,000 people) was 2.2.

Factors in Divorce

Regardless of how prevalent or rare it is, divorce is the best known way of leaving a marriage (Ambert 2009). Divorce is a formal and legal mechanism that relates to legal marriages. Many marriages end with separations that become permanent without a divorce. Other intimate relationships, even those that last a long time, do not require a divorce; they end as informally as they began.

Divorce is often the result of a litany of family problems, for example violence and abuse, that may have occurred over a long period of time before a divorce is ever contemplated, let alone takes place. Divorce itself can be seen as a problem, as well as one that creates many other problems, but it also can be seen as a solution to many problems. Divorce allows a spouse to get out of a bad, even disastrous, relationship. In fact, to some, it is the relationship, especially a "bad" marriage, that is the problem and not the divorce. Thus, we should not simply assume—as many do—that divorce is in itself a problem.

An important factor in divorce today in Canada, and in the Global North in general, is the increasing emphasis on the self and individualism. This is also linked to the idea of the pure relationship discussed above. As we saw, in such relationships, including marital relationships, the partners do not necessarily feel that they are locked into them for a lifetime,

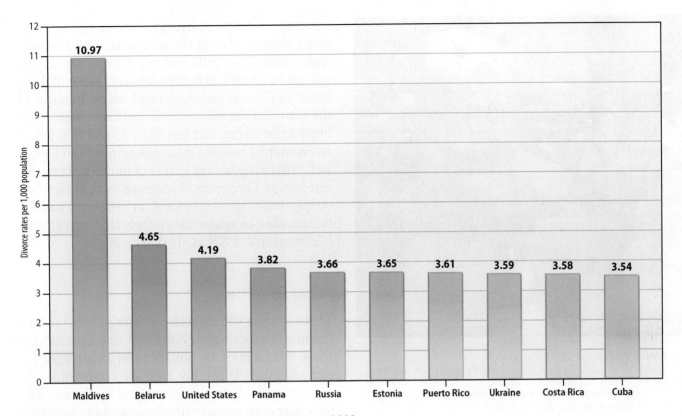

FIGURE 11.10 Countries with the Highest Divorce Rates, 2008

SOURCE: Copyright © 2008–2009, www.mapsofworld.com

or even an extended period of time. Rather, they feel that they are in a relationship as long as it continues to work for *them*. Once individuals come to the conclusion that the relationship is no longer working for them, they are free to leave. Indeed, some take the view that they have an obligation to themselves to leave because they should not jeopardise their own need to have a satisfying life.

In the past, there was a tendency to value positively all marriages that remained intact—that did not end in divorce or in other ways. In many ways, a bad marriage can be a far greater problem than one that ends in divorce. For example, children "in unhappily married families felt the highest levels of neglect and humiliation" (Kimmel 2011:179). As acceptance of divorce has spread, the negative attitudes and social sanctions aimed at those who divorce have declined.

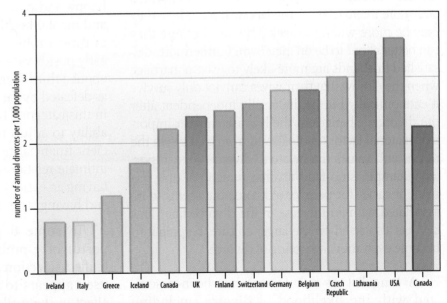

FIGURE 11.11 Crude Divorce Rates for Selected Countries, 2007

SOURCE: Eurostat (2008); Paul R. Amato and Spencer James (2010), "Divorce in Europe and the United States: Commonalities and Differences across Nations," *Family Science* 1(1):2–13; Statistics Canada (2012b).

Carlton the Bear, the official mascot of the Toronto Maple Leafs hockey team, helps Matthew and Andrea Molnar cut their wedding cake. Their first date was to a Leafs game and he proposed before a Leafs game. Their Maple Leaf themed wedding draws another type of linkage between family and consumption.

Not only have negative attitudes, norms, and values as they relate to divorce declined, but so have the material circumstances surrounding divorce. Of prime importance is the fact that women today are likely to be better equipped materially to handle divorce. Among other things, they are better educated and more likely to be in the labour force. Thus, they may be more willing to seek a divorce because they can better afford to be on their own. Furthermore, dissatisfied husbands are more likely to leave a marriage when they know that their wives can not only survive it economically but be financially independent after the divorce. Changes in the law are another important material factor that followed from changes in the norms and values that relate to divorce. One important example is no-fault divorce, which not only has made it easier for people to divorce but seems to be associated with an increase in the divorce rate. This law has also acted on the larger culture, helping it to become even more accepting of divorce.

A long list of risk factors has been associated with the likelihood of divorce, including having relatively little education, marrying as a teenager, whether or not the couple cohabited before marriage, being poor, having divorced parents, infidelity, alcohol or drug abuse, mismanaged finances, and whether domestic violence had occurred. The reasons for divorce in Europe are very similar to those found in Canada and the United States. In terms of the nature of the relationship, marriages were more likely to be stable, and less likely to end in divorce, when couples handled their disagreements and anger well, such as by having a sense of humour about disagreements. Conversely, divorce was more likely when couples were contemptuous of, or belligerent toward, one another, or reacted defensively to disagreements (Gottman et al. 1998; Hetherington 2003).

After Divorce

There is wide variation in the way people react to divorce (Hetherington 2003). At one extreme are those whose lives are enhanced by divorce by, for example, their becoming more successful at work, as parents, in their social lives, and by the fact that they may even remarry (presumably more happily). At the other end of the spectrum various findings indicate that those who divorce are worse off than those who are married, and this is true in many parts of the world (Amato 2000; Mastekaasa 1994). Among other things, they are worse off economically (including women having higher poverty rates), are less well adjusted psychologically, are less likely to be happy, and have more problems related to physical and mental health (Kimmel 2011). However, many of these problems are more likely to occur in the early postdivorce years and to abate over time. While about a third of recently divorced adults can be seen as defeated by the process, only about 10 percent are in this category 10 years after the divorce. A greater ability to adjust to divorce is associated with sufficient financial resources, the development of new intimate relationships, being younger and therefore having an easier time developing such relationships, and having strong social networks.

To some degree, those who are prone to postdivorce problems are more likely to divorce (called selection effect), but the stress of divorce itself appears to play a larger role than selection effect in the well-being, or the lack of well-being, of those who divorce. A major issue is the fate not only of the adults involved in a marriage but also of the children produced by such a marriage who experience a divorce and its aftermath. Most children of divorce function as well as children from intact families; however, it seems clear that many find divorce stressful because of unpleasant experiences during the divorce. Although many twentieth-century experts on child development assumed children of divorce would be at greater risk of developing psychological problems as they grew up (for example, mental health problems and behavioural difficulties), longitudinal studies did not necessarily support this belief. Instead, findings suggested that children's later adjustment depends on the degree and intensity of the conflict between the parents during their marriage, how well the children were parented, the children's relationship with their parents after the divorce, and the family's economic status (Ambert 2009; M. Fine 2007).

Divorce often leads to issues surrounding the custody of a child or children. Issues include where the children will live and with whom, who will handle day-to-day care and the major decisions relating to the children's lives, how much contact the noncustodial parent will have with the children, and finances as they relate to supporting the children, or child support (J. Walker 2007). It is generally considered best for parents to make decisions on these kinds of issues on their own, but these days it often becomes a legal matter involving lawyers and the courts. Historically, fathers were given custody of the children; today, with changes in the roles of women and mothers (including increasing financial independence), this is no longer the case. Mothers are now more likely to get custody of children, and at least some fathers are spending more time with these children. As a result, custody arrangements between mothers and fathers today are much more complex and less clear-cut than they were in the past. One thing that is clear is that children are better off spending time with both parents rather than being in the sole custody of their father or mother.

GLOBAL FAMILIES

Just as the nation-state is eroding in the face of globalisation, it could be argued that the traditional family, deeply embedded in a national context, is also declining. It is no longer necessary that family members live in the same country, have the same passport, be of the same ethnicity, or share a household in a given locale. Characteristics that used to separate people, and make creating global families difficult or impossible, are less important in the global age. National hostilities, religious differences, and even great geographic distances matter less to family formation today than they did in the past (Beck and Beck-Gernsheim 2012).

On the one hand, this clearly makes possible, even highly likely, a wide range of new family types and configurations. For example, it is increasingly possible for family members, even spouses, to live in different countries, even on different continents, and to function quite well (Nobles 2011).

On the other hand, these new realities also create many new possibilities for conflict within the family. That is, family members are now bringing with them to the family new and far broader stresses and strains of various types; clashes of different languages, cultures, religions, and races create all new points of potential conflict and hostility. However, these differences are also likely to enrich the family, as well as the larger society, in various significant ways. As globalisation increases, new hybrid forms of the family will be created, resulting in innovative and interesting differences within and between families. New combinations of, and interactions between, hybrid cultures will result in unforeseen sociological developments, such as wholly new customs and traditions. Another way of putting this is to say that global families are increasingly liquid (Bauman 2000). That is, they no longer—if they ever did—form solid and immutable structures that are impervious to outside, especially global, influences. Families are subject to global flows of all types, and they and their members are increasingly part of those global flows.

While there are great variations in family forms throughout the world, there are also great commonalities. Thus, many of the general ideas discussed throughout this chapter apply globally. It is well beyond the scope of this section to describe similarities and differences in the family throughout the world. There are sociologists engaged in the comparative analysis of families in various societies who spend their entire careers doing just that (W. Goode 1963; Ingoldsby and Smith 2006). Globalisation on the whole is more about global flows and how these flows relate to the family than it is about comparing families across the world (Ritzer 2010c). In this section, then, we will examine at least some of the global flows that involve or affect the family. It is clear that many families are actively involved in global flows of one kind or another and that no family is totally unaffected by those global flows (Karraker 2008; Trask 2010).

GLOBAL FLOWS THAT INVOLVE THE FAMILY

Global flows that involve the family take four major forms. First, entire families, even extended families, can move from one part of the globe to another with relative ease (assuming they have the resources to do so). They can do so on vacation, in relationship to a temporary job change, or permanently.

Second, individual family members can move to a different part of the world and then bring the rest of the family along later. It is ordinarily the case that males are those doing the moving. Once they are secure enough economically in their new location, they are then able to bring over the rest of the family. Of course, it is possible that males make new lives for themselves in the new locale and leave their families behind in their countries of origin. With increasing economic independence, more women are now moving first and then bringing the remainder of their family over (or not). However, many women move globally in low-paying, low-status jobs such as care worker or, by force, in the global sex trade. Such women are unlikely to be in a strong enough economic position to enable other family members to join them.

Third, individuals can immigrate in order to create a new family. For example, there are many marriage bureaus in developed countries that are in the business of bringing together men from those countries with women who are usually from less developed countries. Great differences between such men and women often create enormous problems for the relationship, however. For one, there is great economic disparity between the spouses. For another, the women often come from societies that

are unstable politically and economically, and this makes it difficult to adapt to a more stable environment. Finally, marriage bureaus often portray the women as fitting traditional gender expectations, but when they arrive it may turn out that they do not really measure up to those expectations. Overall, these differences put females in a weak position vis-à-vis the males, and they are therefore more vulnerable to abuse of various kinds.

Fourth, transnational adoptions generally involve the flow of children from less to more developed countries (Marre and Briggs 2009). The United States is the world leader in the adoption of children from other countries, while very few American children are adopted elsewhere. See Global Flow Map 11.1 for international adoptions to Canada. Adopting a child from another part of the world transforms the family in many ways. There are also various problems associated with this, such as the health risks associated with being born, and having spent at least some time, in less developed countries. There are also stresses involved in the differences between the cultures from which the children came and the cultures of the countries to which they have been sent. This is especially a problem if the adopted children are not infants.

While there are great variations in family forms throughout the world, there are also great commonalities. Here, three generations of a Tibetan family walk together along Barkhor Street, a historic pilgrimage site and popular tourist attraction in Lhasa, Tibet.

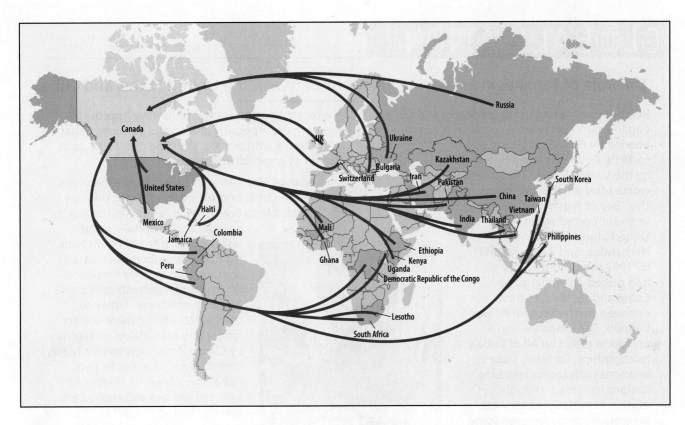

 GLOBAL FLOW MAP 11.1 Major Locales for International Adoptions to Canada, 2010

SOURCE: Citizenship & Immigration Canada, RDM at March 2011, and GCMS on May 31, 2011. Transmitted Oct. 26, 2011.

GLOBAL FLOWS THAT AFFECT THE FAMILY

As a liquid phenomenon in a liquid world, the global family is affected by, and affects, all of the other liquid phenomena that make up the global world. We will examine just a few of them in this section.

Global Migration

The global family is affected by population flows of various kinds. Of utmost importance is the high rate of global migration, both legal and illegal (see Chapter 14). Among other things, this means that very different people from very different parts of the world are coming together in greater numbers than ever before. Some will settle and marry in diasporic communities composed of people like them; many others will not. Those who do not are likely to create families with mates who are very different from themselves in place of origin, race, ethnicity, religion, and the like (Qian and Lichter 2011). As

you recently learned, those entering hybrid families are likely to encounter various difficulties and hostilities. Such problems are likely to be greatest for undocumented immigrants, whose family problems are compounded by the fact that they are in the country illegally.

Global Trafficking

Human trafficking involves selling and buying humans as products. It is likely to affect the family in many ways (T. Harrison 1999; Jakobi 2012). Children are sometimes trafficked for the purpose of illegal adoption. As with legal adoption, the children generally flow from poor, weak countries to those that are rich and powerful. Recall from Chapter 1 that women are trafficked for purposes of prostitution and forced marriage, both of which have the potential of disrupting family life. Then there is the illegal global traffic in human organs. Family members in developed countries who cannot obtain needed organs locally are better able to survive because of this traffic. Poor people in less developed countries sell organs not critical to

GL⊕BALISATION

The Role of Families in Improving Relations Between the United States and Cuba

Relations between the United States and Cuba began to unravel when a communist regime headed by Fidel Castro took power in 1959. Prior to 1959, Cuba was ruled by a dictator supported by the United States. The situation grew much worse after an abortive invasion attempt (at the "Bay of Pigs") by Cuban exiles that had been supported again by the United States (Dominguez, Hernandez, and Barberia 2011). By 1962 the United States had placed an embargo on Cuba, and by 1963 all travel between the two countries was banned. This embargo had a profound effect on all of Cuba's relationships. Early on, Cuba's relations with communist bloc nations increased, though most other relationships were severely limited. However, some noncommunist nations, most notably Canada, retained normal relations with Cuba (Wylie 2010). Most importantly, relations with other Latin American countries were severely limited. Because of U.S. pressure, Cuba's membership in the Organization of American States (OAS) was suspended. It was not until 2009 that Cuba's membership in the OAS was reinstated, and this over the continuing opposition of the United States (Prevost and Campos 2011).

A number of Cubans had fled the country for the United States prior to the travel embargo, and others fled later either illegally or as a result of temporary thaws in the relationship between Cuba and the United States. Most of these Cubans settled in South Florida. Almost a million of them live there today, and they represent a potent economic and political force. Many, especially the early immigrants, were middle-class and opposed to Castro and communism, which sought to redistribute their wealth more equitably among Cubans. For decades they resisted bettering relations with Cuba, but

A painter celebrates Cuba's unique history and culture with a mural located in the Little Havana district of Miami, Florida. While relations between the United States and Cuba have remained frosty over the last 50 years, Cuban Americans have striven to remain in touch with friends and relatives in the small island nation. President Obama loosened restrictions on shipping and travel between the two countries in 2009, perhaps paving the way for warmer relations.

in recent years those relations have improved somewhat, especially among the younger Cuban Americans who arrived after the mid-1990s as a result of a special visa program.

Many Cuban Americans left family members behind in Cuba, and for decades it was difficult or impossible to see them. However, in the last decade, and especially in the last few years, travel restrictions for family members have eased considerably. In 2009 President Obama loosened restrictions on shipping and travel between the two countries; there are no longer any restrictions on flights by Cuban Americans to visit family members in Cuba. For its part, Cuba now allows its citizens to own cell phones and computers, thereby easing contact with family members in the United States.

Cuba has also made it easier for Cubans to buy homes and businesses. As a result, Cuban Americans are sending all sorts of products to their families in Cuba, thus making it possible for those family members to open an array of small businesses. Furthermore, increasing amounts of money are flowing to Cuba to help family members buy (and sell) property.

There are still those in the United States (and undoubtedly in Cuba) who would like to reinstitute restrictions on travel and shipping. Some Americans, especially Cuban Americans in Congress, fear that the Cuban regime is being strengthened by these contacts.

Regardless of politics, it is the drive to connect to family members that is doing much to overcome the lingering hostility between the two nations. As one expert on Cuba put it, "In Washington the whole debate over normalizing relations in Cuba is dead in the water. . . . Meanwhile, in Miami, Cuban-Americans are normalizing relations one by one" (Alvarez 2011:A3).

their lives, which are then transported to developed countries and implanted into well-to-do recipients (Scheper-Hughes 2001). Although the poor in less developed countries do receive some money for their organs, this is but another form of exploitation of the global poor by the global rich. It is a particularly heinous form of exploitation since the poor must sacrifice one or more of the things that make them human in order to survive.

Global Economy

The global economy is likely to affect the family in various ways. For example, a downturn in the increasingly intertwined global economy is likely to disrupt the family by leading to the unemployment of one or more family members. Unemployment in the family might also be related to the increasing outsourcing of work to other countries, leading to the loss of jobs in the country doing the outsourcing. Large corporations are increasingly likely to be multinational, often meaning that high-level employees are likely to move from one part of the world to another on a regular basis. Many high-level jobs require a great deal of movement around the world, and such jobs may even lack a home base. The family lives of those employed in such occupations are likely to be disrupted by the fact that they are home so rarely. Many women, especially mothers, from less developed countries are likely to be involved in global care chains, which means that they will be away from their home countries and their families while they care for someone else's family in a developed country (Yeates 2012). Of course, the existence of such a care worker affects the family in various ways as well.

Global Conflict

Global conflict can affect the family in a number of ways. As combatants, young men are the most likely to die in war. This can create a "marriage squeeze," leaving women without a sufficient number of suitable male partners (Akers 1967). Such a squeeze was found to have occurred in Vietnam in the 1970s and 1980s and in Lebanon, which has been afflicted with armed conflict for decades (Karraker 2008). Although it is not necessarily true for all wars, it was found that those who served in World War II were likely to have higher divorce rates (Pavalko and Elder 1990). It is also likely that civilians in countries that have experienced armed conflict have higher rates of divorce.

The main point is that the family today is an integral part of globalisation, which it is both affecting and being affected by. There is no such thing as a typical global family; at best, there are many global families. More to the point, those people involved in today's families are at the intersection of innumerable global flows and are, as a result, enmeshed in constantly changing intimate relationships of all sorts. This may be as good a definition as any of the family in the global age.

SUMMARY

The family is a crucial social institution that has seen several shifts over the last century. Marriage is a legal union of two people, but can also entail monogamy, polygamy, or cenogamy. An intimate relationship involves partners who have a close, personal, and domestic relationship with one another. Passionate love has a sudden onset, has strong sexual feelings, and tends to involve idealisation of the one who is loved, whereas companionate love develops more gradually, is not necessarily tied to sexual passion, and is based on more rational assessments of the one who is loved.

The traditional nuclear family dropped from 43 percent of all households in 1950 to only about a fifth of all households in 2010. To explain this decline, Andrew Cherlin focused on the deinstitutionalisation of marriage, while Anthony Giddens posited that pure relationships are more fragile than other forms of marriage. Ulrich Beck and Elisabeth Beck-Gernsheim argued that marriage had become only one of many ways of living together, while Georg Simmel suggested that some degree of secrecy is necessary to a successful marriage.

The structure of intimate relationships has changed over time. One reason for this is the rise in cohabitation. There has also been a tremendous rise in nonresident parenting and single-parent households in Canada. Stepfamilies are also increasingly common. The visibility of gay and lesbian families has also increased in recent years. Studies of children of same-sex couples show that these children generally face the same adjustment issues as children growing up in straight families.

Talcott Parsons believed that the family was functional and structurally important to society because of its ability to control adult behaviour and socialise children. Conflict theorists see the family primarily as a place of inequality and conflict, particularly between those of different ages and genders. Feminist theorists view the family as particularly problematic for women because they are oppressed by a system that adversely affects them. Exchange theorists look at the family from a more micro level and examine the rewards and costs associated with the choices individuals make within families.

Conflict is endemic to families; there are five basic models of family conflict: deficit, overload, cultural tensions, conflict of interest, and anomie. Abuse and domestic violence can involve behaviour that is intimidating, threatening, harassing, or harmful. Families can also suffer from poverty, and the recent recession has impacted families greatly, particularly their consumption patterns. Gender inequality takes several forms in marriages, including the time devoted to household tasks, power distribution, and decision making. People react to divorce in a variety of ways. Some people find their lives enhanced by their divorce, whereas others suffer from depression or low self-esteem.

Characteristics that used to separate people, and that make creating global families difficult or impossible, are less important in the global age. Global flows that involve the family take four major forms: Entire families can move from one part of the globe to another with relative ease; individual family members can move to a different part of the world and then bring the rest of the family along later; individuals can immigrate in order to create a new family; and transnational adoptions generally involve the flow of children from less to more developed countries. Global migration, trafficking, economics, and conflict all affect the global family.

KEY TERMS

- Blended family 415
- Cenogamy 400
- Cohabitation 411
- Companionate love 401
- Companionate marriage 404
- Cosmopolitanism 408
- Couples living apart together (LAT) 418
- Deinstitutionalisation 403
- Domestic violence 425
- Endogamy 400
- Exogamy 400
- Extended family 419
- Family 400
- Family household 410
- Individualised marriage 406

- Institutional marriage 404
- Intimacy 401
- Intimate relationship 401
- Marriage 400
- Monogamy 400
- Nonfamily household 409
- Nonresident parents 414
- Nuclear family 403
- Passionate love 401
- Polyandry 400
- Polygamy 400
- Polygyny 400
- Pure relationship 408
- Reflexive modernity 408
- Stepfamily 415

THINKING ABOUT SOCIOLOGY

1. How has the structure of the family changed in Canada since 1900? In what ways is the family as an institution resistant to the McDonaldization of society?

2. What about marriage makes it functionally important? Despite its importance, what are some problems that arise from marriage and the families formed through marriage?

3. What are the five basic models of family conflict? Give an example of conflict; then apply each of the five models in turn. Which rings most true for you? Is it possible that each model applies to family conflict?

4. According to structural-functionalists, why are families so important to society? What criticisms do conflict and feminist theorists have of these theories? In what ways are these criticisms related to ideas about social stratification?

5. What forms can intimate relationships take? Do you think that some forms of relationships in Canada are valued more highly than others? Do you think these values will change in the future? Why or why not?

6. Recent studies show that more relationships are now started on Internet dating sites. In what ways are these dating sites reflective of the changes in the marriage market in Canada? How could one use exchange theories to explain the use of Internet dating sites to find partners?

7. What are the causes and consequences of divorce? What are benefits and disadvantages of divorce?

8. What are some general conclusions sociologists have made about domestic violence? Where is there still debate? What are some other common problems that arise within families?

9. Many sociologists see a close relationship between family structure and poverty. What is this relationship? What role does gender play? What are some contrasting viewpoints?

10. How have the Internet and new social media changed relationships in the family?

APPLYING THE SOCIOLOGICAL IMAGINATION

The television program *Modern Family* depicts a diversity of intimate relationships and family structures. Nontraditional family structures have become increasingly prevalent in Canada. For this exercise, choose two other currently popular television shows and describe how they portray the types of relationships discussed in this chapter. What are the differences in how familial relationships are portrayed in each show? Despite the differences, what similarities do the familial relationships have? What structural factors (such as network, time of day aired, and target audience) could lead to the differences that you noted?

ACTIVE SOCIOLOGY

Genealogy is a hot issue, and sites including www.ancestry.com have helped individuals become prosumers in their quest for family history. Explore as much of the website that you can (some areas are limited to members only, and membership is not free). What assumptions are made about families, according to the website? How does the site normalise certain structures and functions of the family? For example, are nonbiological families represented at all? Start your own family tree on this site. How do the limitations of this site impact your ability to tell your own family story?

STUDENT STUDY SITE

Visit the student study site at **www.sagepub.com/ritzercanadian** for additional web quizzes for further review.

POLITICS AND THE ECONOMY

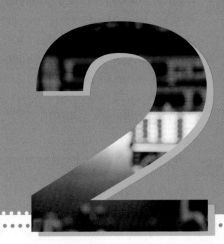

12

The global financial crisis teaches a hard, though perhaps inevitable, lesson about globalisation: As success flows, so too does failure.

The 2008 collapse of complex, unregulated banking practises tied to the U.S. housing market set off a chain reaction that devastated international economic flows and triggered a global recession. Most of the world's advanced economies stumbled dramatically, and several nations (including Ireland, Jamaica, Venezuela, North Korea, Madagascar, and Croatia) even experienced negative economic growth. Because they did not tend to trade in risky economic assets, smaller, less globalised economies have supplanted larger economies as the new drivers of economic growth. According to the International Monetary Fund, emerging and developing countries accounted for 77 percent of global economic growth from 2007 to 2011.

The global financial crisis is an issue not just of economics but also of politics. In many ways, these two fundamental social institutions are inseparable. As you saw in the debt ceiling crisis, a nation's political system—and the individuals who populate it—have an enormous impact on how capital is distributed, spent, and saved at every level of society. At the national level, governments with tighter regulation and less political diversity, such as China and Iran, have not been affected by the global financial crisis as much as those with looser regulation and greater political diversity, such as Canada, the United States, and the European Union.

Within any governing body, political conflict and social change can have serious long-term economic consequences. Cultural differences among the nations that use the euro as a common currency led to an imbalance in economic restraint, making it nearly impossible to draft a debt reduction policy that appeased both fiscally *responsible countries, such as Germany, and those with looser fiscal policies, such as Greece. In the United States, deindustrialisation and consumerism have contributed to unsettling surges in unemployment and personal debt that show no signs of significant abatement. At the extreme, political and economic conflict can lead to terrorism and war—not uncommon phenomena in the current global climate.*

Shortly after downgrading the credit rating of the United States, Standard & Poor's downgraded the ratings of France, Austria, Italy, Spain, and several other European nations. The global financial crisis teaches a hard, though perhaps inevitable, lesson about globalisation: As success flows, so too does failure. When governments allow (or encourage) elite financial institutions to engage in unregulated transnational business, they must consider the potential negative economic consequences. Unfortunately, as many experienced throughout the recent recession, these negative consequences are greatest for those in the middle and lower classes.

POLITICS: POWER AND CONTROL

Society can be seen as a collection of overlapping groups that compete to meet their own objectives. When groups go through established governmental channels to do so, this competition is referred to as **politics**. By using or putting pressure on the **state**—the political body organised for government and civil rule—a group can advance a given position or have enacted a policy that benefits its members. Therefore, politics is one way of exercising power in society.

As you saw in Chapter 8, power is the ability to get others to do what you want them to do, even if it is against their will. It is often expressed through such formal actors as police officers, professors, and business executives. However, it is also expressed in subtler, more informal ways, such as in casual social relationships. When it is legitimated by a social structure such as a government, university, or corporate hierarchy, power is referred to as authority (see Chapter 6). Because authority is a legitimate form of domination, there is a high likelihood that commands will be considered appropriate— and will be obeyed—by subordinates.

TYPES OF GOVERNMENT

For thousands of years humans lived in relatively egalitarian, nomadic hunter-gatherer societies. Karl Marx and Friedrich Engels described these small bands and tribes as existing in **primitive communism** (see Chapter 2) (Engels [1884] 2010). They were *communist* in the sense that property tended to be held in common; no person could "own" land; each worked by hunting, gathering, making temporary shelters, and so forth. People contributed to the group, and the fruits of their labours were held in common. They were *primitive* in that they lacked the basic hallmarks of civilisation. These societies were also *stateless* and without class distinctions. They typically had traditional forms of authority, as represented by chiefs, medicine men, wise women, and healers.

Over time, people began organising into larger and more sedentary groups involved in agriculture. It is at this point that we begin to see the birth of states, although those first states were organised quite differently than they are today. As sedentary groups began to grow, **city-states** developed. These were small proto-states that began institutionalising hierarchical forms of traditional authority extending over large settlements. They eventually reached beyond the confines of the city-state and into the areas immediately surrounding it. As these city-states began battling one another, some were able to extend their rule to larger and larger regions, incorporating other city-states. As people began to identify themselves with these regions, the first states were born.

MONARCHY: THE RISE OF THE STATE

These states were typically **monarchies** (the word *monarch* comes from the Greek meaning "single

DIGITAL LIVING

The State and the Power of the Internet

Power is something that we usually associate with the state, but it is not unusual for that power to be threatened or overthrown in social revolutions. In the last few years, a new threat to the state has arisen in the form of the power of the crowd as manifest in social revolutions made possible in large part by social media, the so-called Twitter and Facebook Revolutions. Of course, revolutions—the French Revolution, the American Revolution, the downfall of the Soviet Union— occurred throughout history and long before social networking. The failed Tiananmen Square revolution in China, for instance, was brought about largely by word of mouth or by people on motorcycles alerting those involved to gather and block troop movements throughout Beijing.

While one of the powers of the state is its ability to set the public agenda, ever-expanding access to the Internet and social media has increasingly allowed crowds to define their own agendas. Faced with this, the state might find itself confronting what Clay Shirky (2011) calls the "conservative dilemma." Interestingly, this is a dilemma not just for autocrats like Hosni Mubarak, the deposed leader of Egypt, but also for more democratic regimes. If threatened with a Twitter Revolution, the state has essentially four choices: repression, censorship, the use of propaganda, or to try to remain off the grid:

1. Muammar Gaddafi sought unsuccessfully to *repress* the revolution in Libya, and at this writing, Bashar al-Assad is attempting to use his military to suppress the simmering revolution in Syria. The problem with repression is that it usually serves to heighten the opposition and to fuel the revolution; it can even serve to radicalise those who are for the regime, or hurt the society in other ways, for example by slowing down the economy.

2. In the old days, newspapers, radio, and television were censored, but such *censorship* was easy to achieve when compared to the difficulties involved in censoring the Internet. China continues to combat dissidents by censoring the Internet, but it seems futile, at least in the long run.

3. The state might resort to *propaganda* delivered via the media, perhaps even the Internet, in an effort to counter the messages being put forth by the rebels.

4. Finally, it is possible, as in the case of North Korea, to stay off the grid completely and to deny people access to the Internet.

While many see social media as a revolutionary force (see, for example, the Chapter 15 *Digital Living* box, "The Role of Social Media in the Arab Spring"), there are those (for example, Gladwell 2010) who see it fostering "slacktivism" rather than activism. Some potential activists might be more inclined to blog than to take to the streets. However, even if these activists are unlikely to become revolutionaries, social media are likely to increase solidarity among those involved (Woods 2011). Another view is that state officials will make better use of social media than the crowd, and the state's position will be strengthened, not jeopardised, by it (Morozov 2011).

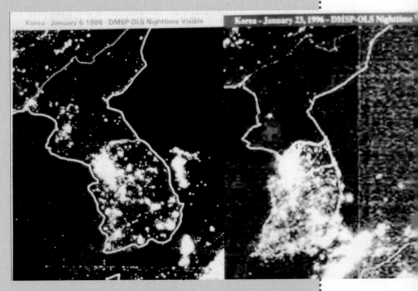

North Korea prevents its citizens from conversing and sharing information on social networks by keeping them off the grid completely. In much of the country, Internet access—even electricity—is reserved for government elites. In these two photographs of electric light at night taken in 1986 (left) and 1996, it is clear that electricity has proliferated throughout South Korea, while North Korea has largely remained dark.

ruler") ruled by a hereditary head of state and based on the traditional form of authority outlined in Chapter 6. This traditional form of authority was closely associated with birthrights and royal families. The monarchs' authority derived not just from the state over which they ruled but also, typically, from some divine source. Thus, monarchs usually served a sacral function within the societies they ruled, either as divinely ordained ruler-priests, as in the "divine right of Kings" in the Christian Middle Ages, or as actual gods or goddesses, such as the monarchs who ruled over Japan until the end of World War II.

DEMOCRACY: CITIZENSHIP AS A RADICAL IDEA

Monarchies can be contrasted with **democracies**, or political systems in which people within a given state vote to choose their leaders and, in some cases, might be able to vote on legislation as well. *Democracy* comes from the Greek meaning "rule of the people." In modern democracies, that typically means that people vote to choose their legislators rather than

actually effectively managing their own affairs and directly making decisions about the things that affect their lives. Nevertheless, contemporary theorists of democracy often suggest that the power to rule in democracies comes from the *consent* of the people.

Sometimes these systems are called **representative democracies**, as the people, as a whole body, do not actually rule themselves but rather have some say in who will best represent them in the state. By comparison, in **direct democracies** the people have a say in decisions that directly affect them. Democracy was a radical idea. It represented a vast change from living under a ruling family, whereby people had no say in who represented them and legislated the decisions that affected their lives.

The Democratic State

Democratic states are organised into bureaucracies (see Chapter 6) with clear hierarchies, as well as established and written codes, laws, and rules. The authority that legislators have under democracies is based on legal codes that confer that authority on them. Democracies tend to extend rights to **citizens**, the people represented by a given state, most often born within its territories. **Citizenship** means that the people of a given state can vote for their representatives and that they have rights and responsibilities as citizens (B. Turner 2011). It should be noted, however, that citizenship was not always universal and in the past was often conferred only on men or property owners. Under *universal citizenship* these rights are generally conferred on most people residing in a given state's territory; at times, however, citizenship is still denied to groups of immigrants residing within it. In Canada citizens over the age of 17 on voting day, but only citizens and not simply residents, can vote in federal elections. Citizens who are serving a sentence of two or more years in a correctional facility are the key group that is not allowed to vote (Elections Canada 2000).

Most democratic states guarantee citizens the right to freely express dissent, the right to due process and equality before the law, freedom of speech and press, and the right to privacy. These rights and others are sometimes extended to noncitizens. This idea of citizenship is radically different from what existed in the monarchies of the past. Nobility tended to wield much more power than politicians do in contemporary societies, and workers and peasants, at times, were given no rights at all. Even in modern liberal democracies, these "rights" are highly contextual. For example, although Canada proclaims the right to free expression, many people who protested against globalisation in Vancouver (APEC, 1997), Quebec City (3rd Summit of the Americas, 2001), and Toronto (G20, 2010) were arrested for their dissent, sometimes unlawfully arrested (Pue 2000). Similarly, consider how elements of the current Anti-Terrorism Act in Canada or its U.S. counterpart, the PATRIOT Act, impact the right to privacy. As a final example, consider how wealth and differences of social class impact "equality before the law," given differences in access to legal services and capital.

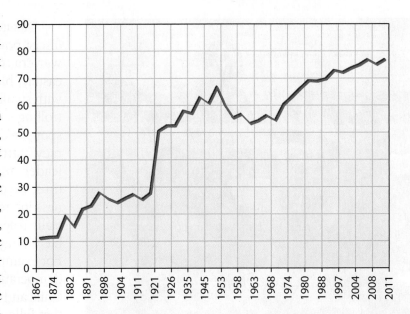

FIGURE 12.1 Percentage of the Canadian Population Eligible to Vote in Federal Elections, 1867–2011

SOURCE: Elections Canada, retrieved December 21, 2012 (http://www.elections.ca/content.aspx?section=el e&dir=turn&document=index&lang=e).

The democratic rights we now enjoy, including the right to vote, were the result of struggles waged by our ancestors. Of course in the earliest democratic states, only men, and then only men with economic resources, were allowed to vote. This was the case in Greece, about 2,500 years ago, the birthplace of democracy. In the earliest national elections in Canada just over 10 percent of the population was eligible to vote (see Figure 12.1). Much as in early Greece, in Canada's 1867 federal election "only males over the age of 21 who met certain property qualifications were eligible to vote" (Elections Canada 2000). This percentage gradually increased as women were allowed to vote (1918), as ethnic exclusions were eliminated (1948 for people of Asian descent), as all Aboriginal peoples gained the right to vote (1960), and as the voting age declined (1970). After World War II the percentage of the population eligible to vote declined because of the baby boom and because of postwar immigration, as immigrants had to wait at least five years after landing in Canada to be eligible to vote.

Democracies are not without their critics, even from within. For example, it is argued that voters are typically uninformed about many political issues. Similarly, there is the belief that liberal democracies extend *too many* rights and tend to allow too much diversity of thought and interest, making them unstable.

DICTATORSHIP: THE SEIZURE OF POWER

If the authority of rulers in democracies comes from the consent of the people, then **dictatorships**, states that are usually totalitarian and ruled either by a single individual or by a small group of people, are governments *without* the consent of the people being governed. In the modern period, dictatorships are often formed in formerly democratic states seized by small groups of political fanatics.

In the years just before and during World War II, the world saw an alliance of dictatorships based on fascist principles. The dictator of Italy, Benito Mussolini, saw the state as an institution on whose behalf its people should sacrifice themselves. He believed that no political organisation, no business, and no union should be organised outside

In Robert A. Heinlein's politically charged 1959 science-fiction novel *Starship Troopers*, citizenship and the right to vote are granted only to individuals who volunteer for military service. Sometimes criticised for promoting fascism and militarism, the book was the first science-fiction novel added to the reading lists of three of the five U.S. military branches. The novel was loosely adapted into a film in 1997.

the purview of the state. He also felt that the state should heavily regulate the economy, merging the state and business to a degree, in what is referred to as **corporatism**. Upon being voted into power, Germany's Adolf Hitler seized the state with his National Socialist Party. Like Mussolini, Hitler saw the state as an overarching institution that should control all social life.

These dictatorships shared some very basic institutional arrangements and principles:

- They were totalitarian in the sense that they attempted to control every facet of social life under their regimes.

- They had a **cult of masculinity** that organised political life and the public sphere around men and punished perceived deficiencies in masculinity, such as homosexuality.

- They saw conflict and war as natural states and methods for human betterment.

- They were viciously opposed to liberalism, Marxism, anarchism, and any form of socialism or communism.

Dictatorships did not end with the defeat of the fascist powers in World War II. Indeed, in the post-war era, the Soviet Union and its satellites in the eastern bloc were often organised as dictatorships, with small groups of Communist Party officials controlling society. Further, the United States has often sponsored dictatorships and fought against democracy, particularly where a democratically elected leader might make a turn toward socialism and, thus, become a thorn in the side of American business interests (Chomsky 1985). This has been especially true in Latin America, where the United States has a long history of supporting dictatorial regimes. For example, in 1973, the United States helped oust democratically elected Marxist Salvador Allende in Chile and supported the brutal military dictatorship that followed under Augusto Pinochet.

All three of these types of government—monarchies, democracies, and dictatorships—continue to exist throughout the world. Indeed, while Canadians are typically proud to live in a democratic country, the bulk of the world's population lives in countries where representative democracy involving the majority of the population is not practised (e.g., China, Iran, Saudi Arabia).

THE CANADIAN POLITICAL SYSTEM

The Canadian political system is a **multiparty system** in which more than two parties hold political office. This is similar to other countries, such as Germany, India, and Taiwan. This contrasts with a **two-party system**, as in the United States and Jamaica, in which members of two parties hold nearly all positions of political power. It is also, of course, quite different from **single-party systems**, where the ruling party holds all offices, such as in China, Singapore, and the former Soviet Union. The single-party system outlaws, or heavily restricts, opposing parties.

Single-party systems typically restrict discussion, debate, and policy choices. Two-party and multiparty systems provide opportunities for more debate, although even in these systems there is often a "race to the centre," whereby parties compete for the majority of the vote without alienating

Political Party	% of Valid Votes	% of Seats in Parliament
Conservative Party	39.6	53.9
New Democratic Party	30.6	33.4
Liberal Party	18.9	11.0
Bloc Québécois	6.1	1.3
Green Party	3.9	0.3
Other	0.7	0.0

FIGURE 12.2 Percentage of Votes and Percentage of Seats by Political Party in Canada's 2011 Federal Election

SOURCE: Elections Canada, Tables 7 and 9; retrieved December 22, 2012 (http://www.elections.ca/scripts/ovr2011/default.html).

voters with extreme positions. In two-party systems this means that minority points of view are often left unexpressed by the ruling parties. In multiparty systems parties work harder to differentiate themselves from one another, so a greater diversity of opinions is represented. However, multiparty systems are often understood as being less stable because of this diversity. Governing requires a majority of votes in a legislative assembly, and when parties have divergent views, establishing a working consensus among representatives from various parties is sometimes very difficult.

It is not obvious what the best way is to organise the political system when two or more political parties coexist. Canada, like the United Kingdom and the United States, uses a form of district representation whereby elected politicians are chosen from geographic areas containing roughly equal populations. This ensures representation from across the country. One of the problems with this form of democracy is that the party in power does not necessarily have electoral support from the majority of voters. For example, in 2011 the Conservative Party was supported by 39.6 percent of Canadians, yet the party holds 53.9 percent of seats in the House of Commons (see Figure 12.2). Alternatively, 572,095 Canadians voted for the Green Party, but only one of their members was elected. Over 500,000 votes were required to elect one member of the Green Party, but the 166 successful Conservatives needed, on average, only about 35,000 votes. While this illustration overly simplifies the electoral process, it does throw into sharp relief a problem with this "winner take all" type of democratic system. Effectively, the voices of minority interest groups can be eclipsed.

An alternative strategy, used in Brazil, Finland, Israel, and Sweden, is known as proportional representation. Under this system, a number of parties compete for a share of seats in the legislature, but the share is decided based on the overall popular vote for the party and is not constrained by geography. For example, had such a scheme been in place in Canada in 2011, the Conservative Party would have received about 40 percent of the seats, the New Democratic Party (NDP) about 30 percent, and the Greens about 4 percent (or 12 seats as opposed to 1). Proportional representation is touted as an alternative system that is better because it more often ensures that diverse voices are elected. A final alternative, used in Germany, is a mixed model, whereby some seats are elected using proportional representation and others are elected using the single-member district representation model.

Further complicating politics in Canada are the differing levels of government and regional particularities. Three main levels of government operate in Canada. The federal government is responsible for things affecting the entire country, such as defence, immigration, foreign affairs, and international trade. The provincial and territorial governments have responsibility for education, health, and most transportation. Finally, municipal governments, for cities, towns, or villages, are responsible for business licenses, firefighting, and building permits. In practise all levels of government have some involvement in almost every issue, so intergovernmental cooperation is important.

Political practises and political cultures vary regionally, and this further complicates things. For example, in Newfoundland and Labrador the provincial Conservative and Liberal Parties have dominated most elections in the post–World War II era, while in nearby Nova Scotia it is more frequently the Conservatives, Liberals, and New Democrats who vie for power provincially and federally. Conversely, in Quebec, it is the separatist Parti Québécois that competes most directly with the Liberal Party in provincial politics, but the latter has most recently been led by a former member of the federal Conservative Party. At the federal level in Quebec it is the Bloc Québécois competing against the Conservatives, the Liberals, and the NDP. In Alberta the Conservative Party has dominated for many decades, both federally and provincially, and most recently at the provincial level had to fend off the aspirations of the Wildrose Party, seen by many as even more conservative than the Conservative Party. The upshot of this is that alliances between national political parties are only loosely coupled with provincial parties, and neither of these are strongly aligned with any parties that vie for municipal office. As a consequence, many provinces find good political mileage in bashing the federal government, although creating alliances with other provincial politicians is often tricky because they represent different political persuasions.

Much of politics is also ritual, and this too must be understood. Currently the formal head of state in Canada is Elizabeth II, the Queen of Canada (and also the Queen of England). She is represented in Canada at the federal level by the governor general, and all of the provinces and territories also have their lieutenant governors or territorial commissioners, including Pierre Duchesne, the current lieutenant governor of Québec. There is also a Canadian senate, although many people feel it plays a largely symbolic role since it wields little effective legislative power. Its members are appointed by the prime minister as vacancies open.

FEDERAL POLITICAL PARTIES AND ELECTIONS

In keeping with Canada's roots in British parliamentary democracy, Canadians vote for representatives who champion their views in Ottawa, the nation's capital. Currently there are 308 elected representatives who occupy seats in the Canadian parliament. If one political party wins the majority of seats, as the Conservative Party did in 2011, then

that party forms the government. If no party wins a majority of seats, then either the party with the most seats forms a formal coalition with another party and governs, or the party with the most seats establishes alliances with other parties on an ad hoc basis and tries to stay in control of government as long as possible (as the Conservative Party did from 2008 until 2011, with support at different times from both the NDP and the Liberal Party).

It is customary to think of politics in terms of left and right. That is, where two or more parties compete for votes, some parties are more likely to support left-wing or progressive issues such as larger and more generous welfare and social assistance programmes such as universal health care. These same parties often support gay marriage and the right of women to have access to abortions. Parties on the political right, or more conservative, seek less government spending, fewer regulations, and less waste. They also often resist gay marriage and support restrictions on abortions.

For Canadian parties seeking to form the government by winning a majority of electoral seats, or to be a viable part of a coalition government, political pragmatism plays an essential role. Because of the race to the centre, the parties haven't historically looked that much different when it comes to the legislation that they support or sign into law. While many members of the Conservative Party would like to see the issue of abortion revisited, Prime Minister Stephen Harper urged his members not to make this a key issue in the 2011 election because Harper knew that this would make winning a majority government next to impossible. Similarly, Jack Layton, the leader of the New Democratic Party, and the party that won the second most seats in 2011, worked hard to establish the party's credentials as fiscally prudent and not wild-eyed socialists, as left-wing parties are sometimes characterised. In this way both the Conservatives and the NDP moved to the centre, trying to capture as many votes as they could. The consequence is an election campaign where the parties are promoting policies that are not radically different. For this reason, the simple binary understanding of politics as left or right disguises more than it illuminates.

Once the election campaign is over, parties revert to being more distinctive. The Conservatives want to cater to their grassroots supporters, so

McDONALDIZATION *Today*

McPolitics

McDonaldization tends to lead to "thin" politics, that is, political activity that is "superficial, transient, and simple." It also leads to "cool" politics, whereby people are not deeply committed to their political views. This stands in contrast to "hot" politics that involve "hysteria, effervescence, mystical trances, and spiritual possession" (B. Turner 2010:230). Modern hot politics are associated with the ethnic political conflicts found in Northern Ireland, Kosovo, Afghanistan, and Iraq. Most modern societies, however, are characterised by cooler politics. Such politics might be described as a "drive-in democracy," promoting the assumption that people's commitments to political causes should be "cool." The latter can also be associated with "ironic liberalism." Ironic liberals refuse to be committed to grand political visions and ambitious efforts at social reform. They are opposed to inflicting pain in the name of a political cause. Thus, there is a positive side to McDonaldization, at least in the political sphere, if not in all spheres: Hot politics can be extremely hazardous in the contemporary world. They are likely to lead to dangerous conflagrations at the local level that have the potential to become much wider conflicts, as is the case in Afghanistan, Pakistan, and Yemen today. Those who wish to avoid such conflicts can turn to McDonald's for their political models. A McDonaldized model of politics would lead to "cool cosmopolitans" who not only would be averse to actions that might lead to political conflagration but would in fact act as preventatives to such conflagrations. There are strong similarities between the perspective outlined above and Benjamin Barber's (1995) in *Jihad vs. McWorld*. Barber juxtaposes cool McWorld, which is very similar to the idea of a McDonaldized world, to hot jihad. The term *jihad*, literally "struggle," is derived from Islam, wherein it is seen as battles against those who threaten the faith. However, Barber discusses many different nations that are experiencing jihad-like movements, such as the Basque separatists in Spain. Barber's work seemed to anticipate the cataclysmic events of September 11, 2001; the U.S. attacks on the Taliban in Afghanistan; the "war" against the terrorist organisation al-Qaeda; and the declaration of a jihad against the United States by the leadership of the Taliban and al-Qaeda. In the early twenty-first century, we are involved in a struggle that is well described as jihad versus McWorld. The cool McWorld would seem to have most of the advantages in today's world, but the heat and passion behind jihad make it a formidable and dangerous alternative.

This video frame shows three unidentified people seated at a table in front of an ETA flag with a Basque Country symbol in foreground. In October 2011, the armed Basque separatist group ETA issued a message stating its intent to end its armed campaign and calling on Spain and France to open talks.

they seek to pass legislation that their political base expects them to champion (e.g., a watering down of regulations on businesses). Likewise, the New Democratic Party, as the official opposition, castigates the Conservatives at every opportunity by playing up issues that their supporters can rally around (e.g., injustices against First Nations peoples). Even here, though, pragmatism and electoral politics play a role in tempering radical change. For example, while the Conservatives might like to rewrite abortion law in Canada, to do so could make it difficult for them to win the next election.

Likewise, the NDP must be prudent about how much spending it should urge the government to undertake because this could undermine the party's claim to being fiscally responsible and damage its chances in the next election.

This highlights a weakness of democracy. Long-term planning often does not have electoral payoffs. Implementing farsighted policy is therefore not high on any political party's agenda. Short-term electoral success is the payoff that most political parties yearn for. In *The Republic*, this was one of Plato's key arguments against democracy—ultimately the ability to win elections is prized over the ability to implement policy that over the long term will be best for the electorate. Furthermore, elections have become orchestrated campaigns that involve little deep and substantial debate. Voters are often apathetic and uninformed about core issues. Politicians frequently stand accused of saying one thing during a campaign and doing other things once elected. The concept of a democratic deficit, the gap between public expectations for good governance and the actual performance of government, captures this frustration (P. Norris 2011).

Still, as the English statesman Winston Churchill argued in the British House of Commons on November 11, 1947:

> No one pretends that democracy is perfect or all-wise. Indeed, it has been said that democracy is the worst form of government except for all those other forms that have been tried from time to time.

One strategy in defending democracy as a form of governance is to compare the outcomes of democratic and nondemocratic governance. In making such a comparison, Amartya Sen (1999) argues for democracy by noting that "no substantial famine has ever occurred in any independent country with a democratic form of government and a relatively free press" (p. 152). On a range of such comparisons he believes democratic forms of government demonstrate they are superior. Furthermore, relative to other forms of decision making, democracy encourages the critical assessment of policy decisions from a variety of interests. By promoting the free exchange of ideas, democratic decision making yields more reliable outcomes since decisions

depend on a broader range of input. This is exactly why the defence of free speech, freedom of assembly, and a free press, for example, is seen as so essential.

Demographics and Voting Patterns

Supporters of representative democracies typically point to the vote as a critical source of power for citizens. It is curious, then, that so few people in Canada actually go to the polls. Even in the elections where the most eligible Canadians vote—federal elections—little more than half of eligible voters typically bother casting a ballot. The turnout in provincial elections is lower still, and at the municipal level turnouts are even smaller (Nakhaie 2006).

As Figure 12.3 illustrates, voter turnout varies over time. Studies of voter turnout ask questions about who votes, why or why not, and what exactly election processes offer citizens in terms of concrete power over their lives and the political direction(s) of the nations in which they live and work. In Canada, this often means looking at groupings of people to see what sense we might make of voting patterns. This also allows political sociologists to formulate theories about why people may or may not vote and whether people feel invested in the political process or, perhaps, feel disenfranchised from it and alienated to the extent that they may not participate.

One might be tempted to believe that the people most likely to vote are those most disadvantaged in a given society. If voting is a way an engaged citizenry exercises its power, then voting allows those people to attempt to improve their lot. By most measures, the exact opposite is the case with voting patterns in Canada. Indeed, those with jobs, those with higher incomes, older people, those with more education, and women are more likely to cast ballots than are their counterparts (Blais and St-Vincent 2011). With the exception of women, this means that the most advantaged are the most likely to vote.

This leaves sociologists with the task of explaining why, first of all, there is low voter turnout in general and why political participation and turnout tend to be lower in disadvantaged groups (Hajnal and Lee 2011). Some studies have suggested that participation in organisations linked with electoral processes allows for political education for the organisations' members, and this might translate into larger rates of voter participation. For example, belonging to unions might provide important political education for working-class people, and the decline of unions might also explain decreases in working-class participation in electoral processes (Radcliff 2001).

However, organisational participation can lead to forms of political activity outside of the electoral process, such as protests or community and workplace organising (R. McVeigh and Smith 1999). This could point to alienation from the electoral process, as individuals who take the time to learn about politics within these organisations often tend to put their energies elsewhere. Some potential voters may feel alienated from the process as a result of the lack of community structures that encourage meaningful political participation (Docherty, Goodlad, and Paddison 2001). Still others, due to their disenfranchisement, widespread unemployment, political scandals, and the like, might question the very legitimacy of the political institutions under which they live (A. Bay and Blekesaune 2002).

One of the clearest findings, not only in Canada but in other western democracies as well, is that young people are less likely to vote. Younger Canadians, in keeping with their peers in other countries, are less likely to engage in formal politics such as voting (see Figure 12.4) or belonging to political parties (Milner 2010). In contrast, younger Canadians are more likely to be engaged with environmental issues or issues of global trade.

MONEY AND ELECTIONS

But the vote isn't the only way to influence politics in a representative democracy, and neither is participation in social protest and organising. Indeed, people use other methods to influence the outcomes of elections and the positions of politicians already in office. These methods often centre on the use of money, sometimes supporting candidates, other times supporting specific parties, and still other times supporting a specific position.

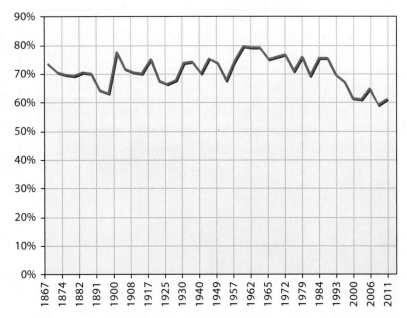

FIGURE 12.3 Voter Turnout in Canadian Federal Elections, 1867–2011

SOURCE: Elections Canada, retrieved December 21, 2012 (http://www.elections.ca/content.aspx?section=ele&dir=turn&document=index&lang=e).

Funding for Federal Political Parties

Federal political parties in Canada get money in one of two ways. They can obtain financial donations from individual contributors (political contributions),

There is increasing concern in Canada, and many other nations, about declines in the number of people voting. Campaigns to educate members of the public about political responsibilities and to mobilize voter turnout are common in all of these countries.

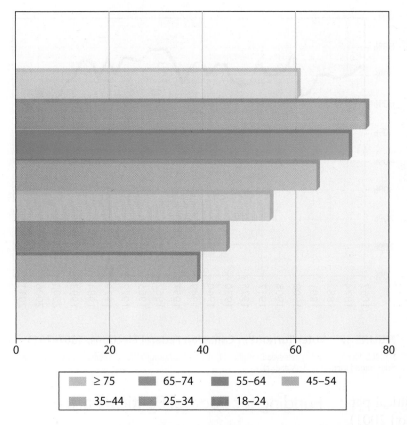

FIGURE 12.4 Voter Turnout (%) by Age Group, Canada, 2011

SOURCE: Elections Canada, retrieved December 21, 2012 (http://www.elections.ca/content.aspx?section=ele&dir=turn&document=index&lang=e).

or they can receive funding from taxpayers based on the number of votes they won in the previous election (per-vote subsidies). Examining each of these in turn reveals how political financing has changed over time and how it may change in the future.

Until 2004, both corporations and unions could make financial contributions to political parties. Figure 12.5 shows financial contributions to the three major national parties by the source of contribution. Corporations contributed 41 percent of all donations parties received, but notice that this funding went largely to two of the three parties, the Conservatives and the Liberals. Conversely, union donations went almost exclusively to the NDP. Even though the major source of funding was individuals, many felt that corporation and union funding provided too strong a tie between these organisations and political parties. In 2004 the law was changed so that only individual citizens could make contributions to any party, and even then there were caps placed on how much they could contribute. This effectively ended the direct subsidies to political parties from both corporations and unions, a beneficial

outcome since it ended any possibility that parties might support legislation that benefitted either of these organisations.

One controversial issue with these financial contributions, which are tax deductible, is that different income groups have more or less ability to make donations. The wealthy have more discretionary income than the poor. Contributions to political parties tend to come from the more well-off. In turn, the people with greater financial resources tend to support those parties that cater to their interests. Put another way, the poor, lacking the income to do so, are less able to donate financially to any parties that support policies beneficial to their disadvantaged position.

Effectively, per-vote subsidies, the second source of funding noted above, made up for the lost dollars that no longer flowed from corporations and unions. As a means of financing political parties this has both advantages and disadvantages. The per-vote subsidy is paid for by tax revenue. Parties that are able to attract votes are rewarded with funding to continue their operations. The funding level they receive is tied directly to the votes they receive and is thus highly democratic as a way of distributing revenue. This is also advantageous in that it provides for a very transparent way of seeing from exactly where party finances flow. Conversely, the per-vote subsidy favours those parties that do well. A party that does well receives more funding and is therefore more likely to do well in the future because it has greater financial resources.

Recently the Conservative government has tabled legislation to rescind the per-vote subsidy and require parties to rely on the donations of individual Canadians as the main source of their financing. The major problem with using political party donations as the way to finance party politics is that it privileges those parties that appeal to the rich while penalising any party that tailors its policies to the less advantaged. The rightmost column in Figure 12.5 shows why a political party that can attract financial support from donors might want to scrap the per-vote subsidy. Both the Liberals and

Parties	1989–1993						2007–2011	
	Corporation	Individuals	Unions	Other	Total	% of Total	Individuals	% of Total
Conservatives	$39,961,798	$30,712,738	$790	$27,610	$70,702,936	45	$96,020,135	61
Liberal	$23,720,001	$23,443,813	$53,120	$200,118	$47,417,052	30	$35,866,430	23
NDP	$764,674	$30,106,760	$7,632,566	$1,560,831	$40,064,831	25	$25,171,059	16
Total (All Parties)	$64,446,473	$84,263,311	7,686,476	$1,788,559	$158,184,819	100	$157,057,624	100
Column %	41	53	5	1	100%		100%	

FIGURE 12.5 Financial Contributions to Political Parties, 1989–1993 and 2007–2011

SOURCE: Elections Canada, Political Financing, Financial Reports and Contributions and Expenses Data Base available at www.elections.ca.

NOTE: See text for an explanation of why the 1989–1993 versus 2007–2011 difference in the source of contributions occurs.

the NDP do not attract the financial dollars from donors that the Conservatives do, so the former depend more on the per-vote subsidy than do the Conservatives.

MEDIA AND THE POLITICAL PROCESS

The media influence what people consider "important political issues" or even "issues" at all, as well as pointing out who is responsible for social conflicts (Barnhurst and Wartella 1998; Iyengar 1990). Therefore, through media concentration, wealthy and powerful people are given much more access to this primary means of socialisation *and* persuasion in our society. In this way, they are able to set the political agenda and create news that reflects the interests of the elite. Herman and Chomsky (1988; Downing 2011) noted how news media concentration allows elites to set the public agenda, but also how it serves to legitimate our class system. This is certainly a boon to the wealthy, who benefit from people seeing the kinds of material inequalities present in our society as natural and normal.

In addition to wealthy interests exerting inordinate control over the news media, *political* elites have great power over, and access to, the media. News media rely on the state's acceptance of their activities and are regulated by the political system in terms of both ownership and content. News media also rely on the state for source material. Studies have consistently shown that government officials are the source of most news, in many cases subtly and not so subtly shaping the content (Gans 1979, 2003; Herman and Chomsky 1988; McKercher 2011; Shehata 2010).

Similarly, government officials rely on news media to circulate information for them. Politicians seeking votes or a particular public image, legislators seeking support for political decisions, and governments with the desire to inform citizens about social policy, conflict, or in some cases public hazards all rely on news media to disseminate information in a way that clearly articulates their position. Thus, the relationship between news media and government is *symbiotic*, each relying on the other in important ways. The wealthy corporations that own most news media also exist in a symbiotic relationship with

While debate continues in Canada about the best way to finance party politics, it is important to note how different the Canadian system is to the powerful political action committees that operate in the United States. These committees are effective ways for rich individuals and organisations to lobby political actors in the hope of influencing legislation and votes.

GL🌐BALISATION

Rupert Murdoch and the British Government

Rupert Murdoch is the archconservative founder and CEO of News Corp., the second largest media conglomerate in the world and the world's largest producer of English-language newspapers (McKnight 2011). He began with Australian newspapers, and he now owns many newspapers in Australia, as well as in Fiji and Papua, New Guinea. He achieved fortune and international fame on the basis of his ability to produce best-selling tabloid newspapers (*The Sun* in the United Kingdom, the *New York Post*), as well as taking famous old papers (*The Wall Street Journal*, *The Times* of London) and radically diminishing their level of sophistication in order to sell more newspapers and earn more money. Among News Corp.'s many other media assets are 20th Century Fox (movies), Fox Broadcasting Company, including Fox Business, and DirecTV in the United States;

a significant amount of the BSkyB pay-television system in Great Britain; all of Sky Italia; and the Satellite Television Asian Region based in Hong Kong. News Corp. is truly a global media colossus. See Global Flow Map 12.1 for a visualisation of the News Corp. empire; see also Figure 12.6.

Murdoch made headlines in mid-2011 because of abuses and illegalities associated with his best-selling British tabloid, *News of the World* (Prall 2011). In fact, the scandal was so great that Murdoch abruptly shuttered the highly profitable newspaper in order to contain the damage that threatened the entire News Corp. empire. The scandal itself focused on the fact that reporters had hacked into the voice mail of a 13-year-old murder victim, the relatives of members of armed forces who had died in Afghanistan, the actor Hugh Grant, and Princess Diana's onetime lover.

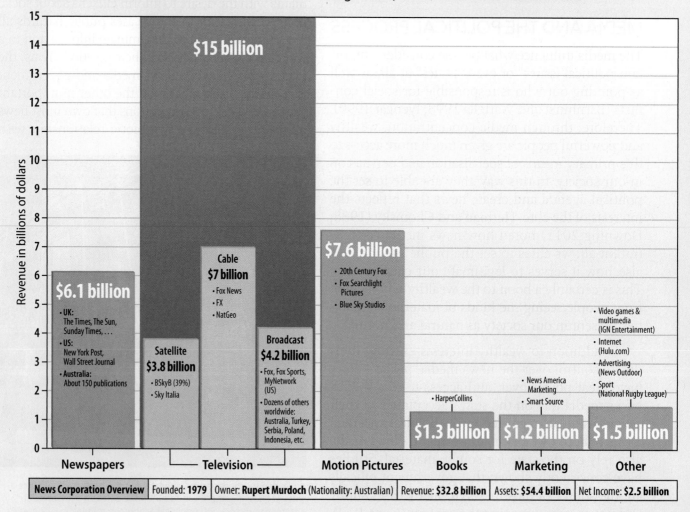

FIGURE 12.6 Rupert Murdoch's Media Empire, 2010
SOURCE: From 2Space Network, World News, Fact file on Rupert Murdoch's media empire News Corporation.

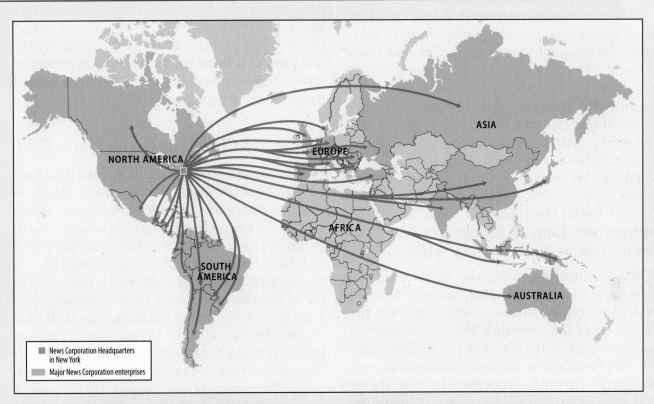

GLOBAL FLOW MAP 12.1 Reach of the News Corporation Media Empire

SOURCE: Forbes. 2007, January 24. "Rupert Murdoch's Global Reach." Available from www.forbes.com/2007/01/24/murdoch-biz-international-tech-media-cz_0125murdochmap_magcover.html?boxes=custom

Legend:
- News Corporation Headquarters in New York
- Major News Corporation enterprises

However, what is of most interest in the context of this chapter is the political implications of these actions as well as of Murdoch's empire more generally. Beyond general allegations of undue, if not illegal, influence on the British government, it turned out that Andy Coulson, a high senior aide and director of communications to Prime Minister David Cameron, was implicated in the scandal. Coulson had been an editor of *News of the World* before entering the government. His presence in the government raised suspicions about the relationship between Murdoch's empire and the British government. In fact, Coulson continued to receive severance pay from the newspaper after he became the director of communications in the Conservative Party headed by Cameron. Murdoch used his political connections to get media regulations that were favourable to his company and its profits (D'Arma 2011). Furthermore, Cameron was endorsed not only by *News of the World* but by other British newspapers controlled by Murdoch as well. Murdoch used the newspaper to help shape public opinion toward those he supported, and his support was ultimately returned to him in the form of political favours.

Until the late 1990s, media systems were largely national in scope, and therefore their influence was mostly national (McChesney 2003). Using a combination of Murdoch's political connections and the company's vast financial resources, News Corp. could influence regulatory bodies and establish dominance in various countries (D'Arma 2011). News Corp.'s global media presence gave it extraordinary clout, as well as the ability to corrupt many other political systems.

Protesters wore masks depicting Prime Minister David Cameron (left) and Rupert Murdoch in bed together after the British government approved plans by News Corp. to buy full control of satellite TV operator BSkyB on March 3, 2011. News Corp. dropped its bid to purchase BSkyB in the wake of the *News of the World* scandal.

government, further solidifying the links between political elites and the wealthy.

The tendency of media to showcase ideas that are acceptable to wealthy and powerful elites, especially those who are conservative, may seem obvious. Most Canadian media, for example in newspapers or on news websites, have a section on business that discusses corporate economic issues, almost always from the perspective of ownership. Not only is there no section on labour, but labour news rarely takes a perspective that is sympathetic to labour. We see daily reports on the ups and downs of the stock market (an interest of corporate owners), but we learn much less about wage settlements or how changes in earnings are related to the cost of living (an interest of working families).

David Roberts and Minelle Mahtani (2010) show how *The Globe and Mail*, Canada's national newspaper, portrays issues of immigration to the advantage of the powerful. They argue that the main story line, in the 800-plus articles they examine, emphasises how increased immigration will benefit the Canadian economy. The main theme is that Canadians should embrace immigration because immigrants will add value to the Canadian

economy. They argue that this not only benefits the powerful who benefit from the low wages paid to new immigrants, but it also "effectively eradicates histories of injustice facing immigrants in Canada" (Roberts and Mahtani 2010:255). Effectively the news media is being used, in subtle and nuanced ways, to spin a particular story that ultimately will benefit some more than others.

Media as a Challenge to the Status Quo

Despite unequal access to media and the great concentrations of ownership of mass media, this in no way guarantees the delivery or acceptance of the messages of elites. The media can be, and are, used to challenge rather than buttress the status quo (Black and Allen 2001). Television news showing the toll of the Vietnam War in graphic ways is often cited as one of the reasons that such a strong antiwar movement grew in the United States and Canada during the late 1960s and early 1970s. News images of protesters being beaten, arrested, and sprayed with powerful fire hoses led many to sympathise with the civil rights movement (see Chapter 15). Pictures of innocent children in Afghanistan and Iraq injured or killed by the missile and drone attacks of western forces fuelled opposition to the wars in these countries. And although critics of society's dominant institutions, such as capitalism and the state, are most often relegated to independent media, there are times when they slip through into mass media. One example is the 2006 film *V for Vendetta*, based on a graphic novel written by an anarchist writer, Alan Moore, with anarchist-inspired themes in opposition to capitalism and the state (see Chapter 2).

Elites also have little control over how their perspectives are received. For example, S. Hall (1980) notes that despite attempts at "encoding" a given message into media, oftentimes people "decode" those messages in widely divergent ways. Likewise, Gans (2003) notes that political messages in media "can neither produce a single and homogenous audience nor create a single effect on people" (p. 70).

WHO RULES CANADA?

The issue of who rules Canada is a source of continuing debate among sociologists. Is it fair to say

In late 2011 and early 2012, nearly 20 Tibetan monks and nuns self-immolated in protest of China's continuing occupation of Tibet and exile of the Dalai Lama. The global dissemination of graphic images and media reports brought attention to the protests, pressuring the Chinese government to address the issue, which it called "separatist propaganda."

that representative democracy is government by the people, for the people, or is there something being left unsaid? Do elected officials reflect the general citizenry of Canada? Such questions can serve as lenses into this larger debate among sociologists about the nature of political power, dominance, and control.

THE STRUCTURAL/FUNCTIONAL PERSPECTIVE: PLURALISM

Within structural-functionalism, the typical position put forward regarding who rules Canada is **pluralism**. This is the view that Canada is characterised by a number of powerful competing interest groups, but no one of them is in control all of the time. In other words, there is a kind of balance of power among these interest groups. In addition, there is a **separation of powers** in the government. Even majority governments are constrained in what they can do, by other parties in opposition, by the courts and the constitution, by a civil service bureaucracy, and by a free press that helps promote accountability.

Among pluralists, there are two major strands of thought. **Group pluralism** focuses on society's many different interest groups and organisations and how they compete for access to political power to attempt to further their interests (Drache 2008; Fung 2004). For group pluralists, this jockeying for power by various organisations provides stability for society. They see a *balance of group power,* where no one group retains power indefinitely and any group can always be challenged by another group. Further, there are *crosscutting group memberships,* by which group members belong to a variety of organisations that see to their needs and interests. This allows people to be political actors in a variety of collective processes. Group pluralists also believe that there tends to be a general *consensus of values* in society, so that the state is expected and pressured to legislate according to the common good and according to the cultural values largely held in common by members of society.

Group pluralists not only focus on existing organisations and groups that act for their political interests in society but also see *potential groups* as a source of stability. Accordingly, if, for example, the state expects that legislation might mobilise people

in opposition to it, that threat might hold political actors back from taking action. This might not yet be an interest group, but this *mobilisation of latent interests* can serve to pressure politicians to legislate in the common good. To group pluralists, then, organisations do not have to exist in order to help create societal stability—the mere threat of the *possibility* of future organisations can have the same effect.

Elite pluralism focuses specifically on how political elites form similar interest groups and organisations that vie for power (Highley and Burton 2006; Lipset 1981). This theory is an attempt to account for the fact that while voters may decide which elites represent them through the vote, the ultimate decision-making power still rests in the hands of those elites. Similar to group pluralists, elite pluralists look at political elites as a diverse social body that organises into groups to compete with one another for votes. This competition for votes ensures that no one group retains political power indefinitely. Stability is achieved in the system because these political elites must forge agreements with one another in order to pass legislation. This allows for a diversity of interests to be satisfied through those agreements, which tend to represent the common values of the larger society.

THE CONFLICT/CRITICAL PERSPECTIVE: THE POWER ELITE

Pluralism is often juxtaposed with a theory produced by conflict/critical theorists. C. Wright Mills's (1956) **power elite theory** holds that power is not dispersed throughout a stable society—either among citizen groups or among elite groups. Rather, power is concentrated among a small number of people who control the major institutions of the state, the corporate economy, and the military. The powerful people who make up these institutions might have minor disagreements about policy but for the most part are unified in their interests and in the business of owning and operating Canada (Carroll 2010; Porter 1965).

These elites develop a common worldview. First, elites undergo a process of *co-optation* whereby they are taught the common ideology of the elite. Further, these elites forge a shared ideology through their common *class identity*. That is, members of the power elite tend to come from wealthy families (the Irving family or the Thomsons), go to similar schools (Upper Canada College), and belong to similar clubs (the Calgary Petroleum Club). The clubs provide a private space where friendships and common policies are forged (Clogher 1981; Domhoff 1974).

William Carroll (2010) has updated the earlier work of John Porter (1965) and Wallace Clement (1976), demonstrating the tight interlocks that exist among this Canadian elite and their international peers. Carroll's work demonstrates the extent to which, in what is publicly touted as a free enterprise economy, there are strong interlocks between all of the dominant corporations in Canada. Members of the boards of directors of one corporation are often on other boards, and ex-politicians also find their way onto multiple boards. Carroll also shows how these interlocks have changed over the last 50 years, especially in the context of globalisation.

In sum, to power elite theorists, the state is not some neutral institution existing in a stable society where everyone (or every group) has an equal chance of having his or her interests met. Rather, the state is an institution that is controlled by the elites.

WHICH PERSPECTIVE IS CORRECT?

Looking critically at both theories—pluralism and power elite theory—one can see strengths and weaknesses to both approaches. For pluralism, the idea of latent interests influencing politicians cannot be verified empirically. The assumption that society is stable is problematic as well—it avoids questions such as for whom society might be stable and in which contexts. Finally, pluralism assumes that the state is a neutral institution rather than an institution with its own interests and one that tends to be controlled by wealthy elites.

Power elite theory also has various problems. For example, it assumes that elites share a common worldview and interests to an extent that may not match reality. Indeed, can we assume that the power elite is monolithic and has little diversity of thought? Further, is this power elite untouchable by the masses of people? Does it control society to the extent that power elite theorists would have us believe, or are there avenues for changing society from below that those theorists are ignoring? And if the power elite all but control our society, how is it that legislation that benefits some sections of society at their expense is passed? How did we end up with minimum wage laws, social welfare, publicly funded health care, and so on?

IMPLEMENTING POLITICAL OBJECTIVES: LEGITIMATE VIOLENCE, WAR, AND TERRORISM

When authority rests in the hands of the state, it maintains order through its claim to the legitimate use of violence in a given territory. Thus, through the police force and the military, the state is able to legitimate violence to enforce order. Much of the power of the state rests in this monopoly on legitimate violence. Stripped of their legitimacy, police activities might look like beating people, kidnapping them and putting them in cages, and even killing them. Indeed, these are the very things that police do!

The state also legitimates the forms of violence that might be used by people not directly acting as its agents. Private security firms can legitimately use violence, provided the state sees this use as legitimate. These firms operate both domestically, as in security details for private corporations, and abroad. The state also determines when private

Skull and Bones is an elite secret society located at Yale University in New Haven, Connecticut. Renowned for its exclusivity and occultist traditions, Skull and Bones has served as a networking base for such individuals as U.S. Presidents George H. W. Bush (pictured back row, sixth from left) and George W. Bush.

citizens have the right to use violence. If someone uses violence against another and it is deemed self-defence by the courts, then that violence is seen as legitimate. The state creates and maintains the regulations and rules that one must abide by in order to commit an act of violence—at times in defence of oneself, but also in some cases in the defence of one's property. There are also legal codes dealing with when people can use violence in defence of someone else or someone else's property.

WAR

War occurs when nations use their military to attempt to impose their will on others outside of their nation or, in cases of civil war, when a nation uses the military to impose its political will within the nation. War is one method of "doing politics" or dealing with political disagreements. Why does war occur? First, there needs to be a cultural tradition of war. Second, a situation must exist in which two political actors have objectives that are incompatible. Finally, a "fuel" must bring the situation from thinking about war to actually *making war* (Timasheff 1965).

In Canada, the cultural tradition of war is all around us. We are often taught in our history classes about our involvement in foreign wars in which we are depicted as saviours, the bringers of democracy, and so on. In our own history, we can see antagonistic situations, such as between the Axis powers and the Allies during World War II. Canada's involvement in Afghanistan has brought us into military conflict with other nations or peoples.

TERRORISM

War is often compared to terrorism, which typically refers to nongovernmental actors engaging in acts of violence targeting noncombatants, property, or even military personnel in order to influence politics. *Terrorism* is often a controversial term because it is usually the powerful who get to define who is or is not a terrorist. Consider, for example, that if property destruction as a way to express political grievances is terrorism, then the people who were part of the Boston Tea Party fit the description. And where is the line drawn between terrorists and revolutionaries fighting against invading or occupying

Private security firm Academi (nee Blackwater USA) underwent a series of name changes after coming under public scrutiny for several indictments and governmental investigations, such as for supplying military equipment to Jordan and killing 17 Iraqi civilians in 2007. Here, contractors working for Blackwater USA take part in a firefight as Iraqi demonstrators attempt to advance on a facility being defended by U.S. and Spanish soldiers in 2004.

armies? Who gets to draw that line, and why? Can states be terrorists?

Nevertheless, all over the world, people refer to acts like suicide bombings and the targeting of civilians of enemy nations or groups as examples of terrorism. These kinds of attacks are quite common and don't seem to be on the decline—particularly where there are occupations of land by foreign nations attempting to police a given population.

GLOBAL POLITICS

In a way, politics has long been global, but it might be convenient to trace modern political globalisation to the end of the First World War in 1918. After the war, efforts at peace led to the creation of the League of Nations in 1920 (see Figure 12.7). While the league was weak, in part because the United States never joined, it created an important forum for global political dialogue and relationships. Of course, peace failed, leading to the start of the Second World War in 1939. This global conflict immersed many of the world's nations in warfare. While the war had disastrous consequences for much of the globe, it did lead to formation of the United Nations (UN) in 1945 (see Figure 12.8). While not an unmitigated success, the UN persists to this day as an important site and source of political globalisation. Many other global political organisations have been formed within the United Nations (for example, the UN Educational, Scientific and Cultural Organization) or alongside it (for example, the European Union).

While these organisations have helped bring about greater dialogue among the world's nations, they have not led to world peace. Since the formation of the UN, there have been a number of major wars, including the Korean War, the war in Vietnam, the various wars involving Israel and its Arab neighbours, and the conflicts in Iraq and Afghanistan. In addition, especially since September 11, 2001, the world has been plagued by a number of terrorist and antiterrorist incidents. While many of the nations of the world talk to one another in various global forums, they still manage to conflict and to slaughter each other's citizens.

GEOPOLITICS

As the previous section indicates, geopolitics continues to define global political relationships

(G. Steinmetz 2012). **Geopolitics** entails political relationships that involve geographic areas—sometimes broad geographic areas—including the globe as a whole. On the one hand, geopolitics is concerned with how politics affects geography (for example, the ways in which national borders are redrawn after the end of a war). On the other hand, geopolitics is concerned with the ways in which geography affects politics. One example is the constant low-level warfare between Israel and its neighbours. This conflict occurs, at least to some degree, because Israel is a tiny nation surrounded by much larger hostile nations. After World War II, much of geopolitics focused on the relationship between the United States and its allies and the Soviet Union and its allies. There was great concern over the global expansion of communism; the United States and the Soviet Union clashed, usually indirectly, over their respective political influences in Germany, Korea, Cuba, Vietnam, and so on. While the Soviet Union sought to expand geopolitically, the United States followed a policy of containment of Soviet efforts to expand communism. For decades, the United States adopted what was known as the *domino theory:* If one nation was allowed to fall to communism, many

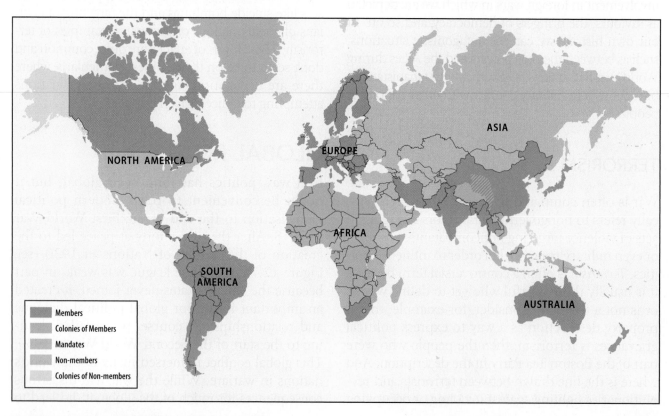

FIGURE 12.7 League of Nations Members, 1920

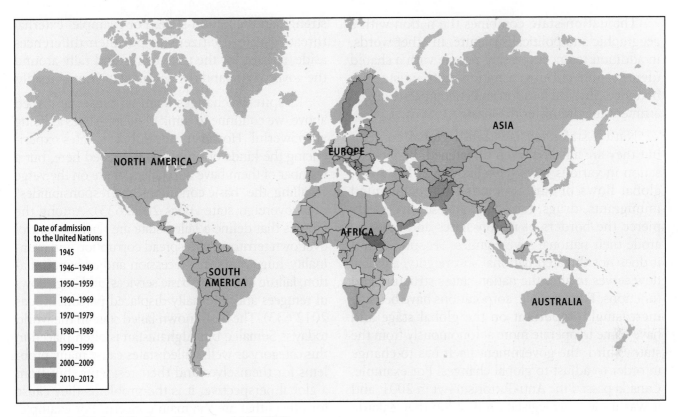

FIGURE 12.8 United Nations Members, 1945–2012

neighbouring nations would also fall. For example, the United States feared that if Vietnam fell to the communists, neighbouring countries, including Laos and Cambodia, would be next.

THE NATION AND THE NATION-STATE

As discussed in Chapter 6, the issue of geopolitics relates to what are perhaps the core concerns in the global age: the future of the nation and the nation-state. A **nation** is a group of people who share, often over a long period of time, similar cultural, religious, ethnic, and linguistic characteristics (Chernilo 2012). Jews are a nation by this definition, and, ironically, so are their frequent geopolitical enemies, the Palestinians. While many Jews and Palestinians live in the Middle East, many others, especially Jews, are spread throughout the world. They are scattered or dispersed; as described in Chapter 9, they exist in a *diaspora* (Fiddian-Qasmiyeh 2012). All diasporas share certain characteristics. First, they involve people who have been dispersed from their homeland. Second,

the people in the diaspora retain a collective and idealised memory of the homeland that they transmit to their offspring as well as to other members of the diaspora. Third, as a result of this idealisation, they are often alienated from their host country; the realities of the latter cannot measure up to the idealisations associated with the homeland. Fourth, those in the diaspora often take as a political goal the idea and the objective of returning to the homeland (R. Cohen 1997).

Many of those involved in a nation, especially those in the diaspora, may have no direct contact with the homeland or with those who live there; their linkages to them may be largely or purely imaginary. In other words, they exist in what Benedict Anderson (1991; Roudometof 2012) called **imagined communities**, or communities that are socially constructed by those who see themselves as part of them. Thus, Jews who have never been to Israel or who may never even want to visit there may still be part of an imagined community rooted in Israel. The same is true of the relationship between Palestine and many Palestinians scattered throughout the world.

The **nation-state** combines the nation with a geographic and political structure. In other words, in addition to encompassing people with a shared identity and culture, a nation-state exists in a bounded physical location and encompasses a government to administer the locale.

Nation-states exist within a global context, but they are affected, even threatened, by globalisation in various ways (Hershkovitz 2012). First, global flows of various kinds—undocumented immigrants, drugs, terrorists, and so on—easily pierce the borders of nation-states and serve to erode their national sovereignties. Second, even if it does not threaten national sovereignty, a global flow serves to alter the nation-state's structure and functions. For example, corporations have become increasingly important on the global stage and have come to operate more autonomously from the state. Third, the government itself has to change in order to adjust to global changes. For example, Canada passed the Anti-Terrorism Act in 2001, and it was under this legislation in 2006 that Zakaria Amara was charged with terrorism as one of the 17 Toronto-area people originally arrested in the largest and most recent terrorism scare in Canada. Fourth, there is the possibility that global flows can

strengthen the nation-state. For example, external threats can lead citizens to put their differences aside, at least for the time being, and rally around the government and the nation-state more broadly.

In spite of changes such as those described above, we continue to think of nation-states as being all-powerful. However, not only are states experiencing the kinds of problems described here, but a number of them have also failed, or are on the verge of failing, the "basic conditions and responsibilities" of a sovereign state (Boas 2012:633). Among the failures that define a failed state are "lack of control over own territory, widespread corruption and criminality, huge economic recession and/or hyperinflation, failure to provide basic services, and large flows of refugees and internally displaced persons" (Boas 2012:633). The best known failed state in the world today is Somalia, but Afghanistan is often placed in this category as well. Failed states cause many problems for themselves and their residents, but from a global perspective, it is the problems they cause for others that are the main concern. For example, pirates based in Somalia roam the high seas and have succeeded in a number of acts of high-stakes piracy, such as holding huge oil tankers for millions of dollars in ransom. The Somali government, to the extent that it exists, is unable to control the pirates or their activities.

Given the problems being experienced by nation-states, especially failed states, there is great interest in the issue of **global governance**, organisations that operate beyond the reach of nation-states yet guide and constrain the actions of those states as well as of individuals in them (R. Cox and Schilthuis 2012). There are three basic types of global governance (Koppell 2010). First are classic organisations that derive their authority from the nation-states. They involve settings in which discussions are held and international agreements are hashed out. The UN is a major example of the first type of global governance. Second are international cartels, which, although their membership is restricted, are able to enforce compliance with their decisions. One example is the Organization of the Petroleum Exporting Countries (OPEC), a cartel in which various oil-producing nations work together to manage the global market for oil. Third are organisations that are not based in nation-states or dependent on them for their authority. They are

American Jews who have never been to or even had contact with anyone from Israel may still be part of an imagined community rooted in the small Middle Eastern republic. Because of this imagined community, their country's ongoing support of Israel is an important subject for many throughout the United States. Here, a man wears a hat with U.S. and Israel flags at a 2010 rally in Washington, DC's Lafayette Park.

usually private organisations operating in a highly delimited domain. One example is the Internet Corporation for Assigned Names and Numbers (ICANN), whose major task is to assign Internet addresses. All of these organisations are handling global governance tasks that nation-states alone cannot, or will not, handle. A major factor in the rise of organisations involved in global governance is the sheer increase in the number and diversity of tasks that require global cooperation.

One of the problems associated with global governance organisations is that they are not accountable to the people they serve. While this lack of accountability is a problem even for major nation-states, it is especially problematic for those smaller countries that are less well developed. The key point here is that as a result of globalisation, nation-states and their interrelationships are no longer the only political entities that matter in the world. Global governance organisations are handling tasks formerly performed by nation-states, *and* they are taking on tasks that were never performed before, such as the assignment of Internet names.

THE ECONOMY: PRODUCTION, CONSUMPTION, AND LEISURE

The **economy** is the social system involved in the production and distribution of goods and services. The devastating effect of the recent recession has reminded us that the economy is of overwhelming importance to everyone (Orr 2012; David Smith et al. 2011). For those who had forgotten or who might have grown complacent about the economy because of the economic boom throughout most of the first decade of the twenty-first century, the onset of the recession was a rude awakening.

SOCIOLOGY OF THE ECONOMY

The economy is, of course, the focal topic in the discipline of economics. So, what distinguishes the sociological approach to the economy from the economic? Economists focus on the economic

behaviour of individuals and take such behaviour as the basis for more general analyses of, and arguments about, the economy. Sociologists are also concerned with individual economic behaviour, but they are more focused on the economy as a whole—its basic components (for example, labour unions, corporations, occupations, financial institutions) and the ways in which they interrelate—as well as global economic systems. More importantly, sociologists devote greater attention to the linkage between the economy and noneconomic macro-phenomena, such as politics, the family, and culture (Fourcade-Gourinchas 2007). Sociologists are also often more concerned with the micro-macro link as it relates to the economy. Sociologists would deal with how the global recession affects individuals who lose their jobs as a result of an economic downturn. For example, Matthew Desmond (2010) has shown how evictions during the recession have disproportionately affected black women.

The economy is the first and longest-running concern of sociology (Ramella 2007). All of the major figures in early sociology had a focal interest in the economy: Marx, of course, was interested in capitalism, Weber in the rationalisation of the economy, Durkheim in the economic division of labour, Simmel in money, and Veblen in consumption (see Chapter 2). Today, the subfield of economic sociology continues to be quite vibrant (Swedberg 2007).

HISTORICAL CHANGES IN THE ECONOMY

INDUSTRIAL REVOLUTION

The key development in the emergence of the modern economy was the nineteenth-century Industrial Revolution (see Figure 12.9), which introduced the factory system of production (Hobsbawm and Wrigley 1999). Instead of making products alone at home or in small groups in workshops, large numbers of workers were brought together in factories. Eventually, manual factory work with hand tools gave way to work in conjunction with machines. In addition, human and animal power was replaced by power supplied by steam and other energy sources. While there were skilled workers in these early factories, they tended over time to be replaced because skills were increasingly likely to be built into the machinery. This meant that less skilled or even unskilled workers, less well-trained and lower-paid workers, and even children could be—and were—hired to do the work. They tended to work increasingly long hours in harsh working conditions and at ever-lower pay. Another defining characteristic of this factory system was an elaborate division of labour, with a single product being produced by a number of workers, each performing a small step in the overall process.

The factories of the early Industrial Revolution were quite primitive, but over time they grew much larger, more efficient, more technologically advanced, and more oriented toward the mass production of a wide variety of goods. **Mass production** has a number of defining characteristics, including large numbers of standardised products, highly specialised workers, interchangeable machine parts, precision tools, a high-volume mechanised production process, and the synchronisation of the flow of materials to and of products from the machines, with the entire process made as continuous as possible. The logical outcome of this was the assembly line, which came to fruition in the early twentieth century in the mass production of Ford automobiles. By the mid-twentieth century these systems had reached their fullest application in the United States and had spread to many other parts of the world. After World War II the Japanese adopted

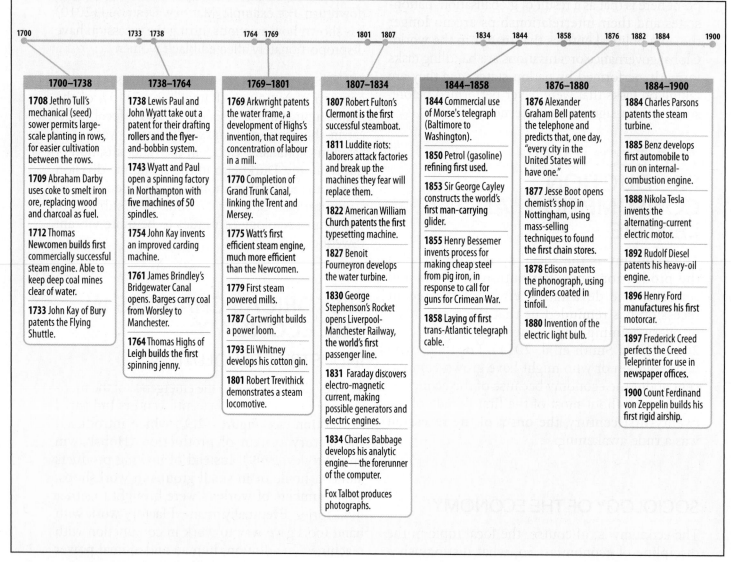

FIGURE 12.9 Timeline of the Industrial Revolution, 1700–1900

SOURCE: Adapted from *Industrial Revolution: Timeline, Facts, and Resources*. Research by B. Sobey, TheFreeResource.com.

these American innovations and later came to outstrip the United States in many areas, most notably the production of electronics and automobiles.

CANADIAN ECONOMIC CHANGE

If the primary economic engine of the Industrial Revolution moved from England to the United States and then to Asia, as it arguably has, then Canada can best be understood as a key supplier to this engine. Canadian fuel, in a variety of forms, helped power the industrial engine. In important ways the economic development of Canada was set from its earliest days as a supplier of key raw materials to the more powerful industrial economies of England and more recently the United States. The phrase "hewers of wood and drawers of water" captures this Canadian focus.

The Canadian economy has been usefully described as a **staples economy**. Flour, milk, rice, and/or corn are often considered as staples for many households, key ingredients that are essential for, or core to, the production of foodstuffs in the home. In describing Canada as a staples economy, scholars point to the production of fish and wheat as key ingredients that feed workers in England and the United States. Similarly, timber and minerals, such as iron ore, copper, and nickel, are core raw materials essential for industrial production lines. More recently the Canadian economy has exported high volumes of hydroelectric power and oil and natural gas. Each of these products is a staple, a core ingredient required as essential raw material input for manufacturing.

Unlike England, the United States, Japan, Korea, or China, Canada has never put manufacturing at the core of its economy. Certainly Canada has some large automobile production facilities, mainly in Ontario and Quebec, as well as a few automobile parts producers, but Canada has always been a net importer of finished products (i.e., manufactured goods) and a net exporter of raw materials. A Canadian company such as Bombardier, producing planes and trains, is the manufacturing exception that proves the raw material rule. Furthermore, a significant proportion of Bombardier's production occurs in foreign locales, mainly in Europe and Asia. The reverse is also true in that the automobile assembly lines in Oshawa, Windsor, and Woodstock are the branch

Lewis Hine (1874–1940) was a sociologist who used photography to bring attention to early twentieth-century social problems such as child labour, poverty, and dangerous working conditions. Hine's 1920 photograph *Power House Mechanic Working on Steam Pump* captured the struggle of the working-class American at the turn of the century, quickly becoming an iconic image of the Industrial Revolution.

plants of companies such as General Motors, Chrysler, and Toyota. Notice too that this manufacturing is regionally specific, with Ontario, and to a lesser extent Quebec, the core locale. This links as well to politics, discussed earlier in the chapter, because regions have different economic interests. For example, a Canadian dollar whose value is relatively low in comparison to other currencies makes exporting manufactured goods easier because they are less costly for consumers elsewhere, but it means that raw material exporters, say, in lumber or oil, receive less for their sales.

In part because manufacturing has not been as central to the Canadian economy as it has been in other countries, particularly England and the United States, the deindustrialisation that has buffeted these two countries has been less intense in Canada's (Baldwin and Macdonald 2009). Indeed, like most western economies, Canada's has now evolved to being a service economy, with by far the largest concentration of economic activity being centred on the production and distribution not of material goods, but of services. That is, the production of staples (raw materials) and finished products (manufacturing goods) is a relatively minor economic activity in comparison to service activities. The service sector, as the name implies, refers to the provision of services or assistance to others. Examples of the service sector include advertising, banking, communications, food service, health care, law, secretarial work, and teaching.

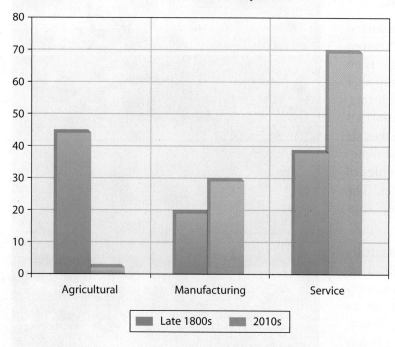

Figure 12.10 provides two different indicators, economic activity and jobs, showing how Canadian economic activity has changed over time and how dominant the service sector has become. Notice first that manufacturing has never been central to the Canadian economy. Second, both sections of the figure demonstrate the transition from an agricultural (or harvesting) economy, including fish and wood, to a service economy. Finally, the dominance of the service sector is clearly shown by both indicators, contribution to economic activity and employment.

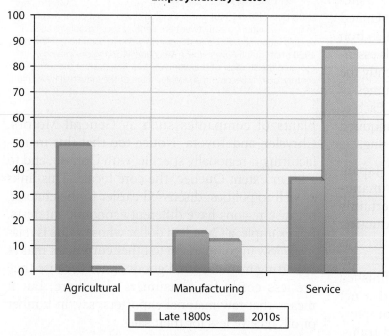

FIGURE 12.10 **Percentage Distribution** of Canadian Economic Production (top graph) and Employment (bottom graph) by Sector and Period

SOURCES: Estimated from K. A. H. Buckley and M. C. Urquhart, *Historical Statistics of Canada* (Toronto: Macmillan, 1965); Statistics Canada, *The Labour Force*, Cat. no. 15–001–XIE; Statistics Canada, CANSIM Table 282–0008.

SCIENTIFIC MANAGEMENT

Economic production and distribution has been dominated by principles created in the late nineteenth and early twentieth centuries, primarily by Frederick W. Taylor. Taylor championed **scientific management**, or the application of scientific principles and methods to management. These principles came to be known as "Taylorism" (Prechel 2007) and were designed to rationalise work by making it more efficient. Those who applied these ideas were called "efficiency experts," and they sought to discover the "one best way" to do a job.

Scientific management certainly helped rationalise work and make it more efficient, but it had its irrationalities. Above all, it separated the conception of work from its execution.

That is, managers—with the help of efficiency experts—were to conceive how the work was to be done while the workers were expected to do what they were told to do in an unthinking manner. Because workers were asked to do only one or a few repetitive tasks, most of the skills and abilities, including the ability to think, that made them human were not used. This was an inherently dehumanising system in which workers were considered expendable and were treated in that way; they were hired and fired at will. In the long run, this had a series of disastrous consequences. For example, workers' full capabilities were ignored, dissatisfied employees performed poorly and sabotaged the production process, and workers quit in large numbers, leading to high costs associated with significant turnover. For this reason, and many others, by the 1980s at least some aspects of North American industry found themselves outstripped by Japanese industry, which had discovered ways of using the abilities of its workers more fully. Today, as Japan declines as an industrial power, its neighbour China rises markedly (see Figure 12.11).

Although one hears little these days about Taylor and scientific management, their impact remains strong in various sectors of the economy. One recent study found that a variety of current practises, such as employee involvement in manual production, temporary outsourcing (see below), project-based teams, and layoffs, can be seen as consistent with Taylorism (M. Crowley et al. 2010). In fact, they represent an extension of those principles. Taylor's principles are highly influential in manual work and have been extended to managers and professionals. As a result of these new forms of Taylorism, manual workers are found to work harder, and managers and professionals experience greater pressure on the job. In the fast-food industry, restaurants strive to discover and implement the "one best way" to grill hamburgers, cook French fries, prepare donuts, and process customers. The most efficient ways of handling a variety of tasks have been codified in training manuals and taught to managers, who, in turn, teach them to new employees. The design of the fast-food restaurant and its various technologies have been put in place to aid in the attainment of the most

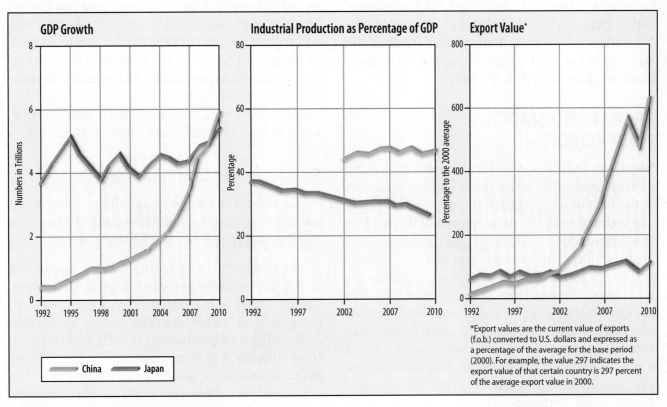

FIGURE 12.11 **GDP Growth, World Bank**

SOURCE: World Bank.

Henry Ford is generally credited with the development of the modern mass-production system, primarily through the creation of the automobile assembly line. Here, a row of Ford Model As is assembled at the Rouge plant in Dearborn, Michigan, in 1932.

efficient means to the end of feeding large numbers of people. This could be called "McDonaldism" rather than Taylorism. Whatever it is called, the basic ideas of scientific management are alive and well in the fast-food restaurant, as well as in many other work settings (Ritzer 1997).

FROM FORDISM TO POST-FORDISM

Fordism includes the ideas, principles, and systems created by Henry Ford and his associates at the turn of the twentieth century. Ford is generally credited with the development of the modern mass-production system, primarily through the creation of the automobile assembly line. Among the characteristics associated with Fordism are mass production of homogeneous products; reliance on inflexible technologies such as the assembly line; use of Tayloristic, standardised work routines; economies of scale; and the creation of a mass market for the products, like automobiles, that flowed from the assembly line (Beynon and Nichol 2006; Bonanno 2012).

Fordism dominated much of the twentieth-century North American automobile industry and many others, but declined beginning especially in the 1970s with the 1973 oil crisis and the rise of the Japanese automobile industry. It was also done in by the fact that consumers were no longer content with homogeneous products and demanded greater choice in their automobiles and their components. **Post-Fordism** is associated with smaller production runs of more specialised products, especially those high in style and quality, more flexible machinery made possible by advances in technology largely traceable to the computer, more skilled workers with greater flexibility and autonomy, less reliance on economies of scale, and more differentiated markets for those more specialised products (Amin 1994; Prechel 2007).

CAPITALISM, SOCIALISM, AND COMMUNISM

From its inception, the Industrial Revolution was capitalist in nature. As is the case with heavy industries such as automobile manufacturing, the United States is beginning to lose its grip on the position of being the preeminent capitalist society in the world. China is already outstripping the United States in many areas, and it is projected that China will replace the United States as the dominant force in global capitalism by the middle of the twenty-first century (Jacques 2009). This is ironic because of China's recent history as a communist power and the fact that it continues to think of, and describe, itself, as least politically, as a communist nation.

Socialism and Communism

Socialism and communism are often confused and are used more or less interchangeably. However, it is important to differentiate between them.

In Chapter 2, you learned that communism is a social system associated with Karl Marx. Communism is an economic system oriented to the collective, rather than the private, ownership of the means of production (Lovell 2007). Recall from Chapter 8 that the means of production are the tools, machines, and factories that in capitalism are owned by the capitalists and are needed by the workers—the proletariat in Marx's terms—in order to produce. Marx hoped that the exploitation of the proletariat would lead workers to revolt against the capitalist system, and that, in turn, would lead to the collective rather than private ownership of the means of production, resulting in a communist economy. Control of the economic base would lead to the control of everything else of importance, including the political system.

From a Marxian perspective, **socialism** can be seen as a historical stage following communism, involving the effort by society to plan and organise production consciously and rationally so that all members of society benefit from it (L. Cox 2007; Shevchenko 2012). The collective control of the means of production in communism is a first step, but in itself is not enough to run a society. Once in control of the means of production, the collective must set about the task of creating a rational centralised economy (and society) that operates for the good of all and creates social and economic equality.

The ideas associated with communism and socialism are less important today than they were only a few decades ago before the fall of the Soviet empire in late 1991. With the demise of the Soviet Union, there is little that passes for communism in the world today. Cuba continues to see itself as a communist society, and China does as well, even though it is, as we have seen, on the cusp of becoming the most powerful capitalist country in the world. A political commitment to communism exists uncomfortably side by side in China with a highly capitalistic economic system.

Welfare States

Socialism is more vibrant in the contemporary world than communism. However, even Israel, not long ago a strongly socialist economy, has moved decidedly in the direction of capitalism (Ram 2007; Zilberfarb 2005). Although there are no fully socialist societies in the world today, many societies have elements that can be considered socialistic. For example, many of the countries of Western Europe, although there is great variation among them, have become "welfare states" (Cousins 2005). They have powerful social welfare programmes that are socialistic in nature because they are run consciously and rationally by centralised authorities. **Welfare states** seek both to run their economic markets efficiently, as capitalism does, and to do so equitably, which capitalism does *not* do (Esping-Anderson 1990; Gangl 2007). Their goal is to provide for the welfare, the well-being, of their citizens (Peoples 2012). There are many examples of social welfare programmes, including national health plans, old age plans, child care and parental leave systems, and social safety nets of one kind or another (for example, unemployment insurance).

Even the United States has social welfare programmes, such as unemployment insurance, Social Security, and Medicare. However, the United States lags far behind the leaders in Western Europe and Canada in these kinds of programmes. And there are powerful forces aligned with capitalism that strongly encourage the shrinkage of social welfare programmes. In Canada there have been various new laws, both federal and provincial, offering less generous benefits and programmes, making it more difficult for people to qualify for them, and making people take greater responsibility for providing for their own welfare. Changes to employment insurance eligibility and benefits exemplify this retrenchment (van den Berg et al. 2008). Threats to, and declines in, social welfare programmes have spread throughout Europe as well as a result of both the recent recession and the euro crisis (see below) that threatened the European economies in 2011–13. Those countries worst hit by the latter—Greece and Spain—have had to cut back on these programmes. Programmes are even in danger in countries such as Sweden, which have long been at the forefront of such social welfare programmes.

Welfare states have been threatened before. However, they are much more threatened today by the realities of the global economy. With today's markets for virtually everything increasingly global and highly competitive, the lion's share of global business is very likely to go to the countries, and the industries in them, where the costs are lowest (see Chapter 8). This advantages countries, including China, India, and Vietnam, where social welfare costs are minimal or nonexistent. By contrast, the costs of production in Western European countries are far higher, in part because of the extraordinary social welfare expenses that must be factored into their cost structure. This has made Western Europe, Canada, and the United States, to a lesser degree, less competitive or even uncompetitive in various global markets. This is seen by many as a profound threat to

GLBALISATION

Fordlandia in Brazil

Beginning in the late 1920s, Henry Ford decided he needed greater control over the supply of rubber required for his tires. The best and closest source of rubber was a remote jungle area near the Amazon River in Brazil. This was a wild and untamed area inhabited by people unaccustomed to the modern, standardised, and rationalised world that Ford, his assembly line, and his automobile had played such a huge role in creating.

Ford sought to apply to his Brazilian rubber plantations the principles and methods that had made him successful in the production of automobiles in Detroit. However, the wilds of the Amazon were far from the urban realities of Detroit, and they proved far more resistant to Ford's methods of operation.

Ford created a town—"Fordlandia"—as the hub of rubber operations in Brazil (Grandin 2010). Created there was a version of small-town America with suburban-type houses built in perfect rows along neatly laid-out streets. This was out of place in the jungles of Brazil. For example, the houses that already existed there had thatched roofs that, because they allowed hot air to escape, functioned reasonably well in the extremely hot and humid climate. Ford had his new houses built with modern metal roofs lined with asbestos. However, Ford's houses retained much more heat than did those with thatched roofs and were transformed into ovens.

In the wild, rubber trees tend to grow in a haphazard manner and at some distance from one another. This makes obtaining the rubber very time-consuming. However, it is also more difficult for diseases and insects to attack trees that are widely dispersed throughout the jungle. The Ford people had their rubber trees planted close to one another in neat rows. This made it much easier for them to contract disease and to be assaulted by insects. Many of the rubber trees died, and Ford's rubber plantation eventually failed.

Ford management also decided that it would be more efficient for Fordlandia employees to be fed cafeteria-style. However, the native workers were unfamiliar with this modern mode of food service. A resulting riot by the workers destroyed much of Fordlandia, although it was later rebuilt.

Fordlandia represented a battle between Ford's efforts to apply modern techniques to a wilderness and its people who operated on the basis of their own, very different, principles. In the short run, the wilderness and the natives and their ways won out. However, in more recent years, Brazil has become one of the world's rising economic powerhouses, a good portion of the Amazon has undergone deforestation, and a major metropolis has burst forth out of the forest. It may be that Henry Ford was just way ahead of his time.

The Fordlandia experiment failed after a few years, and the factories were closed down, leaving many thousands out of work.

these economies and societies, and some argue that these countries must reduce social welfare expenditures in order to compete in the global marketplace. Others argue that their more generous welfare states lower costs of business in some sectors and help make the workforce more productive (P. Hall and Soskice 2001). From this perspective, greater spending on social welfare programmes can contribute to a more educated, healthy, and flexible workforce.

Capitalism

Recall from Chapter 2 that, based on Marx's work, capitalism is an economic system based on one group of people—the capitalists— owning what is needed for production and a second group of people—the proletariat—owning little but their capacity for work. Marx's basic analysis of this economic system, as well as that of the relationship between capitalists and the proletariat, remains relevant today. However, capitalism has changed in many ways since the nineteenth century, and it is important to update our sense of capitalism.

Marx lived during the era of **competitive capitalism**. That is, there were a large number of relatively small firms. No single firm or small subset of firms could completely dominate and control a given area of the economy. In other words, the capitalism of Marx's day was highly competitive.

However, by the late nineteenth century and into much of the twentieth century, this situation changed as huge corporations emerged and alone, or in combination with a few other similarly sized corporations, came to dominate, or monopolise, a market. This came to be known as **monopoly capitalism** (Baran and Sweezy 1966). Perhaps the best example is the North American automobile industry, which for much of the twentieth century was dominated by three huge corporations— General Motors, Ford, and Chrysler.

Of course, capitalism has changed once again, as is clear in the recent misfortunes of these automobile companies. It is also clear in the fact that there are, as we have seen, a number of other companies (Toyota, Honda, Hyundai, BMW, Mercedes) competing successfully with the older North American firms. While we may have

A woman carries shopping bags as she passes homeless people outside the Monastiraki metro station in Athens, Greece, on January 24, 2012. Though Greece has long boasted generous social welfare programmes, the euro crisis forced a number of austerity measures across Europe, including cuts to Greece's welfare efforts. These cuts left holes in Greece's security net, especially for those who were already suffering from the downturned economy.

seen the end of monopoly capitalism in certain key business sectors, it is likely that in the future we will see the emergence of a global system of monopoly capitalism where a small number of corporations come to dominate a global, not just a national, market.

Whether or not capitalism once again becomes monopolistic, in recent years it has certainly become increasingly global. This can be seen as **transnational capitalism** where no longer national, but transnational, economic practises dominate (Sklair 2002). Thus, the global flow of automobiles and even money have become far more important than their existence and movement within national boundaries. The key actors in this global economic system are **transnational corporations**, also referred to as multinational corporations, that exist in various places throughout the world and that cannot be identified and that do not identify themselves, with any specific country (Sklair 2012c). In fact, capitalism has moved away not only from being a national system but also from merely being an international system to becoming a truly global system that encompasses myriad relationships among most, if not all, of the nations of the world. That is, it is an economic system that has decoupled from any specific geographic territory or nation-state, or any simple linkage among a small number of nation-states.

At the heart of global capitalism, and transnational corporations, is a **transnational capitalist class** (TCC)—recall the opening vignette from Chapter 8 (Carroll and Carson 2003; Sklair 2012b). Included in the TCC are executives of transnational corporations, state bureaucrats and politicians, professionals and technical personnel, and those focally concerned with consumption rather than production, such as merchants and media executives. However, this social class is not made up of capitalists in the traditional Marxian sense of the term. That is, unlike Marx's capitalists, the TCC does not necessarily own the means of production.

The TCC may not be capitalist in a traditional sense, but it *is* transnational, even global, in various ways. First, its members tend to share global as well as local interests. Second, they seek to exert various types of control across nations and globally. That is, they exert economic control in the workplace, political control in both domestic and international politics, and ideological control in everyday life across international borders. Third, they tend to share a global rather than a local perspective on a wide range of issues. Fourth, they come from many different countries, but increasingly they see themselves as citizens of the world and not of their country of origin. Finally, wherever they may be at any given time, they share similar lifestyles, especially in terms of the goods and services they consume.

The **culture-ideology of consumerism** is of great importance in transnational capitalism (Sklair 2012a). This encompasses the central role played by consumption in the economy, by the culture of consumption, and by the ideologies that are an integral part of that culture. It is increasingly important to get large numbers of people scattered widely throughout the globe interested, and involved, in consumption. Such interest has increased dramatically primarily through the growing global reach and sophistication of the proconsumption ideologies expressed in advertising, the media, and culture as a whole. This, of course, is buttressed by the bewildering array of consumer goods that are marketed by and through them. Ultimately, they all serve to create a global desire to consume what benefits transnational corporations, as well as the advertising and media corporations that profit from them.

It could be argued that the centre of capitalism lies no longer in production but rather in **consumption**—in inducing large numbers of people throughout the world to consume at high levels. While the capitalism of Marx's day was described as producer capitalism, it could be argued, we now live in the era of consumer capitalism. Of course, we cannot have consumption without production, but it is at least arguable that the success of capitalism today lies more on the spread of consumerism than it does on the growth and spread of production.

Within the realm of consumption, some of the leading transnational corporations are Walmart, IKEA, H&M clothing, and McDonald's. Their top-level executives are part of the TCC and frequently interact with their peers as well as politicians and media executives. Needless to say, these corporations are actively involved in the dissemination of the culture-ideology of consumerism, especially through their massive expenditures on advertisements that appear throughout much of the world.

DEINDUSTRIALISATION IN THE INDUSTRIAL WEST

Industry and industrial employment were clearly crucial to economic development in the western world. Indeed, developed nations were once considered only those with industrial muscle. However, a number of developed nations, especially the United States, have been undergoing a process of deindustrialisation. **Deindustrialisation** involves the decline of manufacturing, as well as a corresponding increase in various types of services (Bluestone and Harrison 1984; Dandaneau 2012; N. Flynn 2007). Most pronounced has been the decline in manufacturing *jobs*, even while in some countries, such as Canada, manufacturing output has been maintained, largely through mechanisation.

We tend to think of deindustrialisation as a process that has been going on for decades, is now far advanced, and may even be near completion. For example, in the *Rust Belt* in the middle part of the United States the demise began in the 1960s.

Cities, including Cleveland, Detroit, and Pittsburgh, have suffered, as have their industries in auto manufacturing and steel. Deindustrialisation in the United States has not yet run its course, and other industries, such as the glass industry, are now experiencing this process (Uchitelle 2010). The process has also been regionally specific in many countries, as the Rust Belt example implies in the United States. In Canada, a similar phenomenon has occurred in the so-called golden horseshoe, stretching from just east of Toronto to Windsor, where there has been a slump in industrial employment.

Factors in Deindustrialisation

There are several factors responsible for deindustrialisation. First, at least historically, was the aging technology in many industries. This made them vulnerable to foreign competitors that were often building new state-of-the-art factories with the latest technology. Many American industries in the Rust Belt, especially steel, suffered from having been in business for decades and therefore having become reliant on antiquated technologies and factories. Another aspect of the technological factor was the rise of automation, which greatly reduced the need for many industrial blue-collar workers (D. Noble 2011). For example, the automobile plants of Oakville (Ford) and Oshawa (General Motors), in Ontario, are now far more mechanised than they once were. Furthermore, the increased efficiency of automated technologies made it possible to close redundant factories, thus cutting many more jobs.

A second factor in deindustrialisation was the expansion of globalisation, which, among other things, brought with it industrial competition from low-wage workers in less developed countries. This was especially true in the early years of the emergence of South Korea and China as industrial powers. Now, of course, China is developing rapidly, but its low wages and seemingly endless stream of workers will make it nearly impossible for western industries to compete with Chinese industries.

For example, most of the work on Apple's iPhone is done in China at Foxconn City (Duhigg and Bradsher 2012). About 230,000 people work there, often six days a week and for as many as 12 hours a day. Workers sleep in barracks on site provided by the company, and many

earn less than $17 a day. How many western workers would be willing to work in such enormous factories, to work such long hours, and to live in company barracks, all for $17 a day? This process is sometimes referred to in the popular press as offshoring. Apple, while headquartered in the United States, is doing increasing amounts of its manufacturing offshore.

A third factor was the rise of consumer society and the increasing demand for goods of all types. While this should have helped western industries, it had the effect of leading to the development of many more foreign manufacturers anxious to sell products to that consumer market. Western industries have had great difficulty competing with them. In terms of the demand for goods, there arose, partly as a result of the low prices offered by foreign manufacturers, a mania among consumers for ever-lower prices. This worked to the advantage of foreign manufacturers because of their much lower cost structures, especially, and, most importantly, their lower labour costs. The consumer obsession with lower prices has led to what has been called the *high cost of low price* (Spotts and Greenwald 2005), or the unfortunate unanticipated consequences of such low prices. Among those consequences is

In late 2011, the housing market in Detroit, Michigan, showed signs of stabilising—even rebounding—after years of decline. While still down almost 45 percent from its precollapse peak, Detroit home prices jumped 3.8 percent in the last six months of 2011—2.9 percent better than the average of the 20 largest metropolitan areas. Windsor, across the river from Detroit, did not suffer as much, although there too the economy remains depressed.

the heightened exploitation of foreign workers, an increasing preference for goods produced by low-cost foreign manufacturers, and the resulting decline in western manufacturers and the jobs they offered.

A fourth factor responsible for deindustrialisation was the rise of the service sector. In the last half of the twentieth century, an increasingly affluent western population demanded not only more and cheaper goods but also a dramatic increase in services of all types (Kollmeyer 2009). People began spending their newfound money on services rather than on industrial products. Among other things, this led to the expansion of service industries such as health, education, and personal and social services. More recently, other service industries have come to the fore, such as financial, real estate, tourism, and hospitality—for example, those who work at Canada's Wonderland, in the casino hotels across the country, and on cruise ships. As job possibilities contracted in manufacturing, they increased dramatically in these and other service sectors (Figure 12.10). In some cases, these jobs were more attractive. Early higher-status service jobs were considered white- or pink-collar jobs rather than the blue-collar jobs in the factories. Now, however, much work in the service sector is better described as "no-collar jobs."

As this process occurred, many other service jobs proliferated that were not so desirable, but that opened up new possibilities for work for many, especially young people. The best example is the millions of jobs in the fast-food industry (Leidner 1993). In addition, millions of jobs created for Canadians of all age groups, even senior citizens, opened in the retail sector, most notably in retail giants such as Walmart and Shoppers Drug Mart. Women are disproportionally represented in these service careers.

The surge in the service sector of the Canadian economy is readily apparent, but notice that Canada has not suffered from deindustrialisation as much as the U.S. Northeast. This is largely because manufacturing was never so central to the Canadian economy. Industrial jobs have declined in Canada as a percentage of employment (Figure 12.10), but manufacturing's contribution to economic output has increased over the last century (see also Baldwin and Gu 2009; Baldwin and Macdonald 2009).

Canadian Labour Unions

Related to deindustrialisation, and sometimes considered part of it, is the decline of labour unions and the weakening of the labour movement in general (Fantasia and Voss 2007; Timms 2012). Caution is necessary here, however, because unionisation has actually remained relatively steady in many western countries, including Canada (Figure 12.12), as well as countries such as Belgium, Finland, and Spain. Union membership rates fell in the United States, where deindustrialisation has been most apparent, as did rates in places including Australia, France, and Germany. The puzzle comes in figuring out what is common in the countries with the declining rates, which sets them apart from the countries where no, or only modest, union decline has occurred.

One set of explanations has focused on either or both globalisation and technological change. Globalisation might dampen union membership because national economies in the West have had to become competitive with emerging market economies such as Brazil, China, and India. This international competition, especially over wages paid, might have weakened the power unions have to leverage better deals for their members. Technological change could have eroded union membership because machines have come more and more to replace people in the workplace. Machines don't unionise, so as

Deindustrialization opened up new possibilities for service industry work for many, including senior citizens.

workers are pushed out by automated processes, the power of collective union action weakens. However, for the most part globalisation and technological change are social forces that have affected all western nations, and it is hard to see these as explanations that help us understand differences between Canada and the United States. Both of these countries have experienced the competitive impact of globalisation, and both have experienced technological change, even if the latter has been somewhat more prevalent in the United States.

One factor that might be common, though, for countries where labour unions have lost power is politics. In many countries, such as the United States and France, where union rates are down, a more conservative, antiunion government has held power at important times. These governments have enacted legislation that weakens union power (Schmitt and Mitukiewicz 2012). A good example here is the aggressive antiunion activism that led to the breaking of the Professional Air Traffic Controllers Organization (PATCO) in 1981 by U.S. President Ronald Reagan. There had always been a powerful current of antiunionism in the United States, but it was emboldened by many things, including a more conservative mood in the United States and the decline of the union movements' traditional industrial power base. Laws were put in effect to expedite the decline of unions. Companies pushed antiunionism by hiring management consultants to find ways to avoid unions as well as employing lawyers highly skilled in "union busting." In contrast, countries such as Canada and Belgium have not had a sustained period in which governments with antiunion agendas have held power. That might change, though, in Canada with the majority Conservative government that was recently elected.

The rise of jobs in the service sector also relates to this issue. In Canada, public sector unions, that is, people working for governments, have compensated for some of the erosion of union membership in the manufacturing sector. These public sector jobs are service jobs, but this has been the only part of the service sector where strong unionisation has taken hold. For their part, unions

were very slow to adopt the new methods needed to appeal to and organise workers in the service sector. For example, among these new workers were large numbers of young people, especially in service jobs like those in the fast-food industry. However, unions had grown rigid and could not find effective ways to attract and organise these young, part-time workers who were likely to stay on the job for only a few months (Freeman and Medoff 1984).

THE POSTINDUSTRIAL SOCIETY

The Postindustrial Society shift toward service work has ushered in postindustrialism in the developed world. An increasing emphasis on consumption and the dramatic growth in service jobs, many of which exist to serve a consumer-oriented society, pushed Canada even further from industrialisation and toward a truly postindustrial society (Bell 1973; Cohen 2008; Hage and Powers 1992; Smart 2011).

A **postindustrial society** is one that was at one time industrial but where the focus on harvesting or mining industrial raw materials and the manufacture of goods has been eclipsed by the prominence of service work. The latter is work which people provide services for one another rather than producing goods. This encompasses a wide range of service-oriented occupations, including lawyers, physicians,

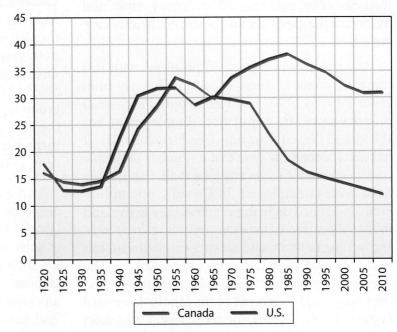

FIGURE 12.12 **Union Membership in Canada and the United States, 1920–2010 (in %)**

SOURCE: HRSD Canada (2012b) and Riddell (1993); U.S. adapted from Hirsch and Macpherson (2003).

teachers, financial advisors, and computer geeks, as well as salespeople, clerks, and counter people in fast-food restaurants. Employment in such occupations has increased dramatically in Canada in the last century, while there has been a decline in work relating to goods production; agricultural work had declined earlier and even more steeply.

WORK, WORKING, AND NOT WORKING

Much of the preceding deals with the economy in terms of general trends and developments. However, most people connect to the economy either through their work or through the process of consumption, to be discussed below. The relationship between people and their work is undergoing rapid change.

EMPLOYMENT, UNEMPLOYMENT, AND UNDEREMPLOYMENT

Not long ago, we tended to think of people as taking a job, perhaps in a large and stable organisation, and embarking on a lifelong career that entailed at least some upward mobility, enough earnings for them and their families to live on, retirement in their early 60s, and a period of security, supported by an ample pension and a sound health care system.

However, there are several problems with this romantic scenario. First, even in its heyday from about 1950 to 1990, it applied to only a very small proportion of the population. Employment has ebbed and flowed over time (see Figure 12.13). It has always been the case that a number of people have been unable to get any jobs at all; that is, they have been unemployed. In Canada, **unemployment** is defined as being economically active and in the labour force (for example, not retired), able and willing to work, and seeking employment, but unable to find a job (Statistics Canada 2010). The unemployment rate in Canada has generally run at between 6 and 8 percent of the labour force (see Figure 12.14). During the most recent recession the rate increased to a peak of about 8.5 percent in August 2009, and has subsequently declined to nearer 7 percent. The most recent increase was

especially noticeable for younger workers, for men, for people with less education, and for workers in industrial jobs (e.g., manufacturing).

However, the statistics on unemployment understate the problem of lack of work because they deal only with those who are in the labour force and who are actively seeking work. There is another large group of people, marginally attached to the workforce, including **discouraged workers**. To be categorised as such, people must have sought work within the last year or since their last job ended, if that was less than a year previous, and must have not sought work in the last four weeks (and therefore not be in the labour force). Other reasons to be considered marginally attached to the labour force include being prevented from working because of family responsibilities or because of a lack of transportation.

The number of marginally employed, especially discouraged, workers is, like unemployment, a chronic problem. Even worse, both marginal employment and unemployment increase in recessionary times. In 2010 about 30,000 Canadians could be defined as discouraged workers, individuals who had given up looking for work because they believed no work was available (Gilmore and LaRochelle-Coté 2011). An additional 65,000 Canadians had been laid off because of the recession and were not actively looking for work, even though they felt work might be available. In essence people in this latter group were not technically defined as discouraged because they believed jobs were available but had chosen not to search. Combined, this group would have added about 100,000 people to the rolls of the unemployed, and the unemployment rate would have increased to about 7.3 percent, from 7.2 percent, had they been included.

An even larger number of Canadians must also cope with the problem of **underemployment** (Dooley and Prause 2009). This involves (1) being in jobs that are beneath one's training and ability, such as a college professor working as a day labourer; (2) being an involuntary part-time worker, a person who works part-time because she cannot find full-time work; and (3) working, but in jobs that do not fully occupy the workers, such as in a seasonal industry like agriculture or fishing, where work slows down dramatically or disappears in the

PUBLIC SOCIOLOGY

Barbara Ehrenreich and Being "Nickel and Dimed" at Work

Barbara Ehrenreich (1941–) has written numerous pieces for magazines (*Time,* for example) and newspapers (especially *The New York Times*). Her greatest fame and influence have been derived from a series of books, most notably *Nickel and Dimed: On (Not) Getting by in America* (2001). In this book, Ehrenreich is primarily interested in the low-paying jobs that millions of American women (and men) are forced to take, and whether they can actually survive on what they are paid. She is also interested in the actual experiences, both on and off the job, of the people who do this work.

In doing the research for this book, Ehrenreich adopted the time-honoured sociological research method of becoming a participant observer in a number of low-paying, entry-level American jobs. Indeed, she actually worked in several of them, including being a waitress, working for a cleaning service, and working for Walmart. In these jobs, she was often paid between $6 and $7 an hour, and she earned much less when she worked as a waitress and depended mainly on tips. One of her goals was to determine whether this work truly paid a living wage. What she found, of course, was that it did not. In fact, it provided only about a quarter of the income needed to live in the United States. In no state can a minimum-wage worker afford a two-bedroom unit at fair market rent, working a standard 40-hour workweek. On one occasion she was forced, as many people—especially women—are, to take a second job in order to get by. Living conditions on such an income were dismal, eating well was problematic, and there was little if anything left for savings or for leisure activities. The work was often hard, even backbreaking.

Perhaps worst of all, there were innumerable humiliations along the way. For one thing, Ehrenreich filled out lots of applications, but few potential employers even bothered to respond. For another, supervisors could be harsh, and they had the power to embarrass her or even to fire her at will. As a waitress, Ehrenreich found that her customers could be difficult and would often leave her a minimal tip or even no tip at all. As a house cleaner, she found herself in a humiliating relationship with the "woman of the house," who closely watched what she did and insisted that she do such things as wash the floor on her hands and knees.

Often unable to survive on their own, the women in these jobs were frequently dependent on others, but the necessary aid was often limited or nonexistent. Some women could not afford to live on their own and had to live with roommates or with extended family members. Those who lived alone might, as Ehrenreich did, find themselves living in trailers or in fly-by-night motels. It was often difficult for those with children to get reliable day care, and much of it was far too expensive given their meagre wages. Most women found that they could not rely on various social services to help them solve their problems. The social safety net, at least for them, was shredded. Normal medical care was out of the question, and the free care that was available was difficult to obtain. Charitable agencies existed, but help from them was often humiliating and insufficient. Living costs were often higher for Ehrenreich's fellow workers than they were for more well-to-do members of society because, for example, their humble living arrangements might lack a kitchen or provide only a hot plate. As a result, they often had to rely on comparatively expensive (and unhealthy) junk food and fast food.

In sum, Ehrenreich found that the "nickels and dimes" that millions of American women and men are paid to work are grossly inadequate. This forces them to, and even beyond, the edge of poverty and into a wide variety of humiliating circumstances and experiences.

Low-paying entry-level service work such as serving can be humiliating, unstable, and backbreaking, and often does not pay a living wage.

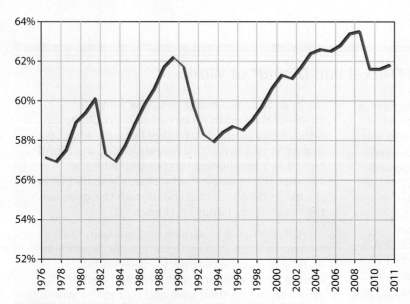

FIGURE 12.13 Canadian Employment Rate, 1976–2011

SOURCE: Authors' calculations from Statistics Canada, CANISM Table 282-0002.

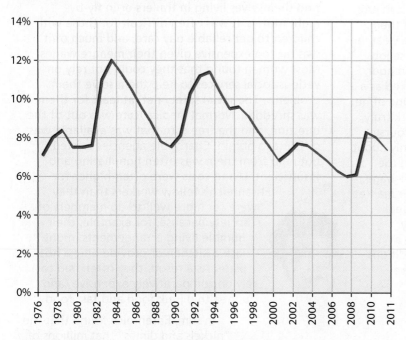

FIGURE 12.14 Canadian Unemployment Rate, 1976–2011

SOURCE: Calculations by authors based on Statistics Canada, CANISM Table 282-0002.

off-season (Fuller and Vosko 2008). This appears to be an even larger problem in Canada than is the discouraged worker rate (although 100,000 discouraged workers are clearly an important issue). Gilmore and LaRochelle-Coté (2011) estimate the number of underemployed by examining people who are working part-time who would prefer to be working full-time (i.e., involuntary part-time

workers). In 2010 about 840,000 people were in this predicament. It is more difficult to measure the underutilisation of workers' skills, and there are no robust national measures of this type of underemployment available in Canada.

The welfare states of Europe seem to have done better in dealing with these problems, but even there, these problems and others are on the rise. In part, this is because of the large influx of immigrants, many of them illegal, who are much more likely to have difficulty finding work. For example, in early 2010, riots occurred among African immigrants in southern Italy. These riots were motivated, at least in part, by a lack of work and low pay ($30 a day) for the jobs, largely in agriculture, such as picking fruit, that were available (Donadio 2010). Greater unemployment difficulties in Europe are also related to the continent-wide economic crisis and the myriad problems being experienced with the euro—but more on that later.

Being without a job is a major problem; however, as pointed out above, most people in Canada who want jobs have them, although they might not always have the jobs that they want. An even bigger problem is that many jobs that exist (especially service jobs) do not pay a *living wage,* an income that is high enough to meet the most basic expenses to provide for a family.

CHANGING NATURE OF THE CANADIAN LABOUR FORCE

A number of dramatic changes in the labour force have been mentioned in the previous sections, including the following:

- In the late 1800s, slightly less than 50 percent of the Canadian labour force was on the farm or in farm-related work; today less than 2 percent are so employed.

- After increasing through the first half of the twentieth century, the number of people who work in manufacturing (production)—that is, in blue-collar jobs—has undergone a noticeable decline, and that decline continued in the first decade of the twenty-first century. There was a drop of over 500,000 workers in manufacturing between 2002 and 2012—to about 10 percent of the labour force—while the labour force as a whole increased by over 2 million people in that period (see Figure 12.15).

- Service work of various types has increased substantially. Among the leaders here are educational services (adding nearly 2 million jobs between 2000 and 2008), health care and social assistance (up almost 3.5 million jobs in that period), and leisure and hospitality, with an increase during that period of over 1.5 million jobs, with most of the increase (almost 1.2 million jobs) coming in accommodation (for example, hotel work) and food services (for example, fast-food restaurants).

These are but a few of the changes in the labour force in Canada. Many of the trends mentioned above will continue, and others will come to the fore as the work world and the labour force continue to change.

One key consequence of the latest economic recession is the closing of businesses. Small businesses are often hardest hit by recessions because they have smaller reserves and weaker safety nets.

In the case of unemployment, a person is able and willing to work but cannot find a job. At left, thousands of job seekers attend a job fair at the International Exhibition Center in Nanjing, China. In the case of underemployment, a person has a job that does not meet the individual's qualifications or desired time commitment.

GLOBALISATION AND THE ECONOMY

Globalisation is associated with many changes in the economy. In this section, we will discuss macrofinance and microfinance, two areas of marked change brought about by globalisation.

MACROFINANCE: GLOBALISATION OF MONEY AND FINANCE

One of the most remarkable changes associated with the global economy is in **macrofinance**, or globalisation as it relates to money and finance. Not long ago, money and finance were closely tied to the nation-state that issued the money and to the financial transactions that took place therein. Moving money and financial instruments—for example, stocks and bonds, as well new instruments such as derivatives—from one part of the world to another was difficult and cumbersome. Not too long ago, travellers would need to change their own country's currency into the currency of a country to which they were travelling. And if they were going to many different countries, this transaction had to be repeated over and over. Now, however, all a traveller needs is a debit card that can be used in most nations in the world to

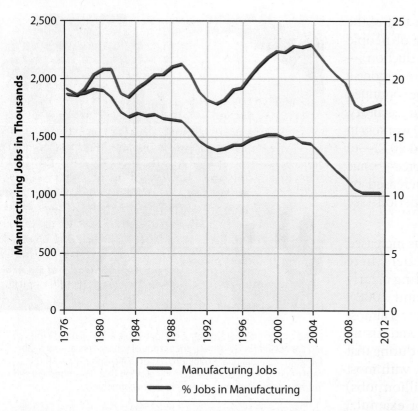

FIGURE 12.15 Number of Manufacturing Jobs (in 2000s) and Percentage of Labour Force

SOURCE: Authors' calculations from Statistics Canada, CANISM Table 282-0088.

NOTE: Left y-axis is Manufacturing Employment in Thousands; Right y-axis is Manufacturing Employment as percentage of all employment.

rapidly and efficiently obtain the currencies of each of the nations visited. As Dodd (2012) puts it, "We are witnessing the end of money's geography" (p. 1446).

As a result, money is increasingly liquid, and it flows around the world quite readily. This is clearly true for tourists and businesspeople, but it is true in other ways as well: Substantial flows of money are associated with the informal economy, criminal networks, the international drug trade, and money laundering. To take another example, much money flows in the form of remittances, largely from migrants in the Global North to family and friends back home in the Global South. In fact, in 2010, recorded remittances—much more probably went unreported—totalled $325 billion (Ratha and Mohapatra 2012). While this sounds like a great deal of money, it pales in comparison to other types of global financial transactions. For example, in only one aspect of the global financial market, the market for the world's currencies, about $4 trillion changes hands *every day* (Knorr-Cetina 2012).

By far the greatest amounts of money flow easily and quickly through electronic transmissions associated with global financial markets (Knorr-Cetina 2012). People and businesses are increasingly dependent on electronic transfers for the credit they need, or think they need, in today's world. Individuals usually need credit to purchase such things as homes and automobiles; credit is also central to the growth and investments of corporations and governments.

Even more important is global trade in a series of obscure financial instruments, such as *credit default swaps,* a kind of insurance policy in case a loan defaults. Recall from the chapter's opening vignette that banking practises tied to the U.S. housing market—including credit default swaps—set off a chain reaction that devastated international economic flows and triggered a global recession. Central to these problems was the fact that financial markets in both the United States and much of the rest of the world were deregulated to a great degree. Without governmental oversight, many of these markets were allowed to run wild. For example, there was wild speculation in exotic financial instruments, producing an economic bubble that burst violently, causing the recession to develop and gather momentum.

The bursting of the bubble created a global liquidity crisis because nations and their banks were reluctant to lend to one another. They were afraid the economic crisis would render other nations and banks unable to repay their loans. Without these loans, and the high interest rates paid on the loans, many nations were plunged into deep recessions. This was especially true among the European countries that comprise the *eurozone,* the 17 of 27 European nations that use the euro as a common currency.

Over the years, this led to the *euro crisis,* which grew particularly intense in late 2011 and throughout

McDONALDIZATION *Today*

McJobs

Work was highly rationalised long before the advent of McDonald's and McDonaldization. Classic examples were jobs on the automobile assembly line that were rationalised as a result of, among other things, Fordism and Taylorism. However, the rise of lower-level, service-sector jobs, especially the millions created by the fast-food industry, led to the emergence of a new term to describe much of the work in that sector of the economy: *McJobs* (J. Newman 2007; Ritzer 1997). McJobs have all of the basic characteristics of McDonaldization: They are to be done efficiently, the focus is on speed and quantity of output, they are to be performed the same way over and over, and they are highly controlled by various technologies. As a result, McJobs tend to be dehumanising and degrading to the people who hold them, and constitute dead ends from a career point of view.

Some of the work in McDonaldized service settings closely resembles work on the assembly line. For instance, hamburgers are assembled in much the same way as automobiles. On the other hand, a great deal of such service work involves human interaction with the public, and such interaction is more difficult to McDonaldize. Nevertheless, it has been McDonaldized to some degree by creating scripts for employees ("May I help you?" "Would you like a dessert to go with your meal?" and "Have a nice day!") and insisting that they be followed during each interaction (Leidner 1993). Thus, one of the distinctive aspects of McJobs is that they McDonaldize not only what people do but also what they say. This leads to new depths in *de-skilling,* taking skills out of jobs and away from employees. Lost is the ability to speak and to interact with people on one's own.

McJobs are clearly linked to social class; those in the lower class are far more likely to hold such positions, at least for a length of time, than those in the middle and upper classes. While more and more work is being McDonaldized, a whole other sector of the economy, the postindustrial sector, offers well-paid, highly skilled, non-McDonaldized service-sector jobs—for example, financial advisors and computer programmers. Thus, we are increasingly moving to a two-tiered occupational system differentiated between the postindustrial work of the middle and upper classes and the McDonaldized work of the lower classes.

McJobs are to be done efficiently, the focus is on speed and quantity of output, they are to be performed the same way over and over, and they are highly controlled by various technologies. The archetypical example of a McJob is a food service position in a fast-food restaurant.

2012 (Riera-Crichton 2012). The wealthier European societies, especially Germany, were able to deal with the recession well. Other countries, especially Greece, Portugal, Ireland, Spain, and later Italy, were not. They suffered huge economic problems, such as the collapse of their housing markets and high unemployment. Recall from the chapter's opening vignette that several of these countries have had their credit scores diminished. In such a situation, the typical course of action for a country is to devalue its currency, thereby reducing its costs. This makes its products cheaper and more competitive in the global economy, allowing the economy to begin to be able to grow again. However, because those troubled countries were part of the eurozone, no one country was able to devalue its currency,

GL🌐BALISATION

Chinese Textile Workers in Italy

There was a time when textiles produced in Italy and made by Italian workers, most notably in the town of Prato, meant something special. However, in recent years, Italian textile manufacturers and many others have had difficulty competing on a price basis with textiles manufactured in China. More recently, tens of thousands of mostly undocumented Chinese workers emigrated to Prato and other areas in Italy, transforming the town into a centre of low-end garment manufacturing (Donadio 2010).

Chinese migrants work for a large number of relatively small manufacturers, which often use materials imported from China to produce price-competitive textiles. Instead of textiles produced slowly and with care, the Chinese are focusing on the production of "fast fashion," which seeks to rapidly deliver designer fashion for cheaper, mass-market consumption. In the process, the differences between "Made in Italy" and "Made in China" have blurred, with an adverse effect on the once prestigious "Made in Italy" label. In fact, the Chinese manufacturers are selling their lower-quality goods with "Made in Italy" labels, or wholesalers and retailers are sewing such labels into garments.

Prato now has the highest concentration of Chinese, both documented and undocumented immigrants, in not only Italy, but all of Europe. Further, there are more Chinese than Italian factories in Prato. This has changed not only the nature of the manufacturing process in Prato, but also the culture of the town. It is beginning to look more like a Chinatown with signs in Chinese and Chinese grocery stores selling food imported from China.

There are certainly problems, especially for Italians, associated with Chinese businesses and business practises. Furthermore, Chinese workers in these factories remain very vulnerable and are subject to a variety of abuses and poor working conditions (Wu and Sheehan 2011). However, it is also the case that the Italians have been slow to innovate and the Chinese have been highly innovative. Drawing from their unique cultural heritage, the Chinese have blended their entrepreneurial orientation with Italian fashion to create new hybrid forms of global culture and production (Santini, Rabino, and Zanni 2011). They produced the fast fashion system and, in the process, probably created many more jobs, even for Italians, than would otherwise have been created.

Chinese-born model maker Xu Qiu Lin measures a design inside Giupiel Factory in Prato, Italy. Giupiel Factory is a fashion design firm specialising in leather clothing that counts 28 workers—only 14 of whom are Italian.

and the troubled European economies were left without the traditional method of dealing with recessions and depression.

Further worsening the situation for these countries was that it became more difficult for them to borrow money to keep their economies functioning. Lenders increasingly believed that the troubled nations might default on those loans. The result was that the troubled eurozone countries had to pay ever-higher interest rates in order to get the loans. The higher interest rates threatened the economic futures of these countries. In the short run, countries including Ireland and Greece had to get bailouts from European sources. In exchange for those bailouts, they had to agree to practise greater austerity—for example, by firing government employees and cutting back welfare programmes. Paradoxically, this austerity further weakened their economies, at least in the short run, because many people had less money to spend.

While the dangers associated with the euro crisis ebbed in early 2012 with the bailout of Greece, the basic problems with the euro remain, and the crisis could flare again. There are many fears associated with a euro crisis. First, those living in the countries most affected by the crisis would face unavoidable economic hardships. Second, at least some of the affected countries might find it necessary to abandon the euro and return to the currencies they used before the creation of the euro, which began circulating in 2002. This could lead to huge internal economic problems for those countries in the short term and, in the long term, to the collapse of the eurozone and perhaps a return to the era in which European nations fought horrendous wars against one another. Third, there is a fear that affected countries would drag the rest of the eurozone countries, and eventually much of the rest of the world, down economically. That could lead to the second dip in a "double-dip" recession begun in late 2007, or it could be the beginning of a global depression. Fourth, there is the fear that people in the worst affected countries could grow increasingly disaffected, leading to political revolutions. Among the fears is the possibility, in the face of looming insurrections, of the rise of right-wing governments and possibly the emergence of new dictatorships. The latter is already of concern in Hungary, and right-wing parties seem to be gaining strength throughout Europe. This is what happened as a result of economic disruption after World War I and the Great Depression, which, among other things, led to the rise of fascism in Europe and eventually to World War II (L. Thomas 2011).

MICROFINANCE: SMALL-SCALE LENDING

Much of the above relates to the financial situation confronting the Global North, especially Europe. The Global South is certainly affected by these problems and would be hugely affected by a meltdown in the eurozone, another global recession, or a depression. However, it should be noted that there are financial issues that are largely specific to the Global South.

Currency exchange rates are one simple indicator of the tightened financial network that is part of the global flows of money. Currency traders play a vital role in the global processes that are part of the increasingly interlocked world economy - and risks of financial uncertainty can have catastrophic consequences.

The best known issue facing the Global South is **microfinance**, or local, grassroots efforts to lend small sums of money to poor people (Offutt 2012). Unlike the trillions involved in global financial markets, microfinance generally involves tiny sums of money, perhaps as little as a hundred dollars, to start or sustain very small businesses. Lending microcredit to the poor was developed by Nobel Peace Prize winner Muhammad Yunus. The idea of microfinance is to support not only small businesses but also the communities in which they exist. One example, "Village Phone," involves the placement of mobile phones in communities without phone service. One member of the community starts a business in which she loans a phone

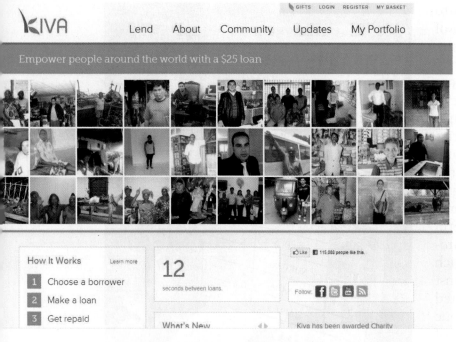

Online microfinance companies such as Kiva.org connect those who seek microfinance loans with those who want to give them. By simply browsing borrowers and making a loan through PayPal, a user in the Global North can easily and instantly participate in microfinance.

to community members for a small fee. Through phone contacts, small businesses become possible, and other businesses, as well as other opportunities, become available to community members for the first time. Microfinance has made possible numerous small businesses, such as crop diversification, nursery schools, and the provision of transportation.

As microfinance has matured, it has grown into a global business valued at $20 billion. This has attracted for-profit institutions interested in earning money from financing the poor. This stands in contrast to the early years of microfinance dominated by nonprofits interested in helping the poor and their communities. An interest in profits tends to mean that social programmes that do not earn a profit will not be funded, even if that adversely affects the local community. The counterargument is that involving global profit-making organisations would lead to much more money available to the global poor. While that may be the case, the fear remains that the most needed programmes,

for example in health education, will go unfunded or underfunded because of the fact that they can produce little if any profit for companies or their investors.

In the early years, poor women were prioritised by microfinance programmes, but there is concern that women's needs will be a lesser priority for profit-making organisations. Women were the focus because they were traditionally excluded from traditional sources of capital. It was also believed that they were more likely than men to accept accountability to peers and to invest the money in productive enterprises, and that there would be large benefits in helping women because of their greater interest in their children and families. Assuming that some or all of this is true, much would be lost if for-profits were, in fact, to target less of their funding at women.

Critics of microfinancing suggest that it may not give women more power because the money they receive might, in fact, be taken from them by men. This would reduce or eliminate the ability of the funding to lead to greater gender equality. Microfinancing could complicate the lives of poor women who would then have to manage both their homes and their businesses. Funding may go not to the poorest members of the community, but to those thought to be best able to use the money successfully. These are likely to be the better-off members of the community, and therefore, instead of increasing equality in communities, microfinance may well support or even enhance inequality.

CONSUMPTION

While aspects of consumption have been mentioned throughout this chapter and throughout this book, especially in the discussion of the culture-ideology of consumerism, in this section we focus more directly on consumption itself (Brandle and Ryan 2012; Sassatelli 2007). Too often, discussions of the economy focus only on production and work, ignoring the increasingly important process of consumption.

Recall from Chapter 1 that consumption is the process by which people obtain and utilise goods and services. More specifically, it is a highly complex process involving the interrelationship among consumer objects and services, consumers, the consumption process, and consumption sites (Ritzer, Goodman, and Wiedenhoft 2001). First, consumption involves what is to be consumed, largely consumer objects (clothes, cars, electronic gear) and services (help from computer experts, medical services). Second, consumption requires consumers or those people who do the consuming. Third, there must be a process of consumption. Fourth, this process often takes place in relation to a physical site—shopping at a farmers' market, wandering through a shopping mall, enjoying yourself at a theme park, or setting off on a cruise ship.

The latter three sites can be seen as **cathedrals of consumption** (Ritzer 2010a), the large and lavish consumption sites created in the last half of the twentieth century and into the early twenty-first century, first in western industrial nations but now increasingly around the globe. The use of the term *cathedrals* is meant to indicate the fact that consumption has in many ways become today's religion. We go to the cathedrals of consumption to practise that religion. Thus, for example, many middle-class children make a pilgrimage to Disney World or Disneyland at least once in their lives.

Outdoor strip malls are traceable to the 1920s, and the first indoor malls were built in the 1950s, but it is the megamall, which arrived in the 1980s and 1990s (for example, the West Edmonton Mall, opened in 1981 and for about 20 years the world's largest shopping mall), that is the crucial innovation here. What defines the megamall is the combination under one roof of a number of cathedrals of consumption, especially a shopping mall and a theme park. The theme park itself is a second cathedral of consumption; the first landmark development was the opening of Disneyland in southern California in 1955. Third is the modern cruise ship, the first of which set sail in 1966. The goal of the cruise ship is not really to go anywhere, but simply to cruise around, say, the Caribbean or the Mediterranean (Clancy 2012). The final major cathedral of consumption is the casino hotel, most notably those that define Las Vegas. The first of these—the Flamingo—was built in 1946. It was the idea of the mobster Bugsy Siegel, as dramatised in the 1991 movie *Bugsy*.

Of course, there are many other important cathedrals of consumption—superstores such as Bed Bath & Beyond and Future Shop, huge discounters such as Walmart and Costco, and now online retailers and malls of various types such as Amazon.ca and Craigslist. These cathedrals, along with other consumption sites, especially chain stores such as McDonald's, Starbucks, and Tim Hortons, have come to define not only the sites themselves, but much consumption as a whole.

CONSUMPTION AND POSTMODERN SOCIETY

Consumption is generally considered to be the hallmark of postmodern society. That is, while modernity is defined by production and work, postmodernity is defined by consumption. This change is best seen in the United States, which moved from being the preeminent industrial society in the world in the mid-twentieth century to being the world's most important consumer society in the late twentieth and early twenty-first century. This is reflected, for example, in the fact that consumption accounts for approximately 70 percent of the U.S. economy today. Canada is not far behind.

Consumption is central to the idea of a postmodern society precisely because it represents a shift from the focus on production in modern society. However, in another sense, there is such a thing as postmodern consumption that is different from, and stands in contrast to, modern consumption (A. Venkatesh 2007). In modernity, consumption is seen as a secondary activity, as well as something to be avoided as much as possible so that people can focus on the far more important activities of production and work. This, of course, was the view associated with Max Weber's ([1904–1905] 1958) famous conception of the Protestant ethic. According to this ethic, people were to concentrate on work because it was there, especially in being successful in one's work, that the signs of religious salvation could be found. People were expected to consume minimally, to be frugal, to save their money, and to reinvest what they earned from productive activities.

Postmodern consumption is best thought of as **consumerism** (see above discussion of the culture-ideology of consumerism), an obsession with consumption (B. Barber 2007). We have become consumed by consumption. This reflects the view, outlined in Chapter 2, that postmodern theory can be seen as a new kind of critical theory. For example, Baudrillard ([1970] 1998) argues against the conventional view that consumption is about the satisfaction of needs. He contends that if that were the case, consumption would cease when one's needs were satisfied. However, in contemporary consumerism, as soon as one need is satisfied, a new and different need comes to the fore, requiring additional consumption. Baudrillard further argues that what consumption is really about is difference. That is, it is through consumption that people seek to demonstrate that they are different from others in, for example, their taste in clothes or in cars. In the postmodern world, where an endless and ever-expanding set of differences is created, consumption becomes a never-ending process of demonstrating those differences.

Postmodernists are very prone to append the prefix *hyper-* to many things (Lipovetsky 2005). Appending *hyper-* to any modern characteristic tends to turn it into something associated with, and critical of, the postmodern world. For example, the postmodern world is associated with **hyperconsumption**, or buying more than you want, need, and can afford (Ritzer 2001a). Related to the idea of hyperconsumption, especially consuming more than you can afford, is the idea of **hyperdebt**, or borrowing more than you should, thereby owing more than you will be able to repay. These concepts are addressed more extensively in Chapter 15. However, some postmodernists have a complex view of consumption, whereby a more positive perspective coexists with this critical orientation (A. Venkatesh 2007). For example, some postmodernists tend to see consumption as an aesthetic undertaking, as a kind of work of art. Consumers are seen as artists in, for example, buying, and putting together in highly creative ways, the various elements of an outfit. This is particularly related to the postmodern idea of *pastiche* (see Chapter 2), or the mixing together of various elements, especially those that most would

not see as fitting together. While a modern consumer might purchase an outfit composed of matching elements (for example, skirt and top) predesigned and preselected by the manufacturer, the postmodern consumer is seen as creatively and artistically putting together components from a wide range of manufacturers and styles. Furthermore, new and used clothing, or clothing from different time periods, is combined in unique ways to create outfits that can be seen as works of art.

LEISURE

One of the dominant trends of our time is that more and more of our leisure time is devoted to consumption. Leisure time often involves activities that require consumption. For example, in golf, consumption includes the equipment, the proper clothing, greens fees, and perhaps even membership in a country club. Leisure time also takes place in settings such as a cruise ship, entirely devoted to consumption. Furthermore, for many people consumption *is* leisure. Going to the shopping mall and making a variety of purchases can be very relaxing for some.

Leisure is defined as a means of escape from the obligations associated with work and family. It involves social activities that are not coerced—that are relaxing, perhaps informative, and set apart in time and often in space (Dumazadier 1967; S. Parker 1971; Rojek 2005, 2007; Scraton 2007; Stebbins 2007). The focus of much research on leisure is on what people think and do when they are at leisure. That is, they are not just free from their usual obligations, but they are also free to think differently and to do different things. It is presumed that when they are at leisure, people have much more freedom of choice than they do at work or at home, perhaps with the family.

However, much leisure activity takes place in settings that are designed to control and to limit the thoughts and actions of those at leisure. The best example is Disney World, where all sorts of conveyances are provided to force people to move around the park and its attractions quickly, efficiently, and in given directions. Even during the times that one seems to be wandering around the park on one's own, the fact is that more subtle

GL BALISATION

Billboards on the Piazza San Marco in Venice, Italy

In our consumer society, we are certainly accustomed to seeing all sorts of advertisements, including in-your-face billboards in cities and on roads and highways. However, we are shocked when our most important and valued cultural icons are used as sites to advertise products. This became clear once again in 2010 when huge billboards appeared in and around one of the world's most revered sites and tourist attractions—the ancient Piazza San Marco in Venice, Italy. The reason for the appearance of the signs is, not surprisingly, money. In this case, however, the revenue is to be used to help repair the decaying structures in and around the piazza that attract hordes of tourists every year.

The Palazzo Ducale is being repaired by Dottor Group, an Italian restoration firm. To pay for the work, part of the palazzo has been wrapped in tarpaulin emblazoned with huge ads for global corporations including Coca-Cola and Italian luxury retailers including Bulgari. As people from around the world visit this uniquely local cultural centre, they are now greeted with a mixture of global icons and corporate logos. Dottor Group claims that such

Massive Bulgari advertising featuring actress Julianne Moore can be seen on the Palazzo Ducale, the Bridge of Sighs, and other historic Piazza San Marco attractions along the Rio di Palazzo in Venice, Italy. As people from around the world visit this uniquely local cultural centre, they are now greeted with a mixture of global icons and corporate logos.

ads are paying for the repairs, and as a result, the city of Venice is incurring no expense for the work. One representative of a heritage organisation recognised the need for such ad income, especially since public funding has been cut, but worried about the "invasiveness of ads in delicate places, like Piazza San Marco." Furthermore, she argued that because of the uniqueness of Venice, "a special dialogue exists between architecture, stones, water and man, which the ads shatter" (Povoledo 2010:18).

From this point of view, Venice is reduced to a "location" like any other, and like any other, it is to be "sold" better. That is, it is to be used to sell more products and in the process to further expand and entrench consumer culture. It is valued not for its cultural beauty and distinctiveness but as a profit-making centre in the global economy. In the process, the historic architecture and ambiance of Venice is sullied and reduced to a backdrop for the sale of consumer goods (Perkins and Thorn 2011).

kinds of controls are exercised over the visitor—for example, preset paths, directional arrows, and signs. Most interesting from this perspective is what Walt Disney called "weenies," or highly visible attractions—mountains, castles, and the like—to which virtually all visitors will find themselves drawn. Thus, they move in the direction of the weenies, the way that Disney management wants them to move. They do so without anyone telling them where they should go and how they should get there. This allows for the efficient movement of large numbers of visitors. On the way, they are led past many kiosks, shops, restaurants, and the like, where they can spend even more money.

A cruise ship is a vast world unto itself where tourists have a wide array of options open to them from early morning until late at night. Leisure activities aboard cruise ships (such as elegant dinners, scuba diving outings, and ship-wide parties) take place in settings that are designed to control and to limit the thoughts and actions of those at leisure.

This controlled and limited image of leisure seems at variance with the increasing diversity of experiences available to those at leisure. For example, there is a world of global choices now open to people who can afford the high costs involved. Thus, a cruise ship is a vast world unto itself where tourists have a wide array of options open to them from early morning until late at night. While this greater choice exists, it is also the case that the settings involved have not given up on their efforts to control those at leisure. Rather, the controls have become more varied and sophisticated. Thus, on a cruise ship, numerous TV cameras monitor virtually everything that passengers do aboard ship.

Ultimately, the success of a cruise ship, and any other setting in which leisure takes place, depends on how much people can be induced to spend on consumption. Cruise ships are very expensive to build and operate, and the costs of a cruise are rarely covered by the up-front cabin fees paid by travellers. Whether a cruise is economically successful depends on how much people lose in the casino, how much they spend on alcohol (not covered in the up-front payment for the cruise, although food is), how much they buy in the shops in the onboard mall, and how many costly side trips they take during the voyage.

Leisure time is strongly affected by social class. Many leisure activities are very expensive, and those in the lower rungs of the stratification system in the Global North, and most of those in the Global South, are largely excluded from them. Of course, there are many inexpensive and even free forms of leisure available to virtually everyone, but these are not generally deemed the most desirable forms in today's world. Furthermore the demands of work, and even of survival, make it difficult for the have-nots of the world to have much time for, or to get great enjoyment from, their leisure-time activities.

Women's leisure has also tended to be more constrained by economic factors than men's, but that too is changing, as women in the middle classes are more likely to have incomes associated with occupations of their own (see Chapter 15). The latter also tends to give them more of the demarcated time for leisure, for example vacations, which historically have been the province of men. Yet because women still spend more hours a week on child care and household maintenance than do men (see Chapter 11), a gendered leisure divide remains.

SUMMARY

Politics are one way to advance a given position or policy through the use of, or by putting pressure on, the state. Various types of governments can be seen throughout history. Small city-states expanded, leading to the birth of the first nation-states. These states were often monarchies. Democracy is a political system in which people within a given state vote to choose their leaders and, in some cases, might

be able to vote on legislation. This is in contrast to dictatorships, which are usually totalitarian.

Canada is an example of a democracy with a multiparty system. Voting is one way of influencing politics, but there are several others. Functionalist sociologists emphasise pluralism, while conflict sociologists focus on power elite theory. One way of dealing with political disagreements is through war. Terrorism refers mainly to nongovernmental actors who engage in acts of violence targeting noncombatants, property, or military personnel.

Sociologists define the economy as the social system involved in the production and distribution of goods and services. There have been several major historical changes in the capitalist Canadian economy over the last 200 years, from the United Kingdom's Industrial Revolution in the nineteenth century to global changes in sites of industrialisation. Communism is an economic system oriented to the collective, and socialism can be seen as a historical stage following communism involving the effort by society to plan and organise production consciously and rationally. Canada has some important social welfare programmes, such as health care and employment insurance, but still lags behind some European welfare states in what it provides.

Recently, capitalism has become increasingly global in that transnational, not national, economic practises predominate. Also important in transnational capitalism is the cultural ideology of consumerism, which encompasses the central role played by consumption in the economy, the culture of consumption, and the ideologies that are an integral part of that culture. In Canada, the growth of service jobs and an increasing focus on consumption set the stage for a postindustrial society, a society in which the focus on the manufacture of goods and the exporting of industrial raw material have been eclipsed, to an important extent, by an increase in service work.

In addition to these general shifts in the economy, there have been dramatic changes in the Canadian labour force. The number of discouraged workers, people who have sought work within the last year but have not sought work in the last four weeks, has risen with the current recession. Other Canadians are dealing with underemployment. Globally speaking, the eurozone has faced, and may again confront, a euro crisis that threatens to destabilise Europe and, possibly, the world. These problems impact both individuals and large-scale—even global—society.

Consumption is generally considered to be the hallmark of postmodern society. Consumerism indicates an obsession with consumption. Baudrillard argues that consumption is not about the satisfaction of needs but about being able to differentiate oneself from others. Cathedrals of consumption indicate how consumption has in many ways become today's religion. The postmodern world is also associated with hyperconsumption and hyperdebt. One of the dominant trends of the last several decades is the increasing amount of leisure time that is devoted to consumption.

KEY TERMS

- Cathedrals of consumption 487
- Citizens 446
- Citizenship 446
- City-states 444
- Competitive capitalism 473
- Consumerism 488
- Consumption 474
- Corporatism 448
- Cult of masculinity 448
- Culture-ideology of consumerism 474
- Deindustrialisation 474
- Democracies 446
- Dictatorships 447
- Direct democracies 446
- Discouraged workers 478
- Economy 465

- Elite pluralism 459
- Fordism 470
- Geopolitics 462
- Global governance 464
- Group pluralism 459
- Hyperconsumption 488
- Hyperdebt 488
- Imagined communities 463
- Leisure 488
- Macrofinance 481
- Mass production 466
- Microfinance 485
- Monopoly capitalism 473
- Monarchy 444
- Multiparty system 448
- Nation 463

THINKING ABOUT SOCIOLOGY

1. What factors help explain the emergence of democratic political systems? How is democracy related to bureaucracy and rational-legal concepts you learned in previous chapters?

2. In what ways is citizenship an important component of a democratic political system? Do you think that low voter turnout in Canada is due to a failure of its citizens? Or do nonvoters in Canada express their political interests in other ways? In what ways could new technologies facilitate political involvement?

3. The question of who rules Canada is still being debated. In what ways does a pluralist understanding of power and politics in Canada differ from the power elite perspective? Do you think globalisation has an effect on who rules Canada? Why or why not?

4. How are socialism and communism alternatives to capitalism? What elements of welfare states are socialistic, and what forces in Canada are resistant to social welfare programmes?

5. What factors help explain deindustrialisation, and how does deindustrialisation relate to the decline of unions? How does Canada fare on deindustrialisation and on unionisation? What effects has deindustrialisation had on other countries, especially the United States?

6. How has work in postindustrial societies become increasingly McDonaldized? Has the McDonaldization of work affected all groups in the same way? Why or why not?

7. In what ways has the Internet changed the nature of work? What are some examples of how you use the Internet as a producer and/or a consumer?

8. How is our society characterised by rampant and insatiable consumerism? How do we use consumption to satisfy our needs in the world today? Do you agree that we tend to consume beyond our needs?

9. In what ways is consumption today the new religion?

10. How do leisure activities create distinctions between groups of people? In what ways are these distinctions reflective of the system of stratification?

APPLYING THE SOCIOLOGICAL IMAGINATION

1.   This chapter poses the question "Who rules Canada?" According to the power elite perspective, power is concentrated in the hands of a small number of people who control the major institutions of the state, the corporate economy, and the military. The powerful people who make up these institutions might have minor disagreements about policy but for the most part are unified in their interests and in owning and operating much of Canadian society.

For this activity, choose an organisation from the top 10 Canadian corporations. Use the Internet to find the most up-to-date data. After selecting the company, go to its website to find information on its board of directors. A good place to start is the company's annual report. For the most part, annual reports are made available on a company's website or its "About Us" tab. Finally, select two members from the company's board of directors and answer the following questions:

- What are their racial or ethnic backgrounds?

- What are their educational backgrounds? Where did they go to school?

- What are their primary occupations?

- Have they held formal positions in government?

- Do they have affiliations with other organisations? If so, which ones?

- Are they outspoken members of particular political parties?

- Do they belong to any specific social clubs?

- Are they often mentioned in news reports? What types of mention?

Do you think the answers to these questions provide evidence for or against the power elite perspective? How might a group pluralist or elite pluralist respond to the limited evidence you have compiled here?

2.   How can you use the clothes on your back to understand the nature of globalisation? As has been explored throughout the textbook, the things we consume say a lot about who we are and how we want others to perceive us. Rarely, however, do we pay attention to how these individual choices are situated within larger global processes. For this activity, choose five of your favourite articles of clothing and check their tags to see where they were made. Then, do research on the companies and their production sites in these various countries. In what ways are the clothes you wear part of an increasingly globalised economy? What are the benefits of such an economy for you? What are the benefits and disadvantages for the workers producing the clothes? What are the consequences for each of the different countries?

ACTIVE SOCIOLOGY ··

As Chapter 12 has pointed out, the nature of work changes in response to shifts in the economy. Technology plays a major role in this. One benefit of the Internet is that it allows for the growth of entrepreneurs. Those people with business ideas can virtually market their products and services to anyone in the world. This means that even small businesses can grow in a global society. One way this is seen is in the growth of the website Etsy (www.etsy.com). Examine the Seller Handbook at www.etsy.com/blog/en/2012/

the-seller-handbook. Then explore the sellers. What kinds of goods and services are for sale? Whom does a site like Etsy benefit most? What is the function of the business owner/seller? What roles or tasks must he or she perform? How is this different from the typical job? Consider a product or service that you could make or provide for sale on Etsy. What steps would you have to take to begin your business? What would you need in order for it to be successful? Would you be able to do this as your full-time job? Why or why not?

STUDENT STUDY SITE ··

Visit the student study site at **www.sagepub.com/ritzercanadian** for additional web quizzes for further review.

Cathedrals of Consumption

Elaborate outdoor markets, bazaars, and arcades have long been centres of consumption. However, consumption centres were revolutionized in post—World War II America with the creation of many modern cathedrals of consumption. Recall from Chapter 12 that cathedrals of consumption are the large, lavish sites where we go to celebrate and practise consumption— a practise that in many ways has become today's most prominent religion.

The shopping mall came to be the archetypical symbol of American consumption throughout the latter half of the twentieth century. While suburban malls remain popular destinations for many, they seem almost quaint when compared to some of the more modern cathedrals of consumption, such as megamalls, cruise ships, and casino hotels.

Encompassing 61 covered streets and dating back to 1455 CE, Istanbul's Grand Bazaar is one of the largest and oldest covered markets in the world, drawing upwards of 400,000 visitors a day. More than 3,000 retail shops line the ornate corridors of the bazaar, selling everything from furniture to falafel.

Dubbed the Love Boat National Holiday, more than a thousand couples renewed their vows at sea aboard the cruise ship *Grand Princess* as part of a seven-day Caribbean cruise. These floating cathedrals of consumption often offer special events, day trips, and promotions to customers who have already paid for room and board.

The Galaxy Macau is a large casino resort on the Cotai Strip in Macau, China. Casinos such as the Galaxy Macau encourage gambling (a form of consumption) through free alcoholic drinks, inexpensive hotel rooms, flashy designs, and live entertainment. Many casinos "forgo" clocks and windows so that gamblers lose track of time.

The Mall of America, located near Minneapolis, Minnesota, boasts four floors, 4.2 million square feet, more than 500 retail outlets, and more than 40 million visitors a year. Beyond its many restaurants and boutiques, the mall features an indoor theme park with several roller coasters, an 18-hole miniature golf course, and an aquarium.

Premier online auction and shopping website, eBay is a virtual bazaar where an unfathomably diverse array of new and used products are auctioned and sold around the world. With the advent of persistent wireless Internet technology, one can carry this cathedral of consumption at all times in a pocket or purse.

Supermarket chain Woolworth's launched the world's first virtual supermarket in Town Hall Station, Sydney, Australia's busy commuter railway hub. Using the Woolworth's smartphone app, customers could browse products, scan bar codes from the virtual supermarket wall, pay for their orders, and have the products delivered directly to their homes or places of work.

Women shop for jewellery at a large open-air market located in a predominantly Muslim area of Delhi, India. Unlike in most western markets, bartering plays a significant role in consumption throughout the Middle East and South Asia—especially in the informal market setting.

THE BODY, MEDICINE, HEALTH, AND HEALTH CARE

The way one perceives and treats one's physical form is a reflection of socialisation and cultural norms. Some will endeavour to maximise their bodies' functionality and aesthetic; others will burden them with risky, sometimes self-destructive, behaviour. Many will dabble in both extremes.

Almost unheard of until 2009, designer drugs with brand names such as K2 and Spice have exploded as popular—and often legal—alternatives to marijuana in many western nations. Similar to the organic drugs in composition, use, and effect, synthetic blends sold as incense or bath salts and labelled "not for human consumption" have been available for purchase at Internet retailers, specialty stores, and even some gasoline stations since 2006. While law enforcement agencies around the world struggle to understand and control the myriad chemicals found in synthetic marijuana blends, a growing number of users are quickly finding out on their own that legality and availability do not always imply safety.

The psychoactive compounds contained in synthetic marijuana are so new to the scientific community that most compounds have not been tested for carcinogenicity or other long-term health effects. Still, as the popularity of synthetic marijuana has risen, so too have related reports of dangerous short-term side effects. In 2009, the American Association of Poison Control Centers received 14 calls regarding synthetic marijuana exposure. By October 2011, the organisation had received almost 9,000 calls. In November 2011, three 16-year-old boys were hospitalised after suffering heart attacks—apparently caused by the ingestion of a synthetic incense blend.

According to Rick Broider, president of the North American Herbal Incense Trade Association, the sale of synthetic marijuana generates nearly $5 billion annually. Clearly, though it can be extremely dangerous to one's health, there is interest in the synthetic drug, as there is in other forms of risky behaviour—extreme sports, binge drinking, texting while driving, and having unprotected sex with *multiple partners, for example. And just as each of these risky activities has come under the scrutiny of the U.S. and Canadian health care systems, so too have synthetic blends.*

Researchers have begun studying some of the most prevalent active chemicals found in synthetic marijuana. However, for-profit laboratories are continually developing new compounds with slightly modified chemical structures and shipping them to Internet-based distributors around the world. This efficient, interconnected global network is maddening not only to law enforcement agencies working to ban specific compounds but also to health care professionals who seek to understand the chemicals, effects, and dangers associated with synthetic marijuana.

The way one perceives and treats one's physical form is a reflection of socialisation and leading cultural norms. Some will endeavour to maximise their bodies' functionality and aesthetic; others will burden them with risky, sometimes self-destructive, behaviour. Many will dabble in both extremes. Synthetic marijuana use is a behaviour shaped by social phenomena such as the illegality of organic marijuana, the depressed economy, and the convenience and confidentiality of online consumption. It is a considerable national and international health concern, but it is far from the only one. In the following pages, you will learn about a number of other health- and health care–related challenges facing patients and medical professionals today.

The central concerns of this chapter—the body, medicine, health (including, albeit briefly, mental health), and health care—are at the top of the social, as well as almost everyone's personal, agenda. Globally, there is much concern for epidemics such as AIDS, malaria, and the flu, as well as the great inequalities in health and health care that exist throughout the world. At the societal level, debate in Canada continues about reforming health care. Among other things, advocates of reform have sought to address flagrant inequalities and rapidly increasing costs in health care. Of particular note, as discussed below, is the rise of privatised medicine in the context of one of the world's most developed and publicly funded health care systems. These global and societal issues affect the health and health care of individuals. Among those who are most concerned about such issues are those who are or will be patients—that is, virtually everyone—as well as the large and growing number of people who work in health care.

Ultimately, much of the concern with health comes down to a growing focus on, and concern about, the state of our bodies. However, interest in the body manifests itself in different ways for various social groups. Given your age, the main concerns for you and your friends are likely to be how to remain good-looking, healthy, and fit through diet, exercise, and perhaps even a nip or a tuck here or there. While these are likely to be lifelong concerns, as you age your focus will shift to the increasing likelihood of various diseases—breast cancer for women and prostate cancer for men, as well as heart disease for both men and women. You will also become increasingly concerned about how to avoid those diseases, if possible, and, if you contract one, how to deal with it—if it can be dealt with. Gender affects the types of health-protective behaviours that you employ. Women tend to be more active participants in their health maintenance than men. These health-protective behaviours include screenings, self-examinations, and regular checkups.

While some of you will fall ill, be hospitalised, and perhaps die in middle age (or even earlier), most of you will face these issues with increasing frequency and intensity as you move into old age. New health-related concerns will emerge when you attain that age, such as the possibility of Alzheimer's disease. As is shown in Figure 13.1, the estimated number of people with Alzheimer's disease, or dementia, will triple between 2000 and 2050. The number of people 85 years of age and over with the disease—and there will be many more in that age group in the coming years—will quadruple. As you age, there will also be increasing worry about how you will die and whether

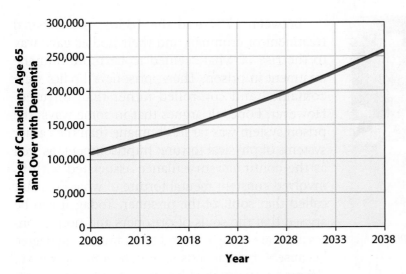

FIGURE 13.1 Current and Projected Numbers of People Age 65 and Over in the Canadian Population with Dementia, 2008–2038

SOURCE: Authors' estimates based on Dudgeon (2010).

you will be able to die with dignity. Then there are issues of whether you are going to be able to access the quality of medical care that you desire, in a timely manner.

For some of these reasons, as well as others, the body has emerged in recent years as a major concern in sociology (L. Moore and Kosut 2010; B. Turner 2008). However, before discussing the body, it is important to remember that the mind and mental processes have long been of concern and of interest to many sociologists. For example, see the discussion of Mead's work on these topics in Chapter 5. Furthermore, while the introduction to this chapter has focused on physical illnesses, mental illnesses such as depression, schizophrenia, and attention deficit/hyperactivity disorder (ADHD) are also major concerns at the global, national, and individual levels (A. Rogers and Pilgrim 2010). There is no clear line between the mind and the body; the brain, which houses the mind, is, after all, a body part. Mental processes affect the body (such as through psychosomatic illnesses), and the body affects the mind. Examples of the latter include the emergence of postpartum depression caused, at least in part, by resulting hormonal imbalances (Benoit et al. 2007) and depression developed after one learns of a diagnosis of prostate cancer or heart disease (Luo 2010). However, it is important to remember that mental processes can also have a positive effect on the body and its well-being. A strong sense of

self-efficacy can help when quitting smoking, losing weight, or recovering from a heart attack, among other things.

THE BODY

While sociology has always had some interest in the body, the explosion of interest in it is largely traceable to the work of the French social theorist Michel Foucault.

THE THINKING OF MICHEL FOUCAULT

The body is a central issue in several of Foucault's most important works. In *Discipline and Punish: The Birth of the Prison*, Foucault ([1975] 1979) is concerned, at least

While it may not concern those in their young adult years, Alzheimer's disease becomes a real concern as people age. Here, an inhabitant of a German residential care home for patients with Alzheimer's disease and dementia experiences the sound and vibrations of a singing bowl during a therapy session.

Michel Foucault
(1926–1984, French)

- Foucault held a chair at the prestigious Collège de France.

- His work influenced those in many fields, including sociology.

- His best known book is *Discipline and Punish* (1975).

- In the last years of his life he published a set of three books devoted to sexuality, including *The History of Sexuality* (1978).

- He was most interested in the relationship between power and knowledge—how knowledge leads to power and how those in power are better able to gain knowledge.

- He believed in the importance of "limit experiences" both intellectually and personally.

- Among his own limit experiences were trying LSD and experiencing gay sex in the infamous bathhouses of San Francisco in the early 1980s—a limit experience that may have cost him his life (he died later from AIDS).

initially, with the punishment of the criminal's body. The book opens with a description of the punishment inflicted on a condemned murderer in 1757:

> [His flesh was] . . . torn from his breasts, arms, thighs and calves with red-hot pincers, his right hand . . . burnt with sulphur, and, on those places where the flesh will be torn away, poured molten lead, boiling oil, burning resin, wax and sulphur melted together and then his body drawn and quartered by four horses . . . when that did not suffice, they were forced to cut off the wretch's thighs, to sever the sinews and hack at the joints. (Foucault [1975] 1979:3)

Clearly, at this point in the history of punishment, the focus was on the body.

Between 1757 and the 1830s, the abysmal treatment of criminals and their bodies gave way to the rise of what seemed to be more humane treatment in prison. There, prisoners' bodies were contained and controlled rather than tortured. However, Foucault argues that in some ways, the prison system was far *less* humane than the earlier systems of physical torture. Imprisonment, as well as the continual surveillance associated with it, involved constant mental torture of what Foucault called the "soul" of the prisoner. Today, it can be argued that the souls of prisoners and nonprisoners alike are being tortured to an increasing degree because surveillance is so much more pervasive. We are being watched by omnipresent video cameras, through scanners at airports, and on the computer, where Google and others keep tabs on the websites we visit (Andrejevic 2009).

In *The Birth of the Clinic* (1975), Foucault begins with an analysis of medicine prior to the nineteenth century. At this time, in order to diagnose a disease, doctors focused on lists of diseases and their associated symptoms. However, in the nineteenth century, the gaze of doctors shifted from such lists to human beings, especially their bodies and the diseases that afflicted them. Of great importance was the ability to see and touch diseased or dead bodies. In terms of the latter, the focus shifted to performing autopsies, cutting into bodies and body parts, in order to learn about diseases, their courses, and their effects on those bodies and their organs.

The Sexual Body

In *The History of Sexuality*, Foucault (1978) emphasises the importance of sexuality and the role of the body in obtaining sexual pleasure. He believed that society used sexuality, and restrictions on it, to gain access to the body in order to control, discipline, and govern it. He urged people to reject such constraints on the body as well as constricted forms of sexuality and, instead, to focus on sexuality that was about "bodies and pleasures" (Foucault 1978:157). One way to do that was to push one's body to the limit in sexual experiences, to make sexuality a limit experience. While most people do not come close to Foucault's limit experiences in the realm of sexuality, there is today much more openness and freedom as far as sexuality is concerned. These often include, for example, oral and anal sex, as well as sex with multiple partners. Although these behaviours were certainly practised a generation or two ago, they would have caused most people to blush, or at least to pretend to be shocked.

Even though we emphasise sexual relations between two or more people here, it is worth remembering that sexual pleasure can be, and often is, achieved in many other ways. These include sex with animals, as well as with one's own body. Masturbation is common for both males and females. Feminists have come to emphasise the importance of pleasuring oneself. Also worth mentioning in this context is objectophilia, whereby people derive sexual satisfaction from or with various objects. There is even an organisation for those who love objects called OS (Objectùm-Sexuality) Internationale. One of its leaders is Erika LaBrie. She is now known as Erika "Aya" Eiffel because of her love of the Eiffel Tower, which she "married" in 2007. Such love can involve sexual relations with the object itself or with a facsimile of it. In the case of the Eiffel Tower, it could be a souvenir or even a copy of the tower built by a lover.

With the work of Foucault and many others as a base, the study of the body has become increasingly important. It is defined by a general focus on the relationship between the body, society, and culture (B. Turner 2007a, 2007b). It also includes a wide range of more specific concerns, including the gendered body, sexuality, body modifications such as tattooing, bodily pain, abominations of the body (such as stigmas; see Chapter 7), and so on. Of course, the issue of the body is also central to the main focus of this chapter, the sociology of health and medicine.

THE HEALTHY BODY: LIFESTYLE, BEAUTY, AND FITNESS

You live in an increasingly reflexive society. In the context of health, reflexivity involves a heightened awareness of your body and yourself more generally. This also entails a responsibility to take care of yourself, especially doing everything possible to avoid becoming sick and dying. Your body and its health have become "projects" to be worked on continually. In spite of this, there is no shortage of times—that trip to the fast-food restaurant, one too many beers on Saturday night—during which health and the body take a backseat. You are likely to mould, and perhaps even alter, your body throughout the course of your life. While this is increasingly true for most people in the developed North, it is particularly characteristic of adolescent girls (Brumberg 1998).

Reflexivity often leads to dissatisfaction with one's body, especially in comparison to those one sees portrayed by the media. This is particularly true of women who are likely not to see themselves as thin enough. Adolescent girls are often dissatisfied with their bodies—this is true of preadolescent girls age 8 to 11 and even girls 5 to 8 years of age (Dohnt and Tiggemann 2006). Among the latter, there is a significant increase in the desire for thinness among 6-year-old girls, perhaps reflecting the influence of peers during the first year of school.

Reflexivity is manifest in many other ways in the contemporary world, but here we are concerned with the fact that you are increasingly likely to reflect on the way you live your life and how that affects your appearance and your physical fitness. Many people, as we will soon discuss, engage in risky behaviours that endanger their health, as well as the way they look and their physical fitness. However, many others focus on creating a lifestyle that they hope will make them fit, attractive, and healthy.

Beauty: The Myth

The issue of beauty became a much more popular topic in society and in sociology after the publication of Naomi Wolf's ([1991] 2002) The Beauty Myth. Wolf argues that the media confront the vast majority of people with an unattainable standard of beauty. Michael Kimmel (2009) refers to this standard of beauty as the "male gaze," as it is males who dominate the media. This standard is rooted in patriarchal and Eurocentric ideals of beauty and attractiveness.

Some argue that the importance of beauty has its roots in evolution (Singh and Singh 2011). That is, beauty may be an indicator of health and fertility with the result being that women with those characteristics are more likely to be selected for mating. They are also more likely to have children

Our society is increasingly reflexive—we judge and alter ourselves based largely on how we want to be viewed by others. This causes people to pursue unattainable standards of beauty, especially as portrayed in popular media.

who are beautiful and who may have a greater chance of survival and success. In any case, both women and men use beauty as a means of determining who is attractive and how to be attractive to the opposite sex, as well as to members of the same sex. For most women, efforts to attain a high standard of beauty (including excessive dieting, bingeing, and purging) lead to failure, a negative self-image, and low self-esteem (Daniels 2009; Rosenberg 1979). Similarly, increased attention to men's bodies in the media leads to a preoccupation with ideas about the male form. Consequently, many men feel ashamed to enter locker rooms for fear of body criticisms; and some homosexual men feel compelled to excessively diet in order to fit the "twink" body type, a very slender form that is often deemed more attractive within the queer community (Kimmel 2009).

The Quest for the Ideal

Yet the rewards for being beautiful are so great that many continue to try to at least approximate the mythic ideal as best they can. This is clear, for example, in the enormous sums of money spent on cosmetics, on fitness workouts and in fitness centres, on clothing, and, most extremely, on cosmetic surgeries of all sorts (see the TV series *Nip/Tuck*) (Gimlin 2007). As is clear in Figure 13.2, the most popular cosmetic surgeries are breast augmentation and reduction, lipoplasty (liposuction), blepharoplasty (cosmetic eyelid surgery), and rhinoplasty (nose job). Less common are rib resections that produce tighter rib cages and therefore smaller waists, removal of pinkie toes in order to allow one to fit into one's favourite shoes, and, for fantasy fiction fans, having one's ears transformed into pointed elfin ears. Genital reconstruction is a cosmetic surgery that is increasing in frequency among both women and men (Kimmel 2009)—one example is the vulvectomy, a procedure to obtain the "perfect vagina."

The Consumption of Beauty

In our consumer culture, beauty has become a commodity that can be bought, or at least we think it can, through great effort, often pain, and almost always expenditures of large sums of money. Naomi Johnson (2010) found that the importance of beauty consumption pervades teen romance novels. The stories therein link a young woman's desirability as a romantic and sexual partner to various brand-name products and product lines, and brand consumption is

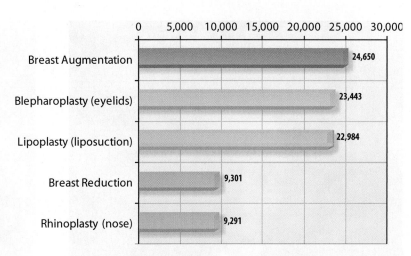

FIGURE 13.2 Canada's Five Most Popular Cosmetic Surgery Procedures, 2010

SOURCE: ISAPS *International Survey on Aesthetic/Cosmetic Procedures Performed in 2010* (http://www.isaps.org/files/html-contents/ISAPS-Procedures-Study-Results-2011.pdf).

woven into the story lines more generally. The books, like movies, engage in *product placement* in order to earn money and to sell advertisers' products. Products emphasised in the books included clothing (Valentino tank), negligees (La Perla), shoes (Jimmy Choo high-heel mules), cosmetics (Chanel Vamp lip gloss), and body modifications (Brazilian body waxes).

All of this interest in how we look, while not new, has grown dramatically in this era of increasing reflexivity. We are more aware of how we (and others) look, and we are more conscious not only that we can do things to improve our appearance but also of what alternatives are available to us for doing so. The increase in pure relationships (see Chapter 11) also adds greater importance to this focus on appearance since others are more likely to leave a relationship with us if they are dissatisfied with how we look (and vice versa).

Fitness and the Healthy Body

Closely related to the emphasis on beauty is the focus on both female and male physical activity, physical fitness, sports, and bodybuilding (A. Klein 1993; Amy Scott 2011). All of these are seen, at least in part, as ways of obtaining not only a more beautiful body but also one that is healthier (Waddington 2007)—or at least appears that way. However, it is important to distinguish among the methods employed to achieve a healthy body. The clearest linkage is between physical activity and a healthy body. Walking, cycling, and

A man waves to the crowd during the 2007 Gay Pride Parade in Paris, France. Some gay men feel compelled to diet in order to fit the slender "twink" body type, a physique deemed more attractive among some within the gay community.

Actress Lara Flynn Boyle, known for her work in television series *Twin Peaks* and *The Practice*, is reported to have undergone several plastic surgery procedures between 1990 (left) and 2008 (right). According to reconstructive surgeon Dr. Paul S. Nassif, "Lara Flynn Boyle appears to have had rhinoplasty, lip augmentation, Botox, facial fillers, and possibly a browlift and facelift."

jogging are clearly good for one's health. These sports typically do not involve competition. While one may develop a better-looking body as a result of involvement in sports, the increasingly competitive nature of many sports may actually adversely affect the health of one's body and its appearance. Such sports require great exertion and are often violent; they can be damaging, even dangerous, to the body. There is an increase in exercise-related injuries in sports, especially in "contact sports." This is clear in the increasing alarm over concussions in various sports, especially professional hockey. A recent study in the *Canadian Medical Association Journal* outlines how rule changes could reduce head injuries in ice hockey (Cusimano, Nastis, and Zuccaro 2013).

Some contact sports, such as wrestling and boxing, require competitors to qualify for, and remain in, very restrictive weight classes. This can lead to bouts of starvation and dehydration in order to "make the weight." This can evolve into what

has been called "manorexia," a male analogue to the mainly female practise of anorexia in order to maintain a slimmer body (Kershaw 2008). There is also a phenomenon known as "bigorexia" or the Adonis complex (Kimmel 2009). This involves men who might have grown up with G.I. Joes or photos of Arnold Schwarzenegger as a bodybuilder (before his 2003–2011 reincarnation as governor of California) and who aspire to having similar physiques. They are likely to feel that their biceps, to take one example, are inadequate in comparison to those of such idealised models. Such men might be led to lift weights obsessively, while consuming mainly, or only, proteins. Such practises are especially rampant among competitive bodybuilders. In addition, bodybuilders might binge on sugars on the day of a competition. This causes their veins to become more prominent; such veins are one sign of fitness, even beauty, in such competitions. All of these examples illustrate the fact that involvement in sports can have a variety of deleterious effects on the body in both the short and the long term.

Walking, cycling, jogging, and other noncompetitive sports are clearly good for one's health. In this photo taken September 22, 2011, residents of Paragominas, Brazil, take part in a nightly aerobics class on a main city avenue. The communal nature of such events can be a strong motivator to improve one's health and fitness.

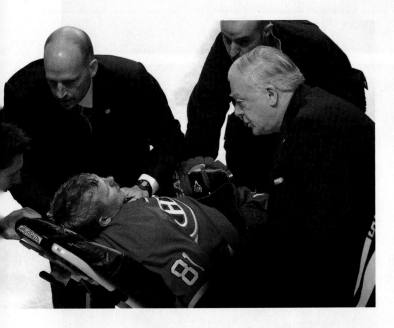

The competitive nature of some sports may actually adversely affect health. In this photo, taken May 2, 2013, Montreal Canadiens' player Lars Eller is taken off the ice. Eller suffered facial fractures and a concussion.

Exercise, sport, and physical activity often take as their goal the improvement of the body and of one's health more generally. They are increasingly oriented toward *outcomes* such as losing weight and strengthening muscles. However, what is often forgotten these days is the importance of the fun associated with exercise (Wellard 2012). As a result, people do not explore the full potential of various kinds of physical activities.

BODY MODIFICATIONS

Body modifications (Ferreira, forthcoming; Pitts 2003) have been nearly universal across societies and throughout history. However, in recent years, there has been something of a boom in such modifications in Canada and elsewhere. There are several major forms of body modification, including tattooing (M. Atkinson 2003; Dukes and Stein 2011), scarification (scarring or cutting the skin; see Inckle 2007), and piercing (Vail 2007). At one time, body modification was associated with deviants (see Chapter 7) of various types, including gangbangers, outlaw motorcycle gang members, prisoners, and prostitutes. It was also associated with some conventional groups, such as those in the military and, in particular, the navy.

Today, body modifications, especially tattoos, have not only become more widespread and common, but are now even mainstream (J. Adams 2009). For example, tattooing occurs these days in tattoo parlours found in shopping malls. The media are full of images of movie stars and especially star athletes adorned, if not covered, with tattoos. Consider, for example, hockey player Jose Theodore, baseball player Brett Lawrie, football player Chris Johnson, and Toronto Raptors basketball player DeMar DeRozan. Usually associated with men, body modification now seems to be much more common among women (Laumann and Derick 2006). Parents seem less likely to reject the idea of tattoos on their children. They may even have tattoos themselves, though perhaps concealed most of the time by clothing. They are likely more concerned with whether their tattoos, or those of their children, are concealable or aesthetically pleasing. In many ways, body modification is now in fashion, and is itself a fashion statement.

Body modification reflects the increase in reflexivity. Ever-greater reflexivity is required with each succeeding decision about which new form or style of body modification to have. Among the issues to be decided are whether the modification, say, a new tattoo, should be visible; where it should be placed; and how traditional or creative and unique it should be. Furthermore, a variety of different tastes in tattooing have emerged. For example, gang members prefer tattoos that identify them as such and that have autobiographical elements. Bikers often want tattoos that not only distinguish them from the general population but also tend to intimidate or frighten people. Collectors of tattoos are likely to prefer personalised and highly distinctive designs (Vail 1999). Various groups also gain status for

Distinct body modifications differentiate groups and societies from each other. Depending on the context, modification can imply proof of achievement or adulthood, allegiance to a group, forced ownership or domination, artistic expression, self-mastery, or any number of other social facets.

different types of tattoos. For example, a full-back tattoo, a "back piece," is highly valued in artistic circles.

As tattoos have grown more mainstream, even common in some circles, the people originally drawn to them have sought to find other ways of distinguishing their bodies from those of others. Many have been drawn to piercings of various types (Schorzman et al. 2007). Most common are tongue and eyebrow piercings, but as those, too, have become more common, there are more piercings of other parts of the body, even the genitals, and an increase in the number of piercings adorning one's body.

Dukes and Stein (2011) compared 9th- to 12th-grade U.S. students in terms of preferences for tattoos or piercings. Slightly more boys than girls reported having tattoos, but a much higher percentage of girls (42 percent) than boys (16 percent) had piercings (other than earlobes). Tattoos were less prevalent than piercings perhaps because they are more or less permanent. The scars left by piercing are likely to heal and less likely to be obtrusive than tattoos. Overall, girls reported fewer deviant behaviours than boys. However, girls with piercings reported more deviant behaviour than girls who were not pierced. Those with piercings were also less school-oriented than girls with tattoos. The older students became, the more likely

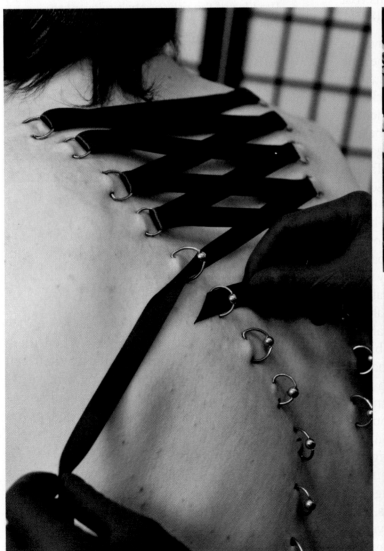

Often performed for self-exploratory, religious, and purely aesthetic reasons, piercing is one of the oldest and most globally ubiquitous forms of body modification. In fact, the oldest mummified body discovered to date—the 5,300-year-old Ötzi the Iceman—was found with an ear piercing.

they were to have body modifications. Body modification has been linked to a variety of risky behaviours, such as self-cutting, drinking, and drug use.

RISKY BEHAVIOUR

The German sociologist Ulrich Beck (1992) argues that we live in a "risk society." The idea of risk has become a central concern in many areas of sociology, and one of those is the way in which it relates to the body and to health. Interestingly, this meshes well with Foucault's ideas on limit experiences since it is in such experiences that the risks are greatest. Indeed, risks are what draw people to them. Few go to the extremes of Foucault, but many people take risks that endanger their health, their bodies, and their lives. That is, they take actions that adversely affect all of these things (Lupton 2007).

People take a wide range of risks that have the potential to jeopardise their health. On the one hand, there are the things people do *not* do, such as seeing their physicians, having regular checkups, being vaccinated, and taking required medicines. On the other hand, people engage in many behaviours that they know pose health risks, cigarette smoking is at, or near, the top of the list. Taking illegal drugs of various sorts, especially those that are addictive, is clearly very risky, as are the illegal activities often required to support a drug habit. Another important form of risky, behaviour is drinking alcohol to excess or driving (or boating) under the influence of alcohol. Especially dangerous is the combination of alcohol and caffeine (Goodnough 2010). While many commercial beverages such as Four Loko have removed caffeine from their ingredients lists, cocktails combining alcohol and caffeine remain popular. The natural inclination with alcohol consumption is to grow sleepy and stop drinking, but it is counteracted by the caffeine. The result is that some people go on drinking well beyond normal inebriation and, as a result, have ended up in hospital emergency rooms. Having unprotected sex is highly risky, especially with multiple partners, and having such sex has been linked to other risky behaviours, such as drug and alcohol abuse. Many people overeat, allow themselves to become obese, and stay that way even though there is overwhelming evidence

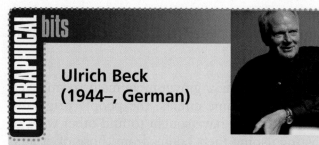

BIOGRAPHICAL bits

Ulrich Beck (1944–, German)

- Beck received his PhD from the University of Munich.

- He is Professor Emeritus at Munich and also holds an appointment at the London School of Economics.

- He is best known for his book *Risk Society* (1992), although he has published many books and articles on that topic and others, especially globalisation.

- The idea of the risk society is relevant to many issues in the contemporary world, including health and illness.

- He is also known for his work on modernity, and argues that we continue to live in the modern world, albeit in a late stage he calls "second modernity."

- Also in this realm is his work on "reflexive modernity," or the idea that second modernity is being built on the basis of critical reflection on first modernity and its central weaknesses.

- In 2010 Beck became involved with the Spinelli Group in the European Parliament, oriented to reinvigorating the efforts to federalise the European Union.

linking obesity to various illnesses. Then there is the propensity of people to talk on their cell phones, or to engage in text messaging, while driving. They do so even though the increased risk of having an accident associated with such actions has received a great deal of publicity (see, for example, A. Newman 2011 and Watkins 2009).

In some cases, the nature of one's work is risky. One example involves nuclear workers and their exposure to radiation that can make them ill and perhaps kill them (Cable, Shriver, and Mix 2008). Of course, there are many occupations that carry with them a variety of health risks.

Some careers carry an element of risk—even risk of death. Here, workers wearing protective suits and masks build water tanks at the tsunami-crippled Fukushima Daiichi nuclear power plant in Fukushima, Japan.

It is worth noting that there is another side to risky behaviour. It may well be that taking some risks makes one happier and mentally, and perhaps even physically, healthier. This may help to account for the growing interest in extreme sports such as surfing and ice climbing. This, of course, does not deny the fact that such sports involve extraordinary physical and health risks.

THE SOCIOLOGY OF HEALTH AND MEDICINE

Medical sociology, the largest specialty area within sociology (Cockerham 2012), is concerned with the "social causes and consequences of health and illness" (Cockerham 2007:2932). Social factors are also deeply involved in the delivery of health care, and this has become an increasingly important issue in Canada and much of the rest of the world. Medical sociology addresses a wide variety of specific issues, including racial/ethnic differences in health care; the basic causes of health inequalities by social class, gender, and race/ethnicity; the linkage between stress and health; the relationship between patients and health care providers; the increasing use of advanced medical technology; the astronomical and spiralling cost of medical care; and the changing nature of the medical profession (Hankin and Wright 2010). Among the changes in the medical profession are its declining status, the more active role of patients in their own health care, the more complicated relationship between patients and health care providers, and the fact that those relationships are likely to last longer because people are living longer and suffering from more chronic ailments.

THE SICK ROLE

Having a body and focusing on it is one thing, but having a sick body is quite another thing. An important link between a concern for the body, its sicknesses, and the sociology of this phenomenon is the concept of the **sick role**, or the expectations about the way sick people are supposed to act (Parsons 1951; Twaddle 2007). Clearly this concept is derived from the broader concept of *role* discussed in Chapter 5. As is true of all roles, the sick role is defined by the expectations associated with it. A sick person is:

- Exempted, within limits, from normal role obligations. That is, if you are sick, you can stay home from school or ignore some family responsibilities, at least for a time. This exemption varies with the severity of the illness.
- Not expected to take responsibility for being ill; the sick person did not cause the illness and needs help in dealing with it.
- Expected to want to get well.
- Expected to seek help from those with the appropriate medical expertise (see the next *McDonaldization Today* box).

The idea of the sick role offers a useful sociological approach to illness, but it has been criticised on various grounds. For one thing, many people clearly do not conform to the sick role. For example, they may ignore the exemptions associated with being sick and insist on handling their usual responsibilities, blame others for making them sick, not want to get well because of the benefits of being considered sick (for example, escaping certain responsibilities), and not seek help or seek the "wrong" kind of help, such as that of a medical "quack." However, the biggest

McDONALDIZATION *Today*

McBirth

One measure of the McDonaldization of giving birth is the decline of midwifery, a very human practise (Ritzer 2013; S. Thomas 2009). Midwives are not physicians; they are traditionally women trained in handling most aspects of the birth process. In 1900, midwives attended about half of all births in Canada, but by the first decade of the twenty-first century less than 10 percent of births were handled by midwives (P. Janssen et al. 2009). When asked why they seek out midwives today, women often express concern about the impersonal and callous treatment they receive from hospital staff. They generally feel that the process of giving birth in the hospital is dehumanised; one physician is willing to admit that hospital birth can be a dehumanised process (M. Harrison 1982).

Historically, giving birth took place in the home, with relatives and friends in attendance. Now, childbirth takes place almost exclusively in hospitals, "alone among strangers" (J. Leavitt 1986:190). In 1900, less than 5 percent of Canadian births took place in hospitals, but by 1960 nearly 100 percent of births occurred in them.

Over the years, hospitals and the medical profession have developed many standardised—that is, McDonaldized—procedures for handling and controlling childbirth. One of the best known of such procedures views motherhood as a sick role and childbirth as a sickness, as a pathologic process. Until quite recently, the routine even for low-risk births involved the following procedures:

1. The patient is supine, with legs in the air, bent and wide apart, supported by stirrups.

2. Sedation is used beginning in the first stage of labour.

3. An episiotomy is performed to enlarge the area through which the baby must pass.

4. Forceps are used to make the delivery more efficient.

Describing this procedure, one woman wrote, "Women are herded like sheep through an obstetrical assembly line" (Mitford 1993:61).

Then there is the Friedman curve, with three rigidly prescribed and calculable stages of labour. For example, the first stage is allocated exactly 8.6 hours, during which cervical dilation is to proceed from 2 to 4 centimeters.

The moment babies come into the world, they are greeted by a scoring system, the Apgar test. Babies receive scores of 0 to 2 on each of five factors, such as heart rate and colour; 10 is the healthiest total score. One minute after birth most babies score between 7 and 9 and have scores of 8 to 10 after five minutes. Babies with scores of 0 to 3 are considered to be in very serious trouble. Subjective, nonquantifiable dimensions, such as the infant's curiosity and mood, are not of concern in the Apgar test.

Caesareans are surgical procedures in which incisions are made through the abdomen and uterus in order to remove a baby rather than letting the mother go through the entire natural birth process. The first modern caesarean took place in 1882; as late as 1970, only 5 percent of all births were by caesarean, but by 2009 over 25 percent of births were of this type (Organisation for Economic Co-operation and Development [OECD] 2011c). The dramatic increase in caesareans meshes well with the McDonaldization of society as a whole:

- Their occurrence is much more predictable than the normal birth process, which can occur a few weeks or even months early or late.

- As a comparatively simple operation, the caesarean is more efficient than natural childbirth, which may involve many more steps and unforeseen contingencies.

- Caesareans normally take 20 to 45 minutes. The time required for a normal birth is much more variable and can often be much longer.

- There are various irrationalities associated with caesareans, including the risks associated with surgery, a longer period of recuperation, a higher mortality rate, and greater expense. The wonders of childbirth are reduced to the routines of a minor surgical procedure.

problem with the concept is related to the theory from which it is derived—structural-functionalism (see Chapter 2). That is, it gives too much power to the larger social structure, the roles that are part of it, and the expectations associated with those roles. It is as though the sick role prescribes how people should act. Of special importance is the fact that it accords too much importance to the expectations of the medical profession; it grants it too much power over the patient. That means that the idea of the sick role gives *too little power* to those who occupy that role: the patients. As we saw above, patients today, and to a lesser extent those in the past, do not simply conform to the expectations of medical professionals, but often actively create their own, individualised, versions of the sick role.

THE MEDICAL PROFESSION

The idea of the sick role reflects the era in which the idea was created—the mid-twentieth century.

That was a time when a great deal of power was accorded to the health care system, especially to the medical profession, the key player in that system. Physicians had many expectations of those in the sick role, but more generally they had accrued and exercised great power over virtually everyone else involved in the health care system—nurses, hospital administrators, and so on (Hafferty and Castellani 2011). They also gained and retained great power over birth and death (see both *McDonaldization Today* boxes in this chapter). This was an era in which the professions of medicine, law, and other fields not only exercised great power but also acquired great autonomy. In fact, a **profession** is distinguished from other occupations by its great power and considerable autonomy.

Physicians have been disproportionately male. It was less than two decades ago that the number of women graduating from medical school was equal to the number of men (Figure 13.3). Women

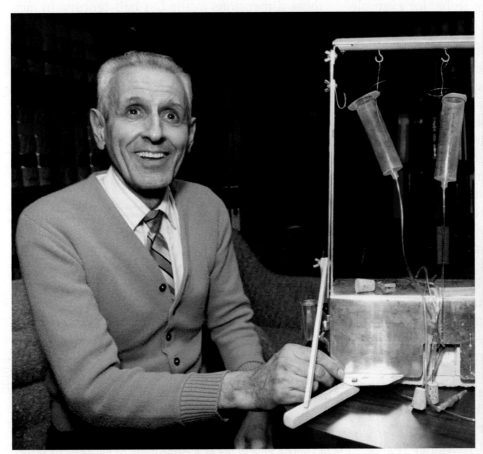
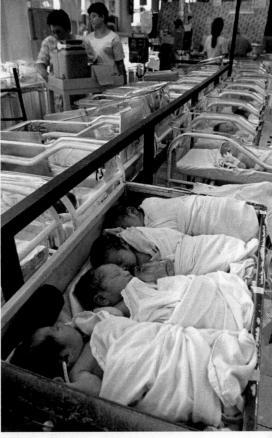

In the past, coming into the world—and leaving it—often took place in the home in the presence of relatives or friends. Over the years, hospitals and the medical profession have developed many McDonaldized procedures for handling and controlling birth and death. Here, newly born babies are lined up in a San Salvador, El Salvador, hospital nursery, and Dr. Jack Kevorkian poses with his assisted suicide device.

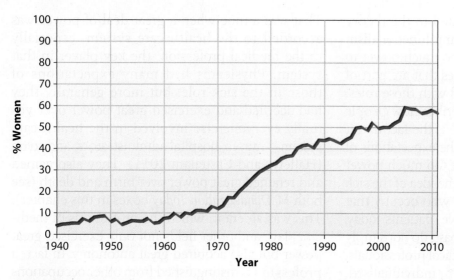

FIGURE 13.3 Percentage of Canadian Medical Degrees Earned by Women, 1940–2011

SOURCE: The Association of Faculties of Medicine of Canada (http://www.afmc.ca/publications-statistics-e.php).

men. These shorter hours are largely a function of women taking on somewhat greater shares of work in the home, especially care work involving both young children and elderly parents (see Chapter 11). As Figure 13.4 clearly illustrates, women's share of physician revenue has stayed almost constant at the 70 percent plateau, and even appears to have dropped by about 5 percent among medical specialists (72 percent down to 67 percent).

While the professions generally, and the medical profession in particular, continue to enjoy considerable power, autonomy, and high status, there has been a marked decline in all of those dimensions in the last half-century. In fact, what has characterised professions in the last several decades has been a process of **deprofessionalisation**, whereby their power and autonomy, as well as their high status and great wealth, have declined, at least relative to the exalted position they once held (Brooks 2011). There are a variety

continue, relative to men, to be overrepresented as general practitioners versus specialists, and even when they are specialists, in for example surgery, they are less likely than men to be, for example, orthopaedic surgeons.

Although more women have graduated from medical schools recently, the ability of women to turn their medical credentials into earnings that are on a par with the earnings of men appears to have been difficult. Salaries are, of course, confidential, but the revenue physicians receive from the government is available. When comparing women and men who work either as general practitioners (i.e., family medicine) or as medical specialists such as neurosurgeons or cardiologists, women receive only about 70 percent of the revenue that men do. This is revenue, and deductions of office expenses are necessary to get to net earnings, but it is hard to imagine that physician overheads would differ markedly by gender. The gap in revenue, and presumably in net earnings, is partly because women work somewhat shorter hours than do

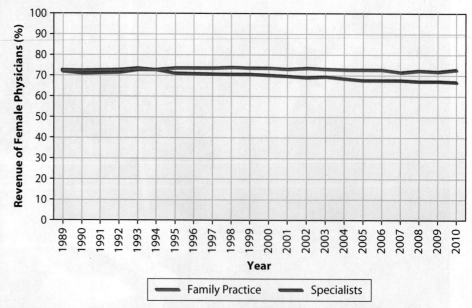

FIGURE 13.4 Revenue of Female Physicians as a Percentage of Revenue of Male Physicians, by Medical Field and Year

SOURCE: Authors' calculations from National Physician Database, Canadian Institute for Health Information (custom tabulation).

McDONALDIZATION *Today*

McDeath

In the natural order of things, the final phase of the body's breakdown can be hugely inefficient, incalculable, unpredictable, and above all uncontrollable. Many dying people have confounded physicians and loved ones by rallying and living longer than expected or, conversely, passing away sooner than anticipated.

Nevertheless, we have found ways to McDonaldize the dying process, giving us at least the illusion of control over it (Nuland 1994). There is, for example, the increasing array of nonhuman technologies such as respirators designed to keep people alive longer. However, they are often used even though some patients would not want to stay alive under such conditions. Unless physicians are following advance directives such as living wills that explicitly state that "no heroic measures" are to be taken, people lose control over their own dying process. We can expect increasing reliance on nonhuman technologies in the dying process. Computer systems may be used to assess a patient's statistical chances of survival at any given point in that process. The actions of medical personnel are likely to be influenced strongly by such assessments.

The decision about when a patient dies is left to physicians and medical bureaucrats. They are making considerable progress in stretching out the time a patient is able to remain alive. However, they have been slower to improve the quality of life during that extra period of time.

Death has followed much the same path as birth (see the previous *McDonaldization Today* box). It has been moved out of the home and beyond the control of the dying and their families. Physicians have gained a large measure of control over death, just as they took control of birth. Death, like birth, is increasingly likely to occur in hospitals, nursing homes, and hospices. The growth of chains of hospices and nursing homes signals the further McDonaldization of death in the future.

The McDonaldization of the dying process has spawned a series of counterreactions. For example, suicide societies and books such as Derek Humphry's (2002) *Final Exit* give people instructions on how to kill themselves. There is the growing interest in, and acceptance of, euthanasia. Finally, many people are choosing to die at home, and some are even opting to be buried in their backyard.

---

of factors involved in the declining power of the medical profession, especially the increasing power of patients, third-party payers such as the government through Medicare, and the pharmaceutical industry. However, while the medical profession is weaker than it once was, it remains a powerful force in the practise of medicine and in the larger society. In other words, the medical profession has proven itself to be quite resilient (Timmermans and Oh 2010).

How do we account for the deprofessionalisation of physicians? First, they simply had acquired too much power a half-century ago to be able to sustain it at that level for very long. Second, the public, which had granted the medical profession that power and autonomy, or had at least conceded those characteristics to it, came to question the medical profession. One basis of this increasing doubt was a

growing awareness of the extraordinary wealth and power acquired by many physicians. Another was the revelation of medical malpractise, which demonstrated that physicians did not always adhere to their own code of ethics (Ocloo 2010). Two other professions, journalists and lawyers, have helped to highlight the incompetence of some physicians. Third, the government has come to exert more power over the medical profession through, for example, Medicare, first introduced across Canada in 1972. Fourth, as is discussed in the coming pages, patients became much more active and aggressive consumers of physician services as well as of other aspects of the medical system. Fifth, medical associations in each of the provinces and territories have become much like labour unions, negotiating with governments for better remuneration for physicians (Clarke 2012).

Overall, medicine has in recent years become a much less powerful and rewarding profession with the result that many young people are reconsidering a medical career, older physicians are retiring early, others are moving to the United States, and still others are moving to what are called "concierge" or "boutique" practises. Concierge clinics or boutique practises allow physicians to tailor the patients they see to a select group, perhaps patients with back pain or who require some form of eye surgery. This latter practise has meant that an increasing fraction of the health care system is experiencing what might be called "creeping privatisation." If you have a painful shoulder injury and require a magnetic resonance imaging (MRI) scan, you can obtain this through the publicly funded system (but with a wait time of at least several weeks), or you can purchase the scan privately through a clinic where you pay for the service. For most basic health care, and for emergency procedures, the publicly funded system works extremely well. Where friction is mounting is with patients who believe their ailment is an emergency.

What is defined as "medically necessary" care and what constitutes an emergency are judgment calls. In a system where demand is outstripping supply, these judgments become very contentious, especially when your very sore knee is not judged to be an emergency that moves you toward the front of the line.

Obviously any purchases of private medical services are more affordable to the well-off than to others, especially when a single MRI scan can cost upwards of $1,000. To the extent private medicine continues to expand in Canada, it serves to widen the gap further between the wealthy and the poor in terms of health care. The poor often lack the means of accessing private clinics and are relegated to using hospital emergency rooms for everyday medical concerns, or to having no medical care at all. The well-to-do, who use concierge services or other elite medical practises without concern for costs, have high-quality physicians and other medical services at their disposal at virtually all times.

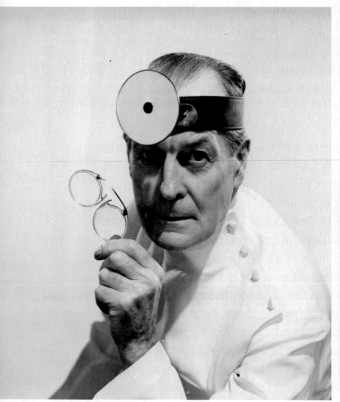
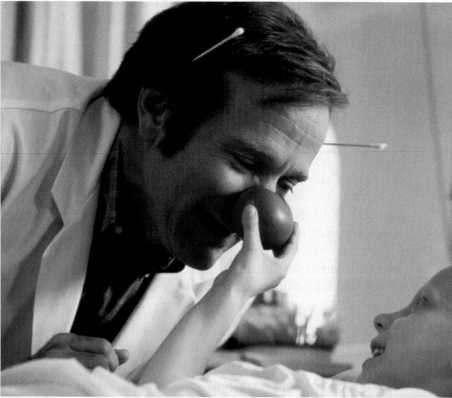

Medical practitioners continue to enjoy considerable power, autonomy, and high status, although there has been a marked decline in all of those dimensions in the last half-century. Some doctors have adopted humbler attitudes in light of these changes—in the 1998 film *Patch Adams*, Robin Williams portrays Hunter Doherty "Patch" Adams, a physician and social activist who organises groups of doctors to dress as clowns and visit medical patients, orphans, and other children.

Nurses

Of course, there are many other occupations in the health care system—most notably nurses (Riska 2007). Historically, nurses were unable to achieve full professional status, and nursing was often thought of as a semiprofession (Etzioni 1969). It lacked anything approaching the power, status, income, and autonomy of the medical profession. Much of this failure had to do with the enormous power wielded by the medical profession and its desire to keep occupations that had the potential to compete with it in a subordinate position (Ocloo 2010). However, a more important factor was the fact that nursing is an occupation that was—and still is—dominated by females (Apesoa-Varano 2007). Males in powerful positions, not only as physicians but also as high-level executives such as hospital administrators, were generally opposed to according professional status to occupations dominated by women; schoolteachers and social workers suffered much the same fate as nurses.

Nevertheless, doctors have come to rely heavily on nurses because nurses engage in, among many other things, "emotion work" or the emotional maintenance of patients (Lorber and Moore 2002). This reliance on nurses is reinforced by the fact that "most people believe that caring comes naturally to women" (Weitz 2010:308). The result has been that while physicians have almost all of the formal power, nurses often have a great deal of informal power over the day-to-day decisions and operation of a hospital (as is clear in the behaviour of Jackie Peyton, protagonist of the Showtime television series *Nurse Jackie*) or a doctor's office.

Of course, patients and the health care professions and occupations are only a small part of the Canadian health care system, which also includes, among many other elements, medical schools, hospitals, insurance companies, pharmaceutical companies, an array of alternative health care providers (e.g., midwives), and state and federal government involvement, especially through Medicare.

WEAKNESSES IN THE CANADIAN HEALTH CARE SYSTEM

There is broad consensus that the Canadian system of health care is world class although continually flailed by those both inside and outside the

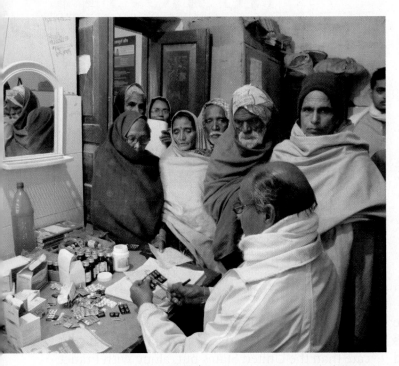
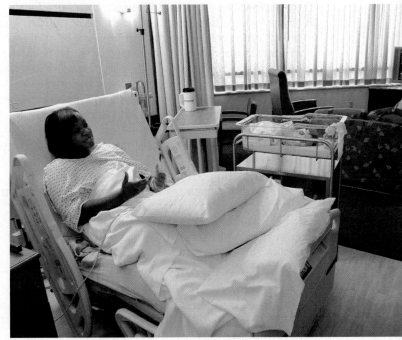

The poor often are relegated to using hospital emergency rooms for everyday medical concerns (if they seek out medical care at all). The well-to-do can afford concierge services and other quality medical services without concern for cost, including travelling abroad for medical procedures.

PUBLIC SOCIOLOGY

Paul Starr on Medicine and Health Care

As a young untenured assistant professor of sociology at the prestigious Harvard University, Paul Starr burst upon the academic and public scene with the publication of *The Social Transformation of American Medicine* in 1983. Within a year Starr had become the first sociologist in American history to win a Pulitzer Prize and the Bancroft Prize, as well as other awards. His career seemed assured as tenure and promotion at Harvard awaited him, but the academic world was shocked when he did not get a lifetime position at Harvard. That meant he had to leave Harvard, and while that was shocking and humiliating, he landed on his feet with a position in sociology at the similarly prestigious Princeton University, where he remains to this day.

The Social Transformation of American Medicine was an important contribution to a number of fields, including the sociology of health and medicine, especially to a historical understanding of the powerful medical profession. Among other things, Starr was interested in exploring historically why the United States was dominated by private rather than public health care.

In 1990 Starr teamed up with academic superstars and important public figures Robert Kuttner and Robert Reich to cofound a monthly magazine, *The American Prospect.* It adopted a liberal orientation and dealt with ideas, politics, and policy, with which it attracts an important audience of literate liberals who are likely to have a powerful voice on various public issues. The magazine in general and Starr in particular have devoted a great deal of attention to health and medicine. For example, for the November 2011 issue Starr wrote an essay titled "The Medicare Bind," in which he recognises the importance of both Medicare and the need to reform it in various ways. A key problem is the escalating costs of Medicare to American society. Starr believes that it was a mistake to set up a separate programme for seniors, and he argues for the need to bring seniors under the same rules as everyone else. Starr favours a fair and universal health care system.

Starr published widely on health care reform during the presidency of Bill Clinton, and he has continued to be an active voice on "Obamacare" in both *The American Prospect* and other venues. At a decisive point in the debate over Obama's health care reforms, he wrote an op-ed piece in *The New York Times* in which he argued that Democrats should sacrifice the *public option*—a government-run health insurance plan that would compete with private plans—in exchange for provisions that help lead to the success of reforms (Starr 2009). After the bill was passed—*without the public option*—Starr (2011a) wrote of the more practical need to get health care reform implemented.

Starr's (2011b) most recent book is *Remedy and Reaction: The Peculiar American Struggle Over Health Care Reform.* He deals with this history of the Clinton and Obama health care plans and with the reasons why health care is such a controversial issue.

Canada's universal health care system, known as Medicare, provides inclusive, comprehensive coverage for medically necessary services. This universality is especially important to key groups of citizens, including elderly women whose incomes are sometimes low.

system (Clarke 2012; Fierlbeck 2011). Because of its centrality to life and death, health care is highly politicised. One major problem is high and rising costs. Canada spends about 12 percent of its gross domestic product on health care, about $200 billion or almost $6,000 per person. On a per capita basis Canada spends less on health care than the United States but, along with France and Germany, is among a second tier of countries ranked on health spending. Among the reasons for the increasing costs is Canadians' love affair with expensive advanced medical technologies, including MRI, rising prices throughout the health care system, the cultural notion that Canadians have a right to the best health care possible, and an aging population that spends more on, and costs more for, health care than other age groups.

The Canadian health care system fares reasonably well in comparison to the health care systems in other countries. Life expectancy for Canadians is two years longer than for our American peers (OECD 2012b), while infant mortality is higher than the rate in France and Germany but below that of the United States (OECD 2012a).

Inequalities in Canadian Health Care and Health

The system of universal health care coverage in Canada (i.e., Medicare) implies that all Canadians have equal access to health services. In theory this is true. In practise, however, access differs across a variety of social categories, including urban/rural, social class, gender, and race/ethnicity/ancestry. For example, the well-off in Canada can afford any medical care they wish and will, if necessary, pay for private care or leave the country to seek services elsewhere. Many poor Canadians have little option but to use emergency rooms or urgent care centres as their first line of access. Two key issues are worth catching here. First, access to and utilisation of health care services are distinct. You might have the right to access something, but for a variety of reasons you might not utilise that right (e.g., distance from access point, availability of discretionary time, awareness of benefits of access). Second, even if you utilise your right of access, the benefits or outcomes of access might not be equitable. For example, you might need much more or much less of something than do others, so simple utilisation does not guarantee equitable outcomes. It is easy to imagine two people with flu ailments seeing a health care provider. If one person returns to a home with nutritious meals and strong central heating while someone else lives in poverty, struggling both with food and with heating, the outcomes are not likely to be equal with respect to well-being, in either the short or the long term.

Social Class and Health. There is a largely invariant relationship between social class and health—the lower one's social class, the poorer one's health is likely to be (Warren and Hernandez 2007). This relationship holds across countries (although there are variations from country to country) and over time; in fact, inequalities have generally widened over the years. In Canada we know that people from less advantaged backgrounds suffer from shorter life expectancy than their peers who are better off. For example, Carrière and Galarneau (2012) found that "less-educated workers have a post-retirement life expectancy of 18 years, compared with 20 and 21 years for their more-educated counterparts" (p. 3). After retirement, would you want to live 10 percent longer than your peers?

There are a number of causes of social class differences in health (Lahelma 2007; Veenstra 2009). First, there are the conditions in which children live since early differences may have long-lasting health consequences. Thus, living in poverty or in a broken home can contribute to ill health in childhood and therefore later in life (Boivin and Hertzman 2012; Duncan, Ziol-Guest, and Kalil 2010). Second, conditions in the adult years also affect health. Contributors to poor physical and mental health among adults include poor living conditions, especially those associated with living in unhealthy urban neighbourhoods (Cockerham 2012), working lives that are unrewarding economically and psychologically, and high levels of stress. Third, a variety of health-related behaviours contribute to inequalities in health. These include the greater likelihood of those in the lower classes using illegal drugs, smoking, drinking to excess, and being obese as a result of poor eating habits and a lack of exercise. Finally, the presence or absence of health care in general, and high-quality health care in particular, can play a huge role in health inequalities. Those who see physicians in concierge practises are likely to have better health than those who get no health care or get it sporadically from hospital emergency rooms (Gawande 2011).

A good example of the relationship between social class and health is to be found in the adverse health consequences associated with smoking (Marmor 2005). In the 1950s those in the upper social classes were more likely than those in the

GL◉BALISATION

Health Care in Mexico

Health care in the United States is a hot political issue and one that is likely to continue to be hot as health care costs continue to rise dramatically and an aging population needs more and more health care. The lack of universal health care in the United States, even with the reforms begun under the administration of Barack Obama, is often compared unfavourably to the more universal health care available in other countries, especially in Canada and Europe (Russell 2006). Mexico also has, at least theoretically, a universal health plan.

In 2000, about half of all Mexicans were not covered by health insurance. While those who held salaried jobs were covered by the Mexican Social Security Institute and a small number of the wealthiest Mexicans had private insurance, excluded were many people including farmers, those who were self-employed, part-time workers, and the like. However, in 2006 the government passed legislation that had as its goal the provision of health care for all Mexicans. At least on paper, all Mexicans who have been without health care coverage are, or soon will be, enrolled in the health insurance plan. In fact, many poor Mexicans are already receiving medical treatment that they would not have been able to afford in the past.

The issue is whether millions of Mexicans are getting, or will be able to get, the health care promised to them by the government. The budget for health care for the entire country is only $12 billion. This is mitigated, however, by the fact that the population of Mexico is comparatively young; less than 10 percent of Mexicans are over 60 years of age. A more youthful population is less likely to need health care, especially the very expensive forms needed by the aging populations in Canada, the United States, and Europe.

All Mexicans have had the option since 2004 of signing up for the Seguro Popular, "popular insurance," which covers a wide range of medical services and medicines, as well as offering some coverage in case of a catastrophic illness. People are supposed to pay an annual fee for the programme, but in fact few do. The programme is underfunded, and its budget allows for only about $200 per patient. Furthermore, the money is not distributed equally throughout the country. The money is allocated to the states based on the numbers enrolled in the programme in each state. It is in the states' interest to sign up as many people as possible, but they are not held accountable for how the money is spent. As a result, as the director of a watchdog group said, "You have people signed up on paper, but there are no doctors, no medicine, no hospital beds" (Malkin 2011). As a result, there is great variability in health care from one Mexican state to another. In order to get adequate care, some people may have to go to another state and camp out there until care is available and until it is completed. As a result, the health care facilities in some states are overwhelmed by people who come there from other states. Health care in Mexico is still far from universal; it is still a work in progress.

Such health care systems are best viewed in comparative perspective (World Heath Organization 2000, 2010b). While Mexico continues to struggle to implement its attempt for universal health care, both developed and developing countries have provided universal care much more effectively. For example, Thailand is able to provide universal coverage to its citizens for an average of $136 per capita—offering broader care for a cheaper price than Mexico or the United States (World Health Organization 2010b). Because of the quality of care in Thailand and some other developing countries, they are now major destinations in a global system of "medical tourism," where patients from developed countries travel to these countries for more affordable, high-quality health care (L. Turner 2007).

Today, many poor Mexicans are receiving medical treatment that they would not have been able to afford in the past, thanks to "popular insurance." Here, a poor *campesino* receives medical attention for a terrible burn on his leg.

lower classes to be smokers. This difference was due, in part, to the influence of cinema that glamourised smoking, travel, and romance (Kimmel 2009). However, by the 1960s it was those in the lower social classes who were more likely to smoke. It was during this period that medical knowledge about the adverse health effects of smoking became better known and publicised. However, while that knowledge was disseminated quickly in the upper classes, it had a much harder time working its way to and through the lower classes (Phelan et al. 2004; Phelan, Link, and Tehranifar 2010). A key factor here is the lower educational levels in the lower classes and a greater inability to access and understand the research and data available on the negative effects of smoking. In any case, to this day the lower classes suffer much more from the ill effects of smoking than do the upper classes. Later in the chapter we will discuss the relationship between globalisation and smoking.

Another example of the relationship between health and social class involves the likelihood of participating in clinical trials for new surgical procedures, disease screenings, or drug therapies. The fact is that the vast majority of people who participate in such trials are people from the middle and upper classes. It is they who are most likely to benefit from them at an early stage in their development and to disseminate knowledge about them, most likely to others in their social classes (Braveman et al. 2005; Clougherty, Souza, and Cullen 2010).

Addressing this linkage between health and social class with strong social policy is challenging, but Clyde Hertzman and his colleagues at Canada's *Human Early Learning Partnership* have championed an intriguing idea. They argue for **proportionate universality**, the idea that a programme, service, or policy should be universal, but with a scale or intensity that is proportionate to the level of disadvantage a person or family endures (Hertzman 2011).

Ancestry/Ethnicity/Race and Health. The relationship between ancestry/ethnicity/race and health is closely related to that between social class and health. In Canada, for example, whites are more likely to be in the middle and upper classes while Aboriginal peoples and recent immigrants of visible minority background are disproportionately

in the lower classes. Overall, whites tend to have better health than other Canadians, although this is, at least in part, a social class effect. For example, Aboriginal men have a life expectancy of about seven years less than non-Aboriginals, while for women the corresponding gap is about five years (Veenstra 2009). As a second example, Inuit families are more likely to have higher rates of infant mortality than non-Inuit families (Lou et al. 2010). In both cases, at least part of the difference in longevity and infant mortality is due to negative effects of social class background on health outcomes.

Indigenous people are sensitive to power imbalances in their interactions with health care services. This is intimately linked with the dominance of the biomedical paradigm and the view that noncompliant behaviours by indigenous people are the cause of poor health outcomes. By contrast, when care providers promote a nonbiomedical approach to

The influence of 1950s cinema, which glamourised smoking, was much to blame for the increasing number of smokers in the nation. By the 1960s, those in the lower social classes were more likely to smoke than those in the upper class, who were more likely to heed the new medical warnings that smoking was hazardous to one's health.

health care interactions, through trust, reciprocity, and shared decision-making, they can empower recipients and more effectively deliver interventions to reduce the gap in health outcomes. Much work focuses on miscommunication as an access barrier (Peiris, Brown, and Cass 2008). Relevant factors include communication dynamics and sharing of health information, language, and literacy. In health care for indigenous people, the power dynamic directly affects communication.

Wenman and her collaborators (2004) compared the pregnancy outcomes of First Nations and Métis women to other non-Aboriginal women in Edmonton, Alberta. They discovered, consistent with an extensive research literature, that Aboriginal women have greater rates of premature babies, still-births, babies with low birth weight, and infant mortality. However, when they accounted for the socioeconomic differences and the higher prevalence of other risk factors among First Nations and Métis women, they found that all of these pregnancy outcome differences vanished. Stated another way, if non-Aboriginal women lived in the same conditions as do most Aboriginal women, then they too would experience the poorer pregnancy outcomes.

Alan Cass (2004) poses an interesting question. "Why do Aboriginal Canadian, Maori New Zealander, Aboriginal Australian and Native American babies born today share a pattern of premature morbidity and mortality rather than the expected healthy life-course of the nonindigenous baby in the next crib?" (p. 597). He suggests two approaches to the answer. The first approach, which he sees as consistent with a biomedical perspective, emphasises explanations that focus "inside the body." Here the explanatory factors might be genetic or behavioural. The explanatory factors are understood as individual, the traits or behaviours of that person. The second approach, which he sees as consistent with a sociocultural perspective, emphasises explanations that focus "outside the body." Here the explanatory factors might be community or cultural. Here the explanatory factors are understood as having to do with the social context in which the individual lives, the community in which the individual is embedded.

The biomedical perspective is the dominant lens through which the health outcomes of all people are understood by most people in the health care community. From this vantage point it is the noncompliant behaviours of Aboriginal people that are the main explanation for their inferior health outcomes. If only indigenous people did not smoke so much or exercised more. In recent years this view has begun to change. Now more and more health care providers are recognising that cultural and power differences influence issues of communication and health literacy between Aboriginals and non-Aboriginals. Building relations of reciprocity and mutual trust are understood as positive ways of enhancing health care. Ignoring the stress of living in conditions of poverty, and treating all individuals from whatever background as equal, contributes to perpetuating inequality.

Why do Aboriginal peoples in Australia, Canada, and the United States have poorer health than whites? Discrimination and stereotype, both today and as a legacy of the past, plays a major role. First Nations, Inuit, and Métis Canadians have never had easy, unencumbered access to any of the major institutions of Canadian society, including health care. Aboriginal Canadians have great difficulty getting the education they need to gain higher-status occupations and the higher incomes associated with them (S. Davies and Guppy 2013). Even if they are able to get such an education, they may still not be able to obtain those jobs and the income that comes with them. As a result, they are less likely to have the ability and the money to visit health care professionals, at least on a regular basis. The health care they do get from hospital emergency rooms, public hospitals, or more marginal physicians is likely to be inferior. Even if they can afford better care, offices and centres that offer such health care may be far away and/or in forbidding white middle- and upper-class neighbourhoods. Aboriginal people are also more likely to be poorly treated, or even mistreated, by the health care system (Reading and Wien 2009). As a result, they are more likely to underutilise that system, to not utilise it at all, or to use alternative medicines (such as folk and faith healers). They are also likely to be put off by the underrepresentation of indigenous people in health care positions and occupations, whether as physicians or nurses or other health care providers. Aboriginal people are more likely to be relegated to neighbourhoods and conditions that adversely affect their health, such as living near waste dumps where the land, air, and water are contaminated and in apartments or houses with lead-based paint that poses a health risk, especially to young children (Crowder and Downey 2010). Veenstra (2009) also points to the "immigrant health effect" (p. 357). This is the recurrent finding that newcomers to Canada typically see their health decline. In part this is a selection effect, with western countries admitting only immigrants who are healthy. A more pronounced effect, though, comes from new Canadians having to adapt to a new health care system, often in circumstances of stress because of migration and economic challenges, coupled with cultural and language barriers. Furthermore, for many immigrants the Canadian lifestyle of diet and exercise poses obstacles to maintaining good health.

Gender and Health. On the surface, inequality in health does not appear to be a problem that afflicts females since their life expectancy throughout the western world exceeds that of males by a significant margin. In Canada, among the leading causes of death, the rates of male mortality are higher than the corresponding rates for women in all of the disease categories (Veenstra 2009). However, as we saw in Chapter 10, while women live longer, there is a widespread, although not fully accepted,

view that they have poorer health during their lifetimes than men (Shinberg 2007). Lorber and Moore (2002) catch this in their phrasing "women get sicker but men die quicker" (p. 13).

But do women actually get sicker than men, or are women simply better judges of their own bodies and not as burdened as are men with socialisation pressures to "be tough"? It could be that women and men have equitable health, but women are more prone to talk about their ailments and be treated by others as "needy" (Chappell and Penning 2009). Conversely, women's health may indeed be worse because of the greater stress associated with their lives, earning less money than men on average, and having the double jeopardy of work at home and the office.

Women have experienced a process of the medicalisation of aspects of their lives that are specific to them. **Medicalisation** involves the tendency to label as an illness a phenomenon or syndrome that was not previously considered an illness. It also involves a tendency to exaggerate the ability of medicine to deal with that phenomenon or syndrome (Conrad 1986; Conrad, Mackie, and Mehrota 2010; Conrad and Schneider 1980). As discussed above, medicalisation is particularly clear in the case of childbirth. Perhaps the most infamous example of a female condition being medicalised is the female orgasm. This was long seen not as a natural aspect of female sexuality, but rather as a "hysterical" disease that required medical attention (Maines 2001). Many other aspects of women's health have been medicalised in recent years, including premenstrual syndrome (PMS), infertility, and menopause. The pharmaceutical industry has also been quick to pick up on the idea that women are more in need of their drugs than are men, so they have targeted more of their products to women. For example, pills to deal with depression were largely marketed, in the beginning, for women as opposed to men, largely on the stereotyped assumption that men are much less likely to suffer from depression. As a second example, only recently has the pharmaceutical industry given stronger attention to a birth control pill for men.

Sexual Orientation and Health. Especially in the light of HIV/AIDS it is not difficult to understand that health and health care are differentially organised around sexual orientation (see below). Even

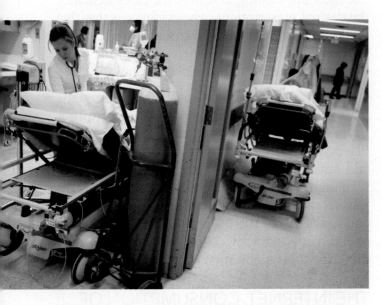

One challenge continually confronting the Canadian health care system is ease of patient access. Many citizens, including in rural areas or in our inner cities, lack direct access to personal physicians, relying instead on emergency room medicine.

more generally, though, how a person's sexual orientation is understood within the health care system has progressed through a convoluted social process. In Canada's early history, homosexuality was illegal. It was dealt with as a crime, and only in 1969 was private homosexual activity between consenting adults removed from possible criminal prosecution. Even then, emotional abuse and mental stress were still directed at gay and lesbian couples. Indeed, the bible of psychiatrists, the *Diagnostic and Statistical Manual of Mental Disorders* (DSM), did not remove homosexuality as a mental illness until 1973. Further, the World Health Organization's *International Classification of Diseases* listed homosexuality as a mental disorder until 1990. Many Canadian provinces apparently continued to use these classification codes for billing purposes up until just a few years ago. According to the *Edmonton Journal* (Kleiss 2010), "until Tuesday [December 2010], section 302.0 of Alberta's diagnostic codes listed homosexuality under the heading 'Mental Disorders: Sexual Deviations and Disorders.'" Of course, to this day, despite a more tolerant attitude on the part of most Canadians toward gays and lesbians, reports in the media regarding "gay bashing" are unfortunately a relatively common occurrence. Furthermore, the slow progress that has been made in more accepting health care legislation for the sexual preferences of gays and lesbians has not been as forthcoming for individuals who are transsexual.

CONSUMERISM AND HEALTH CARE

Historically, thinking about health care involved a tendency to focus on the "producers" of health care, especially physicians, nurses, other health care workers, and government agencies. Also included here are the insurance companies and Medicare. While much attention continues to be paid to all of those producers of health care, the focus began to shift several decades ago in the direction of the consumers of that care. Larger numbers of patients began to realise that they did not simply have to accept what was offered to them by physicians, hospitals, and others. They came to the recognition that they were consumers of those services in much the same way that they were of many other services (and goods).

This was due, in part, to the deprofessionalisation of physicians. As physicians came to be seen as less powerful professionals, it was increasingly easy for patients to question them. At the same time, the increasing questioning furthered the decline in status and power of physicians. The entry of consumerism into medicine led to an increase in shopping around for physicians and in questioning their diagnoses and treatment recommendations.

The best example of increasing consumerism in contemporary medicine is associated with the decision by the pharmaceutical companies to increase the sales of prescription drugs through a direct appeal to consumers using catchy advertisements in newspapers, in magazines, online, and on television. The avalanche started in 1997 when in the U.S. Food and Drug Administration (FDA) began to relax restrictions on direct-to-consumer prescription drug advertisements. The pharmaceutical companies have increasingly supplemented their marketing to physicians through advertisements in medical journals, salespeople, free samples, and other media. Direct marketing is to the ultimate consumer of the pharmaceuticals—the patients (S. G. Morgan 2007). The irony is that, in general, patients cannot go out and obtain these drugs on their own—they need prescriptions from their physicians. Thus the idea is to motivate patients to ask their doctors for, and in some cases demand, the desired prescriptions. The evidence is that this works, and as a result the pharmaceutical companies have become increasingly ubiquitous presences in the media (for example, N. Singer 2009).

We are all familiar with endless advertisements for the leading and most profitable prescription drugs, such as Lipitor (to treat high cholesterol), Plavix (a blood thinner), Nexium (for heartburn), and Advair (an asthma inhaler), and especially the seemingly ubiquitous advertisements for the drugs that treat erectile dysfunction, especially Viagra and Cialis. All of these ads suggest either directly or indirectly that viewers ask their physicians to prescribe these medications for them.

THE INTERNET, CONSUMPTION OF HEALTH CARE, AND TELEVISITS

The Internet has become implicated in the consumption of health care (e-health) in various ways.

The first, and most obvious, is in allowing people to find health care providers of all sorts more easily. The Internet is a vast resource for finding providers, by specialty, on the local, national, and even global levels.

It is not only possible to find the names and addresses of providers on the Internet, but more importantly lots of information about them is available there. For example, one can get rankings of health care providers as well as information from previous patients about their experiences and recommendations. There is also a wealth of information and evaluation available on pharmaceuticals, medical technologies, and alternative treatments.

The increasing amount of health care–related data of all sorts on the Internet allows the consumer-patient to become a much more knowledgeable consumer of health care services and products. At the moment, most of the information is scattered, widely and unsystematically, across the Internet. Another problem is that it is not linked to individuals, their diseases, and their specific needs. There is, however, a start-up company—Keas—that seeks to link individuals and their diseases to available information. Thus, a patient with diabetes would, under this system, receive personalised reminders, questions relating to the condition, and advice regarding variables such as age, gender, and weight (Lohr 2009).

The Internet has become a global source of medical information. One specific example involves a website—www.malecircumcision.org—designed to deal with the lack of information about, and the myths relating to, circumcision and HIV/AIDS (McNeil 2009). This is especially important in Africa, where HIV/AIDS, as we will discuss later, is rampant. It is important, especially for Africans, to know that studies based there have shown that circumcision reduces the risk of sexually transmitted HIV/AIDS by as much as 60 percent. However, one myth that is dealt with on the website is that after circumcision men no longer need to use condoms to prevent HIV/AIDS. Of course, the existence of the digital divide (see Chapter 8) and the lack of access to computers and the Internet make it much more difficult for such information to make its way to the people in Africa—and elsewhere—who are most in need of it.

Pharmaceutical companies are largely responsible for the increasing consumerism in medicine today. Using catchy advertisements and direct appeals to consumers to increase sales of prescription drugs has produced astounding sales numbers—for better or worse.

The Internet also opens a global range of views, possibilities, and alternatives to the consumers of medical goods and services. Consumers are better able to make themselves aware of alternatives available elsewhere in the world, obtain information and advice about them, and find ways of obtaining them. On the positive side, this gives medical consumers better access to most goods and services and many more choices and options. There is also a wider range of alternative medical goods and services to be found on the Internet, and they could prove to be useful, even life-saving. On the negative side, this is relatively new and unregulated global territory, and the consumer is much more likely to obtain fraudulent medical products and services.

The net result of the above is that a patient who uses these resources will become a much better, more sophisticated, knowledgeable, and independent consumer of medical services and products. For example, many products and services can be obtained legally and illegally—and often more inexpensively—through the Internet without going through an intermediary associated with the health care system (Krauss 2004; Napoli 1999). Also available online are a variety of tests that can be done at home. One is a DNA test that can be had for $349 for an individual and $698 for a couple (Pollack 2010). These tests can be used by individuals and couples to determine on their own whether they are carriers of life-threatening diseases, such as cystic fibrosis, that could show up in their children. However, there are concerns that these tests may not be reliable, they may give test takers a false sense of assurance, the costs are too high, the privacy of the test results may not be assured, and those who rely on these tests will not get the expert advice of trained medical professionals (Brody 2009).

There are other problems associated with using the Internet for health-related consumption. For example, there is the possibility of getting counterfeit, and perhaps ineffective, medications, as well as bogus services and information of various types. At the height of the global scare over an H1N1 flu pandemic (see page 531), the Internet was rife with false claims for healing gels and "ionic silver" sprays, as well as ads for fake Tamiflu, an antiviral medication (Wayne 2009). While consumers may become more sophisticated by exploring the medical information on the Internet, they are not trained in medicine and therefore likely unable to understand fully the advantages and disadvantages of what is available. As a result, they are more likely to be duped in various ways.

The Internet is also an increasingly important resource for health care providers. It is possible for them to obtain information on new research, pharmaceuticals, and technologies on the Internet. There are a variety of computer programmes and apps available to medical professionals that can be used to improve medical care. For example, in cases where patients have been exposed to the AIDS virus, a screening process has been developed that allows physicians to ask the right questions and get needed information quickly. It is important to know when exposure to the virus took place and to start treatment quickly (Rabin 2009). Another example involves online registries for various diseases (such as cystic fibrosis), which can be important sources of information on the effectiveness of medications and physical therapy (Freudenheim 2009).

Digitising Medical Records and Televisits

The digitisation of medical records is likely to grow in importance in the coming years. Denmark took

The Internet is an increasingly important resource for health care consumers and providers, making it easier to obtain information on new research, pharmaceuticals, and technologies that can improve medical care. Here, a doctor and patient at Sonam Norbu Memorial Hospital in Leh, India, consult another hospital via video chat.

the lead in digitising medical records while Canada lags far behind; digitising medical records has been a major concern of most provincial governments, but so far progress has been slow, and worries about privacy remain high.

Denmark is also at the forefront of telemedicine. Telemedicine makes it possible for patients, from the comfort of their homes, to use a few simple medical technologies (for example, blood pressure monitors), take various readings with them, have them sent by Bluetooth to the doctor, and then have a consultation via webcam with the physician (Bhanoo 2010). In spite of its obvious utility and advantages, especially for large rural areas of Canada, telemedicine is only in its infancy in Canada. Part of the reason seems to be the resistance of physicians and other professionals.

GLOBALISATION AND HEALTH

There is a near endless array of issues that could be discussed under the heading of globalisation and health (Linn and Wilson 2012). We can do little more than touch on a few of them in this section.

Health 2.0/Medicine 2.0

Web 2.0 is still relatively new; the term itself was introduced by Tim O'Reilly at a conference in 2004. Its use has boomed in many areas, including health and medicine. A review of the literature on Web 2.0 as it relates to health and medicine—Health 2.0/Medicine 2.0—revealed several key facts (Van De Belt et al. 2010):

- Professionals, patients or consumers, and other stakeholders such as medical students and researchers are empowered by Web 2.0 technologies.

- Social networking and social media tools are of central importance on Health2.0/Medicine 2.0.

- Prosumers, as discussed in Chapter 4, both produce and consume content, and both professionals and patients are prosumers when they actively collaborate in producing and consuming health care. Among other things, this serves to elevate the status of patients, in some cases to the same level as medical professionals.

- Medical content continues to be of great importance, although the content is less likely to be "owned" by the professional, but rather is user-owned content. However, increasingly, no one "owns" medical content—it is produced and shared collaboratively.

One example of prosumption on Health 2.0/Medicine 2.0 is the website www.lamsight.org, where patients can report their experiences with lymphangioleiomyomatosis (LAM), a rare and fatal disease that slowly destroys the lungs (Arnquist 2009). Basically, the victims themselves aggregate and report the data on the disease that in the past researchers had to collect and report. The result is a self-reported database that can be utilised by researchers around the world. It is an example of *crowdsourcing* and *open-source* research, whereby, in this case, patients as a whole are in control of their data, and they help build relationships between researchers, patients, and physicians. This can also be seen as members of an online community sharing information about their disease. Another is www.patientslikeme.com, developed for those with epilepsy. However, there are questions about the reliability of the data reported to, and found on, these websites. For example, one study of Facebook communities of diabetes sufferers found that many posts were promotions for non-FDA-approved drugs or remedies (E. Moore 2010).

Prosumption is manifest in many other ways on Health 2.0/Medicine 2.0. For example, patients are increasingly writing reviews, often in the form of blogs, of physicians, hospitals, and the like. Those reviews are being read by other prospective patients—as well as health professionals—who then might write their own blogs based on their experiences. There are websites such as www.rateMDs.com where patients are posting their experiences and evaluations and others are reading them. The Internet is also being used by prosumers to raise awareness about, contribute to, and raise funds for research on many different diseases. See, for example, the stories hosted on www.giveforward.com, which detail individual efforts to help raise funds for medical care.

Growing Global Inequality

While globalisation has been associated with increased aggregate life expectancy, it also has tended to widen global disparities in health (Yach and Yashemian 2007). Women and children tend to be the most vulnerable populations globally due to their lower social positions and poor access to health care (Fillipi et al. 2006). People in poor nations tend to have poorer health as a result of limited access to health care services, education, sanitation, and adequate nutrition and housing. Conversely, poor health tends to limit economic growth in those nations mainly by adversely affecting productivity. Developing countries have a disproportionate share of mortality and morbidity, much of which could be prevented inexpensively and treated effectively if the money were available. Of the total burden of disease, 90 percent is concentrated in low- and middle-income countries. Yet, only 10 percent of total global health care expenditures occur in those countries, the ones that need the money the most. Only 10 percent of the research money in the United States is devoted to the health problems that account for 90 percent of the global disease burden (Al-Tuwaijri et al. 2003).

For these and other reasons, there is a 19-year gap in life expectancy between high- and low-income countries. The improvements in developing countries tend to be in those countries more deeply and successfully involved in economic globalisation, such as Brazil, Egypt, and Malaysia. However, for most of the rest, especially the least developed countries in the Global South, globalisation has brought with it a decline in economic growth, an increase in poverty, and, as a result, a decline in health.

Disease. The vast majority of not only acute, but also chronic, diseases occur at younger ages and in low- and middle-income countries. The rising cost of dealing with chronic diseases in developing countries will adversely affect their ability to deal with acute infectious diseases. Of special importance from the point of view of globalisation is the increasing global marketing of tobacco, alcohol, sugar, and fat—the latter two especially aimed at children—and the consequent global spread of the diseases associated with these products.

Although most observers see an increase over time in health disparities between the developed and the less developed countries, at least two observers (Firebaugh and Goesling 2007) see a decline in recent years in between-nation inequality in health. However, they do recognise that the continuation of that decline is threatened by the HIV/AIDS epidemic. Even if we accept the argument about the decline, great disparities remain between and within nations in terms of health.

Malnutrition. Countries in the Global South suffer disproportionately from hunger and malnutrition (Van de Poel et al. 2008). Roughly 850 million people there are affected by these problems. The causes include inadequate, or totally unavailable, food supplies, and poor and unbalanced diets. Dealing with hunger and malnutrition is especially important for children because those who are underweight are, as adults, likely to be less physically and intellectually productive and to suffer more chronic illnesses and

disabilities. This carries on across generations as the ability of such adults to provide adequate nutrition for their children is compromised.

Undernutrition is a form of malnutrition involving an inadequate intake of nutrients, including calories, vitamins, and minerals. The other form of malnutrition involves obesity caused by an excessive intake of nutrients, especially calories. Developing countries now increasingly suffer from a "double nutritional burden"—those who do not have enough to eat and those who eat too much, especially of the wrong kinds of food (for example, food that is high in fat and cholesterol) (Kelishadi 2007; Prentice 2006). However, although the latter is increasing in the less developed world, undernutrition is the greatest problem there. It is especially a problem for mothers and children. Problems stemming from undernutrition continue through the life cycle and are responsible for stunted growth, less schooling, lower productivity, mothers having children with lower birth weight, and chronic diseases. It is even linked to rapid weight gain and obesity among formerly underweight children (Serra and Ngo 2012).

Undernutrition is related to problems not only for individuals but also for societies as a whole. It is related to underdevelopment and tends to perpetuate poverty. Without adequate nutrition the human capital needed for economic development cannot develop.

Food insecurity is an important cause of undernutrition. Such insecurity exists when people do not have sufficient access to safe and nutritious food—a condition necessary to lead a healthy and productive life. There are many causes of food insecurity, but one of the most important is a lack of adequate agricultural development. A number of global programmes have been undertaken to help deal with the problem, such as the creation of community gardens, farmers' markets, agricultural diversification programmes, and the like.

Smoking

Smoking is an important cause of health problems around the world. In spite of those health problems, though, a highly profitable tobacco industry continues to be central to the global economy (Fulbrook 2007). According to a 2011 World Health Organization estimate, nearly 6 million people die each year from tobacco use, and unless there are dramatic

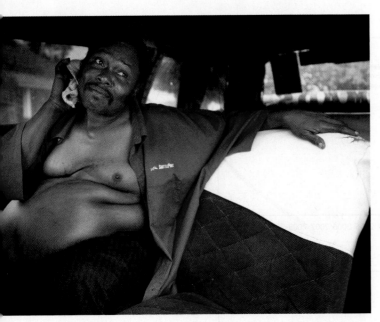

Many developing countries suffer from a "double nutritional burden"—a coexistence of those who do not have enough to eat and those who eat too much. Fifty-nine-year-old Ugandan dancer and chairman of the Sanyu African Music and Dramatic Society Moses Kawooya takes pride in his enormous belly. Kawooya weighs 110 kilograms—roughly 242 pounds.

changes that number will rise to 8 million by 2030. Also projected is that 1 billion people will die in the twenty-first century from smoking-related diseases.

With the western market for cigarettes shrinking because of growing awareness of the risks associated with smoking, the tobacco corporations have shifted their focus to Africa and Asia. India accounts for almost a third of the world's tobacco-related deaths. China is now the world's biggest market for cigarettes (Gu et al. 2009), with 1.7 trillion cigarettes smoked every year. The Chinese consume about 30 percent of the world's cigarettes, though China has about 20 percent of the world's population. Many Chinese appear to have little knowledge of the health hazards associated with smoking (World Health Organization 2010a). For their part, the western powers are the major exporters of cigarettes to the rest of the world. In keeping with much of the Canadian economy, cigarette manufacturing in Canada is largely done by local branches of transnational companies. Of the some 30 billion cigarettes annually produced in this country, the majority are sold locally.

Borderless Diseases

Another negative aspect of globalisation as far as health is concerned is the flow of borderless

diseases (S. Ali 2012). While borderless diseases have become much more common in recent years, they are not a new phenomenon. Tuberculosis (TB) was known in ancient times, and today the World Health Organization (WHO) estimates that more than a third of the world's population is infected with the cause of the disease—the TB bacillus (Linn and Wilson 2012). Sexually transmitted infections (STIs) of various types have long diffused globally. A specific example of the latter is syphilis, which has spread globally, and continues to circulate, especially throughout a number of less developed countries. However, the roots of the disease were probably in Europe, and it was spread by European colonialism and military exploits. In fact, for many in the less developed world the disease was closely associated with French soldiers and came to be known in some parts of the world as the "French disease."

Then there is the increasing prevalence of other borderless diseases, many of them relatively new. Examples include severe acute respiratory syndrome (SARS); bovine spongiform encephalopathy (BSE, or "mad cow disease"), which is often found in cattle and can cause a brain disease in humans (P. Ong 2007); avian flu; Ebola virus; and HIV/AIDS. The nature of these diseases and their spread, either in fact (HIV/AIDS) or merely, at least so far, as a frightening possibility (avian flu), tells us a great deal about the nature and reality of globalisation in the twenty-first century. The pathogens that cause these diseases flow, or have the potential to flow, readily throughout the globe.

Several factors help explain the great and increasing global mobility of borderless diseases. First, there is the increase in global travel and the increasing rapidity of that travel (Rosenthal 2007b). Second, there is growing human migration and the ease with which people can cross borders. As a result, they often bring with them diseases that are not detected at the nation's borders. Third, the expansion of massive urban areas such as Lagos, Nigeria (see Chapter 14), has created vast mixing bowls where large numbers of people in close and frequent proximity can easily infect one another. Fourth is increasing human involvement in natural habitats previously untouched by human beings. There, people can have contact with pathogens for which they have no immunity and that they can spread rapidly throughout the world (S. Ali 2012).

Individuals Living With HIV

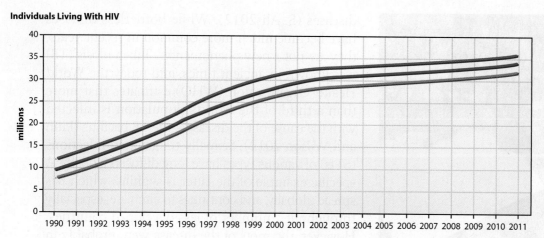

Newly Infected With HIV

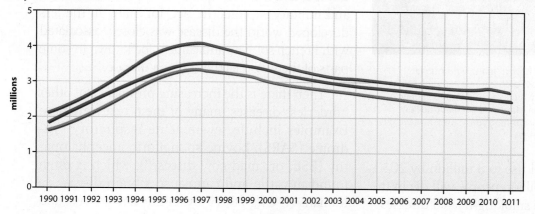

Deaths Due to AIDS

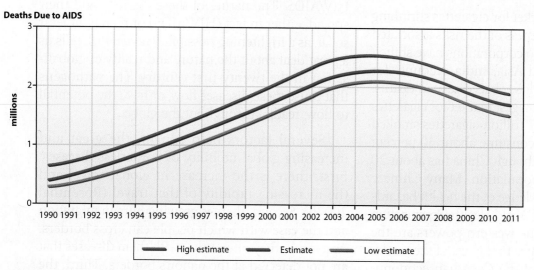

High estimate — Estimate — Low estimate

FIGURE 13.5 Individuals Newly Infected and Living with HIV Globally, 1990–2011

SOURCE: UNAIDS, "Report on the Global AIDS Epidemic," 2012 (http://www.unaids.org/en/media/unaids/contentassets/documents/epidemiology/2012/gr2012/20121120_UNAIDS_Global_Report_2012_en.pdf).

have proven unable or unwilling to be responsive to this global need. For example, China and Vietnam were unwilling to provide the WHO with samples of the avian flu that had become a serious problem in those countries. Such samples were needed in order to study the spread of the disease and the ways in which the flu was evolving. This information could have been useful in heading off the further spread of the disease and might have speeded up the development of a vaccine to prevent it.

HIV/AIDS. HIV/AIDS was first recognised in the United States in 1981 and has since been acknowledged as a scourge throughout much of the world (Whiteside 2008, 2012). In 2010, it was estimated that 25 million people had died from AIDS while another 33 million, many of whom will die from the disease, were suffering from AIDS. The numbers of people infected with HIV and those living with AIDS vary greatly around the world (see Figure 13.5).

The flow of efforts to deal with these diseases must be equally global. That is, there is a need for global responses to the increasing likelihood of the spread of various diseases. However, some nations

HIV/AIDS cannot be contracted through casual contact with people who have the disease. The disease spreads only through intimate human contact with body fluids, especially through unprotected sex and intravenous drug use. Thus, in spite of the large numbers of people with AIDS, it is *not* an easy disease to contract. For instance, fellow passengers on an international flight will not contract AIDS simply because they sit next to, or talk with, a fellow passenger with the disease.

The spread of AIDS is linked to globalisation, especially the increased global mobility associated with tourism (notably, sex tourism), the greater migration rates of workers, increased legal and illegal immigration, much greater rates of commercial and business travel, the movement (sometimes on a mass basis) of refugees, military interventions and the movement of military personnel, and so on.

People who have the disease can travel great distances over a period of years without knowing they have the disease and therefore have the ability to transmit the disease to many others in widely scattered locales. Thus, when people with HIV/AIDS have sexual contact with people in other countries, they are likely to transmit the disease

to at least some of them. Similarly, those without the disease can travel to nations where HIV/AIDS is prevalent, contract it, and then bring it back to their home country. In either case, the disease moves from region to region, country to country, and ultimately globally, carried by human vectors.

More and more people, especially in the Global South, are contracting the disease. Sub-Saharan Africa is especially hard-hit (Nolan 2006). About two thirds of all adults and children living with the disease live in sub-Saharan Africa (see Figure 13.6). Auguring poorly for the future of sub-Saharan Africa is the fact that about two thirds of all new HIV/AIDS infections in 2009 occurred there. One well-known way in which the disease has spread across the African continent is through truck drivers who work their way from country to country. If they have the disease, they may infect those who live in areas that were to that point free of the disease. The data on specific countries in the southern part of Africa are sobering. For example:

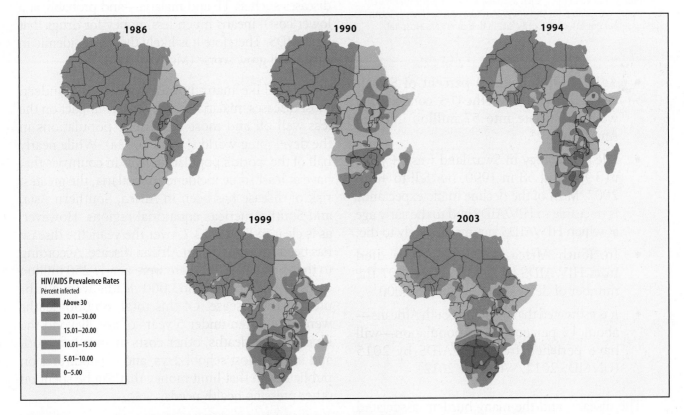

FIGURE 13.6 The Prevalence of AIDS in Sub-Saharan Africa, 1986–2003

SOURCE: Adapted from "Tragedy and Progress Amid the African HIV/AIDS Pandemic," Ezekiel Kalipeni, *The Illinois International Review,* International Programmes and Studies: University of Illinois at Urbana-Champaign. May 21, 2007.

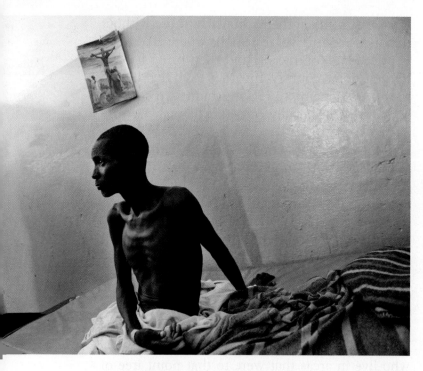

No area of the world has been more devastated by AIDS than sub-Saharan Africa, a region spanning 36 countries and nearly 60 million people. It is estimated that as many as two thirds of all AIDS cases in the world are located in sub-Saharan Africa. And things will soon grow worse: The global recession and the lower-cost treatments for other global epidemics, such as malaria, have meant that much less money is available for the drugs that treat AIDS. Here, a South Sudanese patient affected by HIV sits in bed at N'zara Hospital.

- As of 2008, about 19 percent of Swazis were HIV positive; in the U.S. context, that would translate into 57 million infected Americans.

- Life expectancy in Swaziland was 54 years in 1980 and 58 in 1990, but fell to 40 in 2007. Most of the decline in life expectancy is traceable to HIV/AIDS and to the early age at which HIV/AIDS victims are likely to die.

- In South Africa, 180,000 people died from HIV/AIDS in 2000, but by 2007 the number of deaths had risen to 350,000.

- It is estimated that 6 million South Africans—about 13 percent of the population—will have perished from HIV/AIDS by 2015 (UNAIDS 2012; Whiteside 2012).

The disease, and the many burdens associated with it, is having an adverse effect on all aspects of social and economic life throughout Africa. Some observers predict the failure of African states and the complete economic collapse of some as a result of the spread of the disease. The economies of many African nations have already contracted as average life expectancy declines and it becomes harder to find healthy adults to perform basic tasks.

The greater prevalence of AIDS in Africa is just one example of the greater vulnerability of the world's have-nots to this and many other borderless diseases. This is a question not just of economic marginality but also of social and political marginality. Compounding the problem is the fact that it is precisely this *most* vulnerable population that is also *least* likely to have access to the high-quality health care and the very expensive drugs that can slow the disease for years, or even decades.

In fact, things will soon grow worse for AIDS patients in Africa. In recent years, economic aid, largely from the United States, had allowed many African victims to obtain the needed drugs. However, the global recession, as well as a sense that the money could be better and more efficiently spent on other diseases (for example, more lives could be saved from diseases such as TB and malaria—and probably at a lower cost), means much less money for drugs that treat AIDS. Therefore it is likely that the epidemic in Africa will grow worse (McNeil 2010).

Malaria. Like many borderless diseases, indeed most diseases, malaria has its greatest impact on the less well-off and most vulnerable populations in the developing world (J. Hall 2012a). While nearly half of the world's population lives in countries that have at least some incidence of malaria, the greatest risk of disease has been in Africa, Southern Asia, and South America's equatorial regions. However, as is clear in Figure 13.7, over the years the disease has become primarily an African disease. According to the WHO, in 2008 there were nearly 250 million cases of malaria, and 863,000 deaths were attributed to the disease. Of this total, 85,000 deaths were of children under 5 years of age. Beyond the illnesses and deaths, other costs involve lost work and income, lost school days, and expenditures on public health that limit money that can be spent on other pressing health needs.

There is no vaccine for malaria, but efforts to control the mosquitoes that carry the disease can help. Insecticide-treated nets reduce the number of

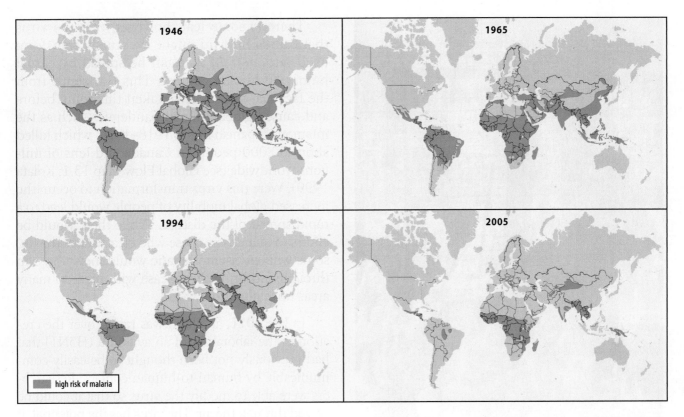

FIGURE 13.7 Areas at High Risk for Malaria, 1946–2005

SOURCE: Maps from *Globalization: A Basic Text* by George Ritzer. Wiley-Blackwell, 2010. Originally adapted from *Power of Place: Geography, Destiny, and Globalization's Rough Landscape* by H. J. de Blij. Copyright © 2008 Oxford University Press; "The Economic Burden of Malaria," John Luke Gallup and Jeffrey D. Sachs in *American Journal of Tropical Medicine and Hygiene* 2001, vol. 64, no. 1, 85–96. Copyright © 2001 by The American Society of Tropical Medicine and Hygiene.

bites while people are asleep, and indoor spraying of homes helps a great deal. However, it is possible that mosquitoes can develop resistance to the chemicals.

Dealing with malaria is complicated by the great mobility characteristics of the global age. New arrivals, especially those without immunity, have a higher risk of contracting the disease. New centres of disease can develop as the disease is passed from infected individuals to previously uninfected mosquitoes, which then are able to infect other humans in a new area. This can lead to renewed outbreaks in areas that had previously been cleared of the disease. The global health community has engaged in a concerted effort to reduce the incidence of malaria. Progress has been made, but elimination of the disease is a distant hope.

Tuberculosis. Tuberculosis is another, even more deadly, disease that largely affects poor people in the poorest areas of the world (J. Hall 2012b). Of the cases 85 percent occur in Southeast Asia, Africa, and the western Pacific. There are not

nearly as many cases of TB each year as there are of malaria; however, TB is far more deadly, killing about twice as many people in a given year. People contract the disease by inhaling airborne bacteria. There is a vaccine for the disease, and treatment can be effective, although it can take up to a year. Those with vulnerable immune systems, such as those with HIV/AIDS, are particularly prone to TB. Some progress has been made globally in fighting the disease, but it lingers on, especially in Africa because of the high rates of HIV/AIDS there.

Avian Flu. In 2009 and 2010 the world witnessed a flu pandemic (H1N1), but it proved to be a relatively mild form of the disease. Prior to that, there had been fear of a pandemic of a potentially far more deadly strain of the flu, and because we live in a global age, its spread would be faster and more extensive than earlier pandemics. However, it is also the case, as will be discussed in a moment, that the ability to deal with such a pandemic is enhanced as a result of globalisation. For example, global monitoring has increased, and there is greater

There is little evidence of human-to-human spread of the avian flu virus; most people have contracted the disease through direct contact with infected birds. Here, a farmer feeds chickens at his farm in Chaungtha Village, some 200 miles southwest of Yangon, Myanmar.

ability to get health workers and pharmaceuticals rapidly to the site of an outbreak.

Some flu subtypes can spread through casual human contact with an infected animal, but there is little evidence of human-to-human spread of the avian flu virus. The relatively small number of humans in the world who have gotten the disease, and the even smaller number who have died from it, contracted the disease through direct contact with birds infected with the disease. Those in less developed nations are more likely to have such direct contact with their birds—some literally live with the birds—since consuming them and their eggs is central to their food supply and/or birds and their eggs may be an important business for them. In contrast, relatively few people in the developed world have direct contact with birds, so they are highly unlikely to contract bird flu in this way.

There is some fear, however, that the virus that causes bird flu might eventually transform itself into a strain that can be spread by casual human-to-human contact. This fear stems from the fact that viruses have taken this route before and caused global human pandemics such as the infamous "Spanish flu" of 1918–1920, which killed about 50,000 people in Canada and tens of millions worldwide (see Global Flow Map 13.1; Kolata 1999). Were this virus transformation to occur, the increased global mobility of people would lead to a rapid spread of the disease. While there would be efforts to quarantine those who clearly have the flu, some who are asymptomatic would inevitably slip through and bring the disease with them to many areas throughout the world.

In late 2011, an alarm was raised over the creation in the laboratory of an avian flu (H5N1) that had previously not been thought to be easily communicable by human-to-human contact. Researchers were able to modify the virus so that it could be spread through the air. The virus has the potential, if it gets out of control, to spread around the world, and it could prove far more deadly than even the Spanish flu since it has an extraordinarily high death rate (Grady and Broad 2011). In fact, the U.S. government made highly unusual and controversial efforts to limit publication of the full results of the research because it was feared that the information could be used by terrorists to create a global pandemic. The argument against such censoring is that access to the results of the research could lead to greater understanding of the virus and better ways to prevent and treat the disease. In early 2012, a decision was made to allow the research results to be published. The argument was that the danger of terrorists being able to use the information to start an epidemic was less than the danger posed by the virus itself undergoing a mutation that could cause an epidemic. The hope is that the publication of the results will lead to methods of preventing or ameliorating such an epidemic.

THE IMPACT OF WAR ON HEALTH

War and the preparations for it have a profound effect on the health and well-being of people, again especially in developing countries. For example, four times as much is spent in the developing world on the military than is spent on health and education. Of

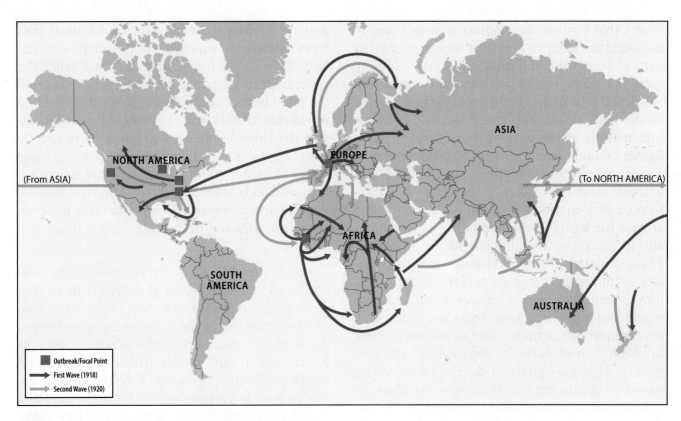

GLOBAL FLOW MAP 13.1 The Spread of Spanish Flu, First and Second Waves, 1918, 1920

SOURCE: Inverness Medical Innovations, Inc. Spanish Flu 2009.

the casualties in war, 90 percent are civilians, many of whom are severely wounded and need significant amounts of long-term health care. Warfare also affects the nutrition of all as agricultural lands and crops are overrun, and the ability of the economy as a whole to function is adversely affected. People, in the form of the human capital they have to offer to the economic system, are diminished, and the result is a decline in the quantity and quality of the labour force.

Warfare also has a measurable impact on mental health. For example, child soldiers in Africa are more likely to exhibit antisocial behaviour, depression, and paranoia as a result of participation in battle (Honwana 2007). Children who do not fight in battle but live near war zones are more likely not only to be wounded but also to feel that they have less control over their surroundings. This can lead to greater feelings of insecurity and depression and to an increased inability to make meaningful connections with others (Sagi-Schwartz 2008). Children, as well as many others in or close to battle, can suffer from posttraumatic stress disorder

(PTSD). For example, among American soldiers returning from Afghanistan, PTSD has been associated with such problems as alcohol and drug abuse, depression, violence toward others, and thoughts of suicide (www.va.gov).

GLOBALISATION AND IMPROVEMENTS IN HEALTH AND HEALTH CARE

We have focused in the last few sections on the negative effects of globalisation on health; it is clear, however, that globalisation has brought with it an array of developments (for example, the growth of global health-related organisations [Inoue and Drori 2006]) that have, or at least should have, improved the quality of health throughout the world. Of course, as with much else about globalisation, the effects have been uneven and affected by a variety of local circumstances.

Increasing interpersonal relations among and between various regions throughout the world means that positive developments in one part of the world are likely to find their way to most other parts of the world, and quite rapidly. In addition, there is a ready flow of new ideas associated with health and health care. In the era of the Internet and online journals—in this case medical journals— information about new medical developments flashes around the world virtually instantaneously. Of course, how those ideas are received and whether, and how quickly, they can be implemented vary enormously. There is great variability around the world in the number of professionals able to comprehend and utilise such information. Thus, surgeons in the developed world might be able to implement a new surgical technique almost immediately, but those in less developed countries would find it harder to learn about and utilise such a technique. Furthermore, the institutions in place in which such ideas can be implemented also vary greatly. Thus, hospitals in developed countries would be able to implement changes to reduce the risks of hospital-based infections, but those in less developed countries would find such changes difficult or impossible because of the costs involved.

New medical products clearly flow around the world much more slowly than new ideas, but because of global improvements in transport they are much more mobile than ever before. Included under this heading would be pharmaceuticals of all types. Clearly, the superstars of the pharmaceutical industry are global phenomena. In fact, while the United States accounted for about $325 billion of the $880 billion in pharmaceutical sales expected worldwide in 2011, sales in emerging markets outside the United States are growing more rapidly than U.S. sales (Alazraki 2010; Herper and Kang 2006). The key point is that as these drugs are approved and come to be seen as effective, they are likely to flow around the world, especially to developed countries and to the elites in less developed countries.

Of course, the drugs that are most likely to be produced and distributed globally are those that are considered likely to be most profitable. Those are the drugs that address the health problems of the wealthier members of global society, such as hypertension, high cholesterol, arthritis, mental health problems, impotence, hair loss, and so on. The well-to-do are most able to afford the diets that lead to high cholesterol, acid reflux, and heartburn, and they are therefore the likely consumers of Lipitor, Zocor, Nexium, and Prevacid. Because they produce the greatest earnings for pharmaceutical companies, these drugs are most likely to achieve global distribution.

Conversely, drugs that might save many lives are not apt to be produced (Moran et al. 2009). Figure 13.8 demonstrates that few, if any, of the pharmaceutical companies surveyed in the United States, Europe, and Japan devote research and development money to creating drugs that would help those in less developed countries who suffer from diseases such as sleeping sickness and malaria. Such drugs are unlikely to yield great profits because those who need them are mainly the poor in less developed countries. If the drugs are produced, their flow to those parts of the globe is likely to be minimal. Thus, as we've seen, Africa is a hotbed of many diseases, such as malaria, some of them killing millions of people each year. However, because these are largely poor people in impoverished countries, the major drug companies based primarily in the West and wealthy developed countries are little interested in doing the research and paying for the start-up and production costs necessary to produce drugs that are not likely to be profitable and may even lose money.

A boy runs toward a relief convoy as it arrives in a village 15 miles northwest of Baidoa, Somalia. A French legionnaire sits in firing position to ensure the safe arrival of the food.

Number of companies (out of 11 respondents) with research and development activities targeting drugs for neglected diseases				
Disease	**R&D Spending**	**Screening**	**Pre-clinical or Clinical Development**	**Product to market in last five years**
sleeping sickness	0	0	0	0
Chagas disease	1	0	1	0
ieishmaniasis	1	0	1	0
malaria	2	1	2	2
tuberculosis	5	4	3	1
Other infectious diseases (Includes viral, bacterial and fungal diseases)	9	N/A	8	6

Methodology: The survey was sent to the CEOs and/or Directors of Research of 20 pharmaceutical companies in Europe, Japan, and the United States. The questionnaire inquired about overall resources devoted to infectious diseases, and specific resources devoted to particular neglected diseases. The survey stated that individual company names would not be disclosed when reporting the results. Results relied on self-reporting and reports were not independently validated.

FIGURE 13.8   Leading Pharmaceutical Companies' Neglect of Certain Diseases

SOURCE: From *Fatal Imbalance: The Crisis in Research and Development for Drugs for Neglected Diseases.* Published by Médecins Sans Frontières Access to Essential Medicines Campaign and the Drugs for Neglected Diseases Working Group I, September 2001.

A similar point can be made about the flow of advanced medical technologies, including MRIs, CAT scans, and PET scans, throughout the world. These are extraordinarily expensive technologies found largely in the wealthy developed countries of the Global North. The machines are not only more likely to exist in these developed countries, but they are more likely to be used intensively because patients, either on their own or because of health insurance, are able to afford the very expensive scans and tests associated with them. Figure 13.9 shows the 2010 world leaders in number of MRI exams per 1,000 people. The United States is at the top with 91.2 per 1,000; Canada offers 46.7 per 1,000; all of the other countries and groups of countries (OECD) are in the Global North. Also concentrated in developed countries are the highly trained personnel needed to administer and interpret the results of, say, an MRI. In contrast, relatively few of these technologies flow to less developed, southern countries; they are used there less intensively; and there are relatively few trained people there

capable of conducting the tests and interpreting the results (Debas 2010; WHO 2010).

In terms of networks of people, much the same picture emerges. Medical and health-related personnel in the North are tightly linked through an array of professional networks. As a result, personnel

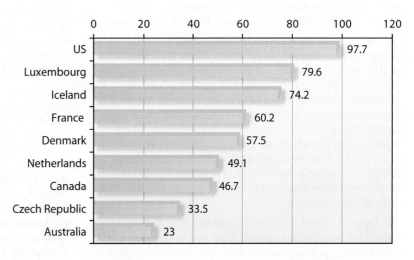

FIGURE 13.9   MRI Exams, per 1,000 People, by Country, 2010

SOURCE: http://www.oecd-ilibrary.org/social-issues-migration-health/magnetic-resonance-imaging-mri-exams-total_mri-exam-total-table-en

A doctor with few if any advanced technologies treats patients in the country of Georgia.

can move about within those networks. More importantly, the latest findings and developments in health and medicine are rapidly disseminated through those networks. The problem in the Global South is that not only are there fewer professionals involved in these networks, but the flow of new information to them is more limited (Godlee et al. 2004; Horton 2000). More importantly, even if they are able to get the information, they generally lack the resources and infrastructure to use it, or to use it adequately.

At a more general level, we can say that the health and medical institutions in the North are highly interconnected while those in the South are only weakly interconnected with those in the North, as well as with one another (Buss and Ferreira 2010). This is another, more general, reason for the fact that important new developments in health and medicine do not flow rapidly to the Global South.

SUMMARY

In many ways beauty has become a commodity that can be bought. The emphasis on beauty has also placed more attention on physical activity and its linkages to healthy bodies. Body modification, such as tattoos and piercing, is another example of society's increase in reflexivity and has become more common over the last several decades. The explosion of sociological interest in the body can be traced back to Michel Foucault, whose work formed the foundation of the sociological study of the body. This field is defined by a general focus on the relationship between the body, society, and culture. It encompasses a wide range of concerns, such as the gendered body, sexuality, and bodily pain.

Medical sociology is concerned with the social causes and consequences of illness. Since the middle of the twentieth century the medical profession, along with other professions, has gone through a process of deprofessionalisation, whereby its power and autonomy, as well as its high status and great wealth, have declined relative to the very high place it once held. Unlike doctors, nurses were never able to achieve full professional status, mainly because of the predominantly male medical profession's desire to keep the predominantly female nursing profession in a subordinate position.

Overall, there is broad consensus that the Canadian health care system is strong on quality but challenged by quantity. For example, on two strong indicators of health care, life expectancy and infant mortality, Canada ranks high among all of the world's nations. Not all groups experience longevity and low infant mortality, however. Disadvantages are often linked with one's social class and ancestry. There have been attempts to address these inequalities with health care reform, though especially for Aboriginal peoples these changes have not been very effective.

In line with the deprofessionalisation of medicine, the focus in health care has shifted from the producers to the consumers of care. People are also being asked, and desiring themselves, to be prosumers in the health care system. The Internet has become involved in the consumption of health care in various ways. It provides, at least to people who have Internet access, a quick and easy way to locate doctors, shop for the lowest prices on procedures, read fellow patients' reviews, and become more knowledgeable about health and health care.

As with the inequality in Canada regarding health care, there are global disparities in health. These disparities have often been tied to globalisation. Individuals in the Global South suffer disproportionately from hunger and malnutrition, including obesity and undernutrition. The spread of AIDS is linked to globalisation and increased global mobility. This is particularly problematic in Africa, where over two thirds of all AIDS cases are located. However, globalisation also allows information about new medical developments to flow faster around the world, though the ability to implement new technologies and afford new pharmaceuticals clearly varies by geographic location.

KEY TERMS

- Deprofessionalisation   512
- Food insecurity   526
- Medical sociology   509
- Medicalisation   521

- Profession   511
- Proportionate universality   519
- Sick role   509
- Undernutrition   526

THINKING ABOUT SOCIOLOGY

1. We live in an increasingly reflexive society with a heightened awareness about our bodies. According to Naomi Wolf, how does the beauty myth perpetuate such reflexivity?

2. How is risk-taking behaviour related to Michel Foucault's idea of limit experiences? What satisfaction do people get out of risk-taking behaviour?

3. You decide to go to a party with friends on the night before a big exam. You end up drinking too much and sleep through the sound of your alarm clock. According to Parsons's idea of the sick role, why would your professor be justified in deciding not to give you a makeup exam? What would you have to change in order to be excused?

4. What are the characteristics of a profession? What factors can help explain why physicians have become increasingly deprofessionalised?

5. What are the weaknesses of the health care system in Canada? How are these weaknesses related to systems of stratification?

6. How is the McDonaldization of childbirth related to the increasing medicalisation of society? What consequences has this had for the birthing process?

7. How have the Internet and new social media technologies affected the consumption of health care? What are some of the disadvantages of having access to more information about health care?

8. In what ways are patients increasingly prosumers of health care? How has this affected the power of physicians?

9. How has globalisation tended to widen global disparities in health care? What kinds of health problems are you most likely to find in the Global South? What could be done to avoid some of these problems?

10. How has globalisation improved the quality of health care around the world? In what ways has technology been an important factor in the improvement of global health? Are the benefits of globalisation evenly distributed with respect to health care? Why or why not?

APPLYING THE SOCIOLOGICAL IMAGINATION

This chapter highlights the inequalities in Canadian health care and health care around the world. For this activity, compare Canada to two other countries—one from the Global North and one from the Global South—based on their health care spending and health outcomes (such as life expectancy and infant mortality). Use the Internet to locate data from the World Health Organization. What do the data suggest about health in each of the countries? How is this reflective of global stratification? How could globalisation be used to help change the outcomes in each of these countries?

ACTIVE SOCIOLOGY

Many websites provide information about health and wellness. One of these is WebMD. Go to the site (www.webmd.com) and describe the way health is constructed. What is considered healthy, and what is considered sick? What types of illnesses are presented, and how are they described? How are constructions of beauty embedded in the site? From a sociological perspective, why might someone use a site like WebMD instead of going to a doctor? Read through the interactive pages, such as the Top Trends, Expert Blogs, and so on. Who is sharing information here?

How does this site reflect the prosumer perspective? To participate in this, create your own account. Based on your membership, what knowledge can you add to this page? That is, how and where are you allowed to create or contribute to medical advice on this site?

STUDENT STUDY SITE ······························

Visit the student study site at **www.sagepub.com/ritzercanadian** for additional web quizzes for further review.

Spice

ARCT

SPICE IS AN EXOTIC INCENSE BLEND THAT RELEASES
ENJOY THE ENCHANTING AROMA OF SPICE. NOT F
ER OUT OF REACH OF CHILDREN.

EXOTISCHE GERUCHSMISCHU
GENIESSEN SIE DAS
FÜR KINDER U

POPULATION, URBANISATION, AND THE ENVIRONMENT

Efforts to reduce fertility have had some effect on the growing population, but not enough to reverse projected gains. As long as new births outpace deaths and the global population climbs, the environment will be challenged.

14

At two minutes to midnight on October 30, 2011, the world's population reached 7 billion. While the actual 7 billionth living human would be impossible to pinpoint among the several hundred born every minute, Danica May Camacho, born in Manila, Philippines, was the first of several babies chosen by the United Nations to represent the major milestone in population growth. A series of media events and press conferences was held throughout the following day, which the United Nations dubbed the Day of 7 Billion in an effort to draw attention to the challenges posed by an ever-growing population.

For many individuals and media outlets around the world, breaching the 7 billion mark proved a fascinating, but passing, diversion. Some were celebratory, others contemplative, but most forgot about the event once the next big news story broke. For sociologists, demographers, ecologists, and other scientists, however, the growing global population is an important, ongoing social phenomenon that has had—and will continue to have—enormous consequences for where and how people live.

As the population grows, the environment must shift and adapt to accommodate its new residents. Demographic changes occurring over the last 150 years have helped give rise to new patterns of urbanisation, such as the emergence of megacities, edge cities, and megalopolises. The proliferation of urbanisation, population, and consumption has contributed to several global environmental problems—such as global warming and a decline in potable water—that have further changed how people perceive and interact with their environments, both natural and social.

While Danica May Camacho's birth will not have a direct effect on urbanisation trends or the environment, the rapid growth of the global population that her birth represents most certainly will. Efforts to reduce *fertility have had some effect on the growing population, but not enough to slow or reverse projected gains. Simply put, as long as new births outpace deaths and the population climbs, the environment will be challenged and will need to adapt.*

This chapter covers three broad topics—population, urbanisation, and the environment. While each is important in its own right, they are covered together here because of the many ways in which they interrelate.

POPULATION

Demography is the scientific study of population (Suzanne Bianchi and Wight 2012; Weeks 2011; Wight 2007), especially its growth and decline, as well as the movement of people. Those who study these population dynamics are **demographers**. Demography is both a distinct field of study and a subfield within sociology. Many demographers are sociologists, but there are those in other fields such as economics who also consider themselves demographers.

POPULATION GROWTH

A great deal of attention has been devoted to population growth and the idea, popularised by Paul Ehrlich (1968), of a population explosion, or what he called the "population bomb." Much of that fear, although not all of it, has dissipated in recent years. This is, at least in part, because of the ability of the world's most populous country, China, to slow its population growth through, among other things, its famous one-child policy. Nevertheless, China's population is huge and continues to grow, and, as we will see, China will soon be surpassed by India in population size. Population increases are important and of interest not only in themselves but also because of the need for greater resources to support a growing population. Also of concern is the strain such increases place on national and city services, as well as on the environment.

Trends and Projections

While overall fertility rates are dropping globally, the world's population continues to increase, although at a declining rate. It was not until the early 1800s that the global population exceeded 1 billion people; it reached 2 billion in just one century (1930), then 3 billion by 1960. In the next 14 years it reached 4 billion (1974), 13 years more and it was 5 billion (1987), and in another 12 years it reached 6 billion (1999) (S. Roberts 2009). As pointed out in the introduction to this chapter, in 12 more years the world's population exceeded 7 billion people (2011)—37 percent of them in China and India alone (Population Reference Bureau 2010). Projections are that it will likely take only another 12 years to achieve the next milestone of 8 billion people by 2025. While the overall trend is for slowing population growth, there remain many countries (for example, Ethiopia and Niger) where population growth continues to be very rapid. In fact, in spite of the ravages of warfare and of diseases such as malaria and AIDS, the population of Africa as a whole is expected to double by 2050. As shown in Figure 14.1, 49 percent of the global population growth between 2010 and 2050 will occur in Africa, with another 41 percent in Asia. The rest of the world population will increase by only 10 percent; Europe's population will shrink by 1 percent.

This recent slowdown in population growth is in stark contrast to the rapid growth after World War II. It was the latter that led to dire predictions about the future of population growth. At one time, projections were for a global population of about 16 billion people by 2050. However, it is now estimated that *only* 9.4 billion people will be in the world by that time (Suzanne Bianchi and Wight 2012). While this is a dramatic reduction in future estimates, it still represents a major increase in the world's population (almost 2.5 billion more souls in the next four decades). This growth is occurring, and will continue to occur, in spite of high death rates in many parts of the world due to high infant mortality, war, starvation, disease, and natural disasters. The death rate may increase dramatically in the twenty-first century if, as many expect, the disastrous effects of global warming accelerate (see page 575), although that increase is unlikely to have much of an impact on overall population

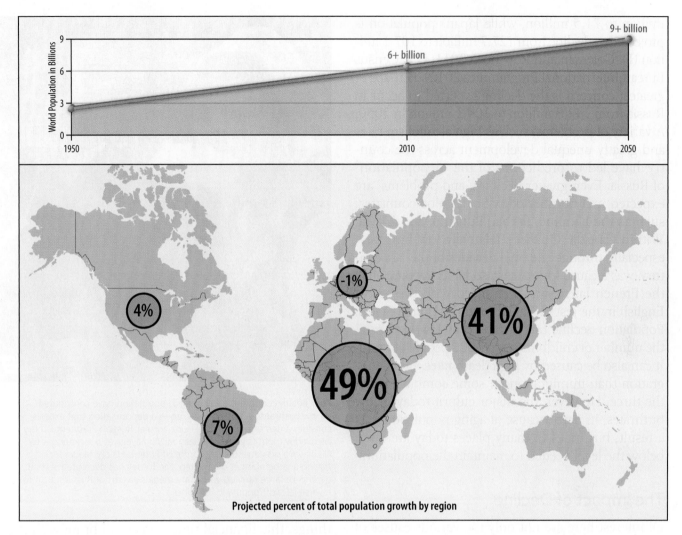

FIGURE 14.1 World Population Growth and Percent of Total Population Growth by Region, 2010–2050

SOURCE: From "World Population Prospects: The 2010 Revision," Department of Economic and Social Affairs, Population Division, United Nations.

projections. Nevertheless, though there is less talk these days about a population explosion, there is little doubt that the world's population is increasing, perhaps at an unsustainable rate.

POPULATION DECLINE

Historically, population decline has not been considered as important as growth, but it has recently come to the fore in various parts of the world, especially in a number of European countries (Italy, Germany, Russia), Japan (D. Coleman and Rowthorn 2011), and Quebec (Pettinicchio 2012). By 2050 the population of Germany is projected to *drop* from 82.4

Many urban areas, such as Kolkata (Calcutta), India, are becoming increasingly crowded places.

million to 71.5 million, while Japan's population is projected to decline from 127.7 million to 107.1 million (D. Coleman and Rowthorn 2011; U.S. Census Bureau International Programmes 2012). Perhaps of greatest concern is the decline expected to occur in Russia from 142.8 million to 109.1 million in 2050. A variety of problems, such as high alcoholism rates and greatly unequal development across the country, have led to predictions of the "depopulation" of Russia. Even greater declines, and problems, are expected in a number of ex-Soviet bloc countries, such as the Ukraine, Serbia, Bulgaria, and Latvia. Within Canada, Quebec's relatively low birthrate, especially through the final decades of the last century, was a cause for concern so far as keeping alive the French language when faced with the sea of English in the rest of Canada and the United States. Population decline can be caused by low **birthrate**, the number of childbirths per 1,000 people per year. It can also be caused by high death rates, more emigration than immigration, or some combination of the three. However, the major culprit today is low birthrates, in part because of aging populations. As a result, birthrates in many places today are often below the level needed to maintain the population.

The Impact of Decline

Of interest here are not only the various causes of such declines but also their impact on society as a whole. For one thing, population decline can weaken nations in various ways, including militarily. This is because the power of nations such as China and the United States is often associated with having large populations; a smaller population generally translates into a smaller military (Israel is an exception). For another, population decline can weaken a nation's economy because the total number of productive workers declines and the productivity of older workers decreases. Third, the fact that population decline is generally accompanied by an aging population brings with it various problems, including a "financial time bomb." This is because of a dramatic increase in the cost of caring for the elderly—especially government pensions and health-related expenses. This is occurring at the same time as a decline in the number of younger people in the labour force who are able to help pay those costs, through taxes, for example (Foot and Venne 2011). Among other

Poor health conditions and an aging population have contributed to low birthrates in Russia, resulting in a depopulation that experts consider a demographic crisis. Here, former Russian President Dmitry Medvedev (right) sits near Nadezhda Nikolayeva at a reception after Nikolayeva was awarded the Order of Parental Glory Medal for having a large number of children. Medvedev has decorated several parents of large families with state medals as part of Russia's push to reverse its swift population decline.

things, this financial time bomb will bring with it a great increase in national debt. This, of course, is already a great concern in many countries throughout the world. However, there are actions that can be taken to mitigate this problem, such as raising the retirement age so that older people can support themselves longer. Another possibility, although it is difficult politically, is for nations to reduce pensions as well as support for the health-related expenses of the aged.

It would be wrong to conclude that population decline brings with it only a series of problems. Among the gains would be a reduction of the ecological problems caused by a growing population. For example, a smaller population would produce fewer automobile emissions and create less pollution. In addition, the pressure on the world's diminishing supplies of oil, water, and food would be reduced.

While some nations will be hurt by an aging population, others, especially developing countries, will get a "demographic dividend" (Desai

According to the Center for Strategic and International Studies, China's social stability and economic growth could come under threat if its population grows old before it becomes wealthy. By 2050, China will have more than 438 million people above the age of 60. This means there will be just 1.6 million working-age adults, largely because of the one-child policy, to support every person above the age of 60—as compared to 7.7 million in 1975.

2010; R. Lee 2007). This results from a favourable ratio in those nations of the employed relative to dependents, such as the aged and children. Nations with more active workers and fewer seniors and children will reap the demographic dividend. The dividend is due, in part, to a large younger

A young Yemeni protester shouts slogans during an Arab Spring demonstration. The median age of Yemen's population is just 16.4. Nations with young, vibrant populations (such as Yemen) will reap a demographic dividend as its young citizens enter the workforce.

population able to work and earn money. At the same time, there are relatively few in need of their support.

THE PROCESSES OF POPULATION CHANGE

Beyond some of the more specific and contemporary issues outlined above, three basic processes are of concern to demographers. The first is **fertility**, or people's reproductive behaviour, especially the number of births. Key to understanding fertility is the birthrate. Second is **mortality**, or deaths and death rates within a population. Finally, there is **migration**, or the movements of people, or *migrants,* and the impact of these movements on both the sending and the receiving locales (Suzanne Bianchi and Wight 2012). While these are dynamic processes, demographers are also concerned with more structural issues, such as population composition, especially the age and sex characteristics of a population.

Fertility

Theoretically, women could average over 20 births throughout their reproductive years. In reality, women rarely reach that number. Today, fertility levels vary widely around the globe, from less than one per woman in Macao to almost eight per woman in Niger. In this section, we deal with the economic and social factors affecting fertility, regional differences in fertility, and some thoughts on fertility trends in Canada.

Economic Factors. Fertility is affected by a variety of economic factors. For example, though it remains to be seen what impact the most recent recession will have on population growth in Canada and elsewhere, we know that record low points in population growth were associated with the Depression of the 1930s. Low points were also recorded in the 1970s, when an oil crisis led to a dramatic jump in oil prices and, more generally, rampant inflation. Time will tell as far as the impact of the current recession is concerned, but its effect on fertility will clearly depend on its length and depth—as of early 2013 it is already quite long and deep—and especially whether the world economy turns down again in a "double dip" recession.

Social Factors. Fertility is also affected by a variety of social factors. For instance, there is the obvious impact of age on fertility. Most childbearing involves women between the ages of 15 and 45. Especially important in the context of age is the fertility and childbearing of adolescents (less than 20 years old). Globally, adolescents give birth to an estimated 15 million babies a year: The rate is as high as 200 per 1,000 births in some African countries, 24 per 1,000 in most developed countries, and only 5 or fewer per 1,000 in China, Japan, and Korea (Cooksey 2007). According to Michael Kimmel (2011), "the United States has the highest rates of births to teenage mothers of all industrial nations—double that of the next highest country, the United Kingdom" (p. 170). The Canadian rate is slightly below the rate for the United Kingdom but ranks above most other western European nations. Among the concerns about a high birthrate among adolescents is that they, as well as their children, experience more birth-related health complications and may not be ready to care for their children. This lack of knowledge is also largely tied to a lack of proper sex education as well as adolescent mothers' subordinate gender roles

(Weiss and Lonnquist 2009). As a result, adolescent mothers generally lack the knowledge and power needed to make informed decisions on childbearing and child rearing.

A second, and related, issue is the broader category of nonmarital fertility; not all of such fertility is accounted for by adolescents (Musick 2007). Nonmarital fertility has increased dramatically in Canada so that now about 25 percent of all births are outside of wedlock, although this percentage is still below the Organisation for Economic Co-operation and Development average and is less than in the United States (38 percent) and much less than in France (52 percent) (OECD 2012b). Canada is not unique among western industrialised countries; its rate of nonmarital fertility is higher than some, such as Japan and Italy; and lower than others, such as the United Kingdom and Sweden. For a look at fertility rates around the world see Figure 14.2.

Regional Factors. While those in many less developed areas of the world still worry about high

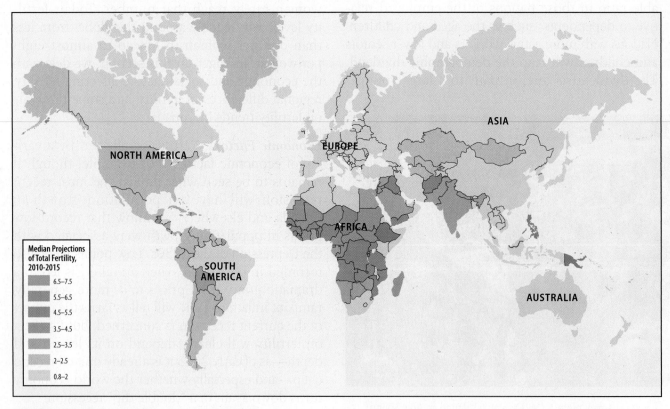

FIGURE 14.2 Global Fertility Rates, 2010–2015

SOURCE: Population Division of the Department of Economic and Social Affairs of the United Nations Secretariat (2007). *World Population Prospects: The 2006 Revision, Highlights.* New York: United Nations.

birthrates, officials in many developed countries have grown increasingly concerned about their *low* birthrates. A birthrate of 2.1 is needed to replace an existing population (it is 2.1, and not 2.0, because of infant mortality). However, in the early twenty-first century the average fertility in developed countries was 1.6 children for each woman; in some of those countries it approached "lowest low fertility" of fewer than 1.3 children; in Russia it was 1.1. In other words, the birthrates there are inadequate to replace the current population. This is a particular concern throughout Western Europe and has led to worry over the same issues discussed above in terms of an aging population. Another concern is the future of the indigenous cultures of various European countries where the birthrates of immigrants (especially Muslims) far exceed those of "natives" (Caldwell 2009). As a result of this, at least in part, there is increasing animosity between natives and immigrants and a growing likelihood of conflict between them.

Canadian Fertility Trends. When Canada was founded, the average birthrate was approximately 8 children per woman; that rate declined throughout the nineteenth century and up until the end of the Depression in the late 1930s (Human Resources and Development Canada 2013). Then World War II led to an increase in the birthrate, and it remained high throughout the 1950s. In fact, the rise in the birthrate between 1948 and 1960 is referred to as the *baby boom*. The peak in fertility in Canada was reached in the late 1950s, with more children born in 1959 than in any year before or after. The fertility rate reached a low of 1.5 in the early 2000s, and has gradually increased since then so that today the birthrate is 1.7. In other words, fertility in Canada remains below "replacement level"—the number needed to replace its population. The Quebec rate is only slightly above the national average.

Mortality

As an indicator of change, a population's mortality—or death rate—is certainly as important to demographers as its birthrate. A population's death rate is measured as the number of deaths per 1,000 people. Life expectancy is the number of years an individual can be expected to live, given the population's mortality rate.

Strong economic growth fuelled in part by pent-up consumer demand led to a housing boom and a rising standard of living for the soldiers returning from World War II. The subsequent dramatic increase in the number of postwar births came to be known as the "baby boom."

Life Expectancy. In prehistoric times, life expectancy in the world was between 20 and 30 years; by 1900, that number had hardly increased at all, but today it has reached 69 years. Nearly half of the decline in mortality in developed countries took place in the twentieth century. Life expectancy is now 77 years in the more developed countries, 67 years in less developed countries, and 56 years in the least developed countries (Suzanne Bianchi and Wight 2012) (see Figure 14.3). Life expectancy in Africa is only 50 years (Elo 2007). The highest life expectancy is found in Japan, where women are likely to live an average of 84.6 years, and men are apt to live 77.6 years (Elo 2007). As we saw in Chapter 10, life expectancy for women in Canada is 83 years; for men it is 79 years. By 2031, life expectancy at birth is projected to be 86 years for women and 82 years for men.

Macro-Social Factors. Though death is, of course, a biological inevitability, increased life expectancy and lower death rates in a population

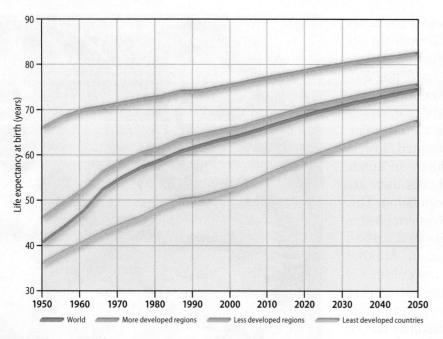

FIGURE 14.3 Global Life Expectancy, 1950–2050

SOURCE: United Nations, Department of Economic and Social Affairs, Population Division (2007). *World Population Prospects: The 2006 Revision, Highlights,* Working Paper No. ESA/P/WP.202. Figure 4, p. 19.

- A general improvement in standards of living (quality of housing and nutrition)
- Better public health (improved sanitation and cleaner drinking water)
- Cultural and behavioural factors (stronger norms about losing weight and stopping smoking)
- Advances in medicine and medical technologies (antibiotics and newer drugs, immunisations, and improved surgical techniques)
- Government actions (control of diseases such as malaria) (Elo 2007).

can be affected by a variety of macro-social factors. Major factors in the decline in mortality (with a few examples) include the following:

Of course, important factors that keep death rates high continue to exist (including infectious diseases such as malaria and AIDS), and there are

A population's improved life expectancy and lower death rates are influenced by a variety of macro-level social factors, including advances in medicine and favourable government actions. In 2012, Bill Gates (left) announced a $750 million contribution to the Global Fund to Fight AIDS, Tuberculosis and Malaria. A year earlier, the Philippines capital city of Manila enacted a strict citywide ban on smoking in public places (right). These actions may have significant effects on global life expectancy and death rates in years to come.

others that loom on the horizon that could increase the death rate, including global flu epidemics.

Mortality is greatly affected by one's position in the system of social stratification (see Chapter 8). In Canada, those in less advantaged positions are likely to have higher death rates and shorter life spans than those who rank higher in on the hierarchy of privilege. Ancestry also has a significant impact on life expectancy, with First Nations, Inuit, and Métis people experiencing some of the lowest life expectancies in Canada. As noted earlier, these lower life expectancies among indigenous peoples are the result of the fact that they are less likely to seek health care, are at higher risk of violent death, and are more likely to engage in substance abuse and other risky life behaviours.

In terms of gender, females have a longer life expectancy than males in spite of the various disadvantages they confront stemming from the system of gender inequality (see Chapter 10). This difference is due, in part, to women engaging in more health-protective behaviours than men, such as visiting physicians more often. Gender roles also tend to protect women from fatal disease and injury (Rieker and Bird 2000). For example, women are less likely than men to engage in potentially disabling or deadly activities such as using illegal drugs, driving dangerously, and engaging in violent behaviour. Higher death rates for male foetuses, as well as for male infants in the first four months of life, suggest that females may be more viable organisms than males. However, in general "women now live longer than men not because their biology has changed, but because their social position and access to resources have changed" (Weitz 2010:52). Nevertheless, there are some parts of the world, such as India and Pakistan, in which females have a lower life expectancy than males. This is traceable, at least in part, to the fact that females in some regions are more likely to die in infancy, perhaps because of parental neglect or female infanticide (Siwon Anderson and Ray 2010).

Micro-Social Factors. Mortality is also affected by a number of micro-social factors, especially those associated with poor lifestyle choices, including smoking or failing to exercise. Another poor lifestyle choice involves overeating or eating the wrong foods such as those that are high in calories, fat, and sugar. Obesity has long been related to higher death rates from heart disease and stroke. A more recent discovery is the linkage of obesity to death from various forms of cancer, including breast and endometrial cancer. More than 100,000 new cases of cancer per year in the United States, and perhaps more, can be traced to obesity. Conversely, healthy lifestyle choices can lead to longer lives. For example, religious groups such as the Mormons that restrict the use of tobacco products, alcohol, coffee, and addictive drugs tend to have extraordinarily low death rates and longer life expectancies. Globally, the lifestyle of the Japanese, which includes eating more fish and less red meat, is closely related to their greater longevity.

The Demographic Transition

The issues of fertility and mortality are central to a major theory of population—demographic transition theory. According to *demographic transition* theory, population changes are related to the shift from an agricultural society to a more industrialised and urbanised society (K. Davis 1945; Weeks 2007). Three stages are associated with the demographic transition (see Figure 14.4). In the first, or agricultural, stage, there is a rough balance between high death rates (mortality) and high birthrates (fertility). As a result, the population is fairly stable or grows only very slowly. In the second, or transitional, stage, the death rate declines while the birthrate remains high or declines more slowly than the death rate. The total population grows rapidly under these circumstances. In this stage, death rates decline first in developed countries for various reasons, including improvement in the standard of living, a better-informed population, improved hygiene, better health care, and so on. This was the situation in most of the developed countries of Europe beginning in the eighteenth century. In the final, stabilising stage, the decline in the death rate leads to more children in the family and the community. As a result, people begin to think about limiting the number of children. In addition, fewer children are required because not as many workers are needed on the family farms. Many family members move into the cities and take jobs in industries and other organisations. For these and other reasons, it is to the family's advantage to limit family size. Eventually, the birthrate drops to a level roughly equal to the death rate. As a result, in this third stage population growth once again slows or stabilises.

As a general rule, birthrates drop more slowly than death rates largely because it is difficult to overcome the positive value individuals and cultures place on children and on life more generally. In contrast, reducing the death rate is relatively easy, at least when the means to do so exist, because postponing death *is* consistent with valuing life. This contradicts the myth that a population grows because of a rise in the birthrate. Rather, such growth is better attributed to a decline in death rates, with birthrates remaining largely unchanged.

In Western Europe, the entire demographic transition took about 200 years from the mid-1800s until the mid-twentieth century. The process continues today in much of the rest of the world. However, in recent years, in less developed countries, the process has taken much less time. This is traceable to the much more rapid decline in the death rate because of the importation of advanced, especially medical, technologies from developed countries. Since birthrates have remained high while death rates have declined, population growth in less developed countries has been extraordinarily high.

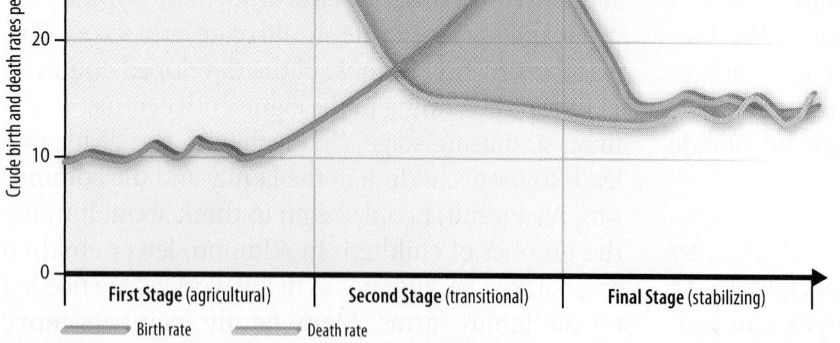

Given this recent rapid population growth in less developed countries, the issue is what can be done about it, especially in the areas of the world where fertility remains high. In other words, how can the birthrate be reduced in those areas?

Reducing Fertility. Adopting the view that development is the best contraceptive, one approach to reducing fertility is to stress economic development. This follows from what was learned from the demographic transition in Europe, the United States, and Canada, where economic development did lead to lower fertility. A second approach is voluntary family planning. This includes providing people with information about reproductive physiology and the use of contraceptive techniques, actually providing such things as birth control pills and condoms, and developing societal or local informational programmes to support the use of contraception and the ideal of a small(er) family. The third approach involves a change in the society as a whole, especially where large numbers of children have been considered both advantageous and desirable by social institutions and cultural values. In many societies children are still needed to work in order for the family to survive and to provide for the parents in their old age. Changes such as compulsory childhood education and child labour laws can counter the fact that these realities lead families to have large numbers of children. They serve to make children less valuable economically because they cannot work when they are in school and they are kept out of the labour force for years by child labour laws. As result, at least some parents have fewer children. Another important step is to be sure that women have important roles in society beyond those associated with motherhood. When women have greater educational and occupational opportunities, their fertility declines, and families have fewer children. Moreover, improvement in women's education and occupations not only contributes to declines in fertility but also creates a variety of other positive outcomes for women

FIGURE 14.4 The Three Stages of Demographic Transition

SOURCE: Adapted from *A Dictionary of Geography,* 2nd edition by Susan Mayhew (1997). Figure 20, p. 122. By permission of Oxford University Press.

(Fillipi et al. 2006). However, solutions that involve changing cultural ideas about women and reproduction can be difficult, particularly when women occupy a lower status within society and child rearing and domestic tasks are their central roles.

Infanticide is an unfortunate measure that also contributes to fertility. The selective killing of female foetuses, also known as *femicide,* directly affects fertility because of the reduction of females in a population (Siwon Anderson and Ray, 2010; Bhatnagar, Dube, and Dube 2006). Infanticide is most common in South and East Asia, although it is also found in other areas of the world, including North Africa and the Middle East (United Nations 2006).

A Second Demographic Transition. In the 1980s some scholars began thinking in terms of a second demographic transition to describe the general decline in the fertility rate and of population growth, especially in developed countries (Lesthaeghe 2010; Lesthaeghe and van de Kaa 1986). This decline is linked to parents coming to focus more on the quality of life of one child, or a few children, as well as on the quality of their own lives. Better occupational prospects, and therefore a more affluent lifestyle, have come to be associated with having fewer children.

Like the first demographic transition, the second is seen as involving three stages, but it is the first stage, between 1955 and 1970, that is of greatest importance. The key factor during this period was the end of the baby boom aided by the revolution in contraception that made it less likely that people would have unwanted children. Also beginning at this time was the gender revolution, which meant, among other things, that women began to marry later and to divorce more. They also entered the work world in greater numbers. This tended to reduce the birthrate, as did the fact that there were fewer women at home to care for children. These and other factors can be said to be associated with a second demographic transition associated with subreplacement fertility, lower birthrates, and a declining rate of population growth (Lesthaeghe 2007). It is also associated with the proliferation of a variety of living arrangements other than marriage and an increasing disconnect between marriage and procreation (Klinenberg 2012).

Migration

Although migration certainly takes place within national borders (for example, from east to west in Canada), our primary concern here is with cross-border, international (Kritz 2007), or global migration—with migration as a central aspect of globalisation (Faist 2012; Scherschel 2007).

Controlling Migration. Prior to the beginning of the fifteenth century, people crossed borders rather freely, although they were greatly hampered by limitations in transportation. However, with the rise of the nation-state in the fifteenth century much more notice was taken of such movement, and many more barriers were erected to limit and control it (Hollifield and Jacobson 2012). Nevertheless, as late as the end of the nineteenth century, there was still much freedom of movement, most notably in the great Atlantic migration to North America from Europe. It is estimated that about 50 million people left Europe for North America between 1820 and the end of the nineteenth century (Moses 2006). The American Civil War forced the earliest forms of Canadian passports to be issued, in 1862, largely to regulate movement between Canada and the United States (Passport Canada 2012). More generally, in 1889 an international emigration conference declared, "We affirm the right of the individual to the fundamental liberty accorded to him by every civilised nation to come and go and dispose of his person and his destinies as he pleases" (cited in Moses 2006:47). It was World War I that changed attitudes and the situation dramatically; nation-states began to impose drastic restrictions on the global movement of people. Today, while there is variation among nation-states, "there is not a single state that allows free access to all immigrants" (Moses 2006:54). In some cases, nations have laws requiring them to accept refugees escaping war, political persecution, and so on (see page 555). With legal migration restricted in various ways, there seems to have been an increase in illegal immigration (Hadjicostandi 2007), even in the smuggling of people into and out of various nations (Shane and Gordon 2008).

There has undoubtedly been a great deal of population movement associated with globalisation (Kritz 2008; Kritz, Lim, and Zlotnik 1992). In the early twenty-first century, about 3 percent of the global population was on the move ("Keep the Borders Open" 2008). To some observers, this represents a large and growing number and, in fact, constitutes a substantial increase of 36 percent since 1990. However, to other observers, the sense that we live in a global era of unprecedented international migration is exaggerated (Guhathakurta, Jacobson, and DelSordi 2007). While international migration has ebbed and flowed over time, the current rate is unspectacular in comparison to much of the nineteenth century. Further, rates of migration in order to find work, while high and the subject of much media interest, lag behind the mobility rates for goods, services, and technologies.

Although the contemporary numbers may not be impressive in comparison to the past, migrants do make up a significant percentage of the population of many countries. For example, in 2005 migrants accounted for almost a quarter of the population of Australia and Switzerland (Department of Immigration and Citizenship 2011; Federal Statistical Office 2012), just under 20 percent of Canada's and Germany's population, and 12 percent of the U.S. population (S. Roberts

New immigrants sing the Israeli National Anthem upon arrival at Ben Gurion International Airport in Lod, Israel. People migrate to different regions of the world for a variety of reasons: economic (to escape poverty); professional (to find employment); political (to escape oppression); retirement (lower cost-of-living); and sentimental (to reunite with family).

2008), while in Great Britain and France migrants represent just under 10 percent of the population ("Keep the Borders Open" 2008).

There are several interesting and important changes in the nature of today's international migrants. For one thing, the proportion of such migrants from the developed world has actually declined. For another, there has been a large increase in the number of migrants from the developing world, and a very significant proportion of them (70 to 90 percent) are moving to North America.

Figure 14.5 offers a more general view of global migration. It shows the countries taking in the most immigrants, those with the most migrants leaving, and those with both migrants and immigrants. Canada remains as one of the world's leading destinations for immigrants. It also shows that while we almost always focus on migration from the Global South to the Global North, there is also some North to South migration. Perhaps more importantly, there is almost as much North-to-South migration as there is South-to-North migration.

Unlike much else in the modern world (trade, finance, investment), restrictions on the migration of people, especially labour migration, have *not* been liberalised (Tan 2007). The major exception is in the European Union, but elsewhere in the world restrictions on migration remain in place. In some places, and for some less welcome migrants, restrictions have not only been increased but also in some cases been militarised. In addition, restrictions on migration have been privatised. Putting this control in the hands of the military and private corporations makes it more difficult for the government to exert oversight over those agencies and to protect the human rights of migrants (Schuster 2012b).

However, there are daunting problems involved in attempting to control global human migration. For one thing, there is the problem of the sheer number of such people. According to one estimate, "tens of millions of people cross borders on a daily basis" (Hollifield and Jacobson 2012:1390). The greatest pressure is on the United States and Europe, which are the

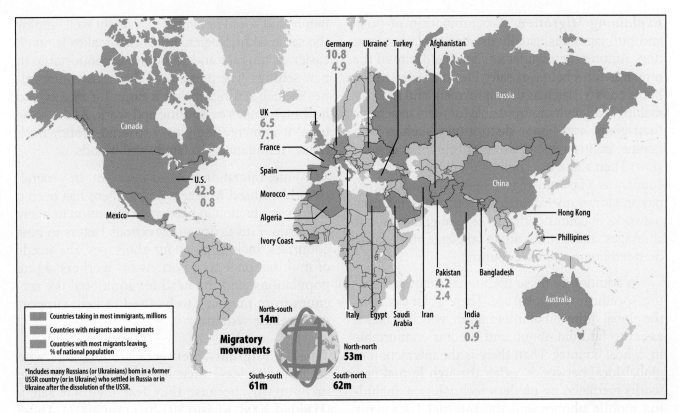

FIGURE 14.5 A General View of Global Migratory Movements

SOURCE: Adapted from "US Is Still the World's Leading Destination for Immigrants," Brigitte Perucca, *Guardian Weekly,* December 14, 2010.

most desirable destinations for migrants, both legal and illegal. For another, controls are very costly, and few nations can afford to engage in much more than token efforts. Then there is the fact that attempts to control migration inevitably lead to heightened and more sophisticated efforts to evade those controls. A lucrative market opens up for those, such as smugglers, who are in the business of transporting people across borders illegally. Finally, the increased efforts at control lead to increasingly desperate efforts to evade it. This, in turn, leads to more deaths and injuries. For example, in 2009 there were 419 known deaths of those who sought to cross the U.S.-Mexico border illegally.

In order to prosper economically, a nation-state must try to retain its own labour force, both highly paid skilled workers and professionals of various types as well as masses of low-paid semiskilled and unskilled workers. If a nation-state routinely lost large numbers of either of these types of workers, but especially the former, its ability to compete in the global marketplace would suffer. However, nation-states also need both skilled and less skilled workers from other locales, and it is in their interest to allow these workers entry either legally or illegally.

While various migrants are welcome, even needed, the influx of large numbers of migrants into a country often leads to conflict of various types. Conflict usually occurs between the newcomers and those who have been in place for quite some time, although there also may be conflict between different groups of newcomers. Thus, in order to limit such conflict, many nations prefer to maintain significant barriers to migration.

The concern over terrorism in many parts of the world, especially in the United States and in many European nations, has served to reinforce, if not increase, the restrictions on migration. This is especially clear in the immense difficulties the United States has created for those wishing to migrate there. And because of the long border Canada shares with the United States, this has become a major issue for Canada as well.

Explaining Migration. A combination of push and pull factors is usually used to explain migration. Among the *push* factors are the desire of the migrants for a better or safer life, problems in the home country, such as unemployment and low pay, making it difficult or impossible for them to achieve their goals, and major disruptions, such as war, famine, political persecution, or economic depression. Then there are such *pull* factors in the host country as a favourable immigration policy, higher pay and lower unemployment, formal and informal networks in countries that cater to migrants, labour shortages, and a similarity in language and culture between home and host country.

In addition to these traditional factors are factors specific to the global age. There is, for example, the global diffusion of information, which makes it easier to find out about, and become comfortable in, a host country. Then there is the interaction of global-local networks, either through formal networks mediated by modern technologies, including mobile phones and the Internet (especially e-mail and Skype), or through more informal family and social networks that might well employ the same technologies. All of this makes it much easier to migrate and to be more comfortable in new settings. The presence of diasporic communities in such settings makes it easier for migrants to find such things as housing and work. At the same time, it is increasingly easy to send money back home (remittances) to family and friends.

While migration policies have not, in general, been liberalised in recent years, there has been a selective reduction in barriers to migration in many countries. This is driven by various factors in host countries, including labour shortages, the needs of multinational corporations for workers, aging populations, and the need for additional tax revenues from migrants to be used to help support state welfare systems.

Types of Migrants. **Refugees** are migrants who are forced to leave their homeland, or who leave involuntarily because they fear for their safety (Haddad 2008; Kivisto 2012b; Loyal 2007). Those who fled their home countries because of

A combination of push and pull factors can help explain migration. A push away from one's home country might come from a desire for a better or safer life. A pull might come from a host country's liberal immigration policy or a similarity in language and culture. Here, immigrants from Europe travel to North America in the early part of the twentieth century.

World War II or recent wars in the Middle East (e.g., Syria) would be considered refugees. More controversial is whether the nearly 3 million Palestinians should be seen as refugees. They are not so designated by the United Nations, but Palestinians and their supporters see them as refugees. Needless to say, the Israeli government disagrees.

Asylum seekers are people who flee their home country usually in an effort to escape political oppression or religious persecution. They seek to remain in the country to which they fled. They are in a state of limbo until a decision is made on their request for asylum (Schuster 2012a). If and when that claim is accepted, the asylum seeker is then considered a refugee. If the claim is rejected, it is likely that the asylum seeker will be returned to the home country.

Labour migrants are those who move from their home country to another country because they are either driven by "push" factors such as a lack of work and low pay in their homeland or attracted by "pull" factors, including the existence of jobs and higher pay elsewhere (Kritz 2008), or both. An example of labour migrants is the Filipino women who immigrate to Canada to be employed as domestics, often caring for the children or the elderly of Canadian families. Among the push factors for such women are "tenuous and scarce job opportunities," civil wars, and economic crises in their home countries. Of course, the major pull factor is the existence of jobs with higher wages in Canada.

Of great interest these days are **undocumented immigrants**, those who either migrate to a receiving country without valid authorisation, usually a passport, or remain in a receiving country after their authorised permits expire (Torpey 2012; Yamamoto 2012). This category overlaps with some of the above types of migrants. Both refugees and labour migrants could be undocumented immigrants, but it is unlikely that asylum seekers would be in their country of destination illegally. There are three broad types of undocumented immigrants. The first are those who manage to gain entry without passing through a checkpoint or without undergoing the required inspection. The second type are those who gain entry legally, but then stay beyond the period of time permitted by their visa. Third, there are those who immigrate

on the basis of false documents. Obviously, it is very difficult to get a precise sense of the number of undocumented immigrants in the world, but estimates range from several million to as many as 40 million people.

Unwelcome Migrants. At least some types of migrants are unwelcome by some people in their receiving countries. Of interest in this section are the often unwelcome less skilled and unskilled migrants to the more developed world (there is also significant migration from one less developed country to another). Those who are undocumented migrants are usually especially unwelcome (Hadjicostandi 2007). Unwelcome migrants are likely to exist at the margins of the more developed world and are apt to fare poorly there. Since the 1970s the number of such migrants has increased dramatically.

Many of these migrants arrived after a(nother) great boom in immigration (Barkan, Diner, and Kraut 2008) that began in the early 1990s. Many, for example, entered the United States illegally. They came from various countries (Philippines, China, El Salvador), but the largest number, at least one third, came from Mexico. It is estimated that more than 10 percent of Mexico's total population of 116 million live in the United States.

As of 2009, about 6.7 million Mexicans, the majority of Mexican immigrants, were in the United States illegally (Hoefer, Rytina, and Baker 2010). They continue to come because although they may be paid poverty wages by U.S. standards (approximately $300 per week), that may be as much as four times what they could earn in Mexico (Preston 2006a). Furthermore, there are more jobs and better future job opportunities in the United States than in Mexico (although there were a lot fewer after the onset of the recent recession).

As is the case in other parts of the world, there has been some backlash against migrants in Canada (Wilkes, Guppy, and Farris 2008). However, a strong case can be made against this backlash.

The Case Against Migration Restrictions. The case against restrictions on international migration can be divided into economic, political, and moral arguments (Moses 2006).

GL⊕BALISATION

Irish Migrants on the Move Again

One of the best known mass migrations occurred in the mid-nineteenth century when Ireland experienced a famine resulting from the failure of its potato crops, a key source of food for the Irish. Over a million people migrated to several countries throughout the world (many to Canada and the United States), and another million died, leading to a sharp drop in Ireland's population. The out-migration was so large that the leading Irish statesman of the day hoped that in the future Irish children would no longer, "like our cattle, be brought up for export" (cited in Daley 2010b:4). While this was the most significant Irish migration, others occurred much earlier as well as later as a result of economic downturns in the 1930s, 1950s, and 1980s (Fitzgerald and Lambkin 2008).

Conditions seemed to have changed dramatically beginning in the late 1980s and early 1990s. Ireland's economy boomed, and that boom continued until the beginning of the latest world recession. In fact, in the decade leading up to 2007, property values in Ireland grew more than those in any other developed country in the world. In terms of population dynamics, this means that migration remained low and stable during this period as most of the Irish stayed in the country. In addition, immigration into Ireland rose dramatically, peaking between 2006 and 2008. Many of the immigrants had come from central Europe and were drawn by Ireland's stronger economic prospects than those back home and by the European Union's increasingly lenient immigration policies.

However, the latest recession has had an enormous effect on Ireland; the Irish economy shrank by 20 percent between 2007 and 2010 ("Irish Economy Shrank by One Fifth During Recession" 2011). Home values dropped 50 percent from their peak in 2007. In late 2010, Ireland had to borrow 85 billion euros from regional and global lending institutions, such as the European Union and the International Monetary Fund, in order to stay afloat economically. As its economy tanked, immigration to the country dropped dramatically; there was little work to draw people in. On the other hand, migration from Ireland rose substantially. At first, many of these migrants were those who had come from elsewhere earlier and were returning to their home countries. However, more recently, it is the Irish themselves who are, once again, leaving Ireland. Many feel that they have little economic future there. The economy is shrinking and will shrink further as the government implements an increasingly austere budget in order to satisfy those who have been lending it money.

Although migration is difficult, especially when it is forced by such things as economic hardship, the Irish may be better able to cope with it than others. Said an Irish economist, "Emigrating is a cultural norm, even if it is not a cultural preference. . . . The Irish know how to do it. They build networks and take care of each other" (cited in Daley 2010b:4). Also aiding migration today are the new global technologies. Said one woman, "It's not like when we were waving goodbye from a dock. . . . There are lots of ways to stay in touch—Google, Facebook" (cited in Daley 2010b:4). These social networks are increasingly embedded in transnational networks that tie people more closely to communities in multiple countries around the world (Krings et al. 2009).

Economically, immigration has had a positive, *not* a negative, effect on the economy of Canada, as well as other developed nations. A further increase in foreign workers would lead to even greater global economic gains. Contrary to what many believe, it is not clear that immigrants compete with the Canadian-born for jobs. It is also not clear that immigrants have less skill than the native-born. While the wages of Canadian-born, less skilled workers may be negatively affected, wages overall are not affected, or may even increase. Immigrants are not a drain on public finances, at least not over the long run, and may even pay more in taxes than they cost in services. A very strong economic argument in support of more open immigration in developed countries is the fact that because they are dominated by aging workforces, they need an influx of young, vibrant, and "hungry" workers. Yet another economic argument relates to the high, and increasing, cost of border controls to restrict immigration. If border controls were eased, this money could be put to other uses.

Politically, freer immigration can contribute in various ways to greater democratisation, to less

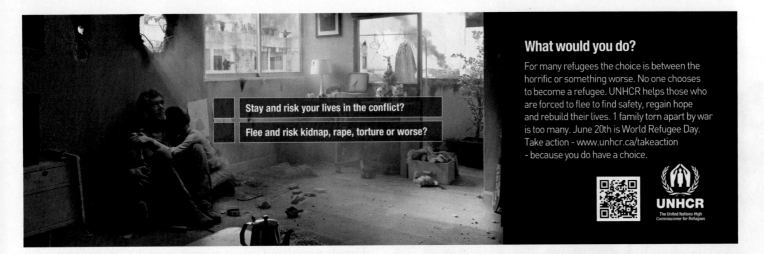

What would you do?

For many refugees the choice is between the horrific or something worse. No one chooses to become a refugee. UNHCR helps those who are forced to flee to find safety, regain hope and rebuild their lives. 1 family torn apart by war is too many. June 20th is World Refugee Day. Take action - www.unhcr.ca/takeaction - because you do have a choice.

Stay and risk your lives in the conflict?

Flee and risk kidnap, rape, torture or worse?

UNHCR
The United Nations High Commissioner for Refugees

The United Nations High Commission for Refugees seeks to assist the many people around the globe whose lives are disrupted by persecution and violence. Canada is a major recipient of refugees, accepting more people per capita than most nations in the world.

authoritarianism. In terms of sending countries, the fact that people, especially the most highly educated and skilled, can and do leave because of a lack democracy puts pressure on their political systems to reform themselves. More generally, it strengthens the ability of individuals to influence political regimes and to push them in the direction of increased democratisation. In a world of freer movement, nation-states would also compete with one another in order to be better able both to keep their best people and to attract those from elsewhere. This could make nation-states the world over more democratic and enhance international exchanges.

There are two basic moral arguments in support of freer migration. First, as an end in itself, free mobility is "a universal and basic human right" (Moses 2006:58). Second, instrumentally, free migration is a means to achieve greater economic and political justice. In terms of the latter, greater freedom of movement would lead to a reduction in global economic inequality and would mitigate global tyranny.

Of course, all of this challenges much conventional wisdom today about migration and open borders. However, it could be argued that most of that conventional wisdom is erroneous or, at best, only partially correct. Recent immigrants to Canada have experienced more challenges than in previous decades, and some immigrants experience discrimination upon arrival, but for many even these hardships are easier to endure than the situations in their homelands, a case that is especially true of refugees. Furthermore, although Canada is a relatively good haven for immigrants, in comparison to experiences in some other jurisdictions where anti-foreigner sentiment runs higher (Wilkes, Guppy, and Farris 2008), new migrants to Canada do face hardships, and those hardships have increased in recent years (Reitz 2012).

We turn now to a discussion of urban areas, the destination for many migrants and the locales most affected by population changes of various types.

URBANISATION

The world has, until very recently, been predominantly rural; even by 1800 there was only a handful of large urban areas in the world. As late as 1850 only about 2 percent of the world's population lived in cities of more than 100,000 residents. Urban areas have, of course, grown rapidly since then. Between 2000 and 2010 a "watershed in human history" occurred as for "the first time the urban population of the Earth" outnumbered the rural population (M. Davis 2007:1). However, there are great differences among the nations of the world in terms of their degrees of urban development: In the United Kingdom, 90 percent of the population is urban, and in Canada it is 81 percent, while only 5 percent of Rwanda's population is urban.

Austrian-born actor and former governor of California Arnold Schwarzenegger is one of many immigrants to the United States who has had a significant and positive impact on that country's economy. In general, freer migration can be a means to achieve a reduction in both global economic inequality and political tyranny.

It is projected that by 2050, 70 percent of the world's population will live in urban areas (see Figure 14.6). For the more developed areas of the world, 86 percent of the population will live in cities, and 67 percent of those in the less developed world will be urban dwellers. Figure 14.6 offers other useful information, such as the tipping point—the point at which the urban population exceeded or will exceed 50 percent—for various parts of the world.

The importance of **cities**, or large, permanent, and spatially concentrated human settlements, has progressively increased. Even when there were not very many of them, cities were at the heart of many societies. Max Weber ([1921] 1968) accorded great importance to the rise of the city in the West in the Middle Ages. The western (occidental) city had a number of distinctive characteristics, including being surrounded by walls, having political autonomy, and having a distinctive urban economy (Le Gales 2007). The city became increasingly central, and it has become much more important in today's "global" and "world" cities (see page 566).

The term *urban* generally refers to city dwelling (Coward 2012). However, the term has a more specific and technical meaning, although what is considered urban varies in different societies (Parrillo 2007). To be considered **urban** in Canada, an area must have a population of at least 1,000 with no fewer than 400 persons per square kilometre. In other words, density is a key attribute in Canada. In comparison, to be classified as urban in, say, Iceland, an area need have only 200 residents while in the United States the population must exceed 50,000. **Urbanisation** is the process by which an increasing percentage of a society's population comes to be located in relatively densely populated urban areas (Orum 2007). It's clear that urbanisation occurred even in ancient times when large numbers of people moved to Rome, Cairo, and Peking; however, it has accelerated greatly in the modern era. **Urbanism** is the distinctive way of life that emerges in, and is closely associated with, urban areas. That way of life includes distinctive lifestyles, attitudes, and social relationships. In terms of the latter, one example is the greater likelihood of relating to strangers (D. Elliott 2012).

SIMMEL, WIRTH, PARK, AND BURGESS ON THE CITY

Georg Simmel ([1903] 1971) offered early sociological insight into the way of life in the city. He saw the city as the centre of the money economy, and money has a profound effect on many things, including a decline in genuine human relationships. Rationality and calculability come to dominate many things, including social relationships, in the city. Because so much of virtually everything is available in the city, people tend to become quite blasé. To them, all things acquire "an equally dull and grey hue" (Simmel [1907] 1978:256). Nothing tends to matter very much one way or the other to urbanites. They have "seen it all"; there is no reason to get very excited or very depressed over anything.

Furthermore, because virtually anything can be bought (and sold) in a money economy, those who have the needed funds develop a highly cynical attitude toward life. It isn't the quality of an object or a relationship (beautiful or ugly, for example) that matters; the only thing that is really important is how much it costs. In

Level of urbanization per region and tipping points urban vs. rural				
Region	Tipping point before 2010 (Year)	2010 urban (%)	Tipping point after 2010 (year)	2050 urban (%)
World		**50.6**		**70**
MORE DEVELOPED REGIONS	**before 1950**	**75**		**86**
Europe	before 1950	72.6		83.8
Eastern Europe	1963	68.8		80
Northern Europe	before 1950	84.4		90.7
Southern Europe	1960	67.5		81.2
Western Europe	before 1950	77		86.5
LESS DEVELOPED REGIONS		45.3	2020	67
Africa		40	2030	61.8
Sub-Saharan Africa		37.3	2032	60.5
Eastern Africa		23.7		47.6
Northern Africa	2005	52		72
Southern Africa	1993	58.8		77.6
Western Africa		44.6	2020	68
Asia		42.5	2023	66.2
Eastern Asia		48.5	2013	74.1
South-central Asia		32.2	2040	57.2
South-eastern Asia		48.2	2013	73.3
Western Asia	1980	66.3		79.3
Latin America and the Caribbean	1962	79.4		88.7
Central America	1965	71.7		83.3
Rest of the World				
South America	1960	83.7		91.4
Northern America	before 1950	82.1		90.2
Oceania	before 1950	70.6		76.4

FIGURE 14.6 Urbanization Around the World

SOURCE: From UN Habitat, *State of the World's Cities 2010/2011. Bridging the Urban Divide. Urban Trends: Urbanization and Economic Growth, 2011.*

this way, the city is a "frightful leveller," with everything reduced to its cost. Human relationships are levelled, as well, as they are reduced to deliberate calculations of how much, or how little, can be gotten from each of them. People tend to deal with positions—police officer, counterperson at Starbucks—rather than the individuals who occupy those positions. The crowded nature of the city also leads people to adapt to it in various ways, including developing a very reserved stance toward the people around them. There are simply too many of them to allow oneself to get very involved with most of the people one meets in the city. In any case, such involvement is too time-consuming and carries with it small risks such as neediness and great risks posed to oneself, for example, by muggers.

However, Simmel also noted the positive sides of life in the city. For example, people are often highly restricted by life in a small town or a rural area. They are likely to be known by many people, and their actions are apt to be closely watched. Any errant behaviour is likely to become widely known very quickly. On the other hand, in the modern city people are much freer because they are personally acquainted with few of the people with whom they come into contact. What happens between them is not likely to come to be known by family members or close friends in other parts of the city, let alone elsewhere in the country and the world. Las Vegas epitomises this aspect of city life, as is clear in its onetime slogan, "What happens in Vegas stays in Vegas." The idea is that people are free to do anything they want in Las Vegas. This applies, in general, to any city, especially in comparison to small towns and rural areas.

A few decades after Simmel's work on the city, Louis Wirth (1938) authored another classic on the city, aptly titled "Urbanism as a Way of Life." Wirth was strongly influenced by Simmel, and he used a variety of terms to describe city life that are similar to Simmel's more critical view of the city. Thus, Wirth described urban social relations as "superficial" and "anonymous." Urbanites were seen as being characterised by "indifference," "reserve," and, as Simmel had argued, "a blasé attitude." However, also like Simmel, Wirth saw a positive side to the city with its diversity leading to internal differentiation and competition. Out of that milieu emerge at least some people who are quite unique and inventive. The rationality of the city is also associated with the fact that many who live there go about their lives, and especially their work, very efficiently. A good deal of what has come to be called **urban sociology** has concerned itself with the issue of the way of life in the city.

Wirth was a member of the Chicago School of Sociology that flourished in the 1920s and 1930s. Two other, even more famous, members of that school, Robert Park and Ernest Burgess, made a variety of other contributions to the study of the city. As we saw in Chapter 3, Park had been a reporter, and with that background he urged his students to go out and observe various aspects of life in the city. They produced a wide range of

BIOGRAPHICAL bits

Louis Wirth (1897–1952, German American)

- Wirth emigrated to the United States from Germany in 1911.

- He earned a PhD from the University of Chicago in 1926.

- Wirth became an assistant professor in the Department of Sociology at Chicago in 1931.

- He was skilled in relating empirical facts to social theory.

- One of his best known works is *The Ghetto* ([1928] 1997), in which he combined his interests in the city with race and culture.

- He believed that sociologists had to do more to educate policymakers in various fields—in other words, to do more "public sociology."

- He felt that sociologists had to demonstrate the applicability of their ideas to the "real world."

- Wirth was elected president of the American Sociological Society (later Association) in 1947.

ethnographic studies that cast much light on the nature of the city. Burgess was also especially interested in the social geography of the city and studied its spatial character. He is best known for his concentric zone theory of the city (Park, Burgess, and McKenzie [1925] 1967). At the heart of the city and its concentric zones is the city's central business district. Radiating out from it is a series of concentric spatial areas. Each of those areas has a specialised function. The area closest to the central business district is devoted to industry. Beyond that are zones where the working class, the middle class, and commuters live. Cities have changed a great deal since they were studied by Burgess and the other Chicago urban sociologists. Thus, the concentric zone theory no longer applies, but what does continue is the study of the spatial nature and character of cities (D. Harvey 2000; Soja 1989).

EVER-LARGER URBAN AREAS

Over the years, in Canada and throughout the world, urbanisation has proceeded at a rapid pace, and this has required the creation of new concepts to describe the development of ever-larger urban areas. After 1920 in the United States (and later elsewhere) there emerged a new urban form—the metropolis—a large, powerful, and culturally influential urban area that contains a central city and surrounding communities that are economically and socially linked to the centre. Suburbs are the surrounding communities that are adjacent to, but outside the political boundaries of, large central cities (J. Friedman 2007). They often create band-like structures around cities. While suburbs in Canada have tended to be middle class, in other societies, such as France and the suburbs that ring Paris, they are more likely to be dominated by the lower class, including many recent immigrants. A megalopolis is a cluster of highly populated cities that can stretch over great distances (Gotham 2007; Jean Gottman 1961). There are currently 18 megalopolises in the United States, with the area between Boston and Washington, DC, being the classic example. Another now stretches from San Diego to San Francisco and ultimately may extend as far as Seattle and even Vancouver. The area between Toronto and Buffalo, or even Detroit, is another cross-border megalopolis.

Figure 14.7 offers another, broader view of urbanisation. *Mega-regions* consist of several interconnected and integrated cities, as well as their surrounding areas. These are regions across which, at low cost, labour and capital can be reallocated (Florida, Gulden, and Mellander 2007). Depicted here are mega-regions in the United States, Europe, and Asia.

SUBURBANISATION

Canadian cities have been affected by a variety of social trends and developments. One, of course, is the process of suburbanisation, whereby large numbers of people move out of the city and into those nearby, less densely populated, environs. They are often impelled by urban problems, such as crime, pollution, poverty, homelessness, and poor schools. The "American dream" of the last half of the twentieth century of an affordable one-family home was more likely to be found in the suburbs than in the city. A key event in turning this dream into a reality occurred in 1947 in the United States with the building of the first of three suburban developments known as Levittowns. They acquired that name because they were built by the Levitt family. In each of the three Levittowns, identical and affordable tract houses were erected quickly, efficiently, and inexpensively on green parcels of land. This was accomplished by bringing the principles of the automobile assembly line—for example, a division of labour among workers—to the site on which the homes were to be built. During this time period, the building of suburban homes was bolstered by "massive government expenditures in highway and school construction." In addition, "the G. I. Bill made single-family suburban home ownership a reality for an increasing number of American families" (Kimmel 2011:147). The TV series *Weeds* spoofs such suburban communities. In its initial seasons it even opened with various renditions of the Malvina Reynolds song "Little Boxes"—"Little boxes on the hillside, little boxes made of ticky-tacky . . ." The music was accompanied by shots of identical houses and identically dressed people getting into identical cars. Of course, *Weeds* is about a highly unusual suburban woman who earns her living by dealing in drugs.

Various criticisms have been directed at suburbanisation. One is that it led to the creation of vast areas characterised by a seemingly endless sprawl of tract houses and the businesses that are created to serve them (Duány, Plater-Zyberk, and Speck 2010). Another critique renamed suburbia "Disturbia," describing the suburban home as a "split-level trap" (Gordon, Gordon, and Gunther 1960). More recently, many others have noted the problem of suburban sprawl, which promotes high levels of traffic congestion and environmental degradation. However, others, especially many who lived in such homes and communities, found much merit in Levittowns and suburbia. For example, a well-known urban sociologist, Herbert Gans (1967), concluded his study of the third Levittown built in New Jersey by arguing that "whatever its imperfections, Levittown is a good place to live" (p. 432).

Suburban developments such as Levittown have changed over the years and are no longer the

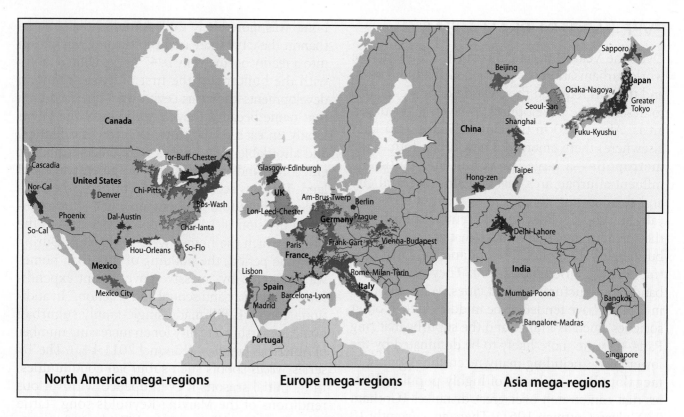

FIGURE 14.7 Mega-regions in North America, Europe, and Asia

SOURCE: From "The Rise of the Mega-Region," Richard Florida, Tim Gulden, and Charlotta Mellander, University of Toronto. October 2007.

homogeneous communities they once were. For example, many residents of Levittown customised their homes so that they are now significantly different from one another (Dullea 1991). More importantly, many suburban developers have learned from previous mistakes. They have, among other things, created communities in which the houses have at least several different looks and have different styles, even though they may at base and in their fundamental structure be similar or even identical.

A more recent suburban development has been the emergence of **gated communities**. In these communities, gates, surveillance cameras, and guards provide the homeowners with greater security from the problems that they thought they had left behind in the city, such as crime and panhandling (R. Atkinson and Blandy 2005; Blakely and Snyder 1997). However, Setha Low's (2003) *Behind the Gates: Life, Security, and the Pursuit of Happiness in Fortress America* finds that such communities tend to produce a heightened sense of fear and insecurity among community members.

While the early suburban communities had small ranch-style houses, the boom years running up to the late 2007 recession witnessed the birth and expansion of suburban communities populated by "McMansions" (R. Lowell 1998; P. Rogers 1995). These are huge private homes that have 5,000 square feet of living space, and often much more. They are built on tracts of land of one, two, or even more acres. They are dubbed McMansions because even though they are expensive ($1 million–$2 million, and more), they are built on the same principles (efficiency and predictability) as the early Levittown houses. In the end, McMansions are little more than huge and luxuriously appointed tract homes built on the basis of a limited number of models.

The early suburbs were primarily residential "bedroom communities" for those who worked, shopped, and enjoyed leisure activities in the city. "Don Draper," the advertising executive who is at the centre of the hit television show *Mad Men* set in the late 1950s and early 1960s, lives in such a community and commutes by train to his job in Manhattan. After he and his wife divorce, his wife and children continue to live in the suburbs.

Suburbanisation was first associated with the United States, though it is now a global phenomenon. However, there is considerable variation around the world in this process and the nature of suburbs. It would be a mistake to simply assume the American model fits suburbs elsewhere in the world, although it is a fairly good fit with much of Canada (Clapson and Hutchison 2010).

The Post-suburban Era

Suburbanisation in Canada peaked in the late twentieth century. Today, there is much talk about the decline of the suburbs and the idea that we live in a postsuburban era. In part, this is related to the growing realisation that a way of life that includes large, energy-devouring private homes and vast thirsty lawns is ecologically unsustainable. Renting apartments, buying condominiums, and moving back into or close to the city are back in vogue. Related to this are high gasoline prices and home heating and air-conditioning costs that help to further make the cost of a suburban home prohibitive for many. Smaller family sizes also mean that large suburban homes are no longer so essential.

Exurbia. Cities and suburbs continue to push outward where land and housing costs are lower. Developments in these outlying areas between the suburbs and rural areas are called **exurbia** (Crump 2007). At their outer edges they blend into the rural countryside and agricultural areas. These are generally upper-middle-class communities and may have enormous, custom-built homes (rather than McMansions) on large, heavily treed lots. Milton near Toronto and Okotoks near Calgary, the fastest-growing urban areas in Canada, are examples of exurbias. Beyond exurbia stretches the rural hinterlands, regions with varying levels of population by province, as shown in Figure 14.8. Although 4 out of every 5 Canadians live in urban areas (81.1% of all Canadians in 2011), notice in the figure that the experience of rural (or urban) living varies sharply by province or territory. Substantial percentages of Canadians live in rural areas, save for Alberta, British Columbia, Ontario, and Quebec.

Edge Cities. Associated with the rise of exurbia, and another aspect of postsuburbanisation, is the emergence of what have come to be called **edge cities** (Garreau 1991; N. Phelps and Wood 2011). As the name suggests, **edge cities** are developments at the outermost rings surrounding large cities, are even further away from major cities, exist beyond suburbs, and in many ways are more like cities than suburbs. As part of exurbia, edge cities become indistinguishable from the hinterlands, giving rise to the idea of the "edgeless city." And just as with suburbanisation, the phenomenon of

Suburbs are the surrounding communities that are just outside the boundaries of large central cities. Suburbs in Canada tend to be middle class and popular among families, while in some societies (such as Paris, France), they tend to be lower class and popular among recent immigrants.

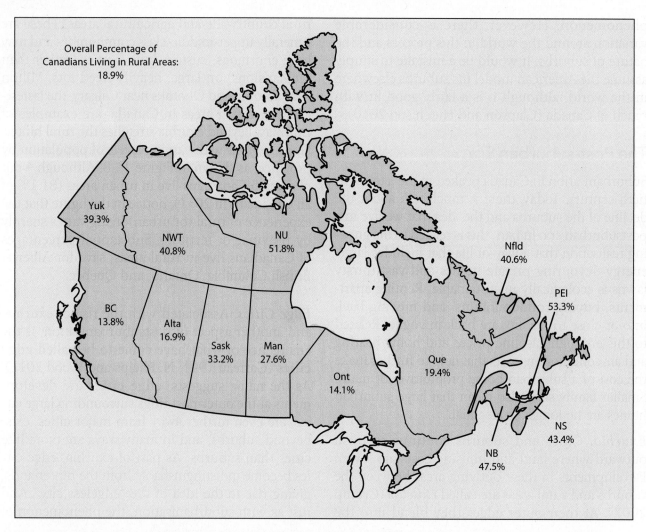

FIGURE 14.8 Percentage of Canadian Population Living in Rural Areas, 2011

SOURCE: Statistics Canada, population counts, for Canada, provinces and territories, census divisions, population centre size groups and rural areas, 2011 census.

edge cities originated in the United States, but there are signs that they are becoming increasingly global (Bontje and Burdack 2011). Cities such as Oshawa in Ontario, now the fifteenth largest city in Canada, or Abbotsford in British Columbia (the 21st largest), are Canadian examples of growing edge cities.

Shopping Malls. Edge cities are on, or near, major highways, have corporate offices that offer employment to many, and have important commercial and consumption centres, most importantly shopping malls. The early malls tended to be strip malls, and while there are still many of them, they have come to be supplanted in importance by fully enclosed malls. Not only are these malls attractive to suburbanites, but urban residents are often drawn to them for the convenience of having so many different shops in one location. More recent suburban attractions are

stand-alone discount giants such as Costco, Réno-Dépôt, and especially Walmart. Renovating malls has now become big business as places, including the Don Mills Shopping Centre in Toronto, have had major makeovers.

New Urbanism. New suburban forms continue to emerge, and one is the shopping mall designed to look and to function like a small town. Combined in one setting might be a few streets with shops, an indoor mall, and apartments and condominiums. These settings are supposed to look and feel more like towns than shopping malls and to overcome the separation between living and shopping that exists in most of suburbia. These developments are related to a movement known as "new urbanism" where the goal is the creation of a simulation (a fake copy) of a traditional small town with neighbourhoods, "walkability," and various facilities within close proximity for residents (Duány and Plater-Zyberk 1990). Two of British Columbia's biggest universities, the University of British Columbia and Simon Fraser University, have created new urban footprints to attract residential housing to campus lands complete with public schools, parks, and shopping districts.

The Aerotropolis Model. Mention should also be made here of one more new postsuburban form— the aerotropolis—a planned city that is built around a vast international airport and its associated shipping facilities and business hubs (Kasarda and Lindsay 2011). This stands in contrast to the model of the recent past, where airports were constructed in, and later around, cities. It is consistent, however, with the fact that cities have long been constructed at central transit points, such as on rivers, near ports, on rail lines, or near highways. Today, in the era of globalisation, the major transit points for both people and products are increasingly airports. The key today is the mobility of people and products, and the aerotropolis is designed to maximise that mobility (Urry 2007). Aerotropolises are currently under construction in New Songdo, South Korea, and in Dubai, and we can expect to see more of them, especially in China. We are clearly witnessing the emergence of a new form of living where people will be increasingly living around, and in some cases literally in, airports.

Renovating Cities. In some cases, cities have rebuilt at least some of their infrastructure in a process of urban redevelopment and renewal (G. Crowley 2007). This has been a major challenge in Canada, where urbanisation is increasing but infrastructure budgets have been tight. The consequence, sometimes tragic, has been the collapsing of bridges, the bursting of water mains, and the toxicity of inadequate sewage treatment. Especially in an era where tax cutting has been politically popular, finding sufficient resources to replace aging equipment and facilities has become a major challenge for municipal politicians.

Gentrification, in which real estate capital is reinvested in blighted inner-city areas in order to rebuild residences and create a new infrastructure for the well-to-do, has been one significant form of urban renovation (Lees, Slater, and Wyly 2010; Walks and Maaranen 2008). Old Montreal, Yorkville and the Annex in Toronto, and Fairview Slopes and

On September 15, 2006 a highway overpass collapsed in Laval, Quebec. Increasingly municipal infrastructure, including roads, sewage, water, and public transit, is deteriorating as politicians are challenged to find revenue in an era of tax cutting.

Granville Island in Vancouver have all had major facelifts recently, where new money has flowed into older, deteriorating neighbourhoods to provide newer, posher, more modern town homes and condominiums. Restaurants, bars, and exercise centres have proliferated as younger professionals, gays, and artists have migrated to these locales. In the process, working-class and poor residents are often forced out or unable to move in, because housing prices rise as a result of gentrification. Those who remain suffer from a variety of problems, such as the loss of their neighbourhood-based support networks. They are left largely on their own in an environment that is increasingly foreign to them and that they are increasingly unable to afford (Betancur 2011).

The development of suburbs, megalopolises, exurbs, edge cities, gentrification, and so on makes it clear that our old notions of the city need to change. We used to think of a city as having a nucleus around which all other areas revolved. Now, it is best to think of a city as having a number of different nuclei that sprawl over a large geographic area. The central city, the central business district, is no longer a magnet for many people. Instead, many separate and specialised centres are found across a wide area, and different types of people are drawn to different areas (Gotham 2012).

CITIES AND GLOBALISATION

From the beginning, cities have been central to both scholarly and popular work on globalisation (Sassen 2012; Timberlake and Ma 2007). Cities are seen as being *cosmopolitan*, or open to a variety of external and global influences (see Chapter 11) (Beck 2007).

Neighbourhoods once known as downtrodden and poor, such as some parts of Vancouver's Downtown Eastside, have been transformed with pricey condominiums, restaurants, and other amenities for their new wealthy residents. The working-class and poor residents who remain face an increasingly unaffordable environment.

In contrast, small towns and rural areas are more likely to be viewed as **local**, or inward- rather than outward-looking. Cities therefore came to be seen as inherently global, and they grew more so as they came to encompass a range of populations, cultures, ethnicities, languages, and consumer products from around the world. Cities also exerted a powerful influence (cultural, political, and economic) over surrounding areas.

However, it would be a mistake to think of cities today as isolated entities within a global environment. Rather, cities are increasingly part of, and open to, innumerable global flows of people, products, information, and much more. A recent work in this area has described this as "mobile urbanism" (E. McCann and Ward 2011). Urban policies and ideas on how to improve the city flow easily throughout the world's urban areas. The many city-based organisations are linked through elaborate networks to organisations in other cities throughout the home country and the world. Furthermore, the people in those cities are themselves involved in a wide range of global networks and are linked to people throughout the world. These include flows of people into and out of urban areas, as well as Internet-based ties via e-mail, Skype, and Facebook. It is also the case that the system of global cities is hierarchical with substantial flows of people, information, and objects moving not only between them but, in a sense, both "up" and "down" the hierarchy.

Global and World Cities

At the top of the world's hierarchy of cities are the global cities (Sassen 1991). Only New York City, London, and Tokyo are generally included in this elite category. Sassen clearly embeds her notion of global cities in the process of globalisation, especially economic (capitalistic) globalisation. In this context, she accords priority to the three cities mentioned above on the basis of their place in the world economy. Specifically, they are **global cities** because they are

- the key locations for leading industries and marketplaces and the high-level management and specialised services they require;
- the centres of the production and creation of innovative, cutting-edge financial services;

- the homes of new financial, legal, and accountancy products; and
- the settings from which businesses and organisations exercise global command and control.

Much of what global cities achieve is enabled by a wide range of new electronic technologies. In light of the recent world recession, we also know that these cities, with their great financial centres, are likely to be at the epicentre of monumental collapses in the global economy and, presumably, of renaissances in that economy.

To Sassen, and others, global cities are central nodes in a new international division of labour. Of great importance are the linkages among and between these global cities and the flows, both positive and negative, among and between them. In many ways the global cities have more in common with one another than with the smaller cities and the hinterlands within their own country. They are also more integrated into the global economy than those hinterlands. The direct linkages between global cities point to the fact that nation-states are less important in the global age than previously. They are unable to control the flows between global cities. As Sassen (2012) puts it, the global city "engages the global directly, often bypassing the national" (p. 189). In addition, the nation-state is unable to stem such other global flows as undocumented immigrants and illegal drugs.

A similar, but somewhat more expansive, concept is **world cities,** a much larger group of cities that perform most of the same functions as global cities (Jonathan Friedman 1986, 1994; J. Lin 2012). They are important, but perhaps not yet as important as global cities. Friedman includes a total of 30 cities under the heading of world cities. Tokyo, New York, and London are included in his lists, but so are a number of other cities of note, such as Toronto, Paris, Los Angeles, and Chicago. Excluded, however, are the now-booming Chinese cities, including Shanghai and Beijing. Any contemporary listing of world cities would likely include them, as well as perhaps other exploding Chinese cities. Also of increasing note are Indian cities such as Mumbai and Bangalore.

Like global cities, world cities are centres of communities of immigrants who interact with family and friends in their homeland, as well as in many other parts of the world. For example, a study of care workers from the Philippines shows the many linkages these women typically have with people back home, especially in sending back remittances from Canada (Pratt 2012). Another study focuses on the mobility of people and money between Canada and China, and especially Hong Kong (Ley 2013).

Megacities (and Beyond)

Megacities are defined as cities with a population greater than 8 million people. Of course, the global cities discussed above meet that criterion, but what is striking is the large and growing number of cities in the less developed world that can be defined as megacities (F. Krass 2012). The largest megacities are Tokyo with 32.45 million people, Seoul with 20.55 million, and Mexico City with 20.45 million, but others of note are Mumbai (Bombay) with 19.2 million, Cairo with 14.45 million, and Lagos with 13.48 million inhabitants (Worldatlas 2010). And these cities are expected to grow dramatically in the coming years. For example, Mumbai will have 33 million people by 2025, and Mexico City will reach a population of 50 million by 2050 (M. Davis 2007).

Such population concentrations bring with them enormous problems associated with the large number of very poor people living in these cities, especially in the third world. Indeed many of those problems already exist (see next *Globalisation* box). More generally, Mike Davis (2007) envisions a planet of urban slums that are a far cry from what early urban visionaries had in mind:

The cities of the future, rather than being made out of glass and steel as envisioned by earlier generations of urbanists, are instead largely constructed out of crude brick, straw, recycled plastic, cement blocks and scrap wood. Instead of cities of light soaring toward heaven, much of the twenty-first-century urban world squats in squalor, surrounded by pollution, excrement, and decay. (P. 19)

Of course, these megacities, even the most blighted of them, have wealthy residents as well, and thus they are sites of some of the most profound inequalities in the world. A stunning example of this inequality is found in Mumbai, where in 2010 the richest person in India completed building a 27-story, single-family home that may be valued at as much as $1 billion. Among other things, it has nine elevators, a six-level garage, helipads, "airborne swimming pools," a spa, hanging gardens, a 50-person theatre, and a grand ballroom. To function, the structure will require hundreds of servants and staff. All of this is found in a city noted for its poverty, where about 60 percent of the population lives in slums (Yardley 2010).

The Main Site of Global Problems

Global or world cities are generally rich, powerful, prestigious, and the main beneficiaries of globalisation, such as the income and other benefits derived from being at the heart of global financial flows. However, it is also the case that cities, including the global or world cities, are especially hard hit by a wide range of global problems. Among other things, it is some of the world's great cities—New York, London, Madrid—that have been the main targets of major terrorist attacks; the destination for large numbers of immigrants, many of them undocumented, who are impoverished and in need of public assistance; the settings where large numbers of those affected by

Mukesh Ambani, a scion of Indian industry whose personal wealth is estimated at $27 billion, built the most opulent home owned by an individual anywhere in the world. Ambani's home is a tower that stands about 174 metres tall. More than 160 cars can be parked in its parking garage, and there are three helipads on the top floor.

global health problems are likely to end up in search of medical help; and so on. This has led Zygmunt Bauman (2003) to contend that "cities have become dumping grounds for globally forgotten problems" (p. 101).

In spite of their global nature and source, dealing with these problems becomes a political problem for the city. They represent a huge difficulty for city officials who often lack the economic resources even to begin to deal with most of them. Furthermore, since the sources of many of these problems are global, whatever city officials seek to do is doomed to failure. Thus, for example, the mayor of London is helpless in dealing with the forces that lead many to migrate to his city, the roots of terrorism in the tribal territories of Pakistan, the global epidemic of HIV/AIDS, or the air pollution being generated in nearby cities on the continent. To quote Bauman (2003) again: "Local politics— and particularly urban politics—has become hopelessly overloaded" (p. 102).

The Centre of Culture and Consumption

Much of this discussion of the city tends to emphasise its problems, or dark side. However, it is also the case that cities have played a highly positive role in the development of societies throughout the world. Much of what we think of as culture, especially "high culture," has its origins, and has become centred, in the city. Thus, a great number of the world's great universities, museums, symphony orchestras, opera companies, theatres (especially in New York and London), restaurants, and so on are found in the world's great cities. It is also the case that much of pop culture—the Beatles from Liverpool, England; hip-hop from many American urban areas; the pop art of Andy Warhol from New York City—emanates from the city.

The city is also the source of many developments in the world of consumption. For example, shopping arcades (Benjamin 1999), world's fairs, and department stores had their origins in nineteenth-century Paris and other European cities (R. Williams [1982] 1991). In the twentieth century, U.S. cities became the world leaders in such consumption sites, most notably New York City with its world-famous

Cities have played a very positive role in the development of societies throughout the world. Much of what we think of as culture—exquisite architecture, higher learning, great music and art—has its origins, and has become centred, in the city. The Guggenheim Museum Bilbao, located in Bilbao, Spain, not only houses masterful works of art, but the Frank Gehry–designed building is a work of art itself.

department stores (Macy's and Gimbels), as well as the 1939 and 1964 World's Fairs. When those who lived outside the city could afford to tavel and wanted to consume, they often made regular treks to the city to shop, go to the theatre, and so on. Cities such as Paris and New York also played other key roles in consumption, such as being national and global centres of fashion (Lipovetsky [1987] 2002; Simmel [1904] 1971). Furthermore, cities, especially New York and its famed Madison Avenue, became the centres for the advertising industry that played, and continues to play, a central role in driving consumption throughout the United States and the world (Schudson 1987). A number of cities have become more specialised centres of consumption, the most notable examples being gambling centres such as Las Vegas and Macau. Although it ran into deep economic problems in the recent recession, Dubai has undergone a massive building boom in an effort to become the commercial and consumption centre for a good part of the world stretching from Cairo to Tokyo.

Fantasy City. A **fantasy city** is one in which great emphasis is placed on creating a spectacle, especially in the areas of consumption, leisure, tourism, and real estate dominated by impressive buildings and other developments. Hannigan (1998, 2007)

sees only two cities as full-scale fantasy cities: Las Vegas, Nevada, and Orlando, Florida (home of Disney World and many other tourist attractions). However, many others, especially Dubai, have moved more in that direction (see the next *Globalisation* box).

Fantasy cities are characterised by an infrastructure dominated by such "cathedrals of consumption" (Ritzer 2010a) as "themed restaurants, nightclubs, shopping malls, multiplex cinemas, virtual reality arcades, casino-hotels . . . sports stadiums and arenas, and other urban entertainment centers" (Hannigan 2007:1641). The whole idea is to draw people, especially tourists, to fantasy cities and once they are there to lure them into the various cathedrals of consumption where they will spend large sums of money. Like many developments in the realm of consumption, the fantasy city was largely a U.S. creation, but it has now become increasingly global, and it is possible to identify fantasy cities in Australia, Singapore, Malaysia, and China, as well as the United Arab Emirates.

Although people are drawn to fantasy cities to consume goods and services, what they find especially attractive is the spectacle of the city. For example, many American cities have built huge and spectacular new sports arenas (the new $1 billion–plus Yankee Stadium in New York is a prime example) as places in which to spend large sums of money (Hoffman, Fainstein, and Judd 2003). In Las Vegas the spectacle is the famous Strip, Las Vegas Boulevard, with its incredible themed casino-hotels, such as the Paris (with both its replica Eiffel Tower and its Arc de Triomphe), the Venetian (with its canals and gondolas), Bellagio (including its famous fountains), and Treasure Island (with its regular outdoor sea battles). In Orlando, the spectacle is Disney World and its many parks and attractions, as well as other theme parks (Universal Studios, Busch Gardens, SeaWorld). Other cities have sought to draw tourists and consumers in similar ways.

Decline. In recent years the central role of cities, especially in consumption, has been reduced. Suburban shopping malls supplanted urban shopping centres and department stores as the prime destination for many shoppers. More recently, the shopping malls themselves are being supplanted by online shopping (Amazon.ca, eBay.ca). Many of the

GL⊕BALISATION

Lagos, Nigeria

Lagos is not on the list of global or world cities. However, it is enormous. It is the fastest-growing megacity in the world with, about 600,000 people moving there every year. Lagos had only 300,000 inhabitants in 1950 (Packer 2006), but it is currently the sixth largest city in the world with about 13.48 million people (Ahemba 2007).

Based on size alone, one might think of Lagos as a world city, but the city and the country of Nigeria are relatively undeveloped economically and in many other ways. Despite Nigeria's large oil reserves—it is Africa's highest oil-producing country and the ninth largest exporter in the world—the country has struggled continuously with corruption and mismanagement. Among its many problems, Nigeria has the second highest HIV/AIDS rate in the entire world (second only to South Africa), resulting in a very high death rate among Nigerians. As in the rest of Nigeria, these problems plague Lagos and its people. Lagos is one of the main examples of a city that has been overwhelmed by poverty and its slums (M. Davis 2007). Among its more appalling characteristics are

- a deteriorating infrastructure that was built for a much smaller population;

- city services, including power, that are unreliable if not nonexistent;

- slums floating over polluted water;

- massive conventional slums;

- difficulty obtaining clean, inexpensive drinking water;

- enormous growth, but growth that is largely unplanned and building that is uncontrolled;

- many half-built and abandoned skyscrapers;

- ubiquitous garbage dumps that "steam" as a result of the combustion of natural gases and that serve as a source of income for scavengers;

- fires from fuel spills that blaze in auto yards;

- enormous traffic jams and a sometimes overwhelming cacophony of noises;

- economic activity that takes place mainly on the streets;

- large numbers of people sleeping outdoors or sharing tiny flats; and

- gang violence.

Nevertheless, Lagos remains a lure for those outside the city who are impressed with what new residents can acquire there compared to what can be acquired in rural Nigeria, as well as elsewhere in rural Africa. In other words, rural Nigeria is even poorer and worse off than Lagos. Thus, hundreds of thousands more people come to Lagos every year, and, as the numbers swell, living conditions grow worse.

Lagos is a megacity in Nigeria and a prime example of an urban environment that is produced by explosive population growth. Here, pedestrians push their way through a traffic jam in downtown Lagos. Traffic jams, or "Go Slows" as locals call them, can last for hours in the overpopulated city.

new consumption giants (Walmart, Target, Costco, McDonald's) were once mainly rural, small-town, or suburban phenomena. Globally, such major players in the world of consumption as IKEA (from Sweden with Dutch ownership) and Carrefour (French) are most likely to be located outside the city. Entertainment giant Disney has placed its theme parks outside of some of the world's great cities—Los Angeles, Orlando, Paris, Tokyo, Hong Kong, and Singapore (in 2014).

In many ways, roles have been reversed, and instead of being the source of innovations in consumption, external developments are increasingly finding their way into the cities. They are making the distinction between cities, suburbs, edge cities, and other geographic areas less clear and meaningful. For example, fast-food restaurants (especially McDonald's) were originally suburban and small-town phenomena, but they have increasingly become urban phenomena, as well. In the process, they have tended to displace distinctive urban cafes and restaurants, driving many of the latter out of business and into oblivion. Similarly, discount chains (Target and Kohl's) have increasingly made their way into American cities. Even New York City, long known for its highly distinctive consumption sites, has come to look more and more like the rest of the United States (and much of the world) with its large numbers of McDonald's, Kentucky Fried Chicken, and now even Kohl's stores.

THE ENVIRONMENT

A concern for the natural environment is part of a broader concern with **ecology**, or the study of people and their relationship to one another as well as to the larger context in which they live (Sanford 2007). Interestingly, one variant of ecology, human ecology, gained a foothold in the early Chicago School of Sociology (1914–1945) and its concern with relationships within and between communities, especially cities. A separable field of human ecology, influenced by the work of the Chicago School, is traceable to Amos Hawley's (1950) *Human Ecology*. Hawley argued for the study of the relationship between individuals, organisations, and the larger social setting (M. White and Kim 2007). However, the environment in the sense

One of the attractions of the modern city is a huge (and hugely expensive) sports arena. The new Yankee Stadium, which opened in 2009, cost approximately $1.5 billion to build. The stadium's Great Hall, featuring 31,000 square feet of retail space and seven-story ceilings, provides fans with plenty of entertainment—and plenty of ways to spend their money.

of the natural world and issues such as climate was not a primary concern of the *human* ecologists.

Given the powerful impact of Émile Durkheim's ([1895] 1982) contention that sociology is the study of *social* facts, sociologists were slow to shift their attention to the natural world and environmental issues (Preisendorfer and Diekmann 2007). This is a bit surprising because, as pointed out above, one of the basic concerns of the early Chicago School of Sociology was ecology. These sociologists were influenced by, and borrowed from, natural scientists such as botanists and biologists who looked at the relationship between, for example, vegetation and climate. The Chicago sociologists saw great similarities between these concerns and human societies, although they viewed such societies as much more complex than the natural world. They involved, for example, the relationship between ethnic groups in

GL⊕BALISATION

Dubai as a Fantasy City

Dubai is a major city in the United Arab Emirates (UAE), a federation of states in the Middle East. Of particular note is the ambitious effort by Dubai to become a fantasy city. It did so by building several cathedrals of consumption, including an impressive set of skyscrapers. These are highlighted by the tallest building in the world, the 211-story Burj Khalifa, which opened in late 2009 and was scaled by Tom Cruise in the 2012 movie *Mission: Impossible— Ghost Protocol.* Dubai is also noted for its grand hotels, such as the Burj Al Arab, which proclaims itself the most luxurious and highest-rated hotel in the world. (See *Globalisation* box, "The Shopping Malls of Dubai," in Chapter 1.)

However, perhaps the most spectacular development, and the greatest fantasy, in Dubai is the Palm Islands—Palm Jumeirah, Palm Jebel Ali, and Palm Deira. These are to be the world's three largest artificial (simulated) islands and the result of the largest land reclamation project ever undertaken. All three are to be shaped, albeit somewhat differently, as palm trees. All three are spectacular because of their size; the largest, Palm Deira, is planned to be bigger than Paris. Also spectacular is the way in which they were, and are, being created by massive and unprecedented dredging of sand from the bottom of the Persian Gulf and by hauling it in from the surrounding desert. Of course, the developers are not content with the spectacle of the islands themselves, but they are each to have their own

cathedrals of consumption—luxury hotels, theme parks, shopping malls, and the like.

The massive development projects have been fuelled by the UAE's enormous oil wealth—the country is the fourth largest exporter of oil in the world. Much of the labour to build the fantasy city has been performed by immigrants from South Asia. This made Dubai a major destination for migrant labour during its rapid expansion in the early 2000s and contributed to the UAE's massive immigration flows (the third largest in the world). Because of Dubai's growth, its standard of living now rivals that of many developed nations in the world, but migrant labourers have been exploited throughout the development process (M. Davis 2006).

More recently, Dubai was badly hurt by the recession. It was announced at the end of 2009 that Dubai was unable to make payments due on an estimated $100 billion debt incurred to build the fantasy city. Planned projects are on hold, construction cranes are stilled, and the city is littered with many unfinished buildings and other projects. Many of the migrant labourers have left the city and returned to their home countries (Worth 2009). As of late 2013, Dubai's future is still cloudy; it depends, as do the futures of all the fantasy cities, on the emergence of the global economy from the recession and the ability of the city to boom once again. A specific factor in Dubai's case is the willingness of oil-rich neighbours such as Abu Dhabi—Dubai itself has little oil—to continue to bankroll it.

The world's tallest building, the Burj Khalifa, appears in the distance as devout Muslims break their fasts outside a mosque in the Gulf emirate of Dubai during the Muslim holy month of Ramadan in 2011. At more than 820 metres, the Burj Khalifa is not merely the world's tallest building—it is taller than any other building by more than 300 metres.

the city and the ways in which one ethnic group invaded an area of the city and succeeded another in coming to dominate that area (Sanford 2007; Schwirian 2007). The Chicago ecologists devoted little or no attention to the relationship between human societies and the natural environment.

Because of the explosive growth of a wide range of environmental problems in recent years, as well as the growing attention to, concern over, and even fear of those problems since the 1970s, many sociologists have been drawn to the study of the environment, especially to an analysis of environmental problems (Antonio and Brulle 2012; Dunlap 2007; Dunlap and Jorgenson 2012). They were inspired, as was the public as a whole, by such highly influential books as Rachel Carson's (1962) *Silent Spring*, which focused on poisons such as insecticides and weed killers and the threats they posed to agriculture, including our most basic sources of food, as well as to nature more generally. There is now a large and growing group of environmental sociologists and a relatively new specialty, environmental sociology (York and Dunlap 2012). Some environmental sociologists have been concerned with how various environmental matters come to be defined as problems, but there is an increasing shift in the direction of conceiving of these problems as "real" (not just in people's minds as social definitions) and in need of serious empirical study. Those problems, and sociological attention to them, are likely to increase dramatically in the coming years.

THEORIES OF THE ENVIRONMENT AND ITS PROBLEMS

Sociological approaches to the environment, and much else, differ depending on the theoretical perspective employed (Preisendorfer and Diekmann 2007). Structural/functional theories tend to focus on large-scale structures and systems and their impact on environmental problems, as well as the ability to deal with them. For example, one line of thinking is that because large-scale structures are differentiated functionally (politically, economically, legally), they have difficulty coming together in order to deal in a unified fashion with environmental problems. The conflict/critical perspective focuses on capitalism and the need for

corporations to grow and to show ever-increasing profits. In other words, capitalism creates a **treadmill of production** in which everyone in the system depends on continuous growth in production and in the economy more generally (K. Gould, Pellow, and Schnaiberg 2008). Such capitalistic needs lead to the reckless exploitation of nonrenewable natural resources and to high levels of production and consumption that have other negative effects on the environment. Among the inter/actionists, some sociologists, especially symbolic interactionists, focus on the ways in which we come to define various environmental issues as problems. Rational choice theorists focus on the fact that there have been great rewards, such as high profits and pay, for those who adversely affect the environment. Conversely, there have been weak, or nonexistent, rewards and even high costs (lower profits, lower wages, higher prices for environmentally friendly products) for those who are interested in being more environmentally responsible. Clearly, from this perspective, the reward and cost structures need to be changed if we hope to induce people to change their behaviour and to take actions that help, rather than hurt, the environment.

URBAN AREAS AND THE ENVIRONMENT

Worth discussing at this point is the relationship between the city and the environment, both because it is a link to the preceding section and because it is an issue of great importance in itself (York and Rosa 2007).

Environmental problems can lead to urbanisation. The extraordinary demands placed on the rural environment by large urban populations can lead to a decline in the ability of rural areas to support those who live there. For example, the need for more natural resources in the city can lead to the depletion of those resources in rural areas. Insatiable need for timber for building purposes can lead to deforestation and the elimination of jobs in the rural lumber industry. Similarly, overuse and abuse of farmland can lead to declining productivity and less farm-related work in rural areas. As a result, many rural residents are forced to move to the city in search of work, thereby increasing urbanisation.

There are also many ways in which cities contribute to environmental degradation. Environmental problems associated with the city include

- pollution from carbon dioxide, or greenhouse gases, through emissions from the large numbers of motor vehicles and centralised power plants that characterise modern cities;

- the paving over of natural habitats associated with increasing urbanisation;

- the encroachment, via urban sprawl, on viable agricultural farmland;

- heat retention in the "treeless concrete jungles of cities" that can greatly worsen the negative health effects of heat waves (York and Rosa 2007:1423); and

- the massive creation of waste, such as organic matter rich in nutrients, that could be used as fertiliser to benefit the environment in rural areas but that becomes by-products in need of disposal in the cities (sewage treatment plants that use a lot of energy).

In addition, environmental toxins spread within the cities, and the presence of environmental pollutants has led to increasing numbers of health problems, such as rising rates of respiratory illnesses (asthma) among children and adults—especially the urban poor.

Although the city has been the cause of these and many other environmental problems, this linkage is not inevitable. New forms of urban development could be less ecologically destructive. Majora Carter, founder of the Majora Carter Group (MCG), states that "it was a pollution-based economy that brought us to the environmental breaking point we face today. [And she advises that we] restructure that system so that a new green economy will benefit us in many more ways than simply raising our GDP [gross domestic product]" (Majora Carter Group 2009). Her consulting group works to create simple green projects that not only physically improve urban neighbourhoods but also foster local community economies, provide "green" and sustainable jobs, and reduce health and social problems. And by creating green spaces, community residents develop a stronger sense of their ability to accomplish important tasks.

GLOBALISATION AND THE ENVIRONMENT

The environment performs three general functions for humans and other species, but overuse and abuse can create great environmental problems (Dunlap and Catton 2002; Dunlap and Jorgenson 2012). First, the environment is kind of a "supply depot" that provides us with the natural resources needed for life to exist. Among the renewable and nonrenewable resources provided are air, water, food, shelter, and the resources needed for industries to operate. However, overuse of such renewable resources as water and such nonrenewable resources as fossil fuels can deplete, if not empty, the supply depot.

Second, in consuming those resources humans produce wastes of various kinds. In this case, the environment serves as a "sink" to absorb or dispose of the waste. However, it is possible to produce so much waste that the environment cannot absorb it all. For example, too much sewage can lead to water pollution.

Third, the environment provides us with living space, or "habitat—where we live, work, play, and travel" (Dunlap and Jorgenson 2012:530).

Smog and air pollution blanket Mong Kok, one of Hong Kong's busiest districts. Human activity and the crowding of modern cities have led to rising levels of carbon dioxide, methane, and other greenhouse gases in the atmosphere, worsening air pollution and contributing to illness and death.

However, having too many people in a living space creates numerous problems associated with over-crowding and overpopulation.

In terms of all three functions, it could be argued that humans are beginning to exceed the "carrying capacity" of Earth. Our **ecological footprint**, the demands we place on the Earth's ecology, has come to exceed what the planet can supply. We are, in effect, eating our host, Planet Earth (Rees 1992).

There is great global inequality in these three functions and in who benefits from the size of our ecological footprint. Basically, the developed nations adversely affect the ability of the less developed nations to perform these functions. For example, they use less developed nations as supply depots for natural resources for which they have historically underpaid. In the process, they often adversely affect the ability of the less developed nations to continue to produce these resources. Developed nations also often ship e-waste—that is, discarded electronic equipment—to developing countries, polluting them and their people with the minerals and chemicals in this dangerous debris. This, in turn, despoils the living space and the eco-system of those developing countries.

While environmental problems can and do affect specific countries, the vast majority of these problems are global in nature and scope. As a result, one of the most enduring and important issues in the study of the environment involves its relationship to globalisation (Stevis 2005). The environment is inherently global. That is, we all share the atmosphere, are warmed by the sun, and are connected by the oceans (Yearley 2007). Further, much that relates to the environment has an impact on and flows around the world, or at least large portions of it (for example, through weather patterns).

In spite of this, the earliest work on globalisation, as in sociology, tended to ignore the natural environment, or at least to underplay its significance (Munton and Wilkening 2007). However, in the 1980s and 1990s the environmental movement (Rootes 1999) made great progress; a number of notable problems, especially the depletion of the ozone layer (Liftin 2007) and global climate change, brought the environment to the fore as a global issue.

A young boy separates various parts of discarded computers in a recycling garage in New Delhi, India. The world is headed for a devastating deluge of electronic waste as new products replace old ones at a dizzying pace. In some countries, the amount of e-waste being produced could increase 500 percent over the next decade, posing environmental and health hazards from the decay of toxic materials.

In the case of these two problems, it is clear that many throughout the world play a major role in their creation and that virtually everyone in the world will suffer their diverse consequences. In that sense they are global in nature.

Global Issues Challenged

However, though the idea that environmental problems are global issues may seem indisputable, this view has been challenged in various ways:

- Not everyone or every part of the world is equally to blame for the most pressing global environmental problems. It is clear that those from the most developed countries are disproportionately responsible for them.

- Such problems do not, and will not, affect everyone and all areas of the world in the same way. For example, the rise of the level of the seas as a result of global warming will mostly affect those who live in coastal areas or on islands. Such areas will also be most affected by the expected increase in the number and severity of hurricanes.

Tornadoes are also expected to increase, although they are likely to affect some geographic areas, such as the American Midwest, more than others. To take another example, because of their greater wealth, those in the Global North will be better able to find ways of avoiding or dealing with all but the most catastrophic of the problems caused by global warming. On the other hand, those in the Global South will be far more defenseless and have fewer options. Therefore, they will suffer more from environmental problems of various kinds.

- There are global differences in the importance accorded to, and the dangers associated with, these problems. For example, many in the developed North are highly concerned about global warming, while many in the Global South feel that they are faced with many more pressing problems, such as health problems related to disease and malnutrition, as well as the decline of available drinking water. As a result, in the South global warming seems, at best, a remote difficulty that will need to be confronted later, if at all.

- The main sources of environmental problems change. For example, the centre of manufacturing, with its associated pollutants, has been moving from the United States to China.

THE LEADING ENVIRONMENTAL PROBLEMS

There are many important environmental problems, and we touched on several in the preceding sections. In this section we deal with a few in more depth, including the depletion of the ozone layer, the destruction of natural habitats, the adverse effects on marine life, the decline in fresh water, and global warming.

Ozone Depletion

A layer of ozone exists in the stratosphere that absorbs between 97 percent and 99 percent of the sun's ultraviolet light. Without that level of protection, excessive ultraviolet light would cause many health problems in humans, such as increases in skin cancer and cataracts. However, since the 1970s scientists have observed a significant deterioration of the ozone layer. Furthermore, a much greater degree of depletion—an "ozone hole"—has been observed in Earth's polar regions. A major cause of ozone depletion was the increasingly wide-scale use of Styrofoam and the chlorofluorocarbons used in refrigeration and air-conditioning units, as well as in the propellant in aerosol cans. Because of growing alarm over the negative effects of ozone depletion, an aggressive campaign was mounted to reduce the use of those products thought to cause the problem. As a result of the success of that campaign, many of the causes of ozone depletion have been or are being phased out. In the eyes of one expert, "ozone depletion has stabilized globally and long-term recovery seems underway" (Ungar 2012). Time will tell whether we have, in fact, actually solved the problem of ozone depletion.

Destruction of Natural Habitats

Natural habitats such as the "forests, wetlands, coral reefs, and the ocean bottom" are being destroyed across the globe, often as the result of population growth and conversion of some of those natural habitats into human habitats (Diamond 2006:487). Today, the most notable deforestation in the world is taking place in the Amazon rain forest (mostly in Brazil) ("Welcome to Our Shrinking Jungle" 2008), but other parts of the world are also destroying/losing their forests. The Amazon forest is being decimated to allow the area to be "developed"—to create farms and areas for livestock to graze—and for the creation of more human settlements. Brazil's forests are so huge and they play such a large role in the global ecology, that their destruction will have negative effects on the world as a whole. For example, the burning of all of those felled trees releases large amounts of carbon dioxide that drift into the atmosphere and flow around the globe, contributing to global warming. The loss of the forest leads to other problems for humans, including a diminished supply of timber and of other raw materials. It is also of great concern, especially in the areas undergoing deforestation, because forests protect against soil erosion, are essential to the water cycle, and provide habitats for many plants and animals. The loss of the other natural habitats, such as wetlands, coral reefs, and the ocean bottom, will also have a variety of negative consequences for life on Earth. For example, the decline of coral reefs due to runoff from agriculture adversely affects the sea life that exists in and around them.

Adverse Effects on Marine Life

A large fraction of the protein consumed by humans comes from fish and, to a lesser extent, shellfish. Without seafood, more people would need to rely on meat for protein, and livestock can be grown only at great cost and with great damage to the environment as well as human health. Aquaculture, which involves growing seafood under controlled conditions such as fish farms, is not an adequate replacement for the loss of natural fishing areas because it causes a whole series of ecological and other problems (Goldburg 2008; Young and Matthews 2010).

Marine life in the world's oceans has been greatly diminished by overfishing. According to the United Nations Food and Agriculture Organization, 69 percent of the world's most important fisheries can be considered either "fully exploited" or "overexploited." An early twenty-first-century study concluded that industrial fishing had led to a 90 percent decline in swordfish, tuna, and marlin populations. In 2007, more than 100 scientists signed a letter saying that unless subsidies to the fishing sector were scaled back, the damage to the oceans would become irreversible in only a few decades (Khatchadourian 2007).

A major culprit in the decimation of marine life is industrial fishing. As the amount of sea life declines, the fishing industry compensates by using much more industrialised and intensive techniques. Among these industrial techniques is the use of huge dragnets that catch large numbers of fish, including many that are not wanted and are discarded. Bottom trawling involves dragging nets along that seafloor, a process that can destroy the ocean bottom. Modern industrial fishing is also characterised by the use of factory ships that process the fish on board rather than waiting until

Manufacturing and mining processes contribute vast amounts of pollutants to water sources such as this Colorado drainage reservoir.

the ships return to port. These technologies contribute to overfishing and in the process destroy complex ecosystems.

Decline in Fresh Water

Water is becoming an increasingly important global issue, or rather raising a number of different issues (Conca 2006; Hoekstra 2012). In fact, there are many today who talk in terms of an imminent "water crisis" in some parts of the world, including California and Nevada in the United States (Subramaniam, Whitlock, and Williford 2012). However, it is the less developed countries in the world that are most likely to be affected by a water crisis because more and more manufacturing, a process that requires large amounts of water, takes place there. In addition, they are the least likely to have environmental regulations to prevent problems or to be able to do very much about the problems once they begin. Among the concerns about water are the following:

- *Water inequality.* Canada and the United States have water footprints double that of the world average and four times that of China. While many in the world have little access to water, many Canadians and Americans "water their gardens, fill their swimming pools, and . . . consume a lot of meat, which significantly enlarges their water footprint" (Hoekstra 2012:2207).

- *Water pollution.* Humans contribute to the pollution of water through manufacturing processes, mining, agriculture, and not adequately treating and managing waste (especially fecal matter). One result of this pollution is an increase in waterborne diseases, especially those that affect children (Jorgenson and Givens 2012).

- *Marine pollution.* This involves "a disruption to the *natural ecology* of water systems, particularly oceans, as a direct or indirect result of human activity" (T. Burns 2012:1324). Among the most important causes of marine pollution is the dumping into the oceans of the herbicides, pesticides, and fertilisers used in modern industrial agriculture.

- *Flooding.* Experts contend that because warmer air holds more moisture, heavy precipitation is expected to increase in some regions as a result of global warming.

- *Increasing scarcity of water.* There is a possibility that the flow of water could slow or stop completely, at least in some locales. Some nations are forced to choose between the uses of water, for example, whether more of the available supply should be allocated for drinking or for irrigating crops (Martin 2008). There are tensions within nations (such as Ethiopia) and between nations (India and Pakistan)—even the possibility of war—over increasingly scarce water supplies. There is likely to be an increase in the number, and an escalation of the actions, of social movements involved in efforts to

deal with water scarcity, as well as other issues that relate to water.

Desertification is the decline in the water supply as a result of the degradation and deterioration of soil and vegetation (Glantz 1977). Water, once considered a public good, is increasingly becoming a valuable and privatised commodity as many places run low on drinkable water. Another preventable decline in water supply is caused by wasting those supplies; for example, nearly two thirds of all water used for irrigation, and as much as half of city water supplies, is wasted due to leaky pipes.

Although we usually think of water as abundant and readily accessible, the fact is that over a billion people do not have reliable sources of safe drinking water and more than 2 billion do not have adequate sanitation systems (Conca 2007). The poorest areas of the globe (largely in the South), and the poorest people within those areas, especially children and women, experience a disproportionate share of water-related problems. The situation is apt to grow worse in coming years; it is possible that half the world's population will be faced with water-related problems by the 2030s.

Freshwater ecosystems (rivers, lakes, wetlands) are under increasing stress from dams and pollution. Also threatened are the invaluable services those ecosystems provide, such as controlling floods and filtering water supplies.

A less visible water problem involves international trade, especially in agricultural and industrial products. For example, when Japan buys crops (which are water-intensive) produced in Canada, pressure is put on Canadian water supplies. People throughout the world are using water from elsewhere on the globe. This is called "virtual water" because almost all the water has been used in production of some commodity—wheat, for example—and no longer exists in the product when it arrives in its destination country. If people do not realise they are using or abusing water, how can they do anything about it?

Astounding quantities of water can be used to produce commodities consumed as much as halfway around the world. For example, according to one estimate, it takes about 140 liters of rainwater to produce enough coffee beans to make one cup of coffee. We begin to get a sense of the magnitude of the water problem produced by the consumption of virtual water when we multiply that level of water consumption by the many cups of coffee, to say nothing of all the other commodities, that people consume on a daily basis throughout the world (Hoekstra and Chapagain 2008).

Global warming (see next page) will make some parts of the world wetter, but other parts will grow drier. As a general rule, already wet areas will grow wetter, already dry areas drier; both floods and droughts will intensify. It is in the latter that we are likely to see increasingly desperate and expensive efforts to find water by, for example, drilling ever deeper for underground water supplies (Struck 2007). Among the areas likely to grow drier are southern Europe, the Middle East, South Australia, Patagonia, and the southwestern United States. In May 2008, Barcelona became the first major city in the world to begin importing large amounts of water by ship to help deal with a long-term drought and a precipitous drop in water resources. There are predictions of Dust Bowl–like conditions in the American Southwest and the resulting possibility of mass migrations. In Mexico similar conditions may lead to mass migrations to Mexican cities *and* to still more migration to the United States. Such an increase threatens to create even far greater problems and animosities than already exist in the United States as a result of legal, and especially undocumented, immigration from Mexico. In more general terms, we are increasingly likely to see the emergence of an entirely new group of people in the world— climate refugees.

Another problem traceable to global warming is the melting of mountaintop glaciers that are an important source of the supply of drinking water to many people in the world. As those glaciers melt and fail to re-form fully, they will produce less and less water for those who need the water to survive. The affected populations, too, are likely to become climate refugees, and they are apt to come into conflict with residents of the still water-rich areas to which they are likely to move. In Canada the impact on the Inuit people will be especially debilitating because so much of their livelihood, and culture, depends upon the environment, and massive changes are expected via global warming in Canada's North.

Global Warming

Humans and their industries have produced greenhouse gases that have damaged the atmosphere and in the view of most experts are leading to a dramatic rise in the temperature of the Earth. During the twentieth century Earth's temperature rose by about 0.74 degrees centigrade; projections for the twenty-first century are for a rise of between 2 and 8 degrees centigrade. Because of the accumulation of greenhouse gases, heat generated by the sun that would ordinarily be reflected back into the atmosphere is trapped and "radiated back to the Earth at a greater rate than before" (T. Beer 2012). Great concern these days is focused on the burning of fossil fuels (coal, gas, oil), the resulting emission of gases (carbon dioxide), and the role they play in the accumulation of greenhouse gases and global warming. Rates of carbon dioxide emissions, mainly from industrialised countries, increased by 80 percent between 1970 and 2004 and have grown by 3 percent a year since 2000.

There is little or no doubt, at least among scientists, that global warming is a real phenomenon with human-induced causes, most notably the huge increase in greenhouse gases. Furthermore, the dominant view is that global warming is already

Global activist organisations have taken steps to reduce the magnitude of environmental problems around the world. In 2008, members of the Canadian-born environmental group Greenpeace protested the Japanese government's support of commercial whaling—a practice opposed by many western nations.

GL⦻BALISATION

The Paradox of Fiji's Bottled Water

We have increasingly witnessed the "commodification of water" (Hoekstra 2012:2206). As many places in the world run low on drinkable water, water is becoming an increasingly important commodity to be bought and sold like any other commodity. For example, there are now large global water companies that control vast reserves of water. This leads to the fear of huge increases in the price of water and increasing inequality, such that the rich can afford all the water they want while the poor are increasingly forced to ration their water consumption. Profit-making water companies would also be inclined to overexploit water supplies in order to increase profits, thereby diminishing the global supply of water (Shiva 2002).

There has been an enormous growth in the global distribution and sale of one type of commodified water—bottled water. Bottled water has become a global commodity, commanding relatively high prices. However, it is too expensive for the poorest people in the world, who may be most in need as a result of the decline in available water supplies. Sales of bottled water are most likely to thrive in the relatively well-to-do areas of the world, where there is still plenty of free drinkable water (Wilk 2006a). But instead of using this inexpensive and accessible water, increasing numbers of people, especially in the Global North, are buying bottled water, which is sometimes shipped in, at great cost and with profoundly negative effects on the environment, from distant locales. All sorts of environmental problems are related to, for example, the great use of fuel by airplanes and ships that transport the bottled water around the world.

One of the most outrageous examples of this is Fiji Water, with $150 million in sales per year. The water is literally produced and bottled in Fiji in the South Pacific and transported thousands of miles to places including New York and London. Aware of the danger it poses to the environment, Fiji Water has announced plans to use renewable energy (build a windmill to power its bottling plant), preserve forests, and cut its carbon footprint by, for example, shipping its bottles of water by sea to the East Coast of North America, rather than by truck from the Pacific (after it gets there by ship). Of course, this says nothing about the environmental cost of shipping to either coast. In spite of actions such as these, the executive director of the Rainforest Action Network said, "Bottled water is a business that is fundamentally, inherently and inalterably unconscionable" (C. Deutsch 2007:C3).

well advanced and is progressing rapidly. Many scientists have further added that some negative effects of global warming, such as the thawing of *permafrost*, soil that has been at or below the freezing point of water for more than two years, will be irreversible once they start.

However, there are still a few scientists and many lay dissenters who take the view that global warming and the resulting climate changes that are now occurring are not the result of human actions but simply part of a natural cycle. Further, they argue that we will soon return to the cold part of the cycle when, for example, much of the ice in the Arctic and Antarctica will refreeze, as will the glaciers atop the world's highest mountains. Some believe that the rise in global temperature is traceable to changes in the energy output of the sun; they also question the computer models that are being used to make future projections about temperature rise. However, scientific data that measure global surface temperatures

650,000 years into the past show that our world is warmer now (and likely to get warmer) than it ever has been through the many cycles of warming and cooling in the past (Lüthi et al. 2008).

Global warming is expected to adversely affect humans in a number of different ways (D. Brown 2007). It will bring with it more, and more intense, heat waves, and excessive heat can be deadly. A heat wave in Europe in 2003, the worst in almost 500 years, caused about 30,000 deaths from heat-related illnesses. The aging of the population throughout much of the developed world makes more people vulnerable to being made ill and dying due to excessive heat. Urbanisation also increases the likelihood of death since cities can become heat islands. Other factors making death from excessive heat more likely are being very young, ill, poor, and among those who lack the ability to move away from super-heated areas. However, there are things that can be done to mitigate the dangers of heat stress, such as greater use of air-conditioning (although many people in the world have no access to it or cannot afford it; furthermore, it causes other problems, such as a huge demand on energy sources), greater awareness of the dangers associated with excessive heat, and better medical treatment of those afflicted with heat stress. Of course, those in the North are much more likely to be able to avail themselves of these mechanisms.

Sea levels are projected to rise dramatically, especially as the glaciers melt. During the twenty-first century a conservative estimate is that sea levels will rise about one meter. Approximately 100 million people in the world, mostly in Asia and on island nations, live within a meter of sea level, and their homes would be washed away by such a rise in the sea level. However, this does not take into account the melting of the Greenland and West Antarctic ice sheets, which could add 10 or more meters to the rising seas. In such a case, much larger areas of both the less developed and developed worlds would be inundated.

More severe storms will lead to more deaths, especially from increased flooding due to those storms. One example of this phenomenon is the death of almost 140,000 people in Myanmar as a result of a typhoon, especially its storm surge, in May 2008. The residents of coastal areas are in particular danger due to storm surges. Extreme variations in weather may lead to more droughts and shortages of water. Food production may not increase as rapidly as expected, with the result that the number of the world's hungry will increase.

Rising temperatures will speed up chemical reactions and worsen pollution from ozone and soot. Deaths from ozone pollution (mostly among those with lung or heart problems) could increase by 5 percent by 2050. Pollen production could increase, adversely affecting those with asthma and other allergies.

Waterborne diseases (cholera) will increase with higher temperatures and more torrential rains. Food-borne infections (salmonella) will also increase with hotter weather.

Diseases caused by animals and insects may increase. For example, it is expected that there will be an increase in malaria and dengue borne by mosquitoes. Exposure to malaria is expected to increase by 25 percent in Africa by 2100. However, as noted in Chapter 13, actions can be taken to mitigate the problem, such as controlling the mosquito population with pesticides (although they pose many other hazards [Carson 1962]), greater use of bed nets (especially by pregnant women and children), and better medical care. Other diseases of this type that are likely to become more prevalent are yellow fever, also carried by mosquitoes, and Lyme disease, carried by ticks (D. Brown 2007).

GLOBAL RESPONSES

Many global environmental problems, especially global warming, are traceable to capitalist economic development (Antonio and Brulle 2012). That is, as economies grow larger and more successful, they are likely to do increasing damage to the environment in the ways in which they produce things (factories that pollute) and what they produce (automobiles that pollute still further), for example. As concerned as nation-states are becoming about damage to the environment, they are not about to either give up the fruits of economic development or cease seeking to become more developed.

PUBLIC SOCIOLOGY

Robert J. Brulle on the Environment, in His Own Words

Over the last four years, I have been engaged in examining the cultural and political dynamics of climate change in the United States. As a highly contentious issue, this topic has attracted a lot of press attention. In addition, it has spawned a spirited and sometimes nasty series of blogs. Given my topic of research, it was only a matter of time until I was contacted by *The New York Times* for an interview.

Having never been interviewed by the elite press, I was quite unprepared for the experience. I was asked a whole series of specific questions, and the reporter drove the entire conversation. I was unable to really provide an overall perspective on my work, and, in the end, the reporter found a sentence or two that complemented the story idea that he had already developed. In effect, I became a footnote used to legitimate the story's frame.

I learned a great deal from this experience. Reporters are under great time pressure to create an interesting story. The days of long investigative journalism have disappeared. Additionally, the print news has to compete with blogs for readership. To be effective in this arena, scholars need to take this into account and be prepared for an interview. Having been interviewed dozens of times now, I regularly prepare for every interview to ensure that my viewpoint is accurately conveyed.

Whenever I get a press inquiry, I do not agree to an interview on the spot. Rather, I set a time in the very near future. This allows me to do some preparation. I then research the media outlet, and see what sort of things the reporter has written in the past. This prepares me for the kinds of interview questions I will receive. Then I figure out what I want the reporter to take away from the interview. Basically, this is a one-line summary of the narrative I want to tell to the reporter. I then develop talking points to back up this narrative.

For example, in one interview, I was asked about my opinion of a climate change television advertising campaign. The actual sociological literature on this topic is quite complex and discusses the role of media in the public sphere, the psychological processing of messages, public opinion formation, and the public reception of scientific information. If I went with the seminar response, I knew I would get nowhere. So I developed a metaphor about toothpaste advertising. There is a lot of competition out there, and so each toothpaste needs to develop and maintain its own brand. Additionally, the advertisements need to be repeated, as the information provided fades quickly over time. Applying this to advertising to create interest in climate change, I maintained that it would probably only create a short-lived interest level, and interest would fade. In addition, it wouldn't work to create real knowledge and commitment to action to address climate change. Here I focused on the need for face-to-face engagement and creation of a community learning experience. So I brought concepts of media attention, civil society, and democratic deliberation into the interview, but never used those terms. You can see it for yourself in *The New York Times* (Broder 2009). For all that effort, my comments received about six lines of text in the article. That is actually quite a bit of coverage. Generally, the reporter accepted my framing.

Most sociologists will never really function directly as journalists. Rather, they will be in the role that I was in—a knowledgeable source. With a little effort and thought, sociologists can use those opportunities to convey sociological knowledge to the public.

SOURCE: Printed with the permission of Robert J. Brulle, PhD.

As a result, a variety of efforts have arisen to at least reduce the magnitude of environmental problems. We have seen the emergence of a variety of environmental movements, such as Greenpeace, oriented to this goal (Caniglia 2012). Involved in these movements, but more general in nature, is the increase in environmental activism (D. Fisher 2012). Activists are generally interested in either protecting some aspect of the environment such as a coral reef or a virgin forest, or protesting environmental hazards such as toxic waste or the site of a garbage dump. In terms of globalisation, either activists can oppose the global exportation of environmental problems, or they can support international efforts and treaties to mitigate these problems. While some environmental movements and activists may want to slow or stop economic development, many favour sustainable development.

Sustainable Development

Sustainable development involves economic and environmental changes that meet the needs of the present, especially of the world's poor, without jeopardising the needs of the future. While the focus of sustainable development is on physical sustainability, there must also be a concern for equity within the current generation and for future generations.

Globalisation can be seen as either a threat or a boon to sustainability. As a threat, globalisation can lead to unsustainable development by reducing the regulatory capacities of governments over environmental threats. Globalisation can aid sustainable development by the spread of modern, less environmentally destructive technologies and the creation of standards for more efficient resource utilisation. Globalisation can also lead to a greater demand for cleaner environments.

There are a number of dimensions to the relationship between globalisation and sustainability. First, there is the *economic* dimension and the issue of whether economic development irretrievably destroys the environment or whether with economic development comes the desire and the ability to better control the factors that are adversely affecting the environment. Second, *technology* can be seen as both producing environmental degradation and creating the possibility of limiting the damage. It can do so through the dissemination of information about environmental problems and their causes via the mass media or the global spread of green technologies. Third, there is the dimension of *awareness* and whether the global media create greater awareness of environmental problems and their causes, or whether consumerism, also pushed by the global media, increases people's blindness to these issues. Finally, there is the *politics* of environmentalism with some global organisations, such as the World Trade Organization (WTO), pushing for more economic growth, while many others, such as Greenpeace, are seeking to reduce it or to limit its negative impact on the environment. Overall, then, many aspects of globalisation adversely affect efforts at sustainable development.

A Technological Fix

There is growing interest these days in a "technological fix" for at least some global environmental problems such as global warming. There is a long-standing attraction to finding technological solutions to all social problems. To many, finding new technologies seems far easier and less painful than the much harder task of getting large numbers of people to change their behaviour. That is, people tend to be reluctant to change their consumption patterns and thus prefer the hope of technological fixes to any resultant ecological problems. Furthermore, many industries have vested interests in the continuation of high levels of consumption. Thus, even though a major cause of global warming is the ever-increasing burning of fossil fuels, innumerable industries and people are wedded to it, and many people in other parts of the world would dearly like to do more of it. This is especially the case with the use in highly developed countries of gasoline in automobiles, the increasing number of people in countries such as China and India who can now afford them, and the large numbers in less developed countries who would like to own and drive automobiles. In the face of this huge and growing demand, it is unlikely that calls to cut back on gasoline use are going to be heeded, although much higher oil prices would reduce demand for gasoline—hence the attraction of the search for a technological fix that will solve the problems caused by the burning of gasoline and, more generally, fossil fuels. With such a fix, production and consumption throughout the world can not only continue, but expand further.

Enter "geoengineering" and a series of relatively new proposals for dealing with global ecological problems while leaving untouched and unaddressed the underlying and growing causes of global warming. Among the ideas being discussed are cooling the Earth's poles by injecting chemicals into the upper atmosphere, making clouds more reflective in order to block sunlight, and putting mirrors in space (Dean 2007). Scientific support for these possibilities has been muted for several reasons:

- There is fear that talk of such solutions would encourage people to continue, if not increase, their use of fossil fuels.

- There is great fear that even if some of the proposals do work, they might have a series of unanticipated consequences that will pose problems as great as, or greater than the problems they are designed to help solve.

- These innovations in geoengineering are untried, incredibly difficult, and likely to be extraordinarily expensive.

- There are many other climate-related problems, such as the increasing acidity of the oceans, which would be unaffected by global climate changes produced by such technologies.

Undertaking such projects would require truly global efforts and a massively funded global governance structure. The hope is that already functioning global governance, such as that which organises air traffic control, will be a model for what is needed to deal with global climate problems (Dean 2007).

SUMMARY

This chapter deals with the interrelated issues of population, urbanisation, and the environment. A great deal of attention has been devoted to population growth and the fear of a population explosion. Much of that fear, though not all, has dissipated in recent years. While overall fertility rates are dropping globally, the world's population continues to increase, though at a declining rate. Historically, population decline has not been considered as important as growth, but it has recently come to the fore in various parts of the world. Population decline can weaken nations in various ways, but it can also have benefits. Demography is the scientific study of population, especially its growth and decline. Demographers focus on three main processes: fertility, people's reproductive behaviour, mortality, death or death rates within a population, and migration, the movements of people and the impact of these movements on both sending and receiving societies.

Urbanisation is the process by which an increasing percentage of a society's population comes to be located in relatively densely populated urban areas. Urbanism is the distinctive way of life that emerges in, and is closely associated with, urban areas. Simmel and Wirth were among the earliest sociologists to examine both the positive and negative aspects of city life. Cities are large, permanent settlements that are cosmopolitan in that they are open to a variety of external, including global, influences. The most important of the world's cities are global cities. Megacities are cities with populations greater than 8 million. While cities often deal with global problems of terrorism and overcrowding, they also play a positive role in the development of societies around the world.

Suburbs are the surrounding communities that are adjacent to, but outside the political boundaries of, central cities. Early suburbs were generally quite homogeneous. Edge cities are on or near major highways, have corporate offices that employ many people, and have important commercial and consumption centres, such as shopping malls. Looking for cheaper land and housing, people have pushed even farther out into areas between the suburbs and rural areas, known as exurbia. In some cities, gentrification has lured some middle-class residents back to those cities' urban centres.

Ecology is the study of people and their relationship to one another as well as to the larger context in which they live. Increasing environmental problems have led sociologists to examine the environment more closely. Structural/functional theorists examine the ability of large-scale structures to deal with these problems. Conflict/critical theorists focus on capitalism and the impact on the environment of corporate expansion and the increasing use of natural resources. Inter/actionists focus more on the ways in which we come to define various environmental issues as problems. The majority of environmental problems are global in nature and scope.

Scientists agree that global warming is a human-induced phenomenon that is deeply impacting the globe. Global climate change is likely to make already wet parts of the world wetter, while already dry places are likely to get even drier. One way people have tried to stem the causes of global environmental problems has been to engage in sustainable development. The relationship between globalisation and sustainability has a number of dimensions, including economic, technological, and political, as well as that of media awareness. While geoengineering provides some hope that technological advances might be able to deal with some of the problems associated with global warming, the cost and potential consequences of geoengineering mean that technological solutions are still a long way off, if ever viable.

KEY TERMS ···

- Aerotropolis   565
- Asylum seekers   555
- Birthrate   544
- Cities   558
- Demography   542
- Demographers   542
- Desertification   578
- Ecology   571
- Ecological footprint   575
- Edge cities   563
- Exurbia   563
- Fantasy city   569
- Fertility   545
- Gated communities   562
- Gentrification   565
- Global cities   566
- Labour migrants   555

- Local   566
- Megacities   567
- Megalopolis   561
- Metropolis   561
- Migration   545
- Mortality   545
- Refugees   554
- Suburbanisation   561
- Suburb   561
- Sustainable development   583
- Treadmill of production   573
- Undocumented immigrants   555
- Urban   558
- Urban sociology   560
- Urbanism   558
- Urbanisation   558
- World cities   567

THINKING ABOUT SOCIOLOGY ···

1. How does the "demographic dividend" differ from the "financial time bomb"? Overall is Canada in a period of a demographic dividend or a financial time bomb? Why?

2. What social factors can impact a country's fertility rate? How are fertility rates related to the level of development of a country?

3. According to demographic transition theory, what role do technological advances play in changing demographics? Why is "development the best contraceptive"?

4. How does the nature of today's migrants differ from the nature of migrants in the past? In contrast, how are the barriers to migration consistent with those of the past? How have the "push" and "pull" factors changed in the global age?

5. What are the arguments against restrictions on international migration? How do these fit into today's popular and political dialogue regarding immigration in Canada?

6. Georg Simmel calls the city a "frightful leveller." How does this "levelling" allow for more freedom than a small town or a rural area? Do you agree or disagree?

7. How are McMansions, strip malls, and edge cities a sign of the McDonaldization of society? How are originally suburban models making the distinction between these areas less clear and meaningful? How has gentrification worked in a city with which you are familiar?

8. What makes cities cultural and consumption centres? How is a "fantasy city" different from a traditional urban area? In what ways are fantasy cities related to processes of Americanisation?

9. The chapter cites environmental problems arising in cities, yet points to the possibility of new forms of urban development that could be less ecologically destructive. How can sustainable

development create a more ecologically friendly city? How would this development differ from that of the last 200 years?

10. Do you think that globalisation is ultimately a threat or a boon to sustainability? What current evidence would you cite to support your position?

APPLYING THE SOCIOLOGICAL IMAGINATION

This chapter examines global differences in perception of environmental issues. For this activity, choose one highly developed and one less developed country, and compare and contrast their environmental policies with those of Canada. How does each country approach global warming?

Based on the chapter, why do you suppose these countries have similar or different approaches to environmental policy? How does this reflect their positions in a global system of stratification? What are the potential consequences of their positions?

ACTIVE SOCIOLOGY

One thing that sociologists are interested in regarding the environment is how our understanding of environmental issues impacts social behaviour, norms, and policies. Considering that, how do you suppose websites such as Craigslist, eBay, and Listia have been influenced by our awareness of environmental issues? As our society has become increasingly materialistic, there is a need to do something with our discarded items. How do the sites, including those listed above, serve an environmental function? Go to each of these sites and explore the types of used items that are for sale. Choose one type of item (electronics, clothing, toys, etc.) and track examples of what is for sale in those areas on these sites. What is the age and condition of the items? How much do they end up selling for? If there are many items in these categories, why do you think people still buy new instead of used? Do you think an increasing awareness of environmental issues encourages people to buy used? Why or why not? List an item that you no longer need on one of these sites. Does there appear to be high demand for the item? Explain.

STUDENT STUDY SITE

Visit the student study site at **www.sagepub.com/ritzercanadian** for additional web quizzes for further review.

Resistance Worldwide

Recent years have seen a marked increase in the prevalence, significance, effectiveness, and impact of protests around the globe. The Arab Spring blossomed across the Middle East and Northern Africa, Europeans opposed austerity measures, Occupy movements set up camp in nearly a hundred countries, and protesters cried out against corrupt Russian elections and Chinese land grabs — and that was just in 2011 and 2012. Time will tell the total impact of these resistance movements, but for some, the consequences will be much more immediately felt.

During the December 2011 trial of Hosni Mubarak in Cairo, Egypt, protesters held posters displaying images of people allegedly killed during the country's bloody revolution. Mubarak was charged with ordering the killing of approximately 850 people during the 18-day uprising that ousted him from power in February 2011.

Originating in New York City's Zuccotti Park, the Occupy movement was quickly joined by frustrated citizens around the world. Here, police disperse protesters attempting to occupy the historic Mendiola Bridge in downtown Manila, Philippines, in reaction to anti-poor policies implemented by President Benigno Aquino III.

A resident holds up a placard that reads, "Return my civil rights" as he listens to speakers during a rally in Wukan, China. Residents of Wukan staged an uprising over land sales for which they were not appropriately reimbursed. The protests were inflamed after the suspicious death of a village representative being held by the police.

An estimated 50,000 demonstrators faced police in London, England's Parliament Square as students protested planned tuition fee increases in December 2011. Students were incensed at the proposal to increase the cap on tuition fees from £3,290 to £9,000. Such a move, argued protesters, would prevent many lower-income students from attending university.

In August 2011, tent cities sprang up in parks along stylish boulevards in Tel-Aviv, Israel, in an attempt to force issues like housing shortages and rising prices onto the government's agenda. The protest rallied more than 300,000 Israelis, the largest protest in Israel's history. The cost of fundamental needs like housing and gas, coupled with high taxation, has placed unprecedented burdens on Israeli households.

Protestors in Athens, Greece, demonstrate in response to the latest round of strict austerity measures proposed by the International Monetary Fund and the European Union. The protest was curated by the Facebook page "Indignants at Syntagma," which had 90,000 fans on the day of the protest.

Demonstrating women wear masks that say "My voice was stolen." The protests, called For Fair Election, were spurred by reports of widespread voter fraud, election irregularities, and illegal campaigning in Russia's 2011 elections.

SOCIAL CHANGE, SOCIAL MOVEMENTS, AND COLLECTIVE BEHAVIOUR

The nearly instantaneous dissemination of up-to-the-minute news and videos across social media networks, combined with the sheer number of interconnected protests, marked Occupy as a truly global social movement.

15

On September 17, 2011, social and political activists took to New York City's Zuccotti Park with supplies, sleeping bags, tents, and a mission to bring attention to the mounting struggles of the lower classes and to end governmental partiality toward corporate and upper-class interests. Representing a budding social movement called Occupy Wall Street, activists established a semipermanent encampment—reminiscent of the shanties and tents set up for the poor during the Great Depression and called Hoovervilles—that served as home base for an ongoing series of demonstrations, marches, and speeches in New York's bustling financial district.

The idea of occupying Wall Street was begun as a "Day of Rage" fashioned after the uprisings that were occurring in the Middle East in 2011. The Vancouver-based nonprofit group Adbusters has been credited in the local Vancouver press as being the originator of the concept "Occupy Wall Street."

Media attention and support from large labour unions, such as the American Federation of Labor and Congress of Industrial Organizations (AFL-CIO) and the Service Employees International Union (SEIU), bolstered the Occupy Wall Street encampment's legitimacy—and its numbers. Large crowds gave rise to new modes of communication, such as the human megaphone, an amplification technique whereby members of a crowd repeat a single speaker's words in unison (often in waves) so that those just out of earshot can hear. The Occupy Wall Street encampment quickly developed a unique culture of its own, with distinct roles, norms, values, and social institutions.

As the Occupy Wall Street encampment endured, Occupy movements fashioned after the original began to appear across the United States and—soon after—the world. Nearly 1,000 Occupy protests *have been documented globally, including several dozen large encampments across the Americas, Europe, Australia, and Asia. Though they upheld the major motivations and organisational structures of the Zuccotti Park protesters, splinter encampments' diverse regional cultures played a significant role in shaping how local encampments operated, what they valued, and how they were perceived by local populations and authority figures.*

Just as regional cultures shape local encampments, the actions of—and reactions to—local encampments flowed outward to shape other encampments and the Occupy movement as a whole. Clashes between police and activists at several Occupy protests, as caught by viral videos depicting police use of riot gear, pepper spray, and semiautomatic weapons, garnered international media attention and affected how some perceived the movement. The nearly instantaneous dissemination of up-to-the-minute news and videos across social media networks, combined with the sheer number of interconnected protests, marked Occupy as a truly global social movement.

Some of the largest Occupy encampments, including Occupy Wall Street and many in Canadian cities, were forcefully emptied by police—though some re-formed in different locations. Whether or not it proves an agent of significant social change, the Occupy movement has certainly been successful in bringing the concerns of those involved to the forefront of public attention. Perhaps more importantly, it has confirmed that we have entered the era of the global social movement. What that means is yet to be seen—we as sociologists have much to learn in the months and years ahead.

as a whole (Sekulic 2007b; Sztompka 1993; Weinstein 2010). Sociologists are concerned with social changes affecting the self-concepts of individuals, the structures of Canada, the global economic and political systems, and much more.

The issue of social change has been at the heart of sociology since its inception. This trend continues to this day, and will be at least as true, if not more true, in the future. Sociology emerged during periods of great social upheaval in the nineteenth century. Early research was shaped by the aftermath of great political and social revolutions in France and America and by the major economic transformation wrought by the Industrial Revolution and the rise of capitalism. For example, Alexis de Tocqueville focused on the nature of democracy brought about by revolution in America (see Chapter 4), while Karl Marx sought to understand the economic changes associated with capitalism (see Chapter 2). The changing nature of the polity and the economy—specifically regarding democracy and capitalism—will continue to be of prime interest to sociologists.

While there has been little social change, at least as yet, as a result of the Occupy movement, social movements in Arab countries that began in late 2010 and continued into 2012 have dramatically changed much of the world. These movements are referred to collectively as the "Arab Spring" (Khondker 2011) and have been discussed several times throughout this text. In Figure 15.1, a macroscopic view of the Occupy movement illustrates its broad impact.

However, it is not just the Arab world that is affected, and perhaps threatened, by the Arab Spring. The Occupy movement was inspired by it, as were protests against the governments in England and Russia. Arab Spring protests reached the borders of Israel, where violent clashes erupted, and could potentially come to Israel's occupied territories. The always tenuous peace between Israel and its Arab neighbours seems far more fragile today than ever before. A new war in that region would have destabilising, if not disastrous, consequences for a large portion of the world.

What is most important for our purposes is that the Arab Spring is an excellent illustration of the major sociological ideas to be discussed in this chapter. It brought about *social change*, and it was

S**ocial change** involves variations over time in every aspect of the social world, ranging from changes affecting individuals to transformations having an impact on the globe

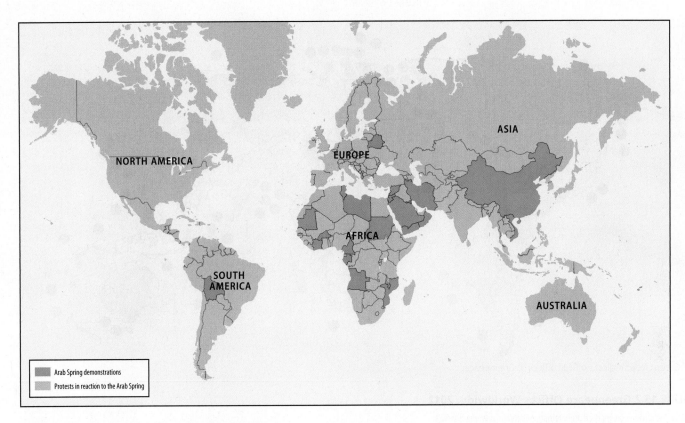

FIGURE 15.1 The Global Impact of the Arab Spring

an excellent illustration of both *collective behaviour* and *social movements*. We begin this discussion with the latter idea.

SOCIAL MOVEMENTS

A **social movement** is a sustained and intentional collective effort, usually operating outside established institutional channels, either to bring about or to retard social change (Cross and Snow 2012; Jasper 2007; Snow, Soule, and Kriesi 2008). Having already touched on both the Occupy and Arab Spring movements, we discuss other examples of social movements later—Greenpeace, the women's movement, the gay and lesbian movements, and the civil rights movement. Following brief overviews of those movements we will discuss various sociological concepts and ideas that help us to better understand these social movements. Finally, although we will not deal with them here, it is worth noting, given the focus in this book on consumption, that there have also been important *consumer* social movements, such as the Consumers' Association

of Canada and the Consumers Union (Glickman 2009).

GREENPEACE

Greenpeace (www.greenpeace.org) is a global environmental movement dedicated to being a voice for our fragile planet (see Figure 15.2). *Green* captures the environmental ethos of the organisation, while *peace* stresses the group's initial focus on combating nuclear weapons testing. Greenpeace was spawned out of protests against U.S. nuclear weapons tests in Alaska.

Formed in the late 1960s and early 1970s, Greenpeace gradually defined its purpose over several years. It began life as a coalition of ideas, protesters, and ideals, fashioned in the hippie haven of Kitsilano in Vancouver, British Columbia (Weyler 2004). Although its precise origins are murky and debated, clarity illuminates its name and initial vision. In the flower-power era of the late 1960s, peace signs and symbols were everywhere. An inspirational figure for Greenpeace, Irving Stowe,

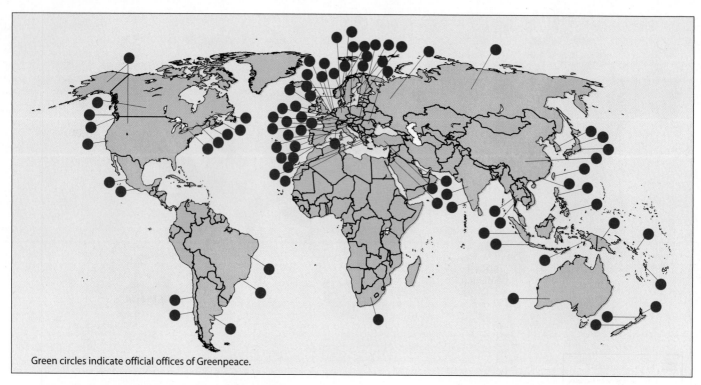

Green circles indicate official offices of Greenpeace.

FIGURE 15.2 Greenpeace Offices Worldwide, 2012

SOURCE: http://www.greenpeace.org/international/en/about/worldwide/#a1

left an early meeting saying "Peace" and flashing a peace sign with his fingers. Bill Darnell, another early group member, responded offhandedly, "Make it a green peace." The two words stuck, getting fused together on badges that were sold as the group's first fundraising initiative.

The initial vision, suggested by Marie Bohlen, was to confront the U.S. military, who were testing a nuclear bomb on Amchitka Island off of Alaska—"Why not sail a boat up there and confront the bomb?" (Weyler 2004:65). Over morning coffee she had captured the defining spirit of the Greenpeace creed, *direct action*. Sailing a boat from Vancouver to Alaska, in the fall of 1971, was not going to be financed by selling badges, so an early obstacle was raising more money. Direct action prevailed—the group made a cold call to Joan Baez, an inspirational folk singer of the 1960s. Baez couldn't help directly, but she sent $1,000 and the phone number of Joni Mitchell. Mitchell agreed to stage a concert at the Pacific Coliseum, to which she brought her boyfriend at the time, James Taylor. Thousands of people attended, with enough money raised to rent a boat to sail to Alaska. However, the boat, dubbed *The Greenpeace*

for the voyage, was intercepted by the U.S. Navy, never getting close to Amchitka.

The news outlets nevertheless had been alerted to the sailing. The audacity of a group of hippies sailing off to "confront the bomb" grabbed the media's attention. The direct action was a "media mindbomb," as Greenpeace dubbed it, with media stories, print, TV, and radio dominating significant portions of the news coverage for weeks. Although the bomb they sought to confront was detonated, subsequently the United States cancelled the rest of the Amchitka testing programme. This was Greenpeace's first success.

Other nations were at the time also testing nuclear weapons. Greenpeace next targeted France and tried to disrupt that country's nuclear weapons programme of atmospheric testing in French Polynesia, in the southern Pacific Ocean. The members of Greenpeace did this by sailing into the area repeatedly to once again confront the bomb. The French navy tried to intercept the Greenpeace vessel, but by now Greenpeace was filming its voyages, with footage supplied to media outlets, and using smaller zodiacs, sailing from the mother ship, to try

DIGITAL LIVING

The Role of Social Media in the Arab Spring

The self-immolation of Mohamed Bouazizi in Tunisia that started the Arab Spring movement, as described in Chapter 1, was preceded by a similar incident three months before (Khondker 2011). However, since that event was not filmed, it could not appear on any social media. The filming of Bouazizi's suicide made possible its wide dissemination through social media. Further, social media had boomed in Tunisia, going from about 28,000 users of Facebook in 2008 to 2 million users in 2010. As a result, at least in part, of this explosion in social media, the 2010 protest led to the downfall of the government while a 2008 protest had been crushed. Although social media triggered the revolution, other factors were also important. For one thing, old media, especially television coverage by Qatar-based Al Jazeera, were a significant force in the revolution. Second, the social and economic conditions in Tunisia were ripe for revolution. Finally, the police and the military were no longer able to contain the revolutionary activities.

The revolution spilled over into Egypt, where social media may have played an even larger role (see Chapter 3). As one leading figure in cyber-activism in Egypt put it, "If you want to free a society just give them Internet access" (cited in Khondker 2011:676). While that may be something of an exaggeration, it did not stop at least one Egyptian parent from naming his daughter "Facebook" in recognition of its role in the revolution. Al Jazeera also played an important role in Egypt, especially since the Egyptian mainstream media there were muffled, if not silenced, by the regime of Hosni Mubarak. A good example of the role of social media occurred in the case of Khaled Said, an Egyptian blogger. In mid-2010, Said was dragged from a cybercafé in Alexandria and beaten to death by police officers. Afterward, the café owner gave a filmed interview that appeared online along with pictures of the blogger's shattered face. Soon an Egyptian and Google executive created a Facebook page titled "We Are All Khaled Said." Within six months it had 350,000 members.

Not only were the social media of great importance in Egypt, but they came to play specialised roles there and elsewhere. As an Egyptian activist indicated in a tweet, "We use Facebook to schedule the protests, Twitter to coordinate, and YouTube to tell the world" (cited in Khondker 2011:677). There is no question that social media are of great importance in contemporary social movements and revolutions, although there is some debate about their importance relative to a variety of other factors (see the next *Digital Living* box).

A Tunisian protester stands next to graffiti praising Facebook and a local radio network during a 2011 demonstration in Tunis, Tunisia's Government Square.

to evade interception. The French also allegedly beat up one of the Greenpeace protesters, a beating that was captured on film. The photographed incident was broadcast worldwide. The French secret service also planted a bomb on a Greenpeace vessel, and the subsequent explosion killed someone on the ship. This increased the visibility and support that Greenpeace was receiving internationally.

Greenpeace has unleashed many spectacular protests. Here two supporters unfurl a climate change banner on the side of the CN Tower in Toronto, on the occasion of a George Bush visit to the city.

Greenpeace also began to expand its focus, still targeting nuclear weapons testing and nuclear energy, but also protesting the killing of whales, the spread of toxic chemicals, the drilling for oil in the Arctic, and much, much more (see www.greenpeace.org). The tactics still involve direct action, with media outlets tipped off about protests. The tactics also frequently involve what the group calls "witnessing" or "bearing witness." The presence of Greenpeace protesters highlights an activity that they find objectionable, offering a form of passive resistance to the planetary threat of military conflict, of resource exploitation, or of human-induced ecological disaster. The overheated media coverage Greenpeace has consistently generated has brought it a degree of attention and influence far out of proportion to the number of active members of the group.

As an organisation Greenpeace now has an international presence, as it must if it is to successfully confront a set of global issues. Figure 15.2 shows the various locations, around the globe, from where Greenpeace organises campaigns of direct action. Its size and its methods are not without criticism, and dissent within the ranks has been an issue. Local, direct action was the movement's early focus, a focus that is still maintained, but now this local action must be coordinated within a global organisation where the centre and the local don't always see eye to eye on priorities and strategies. Greenpeace is often also criticised for merely staging events of a sensational nature but not offering anything viable by way of concrete, plausible steps toward policies and practices that would be sustainable. The sizzle of sensational escapades can eclipse the policy agenda of the organisation.

Like the other examples to be discussed later, Greenpeace has the basic characteristics of a social movement:

- It is a collective effort directly involving thousands of people from around the world in the organisation, and thousands more as supporters and donors.
- It has been sustained for several years.
- It was brought into being intentionally.
- It is outside established institutional channels since it is not formally affiliated with any political party, religion, or business organisation.

A Sociologist Debates a Journalist: The Internet and Social Movements

Malcolm Gladwell is a journalist who draws on many different fields in his work, especially a number of social sciences, including sociology. (See Chapter 5 for a discussion of his work on the "tipping point" in social change.) Gladwell ranges across not only a number of different academic disciplines but also a great number, and an incredibly wide variety, of social phenomena. In October 2010, before the height of the Arab Spring, he wrote an essay for the *New Yorker* titled "Small Change: Why the Revolution Will Not Be Tweeted." He argued *against* the notion that social activism had been radically transformed by the new social media. More generally, he contested the idea that "Facebook and Twitter and the like upended the traditional relationship between political authority and popular will, consequently making it easier for the less powerful to engage in collective action."

Gladwell based this view on the sociological argument that social media are built on the basis of people who have only "weak ties" with one another (Granovetter 1973; see Chapter 5). He went on to argue that people who are not strongly related to one another are unlikely to come together to engage in high-risk behaviours such as a social revolution. Since part of my research (Tufekci 2010) deals with how Internet use interacts with the composition of people's social networks, I knew that the assertion that social media relationships involve only people with weak ties to one another was wrong. In fact, extensive research shows that people use social media to relate to those with whom they

have *both* strong and weak ties. The telephone is used mostly to talk with close friends and family and not only to talk to acquaintances who live far away. Similarly, most people use Facebook to interact with close friends and family as well as with acquaintances with whom they do not have close ties.

Seeking to correct such errors, I penned a reply to Gladwell on my blog, www .technosociology.org. I argued that social media could well be a major contributor to social change by facilitating connections and collective action among ordinary people, which would otherwise be very hard to coordinate. Also, the Internet allows citizens to circumvent censorship and to express their preferences. Unlike television, which is primarily a one-way medium, ordinary citizens can have a voice via the Internet.

Just a few months after I wrote this blog entry, revolutions in Tunisia and Egypt burst onto the world scene. It was clear that the activists involved in these revolutions were using Facebook, Twitter, YouTube, and other platforms to disseminate information that would otherwise be censored. They were communicating with people with whom they were weakly *and* strongly connected to mobilize the masses in order ultimately to overthrow the existing regimes. Contrary to Gladwell's argument, it was clear in these instances, and in many others, that social media can enable collective change and facilitate social change.

SOURCE: Printed with the permission of Zeynep Tufekci.

- It is an effort to sustain the natural diversity of Planet Earth and support life.

- It is an attempt to bring about substantial social change in how humans act. The immediate goal of most Greenpeace activism is to raise the consciousness of people about activities that undermine the viability of sustaining planetary life, with the longer-term objective of ending human domination of the planet and refashioning the way we live our lives.

THE CIVIL RIGHTS MOVEMENT

Arguably, one of the most notable social movements (others would argue that the labour movement was of greatest importance), at least for its impact on Canada, was, and may still be, the U.S. civil rights movement (Morris 1984, 2007). Perhaps the key event in its history was the successful 1955 Montgomery, Alabama, boycott of segregated city buses. At the time, blacks had to ride in the back of public buses. Organised locally, it was led by Martin Luther King Jr. (King [1958]

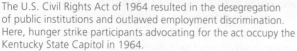

The U.S. Civil Rights Act of 1964 resulted in the desegregation of public institutions and outlawed employment discrimination. Here, hunger strike participants advocating for the act occupy the Kentucky State Capitol in 1964.

Nelson Mandela is widely accepted as the most significant black leader in South Africa. While imprisoned, he became a potent symbol of resistance as the antiapartheid movement gathered strength. Here, women participate in a 1962 demonstration on the steps of the Johannesburg City Hall demanding Mandela's release.

2010). His success there catapulted him into the leadership position within the national civil rights movement. The Montgomery boycott served as a model for future civil rights action and all other subsequent social movements. It emphasised non-violent action, stressed the importance of language, or messaging, especially in what is now called "rights talk," made it clear that internal divisions could be overcome in bringing about effective change, showed the central role of strong leadership linked fundamentally with grassroots support, and demonstrated that the movement could achieve success with little or no outside financial help. And, most importantly, the civil rights movement was successful, which made it an important beacon for other movements that began at the same time or shortly thereafter.

The success of the Montgomery bus boycott led black organisations to become more involved in civil rights organisations. These included the National Association for the Advancement of Colored People (NAACP) formed in 1910, and the Congress of Racial Equality (CORE), organised in 1942. It also led to the formation of new organisations, especially the Southern Christian Leadership Conference (SCLC), and to the creation and active involvement

of innumerable local groups. The actions spurred on by these groups and organisations encountered significant opposition from whites, sometimes leading to violence. A key development in 1960 was the large-scale involvement of black college students in sit-ins at segregated lunch counters throughout the South. These students were crucial to the formation of another new organisation, the Student Nonviolent Coordinating Committee (SNCC), in 1960; in turn, it drew many white students into the movement.

In the 1960s the civil rights movement became a significant force through boycotts, sit-ins, free-dom rides, mass marches, and mass arrests. These involved both blacks and their white allies. In some cases, vicious attacks against black activists gave the movement great visibility and elicited much sympathy from those not initially inclined to support it (just as happened with Greenpeace).

Many of the "invisible leaders" of the civil rights movement were black women, such as Fannie Lou Hamer, Septima Poinsette Clark, and Ella Baker. Their invisibility in leadership positions was an unfortunate by-product of the gender hierarchy as it existed in the 1950s. When women spearheaded successful civil rights campaigns, more "visible" men in the movement took the credit and usurped women's leadership positions (Olson 2002). The many women who participated in the movement served as volunteers, and their numbers far outweighed those of their male counterparts. Even within the radical Black Panther Party, female leadership was greatly limited despite the fact that women, including Elaine Brown, were prominent participants in the party's outreach and advocacy programmes (Brown 1992).

The movement had great success, especially the Civil Rights Act of 1964 banning discrimination on the basis not only of race but also of sex, religion, and national identity. Of course, the larger goal of eliminating racism in America eluded the civil rights movement and continues to elude it to this day (Pager, Western, and Bonikowski 2009).

The global nature of the civil rights movement is especially clear in the antiapartheid movement led by Nelson Mandela in South Africa. Apartheid was a system of racial separation that had been made legal in 1948. Soon thereafter a social movement against it emerged, led by the African National Congress. It garnered great international support and succeeded in achieving its goals in less than a half-century (Waldmeir [1997] 2001). By 1994 both apartheid and white hegemony in South Africa had ended.

THE WOMEN'S MOVEMENT

The women's movement is based on **feminism**, or the belief that women are equal to men, especially socially, politically, and economically (see Chapter 10). It has all of the characteristics of a social movement. It certainly was the intention of many of the (primarily) women involved to bring into being and to maintain the movement. The women's movement has, at least until recently, had to work outside established institutional channels because women were generally denied access to these channels by the men in control of the institutions. The movement has certainly demonstrated, as you will soon learn, that it is sustained both in Canada and around the world (Basu 2010). And it is oriented to improving

dramatically the position of women throughout the world.

The Women's Movement in Canada

The first wave of the women's movement is most concretely traceable to Mary Wollstonecraft's book, published in 1792 as *A Vindication of the Rights of Woman*. Here Wollstonecraft responded directly to debates flowing from the French Revolution (1789–99). One of her central themes was that women deserved a full education so that they could be even more effective in raising their children and in contributing to community welfare. More broadly, and in line with Wollstonecraft's main message, the first wave of the women's movement focused on the recognition of women as subjects worthy of respect, as members of society whose experiences and voices should be both heard and acknowledged. In Canada the "Persons Case" famously highlights this need for recognition.

The British North America Act of 1867 used the word *he* to refer to individuals but *persons* to refer to more than one individual. What did *persons* mean? A British court ruled that "women are persons in matters of pains and penalties, but are not persons in matters of rights and privileges." In 1916 when Emily Murphy was appointed as a chief magistrate in Alberta, her appointment was challenged on the grounds that she was not a person who had "rights and privileges." The Alberta Supreme Court ruled that she was a person and that she could be a chief magistrate, although their ruling applied only in Alberta. Subsequently Murphy was nominated as a candidate for the Senate of Canada, but then–Prime Minister Robert Borden denied her admission on the grounds that she was not a person (at least not in Canada!). The Canadian Supreme Court agreed with Borden, and Murphy was denied a Senate appointment. She and her supporters challenged this ruling at the Judicial Committee of the Privy Council in England. The council, in 1929, ruled that Murphy was indeed a person. This was a significant legal recognition for women in Canada, although a recognition that was very hard fought.

A second wave of the women's movement began in the 1960s, linked to some degree with other protest movements of the time, including the U.S. civil rights movement and the anti–Vietnam War protests. It drew from the first wave but went beyond it in various ways. Several key books, including Simone de Beauvoir's ([1949] 1957) *The Second Sex* and Betty Friedan's (1963) *The Feminine Mystique,* had a strong effect on the movement and articulated a number of its key ideas. More practically, the second wave grew out of women's changing roles during the Second World War (Pierson 1986). Toward the end of World War II over 1 million women were working full-time in the Canadian workforce, a number much, much higher than before the war when mainly young, single women worked full-time. During the war women were recruited to the workforce by the Women's Division of the National Selective Service to fill a void created by so many men and women in active military service in Europe. As a consequence many more women began earning a wage over which they had some control, now being less reliant on a breadwinning man to provide money for household support. As well, day cares were created so children could be cared for while women took on employment. When the war ended, many women went back to being full-time homemakers, but the seeds of change had been sown. Increasing numbers of women continued to seek paid employment after the war ended, and families came increasingly to depend upon two wages.

Fuelled in part by the same sense of injustice that inspired Greenpeace—the feeling that the world was not as fair and equitable as it should be, or that it was too exploitative—the women's movement began to question the treatment of women as second-class citizens, as wage earners of a second order whose pay was not fair in comparison to what male colleagues were earning. Sex discrimination in the workplace became an issue. Sexist language and assumptions that made the contributions of women invisible were increasingly questioned. The unrecognised contribution of women's housework was especially highlighted. In a nutshell, whereas wave one dealt with recognition, wave two highlighted inequality.

The second wave reached its peak between 1965 and 1975. A number of Canadian developments occurred during this period, including the release of the federal report of the Royal Commission on the Status of Women (1970); the appearance of women's studies programmes on university campuses; workplace fights for women's rights to equal pay for work of equal value; and a lengthy pro-choice campaign to legalise early-term abortion. Similar changes in the United States and throughout Europe added to significant changes that altered radically, although did not eclipse, the inequalities women had endured.

The very idea that the women's movement, and feminism more generally, could be understood through the phasing that "waves" imply was itself part of a critique that led to a third wave, or, if you prefer, a more recent reorientation of feminist priorities. The first two waves focused mainly on recognition and inequality as experienced by white middle- and upper-class western women. In Canada a history of the women's movement, based on the first two waves as described above, misrepresents in particular the experiences of women in Quebec, of Aboriginal women, of lesbian and bisexual women, and of women of colour. For example, women in Quebec did not have the right to vote until 1940, long after this had occurred in other provinces. As well, many Aboriginal women and women in Quebec saw issues of colonialism and national sovereignty as closely tied to issues of women's rights, a linkage that was not at all made by most second-wave feminists in the rest of Canada.

The third wave, or reorientation of the women's movement, took much more seriously issues of inclusion. The voices and priorities of minority women—women of colour, lesbians, working-class women—were championed (B. Roth 2004). If the first two waves highlighted recognition and inequality, the third emphasised inclusion.

Some have argued that recent internal conflicts within the movement have led to polarisation. More conservative feminists, the reformists, were primarily concerned with gender equality in the workplace (hooks 2000). Revolutionary feminists criticised the limited goals of the reformists, who focused primarily on the concerns of white middle-class women. They also emphasised the ways in which conservative feminists often acted in a patriarchal and sexist manner toward other women.

In addition, feminism lost its edge because of a decline among women engaging in feminist dialogue in "consciousness-raising" groups (hooks 2000). University campuses had served as one of the few arenas in which feminist politics were discussed. Consequently, feminist politics grew stunted, and some dissatisfied radical feminists left the movement. The rise of opposition groups (REAL Women of Canada) and the emergence of a more powerful conservative movement in federal Canadian politics, the Reform Party initially and then a rebranded Conservative Party, contributed to the development of a sense, at least among some observers and participants, that we had entered a postfeminist era (E. Hall and Rodriguez 2003).

By the early 1990s it was clear that feminism was once again alive and well as the third wave of the women's movement emerged. It has been marked by a reaction against the problems confronted by the movement in the 1980s. The defining characteristics of the third wave have been greater racial, ancestral, and ethnic inclusivity and more of a focus on the problems of minority women, such as racism, classism, and homophobia. The focus has also shifted more in the direction of the place of women in the larger culture and to a variety of specific issues, such as sexual harassment, violence against and sexual abuse of women, and women's body image. The turn to the Internet, and the rise of cyberfeminism (Haraway 1991; Wajcman 2010), can also be seen as part of the third wave. While it is using the latest technologies and is far more internally differentiated than ever before, the third wave continues to draw on the first two waves (R. C. Snyder 2008). It is fusing the old and the new in an effort to adapt feminism to the rapidly changing realities of the twenty-first century.

The Global Women's Movement

Organising women on a transnational basis began between the 1830s and the 1860s (Berkovitch

"Empowered Women, Strong Pakistan" on February 19, 2012, in Karachi, Pakistan. The rally, organised by Pakistan's ruling Muttahida Quami Movement coalition, sought to boost women's political involvement and highlight increasing levels of violence against women in Pakistan.

1999, 2012). At first this was highly informal, but formal organisations did emerge, such as the World Woman's Christian Temperance Union (WWCTU), founded in 1874. While the WWCTU focused on the problem of alcohol, it was concerned with other issues, such as political equality for women. By the time of its first international convention in 1891, the WWCTU had branches in 26 countries. Members adopted the view that "universal sisterhood" existed and that women throughout the world experienced a common fate. Suffrage became an increasingly important issue globally, and that led to the founding of the International Woman Suffrage Alliance (IWSA) in 1904 (Rupp and Taylor 1999). One of the most striking events in the early twentieth century was the gathering of more than a thousand women in the Netherlands in 1915 at an International Congress of Women. This meeting took place in spite of the fact that World War I raged around the attendees, which made it very difficult to traverse national borders. The main goal of the meeting was to find ways to resolve conflicts and prevent future wars. After World War I, the founding of the League of Nations and the International Labour Organization (ILO) created new opportunities for global action by women (and others).

However, women's activities in and through these organisations achieved few tangible results, in part because leaders within these organisations tended to be "elite, White, Christian women from Northern and Western Europe" (Freedman 2009:48). Many women within these groups supported colonialism despite the presence of fellow members who suffered under colonial rule. Moreover, the reproduction of colonial relationships within the movement was yet another facet of the contentious beginnings of an international women's movement. In reaction to this, black women from Africa and the United States formed the International Council of Women of the Darker Races in 1920. It called for support of a struggle not only for personal but also for national independence from colonial domination (Freedman 2009).

Much greater strides were made as a result of the founding of the United Nations (UN) after World War II. Instrumental in this progress was the UN Commission on the Status of Women. Its initiative led to a world conference on women held in 1975 and to that year being declared the UN International Women's Year. Yet at the 1975 conference, men dominated the speeches and leadership positions; they tended to represent the interests of their respective governments rather than those of women's organisations. But women continued to press for equality and were eventually granted more leadership roles to foster discussions about the gaps between male and female opportunities. This was followed by the UN Decade for Women (1976–1985), conferences during that decade, and follow-up conferences held in 1995 (30,000 people attended the UN Fourth World Conference on Women in Beijing) and 2005. Because of such meetings, women from all over the world were able to interact on a face-to-face basis and to develop various transnational interpersonal ties (F. Davis [1991] 1999). As a result of these associations, many local and transnational women's organisations emerged. In addition to these formal organisations, many transnational feminist networks have developed in recent years (Marx Ferree and Tripp 2006). These are more fluid organisational forms, which lack formal membership and a bureaucratic structure. They have been aided in their formation

and interaction by new communication technologies, especially the Internet. However, rather than leading to a single global sisterhood, fractures and divisions have grown stronger in the global women's movement. For example, women of the Global South often resist initiatives from women of the Global North. This resistance is due in part to a need to prevent the imposition of northern notions of superiority and to recognise that injustice and emancipation can take various forms (Freedman 2009). In spite of this, the women's movement is far more global than ever and is not only having an impact on the position of women throughout the world but also shaping, and being shaped by, globalisation (Basu 2010). This can be seen, for example, in arguments over the meaning(s) of feminism and women's rights during the war in Afghanistan and western participation in other international conflicts (A. Ali 2010).

THE GAY AND LESBIAN MOVEMENTS

In 1969 consensual homosexual activity was illegal in Canada. Most lesbians and gay men felt compelled to hide their sexual orientation. Now in Canada same-sex couples can marry, adopt children, and serve openly in the military, and lesbians can make use of in vitro fertilisation. Canada has become one of the most progressive nations in the world on matters of sexual orientation, and in large measure this has been due to the lesbian and gay movement. This social change is a remarkable achievement in many ways. Clearly in comparative perspective, not only are Canadians more tolerant of diverse sexual orientations (see Figure 15.3), but their elected politicians have put in place a set of progressive legal protections and structural supports for the gay and lesbian movement. The success has come against the resistance of many, and violence against both gays and lesbians continues. The success has also come from a movement whose internal divisions have been sharp at certain junctures. For lesbians and gays to work together, this has meant first overcoming the sexual inequality between women and men that feminists were struggling to overthrow. No doubt a common objective of the rights for homosexual choice helped the focus. But the movement also had to deal with issues of social class divisions; racial, ancestral, and ethnic tensions; and the inclusion or not of bisexual and transgender individuals. As portrayals of the movement make clear, internal tensions were high (Ross 1995; Smith 1999; Staggenborg 2011). What were the right political strategies, with whom should a group build alliances (especially debated were linkages with men's groups), and who should be included within a group's membership (e.g., bisexuals?)? Becki Ross's *The House That Jill Built: A Lesbian Nation in Formation* charts the rise and demise of LOOT (the Lesbian Organization of Toronto). LOOT's rallying cry was "feminism is the theory and lesbianism is the practice." Heterosexuality was rejected, and with it the institutions on which it depended, such as the traditional family. But despite playing an enormously important role in raising awareness and pressing for essential change, LOOT withered, in large part because one organisation could not represent the diverse array of lesbian interests that ranged across social classes, race, ancestry, and ethnicity, as well as political and social identities.

More broadly lesbian and gay activists were particularly successful in Canada by making use of the legal system to bring about change. The impact of the 1982 Canadian Charter of Rights and Freedoms is one of the main reasons that Canada is at the forefront of recognition of sexual orientation rights (Smith 1999). The LGBTQ (lesbian, gay, bisexual, transgender, and queer) movement, as it is now commonly called, used the concept of "rights talk," the idea that individuals are equal before the law, to make effective use of charter provisions. In particular the Canadian Charter, under equality rights, seeks to ensure that all people share basic freedoms and that essential human dignity is preserved equally for everyone (see Figure 15.4).

You might note immediately that sexual orientation is not included in the listing of personal characteristics. However, notice the "and, in particular" phrasing. This has been interpreted by the courts to mean that the list of personal characteristics was not meant to be exhaustive. Other personal characteristics could be included as "analogous" grounds. Sexual orientation, marital status, and citizenship have all been identified as characteristics not explicitly included in Section 15 but that are nevertheless protected categories. The LGBTQ movement has successfully used this charter rovision to press for the legal recognition of the rights of gays and lesbians (M. Smith 1999), including, among other victories, the right to same-sex marriage.

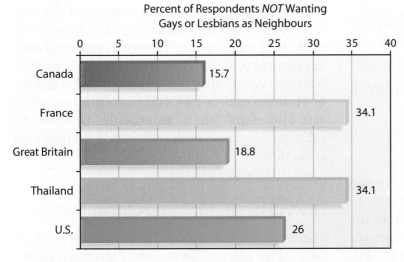

FIGURE 15.3 **Attitudes Toward Sexual Orientation in Five Countries, 2006 and 2007 (World Values Survey)**

SOURCE: www.worldvaluessurvey.org

NOTE: For some countries the survey was done in 2006 and others in 2007. The World Values Survey is not consistent in reporting exactly when the data was collected by country.

The Fight for Marriage Equality

Same-sex couples currently enjoy the legal right to marry in the Netherlands, Spain, South Africa, Belgium, Norway, Sweden, and Canada, and in 12 U.S. states and the District of Columbia. Lesbian and gay marriages were first allowed in Canada in 2001. On June 10, 2003, a decision by the Court of Appeal for Ontario ruled that the common law definition of marriage, which defined marriage as between a woman and a man, violated Section 15 of the charter. It is also the case that federal and provincial benefits, related, say, to pension provisions, that are automatically

Equality Rights
Equality before and under law and equal protection and benefit of law
• 15. (1) Every individual is equal before and under the law and has the right to the equal protection and equal benefit of the law without discrimination and, in particular, without discrimination based on race, national or ethnic origin, colour, religion, sex, age or mental or physical disability.

FIGURE 15.4 Equality Rights

SOURCE: Canadian Charter of Rights and Freedom, http://laws-lois.justice.gc.ca/eng/Const/page-a5.html

conferred upon heterosexual couples also accrue to homosexual couples.

Resistance to the legalisation of gay marriage came from both outside and within the gay and lesbian rights movements. Religious conservatives opposed same-sex marriages, arguing that they threaten the sanctity of marriage and the traditional family. But queer-identified groups have also offered criticisms of gay marriage. For example, emphasising the central importance of securing legal marriage is criticised for failing to address the inequalities inherent in the institution of marriage itself (www.beyondmarriage.org). The rights associated with marriage do not benefit everyone equally. In order to challenge the institution of marriage and to address the needs of varied family forms across the LGBTQ community, a number of alternatives to the mainstream LGBTQ movement's focus on marriage are suggested:

- Legal recognition for a diverse range of relationships and family forms

- Separation of church and state in all matters

- Freedom from state regulation of sexual lives and gender choices

Homosexuality in the DSM

One of the early political victories of the gay and lesbian movement was the removal of homosexuality as a category of mental illness from the American Psychiatric Association's (APA) *Diagnostic and Statistical Manual of Mental Disorders (DSM)*. Throughout the latter half of the twentieth century (as well as today), the *DSM* has served as the definitive differential diagnostic guide for psychiatrists, psychologists, and other mental health professionals. It has therefore been influential in medicalising and pathologising behaviours and identities. The *DSM*'s inclusion of homosexuality as a mental illness framed same-sex behaviour and desire not only as a disease but as one that is treatable as well.

The efforts of both social scientists and gay and lesbian activists fostered the removal of homosexuality from the 1973 edition of the *DSM*. Radical and moderate activist groups employed a variety of strategies to express their opposition to the APA's pathologising of homosexuality.

However, homosexuality was replaced with "ego-dystonic homosexuality" in the 1980 *DSM-III* revision. This new diagnosis could be applied to those who claimed to feel distress as a result of their unwanted homosexuality. However, opposition to this diagnosis led to its later removal from the *DSM-III-R*. The APA has since adopted numerous formal policies in support of the dignity of gay men and lesbians and in opposition to their stigmatisation. However, both individual clinicians and organisations such as the U.S. National Association for Research and Therapy of Homosexuality (NARTH) continue to advocate clinicians' "right" to provide "psychological care" for those with "unwanted homosexual attraction."

HIV/AIDS, ACT UP, and Queer Nation

The recognition of HIV/AIDS in 1981 by the U.S. Centers for Disease Control and Prevention (CDC) had a tremendous impact on gay and lesbian politics and communities. The activism that emerged from this period was embodied in the early efforts of the AIDS Coalition to Unleash Power (ACT

UP). In 1989, ACT UP pressured the pharmaceutical company, Burroughs Wellcome, to make its new antiretroviral drug, AZT, more affordable for HIV-positive patients. ACT UP embodied a new kind of activism, which included civil disobedience, activist art, and other forms of creative activities and representations. ACT UP chapters opened throughout the nation. In 1990, some ACT UP activists formed a new group, Queer Nation, that, although short-lived, served as the beginning of a public and direct representation of LGBTQ issues. Out of HIV/AIDS activism and via the efforts of Queer Nation, the gay and lesbian movement shifted into a politics of queer spaces and identities.

The gay marriage debate and activist efforts relating to it continue to be fraught with tension both within and beyond the LGBTQ community. While the gay and lesbian movements discussed in this section are global in scope, the movements have had mixed success globally. While at least some forms of homosexuality are legal in some parts of the world, either it is illegal or same-sex couples are not recognised in a much larger part of the world. There are even parts of the world, mostly Islamic, where homosexuality is subject to large penalties, life in prison, or even death.

EMERGENCE, MOBILISATION, AND IMPACT OF SOCIAL MOVEMENTS

A variety of conditions determine whether or not a social movement will emerge. To start with, there must be grievances, such as those against weapons testing, the killing of whales, or the exploitation of planetary resource of concern to Greenpeace. The grievances about the unfair treatment of women, gays and lesbians, and blacks animated the other social movements discussed above. However, grievances alone are not sufficient for a social movement to arise; individuals and organisations must be mobilised in order to do something about them. All of the movements discussed above were successful in mobilising people to act.

Gay pride parades are now a fixture in all of Canada's largest cities, annually attracting tens of thousands of spectators and thousands of participants.

Svend Robinson was an effective gay rights activist, and human rights advocate. He was one of the first openly gay men to be elected in federal politics and served in the House of Commons from 1979 to 2004.

Factors in the Emergence of a Social Movement

Assuming a set of grievances and efforts at mobilisation, certain other conditions must exist in order for a social movement to emerge. First, there must be openings or opportunities within the political system. For example, the lengthy and expanding protests against the Vietnam War, the growing awareness of ecological damage, and the context of challenges to ingrained authority by a younger generation all provided an opening for the formation of Greenpeace (M. Brown and May 1991; Weyler 2004). That opening was widened as these and related problems, as well as public concern about them, increased.

A second factor involves various spatial arrangements, such as the physical proximity of those involved. Clearly, social movements develop more easily when those who at least have the potential to become involved come into contact with one another fairly easily or on a regular basis. Another spatial factor is whether or not there are "free spaces" where those involved can meet. It is in such spaces that the movement can develop out of the limelight and free of external surveillance and control. Women on college campuses existed in close proximity to one another, and this helped in the formation of the women's movement, while free spaces such as churches were especially important to the development of the civil rights movement.

A third factor is the availability of resources. This is the concern of **resource mobilisation theory**, one of the most popular approaches to understanding social movements today (B. Edwards 2007; Jenkins 1983; Walder 2009). The focus is on what groups of people need to do in order to mobilise effectively to bring about social change. This theory assumes that there is some strain within the larger society and that there are groups of people who have grievances that result from those strains. One of the most important works in this tradition is that of Jack Goldstone (1991) on *revolutions*—a kind of social movement in which the strains produced by state breakdown (failure of the government to function properly, fiscal distress) play a key role in the development of

Activists of a French branch of ACT UP demonstrate in front of the Health Ministry in Paris on May 19, 2010. Activists covered the steps with animal livers to protest against French health care policies regarding AIDS (SIDA in France) and hepatitis. According to the World Health Organization, more than 33 million people are infected by AIDS worldwide.

revolutionary movements. Once a strain exists, the issue is what resources are needed for these groups to become social movements, perhaps even successful social movements.

Resources and Mobilisation of Social Movements

Five types of resources have been identified as important to the mobilisation of social movements. First are *material resources,* such as money, property, and equipment. It is costly to mount a successful social movement, and money and other material resources are mandatory (Snow, Soule, and Cress

Giles Muhame, managing editor of the Ugandan publication *Rolling Stone,* holds the latest issue of his newspaper on the streets of Kampala. This issue published the names and photos of 14 men it identified as gay in a country where homosexuality can lead to lengthy jail terms and has even prompted calls for the death sentence. Homosexuality in Uganda is punishable by life imprisonment in some instances, and a lawmaker in 2009 introduced a bill calling for some homosexual acts to be punished with death.

2005). Notable in this regard is the backing of Greenpeace by like-minded counterculture entertainers. Second are *organisational resources,* which include infrastructure (Internet access is especially important today; see page 623), social networks (insiders with access to important groups and organisations), and the organisations and alliances that are formed by the social movement. Third are *human resources,* such as the leadership, expertise, skills, and day-to-day labour of those in the organisation (Tsutsui and Wotipka 2004). More specific resources might be dynamic public speakers (such as Martin Luther King Jr.) and spokespersons, skilled web designers, or those skilled in organisational dynamics. Fourth are *moral resources,* such as the degree to which the larger public regards the movement as legitimate. Other moral resources involve a sense that there is a high level of integrity among the leaders, as well as in the membership as a whole (B. Lowe 2002). Finally, there are *cultural resources,* such as bodies of knowledge or skills that are tacitly shared by at least some members of the movement. These might include knowledge of how to organise a protest, hold a news conference, or run a meeting. Overall, the keys to the success or failure of a social movement are the available resources and the ability to use some or all of them in order to mobilise effectively to pursue desired social change.

Another important issue is the source of such resources. One source is simply having members who are themselves able to produce the resources by, for example, raising money, developing networks, or socialising their children to become part of the movement as adults. Another is aggregating external resources such as soliciting donations from a wide range of donors. Also of importance is the need to locate patrons and the ability to rely on them to support the group monetarily and in many other ways (by providing staff members). Finally, a social movement can co-opt the resources of other organisations. For example, social movements in Canada have often used the labour movement and university students and faculty as allies for their causes.

Participation. Once a social movement is under way, methods need to be found to ensure member participation. First, people need to be asked to participate. For that to occur they need to be embedded in social networks involving other movement members. Second, a variety of social psychological factors are involved, including personally identifying with the movement and its causes, being aroused emotionally by the issues involved and becoming committed to dealing with them, and being at a point in life—retired, unemployed, in college—where one is available to participate in the movement. Third, incentives need to be offered so that the gains to members for their involvement outweigh the risks and costs. For example, the achievement of greater rights for blacks outweighed the risk of being beaten or murdered and the cost of time and income for participants in the civil rights movement. While material incentives are important, of far greater importance are the social incentives associated with joining with others as part of the movement, as well as the moral incentives of being involved in something one believes in strongly (Quadagno and Rohlinger 2009).

Goals, Strategy, and Tactics. Once formed, a social movement needs to have goals, a strategy, and a variety of tactics in order to succeed. Goals relate to what the movement seeks to do, such as cutting taxes or making society more equal. Strategy involves the movement's long-term plan for achieving its goals. Once a strategy is in place, tactics become important. Tactics are more short-term in nature. They need to be quite fluid and able to adapt quickly in light of changes taking place in the immediate or larger environment. Of particular importance are the actions of countermovements and government officials. For example, the civil rights movement had to adapt to the hostile actions of both white supremacists and hostile local government officials.

Factors in Success. A variety of factors help to determine whether or not a social movement will succeed (Cross and Snow 2012; Rochon 1990). One is its sheer size. All social movements start small, but those that succeed are likely to have recruited large numbers of activists and supporters. Another is *novelty,* or the uniqueness of the movement and its goals. Uniqueness (and size) is important because it leads to a great deal

of media attention, which, in turn, is likely to generate additional supporters and funds. The latter are two of the many *resources* social movements need in order to succeed (see above). *Violence,* as for example in the case of Greenpeace and France, can be useful, if unintended, in achieving results. However, it also can be counterproductive by turning off potential supporters and members if the movement uses violence in ways that are judged to be inappropriate. Perhaps more importantly, it can lead to violent reactions that can end in the suppression of the movement. *Militancy* can also be double-edged since a highly militant social movement might be able to achieve its goals quickly, but militancy, like violence, can lead to counterreactions and suppression (a reaction by some to the World Trade Organization protests). *Nonviolence* has been a successful method for social movements because it avoids the powerful counterreactions engendered by violent and militant social movements. The nonviolent approach is traceable largely to Mahatma Gandhi and his use of such means as noncooperation with the British-controlled government to gain Indian independence in 1947. Today, a large number of social movements, including Greenpeace and the women's, civil rights, and gay and lesbian movements, have adopted a nonviolent approach. Globally, many organisations associated with the environmental movement, as well as those associated with the World Social Forum (see page 617) and operating in opposition to at least some aspects of globalisation, rely almost exclusively on nonviolent methods.

Although various aspects of social movements themselves strongly affect whether they will be successful, many other factors are involved in this. Of great importance is the ability of individuals, groups, or the state (especially the police and the military) to suppress a social movement (Earl 2007). Efforts at suppressing social movements can be covert as, for example, the FBI wiretapping the phones of members of dissident, especially suspected communist and civil rights, groups in Canada in the mid-1950s through the early 1970s. They can also be overt, with a major example being the

Vancouver's Lions Gate Bridge, prior to and during "Earth Hour," a World Wide Fund for Nature event where non-essential lights are extinguished around the world. Material resources—money, property, and equipment—are critical to the successful mobilization of social movements. Without such resources it is impossible to mount the kinds of effective campaigns necessary to influence public opinion and influence political decision-making.

violent suppression in 1989 of antigovernment protests in Tiananmen Square by the Chinese government and the military. Another example is the violence committed by local law enforcement officers and white supremacists against civil rights activists in the United States in the 1960s. Yet another example is the police raids of public bathhouses frequented by homosexuals in the 1960s (Clendinen and Nagourney 1999).

Impact of Social Movements

Whether or not they are successful, social movements often leave their marks, sometimes quite powerful marks. A government might be able to suppress a social movement, but it is likely that aspects of the government and the way it operates will be affected by the movement as well as the efforts to suppress it. For example, in the 1940s and 1950s the U.S. government was able to suppress efforts to increase the influence of communism throughout the country. However, while it was successful in those efforts, it engaged in a variety of highly questionable actions. The major examples are the activities of the House Un-American Activities Committee (HUAC) and especially those of the infamous Senator Joseph McCarthy. Recall from Chapter 7 that McCarthy conducted hearings with the ostensible goal of rooting communists out of the government and elsewhere, most notably Hollywood and the U.S. Army. McCarthy and his associates often made wild public accusations without presenting any supporting evidence. Long-lasting changes were brought about in the government by the public's revulsion toward the reprehensible tactics used by McCarthy and his supporters. Since that time, government actions that even hint at the kind taken during the 1940s and 1950s are labelled "McCarthyism" and, as a result, are unlikely to succeed.

Social movements, especially those that achieve some success, often leave a strong legacy for, and have a powerful impact on, later movements. For example, the civil rights movement was an inspiration and a model for many later movements in Canada and the United States, such as

Firefighters bear in on a group of demonstrators seeking shelter in a doorway as an antisegregation protest is dispersed. A social movement's tactics need to be able to adapt quickly to changes taking place around them. For example, members of the civil rights movement were often subjected to hostile actions by white supremacists and local government officials.

The success of a social movement can be determined by the results it achieves. Violence and militancy might enable a movement to achieve its goals quickly but can lead to a loss of support and even suppression. Nonviolence, such as that advocated by the Dalai Lama (left) and Archbishop Desmond Tutu, has been a successful method because it avoids powerful counterreactions.

the student, antiwar, environmental, gay and lesbian, and disabled movements. Social movements outside North America—for example, South Africa's antiapartheid movement, the Solidarity movement in Poland, and the pro-democracy movement in China—were also strongly affected by the U.S. civil rights movement.

While social movements are oriented toward changing society, they also have a strong impact on the individuals involved in a social movement, either members of the movement or those who oppose it. The greatest impact is usually on the large numbers of people actively involved in the movement (S. Roth 2007). Their attitudes, and perhaps the entire course of their lives, are often altered greatly by active involvement in social movements (Corrigall-Brown 2011). Much the same is true of those who take an active role in opposing social movements. Senator McCarthy, for example, was embittered by his failures and died soon after he was discredited.

The aggressive tactics used by Senator Joe McCarthy (right) to root out communism destroyed his reputation.

THE INTERNET, GLOBALISATION, AND SOCIAL MOVEMENTS

Two of the most important recent developments as far as social movements are concerned relate to globalisation (Maiba 2005) and the Internet, as well as other new media, such as iPhones (Castells 2008).

On the one hand, the Internet has proven to be an important way of involving and organising large numbers of people, perhaps millions of them, who are widely separated from one another, perhaps even in different parts of the world. In other words, people no longer need to be in close physical proximity in order to be involved in social movements. People can also now communicate more easily through the use of mobile phones, even from the site of an event that has the possibility of mobilising those involved in a social movement. It is possible not only to communicate verbally with others in the movement but to snap pictures or shoot videos with one's smartphone and send them instantaneously via YouTube or Facebook to large numbers of interested parties who can then see for themselves what is transpiring.

The Internet and other technologies enable social movements to cover wide geographic areas, and even to become global. Like much else in the world today, social movements are less constrained than ever before by national borders. It seems likely that the future will bring with it an increasing number of global social movements.

COLLECTIVE BEHAVIOUR

Collective behaviour is action generated or engaged in by a group of people. A social movement is one kind of collective behaviour; others include crowds, riots, and disasters. Like all other forms of collective behaviour, social movements usually occur outside of established institutional channels, and they can bring about or retard social change. However, social movements are different from all other forms of collective behaviour in at least two ways. First, most forms of collective behaviour are short-lived compared to social movements. Thus, a crowd, for example, can come together and disperse within hours, but a social movement can be sustained for years or decades. Second, a social movement is intentional; a collective behaviour is not. A community that comes together because of a disaster such as an earthquake or a flood does not do so intentionally; it has been brought together and goes into action because of some unanticipated external event. For example, after the 2011 earthquake and tsunami in northern Japan, newspapers reported on the strong sense of community that emerged and helped people survive the aftermath (Fackler 2011).

While social movements have been theorised separately and somewhat differently (resource mobilisation theory), the dominant approach to thinking about other forms of collective behaviour is **emergent norm theory** (Arthur 2007; R. Turner and Killian 1987). This theory is based on the idea that new norms emerge in light of some precipitating event, and they guide the often nontraditional actions that characterise collective behaviour. Implicit in this theory is the idea that

in collective behaviour, conventional norms cease to be as effective or as important, at least to some degree. Contrary to popular opinion, however, collective behaviour is not irrational, random, or out of control; it is guided by the new norms that develop in the situation.

This conclusion was recently supported in a study of a 2003 Rhode Island nightclub fire in which 100 people were killed and nearly 200 people were injured (Aguirre et al. 2011). There was little evidence of irrational panic or panic-like behaviour among those seeking to escape the fire. They didn't follow their impulses and try to save their own lives without regard for the lives of others. Instead, a norm quickly emerged that rather than save themselves, people had to help one another in this situation, even when there was a dire, life-threatening emergency. This was especially true of those close to those involved. People put themselves in danger of injury or even death in order to try to help those people who were important to them. More generally, people's behaviour in such situations is affected by commitments that they had to one another prior to the fire.

CROWDS

The clearest application of emergent norm theory to collective behaviour involves the case of a **crowd**, a temporary gathering of a relatively large number of people in a common geographic location and in a given period (McPhail 2007). We are all familiar with all sorts of crowds, such as those that gather at the site of a celebration or a catastrophe, but a relatively new type is the flash crowd (or flash mob). Flash crowds have become easier to generate as a result of the Internet and e-mails and social networking sites. A flash crowd might gather, for example, to engage in a pillow fight. In fact, in 2008 a kind of a global pillow fight took place involving participants in two dozen cities around the world. In recent years largely teenage flash crowds have come together in Philadelphia and been disorderly, gotten into fights, attacked bystanders, and been cracked

Demonstrators in London, England's Trafalgar Square hold their smartphones up with victory hand signs as they celebrate in a day of solidarity with those protesting in Cairo, Egypt's Tahrir Square. The Internet, social media, and other technologies enable social movements to cover wide geographic areas, and even to become global.

In a 2003 Rhode Island nightclub fire that killed at least 50 attendees, there was little evidence of irrational behaviour (panic) among those seeking to escape. Instead, a norm quickly emerged that people had to help others. Here, rescue workers clear debris behind a tarp at the burned-down nightclub.

down upon in an unnecessarily aggressive way by the police (Massarro and Mullaney 2011).

One concern in the literature on crowds is the degree to which individuals behave differently in crowds than they do in other social contexts. Emergent norm theory suggests that they do behave differently, but that is because they are conforming to a different set of norms than exist elsewhere in the social world. That is more comforting than the alternative view, which sees people in crowds as losing control of their cognitive processes, complying blindly with the suggestions of crowd leaders, and copying mindlessly what is done by those around them in the crowd. A large body of research has failed to find any support for this alternative view (Postmes and Spears 1998).

However, it is possible that flash crowds brought together by messages on Twitter do operate differently and may be more in line with the alternative, discomforting view of crowds. It might be that because the individuals in a crowd have been brought together so impersonally and might well not know one another when they do come together, they do not have time to develop norms.

RIOTS

A **riot** is temporary unruly collective behaviour that causes damage to persons or property (Myers 2007). Canadian riots have often been related to sports, when a team either wins (Montreal, 1993) or loses (Vancouver, 1994, 2011). Other Canadian riots have involved student protest (at Sir George Williams University in 1969) or antiglobalisation protests (Quebec City, 2001). Of course, exactly what gets labelled as a riot is a social decision, and some would include the Winnipeg General Strike of 1919, whereas others would see this as a social movement protest, even though people and property were harmed. In Canada there have been

Belarusian youth activists attend a pillow fight flash crowd to commemorate the anniversary of the Battle of Grunwald in Minsk, Belarus, on July 15, 2010.

Vancouverites rioted after the Canucks lost to the Boston Bruins in the 2011 Stanley Cup playoffs. Many people in attendance and many watching on TV were stunned by the violence that erupted after the loss, with crowds in the thousands either participating or consuming the spectacle as by-standers.

protests and blockades involving racial, ancestral, or ethnic discord but nothing like the U.S. race riots such as occurred after the beating of Rodney King in 1992 in Los Angeles. Recall from Chapter 6 that significant rioting and extensive looting and arson took place in London and in other cities in England in August 2011 (see Figure 15.5). Five people died in the riots (see the next *Globalisation* box).

Negative Views of Riots

We are likely to have negative views of riots and rioters. However, riots may not be irrational outbursts but rather motivated by frustrations over various kinds of abuses and the inability to do much about them under normal circumstances (Auyero and Moran 2007). It is hard to generalise about rioters, but there is little support in the research for the idea that rioters are more likely to be criminals, unemployed, or uneducated. A few things seem clear about those who participate in

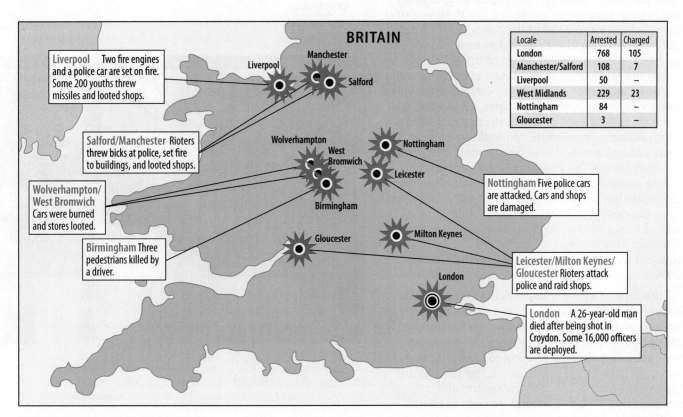

Locale	Arrested	Charged
London	768	105
Manchester/Salford	108	7
Liverpool	50	–
West Midlands	229	23
Nottingham	84	–
Gloucester	3	–

Liverpool Two fire engines and a police car are set on fire. Some 200 youths threw missiles and looted shops.

Salford/Manchester Rioters threw bicks at police, set fire to buildings, and looted shops.

Wolverhampton/ West Bromwich Cars were burned and stores looted.

Birmingham Three pedestrians killed by a driver.

Nottingham Five police cars are attacked. Cars and shops are damaged.

Leicester/Milton Keynes/ Gloucester Rioters attack police and raid shops.

London A 26-year-old man died after being shot in Croydon. Some 16,000 officers are deployed.

FIGURE 15.5 The 2011 British Riots

SOURCE: "We Will Use Water Cannons on Them: At Last Cameron Orders Police to Come Down Hard on the Looters," Emily Allen, *Daily Mail News,* August 2011.

GL⊕BALISATION

Riots in Paris, France

Riots broke out in the Paris suburbs of Argenteuil in 2005 and in Villiers-le-Bel in late 2007. They occurred in areas dominated by the working and lower classes associated with large immigrant groups, especially Arab and African (Sciolino 2007). The riots revealed the fact that racism, long most associated with the United States, was also a French, if not a global, problem. In fact, racism in France is much more blatant now than it is in the United States. Great Britain has also witnessed the development and emergence of a major race problem (Bennhold 2008). Racism in France resembles the racism that existed in the United States decades ago. Among other things, at the behest of landlords, French real estate agents seek out white-only tenants, *patisseries* sell cakes covered in chocolate called *tête de nègre* (head of Negro), TV programmes are dominated by white actors and actresses, and women from Africa and Asia are seen in the wealthy areas of town as "nannies" accompanying well-dressed children to and from school. Racial and ethnic minorities in France primarily work in poorly paid manual jobs that are likely to involve cleaning, pushing, serving, digging, or carrying. They are crucial to the health service since they perform virtually all of the "dirty work" (Ritzer 1972:275) associated with it. Higher-level, higher-paid positions in virtually every sector of the economy are out of the reach of most minorities, even those with adequate education and training—the unemployment rate for French university graduates is 5 percent; it is more than 25 percent for university graduates from North African communities. Minorities are almost totally absent among the elites in almost every walk of life in France. The situation facing minorities in France shows no signs of improving—while the French electorate has (so far) not elected far-right politicians to its top positions, many of France's politicians, as well as its public philosophers, have moved in the direction of right-wing ideas that stand in opposition to social welfare and public assistance (G. Murray 2006).

Racial and ethnic minorities in France experience a variety of other problems. They generally are housed in suburban, government-run "projects," many built in the 1960s. These are not American-style suburbs with well-manicured lawns but dull expanses of concrete and asphalt. The suburbs are generally isolated from the city centre, and it takes a great deal of time and several changes of buses and/or trains to get there.

Jobs are few in the suburbs, especially since many factories have been shuttered as a result of globalisation, and operations have been moved to places including Tunisia, Slovakia, and Southeast Asia. Unemployment in the suburbs can be as high as 40 percent. The result is poverty and hopelessness, especially among the young who represented the vast majority of the rioters in the Paris suburbs. There is great tension with the police, who are apt to harass minority group members, address them rudely, call them names, treat them brutally, and on occasion kill them.

These riots can be seen as being linked to globalisation, especially large-scale migration, at least some of it undocumented. Thus, the rioting by the minorities outside Paris can be seen as resistance both to the way they are treated in France and more generally to the negative effects and consequences of globalisation. This unplanned collective behaviour, therefore, is underpinned by dramatic structural inequality as a result of both national and global processes.

In November 2007, teenagers Lakamy Samoura and Mohsin Sehhouli were killed in Villiers-le-Bel, France, when the motorbike they were riding collided with a police car—an incident widely blamed on police negligence. Following days of rioting, some 300 mourners demanding truth and justice marched through Villiers-le-Bel on November 30.

riots—they are more likely to be men, to be young, to have been physically close to where the riots occur, and to feel that their actions can make a difference. The literature on police involvement is also ambiguous, with the police seen as being able both to quell riots and to incite them further with their repressive actions.

It is also worth noting that the mass media can contribute to rioting in the ways in which they treat riots. For one thing, live coverage of riots can inflame them by drawing others into them. Live, immediate media reports are also more likely to be inaccurate and to involve inflammatory reporting. For another thing, media reports of riots can suggest this is a form of action to be emulated at other places and times. Social media can also quickly draw large numbers of people to a riot site (C. Schneider and Trottier 2012).

Positive Effects of Riots

Riots can have positive effects. The Rodney King riots of 1992 undoubtedly led to changes and improvements in the way the police deal with suspects and the general public, although similar incidents continue to be reported. More generally, riots have at times led to various programmes designed to deal with the conditions that were seen to be at their source, such as poverty and unemployment. However, the lasting power of these changes is unclear, and, in any case, people are injured and die, and communities are ruined in riots. In some cases, it takes decades for riot sites to recover (Cannon 1997; Schoch and Il 2007; Spencer 2004).

DISASTERS

Disasters are events that suddenly, unexpectedly, and severely disrupt and harm the environment, the social structure, people, and their property (Silver 2007). They are distinguished from accidents (automobile, airplane) by their far greater impact. One disaster much in the news in 2010 was the earthquake in Haiti that decimated a significant portion of that Caribbean nation, which shares an island (Hispaniola) with the Dominican

Republic. No one knows the exact numbers, but it is estimated that more than 200,000 people were killed and another 300,000 were injured. Innumerable poorly constructed homes, schools, and other buildings were destroyed. The government virtually ceased functioning as its offices collapsed, literally and figuratively, and many officials were killed or injured (Bhatty 2010). As of late 2013, little progress had been made in rebuilding homes and the Haitian infrastructure. While it is a stark example, the earthquake in Haiti represents just one of many natural disasters that occurred in 2010. As is evident in Figure 15.6, such disasters occur all around the world every year.

Human Involvement in Disasters

Disasters such as earthquakes are natural phenomena, but humans often play a role in bringing them about and in exacerbating their consequences. People frequently build in areas—on geological fault lines, on floodplains—where there should be no significant building. Furthermore, what they build is often quite flimsy and likely to be destroyed in a natural disaster. Building stronger structures can be very costly, and impoverished nations such as Haiti simply cannot afford it (*Newsweek* 2010). Global warming, which has been largely human-induced, has warmed the oceans, and therefore the ferocity of hurricanes and typhoons has intensified as a consequence of the winds passing over increasingly warmer water.

There are, of course, disasters that are the result of human error or corruption. Recall that on April 20, 2010, a huge explosion on the BP/Deepwater Horizon oil rig in the Gulf of Mexico killed 11 workers and unleashed a gusher of oil (*Telegraph* 2010). There have been warnings for decades about the dangers associated with deep sea drilling and oil wells. However, they were pushed forward by the desire for ever-escalating profits by corporations such as BP and the voracious need for oil in Canada, the United States, and other developed nations. Once the oil gusher occurred, it became clear that no one quite knew how to go about stopping it. The well was finally capped on July 15; however, by that time about 5 million barrels of oil had flowed into the surrounding waters (CBS News 2010). The oil caused great damage to the Gulf's marine life, its beaches, and the businesses that depend on tourists drawn to the area.

Recall from Chapter 6 that the space shuttle *Challenger* disintegrated a little over a minute into its flight, killing all seven crew members (Vaughan 1996). In order to get needed funds and to launch space shuttles in a timely manner, NASA ignored warnings, took risks, and tolerated mistakes and deception. While Vaughan saw this disaster as a unique occurrence, Charles Perrow (1999) sees such accidents as "normal." That is, highly complex systems such as those associated with NASA and the space shuttle will inevitably lead to such disasters, although they happen only rarely.

Human-made disasters also can be political in nature, and they are associated with revolutions, riots, and acts of terrorism. For example, in mid-2010 the centre of Bangkok, Thailand, was ravaged by riots aimed at overthrowing the government. And then, of course, there was the 9/11 disaster caused by hijackers crashing planes into the World Trade Center towers and the Pentagon, as well as downing one plane before it reached its target. These terrorist attacks resulted in the deaths of nearly 3,000 people.

The Effects of Disasters

Disasters have enormous negative long-term consequences for the people and areas involved. Individuals and collectives are traumatised for long periods after a disaster (K. Erikson 1978). People's lives are disrupted for years, if not decades, as are the social networks in which they are enmeshed. Disasters also worsen existing inequalities. For example, females in Haiti have suffered disproportionately from the effects of the 2010 hurricane. Furthermore they have been less likely than males to receive humanitarian aid in the aftermath of the hurricane. Haitian women are more likely to live in tents that, among other

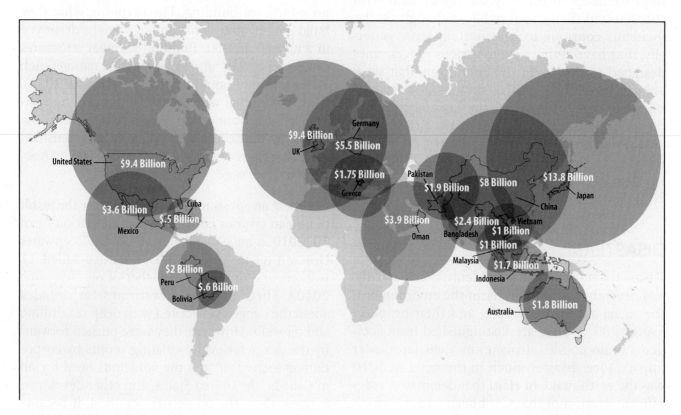

FIGURE 15.6 **Most Costly Natural Disasters around the World, 2007**

SOURCE: Centre for Research on the Epidemiology of Disasters (CRED) and Prevention Web, 2008.

Disasters worsen existing inequalities. For example, in the aftermath of the 2010 earthquake that brought Haiti to the brink, females have received less humanitarian aid than males. More than half a million Haitians are still homeless years after the quake, and many who have homes are worse off than they were before.

things, provide them little protection and security. They are especially vulnerable to "unwanted sexual advances and assault" (Jean-Charles 2010).

However, some people and groups are in a position to handle disasters better than others. Disaster can be a time when people and communities come together in unprecedented ways to deal with the disaster and its aftereffects (Wines 2011). The heroism of many of those involved with the 9/11 disaster—firefighters, police officers, and citizens—is one example of this (Fritsch 2001; Rozdeba 2011; Saxon 2003). Within Haiti, a number of aid agencies are working to continue to provide aid to women and girls, such as the UN Population Fund, the World Food Programme, and World Vision. In addition, "cash for work" programmes, instituted by the Haitian Ministry of Women's Affairs, have helped 100,000 women living in the camps to survive (Jean-Charles 2010). Moreover, in response to the increased vulnerability of women and girls, the Femmes Citoyennes Haiti Solidaire, or Women Citizens Haiti United, formed an alliance of activists to continue addressing gender inequality and injustices within Haiti.

GLOBALISATION AND CYBER-ACTIVISM

The existence of the Internet has given those opposed to globalisation in general, or some specific aspect of it, a powerful tool with which to mount their opposition on a regional and even a global basis. Indeed the origins of the antiglobalisation social movement at the World Trade Organization meetings in Seattle in late November 1999 were based on cyber-activism, as were the ensuing protests in Washington, DC (April 2000), Prague (September 2000), Genoa (July 2001), and other cities (Pleyers 2010). Further, the World Social Forum was made possible by such activism (W. Fisher and Ponniah 2003; J. Sen, Anand, Escobar, and Waterman 2004).

World Social Forum

The World Social Forum (WSF) was formed in 2001 and had its roots in the 1999 protests against the World Trade Organization in Seattle. A key concern was the lack of democracy in global economic and political affairs. The WSF was born of the idea that protests about this problem were insufficient. That is, there was a need for more positive and concrete proposals to deal with such issues, as well as for a forum in which they could be generated. The WSF's slogan has been "Another World Is Possible" (Teivainen 2007). That is, there must be, and there is, an alternative to the free-market capitalism (J. Smith 2008) that has dominated the world economically and politically. Although the slogan is powerful and has facilitated the coordination of large and diverse groups, the WSF has not yet produced concrete actions and policies to make "another world" a reality.

The initial, 2001 meeting of the WSF in Porto Alegre, Brazil (Byrd 2005), drew about 5,000 participants, and the number of participants grew to 100,000 at the meetings in 2004 in Mumbai, India, and in 2005 in Porto Alegre. In 2006 the meeting was decentralised and held on three continents, and many local, national, and regional meetings have developed. In 2011 a centralised meeting in Dakar, Senegal, drew 75,000 participants.

The WSF is, by design, not a social movement, but merely an arena in which like-minded people can exchange ideas on specific social movements and global issues. The very diversity of the movements and people involved in the WSF makes the development of concrete political proposals, let alone actions, difficult. The WSF continues to struggle with this issue and its identity and role in globalisation.

The WSF is a huge social network, and it is based on the "cultural logic of networking" (see Chapter 6 for a discussion of network organisations). Such networking includes the creation of horizontal ties and connections among diverse and autonomous elements, the free and open communication of information among and between those elements, decentralised coordination among the elements that involves democratic decision making, and networking that is self-directed (Juris 2005).

World Huaren Federation

A more specific case of the power of cyber-activism involves a series of events following the 1997 Asian financial crisis, specifically in Indonesia, where anger over the crisis was aimed at ethnic Chinese (A. Ong 2003). By May 1998, Chinese stores in Indonesia had been looted and burned in riots, and Chinese residents had been attacked and women raped. Vigilante groups were said to have hunted Chinese, killed them, and paraded about with their victims' heads on the ends of spikes. The police were reported to have looked on. There has been a long history of anti-Chinese feeling in Indonesia, and the government, as well as the international community, has been seen by Chinese in Indonesia and around the world as having done little or nothing to help the victims of anti-Chinese violence.

Beginning in August 1998, rallies—another form of collective behaviour—against the violence aimed at Chinese residents in Indonesia were held in many cities in the United States, as well as in Canada, Australia, and Asia. This collective behaviour was made possible and coordinated through the creation of a website, www.huaren.org, and the formation of a new social movement, the World Huaren Federation (D. Parker and Song 2006).

There are approximately 50 million people of Chinese ancestry in the Chinese diaspora, and they are scattered throughout more than 100 countries in the world. A large number of them are computer users with access to the Internet. Their great numbers and their high level of computer literacy make them an ideal group for forming a social movement based on cyber-activism.

In effect, the World Huaren Federation created a global Chinese social movement where one had not previously existed. Further, it became a global watchdog for Chinese interests. It was not located in any particular geographic location, existing solely on the Internet; it was a "virtual social movement." Yet another way of saying this is that unlike most other social movements, it was *placeless*. That is, it existed in no single place; it had no headquarters. We are

The WSF is an arena in which like-minded people can exchange ideas on specific social movements and global issues. Senator and Former Environment Minister of Brazil Marina Silva participates in a debate titled "Novos parametros para o Desenvolvimento" ("New Policies for Development") as part of the 10th World Social Forum, held January 2010 in Porto Alegre, Brazil.

McDONALDIZATION *Today*

McDonaldization and Collective Behavior/Social Movements

There are a number of examples of collective behaviour/social movements in various parts of the world, especially Great Britain, France, and Italy, that target McDonald's as well as the larger process of McDonaldization.

In Great Britain, a movement spearheaded by the McSpotlight group grew out of the now infamous McLibel trial (Vidal 1997). McDonald's sued two activists associated with London Greenpeace for passing out a leaflet critical of McDonald's. The trial began in 1994 and ultimately became the longest-running trial in British history. McDonald's "won" the case, although the judge found for the defendants on several grounds. Even so, it was a public relations disaster for the company.

The McSpotlight group is now in the forefront not only of anti-McDonald's activity but also of opposition to many different multinational corporations. Its website (www.mcspotlight.org) has become a global centre for communicating about activities being mounted against McDonald's and other corporations around the world. The McSpotlight group is a social movement as well as a spur to other movements.

In France, José Bové, a sheep farmer and spokesperson for a large farmer's union, Confédération Paysanne, achieved international fame in 1999 by leading a group that dismantled a McDonald's—the group called it "McDo"—under construction in a small town in France. At his trial for his involvement in this action, Bové shouted, "Down with junk food!" Bové's opposition to McDonald's is part of his broader opposition to globalisation. More specifically, he is deeply opposed to the globalisation of food as an industrial commodity and the threat such food poses to traditional French food and culture. McDonald's, and fast-food restaurants in general, has proliferated in France in spite of that nation's association with fine cuisine. Bové's actions were designed to oppose the "McDomination" of France, as well as of many other parts of the world. They were also designed to counter the growing power of multinational corporations and global capitalism (Karon 2001). Bové is defending not only France's food traditions and its organisations but its distinctive identity as well. He is a charismatic individual who has come to serve as an icon for those involved in social movements opposed to McDonaldization and much else about globalisation (Daley 1999).

In Italy, the Slow Food movement was founded by Carlo Petrini (G. Andrews 2008). While it had much earlier roots, a key development in the history of Slow Food was a 1985 protest against the opening of a McDonald's restaurant near the foot of the historic Spanish Steps in Rome. Since that time Slow Food has grown into both a global organisation and a social movement. It opposes the globalised foods offered by McDonald's and the decline in agrodiversity that such foods encourage and accelerate. Slow Food has focused its efforts on championing local foods and more generally the local in the face of the growing power of the global (Leitch 2003, 2010). Although Slow Food is an important and influential social movement, it and the other oppositional movements are quite small and underfinanced in comparison not only to McDonald's, but to the plethora of McDonaldized businesses and other systems throughout the world.

Eugenia Borgna sits among her Raschera cheese-maturing shelves at her family farm in Valcasotto, Italy. Makers of traditionally aged Raschera cheese such as Borgna are championed by the Italian-originated Slow Food movement, which stands against McDonaldized ingredients, preparation, and dining.

likely to see more such global social movements as cyber-activism continues to proliferate.

SOCIAL CHANGE: GLOBALISATION, CONSUMPTION, AND THE INTERNET

Although social change occurs throughout the social world, it is particularly characteristic of the three areas that are the signature concerns of this book—globalisation, consumption, and the Internet. Globalisation is, of course, a social process of relatively recent origin; it is changing the world in which we live and likely to lead to a variety of even more dramatic changes in the future. For example, the changing nature of the global economy, especially the shift of its centre away from the United States and in the direction of China and Asia more generally, means that the job prospects of North Americans are changing and apt to change even more in the future. As some economic prospects have declined—especially those that relate to the production of goods and the jobs associated with it—others have improved. New jobs have arisen—especially those that involve computers and the Internet. Not only is the Internet clearly important in this sense, but it is also, in itself, an arena where great and extremely rapid change has taken place in recent years—change that will certainly continue and to affect your lives in innumerable ways. The changes discussed here—globalisation, the economy, and the Internet—are related to the changing nature of our other core concern—consumption. Consumption has itself become increasingly global, as, for example, more of the things we buy come from outside North America. Our economy has shifted away from one dominated by production to one dominated by services and consumption. It is clear that more consumption is taking place through the Internet, and that trend can only accelerate in the future.

GLOBALISATION AS THE ULTIMATE SOCIAL CHANGE

It could be argued that, prior to the current epoch of globalisation, one of the things that characterised people, things, information, places, and much else was their greater solidity. That is, all

BIOGRAPHICAL bits

Zygmunt Bauman (1925–, Polish)

- Bauman was born in Poznan, Poland.

- He fled to Russia when the Nazis invaded Poland, served in the Red Army during World War II, and was awarded the military Cross of Valour.

- He was a committed communist after the war and in Poland served in military intelligence in the Internal Security Corps.

- He was dishonourably discharged in 1953 when his father sought to emigrate to Israel.

- He had begun studying sociology while still in military intelligence, although sociology was abandoned for a time in Poland because it was considered a "bourgeois science."

- Bauman taught at the University of Warsaw until 1968, when an anti-Semitic campaign forced him to move first to Tel Aviv University and then to Leeds University in England, where he taught until he retired in 1990.

- He became increasingly prolific at Leeds as well as after his retirement; he has written about 20 books since 2000 and after he turned 75 years of age.

- He is best known for his work on the Holocaust, modernity, rationality, consumption, and the increasing liquidity of the contemporary world.

of them tended to harden (metaphorically or figuratively, not literally, of course) over time and therefore, among other things, to remain largely in place. As a result, either people did not go anywhere, or they did not venture very far from where they were born and raised; their social relationships were restricted to those who were nearby. Much the same could be said of most objects (tools, food), which tended to be used where they were produced. The solidity of most material manifestations of information (stone tablets, books) also made them at least somewhat difficult to move very far. Furthermore, since people didn't move very far, neither did information. Places, too, were not only quite solid and immovable but tended to confront solid barriers (mountains, oceans, walls, borders) that made it difficult for people and things to exit or to enter.

Global "Liquids"

At an increasing rate over the last few centuries, and especially in the last several decades, that which once seemed so solid has tended to "melt." Instead of thinking of people, objects, information, and places as being like solid blocks of ice, we need to see them as tending, in recent years, to melt and as becoming increasingly liquid. Needless to say, it is far more difficult to move blocks of ice than to move the water that is produced when those blocks melt. Of course, to extend the metaphor, there continue to exist blocks of ice, even glaciers, in the contemporary world that have not melted, at least not completely. Solid material realities, such as people, cargo, and newspapers, continue to exist, but because of a wide range of technological developments in transportation, communication, and the Internet, they can move across the globe far more readily.

Thus, following the work of Zygmunt Bauman (2000, 2003, 2005, 2006), the perspective on globalisation presented here involves increasing liquidity (Lakoff 2008; Ritzer 2010c). However, there is a constant interplay between liquidity and solidity, with increases in that which is liquid (terrorist attacks launched against Israel from the West Bank) leading to counterreactions and the erection of new solid forms (a fence between Israel and the West Bank). However, at the moment and for the foreseeable future, the momentum lies with increasing and proliferating global liquidity.

Global "Flows"

Closely related to the idea of liquidity, and integral to it, is another key concept in thinking about globalisation, the idea of "flows" (Appadurai 1996). After all, liquids flow easily, far more easily, than solids. Because so much of the world has "melted" or is in the process of "melting," globalisation is increasingly characterised by great flows of increasingly liquid phenomena of all types, including people, objects, information, decisions, places,

and so on. In many cases, the flows have become raging floods that are increasingly less likely to be impeded by place-based barriers of any kind, including the oceans, mountains, and especially the borders of nation-states. This was demonstrated once again in late 2008 in the spread of the American credit and financial crisis to Europe and elsewhere: "In a global financial system, national borders are porous" (Landler 2008a:C1).

Looking at a very different kind of flow, as we saw in Chapter 14, many people in many parts of the world believe that they are being swamped by migrants, especially poor undocumented migrants (Moses 2006). Whether or not these are actually floods, they have come to be seen as such by many people, often aided by politicians and media personalities who have established their reputations by portraying migrants in that way. Places, too, can be said to be flowing around the world, for example, as immigrants re-create the places from which they come in new locales (Logan, Alba, and Zhang 2002). See Global Flow Map 15.1 for a visualisation of the "flow" of prominent Chinatowns around the world.

Undoubtedly because of their immateriality, ideas, images, and information, both legal (blogs) and illegal (child pornography), flow everywhere through interpersonal contact and the media, especially now via the Internet. Much of what would have been considered the height of global liquidity only a few years ago now seems increasingly sludge-like. This is especially the case when we focus on the impact of the computer and the Internet on the global flow of all sorts of things. Instead of scouring an import VHS catalogue and waiting weeks for an anime movie to ship from Japan, a person can simply open the Netflix app on her Xbox 360 and stream any number of anime movies instantly.

GLOBALISATION AND THE INTERNET

Since its birth in the 1990s, the Internet has profoundly affected almost every aspect of life, especially in the developed world. The Internet has expedited the globalisation of many different things and is, itself, a profound form and aspect of globalisation. The Internet is global in several senses, but the most important is that while its users are not equally divided between North and South, rich and poor, and so on, they *do* exist virtually

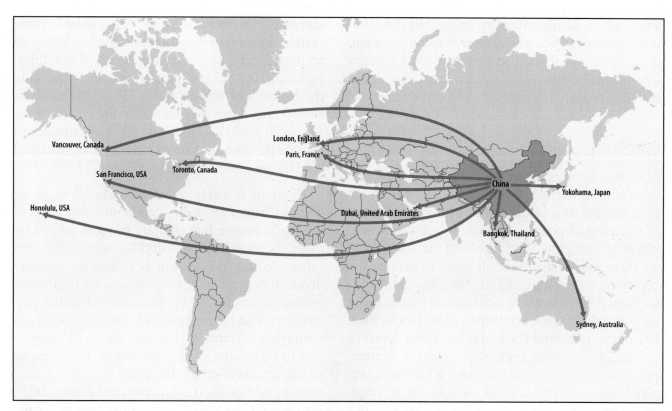

GLOBAL FLOW MAP 15.1 Prominent Chinatowns around the World

An Asian foods supermarket in the Barrio Chino (Chinatown) in Mexico City.

everywhere in the world (Drori 2006). It is also global in the sense that it was produced and is maintained by a number of global and transnational corporations and organisations, including multinational corporations (such as Intel), intergovernmental organisations, and international nongovernmental organisations. For instance, the World Intellectual Property Organization regulates intellectual property rights; the Internet Corporation for Assigned Names and Numbers coordinates domain names; and the UN Educational, Scientific and Cultural Organization promotes computer and Internet use in schools throughout the world.

Spam

It is argued, quite ironically, that "spam is one of globalization's true success stories" (Spector 2007:41). The main form of spam is, of course, unsolicited bulk e-mail, often of a commercial nature, such as offers of products to enhance sexual performance. While it is a bane to the web, spam is a global "success" in the sense that it stems from virtually everywhere on the globe (especially Eastern Europe, Russia, China, and Nigeria), goes everywhere, and is almost impossible to contain, let alone stop. It is one of the *flows* that are a defining feature of globalisation. Virtually as soon as methods are devised to stop the influx of spam, spammers find ways to get around those defenses. Programmes are for sale widely on the Internet that permit anyone from anywhere to get into the spam "business." And one needs virtually no computer expertise in order to become a contributor to the increasing avalanche of spam around the world. Since spam may now represent as much as 90 percent of all e-mails—more than 100 billion of them—it represents a real threat to the web (Symantec 2009). The faith of at least some in the entire system is being shaken because of the mass of useless and sometimes offensive messages that one must wade through in order to get to legitimate messages.

Computer Viruses

The idea of a computer virus made its first appearance in science fiction in the late 1960s and early 1970s. Over a decade later a graduate student wrote the first programme that was able to replicate and propagate itself. His professor, seeing its similarity to a biological phenomenon, suggested it be called a "computer virus." The first global computer virus was likely created in Pakistan in 1986. Since then, of course, many different viruses—some benign, some malicious

("malware")—have been created, circled the globe, and in some cases caused great damage to computer systems. For example, some of these viruses (Win32/Fareit; Mariposa) "infect" personal computers and access users' information, such as credit card numbers, which the cyberthief then uses to purchase all sorts of goods and services illegally. At the same time, global organisations, including law enforcement agencies, have emerged to try to warn people about new viruses and malware—the so-called *trojans* and *worms*—and to develop countermeasures to protect against them (Chanda 2007). To the degree that they are successful, the latter are barriers to the largely free flow of computer viruses around the globe.

It is clear that no change has done more to further the process of globalisation than the Internet. It occupies pride of place in many analyses of globalisation. Perhaps the most famous is Thomas Friedman's (2005) analysis of globalisation as involving a "flat world" (see the *Public Sociology* box in Chapter 6); the major example of such a world is the Internet. The Internet is flat in the sense that virtually anyone anywhere can, at least theoretically, become involved in it—although many poor and undeveloped communities still lack Internet access.

Spam text messages, largely consisting of real estate offers, ads for English lessons, fake tax receipts, and other frauds, have flourished in China in recent years—it is not unusual for Chinese citizens to receive dozens of unsolicited messages a day. China's three main mobile network operators signed an agreement in 2009 limiting the number of messages a mobile number could send per day to 1,000.

CONSUMPTION AND GLOBALISATION

There has been a tendency to associate consumption with America and, as far as the globe is concerned, with Americanisation. This is largely traceable to the affluence of the United States after the close of World War II and the economic difficulties encountered by most other societies in the world during this period. Thus, the United States developed an unprecedented and unmatched consumer society for several decades after the end of the war and at the same time began exporting it—and its various elements—to much of the rest of the world. While much of American consumer society came to be adopted elsewhere, it was also modified in various ways, even in the immediate aftermath of World War II in the European nations ravaged by the war and being aided through America's Marshall Plan (Kroen 2006).

The latter point brings us to the issue of globalisation and consumption. The emphasis in the global economy is to greatly increase flows of everything related to consumption and to greatly decrease any barriers to those flows. Especially important is the expediting of global flows of consumer goods and services of all types and of the financial processes and instruments that facilitate those flows. Thus, for example, the relatively small number of credit card brands with origins in the United States, especially Visa and MasterCard, are increasingly accepted and used throughout the world (Ritzer 1995). This serves to expedite not only global consumption but also the flow of global consumers, including tourists as well as the expansion of Americanisation.

Local and Regional Differences

While there was, and continues to be, an important American component to the globalisation of consumption, it is important to recognise that the heyday of the United States in this area is long past. In any case, there has always been much more to the globalisation of consumption than Americanisation (Brewer and Trentmann 2006). That is, local areas have certainly not always, or perhaps ever, been overwhelmed by American imports, but have integrated them into local cultural and economic realities. Furthermore, other nations and regions have been significant exporters of important aspects of consumer society, such as Mercedes-Benz and BMW automobiles from Germany. Finally, much consumption remains largely, if not totally, local in character. One example is the growing consumption of a mild stimulant, khat, or *qat,* in Kenya, where it is defined in a highly positive way locally. In addition, there is active resistance to external definitions of it, especially the U.S. definition of khat as a dangerous drug (D. Anderson and Carrier 2006).

Consumption also plays itself out differently in different parts of the world. For example, both the United States and Japan can be seen as consumer societies, but Japanese consumers differ from their U.S. counterparts in many ways, including the fact that they never fully embraced the idea of a consumer society and, more specifically, continue to manage to save a significant amount of money (see Figure 15.7; Garon 2006). Canada has historically had savings rates higher than the United States, but not as high as Japan.

While many consumer objects and services remain highly local (such as khat, mentioned above; the services of street-based letter writers for illiterate Indians), an increasing number have been

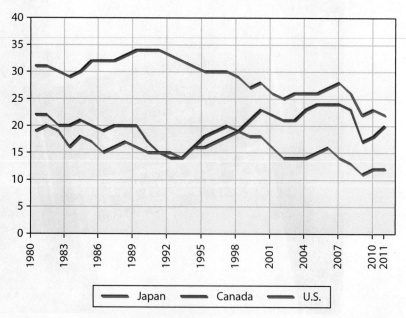

FIGURE 15.7 **Gross Savings as Percentage of GDP in Canada, Japan, and the United States, 1980–2011**

SOURCE: Adapted from the World Bank, Data: Gross Savings (% of GDP). http://data.worldbank.org/indicator/NY.GNS.ICTR.ZS

globalised. On the one hand, there are, for example, the global objects such as automobiles from the United States, Germany, and Japan. On the other hand, there are global services such as those offered by accounting firms, including KPMG International, as well as package delivery services such as DHL.

The Globalisation of Consumers

Increasing numbers of people throughout the world are spending more and more time as consumers. Not long ago it was very different, as most people spent most of their time as producers, or workers. Not only do more people spend more time consuming, but they are increasingly more likely to define themselves by what they consume, such as Bimmers, Patek Philippe watches, and so on, than by their jobs or the companies for which they work. Furthermore, consumers are on the move throughout the world, often as tourists. Not only is tourism a form of consumption, but much tourism is undertaken in order to consume the goods and services on offer at other locales throughout the world.

Increasing numbers of people throughout the world know what is expected of them as consumers; they generally know what to do in the consumption process wherever they happen to be in the world. This includes knowing how to work their way through a tourist resort or a shopping mall, use a credit card, or make a purchase online. Others have not yet encountered, let alone learned how to handle, these processes, but many of them certainly will in the not-too-distant future. Where these processes are known, there is a remarkable similarity throughout the world in the process of consuming in a resort, a supermarket, a shopping mall, or a fast-food restaurant.

Global Brands

A **brand** is a symbol that serves to identify and differentiate one product or service from the others. A brand can be contrasted with, and seeks to contrast itself to, generic commodities such as flour or soap (Holt 2004; Muniz 2007). The process of branding a product or service is undertaken because, if successful, a brand is not only distinguished from the basic commodity but can be sold in greater quantity and at a higher price. We are all familiar with the most

successful brands in the world (BlackBerry, Coca-Cola, McDonald's, Mercedes-Benz, Walmart, and the like), and much consumption is oriented to the purchase of brand-name products and services. Furthermore, even people come to be brand names (David Beckham, Angelina Jolie) and as such are "consumed" globally to a large degree. As brands themselves, they come to be closely associated with various brand-name products, with the best known examples, at least until recently, being the association of Michael Jordan and Tiger Woods with Nike.

Nike is a brand that has made itself so important that it can be said to have created a Nike culture and that has so influenced us that, to some degree, we can be said to live in such a culture (Goldman and Papson 1998; Hollister 2008). However, it is but a part of the larger *brand culture* in which we live.

Nike, a brand known worldwide, has been marketed so heavily and made so important that the company has in effect created a global Nike culture. Here, a man looks at a Nike advertisement and holds a Nike shoe in Beijing, China. Nike intends to reach $4 billion in annual sales in China by 2015, doubling its current numbers.

PUBLIC SOCIOLOGY

Naomi Klein: *No Logo*

Naomi Klein (1970–) is a Canadian journalist who is best known for books that have contributed to our understanding of consumption and globalisation. While there is significant sociological analysis in her work, it is most defined by her strong, perhaps sometimes hyperbolic, criticism of many aspects of both of these phenomena.

In *No Logo*, Klein ([2000] 2010) offers an unrelenting critique of the role of branding in the world of consumption. Among Klein's favourite targets are Nike, McDonald's, Microsoft, and Tommy Hilfiger, as well as celebrity brands such as Michael Jordan. In the context of a society that has shifted from the dominance of production to the preeminence of consumption, corporations have discovered that the key to success is no longer what they produce, but the creation and dissemination of a brand. While it concentrates on its brand, the modern corporation often outsources production to subcontractors in less developed parts of the world. Those who do the work in such places are paid a small percentage of what their counterparts in more developed nations would be paid. Klein is especially critical of the work done in free-enterprise zones in less developed countries where corporations and subcontractors are able to do as they wish, free of local government control. In those settings, wages are particularly low and working conditions especially harsh.

Given these realities in less developed countries, it is clearly in the interest of corporations to produce little or nothing in high-wage, developed countries. With production costs minuscule in less developed countries, these corporations can spend lavishly on their brands and the associated logos, such as Nike's swoosh and the McDonald's Golden Arches. Low production costs also allow for great profits and make it possible for corporate leaders to be paid unconscionable sums of money. Especially egregious is the contrast between someone such as Phil Knight, founder and chairman of Nike, and the economic situation experienced by those who work in development zone factories to produce Nike products, including some trafficked workers who function as modern-day slaves and are forced to work in Nike factories against their will. Similarly egregious are the sums of money paid to celebrities, are including Michael Jordan, to advertise products and, in the process, to become brands themselves. Once someone like Jordan achieves such a status, a synergy develops between the person and the corporation so that viewing one immediately brings to mind the other. Michael Jordan and Nike have become brands that have mutually supported and literally enriched one another.

Naomi Klein is one of the leading critics of branding and consumption in North America. Here, Klein speaks to a large Occupy Wall Street crowd at Zuccotti Park in October 2011.

That is, brands are a key part of the larger culture, they infuse it with meaning, and contemporary society as a whole is profoundly affected by brands (Schroeder 2007).

Brands are of great importance not only within Canada and many other nations but also globally. Indeed, much money and effort are invested in creating brand names that are recognised and trusted throughout the world. In her best-selling book *No Logo: Taking Aim at the Brand Bullies*, Naomi Klein ([2000] 2010) details the importance of brands in the contemporary world and the degree to which they are both globalised—corporate logos are virtually an international language—and having a global impact.

SUMMARY

Social change involves variations over time in every aspect of the social world, ranging from those changes affecting individuals to those that have an impact on the globe as a whole. Social change is all around you. For example, social movements and collective behaviour involve social change, are caused by other social changes, and are likely to lead to still other, broader social changes. Social movements are sustained and intentional collective efforts, usually operating outside of established institutional channels, either to bring about social change or to retard it. Prominent social movements include Greenpeace, the women's movement, the civil rights movement, and the gay and lesbian movement.

There are several conditions that must be met in order for a social movement to emerge. These include a set of grievances, efforts at mobilisation, opportunities within the political system, the proximity of people, the availability of free space to meet, and the availability of resources. Resource mobilisation theory relates to the latter point and focuses on what groups of people need to do in order to mobilise effectively to bring about social change. Once under way, methods must be utilised to ensure participation in a movement. There are a variety of factors that impact the success of a social movement, including its size and uniqueness as well as other groups' ability to suppress the movement. When successful, social movements can leave a lasting legacy.

A social movement is one type of collective behaviour. Collective behaviour is action generated, or engaged in, by a group of people. Emergent norm theory, based on the idea that new norms emerge in light of some precipitating event and guide the often nontraditional actions that characterise behaviour, is the dominant theoretical approach to examining types of collective behaviour. Other types of collective behaviour include crowds and riots. Disasters also impact people collectively. While disasters are sometimes natural phenomena, humans often play a significant role in bringing them about and exacerbating their consequences.

Social change occurs throughout the world, but it is particularly characteristic of globalisation, consumption, and the Internet, which we have focused on extensively in this book. Globalisation is arguably the most important change in human history. Globalisation is increasingly characterised by great flows of liquid phenomena across the globe. The Internet itself is both a form and an aspect of globalisation and has expedited the globalisation of many different things. In terms of consumption, the global economy focuses on increasing the flows of everything related to consumption and decreasing the barriers to these flows. While this does have some advantages, it also has distinct disadvantages, such as leading more societies to experience levels of hyperconsumption and hyperdebt. Increasing numbers of people across the globe are spending more time as consumers and not as producers. Additionally, global brands have become more prominent over the last several decades.

KEY TERMS

- Brand   625
- Collective behaviour   610
- Crowd   611
- Disasters   615
- Emergent norm theory   611

- Feminism   599
- Resource mobilisation theory   606
- Riot   612
- Social change   592
- Social movements   593

THINKING ABOUT SOCIOLOGY

1. What about Greenpeace makes it a social movement? What were the conditions or the context that facilitated the emergence of the Greenpeace movement?

2. What are the three different waves of the women's movement? How did the goals and strategies of the women's movement change during each of these three waves?

3. How have new communication technologies such as the Internet and social networking sites (Facebook and Twitter) aided global social movements? What types of resources move more easily because of these new technologies?

4. According to resource mobilisation theory, what do groups of people need in order to mobilise effectively? How can we apply this theory to the

discussion of the civil rights movement earlier in the chapter?

5. What mechanisms do social movements use to ensure member participation? How can you apply these mechanisms to the gay and lesbian movement discussed earlier in the chapter?

6. What factors are used to determine whether a social movement is successful? How has Greenpeace been successful to date? Has there been any resistance to the movement? How might this affect the movement's future success?

7. According to emergent norm theory, why are individuals likely to behave differently when they are in crowds? How can we explain some deviant

behaviour in bars (such as fighting or public displays of affection) using emergent norm theory?

8. The 2011 earthquake and tsunami in Japan is an example of a disaster. In what ways did humans exacerbate the consequences of this natural disaster? What sorts of negative long-term consequences can be expected from a disaster like this?

9. In what ways is globalisation the "ultimate social change"? How has the world become more liquid because of globalisation? What role have new communication technologies played in making the world more liquid?

10. Why is branding an important process to transnational corporations? In what ways is branding reflective of the process of Americanisation?

APPLYING THE SOCIOLOGICAL IMAGINATION ·····························

In many ways, 2011 was an important year for social movements around the world. Using what you have learned about social movements in this chapter, do some research on one of the social movements in the Arab world. What are some of the reasons that the social movement emerged? What resources was the social movement able to mobilise? What

mechanisms did the social movement use to encourage member participation? How did the processes of globalisation affect the movement? How has the movement been affected by new communication technologies such as the Internet and social networking sites? As it stands now, was the social movement successful?

ACTIVE SOCIOLOGY ···

If it wasn't already apparent, the Arab Spring (2011) brought to light the influence of social media on collective action and social movements. Information that used to take hours or even days to spread is now able to be shared in real time, or at least minute-by-minute updates. Social media sites including Twitter and Facebook make it easy to share and learn about issues of injustice and a push toward social change. Change.org is a site that promotes active citizenship by allowing you, the user, to create positions and gain support for your cause. Visit this site (www.change.org)

and view current petitions. What are the current top causes? Choose one that you think is important. Sign it and share it with your friends via Facebook and/or Twitter. Track the petition to see its outcome. How does this site allow for individual participation in social change? What are the pros and cons of this site's ease of use? After you sign and track a petition, will you continue following that cause? Why or why not? Think about a current issue (local, national, or global) that you think is unjust. Start a petition on this site and see where it goes.

STUDENT STUDY SITE ·······································

Visit the student study site at **www.sagepub.com/ritzercanadian** for additional web quizzes for further review.

RELIGION AND EDUCATION

Advocates of evolution-only science programmes cite the First Amendment to the U.S. Constitution's Establishment Clause and the importance of scientific validity in the classroom, while intelligent design proponents believe that evolution and intelligent design should be taught equally and that students should be encouraged to decide the truth for themselves.

16

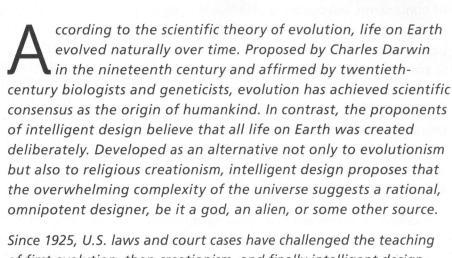

A ccording to the scientific theory of evolution, life on Earth evolved naturally over time. Proposed by Charles Darwin in the nineteenth century and affirmed by twentieth-century biologists and geneticists, evolution has achieved scientific consensus as the origin of humankind. In contrast, the proponents of intelligent design believe that all life on Earth was created deliberately. Developed as an alternative not only to evolutionism but also to religious creationism, intelligent design proposes that the overwhelming complexity of the universe suggests a rational, omnipotent designer, be it a god, an alien, or some other source.

Since 1925, U.S. laws and court cases have challenged the teaching of first evolution, then creationism, and finally intelligent design, in public schools. Advocates of evolution-only science programmes cite the First Amendment to the U.S. Constitution's Establishment Clause and the importance of scientific validity in the classroom, while intelligent design proponents believe that evolution and intelligent design should be taught equally and that students should be encouraged to decide the controversy for themselves. Even though intelligent design was developed to sidestep the religious nature of creationism, the debate over its teaching is deeply rooted in religious belief. Humans have explained life as the work of an omnipotent, sentient god (or set of gods) since before recorded history. While evolutionary biology is a relatively recent development in the timeline of human understanding, creation myths that centre on God have been passed down across centuries—in some cases millennia—of socialisation. Proponents of intelligent design may allow for an architect outside of an established religious tradition, but their acceptance of any otherworldly, untestable *force is inherently informed by and rooted in a nonscientific framing of the world. While intelligent design may serve a philosophical or sociocultural purpose, many advocates of evolution contend that it has no place in educational courses dedicated to evidence-based knowledge. People who value particular religious holidays, rituals, and beliefs (such as the Judeo-Christian six-day creation story) want their children to share these values. If an external socialising agent as influential as the public school system presents an entirely different perspective on the origins of humankind, advocates of intelligent design contend, this meaningful religious belief could be subverted, even abandoned, in generations to come. In Canada the New Democratic Party government of British Columbia issued an edict, in 1995, to stop the practise of teaching creationism, alongside the theory of evolution, as an explanation for the origin of life in science classes, a practise that had been followed in the Abbotsford School District for some time.*

The debate is important in its own right and symbolic of larger cultural issues. However, as you will learn in this chapter, the provincial education systems have far more difficult issues to deal with than the treatment of the origin of humans.

RELIGION

Religion is one of sociology's longest-running concerns. The early giants in the field were all affected by, and interested in, religion:

- The founder of sociology, Auguste Comte, was raised by a father who was an ardent Catholic, but he turned away from religion and toward science, especially a science of sociology. However, Comte transformed his science into a religion that resembled Catholicism, and he saw himself as its leader—the "Pope" of the new religion. (See Chapter 2.)

- Émile Durkheim was raised in a religious Jewish family; in fact, his father was a rabbi. Durkheim came to reject religion, but it, and morality more generally, became a subject of study for him, especially in the famous *Elementary Forms of Religious Life* (Durkheim [1912] 1965). (See Chapter 2.)

- Max Weber was torn between his highly religious mother and his secular father, who was a modern bureaucrat. Weber had a nervous breakdown when his father died soon after they had a violent argument. After he recovered, Weber spent the rest of his personal and professional life wrestling with the relationship between faith in religion and the rationalisation of the modern world epitomised by the bureaucracy. (See Chapter 2.)

- Sigmund Freud was victimised by anti-Semitism. He came to see religion as a psychological defence mechanism used by people to defend themselves against deprivations, especially of a sexual nature, caused by society. (See Chapter 5.)

- Although his father had converted to Christianity, Karl Marx, like Durkheim, came from a religious Jewish family and a long line of rabbis. However, Marx rejected all religions because he came to see them as tools used by the capitalists to control the proletariat. Religion distracted the workers from the need for social revolution. (See Chapter 2.)

Given this history, and the importance of religion to society, it is not surprising that religion became a central concern within sociology.

WHAT IS RELIGION?

Many scholars see religion as difficult or impossible to define because it is so complex and perceived differently by societies and even by individuals within any given society (James [1902] 1960; Weber 1963). Nevertheless, we need a definition to shape our discussion and analysis of religion (Hargrove 1989).

The best definition of religion is still the one derived from Émile Durkheim's ([1915] 1965) classic statement: **Religion** is a social phenomenon that consists of beliefs about the sacred; the experiences, practises, and rituals that reinforce those beliefs; and the community that shares similar beliefs and practises (Kurtz 2012).

COMPONENTS OF RELIGION

The major components of religion are beliefs, rituals, and experiences. Beliefs and rituals have grown out of and acted back on each other for millennia. They have persisted but also changed as believers of various religious traditions diffused globally and interacted with other religions in the lands they passed through and in which they settled. Moreover, neither belief nor ritual is created in isolation, but both are created as a response to people's experiences. Beliefs and rituals, in turn, shape these experiences.

BELIEF

Every religion has a set of interrelated **beliefs**, or ideas that explain the world and identify what should be sacred or held in awe, that is, the religion's "ultimate concerns." Religious beliefs have been shaped over thousands of years and are embedded in religious traditions.

Émile Durkheim argued that all human experience could be divided into two categories, the **sacred**, or what is of ultimate concern, and the **profane**, or the ordinary and mundane. People can come to *believe* that virtually anything is sacred—a deity, a place (such as Jerusalem), a particular time or season (for example, Ramadan or Diwali), an idea (such as freedom), or even a thing (for example, an animal, a mountain, a tree, a canyon, a flag, or a rock). The sacred is treated with respect, and one's relation to it is often defined in rituals: You might genuflect when passing in front of an altar or

take off your shoes when entering a temple. People believe that anything that is not considered sacred is profane.

Each religious tradition weaves together a fabric of many different and interdependent beliefs. These include beliefs about creation and suffering, as well as ethical standards for judging proper behaviour. When Muslims declare in their daily prayers, for example, that they believe that God is the Most Merciful and the Most Compassionate, it means that their behaviour must reflect God's mercy: "The imperative to be merciful—to bring benefit to the world and avert harm—must underlie a Muslim's understanding of reality and attitude toward society" (Abd-Allah 2005).

Beliefs are often presented in sacred stories and scriptures, which address questions about the origin and meaning of life, theories about why the world was created, and explanations of suffering and death. They first express a *worldview*—that is, a culture's most comprehensive image of the ways in which life—nature, self, and society—is ordered (Geertz 1973). That worldview in turn shapes an *ethos* (see page 644), which "expresses a culture's and a people's basic attitude about themselves and the world in general" (Geertz 1973:173).

These beliefs are at the same time models of and models for reality. They provide believers with information and a framework for interpreting the world around them. As models *for* reality, however, beliefs show how the world should be versus how it really is, often prompting the believer to act. Mahatma Gandhi believed that the world was ultimately grounded in truth and nonviolence and that a just god ruled the world. His noncooperation with the British Empire on behalf of the struggle for Indian independence was not only political resistance but also an act of faith. He saw no reason to be fearful of unjust political powers who were simply under the illusion that they were in control of the world. Hindu and Buddhist theories of *ahimsa*, nonharmfulness or nonviolence, not only explained the real power behind the universe for Gandhi but also gave him a guide for how to act.

Most religious belief systems include a *cosmogony*, a story about how and why the world was created, which usually links the believers to the act of creation.

Finally, every religious tradition provides a *theodicy,* an explanation for the presence of evil, suffering, and death. Most theodicies identify the source of evil in the world. How a religion recommends confronting evil may affect everything from individual beliefs and decisions to a nation's foreign policy. We can find a wide range of explanations in the world's religions for the existence of suffering: It may be seen as punishment for sinful behaviour, a result of a battle between evil and good, or just part of the natural cycles of life and death.

One of the most difficult dilemmas for any religion is to explain why good people suffer and bad people sometimes flourish. While the suffering of the righteous is problematic, most theodicies suggest that ethical behaviour will eventually be rewarded. Most mainstream religions suggest that suffering is just part of the way the universe functions, so that everyone is subject to it at one time or another. It is how you deal with suffering that is most important.

RITUAL

In most religious traditions, simply believing is never enough; one also has to act. The belief systems of religious traditions are replete with rituals that reinforce those beliefs, serve as reminders, and help believers enact their beliefs in the world. A **ritual** is a set of regularly repeated, prescribed, and traditional behaviours that serve to symbolise some value or belief (Kurtz 2012). Rituals are enacted during ceremonies and festivals, such as funerals and weddings or other **rites of passage—** rituals that surround major transitions in life: birth, puberty, marriage, and death, and conversion rituals such as baptism. Also included are ongoing spiritual practises, such as personal prayer and attending worship services of faith communities, as well as elements of everyday language that serve as religious reminders for many people.

Rituals come in many forms. Some, such as prayer, chanting, singing, and dancing, help

people communicate or show devotion to the gods. Some, such as mantras and meditations, help believers organise their personal and social lives. Some frame daily life, including those relating to diet, hygiene, and sexual practises, while others celebrate cycles of nature and build community, including holidays, seasonal festivals, and processionals.

Rituals solve problems of personal and collective life by providing time-tested actions, words, and sentiments for every occasion. When addressing serious problems, such as death, violence, natural disasters, or social crises, people often use rituals to (1) identify the source of the problem, (2) characterise it as evil, (3) mark boundaries between "us" and "them," and (4) give themselves some means of working toward a solution, or at least the satisfaction that they are doing something about the problem. In times of crisis, rituals can help people transform tragedy into opportunity. They build a sense of solidarity that provides support for the suffering and reinforces the authority of the social order and the institutions that sponsor the rituals, especially when they are being threatened. Rituals provide a theory of evil and focus participants' attention on some abstract issue, a personified devil or mythical figure, or a human enemy who needs to be denounced or attacked.

Participants usually believe that the rituals are effective and remember the stories from their culture or religion that remind them of their efficacy. Although partly a rational process, rituals as symbols also evoke sentiments and emotions that go beyond rationality. When a traditional ritual is used to solve personal or social troubles, it gains new authority and helps to sustain old habits and preserves the society and its institutions.

Religious rituals are also crucial for social change and cultural innovation, especially when traditional rituals can be transformed for revolutionary purposes. One example is Gandhi's use of religious processions, prayers, and scripture readings to mobilise his fellow Indians to demand their freedom from the British Empire, as brothers and sisters of the same god. In another example,

Though they may be widely accepted and normalised among believers, some religious rituals seem odd—even unsettling—to those outside the practising cultures. Here, Shi'ite Muslims flagellate themselves with knives to mark the martyrdom of Husayn ibn Ali during a Day of Ashura celebration in Karachi, Pakistan (left), and a preacher handles a poisonous snake at Camp Creek Holiness Church in Madison, West Virginia, to demonstrate full and literal adherence to the scripture.

in 1989 the Christian rituals of Eastern Europe provided spaces for nonviolent political resistance against communist regimes. And in 2011 the Muslim Friday prayers in Egypt became occasions for large gatherings on Friday afternoons that moved from prayer to protest.

Moreover, religious rituals often mark a **liminal** period, or a special time set apart from ordinary reality (V. Turner 1967). The sacred time during a religious ceremony may involve an inversion of apparent reality, giving hope for the oppressed that they will be liberated, for the sad that they will be comforted, and for the last that they shall be first. In the traditional Catholic Carnival ritual preceding Lent (a period of penitence), Old Man Winter is dethroned by the young Princess Spring. The norms of appropriate behaviour appear to be suspended as the celebrants sing, dance, and drink to excess. This helps encourage the revellers to overthrow

masculine authority. In the liminal period when stodgy patriarchy is defeated by youthful feminine energy, the cycles of nature replace winter with spring, resurrecting hope in the hearts of the celebrants.

EXPERIENCE

The combination of beliefs, rituals, and other practises forms the variety of religious experiences for believers regardless of which tradition they celebrate. Much of the human community views the world through a religious lens and constructs an identity around religious affiliation and experiences, such as prayer or attendance at religious services. In a survey of 44 countries, large numbers of people, especially in Africa, Latin America, and parts of Asia, reported religion and religious experiences to be very important in their lives (see Figure 16.1).

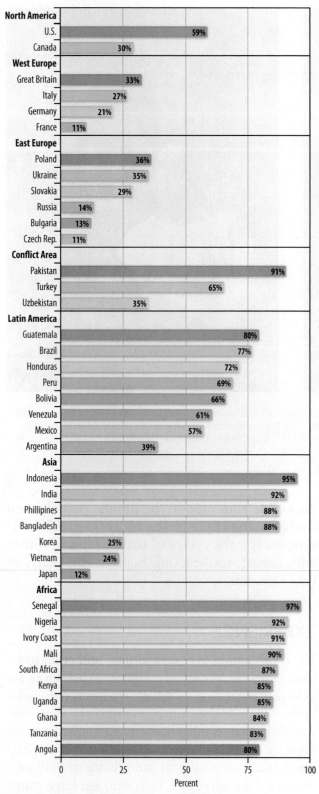

FIGURE 16.1 Percentage of Respondents Reporting "Religion Is Very Important" in Their Lives, 2002

SOURCE: *U.S. Stands Alone in Its Embrace of Religion among Wealthy Nations*, December 19, 2002. Pew Global Attitudes Project, Pew Research Center.

When asked about significant issues in their lives, about a fifth of Canadian young people between the ages of 15 and 29 report that religion is "very important" (see Figure 16.2). The percentage of Canadians over 50 who see religion as very important is twice as high. Among American young people, about 43 percent report that religion is "very important," a percentage only a little lower than for Americans 50 and over (50 percent). Canadians are more typical of the pattern of religious commitment in industrial countries, whereas the powerful grip of religion for many in the United States is anomalous among western nations.

Interestingly, a negative relationship exists between wealth and religiosity, with people living in poorer nations being more religious than those in wealthy countries (see Figure 16.3). The major exception is the United States. Religion is much more important to Americans than it is to people living in other wealthy nations. In African countries, no fewer than eight in ten report religion as very important, as do a majority of all Latin Americans except the Argentinians. Nine in ten of those in the predominantly Muslim countries (such as Indonesia, Pakistan, Mali, and Senegal) view religion as very important.

Religion, Aboriginal Spirituality, and the Courts

The experiences discussed to this point in this section relate to organised religion. However, many religious experiences occur outside of, and side by side with, those that occur in the context of those religions. One set of such experiences involves Aboriginal peoples. Notice the subheading reference to spirituality. This is intentional because the way we often think of religion, as involving churches, prayers, and Sunday attendance, does not capture how Aboriginal peoples practise religion. **Spirituality** is all-pervasive for Aboriginal people—it is integral to everything that they do, to every action they undertake. Certainly spiritual practises vary from tribe to tribe and person to person, but in Aboriginal culture spirituality is not separate from the rest of life, not confined to prayer time or church attendance.

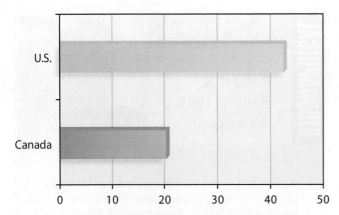

FIGURE 16.2 Percentage of Youth (15–29) Living in Canada and the U.S. Reporting "Religion Is Very Important" in Their Lives, 2006

SOURCE: Authors' calculations from the World Values Survey (www.worldvaluessurvey.org).

This becomes clearer perhaps in the context of an example about how the Canadian courts have dealt with Aboriginal spirituality (Beaman 2002; Ginn 1986). In 1985 Anderson Jack and his brother-in-law were convicted of shooting a deer out of season. The deer meat was to have been used as part of a religious cleansing ritual to honour Mrs. Jack's great grandfather. A Lower Court judge had argued that this practise of hunting and killing a deer was a long-standing religious tradition among Coast Salish people and should have been protected by the freedom to practise religion. The Supreme Court of Canada disagreed and effectively ruled that the motive for shooting the deer did not excuse the crime. That is, the need for the meat (motive) did not excuse the crime of killing the deer. They also ruled that the killing of the deer was not part of the religious ceremony. Instead meat that had been kept in a deep freezer, for instance, could have been used. Although Coast Salish people do not segment their lives into discrete activities such as hunting, honouring the dead, and religion, the courts used these categorical distinctions to delineate the activity of hunting as separate from any religious act. This example reinforces the opening note about the complexities in understanding religion, although notice that all of Durkheim's defining features are part of

the Aboriginal worldview as exemplified by the deer meat instance.

Secularisation

Secularisation refers to the declining significance of religion (Dobbelaere 2007). Secularisation occurs at both the societal and individual levels. At the societal level, it can involve the declining power of organised religion, as well as the loss by religion of functions such as education to the state. At the individual level, secularisation means that individual experience with religion is less intense and less important relative to other kinds of experiences.

The importance of religion among older, relative to younger, Canadians is one example of the declining significance of religion. So too is the significantly lower number of young women and men who now become nuns or priests. For some religion is still an important guide in their lives, but even here religious views now guide people's private lives more than they guide the direction of Canadian society. This is perhaps most noticeable in Quebec, where we have seen in a few examples that prior to the Quiet Revolution of the 1960s

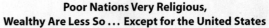
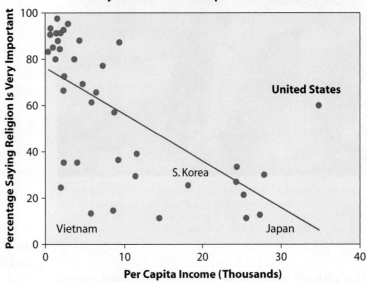

FIGURE 16.3 Religiosity and Income

SOURCE: "U.S. Stands Alone in Its Embrace of Religion among Wealthy Nations," December 19, 2002. Pew Global Attitudes Project, Pew Research Center.

Beliefs, rituals, and other practises form a believer's religious experience, regardless of which tradition that person celebrates. Here, a Buddhist monk prays at Dhamekh Stupa, a massive reliquary near Varanasi, India, where the historical Buddha allegedly taught his first sermon.

The sweat lodge is a tradition of many First Nations peoples, a ritual purification practice that would be recognized by a sociological definition of religious spirituality. The experience is meant to be a cleansing of the mind, the body, and the spirit.

BIOGRAPHICAL bits

Robert N. Bellah (1927–, American)

- Bellah obtained his doctorate from Harvard University; his doctoral dissertation was published in 1957 under the title *Tokugawa Religion.*

- His PhD was in both sociology and Far East languages.

- He taught for a decade at Harvard and then for three decades at the University of California, Berkeley, as Ford Professor of Sociology.

- Over the years he published many books on religion and morality, including one on Émile Durkheim's work on morality.

- In addition to his work on civil religion, he is perhaps best known for a coauthored book, *Habits of the Heart: Individualism and Commitment in American Life,* published in 1985.

- As the subtitle suggests, *Habits of the Heart* analyzes the conflict between individualism and community, including the kind of community offered by religion.

- U.S. President Bill Clinton awarded him the National Humanities Medal for his work on community in American society and the dangers of unchecked individualism.

- Although he has been retired for well over a decade, Bellah continues to be active, and in 2011 Harvard University published *Religion in Human Evolution: From the Paleolithic to the Axial Age*—the result of 13 years of research by Bellah.

the church was more integral to broad social decisions in both politics and education. However, while at one time a strong argument was made for increasing secularisation, the dominant view now is that contradictory trends are occurring, with increasing religiosity coexisting with entrenched and expanding secularisation (Goldstein 2009). The rise of evangelical Christianity and the prominence of religion among supporters of the Conservative Party of Canada speak to this revival. For some religion is more central to their lives, and at the collective level religion once again has come to animate more and more of political decision making.

Religion as a Form of Consumption

One measure of the degree to which religion has been secularised is the extent to which it has come to be associated with such a seemingly secular activity as consumption. In fact, religion has increasingly become just another arena in which to market religious experiences (Drane 2008). As with all other aspects of consumer culture, religions need to respond to the demands of those who consume them and what they have to offer (Roof 2001). Even more blatant are the efforts to sell all sorts of goods and services linked to religion (R. Moore 1997). All major holidays are associated with one form of consumption or another, but this is most clearly true of Christmas (Belk 1987). There are even religious theme parks devoted to consumption (O'Guinn and Belk 1989). Less obvious is the fact that religion itself has become just another form of consumption. That is, in Canada and elsewhere, people "shop" for religion much as they shop for most other things (Gonzalez 2010; Warner 1993). In this context, religions must compete for consumers of religion in much the same way that manufacturers and shopping malls compete for customers. Many churches, especially the large megachurches, are increasingly oriented to making themselves consumer friendly. Thus, they "have created sanctuaries that can only be intended to be entertainment spaces complete with stages, lighting, and even theatre-style seats" (Drane 2000:90–91). The fanciest megachurches may have aerobics classes and bowling alleys, as well as multimedia bible classes that are presented in ways that resemble MTV videos (Niebuhr 1995). At crusades, as well as in some cases in churches themselves (such as Canterbury Cathedral in England), people exit through a bookstore/gift shop that sells all sorts of religious and nonreligious items. On Sunday morning, big screens project scripture verses and lyrics to pop-style religious songs so that everyone in the congregation can see and follow along (Niebuhr 1995). The pastor of one Baptist church sought to make services more "fun"

and in order to do so urged his staff to study the techniques used by Disney World (Barron 1995).

Many Canadian universities have deep religious roots, although in most places this is much less obvious than it was 50 years ago. Nevertheless, the University of British Columbia, the University of Waterloo, and Dalhousie University all have strong religious connections through affiliated religious colleges. While religion has become more like secular forms of consumption, it can be argued that consumption has become our new religion. As a result, shopping malls and fast-food restaurants, among many other settings, have become places where people go to practise their consumer religion. For example, at the opening of a McDonald's in Moscow a worker spoke of it "as if it were the Cathedral at Chartres . . . a place to experience 'celestial joy'" (Keller 1990). A trip to Disney World has been described as the "middle class hajj, the compulsory visit to the sunbaked city" (Garfield 1991).

Shopping malls have much in common with traditional religious centres (Zepp 1997). In line with religious centres, shopping malls fulfill various human needs such as connecting with other

Many of Canada's universities, like the University of Waterloo pictured here, began with strong attachments to the church. In many cases, like Waterloo, some form of these affiliations continue. Other examples include Dalhousie, Western, Laval, and Alberta.

people; gaining a sense of community as well as receiving community services; being in the presence of nature in the form of water, trees, plants, and flowers found in the atriums; and participating in the nonstop festivals that are, and that take place in, shopping malls. Malls also provide the centredness usually associated with temples. They are characterised by a similar balance, order, and symmetry. Play is generally an integral part of religious practise, and malls are certainly a place to play. Similarly, malls offer a place where people can partake of ceremonial meals. In these and other ways, the shopping mall has religious qualities and therefore can truly be considered a "cathedral of consumption" (Ritzer 2010a). It is in those cathedrals, and in the process of consumption, that many people have what can only be described as religious experiences.

TYPES OF RELIGIOUS ORGANISATIONS

In modern secular societies we often think of religion as a private matter, but it is the faith communities that sustain and nurture religious experience in individuals. Religious traditions that persist become institutionalised, and in the twenty-first century, reflecting the societies in which they exist, many have become bureaucratised.

As with all other aspects of religion, its institutions are highly diverse both between and within religious traditions. On the one hand, religious institutions tend to reflect the organisational forms prominent in society. On the other, there is always a tension between the large, established, formalised institutions and newer or less formal religious groups that come and go. Moreover, religious institutions with a pluralistic religious worldview and a diverse population tend to be decentralised institutionally, whereas those with more homogeneous populations and belief systems may tend to be more centralised. Hinduism and Buddhism tend to be less centralised and hierarchical, whereas Christianity has become more formalised, in part as a response to the universalism of its membership.

Sociologists have distinguished between two basic kinds of religious organisations, the *sect* and the *church* (Swatos 2007b, n.d.). These are sometimes conceived as poles along a continuum from the sect at one end and the church on the other.

SECTS

A **sect** is a small group of people who have joined the group consciously and voluntarily in order to have a personal religious experience. That experience, as well as the behaviour of sect members, tends to be spontaneous and unregimented. A sect's leadership is usually composed of laypersons rather than those with specialised training. Sects tend to be antiestablishment, and the members often feel alienated from, and as a result are prone to reject, society and the status quo. Therefore, sects tend to draw their membership largely from the lower classes who are more interested in changing society than they are in maintaining the status quo. Sects tend to set themselves apart

While sect members often set themselves apart from society in terms of such things as dress and diet, there can still be great variation among branches and their members. For example, members of the Ultra-Orthodox Jewish group Neturei Karta stand apart from many Ultra-Orthodox Jews in their opposition to Zionism and belief that Israel should be dismantled as a state. Here, members of Neturei Karta watch as members of the group burn the Israeli flag.

PUBLIC SOCIOLOGY

Andrew M. Greeley: Sociologist, Priest, Novelist

Andrew Greeley is a unique person and a unique public sociologist. He obtained degrees in theology in the early 1950s and served as an assistant priest at a church in Chicago. However, he also began studying sociology at the University of Chicago and received his PhD from there in 1962. Thus, Greeley often fuses theology and sociology in his work, and this allows him to deal with some of the big social issues in the context of religion as well as some of the major questions of theology in the context of contemporary social realities and problems. His involvement in both theology and sociology allows him to fuse imagination with rationality in both his theological and his sociological

Andrew M. Greeley

work. He has held various academic positions and published numerous important academic articles and monographs, but what distinguishes Greeley is the breadth of his public sociology.

As a priest, Greeley has used sociology to raise a variety of social issues that need to be faced by his parishioners, the Catholic Church, and society as a whole. He has given homilies and written religious books and articles that deal with sociological and religious issues confronting the Catholic Church and its members. He has written a weekly column for the *Chicago Sun-Times* and has been a frequent contributor to other newspapers, including *The New York Times.* Greeley has also been a popular interviewee on radio and television.

What most distinguishes Greeley as a public sociologist is the fact that he has published 50 novels—many of them best sellers! Although these are novels and therefore tell good stories, they also often deal with important sociological issues. Most sociological work requires that the authors be good storytellers, but Greeley takes this to its logical conclusion in his novels.

However, it would be wrong to conclude that Greeley's main goal in his novels is to teach sociological lessons. Rather, he remains a priest, and as such his major objective is to teach moral and religious lessons both to laypeople and to those who labour in the church hierarchy. However, our main interest here is in the sociology in Greeley's novels. Among his novels and their sociological themes are the following:

- *The Priestly Sins: A Novel* (2005) takes on the issue of priests who are pedophiles, but is especially critical of the church bureaucracy and those who ignore and even protect those priests.

- In *White Smoke: A Novel of Papal Election* (1997) the election of a new pope is an occasion for Greeley to reflect on the nature of power and the role of old-fashioned politics and succession in the church hierarchy.

- Power and politics, this time in the White House, is the subject of *The Bishop in the West Wing* (2003).

- *Angel Light* (2006) deals with the very contemporary topics of the Internet, cyberspace, and computer hackers.

- Greeley is also concerned with the problems faced by women in society, especially in a series of books, the first of which was *Irish Gold* (1994), that feature a strong female character, Nuala Anne McGrail.

In 2008 Greeley suffered a devastating brain injury when his coat got caught in the door of a taxicab as it pulled away. He is under 24-hour care, has difficulty speaking, and is no longer able to write.

from the larger society and admit only those who rigorously conform to the group's norms. They frequently set themselves apart from society in terms of such things as how they dress and what they eat. In addition, they might even segregate themselves physically and live in areas that are largely isolated from the rest of the community. Two major examples of sects today are Hasidic Jews and the Doukhobors.

CHURCHES

In contrast, a **church** is a large group of religiously oriented people into which one is usually born rather than, as is the case in sects, joining consciously and voluntarily. The church's leadership is composed of professionals who have highly specialised training, and the church as a whole tends to have a highly bureaucratic structure (Diotallevi 2007). Churches tend to draw members from throughout society and across all social classes. While a sect tends to restrict membership to true believers, a church seeks to include as many people as possible. Churches often actively seek out new members, sometimes by employing missionaries. A church's belief systems tend to be highly codified, and rituals are often elaborate and performed in a highly prescribed manner. In comparison to members of sects, church members tend to have a lower level of commitment, and much less is expected of them. While sects tend to reject the status quo, churches are more mainstream and accepting of the status quo. The largest and best known church is the Roman Catholic Church.

While *sect* and *church* are presented here as if they are totally distinct, in reality there is no clear dividing line between them. They are discussed above as "ideal types" (see Chapter 3) in order to be able to distinguish them clearly. In fact, over time there is a tendency for sects to become churches. Among other things, as sects become larger they need ever-larger bureaucratic structures. The behaviour of sect members becomes less spontaneous and more rigid and formal. Examples of sects that have become churches include Baptists, Methodists, and Quakers.

CULTS

A cult resembles a sect in many ways, but it is important to distinguish between them (Stark and Bainbridge 1979). While a sect is a religious group that breaks off from a more established religion as a result of a schism in order to revive it and rediscover the original beliefs and practises of that organisation, a **cult** is a new, innovative, small, voluntary, and exclusive religious tradition that was never associated with any religious organisation. A cult is often at odds with established religions as well as the larger society. Those who found a cult tend to be religious radicals who want to go back to religion's origins, to import ideas from other religions, or to create totally new ideas.

The term *cult* has fallen out of favour in sociology because it is has come to be associated in the popular mind and press with such destructive groups as Charles Manson and his "family," which murdered a number of people, including actress Sharon Tate in 1969, as well as Jim Jones's Peoples Temple and the 1979 mass suicide of 918 of his followers in Guyana. Similarly, in Japan, the Aum Shinrikyo cult was involved in the release of sarin gas in the Tokyo subway system, killing 12 people and injuring thousands of others. However, none of these are true cults in the sense of the definition offered above. Among those that better fit the definition are more benign groups, such as the International Society for Krishna Consciousness, commonly known as *Hare Krishnas,* and Korean Reverend Sun Myung Moon's Unification Church. However, even these cults tend to have a negative connotation. For example, those who are associated with the Unification Church are often belittled as "Moonies." Given the negative connotations associated with the term *cult,* many sociologists today have discontinued using it. However, others continue to view *cult* as a useful sociological concept (Gary Shepard 2007).

NEW RELIGIOUS MOVEMENTS

Some sociologists prefer to use the term *new religious movements* to encompass sects, cults, and a wide array of other innovative religious groups. **New religious movements** are typified by their zealous religious converts, their charismatic leaders, their appeal to an atypical portion of the population, a tendency to differentiate between "us" and "them," distrust of others, and being prone to rapid fundamental changes (Barker 2007). One example is the New Age movement characterised by a belief in the coming of a global renewal in the "age of Aquarius," as well as an individually oriented spirituality (Introvigne 2007). The idea of a new religious movement eliminates the negative connotations associated with cults and emphasises the idea that each unconventional religious organisation should be examined objectively based on its own characteristics.

DENOMINATIONS

New religious movements sometimes move in the direction of greater respectability and public acceptance. Some of them become **denominations**, or organised forms of religious expression that typically support the social order and tend to be tolerant of other denominations (Swatos 2007a). Among major Christian denominations today are Methodists, Presbyterians, and Episcopalians. Denominationalism accepts a pluralistic view of religion and is in line with political pluralism (see Chapter 9).

THEORISING RELIGION

Because religion is such an important sociological subject, it should come as no surprise that researchers have examined it from the perspectives of the major sociological theories. In the following sections, religion will be addressed in terms of the structural/functional and conflict/critical lenses. While the former holds that religion fulfills important social functions—and perhaps simultaneously causes a panoply of dysfunctions—the latter argues that religion serves merely as a distraction from economic and social inequalities.

STRUCTURAL/FUNCTIONAL THEORY AND RELIGION

Early sociologists such as Auguste Comte and Émile Durkheim believed that religion fulfilled important social functions. The structural/functionalist perspective that emerged from their work focuses not only on the functions, or social purposes, served by religion but also on its dysfunctions.

Functions of Religion

In *The Elementary Forms of the Religious Life,* Durkheim ([1912] 1965) emphasises the social functions of religion, especially the solidarity produced by religion: "It is by uttering the same cry, pronouncing the same word, or performing the same gesture in regard to some object, that they become and feel themselves to be in unison" (p. 230). This definition also helps in understanding why hockey is referred to as Canada's religion! In addition to solidarity, religion provides a number of other functions for individuals and societies.

First, as Peter Berger (1969) suggests, religious and cultural traditions become a "sacred canopy" that covers people, provides a sense of security, and

Scientology, founded by science fiction author L. Ron Hubbard in 1953, is the archetypal new religious movement. In 2012, Russian courts upheld a ban on the publication and distribution of Scientologist books, citing them as extremist literature. A similar effort by the German government fell through in 2008, however, and Scientology continues to spread throughout the large central European country. Here, believers stand on a balcony at the Church of Scientology's newly built Berlin headquarters.

answers their questions about *meaning,* or the purpose of life. A religion's answers to these questions include an overall vision of the universe, a worldview, and perceptions of how best to organise life, individually and collectively.

Second, Durkheim ([1912] 1965) observes that religion provides explanations for puzzling aspects of life. Of particular importance are the previously discussed theodicies, theories that help us to better understand and deal with suffering and death.

A third and vital function of religion for any society and its individuals is to provide an *ethos,* or set of ethical guidelines. The ethos identifies taboo lines marking what is unacceptable or immoral behaviour. The ethos also promotes positive action, such as sharing and caring for others. Each religious tradition will also have a theory about what happens when people violate the norms, the most important of which are codified in a society's laws. While there is much variation within each religion, it is interesting to compare the similarities and

differences in the ethics of the founders of the global religions, as shown in Figure 16.4.

Most of these founding fathers begin with something like the Silver Rule of the Buddha and Confucius, or Jesus's Golden Rule: Treat others as you would like to be treated. This ethic is implied in the Decalogue (Ten Commandments) that Moses issues and the prophet Muhammad's insistence on showing mercy and compassion to others because God is the Most Merciful and the Most Compassionate.

In Buddhism, as in Hinduism, the consequences of violating the system's ethics come more or less automatically and are built into the structure of the universe and expressed in the idea of karma, which is actually quite similar to the Christian idea that you will reap what you sow (Galatians 6:7) (Jagannathan 1984:54). The law of karma is basically a law of cause and effect, which has the same status as the law of gravity in western science. The consequences of every thought, word, and deed

Founder	Key Ethical Teaching	Treatment of Violators
Buddha	Silver Rule: Don't do unto others . . . Show compassion to all creatures 10 immoral action, 5 precepts	Karma: Reap what you sow Repent: It can be OK (King Ajatasattu)
Confucius	Silver Rule Filial piety, respect	Reciprocity
Jesus	Golden Rule: Do unto others . . . Love God and neighbour Be perfect	Let the one without sin cast the first stone Judgment: Give food, drink, visit the prisoner
Moses	Decalogue (TenCommandments): Do not kill, steal, envy, etc. Love God and neighbour Follow the law	Pleads with God for mercy Punishes unrepentant
Prophet Muhammad	Love God Follow the law Show mercy to all of creation Hospitality Strict personal discipline	Compassionate with repentant sinners Judgment for those who will not repent Reciprocity of mercy—show it, you get it

FIGURE 16.4 Founders of the Global Religions and Key Ideas

SOURCE: From Lester R. Kurtz, *Comparative Ethics: Gods in the Global Village.* Thousand Oaks, CA: Sage, 2012: p. 147.

grow exponentially: If we harm people, it is very possible that they will not only harm us back but go on to harm others as well. It is also possible that harming others will become a habitual practise for dealing with conflict. Those they harm may, in turn, go on to harm still others so that the entire network in which they interact turns to violence more frequently. If, on the other hand, we show compassion—even to those who harm us—it increases the chances that those we treat well will treat others well and on and on. That is why the Buddha insisted, "Hatreds never cease through hatred in this world; through love alone they cease. This is an eternal law" (Buddha n.d.).

The idea of treating others with compassion and love—including one's enemies—is a theme that runs through all the world's faith traditions, perhaps mitigating intercommunal hatred and violence. Jesus taught, "You have heard that it was said, 'You shall love your neighbor and hate your enemy.' But I say to you, Love your enemies and pray for those who persecute you just as God sends rain on both the just and the unjust" (Matthew 5:43–45). Similar sentiments are in the scriptures of Taoism, Confucianism, Sikhism, Judaism, and Islam (World Scripture n.d.).

A fourth function of religion is to provide guidelines for a better style of life. Recent research has shown that Americans who are actively religious are more likely to have better physical and mental health (Ellison 1999). One way this is accomplished is by helping people develop social support networks and ways of coping with various types of stress.

Fifth, religious systems can provide individuals and groups with hope for the future, including what happens after death, giving believers a sense of self-confidence. If you believe the universe is friendly or at least that you are on the right side of larger forces or that they are protecting you, it is easier to have a sense that the future will turn out well, even if the present seems dark. The Qur'an (9:72) insists, for example, that no matter how difficult life seems at the moment,

> God has promised
> the believing male and the believing females
> gardens beneath which rivers flow,
> to abide in them,
> and pleasant dwellings
> in gardens of eternity. (Cleary 2004:93)

Finally, religion plays a crucial role in the process of social change. Although religious institutions are often intertwined with ruling elites, they also provide the foundation for major changes in a society. Examples include the Rev. Dr. Martin Luther King Jr.'s condemnation of racism in the United States, the antiapartheid movement's challenge to the South African government, and the uprisings in Eastern Europe in 1989 and the Arab world in 2011. In more subtle ways religious groups have been instrumental in sponsoring many refugees who have brought changes to Canada, including the introduction of new religious practises.

Dysfunctions of Religion

Although religion can facilitate the creation of community, it also might lead to ethnocentrism involving intolerance, conflict, and sometimes violence

Sikhism is a monotheistic religion founded in India's Punjab region during the fifteenth century. The fifth-largest world religion, with more than 30 million adherents, Sikhism advocates, among other things, universal brotherhood and the equality of all humankind. Here, Pakistani Sikhs load relief goods to be sent to the earthquake-struck village of Lahore, which straddles the border between Pakistan and India.

between religious groups. This is the "paradox of community": The same things that draw us together tear us apart (Ekland-Olson 2012). Although being a Hindu in South Asia may give one a sense of belonging to a significant community, for some it is at the expense of bonds with Muslims. In forging their identities in terms of negative comparisons, the two communities tend to cultivate disrespect for each other. This mutual disrespect sometimes becomes violent.

Moreover, the very functions of religion may be dysfunctional. What is functional from one point of view is dysfunctional from another. Religion may promote solidarity and order, but to the detriment of oppressed minority groups or those exploited by the system, by helping to keep injustice in place. It may provide explanations for suffering and evil that single out some groups as responsible for a society's problems. It therefore provides a rationale for the subordination of those groups or for hostility against them.

The flip side of social solidarity is antipathy toward the other, which is a hallmark of religious history in many times and places. Exclusivist, "chosenness" theologies that promote the status of one group or society at the expense of another can be functional not only for a given community or society, but for regional and international relations. Those traditions that accentuate differences between "us" and "them," and imbue those differences and their perceived superior status with a sacred endorsement, are almost inevitably going to engage in conflict with others. Religious communities with an ethnocentric view of the world and a belief that they are chosen by God—that only people who follow their beliefs and rituals are God's elect—are more vulnerable to rhetoric of exclusion and the condemnation of outsiders. In the midst of communal conflicts both parties may see the other community as the focus of evil in the world and the source of all their problems. Religious justifications for these social divisions—such as the scapegoating of Jews in Nazi Germany—intensify emotions and sometimes make the conflict itself take on a sacred meaning (Kurtz 2005). Escalating communal conflict can, in short, lead to violence and even war.

The final and perhaps most dangerous dysfunction of religion, therefore, is the fact that it sometimes promotes violence and even evil behaviour. A major reason for this is that religion provides a rationale for the use of violence against others. Individuals who are going to harm others have to use what are called "mechanisms of moral disengagement" in order to avoid having guilty feelings for engaging in such behaviour (Bandura et al. 1996). Among the most effective of those mechanisms, often facilitated by religious beliefs, are the practises of dehumanisation, blaming the victim, and advantageous comparison. That is, if others are evil and condemned by God, they are more easily dehumanised and rationalised as unworthy of respect or dignity.

CONFLICT/CRITICAL THEORY AND RELIGION

A discussion of the dysfunctions of religion leads nicely into the conflict/critical approach to religion. Much of this approach continues to be informed by Karl Marx's original thinking in general, especially on the base and superstructure of capitalist society. To Marx ([1859] 1970), the *base* of capitalist society is the economy, while everything else—ideas, the state, and religion—are part of the

Hindu Brahmins chant mantras and present offering of fire while others gather to pray in Ujjain, India. In Hinduism, Brahmins are priests who officiate religious rites and teach religious principles. At the top of India's caste system, Brahmins have historically been regarded as separate from and higher than most other Indians. This has afforded Brahmins great power, wealth, and respect, and has allowed them as a group to marginalise and take advantage of lower castes.

superstructure. The things that are part of the super-structure in capitalist society are erected on an economic base. Thus, the nature of ideas, the state, and religion is ultimately traceable to that base. As a result, it is the capitalist economy that controls religion—as well as the state and ideas—and religion serves to enhance and protect the economic base.

To Marx, religion performs this function by serving as an ideology that, like all ideologies, distorts and hides the underlying realities of capitalist society. Religious ideologies also serve to distract people and to obscure those economic and social realities. They are like drugs that put people into a daze so that they cannot see the social world accurately. It is this view that leads Marx ([1843] 1970) to his famous idea that religion is the "opium of the people." People who are drugged by religion are not only unable to have an accurate view of social problems but are also unable to act on those problems, let alone overthrow the capitalist social structure that is the source of those problems.

Religion can be seen as what the contemporary critical theorist Jürgen Habermas (1975) called **legitimations**, or systems of ideas generated by the social system to support its own existence. Thus, the ideas associated with religion legitimate not only it, but also the social, economic, and political system in which it exists. To the critical theorists, legitimations serve to "mystify" all of these systems, making it unclear exactly what is happening, especially the negative effects these systems are having on large numbers of people.

Another way of thinking of religion is that its distortions and illusions lead people into *false consciousness* (see Chapter 2). That is, because of religion and many other social forces, large numbers of people do not have a clear and correct sense of their true interests. For example, the working class does not realise that it is being exploited in a capitalist system. To critical theorists, false consciousness, including that induced by religion, prevents people from acquiring *class consciousness,* or a true sense of their interests. Without religion, people would be better able to see that their interests would be furthered by the overthrow of the capitalist system as well as the religious system that supports it (Lukacs [1922] 1968).

The role of churches has long been controversial on the political left. While many Church members have been staunch supporters of human rights, sponsoring refugees to come to Canada for example, the Church is also understood by some on the left as promoting a false consciousness by distracting people from their own exploitation in a capitalist wage system. Or, as Habermas insisted, to "mystify." (Nave and alter of Notre Dame Basilica in Montreal.)

The role of churches has long been controversial on the political left. While many church members have been staunch supporters of human rights, sponsoring refugees to come to Canada, for example, the church is also understood by some on the left as promoting a false consciousness by distracting people from their own exploitation in a capitalist wage system. Or, as Habermas insisted, to "mystify."

RELIGION AND GLOBALISATION

Every major religious tradition was originally a local, even tribal, expression of faith that grew out of a specific environment and then diffused across certain regions and eventually the globe. All of the global religions originated in Asia: The eastern religions, including Hinduism, Buddhism, Confucianism, and Taoism, originated in South Asia and then spread east into China and East and South Asia. The western religions, including Judaism, Christianity, and Islam, came from West Asia, or the Middle East.

Today, three out of ten people in the world might identify themselves as Christians (see Figure 16.5) (Brittanica 2012; Kurtz 2012:46). Two out of the ten would be Muslims, one Hindu, and one Buddhist or a related East Asian religion (such as Taoist). Another one in ten would represent all other religious groups, including Judaism, various folk religions, and tribal and shamanist traditions. Only two of the ten would be unaffiliated or identify themselves as atheists.

The study of the relationship between religion and globalisation is very contemporary, but it is clear that religion globalised before anything else. In fact, by this accounting globalisation is at least 2,000 years old (Beyer 2006). Although religion, like globalisation, is a highly contested concept, we can focus on institutional religion and under that heading on two aspects of its relationship to globalisation.

First, there is the issue of the importance of religion in transnational migration—in the bringing of institutional religion to new locales. Migrants transplant religions into new places, making those places more multireligious. They also generate in those locales new and different versions of the local religions even as the migrants' versions are influenced and altered by local religions. This, in turn, can alter religion in the migrants' homeland. Thus, transnational migration globalises religion spatially and contributes to the further pluralisation of religion around the world. Migrants play a variety of other roles in globalisation. They help to unify various parts of the world by, for example, making pilgrimages to religious sites such as Mecca and the Wailing Wall, posting prayers in cyberspace, and sending money to religious centres in their homelands.

Second is the spread of religious organisations and movements through independent missions. Here the Christian Church, especially the Roman Catholic Church, has played a central role through its missionaries. In fact, Christianity became the first worldwide religion. Messengers for Islam created the most global system prior to the modern era (see page 649).

Many other religions have expanded globally, but special note must be made of Buddhism and Islam and their renewed expansion and the utilisation of new possibilities and technologies.

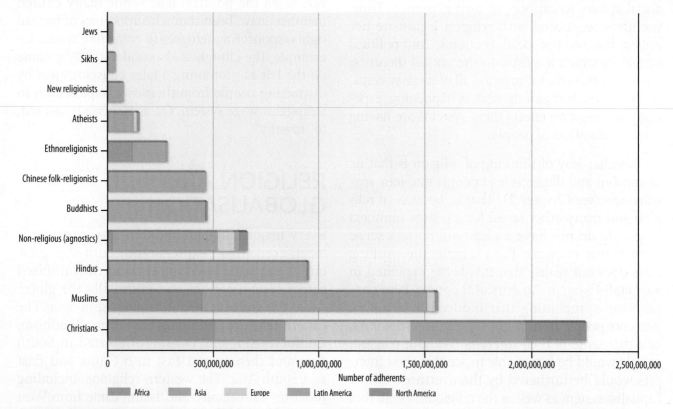

FIGURE 16.5 Worldwide Adherents of Major Religions, Mid-2010

SOURCE: Data from "Religion: Year in Review 2010." *Britannica Book of the Year, Encyclopædia Britannica Online.* Encyclopædia Britannica Inc., 2012.

A Christian missionary watches over children at the end of the school day at Guatemala's Manantenasoa Center. The Christian Church, especially the Roman Catholic Church, has played a central role in bringing institutional religion to new locales through its missionaries. While its prominence declines in parts of the Global North, Christianity continues to grow throughout the Global South in regions first introduced to the religion through missionary work.

It is also important to keep in mind that the spread of institutionalised religion was not unrelated to other institutions and other aspects of globalisation. For example, the spread of Christianity in the sixteenth century through the eighteenth century was closely related to the spread of European political power and influence. Colonialism, as experienced by Aboriginal peoples in Canada, was frequently ministered via the church, whether in residential schools or in missionary schools.

THE MOST SIGNIFICANT GLOBAL RELIGIONS

The religions we will deal with in this section are those that have globalised the most, or have spread furthest throughout the world: Judaism, Buddhism, Hinduism, Islam, and Christianity (see Figure 16.6). Under the heading of Christianity we will give special attention to Mormonism because of its very contemporary efforts to globalise.

Judaism

Founded more than 3,000 years ago, Judaism is today one of the smallest of the world's religions, with roughly 13.4 million people in the world defining themselves as Jews (H. Goldberg 2007; Goldscheider 2012). However, for a variety of reasons Judaism's importance both historically and contemporaneously has been far greater than one would think looking simply at the numbers involved. By the late nineteenth century there were 12 million Jews in the world who had migrated from the Middle East and were spread in small enclaves throughout the world. There was and continued to be a large concentration of Jews in Europe, but migrations to North America, as well as to Israel (then under Ottoman control), began during this period. By World War II the number of Jews in the world had grown to 16.6 million, but the atrocities of the Nazis led to a reduction in the population to about 10 million. The founding of Israel in 1948 marked an important turning point for Jews, and its population is now approaching 6 million people. Another large concentration of Jews—approximately 6 million—lives in North America, mostly in the United States. The vast majority of all of the over 13 million Jews alive today live in either North America or Israel, with fewer than 2 million living elsewhere, especially in Europe. Just a few of the factors that make Judaism of great global significance are the spread of Jews throughout the world, Zionism (which helped lead to the founding of Israel), the Holocaust, anti-Semitism, and the conflict between Israel and its Arab neighbours over Palestine.

Hinduism

Although there is no precise starting date, Hinduism began sometime between 800 and 200 BCE (Abrutyn 2012). While it had ancient origins, Hinduism became firmly established in India as it opposed foreign occupations of Muslims (999–1757) and later the British (1757–1947). Today, the vast majority of Hindus (about 800 million) live in India. Hinduism is strongly defined by the *Vedas*, which are both historical documents and enumerations of incantations needed for successful rituals. Hinduism is also closely associated with the caste system (see Chapter 8).

While it continues to be heavily concentrated in India, Hinduism is a global religion spread across six continents. It is spread by both migrants and itinerant religious teachers (Madan 2007). Although it is

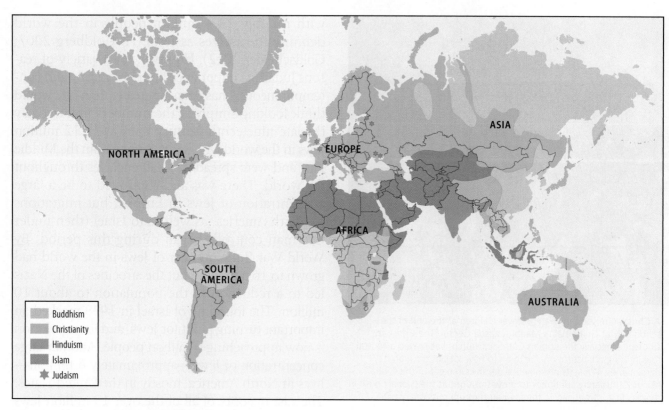

FIGURE 16.6 The Most Globalised Religions

SOURCE: From *Globalization: A Basic Text* by George Ritzer. Copyright © 2010 George Ritzer. Published by Wiley-Blackwell.

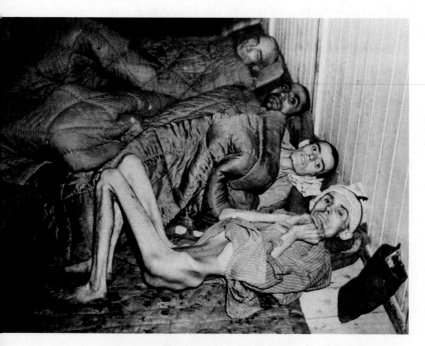

The atrocities of the Nazis led to a reduction in the global Jewish population to about 10 million. Liberated Jewish prisoners of Buchenwald concentration camp, still showing evidence of horrific mistreatment and starvation, struggle to retain warmth in 1945.

heavily concentrated geographically, Hinduism has been important as part of the "Easternization of the West" (Campbell 2007) in, for example, the spread of yoga, transcendental meditation, and so on. However, Hinduism has not been nearly as expansionistic as Christianity, Islam, or even Buddhism.

Buddhism

Buddhism arose in the Indus-Ganges Basin in about the sixth century BCE and began to have a transnational influence about three centuries later (Nichols 2012; J. Taylor 2007). Today, there are somewhere between 230 million and 500 million Buddhists across the globe, although the vast majority are in Asia. China has the largest number of Buddhists, followed by Japan.

Islam

Islam was founded by the prophet Muhammad, who was born on the Arabian Peninsula and lived between 570 and 632 CE. The lands encompassed

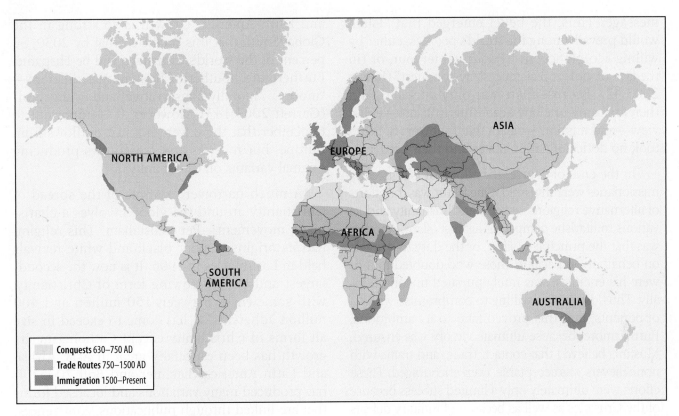

FIGURE 16.7 The Global Reach of Islam

SOURCE: The World of Islam—Version 2.0, 2001, Editor: J. Dudley Woodberry, General Mapping International.

by Islam were seen as the centre of the world, with all else subordinate to it. Important to its spread (see Figure 16.7) was its universalistic worldview; Muslims did not view themselves as a chosen people but believed that they and all of humanity had a common destiny. Islam's universalistic ideas (God-given standards that led everyone to search for goodness) had to be diffused throughout the world. Such beliefs led to a global mission to rid the world of competing idea systems, such as idolatry and superstition. On the other hand, it saw itself as building on, but going beyond, Judaism and Christianity. Thus, "Islam was the first of the world's great religious civilizations to understand itself as one religion among others" (Keane 2003:42).

Believers in Islam, as well as their armies, spread westward into Spain and France and eastward into Byzantium, Persia, and eventually India and China. They travelled with the belief that they were the messengers and that everyone was eagerly awaiting, if not being actively denied, their

Muslim believers at Makhachkala, Russia's central mosque, mark the start of Ramadan in October 2004. Throughout the ninth month of the Islamic calendar, millions of Muslims around the world observe the holy month of Ramadan with fasting and prayer. While Islam's early missionaries did not realise a complete global spread of their religion, they achieved astounding success throughout southwestern Asia and northern Africa.

message. Thus, the belief emerged that "Islam would prevail among the world's peoples, either by willing acceptance, or by spiritual fervour, or (in the face of violent resistances) by conquest" (Keane 2003:42). Because there was only one God, and therefore only one law according to Islam, such a view—and mission—meant that followers of Islam took no notice of nation-states and their borders.

In the end, of course, the efforts of Islam's early missionaries were thwarted. One factor was the efforts of alternative religions, especially Christianity and its various militaristic campaigns against Islam. Another was that the principle of *jihad,* or the duty to struggle on behalf of God against those who doubted him or were his enemies, was rarely pursued unconditionally. Thus, Islam was willing to compromise with its opponents, and this proved fatal to its ambitions. Furthermore, because ultimate victory was ensured, Muslims believed that contact, trade, and traffic with nonbelievers was acceptable, even encouraged. These efforts were ultimately only a limited success because of the Crusades as well as because of military defeats that forced Muslims out of Italy, Spain, and Portugal. However, the history of such efforts remains strong among many devotees of Islam and helps to inform the contemporary thinking of jihadists and Islamic fundamentalists (Sayyid 2012).

Christianity

Christianity and Islam are the two fastest-growing religions in the world today (Garrett 2007; G. Thomas 2012). Christianity spread in the Middle East following the death of Jesus of Nazareth. By 1000 CE, a schism developed between Roman Catholicism in the West and Orthodoxy in the East, with more Christians living in the East than the West. A major series of events in the history of globalisation was the Crusades, which began in 1095 CE and lasted for centuries. The Crusades were designed to liberate the Holy Land from Muslims and others who had gained control of Jerusalem in 638 CE. This is still a sensitive issue for Muslims, as reflected in protests that erupted when American President George W. Bush used the word *crusade* in a speech shortly after the 9/11 terrorist attacks.

Christianity today is declining in Europe, but that is more than compensated for by strong growth in the Global South, including parts of Asia, Africa,

and Latin America. Growth is so strong in the Global South that it is predicted that by 2050, 80 percent of the world's Christians will be Hispanic. Furthermore, southern Christianity is different— "more . . . morally conservative, and evangelical" (Garrett 2007:143). However, it is important to remember that there were not just outflows from Europe, but reverse- and cross-flows producing original variants on Christianity.

A much narrower example of the spread of Christianity around the globe involves a charismatic movement—Pentecostalism. This religion had its origins in poor black and white revivals held in Los Angeles in 1906. It is now the second-largest and fastest-growing form of Christianity, with somewhere between 150 million and 400 million adherents. It has come to exceed in size all forms of Christianity except Catholicism. Its growth has been especially great in Asia, Africa, and Latin America (Lechner and Boli 2005). It has produced many variations and localised forms that are linked through publications, conferences, electronic media, and travel. First Nations communities, as well as in other Canadian locales, have witnessed the growth of Pentecostalism (M. Wilkinson 2009).

Mormonism

Mormonism, or the Church of Jesus Christ of Latter-day Saints, has shown substantial growth in the last 50 years. Founded in the United States in the nineteenth century, Mormonism had fewer than 2 million members in 1960, but today that number has risen to approximately 13 million.

The Church of Jesus Christ of Latter-day Saints is centrally controlled from its headquarters in Salt Lake City, Utah. The organisation exercises considerable oversight over its churches. It also transmits much content, such as conferences and leadership training, via satellite throughout the world. And, of course, it maintains websites for the use of its global members. Global Flow Map 16.1 shows the countries with the most Mormon missions across the globe.

Once almost exclusively an American religion, today it has more members (about 7 million) outside the United States and has 8,400 churches and meetinghouses in 178 countries and territories.

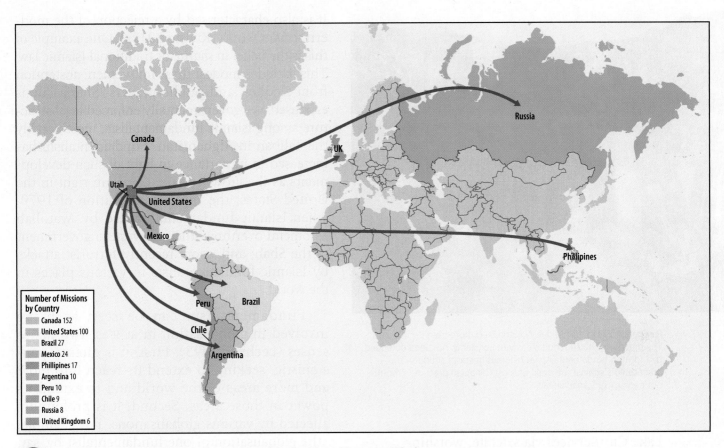

Number of Missions
by Country

Canada	152
United States	100
Brazil	27
Mexico	24
Phillipines	17
Argentina	10
Peru	10
Chile	9
Russia	8
United Kingdom	6

GLOBAL FLOW MAP 16.1 Countries with the Most Mormon Missions

SOURCE: Data from www.mormon.org

Although it had a ban on blacks becoming priests until 1978, today it is growing rapidly in Africa, with about a quarter of a million members there (Jordan 2007).

The global expansion of Mormonism is not only an example of globalisation but also the result of a variety of global processes. First, as noted above, the church has made extensive use of the Internet, especially its well-known website (www.mormon.org). Second, church services, conferences, and leadership training conducted at the church's headquarters are broadcast via satellite to 6,000 of its churches around the world. Third, it continues to follow the traditional path of global and globalising religions by sending tens of thousands of missionaries around the world. The global acceptance and expansion of Mormonism are especially notable because of its sect-like character and practises. For example, the church has a history of polygamy and the marriage of preteen girls to older men—practises that some fundamentalist

branches of Mormonism continue to this day, as in the Mormon settlement in Bountiful, British Columbia. Such traditions are not easily accepted in many cultures and parts of the world. Other unusual practises include having a family "sealed," so that it can stay together after death, and *tithing*, whereby one-tenth of one's income is given to the church.

In contrast to other globally successful religions, Mormonism has not significantly adapted to local customs and realities. For example, unlike the far more rapidly expanding Pentecostalism, Mormonism has *not* incorporated a variety of indigenous customs (such as drumming and dancing) into its African Sunday services. Said one member who had moved to Nigeria and married a Nigerian: "No matter where you go in the world, the service is the same . . . the buildings, baptismal fonts, services and hymns in Lagos were nearly identical to those back home in the United States" (Jordan 2007:A13). Through watching Salt

Pictured in the foreground is Winston Blackmore from Bountiful BC. The practice of having multiple wives, polygamy, has been defended by Mormon fundamentalists as religious freedom although this practice cuts against the grain of most Canadian practice, although not necessarily Canadian law.

Lake City services via satellite, worshippers elsewhere in the world can easily see that the services and the teachings are the same— or at least very similar.

The practise of having multiple wives, polygamy, has been defended by Mormon fundamentalists as religious freedom. The practise cuts against the grain of most Canadian practise, although not necessarily Canadian law.

Fundamentalism

Religious fundamentalism is a strongly held belief in the fundamental or foundational precepts of any religion (Stolow 2004).

It is also characterised by a rejection of the modern secular world (Kivisto 2012a). One example of this is the belief in *sharia,* or traditional Islamic law. This includes modest dress for women, abstention from alcohol, and public prayers. Sharia law is espoused as a governmentally enforced legal structure among Islamic fundamentalists, most notably the Taliban in Afghanistan. Fundamentalism has increased in importance in light of such developments as the growth of the Christian right in the United States, the Iranian Revolution of 1979, when Islamic fundamentalists led by Ayatollah Khomeini overthrew the pro-western government of the Shah, and, more recently, terrorist attacks by Islamic fundamentalists in various places in the world.

Fundamentalism can be seen as being involved in globalisation in at least two major senses (Lechner 1993). First, it is often expansionistic, seeking to extend its reach into more and more areas of the world and to extend its power in those areas. Second, it is profoundly affected by various globalisations. For example, the globalisation of one fundamentalist by, say, Islamic militants, is likely to lead to a counterreaction by, say, Hasidic Jews. Another important reaction involves that against various forces seen as emanating from the modern world, including secularism, popular culture, rationalisation, and the West in general. Much of the momentum for the recent rise of fundamentalism can be seen as traceable to a reaction against such forces. In a

In April 2011, France instituted a ban on covering one's face in public, effectively outlawing the burqa. While proponents of the ban believe that burqas symbolise gender inequality and the oppression of women, opponents suggest that France is acting to limit religious freedom and is itself being oppressive. Here, two women, one wearing a burqa, walk side by side in downtown Marseille, France.

subtler sense, it has become a global expectation that people develop a communal identity through involvement in fundamentalism.

EDUCATION

Education is closely related to the process of social-isation discussed in Chapter 5. In fact there is no clear line between the two, since both involve the learning process. Much socialisation—for example, learning not to eat with one's hands—takes place largely within the family in a child's early years. However, a good deal of education takes place during those years, as well, with children learning to talk and in many cases to read before they begin their formal schooling. In adulthood, much new learning takes place during socialisa-tion processes, such as when starting a new job, but adults also increasingly participate in adult education programmes. Overall, some educa-tion takes place during socialisation processes, and socialisation—for example, orientation when beginning university—occurs in educational settings. As a general rule socialisation tends to be a more informal process while education takes place more formally in schools of various types (Zerelli 2007).

Historically in Canada, when a child reaches about 5 years of age the focus has shifted from the highly informal process of socialisation in the family to the more formal educational pro-cess in schools. It is important to note, however, that an increasing number of Canadian chil-dren, and more recently children elsewhere in the world, are being homeschooled (Arai 2000; Martin-Chang, Gould, and Meuse 2011). This, like many other changes in education, is spurred on by the digital revolution, which is making homeschooling, indeed schooling in any setting, much easier and more effective (A. Collins and Halverson 2009).

While 5 years of age is the norm for start-ing school, increasingly in Canada and in other developed countries much younger children are entering preschools, and infants as young as a few months old are being placed in day care cen-tres. While all schools involve a shift away from parents to others in the processes of socialisation and education, a number of issues arise when large numbers of 2- to 3-year-olds, and especially 2- to 3-month-olds, are turned over to schools for large portions of the day.

Of course, this only touches on the beginnings of the educational process. In Canada, education goes on for many years through grade school, high school, university, graduate school, and professional school, and even beyond in formal adult socialisa-tion programmes (S. Davies and Guppy 2013). Most people do not progress through all of these stages, and where one ends one's formal education has pro-found implications for one's future. Clearly, educa-tional attainment and lifetime earnings are closely related. While there are many other measures of suc-cess in life, levels of education and earnings are obvi-ously of great importance (Blau and Duncan 1967).

Education makes a huge difference not only at the individual level but also at the level of the nation-state. Thus, if we compare nation-states on a global basis, those nations with strong educational systems and high levels of education also tend to be more economically prosperous. In addition, there are other benefits, such as being better-off in terms of overall health and tending to be more open politi-cally (Bills 2007; Buchmann and Hannum 2001). As Figure 16.8 shows, nations with higher levels of schooling in the population are much more likely to have a more prosperous economy, as measured by gross domestic product per person.

THINKING ABOUT EDUCATION

As with religion, analyses of education lend them-selves nicely to the broad theories that inform this book. In the following sections, educa-tion will be discussed in terms of the structural/functional approach, the conflict/critical approach, and the inter/actionist approach.

STRUCTURAL/ FUNCTIONAL THEORY

The structural/functional orientation to education is traceable to one of the founders of sociology, Émile Durkheim. Durkheim was a professor of the

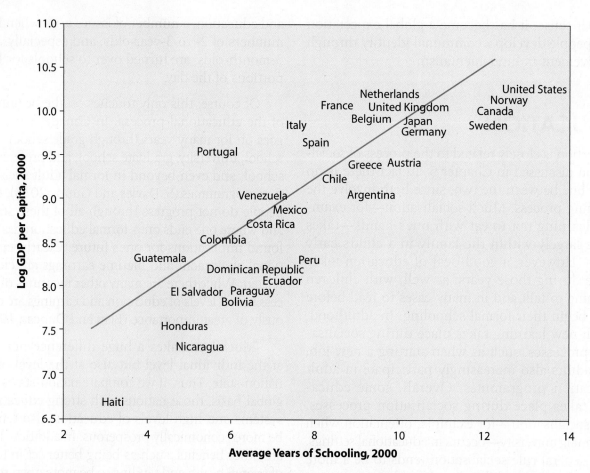

FIGURE 16.8 The Relationship Between National Gross Domestic Product and Average Years of Schooling

SOURCE: Adapted from Campante, Filipe and Edward Glaeser. 2009. "Yet Another Tale of Two Cities: Buenos Aires and Chicago." Working Paper 15104, National Bureau of Economic Research: Cambridge, MA.

science of education and sociology at the famous French university, the Sorbonne. He felt that the task of sociology was to provide the needed theory, while education was a crucial area to which that theory was to be applied. Education was defined by Durkheim as the process by which the individual acquires the physical, intellectual, and moral tools needed to function in society. Thus to Durkheim and to later structural-functionalists, education is a structure that is functional for both individuals and society.

Durkheim on Education

Durkheim (1973) believed that the educational system should provide individuals with two types of training. First, schools should provide individuals with training for life in the broader society. Each society is unique, with its own needs, and

has a culture with its own moral codes, values, and norms. Recall that anomie, a state of "norm-lessness," was a major issue for Durkheim (see Chapter 2). Durkheim hoped that schools would provide those guidelines as well as the social "glue" that would help a highly differentiated society remain normatively coherent.

Second, Durkheim believed that individuals needed specialised training for the specific "milieu" that a person will occupy in life. As regards "milieu," Durkheim was especially concerned with the many diverse occupations that arose in modern societies. Durkheim believed that schools should not provide every member of the society with the same type of education. Individuals needed the technical skills to do their jobs well, and the complex division of labour meant that education should be aligned with one's future occupational aspirations. Schools should help all workers acquire the skills to increase economic productivity in their occupational context. Durkheim also believed that occupations were increasingly a locus of social activity within society. Thus, schools needed to socialise workers for social life within occupations so that they could more easily interact with people at work.

Durkheim argued that educational systems should differ depending on a society's particular circumstances and needs. Thus, we should expect school systems to vary by time and place. For example, Roman society sought to make all students "men of action, devoted to military glory, and indifferent to letters and the arts" (Durkheim 1956:64). In contrast, modern society values individualism and personal autonomy, and the educational system in a modern capitalist society should inculcate those values in younger generations. Durkheim notes such an education would have harmed Roman society and failed to allow it to maintain itself.

A Later Structural/ Functional Approach

Robert Dreeben (1968) provided a later structural/ functional account of the role that educational institutions play in socialising the young into industrial societies. Schools teach students four main values that are critically important for success in such societies. First, schools encourage independence among students. Children must learn that adults in the broader society are less available to them than their parents, and they must learn to function on their own. Second, schools teach children to value achievement. While families tend to accept and value each child unconditionally, a teacher's acceptance of a student often depends on successful performance in the classroom. Third, while families are particularistic and treat each child as a unique person, schools are universalistic, treating children as members of general social categories, such as third graders and honour students. Finally, schools teach the norm of "specificity." While families think of the "whole child," schools are interested only in specific aspects of a given student. Math teachers judge students on their math skills and are uninterested in a student's performance in other

subjects, let alone their behaviour outside the classroom. Together, the daily practises and underlying structure of schooling socialise students for life in the broader society by ensuring that they possess the values considered necessary for society to function properly.

In sum, Durkheim and later structural-functionalists believe that school systems are at worst benign institutions and at best highly positive systems necessary to the successful functioning of society. As we will see, conflict theorists question this assumption and suggest that the educational system serves the interests of some social groups much better than others.

CONFLICT/CRITICAL THEORY

There are two main approaches under this heading that have proposed very different views of the role education plays in society. However, the overarching view of both perspectives is that education serves to reproduce social inequalities and reinforces the system of social stratification. In other words, the education system tends to help those on top and to adversely affect those toward the bottom of the stratification system.

Capitalist Systems and Education

The first conflict/critical perspective is largely inspired by Karl Marx's critique of capitalism. Marx believed that a capitalist society's dominant social institutions, including its schools, support and reproduce the capitalist system, just like religion.

Working within this perspective, Bowles and Gintis (1976) argued that in order to maximise profits, capitalists must find ways to motivate their workers to work hard even though they earn a disproportionately small share of the profits. Schools address this problem by training students to be submissive, docile, punctual, and hardworking— all of the traits that make for "good" workers in the capitalist system. As in the factory and the office, students are required to show up regularly and follow a schedule; follow the orders of an authority figure, such as the teacher; do boring work that has little meaning; and pursue external rewards, or grades, rather than the intrinsic meaning in their work, or learning. Bowles and Gintis labelled this the "hidden curriculum" of schools. Students who displayed the traits of punctuality, dependability, perseverance, and consistency received the highest grades in school.

Bowles and Gintis (1976) also recognised that some workers, such as managers, professionals, and other highly skilled workers, needed different skill sets to perform their role well in the capitalist order. It could be argued that curricular tracking arose in schools in order to deal with this problem. Students who were likely to attain jobs that required creativity, independence, and problem-solving skills were placed in advanced classes with an enriched curriculum that instilled these values. Oakes (2005) studied the curricular content and experiences of students in high- and low-track classes. She found support for Bowles and Gintis's theory: High-track students were exposed to a more sophisticated curriculum and were encouraged to be independent problem solvers, while low-track students were rewarded for rote learning, conformity, and docility.

The 1982 film *The Wall*, based on a 1979 Pink Floyd album of the same name, depicts the construction and eventual demolition of an allegorical brick wall. A portion of the film portrays the educational system as a capitalistic enterprise that promotes uniformity, conformity, and obedience. Lyrics from "Another Brick in the Wall (Part 2)," which plays during this scene, punctuate this message: "We don't need no education / We don't need no thought control . . . All in all, you're just another brick in the wall."

P. Willis (1977; McGrew 2011) offered a different interpretation of how the capitalist system reproduces the economic order. He studied working-class students—"lads"—in Great Britain, and he found that they do not passively submit to the normative climate of schools. Rather, they actively resist attempts to make them docile and subservient to authority. The lads formed an "oppositional culture," and they openly mocked teachers and students who bought into the schooling system. Ultimately, by rejecting school, the lads embraced working-class culture and ended up reproducing the capitalist order by becoming factory workers like their parents. Willis's contribution is to highlight the role of students as *active agents* in the process of social reproduction.

Overall, conflict theorists inspired by Marx conclude that the educational system is a system of **social reproduction**—class relations and the capitalist order are systematically reproduced with each new generation of students.

Industrialised Society and Education

A second conflict/critical perspective on education was largely inspired by the writings of Max Weber. Weber recognised that modern industrialised societies became increasingly dependent on the rise of rationalised bureaucracies. Educational institutions and specialised certifications linked to occupations arose along with the proliferation of bureaucracies. However, Weber did not believe that the main purpose of schooling was to enhance the skills of workers in bureaucratic systems. Rather, schooling helped certain social groups exclude outsiders from entering their trade or profession, and thereby monopolise and control access to these economic positions. In short, Weber saw education as central to a status competition among groups with society.

Randall Collins (1979) extended this idea in focusing on the educational credentials, such as university degrees of all sorts, needed to succeed in society. He examined the expansion of educational institutions in the United States from the late 1800s through the 1930s. Collins found that functionalist accounts of increased skill demands at work did not explain the growth in secondary and postsecondary schooling during that period because the growth in credentials expanded much faster than jobs requiring complex skills. According to Collins, educational expansion was due to credentialing—the linkage between educational degrees and high-status positions. As low- and high-status groups both pursued upward mobility, Collins argued that high-status groups maintained their social position by acquiring more education and more educational credentials. Low-status groups found it more difficult to attain the same credentials as high-status groups, and therefore found it difficult to improve their social position.

It is important to recognise that Collins argued that there is often little substance to these "inflated" credentials—additional schooling does not really make workers more productive; rather, it only serves as a social signal to employers to convince them that an applicant is the "right" kind of person for the job. Thus, Collins believed that educational expansion driven by status competition is inherently wasteful and inefficient for society.

The MBA is often criticised as such a "hollow" degree, and that criticism has picked up since the onset of the latest economic recession. After all, it was those with MBAs who occupied many high-level financial and corporate positions, and they played a key role in plunging the American, and the global, economy into a deep recession. The norms and values taught in MBA programmes— the emphasis on maximising the profits of one's employer as well as one's own income, irrespective of costs—were key factors in overheating the economy and in the emergence of the recession. In fact, in light of the recession, many graduate schools of business are rethinking their MBA programmes in order to make them less hollow—to better equip MBAs to know how to avoid producing the next great recession (Datar, Garvin, and Cullen 2010).

Critical theorists focus on culture rather than the economy, and they see education as part of the larger culture. In capitalism that culture is seen as producing a mass culture that is administered and phony (M. Jay 1973). The ideas associated with that culture are designed to repress, pacify, and stupefy students. In this view, education is designed to keep people in their place and not to teach them the sorts of things that might lead them to think creatively, let alone resist or rebel (Wotherspoon 2009).

Educational systems are also part of what the critical theorists call the "knowledge industry" (Schroyer 1970). The use of the term *industry* here is meant to suggest that education is not that much different from traditional industries, such as the automobile and computer industries. This means, for example, that educational systems such as universities and research institutes have sought to extend their cultural influence throughout society and well beyond their original educational mandate. In recent years the educational system has become increasingly industrial in the sense that more and more of it is characterised and affected by profit-making organisations. We will discuss several of these educational organisations in the section on consumption and education.

INTER/ACTIONIST THEORY

Symbolic interactionism tends to focus more microscopically on the school, the classroom, and interaction between teachers and students, among students, and so on. One concern is how at this level the system of patterned advantages and disadvantages discussed above is reinforced in the classroom. This sometimes becomes an application of labelling theory discussed in Chapter 7. In the classroom, students acquire a variety of labels, such as *good* and *bad*, *smart* and *slow*. Such labels tend to reinforce the students' own previous experience, as well as teachers' experiences with them or what they've heard about the students. Such reinforcement serves to reproduce both positive (*good, smart*) and negative (*bad, slow*) behaviour in the classroom. Students are very much aware of the labels being applied to them and come under enormous pressure from themselves and others to live up to the expectations associated with those labels.

The classroom is an "interaction order" (see Chapter 5), and it is the primary responsibility of the teacher to maintain order in it (Way 2007). However, this involves a delicate balance—too much control can stifle the educational process, and too little can lead to chaos and little or no possibility of any meaningful learning. Student behaviour can be unruly and aggressive, but it often takes much more mundane forms that, nonetheless, can disrupt the class. The following is one example of the kinds of disruptions teachers must deal with: "Being a physically attractive young lady in an extremely short skirt, this jaunt [to the pencil sharpener in the front of the room] captured the attention of everyone in the room, the teacher included. In her seat, she shortly began a whispered conversation with those around her, even though textwork had been given" (Stebbins 1977:45–46). This kind of seemingly trivial everyday classroom behaviour is an important issue for symbolic interactionists, as is what, if anything, teachers and peers do about it. Of course, there are far more serious discipline problems in the classroom, such as delinquency and gang activity, that are of great public concern and also involve the kind of topics of interest to symbolic interactionists.

Ethnomethodologists are interested in the everyday methods that students and teachers employ to accomplish, for example, taking an exam or having a discussion about current events (C. Baker 1997). These are the kinds of things that are taken for granted by most people, including most sociologists, but are the focal concerns of ethnomethodologists. Much of their work involves a detailed analysis of talk and of conversations in the classroom. The key point here, as in many places in their work, is that ethnomethodologists refuse to treat students as **cultural dopes**, that is, as being controlled unthinkingly by a variety of external forces such as school rules or teacher demands. Rather, students—and teachers—are actively and thoughtfully involved in accomplishing the taking of exams or the discussion of, for example, current events. The ethnomethodologist must attend to what the students say and do in the classroom. In fact, in a real sense, what students and teachers say and do in the classroom *is* the class. This is the topic of study for the ethnomethodologist while structural-functionalists and conflict/critical theorists tend to see what transpires in the classroom as being determined largely by such structural forces as the structure of the classroom, the school, and the educational system as a whole.

EDUCATION AND CONSUMPTION

In the broadest sense, students have always been consumers of education, although the expansion of digital, online education means that students will be

More often than not, classroom disruption is relatively mundane. The proliferation of laptops, tablets, and smartphones—coupled with the popularity of wireless Internet access and texting—ensures that there is always something vying for students' attention while teachers are attempting to instruct. Habitual texting during class can earn a student a label of "inconsiderate" or "uninterested," which may affect a teacher's opinion of and willingness to help that student.

less consumers of education and more active producers of the educational process. What is different today is the emergence of an all-encompassing consumer society, as well as the increasing commercialisation of education (T. Norris 2011a). Although students have always consumed education, they have not always done so in ways that yield profits for commercial enterprises.

COMMERCIALISATION AND CONSUMPTION

Education takes place in societies, especially North American society, where consumption is pervasive. Consumption is not restricted to the obvious places, such as shopping malls, supermarkets, and fast-food restaurants, but is manifest throughout society. Students are deeply immersed in that society and can't help but bring its ethos into the educational setting. At the university level, education, or at least the degree, is increasingly seen as a product to be purchased and consumed. As in most consumption, the emphasis is on evaluating educational alternatives in order to find the one that promises the greatest return for the least amount of money. Parents who are likely to foot the bill for most university expenses are especially oriented to looking at university education from this perspective.

As a result, at least in part, of the pervasiveness of consumer culture, we are witnessing the increasing commercialisation of the educational system itself. There is, for example, the increase in for-profit education in corporations such as the University of Phoenix. It is the largest for-profit university in the United States, with over 100,000 students, about a third of whom are online students. The University of Phoenix has physical classrooms in several Canadian cities. For-profit education is most pervasive in Canada in the franchises of firms, including Sylvan Learning, Oxford Learning, and Kumon (Auruni, forthcoming). This is a form of shadow education, outside the formal school system but increasingly used by parents as a way of investing in the educational success of their children. The hope is that this supplemental instruction, similar to hiring private tutors, will enhance the grades of students and increase the likelihood of their success in entering strong universities and selective fields of study such as law and medicine.

Corporate businesses have tried for some time to have a presence in traditional public schools, but this practise is much more common in the United States than in Canada. However, one local retailer of high-tech products donated computers to some schools in the Toronto school system. In return, the retailer required the schools that received the computers to repaint classrooms in the colours and patterns of its logo. In addition, the only schools that received computers were those within shopping distance of one of the retailer's stores (T. Norris 2011b). At the university level this corporate intrusion has been much more visible, with various campuses across the country having buildings or portions of buildings connected with corporate sponsors. Corporations also donate to specific university causes, as did Kinross Gold in giving Queen's University $500,000 to support a professorship in mining and sustainability. These gifts are often controversial because on the one hand they support scholarship while on the other they promote private business interests (Carroll 2010).

INEQUALITY IN EDUCATION

A **meritocracy** is a dominant ideology involving the widely shared belief that all people have an equal chance of succeeding economically, based on their hard work and skills (see Chapter 4). A meritocratic social system also requires that people's social origins, such as class background, and ascribed characteristics, such as ancestry, race, and gender, be unrelated to their opportunities to move up in the social system. Education is a centrally important institution in a meritocracy because it has the potential to level the playing field and provide equal opportunities for students to learn, work hard, and compete to move up in the social hierarchy.

Structural-functionalists see meritocracy as a positive development because society benefits

DIGITAL LIVING

The Digital Revolution in Education

As with much else in the social world, education has been radically transformed in the digital age, and it is likely that it will change even more in the years to come. The most obvious example of this is the changes in schools themselves. To borrow a phrase from industry, schools have gone from "just-in-case" to "just-in-time" learning (A. Collins and Halverson 2009). That is, schools are moving from teaching various things that students might need to know at some point in the future to teaching what students want and need to know at a given point. There is less focus on providing students with a wide range of knowledge that they may never need or use, and more on what is needed and can be used at the moment.

There are a variety of more specific changes in schools that can be linked to digital technology. First, instead of mass-produced and uniform education, digital technology makes it possible to customise learning for the individual student. This can involve offering a virtually unlimited range of content, as well as responding to a given student's particular interests and problems. Second, instead of the teacher being seen as the only expert who presents information through lectures (Koller 2011), information on the Internet is now one of many resources for students. Third, assessment changes as a result of the above, with the result that it, like learning itself, is more individualised rather than the standardised testing that dominates education today. Fourth, instead of focusing on memorisation, teachers need to focus on teaching about, and allowing students to use, outside sources. Fifth, the old notion of covering everything there is to know in a course or through a single textbook—which, itself, is increasingly likely to be digital—students need to

be taught *how* to learn throughout their lifetimes and *where* to find whatever information they might require. Finally, instead of the more passive process of simply acquiring knowledge, digital technologies allow for greater interactivity and "learning by doing."

Digital technology has also allowed more education to take place in settings other than the school. As a result, the nature of the traditional school and classroom is threatened and will need to change radically in the future. Beyond those changes, there will be more education throughout one's lifetime, in the home, at work, on the Internet through distance education, at commercial learning centres, through videos and educational television, and via computer-based learning environments such as The Sims. Furthermore, certification is increasingly possible online, such as finishing high school through a GED programme. It is worth noting, too, that the increasingly important smartphones will allow education to take place on the go and in virtually every setting imaginable. In other words, education, like much else, will be increasingly mobile (Urry 2007).

While much digital education is to be welcomed, it is not without its problems, such as creating or exacerbating the "digital divide" between well-to-do students who can afford various technologies and poorer students who cannot. This, of course, is even truer globally, where the Global South will continue to lag far behind the Global North in access to digital technologies useful in education. Another important unresolved issue is whether, in spite of all the glitz and attention, digital technology really improves learning (Richtel 2011a).

from having the most important positions filled by the most hardworking, skilled, and capable individuals. Conflict theorists argue that advantaged groups will secure better opportunities for their children and thereby be able to reproduce their social and economic status across generations.

WHO SUCCEEDS IN SCHOOL?

In a meritocratic society, we would expect to find that social origins and ascribed characteristics would have little effect on how much students learn and how far they go in school. In all western countries, there is a clear pattern of inequality

GL🌐BALISATION

American Universities Overseas

American universities have long been active overseas, but a relatively recent development is the rush toward the construction by American universities of branch campuses overseas (Clotfelter 2010; Lewin 2008a, 2008b, 2008c). Existing programmes are being expanded and new ones created in various countries, including China, India, and Singapore, and most importantly the Middle East, especially the Persian Gulf area. Why there? The obvious answer is that the nations in that area are awash with oil money and can afford such educational centres, and they can afford to pay the way for many students to attend them. For example, the president of New York University was led to create a branch campus in Abu Dhabi by a $50 million gift from its government.

Universities are headed toward becoming *global universities.* Faculty and students will move back and forth around the globe to the various branch campuses of a university. An educational centre known as Education City has developed in Doha, Qatar. Students from there, and the general region, will be able to study at branch campuses of leading universities, such as Weill Medical College of Cornell University, Georgetown, Carnegie Mellon, Virginia Commonwealth, and Texas A&M.

The expansion of American universities overseas raises a number of other interesting questions from the point of view of globalisation. One issue is to what degree these international campuses will reflect American culture or the culture of the nation in which the branch university exists. Another is the issue of whether it is in the interest of the United States to export its educational systems. That is, there are those who believe that training people from other nations will serve to adversely affect the ability of the United States to compete globally. Then there is the matter of what happens to these campuses, especially as they expand in the future, if, for example, Abu Dhabi falls to a radical Islamic regime hostile to the United States and the North in general. Still another issue is

whether these transplanted universities will come to generate great hostility as simply a new version of American imperialism.

Students converse in the library of the Texas A&M University campus at the Qatar Foundation Education City in Doha, Qatar. The expansion of American universities overseas raises a number of interesting questions about globalisation and American imperialism.

that suggests that the educational system is not meritocratic. Put another way, social origins and ascribed characteristics have an effect on educational outcomes in all western countries. This was captured very clearly in a recent Organisation for Economic Co-operation and Development study, "A Family Affair" (OECD 2010). The report is titled "A Family Affair" because it demonstrates that students do better or worse on educational tests as a function of their family's socioeconomic background. As indicated by grades on an international science test, students from advantaged backgrounds

DIGITAL LIVING

Student Plagiarism in the Internet Age

Plagiarism among students and the role of Internet in it are of huge concern in the educational system, especially in colleges and universities (S. Blum 2009). Students and others, including their professors, have, at least on occasion and perhaps inadvertently, always plagiarised. In the Internet age, plagiarism has become much more common, much easier, and much more difficult to detect (Gabriel 2010). Text can simply be "cut" from an Internet site and "pasted" on a student's paper. However, what is most different today is that it seems less clear, at least to students, what constitutes plagiarism—what is their own work and what is that of others. A key factor here is the idea of "crowdsourcing" (Howe 2008); that is, much of what appears on the Internet has been produced by a number of people, often a large group of people. For example, all entries on Wikipedia are written and rewritten, by hundreds, perhaps thousands, of people. It may even be the case, although it would be highly unusual, that the student plagiarising part of a Wikipedia entry was one of the contributors to it. The "author" of much of the material on the user-generated Internet is unclear. Some students may believe that it is not necessary to cite work for which no author is indicated. If the whole idea of an author is unclear and crowdsourcing is increasingly the norm, then it should come as no surprise that at least some students are not clear about what is their work and what constitutes the illegitimate use of others' work. In addition, there is an increasing sense that what is on the Internet is part of the "commons" and is therefore the common property of all. It therefore seems that all users, including students accused of plagiarism, are free to do what they want with material on the Internet. Even if students are consciously engaging in plagiarism, they may simply believe that it is just not much of a "crime."

It may be that the increase in plagiarism fits well with postmodernity and various ideas associated with postmodern social theory (see Chapter 2). For example, a plagiarised term paper can be seen as a "pastiche" of work that includes some of the student's words, as well as the words of many others. To take another example, postmodern theorists talk about the "death of the author." If there is no author, no original source of the text, then the student is free to borrow freely, and without citation, from many other "nonauthors." Postmodernity may be a defence for plagiarism, and while you might think your professor will admire your sophistication if you claim it, I would not recommend that you do so.

are more likely to have higher science scores than students from disadvantaged backgrounds (see Figure 16.9). In some countries the effect is stronger, for example in France, the United Kingdom, and the United States. In other countries, while there is still an effect, the effect is weaker—in Japan, Canada, and Finland. This evidence of inequality of educational opportunity, by socioeconomic status (or social class), is persistent in these three important senses (S. Davies and Guppy 2013). First, it is a repeatable effect that is robust no matter how either school achievement or socioeconomic status is measured. Second, the effect is persistent over time, with little evidence that it is increasing or decreasing over the previous half-century. Third, the effect does not vanish when researchers introduce other measures, such as gender, or ethnicity, or language. That is, the result holds if only women or only men are considered, or if the comparison is made across a series of different ethnic groups.

An alternative to examining how well students score on tests (Figure 16.9) is to examine how far people persist in school. Figure 16.10 looks at the likelihood of holding a university degree for women and men between the ages of 25 and 39. Notice, first, that women are more likely than men to hold a university degree, a major change that has occurred in the last half-century. Since the early 1980s in Canada more women than men have been graduating from university. Notice, however, that for women and men, the likelihood of holding a university degree rises significantly, depending on how much education their parents received. This latter finding can be stated another way. Your odds of obtaining a university degree are six times greater if your parents have a university degree, as compared to peers whose parents did not attend university. This parental education effect on their children's educational outcomes is the "family affair" to which the OECD (2010) pointed, now displayed in a slightly different way.

Are the odds of holding a university degree higher or lower depending on your ancestral, racial, or ethnic background? It depends. For most students whose families have immigrated to Canada, the odds of holding a university degree are about twice as great in comparison to students who were born in Canada (Turcotte 2011). As Figure 16.11 shows, young people aged 25–39 whose mother tongue was neither English nor French are the most likely to hold a university degree. In other words, younger Canadians who either were born abroad or were born in Canada but first learned a language other than English or French, are doing the best at achieving university degrees in last few decades. Other evidence supports this finding, but in ways that complicate the overall pattern. For example, Scott Davies and Neil Guppy (2013) show that students of Asian background are more likely to complete university than are people of either English or French Canadian backgrounds. However, all three of these groups do better in school attainment than do Aboriginal students or students who are black. This demonstrates that your odds of obtaining a university degree are worse if you are Aboriginal or black, while if you are Asian, your odds of obtaining a degree are greater than if you are either English or French.

Historically it was the case that women were less likely than men to obtain university degrees. This has changed significantly in Canada in recent years (Figure 16.12). Now it is the case that there are about 100,000 more women than men enrolled in undergraduate university programmes.

There are several explanations for this turnaround. First, young men are still able to find well-paying jobs in the resource sector of the Canadian economy, jobs that do not require postsecondary education. Second, for women, many occupations in which they are concentrated have become very competitive, and university degrees have become mandatory. This includes nursing and teaching. We should also note that although more women than men are enrolled in universities now, certain fields still remain tightly gendered. For women, little progress has been made in enrolments in engineering and forestry, whereas for men little progress has been made in enrolments in nursing and social work.

What do these patterns tell us about whether Canadian society is a meritocracy? Clearly, social origins are strongly related to educational outcomes, as are some ascribed characteristics, such as ancestry, and, to many, this suggests that Canadian society is decidedly unmeritocratic. The patterning by ancestry and race, at least for Aboriginal peoples and blacks, suggests that impediments to meritocracy exist, although in general young people of visible minority backgrounds have done relatively well, compared to their English and French Canadian peers.

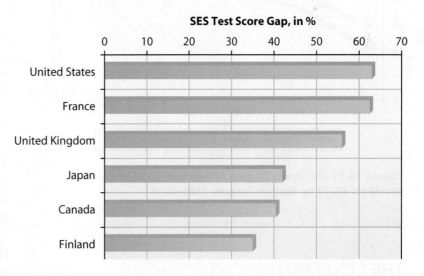

FIGURE 16.9 Differences in PISA Science Test Scores Between Students From Lower and Higher Socioeconomic Backgrounds, 2006, Selected Countries

SOURCE: Authors' adaptations from OECD (2010); retrieved February 2, 2013 (http://www.oecd.org/tax/public-finance/chapter%205%20gfg%202010.pdf).

NOTE: Scores are from the science component of PISA, the Programme for International Student Assessment. The scores reflect the gain in the science test results for every increase of one standard deviation in family socioeconomic background. Socioeconomic background is a composite measure of parental education, occupational status, and family status.

NOTE: Each bar represents the test score gap between high and low SES students.

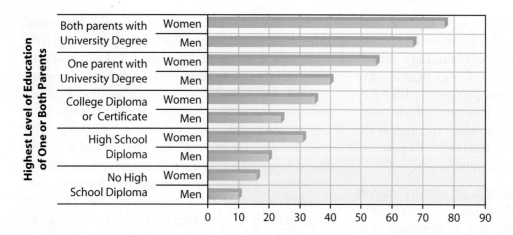

FIGURE 16.10 Percentage of Women and Men Aged 25–39 Who Held a University Degree by Parents' Highest Level of Education, 2009

SOURCE: Authors' calculations from Turcotte (2011), using General Social Survey data from Statistics Canada.

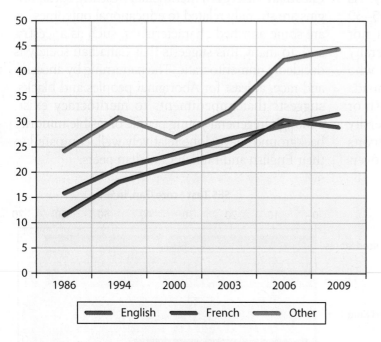

FIGURE 16.11 University Degree Attainment (in %) of Canadian Residents 25–39 by Mother Tongue, 1986–2009

SOURCE: Authors' calculations based on Turcotte (2011), using General Social Survey data from Statistics Canada.

THE COLEMAN REPORT: HOW MUCH DO SCHOOLS MATTER?

In the 1960s the U.S. Congress commissioned the sociologist James Coleman to undertake a study that has had international ramifications. Everyone anticipated that Coleman's findings would support the conventional wisdom of the time: Differences in student learning reflected the inequalities in school quality. Coleman's findings were a great surprise, and they forever changed the way that sociologists understand educational inequality.

First, Coleman (1966) estimated how much schools differ in "quality." Coleman collected data on teachers' salaries, teacher quality, the number of books in the library, the age of school buildings, the curriculum, and numerous other features of schools. On average, schools were much more similar in these respects than was commonly believed. Subsequent research has supported this finding, and reforms in the past half-century have made schools even more similar than they were when Coleman conducted his study.

Second, Coleman found few school characteristics that were related to student learning. School resources, such as per-pupil spending, the books in a library, and so on, did not predict student achievement. In terms of achievement, Coleman found that the most important school characteristics were teacher quality and the family background and racial composition of the students attending the school. Students learned more in schools with better teachers and white, middle-class peers. Finally, Coleman found that the most important predictor of student learning was a student's family background. This, of course, echoes back to the more recent OECD report, "A Family Affair," noted above.

Recent research on "school effects" has generally been supportive of Coleman's conclusion that school differences contribute little to educational inequality. There have been many studies

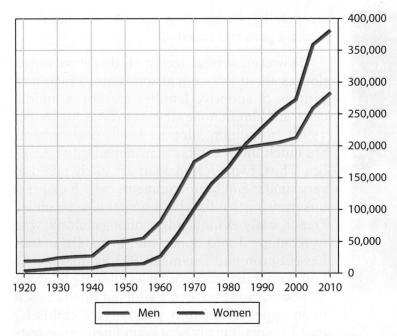

FIGURE 16.12 Full-time University Undergraduate Enrolment for Women and Men, 1920–2010

SOURCE: Historical Statistics of Canada, Series W340-438; Statistics Canada, *Education in Canada*; Education Indicators in Canada, Statistics Canada, Table D.1.4.5.

of the importance of school funding for student learning, and generally the results are inconclusive. Numerous studies of public-private differences in student learning indicate only a small advantage in learning for Catholic high school students, mostly due to more rigorous course work (see Carbonaro and Covay 2010; Davies, forthcoming). In elementary and middle school, U.S. public school students actually outperform private school students in math, and do equally well in reading (Lubienski 2006). Charter schools are alternative public schools that are often run by private (sometimes "for-profit") firms, and typically have fewer regulations governing them than "regular" public schools. Overall, most international studies indicate that charter schools perform about the same as matched public schools in levels of student learning (Berends et al. 2010).

Finally, recent large-scale surveys indicate that socioeconomic differences in student ability are sizable when children *begin* kindergarten. Furthermore, these differences can be detected when children are as young as 2 years of age (Aud and Hannes 2011; Hertzman et al. 2010). Clearly, schools cannot be implicated in producing educational inequalities if the inequalities are present *before students even enter school!* In short, Coleman's study and subsequent research undermine the simplistic explanation that educational inequality merely reflects unequal opportunities available to students while in school.

INTELLIGENCE AND SCHOOL SUCCESS

One possible explanation for Coleman's puzzling findings, and the findings of others, focused on innate differences in intelligence. Richard Herrnstein and Charles Murray (1994) offered the most well-developed and widely cited argument in support of this thesis in their book *The Bell Curve*. They argued that educational inequalities were due mostly to "natural" differences in intelligence in human populations rather than systematic differences in educational opportunities.

Herrnstein and Murray claimed that differences in learning and schooling are largely determined by differences in intelligence. In addition, they argued that differences in intelligence are largely inherited (up to 80 percent) and fixed. Two of those claims will be evaluated here because they are the most relevant to our discussion of meritocracy and schooling. If intelligence determines how much students learn and intelligence is largely inherited and fixed, then efforts to equalise opportunities in schools are futile, and nothing much can be done to eliminate differences in student learning.

Herrnstein and Murray's claim that learning and school success are determined by intelligence is consistent with the finding that students who learn more in school have higher IQs. However, intelligence is by no means the only, or even the most important, predictor of learning. Angela Duckworth and Martin Seligman (2005) conducted a study in which students' "self-discipline," such as their work habits, perseverance, and intelligence, was measured and correlated with their grades at the end of the year. They found that a

Two 8-year-olds in school uniforms walk down a street on their way to St. George's Preparatory School in St. George's Island, Bermuda. Recent research on "school effects" has generally been supportive of James Coleman's conclusion that school differences, at least in the United States, contribute little to educational inequality.

student's self-discipline had a substantially greater impact than intelligence on that student's grades at the end of the year. These findings are consistent with both structural/functional and conflict theories, which suggest that students who master the school's "hidden curriculum" by, for example, developing the best work habits, are the most likely to be rewarded in school.

Herrnstein and Murray's claim that intelligence is largely inherited and fixed has been vigorously challenged by many researchers. Herrnstein and Murray rely on data on identical twins raised in separate families to derive their estimates of the high "heritability" of IQ. The IQs of identical twins raised in different families are almost as similar as those who are raised in the same families. These findings suggest that intelligence is affected more strongly by a person's genes than the family in which a person is raised.

However, several recent studies have raised doubts about this conclusion. First, a high percentage of adoptive families are upper middle class, and almost none are lower class (Stoolmiller 1999). In addition, adoptive family environments are much more similar than nonadoptive families. Thus, twins reared apart are likely raised in very similar family environments, which makes it unsurprising that they have similar IQs. Second, a French study examined IQs among children who were adopted into upper- and lower-class families (Capron and Duyme 1989). Being born to upper-class parents boosted a child's IQ by about 12 points. However, being adopted by and raised in an upper-class family also raised a child's IQ by 12 points. Finally, scores on intelligence tests have increased dramatically in many nations in the past 50 years (N. Flynn 2007). Such dramatic increases in intelligence across generations in so short a time are inconsistent with the claim that intelligence is largely genetically determined and fixed.

CLASS DIFFERENCES IN EARLY CHILDHOOD

If both school-based and "natural" explanations of educational inequality fail, what remains? Many social scientists have turned their attention to inequalities in children's earliest experiences—the home environment. Betty Hart and Toddy Risley (1995) performed a fascinating in-depth study of 42 families and their children. The study began when each child studied was 7 to 9 months old, and the researchers visited each family once every month until the children were 3 years old. For each hourlong visit, Hart and Risley recorded every spoken word and took notes on what happened. They found that the three types of families in their study—professional, working class, and welfare—differed markedly in how they spoke to, and interacted with, their children. By 3 years of age, there were massive differences in the number of words that were addressed to children in these different families: 35 million words in professional families,

20 million in working-class families, and fewer than 10 million in welfare families. Hart and Risley also found that children in professional families experienced the most encouragement and least discouragement by their parents, as well as the greatest diversity in language. In terms of interaction styles, parents in professional families tended to use questions rather than commands to direct children's behaviour, and they were also more responsive to their children's requests.

Did these differences in home environments matter for early learning outcomes? Children's exposure to differences in parenting practises and styles are highly correlated with vocabulary growth, vocabulary use, and intelligence by age 3, and these effects persist when intelligence is measured at ages 9 and 10. In addition, class differences in early cognitive outcomes are almost entirely explained by differences in parenting. Hart and Risley's classic study provides compelling evidence that children enter formal schooling with large differences in ability because they are exposed to very different home environments from an early age.

Preschool

Can we change children's educational outcomes by changing the cognitive culture that they experience when they are very young? Several intensive preschool programmes have shown impressive results. From 1962 to 1967, 123 black children whose families were living in poverty in Ypsilanti, Michigan, participated in a fascinating policy experiment (Schweinhart, Barnett, and Belfield 2005). Half of the children were assigned to an enriched preschool programme ("High Scope— Perry Preschool"), while the other half—the control group—received no preschooling (Stoolmiller 1999). Children who attended the Perry Preschool programme for two years experienced larger gains in intelligence than the control group by the time the programme ended, but this advantage faded away only a few years after the programme ended. However, the Perry students performed better in school because they were more motivated to learn. Researchers followed these two groups of students well into adulthood (age 40), and found that the Perry students did substantially better as adults

than the control group. The Perry students were more likely to finish high school and university and hold a steady job, and had higher earnings than the control group. The control group was more likely to be arrested, to use public assistance, and to have out-of-wedlock children.

James Heckman (2006) has estimated that in the long run every dollar spent on the Perry Preschool programme saved $7 in tax revenue. He attributed the adult success enjoyed by Perry students to the better social skills that they learned in preschool, since the differences in cognitive ability between the two groups were negligible.

SEASONAL LEARNING AND CLASS DIFFERENCES IN ACHIEVEMENT

Differences in early childhood experiences explain why socioeconomic differences are present when children enter school. However, achievement gaps grow larger as children progress through school, and this pattern suggests that unequal learning opportunities in school are important factors driving educational inequality. One method for examining the role of schools in producing educational inequality is to measure learning gains during the school year, and compare them to learning gains during the summer when students are not in school.

Entwisle, Alexander, and Olson (1998) studied children in the Baltimore school system, testing them at the beginning and end of each school year in Grades K through 5. Students clearly learned at a faster rate during the school year than they did during the summer. Students who were high or low in socioeconomic status (SES) learned at roughly *the same* rate during the school year. In contrast, during the summer, high-SES students kept learning while low-SES students did not. When they compared school year and summer gains from kindergarten through fifth grade, they found that virtually all of the growth in the SES gap in learning occurred during the summer. Alexander, Entwisle, and Olson (2007) found that summer learning had a variety of long-term effects, such as whether or not students were placed in university preparatory tracks, whether or not they completed high school, and attendance at university. In Canada, Janice Aurini and Scott Davies (2013) have begun an extensive study of the "summer setback" phenomena, with early results similar to those from the initial Baltimore study.

Why do high-SES students learn more in the summer than low-SES students? Alexander, Entwisle, and Olson (2007) offer the metaphor of schooling as a faucet to explain this pattern. When school is in session, the faucet is open for both high- and low-SES students, and differences in family backgrounds matter little for student learning. However, during the summer, the school spigot is turned off, and inequalities in family resources become much more important for student learning. High-SES students attend summer camp, visit the library, take educational summer vacations, and have many more educational resources in the home. Low-SES families provide far fewer resources for their children during the summer, and consequently they have fewer opportunities to reinforce or expand on learning gains from the school year.

Research on seasonal learning affirms the power of schooling to compensate for differences in family backgrounds and to act as an "equaliser" that actually reduces educational inequality (Downey, von Hippel, and Broh 2004). Coleman was correct in concluding that differences among schools, or "school effects," play a small role in generating educational inequality. However, that conclusion does not mean that schools are unimportant for student outcomes. Indeed, schools reduce inequality in student outcomes because school environments are much more similar than family environments.

INEQUALITY WITHIN SCHOOLS: TRACKING AND STUDENT OUTCOMES

Many studies have examined whether students who attend the same school receive similar learning opportunities. It is common at all levels of schooling in Canada to group students by ability, which is typically measured by standardised test scores and/or grades. This is commonly known as tracking or streaming (A. Taylor and Krahn 2009).

Barr and Dreeben (1983) examined first-grade reading groups in which students were grouped by their reading ability at the beginning of the year. Students in higher-ability groups learned more new words and improved their reading skills more rapidly than students in low-ability groups. Better readers were placed in high-ability groups at the beginning of the year, and they received more instructional time, were exposed to more new words, and experienced a faster pace of instruction than students placed in low-ability groups. In short, higher-performing students received more learning opportunities than lower-performing students, and consequently the gap between high- and low-achieving students grew larger during the year. This process is known as **cumulative advantage**—the most advantaged individuals are awarded the best opportunities, and this increases inequality over time (DiPrete et al. 2006).

As students progress through middle and secondary school, curricular differentiation takes the form of different classes with different content. Traditionally, these curricular tracks are aligned with students' future ambitions: The "high" track entails course work that prepares students for university and professional careers, and the "low" track focuses on basic and/or vocational skills for semiskilled occupations that do not require a university degree. Research consistently finds that high-track classes offer better learning opportunities to students because they are taught by more experienced, higher-quality teachers, who have higher expectations of their students (W. Kelly 2004). Higher-track classes cover more material, and students receive higher-quality instruction (Gamoran et al. 1995). Students in high-track classes are more engaged and exert greater effort in school (Carbonaro 2005), which also helps them learn at a faster rate. Research consistently shows that otherwise similar students learn more when placed in a higher-track class due to higher expectations, greater effort, and better learning opportunities. Ultimately, high-track students are more likely to attend university than low-track students. Programmes such as Advanced Placement and the International Baccalaureate, popular in most Canadian provinces, are examples of high-track streams.

What determines how students are assigned to different ability groups, tracks, and classes? In a meritocracy, achieved characteristics—hard work and prior academic success—should determine which students have access to high-track classes. Most studies show that prior achievement and grades are indeed the most important predictors of track placement. Since students from high-SES families are more likely to be high achievers, they are much more likely to take high-track classes than low-SES students. However, when students with the same test scores and grades are compared, students from higher-SES families are still more likely to be enrolled in high-track classes than low-SES students (Gamoran and Mare 1989). Thus, high-SES students are doubly advantaged in the track placement process.

What accounts for the SES advantage in track placement? Useem (1992) studied how families affected students' placements in middle school math classes. She found that university-educated parents had several key advantages in the placement process that ensured that their children ended up in the high-level classes. First, university-educated parents were much more knowledgeable regarding which classes were the most demanding and which ones were linked to high-level classes in high school. Indeed, some less educated parents seemed unaware that math classes were tracked. University-educated parents also better understood how the placement process worked, and they knew how to intervene successfully on their child's behalf. Second, university-educated parents were also much more integrated into social networks in the school—through parent-teacher associations and volunteering, for example—and they used these connections to gain information about classes and teachers in the school. Finally, university-educated parents influenced their children's choices in selecting classes by encouraging them to challenge themselves and think about the long-term consequences of their choices.

Why does family background matter so much for school success, and university attainment in particular? Studies from the 1950s through the 1980s found that students from high-SES families had a greater likelihood of receiving a university degree. More recent studies, however, suggest that virtually all students—regardless of family background—want and expect to complete some postsecondary credential (Schneider and Stevenson 1999). This trend reflects a "university for all" mentality by policymakers, counsellors, and the general public (Rosenbaum 2001, 2011).

However, higher-SES students are more likely to attend and to graduate from university because they encounter a "university-going habitus" at home and in school. **Habitus** is an internalised set of preferences and dispositions that are learned through experience and social interactions in specific social contexts (Bourdieu and Passeron 1977). For example, children raised in families with highly educated parents may constantly be exposed to justifications regarding how important education is in one's life as an adult. They may also hear dismissive and derogatory comments that devalue people with less education. It may become clear that education is a critical part of being accepted as a member of the group. Ultimately, children in this situation may not see the pursuit of a university degree as "choice"; rather, they see it as an obligation. As students experience different social contexts that correspond with their family backgrounds, they will form different ideas about the importance of

Students prepare for China's yearly national university entrance examination in Zhengzhou. A student's score on the national examination—and just that score—determines whether (and where) a student should enrol in university. While the amount of studying one does in preparation for this crucial exam plays a large role in one's success, the lifelong impact of an advantaged family background cannot be discounted.

Students attend class in Dertu, Kenya's primary school in 2010. Dertu is distinguished from the thousands of other villages that dot the impoverished landscape of sub-Saharan Africa by its cell phone tower, which keeps the village in touch with the outside world. Dertu is one of the United Nations' 14 "Millennium Villages" envisioned as launchpads for a mass leap out of poverty.

university and the role it plays in their life. For working-class students, or students from less economically and socially privileged backgrounds, going to university is often like going to a foreign country. It is an adventure that has risks attached, and often it is a journey made without any, or many, role models who have paved the way and can help in navigating a different, unfamiliar culture (S. Davies and Guppy 2013; Lehman 2009).

GLOBALISATION AND EDUCATION

We have spent much time discussing educational inequality in learning outcomes in the United States. Is the American system typical? How do other school systems differ and with what consequences?

U.S., German, and Japanese Education Systems

As we have seen, the American schooling system does not create inequality in student learning outcomes. Sometimes it compensates for other inequalities, sometimes it reinforces these inequalities, and sometimes it worsens educational

inequality. Other nations have structured their educational systems differently, and these institutional differences have important implications for inequalities in learning among students.

Three schooling systems—Germany, Japan, and the United States—were compared to explore how different nations allocate learning resources to students who will occupy different positions in the social hierarchy.

In Germany, all elementary school students attend Grundschule, which does not practise ability grouping; all children are exposed to the same curriculum. At the end of fourth grade, teachers make a recommendation to families based on test scores and

As in China, advancement through Japan's educational system depends on rigorous standardised placement exams. Here, a Japanese boy wearing a headband reading "struggle" studies intensely at a local juku, or private cram school. Depending on the results of a standardised test taken at the end of ninth grade, students are directed to either a university preparatory programme or a technical or vocational school.

GL🌐BALISATION

Changing Global Models in Education: The Decline of Japan and the Rise of India

Nations often seek to emulate the successful educational models of other nations. In that realm, the United States has long been the world leader, and its various approaches have been copied, at least in part, by many nations. However, other nations have been and are models, and there are regional differences in what nation the model might be.

An interesting case in point today is Japan, which is undergoing something of a crisis of confidence in its educational system because its students no longer score at or near the top on various international tests. Having been the first country in Asia to develop its economy, Japan built an educational system that rose above the rest of the continent. But now many there are coming to see the school system of India as a worthy model to emulate (Fackler 2008). This is a sea change for Japan, which has long seen itself as the dominant power in Asia in general and in education in particular (Ninomiya, Knight, and Watanabe 2009). But, the Japanese are changing their view drawn by such facts as the reality that while Japanese elementary schoolchildren are required to know 9 × 9 multiplication tables, in India that requirement is 99 × 99. The few Indian international schools in Japan are increasingly popular and books on Indian education, such as *Extreme Indian Arithmetic Drills,* are selling well.

Indian schools seem to be excelling at what the Japanese once thought were their educational advantages, including "learning more at an earlier age, an emphasis on memorisation and cramming, and a focus on the basics, particularly in math and science" (Fackler 2008:A9). In one of the Indian schools in Japan "5-year-olds learn to multiply, solve math word problems and write one-page essays in English.

Tasks most Japanese schools do not teach until at least second grade" (Fackler 2008:A9). Said one mother of a 5-year-old: "My son's level is higher than those of other Japanese children the same age . . . Indian education is really amazing. This wouldn't have been possible at a Japanese kindergarten" (Fackler 2008:A9). With European and American international schools having a long-standing presence in Japan, Indian international schools are now rapidly expanding and attracting more Japanese students.

Indian schools have been excelling in recent years, leading to a crisis of confidence among some Japanese educators. Indian students are learning more (especially in the fields of science and math) at a younger age, while Japanese educational attainment has remained steady. Here, Indian students collaborate on a complex group project at the University of Delhi in New Delhi, India.

their subjective assessments of student ability regarding the type of secondary school a given child should attend. There are three types of schools that represent academic and vocational tracks: lower-level "gymnasium" (the university track), "realschule" (the middle track), and "hauptschule" (the lowest track). Each of these schools has its own curriculum, which is designed to correspond with the future occupational trajectories of its students. Only 30 percent of students are placed in the gymnasium level. Transferring to a different track is possible, but it is difficult and rare. Between-school tracking continues at the next level of schooling, and only students who attend upper-level gymnasium can proceed to the university system and attain the equivalent of a baccalaureate degree.

Japan has a very different system of stratification in its educational system. From school entry through ninth grade, there is little or no ability grouping among students either between or within schools. For the first nine years of school, Japanese students are exposed to a remarkably uniform curriculum. At the end of ninth grade, Japanese students take a high-stakes test that determines which type of high school they will attend. About 75 percent of students attend "futsuuka," which has a university preparatory curriculum. The remaining 25 percent of students attend a variety of technical and vocational schools. Family background still plays an important role in educational success for Japanese students because of a "shadow education" system, in which informal schooling opportunities outside of school give more advantaged students a better preparation for both high school and university entrance exams.

The German and Japanese systems highlight key features of the American schooling system. Education in the United States has always been organised around the "common school" ideal: All American students, regardless of their class origins and their future aspirations, attend the same types of schools. In the United States, tracking occurs within schools, not between schools. The United States also has more variability in school quality by geographical region. The German and Japanese systems are much more centralised than the United States, which has 50 different educational systems (one run by each state) with different levels of funding and varying curriculum. In the United States, more so than in Japan and Germany, the quality and character of students' education are likely to be affected by where their family lives.

These differences have implications for achievement outcomes in each nation (Montt 2011). Germany has the highest levels of achievement inequality because of its highly stratified system. Japan has higher average achievement than Germany but much less inequality in outcomes because it does not practise curricular differentiation until very late. The United States actually has the lowest average achievement and the least variability of these three nations.

There are two features of educational systems that are significant for students' outcomes. First, nations with highly differentiated school systems—with between-school tracking—have more unequal learning outcomes for students, and family background tends to matter more for student outcomes (Van de Werfhorst and Mij 2010). Second, standardisation—the degree to which the curriculum and examinations are the same across schools—produces less inequality in student outcomes and a weaker correlation between family background and achievement. Thus, institutions do matter greatly, and the choices nations make have important consequences for how learning is distributed within society.

SUMMARY

Religion has always been a topic of interest to sociologists. Durkheim studied the relationship between religion and society extensively, in particular the distinction between the sacred and the profane. Weber wrestled with the relationship between faith in religion and the rationalisation of the modern world. Marx argued that religion was a tool utilised by those in power to keep the proletarians from seeing clearly and fighting against the inequalities they experienced.

Sociologists have distinguished between two basic kinds of religious organisation, the *church* and the *sect*. Theorists approach the study of religion from different perspectives. Structural-functionalists focus not only on the functions, or social purposes, served by religion, but also on its dysfunctions. Conflict theorists argue that religious ideologies serve to distract people and to obscure economic and social realities.

The spread of religion is not new, but it has accelerated with increased globalisation. The most significant global religions are Judaism, Buddhism, Hinduism, Islam, and Christianity. Judaism is one of the smallest world religions; the two fastest-growing world religions are Christianity and Islam. Christianity is declining in Europe, but it has had strong growth in the Global South. The vast majority of Buddhists reside in Asia, and the majority of Hindus live in India, although both Hinduism and Buddhism have been spreading throughout the globe.

The Mormons have aggressively expanded globally using modern techniques and technologies. Religious fundamentalism can be seen as being involved in globalisation because of its expansionistic nature and ability to be affected by various globalisations.

Education is closely related to the process of socialisation, though it most often takes place more formally in schools. Structural-functionalists view education as a social structure that is functional to both individuals and society. Conflict theorists believe that education serves to reproduce social inequalities and reinforce social stratification. Symbolic interactionists focus on the more micro aspects of education and often analyze how social inequality is reinforced on this level.

James Coleman found that teacher quality, family background, and racial composition of the students attending a school were the most important factors affecting student achievement. Herrnstein and Murray later argued that inherited differences accounted for different levels of achievement. However, other researchers have convincingly shown that it is differences in the home environment of very young children that account for differences in educational ability and attainment.

The use of tracking in schools often leads to cumulative advantage for students placed in higher tracks. These most advantaged students are consequently awarded the best opportunities for learning, which in turn exacerbates inequality over time. Further increasing inequality is the fact that students from higher-SES families are more often placed in higher tracks than their low-SES peers, irrespective of ability. Differences in SES also affect university attainment. There are great differences in educational inequality around the world.

KEY TERMS

- Beliefs   633
- Church   642
- Credentialing   659
- Cult   642
- Cultural dopes   660
- Cumulative advantage   670
- Denominations   643
- Fundamentalism   654
- Habitus   671
- Legitimations   647
- Liminal   635

- Meritocracy   661
- New religious movements   643
- Profane   633
- Religion   633
- Rites of passage   634
- Ritual   634
- Sacred   633
- Sect   640
- Secularisation   637
- Social reproduction   658
- Spirituality   636

THINKING ABOUT SOCIOLOGY

1. Religion is one of sociology's longest-running concerns. How have some of history's greatest sociologists been affected by their own religious upbringing and environment? How might religion have shaped their sociological interests and research?

2. How do we define religion? What are the basic elements and components of religious institutions? In what ways have religions changed over time?

3. What are the major religions of the world? How are people distributed among the major religions of the world? In what ways are religions global?

4. What is the difference between a sect and a cult? What is one example of a sect, and one example of a cult? Why has the term *cult* fallen out of favour with many sociologists?

5. How do structural/functional explanations of education differ from conflict/critical approaches? Which theoretical perspective is best suited to explaining current changes in education?

6. What is a meritocracy, and why is the educational system an important component of a meritocratic society? In what ways is the Canadian education

system meritocratic, and in what ways is it not meritocratic?

7. According to the Coleman Report, how important is the quality of schools for the quality of student achievement? What other factors affect student achievement? What factors have not been found to affect student achievement to any great extent?

8. Aboriginal students do not go to postsecondary institutions as frequently as their non-Aboriginal peers. Why is this? Can you find and describe examples of programmes that are designed to benefit Aboriginal youth in their educational

pursuits? Why do you think these programmes may, or may not, work?

9. Compare and contrast the American, German, and Japanese educational systems. How do these systems' differences affect achievement outcomes in these countries? How do their attitudes toward grouping reflect their respective cultural norms and values? How does the provincial education system with which you are most familiar compare?

10. What are some examples of digital technology in education? How has this technology affected education? What are some of its benefits, and what are some of its problems?

APPLYING THE SOCIOLOGICAL IMAGINATION

This chapter pointed out that a large and increasing number of people in the world today consider themselves nonreligious. For this activity, think of yourself as someone who is nonreligious seeking to become a member of one of the major world religions. Use the Internet (Google search, Twitter hashtag) to learn more about the major world religions and to determine what you might consider the pros and cons of trying to adopt and participate in a specific religion. What do you think would be a to-do in order to facilitate your membership? How is choosing a religion different from choosing to buy a certain product or join a certain gym?

ACTIVE SOCIOLOGY

More and more people are taking a "DIY" approach to home improvement, using the resources available for them online. People can look to YouTube to teach them how to hang, tape, and mud drywall, allowing them to complete a big project on a limited budget. You can easily find a "how-to" video that will teach you what you need to know. Choose a topic that you are interested in learning about. You could consider a home project, an academic topic like sociology or art history, or a hobby or leisure activity like how to play cribbage or make sushi. View several of the videos that teach you about this topic. Who are the sources of information? Are they credible? How do you know? How do you think the information is similar to or different from what you might learn if you took a class on this subject? Now consider the ways in which the spread of information via YouTube is impacting education. While it doesn't give degrees, the information on YouTube might be used as a review or study tool. In addition, it might impact education programmes that have been traditionally offered in community centres and at community colleges. Finally, YouTube is used as a way to present class projects. Consider making a video about something you've learned in Sociology class. Post it on YouTube (make sure the privacy settings are set to "public"). Track the number of views. What are the positive and negative functions of learning from YouTube?

STUDENT STUDY SITE

Visit the student study site at **www.sagepub.com/ritzercanadian** for additional web quizzes for further review.

GLOSSARY

Aboriginal: Sometimes also Indigenous Peoples, refers to individuals who have ancestral ties to people who trace their lineage to the first inhabitants of North America

Absolute poverty: An absolute measure—such as the U.S. poverty line—that makes it clear what level of income people need in order to survive.

Achieved status: A position acquired by people on the basis of what they accomplish or the nature of their capacities.

Achievement: Positions in the stratification system are based on the accomplishments, the merit, of the individual.

Aerotropolis: A planned city that is built around a vast international airport and its associated shipping facilities and business hubs.

Affirmative action: A process aimed at increasing diversity and equal opportunity by taking race and other minority group factors into consideration in making various decisions, especially those relating to personnel matters.

Agents of socialization: Those who do the socializing.

Agency: Individual social power and capacity for creativity.

Alienation: In a capitalist system, being unconnected to one's work, products, fellow workers, and human nature.

Americanization: The importation by other countries of products, images, technologies, practices, norms, values, and behaviors that are closely associated with the United States.

Ancestry: Refers to aboriginal or indigenous populations and differentiates these

populations from other groups defined by ethnic or racial criteria

Anomie: The feeling of not knowing what is expected of one in society or of being adrift in society without any clear, secure moorings.

Anti-Americanism: An aversion to America in general, as well as to the influence of its culture abroad.

Anticipatory socialization: The teaching (and learning) of what will be expected of one in the future.

Ascribed status: A position in which individuals are placed, or to which they move, but where such placement or movement has nothing to do with what people do or the nature of their capacities or accomplishments.

Ascription: Positions in the stratification system are based on certain characteristics (wealth, high status, etc.) that one was born with or inherited.

Asexuality: A lack of sexual desire.

Assimilation: When a minority group takes on the characteristics of the dominant group and leaves its old ways behind; the adaptation of minorities to the dominant culture.

Asylum seekers: People who flee their home country usually in an effort to escape political oppression or religious persecution.

Authority: A particular type of domination: legitimate domination.

Back stage: Part of the social world where people feel free to express themselves in ways that are suppressed in the front stage.

Beliefs: Ideas that explain the world and identify what should be sacred or held in awe, that is, the religion's ultimate concerns.

Birth rate: The number of childbirths per 1,000 people per year.

Bisexuality: Involves a desire to have sexual relations with individuals of both the opposite sex and the same sex.

Blended family: Some combination of children from the partners' previous marriages or relationships, along with one or more children of the currently married or cohabiting couple.

Bounded rationality: Rationality limited by, among other things, instabilities and conflicts within most, if not all, organizations, as well as by the limited human capacities to think and act in a rational manner.

Brand: A symbol that serves to identify and differentiate one product or service from the others.

Bureaucracy: A highly rational organization, especially one that is highly efficient.

Bureaucratic personality: A type of bureaucrat who slavishly follows the rules of the organization to such an extent that the ability to achieve organizational goals is subverted.

Butterfly effect: The far-ranging, even global impact of a small change in a specific location, over both time and distance.

Capitalism: In Marx's view, an economic system based on one group of people—the capitalists (owners)—owning what is needed for production and a second group—the proletariat (workers)—owning little but their capacity for work.

Capitalists: Those who own what is needed for production—factories, machines, tools—in a capitalist system.

Caste: The most rigid and the most closed system of stratification, usually associated mainly with India.

Cathedrals of consumption: The large and lavish consumption sites created, mostly in the United States in the last half of the twentieth century and into the early twenty-first century.

Cenogamy: Group marriage.

Charismatic authority: Authority that is based on the devotion of the followers to what they define as the exceptional characteristics, such as heroism, of the leaders.

Church: A large group of religiously oriented people into which one is usually born rather than, as is the case in sects, joining consciously and voluntarily.

Cities: Large, permanent, and spatially concentrated human settlements.

Citizens: The people represented by a given state, most often born within its territories, and eligible to vote in its elections.

Citizenship: The idea that people of a given state can vote for their representatives within the state, but also that they have access to rights and responsibilities as citizens.

City-states: Small proto-states that began institutionalizing hierarchical forms of traditional authority that extended over large settlements.

Civil religion: The beliefs, practices, and symbols that a nation holds sacred.

Class consciousness: According to Marx, a mental state in which the workers (proletariat) come to truly understand capitalism, their collective role in it, and their relationship to one another, as well as to the capitalist; exists when large numbers of people have a true sense of their interests.

Cohabitation: A couple sharing a home and a bed without being legally married.

Collective behavior: Action generated, or engaged in, by a group of people.

Collective conscience: The set of beliefs shared by people throughout society.

Colonialism: Generally involves settlers as well as much more formal mechanisms of control over geographic areas than imperialism.

Companionate love: Typified by gradual onset and not necessarily tied to sexual passion, but based on more rational assessments of the one who is loved.

Companionate marriage: Predominant model of marriage in the middle twentieth century (see companionate love).

Competitive capitalism: A form of capitalism where there are a large number of relatively small firms with the result that no one, or small subset, of them can completely dominate and control a given area of the economy.

Conflict theory: A set of ideas focusing on the sources of conflict within society.

Conformists: People who accept both cultural goals and the traditional means of achieving those goals.

Consensual sex: Sexual intercourse that is agreed upon by the participants in an informed process.

Conspicuous consumption: The public demonstration of wealth through consumption that one is able to waste money—for example, by flaunting the use of expensive, high-status goods and services (mansions, yachts, personal assistants, etc.).

Constructionist theories: Theories of deviance that seek a greater understanding of the process by which people define and classify some behaviors as normal and others as deviant.

Consumer crime: Crimes related to consumption, including shoplifting and using stolen credit cards or credit card numbers.

Consumer culture: A culture in which the core ideas and material objects relate to consumption and in which consumption is a primary source of meaning in life.

Consumerism: A value-laden term indicating an obsession with consumption.

Consumption: A highly complex process by which people obtain and utilize goods and services; involves the interrelationship among consumer objects and services, consumers, the consumption process, and consumption sites.

Content analysis: Systematic and objective analysis of the content of cultural artifacts in print, visual, audio, and digital media, using both qualitative and quantitative analysis.

Convenience sample: A readily available group of people who fit the criteria for participating, and are conveniently available to participate, in a research project.

Conversation analysis: Concerned with how people do, or accomplish, conversations.

Corporate crime: Involves legal organizations that violate the law including

such illegal acts as antitrust violations and stock market violations.

Corporatism: The idea that the state should heavily regulate the economy.

Cosmopolitanism: The ability to transcend local constraints on thought and action and to take into account many different points of view.

Counterculture: A group whose culture not only differs in certain ways from the dominant culture, but whose norms and values may be incompatible with those of the dominant culture.

Couples living apart together (LAT): Couples who define themselves as a couple without the necessity of living together; they have separate residences within the same geographic area.

Credentialing: The linkage between educational degrees and high-status positions.

Crime: Simply a violation of the criminal law.

Criminalization: The process by which the legal system negatively sanctions some form of deviant behavior.

Criminology: The study of all aspects of crime.

Critical theories of race and racism: A set of ideas arguing that race continues to matter and that racism continues to exist and adversely affect blacks.

Critical theory: A set of critical ideas derived from Marxian theory but focused on culture rather than the economy.

Crowd: A temporary gathering of a relatively large number of people in a common geographic location and in a given period.

Cult: A new, innovative, small, voluntary, and exclusive religious tradition that was never associated with any religious organization.

Cult of masculinity: A social practice that organized political life and the public sphere around men and punished perceived deficiencies in masculinity in men.

Cultural dopes: People who are controlled unthinkingly by a variety of external forces such as school rules or teacher demands.

Cultural hybrid: A cultural phenomenon combining inputs and impositions from other cultures with local realities.

Cultural imperialism: The imposition of one culture, more or less consciously, on other cultures.

Cultural relativism: The idea that aspects of culture such as norms and values need to be understood within the context of a person's own culture or that there are no universally accepted norms and values.

Culture: A collection of ideas, values, practices, and material objects that mean a great deal to a group of people, even an entire society, and that allow them to carry out their collective lives in relative order and harmony.

Culture ideology of consumerism: Acknowledges the central role played by consumption in the economy, by the culture of consumption, and by the ideologies that are an integral part of that culture.

Culture industry: Rationalized and bureaucratized structures that control modern culture.

Culture jamming: The radical transformation of an intended message in popular culture, especially one associated with the mass media, to protest underlying realities of which consumers may be unaware.

Culture war: A conflict that pits subcultures and countercultures against the dominant culture or that pits dominant groups within society against each other.

Cumulative advantage: The most advantaged individuals are awarded the best opportunities, and this increases inequality over time.

Cybercrime: Crime that targets computers, uses computers to commit traditional crimes, and transmits illegal information and images.

Cyberculture: An emerging culture online that has the characteristics of all culture, including distinctive values and norms.

Dangerous giant: An individual who has agency, or the potential to disrupt and destroy the structures in which one finds himself or herself.

Debunking: Looking beneath and beyond the surface of social structures, which are seen as facades that conceal what is truly important.

Deindustrialization: The decline of manufacturing as well as a corresponding increase in various types of services.

Deinstitutionalization: Weakened social norms especially with regard to the institution of marriage.

Democracy: A political system in which people within a given state vote to choose their leaders and in some cases vote on legislation.

Democrats: Members of a political party within the U.S. two-party system, which is typically seen as the liberal party.

Demographers: Those who study population, especially such processes as the growth and decline of populations.

Demography: Concerned primarily with the scientific study of population, especially such processes as the growth and decline of populations.

Denominations: Organized forms of religious expression that typically support the social order and tend to be tolerant of other forms.

Dependent variable: A characteristic or measurement that is the result of manipulating an independent variable.

Deprofessionalization: The process whereby a profession's power and autonomy, as well as high status and great wealth, have declined, at least relative to the exalted position it once held.

Descriptive statistics: Numerical data that allow researchers to see trends over time or compare differences between groups, in order to describe some particular collection of data that is based on a phenomenon in the real world.

Descriptive survey: Questionnaire or interview used to gather accurate information about those in a group, people in a given geographic area, and those in organizations.

Desertification: Involves the decline in the water supply as a result of the degradation and deterioration of soil and vegetation.

Deviance: Any action, belief, or human characteristic that members of a society or a social group consider a violation of group norms and for which the violator is likely to be censured or punished.

Diaspora: Dispersal, typically involuntary, of a racial or ethnic population from its traditional homeland and over a wide geographic area.

Dictatorships: States that are usually totalitarian and ruled either by a single individual or by a small group of people.

Differential association: A theory that focuses on the fact that people learn criminal behavior and therefore that what is crucial is who a person associates with.

Direct democracy: A political system in which people directly affected by a given decision have a say in that decision.

Disasters: Events that suddenly, unexpectedly, and severely disrupt and harm the environment, the social structure, people, and their property.

Discouraged workers: Those who have sought work within the last year or since their last job ended, if that was less than a year previous, and have not sought work in the last four weeks (and are therefore not in the labor force).

Discreditable stigma: Stigma in which individuals involved assume that their stigma is neither known about nor immediately perceivable.

Discredited stigma: Stigma in which individuals involved assume their differentness is known about already or is evident on the spot.

Discrimination: The unfavorable treatment of black Americans and other minorities, either formally or informally, simply because of their race, or some other characteristic.

Distinction: The need to distinguish oneself from others.

Domestic violence: The exertion of power over a partner in an intimate relationship that can involve behavior that is intimidating, threatening, harassing, or harmful.

Domination: The probability or likelihood that commands will be obeyed by subordinates.

Double-consciousness: Among black Americans, the sense of "two-ness," of being both black and American.

Dramaturgy: The view that social life is a series of dramatic performances akin to those that take place in a theater and on a stage.

Dyad: A two-person group.

Dysfunction: An observable consequence that negatively affects the ability of a given system to survive, adapt, or adjust.

Ecology: The study of people and their relationship to one another as well as to the larger context (including the natural environment) in which they live.

Ecological footprint: Is a measure of the amount of demand that a person or community places on earth's ecosystems, including all resources consumed and all waste.

Economy: The social system involved in the production and distribution of a wide range of goods and services.

Economic inequality: Differences among individuals or groups based on their material resources, most specifically income and wealth.

Edge cities: Cities that are on, or near, major highways, have corporate offices that offer employment to many, and have important commercial and consumption centers, most importantly shopping malls.

Electoral College: A method of indirect election of U.S. presidents by which electors in each state designated by the state legislature cast their votes for president according to their state's popular vote.

Elite pluralism: Political elites form similar interest groups and organizations that vie for power and, likewise, provide political stability for society.

Emergent norm theory: Argues that in light of some precipitating event new norms emerge that guide the often nontraditional actions that characterize collective behavior.

Emphasized femininity: A set of ideas about the characteristics of women that accommodates to the interests of men and to patriarchy and involves the compliance of females.

Empiricism: The gathering of information and evidence using one's senses, especially one's eyes and ears, to experience the social world.

Endogamy: Marrying someone with similar characteristics.

Ethics: A set of beliefs concerning right and wrong in the choices that people make and the ways those choices are justified.

Ethnic cleansing: The establishment by the dominant group of policies that allow or require the forcible removal of people of another ethnic group.

Ethnic group: Typically a group defined on the basis of some cultural characteristic such as language, religion, traditions, and cultural practices.

Ethnicity: A sense, shared by members of the group, of belonging to and identifying with a given ethnic group.

Ethnocentrism: The belief that one's own group or culture—including its norms, values, customs, and so on—is superior to, or better than, others.

Ethnography: Observational research, often intensive and over lengthy periods, that leads to an account of what people do and how they live.

Ethnomethodology: A theory focused on what people do rather than on what people think.

Ethnoscapes: Involve the movement, or fantasies about movement, of various individuals and groups.

Exchange relationship: A stable and persistent bond between individuals who interact, generally formed because their interactions are rewarding.

Exchange theory: A set of ideas related to the rewards and costs associated with human behavior.

Exogamy: Marrying someone with characteristics that are dissimilar.

Experiment: The manipulation of a characteristic under study (an independent variable) in order to examine the effect on another characteristic (dependent variable).

Explanatory survey: Questionnaire or interview used to uncover potential causes for some observation.

Explanatory theories: Theories of deviance (or some other social phenomenon) that are concerned with trying to explain why it occurs.

Exploitation: A feature of capitalism in which the workers (proletariat) produce virtually everything but get few rewards while the capitalists, who do little, reap the vast majority of the rewards.

Expulsion: Removal of a minority group from a territory, either by forcible ejection through military and other government action or by "voluntary" emigration due to the majority's harassment, discrimination, and persecution.

Extended family: Two or more generations of a family living in the same household or in close proximity to one another.

Exurbia: Encompasses outlying areas between the suburbs and rural areas.

False consciousness: Regarding the proletariat in capitalism, the lack of understanding of capitalism's nature and the erroneous belief that capitalism operates to workers' benefit; exists when large numbers of people do not have a clear and correct sense of their true interests.

Family: A group of people who are related by descent, marriage, or adoption and that is especially important in socializing children so that they are better able to fit into the larger society.

Family household: A residential unit of one or more people occupying a given domicile who are related by blood, marriage, or adoption.

Fantasy city: A city in which great emphasis is placed on creating a spectacle, especially in the areas of consumption, leisure, tourism, and impressive buildings and other real estate developments.

Felonies: Serious crimes punishable by a year or more in prison.

Female genital mutilation (FGM): Female circumcision, involving the removal of a portion of a girl's genitalia.

Female proletarianization: Involves the increasing number of women who are doing low-status, poorly paid manual work.

Feminism: The belief that women are equal to men, especially socially, politically, and economically.

Feminist theory: A set of ideas critical of the social situation confronting women and offering solutions for improving, if not revolutionizing, their situation.

Feminization of labor: Involves the increasing participation of women in both the global formal and the informal paid labor force.

Feminization of poverty: Involves the increasing numbers of women falling below the poverty line.

Fertility: Relates to people's childbearing behavior (number of children).

Field experiment: Research that occurs in natural situations but that allows researchers to exert at least some control over who participates and what happens during the experiment.

Financescapes: Involve the use of various financial instruments in order to allow huge sums of money and other things of economic value to move into and across nations and around the world at great speed, almost instantaneously.

First Nations: Or First Peoples refers to people who are considered ancestors of the original inhabitants of what is now Canada. The term excludes Inuit (people of the far north) and Metis (mixed Aboriginal and European ancestry).

Folkway: A norm that is relatively unimportant and, if violated, carries few if any sanctions.

Food insecurity: A cause of undernutrition that occurs when people do not have sufficient access to safe and nutritious food.

Fordism: Involves the mass production of homogenous products, reliance on inflexible technologies, use of standardized work routines, economies of scale, and a mass market.

Free-trade zones: Geographic areas that are controlled by corporations rather than the nation-state in which they exist.

Front stage: Part of the social world where the social performance is idealized and designed to define the situation for those who observe it.

Function: An observable, positive consequence that helps a system survive, adapt, or adjust.

Fundamentalism: A strongly held belief in the fundamental or foundational precepts of any religion, or a rejection of the modern secular world.

Game stage: The stage in socialization in which a child develops a self in the full sense of the term because it is then that the child begins to take on the role of a group of people simultaneously rather than the roles of discrete individuals.

Gated communities: Communities in which gates, surveillance cameras, and guards provide the owners of homes, as well as condominiums, greater security from the problems (crime, panhandling) that they think they left behind in the city.

Gemeinschaft societies: Traditional societies characterized by face-to-face relations.

Gender: A social distinction and social definition (although it is obviously strongly affected by biology) that is based on what, given a person's biological category, are considered appropriate physical, behavioral, and personality characteristics.

General deterrence: Deals with whether the population as a whole will be less likely to commit crimes because of fear that they will be punished or imprisoned for their crimes.

Generalized other: Group or community that provides the self with a source of self-definition.

Genocide: An active, systematic attempt at eliminating an entire group of people.

Gentrification: Involves the reinvestment of real estate capital in blighted inner-city areas in order to rebuild residences and create a new infrastructure for the well-to-do.

Geopolitics: Political relationships that involve large geographic areas or the globe as a whole.

Gesellschaft societies: Modern societies characterized by impersonal, distant, and limited social relationships.

Gesture: Movement of one animal or human that elicits a mindless, automatic, and appropriate response from another animal or human.

Global care chain: A series of personal relationships among people, mostly women, across the globe based on the paid or unpaid work of caring.

Global cities: The three key locations (New York City, London, and Tokyo) for leading industries and marketplaces and the high-level management and the specialized services they require.

Global ethnography: A type of ethnography that is "grounded" in various parts of the world and that seeks to understand globalization as it exists in people's social lives.

Global governance: Organizations that operate beyond the reach of nation-states, yet guide and constrain the actions of those states.

Globalization: The social process of increasingly fluid global flows and the structures that expedite and impede those flows.

Group: A relatively small number of people who over time develop a patterned relationship based on interaction with one another.

Group pluralism: Society's various interest groups and organizations compete for access to political power to attempt to further their interests.

Habitus: An internalized set of preferences and dispositions that are learned through experience and social interactions in specific social contexts.

Hate crimes: Crimes that stem from the fact that the victims are in various ways different from, and disesteemed by, the perpetrators.

Hegemonic masculinity: A set of ideas about the characteristics of men that focuses on the interests and desires of men and is linked to patriarchy.

Hegemony: Occurs when one race (or other group) subordinates another more on the basis of dominant ideas, especially about cultural differences, than through material constraints.

Heterosexuality: Involves a desire to have sexual relations with someone of the opposite sex.

Hidden curriculum: A school's unofficial rules, routines, and structures through which students learn various behaviors, attitudes, and values.

High culture: A collection of cultural products that have tended to be associated with societal elites, to be seen as the product of artists or skilled professionals, and to be thought of as aesthetically rich.

Historical-comparative research: A research methodology that contrasts how different historical events and conditions in various societies (or components of societies) lead to different societal outcomes.

Homosexuality: Involves a desire to have sexual relations with someone of the same sex.

Horizontal mobility: Movement within one's social class.

Hyperconsumption: Consumption of, or buying, more than we need, really want, and can afford.

Hyperdebt: Borrowing more than you should, thereby owing more than you will be able to pay back.

Hypodescent rule: Law or judicial ruling that classified persons with even one nonwhite ancestor, or a nonwhite ancestor within a certain number of generations, as black or colored.

"I": The immediate response of an individual to others; that part of the self that is incalculable, unpredictable, and creative.

Ideal culture: Norms and values indicating what members of a society should believe in and do.

Ideal type: An exaggeratedly rational model that is used to study real-world phenomena.

Identity politics: The use of a minority group's power to strengthen the position of the cultural group with which it identifies.

Ideology: A set of shared beliefs that explains the social world and guides people's actions; a set of ideas that distort the reality of social systems, such as capitalism, and conceal the ways in which they really operate.

Ideoscapes: Involve images, largely political images often in line with the ideologies of nation-states.

Imagined communities: Communities that are socially constructed by those who see themselves as part of them.

Imperialism: Control over geographic areas without the creation of colonies.

Impression management: People's use of a variety of techniques to control the image of themselves that they want to project during their social performances.

Income: The amount of money a person earns in a given year from a job, a business, or various types of assets and investments.

Independent variable: In an experiment, a condition that can be independently manipulated by the researcher with the goal of producing a change in some other variable.

Indictable offences: These are serious crimes that have penalties typically longer than six months (known as a felony in the U.S.), see also summary convictions.

Individualized marriage: A shift in the 1960s to a model of marriage with emphasis on satisfaction of individuals involved.

Inequality: The fact that some positions in society yield a great deal of money, status, and power while others yield little, if any, of these.

Inferential statistics: Numerical data that allow researchers to use data from a small group to speculate with some level of certainty about a larger group.

Informal organization: How the organization actually works as opposed to the way it is supposed to work.

Informationalism: Combines forces of production (factories, shopping malls, machines, etc.) with knowledge and information.

Informed consent: Agreement by participants in social research that they understand and accept the true nature and purpose of the study and any sensitive or dangerous aspects of the research.

In-group: A group to which people belong and with which they identify, perhaps strongly.

Innovators: Individuals who accept cultural goals, but reject the conventional means to achieve success.

Institutional marriage: Predominant model of marriage in the early twentieth century; emphasized maintenance of the institution of marriage itself.

Institutional racism: Race-based discrimination that results from the day-to-day operation of social institutions and social structures and their rules, policies, and practices.

Interaction: A social engagement that involves two, or more, individuals who perceive, and orient their actions to, one another.

Interaction order: An area of interaction that is organized and orderly, but the order is created informally by those involved in the interaction rather than by some formal structure.

Intergenerational mobility: The difference between the parents' social class position and the position achieved by their child(ren).

Intersectionality: The fact that members of any given minority group are affected by the nature of their positions in other arrangements of social inequality; the confluence, or intersection, of various social statuses and the inequality and oppression associated with each in combination with others.

Intersexed: Are those who have some combination of the genitalia of both males and females.

Interview: Research method in which information is sought from participants (respondents) who are asked a series of questions (usually face-to-face, but also by phone and increasingly via the Internet) that have been spelled out, at least to some degree, before the research is conducted.

Intimacy: A close and personal relationship.

Intimate relationship: Partners who have a close, personal, and domestic relationship with one another.

Intragenerational mobility: Movement up or down the stratification system in one's lifetime.

Juvenile delinquency: Involves, in most states in the United States, crimes committed by those who are less than 18 years of age.

Labeling theory: Contends that a deviant is someone to whom a deviant label has been successfully applied.

Labor migrants: Those who migrate because they are driven by either "push" factors (a lack of work, low pay) in their homeland or "pull" factors (jobs and higher pay available elsewhere).

Laboratory experiment: Research that occurs in a laboratory, giving the researcher great control over both the selection of the participants to be studied and the conditions to which they are exposed.

Landscapes (scapes): Fluid, irregular, and variable global flows that produce different results throughout the world.

Language: A set of meaningful symbols that makes possible the communication of culture as well as communication more generally within a given culture, and that calls out the same meaning in the person to whom an utterance is aimed as to the person making the utterance.

Latent functions: Unintended positive consequences.

Law: A norm that has been codified, or written down, and is formally enforced through institutions such as the state.

Legitimations: Systems of ideas generated by the social system to support its own existence.

Leisure: Involves means of escape from the obligations associated with work and family involving social activities that are uncoerced, relaxing, and perhaps informative and that are set apart in time and often in space.

Liminal: A period, or a special time, set apart from ordinary reality.

Local: Involves looking inward to one's company rather than looking outward.

Looking-glass self: The self-image that reflects how others respond to a person, particularly as a child.

Low culture: A collection of cultural products, also referred to as popular culture, that have tended to be associated with the masses, to be seen as homogenized and standardized products of massive corporations, and to be viewed as lacking in virtually any redeeming aesthetic qualities.

Macro-: Large-scale; used to describe social phenomena such as groups, organizations, cultures, society, and the globe.

Macrofinance: The globalization of money and finance.

Majority group: A group in a dominant position on the dimensions of wealth, power, and prestige.

Majority-minority population: Where more than 50 percent of the population is part of a minority group.

Manifest functions: Positive consequences that are brought about consciously and purposely.

Marriage: The legal union of two people.

Mass culture: Culture that is administered by large organizations, lacks spontaneity, and is phony.

Mass production: Characterized by large numbers of standardized products, highly specialized workers, interchangeable machine parts, precision tools, a high-volume mechanized production process, and the synchronization of the flow of materials to and of products from the machines, with the entire process made as continuous as possible.

Master status: A position that is more important than any others both for the person in the position and for all others involved.

Material culture: All of the material objects that are reflections or manifestations of a culture.

McDonaldization: A process by which the principles of the fast-food restaurant are coming to dominate more and more sectors of society and more societies throughout the world.

"Me": The organized set of others' attitudes assumed by the individual; it involves the adoption by the individual of the generalized other.

Mechanical solidarity: Cohesion among a group of people, most common in an early form of society, in which people are held together by the fact that they all do essentially the same things.

Mediascapes: Involve the electronic capability to produce and transmit information and images around the world.

Mediated interaction: Social interaction in which some technology comes between the participants, unlike face-to-face interaction.

Medical sociology: A field concerned with the social causes and consequences of health and illness.

Medicalization: The tendency to label as an illness a phenomenon or syndrome that was not previously considered an illness, as well as to exaggerate the ability of medicine to deal with that phenomenon or syndrome.

Megacities: Cities with a population greater than 8 million people.

Megalopolis: A cluster of highly populated cities that can stretch over great distances.

Meritocracy: A dominant ideology involving the widely shared belief that all people have an equal chance of succeeding economically based on their hard work and skills.

Metropolis: A large, powerful, and culturally influential urban area that contains a central city and surrounding communities that are economically and socially linked to the center.

Micro-: Small-scale; used to describe social phenomena such as individuals and their thoughts and actions.

Micro-macro continuum: The range of social entities from the individual, even mind and self, to the interaction among individuals, the groups often formed by that interaction, formally structured organizations, societies, and increasingly the global.

Microfinance: Local, grassroots efforts to lend largely small sums of money to poor people, especially in the Global South.

Migration: The movements of people and their effect on sending and receiving societies.

Mind: An internal conversation that arises, is related to, and is continuous with interactions, especially conversations that one has with others in the social world.

Minority group: A group in a subordinate position in terms of wealth, power, and prestige.

Misdemeanors: Minor offenses punishable by imprisonment of less than a year.

Monarch: Head of state in a monarchy; from the Greek, meaning "single ruler."

Monarchies: Politics ruled by a typically hereditary head of state, usually springing from a royal family, and based on the traditional forms of authority.

Monogamy: A family with one wife and one husband (or two wives or two husbands).

Monopoly capitalism: A form of capitalism dominated by huge corporations that monopolize the market.

Moral entrepreneurs: Individuals or groups who come to define an act as a moral outrage and who lead a campaign to have it defined as deviant and to have it made illegal and therefore subject to legal enforcement.

Moral panic: A widespread, but disproportionate, reaction to a form of deviance.

More: An important norm whose violation is likely to be met with severe sanctions.

Mortality: Relates to a population's deaths and death rates.

Multiculturalism: An environment in which cultural differences are encouraged both by the state and by the majority group.

Multiparty system: A political system in which more than two parties enjoy public support and hold political office in a nation.

Nation: A group of people who share similar cultural, religious, ethnic, linguistic, and territorial characteristics.

Nation-state: The combination of a nation with a geographic and political structure; encompasses both populations that define themselves as a nation with various shared characteristics and the organizational structure of the state.

Natural experiment: An experiment that occurs when researchers take advantage of a naturally occurring event to study its effect on one or more dependent variables.

Netnography: An ethnographic method in which the Internet becomes the research site and what transpires there is the sociologist's research interest.

Network organization: A new organizational form that is flat and horizontal; is intertwined with other organizations; is run and managed in very different ways than traditional organizations; uses more flexible production methods; and is composed of a series of interconnected nodes.

Networks: "Interconnected nodes" that are open, capable of unlimited expansion, dynamic, and able to innovate without disrupting the system in which they exist.

New religious movements: Movements that attract zealous religious converts, follow leaders who are defined as charismatic, appeal to an atypical portion of the population, have a tendency to differentiate between "us" and "them," are characterized by distrust by others, and are prone to rapid fundamental changes.

Nonfamily household: A residential unit where a person lives either alone or with nonrelatives.

Nonparticipant observation: A research method in which the sociologist plays little or no role in what is being observed.

Nonresident parents: Fathers and mothers who live apart from their children.

Norm: An informal rule that guides what a member of a culture does in a given situation and how that person lives.

Nuclear family: A family with two married adults and one or more children.

Observation: A research method that involves systematic watching, listening to, and recording what takes place in a natural social setting over some period of time.

Occupational mobility: Changes in people's work either across or within generations.

Offshore outsourcing: The transfer of work to organizations in other countries.

Oligarchy: An organization with a small group of people at the top obtaining, and exercising, far more power than they are supposed to have.

Organic solidarity: Cohesion among a group of people, most common in a later type of society, in which people are held together by their differences.

Organization: A collective purposely constructed to achieve particular ends.

Organized crime: Can involve various types of organizations, but is most often associated with syndicated organized crime, which uses violence (or its threat) and the corruption of public officials to profit from illegal activities.

Orientalism: A set of ideas and texts produced in the West that served as the basis to dominate, control, and exploit the Orient (the East) and its many minority groups.

Out-group: A group to which outsiders (at least from the perspective of the in-group) belong.

Outsourcing: The transfer of activities once performed by one organization to another organization in exchange for money.

Paradigm: A general model of the world that is accepted by most practitioners in a field.

Parole: Involves the supervised early release of a prisoner for such things as good behavior while in prison.

Participant observation: A research method in which the researcher actually plays a role, usually a minor one, in the group or setting being observed.

Passionate love: Typified by sudden onset, strong sexual feelings, and idealization of the one who is loved.

Pedophilia: Sexual attraction to children.

Play stage: Mead's first stage in the socialization process where children learn to take on the attitudes of specific others toward themselves.

Pluralism: The belief that a representative democracy has a government in which people exercise their power through the vote and get the leadership that they want; where many groups are able to coexist in society without any of them losing their individual qualities.

Political action committees (PACs): Private groups organized to advance a given political perspective or candidate.

Political crime: Either an illegal offense against the state to affect its policies, or an offense by the state, either domestically or internationally.

Politics: Societal competition through established governmental channels to advance a position or enact a policy to benefit its members.

Polyandry: A family with multiple husbands.

Polygamy: A family with multiple spouses.

Polygyny: A family with multiple wives.

Postcolonialism: The era in once-colonized areas after the colonizing power has departed, although postcolonial thinking and work could already be well under way before the colonizing power departs.

Post-Fordism: Associated with smaller production runs of more specialized products, especially those high in style and quality, more flexible machinery made possible by advances in technology largely traceable to the computer, more skilled workers with greater flexibility and

autonomy, less reliance on economies of scale, and more differentiated markets for those more specialized products.

Postindustrial society: A society that was at one time industrial, but where the focus on the manufacture of goods has been replaced by an increase, at least initially, in service work; that is, work in which people are involved in providing services for one another rather than producing goods.

Postmodern theory: A set of ideas oriented in opposition to modern theory by, for example, rejecting or deconstructing the grand narratives of modern social theory.

Postmodernism: The emergence of new and different cultural forms in music, movies, art, architecture, and the like.

Postmodernity: The state of having moved beyond the modern era analyzed by the classic social theorists and into a new postmodern epoch characterized by less rationality and more eclecticism.

Poverty line: The threshold, in terms of income, below which a household is considered poor.

Power: The ability to get others to do what you want them to do, even if it is against their will.

Power elite theory: Power is not dispersed throughout a stable society but is concentrated in a small number of people who control the major institutions of the state, the corporate economy, and the military.

Prejudice: Involves negative attitudes, beliefs, and feelings toward African Americans (and other minorities).

Primary deviance: Early, nonpatterned acts of deviance or an act here or there that is considered to be strange or out of the ordinary.

Primary groups: Groups that are small, are close-knit, and have intimate face-to-face interaction.

Primary socialization: The acquisition of language, identities, gender roles, cultural routines, norms, and values from parents and other family members at the earliest stages of an individual's life.

Primitive communism: Egalitarian, nomadic hunter-gatherer societies.

Probation: A system by which those who are convicted of less serious crimes may be released into the community, but under supervision and under certain conditions such as being involved in and completing a substance abuse program.

Profane: To Durkheim, that which has not been defined as sacred, or that which is ordinary and mundane.

Profession: Distinguished from other occupations by its power and considerable autonomy.

Proletariat: Workers as a group, or those in the capitalist system who own little or nothing except for their capacity for work (labor), which they must sell to the capitalists in order to survive.

Property crimes: Do not involve injury or force, but rather are offenses that involve gaining or destroying property. The major property crimes are larceny-theft, burglary, motor-vehicle theft, and arson.

Prosumer: A consumer who produces value in the process of consumption; one who combines the acts of consumption and production.

Protestant ethic: Belief in hard work, frugality, and good work as means to achieve both economic success and heavenly salvation.

Public sociology: Addresses a wide range of audiences, most of which are outside the academy, including a wide variety of local, national, and global groups. Public sociologists write for these groups, and they can become involved in collaborative projects with them.

Pure relationship: A relationship that is entered into for what each partner can get from it, and those involved remain in it only as long as each derives enough satisfaction from it.

Qualitative research: Any research method that does not require statistical methods for collecting and reporting data.

Quantitative research: Any research method that involves the analysis of numerical data derived usually from surveys and experiments.

Queer theory: A set of ideas that tends to focus on the social realities of gays; lesbians; bisexuals; and individuals who are transgendered, transsexual, intersexed, and so on but that argues more generally against fixed and stable identities that determine who we are.

Questionnaire: A self-administered, written set of questions.

Race: A social definition based on some real or presumed physical, biological characteristic, such as skin color or hair texture, as well as a shared lineage; race is more about what people define it to be than it is about any basic physical differences.

Racism: Involves defining a group as a race and attributing negative characteristics to that group.

Random sample: A subset of a population in which every member of the group has an equal chance of being included.

Rape: A form of domination; violent sexual intercourse.

Rational choice theory: A set of ideas that sees people as rational and as acting purposively in order to achieve their goals.

Rational-legal authority: Authority that is legitimated on the basis of legally enacted rules and the right of those with authority under those rules to issue commands.

Rationalization: The process by which social structures are increasingly characterized by the most direct and efficient means to their ends.

Real culture: What people actually think and do in their everyday lives.

Rebels: Individuals who reject both traditional means and goals and instead substitute nontraditional goals and means to those goals.

Recidivism: The repetition of a criminal act by one who has been convicted for an offense.

Reciprocity: The expectation that those involved in an interaction will give and receive rewards of roughly equal value.

Reference groups: Groups that people take into consideration in evaluating themselves.

Reflexive modernity: The argument that, over time, society is becoming increasingly more self-aware, reflective, and hence reflexive.

Refugees: Migrants who are forced to leave their homeland, or who leave involuntarily, because they fear for their safety.

Relative poverty: A concern for how some people, irrespective of income, are, or feel themselves to be, poor relative to others.

Reliability: The degree to which a given question (or another kind of measure) produces the same results time after time.

Religion: A social phenomenon that consists of beliefs about the sacred; the experiences, practices, and rituals that reinforce those beliefs; and the community that shares similar beliefs and practices.

Representative democracy: A political system in which people, as a whole body, do not actually rule themselves but rather have some say in who will best represent them in the state.

Republicans: Members of a political party within the U.S. two-party system; typically seen as the conservative party.

Resocialization: Involves unlearning old behaviors, norms, and values and learning new ones.

Resource mobilization theory: An approach to understanding social movements that focuses on what groups of people need to do in order to mobilize effectively to bring about social change. What matters most are the resources available to the group and the ability to bring enough of those resources together in order to create an effective social movement.

Retreatists: Individuals who reject both cultural goals and the traditional routes to their attainment; they have completely given up on attaining success within the system.

Reverse socialization: The socialization of those who normally do the socializing—for example, children socializing their parents.

Riot: Temporary unruly collective behavior that causes damage to persons or property.

Rites of passage: Rituals that surround major transitions in life: birth, puberty, marriage, death, and conversion rituals such as baptism.

Ritual: A set of regularly repeated, prescribed, and traditional behaviors that serve to symbolize some value or belief.

Ritualists: Individuals who realize that they will not be able to achieve cultural goals, but they nonetheless continue to engage in the conventional behavior associated with such success.

Role: What is generally expected of a person who occupies a given status.

Role ambiguity: A state in which one is unclear about the expectations of one's role.

Role conflict: Conflicting expectations associated with a given position or multiple positions.

Role overload: A situation in which people are confronted with more expectations than they can possibly handle.

Rule creators: Individuals who devise society's rules, norms, and laws.

Rule enforcers: Individuals who threaten to, or actually, enforce the rules.

Sacred: To Durkheim, that which has been defined as being of ultimate concern.

Sample: A representative portion of the overall population.

Sanction: The application of rewards (positive sanctions) or punishments (negative sanctions) when norms are accepted or violated.

Scientific management: The application of scientific principles and methods to management.

Scientific method: A structured way to find answers to questions about the world.

Secondary data analysis: Reanalysis of data, often survey data, collected by others, including other sociologists.

Secondary deviance: Deviant acts that persist, become more common, and eventually cause people to organize their lives and personal identities around their deviant status.

Secondary groups: Generally large, impersonal groups in which ties are relatively weak and members do not know one another very well, and whose impact on members is typically not very powerful.

Sect: A small group of people who have joined the group consciously and voluntarily in order to have a personal religious experience.

Secularization: The declining significance of religion.

Segregation: The physical and social separation of majority and minority groups.

Self: The sense of oneself as an object, which becomes more defined over time.

Separation of powers: Different branches of government are separate and counter-balance one another so that no one branch of government can wield too much power.

Sex: Mainly a biological distinction between males and females based on fundamental differences in their reproductive functions.

Sexual assault: Encompasses sexual acts of domination usually enacted by men against women.

Sexual harassment: Involves unwanted sexual attention, for example sexually oriented remarks and jokes, advances, and requests, usually by men, that take place in the workplace or other settings.

Sexual orientation: Involves who one desires sexually, with whom one wants to engage in sexual relations, and with whom one feels connected to—typically categorized as heterosexual, homosexual, bisexual, or asexual.

Sexual scripts: Generally known ideas about what one ought to do and not do as far as sexual behavior is concerned.

Sexuality: The ways in which people think about, and behave toward, themselves and others as sexual beings.

Sick role: Expectations about the way sick people are supposed to act.

Significant symbol: A gesture that arouses in the individual the same kind of response, although it need not be identical, as it is supposed to elicit from those to whom the gesture is addressed.

Simulation: An inauthentic or fake version of something.

Single-party system: A political system in which the ruling party outlaws, or heavily restricts, opposing parties.

Slavery: A system in which people are defined as property, involuntarily placed in perpetual servitude, and not given the same rights as the rest of society.

Social change: Variations over time in every aspect of the social world ranging from changes affecting individuals to transformations having an impact on the globe as a whole.

Social class: One's economic position in the stratification system, especially one's occupation, which strongly determines and reflects one's income and wealth.

Social construction of reality: The continuous process of individual creation of structural realities and the constraint and coercion exercised by those structures.

Social control: The process by which a group or society enforces conformity to its demands and expectations.

Social control agents: Those who label a person as deviant.

Social control theory: Theory that focuses on the reasons why people do not commit deviant acts such as social control and the stake people have in engaging in conformist behavior.

Social facts: Macro-level phenomena—social structures and cultural norms and values—that stand apart from and impose themselves on people.

Social mobility: The ability or inability to change one's position in the social hierarchy.

Social movements: Sustained and intentional collective efforts, usually operating outside of established institutional channels, either to bring about or to retard social change.

Social reproduction: A system that systematically reproduces class relations and the capitalist order.

Social stratification: Hierarchical differences and inequalities in economic positions, as well as in other important areas, especially political power and status, or social honor.

Social structures: Enduring and regular social arrangements, such as the family and the state, based on persistent patterns of interaction and social relationships.

Social processes: Dynamic and changing aspects of the social world.

Socialism: A historical stage following communism involving the effort by society to plan and organize production consciously and rationally so that all members of society benefit from it.

Socialization: The process through which a person learns and generally comes to accept the ways of a group or of society as a whole.

Society: A relatively large population that lives in a given territory, has a social structure, and shares a culture, and the complex pattern of social relationships that is bounded in space and persists over time.

Sociological imagination: The ability to look at the social world from a unique sociological perspective.

Sociology: The systematic study of the ways in which people are affected by, and affect, the social structures and social processes that are associated with the groups, organizations, cultures, societies, and world in which they exist.

Soft money: A way of affecting political processes through monetary contributions to party building, especially around specific issues that do not fall under federal regulations for campaign contributions.

Spaces of flows: Settings that are unlikely to have clear and defensible borders; they are likely to be quite fluid and more likely than spaces of places to be temporary in nature.

Spaces of places: Settings that are more likely to have clear borders and to be able to limit flows of all kinds and even stop them from entering completely.

Specific deterrence: Whether the experience of punishment in general, and incarceration in particular, makes it less likely that an individual will commit crimes in the future.

Staples economy: An economy based on raw material extraction or harvesting, including resources such as fish, gas, grain, minerals, oil, and timber.

Statistics: The mathematical method used to analyze numerical data.

State: A political body organized for government and civil rule, with relatively autonomous officeholders and with its own rules and resources coming largely from taxes.

Status: A dimension of the social stratification system that relates to the prestige attached to people's positions within society.

Status consistency (or crystallization): Exists when people have similar positions in the stratification system on class, status, and power; they rank high, medium, or low on all three dimensions.

Status inconsistency: Exists when people occupy positions on one dimension of stratification that are different, perhaps very different, from their positions on the other dimensions of stratification.

Stepfamily: A family in which two adults are married or cohabiting, and at least one of them has a child or children from a previous marriage or cohabitation living with them.

Stereotype: An exaggerated generalization about an entire category of people.

Stratified sample: Created when a larger group is divided into a series of subgroups and then random samples are taken within each of these groups.

Stigma: A characteristic that others find, define, and often label as unusual, unpleasant, or deviant.

Strain theory: Theory based on the idea that the discrepancy between the larger structure of society and the means available to people to achieve that which the society considers to be of value produces strain that may cause an individual to undertake deviant acts.

Structural mobility: The effect of changes in the larger society on the position of individuals in the stratification system, especially the occupational structure.

Structural-functionalism: A set of ideas focused on social structures as well as the functions and dysfunctions that such structures perform.

Structuralism: Social theory interested in the social impact of hidden or underlying structures.

Subculture: A group of people who accept much of the dominant culture but are set apart from it by one or more culturally significant characteristics.

Suburbanization: The process whereby large numbers of people move out of the city and into nearby, less densely populated, environs.

Suburbs: Communities that are adjacent to, but outside the political boundaries of, large central cities.

Summary convictions: Typically these involve less serious crimes that usually have a maximum penalty of six months in jail (known as a misdemeanor in the U.S.), see also indictable offences

Survey research: A research methodology that involves the collection of information from a population, or more usually a representative portion of a population, through the use of interviews and, more importantly, questionnaires.

Sustainable development: Involves economic and environmental changes that meet the needs of the present, especially of the world's poor, without jeopardizing the needs of the future.

Symbolic culture: Aspects of culture that exist in nonmaterial forms.

Symbolic exchange: A process whereby people swap all sorts of things, but most importantly the process of exchange is valued in itself and for the human relationships involved and not because of the economic gains—the money—that may be derived from it.

Symbolic interaction: Interaction on the basis of not only gestures but also significant symbols.

Symbolic interactionism: A set of ideas concerned with the role of symbols whose meanings are shared and understood by those involved in human interaction.

Symbol: A word, gesture, or object that stands in for something, or someone (i.e., a "label").

Technology: The interplay of machines, tools, skills, and procedures for the accomplishment of tasks.

Technoscapes: Involve mechanical and informational technologies, as well as the material that moves quickly and freely through them.

Terrorism: Involves nongovernmental actors who engage in acts of violence that targets noncombatants, property, or military personnel to influence politics.

Theories of colonialism: Systems of thought that address the causes and consequences of a powerful nation-state controlling a less powerful geographic area.

Theory: A set of interrelated ideas that have a wide range of application, deal with centrally important issues, and have stood the test of time.

Total institution: A closed, all-encompassing place of residence and work set off from the rest of society that meets all of the needs of those enclosed in it.

Traditional authority: Authority that is based on the belief in long-running traditions.

Transgender: Umbrella term describing individuals whose gender identity does not conform to the sex to which they were assigned at birth and whose behavior challenges gender norms.

Transnational capitalism: An economic system in which transnational economic practices predominate.

Transnational capitalist class (TCC): A class at the heart of the global capitalist system but not made up of capitalists in the traditional Marxian sense of the term since none of them own the means of production.

Transnational corporations: Corporations, also referred to as multinational corporations, that exist in various places throughout the world and cannot be identified, and do not identify themselves, with any specific country.

Transsexual: An individual whose genitalia are opposite to the sex with which he or she identifies and who may undergo treatment or surgery to acquire the physical characteristics of the self-identified sex.

Treadmill of production: When everyone in the capitalist system depends on continuous growth in production and in the economy.

Triad: A three-person group.

Two-party system: A political system in which two parties hold nearly all positions of political power in a given nation.

Unanticipated consequence: An unexpected social effect, especially a negative effect.

Underemployment: Involves being in jobs that are beneath one's training and ability, being considered an involuntary part-time worker, and working, but in jobs that do not fully occupy the workers (for example, seasonal work).

Undernutrition: A form of malnutrition involving an inadequate intake of nutrients, including calories, vitamins, and minerals.

Undocumented immigrants: Those who either migrate to a receiving country without valid authorization, usually a passport, or remain in a receiving country after their authorized permits have expired.

Unemployment: Being economically active and in the labor force (for example, not retired), able and willing to work, and seeking employment, but unable to find a job.

Urban: In the United States, to be considered urban an area must have more than 50,000 inhabitants.

Urban sociology: The subfield of sociology concerned with the issue of the way of life in the city.

Urbanism: The distinctive way of life (lifestyles, attitudes, social relationships) that emerges in, and is closely associated with, urban areas.

Urbanization: The process by which an increasing percentage of a society's population comes to be located in relatively densely populated urban areas.

Validity: The degree to which a question (or another kind of measure) gets an accurate response, or measures what it is supposed to measure.

Values: General and abstract standards defining what a group or society as a whole considers good, desirable, right, or important—in short, its ideals.

Vertical mobility: Both upward and downward mobility.

Violent crime: The threat of injury or the threat or actual use of force, including murder, rape, robbery, and aggravated assault, as well as terrorism and, globally, war crimes.

War: Armed conflict in which a nation uses its military to attempt to impose its will on others.

Wealth: The total amount of a person's assets (e.g., savings, investments, home, automobile) less the total of various kinds of debts (e.g., amount owed on a home mortgage, car loan, or to the credit card company).

Welfare states: States that seek both to run their economic markets efficiently, as capitalism does, and to do so more equitably, which capitalism does not do.

White-collar crime: Involves crimes committed by responsible and (usually) high-social-status people in the course of their work.

White racial frame: Includes an array of racist ideas, racial stereotypes, racialized stories and tales, racist images, powerful racial emotions, and various inclinations to discriminate against blacks.

World cities: Thirty cities that perform most of the same functions as global cities, as locations for leading industries and marketplaces and the high-level management and the specialized services they require.

World system theory: A system of thought that focuses on the stratification of nation-states on a global scale.

Xenophobia: Involves the beliefs, attitudes, and prejudices that reject, exclude, and vilify groups that are outsiders or foreigners to the dominant social group.

REFERENCES

Abd-Allah, U. F. 2005. "Mercy: The Stamp of Creation." A Nawawi Foundation Paper, p. 6. Retrieved March 28, 2012 (http://www.nawawi.org/downloads/article1.pdf).

Abrutyn, Seth. 2012. "Hinduism." Pp. 932–37 in *The Wiley-Blackwell Enyclopedia of Globalization,* edited by George Ritzer. Malden, MA: Wiley-Blackwell.

Acemoglu, Daron, and Pierre Yared. 2010. "Political Limits to Globalization." Working Paper 15694. Retrieved March 28, 2012 (http://www.nber.org/papers/w15694).

Acierno, Ron, et al. 2010. "Prevalence and Correlates of Emotional, Physical, Sexual, and Financial Abuse and Potential Neglect in the United States: The National Elder Mistreatment Study." *American Journal of Public Health* 100:292–97.

Acker, Joan. 1990. "Hierarchies, Jobs, and Bodies: A Theory of Gendered Organizations." *Gender and Society* 4(2):139–58.

Acker, Joan. 2004. "Gender, Capitalism and Globalization." *Critical Sociology* 30(1):17–41.

Acker, Joan. 2009. "From Glass Ceiling to Inequality Regimes." *Sociologie du Travail* 51(2):199–217.

Acker, Sandra. 1987. "Feminist Theory and the Study of Gender and Education." *International Review of Education* 33(4):419–33.

Adachi, Ken. 1976. *The Enemy that Never Was: A History of the Japanese Canadians.* Toronto, ON: McClelland and Stewart.

Adams, Ann, Christopher D. Buckingham, Antje Lindenmeyer, John B. McKinlay, Carol Link, Lisa Marceau, and Sara Arber. 2008. "The Influence of Patient and Doctor Gender on Diagnosing Coronary Heart Disease." *Sociology of Health & Illness* 30(1):1–18.

Adams, Josh. 2009. "Bodies of Change: A Comparative Analysis of Media Representations of Body Modification Practices." *Sociological Perspectives* 52:103–29.

Adorno, Theodor, and Max Horkheimer. 1997. *Dialectic of Enlightenment.* London: Verso.

Agnew, Robert. 2001. "An Overview of General Strain Theory." Pp. 161–74 in *Explaining Criminals and Crime: Essays in Contemporary Criminological Theory,* edited by R. Paternoster and R. Bachman. Los Angeles: Roxbury.

Aguirre, B. E., et al. 2011. "Normative Collective Behavior in the Station Building Fire." *Social Science Quarterly* 92:100–118.

Ahamad, Liaquat. 2011. "How Bernard Madoff Did It." *The New York Times,* May 13. Retrieved March 28, 2012 (http://www.nytimes.com/2011/05/15/books/review/book-review-the-wizard-of-lies-bernie-madoff-and-the-death-of-trust-by-diana-b-henriques.html?pagewanted=all).

Ahemba, Tume. 2007. "Lagos Rejects Nigeria Census, Says Has 17.5 Million." Reuters, February 6. Retrieved February 28, 2012 (http://uk.reuters.com/article/2007/02/06/nigeria-lagos-idUKL0674057420070206).

Ahituv, Avner, and Robert I. Lerman. 2007. "How Do Marital Status, Work Effort, and Wage Rates Interact?" *Demography* 44(3):623–47.

Ahuvia, Aaron, and Elif Izberk-Bilgin. 2011. "Limits of the McDonaldization Thesis: eBayization and Ascendant Trends in Post-industrial Consumer Culture." *Consumption, Markets & Culture* 14:361–64.

Ajrouch, Kristine A. 2007. "Reference Groups." Pp. 3828–29 in *The Blackwell Encyclopedia of Sociology,* edited by George Ritzer. Malden, MA: Blackwell.

Akers, Donald S. 1967. "On Measuring the Marriage Squeeze." *Demography* 4:907–24.

Alatas, Farid. 2011. "Ibn Khaldun." Pp. 12–29 in *The Wiley-Blackwell Companion to Major Social Theorists: Volume 1. Classical Theorists,* edited by George Ritzer and Jeffrey Stepnisky. Malden, MA: Wiley-Blackwell.

Alazraki, Melly. 2010. "Global Pharmaceutical Sales Expected to Rise to $880 Billion in 2011." *Daily Finance.* Retrieved January 25, 2012 (http://www.dailyfinance.com/2010/10/07/global-pharmaceutical-sales-expected-to-rise-to-880-billion-in/).

Alba, Richard. 2009. *Blurring the Color Line: The New Chance for a More Integrated America.* Cambridge, MA: Harvard University Press.

Albanese, Patrizia. 2009. *Children in Canada Today.* Toronto, ON: Oxford University Press.

Albrow, Martin. 1996. *The Global Age.* Cambridge, UK: Polity Press.

Aleman, Ana M., and Katherine Link Wartman. 2008. *Online Social Networking on Campus: Understanding What Matters in Student Culture.* New York: Routledge.

Alexander, Bayarma, Dick Ettema, and Martin Dijst. 2010. "Fragmentation of Work Activity as a Multi-dimensional Construct and, Its Association with ICT, Employment and Sociodemographic Characteristics." *Journal of Transport Geography* 18(1):55–64.

Alexander, Douglas. 2010. "The Impact of the Economic Crisis on the World's Poorest Countries." *Global Policy* 1:118–20.

Alexander, K., Entwisle, D., and Olson, L. 2007. "Lasting Consequences of the Summer Learning Gap." *American Sociological Review* 72:167–80.

Ali, Ayann Hirsi. 2010. "Not the Child My Grandmother Wanted." *The New York Times,* December 2. Retrieved May 28, 2012 (http://www.nytimes.com/2010/12/02/opinion/global/02iht-GA13ali.html?_r=2).

Ali, S. Harris. 2012. "Diseases, Borderless." Pp. 446–49 in *The Wiley-Blackwell Encyclopedia of Globalization,* edited by George Ritzer. Malden, MA: Wiley-Blackwell.

Allan, Graham. 2007. "Family Structure." Pp. 1618–21 in *The Blackwell Encyclopedia of Sociology,* edited by George Ritzer. Malden, MA: Blackwell.

Allan, Stuart. 2007. "Network Society." Pp. 3180–82 in *The Blackwell Encyclopedia of Sociology,* edited by George Ritzer. Malden, MA: Blackwell.

Allen, I. E., and J. Seaman. 2010. *Learning on Demand: Online Education in the United States, 2009.* Needham, MA: Sloan Center for Online Education.

Allmendinger, Jutta. 2007. "Unemployment as a Social Problem." Pp. 5092–96 in *The Blackwell Encyclopedia of Sociology,* edited by George Ritzer. Malden, MA: Blackwell.

Alter Chen, Martha. 1995. "Engendering World Conference: The International Women's Movement and the United Nations." *Third World Quarterly* 16(3):477–94.

Altman, Dennis. 1996. "Rupture or Continuity? The Internationalization of Gay Identities." *Social Text* 48:77–94.

Altman, Dennis. 2001. *Global Sex*. Chicago: University of Chicago Press.

Al-Tuwaijri, Sameera, Louis J. Currat, Sheila Davey, Andrés de Francisco, Abdul Ghaffar, Susan Jupp, and Christine Mauroux. 2003. *The 10/90 Report on Health Research 2003–2004*. Global Forum for Health Research, Geneva.

Alvarez, Lizette. 2006a. "A Growing Stream of Illegal Immigrants Choose to Remain Despite the Risks." *The New York Times*, December 20.

Alvarez, Lizette. 2006b. "Fear and Hope in Immigrant's Furtive Existence." *The New York Times*, December 20.

Alvarez, Lizette. 2011. "Pull of Family Reshapes U.S.-Cuban Relations." *The New York Times*, November 22, pp. A1, A3.

Alvesson, M., and Y. D. Billing. 2009. *Understanding Gender and Organizations*. 2nd ed. London: Sage.

Amato, Paul R. 2000. "The Consequences of Divorce for Adults and Children." *Journal of Marriage and Family* 62(4):1269–87.

Amato, Paul R. 2004. "Tension Between Institutional and Individual Views of Marriage." *Journal of Marriage and the Family* 66:959–65.

Amato, Paul R., et al. 2007. *Alone Together: How Marriage in America Is Changing*. Cambridge, MA: Harvard University Press.

Amato, Paul R. and Spencer James. 2010. "Divorce in Europe and the United States: Commonalities and Differences across Nations." *Family Science* 1:2–13.

Ambert, Anne-Marie. 2009. *DIVORCE: Facts, Causes & Consequences*. 3rd ed. Ottawa, ON: The Vanier Institute of the Family.

America.gov. 2008. "U.S. Minorities Will Be the Majority by 2042, Census Bureau Says." Archive, August 15. Retrieved April 14, 2011 (http://www.america.gov/st/peopleplace-english/2008/August/20080815140005xlrennef0.1078106.html).

Amin, A., ed. 1994. *Post-Fordism*. Oxford: Blackwell.

Amnesty International. 2004. "Lives Blown Apart: Crimes Against Women in Times of Conflict: Stop Violence against Women." Retrieved March 28, 2012 (http://www.amnesty.org/en/library/info/ACT77/075/2004/en).

Amnesty International. 2011. "Death Sentences and Executions, 2010." London: Author. Retrieved March 28, 2012 (http://www.amnesty.org/en/library/asset/ACT50/001/2011/en/ea1b6b25-a62a-4074-927d-ba51e88df2e9/act500012011en.pdf).

Anderson, Benedict. 1991. *Imagined Communities: Reflections on the Origin and Spread of Nationalism*. 2nd ed. London: Verso.

Anderson, Chris. 2009. *Free: The Future of a Radical Price*. New York: Hyperion.

Anderson, David M., and Neil Carrier. 2006. "'Flower of Paradise' or 'Polluting the Nation': Contested Narratives of Khat Consumption."

Pp. 145–66 in *Consuming Cultures, Global Perspectives: Historical Trajectories, Transnational Exchanges*, edited by John Brewer and Frank Trentmann. Oxford: Berg.

Anderson, Elijah. 1999. *Code of the Street: Decency, Violence, and the Moral Life of the Inner City*. New York: Norton.

Anderson, Nickela, and Karen Hughes. 2010. "The Business of Caring: Women's Self-Employment and the Marketization of Care." *Gender, Work & Organization* 17(4):381–405.

Anderson, Sam. 2010. "The Human Shuffle." *New York Magazine*, February 5. Retrieved May 26, 2011 (http://nymag.com/news/media/63663/).

Anderson, Siwan, and Debraj Ray. 2010. "Missing Women: Age and Disease." *Review of Economic Studies* 77:1262–1300.

Andreas, Peter, and Ethan Nadelmann. 2006. *Policing the Globe: Criminalization and Crime Control in International Relations*. New York: Oxford University Press.

Andrejevic, Mark. 2009. *Spy: Surveillance and Power in the Interactive Era*. Lawrence: University of Kansas Press.

Andrews, Geoff. 2008. *The Slow Food Story: Politics and Pleasure*. Montreal, QU: McGill University Press.

Andrews, J. A., E. Tildesley, H. Hops, and F. Z. Li. 2002. "The Influence of Peers on Young Adult Substance Use." *Health Psychology* 4:349–57.

"Another Addition to Dubai's Malls." 2002. *Gulf News*, October 30. Retrieved May 19, 2011 (http://gulfnews.com/news/gulf/uae/general/another-addition-to-dubai-s-malls-1.402095).

Antonio, Robert. 2007. "The Cultural Construction of Neoliberal Globalization." Pp. 67–83 in *The Blackwell Companion to Globalization*, edited by George Ritzer. Malden, MA: Blackwell.

Antonio, Robert J. 2011. "Karl Marx." Pp. 115–64 in *The Wiley-Blackwell Companion to Major Social Theorists: Volume 1. Classical Theorists*, edited by George Ritzer and Jeffrey Stepnisky. Malden, MA: Wiley-Blackwell.

Antonio, Robert J., and Robert J. Brulle. 2012. "Ecological Problems." Pp. 476–84 in *The Wiley-Blackwell Companion to Sociology*, edited by George Ritzer. Malden, MA: Wiley-Blackwell.

Apel, Robert S., and Daniel Nagin. 2011. "General Deterrence: A Review of Recent Literature." Pp. 411–36 in *Crime and Public Policy*, edited by James Q. Wilson and Joan Petersilia. Oxford: Oxford University Press.

Apesoa-Varano, Ester Carolina. 2007. "Educated Caring: The Emergence of Professional Identity Among Nurses." *Qualitative Sociology* 30:249–74.

Appadurai, Arjun. 1996. *Modernity of Large: Cultural Dimensions of Globalization*. Minneapolis: University of Minnesota Press.

Appelbaum, S. H., N. Asham, and K. Argheyd. 2011a. "Is the Glass Ceiling Cracked in Information Technology? A Quantitative Analysis: Part 1." *Industrial and Commercial Training* 43(6):354–61.

Appelbaum, S. H., N. Asham, and K. Argheyd. 2011b. "Is the Glass Ceiling Cracked in Information Technology? A Quantitative Analysis: Part 2." *Industrial and Commercial Training* 43(7):451–59.

Arai, A. Bruce. 2000. "Changing Motivations for Homeschooling in Canada." *Canadian Journal of Education* 25(3):204–17.

Archibold, R. C. 2009. "Mexican Drug Cartel Violence Spills Over, Alarming U.S." *The New York Times*, March 22.

Archibold, R. C. 2010. "Ranchers Alarmed by Killing Near Border." *The New York Times*, April 4.

Argiero, S. J., et al. 2010. "A Cultural Perspective for Understanding How Campus Environments Perpetuate Rape-supportive Culture." *Journal of the Indiana University Student Personnel Association* 43:26–40.

Aries, Phillipe. 1978. "La Famille et La Ville." *Esprit* 1:3–12.

Aries, Philippe. 1980. "Two Successive Motivations for the Declining Birth Rates in the West." *Population and Development Review* 6(4): 645–50.

Armstrong, Elizabeth, and Suzanna M. Crage. 2006. "Movements and Memory: The Making of the Stonewall Myth." *American Sociological Review* 71(5):724–51.

Armstrong, Pat, and Hugh Armstrong. 2010. *The Double Ghetto: Canadian Women and their Segregated Work*. 3rd ed. Toronto, ON: Oxford University Press.

Armstrong-Coben, Anne. 2009. "The Computer Will See You Now." *The New York Times*, March 6.

Arnold, Tom. 2011. "Major Gain for Dubai Non-oil Trade." *The National*, May 19. Retrieved May 19, 2011 (www.thenational.ae/business/markets/major-gain-for-dubai-non-oil-trade).

Arnquist, Sarah. 2009. "Research Trove: Patients' Online Data." *The New York Times*, August 25, p. D1.

Aronson, Jay D., and Simon A. Cole. 2009. "Science and the Death Penalty: DNA, Innocence, and the Debate over Capital Punishment in the United States." *Law & Social Inquiry* 34:603–33.

Arriola, Elvia R. 2006–2007. "Accountability for Murder in the Maquiladoras: Linking Corporate Indifference to Gender Violence at the U.S.-Mexico Border." *Seattle Journal for Social Justice* 5:603.

Arthur, Mikaila Mariel Lemonik. 2007a. "Race." Pp. 3731–34 in *The Blackwell Encyclopedia of Sociology*, edited by George Ritzer. Malden, MA: Blackwell.

Arthur, Mikaila Mariel Lemonik. 2007b. "Racism, Structural and Institutional." Pp. 3765–67 in *The Blackwell Encyclopedia of Sociology,* edited by George Ritzer. Malden, MA: Blackwell.

Arvidsson, Adam. 2012. "Brands." In *The Wiley-Blackwell Encyclopedia of Globalization,* edited by George Ritzer. Malden, MA: Wiley-Blackwell.

Asch, Solomon Eliot. 1952. *Social Psychology.* New York: Prentice-Hall.

Ashmore, Richard, Lee Jussim, and David Wilder. 2001. *Social Identity, Intergroup Conflict, and Conflict Resolution.* Oxford, UK: Oxford University Press.

Asia Pacific Foundation. 2012. "Canada's Merchandise Trade with China." Retrieved September 8, 2012 (http://www.asiapacific.ca/statistics/trade/bilateral-trade-asia-product/canadas-merchandise-trade-china).

Association of Universities and Colleges of Canada. 2011. *Trends in Higher Education.* Ottawa, ON: Author.

Atkinson, Michael. 2003. *Tattooed: The Sociogenesis of a Body Art.* Toronto, ON: University of Toronto Press.

Atkinson, Rowland, and Sarah Blandy. 2005. "Introduction: International Perspectives on the New Enclavism and the Rise of Gated Communities." *Housing Studies* 20:177–86.

Aud, Susan, and Gretchen Hannes, eds. 2011. *The Condition of Education 2011 in Brief* (NCES 2011-034). Washington, DC: U.S. Department of Education, National Center for Education Statistics.

Aurini, Janice. 2011. "How Upper-Middle Class Canadian Parents Understand the Transmission of Advantages." *Education and Pedagogy* 23(60).

Aurini, Janice. 2012. "Patterns of Loose and Tight Coupling in a Competitive Private Education Marketplace: The Case of Learning Center Franchises." *Sociology of Education* 85(4):373–387.

Aurini, Janice. Forthcoming. "Patterns of Loose and Tight Coupling in a Competitive Private Education Marketplace: The Case of Learning Center Franchises." *Sociology of Education.*

Aurini, Janice, and Scott Davies. 2011. "Do I Have to Go Home Already? A Report on the 2011 Summer Learning Literacy Program in Ontario Schools." Ontario Ministry of Education, Council of Directors of Education.

Aurini, Janice, and Scott Davies. 2013. "Building Confidence, Making Connections: Continuing the Summer Learning Literacy Project in Ontario Schools." Toronto, ON: Council of Ontario Directors of Education.

Auyero, Javier, and Timothy Patrick Moran. 2007. "The Dynamics of Collective Violence: Dissecting Food Riots in Contemporary Argentina." *Social Forces* 85(3):1341–67.

Avishai, Orit. 2007. "Managing the Lactating Body: The Breast-Feeding Project and the Privileged Mother." *Qualitative Sociology* 30:135–42.

Ayanian, John Z., and Arnold M. Epstein. 1991. "Differences in the Use of Procedures Between Men and Women Hospitalized for Coronary Heart Disease." *The New England Journal of Medicine* 325(1):221–25.

Babb, Sarah. 2005. "The Social Consequences of Structural Adjustment: Recent Evidence and Current Debates." *Annual Review of Sociology* 31:199–222.

Babones, Salvatore. 2007. "Studying Globalization: Methodological Issues." Pp. 144–61 in *The Blackwell Companion to Globalization,* edited by George Ritzer. Malden, MA: Blackwell.

Baehr, Peter. 2001. "The 'Iron Cage' and the 'Shell as Hard as Steel': Parsons, Weber, and the Stahlhartes Gehäuse Metaphor in *The Protestant Ethic and the Spirit of Capitalism*" *History and Theory* 40(2):153–69.

Bair, Jennifer, and Gary Gereffi. 2003. "Upgrading, Uneven Development, and Jobs in the North American Apparel Industry." *Global Networks* 3(2):143–69.

Bajaj, Vikas. 2011. "Philippines Replaces India as Companies Seek American English." *The New York Times,* November 26, pp. B1, B4.

Baker, Carolyn. 1997. "Ethnomethodological Studies of Talk in Educational Settings." Pp. 43–52 in *Encyclopedia of Language and Education: Volume 3. Oral Discourse and Education,* edited by B. Davies and D. Corson. Netherlands: Kluwer.

Baker, Maureen. 2009. *Families: Changing Trends in Canada.* 6th ed. Toronto, ON: McGraw-Hill Ryerson.

Baker, Peter. 2010. "Book Says Afghanistan Divided White House." *The New York Times,* September 22, p. A12.

Baldwin, John, and Wulong Gu. 2009. *Productivity Performance in Canada, 1961 to 2008: An Update on Long-term Trends.* Ottawa: Statistics Canada, Catalogue no. 15-206-X—No. 025.

Baldwin, John, and Ryan Macdonald. 2009. "The Canadian Manufacturing Sector: Adapting to Challenges." Ottawa, ON: Statistics Canada, Catalogue no. 11F0027M—No. 057

Bales, Kevin. 1999. *Disposable People: New Slavery in the Economy.* Berkeley: University of California Press.

Bancroft, Angus. 2005. *Roma and Gypsy-Travellers in Europe: Modernity, Race, Space, and Exclusion.* Burlington, VT: Ashgate.

Bandura, Albert, Claudio Barbaranelli, Gian Vittorio Caprara, and Concetta Pastorelli. 1996. "Mechanisms of Moral Disengagement in the Exercise of Moral Agency." *Journal of Personality and Social Psychology* 71: 364–74.

Banks, Russell. 2011. *Lost Memory of Skin.* New York: HarperCollins.

Bannon, Lisa, and Bob Davis. 2009. "Spendthrift to Penny Pincher: A Vision of the New Consumer." *The Wall Street Journal,* December 17, pp. A1, A24.

Bar, Stephen J., Chao-Chin Lu, and Jonathan H. Westover. 2007. "Divorce." Pp. 1206–10 in *The Blackwell Encyclopedia of Sociology,* edited by George Ritzer. Malden, MA: Blackwell.

Baran, Paul A., and Paul M. Sweezy. 1966. *Monopoly Capital: An Essay on American Economic and Social Order.* New York: Modern Reader Paperbacks.

Barber, Benjamin R. 1995. *Jihad vs. McWorld.* New York: Times Books.

Barber, Benjamin R. 2007. *Consumed: How Markets Corrupt Children, Infantilize Adults, and Swallow Citizens Whole.* New York: MTM Publishing.

Barber, Marsha, and Ann Rauhala. 2008. "The Canadian News Directors Study: Role Conceptions of Television Newsroom Decision Makers." *Electronic News* 2(1): 46-60.

Barboza, David. 2008. "China Surpasses U.S. in Number of Internet Users." *The New York Times,* July 26. Retrieved May 23, 2011 (http://www.nytimes.com/2008/07/26/business/worldbusiness/26internet.html).

Barboza, David. 2010. "China Passes Japan as Second-Largest Economy." *The New York Times,* August 15. Retrieved May 29, 2011 (http://www.nytimes.com/2010/08/16/business/global/16yuan.html).

Barkan, Elliott R., Hasia Diner, and Alan M. Kraut, eds. 2008. *From Arrival to Incorporation: Migrants to the U.S. in a Global Era.* New York: New York University Press.

Barker, Eileen. 2007. "New Religious Movements." Pp. 3201–206 in *The Blackwell Encyclopedia of Sociology,* edited by George Ritzer. Malden, MA: Blackwell.

Barnes, Brooks. 2010. "Disney Selling Film Tickets on Facebook." *The New York Times,* June 2, pp. B1, B4.

Barnhurst, K. G., and E. Wartella. 1998. "Young Citizens, American TV Newscasts and the Collective Memory." *Critical Studies in Mass Communication* 15(3):279–305.

Baron, Stephen. 2008. "Street Youth, Unemployment, and Crime: Is It That Simple? Using General Strain Theory to Untangle the Relationship." *Canadian Journal of Criminology and Criminal Justice* 50(4): 399–434.

Barr, Rebecca, and Robert Dreeben. 1983. *How Schools Work.* Chicago: University of Chicago Press.

Barron, James. 1995. "A Church's Chief Executive Seeks the Target Audience." *The New York Times,* April 18, p. A20.

Barstow, David. 2010. "Tea Party Lights Fuse for Rebellion on the Right." *The New York Times,* February 16.

Bartky, Sandra. 1990. *Femininity and Domination.* New York: Routledge.

Basu, Amrita, ed. 1995. *The Challenge of Local Feminisms: Women's Movements in Global Perspective.* Boulder, CO: Westview Press.

Basu, Amrita, ed. 2010. *Women's Movements in the Global Era: The Power of Local Feminisms.* Boulder, CO: Westview Press.

Baudrillard, Jean. [1968] 1996. *The System of Objects.* London: Verso.

Baudrillard, Jean. [1970] 1998. *The Consumer Society.* London: Sage.

Baudrillard, Jean. [1976] 1993. *Symbolic Exchange and Death.* London: Sage.

Baudrillard, Jean. [1983] 1990. *Fatal Strategies.* New York: Semiotext(e).

Baudrillard, Jean. [1991] 1995. *The Gulf War Did Not Take Place.* Bloomington: Indiana University Press.

Bauer, Robin. 2008. "Transgressive and Transformative Gendered Sexual Practices and White Privileges: The Case of the Dyke/Trans BDSM Communities." *Women's Studies Quarterly* 36(3–4):233–53.

Bauman, Zygmunt. 1989. *Modernity and the Holocaust.* Ithaca, NY: Cornell University Press.

Bauman, Zygmunt. 1992. *Intimations of Postmodernity.* London: Routledge.

Bauman, Zygmunt. 1997. *Postmodernity and Its Discontents.* Cambridge, UK: Polity Press.

Bauman, Zygmunt. 1998. *Globalization: The Human Consequences.* New York: Columbia University Press.

Bauman, Zygmunt. 1999. "The Self in Consumer Society." *Hedgehog Review* Fall:35–40.

Bauman, Zygmunt. 2000. *Liquid Modernity.* Cambridge, UK: Polity Press.

Bauman, Zygmunt. 2003. *Liquid Love.* Cambridge, UK: Polity Press.

Bauman, Zygmunt. 2005. *Liquid Life.* Cambridge, UK: Polity Press.

Bauman, Zygmunt. 2006. *Liquid Fear.* Cambridge, UK: Polity Press.

Baumer, Eric P., and Janet L. Lauritsen. 2010. "Reporting Crime to the Police, 1973–2005: A Multivariate Analysis of Long-term Trends in the National Crime Survey (NCS) and National Crime Victimization Survey (NCVS)." *Criminology* 48(1):131–85.

Bay, A. H., and M. Blekesaune. 2002. "Youth, Unemployment and Political Marginalisation." *International Journal of Social Welfare* 11(2):132–39.

Baym, Nancy. 2010. *Personal Connections in the Digital Age.* Cambridge, UK: Polity Press.

BBC News. 2004. "Story of Cricket Part V: India and Pakistan," February 3. Retrieved March 29, 2012 (http://news.bbc.co.uk/sport2/hi/cricket/3447829.stm).

BBC News. 2010. "Timeline: China's Net Censorship," June 29. Retrieved May 23, 2011 (http://www.bbc.co.uk/news/ 10449139).

BBC News. 2011. "Schengen State Denmark to Re-impose Border Controls," May 11. Retrieved March 29, 2012 (http://www.bbc.co.uk/news/world-europe-13366047).

Beagan, Brenda. 2003. "Teaching Social and Cultural Awareness to Medical Students: 'It's All Very Nice to Talk about It in Theory, but Ultimately It Makes No Difference.'" *Academic Medicine* 78(6):605–614.

Beaglehole, Robert, Alec Irwin, and Thomson Prentice. 2003. *World Health Report: Shaping the Future.* Geneva: World Health Organization.

Beaman, Lori. 2002. "Aboriginal Spirituality and the Legal Construction of Freedom of Religion." *Journal of Church and State* 44(Winter):135–49.

Beavon, Daniel, and Paul Maxim. 1993. "The Life Expectancy of Correctional Service of Canada Employees." *Forum on Corrections Research* 5(1):1–5.

Beccaria, Cesare. [1764] 1986. *On Crimes and Punishments.* Indianapolis, IN: Hackett.

Beck, Ulrich. 1992. *Risk Society: Towards a New Modernity.* London: Sage.

Beck, Ulrich. 2007. "Cosmopolitanism: A Critical Theory for the Twenty-first Century." Pp. 162–76 in *The Blackwell Companion to Globalization,* edited by George Ritzer. Malden, MA: Blackwell.

Beck, Ulrich, and Elisabeth Beck-Gernsheim. 1995. *The Normal Chaos of Love.* Cambridge, UK: Polity Press.

Beck, Ulrich, and Elisabeth Beck-Gernsheim. 2002. *Individualization: Institutionalized Individualism and its Social and Political Consequences.* London: Sage.

Beck, Ulrich, and Elisabeth Beck-Gernsheim. 2012. "Families." Pp. 637–39 in *The Wiley-Blackwell Encyclopedia of Globalization,* edited by George Ritzer. Malden, MA: Wiley-Blackwell.

Becker, Gary S. 1992. "Human Capital and the Economy." *Proceedings of the American Philosophical Society* 136(1):85–92.

Becker, Howard. 1953. "Becoming a Marihuana User." *American Journal of Sociology* 59(3):232–42.

Becker, Howard S. 1963. *Outsiders: Studies in the Sociology of Deviance.* New York: Free Press.

Becker, Howard, and Blanche Geer. 1958. "The Fate of Idealism in Medical School." *American Sociological Review* 23:50–56.

Becker, Howard, Blanche Geer, Everett Hughes, and Anselm Strauss. 1961. *Boys in White: Student Culture in Medical School.* Chicago: University of Chicago Press.

Becker, P., and P. Moen. 1999. "Scaling Back: Dual Earner Couples' Work-Family Strategies." *Journal of Marriage and Family* 61:995–1007.

Beer, David, and Roger Burrows. 2007. "Sociology and, of and in Web 2.0: Some Initial Considerations." *Sociological Research Online* 12(5). Retrieved March 29, 2012 (socresonline.org.uk/12/5/17.html).

Beer, Todd. 2012. "Global Warming." Pp. 841–44 in *The Wiley-Blackwell Companion to Sociology,* edited by George Ritzer. Malden, MA: Wiley-Blackwell.

Belk, Russell W. 1987. "A Child's Christmas in America: Santa Claus as Deity, Consumption as Religion." *Journal of American Culture* 10(1):87–100.

Belk, Russell W. 2007. "Consumption, Mass Consumption, and Consumer Culture." Pp. 737–46 in *The Blackwell Encyclopedia of Sociology,* edited by George Ritzer. Malden, MA: Blackwell.

Bell, Daniel. 1973. *The Coming of Post-Industrial Society: A Venture in Social Forecasting.* New York: Basic Books.

Bell, David. 2007. "Sexualities, Cities and." Pp. 4254–56 in *The Blackwell Encyclopedia of Sociology,* edited by George Ritzer. Malden, MA: Blackwell.

Bell, Kerryn. 2009. "Gender and Gangs: A Quantitative Comparison." *Crime & Delinquency* 55:363–87.

Bell, Sheri. 2011. "Through a Foucauldian Lens: A Genealogy of Child Abuse." *Journal of Family Violence* 26:101–08.

Bellah, Robert N., et al. 1957. *Tokugawa Religion.* PhD dissertation, Harvard University.

Bellah, Robert N. 1967. "Civil Religion in America." *Daedalus* 96:1–21.

Bellah, Robert N. 1985. *Habits of the Heart: Individualism and Commitment in American Life.* Berkeley: University of California Press.

Bellah, Robert N. 2011. *Religion in Human Evolution: From the Paleolithic to the Axial Age.* Cambridge, MA: Harvard University Press.

Bendix, Reinhard, and Seymour Martin Lipset, eds. 1966. *Class, Status and Power.* 2nd rev. ed. Glencoe, IL: Free Press.

Benitez, Jose Luis. 2006. "Transnational Dimensions of the Digital Divide among Salvadoran Immigrants in the Washington DC Metropolitan Area." *Global Networks* 6(2):181–199.

Benjamin, Walter. 1999. *The Arcades Project.* Cambridge, MA: Belknap.

Bennett, Isabella. 2011. "Media Censorship in China." Council on Foreign Relations. Retrieved May 23, 2011 (http://www.cfr.org/china/media-censorship-china/p11515).

Bennett, M. D., and M. W. Fraser. 2000. "Urban Violence among African American Males: Integrating Family, Neighborhood, and Peer Perspectives." *Journal of Sociology and Social Welfare* 27:93–117.

Bennett, Tony, et al. 2009. *Culture, Class, Distinction.* London: Routledge.

Bennhold, Katrin. 2008. "A Veil Closes France's Door to Citizenship." *The New York Times,* July 19, pp. A1, A2.

Bennhold, Katrin and Stephen Castle. 2010. "E.U. Calls France's Roma Expulsions a 'Disgrace.'" *The New York Times,* September 14.

Benoit, Cecilia, et al. 2007. "Social Factors Linked to Postpartum Depression: A Mixed-methods Longitudinal Study." *Journal of Mental Health* 16:719–30.

Ben-Yehuda, Nachman. 1980. "The European Witch Craze of the 14th to 17th Centuries: A Sociologist's Perspective." *American Journal of Sociology* 86(1):1–31.

Ben-Yehuda, Nachman. 1985. *Deviance and Moral Boundaries.* Chicago: University of Chicago Press.

Ben-Yehuda, Nachman. 2012. "Deviance: A Sociology of Unconventionalities." Pp. 197–211 in *The Wiley-Blackwell Companion to Sociology,* edited by George Ritzer. Malden, MA: Wiley-Blackwell.

Berard, T. J. 2007. "Deviant Subcultures." Pp. 4872–77 in *The Blackwell Encyclopedia of Sociology,* edited by George Ritzer. Malden, MA: Blackwell.

Berends, Mark, Ellen Goldring, Marc Stein, and Xiu Cravens. 2010. "Instructional Conditions in Charter Schools and Students' Mathematics Achievement Gains." *American Journal of Education* 116:123–56.

Berger, Joseph, Anne Motte, and Andrew Parkin. 2009. *The Price of Knowledge: Access and Student Finance in Canada.* Montreal, QU: Canada Millennium Scholarship Foundation.

Berger, Joseph, and Andrew Parkin. 2009. "The Value of a Degree: Education, Employment and Earnings in Canada." In *The Price of Knowledge: Access and Student Finance in Canada,* edited by Joseph Berger, Anne Motte, and Andrew Parkin. Montreal, QU: Canada Millennium Scholarship Foundation.

Berger, Peter. 1963. *Invitation to Sociology.* New York: Doubleday.

Berger, Peter. 1969. *The Sacred Canopy: Elements of a Sociological Theory of Religion.* New York: Doubleday.

Berger, Peter L., and Thomas Luckmann. 1967. *The Social Construction of Reality: A Treatise in the Sociology of Knowledge.* New York: Anchor Books.

Bergquist, Magnus. 2003. "Open-Source Software Development as Gift Culture: Work and Identity Formation in an Internet Community." In *New Technologies at Work: People, Screens, and Social Virtuality,* edited by C. Garsten and H. Wulff. New York: Berg.

Berkovitch, Nitza. 1999. *From Motherhood to Citizenship: Women's Rights and International Organizations.* Baltimore: Johns Hopkins Press.

Berkovitch, Nitza. 2012. "Women's Movement(s), Transnational." Pp. 2233–42 in *The Wiley-Blackwell Encyclopedia of Globalization,* edited by George Ritzer. Malden, MA: Wiley-Blackwell.

Bernard, André. 2009. "Trends in Manufacturing Employment" *Perspectives on Labour and Income.* February, Statistics Canada: Catalogue no. 75-001-X.

Bernard, Jessie. 1972. *The Future of Marriage.* 2nd ed. New Haven, CT: Yale University Press.

Berton, Justin. 2007. "Continent-size Toxic Stew of Plastic Trash Fouling Swath of Pacific Ocean." *San Francisco Chronicle,* October 19. Retrieved May 25, 2011 (http://www.sfgate.com/cgi-bin/article.cgi?f=/c/a/2007/10/19/SS6JS8RH0.DTL).

Bertrand, Marianne, and Sendhil Mullainathan. 2004. "Are Emily and Greg More Employable than Lakisha and Jamal? A Field Experiment on Labor Market Discrimination." *The American Economic Review* 94(4), 991–1013.

Best, Amy L. 2007. "Consumption, Girls' Culture and." Pp. 724–27 in *The Blackwell Encyclopedia of Sociology,* edited by George Ritzer. Malden, MA: Blackwell.

Bestor, Theodore C. 2005. "How Sushi Went Global." Pp. 13–20 in *The Cultural Politics of Food and Eating: A Reader,* edited by James L. Watson and Melissa L. Caldwell. Malden, MA: Blackwell.

Betancur, John. 2011. "Gentrification and Community Fabric in Chicago." *Urban Studies* 48:383–406.

Betegeri, Aarti. 2011. "Cricket World Cup Final: You May Not Care, But India Sure Does." *Christian Science Monitor,* March 29. Retrieved March 29, 2012 (http://www.csmonitor.com/World/Global-News/2011/0329/Cricket-World-Cup-final-You-may-not-care-but-India-sure-does).

Beyer, Peter. 2006. *Religion and Globalization.* London: Sage.

Beynon, Huw, and Theo Nichol, eds. 2006. *The Fordism of Ford and Modern Management: Fordism and Post-Fordism.* Cheltenham, UK: Elgar.

Bhambra, Gurminder K. 2007a. *Rethinking Modernity: Postcolonialism and the Sociological Imagination.* Houndsmills, UK: Palgrave Macmillan.

Bhambra, Gurminder K. 2007b. "Sociology and Postcolonialism: Another 'Missing' Revolution?" *Sociology* 41:871–84.

Bhanoo, Sindya N. 2010. "Denmark Leads the Way in Digital Care." *The New York Times,* January 12, p. D5.

Bhatnagar, Rashmi, Renu Dube, and Reena Dube. 2006. *Female Infanticide in India: A Feminist Cultural History.* New York: SUNY Press.

Bhatty, Ayesha. 2010. "Haiti Devastation Exposes Shoddy Construction." BBC News. Retrieved March 31, 2012 (http://news.bbc.co.uk/2/hi/8460042.stm).

Bhaumik, Subir. 2010. "India to Deploy 36,000 Extra Troops on Chinese Border." BBC News. Retrieved May 26, 2011 (http://www.bbc.co.uk/news/world-south-asia-11818840).

Bian, Y. J. 1997. "Bringing Strong Ties Back In: Indirect Ties, Network Bridges, and Job Searches in China." *American Sociological Review* 62:366–85.

Bianchi, Stefania. 2010. "Leak at Dubai Mall Aquarium Forces Evacuation." *The Wall Street Journal,* March 1. Retrieved May 19, 2011 (http://online.wsj.com/article/SB10001424052748704479404575087122447511764.htm).

Bianchi, Suzanne, and Melissa Milkie. 2010. "Work and Family Research in the First Decade of the 21st Century." *Journal of Marriage and Family* 72:205–225.

Bianchi, Suzanne M., and Vanessa Wight. 2012. "Population." Pp. 470–87 in *The Wiley-Blackwell Companion to Sociology,* edited by George Ritzer. Malden, MA: Wiley-Blackwell.

Biblarz, Timothy J., and Judith Stacey. 2010. "How Does the Gender of Parents Matter?" *Journal of Marriage and Family* 72(1):3–22.

Bigge, Ryan. 2003. "One Beer, Two Solitudes." *Marketing Magazine,* May.

Bihagen, Erik. 2007. "Class Origin Effects on Downward Career Mobility in Sweden 1982–2001." *Acta Sociologica* 50(4):415–30.

Bilefsky, Dan. 2010. "Dark Film on Teenagers Echoes From Mall to Church." *The New York Times,* March 4, p. A8.

Bills, David. 2007. "Educational Attainment." Pp. 1333–36 in *The Blackwell Encyclopedia of Sociology,* edited by George Ritzer. Malden, MA: Blackwell.

Binkley, Sam. 2007. "Counterculture." Pp. 809–10 in *The Blackwell Encyclopedia of Sociology,* edited by George Ritzer. Malden, MA: Blackwell.

Binnie, Jon. 2004. *The Globalization of Sexuality.* London: Sage.

Bishop, Ryan. 2006. "The Global University." *Theory, Culture and Society* 23:563–66.

Black, A. E., and J. L. Allen. 2001. "Tracing the Legacy of Anita Hill: The Thomas/Hill Hearings and Media Coverage of Sexual Harassment." *Gender Issues* 19(1):33–52.

Blackman, Shane. 2007. "'Hidden Ethnography': Crossing Emotional Borders in Accounts of Young People's Lives." *Sociology* 41:699–716.

Blair-Loy, Mary. 2003. *Competing Devotions.* Cambridge, MA: Harvard University Press.

Blais, André, and Simon Labbé St-Vincent. 2011 "Personality Traits, Political Attitudes and the Propensity to Vote." *European Journal of Political Research* 50(3):395–417.

Blakely, Edward J., and M. G. Snyder. 1997. *Fortress America: Gated Communities in the United States.* Washington, DC: Brookings Institution Press.

Blanchflower, David. 2007. "International Patterns of Union Membership." *British Journal of Industrial Relations* 45(1):1–28.

Blass, Thomas. 1999. "The Milgram Paradigm After 35 Years: Some Things We Now Know about Obedience to Authority." *Journal of Applied Social Psychology* 29(5):955–78.

Blass, T., and A. Krackow. 1991. "The Milgram Obedience Experiments: Students' Views vs. Scholarly Perspectives and Actual Findings." Paper presented at the annual convention of the American Psychological Society, Washington, DC, June 14.

Blatt, Jessica. 2007. "Scientific Racism." Pp. 4113–15 in *The Blackwell Encyclopedia of Sociology,* edited by George Ritzer. Malden, MA: Blackwell.

Blau, Peter. 1963. *The Dynamics of Bureaucracy.* Chicago: University of Chicago Press.

Blau, Peter. 1964. *Exchange and Power in Social Life.* New York: Wiley.

Blau, Peter, and Otis D. Duncan. 1967. *The American Occupational Structure.* New York: Wiley.

Blauner, Robert. 1964. *Alienation and Freedom: The Factory Worker and His Industry.* Chicago: University of Chicago Press.

Blee, Kathleen. 2002. *Inside Organized Racism.* Berkeley: University of California Press.

Blee, Kathleen M. 2007. "Racist Movement." Pp. 3767–71 in *The Blackwell Encyclopedia of Sociology,* edited by George Ritzer. Malden, MA: Blackwell.

Blight, James G., and Janet M. Lang. 2005. *The Fog of War: Lessons from the Life of Robert S. McNamara.* Lanham, MD: Rowman and Littlefield.

Bloom, Harold. 1992. *The American Religion: The Emergence of a Post-Christian Nation.* New York: Simon and Schuster.

Bluestone, Barry and B. Harrison. 1984. *The Deindustrialization of America: Plant Closings, Community Abandonment, and the Dismantling of Basic Industry.* New York: Basic Books.

Blum, Linda. 2000. *At the Breast: Ideologies of Breastfeeding and Motherhood in the Contemporary United States.* Boston: Beacon Press.

Blum, Susan. 2009. *My Word! Plagiarism and College Culture.* Ithaca, NY: Cornell University Press.

Blumenberg, Werner. 2008. *Karl Marx: An Illustrated Biography.* New York: Verso.

Boas, Morten. 2012. "Failed States." Pp. 633–35 in *The Wiley-Blackwell Encyclopedia of Globalization,* edited by George Ritzer. Malden, MA: Wiley-Blackwell.

Bocian, Debbie Gruenstein, Wei Li, and Keith S. Ernst. 2010. *Foreclosures by Race and Ethnicity: The Demographics of a Crisis.* Durham, NC: Center for Responsible Lending.

Bodinger-deUriarte, Cristina. 1992. *Hate Crime Sourcebook for Schools.* Philadelphia: RBS.

Boehlin, W. 1992. "Street Corner Society: Cornerville Revisited." *Journal of Contemporary Ethnography* 21:11–51.

Bogdanich, Walt. 2007. "Free Trade Zones Ease Passage of Counterfeit Drugs to US." *The New York Times,* December 17.

Bogle, Kathleen. 2008. *Hooking Up: Sex, Dating, and Relationships on Campus.* New York: NYU Press.

Boivin, Michel, and Clyde Hertzman, eds. 2012. "Early Childhood Development: Adverse Experiences and Developmental Health." Royal Society of Canada, Canadian Academy of Health Sciences Expert Panel (with Ronald Barr, Thomas Boyce, Alison Fleming, Harriet MacMillan, Candice Odgers, Marla Sokolowski, and Nico Trocmé). Ottawa, ON: Royal Society of Canada. Retrieved May 14, 2013 (https://rsc-src.ca/sites/default/files/pdf/ECD%20Report_0.pdf).

Bolton, Kenneth, and Joe Feagin. 2004. *Black in Blue: African American Police Officers and Racism.* New York: Routledge.

Bonanno, Alessandro. 2012. "Fordism Post Fordism." Pp. 680–82 in *The Encyclopedia of Globalization,* edited by George Ritzer. Malden, MA: Wiley-Blackwell.

Bongaart, John. 2007. "Fertility and Public Policy." Pp. 1737–41 in *The Blackwell Encyclopedia of Sociology,* edited by George Ritzer. Malden, MA: Blackwell.

Bonilla-Silva, Eduardo. 1997. "Rethinking Racism: Toward a Structural Interpretation." *American Sociological Review* 62:465–80.

Bonilla-Silva, Eduardo. 2009. *Racism Without Racists: Color-Blind Racism and the Persistence of Racial Inequality in the United States.* Lanham, MD: Rowman and Littlefield.

Bontje, Marco, and Joachim Burdack. 2011. "Edge Cities, European-style: Examples from Paris and the Randstad." *Urban Studies* 48:2591–610.

Bordo, Susan. 1993. *Unbearable Weight: Feminism, Western Culture, and the Body.* Berkeley: University of California Press.

Bose, Christine E., and Edna Acosta-Belen, eds. 1995. *Women in the Latin American Development Process.* Philadelphia: Temple University Press.

Bosick, Stacey. 2009. "Operationalizing Crime Over the Life Course." *Crime & Delinquency* 55:472–96.

Boswell, A. Ayres and Joan Z. Spade. 1996. "Fraternities and Collegiate Rape Culture: Why Are Some Fraternities More Dangerous Places for Women?" *Gender & Society* 10(2):133–47.

Bourdieu, Pierre. 1984. *Distinction: A Social Critique of the Judgment of Taste.* Cambridge, MA: Harvard University Press.

Bourdieu, Pierre. 1992. *The Logic of Practice.* Palo Alto, CA: Stanford University Press.

Bourdieu, Pierre, and Jean-Claude Passeron. [1970] 1990. *Reproduction in Education, Society and Culture.* London: Sage.

Bourdieu, Pierre, and Jean-Claude Passeron. 1977. *Reproduction: In Education, Society, and Culture.* Beverly Hills, CA: Sage.

Bourgeois, Phillippe. 2003. *In Search of Respect: Selling Crack in El Barrio.* Cambridge, UK: Cambridge University Press.

Boushey, Heather. 2008. "Motherhood Penalty and Women's Earnings, Opting out? The Effect of Children on Women's Employment in the United States." *Feminist Economics* 14(1):1–36.

Bowen, Ted Smalley. 2001. "English Could Snowball on Net." *Technology Research News,* November 21. Retrieved January 3, 2012 (http://www.trnmag.com/Stories/2001/112101/English_could_snowball_on_Net_112101.html).

Bowles, Samuel, and Herbert Gintis. 1976. *Schooling in Capitalist America: Educational Reform and the Contradictions of Economic Life.* New York: Basic Books.

Bowling, Ben, and James W. E. Sheptycki. 2012. *Global Policing.* London: Sage.

Bowman, John R., and Alyson Cole. 2009. "Do Working Mothers Oppress Other Women? The Swedish 'Maid Debate' and the Welfare State Politics of Gender Equality." *Signs* 35(1):157–84.

boyd, danah. 2010. "White Flight in Networked Publics? How Race and Class Shaped American Teen Engagement With MySpace and Facebook." In *Digital Race Anthology,* edited by Lisa Nakamura and Peter Chow-White. New York: Routledge.

Boykoff, Jules, and Eulalie Laschever. 2011. "The Tea Party Movement, Framing, and the U.S. Media." *Social Movement Studies* 10:341–66.

Brady, David, and Denise Kall. 2008. "Nearly Universal, but Somewhat Distinct: The Feminization of Poverty in Affluent Western Democracies, 1969–2000." *Social Science Research* 37(3):976–1007.

Braga, Anthony A., and David L. Weisburd. 2011. "The Effects of Focused Deterrence Strategies on Crime: A Systematic Review and Meta-Analysis of the Empirical Evidence." *Journal of Research in Crime and Delinquency.* Retrieved March 29, 2012 (http://jrc.sagepub.com/content/early/2011/09/08/0022427811419368.abstract).

Braithwaite, John. 1997. "Conferencing and Plurality—Reply to Blagg." *British Journal of Criminology* 37:502–06.

Braithwaite, John. 2010. "Diagnostics of White-collar Crime Prevention." *Criminology & Public Policy* 9:621–26.

Brandle, Gaspar and J. Michael Ryan. 2012. "Consumption." Pp. 289–95 in *The Encyclopedia of Globalization,* edited by George Ritzer. Malden, MA: Wiley-Blackwell.

Branisa, Boris, Stephan Klasen, and Maria Ziegler. 2009. "New Measures of Gender Inequality: The Social Institutions and Gender Index (SIGI) and Its Subindices." Courant Research Centre Discussion Paper #10. Retrieved March 29, 2012 (http://www2.vwl.wiso.uni-goettingen.de/courant-papers/CRC-PEG_DP_10.pdf).

Braveman, P. A., C. Cubbin, S. Egerter, S. Chideya, K. S. Marchi, M. Metzler, and S. Posner. 2005. "Socioeconomic Status in Health Research: One Size Does Not Fit All." *Journal of the American Medical Association* 294(22):2879–88.

Brennan, Denise. 2002. "Selling Sex for Visas: Sex Tourism as a Stepping-stone to International Migration." In *Global Woman: Nannies, Maids, and Sex Workers in the New Economy,* edited by Barbara

Ehrenreich and Arlie Hochschild. New York: Henry Holt.

Brennan, Denise. 2004. *What's Love Got to Do with It? Transnational Desires and Sex Tourism in the Dominican Republic.* Durham, NC: Duke University Press.

Brennan, Shannon. 2012. "Police-reported Crime Statistics in Canada, 2011." *Juristat* 32(2). Statistics Canada Catalogue no. 85-002-X.

Brents, Barbara, Crystal A. Jackson, and Kate Hausbeck. 2009. *The State of Sex: Tourism, Sex and Sin in the New American Heartland.* New York: Routledge.

Breton, Raymond. 1964. "Institutional Completeness of Ethnic Communities and the Personal Relations of Immigrants." *American Journal of Sociology* 70(2):193–205.

Brewer, John, and Frank Trentmann. 2006. "Introduction: Space, Time and Value in Consuming Cultures." Pp. 1–17 in *Consuming Cultures, Global Perspectives: Historical Trajectories, Transnational Exchanges,* edited by John Brewer and Frank Trentmann. Oxford, UK: Berg.

Brim, Orville. 1968. "Adult Socialization." Pp. 182–226 in *Socialization and Society,* edited by John A. Clausen. Boston: Little, Brown.

Brimeyer, T. M., J. Miller, and R. Perrucci. 2006. "Social Class Sentiments in Formation: Influence of Class Socialization, College Socialization, and Class Aspirations." *The Sociological Quarterly* 47:471–95.

Brinkley, Douglas. 2006. *The Great Deluge: Hurricane Katrina, New Orleans, and The Mississippi Gulf Coast.* New York: Harper Perennial.

Brittanica. 2012. "Religion: Year in Review 2010." In *Britannica Book of the Year.* Retrieved May 29, 2012 (http://www.britannica.com/EBchecked/topic/1731588/religion-Year-In-Review-2010).

Broder, John M. 2009. "Seeking to Save the Planet, With a Thesaurus." *The New York Times,* May 1. Retrieved March 29, 2012 (http://www.nytimes.com/2009/05/02/us/politics/02enviro.html).

Brody, Jane E. 2009. "Buyer Beware of Home DNA Tests." *The New York Times,* September 1, p. D6.

Bronfenbrenner, Kate, ed. 2007. *Global Unions: Challenging Transnational Capital through Cross-Border Campaigns.* Ithaca, NY: Cornell University Press.

Bronner, Ethan. 2011a. "Protests Force Israel to Confront the Wealth Gap." *The New York Times,* August 11. Retrieved March 29, 2012 (http://www.nytimes.com/2011/08/12/world/middleeast/12israel.html?pagewanted=all).

Bronner, Ethan. 2011b. "Virtual Bridge Allows Strangers in Mideast to Seem Less Strange." *The New York Times,* July 10. Retrieved March 29, 2012 (http://www.nytimes.com/2011/07/10/world/middleeast/10mideast.html).

Brookings Institution. 2013. *OECD Factbook 2013: Economic, Environmental and Social Statistics.* Retrieved April 29, 2013 (http://www.brookings.edu/research/books/2013/oecdfactbook2013).

Brooks, Robert A. 2011. *Cheaper by the Hour: Temporary Lawyers and the Deprofessionalization of the Law.* Philadelphia: Temple University Press.

Brown, David. 2007. "As Temperatures Rise, Health Could Decline." *Washington Post,* December 17, p. A7.

Brown, Elaine. 1992. *A Taste of Power: A Black Woman's Story.* New York: Doubleday.

Brown, Michael Harold, and John May. 1991. *The Greenpeace Story.* New York: Dorling Kindersley.

Brown, Stephen E. 2007a. "Criminology." Pp. 856–60 in *The Blackwell Encyclopedia of Sociology,* edited by George Ritzer. Malden, MA: Blackwell.

Brown, Stephen E. 2007b. "Ethnocentrism." Pp. 1478–79 in *The Blackwell Encyclopedia of Sociology,* edited by George Ritzer. Malden, MA: Blackwell.

Brownmiller, Susan. 1975. *Against Our Will: Men, Women, and Rape.* New York: Simon and Schuster.

Broyard, Bliss. 2007. *One Drop: My Father's Hidden Life.* New York: Little, Brown.

Brumberg, Joan Jacobs. 1998. *The Body Project: An Intimate History of American Girls.* New York: Vintage.

Bryant, Melanie, and Vaughan Higgins. 2010. "Self-confessed Troublemakers: An Interactionist View of Deviance During Organizational Change." *Human Relations* 63:249–77.

Bryk, Anthony, Valerie Lee, and Peter Holland. 1993. *Catholic Schools and the Common Good.* Cambridge, MA: Harvard University Press.

Brym, Robert, and Rhonda Lenton. 2001. "Love Online: A Report on Digital Dating in Canada." Toronto: MSN. Retrieved September 18, 2012 (http://projects.chass.utoronto.ca/brym/loveonline.pdf).

Bryman, A. 2004. *The Disneyization of Society.* London: Sage.

Buchmann, Claudia, and Thomas DiPrete. 2006. "The Growing Female Advantage in College Completion: The Role of Family Background and Academic Achievement." *American Sociological Review* 71(4):515–41.

Buchmann, C., and E. Hannum. 2001. "Education and Stratification in Developing Countries: A Review of Theories and Research." *Annual Review of Sociology* 27:77–102.

Buckingham, David, ed. 2008. *Youth, Identity and Digital Media.* Cambridge, MA: MIT Press.

Buckley, Cara. 2009. "For Uninsured Young Adults, Do-It-Yourself Medical Care." *The New York Times,* February 18.

Buddha, Gautama. n.d. "Dhammapada 1: The Twin Verses (Yamakavaggo)," translated by Ven Nàrada. Retrieved March 29, 2012 (http://www.metta.lk/tipitaka/2Sutta-Pitaka/5Khuddaka-Nikaya/02Dhammapada/01-Yamakavaggo-e2.html).

Bulman, Philip. 2009. "Using Technology to Make Prison Safer." *National Institute of Justice Journal* 262.

Burawoy, Michael. 1979. *Manufacturing Consent: Changes in the Labor Process under Monopoly Capitalism.* Chicago: University of Chicago Press.

Burawoy, Michael. 2000. "Introduction: Reaching for the Global." Pp. 1–40 in *Global Ethnography: Forces, Connections, and Imaginations in a Postmodern World,* edited by Michael Burawoy et al. Berkeley: University of California Press.

Burawoy, Michael. 2005. "For Public Sociology." *American Sociological Review* 70(1):4–28.

Burger, Jerry. 2009. "Replicating Milgram: Would People Still Obey Today?" *American Psychologist* 64(1):1–11.

Burgess, Ernest W., and Harvey J. Locke. 1945. *The Family: From Institution to Companionship.* New York: American Book.

Burke, Peter J. 1991. "Identity Processes and Social Stress." *American Sociological Review* 56:836–49.

Burke, P. J., and D. C. Reitzes. 1981. "The Link between Identity and Role Performance." *Social Psychology* 44:83–92.

Burke, P. J., and D. C. Reitzes. 1991. "An Identity Theory Approach to Commitment." *Social Psychology* 54(3):239–251.

Burke, Peter J. and Jan E. Stets. 1999. "Trust and Commitment through Self-Verification." *Social Psychology Quarterly* 62:347–66.

Burns, John F. 2011. "Founder Says Wikileaks, Starved of Cash, May Close." *The New York Times,* October 24. Retrieved March 29, 2012 (http://www.nytimes.com/2011/10/25/world/europe/blocks-on-wikileaks-donations-may-force-its-end-julian-assange-warns.html?_r=1&ref=wikileaks).

Burns, John F., and Ravi Somaiya. 2010a. "Hackers Attack Sites Considered WikiLeaks Foes." *The New York Times,* December 9, p. A1.

Burns, John, and Ravi Somaiya. 2010b. "Wikileaks Founder on the Run, Trailed by Notoriety." *The New York Times,* October 23. Retrieved March 29, 2012 (http://www.nytimes.com/2010/10/24/world/24assange.html).

Burns, Thomas J. 2012. "Marine Pollution." Pp. 1324–25 in *The Wiley-Blackwell Companion to Sociology,* edited by George Ritzer. Malden, MA: Wiley-Blackwell.

Buse, Kent. 2007. "World Health Organization." P. 1277 in *Encyclopedia of Globalization,* edited by Jan Aart Scholte and Roland Robertson. New York: MTM Publishing.

Bushell-Embling, Dylan. 2010. "US Blocks Chinese Fiber Deal Over National Security Fears." *TelecomsEurope,* June 30. Accessed December 7, 2011 (www.telecomseurope.net/content/us-blocks-chinese-fiber-deal-over-national-security-fears).

Businessweek. 2006. "Are 'Liars' Loans' Bad for America?" Retrieved March 29, 2012 (http://www.businessweek.com/the_thread/hotproperty/archives/2006/07/are_liars_loans_bad_for_america.html).

Buss, Paulo, and Jose Roberto Ferreira. 2010. "Developing Global Public Health Links." *UN Chronicle* XLVII(2). Retrieved March 29, 2012 (http://www.un.org/wcm/content/site/chronicle/cache/bypass/home/archive/issues2010/achieving_global_health/developingpublichealthlinks?ctnscroll_articleContainerList=1_0&ctnlistpagination_articleContainerList=true).

Butler, Judith. 1990. *Gender Trouble: Feminism and the Subversion of Identity*. New York: Routledge.

Byles, Jeff. 2003. "Profile of the President. Tales of the Kefir Furnaceman: Michael Burawoy." *Footnotes* 21(7).

Byrd, Scott. 2005. "The Porto Alegre Consensus: Theorizing the Forum Movement." *Globalizations* 2(1):151–63.

Cable, Sherry, Thomas E. Shriver, and Tamara L. Mix. 2008. "Risk Society and Contested Illness: The Case of Nuclear Weapons Workers." *American Sociological Review* 73:380–401.

Cagatay, Nilufer, and Sule Ozler. 1995. "Feminization of the Labor Force: The Effect of Long Term Development and Structural Adjustment." *World Development* 23(11):1827–36.

Caine, Alex. 2008. *Befriend and Betray: Infiltrating the Hells Angels, Bandidos and Other Criminal Brotherhoods*. Toronto, ON: Random House.

Calasanti, Toni, and Kathleen Slevin. 2001. *Gender, Social Inequality and Aging*. Walnut Creek, CA: Altamira Press.

Caldwell, Christopher. 2009. *Reflections on the Revolution in Europe: Immigration, Islam, and the West*. New York: Doubleday.

Callinicos, Alex. 2004. *The Revolutionary Ideas of Karl Marx*. London: Bookmarks.

Calvin, John. 1536. *Institutes of the Christian Religion*. Basel, Switzerland.

Cameron, David. 2011. "PM Statement on Disorder in England." Released August 11, 2011. Retrieved April 29, 2013 (https://www.gov.uk/government/news/pm-statement-on-disorder-in-england).

Campbell, Colin. 1987. *The Romantic Ethic and the Spirit of Modern Consumerism*. Oxford, UK: Blackwell.

Campbell, Colin. 2007. *The Easternization of the West: A Thematic Account of Cultural Change in the Modern Era*. Boulder, CO: Paradigm Press.

Caniglia, Beth. 2012. "Environmental Protection Movement." Pp. 536–41 in *The Wiley-Blackwell Encyclopedia of Globalization*, edited by George Ritzer. Malden, MA: Wiley-Blackwell.

Cannon, Lou. 1997. "Scars Remain Five Years after Los Angeles Riots." Special to *The Washington Post*, April 28. Retrieved March 28, 2012 (http://www.washingtonpost.com/wp-srv/national/longterm/lariots/lariots.htm).

Cao, Liqun. 2011. "Visible Minorities and Confidence in the Police" *Canadian Journal of Criminology and Criminal Justice* 53(1): 1–27.

Caprile, Maria, and Amparo Serrano Pascual. 2011. "The Move towards the Knowledge-based Society: A Gender Approach." *Gender, Work & Organization* 18:48–72.

Capron, Christiane and Michel Duyme, 1989. "Assessment of the Effects of Socioeconomic Status on IQ in a Full Cross-fostering Study." *Nature* 340:552–54.

Carbonaro, William. 2005. "Tracking, Student Effort, and Academic Achievement." *Sociology of Education* 78:27–49.

Carbonaro, William, and Elizabeth Covay. 2010. "School Sector and Student Achievement in the Era of Standards Based Reforms." *Sociology of Education* 83:160–82.

Cardinal, Harold. 1969. *The Unjust Society*. Vancouver: Douglas & McIntyre.

Carey, Stephen. 2011. *A Beginner's Guide to Scientific Method*. Boston: Wadsworth.

Carmichael, Stokely, and Charles V. Hamilton. 1967. *Black Power: The Politics of Liberation*. New York: Vintage Books.

Carmody, Dianne Cyr. 2007. "Domestic Violence." Pp. 1219–20 in *The Blackwell Encyclopedia of Sociology*, edited by George Ritzer. Malden, MA: Blackwell.

Carrara, Sergio. 2007. "Sexual Minorities." In *Encyclopedia of Globalization*, edited by Jan Aart Scholte and Ronald Robertson. New York: MTM Publishing.

Carrière, Yves, and Diane Galarneau. 2012. "How Many Years to Retirement?" *Insights on Canadian Society*. Ottawa, ON: Statistics Canada.

Carroll, William. 2010. *Corporate Power in a Globalizing World*. Revised edition. Toronto, ON: Oxford University Press.

Carroll, W. K., and C. Carson. 2003. "The Network of Global Corporations and Elite Policy Groups: A Structure for Transnational Capitalist Class Formation?" *Global Networks* 3(1):29–57.

Carson, Rachel. 1962. *Silent Spring*. New York: Houghton Mifflin.

Carter, Bill, and Tanzia Vega. 2011. "In Shift, Ads Try to Entice Over-55 Set." *The New York Times*, May 13.

Casey, Emma. 2006. "Domesticating Gambling: Gender, Caring the UK National Lottery." *Leisure Studies* 25(1).

Casper, Lynne M. 2007. "Family Demography." Pp. 1583–89 in *The Blackwell Encyclopedia of Sociology*, edited by George Ritzer. Malden, MA: Blackwell.

Cass, Alan. 2004. "Health Outcomes in Aboriginal Populations." *Canadian Medical Association Journal* 171(6):597–98.

Castells, Manuel. [1972] 1977. *The Urban Question: A Marxist Approach*, translated by Alan Sheridan. London: Edward Arnold.

Castells, Manuel. 1996. *The Information Age*. Oxford, UK: Blackwell.

Castells, Manuel. 1997. "The Power of Identity." *The Information Age: Economy, Society, and Culture*. Vol. 2. Oxford, UK: Blackwell.

Castells, Manuel. 1998. "End of Millennium." *The Information Age: Economy, Society, and Culture*. Vol. 3. Oxford, UK: Blackwell.

Castells, Manuel. 2008. *The New Public Sphere: Global Civil Society, Communication Networks, and Global Governance*. Los Angeles: University of Southern California.

Castells, Manuel. 2010. "The Rise of the Network Society." *The Information Age: Economy, Society and Culture*. Vol. 1. Malden, MA: Wiley, Blackwell.

Castle, Stephen. 2010. "France Faces European Action After Expulsions." *The New York Times*, September 29.

Cavanagh, Allison. 2007. *Sociology in the Age of the Internet*. Maidenhead, UK: Open University Press.

Cave, Damien. 2010. "In Recession, Americans Doing More, Buying Less." *The New York Times*, January 3.

Cave, Damien. 2011. "Mexico Turns to Social Media for Information and Survival." *The New York Times*, September 25, p. 5.

CBS News. 2009. "Sexual Assault Permeates U.S. Armed Forces," March 18. Retrieved March 29, 2012 (http://www.cbsnews.com/stories/2009/03/17/eveningnews/main4872713.shtml).

CBS News. 2010. "Gulf Oil Spill Declared 'Effectively Dead,'" September 20. Retrieved March 29, 2012 (http://www.cbsnews.com/stories/2010/09/19/national/main6881308.shtml).

Central Intelligence Agency. 2012a. "East & Southeast Asia: Singapore." *The World Factbook*, March 22. Retrieved March 29, 2012 (https://www.cia.gov/library/publications/the-world-factbook/geos/sn.html).

Central Intelligence Agency. 2012b. "North America: United States." *The World Factbook*. Retrieved March 29, 2012 (https://www.cia.gov/library/publications/the-world-factbook/geos/us.html).

Central Intelligence Agency. 2012c. "Qatar." *The World Factbook*, March 20. Retrieved March 29, 2012 (https://www.cia.gov/library/publications/the-world-factbook/geos/qa.html).

Central Intelligence Agency. 2013a. "Country Comparison: GDP Per Capita (PPP)." The World Factbook. Retrieved May 6, 2013 (https://www.cia.gov/library/publications/the-world-factbook/rankorder/2004rank.html?countryName=Kuwait&countryCode=ku&regionCode=mde&rank=18#ku).

Central Intelligence Agency. 2013b. "Death Rate: Country Comparison to the World." The World Factbook. Retrieved May 3, 2013 (https://www.cia.gov/library/publications/the-world-factbook/fields/2066.html#xx).

Central Intelligence Agency. 2013c. "Japan." *The World Factbook*, May 7. Retrieved May 11, 2013 (https://www.cia.gov/library/

publications/the-world-factbook/geos/ja.html).

Central Intelligence Agency. 2013d. "Malawi." *The World Factbook,* May 7. Retrieved May 11, 2013 (https://www.cia.gov/library/publications/the-world-factbook/geos/mi.html).

Central Intelligence Agency. 2013e. "Qatar." *The World Factbook,* May 7. Retrieved May 11, 2013 (https://www.cia.gov/library/publications/the-world-factbook/geos/qa.html).

Central Intelligence Agency. 2013f. "Singapore." *The World Factbook,* April 16. Retrieved April 29, 2013 (https://www.cia.gov/library/publications/the-world-factbook/geos/sn.html).

Cerkez, Aida. 2010. "UN Official: Bosnia War Rapes Must Be Prosecuted." *The Washington Post,* November 26. Retrieved May 16, 2013 (http://www.peacewomen.org/news_article.php?id=2506&type=news).

Cerny, Phillip G. 2007. "Nation-state." In *Encyclopedia of Globalization,* edited by Jan Aart Scholte and Roland Robertson. New York: MTM Publishing.

Chakravorti, Robi. 1993. "Marx the Journalist." *Economic and Political Weekly* 28(September 4):1856–59.

Chambers, Erve. 2010. *Native Tours: The Anthropology of Travel and Tourism.* Prospect Heights, IL: Waveland Press.

Chambliss, William J. 1964. "A Sociological Analysis of the Law of Vagrancy." *Social Problems* 12:67–77.

Chammartin, Gloria Moreno-Fontes. 2005. "Domestic Workers: Little Protection for the Underpaid." *Migration Information Source.* Retrieved June 2, 2011 (http://www.migrationinformation.org/Feature/display.cfm?id=300).

Chanda, Nayan. 2007. *Bound Together: How Traders, Preachers, Adventurers, and Warriors Shaped Globalization.* New Haven, CT: Yale University Press.

Chandy, Laurence, and Geoffrey Gertz. 2011. "Poverty in Numbers: The Changing State of Global Poverty from 2005 to 2015." Washington, DC: The Brookings Institution. Retrieved March 29, 2012 (http://www.brookings.edu/~/media/Files/rc/papers/2011/01_global_poverty_chandy/01_global_poverty_chandy.pdf).

Chant, John. n.d. "The ABCP Crisis in Canada: The Implications for the Regulation of Financial Markets." Research Study Prepared for the Expert Panel on Securities Regulation, Ottawa: Department of Finance. Retrieved September 30, 2012 (http://investisseurautonome.info/PDF-Downloads/COMMENT-INVESTIR-RENDEMENT-INDEX/doc.1495-%20Chant%202009%20ABCP%20report%20.pdf

Chapman, John, and Alan Wertheimer, eds. 1990. *Majorities and Minorities: Nomos XXXII.* New York: New York University Press.

Chappell, Neena, and Margaret Penning. 2009. *Understanding Health, Health Care, and Health Policy in Canada.* Toronto, ON: Oxford University Press.

Charles, Maria, and Karen Bradley. 2009. "Indulging Our Gendered Selves: Sex Segregation by Field of Study in 44 Countries." *American Journal of Sociology* 114:924–76.

Cheal, David. 2007. "Family Theory." Pp. 1630–34 in *The Blackwell Encyclopedia of Sociology,* edited by George Ritzer. Malden, MA: Blackwell.

Cheever, Susan. 2002. "The Nanny Dilemma." Pp. 31–38 in *Global Woman: Nannies, Maids and Sex Workers in the New Economy,* edited by Barbara Ehrenreich and Arlie Hochschild. New York: Henry Holt.

Chen, Pauline W. 2010. "Are Doctors Ready for Virtual Visits?" *The New York Times,* January 7.

Cherlin, Andrew J. 1978. "Remarriage as an Incomplete Institution." *American Journal of Sociology* 84:634–50.

Cherlin, Andrew J. 2004. "The Deinstitutio-nalization of American Marriage." *Journal of Marriage and the Family* 66:848–61.

Cherlin, Andrew J. 2009. *The Marriage-Go-Round: The State of Marriage and the Family in America Today.* New York: Knopf.

Cherlin, Andrew J. 2010. "The Houswife Anomaly." *The New York Times,* January 24.

Cherlin, Andrew J., Frank F. Furstenberg, P. L. Chase-Lansdale, K. E. Kiernan, P. K. Robins, D. R. Morrison, and J. O. Teitler. 1991. "Longitudinal Studies of the Effects of Divorce on Children in Great Britain and the United States." *Science* 252:1386–89.

Chernilo, Daniel. 2012. "Nation." Pp. 1485–92 in *The Wiley-Blackwell Encyclopedia of Globalization,* edited by George Ritzer. Malden, MA: Wiley-Blackwell.

Chiang, O. 2009. "The Challenge of User-Generated Porn." Forbes.com. Retrieved October 18, 2010 (http://www.forbes.com/2009/08/04/digital-playground-video-technology-e-gang-09-ali-joone.html).

Chilton, Roland, and Ruth Triplett. 2007a. "Class and Crime." Pp. 542–45 in *The Blackwell Encyclopedia of Sociology,* edited by George Ritzer. Malden, MA: Blackwell.

Chilton, Roland, and Ruth Triplett. 2007b. "Race and Crime." Pp. 3734–37 in *The Blackwell Encyclopedia of Sociology,* edited by George Ritzer. Malden, MA: Blackwell.

Chin, Elizabeth. 2007. "Consumption, African Americans." Pp. 706–09 in *The Blackwell Encyclopedia of Sociology,* edited by George Ritzer. Malden, MA: Blackwell.

China Internet Network Information Center. 2010. "Statistical Report on Internet Development in China," July. Retrieved June 17, 2011 (http://www.cnnic.cn/uploadfiles/pdf/2010/8/24/93145.pdf).

Chodorow, Nancy. 1978. *The Reproduction of Mothering.* Berkeley: University of California Press.

Chodorow, Nancy. 1988. *Psychoanalytic Theory and Feminism.* Cambridge, UK: Polity Press.

Chomsky, N. 1985. *Turning the Tide: U.S. Intervention in Central America and the Struggle for Peace.* Boston: South End Press.

Choy, Wayson. 1995. *The Jade Peony.* Vancouver: Douglas and McIntyre.

Chriqui, James F., Rosalie Liccardo Pacula, Duane C. McBride, Deborah A. Reichmann, Curtis J. Vanderwaal, and Yvonne Terry-McElrath. 2002. *Illicit Drug Policies: Selected Laws from the 50 States.* Princeton, NJ: Robert Wood Johnson Foundation.

Chriss, James J. 2007. "Networks." Pp. 3182–85 in *The Blackwell Encyclopedia of Sociology,* edited by George Ritzer. Malden, MA: Blackwell.

Chui, Tina. 2011. "Immigrant Women." Statistics Canada, Retrieved December 17, 2012 (http://www.statcan.gc.ca/pub/89-503-x/2010001/article/11528-eng.pdf)

Chun, Jennifer. 2009. *Organizing at the Margins: The Symbolic Politics of Labor in South Korea and the United States.* Ithaca, NY: Cornell University Press.

Clammer, John. 1997. *Contemporary Urban Japan: A Sociology of Consumption.* Oxford, UK: Blackwell.

Clancy, Michael. 2012. "Cruise Tourism." Pp. 360–62 in *The Wiley-Blackwell Encyclopedia of Globalization,* edited by George Ritzer. Malden, MA: Wiley-Blackwell.

Clapson, Mark, and Ray Hutchison, eds. 2010. *Suburbanization in Global Society.* United Kingdom: Emerald Publishing Group.

Clark, Nancy L., and William H. Worger. 2004. *South Africa: The Rise and Fall of Apartheid.* New York: Longman.

Clarke, Juanne. 2012. *Health, Illness, and Medicine in Canada.* 6th ed. Toronto, ON: Oxford University Press.

Clawson D., A. Neustadtl, and M. Weller. 1998. *Dollars and Votes: How Business Campaign Contributions Subvert Democracy.* Philadelphia: Temple University Press.

Clawson, Dan, Robert Zussman, Joya Misra, Naomi Gerstel, and Randall Stokes. 2007. *Public Sociology: Fifteen Eminent Sociologists Debate Politics and the Profession in the Twenty-first Century.* Berkeley: University of California Press.

Cleary, Thomas, trans. 2004. *The Qur'an: A New Translation.* Chicago: Starlatch Press.

Clegg, Stewart. 2007. "Ideal Type." Pp. 2201–202 in *The Blackwell Encyclopedia of Sociology,* edited by George Ritzer. Malden, MA: Blackwell.

Clegg, Stewart, and Michael Lounsbury. 2009. "Sintering the Iron Cage: Translation, Domination and Rationalization." Pp. 118–45 in *The Oxford Handbook of Sociology and Organization Studies: Classical Foundations,* edited by Paul S. Adler. Oxford, UK: Oxford University Press.

Clement, Wallace. 1975. *The Canadian Corporate Elite: an Analysis of Economic Power.* Toronto: McClelland and Stewart.

Clendinen, Dudley, and Adam Nagourney. 1999. *Out for Good: The Struggle to Build a Gay Rights Movement in America*. New York: Simon & Schuster.

Clogher, R. 1981. "Weaving Spiders Come Not Here: Bohemian Grove: Inside the Secret Retreat of the Power Elite." *Mother Jones* (August):28–35.

Clotfelter, Charles T. 2010. *American Universities in a Global Market*. Chicago: University of Chicago Press.

Clougherty, J. E., K. Souza, and M. R. Cullen. 2010. "Work and Its Role in Shaping the Social Gradients in Health." *Annals of the New York Academy of Sciences* 1186:102–124.

Cockerham, William C. 2007. "Medical Sociology." Pp. 2932–36 in *The Blackwell Encyclopedia of Sociology*, edited by George Ritzer. Malden, MA: Blackwell.

Cockerham, William. 2012. "Current Directions in Medical Sociology." Pp. 385–401 in *The Wiley-Blackwell Companion to Sociology*, edited by George Ritzer. Malden, MA: Wiley-Blackwell.

Cohen, Daniel. 2008. *Three Lectures on Post-industrial Society*. Cambridge, MA: MIT Press.

Cohen, Lizabeth. 2004. *A Consumer Republic: The Politics of Mass Consumption in Post War America*. Chicago: University of Chicago Press.

Cohen, Noam. 2011. "Define Gender Gap? Look Up Wikipedia's Contributor List." *The New York Times,* January 30. Accessed on December 3, 2011 (http://www.nytimes.com/2011/01/31/business/media/31link.html).

Cohen, Patricia. 2010. "'Culture of Poverty' Makes a Comeback." *The New York Times,* October 17. Retrieved March 29, 2012 (http://www.nytimes.com/2010/10/18/us/18poverty.html).

Cohen, R. 1997. *Global Diasporas: An Introduction*. London: Routledge.

Cohen, Richard. 2008. "The Election That LBJ Won." *The Washington Post,* November 4, p. A17.

Cohen-Cole, Ethan, Steven Durlauf, Jeffrey Fagan, and Daniel Nagin. 2009. "Model Uncertainty and the Deterrent Effect of Capital Punishment." *American Law and Economics Review* 11:335–69.

Cole, E., and J. D. Henderson. 2005. *Featuring Females: Feminist Analyses of Media*. Washington, DC: American Psychological Association.

Coleman, David, and Robert Rowthorn. 2011. "Who's Afraid of Population Decline? A Critical Examination of Its Consequences." *Population and Development Review* 37:217–48.

Coleman, James. 1966. *Equality of Educational Opportunity*. Washington, DC: U.S. Department of Health, Education, and Welfare.

Coleman, James. 1990. *Foundations of Social Theory*. Cambridge, MA: Belknap Press of Harvard University Press.

Coleman, Marilyn, and Lawrence H. Ganong. 2007a. "Stepfamilies." Pp. 4765–68 in *The Blackwell Encyclopedia of Sociology*, edited by George Ritzer. Malden, MA: Blackwell.

Coleman, Marilyn, and Lawrence H. Ganong. 2007b. "Stepmothering." Pp. 4770–72 in *The Blackwell Encyclopedia of Sociology*, edited by George Ritzer. Malden, MA: Blackwell.

Collier, Paul. 2007. *The Bottom Billion: Why the Poorest Countries Are Failing and What Can Be Done about It*. New York: Oxford University Press.

Collier, Paul. 2012. "The Bottom Billion." Pp. 126–30 in *The Wiley-Blackwell Encyclopedia of Globalization,* edited by George Ritzer. Malden, MA: Wiley-Blackwell.

Collins, A., and R. Halverson. 2009. *Rethinking Education in the Age of Technology: The Digital Revolution and the Schools*. New York: Teachers College Press.

Collins, Chiquita, and David R. Williams. 2004. "Segregation and Mortality: The Deadly Effects of Racism?" *Sociological Forum* 45:265–85.

Collins, J. 2009. "Social Reproduction in Classrooms and Schools." *Annual Review of Anthropology* 38:33–48.

Collins, Jane L. 2003. *Threads: Gender, Labor, and Power in the Global Apparel Industry*. Chicago: University of Chicago Press.

Collins, Patricia Hill. 1990. *Black Feminist Thought: Knowledge, Consciousness, and the Politics of Empowerment*. Boston: Unwin Hyman.

Collins, Patricia Hill. 2000. *Black Feminist Thought: Knowledge, Consciousness, and the Politics of Empowerment*. 2nd ed. New York: Routledge.

Collins, Patricia Hill. 2004. *Black Sexual Politics: African-Americans, Gender and the New Racism*. New York: Routledge.

Collins, Patricia Hill. 2009. *Another Kind of Public Education: Race, the Media, Schools, and Democratic Possibilities*. Boston: Beacon Press.

Collins, Patricia Hill. 2012. "Looking Back, Moving Ahead Scholarship in Service to Social Justice." *Gender & Society* 26:14–22.

Collins, Randall. 1975. *Conflict Society: Toward an Explanatory Science*. New York: Academic Press.

Collins, Randall. 1979. *The Credential Society: An Historical Sociology of Education and Stratification*. New York: Academic Press.

Collins, Randall. 1990. "Conflict Theory and the Advance of Macro-Historical Sociology." In *Frontiers of Social Theory,* edited by George Ritzer. New York: Columbia University Press.

Collins, Randall. 2008. *Violence: A Micro-sociological Theory*. Princeton, NJ: Princeton University Press.

Collins, Randall. 2009. "Micro and Macro Causes of Violence." *International Journal of Conflict and Violence* 3:9–22.

Comaroff, John L., and Jean Comaroff. 2009. *Ethnicity, Inc.* Chicago: University of Chicago Press.

Comstock, G., and E. Scharrer. 2007. *Media and the American Child*. Burlington, MA: Academic Press.

Conca, Ken. 2006. *Governing Water: Contentious Transnational Political and Global Institution Building*. Cambridge, MA: MIT Press.

Conca, Ken. 2007. "Water." In *Encyclopedia of Globalization,* edited by Jan Aart Scholte and Ronald Robertson. New York: MTM Publishing.

Conference Board of Canada. 2009. "Intergenerational Income Mobility" Retrieved October 9, 2012 (http://www.conferenceboard.ca/hcp/details/society/intergenerational-income-mobility.aspx).

Conley, Dalton. 2001a. "The Black-White Wealth Gap." *The Nation,* March 26. Retrieved March 29, 2012 (http://www.thenation.com/article/black-white-wealth-gap).

Conley, Dalton. 2001b. *Honky*. New York: Vintage Books.

Conley, Dalton. 2004. "For Siblings, Inequality Starts at Home." *The Chronicle Review,* March 4. Retrieved March 29, 2012 (http://chronicle.com/article/For-Siblings-Inequality/7314/).

Conley, Dalton. 2008. "Rich Man's Burden." *The New York Times,* September 2. Retrieved March 29, 2012 (http://www.nytimes.com/2008/09/02/opinion/02conley.html).

Connell, Robert W. 1987. *Gender and Power: Society, the Person, and Sexual Politics*. Palo Alto, CA: Stanford University Press.

Connell, Robert W. 1995. *Masculinities*. Berkeley: University of California Press.

Connell, Robert W. 1997. "Hegemonic Masculinity and Emphasized Femininity." Pp. 22–25 in *Feminist Frontiers IV,* edited by L. Richardson, V. Taylor, and N. Whittier. New York: McGraw-Hill.

Connell, Robert. W. 2005. *Masculinities*. 2nd ed. Berkeley: University of California Press.

Connidis, Ingrid. 2010. *Family Ties and Aging*. 2nd ed. Thousand Oaks, CA: Sage.

Conrad, Peter. 1986. "Problems in Health Care." Pp. 415–50 in *Social Problems,* edited by George Ritzer. 2nd ed. New York: Random House.

Conrad, Peter, Thomas Mackie, and Ateev Mehrota. 2010. "Estimating the Costs of Medicalization." *Social Science & Medicine* 70:1943–47.

Conrad, Peter, and Joseph W. Schneider. 1980. *Deviance and Medicalization: From Badness to Sickness*. St. Louis, MO: Mosby.

Considine, Austin. 2012. "Gay Marriage Victory Still Shadowed by AIDS." *The New York Times* Sunday Styles, January 1, pp. 1, 2.

Cook, Daniel T. 2004. *The Commodification of Childhood: The Children's Clothing Industry and the Rise of the Child Consumer*. Durham, NC: Duke University Press.

Cook, Daniel Thomas. 2007. "Consumer Culture, Children's." Pp. 693–97 in *The Blackwell Encyclopedia of Sociology,* edited by George Ritzer. Malden, MA: Blackwell.

Cook, Karen S., Richard M. Emerson, Mary B. Gilmore, and Toshio Yamagishi. 1983.

"The Distribution of Power in Exchange Networks: Theory and Experimental Results." *American Journal of Sociology* 89:275–305.

Cooksey, Elizabeth. 2007. "Fertility: Adolescent." Pp. 1725–29 in *The Blackwell Encyclopedia of Sociology,* edited by George Ritzer. Malden, MA: Blackwell.

Cool, Julie. 2010. "Wage Gap between Women and Men." Background Paper, Library of Parliament, Ottawa: Publication # 2010 30-E.

Cooley, Charles Horton. 1909. *Social Organization: A Study of the Larger Mind.* New York: Charles Scribner's Sons.

Correll, Shelley L. 2004. "Constraints into Preferences: Gender, Status, and Emerging Career Aspirations." *American Sociological Review* 69(1):93–113.

Correll, S. J., S. Benard, and I. Paik. 2007. "Getting a Job: Is There a Motherhood Penalty?" *American Journal of Sociology* 112:1297–1338.

Corrigall-Brown, Catherine. 2011. *Patterns of Protest: Trajectories of Participation in Social Movements.* Palo Alto, CA: Stanford University Press.

Corrigall-Brown, Catherine, and Rima Wilkes. 2012. "Picturing Protest: The Visual Framing of Collective Action by First Nations in Canada." *American Behavioural Scientist* 56(2):223–43.

Corsaro, William A., and Peggy J. Miller, eds. 1992. "Interpretive Approaches to Children's Socialization." Special Edition of *New Directions for Child Development* 58(Winter).

Corwin, Zoe Blumberg, and William G. Tierney. 2007. "Institutional Review Boards and Sociological Research." Pp. 2345–51 in *The Blackwell Encyclopedia of Sociology,* edited by George Ritzer. Malden, MA: Blackwell.

Cosenza, Vicenzo. 2011. "World Map of Social Networks." Retrieved August 27, 2011 (www.vincos.it/world-map-of-social-networks/).

Coser, Lewis. 1956. *The Functions of Social Conflict.* New York: Free Press.

Cotter, David A., Joan M. Hermsen, Seth Ovadia, and Reeve Vanneman. 2001. "The Glass Ceiling Effect." *Social Forces* 80(2):655–82.

Coulmont, Baptiste, and Phil Hubbard. 2010. "Consuming Sex: Socio-legal Shifts in the Space and Place of Sex Shops." *Journal of Law and Society* 37(1):189–209.

Cousins, Mel. 2005. *European Welfare States: Comparative Perspectives.* London: Sage.

Coventry, Martha. 2006. "Tyranny of the Esthetic: Surgery's Most Intimate Violation." Pp. 203–11 in *Estelle Disch's Reconstructing Gender: A Multicultural Anthology.* New York: McGraw-Hill Education.

Coward, Martin. 2012. "Urban." Pp. 2130–34 in *The Wiley-Blackwell Encyclopedia of Globalization,* edited by George Ritzer. Malden, MA: Wiley-Blackwell.

Cox, Lloyd. 2007. "Socialism." Pp. 4549–54 in *The Blackwell Encyclopedia of Sociology,* edited by George Ritzer. Malden, MA: Blackwell.

Cox, Richard Henry, and Albert Schilthuis. 2012. "Governance." Pp. 885–88 in *The Wiley-Blackwell Encyclopedia of Globalization,* edited by George Ritzer. Malden, MA: Wiley-Blackwell.

Crawford, Allan, and Umar Faruqui. 2011–12. "What Explains Trends in Household Debt in Canada." *Bank of Canada Review* Winter: 3–15.

Creese, Gillian. 1999. *Contracting Masculinity: Gender, Class and Race in a White-collar Union, 1944–1994.* Toronto, ON: Oxford University Press.

Creese, Gillian, and Brenda Beagan. 2009. "Gender at Work: Strategies for Equality in Neo-liberal Times." Pp. 224–36 in *Social Inequality in Canada*, edited by Ed Grabb and Neil Guppy. Toronto, ON: Pearson.

Creswell, John. 2008. *Research Design: Qualitative, Quantitative, and Mixed Methods Approaches.* Thousand Oaks, CA: Sage.

Cross, Remy, and David Snow. 2012. "Social Movements." Pp. 522–44 in *The Wiley-Blackwell Companion to Sociology,* edited by George Ritzer. Malden, MA: Wiley-Blackwell.

Crothers, C. 2011. "Robert K. Merton." Pp. 65–88 in *Major Social Theorists: Volume II. Contemporary Social Theorists,* edited by G. Ritzer and J. Stepnisky. West Sussex, UK: Wiley-Blackwell.

Crothers, Lane. 2010. *Globalization and American Popular Culture.* 2nd ed. Lanham, MD: Rowman Littlefield.

Crouse, Janice Shaw. 2010. "Cohabitation Nation." *The Washington Times,* November 22, p. 1.

Crowder, Kyle, and Liam Downey. 2010. "Interneighborhood Migration, Race, and Environmental Hazards: Modeling Microlevel Processes of Environmental Inequality." *The American Journal of Sociology* 115(4):1110–49.

Crowder, Kyle, and Matthew Hall. 2007. "Migration, Internal." Pp. 3014–19 in *The Blackwell Encyclopedia of Sociology,* edited by George Ritzer. Malden, MA: Blackwell.

Crowley, Gregory J. 2007. "Urban Renewal and Development." Pp. 5128–32 in *The Blackwell Encyclopedia of Sociology,* edited by George Ritzer. Malden, MA: Blackwell.

Crowley, Martha, Daniel Tope, Lindsey Joyce Chamberlain, and Randy Hodson. 2010. "Neo-Taylorism at Work: Occupational Change in the Post-Fordist Era." *Social Problems* 57:421–47.

Cruikshank, Julie. 1992. "Invention of Anthropology in British Columbia's Supreme Court: Oral Tradition as Evidence in *Delgamuukw v. B.C.*" *BC Studies* 95, Autumn, 25–42.

Crump, Jeff. 2007. "Exurbia." Pp. 1549–51 in *The Blackwell Encyclopedia of Sociology,* edited by George Ritzer. Malden, MA: Blackwell.

Crutsinger, Martin. 2010. "G20 Leaders Facing Worries About Rising Deficits," June 24. Retrieved March 29, 2012 (http://www.businessweek.com/ap/financialnews/D9GHNNI81.htm).

Cullen, Francis T., Cheryl Lero Jonson, Daniel S. Nagin. 2011. "Prisons Do Not Reduce Recidivism: The High Cost of Ignoring Science." *The Prison Journal* 91:48S–65S.

Culver, Leigh. 2007. "Criminal Justice System." Pp. 851–56 in *The Blackwell Encyclopedia of Sociology,* edited by George Ritzer. Malden, MA: Blackwell.

Currie, Dawn. 1997. "Decoding Femininity: Advertisements and Their Teenage Readers." *Gender and Society* 11(4):454–78.

Curtiss, Susan. 1977. *Genie: A Psycholinguistic Study of a Modern-day "Wild Child."* New York: Academic Press.

Cusimano, Michael, Sofia Nastis, and Laura Zuccaro. 2013. "Effectiveness of Interventions to Reduce Aggression and Injuries among Ice Hockey Players: A Systematic Review." *Canadian Medical Association Journal* 185(1):E57–E69.

Cyert, Richard Michael and James G. March. 1963. *A Behavioral Theory of the Firm.* Englewood Cliffs, NJ: Prentice-Hall.

D'Arma, Alessandro. 2011. "Global Media, Business and Politics: A Comparative Analysis of News Corporation's Strategy in Italy and the UK." *International Communication Gazette* 73(8):670–84.

D'Elia, Valarie. 2011. "Developers Have Big Plans for NJ Mega Mall." *NY1,* May 19. Retrieved May 19, 2011 (http://bronx.ny1.com/content/ny1_living/travel/139387/developers-have-big-plans-for-nj-mega-mall).

Dahl, Darren, Jaideep Sengupta, and Kathleen D. Vohs. 2009. "Sex in Advertising: Gender Differences and the Role of Relationship Commitment." *Journal of Consumer Research* 36(2):215–31.

Dahrendorf, Ralf. 1959. *Class and Class Conflict in Industrial Society.* Stanford, CA: Stanford University Press.

Daley, Suzanne. 1999, October 12. "Montredon Journal; French See a Hero in War on 'McDomination.'" Retrieved March 29, 2012 (http://www.nytimes.com/1999/10/12/world/montredon-journal-french-see-a-hero-in-war-on-mcdomination.html).

Daley, Suzanne. 2010a. "A Dutch City Seeks to End Drug Tourism." *The New York Times,* August 18, pp. A1, A12.

Daley, Suzanne. 2010b. "The Hunt for Jobs Send the Irish Abroad, Again." *The New York Times,* November 21, p. 4.

Dandaneau, Steven P. 2007. "Norms." Pp. 3229–32 in *The Blackwell Encyclopedia of Sociology,* edited by George Ritzer. Malden, MA: Blackwell.

Dandaneau, Steven P. 2012. "Deindustrialization." Pp. 385–87 in *The Wiley-Blackwell Encyclopedia of Globalization,* edited by George Ritzer. Malden, MA: Wiley-Blackwell.

Daniels, Jessie. 2009. *Cyber Racism: White Supremacy Online and the New Attack on Civil Rights.* Lanham, MD: Rowman and Littlefield.

Dann, Gary Elijah, and Neil Haddow. 2008. "Just Doing Business or Doing Just Business: Google, Microsoft, Yahoo! and the Business of Censoring China's Internet." *Journal of Business Ethics* 79:219–34.

Dant, Tim. 2007. "Material Culture." P. 2835 in *The Blackwell Encyclopedia of Sociology,* edited by George Ritzer. Malden, MA: Blackwell.

"The Dark Side of Organizations: Mistake, Misconduct, and Disaster." 1999. *Annual Review of Sociology* 25:271–305.

Darwin, Charles. [1859] 2003. *On the Origin of Species.* London: Signet Classics.

Datar, Srikant, David A. Garvin, and Patrick G. Cullen. 2010. *Rethinking the MBA: Business Education at a Crossroads.* Cambridge, MA: Harvard Business Review Press.

Dauvergne, Mia. 2012. *Adult Correctional Statistics in Canada 2010/2011.* Ottawa, ON: Statistics Canada, Canadian Centre for Justice Statistics.

Davidson, Christopher M. 2008. *Dubai: The Vulnerability of Success.* New York: Columbia University Press.

Davidson, Julia O'Connell. 2005. *Children in the Global Sex Trade.* Cambridge, UK: Polity Press.

Davies, James. 2009. "The Distribution of Wealth and Economic Inequality." Pp. 92–105 in *Social Inequality in Canada,* edited by Edward Grabb and Neil Guppy. Toronto, ON: Pearson Prentice Hall.

Davies, Scott. Forthcoming. "Are There Catholic School Effects in Ontario, Canada?" *European Sociological Review.*

Davies, Scott, and Janice Aurini. 2011. "Determinants of School Choice in Canada: Understanding Which Parents Choose and Why." *Canadian Public Policy* 37(4):459–77.

Davies, Scott, and Neil Guppy. 2013. *The Schooled Society.* 3rd ed. Toronto, ON: Oxford University Press.

Davis, F. James. 1991. "Who Is Black? One Nation's Definition." Retrieved January 27, 2012 (http://www.pbs.org/wgbh/pages/frontline/shows/jefferson/mixed/onedrop.html).

Davis, F. James. 1991. *Who Is Black? One Nation's Definition.* Philadelphia: Penn State University Press.

Davis, Flora. [1991] 1999. *Moving the Mountain: The Women's Movement in America Since 1960.* New York: Simon and Schuster.

Davis, Kingsley. 1940. "Extreme Social Isolation of a Child." *American Journal of Sociology* 45(4):554–65.

Davis, Kingsley. 1945. "The World Demographic Transition." *Annals of the American Academy of Political and Social Science* 237:1–110.

Davis, Kingsley. 1947. "Final Note on a Case of Extreme Isolation." *American Journal of Sociology* 50:432–37.

Davis, Kingsley, and Wilbert E. Moore. 1945. "Some Principles of Stratification." *American Sociological Review* 10.

Davis, Mike. 2006. "Fear and Money in Dubai." *New Left Review* 41(September/October).

Davis, Mike. 2007. *Planet of Slums.* London: Verso.

Davis-Blake, Allison and Joseph P. Broschak. 2009. "Outsourcing and the Changing Nature of Work." *Annual Review of Sociology* 35:321–40.

Day, Jennifer Cheeseman, and Eric C. Newburger. 2002. "The Big Payoff: Educational Attainment and Synthetic Estimates of Work-Life Earnings." *Current Population Reports* (July):1–13.

de Beauvoir, Simone. [1949] 1957. *The Second Sex.* New York: Vintage.

de Beauvoir, Simone. 1952. *The Second Sex,* translated by H. M. Parshley. New York: Vintage.

de Beauvoir, Simone. 1973. *The Second Sex.* New York: Vintage.

de Beauvoir, Simone. [1980] 1989. *The Second Sex.* New York: Vintage.

De Graaf, Paul M. 2007. "Stratification: Functional and Conflict Theories." Pp. 4797–99 in *The Blackwell Encyclopedia of Sociology,* edited by George Ritzer. Malden, MA: Blackwell.

de la Dehesa, Rafael. 2010. *Queering the Public Sphere in Mexico and Brazil: Sexual Rights Movements in Emerging Democracies.* Durham, NC: Duke University Press.

De Lollis, Barbara, and Laura Petrecca. 2005. "Four Years after 9/11, New York Is Back." *USA Today,* September 8. Retrieved March 31, 2012 (http://www.usatoday.com/travel/news/2005-09-08-new-york-usat_x.htm).

de Regt, Marina. 2009. "Preferences and Prejudices: Employers' Views on Domestic Workers in the Republic of Yemen." *Signs* 34(3):559–81.

De Silva, Dakshina G., Robert P. McComb, Young-Kyu Moh, Anita R. Schiller, and Andres J. Vargas. 2010. "The Effect of Migration on Wages: Evidence From a Natural Experiment." *American Economic Review: Papers & Proceedings* 100(May):321–26.

Dean, Cornelia. 2007. "Experts Discuss Engineering Feats, Like Space Mirror, to Slow Climate Change." *The New York Times,* November 10, p. A11.

Debas, Haile T. 2010. "Global Health: Priority Agenda for the 21st Century." *UN Chronicle* XLVII(2). Retrieved March 29, 2012 (http://www.un.org/wcm/content/site/chronicle/cache/bypass/home/archive/issues2010/achieving_global_health/globalhealth_priorityagendaforthe21stcentury?ctnscroll_articleContainerList=1_0&ctnlistpagination_articleContainerList=true).

Decker, Scott H., and G. David Curry. 2000. "Addressing Key Features of Gang Membership: Measuring the Involvement of Young Members." *Journal of Criminal Justice* 28:473–82.

DeGraaf, N. D., et al. 2000. "Parental Cultural Capital and Educational Attainment in the Netherlands." *Sociology of Education* 73:92–111.

Dei, George. 2008. "Schooling as Community Race, Schooling, and the Education of African Youth." *Journal of Black Studies* 38(3):346–66.

Dei, George. 2010. *Learning to Succeed: The Challenges and Possibilities of Educational Achievement for All.* New York: Teneo Press.

Dentler, Robert A., and Kai T. Erickson. 1959. "The Function of Deviance in Small Groups." *Social Problems* 7:98–107.

Department of Immigration and Citizenship. 2011. "Trends in Migration: Australia 2010–11." Australian Government. Retrieved February 28, 2012 (http://www.immi.gov.au/media/publications/statistics/trends-in-migration/trends-in-migration-2010-11.pdf).

Desai, Sonalde. 2010. "The Other Half of the Demographic Dividend." *Economic & Political Weekly* 14:12–14.

Desmond, Matthew. 2010. PhD dissertation, University of Wisconsin.

Deutsch, Claudia H. 2007. "For Fiji Water, a Big List of Green Goals." *The New York Times,* November 7, p. C3.

Deutsch, Nancy, and Eleni Theodorou. 2010. "Aspiring, Consuming, Becoming: Youth Identity in a Culture of Consumption." *Youth & Society* 42(2):229–54.

DeVault, Marjorie. 1991. *Feeding the Family: The Social Organization of Caring as Gendered Work.* Chicago: University of Chicago Press.

Dewing, Michael, and Mark Leman. 2006. "Canadian Multiculturalism." Current Issue Review—Parliamentary Research Branch, Library of Parliament Research Publications (93-6E). Retrieved September 25, 2010 (http://www2.parl.gc.ca/content/lop/researchpublications/936-e.htm).

Dey, EL. 1997. "Undergraduate Political Attitudes: Peer Influence in Changing Social Contexts." *Journal of Higher Education* 68:398–416.

Diamond, Jared. 2006. *Collapse: How Societies Choose to Fail or Succeed.* New York: Penguin.

Dicke, Thomas S. 1992. *Franchising in America: The Development of a Business Method, 1840–1980.* Chapel Hill: University of North Carolina Press.

Dikötter, Frank. 2008. "The Racialization of the Globe: An Interactive Interpretation." *Ethnic and Racial Studies* 31(8):1478–96.

Dilworth-Anderson, Peggye, and Gracie Boswell. 2007. "Cultural Diversity and Aging: Ethnicity, Minorities and Subcultures." Pp. 898–902 in *The Blackwell Encyclopedia of Sociology,* edited by George Ritzer. Malden, MA: Blackwell.

DiMaggio, Paul. 1987. "Classification in Art." *American Sociological Review* 52:440–55.

DiMaggio, Paul, Eszter Hargittai, W. Russell Neuman, and John P. Robinson. 2001.

"Social Implications of the Internet." *Annual Review of Sociology* 27:307–36.

DiMaggio, P. J., and W. Powell. 1983. "'The Iron Cage Revisited': Institutional Isomorphism and Collective Rationality in Organizational Fields." *American Sociological Review* 48.

Diotallevi, Luca. 2007. "Church." Pp. 483–89 in *The Blackwell Encyclopedia of Sociology,* edited by George Ritzer. Malden, MA: Blackwell.

DiPrete, Thomas A., Gregory M. Eirich, Karen S. Cook, and Douglas S. Massey. 2006. "Cumulative Advantage as a Mechanism for Inequality: A Review of Theoretical and Empirical Developments." *Annual Review of Sociology* 32:271–97.

Disch, L. J. 2002. *The Tyranny of the Two-Party System.* New York: Columbia University Press.

Dobbelaere, Karel. 2007. "Secularization." Pp. 4140–48 in *The Blackwell Encyclopedia of Sociology,* edited by George Ritzer. Malden, MA: Blackwell.

Docherty, I., R. Goodlad, and R. Paddison. 2001. "Civic Culture, Community and Citizen Participation in Contrasting Neighbourhoods." *Urban Studies* 38(12):2225–50.

Dodd, Nigel. 2012. "Money." Pp. 1444–48 in *The Wiley-Blackwell Encyclopedia of Globalization,* edited by George Ritzer. Malden, MA: Wiley-Blackwell.

Dohnt, Hayley K., and Marika Tiggeman. 2006. "Body Image Concerns in Young Girls: The Role of Peers and Media Prior to Adolescence." *Journal of Youth and Adolescence* 35:21–33.

Dombrink, John, and Daniel Hillyard. 2007. *Sin No More: From Abortion to Stem Cells, Understanding Crime, Law, and Morality in America.* New York: New York University Press.

Domhoff, G. W. 1974. *The Bohemian Grove and Other Retreats: A Study in Ruling-Class Cohesiveness.* New York: Harper and Row.

Dominguez, Jorge I., Rafael Hernandez, and Lorena Barberia, eds. 2011. *Debating U.S.-Cuban Relations: Shall We Play Ball?* Contemporary Inter-American Relations Series. London: Routledge.

Donadio, Rachel. 2008. "Italy's Attacks on Migrants Fuel Debate on Racism." *The New York Times,* October 2.

Donadio, Rachel. 2010. "Looking Past the Façade of Italian City after Riots." *The New York Times,* January 13, p. A6.

Dooley, David, and JoAnn Prause. 2009. *The Social Costs of Underemployment: Inadequate Employment as Disguised Unemployment.* Cambridge, UK: Cambridge University Press.

Dorius, Shawn, and Glenn Firebaugh. 2010. "Trends in Global Gender Inequality." *Social Forces* 88(5):1941–68.

Dotter, Daniel L., and Julian B. Roebuck. 1988. "The Labeling Approach Re-examined: Interactionism and the Components of Deviance." *Deviant Behavior* 9(1):19–32.

Doucet, Andrea. 2006. *Do Men Mother? Fathering, Care and Domestic Responsibility.* Toronto, ON: University of Toronto Press.

Doucet, Andrea. 2009 "Gender Equality and Gender Differences: Parenting, Habitus and Embodiment." *Canadian Review of Sociology* 48(2):99–117.

Douglas, Susan J., and Meredith W. Michaels. 2006. "The New Momism." Pp. 226–38 in *Reconstructing Gender: A Multicultural Anthology,* edited by Estelle Disch. New York: McGraw-Hill Education.

Downes, David, and Paul Rock. 2011. *Understanding Deviance: A Guide to the Sociology of Crime and Rule-Breaking.* Oxford, UK: Oxford University Press.

Downey, Douglas B., Paul T. von Hippel, and Beckett A. Broh. 2004. "Are Schools the Great Equalizer? Cognitive Inequality during the Summer Months and the School Year." *American Sociological Review* 69:613–35.

Downing, John D. H. 2011. "Media Ownership, Concentration, and Control: The Evolution of Debate." In *The Handbook of Political Economy of Communications*, edited by Janet Wasko, Graham Murdock, and Helena Sousa. Oxford, UK: Wiley-Blackwell.

Doyle, Thomas P. 2003. "Roman Catholic Clericalism, Religious Duress, and Clergy Sexual Abuse." *Pastoral Psychology* 51(3):189–231.

Drache, D. (with M. D. Froese). 2008. *Defiant Publics: The Unprecedented Reach of the Global Citizen.* Cambridge, UK: Polity Press.

Drane, John. 2001. *The McDonaldization of the Church.* London: Darton, Longman, Todd.

Drane, John. 2008. *After McDonaldization: Mission, Ministry, and Christian Discipleship in an Age of Uncertainty.* Grand Rapids, MI: Baker.

Dreeben, Robert. 1968. *On What Is Learned in School.* Reading, MA: Addison-Wesley.

Drew, Christopher. 2010. "The War Chatroom." *The New York Times,* June 8, p. B1.

Drolet, Marie. 2002. "Can the Workplace Explain Canadian Gender Pay Differentials?" *Canadian Public Policy* 28:S41–S63.

Drori, Gili. 2006. *Global E-litism: Digital Technology, Social Inequality, and Transnationality.* New York: Worth.

Drori, Gili S. 2010. "Globalization and Technology Divides: Bifurcation of Policy Between the 'Digital Divide' and the 'Innovation Divide.'" *Sociological Inquiry* 80:63–91.

Duány, Andrés, and Elizabeth Plater-Zyberk. 1990. "Projects of Villages, Towns and Cities, Territories, and Codes." In *Towns and Town-making Principles,* edited by A. Krieger and W. Lennertz. New York: Rizzoli.

Duány, Andres, Elizabeth Plater-Zyberk, and Jeff Speck. 2010. *Suburban Nation: The Rise of Sprawl and the Decline of the American Dream.* 10th anniversary ed. North Point Press.

"Dubai Mall Set for August 28 Opening." 2008. *Gulf News,* April 9. Retrieved May 19, 2011 (http://gulfnews.com/business/construction/dubai-mall-set-for-august-28-opening-1.97114).

Duberman, Martin B. 1994. *Stonewall.* New York: Plume.

Du Bois, W. E. B. [1899] 1996. *The Philadelphia Negro: A Social Study.* Philadelphia: University of Pennsylvania Press.

Du Bois, W. E. B. [1903] 1966. *The Souls of Black Folk.* New York: Modern Library.

Duckworth, Angela, and Martin Seligman. 2005. "Self-Discipline Outdoes IQ Predicting Academic Performance in Adolescents." *Psychological Science* 16:939–44.

Dudgeon, Scott. 2010. *Rising Tide: The Impact of Dementia on Canadian Society.* Toronto, ON: Alzheimer Society of Canada.

Duhigg, Charles and Keith Bradsher. 2012. "How the U.S. Lost Out on iPhone Work." *The New York Times,* January 22, pp. A1, A22.

Dullea, Georgia. 1991. "The Tract House as Landmark." *The New York Times,* October 17, pp. C1, C8.

Dukes, Richard L., and Judith A. Stein. 2011. "Ink and Holes Correlates and Predictive Associations of Body Modification among Adolescents." *Youth & Society* 43:1547–69.

Dumazadier, Joffre. 1967. *Toward a Society of Leisure.* New York: Free Press.

Duncan, Greg J., Kathleen M. Ziol-Guest, and Ariel Kalil. 2010. "Early-Childhood Poverty and Adult Attainment, Behavior, and Health." *Child Development* 81:306–25.

Duneier, Mitchell. 1999. *Sidewalk.* New York: Farrar, Straus & Giroux.

Dunlap, Riley E. 2007. "Environment, Sociology of the." Pp. 1417–22 in *The Blackwell Encyclopedia of Sociology,* edited by George Ritzer. Malden, MA: Blackwell.

Dunlap, Riley E., and William R. Catton Jr. 2002. "Which Functions of the Environment Do We Study? A Comparison of Environmental and Natural Resource Sociology." *Society and Natural Resources* 15:239–49.

Dunlap, Riley E., and Andrew K. Jorgenson. 2012. "Environmental Problems." Pp. 529–36 in *The Wiley-Blackwell Companion to Sociology,* edited by George Ritzer. Malden, MA: Wiley-Blackwell.

Dunn, Jennifer L. 2005. "'Victims' and 'Survivors': Emerging Vocabularies of Motive for 'Battered Women Who Stay.'" *Sociological Inquiry* 75:1–30.

Dunning, Eric, P. Murphy, and J. Williams. 1986. *The Roots of Football Hooliganism.* London: Routledge and Kegan Paul.

Durkheim, Émile. [1893] 1964. *The Division of Labor in Society.* New York: Free Press.

Durkheim, Émile. [1895] 1982. *The Rules of Sociological Method.* New York: Free Press.

Durkheim, Émile. [1897] 1951. *Suicide.* New York: Free Press.

Durkheim, Émile. [1912] 1965. *Elementary Forms of Religious Life.* New York: Free Press.

Durkheim, Émile. 1956. *Education and Society.* Glencoe, IL: Free Press.

Durkheim, Émile. 1973. *Moral Education.* New York: Free Press.

Duster, Troy. 2003. *Backdoor to Eugenics*. New York: Routledge.

Dustin, Donna. 2007. *The McDonaldization of Social Work*. Burlington, VT: Ashgate.

Dworkin, Andrea. 1974. *Woman Hating*. New York: E. P. Dutton.

Earl, Jennifer. 2007. "Social Movements, Repression of." Pp. 4475–79 in *The Blackwell Encyclopedia of Sociology*, edited by George Ritzer. Malden, MA: Blackwell.

Eckholm, Erik. 2010. "Recession Raises U.S. Poverty Rate to a 1-Year High." *The New York Times*, September 17, pp. A1, A3.

The Economist. 2006. "DP Seeks to Calm the Storm over Ports," March 10. Retrieved March 29, 2012 (http://www.economist.com/node/5620236).

The Economist. 2008. "The Internet in China," January 31. Retrieved March 29, 2012 (http://www.economist.com/node/10608655).

Edin, Kathryn, and Laura Lein. 1997. *Making Ends Meet: How Single Mothers Survive Welfare and Low-Wage Work*. New York: Russell Sage.

Edwards, Bob. 2007. "Resource Mobilization Theory." Pp. 3893–98 in *The Blackwell Encyclopedia of Sociology*, edited by George Ritzer. Malden, MA: Blackwell.

Edwards, Rosalind, and Lucy Hadfield. 2007. "Stepfathering." Pp. 4768–70 in *The Blackwell Encyclopedia of Sociology*, edited by George Ritzer. Malden, MA: Blackwell.

Ehrenreich, Barbara. 2001. *Nickel and Dimed: On (Not) Getting by in America*. New York: Henry Holt.

Ehrenreich, Barbara. 2002. "Maid to Order." In *Global Woman: Nannies, Maids, and Sex Workers in the New Economy*, edited by Barbara Ehrenreich and Arlie Hochschild. New York: Henry Holt.

Ehrenreich, Barbara. 2008. *Nickel and Dimed: On (Not) Getting By in America*. New York: Holt Paperbacks.

Ehrenreich, Barbara, and Arlie Hochschild. 2002. "Introduction." In *Global Woman: Nannies, Maids, and Sex Workers in the New Economy*, edited by Barbara Ehrenreich and Arlie Hochschild. New York: Henry Holt.

Ehrlich, Paul. 1968. *The Population Bomb*. New York: Ballantine.

Eichler, Margrit. 1991. *Nonsexist Research Methods: A Practical Guide*. London: Routledge.

Ekland-Olson, Sheldon. 2012. *Who Lives, Who Dies, Who Decides*. New York: Routledge.

Elections Canada. 2000. "The History of the Vote in Canada." Retrieved December 22, 2012 (http://www.elections.ca/content.aspx?section=med&document=oct2600b&dir=pre&lang=e).

Elections Canada. 2013. "Voter Turnout at Federal Elections and Referendums." Retrieved April 28, 2013 (http://www.elections.ca/content.aspx?section=ele&dir=turn&document=index&lang=e).

Elgin, Duane. 2010. *Voluntary Simplicity: Toward a Way of Life That Is Outwardly Simple, Inwardly Rich*. 2nd ed. New York: Quill.

Elliott, Anthony, and John Urry. 2010. *Mobile Lives*. London: Routledge.

Elliott, David L. 2012. "Urbanism." Pp. 2134–36 in *The Wiley-Blackwell Encyclopedia of Globalization*, edited by George Ritzer. Malden, MA: Wiley-Blackwell.

Elliott, Diana B., Rebekah Young, and Jane Lawler Dye. 2011. "Variation in the Formation of Complex Family Households During the Recession" (SEHSD Working Paper Number 2011-32). Paper presented at the National Council on Family Relations 73rd Annual Conference, Orlando, FL, November 16–19.

Ellison, Christopher G. 1999. "Introduction to Symposium: Religion, Health, Well-being." *Journal for the Scientific Study of Religion* 37:692–93.

Elo, Irma T. 2007. "Mortality: Transitions and Measures." Pp. 3096–102 in *The Blackwell Encyclopedia of Sociology*, edited by George Ritzer. Malden, MA: Blackwell.

Elster, Jon. 1999. *An Introduction to Karl Marx*. New York: Cambridge University Press.

Emerson, R., ed. 2001. *Contemporary Field Research: Perspectives and Formulations*. 2nd ed. Longrove, IL: Waveland Press.

Encyclopedia Brittannica Inc. 2010. *The Encyclopedia Britannica*. Chicago.

Engels, Friedrich. [1884] 1970. *The Origins of the Family, Private Property and the State*. New York: International Publishers.

Engels, Friedrich. [1884] 2010. *The Origin of the Family, Private Property and the State*. New York: Penguin Classics.

England, Paula. 2010. "The Gender Revolution: Uneven and Stalled." *Gender & Society* 24(2):149–66.

England, Paula, and Kathryn Edin. 2009. "Briefing Paper: Unmarried Couples With Children: Why Don't They Marry? How Can Policy-Makers Promote More Stable Relationships?" Pp. 307–12 in *Families as They Really Are*, edited by Barbara J. Risman. New York: Norton.

EnglishEnglish.com. N.d. "The English Language: Facts and Figures." Retrieved January 3, 2012 (http://www.englishenglish.com/english_facts_8.htm).

Entwhistle, Joanne. 2009. *The Aesthetic Economy of Fashion: Markets and Value in Clothing and Modelling (Dress, Body, Culture)*. Berg.

Entwisle, Doris, Karl Alexander, and Linda Olson. 1998. *Children, Schools, and Inequality*. Boulder, CO: Westview Press.

Epstein, Cynthia Fuchs. 1988. *Deceptive Distinctions: Sex, Gender, and the Social Order*. New Haven, CT: Yale University Press.

Epstein, Steve. 2009. *Inclusion: The Politics of Difference in Medical Research*. Chicago: University of Chicago Press.

Eriksen, Thomas Hylland. 2007. "Steps to an Ecology of Transnational Sports." In *Globalization and Sport*, edited by Richard Giulianotti and Ronald Robertson. Malden, MA: Blackwell.

Eriksen, Thomas Hylland. 2010. *Ethnicity and Nationalism: Anthropological Perspectives*. 3rd ed. Sidmouth, England: Pluto Press.

Eriksen, Thomas Hylland. 2012. "Ethnicity." Pp. 551–558 in *The Wiley-Blackwell Encyclopedia of Globalization*, edited by George Ritzer. Malden, MA: Wiley-Blackwell.

Erikson, Erik. 1994. *Identity and the Life Cycle*. New York: Norton.

Erikson, Kai T. 1964. "Notes on the Sociology of Deviance." Pp. 9–22 in *The Other Side: Perspectives on Deviance*, edited by Howard S. Becker. New York: Free Press.

Erikson, Kai. 1978. *Everything in Its Path*. New York: Simon & Schuster Paperbacks.

Erlanger, Steven. 2008. "Tense Rivalries Threaten a Melting-Pot District." *The New York Times*, September 24, p. A11.

Erlanger, Steven. 2010a. "Expulsion of Roma Raises Questions in France." *The New York Times*, August 19.

Erlanger, Steven. 2010b. "A French Castle Built of Stone and Dreams." *The New York Times*, August 1.

Erlanger, Steven. 2010c. "Utopian Dream Becomes Battleground in France." *The New York Times*, August 9, p. A7.

Ertman, Thomas. 1997. *Birth of the Leviathan*. Cambridge: Cambridge University Press.

Esping-Anderson, Gosta. 1990. *The Three Worlds of Welfare Capitalism*. Princeton, NJ: Princeton University Press.

Etzioni, Amitai, ed. 1969. *The Semi-Professions and Their Organization: Teachers, Nurses, and Social Workers*. New York: Free Press.

Eurostat. 2008. *European Statistics Database*. Retrieved May 13, 2013 (http://epp.eurostat.ec.europa.eu/portal/page/portal/eurostat/home).

Ezzy, D. 1993. "Unemployment and Mental Health: A Critical Review." *Social Science and Medicine* 37:41–52.

Fackler, Martin. 2008. "Losing an Edge, Japanese Envy India's Schools." *The New York Times*, January 2, pp. A1, A9.

Fackler, Martin. 2011. "Severed From the World, Villagers Survive on Tight Bonds and To-Do Lists." *The New York Times*, March 23. Retrieved March 29, 2012 (http://www.nytimes.com/2011/03/24/world/asia/24isolated.html?adxnnl=1&adxnnlx=1332612166-pPLwIe5hgFAW4cQM2m4bWQ).

Faderman, Lillian. 1991. *Odd Girls and Twilight Lovers: A History of Lesbian Life in Twentieth Century America*. New York: Penguin.

Fadiman, Anne. 1997. *The Spirit Catches You and You Fall Down: A Hmong Child, Her Doctors, and the Collision of Two Cultures*. New York: Farrar, Straus & Giroux.

Fahim, Kareem. 2010. "Away From Home, Fleeing Domestic Life: Immigrant Maids Suffer Abuse in Kuwait." *The New York Times*, August 2, pp. A4, A8.

Faist, Thomas. 2012. "Migration." Pp. 1384–88 in *The Wiley-Blackwell Encyclopedia of Globalization*, edited by George Ritzer. Malden, MA: Wiley-Blackwell.

"Family Caregiver Role Acquisition: Role-Making Through Situated Interaction." 1995. *Research and Theory for Nursing Practice* 9(3):211–26.

Fantasia, Rick. 1992. "The Assault on American Labor." In *Social Problems,* edited by Craig Calhoun and George Ritzer. New York: McGraw-Hill.

Fantasia, Rick, and Kim Voss. 2007. "Labor Movement." Pp. 2518–21 in *The Blackwell Encyclopedia of Sociology,* edited by George Ritzer. Malden, MA: Blackwell.

Farley, John E. 2007. "Metropolitan Statistical Area." Pp. 2993–96 in *The Blackwell Encyclopedia of Sociology,* edited by George Ritzer. Malden, MA: Blackwell.

Farley, John E. 2009. *Majority-Minority Relations.* 6th ed. New Jersey: Prentice-Hall.

Farmer, Charles M. 2003. "Reliability of Police-Reported Information for Determining Crash and Injury Severity." *Traffic Injury Prevention* 4(1):38–44.

Farr, Kathryn. 2005. *Sex Trafficking: The Global Market in Women and Children.* New York: Worth.

Fassmann, Heinz, and Rainer Munz. 1992. "Patterns and Trends of International Migration in Western Europe." *Population and Development Review* 18:457–80.

Fausto-Sterling, A. 1999. "The Five Sexes: Why Female and Male Are Not Enough." *The Sciences* (March/April):20–24.

Feagin, Joe R. 2006. *Systemic Racism: A Theory of Oppression.* New York: Routledge.

Feagin, Joe R. 2010. *The White Racial Frame: Centuries of Racial Framing and Counter-Framing.* New York: Routledge.

Feagin, Joe R., and Harlan Hahn. 1973. *Ghetto Revolts: The Politics of Violence in American Cities.* New York: Macmillan.

Feagin, Joe, Anthony Orum, and Gideon Sjoberg, eds. 1991. *A Case for the Case Study.* North Carolina: University of North Carolina Press.

Feagin, Joe R., and Brittany Chevon Slatton. 2012. "Racial and Ethnic Issues: Critical Race Approaches in the United States." In *The New Blackwell Companion to Sociology*, edited by George Ritzer. Malden, MA: Wiley-Blackwell.

Federal Bureau of Investigation. 2002–2005. "Terrorism." Retrieved March 29, 2012 (http://www.fbi.gov/stats-services/publications/terrorism-2002-2005/terror02_05).

Federal Bureau of Investigation. 2009. "Crime in the United States 2008." Retrieved April 21, 2010 (http://www.fbi.gov/ucr/cius2008/arrests/index.html).

Federal Statistical Office. 2012. "Swiss Statistics: The Statistical Encyclopedia." Swiss Federal Statistical Office. Retrieved February 28, 2012 (http://www.bfs.admin.ch/bfs/portal/en/index/infothek/lexikon.topic.1.html).

Federation of Medical Women of Canada. 2010. "Report to the House of Commons Standing Committee on the Status of Women" (by Dr. K. Gartke and Dr. J. Dollin), April 19.

Fehr, Ernst, Urs Fischbacher, and Simon Gächter. 2002. "Strong Reciprocity, Human Cooperation, and the Enforcement of Social Norms." *Human Nature* 13(1):1–25.

Fellner, Kim. 2008. *Wrestling with Starbucks: Conscience, Capital, and Cappuccino.* New Haven, NJ: Rutgers University Press.

Ferguson, Ann Arnett. 2001. *Bad Boys: Public Schools in the Making of Black Masculinity.* University of Michigan Press.

Fernandez, Bina. 2010. "Cheap and Disposable? The Impact of the Global Economic Crisis on the Migration of Ethiopian Women Domestic Workers to the Gulf." *Gender and Development* 8(2):249–62.

Ferraro, Emilia. 2011. "Trueque: An Ethnographic Account of Barter, Trade and Money in Andean Ecuador." *The Journal of Latin American and Caribbean Anthropology* 16:168–84.

Ferreira, Vitor Sergio. Forthcoming. "Becoming a Heavily Tattooed Young Body: From a Bodily Experience to a Body Project." *Youth & Society.*

Fiddian-Qasmiyeh, Elena. 2012. "Diaspora." Pp. 430–33 in *The Wiley-Blackwell Encyclopedia of Globalization,* edited by George Ritzer. Malden, MA: Wiley-Blackwell.

Fielding, A. J. 1989. "Migration and Urbanization in Western Europe Since 1950." *The Geographical Journal* 155:60–69.

Fierlbeck, Katherine. 2011. *Health Care in Canada: A Citizen's Guide to Policy and Politics.* Toronto, ON: University of Toronto Press.

Fillipi, Veronique, Carine Ronsman, Oona MR Campbell, Wendy J. Graham, Anne Mills, Jo Borghi, Marjorie Koblinsky, and David Osrin. 2006. "Maternal Health in Poor Countries: The Broader Context and a Call for Action." *The Lancet* 368:1525–41.

Fine, Gary. 1987. *With the Boys: Little League Baseball and Preadolescent Culture.* Chicago: University of Chicago.

Fine, Mark A. 2007. "Children and Divorce." Pp. 467–71 in *The Blackwell Encyclopedia of Sociology,* edited by George Ritzer. Malden, MA: Blackwell.

Firebaugh, Glenn, and Brian Goesling. 2007. "Globalization and Global Inequalities: Recent Trends." Pp. 549–64 in *The Blackwell Companion to Globalization,* edited by George Ritzer. Malden, MA : Blackwell.

Fisher, Dana. 2012. "Environmental Activism." Pp. 517–19 in *The Wiley-Blackwell Encyclopedia of Globalization,* edited by George Ritzer. Malden, MA: Wiley-Blackwell.

Fisher, William F., and Thomas Ponniah. 2003. *Another World Is Possible: Popular Alternatives to Globalization at the World Social Forum.* London: Zed Books.

Fitzgerald, Patrick, and Brian Lambkin. 2008. *Migration in Irish History 1607–2007.* New York: Palgrave Macmillan.

Flanigan, James. 2008. "Passports Essential for the M.B.A.'s." *The New York Times,* February 21, p. C5.

Flavin, Jeanne. 2008. *Our Bodies, Our Crimes.* New York University Press.

Florida, Richard, Tim Gulden, and Charlotta Mellander. 2007. *The Rise of the Mega-Region.* Joseph L. Rotman School of Management, The Martin Prosperity Institute, University of Toronto.

Flynn, Nicole. 2007. "Deindustrialization." Pp. 992–94 in *The Blackwell Encyclopedia of Sociology,* edited by George Ritzer. Malden, MA: Blackwell.

Flynn, Sean. 2011. "The Sex Trade." Pp. 41–66 in *Deviant Globalization: Black Market Economy in the 21st Century,* edited by Nils Gilman, Jesse Goldhammer, and Steven Weber. London: Continuum.

FM Signal. 2010. "Morgan Stanley: Internet Trends." SlideShare, June 7. Retrieved March 31, 2012 (http://www.slideshare.net/CMSummit/ms-internet-trends060710final).

Fogiel-Bijaoui, Silvie. 2007. "Women in the Kibbutz: The 'Mixed Blessing' of Neo-Liberalism." *Nashim: A Journal of Jewish Women's Studies & Gender Issues* 13(Spring):102–22.

Fogiel-Bijaoui, Sylvie. 2009. "Kibbutz." *Jewish Women: A Comprehensive Historical Encyclopedia,* March 1. Jewish Women's Archive. Retrieved September 10, 2011 (http://jwa.org/encyclopedia/article/kibbutz).

Fontana, Andrea. 2007. "Interviewing, Structured, Unstructured, and Postmodern." Pp. 2407–11 in *The Blackwell Encyclopedia of Sociology,* edited by George Ritzer. Malden, MA: Blackwell.

Foot, David, and Rosemary Venne. 2011. "The Long Goodbye: Age, Demographics, and Flexibility in Retirement." *Canadian Studies in Population* 38(3–4):59–74.

Fortin, Nicole, David Green, Thomas Lemieux, Kevin Milligan, and Craig Riddell. 2012. "Canadian Inequality: Recent Developments and Policy Options." *Canadian Public Policy* 38(2):121–45.

Foschi, Martha. 2000. "Double Standards for Competence: Theory and Research." *Annual Review of Sociology* 26:21–42.

Foster, Daniel. 2011. "Koch Responds to Buffett's Call for Tax Hikes." *National Review Online.* Retrieved August 26, 2011 (http://www.nationalreview.com/corner/275099/koch-responds-buffetts-call-tax-hikes-daniel-foster#).

Foucault, Michel. 1975. *The Birth of the Clinic: An Archaeology of Medical Perception.* New York: Vintage.

Foucault, Michel. [1975] 1979. *Discipline and Punish: The Birth of the Prison.* New York: Vintage.

Foucault, Michel. 1978. *The History of Sexuality: Volume 1. An Introduction.* New York: Vintage.

Fourcade, Marion. 2009. *Economists and Societies: Discipline and Profession in the United States, Britain, and France, 1890s to 1990s.* Princeton, NJ: Princeton University Press.

Fourcade-Gourinchas, Marion. 2007. "Culture, Economy and." Pp. 932–36 in *The Blackwell Encyclopedia of Sociology,* edited by George Ritzer. Malden, MA: Blackwell.

"14 Cool Vending Machines from Japan." 2009. Toxel.com, June 8. Retrieved August 25, 2011 (www.toxel.com/tech/2009/06/08/14-cool-vending-machines-from-Japan/).

Fox, Bonnie. 2009. *Family Patterns, Gender Relations.* 3rd ed. Toronto: Oxford University Press.

Fox, Susannah, Kathryn Zickuhr, and Aaron Smith. 2009. "Twitter and Status Updating," October 21. Retrieved March 29, 2012 (http://www.pewinternet.org/Reports/2009/17-Twitter-and-Status-Updating-Fall-2009.aspx?r=1).

Frailing, Kelly, Jr., and Dee Wood Harper. 2010. "The Social Construction of Deviance, Conflict and the Criminalization of Midwives, New Orleans: 1940s and 1950s." *Deviant Behavior* 31:729–55.

France, Anatole. [1894] 2011. *The Red Lily.* Kindle edition.

Francis, Mark. 2011. "Herbert Spencer." Pp. 165–84 in *The Wiley-Blackwell Companion to Major Social Theorists: Volume 1. Classical Theorists,* edited by George Ritzer and Jeffrey Stepnisky. Malden, MA: Wiley-Blackwell.

Frank, David John. 2012. "Sex." Pp. 1843–47 in *The Wiley-Blackwell Companion to Sociology,* edited by George Ritzer. Malden, MA: Wiley-Blackwell.

Frank, David John, and Elizabeth H. McEneaney. 1999. "The Individualization of Society and the Liberalization of State Policies on Same Sex Sexual Relations, 1984–1995." *Social Forces* 77:911–44.

Frank, Robert H., 2011. *The Darwin Economy: Liberty, Competition, and the Common Good.* Princeton, NJ: Princeton University Press.

Frank, Robert H., and Philip J. Cook. 1995. *The Winner-Take-All Society.* New York: Penguin.

Franklin, V. P. 1987. "W. E. B. Du Bois as Journalist." *The Journal of Negro Education* 56(Spring):40–44.

Freedman, Russell. 2009. *Freedom Walkers: The Story of the Montgomery Bus Boycott.* Holiday House.

Freeland, Chrystia. 2011. "The Rise of the New Global Elite." *The Atlantic,* January/February. Retrieved August 26, 2011 (http://www.theatlantic.com/magazine/print/2011/01/the-rise-of-the-new-global-elite/8343/).

Freeman, Carla. 2001. "Is Local: Global as Feminine: Masculine? Rethinking the Gender of Globalization." *Signs: Journal of Women in Culture and Society* 26(4):1007–37.

Freeman, Richard B., and James L. Medoff. 1984. *What Do Unions Do?* New York: Basic Books.

Freidrichs, Robert. 1970. *A Sociology of Sociology.* New York: Free Press.

Freidson, Eliot. 1970a. *Profession of Medicine.* New York: Dodd, Mead.

Freidson, Eliot. 1970b. *Professional Dominance.* New York: Atheron.

French, Howard W. 2008. "Great Firewall of China Faces Online Rebels." *The New York Times,* February 4.

Frenette, Marc. 2005. *Is Post-secondary Access More Equitable in Canada or the United States?* Ottawa: Statistics Canada, Analytical Studies Branch, Catalogue no. 11F0019MIE No. 244.

Frenette, Marc, and Simon Coulombe, 2007 "Has Higher Education among Young Women Substantially Reduced the Gender Gap in Employment and Earnings?", Statistics Canada Catalogue no. 11F0019MIF—No. 301, Analytical Studies Branch Research Paper Series, Ottawa.

Freud, Sigmund. 2006. *The Penguin Freud Reader.* New York: Penguin.

Freudenheim, Milt. 2009. "Tool in Cystic Fibrosis Fight: A Registry." *The New York Times,* December 22, p. D1.

Freudenheim, Milt. 2010. "In Haiti, Practicing Medicine from Afar." *The New York Times,* February 9.

Frideres, Jim, and René Gadacz. 2011. First Nations in the Twenty-first Century. 9th ed. Toronto, ON: Oxford University Press.

Friedan, Betty. 1963. *The Feminine Mystique.* New York: Dell.

Friedman, Debra, and Michael Hechter. 1988. "The Contribution of Rational Choice Theory to Macrosociological Research." *Sociological Theory* 6:201–18.

Friedman, Jonathan. 1986. "The World City Hypothesis." *Development and Change* 17.

Friedman, Jonathan. 1994. *Culture Identity and Global Processes.* London: Sage.

Frieden, Jeffry A. 2006. *Global Capitalism: Its Fall and Rise in the Twentieth Century.* New York: Norton.

Friedkin, N. E. 2001. "Norm Formation in Social Influence Networks." *Social Networks* 23(3):167–89.

Friedman, Judith J. 2007. "Suburbs." Pp. 4878–81 in *The Blackwell Encyclopedia of Sociology,* edited by George Ritzer. Malden, MA: Blackwell.

Friedman, Thomas. 1999. *The Lexus and the Olive Tree.* New York: Farrar, Straus & Giroux.

Friedman, Thomas. 2005. *The World Is Flat: A Brief History of the Twenty-first Century.* New York: Farrar, Straus & Giroux.

Friedrichs, David O. 2007. "Organizational Deviance." Pp. 3303–306 in *The Blackwell Encyclopedia of Sociology,* edited by George Ritzer. Malden, MA: Blackwell.

Friedrichs, Robert. 1970. *A Sociology of Sociology.* New York: Free Press.

Frieze, Irene Hanson. 2007. "Love and Commitment." Pp. 2671–74 in *The Blackwell Encyclopedia of Sociology,* edited by George Ritzer. Malden, MA: Blackwell.

Fritsch, Jane. 2001, September 12. "A Day of Terror: The Response; Rescue Workers Rush In, and Many Do Not Return." *The New York Times,* September 12 .Retrieved March 29, 2012 (http://www.nytimes.com/2001/09/12/us/a-day-of-terror-the-response-rescue-workers-rush-in-and-many-do-not-return.html?ref=sept112001).

Fulbrook, Julian. 2007. "Tobacco." Pp. 1146–49 in *Encyclopedia of Globalization,* edited by Jan Aart Scholte and Roland Robertson. New York: MTM Publishing.

Fuller, Sylvia 2009. "Investigating Longitudinal Dimensions of Precarious Employment: Conceptual and Practical Issues." In *Gender and the Contours of Precarious Employment,* edited by Leah Vosko, Martha MacDonald, and Iain Campbell. London: Routledge.

Fuller, Sylvia, and Leah Vosko. 2008. "Temporary Employment and Social Inequality in Canada: Exploring Intersections of Gender, Race and Immigration Status." *Social Indicators Research* 88(1):31–50.

Fung, A. 2004. *Empowered Participation: Reinventing Urban Democracy.* Princeton, NJ: Princeton University Press.

Gabriel, Trip. 2010. "For Students in Internet Age, No Shame in Copy and Paste." *The New York Times,* August 2, pp. A1, A10.

Gadsden, Gloria. 2007. "Gender, Deviance and." Pp. 1856–58 in *The Blackwell Encyclopedia of Sociology,* edited by George Ritzer. Malden, MA: Blackwell.

Gaio, Fatima Janine. 1995. "Women in Software Programming: The Experience in Brazil." In *Women Encounter Technology,* edited by Swasti Mitter and Sheila Rowbotham. London: Routledge.

Gallegos, Jodi. 2008. "Basic Skateboarding Terminology: Beginner's Terms for Skateboard Tricks and Styles." Outdoor and Recreation Suite 101, ExtremeSports, March 5. Retrieved August 26, 2011 (www.suite101.com/content/basic-skateboarding-terminology-a46799).

Galston, William A., Steven Kull, and Clay Ramsay. 2009. *Battleground or Common Ground? American Public Opinion on Health Care Reform.* Washington, DC: Brookings Institution.

Gamoran, A., M. Nystrand, M. Berends, and P. C. LePore. 1995. "An Organizational Analysis of the Effects of Ability Grouping." *American Educational Research Journal* 32:687–715.

Gangl, Markus. 2007. "Welfare State." Pp. 5242–46 in *The Blackwell Encyclopedia of Sociology,* edited by George Ritzer. Malden, MA: Blackwell.

Gamoran, A., and R. Mare. 1989. "Secondary School Tracking and Educational Inequality: Compensation, Reinforcement, or Neutrality?" *American Journal of Sociology* 94:1146–83.

Gannon, Marie. 2001. "Crime Comparisons between Canada and the United States." *Juristat* 21(11). Statistics Canada Catalogue no. 85-002-X.

Gans, Herbert. 1962. *The Urban Villagers.* New York: Free Press.

Gans, Herbert. 1967. *The Levittowners.* New York: Columbia University Press.

Gans, Herbert. 1979. *Deciding What's News.* New York: Pantheon.

Gans, Herbert. 1999. *Popular Culture and High Culture: An Analysis and Evaluation of Taste.* New York: Basic Books.

Gans, Herbert J. 2003. *Democracy and the News.* New York: Oxford University Press.

Gans, Herbert J. 2009. "First Generation Decline: Downward Mobility among Refugees and Immigrants." *Ethnic and Racial Studies* 32:1658–70.

Gardner, Margo, and Laurence Steinberg. 2005. "Peer Influence on Risk Taking, Risk Preference, and Risky Decision Making in Adolescence and Adulthood: An Experimental Study." *Developmental Psychology* 41:625–35.

Garfield, Bob. 1991. "How I Spent (and Spent and Spent) My Disney Vacation." *The Washington Post,* July 7, p. B5.

Garfinkel, Harold. 1967. *Studies in Ethnomethodology.* Malden, MA: Blackwell.

Garon, Sheldon. 2006. "Japan Post-War 'Consumer Revolution,' or 'Striking a 'Balance' between Consumption and Saving." In *Consuming Cultures, Global Perspectives: Historical Trajectories, Transnational Exchanges,* edited by John Brewer and Frank Trentmann. Oxford: Berg.

Garreau, Joel. 1991. *Edge City: Life on the New Frontier.* New York: Doubleday.

Garrett, William R. 2007. "Christianity." Pp. 139–44 in *Encyclopedia of Globalization,* edited by Jan Aart Scholte and Roland Robertson. New York: MTM Publishing.

Gartner, Rosemary, Cheryl Webster, and Anthony Doob. 2009. "Trends in the Imprisonment of Women in Canada." *Canadian Journal of Criminology and Criminal Justice* 51(2):169–98.

Gates, Katherine. 1999. *Deviant Desires: Incredibly Strange Sex.* New York: Juno Books.

Gawande, Atul. 2011. "The Hot Spotters." *The New Yorker,* January 24.

Geertz, Clifford. 1973. *The Interpretation of Cultures.* New York: Basic Books.

Geis, Gilbert. 2007a. "Crime, Corporate." Pp. 826–28 in *The Blackwell Encyclopedia of Sociology,* edited by George Ritzer. Malden, MA: Blackwell.

Geis, Gilbert. 2007b. "Crime, White-Collar." Pp. 850–51 in *The Blackwell Encyclopedia of Sociology,* edited by George Ritzer. Malden, MA: Blackwell.

Genosko, Gary. 1994. *Baudrillard and Signs: Signification Ablaze.* London: Routledge.

George, Kimberly. 2007. "Women's Movements." Pp. 1257–60 in *Encyclopedia of Globalization,* edited by Jan Aart Scholte and Ronald Robertson. New York: MTM Publishing.

George, Sheba. 2000. "'Dirty Nurses' and 'Men Who Play': Gender and Class in Transnational Migration." Pp. 144–74 in *Global Ethnography: Forces, Connections, and Imaginations in a Postmodern World,* edited by Michael Burawoy et al. Berkeley: University of California Press.

Gerami, Shahin, and Melodye Lehnerer. 2007. "Gendered Aspects of War and International Violence." Pp. 1885–88 in *The Blackwell Encyclopedia of Sociology,* edited by George Ritzer. Malden, MA: Blackwell.

Gereffi, Gary. 2005. "The Global Economy: Organization, Governance, and Development." In *Handbook of Economic Sociology,* edited by Neil Smelser and Richard Swedberg. Princeton, NJ: Princeton University Press.

Gereffi, Gary. 2009. "Development Models and Industrial Upgrading in China and Mexico." *European Sociological Review* 25:37–51.

Gerhardt, H. Carl and Franz Huber. 2002. *Acoustic Communication in Insects and Anurans: Common Problems and Diverse Solutions.* Chicago: University of Chicago Press.

Gershon, Ilana. 2010. *The Break-Up 2.0.* Ithaca, NY: Cornell University Press.

Gerth, Hans, and C. Wright Mills, eds. 1958. *From Max Weber.* New York: Oxford University Press.

Gettleman, Jeffrey. 2010. "4-Day Frenzy of Rape in Congo Reveals U.N. Troops' Weakness." *The New York Times,* October 4, pp. A1, A3.

Giddens, Anthony. 1984. *The Constitution of Society: Outline of the Theory of Structuration.* Berkeley: University of California Press.

Giddens, Anthony. 1992. *The Transformation of Intimacy: Sexuality, Love and Eroticism in Modern Societies.* Stanford, CA: Stanford University Press.

Giridharadas, Anand. 2010. "Getting In (and Out of) Line." *The New York Times,* August 8. Retrieved November 9, 2011 (http://www.nytimes.com/2010/08/07/world/asia/07iht-currents.html).

Giridharadas, Anand, and Keith Bradsher. 2006. "Microloan Pioneer and His Bank Win Nobel Peace Prize." *The New York Times,* October 13.

Gilman, Nils, Jesse Goldhammer, and Steven Weber. 2011. *Deviant Globalization: Black Market Economy in the 21st Century.* London: Continuum.

Gilmore, Jason, and Sébastien LaRochelle-Côté. 2011. "Inside the Labour Market Downturn." *Perspectives on Labour and Income* Statistics Canada 23(1):3–14.

Gilroy, Paul. 1993. *The Black Atlantic: Modernity and Double Consciousness.* London: Verso.

Gimlin, Debra. 2000. "Cosmetic Surgery: Beauty as Commodity." *Qualitative Sociology* 23(1):77–98.

Gimlin, Debra. 2007. "Accounting for Cosmetic Surgery in the USA and Great Britain: A Cross-cultural Analysis of Women's Narratives." *Body and Society* 13:41–60.

Ginn, Diana. 1986. "Indian Hunting Rights: *Dick v. R., Jack and Charlie v. R. and Simon v. R.*" *McGill Law Journal* 31:527–50.

Giroux, Henry, and David E. Purpel, eds. 1983. *The Hidden Curriculum and Moral Education.* Berkeley, CA: McCutchan.

Gitlin, Todd. 1980. *The Whole World Is Watching.* Berkeley: University of California Press.

Gitlin, Todd. 1993. *The Sixties: Years of Hope, Days of Rage.* New York: Bantam.

Gittins, Diana. 1993. *The Family in Question.* New York: Macmillan.

Gladwell, Malcolm. 2000. *The Tipping Point.* New York: Little, Brown.

Gladwell, Malcolm. 2009. *What the Dog Saw.* New York: Little, Brown.

Gladwell, Malcolm. 2010. "Small Change: Why the Revolution Will Not Be Tweeted." *The New Yorker,* October.

Glantz, M. 1977. *Desertification.* Boulder, CO: Westview.

Glasberg, D. S. and D. Shannon. 2011. *Political Sociology: Oppression, Resistance, and the State.* Thousand Oaks, CA: Pine Forge Press.

Glenny, Misha. 2008. *McMafia: A Journey Through the Global Criminal Underworld.* New York: Knopf.

Glickman, Lawrence B. 2009. *Buying Power: A History of Consumer Activism in America.* Chicago: University of Chicago Press.

Gloor, Peter, and Scott Cooper. 2007. *Coolhunting: Chasing Down the Next Big Thing.* New York: AMACOM.

Gmelch, Sharon Bohn, ed. 2010. *Tourists and Tourism: A Reader.* Prospect Heights, IL: Waveland Press.

Godlee, Fiona, Neil Pakenham-Walsh, Dan Ncayiyana, Barbara Cohen, and Abel Packer. 2004. "Can We Achieve Health Information for All by 2015?" *The Lancet* 364:295–300.

Godwyn, Mary, and Jody Hoffer Gittell, eds. 2011. *Sociology of Organizations: Structures and Relationships.* Thousand Oaks, CA: Pine Forge Press.

Goff, Colin, and Charles Reasons. 1978. *Corporate Crime in Canada: A Critical Analysis of Anti-combines Legislation.* Toronto, ON: Prentice-Hall.

Goffman, Erving. 1959. *The Presentation of Self in Everyday Life.* Garden City, NY: Anchor Books.

Goffman, Erving. 1961a. *Asylums: Essays on the Social Situations of Mental Patients and Other Inmates.* Garden City, NY: Anchor Books.

Goffman, Erving. 1961b. *Encounters.* Indianapolis: Bobbs-Merrill.

Goffman, Erving. 1963. *Stigma: Notes on the Management of Spoiled Identity.* Englewood Cliffs, NJ: Prentice-Hall/Spectrum.

Goffman, E. 1979. *Gender Advertisements.* New York: Harper.

Goffman, Erving. 1983. "The Interaction Order." *American Sociological Review* 48:1–17.

Golani, Helena Yakovlev. 2011. "Two Decades of the Russian Federation's Foreign Policy in the Commonwealth of Independent States: The Cases of Belarus and Ukraine." The European Forum at the Hebrew University of Jerusalem. Retrieved March 29, 2012 (http://www.ef.huji.ac.il/publications/Yakovlev%20Golani.pdf).

Goldberg, David Theo. 2009. "Racial Comparisons, Relational Racisms: Some Thoughts on Method." *Ethnic and Racial Studies* 32:1271–82.

Goldberg, Harvey E. 2007. "Judaism." Pp. 690–93 in *Encyclopedia of Globalization,* edited by

Jan Aart Scholte and Roland Robertson. New York: MTM Publishing.

Goldberger, Paul. 2010. "What Happens in Vegas." *The New Yorker,* October 4, pp. 95–96.

Goldburg, Rebecca J. 2008. "Aquaculture, Trade, and Fisheries Linkages: Unexpected Synergies." *Globalization* 5(2):143–50.

Goldfield, Michael. 1987. *The Decline of Organized Labor.* Chicago: University of Chicago Press.

Goldfrank, Walter. 2005. "Fresh Demand: The Consumption of Chilean Produce in the United States." Pp. 42–53 in *The Cultural Politics of Food and Eating: A Reader,* edited by James L. Watson and Melissa L. Caldwell. Malden, MA: Blackwell.

Goldman, R. 2008. "Do It Yourself! Amateur Porn Stars Make Bank." Retrieved October 18, 2010 (http://abcnews.go.com/Business/SmallBiz/story?id=4151592&page=1).

Goldman, Robert, and Stephen Papson. 1998. *Nike Culture.* London: Sage.

Goldscheider, Calvin. 2012. "Judaism." Pp. 1225–34 in *Wiley-Blackwell Enyclopedia of Globalization,* edited by George Ritzer. Malden, MA: Wiley-Blackwell.

Goldstein, Warren. 2009. "Secularization Patterns in the Old Paradigm." *Sociology of Religion* 70:157–78.

Goldstone, Jack. 1991. *Revolution and Rebellion in the Early Modern World.* Berkeley: University of California Press.

Gonzalez, Michelle A. 2010. *Shopping.* Fortress Press.

Goode, Erich. 1996. "Gender and Courtship Entitlement: Responses to Personal Ads." *Sex Roles* 3–4:141–69.

Goode, Erich. 2002. "Sexual Involvement and Social Research in a Fat Civil Rights Organization." *Qualitative Sociology* 25(4):501–34.

Goode, Erich. 2007a. "Deviance." Pp. 1075–82 in *The Blackwell Encyclopedia of Sociology,* edited by George Ritzer. Malden, MA: Blackwell.

Goode, Erich. 2007b. "Deviance: Explanatory Theories of." Pp. 1100–107 in *The Blackwell Encyclopedia of Sociology,* edited by George Ritzer. Malden, MA: Blackwell.

Goode, Erich, and Nachman Ben-Yehuda. 1994. *Moral Panics: The Social Construction of Deviance.* Oxford, UK: Blackwell.

Goode, Erich, and Nachman Ben-Yehuda. 2009. *Moral Panics: The Social Construction of Deviance.* 2nd ed. Malden, MA: Blackwell.

Goode, Erich, and Alex Thio. 2007. "Deviance, Crime and." Pp. 1092–95 in *The Blackwell Encyclopedia of Sociology,* edited by George Ritzer. Malden, MA: Blackwell.

Goode, Erich and, D. Angus Vail. 2007. *Extreme Deviance.* Thousand Oaks, CA: Pine Forge Press.

Goode, William J. 1963. *World Revolution and Family Patterns.* New York: Free Press.

Goode, Williams J. 1959. "The Theoretical Importance of Love." *American Sociological Review* 24:38–47.

Goodlin, Wendi E., and Christopher S. Dunn. 2011. "Three Patterns of Domestic Violence in Households: Single Victimization, Repeat Victimization, and Co-occurring Victimization." *Journal of Family Violence* 26:101–08.

Goodnough, Abby. 2010. "Doctors Point to Caffeinated Alcoholic Drinks' Dangers." *The New York Times,* October 27, p. A12.

Gordon, Richard E., Katherine K. Gordon, and Max Gunther. 1960. *The Split-Level Trap.* New York: Gilbert Geis Associates.

Gorski, Philip S. 2011. "Barack Obama and Civil Religion." Pp. 179–214 in *Rethinking Obama Political Power and Social Theory* (Vol. 22), edited by Julian Go. Emerald Group Publishing.

Gotham, Kevin Fox. 2007. "Megalopolis." Pp. 2942–44 in *The Blackwell Encyclopedia of Sociology,* edited by George Ritzer. Malden, MA: Blackwell:

Gotham, Kevin. 2012. "Urbanization." Pp. 488–503 in *The Wiley-Blackwell Companion to Sociology,* edited by George Ritzer. Malden, MA: Wiley-Blackwell.

Gottdiener, Mark. 2001. *The Theming of America.* 2nd ed. Boulder, CO: Westview Press.

Gottdiener, Mark, Claudia C. Collins, and David R. Dickens. 1999. *Las Vegas: The Social Production of an All-American City.* Malden, MA: Blackwell.

Gottman, Jean. 1961. *Megalopolis: The Urbanized Northeastern Seaboard of the United States.* New York: Twentieth Century Fund.

Gottman, John M., Tames Coan, Sybil Carrere, and Catherine Swanson. 1998. "Predicting Marital Happiness and Stability from Newly Wed Interactions." *Journal of Marriage and the Family* 60:5–22.

Gottschalk, S. 2010. "The Presentation of Avatars in Second Life: Self and Interaction in Social Virtual Spaces." *Symbolic Interaction* 33(4):501–525.

Gould, Kenneth, David N. Pellow, and Allan Schnaiberg. 2008. *The Treadmill of Production: Injustice and Unsustainability in the Global Economy.* Paradigm Publishers.

Gould, Stephen Jay. 1981. *The Mismeasure of Man.* New York: Norton.

Gouldner, Alvin W. 1960. "The Norm of Reciprocity: A Preliminary Statement." *American Sociological Review* 25(2):161–78.

Gouldner, Alvin. 1962. "Anti-Minotaur: The Myth of a Value Free Sociology." *Social Problems* Winter:199–213.

Gove, Walter R. 1980. *The Labelling of Deviance.* Beverly Hills, CA: Sage.

Gove, Walter R. and Michael Hughes. 1979. "Possible Causes of the Apparent Sex Differences in Physical Health: An Empirical Investigation." *American Sociological Review* 44:126–46.

Government of Canada. 2006. *The Human Face of Mental Health and Mental Illness in Canada.* Minister of Public Works and Government Services Canada, Cat. No. HP5-19/2006E

Gowan, Teresa. 2000. "Excavating 'Globalization' from Street Level: Homeless Men Recycle Their Pasts." Pp. 74–105 in *Global Ethnography: Forces, Connections, and Imaginations in a Postmodern World,* edited by Michael Burawoy et al. Berkeley: University of California Press.

Goyder, John. 2009. *The Prestige Squeeze: Occupational Prestige in Canada since 1965.* Montreal: McGill-Queens University Press.

Grabb, Edward. 2007. *Theories of Social Inequality.* 5th ed. Toronto, ON: Thomson Nelson.

Grabb, Edward, and James Curtis. 2010. *Regions Apart: The Four Societies of Canada and the United States.* 2nd ed. Toronto: Oxford.

Grabb, Edward, and Neil Guppy. 2009. *Social Inequality in Canada: Patterns, Problems, and Policies.* 5th ed. Toronto, ON: Pearson Prentice Hall.

Grady, Denise, and William J. Broad. 2011. "Seeing Terror Risk, U.S. Asks Journals to Cut Flu Study Facts." *The New York Times,* December 20. Retrieved May 14, 2013 (http://www.nytimes.com/2011/12/21/health/fearing-terrorism-us-asks-journals-to-censor-articles-on-virus.html?pagewanted=all).

Grandin, Greg. 2010. *Fordlandia: The Rise and Fall of Henry Ford's Forgotten Jungle City.* New York: Picador.

Granovetter, Mark. 1973. "The Strength of Weak Ties." *American Journal of Sociology* 78(6):1360–80.

Granovetter, Mark. 1974. *Getting a Job: A Study of Contacts and Careers.* Cambridge, MA: Harvard University Press.

Gray, Louise. 2009. "McDonald's Waste Makes Up Largest Proportion of Fast Food Litter on Streets." *The Telegraph,* January 13. Retrieved May 26, 2011 (http://www.telegraph.co.uk/earth/earthnews/4223106/McDonalds-waste-makes-up-largest-proportion-of-fast-food-litter-on-streets.html).

Greeley, Andrew M. 1976. "The Ethnic Miracle." *The Public Interest* 45:20–36.

Greenberg, A. 2010. "WikiLeaks' Julian Assange Wants to Spill Your Corporate Secrets." *Forbes* (December):70–86.

Greenberg, Miriam. 2007. *Branding New York: How a City in Crisis Was Sold to the World.* New York: Routledge.

Greenfeld, Lawrence A., and Steven K. Smith. 1999. "American Indians and Crime" (NCJ 173386, Table 3). Office of Justice Programs, Bureau of Justice Statistics. Retrieved March 31, 2012 (http://bjs.ojp.usdoj.gov/content/pub/ascii/aic.txt).

Greenhouse, Steven. 2011. "Union Membership in U.S. Fell to a 70-Year Low Last Year." *The New York Times,* January 21.

Grekul, Jana. 2011. "Building Collective Efficacy and Sustainability into a Community Collaborative: Community Solution to Gang Violence." *Journal of Gang Research* 18(2):23–45.

Gressman, Eugene. 2005. "Judgments Judged and Wrongs Remembered: Examining the Japanese American Civil Liberties Cases on Their Sixtieth Anniversary." *Law and Contemporary Problems* 68:15–27.

Grier, Ronelle. 2010. "Teen Sexting: Technological Trend Can Lead to Tragic Consequences." *Daily Tribune.* Retrieved March 29, 2012 (http://www.dailytribune.com/articles/2010/01/27/news/srv0000007438542.txt?viewmode=fullstory).

Griffin, Sean Patrick. 2007. "Crime, Organized." Pp. 833–34 in *The Blackwell Encyclopedia of Sociology,* edited by George Ritzer. Malden, MA: Blackwell.

Griffith, Alison, and Dorothy E. Smith. 2005. *Mothering for Schooling.* New York: Routledge.

Grigsby, Mary. 2004. *Buying Time and Getting By: The Voluntary Simplicity Movement.* Albany: SUNY Press.

Groenemeyer, Axel. 2007. "Deviant Careers." Pp. 1142–45 in *The Blackwell Encyclopedia of Sociology,* edited by George Ritzer. Malden, MA: Blackwell.

Gronow, Jukka. 2007. "Taste, Sociology of." Pp. 4930–35 in *The Blackwell Encyclopedia of Sociology,* edited by George Ritzer. Malden, MA: Blackwell.

Groseclose, Tim. 2011. *Left Turn: How Liberal Media Bias Distorts the American Mind.* New York: St. Martin's Press.

Gu, Dongfeng, Tanika N. Kelly, Xigui Wu, Jing Chen, Jonathan M. Samet, Jian-feng Huang, Manlu Zhu, Ji-chun Chen, Chung-shiuan Chen, Xiufang Duan, Michael J. Klag, and Jiang He. 2009. "Mortality Attributable to Smoking in China." *New England Journal of Medicine* 360:150–59.

Guhathakurta, Subhrajit, David Jacobson, and Nicholas C. DelSordi. 2007. "The End of Globalization? The Implications of Migration for State, Society and Economy." Pp. 201–15 in *The Blackwell Companion to Globalization,* edited by George Ritzer. Malden, MA: Blackwell.

Guillen, Mario F. 2010. "Classical Sociological Approaches to the Study of Leadership." Pp. 223–38 in *Handbook of Leadership Theory and Practice,* edited by Nitin Nohria and Rakesh Khurana. Boston: Harvard University Press.

Guo, Guang, Michael E. Roettger, and Tianji Cai. 2008. "The Integration of Genetic Propensities into Social-Control Models of Delinquency and Violence among Male Youths." *American Sociological Review* 73(4):543–68.

Guppy, Neil, and George Gray. 2008. *Successful Surveys: Research Methods and Practice.* Toronto, ON: Thomson-Nelson.

Guppy, Neil, and Robin Hawkshaw. 2009. "Defining, Measuring, and Reducing Poverty." Pp. 106–115 in *Social Inequality in Canada: Patterns, Problems, and Policies,* 5th ed., edited by Edward Grabb and Neil Guppy. Toronto: Prentice-Hall.

Guppy, Neil, and Katherine Lyon. 2011. "Multiculturalism, Education Practices, and Colonial Legacies: The Canadian Case." Pp. 114–135 in *The Politics of Education: Challenging Multiculturalism,* edited by Christos Kassimeris and Marios Vryonides. London: Routledge.

Habermas, Jürgen. 1975. *Legitimation Crisis.* Boston: Beacon Press.

Haddad, Emma. 2008. "The Refugee: The Individual Between Sovereigns." *Global Society* 17(3).

Hadden, Wilbur C. and Raul D. Rockswold. 2008. "Increasing Differential Mortality by Educational Attainment in Adults in the United States." *IJHS* 38(1):47–61.

Hadjicostandi, Joanna. 2007. "Migration: Undocumented/Illegal." Pp. 3031–34 in *The Blackwell Encyclopedia of Sociology,* edited by George Ritzer. Malden, MA: Blackwell.

Hafferty, Frederic, and Brian Castellani. 2011. "Two Cultures: Two Ships: The Rise of a Professionalism Movement within Modern Medicine and Medical Sociology's Disappearance from the Professionalism Debate." Pp. 201–20 in *Handbook of the Sociology of Health, Illness, and Healing,* edited by Bernice Pescosolido et al. Dordrecht, Netherlands: Springer.

Hagan, John. 1989. *Structural Criminology.* New Brunswick, NJ: Rutgers University Press.

Hage, Jerald, and Charles H. Powers. 1992. *Post Industrial Lives: Roles and Relationships in the 21st Century.* Newbury Park, CA: Sage.

Haggerty, Kevin. 2001. *Making Crime Count.* Toronto: University of Toronto Press.

Haggerty, Kevin. 2004. "Ethics Creep: Governing Social Science Research in the Name of Ethics." *Qualitative Sociology* 27(4):391–414.

Hajnal, Zoltan L., and Taeku Lee. 2011. *Why Americans Don't Join the Party: Race, Immigration, and the Failure (of Political Parties) to Engage the Electorate.* Princeton, NJ: Princeton University Press.

Hall, Elaine J., and Marnie Salupo Rodriguez. 2003. "The Myth of Postfeminism." *Gender & Society* 17(6):878–902.

Hall, Jason K. 2012a. "Malaria." Pp. 1319–20 in *The Wiley-Blackwell Encyclopedia of Globalization,* edited by George Ritzer. Malden, MA: Wiley-Blackwell.

Hall, Jason K. 2012b. "Tuberculosis." Pp. 2051–53 in *The Wiley-Blackwell Encyclopedia of Globalization,* edited by George Ritzer. Malden, MA: Wiley-Blackwell.

Hall, Peter, and David Soskice, eds. 2001. *Varieties of Capitalism: The Institutional Foundations of Comparative Advantage.* Oxford University Press.

Hall, S. 1980. "Encoding and Decoding." In *Culture, Media, Language: Working Papers in Cultural Studies.* London: Hutchinson.

Halle, David. [1993] 2007. *Inside Culture.* Chicago: University of Chicago Press.

Halle, David. 2007. "Highbrow/Lowbrow." Pp. 2123–26 in *The Blackwell Encyclopedia of Sociology,* edited by George Ritzer. Malden, MA: Blackwell.

Hamilton, Laura, and Brian Powell. 2007. "Hidden Curriculum." Pp. 2116–18 in *The Blackwell Encyclopedia of Sociology,* edited by George Ritzer. Malden, MA: Blackwell.

Hamilton, M. C., D. Anderson, M. Broaddus, and K. Young. 2006. "Gender Stereotyping and Under-representation of Female Characters in 200 Popular Children's Picture Books: A Twenty-first Century Update." *Sex Roles* 55:757–65.

Hammersley, Martyn. 2007. "Ethnography." Pp. 1479–83 in *The Blackwell Encyclopedia of Sociology,* edited by George Ritzer. Malden, MA: Blackwell.

Handelman, Jay M., and Robert V. Kozinets. 2007. "Culture Jamming." Pp. 945–46 in *The Blackwell Encyclopedia of Sociology,* edited by George Ritzer. Malden, MA: Blackwell.

Hankin, Janet R., and Eric R. Wright. 2010. "Reflections on Fifty Years of Medical Sociology." *Journal of Health and Social Behavior* 51:S10–S14.

Hannigan, John. 1998. *Fantasy City: Pleasure and Profit in the Postmodern Metropolis.* London: Routledge.

Hannigan, John. 2007. "Fantasy City." Pp. 1641–44 in *The Blackwell Encyclopedia of Sociology,* edited by George Ritzer. Malden, MA: Blackwell.

Hanser, Amy. 2008. *Service Encounters: Class, Gender, and the Market for Social Distinction in Urban China.* Stanford University Press.

Hanson, Andrew, and Zackary Hawley. 2010. "Do Landlords Discriminate in the Rental Housing Market? Evidence from an Internet Field Experiment in US Cities." *Journal of Urban Economics.* Retrieved March 30, 2012 (http://www.sciencedirect.com/science/article/pii/S0094119008000181).

Hanson, Andrew, and Zachary Hawley. 2011. "Do Landlords Discriminate in the Rental Housing Market? Evidence from an Internet Field Experiment in U.S. Cities." *Journal of Urban Economics* 70(2–3):99–114.

Hanushek, Eric, and Steven Rivkin. 2006. "School Quality and the Black-White Achievement Gap" (Working Paper No. 12651). Cambridge, MA: National Bureau of Economic Research.

Haraway, Donna. 1991. "A Cyborg Manifesto: Science, Technology, and Socialist-feminism in the Late Twentieth Century." Pp. 149–81 in *Simians, Cyborgs and Women: The Reinvention of Nature.* New York: Routledge.

Harder, Lois. 2011. *After the Nuclear Age? Some Contemporary Developments in Families and Family Law in Canada.* Ottawa, ON: The Vanier Institute of the Family.

Hare, Bruce. 2001. "Black Youth at Risk." Pp. 97–113 in *Race Odyssey: African Americans and Sociology,* edited by Bruce Hare. Syracuse, NY: Syracuse University Press.

Hare, Jan. 2007. "First Nations Education Policy in Canada: Building Capacity for Change and Control." Pp. 51–68 in *Multicultural Education Policies in Canada and the United*

States, edited by R. Joshee and L. Johnson. Vancouver: UBC Press.

Hargrove, Barbara. 1989. *Sociology of Religion: Classical and Contemporary Approaches.* 2nd ed. Arlington Heights, IL: Harlan Davidson.

Harmon, Corinne, Glenda Carne, Kristina Lizardy-Hajbi, and Eugene Wilkerson. 2010. "Access to Higher Education for Undocumented Students: 'Outlaws' of Social Justice, Equity, and Equality." *Journal of Praxis in Multicultural Education* 5(1): 67–82.

Harper, Douglas. 1982. *Good Company.* Chicago: University of Chicago Press.

Harrison, B. 1994. *Lean and Mean: The Changing Landscape of Corporate Power in the Age of Flexibility.* New York: Basic Books.

Harrison, Michelle. 1982. *A Woman in Residence.* New York: Random House.

Harrison, T. 1999. "Globalization and the Trade in Human Body Parts." *Canadian Review of Sociology/ Revue canadienne de sociologie* 36:21–35.

Hart, Betty and Todd Risley. 1995. *Meaningful Differences in the Everyday Experience of Young American Children.* Baltimore: Paul H. Brookes.

Hart, Sarah V. 2003. "Making Prison Safer Through Technology." *Corrections Today* 65(2).

Hartmann, Heidi. 1979. "Capitalism, Patriarchy and Job Segregation by Sex." Pp. 206–47 in *Capitalist Patriarchy and the Case for Socialist Feminism,* edited by Z. Eisenstein. New York: Monthly Review Press.

Harvey, Adia Wingfield. 2009. "Racializing the Glass Escalator: Reconsidering Men's Experiences with Women's Work." *Gender & Society* 23(1):5–26.

Harvey, David. 2000. *Spaces of Hope.* Berkeley: University of California Press.

Harvey, David. 2003. *The New Imperialism.* New York: Oxford University Press.

Harvey, David. 2005. *A Brief History of NeoLiberalism.* Oxford, UK: Oxford University Press.

Harvey, David. 2007. "Poverty and Disrepute." Pp. 3589–94 in *The Blackwell Encyclopedia of Sociology,* edited by George Ritzer. Malden, MA: Blackwell.

Haslam, Alexander, and Michelle K. Ryan. 2008. "The Road to the Glass Cliff." *Leadership Quarterly* 19:530–46.

Hatch, Anthony. 2009. *The Politics of Metabolism: The Metabolic Syndrome and the Reproduction of Race and Racism in the United States.* PhD dissertation, University of Maryland.

Haug, Marie. 1973. "Deprofessionalization: An Alternative Hypothesis for the Future." *Sociological Review Monograph.*

Hausbeck, Kathryn, and Barbara G. Brents. 2008. *The State of Sex: Nevada's Brothel Industry.* Routledge.

Hausbeck, Kathryn, and Barbara G. Brents. 2010. "McDonaldization of the Sex Industries? The Business of Sex." Pp. 102–17 in *McDonaldization: The Reader,* 3rd ed., edited by George Ritzer. Thousand Oaks, CA: Pine Forge Press.

Hausmann, Ricardo, Ina Ganguli, and Martina Viarengo. 2009. "The Dynamics of the Gender Gap: How Do Countries Rank in Terms of Making Marriage and Motherhood Compatible with Work." Pp. 27–29 in *Global Gender Gap Report,* edited by Ricardo Hausmann, Laura D. Tyson, and Saadia Zahidi. Geneva: World Economic Forum.

Hawley, Amos. 1950. *Human Ecology: A Theory of Community Structure.* New York: Ronald Press.

Hayes, Dennis, and Robin Wynyard, eds. 2002. *The McDonaldization of Higher Education.* Westport, CT: Bergin and Garvey.

Haynie, L. 2001. "Delinquent Peers Revisited: Does Network Structure Matter?" *American Journal of Sociology* 106:1013–57.

"Head Injuries in Football." 2010. *The New York Times,* October 21. Retrieved March 30, 2012 (topics.nytimes.com/top/reference/ timestopics/subjects/f/football/head_ injuries/index.html).

Heaphy, Brian. 2007a. "Lesbian and Gay Families." Pp. 2606–09 in *The Blackwell Encyclopedia of Sociology,* edited by George Ritzer. Malden, MA: Blackwell.

Heaphy, Brian. 2007b. "Same-Sex Marriage/Civil Unions." Pp. 3995–98 in *The Blackwell Encyclopedia of Sociology,* edited by George Ritzer. Malden, MA: Blackwell.

Hecht, L. M. 2001. "Role Conflict and Role Overload: Different Concepts, Different Consequences." *Sociological Inquiry* 71(1): 111–21.

Heckman, James. 2006. "Skill Formation and the Economics of Investing in Disadvantaged Children." *Science* 312:1900–02.

Hedenus, Anna. 2011. "Finding Prosperity as a Lottery Winner: Presentations of Self after Acquisition of Sudden Wealth." *Sociology* 46(1):22–37.

Heintz, James. 2006. "Globalization, Economic Policy and Employment: Poverty and Gender Implications." Employment Strategy Unit, International Labor Organization. Retrieved March 30, 3012 (http://www.ilo.org/empelm/ pubs/WCMS_114024/lang—en/index.htm).

Heise, David R. 1979. *Understanding Events.* Cambridge, UK: Cambridge University Press.

Heise, David R. 2007. *Expressive Order: Confirming Sentiments in Social Actions.* New York: Springer.

Helft, Miguel. 2007. "Chinese Political Prisoner Sues in U.S. Court, Saying Yahoo Helped Identify Dissidents." *The New York Times,* April 19.

Heller, Joseph. 1955. *Catch-22.* New York: Knopf.

Helmes-Hayes, Richard. 1998. "Everett Hughes: Theorist of the Second Chicago School." *International Journal of Politics, Culture and Sociology* 11(4): 621–73.

Helweg-Larsen, Marie, and Barbara L. LoMonaco. 2008. "Queuing among U2 Fans: Reactions to Social Norm Violations." *Journal of Applied Social Psychology* 38(9):2378–93.

Hendershott, Anne. 2002. *The Politics of Deviance.* San Francisco: Encounter Books.

Henry J. Kaiser Family Foundation. 2010. "Generation M2: Media in the Lives of 8- to 18-Year-Olds." Retrieved March 30, 3012 (http://www.kff.org/entmedia/ mh012010pkg.cfm).

Henry, Stuart. 2007. "Deviance, Constructionist Perspectives." Pp. 1086–92 in *The Blackwell Encyclopedia of Sociology,* edited by George Ritzer. Malden, MA: Blackwell.

Hepburn, Stephanie, and Rita Simon. 2010. "Hidden in Plain Sight: Human Trafficking in the United States." *Gender Issues* 27(1/2):1–26.

Herbert, Bob. 2011. "Losing Our Way." *The New York Times,* March 25. Retrieved March 30, 3012 (http://www.nytimes .com/2011/03/26/opinion/26herbert.html).

Herman, E., and N. Chomsky. 1988. *Manufacturing Consent: The Political Economy of the Mass Media.* New York: Pantheon.

Herrnstein, Richard J., and Charles Murray. 1994. *The Bell Curve: Intelligence and Class Structure in American Life.* New York: Free Press.

Herod, Andrew. 2009. *Geographies of Globalization: A Critical Introduction.* Malden, MA: Wiley-Blackwell.

Herper, Matthew and Peter Kang. 2006. "The World's Ten Best-Selling Drugs." *Forbes,* March 22. Retrieved January 25, 2012 (http:// www.forbes.com/2006/03/21/pfizer-merck-amgen-cx_mh_pk_0321topdrugs.html).

Hershkovitz, Shay. 2012. "Nation-state." Pp. 1492–96 in *The Wiley-Blackwell Encyclopedia of Globalization,* edited by George Ritzer. Malden, MA: Wiley-Blackwell.

Hertzman, Clyde. 2011. "Proportionate Universality." Policy Brief 2011. Retrieved January 11, 2013, (http://earlylearning.ubc.ca/media/uploads/ publications/proportionate_universality_ brief_-_final.pdf).

Hertzman, Clyde, A. Siddiqi, E. Hertzman, L. G. Irwin, Z. Vaghri, T. A. Houweling, R. Bell, A. Tinajero, and M. Marmot. 2010. "Bucking the Inequality Gradient through Early Child Development." *British Medical Journal* 340:c468.

Hesse-Biber, Sharlene. 1996. *Am I Thin Enough Yet? The Cult of Thinness and Commercialization of Identity.* London: Oxford University Press.

Hetherington, E. M. 2003. "Intimate Pathways: Changing Patterns in Close Personal Relationships across Time." *Family Relations* 52:183–206.

Hibel, Jacob, George Farkas, and Paul Morgan. 2010. "Who Is Placed into Special Education?" *Sociology of Education* 83(4): 312–32.

Hier, Sean P. 2011. "Tightening the Focus: Moral Panic, Moral Regulation and Liberal Government" *The British Journal of Sociology* 62:523–41.

Highley, J., and M. Burton. 2006. *Elite Foundations of Liberal Democracy.* Lanham, MD: Rowman and Littlefield.

Hill, Jessica, and Pranee Liamputtong. 2011. "Being the Mother of a Child with Asperger's Syndrome: Women's Experiences of Stigma." *Health Care for Women International* 32:708–22.

Hillman, Arye L., and Eva Jenkner. 2004. "Educating Children in Poor Countries." International Monetary Fund. Retrieved March 30, 2012 (http://www.imf.org/external/pubs/ft/issues/issues33/index.htm).

Hillyard, Daniel. 2007. "Deviance, Criminalization of." Pp. 1095–100 in *The Blackwell Encyclopedia of Sociology*, edited by George Ritzer. Malden, MA: Blackwell.

Himanen, Pekka. 2001. *The Hacker Ethic: And the Spirit of the Information Age.* New York: Random House.

Hindin, Michelle J. 2007. "Role Theory." Pp. 3951–54 in *The Blackwell Encyclopedia of Sociology*, edited by George Ritzer. Malden, MA: Blackwell.

Hindmarsh, J., C. Heath, and M. Fraser. 2006. "(Im)materiality, Virtual Reality and Interaction: Grounding the 'Virtual' in Studies of Technology in Action." *Sociological Review* 54(4):795–817.

Hirsch, Barry, and David A. Macpherson. 2003. "Union Membership and Coverage Database from the Current Population Survey: Note." *Industrial and Labor Relations Review* 56(2):349–54.

Hirschi, Travis. 1969. *The Causes of Delinquency.* Berkeley: University of California Press.

Hirschi, Travis. 2004. "Self-Control and Crime." Pp. 537–52 in *Handbook of Self-Regulation: Research, Theory and Application*, edited by R. F. Baumeister and K. D. Vohs. New York: Guilford.

Hobsbawm, E. J., and Chris Wrigley. 1999. *Industry and Empire: The Birth of the Industrial Revolution.* New Press.

Hochschild, Adam. 2011. "Explaining Congo's Endless Civil War." *The New York Times* Book Review, April 1. Accessed January 29, 2012 (http://www.nytimes.com/2011/04/03/books/review/book-review-dancing-in-the-glory-of-monsters-the-collapse-of-the-congo-and-the-great-war-of-africa-by-jason-k-stearns.html?pagewanted=all).

Hochschild, Arlie R. 1979. "Emotion Work, Feeling Rules and Social Structure." *American Journal of Sociology* 85:551–75.

Hochschild, Arlie. 1983. *The Managed Heart.* Berkeley: University of California Press.

Hochschild, Arlie. 1989. *The Second Shift.* New York: Viking.

Hochschild, Arlie. 1997. *The Time Bind.* New York: Holt.

Hochschild, Arlie. 2000. "Global Care Chains and Emotional Surplus Value." Pp. 130–46 in *On the Edge: Living with Global Capitalism*, edited by W. Hutton and Anthony Giddens. London: Jonathan Cape.

Hochschild, Arlie R. (with A. Machung). 2003. *The Second Shift.* New York: Penguin.

Hodge, David. 2008. "Sexual Trafficking in the US: A Domestic Problem with Transnational Dimensions." *Social Work* 53(2):143–52.

Hodson, Randy. 2001. *Dignity at Work.* Cambridge, UK: Cambridge University Press.

Hoecker-Drysdale, Susan. 2011. "Harriet Martineau." Pp. 61–95 in *The Wiley-Blackwell Companion to Major Social Theorists: Volume 1. Classical Theorists*, edited by George Ritzer and Jeffrey Stepnisky. Malden, MA: Wiley-Blackwell.

Hoefer, Michael, Nancy Rytina, and Bryan C. Baker. 2010. "Estimates of the Unauthorized Immigrant Population Residing in the United States: January 2009." U.S. Department of Homeland Security. Retrieved February 28, 2012 (http://www.dhs.gov/xlibrary/assets/statistics/publications/ois_ill_pe_2009.pdf).

Hoekstra, Arjen J. 2012. "Water." Pp. 2202–10 in *The Wiley-Blackwell Companion to Sociology*, edited by George Ritzer. Malden, MA: Wiley-Blackwell.

Hoekstra, Arjen Y., and Ashok K. Chapagain. 2008. *Globalization of Water: Sharing the Planet's Freshwater Resources.* Malden, MA: Blackwell.

Hoff, E., B. Larsen, and T. Tardiff. 2002. "Socioeconomic Status and Parenting." Pp. 231–52 in *Handbook of Parenting, Volume 2. Biology and Ecology of Parenting*, 2nd ed., edited by M. H. Bornstein. Mahwah, NJ: Erlbaum.

Hoffman, Lily M., Susan S. Fainstein, and Dennis R. Judd, eds. 2003. *Cities and Visitors: Regulating People, Markets, and City Space.* New York: Blackwell.

Hollander, Jason. 2003. "Renowned Columbia Sociologist and National Medal of Science Winner Robert K. Merton Dies at 92." Retrieved April 1, 2012 (http://www.columbia.edu/cu/news/03/02/robertKMerton.html).

Hollifield, James E., and David Jacobson. 2012. "Migration and the State." Pp. 1390–400 in *The Wiley-Blackwell Encyclopedia of Globalization*, edited by George Ritzer. Malden, MA: Wiley-Blackwell.

Hollister, Geoff. 2008. *Out of Nowhere: The Inside Story of How Nike Marketed the Culture of Running.* Maidenhead, UK: Meyer and Meyer Sport.

Holmes, Mary. 2007. "Couples Living Apart Together." Pp. 810–12 in *The Blackwell Encyclopedia of Sociology*, edited by George Ritzer. Malden, MA: Blackwell.

Holt, Douglas. 2004. *How Brands Become Icons: Principles of Cultural Branding.* Cambridge, MA: Harvard Business School Press.

Holt, Douglas B. 2007. "Distinction." Pp. 1189–91 in *The Blackwell Encyclopedia of Sociology*, edited by George Ritzer. Malden, MA: Blackwell.

Holton, Robert. 2011. *Globalization and the Nation State.* 2nd ed. New York: Palgrave Macmillan.

Homans, George. 1961. *Social Behavior: Its Elementary Forms.* New York: Harcourt, Brace, and World.

Hondagneu-Sotelo, Pierette. 2000. *Doméstica: Immigrant Workers Cleaning and Caring in the Shadows of Affluence.* Berkeley: University of California Press.

Hondagneu-Sotelo, Pierette, and Ernestine Avila. 2005. "'I'm Here, but I'm There': The Meanings of Latina Trasnational Motherhood." In *Gender through a Prism of Difference*, edited by Maxine Baca Zinn, Pierette Hondagneu-Sotelo, and Michael Messner. New York: Oxford University Press.

Honwana, Alcinda. 2007. *The Child Soldiers in Africa.* Philadelphia: University of Pennsylvania Press.

hooks, bell. 2000. *Feminist Thought: From Margin to Center.* Cambridge, UK: South End Press.

Horovitz, Bruce. 2002. "Fast-food World Says Drive-thru Is the Way to Go." *USA Today*, April 3. Retrieved May 26, 2011 (http://www.usatoday.com/money/covers/2002-04-03-drive-thru.htm).

Horrey, William J., and Christopher D. Wickens. 2006. "Examining the Impact of Cell Phone Conversations on Driving Using Meta-analytic Techniques." *Human Factors: The Journal of the Human Factors and Ergonomics Society* 48:196–205.

Horrigan, John. 2008. *Online Shopping.* Washington, DC: Pew Internet & American Life Project.

Horrigan, John. 2009. "Wireless Internet Use." Retrieved January 27, 2012 (http://pewinternet.org/Reports/2009/12-Wireless-Internet-Use.aspx).

Horton, Richard. 2000. "North and South: Bridging the Information Gap." *The Lancet* 355(9222):2231–36.

Hou, Feng, and John Myles. 2008. "The Changing Role of Education in the Marriage Market: Assortative Marriage in Canada and the United States since the 1970s." *Canadian Journal of Sociology* 33(2):335–64.

Houck, Davis W., and David E. Dixon, eds. 2011. *Women and the Civil Rights Movement, 1954–1965.* Jackson: University of Mississippi Press.

Howard, I. 2002. "Power Sources: On Party, Gender, Race and Class, TV News Looks to the Most Powerful Groups." Retrieved March 30, 2012 (http://www.fair.org/index.php?page=1109).

Howe, Jeff. 2008. *Crowdsourcing: Why the Power of the Crowd Is Driving the Future of Business.* New York: Three Rivers Press.

Huaco, George. 1966. "The Functionalist Theory of Stratification: Two Decades of Controversy." *Inquiry* 9:215–40.

Huang, Penelope M., et al. 2011. "He Says, She Says: Gender and Cohabitation." *Journal of Family Issues* 32:876–905.

Hughes, Donna M. 1999. "Pimps and Predators on the Internet—Globalizing the Sexual Exploitation of Women and Children." Kingston, RI: Coalition Against Trafficking in Women. Retrieved March 30, 2012 (http://www.uri.edu/artsci/wms/hughes/pprep.pdf).

Hughes, Donna M. 2000. "Welcome to the Rape Camp: Sexual Exploitation and the

Internet in Cambodia." *Journal of Sexual Aggression* 6:1–23.

Hughes, Everett. 1943. *French Canada in Transition.* Chicago: University of Chicago Press.

Hughes, Karen. 2005. *Female Enterprise in the New Economy.* Toronto, ON: University of Toronto Press.

Hull, Kathleen E., Ann Meier, and Timothy Ortyl. 2010. "The Changing Landscape of Love and Marriage." *Contexts* 9:32–37.

Human Resources and Skills Development Canada. 2012a. "Indicators of Well-being in Canada." Retrieved October 7, 2012 (http://www4.hrsdc.gc.ca/.3ndic.1t.4r@-eng.jsp?iid=22).

Human Resources and Skills Development Canada. 2012b. *Union Coverage in Canada.* Ottawa, ON: Author, Workplace Information Division.

Human Resources and Skills Development Canada. 2013. "Canadians in Context—Population Size and Growth." Retrieved January 30, 2013 (http://www4.hrsdc.gc.ca/.3ndic.1t.4r-eng.jsp?iid=35).

Humphreys, Laud. 1970. *Tearoom Trade: A Study of Homosexual Encounters in Public Places.* Chicago: Aldine.

Humphreys, Laud. 1972. *Out of the Closets: The Sociology of Homosexual Liberation.* Prentice Hall Trade.

Humphreys, Laud. 1975. *Tearoom Trade: Impersonal Sex in Public Places.* Enlarged ed. Chicago: Aldine.

Humphry, Derek. 2002. *Final Exit: The Practicalities of Self-deliverance and Assisted Suicide for the Dying.* 3rd ed. New York: Delta.

Hunt, Stephen. 2007. "Social Structure." Pp. 4524–26 in *The Blackwell Encyclopedia of Sociology,* edited by George Ritzer. Malden, MA: Blackwell.

Huntington, Samuel P. 1996. *The Clash of Civilizations and the Remaking of the World Order.* New York: Simon and Schuster.

Hurley, Dan. 2005. "Divorce Rate: It's Not as High as You Think." *The New York Times,* April 19.

Hutson, Brittany. 2010. "Overcoming Gender Differences." *Black Enterprise* 40(8):56–57.

Iceland, John. 2007. "Poverty." Pp. 3587–88 in *The Blackwell Encyclopedia of Sociology,* edited by George Ritzer. Malden, MA: Blackwell.

Illouz, Eva. 2007. *Cold Intimacies: The Making of Emotional Capitalism.* Cambridge, UK: Polity.

Illouz, Eva. 2008. *Saving the Modern Soul: Therapy, Emotions and the Culture of Self Help.* Berkeley: University of California Press.

Inckle, Kay. 2007. *Writing on the Body? Thinking through Gendered Embodiment and Marked Flesh.* Newcastle, UK: Cambridge Scholars.

Inda, Jonathan Xavier and Renato Rosaldo. 2008. *The Anthropology of Globalization: A Reader.* 2nd ed. Malden, MA: Blackwell.

Inglehart, Ronald, and Wayne E. Baker. 2000. "Modernization, Cultural Change, and the Persistence of Traditional Values." *American Sociological Review* 65:19–51.

Inglehart, Ronald, Roberto Foa, Christopher Peterson, and Christian Welzel. 2008. "Development, Freedom, and Rising Happiness: A Global Perspective (1981–2007)." *Perspectives on Psychological Science* 3(4):264–85.

Ingoldsby, B. B., and S. Smith. 2006. *Families in Global and Multicultural Perspective.* 2nd ed. Thousand Oaks, CA: Sage.

Inoue, Keiko, and Gili S. Drori. 2006. "The Global Institutionalization of Health as a Social Concern." *International Sociology* 21(1):199–219.

Insch, Gary S., Nancy McIntyre, and Nancy C. Napier. 2008. "The Expatriate Glass Ceiling: The Second Layer of Glass." *Journal of Business Ethics* 83:19–28.

Institute of International Studies, University of California at Berkeley. 2001. "Conversations with History: Manuel Castells." Retrieved April 1, 2012 (http://globetrotter.berkeley.edu/people/Castells/castells-con0.html).

"Interest Rates: Taking the Lie Out of LIBOR." 2012. Schumpeter [blog]. *The Economist,* September 28. Retrieved April 26, 2013 (http://www.economist.com/blogs/schumpeter/2012/09/interest-rates).

Intergovernmental Panel on Climate Change. 2007. "Summary for Policymakers." In *Climate Change 2007: The Physical Science Basis,* edited by S. Solomon, D. Qin, M. Manning, Z. Chen, M. Marquis, K. B. Averyt, M. Tignor, and H. L. Miller. Contribution of Working Group I to the Fourth Assessment Report of the Intergovernmental Panel on Climate Change. Cambridge, UK: Cambridge University Press.

International Centre for Prison Studies. 2012. "Data." Retrieved September 25, 2012 (http://www.prisonstudies.org/).

International Confederation of Free Trade Unions. 2004. "The Informal Economy: Women on the Frontline." *Trade Union World Briefing* 2, March 2. Retrieved March 30, 2012 (www.ilo.org/public/english/region/ampro/cinterfor/temas/informal/doc/womflin.pdf).

International Federation of the Phonographic Industry. 2012. "Music Market Statistics." March 30, 2012 (http://www.ifpi.org/content/section_statistics/index.html).

International Labour Office. 2005. *A Global Alliance against Forced Labour: Global Report under the Follow-up to the ILO Declaration on Fundamental Principles and Rights at Work: 2005* (Report I [B]), pp. 55–56. International Labour Conference, 93rd Session.

International Monetary Fund. 2011. "WEO Data: April 2011 Edition." Retrieved May 26, 2011 (http://www.imf.org/external/pubs/ft/weo/2011/01/weodata/WEOApr2011all.xls).

International Organization for Migration. 2005. "World Migration 2005: Costs and Benefits of International Migration." Retrieved March 30, 2012 (http://www.iom.int/jahia/Jahia/cache/offonce/pid/1674?entryId=932).

International Pacific Research Center. 2011. "Where Will the Debris from Japan's Tsunami Drift in the Ocean?" April 5. Retrieved May 25, 2011 (http://www.soest.hawaii.edu/iprc/news/press_releases/2011/maximenko_tsunami_debris.pdf).

Intravia, Jonathan, Shayne Jones, and Alex R. Piquero. 2011. "The Roles of Social Bonds, Personality, and Perceived Costs: An Empirical Investigation into Hirschi's 'New' Social Control Theory." *International Journal of Offender Therapy and Comparative Criminology*:1–19.

Introvigne, Masimo. 2007. "New Age." Pp. 3189–92 in *The Blackwell Encyclopedia of Sociology,* edited by George Ritzer. Malden, MA: Blackwell.

Ioffe, Julia. 2010. "Roulette Russian: The Teen-ager Behind Chatroulette." *The New Yorker,* May 17, p. 54.

"Irish Economy Shrank by One Fifth During Recession." 2011. BBC News, September 19. Retrieved February 28, 2012 (http://www.bbc.co.uk/news/uk-northern-ireland-14976439).

Iyengar, S. 1990. "The Accessibility Bias in Politics: Television News and Public Opinion." *International Journal of Public Opinion Research* 2(1):1–15.

Jackson, Shirley A. 2007. "Majorities." Pp. 2701–702 in *The Blackwell Encyclopedia of Sociology,* edited by George Ritzer. Malden, MA: Blackwell.

Jackson-Jacobs, Curtis. 2005. "Hard Drugs in a Soft Context: Managing Trouble and Crack Use on a College Campus." *Sociological Quarterly* 45(4):835–56.

Jacobs, Andrew. 2010. "China Seeks End to Public Shaming." *The New York Times,* July 27, pp. A1, A3.

Jacobs, Jerry. 1996. "Gender Inequality and Higher Education." *Annual Review of Sociology* 22:153–85.

Jacobs, Mark D. 2007. "Interaction Order." Pp. 2365–66 in *The Blackwell Encyclopedia of Sociology,* edited by George Ritzer. Malden, MA: Blackwell.

Jacques, Martin. 2009. *When China Rules the World: The End of the Western World and the Birth of a New Global Order.* London: Penguin.

Jagannathan, S. 1984. *Hinduism: An Introduction.* Bombay, India: Vakils, Feffer, and Simons.

Jakobi, Anja P. 2012. "Human Trafficking." Pp. 953–56 in *The Wiley-Blackwell Encyclopedia of Globalization,* edited by George Ritzer. Malden, MA: Wiley-Blackwell.

Jalali, Rita. 2007. "Caste: Inequalities Past and Present." Pp. 404–406 in *The Blackwell Encyclopedia of Sociology,* edited by George Ritzer. Malden, MA: Blackwell.

James, William. [1902] 1960. *The Varieties of Religious Experience.* New York: Random House.

Jamieson, Kathleen. 1996. *Packaging the Presidency: A History and Criticism of*

Presidential Campaign Advertising. New York: Oxford.

Jamieson, Lynn. 1998. *Intimacy: Personal Relationships in Modern Societies.* Cambridge, UK: Polity Press.

Jamieson, Lynn. 2007. "Intimacy." Pp. 2411–14 in *The Blackwell Encyclopedia of Sociology,* edited by George Ritzer. Malden, MA: Blackwell.

Jansen, Jim. 2010. "Online Product Research." The Pew Research Center, September 29. Retrieved May 27, 2011 (http://www.pewinternet.org/Reports/2010/Online-Product-Research.aspx).

Janssen, I. P. T. Katzmarzyk, W. F. Boyce, C. Vereecken, C. Mulvihill, C. Roberts, C. Currie, and W. Pickett. 2005. "Comparison of Overweight and Obesity Prevalence in School-aged Youth from 34 Countries and Their Relationships with Physical Activity and Dietary Patterns." *Obesity Reviews* 6(2):123–32.

Janssen, Patricia, Lee Saxell, Lesley Page, Michael Klein, Robert Liston, and Shoo Lee. 2009. "Outcomes of Planned Home Birth with Registered Midwife versus Planned Hospital Birth with Midwife or Physician." *Canadian Medical Association Journal* 181(6–7):377–83.

Jasper, James M. 2007. "Social Movement." Pp. 4443–51 in *The Blackwell Encyclopedia of Sociology,* edited by George Ritzer. Malden, MA: Blackwell.

Jay, Karla. 1999. *Tales of the Lavender Menace: A Memoir of Liberation.* New York: Basic Books.

Jay, Martin. 1973. *The Dialectical Imagination.* Boston, Little Brown.

Jean-Charles, Régine Michelle. 2010. "Cracks of Gender Inequality: Haitian Women after the Earthquake." Retrieved March 30, 2012 (http://www.ssrc.org/features/pages/haiti-now-and-next/1338/1428/).

Jefferson, Gail. 1979. "A Technique for Inviting Laughter and Its Subsequent Acceptance Declination." Pp. 79–96 in *Everyday Language: Studies in Ethnomethodology,* edited by G. Psathas. New York: Irvington.

Jeffreys, Sheila. 2005. *Beauty and Misogyny: Harmful Cultural Practices in the West.* New York: Routledge.

Jeffries, Ian. 2011. *Economic Developments in Contemporary Russia.* New York: Routledge.

Jekielek, Susan M., and Kristin A. Moore. 2007. "Family Structure and Child Outcomes." Pp. 1621–26 in *The Blackwell Encyclopedia of Sociology,* edited by George Ritzer. Malden, MA: Blackwell.

Jenkins, J. C. 1983. "Resource Mobilization Theory and the Study of Social Movements." *Annual Review of Sociology* 9:248–67.

Jenness, Valerie. 2004. "Explaining Criminalization: From Demography and Status Politics to Globalization and Modernization." *Annual Review of Sociology* 30:141–71.

Jensen, Gary F. 1988. "Functional Perspectives on Deviance: A Critical Assessment and Guide for the Future." *Deviant Behavior* 9:1–17.

Jerolmack, C. 2009a. "Humans, Animals, and Play: Theorizing Interaction When Intersubjectivity Is Problematic." *Sociological Theory* 27(4):371–89.

Jerolmack, C. 2009b. Special Issue (Part 1). *Ethnography* 10(4):435–57.

Jimenez, Maria. 2009. "Humanitarian Crisis: Migrant Deaths at the U.S.-Mexican Border." Retrieved March 30, 2012 (http://www.aclu.org/files/pdfs/immigrants/human itariancrisisreport.pdf).

Johnson, Carrie. 2009. "Justice Department Turning Attention toward Native American Crime Issues." *The Washington Post,* June 15.

Johnson, C., R. Ford, and J. Kaufman. 2000. "Emotional Reactions to Conflict: Do Dependence and Legitimacy Matter?" *Social Forces* 79(1):107–37.

Johnson, David K. 2004. *The Lavender Scare: The Cold War Persecution of Gays and Lesbians in the Federal Government.* Chicago: University of Chicago Press.

Johnson, Holly, and Myrna Dawson. 2010. *Violence Against Women in Canada: Research and Policy Perspectives.* Toronto, ON: Oxford University Press.

Johnson, M., and M. Hall. 2010. "Officials, Analysts Flay WikiLeaks Release of Key U.S. Security Sites." *USA Today,* December 7, p. 6A.

Johnson, Naomi. 2010. "Consuming Desires: Consumption, Romance, and Sexuality in Best-selling Teen Romance Novels." *Women's Studies in Communication* 33:54–73.

Jordan, Mary. 2007. "The New Face of Global Mormonism: Tech-Savvy Missionary Church Thrives as Far Afield as Africa." *The Washington Post,* November 19, pp. A1, A13.

Jorgenson, Andrew, and Jennifer Givens. 2012. "Pollution, Water." P. 1674 in *The Wiley-Blackwell Companion to Sociology,* edited by George Ritzer. Malden, MA: Wiley-Blackwell.

Joyner, Chris. 2010. "Miss. Prom Canceled." *Signs* 33(4):761–69.

Joyner, Chris. 2010. "Miss. Prom Canceled After Lesbian's Date Request," March 11. Retrieved March 30, 2012 (http://www.usatoday.com/news/nation/2010-03-10-noprom_N.htm).

Juris, Jeffrey. 2005. "The New Digital Media and Activist Networking within Anti-Corporate Globalization Movements." *Annals* 597 (January):189–208.

Kahlenberg, Richard D., ed. 2010. *Affirmatie Action for the Rich: Legacy Preferences in College Admissions.* Washington, DC: Brookings Institution Press.

Kahlenberg, Susan G., and Michelle M. Hein. 2010. "Progression on Nickelodeon? Gender-role Stereotypes in Toy Commercials." *Sex Roles: A Journal of Research* 62(11–12):830–47.

Kahn, Joseph, and Mark Landler. 2007. "China Grabs West's Smoke-spewing Factories." *The New York Times,* December 21.

Kahn, Richard, and Douglas Kellner. 2007. "Resisting Globalization." Pp. 662–74 in *The Blackwell Companion to Globalization,* edited by George Ritzer. Malden, MA: Blackwell.

Kalberg, Stephen. 1980. "Max Weber's Type of Rationality: Cornerstones for the Analysis of Rationalization Processes in History." *American Journal of Sociology* 85.

Kalberg, Stephen. 2011. "Max Weber." Pp. 305–72 in *The Wiley-Blackwell Companion to Major Social Theorists: Volume 1. Classical Theorists,* edited by George Ritzer and Jeffrey Stepnisky. Malden, MA: Wiley-Blackwell.

Kalev, Alexandra. 2009. "Cracking the Glass Cages? Restructuring and Ascriptive Inequality at Work." *American Journal of Sociology* 114:1591–643.

Kalleberg, Arne. 2009. "Precarious Work, Insecure Workers: Employment Relations in Transition." *American Sociological Review* 74:1–22.

Kane, Emily. 2006. "'No Way My Boys Are Going to Be Like That!' Parents' Responses to Children's Gender Nonconformity." *Gender & Society* 20(2):149–76.

Kangas, Olli E. 2007. "Welfare State, Retrenchment of." Pp. 5247–49 in *The Blackwell Encyclopedia of Sociology,* edited by George Ritzer. Malden, MA: Blackwell.

Kanter, Rosabeth Moss. 1993. *Men and Women of the Corporation.* New York: Basic Books.

Karmen, A. 1994. "Defining Deviancy Down: How Senator Moynihan's Misleading Phrase about Criminal Justice Is Rapidly Being Incorporated into Popular Culture." *Journal of Criminal Justice and Popular Culture* (October):99–127.

Karon, Tony. 2001. "Why Courts Don't Deter France's Anti-McDonald's 'Astérix.'" *Time,* February 15. Retrieved March 30, 2012 (http://www.time.com/time/world/article/0,8599,99592,00.html).

Karpowitz, Christopher F., et al. 2011. "Tea Time in America? The Impact of the Tea Party Movement on the 2010 Midterm Elections." *PS* (April):303–309.

Karraker, Meg Wilkes. 2008. *Global Families.* Boston: Pearson.

Karstedt, Susanne. 2007. "Genocide." Pp. 1909–13 in *The Blackwell Encyclopedia of Sociology,* edited by George Ritzer. Malden, MA: Blackwell.

Karstedt, Susanne. 2012. "Genocide." Pp. 793–97 in *The Wiley-Blackwell Encyclopedia of Globalization,* edited by George Ritzer. Malden, MA: Wiley-Blackwell.

Kasarda, John D., and Greg Lindsay. 2011. *Aerotropolis: The Way We'll Live Next.* New York: Farrar, Straus & Giroux.

Kasten, Erich. 2004. *Properties of Culture, Culture as Property: Pathways to Reform in Post-Soviet Siberia.* Reimer.

Katsulis, Yasmina. 2010. "'Living Like a King': Conspicuous Consumption, Virtual

Communities, and the Social Construction of Paid Sexual Encounters by U.S. Sex Tourists." *Men and Masculinities* 27:1–18.

Katz-Gerro, Tally, and Mads Meier Jaeger. 2011. "Top of the Pops, Ascend of the Omnivores, Defeat of the Couch Potatoes: Cultural Consumption Profiles in Denmark 1975–2004." *European Sociological Review.*

Kaufman, Jason, and Orlando Patterson. 2005. "Cross-national Cultural Diffusion: The Global Spread of Cricket." *American Sociological Review* 70:82–110.

Kaufman, M. T. 2003. "Robert K. Merton, Versatile Sociologist and Father of the Focus Group, Dies at 92." *The New York Times* Obituaries, February 24. Retrieved March 30, 2012 (http://www.nytimes.com/2003/02/24/nyregion/robert-k-merton-versatile-sociologist-and-father-of-the-focus-group-dies-at-92.html?pagewanted=all&src=pm).

Kaufman-Scarbrough, Carol. 2006. "Time Use and the Impact of Technology: Examining Workspaces in the Home." *Time & Society* 15(1):57–80.

Kay, Fiona, and John Hagan. 1998. "Raising the Bar: The Gender Stratification of Law-firm Capital." *American Sociological Review* 63(5):728–43.

Kay, Fiona, and Elizabeth Gorman. 2008. "Women in the Legal Profession." *Annual Review of Law and Social Sciences* 4: 299–332.

Keane, John. 2003. *Global Civil Society.* Cambridge, UK: Cambridge University Press.

"Keep the Borders Open." 2008. *The Economist,* January 3. Retrieved March 7, 2012 (http://www.economist.com/node/10430282).

Kefalas, Maria J., et al. 2011. "'Marriage Is More Than Being Together': The Meaning of Marriage for Young Adults." *Journal of Family Issues* 32:845–75.

Kelishadi, Roya. 2007. "Childhood Overweight, Obesity, and the Metabolic Syndrome in Developing Countries." *Epidemiologic Reviews* 29(1):62–76.

Keller, Bill. 1990. "Of Famous Arches, Been Meks and Rubles." *The New York Times,* January 28, Section 1, p. 12.

Kellerhals, Jean. 2007. "Family Conflict." Pp. 1580–83 in *The Blackwell Encyclopedia of Sociology,* edited by George Ritzer. Malden, MA: Blackwell.

Kellner, Douglas, and Tyson E. Lewis. 2007. "Cultural Critique." Pp. 896–98 in *The Blackwell Encyclopedia of Sociology,* edited by George Ritzer. Malden, MA: Blackwell.

Kelly, Deirdre, Shauna Pomerantz, and Dawn H. Currie. 2005 "Skater Girlhood and Emphasized Femininity: 'You Can't Land an Ollie Properly in Heels.'" *Gender and Education* 17(3):229–48.

Kelly, Liz. 2007. "Sexual Violence and Rape." Pp. 4249–54 in *The Blackwell Encyclopedia of Sociology,* edited by George Ritzer. Malden, MA: Blackwell.

Kelly, Mary Bess. 2012. "Divorce Cases in Civil Court, 2010/11." Jurisdat Statistics Canada Catalogue no. 85-002-X.

Kelly, William W., ed. 2004. *Fanning the Flames: Fans and Consumer Culture in Contemporary Japan.* New York: SUNY Press.

Kelly, William W. 2007. "Is Baseball a Global Sport? America's 'National Pastime' as a Global Field and International Sport." Pp. 79–93 in *Globalization and Sport,* edited by Richard Giulianotti and Roland Robertson. Malden, MA: Blackwell.

Kelso, Alicia. 2011. "NRA 2011: McCafé Digital Menu Board Project Largest in World." QSR Web. Retrieved May 25, 2011 (http://www.qsrweb.com/article/181495/NRA-2011-McCaf-digital-menu-board-project-largest-in-world).

Kempadoo, Kamala, and Jo Doezema, eds. 1998. *Global Sex Workers: Rights, Resistance, and Redefinition.* London: Routledge.

Kemper, Theodore D. 1991. "Predicting Emotions from Social Relations." *Social Psychology Quarterly* 54:330–42.

Kennedy, John. 2007. "China: Blogger Goes to Court." *Global Voices.* Retrieved May 23, 2011 (http://globalvoicesonline.org/2007/08/06/china-blogger-goes-to-court/).

Kennedy, M. Alexis, Carolin Klein, Jessica T. K. Bristowe, Barry S. Cooper, and John C. Yuille. 2007. "Routes of Recruitment: Pimps' Techniques and Other Circumstances that Lead to Street Prostitution." *Journal of Aggression, Maltreatment and Trauma* 15(2):1–19.

Kennedy, Randall. 2003. *Nigger: The Strange Career of a Troublesome Word.* New York: Vintage Books.

Kerber, Linda K. 1988. "Separate Spheres, Female Worlds, Woman's Place: The Rhetoric of Women's History." *The Journal of American History* 75(1):9–39.

Kershaw, Sarah. 2008. "Starving Themselves, Cocktail in Hand." *The New York Times,* March 2. Retrieved January 1, 2012 (http://www.nytimes.com/2008/03/02/fashion/02drunk.html).

Kestnbaum, Meyer. 2012. "Organized Coercion and Political Authority: Armed Conflict in a World of States." Pp. 588–608 in *The Wiley-Blackwell Companion to Sociology,* edited by George Ritzer. Malden, MA: Wiley-Blackwell.

Khan, Rana Ejaz Ali, and Muhammad Zahir Faridi. 2008. "Impact of Globalization and Economic Growth on Income Distribution: A Case Study of Pakistan." *IUB Journal of Social Sciences and Humanities* 6(2):7–33.

Khatchadourian, Raffi. 2007. "Neptune's Navy." *The New Yorker,* November 5.

Khondker, Habibul Haque. 2011. "Role of the New Media in Arab Spring." *Globalizations* 8:675–79.

Kilgannon, Corey, and Jeffrey E. Singer. 2010. "Stores' Treatment of Shoplifters Tests Rights." *The New York Times,* June 21. Accessed December 20, 2011 (http://www.nytimes.com/2010/06/22/nyregion/22shoplift.html?pagewanted=all).

Kim, Eunjung. 2011. "Asexuality in Disability Narratives." *Sexualities* 24:479–93.

Kimmel, Michael S. 2004. *The Gendered Society.* New York: Oxford University Press.

Kimmel, Michael. 2009. *The Gendered Society.* New York: Oxford University Press.

Kimmel, Michael. 2011. *The Gendered Society.* New York: Oxford University Press.

King, Martin Luther Jr. [1958] 2010. *Stride Toward Freedom: The Montgomery Story.* Boston: Beacon Press.

Kinney, William J. 2007. "Asch Experiments." Pp. 189–91 in *The Blackwell Encyclopedia of Sociology,* edited by George Ritzer. Malden, MA: Blackwell.

Kirton, Gill. 2007. "Gendered Enterprise." Pp. 1888–91 in *The Blackwell Encyclopedia of Sociology,* edited by George Ritzer. Malden, MA: Blackwell.

Kivisto, Peter. 2012a. "Fundamentalism." Pp. 709–13 in *The Wiley-Blackwell Encyclopedia of Globalization,* edited by George Ritzer. Malden, MA: Wiley-Blackwell.

Kivisto, Peter. 2012b. "Refugees." Pp. 1761–65 in *The Wiley-Blackwell Encyclopedia of Globalization,* edited by George Ritzer. Malden, MA: Wiley-Blackwell.

Klein, Alan. 1993. *Little Big Men: Bodybuilding Subculture and Gender Construction.* Albany: SUNY Press.

Klein, Naomi. [2000] 2010. *No Logo: Taking Aim at the Brand Bullies.* Toronto, ON: Vintage, Canada.

Kleinfeld, J. 1979. *Eskimo School on the Andreafsky: A Study of Effective Bicultural Education.* Praeger.

Kleiss, Karen. 2010. "Alberta Docs Billed for Homosexuality as a Mental Disorder Five Times in 2009." *Edmonton Journal,* December 24, 2010. Retrieved January 14, 2013 (http://www.edmontonjournal.com/news/Alberta+docs+billed+homosexuality+mental+disorder+five+times+2009/4021060/story.html).

Klinenberg, Eric. 2012. *Going Solo: The Extraordinary Rise and Surprising Appeal of Living Alone.* New York: Penguin.

Klingmann, Anna. 2007. *Brandscapes: Architecture in the Experience Economy.* Cambridge, MA: MIT Press.

Knorr Cetina, Karin. 2012. "Financial Markets." Pp. 653–64 in *The Encyclopedia of Globalization,* edited by George Ritzer. Malden, MA: Wiley-Blackwell.

Koch, Jerome R., Alden E. Roberts, Myrna L. Armstrong, and Donna C. Owen. 2010. "Body Art, Deviance, and American College Students." *The Social Science Journal* 47:151–61.

Kochel, Tammy Rinehart, David B. Wilson, and Stephen D. Mastrofski. 2011. "Effect of Suspect Race on Officers' Arrest Decisions." *Criminology* 49:473–512.

Kogawa, Joy. 1981. *Obasan.* Toronto: Lester and Orpen Dennys.

Kohlberg, Lawrence. 1966. "A Cognitive-Development Analysis of Sex-Role Concepts and Attitudes." Pp. 82–173 in *The Development of Sex Differences,* edited by Eleanor Maccoby. Berkeley: University of California Press.

Kohm, Steve. 2009. "Naming, Shaming and Criminal Justice: Mass-mediated Humiliation as Entertainment and Punishment." *Crime Media Culture* 5(2):188–205.

Kohn, Melvin L. (with Joanne Miller, Karen A. Miller, Carrie Schoenbach, and Ronald Schoenberg). 1983. *Work and Personality: An Inquiry into the Impact of Social Stratification.* Norwood, NJ: Albex.

Kohrmann, M. 2008. "Smoking among Doctors: Governmentality, Embodiment, and the Diversion of Blame in Contemporary China." *Medical Anthropology* 27(1):9–42.

Kolata, Gina. 1999. *The Flu: The Story of the Great Influenza Pandemic of 1918 and the Search for the Virus That Caused It.* New York: Touchstone.

Koller, Daphne. 2011. "Death Knell for the Lecture: Technology as a Passport to Personalized Education." *The New York Times,* December 5.

Kollmeyer, Christopher. 2009. "Explaining Deindustrialization: How Affluence, Productivity Growth, and Globalization Diminish Manufacturing Employment." *American Journal of Sociology* 114:1644–74.

Kong, Travis. 2010. *Chinese Male Homosexualities.* London: Routledge.

Konrad, Waleca. 2009. "Seeking the Best Medical Care Prices." *The New York Times,* November 28, p. B5.

Koppell, J. G. S. 2010. *World Rule: Accountability, Legitimacy and the Design of Global Governance.* Chicago: University of Chicago Press.

Korenman, S. D., and D. Neumark. 1991. "Does Marriage Really Make Men More Productive?" *Journal of Human Resources* 26:282–307.

Kortenhaus, C. M. and J. Demarest. 1993. "Gender Role Stereotyping in Children's Literature: An Update." *Sex Roles* 28:219–32.

Kosic, Ankica, Arie W. Kruglanski, Antonio Pierro, and Lucia Mannetti. 2004. "The Social Cognition of Immigrants' Acculturation: Effects of the Need for Closure and the Reference Group at Entry." *Journal of Personality and Social Psychology* 86:796–813.

Kottak, Conrad P. 2010. "What Is Hypodescent?" Human Diversity and "Race" Online Learning, McGraw-Hill. Retrieved April 15, 2011 (http://highered.mcgraw-hill .com/sites/0072500506/student_view0/ chapter5/faqs.html).

Kozinets, Robert V. 1998. "On Netnography: Initial Reflections on Consumer Research Investigations of Cyberculture." Pp. 366–71 in *Advances in Consumer Research,* edited by Joseph Alba and Wesley Hutchinson. Provo, UT: Association for Consumer Research.

Kozinets, Robert V. 2002. "The Field Behind the Screen: Using Netnography for Marketing Research in Online Communities." *Journal of Marketing Research* 39:61–72.

Krahn, H. 2009. "Choose Your Parents Carefully: Social Class, Post-secondary Education, and Occupational Outcomes." Pp. 171–89 in *Social Inequality in Canada: Patterns, Problems, Policies,* 5th ed., edited by Edward Grabb and Neil Guppy. Toronto, ON: Pearson/Prentice-Hall.

Krahn, Harvey, Graham Lowe, and Karen Hughes. 2011. *Work, Industry, and Canadian Society.* Toronto, ON: Nelson.

Kramer, Andrew E. 2011. "Delivering on Demand: American Fast Food Meets a Warm Reception in Russia." *The New York Times,* August 4, pp. B1, B4.

Krass, Frauke, ed. 2012. *Megacities: Our Global Urban Future.* Springer.

Krass, P. 1990. "The Dollars and Sense of Outsourcing." *Information Week* 259 (February 26):26–31.

Krauss, Clifford. 2004. "Internet Drug Exporters Feel Pressure in Canada." *The New York Times,* December 11. Retrieved March 30, 2012 (http://query.nytimes.com/gst/ fullpage.html?res=9F04EED81131F932 A25751C1A9629C8B63&&scp=4&sq= pharmaceutical%20purchase%20over%20 internet&st=cse).

Kreager Derek. 2007. "Unnecessary Roughness? School Sports, Peer Networks, and Male Adolescent Violence." *American Sociological Review* 72(5):705–24.

Krings, Torben, Alicja Bobek, Elaine Moriarty, Justyna Salamonska, and James Wickham. 2009. "Migration and Recession: Polish Migrants in Post-Celtic Tiger Ireland." *Sociological Research Online* 14(2):9. Retrieved March 30, 2012 (http://www .socresonline.org.uk/14/2/9.html).

Kritz, Mary M. 2007. "Migration, International." Pp. 3019–25 in *The Blackwell Encyclopedia of Sociology,* edited by George Ritzer. Malden, MA: Blackwell.

Kritz, Mary M. 2008. "International Migration." In *The Blackwell Encyclopedia of Sociology Online,* edited by George Ritzer. Malden, MA: Blackwell.

Kritz, Mary M., L. I. Lim, and H. Zlotnik. 1992. *International Migration Systems: A Global Approach.* Oxford: Oxford University Press.

Kroen, Sheryl. 2006. "Negotiations with the American Way: The Consumer and the Social Contract in Post-war Europe." Pp. 251–78 in *Consuming Cultures, Global Perspectives: Historical Trajectories, Transnational Exchanges,* edited by John Brewer and Frank Trentmann. Oxford: Berg.

Kuhn, Thomas. [1962] 1970. *The Structure of Scientific Revolutions.* 2nd ed. Chicago: University of Chicago Press.

Kuisel, Richard. 1993. *Seducing the French: The Dilemma of Americanization.* Berkeley, CA: Berkeley University Press.

Kulish, Nicholas. 2007. "Europe Fears that Meth Foothold Is Expanding." *The New York Times,* November 23.

Kurtz, Lester R. 2005. "From Heresies to Holy Wars: Toward a Theory of Religious Conflict." *Ahimsa Nonviolence* 1(March–April):143–57.

Kurtz, Lester. 2012. *Gods in the Global Village.* Thousand Oaks, CA: Sage.

Kurzban. 2006. "Post-Sept. 11, 2001." Kurzban's *Immigration Law Sourcebook* (pp. xxi–xxiii). 10th ed. American Immigration Law Foundation.

Kurzman, Charles. 2002. "Bin Laden and Other Thoroughly Modern Muslims." *Contexts* 1(4):13–20.

Lacey, Marc. 2009. "Money Trickles North as Mexicans Help Relatives." *The New York Times,* November 16, p. A1.

Lacey, Marc. 2011. "Rift in Arizona as Latino Class Is Found Illegal." *The New York Times,* January 7. Retrieved March 30, 2012 (http://www.nytimes.com/2011/01/08/ us/08ethnic.html).

Lachapelle, Réjean, and Jean-François Lepage. 2010. *Languages in Canada: 2006 Census.* Ottawa, ON: Heritage Canada and Statistics Canada, Cat. # CH3-2/8-2010.

Lacharite, Jason. 2002. "Electronic Decentralisation in China: A Critical Analysis of Internet Filtering Policies in the People's Republic of China." *Australian Journal of Political Science* 37(2):333–46.

Lacity, Mary Cecelia, and R. A. Hirschheim. 1993. *Information Systems Outsourcing: Myths, Metaphors and Realities.* New York: Wiley.

Lahelma, Eero. 2007. "Health and Social Class." Pp. 2086–91 in *The Blackwell Encyclopedia of Sociology,* edited by George Ritzer. Malden, MA: Blackwell.

Lakoff, Andrew. 2008. "Diagnostic Liquidity: Mental Illness and the Global Trade in DNA." Pp. 277–300 in *The Anthropology of Globalization: A Reader,* 2nd ed., edited by Jonathan Xavier Inda and Renato Rosaldo. Malden, MA: Blackwell.

Lal, Dinesh. 2008. *Indo-Tibet-China Conflict.* Delhi, India: Kalpaz Publications.

Landler, Mark. 2008a. "Credit Cards Tighten Grip Outside US." *The New York Times,* August 30, p. C1.

Landler, Mark. 2008b. "At Tipping Point." *The New York Times,* October 1.

Landry, Bart. 1988. *The New Black Middle Class.* Berkeley: University of California Press.

Landry, Bart, and Kris Marsh. Forthcoming. "The Evolution of the New Black Middle Class." *Annual Review of Sociology.*

Lane, Harlan. 1975. *The Wild Boy of Aveyron.* Cambridge, MA: Harvard University Press.

Lareau, Annette. [1989] 2000. *Home Advantage: Social Class and Parental Intervention in Elementary Education.* 2nd ed. Lanham, MD: Rowman and Littlefield.

Lareau, Annette. 2003. *Unequal Childhoods: Class, Race, and Family Life.* Berkeley: University of California Press.

Larsen, Ulla. 2007. "Gender, Health, and Morality." Pp. 1864–67 in *The Blackwell Encyclopedia of Sociology,* edited by George Ritzer. Malden, MA: Blackwell.

Lash, Scott, and Celia Lury. 2007. *Global Culture Industry*. Cambridge, UK: Polity Press.

Lauderdale, Pat. 2007. "Deviance, Moral Boundaries and." Pp. 1114–16 in *The Blackwell Encyclopedia of Sociology*, edited by George Ritzer. Malden, MA: Blackwell.

Lauer, Sean, and Carrie Yodanis. 2010. "The Deinstitutionalization of Marriage Revisited: A New Institutional Approach to Marriage." *Journal of Family Theory & Review* 2:58–72.

Lauer, Sean, and Carrie Yodanis. 2011. "Individualized Marriage and the Integration of Resources." *Journal of Marriage and Family* 73:669–83.

Laumann, Anne E., and Amy J. Derick. 2006. "Tattoos and Body Piercings in the United States: A National Data Set." *Journal of the American Academy of Dermatology* 55:413–21.

Laurie, N., C. Dwyer, S. Holloway, and F. Smith. 1999. *Geographies of New Femininities*. London: Longman.

Lauster, Nathan, and Adam Easterbrook. 2011. "No Room for New Families? A Field Experiment Measuring Rental Discrimination against Same-sex Couples and Single Parents." *Social Problems* 58(3):389–409.

Lautard, Hugh, and Neil Guppy. 2011. "Multiculturalism or Vertical Mosaic: Occupational Stratification among Canadian Ethnic Groups." In *Society in Question*. 6th ed., edited by Robert Brym. Toronto, ON: Nelson.

Law, Ian. 2007. "Discrimination." Pp. 1182–84 in *The Blackwell Encyclopedia of Sociology*, edited by George Ritzer. Malden, MA: Blackwell.

Law, Ian. 2010. *Racism and Ethnicity: Global Debates, Dilemmas*. London: Pearson.

Law, Ian. 2012a. "Race." Pp. 1737–43 in *The Wiley-Blackwell Encyclopedia of Globalization*, edited by George Ritzer. Malden, MA: Wiley-Blackwell.

Law, Ian. 2012b. "Racism." Pp. 1743–46 in *The Wiley-Blackwell Encyclopedia of Globalization*, edited by George Ritzer. Malden, MA: Wiley-Blackwell.

Law, John, and John Hassard, eds. 1999. *Actor Network Theory and After*. Oxford, UK: Blackwell.

Leavitt, Alex, and Tim Hwang. 2010. "ChatRoulette: An Initial Survey." Web Ecology Project, March 1. Retrieved March 30, 2012 (http://www.slideshare.net/GuiM_/chatroulette-an-initial-survey).

Leavitt, Judith Walzer. 1986. *Brought to Bed: Childbearing in America*. New York: Oxford University Press.

Lechner, Frank J. 1993. "Global Fundamentalism." In *A Future for Religion?* edited by William H. Swatos. Thousand Oaks, CA: Sage.

Lechner, Frank. 2008. *The Netherlands: Globalization and National Identity*. New York: Routledge.

Lechner, Frank, and John Boli. 2005. *World Culture: Origins and Consequences*. Oxford, UK: Blackwell.

Lee, Ching Kwan. 1999. *Gender and the South China Miracle*. Berkeley: University of California Press.

Lee, Marc. 2007. *Eroding Tax Fairness: Tax Incidence in Canada 1990–2005*. Ottawa, ON: Centre for Policy Alternatives.

Lee, Ronald D. 2007. *Global Population Aging and Its Economic Consequences*. Washington, DC: American Enterprise Institute Press.

Lee, Susan Hagood. 2007. "Female Genital Mutilation." Pp. 1653–57 in *The Blackwell Encyclopedia of Sociology*, edited by George Ritzer. Malden, MA: Blackwell.

Lee, Susan Hagood. 2012a. "Genital Mutilation." Pp. 791–93 in *The Wiley-Blackwell Companion to Sociology*, edited by George Ritzer. Malden, MA: Wiley-Blackwell.

Lee, Susan Hagood. 2012b. "Sex Trafficking." In *The Wiley-Blackwell Encyclopedia of Globalization*, edited by George Ritzer. Malden, MA: Wiley-Blackwell.

Lees, Loretta, Tom Slater, and Elvin Wyly, eds. 2010. *The Gentrification Reader*. New York: Routledge.

Le Gales, Patrick. 2007. "Cities in Europe." Pp. 493–97 in *The Blackwell Encyclopedia of Sociology*, edited by George Ritzer. Malden, MA: Blackwell.

Lehman, Wolfgang. 2009. "University as Vocational Education: Working-class Students' Expectations for University." *British Journal of Sociology of Education* 30(2):137–49.

Leicht, Kevin, and Scott Fitzgerald. 2006. *Postindustrial Peasants: The Illusion of Middle-class Prosperity*. New York: Worth.

Leidner, Robin. 1993. *Fast Food, Fast Talk*. Berkeley: University of California Press.

Leitch, Alison. 2003. "Slow Food and the Politics of Pork Fat: Italian Food and European Identity." *Ethnos* 68(4):437–62.

Leitch, Alison. 2010. "Slow Food and the Politics of 'Virtuous Globalization.'" Pp. 45–64 in *The Globalization of Food*, edited by David Inglis and Debra Gimlin. Oxford, UK: Berg.

Lemert, Charles, and Anthony Elliott. 2006. *Deadly Worlds: The Emotional Costs of Globalization*. Lanham, MD: Rowman and Littlefield.

Lengermann, Patricia Madoo, and Gillian Niebrugge. 2008. "Contemporary Feminist Theory." Pp. 450–97 in *Sociological Theory*, edited by George Ritzer. New York: McGraw-Hill.

Lenin, Vladimir. [1917] 1939. *Imperialism: The Highest Stage of Capitalism*. New York: International Publishers.

Lenski, Gerhard. 1954. "Status Crystallization: A Non-vertical Dimension of Stratification." *American Sociological Review* 19:405–13.

Lenton, Rhonda. 1990. "Techniques of Child Discipline and Abuse by Parents." *Canadian Review of Sociology and Anthropology* 27(2):157–85.

Lepp, Annalee. 2013. "Repeat Performance? Human Trafficking and the 2010 Vancouver Winter Olympic Games." In *Selling Sex: Canadian Academics, Advocates, and Sex Workers in Dialogue*, edited by Emily van der Meulen, Elya M. Durisin, and Victoria Love. Vancouver: UBC Press.

Lesthaeghe, Ron J. 2007. "Second Demographic." Pp. 4123–27 in *The Blackwell Encyclopedia of Sociology*, edited by George Ritzer. Malden, MA: Blackwell.

Lesthaeghe, Ron. 2010. "The Unfolding Story of the Second Demographic Transition." *Population and Development Review* 36:211–51.

Lesthaeghe, Ron, and D. J. van de Kaa. 1986. "Twee Demografische Transities?" Pp. 9–24 in *Bevolking: Groei en Krimp, Mens en Maatschappij* (Book Supplement), edited by Ron Lesthaeghe and D. J. van de Kaa. Deventer: Van Loghum, Slaterus.

Levin, Jack. 2007. "Hate Crimes." Pp. 2048–50 in *The Blackwell Encyclopedia of Sociology*, edited by George Ritzer. Malden, MA: Blackwell.

Levitt, Peggy. 2001. *The Transnational Villagers*. Berkeley: University of California Press.

Levitt, Steven. 1998. "The Relationship between Crime Reporting and Police: Implications for the Use of Uniform Crime Reports." *Journal of Quantitative Criminology* 14(1):61–81. Retrieved March 30, 2012 (http://pricetheory.uchicago.edu/levitt/Papers/LevittTheRelationshipBetweenCrime1998.pdf).

Levitt, Steven D., and Stephen J. Dubner. 2005. *Freakonomics: A Rogue Economist Explores the Hidden Side of Everything*. New York: HarperCollins.

Levy, Frank. 1987. *Dollars and Dreams: Changing American Income Distribution*. New York: Russell Sage.

Levy, Frank. 1999. *The New Dollars and Dreams: American Incomes and Economic Change*. New York: Russell Sage.

Levy, Steven. 2010. *Hackers: Heroes of the Computer Revolution*. 25th anniversary ed. O'Reilly Media.

Lewin, Tamar. 2008a. "Oil Money Cultivates a Mideast Ivy League." *The New York Times*, February 11, p. A12.

Lewin, Tamar. 2008b. "Universities Rush to Set Up Outposts Abroad." *The New York Times*, February 10, pp. 1–8.

Lewin, Tamar. 2008c. "U.S. Universities Join Saudis in Partnerships." *The New York Times*, March 6, p. A19.

Lewin, Tamar. 2010. "Children Awake? Then They're Probably Online." *The New York Times*, January 20, pp. A1, A3.

Lewis, C. S. 1960. *The Four Loves*. New York: Harcourt, Brace.

Lewis, Melissa A., Hollie Granato, Jessica A. Blayney, Ty W. Lostutter, and Jason R. Kilmer. 2011. "Predictors of Hooking Up Sexual Behaviors and Emotional Reactions among U.S. College Students." *Archives of Sexual Behavior*, Online First™, July 28.

Ley, David. 2010. "Multiculturalism: A Canadian Defence." Pp. 190–206 in *The Multiculturalism Backlash: European Discourses, Policies and Practices*, edited by Steven Vertovec and Susanne Wessendorf. London: Routledge.

Ley, David. 2013. *Millionaire Migrants: Trans-Pacific Life Lines*. Malden, MA: Wiley-Blackwell.

Leyton-Brown, Ken. 2010. *The Practice of Execution in Canada.* Vancouver, BC: University of British Columbia Press.

Lichtblau, Eric. 2011. "With Lobbying Blitz, Profit-making Colleges Diluted New Rules." *The New York Times,* December 10, pp. A1, A3.

Lichter, Daniel T. 2007. "Family Structure and Poverty." Pp. 1463–65 in *The Blackwell Encyclopedia of Sociology,* edited by George Ritzer. Malden, MA: Blackwell.

Lichtmann, A. J. 2003. "What Really Happened in Florida's 2000 Presidential Election?" *Journal of Legal Studies* 32(1):221–43.

Liebow, Elliot. 1967. *Tally's Corner: A Study of Negro Streetcorner Men.* New York: Little, Brown.

Liftin, Karen T. 2007. "Ozone Depletion." Pp. 927–30 *Encyclopedia of Globalization,* edited by Jan Aart Scholte and Ronald Robertson. New York: MTM Publishing.

Light, Donald W. 2007. "Professional Dominance in Medicine." Pp. 3656–60 in *The Blackwell Encyclopedia of Sociology,* edited by in George Ritzer. Malden, MA: Blackwell.

Lin, Jan. 2012. "World Cities." Pp. 2254–62 in *The Wiley-Blackwell Encyclopedia of Globalization,* edited by George Ritzer. Malden, MA: Wiley-Blackwell.

Lin, N. 1999. "Social Networks and Status Attainment." *Annual Review of Sociology* 25:467–87.

Lin, N. and Y. J. Bian. 1991. "Getting Ahead in Urban China." *American Journal of Sociology* 97:657–88.

Lin, N., W. M. Ensel, and J. C. Vaughn. 1981. "Social Resources and Strength of Ties: Structural Factors in Occupational-Status Attainment." *American Sociological Review* 46:393–403.

Lind, Amy. 2007. "Femininities/Masculinities." Pp. 1662–66 in *The Blackwell Encyclopedia of Sociology,* edited by George Ritzer. Malden, MA: Blackwell.

Linn, James G., and Debra Rose Wilson. 2012. "Health." Pp. 910–23 in *The Wiley-Blackwell Encyclopedia of Globalization,* edited by George Ritzer. Malden, MA: Wiley-Blackwell.

Lipovetsky, Gilles. [1987] 2002. *The Empire of Fashion: Dressing Modern Democracy.* Princeton, NJ: Princeton University Press.

Lipovetsky, Gilles. 2005. *Hypermodern Times.* Cambridge, UK: Polity Press.

Lipset, Seymour M. 1981. *Political Man.* Expanded ed. Baltimore: Johns Hopkins University Press.

Little, Craig B. 2007. "Deviance, Absolutist Definitions of." Pp. 1082–84 in *The Blackwell Encyclopedia of Sociology,* edited by George Ritzer. Malden, MA: Blackwell.

Livermore, Michelle, Rebecca S. Powers, Belinda Creel Davis, and Younghee Lim. 2011. "Failing to Make Ends Meet: Dubious Financial Success among Employed Former Welfare to Work Program Participants." *Journal of Family Economic Issues* 32:73–83.

Logan, John, Richard Alba, and Wenquan Zhang. 2002. "Immigrant Enclaves and Ethnic Communities in New York and Los Angeles." *American Sociological Review* 67(2):299–322.

Lohr, Steve. 2009. "A Web Site Devoted to Your Health." *The New York Times,* October 6.

Lopez, Steven H., Randy Hodson, and Vincent J. Roscigno. 2009. "Power, Status, and Abuse at Work: General and Sexual Harassment Compared." *The Sociological Quarterly* 50:3–27.

Lorber, Judith. 1967. "Deviance as Performance: The Case of Illness." *Social Problems* 14:302–10.

Lorber, Judith. 1994. *Paradoxes of Gender.* New Haven, CT: Yale University Press.

Lorber, Judith. 2000. "Using Gender to Undo Gender: A Feminist Degendering Movement." *Feminist Theory* 1(1):79–95.

Lorber, Judith, and Lisa Jean Moore. 2002. *Gender and the Social Construction of Illness.* Altamira Press.

Lorenz, Edward. 1995. *The Essence of Chaos.* Seattle: University of Washington Press.

Lou, Z. C., S. Senécal, F. Simonet, E. Guimond, C. Penney, and R. Wilkins. 2010. "Birth Outcomes in the Inuit-inhabited Areas of Canada." *Canadian Medical Association Journal* 182(3):235–42.

Lovell, David W. 2007. "Communism." Pp. 612–17 in *The Blackwell Encyclopedia of Sociology,* edited by George Ritzer. Malden, MA: Blackwell.

Low, Setha. 2003. *Behind the Gates: Life, Security, and the Pursuit of Happiness in Fortress America.* New York: Routledge.

Lowe, Brian. 2002. "Hearts and Minds and Morality: Analyzing Moral Vocabularies in Qualitative Studies." *Qualitative Sociology* 25(1):105–12.

Lowe, Graham. 2003. "Healthy Workplaces and Productivity: A Discussion Paper." Economic Analysis and Evaluation Division, Ottawa, ON: Health Canada.

Lowell, B. Lindsay, Micah Bump, and Susan Martin. 2007. "Foreign Students Coming to America: The Impact of Policy, Procedures, and Economic Competition." Retrieved May 31, 2011 (http://www12.georgetown.edu/sfs/isim/Publications/SloanMaterials/Foreign%20Students%20Coming%20to%20America.pdf).

Lowell, Rebecca. 1998. "Modular Homes Move Up." *The Wall Street Journal,* October 23, p. W10.

Loyal, Steve. 2007. "Refugees." Pp. 3837–38 in *The Blackwell Encyclopedia of Sociology,* edited by George Ritzer. Malden, MA: Blackwell.

Lubienski, Christopher. 2006. "School Sector and Academic Achievement: A Multilevel Analysis of NAEP Mathematics Data." *American Educational Research Journal* 43:651–98.

Lucas, J. W., C. Graif, and M. J. Lovaglia. 2008. "Can You Study a Legal System in a Laboratory?" Pp. 119–36 in *Experiments in Criminology and Law: A Research Revolution,* edited by C. Horne and M. J. Lovaglia. Lanham, MD: Rowman and Littlefield.

Lukacs, George. [1922] 1968. *History and Class Consciousness.* Cambridge, MA: MIT Press.

Lukes, S. 1974. *Power: A Radical View.* London: Macmillan.

Luo, Michael. 2010. "At Closing Plant, Ordeal Included Heart Attacks." *The New York Times,* February 24.

Lupton, Deborah. 2007. "Health Risk Behavior." Pp. 2083–85 in *The Blackwell Encyclopedia of Sociology,* edited by George Ritzer. Malden, MA: Blackwell.

Lutfey, K., and J. Mortimer. 2006. "Development and Socialization through the Adult Life Course." In *Handbook of Social Psychology,* edited by John Delamater. New York: Kluwer Academic/Plenum Publishers.

Lüthi, Dieter, Martine Le Floch, Bernhard Bereiter, Thomas Blunier, Jean-Marc Barnola, Urs Siegenthaler, Dominique Raynaud, Jean Jouzel, Hubertus Fischer, Kenji Kawamura, and Thomas F. Stocker. 2008. "High-resolution Carbon Dioxide Concentration Record 650,000–800,000 Years before Present." *Nature* 453:379–82.

Luttrell, M. 2010. "Never-ending iTunes Sales Tally Hits 10 Billion." *TG Daily.* Retrieved November 6, 2011 (http://www.tgdaily.com/consumer-electronics-brief/48578-never-ending-itunes-sales-tally-hits-10-billion).

Luxton, David D., Jennifer D. June, and Julie T. Kinn. 2011. "Technology-based Suicide Prevention: Current Applications and Future Directions." *Telemedicine and e-Health* 17(1):50–54.

Luxton, Meg. 2009 [1980]. *More than a Labour of Love: Three Generations of Women's Work in the Home.* Toronto, ON: The Canadian Women's Educational Press.

Luxton, Meg. 2011. *Changing Families, New Understandings.* Ottawa, ON: The Vanier Institute of the Family.

"Luxury—Cheaper Suites and Empty Beds." 2009. *Executive,* July 1. Retrieved April 16, 2013, from (http://www.executive-magazine.com/special-report/Luxury-Cheaper-suites-and-empty-beds/994).

Lyall, Sarah. 2011. "Scandal Shifts British Media's and Political Landscape." *The New York Times,* July 7.

Lydaki, Anna. 2012. "Gypsies." In *The Wiley-Blackwell Encyclopedia of Sociology Online,* edited by George Ritzer. Malden, MA: Wiley-Blackwell.

Lyotard, Jean-Francois. [1979] 1984. *The Postmodern Condition: A Report on Knowledge.* Minneapolis: University of Minnesota Press.

Maahs, Jeff. 2007. "Juvenile Delinquency." Pp. 2454–55 in *The Blackwell Encyclopedia of Sociology,* edited by George Ritzer. Malden, MA: Blackwell.

MacDonald, Keith, and George Ritzer. 1988. "The Sociology of the Professions: Dead or Alive?" *Work and Occupations* (August):251–72.

MacDonald, Neil. 2010. "The Tea Party's Freak Show." Retrieved March 31, 2012 (http://www.cbc.ca/news/world/story/2010/09/24/f-rfa-macdonald.html).

MacFarquhar, Neil. 2008. "To Muslim Girls, Scouts Offer a Chance to Fit In." *The New York Times,* November 28.

Mackenzie, Adrian. 2005. "The Problem of the Attractor: A Singular Generality between Sciences and Social Theory." *Theory, Culture and Society:*45–65.

Madan, T. N. 2007. "Hinduism." Pp. 571–73 in *Encyclopedia of Globalization,* edited by Jan Aart Scholte and Roland Robertson. New York: MTM Publishing.

Madood, Tariq. 2007. "Multiculturalism." Pp. 3105–108 in *The Blackwell Encyclopedia of Sociology,* edited by George Ritzer. Malden, MA: Blackwell.

Maguire, Jennifer, and Kim Stanway. 2008. "Looking Good: Consumption and the Problems of Self-production." *European Journal of Cultural Studies* 11:63.

Mahoney, James, and Dietrich Rueschmeyer. 2003. *Comparative Historical Analysis in the Social Sciences.* Cambridge, MA: Cambridge University Press.

Mahony, Tina Hotton. 2011. "Women and the Criminal Justice System." Component of Statistics Canada Catalogue no. 89-503-X *Women in Canada: A Gender-based Statistical Report.*

Maiba, Herman. 2005. "Grassroots Transnational Social Movement Activism: The Case of Peoples' Global Action." *Sociological Focus* 38(1):41–63.

Maines, Rachel. 2001. *The Technology of Orgasm: "Hysteria, the Vibrator and Women's Sexual Satisfaction."* Baltimore: Johns Hopkins University Press.

Majora Carter Group. 2009. "Majora Carter Group." Retrieved February 28, 2012 (http://www.majoracartergroup.com).

Malik, Ved. 2011. "Too Close for Comfort." *Hindustan Times,* April 7. Retrieved May 26, 2011 (http://www.hindustantimes.com/News-Feed/columnsothers/Too-close-for-comfort/Article1-682474.aspx).

Malkin, Elisabeth. 2011. "Mexico's Universal Health Care Is Work in Progress." *The New York Times,* January 29. Retrieved March 30, 2012 (http://www.nytimes.com/2011/01/30/world/americas/30mexico.html?pagewanted=all).

Mall of the Emirates. 2010. "About Mall of the Emirates." Retrieved May 19, 2011 (www.malloftheemirates.com/MOE/En/MainMenu/AboutMOE/tabid/64/Default.aspx).

Mamo, Laura. 2007. *Queering Reproduction: Achieving Pregnancy in the Age of Technoscience.* Durham, NC: Duke University Press.

Mampaey, Luc, and Jean-Philippe Renaud. 2000. *Prison Technologies: An Appraisal of Technologies of Political Control.* Luxembourg: European Parliament.

Manicas, Peter. 2007. "Globalization and Higher Education." Pp. 461–77 in *The Blackwell Companion to Globalization,* edited by George Ritzer. Malden, MA: Blackwell.

Mankekar, Purnima. 2005. "'India Shopping': Indian Grocery Stores and Transnational Configurations of Belonging." Pp. 197–214 in *The Cultural Politics of Food and Eating: A Reader,* edited by James L. Watson and Melissa L. Caldwell. Malden, MA: Blackwell.

Mannheim, Karl. [1931] 1936. *Ideology and Utopia.* New York: Harcourt, Brace, and World.

Manning, Peter. 2005. "Impression Management." Pp. 397–99 in *The Encyclopedia of Social Theory,* edited by George Ritzer. Thousand Oaks, CA: Sage.

Manning, Peter. 2007. "Dramaturgy." Pp. 1226–29 in *The Blackwell Encyclopedia of Sociology,* edited by George Ritzer. Malden, MA: Blackwell.

Manning, Robert D. 2001. *Credit Card Nation: The Consequences of America's Addiction to Debt.* New York: Basic Books.

Mansfield, Louise. 2007. "Gender, Sport and." Pp. 1875–80 in *The Blackwell Encyclopedia of Sociology,* edited by George Ritzer. Malden, MA: Blackwell.

Manzo, John. 2010. "Coffee, Connoisseurship, and an Ethnomethodologically Informed Sociology of Taste." *Human Studies* 33(2):141–55.

Marchak, Patricia. 1981. *Ideological Perspectives on Canada.* Toronto, ON: McGraw-Hill Ryerson.

Marchak, Patricia. 2008. *No Easy Fix: Global Responses to Internal Wars and Crimes against Humanity.* Montreal, QU: McGill-Queen's University Press.

Markoff, John. 2007. "Comparative Analysis." Pp. 193–96 in *Encyclopedia of Globalization,* edited by Jan Aart Scholte and Roland Robertson. New York: MTM Publishing.

Marmor, Michael. 2005. *The Status Syndrome: How Social Standing Affects Our Health and Longevity.* New York: Holt.

Maroto, Michelle Lee. 2011. "Professionalizing Body Art: A Marginalized Occupational Group's Use of Informal and Formal Strategies of Control." *Work and Occupations* 38:101–38.

Marre, Diana, and Laura Briggs. 2009. *International Adoption: Global Inequalities and the Circulation of Children.* New York: New York University Press.

Marron, Donncha. 2009. *Consumer Credit in the United States: A Sociological Perspective from the 19th Century to the Present.* New York: Palgrave Macmillan.

Marsden, Peter V., and Elizabeth H. Gorman. 2001. "Social Networks, Job Changes, and Recruitment." Pp. 467–502 in *Sourcebook on Labor Markets: Evolving Structures and Processes,* edited by I. Berg and A. L. Kalleberg. New York: Kluwer Academic/Plenum Publishers.

Marshall, Catherine, and Gretchen Rossman. 2010. *Designing Qualitative Research.* Thousand Oaks, CA: Sage.

Marshall, Katherine. 2006. "Converging Gender Roles." Perspectives on Labour and Income (Statistics Canada, Catalogue no. 75-001-XIE). August online edition.

Marshall, Kathy. 2009. "The Family Work Week." *Perspectives on Labour and Income.* April. Ottawa, ON: Statistics Canada.

Marshall, Katherine. 2010. "Employment Patterns of Postsecondary Students." *Perspectives on Labour and Income* 11(9):5–17.

Marshall, Kathy. 2012. "Paid and Unpaid Work over Three Generations." *Perspectives on Labour and Income.* Spring. Ottawa, ON: Statistics Canada.

Martin, Andrew. 2008. "Mideast Facing Difficult Choice, Crops or Water." *The New York Times,* July 21.

Martin-Chang, Sandra Odette Gould, and Reanne Meuse. 2011. "The Impact of Schooling on Academic Achievement: Evidence from Homeschooled and Traditionally Schooled Students." *Canadian Journal of Behavioural Science* 43(3:195–202.

Marx, Karl. [1842] 1977. "Communism and the Augsburger Allegemeine Zeitung." P. 20 in *Karl Marx: Selected Writings,* edited by David McLellan. New York: Oxford University Press.

Marx, Karl. [1843] 1970. "A Contribution to the Critique of Hegel's Philosophy of Right." Pp. 3–129 in *Marx/Engels Collected Works* (Vol. 3). New York: International Publishers.

Marx, Karl. [1857–1858] 1964. *Pre-capitalist Economic Formations.* New York: International Publishers.

Marx, Karl. [1859] 1970. *A Contribution to the Critique of Political Economy.* New York: International Publishers.

Marx, Karl. 1938. *Critique of the Gotha Programme.* New York: International Publishers.

Marx, Karl, and Friedrich Engels. 1848. *The Communist Manifesto.* London: Communist League.

Marx Ferree, Myra, and Aili Mari Tripp. 2006. "Preface." Pp. vii–ix in *Global Feminism: Transnational Women's Activism, Organizing, and Human Rights,* edited by Myra Marx Ferree and Aili Mari Tripp. New York: New York University Press.

Massaro, Vanessa A., and Emma Gaalaas Mullaney. 2011. "Philly's 'Flash Mob Riots' and the Banality of Post-9/11 Securitization." *City* 15:591–604.

Massey, Douglas. 2003. *Beyond Smoke and Mirrors: Mexican Immigration in an Era of Economic Integration.* New York: Russell Sage Foundation.

Massey, Douglas, and Amelia Brown. 2010. "New Migration Stream between Mexico and Canada." *Migraciones Internacionales* 6(1):119–44.

Mastekaasa, Arne. 1994. "Marital Status, Distress, and Well-being: An International Comparison." *Journal of Comparative Family Studies* 23:183–206.

Mather, Mark. 2009. *Reports on America; Children in Immigrant Families Chart New Path.*

Washington, DC: Population Reference Bureau.

Matza, David. 1966. "The Disreputable Poor." Pp. 289–302 in *Class, Status, and Power: Social Stratification in Comparative Perspective*, edited by Reinhard Bendix and Seymour M. Lipset. 2nd ed. New York: Free Press.

Mawathe, Anne. 2010. "Haunted by Congo Rape Dilemma." BBC News, May 15. Retrieved January 29, 2012 (http://news.bbc.co.uk/2/hi/africa/8677637.stm).

Mayer Brown. 2010. "The United States Blocks on National Security Grounds a Chinese Investment in a US Telecommunications and Solar Technology Firm." Retrieved December 3, 2011 (http://www.mayerbrown.com/publications/article.asp?id=9297&nid=6).

McAdams, Dan P., Michelle Albaugh, Emily Farber, Jennifer Daniels, Regina L. Logan, and Brad Olson. 2008. "Family Metaphors and Moral Intuitions: How Conservatives and Liberals Narrate Their Lives." *Journal of Personality and Social Psychology* 95:978–90.

McBride, Sarah, and Ethan Smith. 2008. "Music Industry to Abandon Mass Suits." *The Wall Street Journal*, December 19.

McCann, Eugene, and Kevin Ward, eds. 2011. *Mobile Urbanism: Cities and Policymaking in the Global Age*. Minneapolis: University of Minnesota Press.

McCann, P. J., and Peter Conrad. 2007. "Deviance, Medicalization of." Pp. 1110–13 in *The Blackwell Encyclopedia of Sociology*, edited by George Ritzer. Malden, MA: Blackwell.

McChesney, R. W. 1999. *Rich Media, Poor Democracy: Communication Politics in Dubious Times*. New York: New Press.

McChesney, Robert. 2003. "The New Global Media." Pp. 260–68 in *The Global Transformations Reader*, edited by David Held and Anthony G. McGrew. Malden, MA: Wiley-Blackwell.

McCormick, Ken. 2011. "Thorstein Veblen." Pp. 185–204 in *The Wiley-Blackwell Companion to Major Social Theorists: Volume 1. Classical Theorists*, edited by George Ritzer and Jeffrey Stepnisky. Malden, MA: Wiley-Blackwell.

McCurdy, David W., and James P. Spradley, eds. 1979. *Issues in Cultural Anthropology: Selected Readings*. Boston: Little, Brown.

McDiarmid, Garnet, and David Pratt. 1971. *Teaching Prejudice: A Content Analysis of Social Studies Textbooks Authorized for Use in Ontario*. Toronto: Ontario Institute for Studies in Education.

McDonald, Michael. 2010. "Voter Turnout." U.S. Elections Project. Retrieved September 14, 2011 (http://elections.gmu.edu/voter_turnout.htm).

McDonald, Michael. 2011. "2010 General Election Turnout Rates." U.S. Elections Project, January 28. Retrieved September 14, 2011 (http://elections.gmu.edu/Turnout_2010G.html).

McDonald's. 2010. "Financial Highlights." Retrieved August 24, 2011 (http://www.aboutmcdonalds.com/mcd/investors/publications/2010_Financial_Highlights.html).

McEwen, Krista, and Kevin Young. 2011. "Ballet and Pain: Reflections from a Risk-dance Culture." Paper presented at the Annual Meetings of the Pacific Sociological Association, Seattle, March 10–13.

McGrew, Ken. 2011. "A Review of Class-based Theories of Student Resistance in Education." *Review of Educational Research* 81:234–66.

McIntosh, Peggy. 2010. "White Privilege: Unpacking the Invisible Knapsack." Pp. 172–77 in *Race, Class and Gender in the United States*, 8th ed., edited by Paula S. Rothenberg. New York: Worth.

McKercher, Catherine. 2011. *The Canadian Reporter: News Writing and Reporting*. Toronto, ON: Nelson Education.

McKinlay, John B., and Joan Arches. 1985. "Towards the Proletarianization of Physicians." *International Journal of Health Services* 15(2).

McKinley, James C., Jr. 2008. "Cyber-rebels in Cuba Defy State's Limits." *The New York Times*, March 6.

McKinley, James C., Jr. 2010. "Fleeing Drug Violence, Mexicans Pour into U.S." *The New York Times*, April 17.

McKnight, David. 2011. "'You're All a Bunch of Pinkos': Rupert Murdoch and the Politics of HarperCollins." *Media Culture Society* 33:835–50.

McLanahan, S. 1999. "Father Absence and the Welfare of Children." In *Coping with Divorce, Single Parenting and Remarriage*, edited by E. M. Hetherington. Mahwah, NJ: Erlbaum.

McLaren, Angus. 1990. *Our Own Master Race: Eugenics in Canada 1885–1945*. Toronto, ON: McClelland and Stewart.

McNair, B. 2002. *Striptease Culture: Sex, Media and the Democratization of Desire*. London: Routledge.

McNeil, Donald G., Jr. 2008a. "A Pandemic that Wasn't But Might Be." *The New York Times*, January 22, pp. D1, D4.

McNeil, Donald G., Jr. 2008b. "W.H.O. Official Complains of Gates Foundation Dominance in Malaria Research." *The New York Times*, February 16, p. A6.

McNeil, Donald G., Jr. 2009. "New Web Site Seeks to Fight Myths about Circumcision and H.I.V." *The New York Times*, March 3.

McNeil, Donald G., Jr. 2010. "At Front Lines, Global War on AIDS Is Falling Apart." *The New York Times*, May 10.

McNichol, Tom. 2011. "Mint That Kills: The Curious Life of Menthol Cigarettes." *The Atlantic Monthly*, March 25.

McPhail, Clark. 2007. "Crowd Behavior." Pp. 880–83 in *The Blackwell Encyclopedia of Sociology*, edited by George Ritzer. Malden, MA: Blackwell.

McShane, Marilyn D., and Frank P. Williams. 2007. "Beccaria, Cesare (1738–94)."

Pp. 255–56 in *The Blackwell Encyclopedia of Sociology* (Vol. 1), edited by George Ritzer. Malden, MA: Blackwell.

McVeigh, R., and C. Smith. 1999. "Who Protests in America: An Analysis of Three Political Alternatives—Inaction, Institutionalized Politics, or Protest." *Sociological Forum* 14(4):685–702.

McVeigh, Tracy. 2011. "Charity President Says Aid Groups Are Misleading the Public on Somalia." *The Guardian*, September 3. Retrieved March 30, 2012 (http://www.guardian.co.uk/global-development/2011/sep/03/charity-aid-groups-misleading-somalia).

Mead, George Herbert. [1934] 1962. *Mind, Self, and Society: From the Standpoint of a Social Behaviorist*. Chicago: University of Chicago Press.

Meier, Robert F. 2007a. "Deviance, Normative Definitions of." Pp. 1116–17 in *The Blackwell Encyclopedia of Sociology*, edited by George Ritzer. Malden, MA: Blackwell.

Meier, Robert F. 2007b. "Deviance, Positivist Theories of." Pp. 1117–21 in *The Blackwell Encyclopedia of Sociology*, edited by George Ritzer. Malden, MA: Blackwell.

Meikle, James. 2009. "Fast Food Firms Taken to Task after Survey of Street Litter." *The Guardian*, January 13.

Melde, Chris, Terrance J. Taylor, and Finn Aage Esbensen. 2009. "'I Got Your Back': An Examination of the Protective Function of Gang Membership in Adolescence." *Criminology* 47(2):565–94.

Meltzer, David. 2009. *First Peoples in a New World: Colonizing Ice Age America*. Berkeley: University of California Press.

Ménard, France-Pascale. 2011. "What Makes It Fall Apart? The Determinants of the Dissolution of Marriages and Common-Law Unions in Canada." *McGill Sociological Review* 2(April):59–76.

Menkes, Suzy. 2008. "Is Fast Fashion Going Out of Fashion?" *The New York Times*, September 21.

Merriam-Webster. 2008. *Merriam-Webster's Collegiate Dictionary*. 11th ed. Merriam-Webster, Inc.

Mersland, Roy, and R. Øystein Strøm. 2010. "Microfinance Mission Drift?" *World Development* 38(1):28.

Merton, Robert. 1938. "Social Structure and Anomie." *American Sociological Review* 3:672–82.

Merton, Robert. [1949] 1968. *Social Theory and Social Structure*. 3rd ed. New York: Free Press.

Merton, Robert K. 1957. *Social Theory and Social Structure*. Rev. ed. Glencoe, IL: Free Press.

Merton, Robert, and Alice S. Kitt. 1950. "Contributions to the Theory of Reference Group Behavior." In *Continuities in Social Research*, edited by Robert K. Merton and Paul F. Lazarsfeld. Glencoe, IL: Free Press.

Messerschmidt, James W. 2007. "Masculinities, Crime and." Pp. 2818–21 in *The Blackwell Encyclopedia of Sociology*, edited by George Ritzer. Malden, MA: Blackwell.

Meszaros, Istvan. 2006. *Marx's Theory of Alienation.* Merlin Press.

Metzl, Jonathan. 2009. *The Protest Psychosis.* Beacon Press.

Meyer, John, J. Boli, and F. Ramirez. 1997. "World Society and the Nation State." *American Journal of Sociology* 103:144–81.

Michael I. Norton, and Dan Ariely. 2011. "Building a Better America—One Wealth Quintile at a Time." *Perspectives on Psychological Science* January:9–12.

Michels, Robert. [1915] 1962. *Political Parties.* New York: Collier Books.

Milan, Anne, Hélène Maheux, and Tina Chui, 2010. "A Portrait of Couples in Mixed Unions." *Canadian Social Trends* 89(Summer):70–80.

Miles, Andrew, Mike Savage, and Felix Bühlmann. 2011. "Telling a Modest Story: Accounts of Men's Upward Mobility from the National Child Development Study." *The British Journal of Sociology* 62:418–41.

Milgram, Stanley. 1974. *Obedience to Authority: An Experimental View.* New York: Harper & Row.

Milibrandt, Tara, and Frank Pearce. 2011. "Emile Durkheim." Pp. 236–82 in *The Wiley-Blackwell Companion to Major Social Theorists: Vol. 1. Classical Theorists,* edited by George Ritzer and Jeffrey Stepnisky. Malden, MA: Wiley-Blackwell.

Miller, Claire Cain. 2009. "The Virtual Visit May Expand Access to Doctors." *The New York Times,* December 21, p. B4.

Miller, Daniel. 1998. *A Theory of Shopping.* Ithaca, NY: Cornell University Press.

Miller, Daniel, and Donald Slater. 2000. *The Internet: An Ethnographic Approach.* London: Berg.

Miller, Gale, and James A. Holstein, eds. 1993. *Constructionist Controversies: Issues in Social Problems Theory.* New York: Aldine De Gruyter.

Miller, J. Mitchell, and Richard Tewksbury, eds. 2001. *Extreme Methods: Innovative Approaches to Social Science Research.* Boston: Allyn & Bacon.

Miller, Jody. 2001. *One of the Guys: Girls, Gangs and Gender.* New York: Oxford University Press.

Mills, C. Wright. 1951. *White Collar.* New York: Oxford University Press.

Mills, C. Wright. 1956. *The Power Elite.* New York: Oxford University Press.

Mills, C. Wright. 1959. *The Sociological Imagination.* New York: Oxford University Press.

Milner, Henry. 2010. *The Internet Generation: Engaged Citizens or Political Dropouts.* Medford, MA: Tufts University Press.

Mindlin, Alex. 2006. "Seems Somebody Is Clicking on that Spam." *The New York Times,* July 3.

Mirchandani, Kiran. 2004. "Practices of Global Capital: Gaps, Cracks and Ironies in Transnational Call Centres in India." *Global Networks* 4(4):355–73.

Mishell, Lawrence, and Josh Bivens. 2011. "Occupy Wall Streeters Are Right about Skewed Economic Rewards in the United States." Economic Policy Institute Briefing Paper #331, October 26. Retrieved March 31, 2012 (http://www.epi.org/files/2011/BriefingPaper331.pdf).

Mitchell, Juliet. 1975. *Psychoanalysis and Feminism.* New York: Random House.

Mitford, Jessica. 1993. *The American Way of Birth.* New York: Plume.

"Mixed Views of Obama at Year's End." 2009. Pew Research Center for the People and the Press, December 16. Retrieved March 31, 2012 (http://people-press.org/report/572/mixed-views-of-obama-at-year-end).

Modood, Tariq. 2007. "Multiculturalism." Pp. 3105–108 in *The Blackwell Encyclopedia of Sociology,* edited by George Ritzer. Malden, MA: Blackwell.

Moffitt, Terrie E. 1993. "'Life Course-Persistent' and 'Adolescence-Limited' Antisocial Behavior: A Developmental Taxonomy." *Psychological Review* 100:674–701.

Moghadam, Valentine. 1999. "Gender and Globalization: Female Labor and Women's Mobilization." *Journal of World-Systems Research* 5:2.

Molm, Linda D. 2007. "Power-Dependence Theory." Pp. 3598–602 in *The Blackwell Encyclopedia of Sociology,* edited by George Ritzer. Oxford: Blackwell.

Molm, Linda D., and Karen S. Cook. 1995. "Social Exchange and Exchange Networks." Pp. 209–35 in *Sociological Perspective on Social Psychology,* edited by K. S. Cook, G. A. Fine, and J. S. House. Boston: Allyn and Bacon.

Molotch, Harvey. 2003. *Where Stuff Comes From.* New York: Routledge.

Monaghan, Lee F. 2007. "McDonaldizing Men's Bodies? Slimming, Associated (Ir)Rationalities and Resistances." *Body & Society* 13:67–93.

Monaghan, Lee F., Robert Hollands, and Gary Pritchard. 2010. "Obesity Epidemic Entrepreneurs: Types, Practices and Interests." *Body & Society* 16:37–71.

Monbiot, George, and Todd Gitlin. 2011. "How to Be Radical? An Interview with Todd Gitlin and George Monbiot." OpenDemocracy, April 5. Retrieved November 9, 2011 (http://www.opendemocracy.net/democracy-vision_reflections/article_1462.jsp).

Montaigne, Fen. 2009. "The Ice Retreat: Global Warming and the Adelie Penguin." *The New Yorker,* December 21, p. 72.

Montoya, I. D. 2005. "Effect of Peers on Employment and Implications for Drug Treatment." *American Journal of Drug and Alcohol Abuse* 31:657–68.

Montt, Guillermo. 2011. "Cross-national Differences in Educational Inequality." *Sociology of Education* 84:49–68.

Moore, D. 1995. "Role Conflict: Not Only for Women? A Comparative Analysis of 5 Nations." *International Journal of Comparative Sociology* 36(1–2):17–35.

Moore, Dene. 2012. "Hundreds of Women Come Forward in RCMP Harassment Class-action Lawsuit." *The Globe and Mail,* July 30. Retrieved on September 28, 2012 http://www.theglobeandmail.com/news/national/hundreds-of-women-come-forward-in-rcmp-harassment-class-action-lawsuit/article4450218/).

Moore, Elizabeth Armstrong. 2010. "Harvard Health Expert Calls Facebook 'Wild West.'" CNET News. Retrieved February 27, 2012 (http://news.cnet.com/8301-27083_3-20021519-247.html).

Moore, Lisa Jean, and Mary Kosut, eds. 2010. *The Body Reader: Essential Social and Cultural Readings.* New York: New York University Press.

Moore, R. Laurence. 1997. *Selling God: American Religion in the Marketplace of Culture.* Oxford: Oxford University Press.

Moran, Mary, Javier Guzman, Anne-Laure Ropars, Alina McDonald, Nicole Jameson, Brenda Omune, Sam Ryan, and Lindsey Wu. 2009. "Neglected Disease Research and Development: How Much Are We Really Spending?" *PLoS Med* 6(2):e1000030.

Morelli, M. 1983. "Milgram's Dilemma of Obedience." *Metaphilosophy* 14:183.

Morgan, David H. J. 2007. "Marriage." Pp. 2789–91 in *The Blackwell Encyclopedia of Sociology,* edited by George Ritzer. Malden, MA: Blackwell.

Morgan, Stephen G. 2007. "Direct-to-consumer Advertising and Expenditures on Prescription Drugs: A Comparison of Experiences in the United States and Canada." *Open Medicine* 1(1):e37–e45.

Morgan, S. Philip. 2007. "Fertility, Low." Pp. 1729–33 in *The Blackwell Encyclopedia of Sociology,* edited by George Ritzer. Malden, MA: Blackwell.

Morozov, Evgeny. 2011. *The Net Delusion: The Dark Side of Internet Freedom.* Public Affairs.

Morris, Aldon. 1984. *The Origins of the Civil Rights Movement: Black Communities Organizing for Change.* New York: Free Press.

Morris, Aldon. 2007. "Civil Rights Movement." Pp. 507–12 in *The Blackwell Encyclopedia of Sociology,* edited by George Ritzer. Malden, MA: Blackwell.

Morris, Alex. 2011. "They Know What Boys Want: Why Learning about Sex from the Web Comes with Drawbacks." *New York Magazine.* Retrieved March 31, 2012 (http://nymag.com/news/features/70977/).

Morrow, Richard L., E. Jane Garland, James M. Wright, Malcolm Maclure, Suzanne Taylor, and Colin R. Dormuth. 2012. "Influence of Relative Age on Diagnosis and Treatment of Attention-deficit/Hyperactivity Disorder in Children." *CMAJ* 184:755–62. Retrieved April 16, 2013 (http://www.cmaj.ca/search?author1=Richard+L.+Morrow&sortspec=date&submit=Submit).

Moses, Jonathon W. 2006. *International Migration: Globalization's Last Frontier.* London: Zed Books.

Mugarask, Larry. 2011. *Buffalo Law Review* 83(1):1.

Munford, Monty. 2010. "India Digs a Tunnel at the Top of the World as China Bides Its Time." *The Telegraph*, August 11. Retrieved May 26, 2011 (http://blogs.telegraph.co.uk/news/montymunford1/100050206/india-digs-a-tunnel-at-the-top-of-the-world-as-china-bides-its-time/).

Muniz, Albert M., Jr. 2007. "Brands and Branding." Pp. 357–60 in *The Blackwell Encyclopedia of Sociology*, edited by George Ritzer. Malden, MA: Blackwell.

Muniz, Albert M., Jr., and Thomas C. O'Guinn. 2001. "Brand Community." *Journal of Consumer Research* 27:412–32.

Munton, Don, and Ken Wilkening. 2007. "Acid Rain." In *Encyclopedia of Globalization*, edited by Jan Aart Scholte and Ronald Robertson. New York: MTM Publishing.

Murphy, Brian, Zuelin Zhang, and Claude Dionne. 2012. *Low Income in Canada: A Multi-Line Multi-Index Perspective*. Ottawa, ON: Statistics Canada Catalogue #75F0002M—No. 001.

Murray, Graham. 2006. "France: The Riots and the Republic." *Race and Class* 47:26–45.

Murthy, Dhiraj. 2008. "Digital Ethnography: An Examination of the Use of New Technologies for Social Research." *Sociology* 42:837–55.

Musick, Kelly. 2007. "Fertility: Nonmarital." Pp. 1734–37 in *The Blackwell Encyclopedia of Sociology*, edited by George Ritzer. Malden, MA: Blackwell.

Mydans, Seth. 2008. "Indonesian Chickens, and People, Hard Hit by Bird Flu." *The New York Times*, February 1, p. A3.

Myers, Daniel J. 2007. "Riots." Pp. 3921–26 in *The Blackwell Encyclopedia of Sociology*, edited by George Ritzer. Malden, MA: Blackwell.

Nakano-Glenn, Evelyn. 2000. "The Social Construction and Institutionalization of Gender and Race." Pp. 3–43 in *Revisioning Gender*, edited by M. M. Ferree, J. Lorber, and B. B. Hess. Thousand Oaks, CA: Sage.

Nakhaie, Reza. 2006. "Electoral Participation in Municipal, Provincial and Federal Elections in Canada." *Canadian Journal of Political Science* 39(2):363–90.

Nanda, Serena. 1999. *Neither Man Nor Woman: The Hijras of India*. 2nd ed. Belmont, CA: Wadsworth.

Naples, Nancy A. 2009. "Presidential Address: Crossing Borders: Community Activism, Globalization, and Social Justice." *Social Problems* 56:2–20.

Naples, Nancy A., and Manisha Desai. 2002. "Women's Local and Transnational Responses: An Introduction to the Volume." In *Women's Activism and Globalization: Linking Local Struggles and Transnational Politics*, edited by Nancy A. Naples and Manisha Desai. New York: Routledge.

Naples, Nancy A., and Barbara Gurr. 2012. "Genders and Sexualities in Global Context: An Intersectional Assessment of Contemporary Scholarship." Pp. 304–32 in *The Wiley-Blackwell Companion to Sociology*, edited by George Ritzer. Malden, MA: Wiley-Blackwell.

Napoli, Lisa. 1999. "Dispensing of Drugs on Internet Stirs Debate." *The New York Times*, April 6. Retrieved March 31, 2012 (http://query.nytimes.com/gst/fullpage.html?res=9B02E1D61139F935A35757C0A96F958260&scp=8&sq=pharmaceutical%20purchase%20over%20internet&st=cse).

Naquin, Charles E., Terri R. Kurtzberg, and Liuba Y. Belkin. 2008. "E-mail Communication and Group Cooperation in Mixed Motive Contexts." *Social Justice Research* 21:470–89.

Nasar, Jack L., Jennifer S. Evans-Cowley, and Vicente Mantero. 2007. "McMansions: The Extent and Regulation of Supersized Houses." *Journal of Urban Design* 12:339–58.

National Center for Health Statistics. 2011. "Health, United States, 2010." U.S. Department of Health and Human Services. Retrieved February 28, 2012 (http://www.cdc.gov/nchs/data/hus/hus10.pdf).

National Institutes of Health. 2011. "Human Genome Project." Retrieved April 15, 2011 (http://report.nih.gov/NIHfactsheets/ViewFactSheet.aspx?csid=45&key=H#H).

National Oceanic and Atmospheric Administration. 2013. "Japan Tsunami Marine Debris." Washington, DC: U.S. Department of Commerce. Retrieved April 15, 2013 (http://marinedebris.noaa.gov/tsunamidebris/debris_sightings.html).

National Response Team. 2011. "On Scene Coordinator Report: Deepwater Horizon Oil Spill." Retrieved April 29, 2013 (http://www.uscg.mil/foia/docs/dwh/fosc_dwh_report.pdf).

Navarro, Mireya. 2006. "For Divided Family, Border Is Sorrowful Barrier." *The New York Times*, December 21.

Nayyer, Deepak. 2010. "China, India, Brazil, and South Africa in the World Economy: Engines of Growth?" In *Southern Engines of Global Growth*, edited by Amelie U. Santos-Paulino and Guanghua Wan. Oxford.

Nederveen Pieterse, Jan. 2009. *Globalization and Culture: Global Melange*. 2nd ed. Lanham, MD: Rowman and Littlefield.

"Netherlands: High-grade Marijuana to Be Declassified." 2011. *The New York Times*, October 7. Accessed December 20, 2011 (http://www.nytimes.com/2011/10/08/world/europe/netherlands-high-grade-marijuana-to-be-reclassified.html).

Neuendorf, Kimberly A., Thomas D. Gore, Amy Dalessandro, Patricie Janstova, and Sharon Snyder-Suh. 2009. "Shaken and Stirred: A Content Analysis of Women's Portrayals in James Bond Film." *Sex Roles* 62:747–76.

Neuwirth, Robert. 2011. *Stealth of Nations: The Global Rise of the Informal Economy*. New York: Pantheon.

Newman, Andy. 2011. "Go Hands-free, or Risk Points on Your License." *The New York Times*, February 16. Retrieved March 31, 2012 (http://cityroom.blogs.nytimes.com/2011/02/16/go-hands-free-or-risk-points-on-your-license/?ref=andynewman&gwh=E21FA99531426B5BDF47E03EBF34EAF7).

Newman, Jerry. 2007. *My Secret Life on the McJob: Lessons from Behind the Counter Guaranteed to Supersize Any Management Style*. New York: McGraw-Hill.

Newman, Katherine S., Cybelle Fox, David Harding, Jal Mehta, and Wendy Roth. 2004. *Rampage: The Social Roots of School Shootings*. Cambridge, MA: Basic Books.

Newman, Otto. 1968. "The Sociology of the Betting Shop." *The British Journal of Sociology* 19(1):17–33.

Newsweek. 2010. "Why the Palace Fell: Lessons Learned from the Destruction of Haiti's Presidential Home." Retrieved March 31, 2012 (http://www.thedailybeast.com/newsweek/2010/01/20/why-the-palace-fell.html).

Newton, David E. 2009. *Gay and Lesbian Rights: A Reference Handbook*. ABC-CLIO.

Newton, Isaac (with Stephen Hawking). [1687] 2005. *Principia (On the Shoulders of Giants)*. Philadelphia: Running Press.

Newton, Michael. 2002. *Savage Girls and Wild Boys: A History of Feral Children*. London: Faber and Faber.

New York University Institute for Public Knowledge. 2011. "Arjun Appadurai: IPK Senior Fellow." Retrieved December 3, 2011 (http://www.nyu.edu/ipk/people/arjun-appadurai).

New York University Steinhardt School of Culture, Education, and Human Development. 2012. "Arjun Appadurai." Retrieved April 1, 2012 (http://steinhardt.nyu.edu/faculty_bios/view/Arjun_Appadurai).

Nichols, Brian J. 2012. "Buddhism." Pp. 142–45 in *The Wiley-Blackwell Encyclopedia of Globalization*, edited by George Ritzer. Malden, MA: Wiley-Blackwell.

Nicholson, Linda. 2008. *Identity Before Identity Politics*. Cambridge, UK: Cambridge University Press.

Niebuhr, Gustav. 1995. "Where Shopping-mall Culture Gets a Big Dose of Religion." *The New York Times*, April 16, pp. 1, 14.

Ninomiya, Akira, Jane Knight, and Aya Watanabe. 2009. "The Past, Present, and Future of Internationalization in Japan." *Journal of Studies in International Education* 13(2):117–24.

Noble, David F. 2011. *Forces of Production: A Social History of Industrial Automation*. Transaction.

Nobles, Jenna. 2011. "Parenting from Abroad: Migration, Nonresident Father Involvement, and Children's Education in Mexico." *Journal of Marriage & Family* 73:729–46.

Noël, Alain, and Florence Larocque. 2009. "Aboriginal Peoples and Poverty in Canada: Can Provincial Governments Make a Difference?" Paper prepared for the Annual Meeting of the International Sociological Association's Research Committee 19, Montréal, August 20.

Nolan, Stephanie. 2006. "The African State: An AIDS Survivor." *The Globe and Mail* (Toronto), August 10, p. A7.

Nordenmark, Mikael. 2007. "Unemployment." Pp. 5090–91 in *The Blackwell Encyclopedia of Sociology,* edited by George Ritzer. Malden, MA: Blackwell.

Nordland, Rod. 2010. "Taliban Order Stoning Deaths in Bold Display." *The New York Times,* August 17, pp. A1, A10.

Nordland, Rod, and Taimoor Shah. 2010. "Arrest Made in Afghan Disfigurement Case." *The New York Times,* December 7. Retrieved March 31, 2012 (http://www.nytimes.com/2010/12/08/world/asia/08afghan.html).

Nordstrom, Carolyn. 2007. *Global Outlaws: Crime, Money, and Power in the Contemporary World.* Berkeley: University of California Press.

Norris, Dawn. 2011. "Interactions that Trigger Self-labeling: The Case of Older Undergraduates." *Symbolic Interaction* 34:173–97.

Norris, Pippa. 2001. "Global Governance and Cosmopolitan Citizens." Pp. 155–77 in *Governance in a Globalizing World,* edited by Joseph S. Nye and John D. Donahue. Washington, DC: Brookings University Press.

Norris, Pippa. 2010. *Public Sentinel: News Media and Governance Reform.* Washington, DC: World Bank Publications.

Norris, Pippa. 2011. *Democratic Deficit: Critical Citizens Revisited.* Cambridge, UK: University of Cambridge Press.

Norris, Trevor. 2011a. *Consuming Schools: Commercialism and the End of Politics.* Toronto, ON: University of Toronto Press.

Norris, Trevor. 2011b. "Response to David Waddington's Review of *Consuming Schools: Commercialization and the End of Politics.*" *Studies in the Philosophy of Education* 30:93–96.

Nossiter, Adam. 2010. "Shaken by a Promise of Riches." *International Herald Tribune,* August 20, p. 2.

Novek, Joel. 1992. "The Labour Process and Workplace Injuries in the Canadian Meat-packing Industry." *Canadian Review of Sociology and Anthropology* 29(1):17–37.

Nuland, Sherwin. 1994. *How We Die: Reflections on Life's Final Chapter.* New York: Knopf.

Nunn, Samuel. 2007. "Cybercrime." Pp. 960–61 in *The Blackwell Encyclopedia of Sociology,* edited by George Ritzer. Malden, MA: Blackwell.

Nuru-Jeter, Amani, Tyan Parker Dominguez, Wizdom Powell Hammond, Janxin Leu, Marilyn Skaff, Susan Egerter, Camara P. Jones, and Paula Braveman. 2008. "It's the Skin You're In: African American Women Talk about Their Experiences of Racism. An Exploratory Study to Develop Measures of Racism for Birth Outcome Studies." *Maternal Child Health Journal.*

Nyden, Philip W., Leslie H. Hossfeld, and Gwendolyn E. Nyden. 2011. *Public Sociology: Research, Action, and Change.* Thousand Oaks, CA: Sage.

Oakes, Jennie. 2005. *Keeping Track: How Schools Structure Inequality.* 2nd ed. New Haven, CT: Yale University Press.

O'Byrne, Darren, and Alexander Hensby. 2011. *Theorizing Global Studies.* Palgrave Macmillan.

O'Connell Davidson, Julia. 2005. *Children in Global Sex Trade.* Cambridge, UK: Polity Press.

O'Connor, Brendan, and Martin Griffiths. 2005. *The Rise of Anti-Americanism.* London: Routledge.

O'Dell, Jolie. 2010. "12 Chatroulette Clones You Should Try." Mashable. Retrieved April 27, 2011 (http://mashable.com/2010/04/12/12-chatroulette-clones-you-should-try/).

O'Guinn, Thomas C., and Russel W. Belk. 1989. "Heaven on Earth: Consumption at Heritage Village, USA." *Journal of Consumer Research* 16:227–38.

O'Leary, Ann. 1985. "Self-efficacy and Health." *Behaviour Research and Therapy* 23(4):437–51.

O'Reilly, Tim. 2005. "What Is Web 2.0?" Retrieved March 31, 2012 (http://www.oreillynet.com/pub/a/oreilly/tim/news/2005/09/30/what-is-web-20.html).

Oberschall, Anthony. 2012. "Ethnic Cleansing." Pp. 547–51 in *The Wiley-Blackwell Encyclopedia of Globalization,* edited by George Ritzer. Malden, MA: Wiley-Blackwell.

Ocloo, Josephine Enyonam. 2010. "Harmed Patients Gaining Voice: Challenging Dominant Perspectives in the Construction of Medical Harm and Patient Safety Reforms." *Social Science & Medicine* 71:510–16.

Offutt, Michael. 2012. "Microfinance." Pp. 1373–77 in *The Wiley-Blackwell Encyclopedia of Globalization,* edited by George Ritzer. Malden, MA: Wiley-Blackwell.

Ogburn, William F. 1922. *Social Change.* New York: The Viking Press.

Ohlsson-Wijk, Sofi. 2011. "Sweden's Marriage Revival: An Analysis of the New-millennium Switch from Long-term Decline to Increasing Popularity." *Population Studies* 65:183–200.

Olson, Lynn. 2002. *Freedom's Daughters: The Unsung Heroines of the Civil Rights Movements from 1830 to 1970.* New York: Scribner.

Omi, Michael, and Howard Winant. 1994. *Racial Formation in the United States: From the 1960s to the 1990s.* New York: Routledge.

Ong, Aihwa. 2003. "Cyberpublics and Diaspora Politics among Transnational Chinese." *Interventions* 5(1):82–100.

Ong, Paul. 2007. "Bovine Spongiform Encephalo-pathy." Pp. 102–106 in *Encyclopedia of Globalization,* edited by Jan Aart Scholte and Roland Robertson. New York: MTM Publishing.

Onishi, Norimitsu. 2010. "Toiling Far from Home for Philippine Dreams." *The New York Times,* September 19, p. 5.

Oreopoulos, Philip. 2009. "Why Do Skilled Immigrants Struggle in the Labor Market? A Field Experiment with Six Thousand Résumés." Working Paper, Economics, University of British Columbia.

Organisation for Economic Co-operation and Development. 2010. "A Family Affair: Intergenerational Social Mobility across OECD Countries." Retrieved May 15, 2013 (http://www.oecd.org/eco/public-finance/chapter%205%20gfg%202010.pdf).

Organisation for Economic Co-operation and Development. 2011a. *Divided We Stand: Why Inequality Keeps Rising.* Paris: Author.

Organisation for Economic Co-operation and Development. 2011b. "Health at a Glance: OECD Indicators." Retrieved January 7, 2013 (http://www.oecd-ilibrary.org/sites/health_glance-2011-en/index.html?contentType=/ns/Book,/ns/StatisticalPublication&itemId=/content/book/health_glance-2011-en&containerItemId=/content/serial/199913 12&accessItemIds=&mimeType=text/html).

Organisation for Economic Co-operation and Development. 2012a. "Health Policies and Data: OECD Health Data 2012—Frequently Requested Data." Retrieved May 14, 2013 (http://www.oecd.org/els/health-systems/oecdhealthdata2012-frequentlyrequesteddata.htm).

Organisation for Economic Co-operation and Development. 2012b. "OECD Health Data 2012: How Does Canada Compare." Retrieved January 9, 2013 (http://www.oecd.org/canada/BriefingNoteCANADA2012.pdf).

Organisation for Economic Co-operation and Development. 2012c. "Share of Births Out of Wedlock and Teenage Births." Retrieved January 30, 2013 (http://www.oecd.org/els/familiesandchildren/SF2.4_Births%20outside%20marriage%20and%20teenage%20births%20-%20updated%20240212.pdf).

Orkin, Haris. 2011. "Did Dead Island's Powerful Announcement Trailer Misrepresent the Highly Anticipated Video Game?" PRWeb. Retrieved May 27, 2011 (http://www.prweb.com/releases/prweb2011/5/prweb8482799.htm).

Orlikowski, Wanda J. 2010. "Technology and Organization: Contingency All the Way Down." Pp. 239–46 in *Technology and Organization: Essays in Honour of Joan Woodward (Research in the Sociology of Organizations, Volume 29),* edited by in Nelson Phillips, Graham Sewell, Dorothy Griffiths. Emerald Group.

Orloff, Ann S. 1993. *The Politics of Pensions: A Comparative Analysis of Britain, Canada and the United States, 1880s–1940.* Madison: University of Wisconsin Press.

Orr, Martin. 2012. "Great Recession." Pp. 890–91 in *The Encyclopedia of Globalization,* edited by George Ritzer. Malden, MA: Wiley-Blackwell.

Ortiz, S. Y., and V. J. Roscigno. 2009. "Discrimination, Women, and Work: Processes and Variations by Race and Class." *The Sociological Quarterly* 50(2):336–59.

Orum, Anthony M. 2007. "Urbanization." Pp. 5151–54 in *The Blackwell Encyclopedia of Sociology,* edited by George Ritzer. Malden, MA: Blackwell.

Orwell, George. 1949. *Nineteen Eighty-four.* London: Secker and Warburg.

Oshri, Ilan, Julia Kotlarsky, and Leslie Willcocks. 2009. *The Handbook of Global Outsourcing and Offshoring.* Basingstoke, UK: Palgrave Macmillan.

Osman, Suleiman. 2011. *The Invention of Brownstone Brooklyn: Gentrification and the Search for Authenticity in Postwar New York.* New York: Oxford University Press.

Ovaska, Tomi, and Ryo Takashima. 2010. "Does a Rising Tide Lift All the Boats? Explaining the National Inequality of Happiness." *Journal of Economic Issues* 44(1):205–23.

Pace, Julie. 2010. "Obama Takes on Election-year Fears Over Big Debt." Retrieved March 31, 2012 (http://www.cbsnews.com/stories/2010/09/19/national/main6881308.shtml).

Packer, George. 2006. "The Megacity: Decoding the Chaos of Lagos." *The New Yorker,* November 12.

Pager, D. 2003. "The Mark of a Criminal Record." *American Journal of Sociology* 108(5):937–975.

Pager, D., B. Western, and B. Bonikowski. 2009. "Discrimination in a Low-wage Labor Market: A Field Experiment." *American Sociological Review* 74(5):777–99.

Panitch, Leo. 2009. "Thoroughly Modern Marx." *Foreign Policy,* April 15.

Park, Robert E. [1927] 1973. "Life History." *American Journal of Sociology* 79:251–60.

Park, Robert, Ernest Burgess, and R. D. McKenzie. [1925] 1967. *The City: Suggestions for Investigation of Human Behavior in the Urban Environment.* Chicago: University of Chicago Press.

Parker, David, and Miri Song. 2006. "New Ethnicities Online: Reflexive Racialisation and the Internet." *The Sociological Review* 54:575–94.

Parker, Stanley. 1971. *The Future of Work and Leisure.* London: MacGibbon and Kee.

Parreñas, Rhacel. 2001. *Servants of Globalization: Women, Migration, and Domestic Work.* Stanford, CA: Stanford University Press.

Parrillo, Vincent N. 2007. "Urban." Pp. 5101–104 in *The Blackwell Encyclopedia of Sociology,* edited by George Ritzer. Malden, MA: Blackwell.

Parsons, Talcott. 1943. "The Kinship System of the Contemporary United States." *American Anthropologist* 43:22–38.

Parsons, Talcott. 1951. *The Social System.* Glencoe, IL: Free Press.

Parsons, Talcott. 1966. *Societies.* Englewood Cliffs, NJ: Prentice-Hall.

Passel, Jeffrey. 2010. "Race and the Census: The 'Negro' Controversy." Pew Research Center Online, January 21. Retrieved January 16, 2012 (http://www.pewsocialtrends.org/2010/01/21/race-and-the-census-the-%E2%80%9Cnegro%E2%80%9D-controversy/).

Passport Canada. 2012. "History of Passports." Retrieved on February 1, 2013 (http://www.ppt.gc.ca/pptc/hist.aspx).

Patch, Jason, and Neil Brenner. 2007. "Gentrification." Pp. 1917–20 in *The Blackwell Encyclopedia of Sociology,* edited by George Ritzer. Malden, MA: Blackwell.

Patchin, Justin W., and Sameer Hinduja. 2010. "Trends in Online Social Networking: Adolescent Use of MySpace Over Time." *New Media and Society* 12:197–216.

Patchin, Justin W., and Sameer Hinduja. 2011. "Traditional and Nontraditional Bullying among Youth: A Test of General Strain Theory." *Youth Society* 43:727–51.

Patel, Reena. 2010. *Working the Night Shift: Women in India's Call Centers.* Palo Alto, CA: Stanford University Press.

Paternoster, Raymond. 1992. *Capital Punishment in America.* Lexington, MA: Lexington Books.

Paternoster, Ray. 2007. "Capital Punishment." Pp. 385–88 in *The Blackwell Encyclopedia of Sociology,* Vol. 2, edited by George Ritzer. Malden, MA: Blackwell.

Paternoster, Raymond, Robert Brame, and Sarah Bacon. 2007. *The Death Penalty: America's Experience with Capital Punishment.* Oxford: Oxford University Press.

Patterson, Maurice, and Jonathan Schroeder. 2010. "Borderlines: Skin, Tattoos and Consumer Culture Theory." *Marketing Theory* 10:253–67.

Patton, Peter L. 1998. "The Gangstas in Our Midst." *Urban Review* 30:49–76.

Pavalko, E. K., and G. H. Elder. 1990. "World War II and Divorce: A Life-course Perspective." *American Journal of Sociology* 95:1213–34.

Payton, Andrew, and Peggy A. Thoits. 2011. "Medicalization, Direct-to-Consumer Advertising, and Mental Illness Stigma." *Society and Mental Health* 1:55–70.

PBS. 2010. *Frontline: Digital Nation.* Retrieved May 25, 2011 (http://www.pbs.org/wgbh/pages/frontline/digitalnation/view/).

PBS NewsHour. 2006. "Tracking Nuclear Proliferation: Country Profiles." Retrieved May 26, 2011 (http://www.pbs.org/newshour/indepth_coverage/military/proliferation/profiles.html).

Pearlin, Leonard I. 1989. "The Sociological Study of Stress." *Journal of Health and Social Behavior* 30:241–56.

Pearson, Ruth. 1992. "Gender Issues in Industrialization." In *Industrialization and Development,* edited by T. Hewitt, J. Johnson, and D. Wield. Oxford: Oxford University Press.

Pearson, Ruth. 2000. "Moving the Goalposts: Gender and Globalization in the Twenty-first Century." *Gender and Development* 8(1):10–19.

Pegg, Rayne. 2010. "Survey Says: Farmers Markets on the Rise." USDA Blog. Retrieved May 27, 2011 (http://blogs.usda.gov/2010/08/04/survey-says-farmers-markets-on-the-rise/).

Peiris, David, Alex Brown, and Alan Cass. 2008. "Addressing Inequities in Access to Quality Health Care for Indigenous People." *Canadian Medical Association Journal* 179(10). Retrieved May 6, 2013 (http://www.cmaj.ca/content/179/10/985.full#ref-10).

Pendakur, Krishna, and Ravi Pendakur. 2012. "Colour by Numbers: Minority Earnings in Canada 1996–2006." *Journal of International Migration and Integration* 12(3):305–329.

People v. Hall 4 Cal. 399. 1854. Supreme Court of the State of California.

Peoples, Clayton D. 2012. "Welfare State." Pp. 2218–21 in *The Encyclopedia of Globalization,* edited by George Ritzer. Malden, MA: Wiley-Blackwell.

Perchel, Harland. 2007. "Taylorism." Pp. 4939–40 in *The Blackwell Encyclopedia of Sociology,* edited by George Ritzer. Malden, MA: Blackwell.

Perkins, Harvey C., and David C. Thorns. 2001. "Gazing or Performing? Reflections on Urry's Tourist Gaze in the Context of Contemporary Experience in the Antipodes." *International Sociology* 16(2):185–204.

Perloff, Richard M., Bette Bonder, George B. Ray, Eileen Berlin Ray, and Laura A Siminoff. 2006. "Doctor-patient Communication, Cultural Competence, and Minority Health: Theoretical and Empirical Perspectives." *American Behavioral Scientist* 49(6):835–52.

Perna, Laura W. 2006. "Studying College Access and Choice: A Proposed Conceptual Model." Pp. 99–157 in *Higher Education: Handbook of Theory and Research,* Vol. 21, edited by Jean Smart. The Netherlands: Springer.

Perreault, Samuel. 2004. *Visible Minorities and Victimization.* Statistics Canada, Canadian Centre for Justice Statistics Profile Series, Cat. #85F0033MIE—No. 015.

Perreault, Samuel. 2009. "The Incarceration of Aboriginal People in Adult Correctional Services." *Juristat* 29(July). Statistics Canada Catalogue no. 85-002-X.

Perreault, Samuel, and Shannon Brennan. 2010. "Criminal Victimization in Canada, 2009." *Juristat* 30(2). Statistics Canada Catalogue no. 85-002-X.

Perrin, Ben. 2010. *Invisible Chains: Canada's Underground World of Human Trafficking.* Toronto, ON: Penguin.

Perrin, Robin D. 2007. "Deviant Beliefs/Cognitive Deviance." Pp. 1140–42 in *The Blackwell Encyclopedia of Sociology,* edited by George Ritzer. Malden, MA: Blackwell.

Perrow, Charles. 1999. *Normal Accidents.* Princeton, NJ: Princeton University Press.

Pescosolido, B. A., E. Grauerholz, and M. A. Milkie. 1997. "Culture and Conflict: The Portrayal of Blacks in U.S. Children's Picture Books through the Mid- and Late-twentieth Century." *American Sociological Review*:443–64.

Peterson, Richard A., and Roger M. Kern. 1996. "Changing Highbrow Taste: From Snob to Omnivore." *American Sociological Review* 61:900–907.

Pettinicchio, David. 2012. "Migration and Ethnic Nationalism: Anglophone Exit and the 'Decolonisation' of Québec." *Nations and Nationalism* 18(4):719–43.

Pew Research Center for the People and the Press. 2009. "Public More Optimistic about the Economy, But Still Reluctant to Spend," June 19. Retrieved March 31, 2012 (http://pewresearch.org/pubs/1260/more-optimistic-about-economy-but-reluctant-to-spend).

Pfeffer, Max J., and Pilar A. Parra. 2009. "Strong Ties, Weak Ties, and Human Capital: Latino Immigrant Employment Outside the Enclave." *Rural Sociology* 74(2):241–69.

Phelan, Jo C., et al. 2004. "'Fundamental Causes' of Social Inequalities in Mortality: A Test of the Theory." *Journal of Health and Social Behavior* 45:265–85.

Phelan, Jo C., Bruce G. Link, and Parisa Tehranifar. 2010. "Social Conditions as Fundamental Causes of Health Inequalities: Theory, Evidence, and Policy Implications." *Journal of Health and Social Behavior* 51:S28–S40.

Phelps, Nicholas, and Andrew M. Wood. 2011. "The New Post-suburban Politics?" *Urban Studies* 48:2591–610.

Phillips, Leigh, Kate Connolly, and Lizzy Davies. 2010. "EU Turning Blind Eye to Discrimination against Roma, Say Human Rights Groups." *The Guardian,* July 30. Retrieved November 29, 2011 (http://www.guardian.co.uk/world/2010/jul/30/european-union-roma-human-rights).

Piaget, Jean, and Barbel Inhelder. 1972. *The Psychology of the Child.* New York: Basic Books.

Picca, Leslie H., and Joe R. Feagin. 2007. *Two-faced Racism: Whites in the Backstage and Frontstage.* New York: Routledge.

Pickering, Mary. 2011. "Auguste Comte." Pp. 30–60 in *The Wiley-Blackwell Companion to Major Social Theorists: Volume 1. Classical Theorists,* edited by George Ritzer and Jeffrey Stepnisky. Malden, MA: Wiley-Blackwell.

Pierson, Ruth Roach. 1986. *They're Still Women After All: The Second World War and Canadian Womanhood.* Toronto, ON: McClelland and Stewart.

Pinker, Stephen. 2009. "Book Review: 'What the Dog Saw—And Other Adventures,' by Malcolm Gladwell." *The New York Times Book Review,* November 9, p. 12.

Piquero, Alex R., and Zenta Gomez-Smith. 2007. "Crime, Life Course Theory of." Pp. 830–33 in *The Blackwell Encyclopedia of Sociology,* edited by George Ritzer. Malden, MA: Blackwell.

Piquero, Alex R., Raymond Paternoster, Greg Pogarsky, and Thomas Loughran. 2011. "Elaborating the Individual Difference Component in Deterrence Theory." *Annual Review of Law and Social Science* 7:335–60.

Piquero, A. R., T. P. Thornberry, M. D. Krohn, A. J. Lizotte, and N. Leeper Piquero. 2012. *Measuring Crime and Delinquency Over the Life Course.* Springer.

Pitts, Victoria. 2003. *In the Flesh: The Cultural Politics of Body Modification.* New York: Palgrave Macmillan.

Plant, Rebecca F., and Michael S. Kimmel. 2007. "Sexuality, Masculinity and." Pp. 4272–75 in *The Blackwell Encyclopedia of Sociology,* edited by George Ritzer. Malden, MA: Blackwell.

Pleyers, Geoffrey. 2010. *Alter-globalization: Becoming Actors in the Global Age.* Cambridge, UK: Polity.

Plummer, Ken. 1975. *Sexual Stigma: An Interactionist Account.* London: Routledge.

Plummer, Ken. 1992. *Modern Homosexualities: Fragments of Lesbian and Gay Experience.* New York: Routledge.

Plummer, Ken. 2007a. "Sexual Identities." Pp. 4238–42 in *The Blackwell Encyclopedia of Sociology,* edited by George Ritzer. Malden, MA: Blackwell.

Plummer, Ken. 2007b. "Sexual Markets, Commodification, and Consumption." Pp. 4242–44 in *The Blackwell Encyclopedia of Sociology,* edited by George Ritzer. Malden, MA: Blackwell.

Plummer, Ken. 2012. "Critical Sexuality Studies." Pp. 243–68 in *The Wiley-Blackwell Companion to Sociology,* edited by George Ritzer. Malden, MA: Wiley-Blackwell.

Pocock, Emil. 2011. "World's Largest Shopping Malls." Shopping Center Studies at Eastern Connecticut State University. Retrieved May 19, 2011 (www.easternct.edu/~pocock/MallsWorld.htm).

Poff, Deborah. 2010. "Ethical Leadership and Global Citizenship: Considerations for a Just and Sustainable Future." *Journal of Business Ethics* 93:9–14.

Polgreen, Lydia. 2010a. "India Digs Under the Top of the World to Match a Rival." *The New York Times,* August 1. Retrieved May 26, 2011 (http://www.nytimes.com/2010/08/01/world/asia/01pass.html).

Polgreen, Lydia. 2010b. "New Business Class Rises in Ashes of South India's Caste System." *The New York Times,* September 11, p. A4.

Polgreen, Lydia. 2010c. "One Bride for Multiple Brothers: A Himalayan Custom Fades." *The New York Times,* July 17, pp. A4, A6.

Pollack, Andrew. 2010. "Firm Brings Gene Tests to Masses." *The New York Times,* January 29.

Pollock, Jocelyn M. 2001. *Women, Prison & Crime.* New York: Wadsworth.

Polonko, Karen. 2007. "Child Abuse." Pp. 448–51 in *The Blackwell Encyclopedia of Sociology,* edited by George Ritzer. Malden, MA: Blackwell.

Pontell, Henry L. 2007. "Deviance, Reactivist Definitions of." Pp. 1123–26 in *The Blackwell Encyclopedia of Sociology,* edited by George Ritzer. Malden, MA: Blackwell.

Popenoe, David. 1987. "Beyond the Nuclear Family: A Statistical Portrait of the Changing Family in Sweden." *Journal of Marriage and the Family* 49:173–83.

Popenoe, David. 1993. "American Family Decline, 1960–1990: A Review and Appraisal." *Journal of Marriage and Family* 55:527–42.

Popenoe, David. 2009. "Cohabitation, Marriage, and Child Wellbeing: A Cross-national Perspective." *Society* 46:429–36.

Population Reference Bureau. 2010. "World Population Data Sheet." Retrieved October 28, 2010 (www.prb.org/Publications/Datasheets/2010/2010wpds.aspx).

Porter, John. 1965. *The Vertical Mosaic: An Analysis of Social Class and Power in Canada.* Toronto: University of Toronto Press.

Portes, Alejandro. 1993. "The New Second Generation: Segmented Assimilation and Its Variants." *Annals of the American Academy of Political and Social Science* 530:75–96.

Poster, Winifred. 2007. "Who's on the Line? Indian Call Center Agents Pose as Americans for U.S.-Outsourced Firms." *Industrial Relations: A Journal of Economy and Society* 46(2):271–304.

Postmes, T., and R. Spears. 1998. "Deindividuation and Anti-normative Behavior." *Psychological Bulletin* 123:238–59.

Povoledo, Elisabetta. 2010. "Behind Venice's Walls of Ads, the Restoration of Heritage." *The New York Times,* September 19, p. 18.

Powell, Brian, Catherine Bolzendahl, Claudia Geist, and Lala Carr Steelman. 2010. *Counted Out: Same-sex Relations and Americans' Definitions of Family.* New York: Russell Sage Foundation.

Powell, Joe, and Karen Branden. 2007. "Family, Sociology of." Pp. 1614–18 in *The Blackwell Encyclopedia of Sociology,* edited by George Ritzer. Malden, MA: Blackwell.

Prall, Kevin H. 2011. *Rupert Murdoch and the News International Phone Hacking Scandal: How It All Went Down.* Kindle Edition.

Pratt, Geraldine, 2012. *Families Apart: Migrant Mothers and the Conflicts of Labor and Love.* Minneapolis, MN: University of Minnesota Press.

Prechel, Harland. 2007. "Taylorism." Pp. 4939–40 in *The Blackwell Encyclopedia of Sociology,* edited by George Ritzer. Malden, MA: Blackwell.

Preibisch, Kerry L., and Evelyn Encalada Grez. 2010. "The Other Side of el Otro Lado: Mexican Migrant Women and Labor Flexibility in Canadian Agriculture." *Signs* 35(2):289–316.

Preisendorfer, Peter, and Andreas Diekmann. 2007. "Ecological Problems." Pp. 1281–86 in *The Blackwell Encyclopedia of Sociology,* edited by George Ritzer. Malden, MA: Blackwell.

Prell, C., M. Reed, L. Racin, and K. Hubacek. 2010. "Competing Structure, Competing Views: The Role of Formal and Informal Social Structures in Shaping Stakeholder Perceptions." *Ecology and Society* 15(4):34.

Premack, David. 2007. "Human and Animal Cognition: Continuity and Discontinuity." *Proceedings of the National Academy of Sciences* 104:13861–67.

Prentice, Andrew. 2006. "The Emerging Epidemic of Obesity in Developing Countries." *International Journal of Epidemiology* 35(1):93–99.

Presser, Stanley. 1995. "Informed Consent and Confidentiality in Survey Research." *Public Opinion Quarterly* 58:446–59.

Preston, Julia. 2006a. "Low-wage Workers from Mexico Dominate Latest Great Wave of Immigrants." *The New York Times,* December 19.

Preston, Julia. 2006b. "Making a Life in the United States, but Feeling Mexico's Tug." *The New York Times,* December 19.

Prevost, Gary, and Carlos Oliva Campos, eds. 2011. *Cuban-Latin American Relations in the Context of a Changing Hemisphere.* London: Cambria Press.

Prior, Nick. 2011. "Critique and Renewal in the Sociology of Music: Bourdieu and Beyond." *Cultural Sociology* 5:121–38.

Prokos, Anastasia, and Irene Padavic. 2005. "An Examination of Competing Explanations for the Pay Gap Among Scientists and Engineers." *Gender and Society* 19(4):523–43.

Public Culture. 2011. "Arjun Appadurai." Accessed December 3, 2011 (http://publicculture.org/people/view/arjun-appadurai).

Public Health Agency of Canada. 2010. *Canadian Incidence Study of Reported Child Abuse and Neglect— 2008: Major Findings.* Ottawa, ON: Public Health Agency of Canada.

Pue, Wesley. 2000. *Pepper in Our Eyes: The APEC Affair.* Vancouver: University of British Columbia Press.

Pugh, Derek S., David Hickson, C. R. Hinings, and C. Turner. 1968. "The Context of Organizational Structures." *Administrative Science Quarterly* 14:91–114.

Pun, Nagi. 1995. "Theoretical Discussions on the Impact of Industrial Restructuring in Asia." In *Silk and Steel: Asia Women Workers Confront Challenges of Industrial Restructuring.* Hong Kong: CAW.

Qian, Zhenchao, and Daniel T. Lichter. 2011. "Changing Patterns of Interracial Marriage in a Multiracial Society." *Journal of Marriage and Family* 73:1065–84.

Quadagno, Jill, and Deana Rohlinger. 2009. "Religious Conservatives in U.S. Welfare State Politics." Pp. 236–66 in *The Western Welfare State and Its Religious Roots,* edited by K. van Kersbergen and P. Manow. New York: Cambridge University Press.

Putnam, Robert. 2001. *Bowling Alone.* New York: Simon & Schuster.

Rabin, Roni Caryn. 2009. "Tool to Offer Fast Help for H.I.V. Exposure." *The New York Times,* September 8.

Raby, C. R., D. M. Alexis, A. Dickenson, and N. S. Clayton. 2007. "Planning for the Future by Western Planning for the Future by Western Scrub-jays." *Nature* 445:919–21.

Racial Integrity Act of 1924, Article 5. State of Virginia.

Radcliff, B. 2001. "Organized Labor and Electoral Participation in American National Elections." *Journal of Labor Research* 22(2):405–14.

Rafferty, Y. 2007. "Children for Sale: Child Trafficking in Southeast Asia." *Child Abuse Review* 16:401–22.

Ragin, Charles. 1987. *The Comparative Method: Moving beyond Qualitative and Quantitative Strategies.* Berkeley: University of California Press.

Raine, Lee, and Barry Wellman. 2012. *Networked: The New Social Operating System.* Boston: MIT Press.

Raley, Sara. 2010. "McDonaldization and the Family." Pp. 138–48 in *McDonaldization: The Reader,* 3rd ed., edited by George Ritzer. Thousand Oaks, CA: Pine Forge Press.

Ram, Uri. 2007. *The Globalization of Israel: McWorld in Tel Aviv, Jihad in Jerusalem.* London: Routledge.

Raman, Anuradha. 2011. "Dalit Crorepatis: The Other Temple Entry." Outlook, May 2. Retrieved March 31, 2012 (http://www.outlookindia.com/article.aspx?271501).

Ramella, Francesco. 2007. "Political Economy." Pp. 3433–36 in *The Blackwell Encyclopedia of Sociology,* edited by George Ritzer. Malden, MA: Blackwell.

Ramirez, Francisco O., Yasemin Soysal, and Suzanne Shanahan. 1997. "The Changing Logic of Political Citizenship: Cross-national Acquisition of Women's Suffrage Rights, 1890–1990." *American Sociological Review* 62:735–45.

Rao, Leena. 2010. "TinyChat Launches Grouped Version of Chatroulette." TechCrunch. Retrieved May 27, 2011 (http://techcrunch.com/2010/02/16/tinychat-launches-grouped-version-of-chatroulette/).

Rape, Abuse, and Incest National Network. 2009a. "Marital Rape." Retrieved March 31, 2012 (http://www.rainn.org/public-policy/sexual-assault-issues/marital-rape).

Rape, Abuse, and Incest National Network. 2009b. "Who Are the Victims?" Retrieved March 31, 2012 (http://www.rainn.org/get-information/statistics/sexual-assault-victims).

Ratha, Dilip, and Sanket Mohapatra. 2012. "Remittances and Development." Pp. 1782–92 in *The Wiley-Blackwell Encyclopedia of Globalization,* edited by George Ritzer. Malden, MA: Wiley-Blackwell.

Rauscher, Lauren. 2007. "Gendered Organizations/Institutions." Pp. 1892–95 in *The Blackwell Encyclopedia of Sociology,* edited by George Ritzer. Malden, MA: Blackwell.

Rawls, Anne. 2011. "Harold Garfinkel." Pp. 89–124 in *The Wiley-Blackwell Companion to Major Social Theorists: Volume II. Contemporary Sociological Theorists,* edited by George Ritzer and Jeff Stepnisky. Malden, MA: Wiley-Blackwell.

Ray, Larry. 2007. "Civil Society." Pp. 512–13 in *The Blackwell Encyclopedia of Sociology,* edited by George Ritzer. Malden, MA: Blackwell.

Reading, Charlotte Loppie, and Fred Wien. 2009. *Health Inequalities and Social Determinants of Aboriginal Peoples' Health.* Ottawa, ON: National Collaborating Centre for Aboriginal Health.

Reardon, Sean F., and Claudia Galindo. 2008. "The Hispanic-White Achievement Gap in Math and Reading in the Elementary Grades" (Working Paper No. 2008-01). Stanford University, Institute for Research on Education Policy & Practice.

Recording Industry Association of America. 2013. "Piracy Online Facts." Retrieved April 26, 2013 (http://www.riaa.com/physicalpiracy.php?content_selector=piracy-online-scope-of-the-problem).

Rees, W. E. 1992. "Ecological Footprints and Appropriated Carrying Capacity: What Urban Economics Leaves Out." *Environment and Urbanisation* 4(2):121.

Reger, Jo. 2007. "Feminism, First, Second, and Third Waves." Pp. 1672–81 in *The Blackwell Encyclopedia of Sociology,* edited by George Ritzer. Malden, MA: Blackwell.

Reid, Colleen. 2004. "Advancing Women's Social Justice Agendas: A Feminist Action Research Framework." *International Journal of Qualitative Methods* 3(3):1–15.

Reiman, Jeffrey H., and Paul Leighton. 2009. *The Rich Get Richer and the Poor Get Prison: Ideology, Class, and Criminal Justice.* 9th ed. Boston: Prentice Hall.

Reinberg, Steven. 2011. "Survey Finds Many Young Adults Oblivious to Heart Health." *U.S. News & World Report,* May 2. Retrieved May 23, 2011 (http://health.usnews.com/health-news/family-health/heart/articles/2011/05/02/survey-finds-many-young-adults-oblivious-to-heart-health).

Reitz, Jeffrey. 2012. "The Distinctiveness of Canadian Immigration Experience." *Patterns of Prejudice* 46(5):518–38.

Reitz, Jeffrey, Rupa Banerjee, Mai Phan, and Jordan Thompson, 2009. "Race, Religion, and the Social Integration of New Immigrant Minorities in Canada." *International Migration Review* 43(4):695–726.

Reuveny, Rafael, and William R. Thompson. 2001. "Leading Sectors, Lead Economies and Economic Growth." *Review of International Political Economy* 8(4):689–719.

Reverby, Susan. 2009. *Examining Tuskegee: The Infamous Syphilis Study and Its Legacy.* Chapel Hill: University of North Carolina Press.

Reyhner, J. A., and J. M. O. Eder. 2006. *American Indian Education: A History.* University of Oklahoma Press.

Rhinoplasty Online. 2011. "African American (Black) Rhinoplasty." Retrieved March 31, 2012 (http://www.rhinoplastyonline.com/africanamerican.html).

Richard, Jane Garland, James M. Wright, Malcolm Maclure, Suzanne Taylor, and Colin R. Dormuth. 2012. "Influence of Relative Age on Diagnosis and Treatment of Attention-deficit/hyperactivity Disorder in Children." *Canadian Medical Association Journal* 184(7):755.

Richards, John. 2010. *Reducing Lone-parent Poverty: A Canadian Success Story.* Commentary/C. D. Howe Institute; no. 306.

Richer, Stephen. 1988. "Schooling and the Gendered Subject: An Exercise in Planned Social Change." *Canadian Review of Sociology and Anthropology* 25(1):98–107.

Richer, Stephen. 1990. *Boys and Girls Apart: Children's Play in Canada and Poland.* Montreal, QU: McGill Queen's Press.

Richtel, Matt. 2007. "For Pornographers, Internet's Virtues Turn to Vices." *The New York Times,* June 2.

Richtel, Matt. 2010a. "Attached to Technology and Paying a Price." *The New York Times,* June 6.

Richtel, Matt. 2010b. "Hooked on Gadgets, and Paying a Mental Price." *The New York Times,* June 7, pp. A1, A12–13.

Richtel, Matt. 2011a. "In Classroom of the Future, Stagnant Scores." *The New York Times,* September 3.

Richtel, Matt. 2011b. "Egypt Cuts Off Most Internet and Cell Service." *The New York Times,* January 28. Accessed December 3, 2011 (http://www.nytimes.com/2011/01/29/technology/internet/29cutoff.html).

Riddell, Craig. 1993. "Unionization in Canada and the United States: A Tale of Two Countries." Pp. 109–148 in *Small Differences that Matter: Labor Markets and Income Maintenance in Canada and the United States,* edited by David Card and Richard Freeman. Chicago: University of Chicago Press and National Bureau of Economic Research.

Rideout, V. J., U. G. Foehr, and D. F. Roberts. 2010. *Generation M2: Media in the Lives of 8- to 18-year-olds.* Menlo Park, CA: Kaiser Family Foundation.

Rieger, Jon H. 2007. "Key Informant." Pp. 2457–58 in *The Blackwell Encyclopedia of Sociology,* edited by George Ritzer. Malden, MA: Blackwell.

Rieker, Patricia R. and Chloe E. Bird. 2000. "Sociological Explanations of Gender Differences in Mental and Physical Health." In *Handbook of Medical Sociology,* edited by Chloe E. Bird, Peter Conrad, and Alan Freemont. New York: Prentice Hall.

Riera-Crichton, Daniel. 2012. "Euro Crisis." Pp. 566–70 in *The Encyclopedia of Globalization,* edited by George Ritzer. Malden, MA: Wiley-Blackwell.

Rifkin, Jeremy. 1995. *The End of Work.* New York: Putnam.

Riger, Stefanie. 1992. "Epistemological Debates, Feminist Voices: Science, Social Values, and the Study of Women." *American Psychologist* 47(6):730–40.

Riley, Tasha, and Charles Ungerleider. 2012. "Self-fulfilling Prophecy: How Teachers' Attributions, Expectations, and Stereotypes Influence the Learning Opportunities Afforded Aboriginal Students." *Canadian Journal of Education* 35(2):303–333.

Riska, Elianne. 2007. "Health Professions and Occupations." Pp. 2075–78 in *The Blackwell Encyclopedia of Sociology,* edited by George Ritzer. Malden, MA: Blackwell.

Ristau, Carolyn A. 1983. "Language, Cognition, and Awareness in Animals." *Annals of the New York Academy of Sciences* 406:170–86.

Ritzer, George. 1972. *Man and His Work: Conflict and Change.* New York: Appleton-Century-Crafts.

Ritzer, George. 1975. *Sociology: A Multiple Paradigm Science.* Boston: Allyn & Bacon.

Ritzer, George. 1981. "Paradigm Analysis in Sociology: Clarifying the Issues." *American Sociological Review* 46(2):245–48.

Ritzer, George. 1995. *Expressing America: A Critique of the Global Credit Card Society.* Thousand Oaks, CA: Pine Forge Press.

Ritzer, George. 1997. *The McDonaldization Thesis.* London: Sage.

Ritzer, George. 2001a. *Explorations in the Sociology of Consumption: Fast Food, Credit Cards, and Casinos.* London: Sage.

Ritzer, George. 2001b. "Hyperrationality: An Extension of Weberian and Neo-Weberian Theory." In *Explorations in Social Theory,* edited by George Ritzer. London: Sage.

Ritzer, George, ed. 2007. *The Blackwell Encyclopedia of Sociology.* Malden, MA: Blackwell.

Ritzer, George. 2008. *Sociological Theory.* 7th ed. New York: McGraw-Hill.

Ritzer, George. 2010a. "Cathedrals of Consumption: Rationalization, Enchantment, and Disenchantment." Pp. 234–39 in *McDonaldization: The Reader,* edited by George Ritzer. 3rd ed. Thousands Oaks, CA: Pine Forge Press.

Ritzer, George. 2010b. *Enchanting a Disenchanted World: Continuity and Change in the Cathedrals of Consumption.* Thousand Oaks, CA: Sage.

Ritzer, George. 2010c. *Globalization: A Basic Text.* Malden, MA: Wiley-Blackwell.

Ritzer, George, ed. 2010d. *The McDonaldization of Society: The Reader.* 3rd ed. Thousand Oaks, CA: Pine Forge Press.

Ritzer, George. 2013. *The McDonaldization of Society.* 7th ed. Thousand Oaks, CA: Sage.

Ritzer, George, and Zeynep Atalay, eds. 2010. *Reading in Globalization: Key Concepts and Major Debates.* West Sussex, UK: Wiley-Blackwell.

Ritzer, George, Paul Dean, and Nathan Jurgenson. 2012. "The Coming of Age of the Prosumer." *American Behavioral Scientist* 56:379–98.

Ritzer, George, Douglas Goodman, and Wendy Wiedenhoft. 2001. "Theories of Consumption." Pp. 410–27 in *Handbook of Social Theory,* edited by George Ritzer and Barry Smart. London: Sage.

Ritzer, George, and Nathan Jurgenson. 2010. "Production, Consumption, Prosumption: The Nature of Capitalism in the Age of the Digital 'Prosumer.'" *Journal of Consumer Culture* 10(1):13–36.

Ritzer, George, and Craig Lair. 2007. "Outsourcing: Globalization and Beyond." Pp. 307–29 in *The Blackwell Companion to Globalization,* edited by George Ritzer. Malden, MA: Blackwell.

Ritzer, George, and Craig Lair. Forthcoming. *The Outsourcing of Everything.* New York: Oxford University Press.

Ritzer, George, and David Walczak. 1988. "Rationalization and the Deprofessionalization of Physicians." *Social Forces* 67:1–22.

Rivoli, Pietra. 2005. *The Travels of a T-shirt in the Global Economy: An Economist Examines the Markets, Power, and Politics of World Trade.* Hoboken, NJ: Wiley.

Rizvi, Fazal. 2012. "Bollywood." Pp. 120–121 in *The Wiley-Blackwell Encyclopedia of Globalization,* edited by George Ritzer. Malden, MA: Wiley-Blackwell.

Roberts, David, and Minelle Mahtani. 2010. "Neoliberalizing Race, Racing Neoliberalism: Placing 'Race' in Neoliberal Discourses." *Antipode* 42:248–57.

Roberts, Karen, Margot Shields, Margaret de Groh, Alfred Aziz and Jo-Anne Gilbert. 2012. "Overweight and Obesity in Children and Adolescents: Results from the 2009 to 2011 Canadian Health Measures Survey." *Health Reports* 23(3):3–7.

Roberts, Lance, Rodney Clifton, and Barry Ferguson. 2005. *Recent Social Trends in Canada, 1960–2000.* Montreal, QU: McGill Queen's Press.

Roberts, Sam. 2008. "Study Foresees the Fall of an Immigration Record that Has Lasted a Century." *The New York Times,* February 12, p. A11.

Roberts, Sam. 2009. "In 2025, India to Pass China in Population, U.S. Estimates." *The New York Times,* December 16, p. MB2.

Roberts, Sam. 2010. "More Men Marrying Wealthy Women." *The New York Times,* January 19.

Robertson, Craig. 2010. *The Passport in America: The History of a Document.* New York: Oxford University Press.

Robin, M. 1992. *Shades of Right: Nativist and Fascist Politics in Canada, 1920–1940.* Toronto, ON: University of Toronto Press.

Robinson, Matthew B. 2010. "McDonaldization of America's Police, Courts, and Corrections." Pp. 85–100 in *McDonaldization: The Reader,* 3rd ed., edited by George Ritzer. Los Angeles: Pine Forge Press.

Rochon, T. R. 1990. "The West European Peace Movements and the Theory of Social Movements." In *Challenging the Political Order,* edited by R. Dalton and M. Kuchler. Cambridge, UK: Polity Press.

Rockloff, Matthew and Victoria Dyer. 2007. "An Experiment on the Social Facilitation of Gambling Behavior." *Journal of Gambling Studies* 23(1):1–12.

Rogers, Ann, and David Pilgrim. 2010. *A Sociology of Mental Health and Illness.* London: Open University Press.

Rogers, Patricia Dane. 1995. "Building a Dream House." *The Washington Post,* February 2, pp. 12, 15.

Rohlinger, Deana A. 2007. "Socialization, Gender." Pp. 4571–74 in *The Blackwell Encyclopedia of Sociology,* edited by George Ritzer. Malden, MA: Blackwell.

Rojek, Chris. 2005. *Leisure Theory: Principles and Practice.* Palgrave Macmillan.

Rojek, Chris. 2007. *The Labour of Leisure: The Culture of Free Time.* London: Sage.

Romero, Simon. 2010. "Left Behind in Venezuela to Piece Lives from Scraps." *The New York Times,* September 19, pp. 10.

Ronai, Carol R., and Carolyn Ellis. 1989. "Turn-ons for Money: Interactional Strategies of the Table Dancer." *Journal of Contemporary Ethnography* 18:271–98.

Roof, Wade Clark. 2001. *Spiritual Marketplace: Baby Boomers and the Remaking of American Religion.* Princeton, NJ: Princeton University Press.

Room, Graham. 2011. "Social Mobility and Complexity Theory: Towards a Critique of the Sociological Mainstream." *Policy Studies* 32(2):109–26.

Rootes, Christopher, ed. 1999. *Environmental Movements: Local, National and Global.* London: Routledge.

Roscigno, Vincent J., and M. Keith Kimble. 1995. "Elite Power, Race, and the Presistence of Low Unionization in the South." *Work and Occupations* 22.

Rose, Arnold. 1967. *The Power Structure.* New York: Oxford University Press.

Rose, Claire. 2010. *Making, Selling and Wearing Boys' Clothes in Late-Victorian England.* Ashgate.

Rosenbaum, James. 2001. *Beyond College for All: Career Paths for the Forgotten Half.* New York: Russell Sage Foundation.

Rosenbaum, James. 2011. "The Complexities of College for All: Beyond Fairy-tale Dreams." *Sociology of Education* 84:113–17.

Rosenberg, Morris. 1979. *Conceiving the Self.* New York: Basic Books.

Rosenbloom, Stephanie. 2010. "But Will It Make You Happy?" *The New York Times,* August 7.

Rosenfield, Richard. 2011. "The Big Picture: 2010 Presidential Address to the American Society of Criminology." *Criminology* 49:1–26.

Rosenstein, Judith E. 2008. "Individual Threat, Group Threat, and Racial Policy: Exploring the Relationship between Threat and Racial Attitudes." *Social Science Research* 37:1130–46.

Rosenthal, Elisabeth. 2007a. "As Earth Warms Up, Virus from Tropics Moves to Italy." *The New York Times,* December 23, p. 21.

Rosenthal, Elisabeth. 2007b. "W.H.O. Urges Effort to Fight Fast-spreading Disease." *The New York Times,* August 27, p. A9.

Ross, Becki. 1995. *The House that Jill Built: A Lesbian Nation in Formation.* Toronto, ON: University of Toronto Press.

Ross, Becki. 2009. *Burlesque West: Showgirls, Sex, and Sin in Postwar Vancouver.* Toronto, ON: University of Toronto Press.

Rossi, Alice. 1983. "Gender and Parenthood." *American Sociological Review* 49:1–19.

Roszak, Theodore. [1968] 1995. *The Making of a Counter Culture: Reflections on the Technocratic Society and Its Youthful Opposition.* Berkeley: University of California Press.

Roszak, Theodore. 1969. *The Making of a Counter Culture.* New York: Anchor.

Rotella, Carlo. 2010. "Class Warrior: Arne Duncan's Bid to Shake Up Schools." *The New Yorker,* February 10, p. 24.

Roth, Benita. 2004. *Separate Roads to Feminism: Black, Chicana and White Feminist Movements in America's Second Wave.* Cambridge, UK: Cambridge University Press

Roth, Julius A. 1963. *Timetables: Structuring the Passage of Time in Hospital Treatment and Other Careers.* Indianapolis: Bobbs-Merrill.

Roth, Philip. [1969] 1994. *Portnoy's Complaint.* New York: Vintage.

Roth, Silke. 2007. "Social Movements, Biographical Consequences of." Pp. 4451–53 in *The Blackwell Encyclopedia of Sociology,* edited by George Ritzer. Malden, MA: Blackwell.

Rothman, Barbara. 2000. *Recreating Motherhood.* 2nd ed. New Brunswick, NJ: Rutgers University Press.

Roudometof, Victor. 2012. "Imagined Communities." Pp. 996–98 in *The Wiley-Blackwell Encyclopedia of Globalization,* edited by George Ritzer. Malden, MA: Wiley-Blackwell.

Rousseau, D. M., and A. Rivero. 2003. "Democracy: A Way of Organizing in a Knowledge Economy." *Journal of Management Inquiry* 12(2):115–34.

Rowlingson, Karen. 2007. "Lone-Parent Families." Pp. 2663–67 in *The Blackwell Encyclopedia of Sociology,* edited by George Ritzer. Malden, MA: Blackwell.

Roxburgh, S. 2004. "There Just Aren't Enough Hours in the Day: The Mental Health Consequences of Time Pressures." *Journal of Health and Social Behavior* 45:115–31.

Roy, Olivier. 2004. *Globalized Islam: The Search for a New Ummah.* New York: Columbia University Press.

Rozdeba, Suzanne. 2011. "Firefighters Recall Spirit of 9/11 Hero." Retrieved March 31, 2012 (http://eastvillage.thelocal.nytimes.com/2011/01/10/firefighters-recall-spirit-of-911-hero/?scp=3&sq=9/11%20heroism&st=cse).

Ruck, Martin, and Scot Wortley. 2002. "Racial and Ethnic Minority High School Students' Perceptions of School Disciplinary Practices: A Look at Some Canadian Findings." *Journal of Youth and Adolescence* 31(3):185–95.

Rudrappa, Sharmila. 2012. "Rape." Pp. 1748–51 in *The Wiley-Blackwell Encyclopedia of Globalization,* edited by George Ritzer. Malden, MA: Wiley-Blackwell.

Rueschemeyer, Dietrich, Evelyne Stephens, and John Stephens. 1992. *Capitalist Development and Democracy.* Chicago: University of Chicago Press.

Runyon, Anne Sisson. 2012. "Gender." Pp. 725–34 in *The Wiley-Blackwell Encyclopedia of Globalization,* edited by George Ritzer. Malden, MA: Wiley-Blackwell.

Rupp, Leila, J. 1997. *Worlds of Women: The Making of an International Women's Movement.* Princeton, NJ: Princeton University Press.

Rupp, Leila and Verta Taylor. 1999. "Forging Feminist Identity in an International Movement: A Collective Identity Approach to Twentieth-century Feminism." *Signs* 24(2):363–86.

Rush, Curtis. 2011. "Cop Apologizes for 'Sluts' Remark at Law School." *Toronto Star,* February 18. Retrieved May 3, 2013 (http://www.thestar.com/news/gta/2011/02/18/cop_apologizes_for_sluts_remark_at_law_school.html).

Russell, James. 2006. *Double Standard: Social Policy in Europe and the United States.* Lanham, MD: Rowman and Littlefield.

Rutherford, Alexandra, Kelli Vaughn-Blount, and Laura C. Ball. 2010. "Responsible, Disruptive Voices: Science, Social Change, and the History of Feminist Psychology." *Psychology of Women Quarterly* 34(4):460–73.

Rutherford, Paul. 2007. *The World Made Sexy: Freud to Madonna.* Toronto, ON: University of Toronto Press.

Rutledge, Leigh W. 1992. *The Gay Decades: From Stonewall to the Present.* New York: Plume.

Ryan, Barbara. 2007. "Sex and Gender." Pp. 4196–98 in *The Blackwell Encyclopedia of Sociology,* edited by George Ritzer. Malden, MA: Blackwell.

Ryan, J. Michael. 2012. "Homosexuality." Pp. 941–44 in *The Wiley-Blackwell Encyclopedia of Globalization,* edited by George Ritzer. Malden, MA: Wiley-Blackwell.

Ryan, Kevin. 1994. "Technicians and Interpreters in Moral Crusades: The Case of the Drug Courier Profile." *Deviant Behavior* 15:217–40.

Ryan, M. K., and S. A. Haslam. 2005. "The Glass Cliff: Evidence That Women Are Over-represented in Precarious Leadership Positions." *British Journal of Management* 16:81–90.

Ryan, William. 1976. *Blaming the Victim.* New York: Pantheon.

Ryave, A. Lincoln, and James N. Schenkein. 1974. "Notes on the Art of Walking." Pp. 265–75 in *Ethnomethodology: Selected Readings,* edited by R. Tuirner. Harmondsworth, UK: Penguin.

Sabo, Don. 1998. "Masculinities and Men's Health: Moving towards Post-Superman Era Prevention." In *Men's Lives,* edited by Michael Kimmel and Michael Messner. Needham Heights, MA: Allyn & Bacon.

Sabo, Don. 2005. "Doing Time, Doing Masculinity." Pp. 108–12 in *Gender through a Prism of Difference,* edited by Maxine Baca Zinn, Pierette Hondagneu-Sotelo, and Michael Messner. New York: Oxford University Press.

Sack, Kevin. 2009. "Despite Recession, Personalized Health Care Remains in Demand." *The New York Times,* May 11, p. A12.

Sadker, M., and D. Sadker. 1994. *Failing at Fairness: How Our Schools Cheat Girls.* New York: Simon and Schuster.

Sagi-Schwartz, Abraham. 2008. "The Well Being of Children Living in War Zones: The Palestinian-Israeli Case." *International Journal of Behavioral Development* 32(4): 322–36.

Said, Edward W. [1979] 1994. *Orientalism.* New York: Knopf.

Sallaz, Jeffrey. 2010. "Talking Race, Marketing Culture: The Racial Habitus in and out of Apartheid." *Social Problems* 57(2):294–314.

Salkind, Neil. 2004. *Statistics for People who (Think They) Hate Statistics.* Thousand Oaks: Sage.

Saltmarsh, Matthew. 2010. "Sarkozy Toughens on Illegal Roma." *The New York Times,* July 29, p. A7.

Salzman, T. 2000. "Rape Camps, Forced Impregnation, and Ethnic Cleansing." Pp. 63–92 in *War's Dirty Secret: Rape, Prostitution and Other Crimes against Women,* edited by A. L. Barstow. Ohio: Pilgrim Press.

Samnani, Hina, and Lolla Mohammed Nur. 2011. "Crowdmapping Arab Spring—Next Social Media Breakthrough?" Voice of America, June 28. Retrieved August 12, 2011 (www .voanews.com/english/news/middle-east/ Crowdmapping-Arab-Spring-Next-Social-Media-Breakthrough—124662649.html).

Samuel, Laurie. 2007. "Race and the Criminal Justice System." Pp. 3737–40 in *The Blackwell Encyclopedia of Sociology,* edited by George Ritzer. Malden, MA: Blackwell.

Sanders, Teela. 2007. "Becoming an Ex–Sex Worker: Making Transitions Out of a Deviant Career." *Feminist Criminology* 2:74–95.

Sanford, Marc M. 2007. "Ecology." Pp. 1289–91 in *The Blackwell Encyclopedia of Sociology,* edited by George Ritzer. Malden, MA: Blackwell.

Santini, Cristina, Samuel Rabino, and Lorenzo Zanni. 2011. "Chinese Immigrants Socio-economic Enclave in an Italian Industrial District: The Case of Prato." *World Review of Entrepreneurship, Management and Sustainable Development* 7(1):30–51.

Sarlo, Christopher. 2006. Poverty in Canada, update 2006. Retrieved October 10, 2012 (http://www.fraserinstitute.org/research-news/research/display.aspx?id=13293)

Sarroub, Loukia K. 2005. *All American Yemeni Girls: Being Muslim in a Public School.* Philadelphia: University of Pennsylvania Press.

Sassatelli, Roberta. 2007. *Consumer Culture: History, Theory and Politics.* London: Sage.

Sassen, Saskia. 1991. *The Global City: New York, London, Tokyo.* Princeton, NJ: Princeton University Press.

Sassen, Saskia. 2004. "Local Actors in Global Politics." *Current Sociology* 52(4):649–70.

Sassen, Saskia. 2012. "Cities." Pp. 187–202 in *The Wiley-Blackwell Encyclopedia of Globalization,* edited by George Ritzer. Malden, MA: Wiley-Blackwell.

Sassler, Sharon. 2007. "Cohabitation." Pp. 565–69 in *Encyclopedia of Sociology*, Vol. II, edited by George Ritzer. Oxford, England: Blackwell.

Satzewich, Vic, and Nikolaos Liodakis. 2013. *"Race" and Ethnicity in Canada: A Critical Introduction.* 3rd ed. Toronto, ON: Oxford University Press.

Saussure, Ferdinand de. [1916] 1966. *Course in General Linguistics.* New York: McGraw-Hill.

Sauvé, Roger. 2012. *The Current State of Canadian Family Finances.* Ottawa, ON: The Vanier Institute of the Family.

Savage, C. 2010. "U.S. Prosecutors, Weighing WikiLeaks Charges, Hit the Law Books." *The New York Times,* December 8, p. A10.

Saviano, Roberto. 2006/2007. *Gomorrah: A Personal Journey into the Violent International Empire of Naples' Organized Crime System.* New York: Picador.

Sayer, L. C. 2005. "Gender, Time, and Inequality: Trends in Women's and Men's Paid Work, Unpaid Work, and Free Time." *Social Forces* 84:285–303.

Sayyid, Salman. 2012. "Political Islam." Pp. 1202–204 in *The Wiley-Blackwell Encyclopedia of Globalization,* edited by George Ritzer. Malden, MA: Wiley-Blackwell.

Saxon, Wolfgang. 2003. "Adm. Richard E. Bennis, A Hero of 9/11, Dies at 52." *The New York Times,* August 9. Retrieved March 31, 2012 (http://www.nytimes .com/2003/08/09/nyregion/adm-richard-e-bennis-a-hero-of-9-11-dies-at-52.html).

Scaff, Lawrence A. 2011. "Georg Simmel." Pp. 205–35 in *The Wiley-Blackwell Companion to Major Social Theorists: Volume 1. Classical Theorists,* edited by George Ritzer and Jeffrey Stepnisky. Malden, MA: Wiley-Blackwell.

Scambler, Graham, and Frederique Paoli. 2008. "Health Work, Female Sex Workers and HIV/AIDS: Global and Local Dimensions of Stigma and Deviance as Barriers to Effective Interventions." *Social Science & Medicine* 66:1848–62.

Schafer, Markus H., and Kenneth F. Ferraro. 2011. "The Stigma of Obesity: Does Perceived Weight Discrimination Affect Identity and Physical Health?" *Social Psychology Quarterly* 74:76–97.

Schauer, Edward J., and Elizabeth M. Wheaton. 2006. "Sex Trafficking into the United States: A Literature Review." *Criminal Justice Review* 31(2):146–69.

Scheffer, David. 2008. "Rape as Genocide in Darfur." *Los Angeles Times,* November 13.

Scheper-Hughes, Nancy. 2001. "Commodity Fetishism in Organs Trafficking." *Body & Society* 7:31–62.

Scherschel, Karin. 2007. "Migration, Ethnic Conflicts, and Racism." Pp. 3011–14 in *The Blackwell Encyclopedia of Sociology,* edited by George Ritzer. Malden, MA: Blackwell.

Scheuer, Steen. 2011. "Union Membership Variation in Europe: A Ten-country Comparative Analysis." *European Journal of Industrial Relations* 17(1):57–73.

Schlueter, E., and P. Scheepers. 2010. "The Relationship between Outgroup Size and Anti-outgroup Attitudes: A Theoretical Synthesis and Empirical Test of Group Threat and Intergroup Contact Theory." *Social Science Research* 39(2):285–95.

Schilt, Kristen. 2010. *Just One of the Guys? Transgender Men and the Persistence of Inequality.* University of Chicago Press.

Schlosser, Eric. 2002. *Fast Food Nation.* New York: Harper Perennial.

Schmitt, John, and Alexandra Mitukiewicz. 2012. "Politics Matter: Changes in Unionisation Rates in Rich Countries, 1960–2010." *Industrial Relations Journal* 43(3):260–80.

Schmitt, Vanessa, and Julia Fischer. 2009. "Inferential Reasoning and Modality Dependent Discrimination Learning in Olive Baboons (*Papio hamadryas anubis*)." *Journal of Comparative Psychology* 123(3):316–25.

Schneider, Barbara, and David Stevenson. 1999. *The Ambitious Generation: America's Teenagers, Motivated but Directionless.* New Haven, CT: Yale University Press.

Schneider, Christopher J. and Daniel Trottier. 2012. "The 2011 Vancouver Riot and the Role of Facebook in Crowd-Sourced Policing." *BC Studies* 175(Autumn):93–109.

Schneider, S. L. 2008. "Anti-immigrant Attitudes in Europe: Outgroup Size and Perceived Ethnic Threat." *European Sociological Review* 24(1):53–67.

Schoch, Deborah, and Rong-Gong Lin Il. 2007. "15 Years after L.A. Riots, Tension Still High; Promises Made in the Wake of Three Days of Violence Remain Unfulfilled, Residents Tell City Officials at South Los Angeles Events." Retrieved March 31, 2012 (http://pqasb.pqarchiver.com/latimes/ access/1261997281.html?dids=12619972 81:1261997281&FMT=ABS&FMTS=ABS :FT&type=current&date=Apr+29%2C+20 07&author=Deborah+Schoch%3B+Rong-Gong+Lin+II&pub=Los+Angeles+Times&d esc=15+years+after+L.A.+riots%2C+tension +still+high%3B+Promises+made+in+the+wa ke+of+three+days+of+violence+remain+unf ulfilled%2C+residents+tell+city+officials+at+ South+Los+Angeles+events.&pqatl=google).

Schor, Juliet. 1993. *The Overworked American: The Unexpected Decline of Leisure.* New York: Basic Books.

Schor, Juliet. 1998. *The Overspent American: Why We Want What We Don't Need.* New York: Basic Books.

Schor, Juliet. 2005. *Born to Buy: The Commercialized Child and the New Consumer Culture.* New York: Scribner.

Schorzman, Cindy M., et al. 2007. "Body Art: Attitudes and Practices Regarding Body Piercing among Urban Undergraduates." *Journal of the American Osteopathic Association* 107:432–438.

Schroeder, Jonathan E. 2007. "Brand Culture." Pp. 351–53 in *The Blackwell Encyclopedia of Sociology,* edited by George Ritzer. Malden, MA: Blackwell.

Schroyer, Trent. 1970. "Toward a Critical Theory of Advanced Industrial Society." Pp. 210–34 in *Recent Sociology: No. 2,* edited by H. P. Dreitzel. New York: Macmillan.

Schudson, Michael. 1989. "The Sociology of New Production." *Media, Culture and Society* 11:263–82.

Schudson, Michael. 1987. *Advertising, the Uneasy Persuasion: Its Dubious Impact on American Society.* New York: Basic Books.

Schumpeter, Joseph. 1976. *Capitalism, Socialism and Democracy.* 5th ed. London: George Allen and Unwin.

Schuster, Liza. 2012a. "Asylum-seekers." Pp. 89–92 in *The Wiley-Blackwell Encyclopedia of Globalization,* edited by George Ritzer. Malden, MA: Wiley-Blackwell.

Schuster, Liza. 2012b. "Migration Controls." Pp. 1388–90 in *The Wiley-Blackwell Encyclopedia of Globalization,* edited by George Ritzer. Malden, MA: Wiley-Blackwell.

Schutt, Russell K. 2007. "Secondary Data Analysis." Pp. 4127–29 in *The Blackwell Encyclopedia of Sociology,* edited by George Ritzer. Malden, MA: Blackwell.

Schwartz, H. 1986. *Never Satisfied: A Cultural History of Diets, Fantasies and Fat.* New York: Anchor Books.

Schwartz, Pepper. 1971. *The Student Guide to Sex on Campus,* by the Student Committee on Human Sexuality at Yale, edited by Richard Feller, Elaine Fox, and Pepper Schwartz. New York: Signet Books.

Schwartz, Pepper. 2007. *Prime: Adventures and Advice in Sex, Love, and the Sensual Years.* New York: HarperCollins.

Schwartz, Pepper, and Philip Blumstein. 1983. *American Couples: Money, Work and Sex.* New York: Morrow.

Schwartz, Pepper (with Richard Feller, Elaine Fox, and Dr. Philip Sarrel Feller). 1970. *Sex and the Yale Student.* Committee on Human Sexuality, Yale University.

Schweinhart, Lawrence J. W., Steven Barnett, and Clive R. Belfield. 2005. *Lifetime Effects: The High/Scope Perry Preschool Study Through Age 40.* High/Scope Press.

Schwirian, Kent. 2007. "Ecological Models of Urban Form: Concentric Zone Model, the Sector Model, and the Multiple Nuclei Model." Pp. 1277–81 in *The Blackwell Encyclopedia of Sociology,* edited by George Ritzer. Malden, MA: Blackwell.

Schwirtz, Michael. 2010. "In Information War, Documentary Is the Latest Salvo." *The New York Times,* August 1, p. 10.

Sciolino, Elaine. 2007. "Sarkozy Pledges Crackdown on Rioters." *The New York Times,* November 29, p. A8.

Scott, Amy. 2011. "Pumping Up the Pomp: An Exploration of Femininity and Female Bodybuilding." *Explorations in Anthropology* 11:70–88.

Scott, Austin. 1982. "The Media's Treatment of Blacks: A Story of Distortion." *Los Angeles Times* IV(3), September 5.

Scott, Barbara Marliene, and Mary Ann A. Schwartz. 2008. *Sociology: Making Sense of the Social World.* Boston: Allyn & Bacon.

Scott, W. R. 2008. *Institutions and Organisations: Ideas and Interests.* 3rd ed. Thousand Oaks: Sage.

Scraton, Sheila. 2007. "Leisure." Pp. 2588–92 in *The Blackwell Encyclopedia of Sociology,* edited by George Ritzer. Malden, MA: Blackwell.

Scrim, Katie. 2012. "Aboriginal Victimization in Canada: A Summary of the Literature." Department of Justice, Victims of Crime Research Digest No. 3. Retrieved October 4, 2012 (http://www.justice.gc.ca/eng/pi/rs/rep-rap/rd-rr/rd3-rr3/p3.html)

Sedgwick, Eve Kasofsky. 1991. *The Epistemology of the Closet.* London: Harvester Wheatsheaf.

Segal, David. 2010. "Is Italy Too Italian?" *New York Times Business,* August 1, pp. 1, 6.

Segan, Sascha. 2011. "Life behind the Great Firewall of China." PCMag.com, June 27. Retrieved September 12, 2011 (http://www.pcmag.com/slideshow/story/266213/life-behind-the-great-firewall-of-china).

Sekulic, Dusko. 2007a. "Ethic Cleansing." Pp. 1450–52 in *The Blackwell Encyclopedia of Sociology,* edited by George Ritzer. Malden, MA: Blackwell.

Sekulic, Dusko. 2007b. "Social Change." Pp. 4360–64 in *The Blackwell Encyclopedia of Sociology,* edited by George Ritzer. Malden, MA: Blackwell.

Sekulic, Dusko. 2007c. "Values; Global." Pp. 5172–76 in *The Blackwell Encyclopedia of Sociology,* edited by George Ritzer. Malden, MA: Blackwell.

Seltzer, Judith A. 2007. "Intimate Union Formation and Dissolution." Pp. 2414–18 in *The Blackwell Encyclopedia of Sociology,* edited by George Ritzer. Malden, MA: Blackwell.

Sen, A., 1999, *Development as Freedom.* New York: Knopf.

Sen, Amartya. 2011. "Quality of Life: India vs. China." *The New York Review of Books,* May 12. Retrieved June 5, 2011 (http://www.nybooks.com/articles/archives/2011/may/12/quality-life-india-vs-china/).

Sen, Jai, Anita Anand, Arturo Escobar, and Peter Waterman, eds. 2004. *World Social Forum: Challenging Empires.* New Delhi: Viveka Foundation.

Serra-Majum, Luis, and Joy Ngo. 2012. "Undernutrition." In *The Wiley-Blackwell Enyclopedia of Globalization,* edited by George Ritzer. Malden, MA: Wiley-Blackwell.

Serrano, Alfonso. 2006. "E. Coli Outbreak Linked to Taco Bell." CBS News, December 4. Retrieved May 26, 2011 (http://www.cbsnews.com/stories/2006/12/04/health/main2227678.shtml).

Shahbaz, Muhammad. 2010. "Income Inequality, Economic Growth and Non-linearity: A Case of Pakistan." *International Journal of Social Economics* 37(8):613–36.

Shamir, Ronen. 2005. "Without Borders? Notes on Globalization as a Mobility Regime." *Sociological Theory* 23(2):197–217.

Shane, S. 2010. "Keeping Secrets WikiSafe." *The New York Times,* December 12, p. WK1.

Shane, Scott, and Michael Gordon. 2008. "Dissident's Tale of Epic Escape from Iran's Vise." *The New York Times,* July 13.

Shanker, T. 2011. "U.S. Accuses China and Russia of Internet Espionage." *The New York Times.* Retrieved November 6, 2011 (http://www.nytimes.com/2011/11/04/world/us-report-accuses-china-and-russia-of-internet-spying.html?scp=2&sq=china%20russia&st=cse).

Shattuck, Roger. 1980. *The Forbidden Experiment: The Story of the Wild Boy.* New York: Kodansha Globe.

Shauman, K. A. 2010. "Gender Asymmetry in Family Migration: Occupational Inequality or Interspousal Comparative Advantage?" *Journal of Marriage and Family* 72:375–92.

Shavit, Yossi. 1990. "Segregation, Tracking, and the Educational Attainment of Minorities: Arabs and Oriental Jews in Israel." *American Sociological Review* 55:115–26.

Shaw, Susan, and Janet Lee. 2009. *Women's Voices, Feminist Visions.* New York: McGraw-Hill.

Shehan, Constance, and Susan Cody. 2007. "Inequalities in Marriage." Pp. 2301–304 in *The Blackwell Encyclopedia of Sociology,* edited by George Ritzer. Malden, MA: Blackwell.

Shehata, Adam. 2010. "'Marking Journalistic Independence: Official Dominance and the Rule of Product Substitution in Swedish Press Coverage." *European Journal of Communication* 25:123–37.

Sheldon, Jane. 2004. "Gender Stereotypes in Educational Software for Young Children." *Sex Roles* 51(7/8).

Shell, Ellen Ruppel. 2009. *Cheap: The High Cost of Discount Culture.* Penguin.

Shelley, Louise, John Picarelli, and Chris Corpora. 2011. "Global Crime Inc." Pp. 141–69 in *Beyond Sovereignty: Issues for a Global Agenda,* 4th ed., edited by Maryann Cusimano Love. Boston: Wadsworth, Cengage Learning.

Shepard, Gary. 2007. "Cults: Social Psychological Concepts." Pp. 884–87 in *The Blackwell Encyclopedia of Sociology,* edited by George Ritzer. Malden, MA: Blackwell.

Shepard, Gordon. 2007. "Socialization, Anticipatory." Pp. 4569–70 in *The Blackwell Encyclopedia of Sociology,* edited by George Ritzer. Malden, MA: Blackwell.

Shevchenko, Olga. 2012. "Socialism." Pp. 1882–86 in *The Wiley-Blackwell Encyclopedia of Globalization,* edited by George Ritzer. Malden, MA: Wiley-Blackwell.

Shields, Margot, Margaret Carroll, and Cynthia Ogden. 2011. "Adult Obesity Prevalence in Canada and the United States." National Center for Health Statistics, Data Briefs, No. 56.

Shinberg, Diane S. 2007. "Women's Health." Pp. 5275–79 in *The Blackwell Encyclopedia of Sociology,* edited by George Ritzer. Malden, MA: Blackwell.

Shirky, Clay. 2011. "The Political Power of Social Media." *Foreign Affairs* January/February.

Shiva, V. 2002. *Water Wars: Privatization, Pollution, and Profit.* Cambridge, MA: South End Press.

Shock, Kurt. 2007. "Social Movements, Non-violent." Pp. 4458–63 in *The Blackwell Encyclopedia of Sociology,* edited by George Ritzer. Malden, MA: Blackwell.

Shroedel, Jean Reith, and Pamela Fiber. 2000. "Lesbian and Gay Policy Priorities: Commonality and Difference." Pp. 97–118 in *The Politics of Gay Rights,* edited by Craig A. Rimmerman, Kenneth D. Wald, and Clyde Wilcox. Chicago: University of Chicago Press.

Shwirian, Kent. 2007. "Ecological Models of Urban Form: Concentric Zone Model, the Sector Model, and the Multiple Nuclei Model." Pp. 1277–81 in *The Blackwell Encyclopedia of Sociology,* edited by George Ritzer. Malden, MA: Blackwell.

Sica, A. 2008. "Robert K. Merton." Pp. 151–67 in *Key Sociological Thinkers,* 2nd ed., edited by R. Stones. Basingstoke, UK: Palgrave Macmillan.

Siddiqi, A., I. Kawachi, L. Berkman, C. Hertzman, and S. V. Subramanian. 2012. "Education Determines a Nation's Health, but What Determines Educational Outcomes? A Cross-national Comparative Analysis." *Journal of Public Health Policy* 33(1):1–15.

Siebold, G. L. 2007. "The Essence of Military Cohesion." *Armed Forces & Society* 33(2):286–95.

Sigal, Alon and Dafne Gelbgiser. 2011. *Social Science Research* 40(1):107–19.

Siltanen, Janet and Andrea Doucet. 2008. *Gender Relations in Canada: Intersectionality and Beyond.* Toronto, ON: Oxford University Press.

Silver, Hilary. 2007. "Disasters." Pp. 1174–76 in *The Blackwell Encyclopedia of Sociology,* edited by George Ritzer. Malden, MA: Blackwell.

Silvestri, Marisa and Crowther-Dowey Chris. 2008. *Gender and Crime.* Thousand Oaks, CA: Sage.

Simmel, Georg. [1903] 1971. "The Metropolis and Mental Life." In *Georg Simmel: On Individuality and Social Forms,* edited by

D. Levine. Chicago: University of Chicago Press.

Simmel, Georg. [1904] 1971. "Fashion." Pp. 294–323 in *Georg Simmel: On Individuality and Social Forms,* edited by Donald Levine. Chicago: University of Chichago Press.

Simmel, Georg. [1906] 1950. "The Secret and the Secret Society." Pp. 307–76 in *The Sociology of Georg Simmel,* edited by K. H. Wolff. New York: Free Press.

Simmel, Georg. [1907] 1978. *The Philosophy of Money,* edited and translated by Tom Bottomore and David Frisby. London: Routledge and Kegan Paul.

Simmel, Georg. [1908] 1971a. "Domination." Pp. 96–120 in *Georg Simmel: On Individuality and Social Forms,* edited by Donald Levine. Chicago: University of Chicago Press.

Simmel, Georg. [1908] 1971b. "The Poor." Pp. 150–78 in *Georg Simmel: On Individuality and Social Forms,* edited by Donald Levine. Chicago: University of Chicago Press.

Simmel, Georg. [1908] 1971c. "The Stranger." Pp. 143–49 in *Georg Simmel: On Individuality and Social Forms,* edited by Donald Levine. Chicago: University of Chicago Press.

Simmel, Georg. 1950. *The Sociology of Georg Simmel,* edited and translated by K. Wolff. New York: Free Press.

Simon, Bryant. 2009. *Everything but the Coffee: Learning about America from Starbucks.* Berkeley: University of California Press.

Simon, Bryant. 2011. *Everything but the Coffee: Learning about America from Starbucks.* Berkeley: University of California Press.

Simon, David R. 2012. *Elite Deviance.* 10th ed. Boston: Pearson/Allyn & Bacon.

Simon, Herbert A. [1945] 1976. *Administrative Behavior.* New York: Macmillan.

Simon, Rita J. and Jean Landis. 1991. *The Crimes Women Commit, the Punishments They Receive.* Lexington, MA: Lexington Books.

Simons, Marlise. 2010a. "France: Roma Policy Challenged." *The New York Times,* August 28.

Simons, Marlise. 2010b. "International Court Adds Genocide to Charges Against Sudan Leader." *The New York Times.* (http://www.nytimes.com/2010/07/13/world/africa/13hague.html).

Simons, Marlise. 2010c. "Rights Panel Criticizes France over Roma Policy." *The New York Times,* August 27.

Simpson, Colton. 2006. *Inside the Crips: Life Inside L.A.'s Most Notorious Gang.* St. Martin's Griffin.

Simpson, George Eaton and J. Milton Yinger. 1985. *Racial and Cultural Minorities: An Analysis of Prejudice and Discrimination.* 5th ed. New York: Plenum Press.

Simpson, Sally S. 2002. *Corporate Crime, Law, and Social Control.* New York: Cambridge University Press.

Simpson, Sally and David Weisburd, eds. 2009. *The Criminology of White-collar Crime.* New York: Springer.

Sims, Barbara. 2007. "Crime, Radical/Marxist Theories of." Pp. 839–42 in *The Blackwell Encyclopedia of Sociology,* edited by George Ritzer. Malden, MA: Blackwell.

Singer, Natasha. 2009. "Lawmakers Seek to Curb Drug Commercials." *The New York Times,* July 27.

Singer, Natasha. 2010. "The Financial Time Bomb of Longer Lives." *The New York Times,* October 16.

Singer, Peter. 1996. *Marx: A Very Short Introduction.* New York: Oxford University Press.

Singh, Devendra, and Dorian Singh. 2011. "Shape and Significance of Feminine Beauty: An Evolutionary Perspective." *Sex Roles* 64:723–31.

Sisario, B. 2011. "Master of the Media Marketplace, and Its Demanding Gatekeeper." *The New York Times.* Retrieved November 5, 2011 (http://www.nytimes.com/2011/10/07/business/media/master-of-the-media-marketplace-and-its-demanding-gatekeeper.html?scp=5&sq=music%20industry&st=cse).

Sitton, John F., ed. 2010. *Marx Today: Selected Works and Recent Debates.* New York: Palgrave Macmillan.

Sivalingam, G. 1994. *The Economic and Social Impact of Expert Processing Zones: The Case of Malaysia.* Geneva: International Labor Organization.

Skinner, Quentin, ed. 1985. *The Return of Grand Theories in the Human Sciences.* Cambridge, UK: Cambridge University Press.

Sklair, Leslie. 2002. *Globalization: Capitalism and Its Alternatives.* Oxford, UK: Oxford University Press.

Sklair, Leslie. 2012a. "Culture-ideology of Consumerism." Pp. 377–79 in *The Wiley-Blackwell Encyclopedia of Globalization,* edited by George Ritzer. Malden, MA: Wiley-Blackwell.

Sklair, Leslie. 2012b. "Transnational Capitalist Class." Pp. 2017–19 in *The Wiley-Blackwell Encyclopedia of Globalization,* edited by George Ritzer. Malden, MA: Wiley-Blackwell.

Sklair, Leslie. 2012c. "Transnational Corporations." Pp. 2019–21 in *The Encyclopedia of Globalization,* edited by George Ritzer. Malden, MA: Wiley-Blackwell.

Skloot, Rebecca. 2011. *The Immortal Life of Henrietta Lacks.* Broadway Edition.

Slackman, Michael. 2010a. "Citizens of Qatar, a Land of Affluence, Seek What Money Cannot Buy." *The New York Times,* May 14, p. A7.

Slackman, Michael. 2010b. "Piercing the Sky amid a Deflating Economy." *The New York Times,* January 14, p. A10.

Slate, Nico. 2011. "Translating Race and Caste." *Journal of Historical Sociology* 24(1):62–79.

Slater, Don. 1997. *Consumer Culture and Modernity.* Cambridge, UK: Polity Press.

Slatton, Brittany Chevon, and Joe R. Feagin. 2012. "Racial and Ethnic Issues: Critical Race Approaches in the United States." Pp. 287–303 in *The Wiley-Blackwell Companion to Sociology,* edited by George Ritzer. Malden, MA: Wiley-Blackwell.

Smart, Barry, ed. 2011. *Post-industrial Society.* London: Sage.

Smith, Adam. 1776 [1991]. *An Inquiry into the Nature and Causes of the Wealth of Nations.* New York: Knopf.

Smith, Anthony D. 1990. "Towards a Global Culture?" Pp. 171–92 in *Global Culture: Nationalism, Globalization and Modernity.* London: Sage.

Smith, David. et al. 2011. "Mapping the Great Recession: A Reader's Guide to the First Crisis of 21st Century Capita." *New Political Science 33.*

Smith, Dorothy. 2000. "Schooling for Inequality." *Signs* 25(4):1147–51.

Smith, Dorothy. 2005. *Institutional Ethnography: A Sociology for People.* Lanham, MD: AltaMira Press.

Smith, Jackie. 2008. *Social Movements for Global Democracy.* Baltimore: Johns Hopkins University Press.

Smith, Jackie, and Marina Karides. 2008. *Global Democracy and the World Social Forums.* Boulder, CO: Paradigm Publishers.

Smith, Miriam. 1999. *Lesbian and Gay Rights in Canada: Social Movements and Equality-seeking, 1971–1995.* Toronto, ON: University of Toronto Press.

Smith, Oakley. 2012 "Asian/Oriental Rhinoplasty." Retrieved October 17, 2012 (http://droakleysmithrhinoplasty.com/?page_id=1255&/asian-oriental-rhinoplasty/).

Smith, Paula. 2007. "Recidivism." Pp. 3818–19 in *The Blackwell Encyclopedia of Sociology,* edited by George Ritzer. Malden, MA: Blackwell.

Smith, Vicki. 1997. "New Forms of Work Organization." *Annual Review of Sociology* 23:315–39.

Smock, Pamela L., and Wendy Manning. 2004. "Living Together Unmarried in the United States: Demographic Perspectives and Implications for Family Policy." *Law and Policy* 26(1):87–117.

Smyth, Bruce. 2007. "Non-resident Parents." Pp. 3223–27 in *The Blackwell Encyclopedia of Sociology,* edited by George Ritzer. Malden, MA: Blackwell.

Snow, David A., Sarah A. Soule, and Daniel M. Cress. 2005. "Identifying the Precipitants of Homeless Protest Across 17 U.S. Cities, 1980 to 1990." *Social Forces* 83:1183–210.

Snow, David, Sarah A. Soule, and Hanspeter Kriesi. 2008. *The Blackwell Companion to Social Movements.* Malden, MA: Blackwell.

Snyder, Margaret. 2006. "Unlikely Godmother: The UN and the Global Women's Movement." In *Global Feminism: Transnational Women's Activism, Organizing, and Human Rights,* edited by Myra Marx Ferree and Aili Mari Tripp. New York: New York University Press.

Snyder, R. Claire. 2008. "What Is Third-wave Feminism? A New Directions Essay." *Signs* 34(1):175–96.

Soja, Edward W. 1989. *Postmodern Geographies: The Reassertion of Space in Critical Social Theory.* London: Verso.

Song, Miri. 2007. "Racial Hierarchy." Pp. 3360–64 in *The Blackwell Encyclopedia of Sociology,* edited by George Ritzer. Malden, MA: Blackwell.

Southern Poverty Law Center (SPLC). 2012. "Hate Map." Retrieved March 31, 2011 (http://www.splcenter.org/get-informed/hate-map).

"Special Forum on the Arab Revolutions." 2011. *Globalizations* 5(8).

Spector, Michael. 2007. "Damn Spam: The Losing War on Junk E-mail." *The New Yorker,* August 6.

Speicher Muñoz, Lisa. 2011. *Difference, Inequality, and Change: Social Diversity in the U.S.* Dubuque: Kendall Hunt.

Spencer, James H. 2004. "Los Angeles Since 1992: How Did the Economic Base of Riot-torn Neighborhoods Fare after the Unrest?" *Race, Gender & Class* 11(1):94–115.

Spitz, Herman H. 1999. "Beleaguered Pygmalion: A History of the Controversy over Claims that Teacher Expectancy Raises Intelligence." *Intelligence* 27(3):199–234.

Spitz, Vivien. 2005. *Doctors from Hell: The Horrific Account of Nazi Experiments on Humans.* Sentient Publications.

Spotts, Greg, and Robert Greenwald. 2005. *Wal-Mart: The High Cost of Low Price.* New York: Disinformation Press.

Sprott, Jane, and Anthony Doob. 2010. "Gendered Treatment: Girls and Treatment Orders in Bail Court." *Canadian Journal of Criminology and Criminal Justice* 52(4):427–44.

Srinivas, M. N. 2003. "An Obituary on Caste as a System." *Economic and Political Weekly* 38(5):455–59.

Srivastava, Rahul and Matias Echanove. 2008. "Airoots Interviews Arjun Appadurai." Retrieved April 1, 2012 (http://www.airoots.org/2008/09/airoots-interviews-arjun-appadurai/).

Stacey, Judith. 1998. *Brave New Families.* Berkeley: University of California Press.

Staggenborg, Suzanne. 2011. *Social Movements.* 2nd ed. Toronto, ON: Oxford University Press.

Standing, Guy. 1989. "Global Feminization through Flexible Labor: A Theme Revisited." *World Development* 27(3):583–602.

Stark, Rodney, and William Sims Bainbridge. 1979. "Of Churches, Sects, and Cults: Preliminary Concepts for a Theory of Religious Movements." *Journal for the Scientific Study of Religion* 18(2):117–131.

Starr, Paul. 1983. *The Social Transformation of American Medicine.* New York: Basic Books.

Starr, Paul. 2009. "Fighting the Wrong Health Care Battle." *The New York Times,* November 29.

Starr, Paul. 2011a. "The Medicare Bind." *The American Prospect,* September 30. Retrieved March 31, 2012 (http://prospect.org/article/medicare-bind).

Starr, Paul. 2011b. *Remedy and Reaction: The Peculiar American Struggle over Health Care Reform.* New Haven, CT: Yale University Press.

Statistics Canada. 2006. *The Wealth of Canadians: An Overview of the Results of the Survey of Financial Security, 2005.* Ottawa, ON: Author, Cat. #13F0026MIE.

Statistics Canada. 2010. *Guide to the Labour Force Survey.* Ottawa, ON: Author, Cat. #71-543-G

Statistics Canada. 2011a. "Canadian Internet Use Survey." *The Daily,* May 25.

Statistics Canada. 2011b. "General Social Survey—2010 Overview of the Time Use of Canadians." Ottawa, ON: Author, Cat. #89-647-X.

Statistics Canada. 2011c. *Family Violence in Canada: A Statistical Portrait.* Ottawa, ON: Canadian Centre for Justice Statistics, Cat. #85-224-X.

Statistics Canada. 2012a. "The Classification of Visible Minority." Retrieved October 21, 2012 (http://www.statcan.gc.ca/concepts/definitions/minority01-minorite01a-eng.htm).

Statistics Canada. 2012b. "Crude Marriage Rate and Crude Divorce Rate, Canada, 1926 to 2008." Ottawa, ON: Author. Retrieved December 21, 2012 (http://www.statcan.gc.ca/pub/89-503-x/2010001/article/11546/c-g/c-g006-eng.htm).

Statistics Canada. 2012c. "Fifty Years of Families in Canada, 1961 to 2011." Ottawa, ON: Author, Cat. #98-312-X2011003, Census in Brief, No. 1.

Statistics Canada. 2012d. "Leading Causes of Death in Canada, 2009." Ottawa: Statistics Canada.

Statistics Canada. 2012e. "Living Arrangements of Seniors." Ottawa, ON: Author, Cat. #98-312-X2011003, Census in Brief, No. 4.

Statistics Canada. 2012f. "Low Income Lines, 2010–2011." Ottawa, ON: Author, Cat. #75F0002M, No. 002.

Statistics Canada. 2012g. "Portrait of Families and Living Arrangements in Canada." Ottawa, ON: Author, Cat. # 98-312-X2011001.

Statistics Canada. 2012h. "2006 Census: Educational Portrait of Canada," "2006 Census: Aboriginal Population." Retrieved October 21, 2012 (http://www.arcticstat.org/TableViewer.aspx?S=1&ID=11742).

Statistics Canada. 2012. *Deaths and Mortality Rate, 2000–2009, by Selected Causes and Sex, Canada, Provinces and Territories* (CANSIM Table 102-0552). Ottawa, ON: Statistics Canada.

Stearns, Cindy. 2009. "The Work of Breast-feeding." *Women's Studies Quarterly* 37: 63–80.

Stearns, Cindy A. 2011. "Cautionary Tale about Extended Breastfeeding and Weaning." *Health Care for Women International* 32:538–54.

Stebbins, Robert. 1977. "The Meaning of Academic Performance: How Teachers Define a Classroom Situation." In *School Experience,* edited by Peter Woods and Martyn Hammersly. New York: St. Martin's Press.

Stebbins, Robert. 1984. *The Magician: Career, Culture, and Social Psychology in a Variety Art.* New York: Irwin.

Stebbins, Robert. 1996. *The Barbershop Singer: Inside the Social World of a Musical Hobby.* Toronto, ON: University of Toronto Press.

Stebbins, Robert. 2005. *Challenging Mountain Nature: Risk, Motive, and Lifestyle in Three Hobbyist Sports.* Calgary, AB: Detselig.

Stebbins, Robert A. 2007. "Leisure, Popular Culture and." Pp. 2596–600 in *The Blackwell Encyclopedia of Sociology,* edited by George Ritzer. Malden, MA: Blackwell.

Steele, Valerie. 2011. "The Homogenization Effect." *New York Times,* August 21.

Steinberg, L., and K. C. Monahan. 2007. "Age Differences in Resistance to Peer Influence." *Developmental Psychology* 43:1531–43.

Steinfatt, Thomas. 2011. "Sex Trafficking in Cambodia: Fabricated Numbers versus Empirical Evidence." *Crime, Law and Social Change* 56:443–62.

Steinmetz, George. 2012. "Geopolitics." Pp. 800–23 in *The Wiley-Blackwell Encyclopedia of Globalization,* edited by George Ritzer. Malden, MA: Wiley-Blackwell.

Steinmetz, Suzanne K. 1987. "Family Violence." In *Handbook of Marriage and the Family,* edited by Marvin B. Sussman and Suzanne K. Steinmetz. New York: Plenum Press.

Steketee, Gail, and Randy Frost. 2011. *Stuff: Compulsive Hoarding and the Meaning of Things.* Boston: Mariner Books.

Stepan-Norris, Judith, and Caleb Southworth. 2007. "Churches as Organizational Resources: A Case Study in the Geography of Religion and Political Voting in Postwar Detroit." *Social Science History* 31(3):343–80.

Stets, Jan E., and Jonathan H. Turner, eds. 2007. *Handbook of the Sociology of Emotions.* Springer.

Stevens, Mitchell L. 2001. *Kingdom of Children: Culture and Controversy in the Home Schooling Movement.* Princeton, NJ: Princeton University Press.

Stevens, Mitchell L. 2007. "Schooling, Home." Pp. 4032–34 in *The Blackwell Encyclopedia of Sociology,* edited by George Ritzer. Malden, MA: Blackwell.

Stevis, Dimitris. 2005. "The Globalization of Environment." *Globalizations* 2(3):323–33.

Stewart, Lathonia Denise and Richard Perlow. 2001. "Applicant Race, Job Status, and Racial Attitude as Predictors of Employment Discrimination." *Journal of Business and Psychology* 16(2):259–75.

Stigter, Shelley. 2005. *Double-voice and Double-consciousness in Native American Literature.* Master's thesis, University of Lethbridge.

Stoddart, Mark, and David Tindall. 2012. "We've Also Become Quite Good Friends: Environmentalists, Social Networks and Social Comparison in British Columbia." *Social Movement Studies* 9(3):353–71.

Stokoe, Elizabeth. 2006. "On Ethnomethodology, Feminism, and the Analysis of Categorical Reference to Gender in Talk-in-Interaction." *The Sociological Review* 54:3.

Stolow, Jeremy. 2004. "Transnationalism and the New Religio-politics: Reflections on a Jewish Orthodox Case." *Theory, Culture & Society* 21(2):109–137.

Stone, Brad. 2009. "Spam Back to 94% of All E-mail." *The New York Times,* March 31.

Stone, Brad. 2010. "Chatroulette's Creator, 17, Introduces Himself." *The New York Times,* February 13. Retrieved May 26, 2011 (http://bits.blogs.nytimes.com/2010/02/13/chatroulettes-founder-17-introduces-himself/).

Stone, R. 1991. "Will the Real Body Please Stand Up?" In *Cyberspace: First Steps,* edited by M. Benedikt. Cambridge, MA: MIT Press.

Stone, Richard, and Hao Xin. 2010. "Google Plots Exit Strategy as China Shores Up 'Great Firewall.'" *Science* 327:402–403.

Stoolmiller, Michael. 1999. "Implications of the Restricted Range of Family Environments for Estimates of Heritability and Nonshared Environments in Behavior-genetic Adoption Studies." *Psychological Bulletin* 125:392–409.

Straus, Murry A. 1980. "Victims and Aggressors in Marital Violence." *American Behavioral Scientist* 23:681–704.

Strauss, Anselm, and Corbin, Juliet. 1998. *Basics of Qualitative Research.* Thousand Oaks, CA: Sage.

Strobel, Frederick R. 1993. *Upward Dreams, Downward Mobility: The Economic Decline of the American Middle Class.* Lanham, MD: Rowman and Littlefield.

Struck, Doug. 2007. "Warming Will Exacerbate Global Water Conflicts." *The Washington Post,* October 22.

Stryker, Sheldon. 1980. *Symbolic Interactionism: A Social Structural Version.* Menlo Park, CA: Benjamin/Cummings.

Stryker, Sheldon, and Anne Statham Macke. 1978. "Status Inconsistency and Role Conflict." *Annual Review of Sociology* 4:57–90.

Stryker, Sheldon, and Richard T. Serpe. 1994. "Identity Salience and Psychological Centrality: Equivalent, Overlapping, or Complementary Concepts?" *Social Psychology Quarterly* 57:16–35.

Subramaniam, Mangala, David Whitlock, and Beth Williford. 2012. "Water Crisis." Pp. 2210–12 in *The Wiley-Blackwell Encyclopedia of Globalization,* edited by George Ritzer. Malden, MA: Wiley-Blackwell.

Subramanian, Ramesh, and Eddan Katz, eds. 2011. *The Global Flow of Information: Legal, Social, and Cultural Perspectives.* New York: New York University Press.

Sugiman, Pamela. 2009. "'Life Is Sweet': Vulnerability and Composure in the Wartime Narratives of Japanese Canadians." *Journal of Canadian Studies* 43(1):186–218

Sullivan, John. 2010. "Attacks on Journalists and 'New Media' in Mexico's Drug War: A Power and Counter Power Assessment." Retrieved March 31, 2012 (http://smallwarsjournal.com/jrnl/art/attacks-on-journalists-and-new-media-in-mexicos-drug-war).

Sullivan, Robert. 2011. "Swamp Dreams." *New York Magazine,* August 21.

Sumner, Colin. 1994. *The Sociology of Deviance: An Obituary.* New York: Continuum.

Sumner, William Graham. [1906] 1940. *Folkways: A Study of the Sociological Implications of Usages, Manners, Customs, Mores and Morals.* Boston: Ginn.

Suroor, Hasan. 2011. "U.K. to Raise Diplomatic Profile in India, China." *The Hindu,* May 11. Retrieved May 26, 2011 (http://www.thehindu.com/news/article2009518.ece).

Sutherland, Edwin H. 1947. *Criminology.* 4th ed. Philadelphia: Lippincott.

Sutherland, Edwin H. 1924. *Principles of Criminology.* Chicago: University of Chicago Press.

Swatos, William H., Jr. 2007a. "Denomination." Pp. 1051–56 in *The Blackwell Encyclopedia of Sociology,* edited by George Ritzer. Malden, MA: Blackwell.

Swatos, William H., Jr. 2007b. "Sect." Pp. 4135–40 in *The Blackwell Encyclopedia of Sociology,* edited by George Ritzer. Malden, MA: Blackwell.

Swatos, William H., Jr. n.d. "Church-Sect Theory." In the *Encyclopedia of Religion and Society,* edited by William H. Swatos Jr. Retrieved January 25, 2012 (http://hirr.hartsem.edu/ency/cstheory.htm).

Swedberg, Richard. 2007. *Principles of Economic Sociology.* Princeton, NJ: Princeton University Press.

Sykes, Gresham. [1958] 2007. *The Society of Captives: A Study of a Maximum Security Prison.* Princeton, NJ: Princeton University Press.

Symantec. 2009. *MessageLabs Intelligence (Symantec) Report.* Mountain View, CA: Author.

Sztompka, Piotr. 1993. *The Sociology of Social Change.* West Sussex, UK: Wiley-Blackwell.

Tabuchi, Hiroko. 2010. "Beef Bowl Economics: In Japan, a Price War at Popular Restaurants Is the Face of Deflation." *The New York Times,* January 30, pp. B1, B6.

Talbani, Aziz, and Parveen Hasanali. 2000 "Adolescent Females between Tradition and Modernity: Gender Role Socialization in South Asian Immigrant Culture." *Journal of Adolescence* 25:615–27.

Tan, Celine. 2007. "Liberalization." Pp. 735–39 in *Encyclopedia of Globalization,* edited by Jan Aart Scholte and Ronald Robertson. New York: MTM Publishing.

Tansey, Oisín. 2006. "Process Tracing and Elite Interviewing." Paper presented at the annual meeting of the American Political Science Association, Philadelphia, August 31.

Tavernise, Sabrina. 2010. "Pakistan's Elite Pay Few Taxes, Widening Gap." *The New York Times,* July 19, pp. A1, A9.

Taylor, Alison, and Harvey Krahn. 2009. "Streaming in/for the New Economy." Pp. 103–123 in *Canadian Perspectives on the Sociology of Education,* edited by C. Levine-Rasky. Toronto, ON: Oxford University Press.

Taylor, J. L. 2007. "Buddhism." Pp. 108–13 in *Encyclopedia of Globalization,* edited by Jan Aart Scholte and Roland Robertson. New York: MTM Publishing.

Taylor, Paul C. 2011. "William Edward Burghardt Du Bois." Pp. 426–47 in *The Wiley-Blackwell Companion to Major Social Theorists: Volume 1. Classical Theorists,* edited by George Ritzer and Jeffrey Stepnisky. Malden, MA: Wiley-Blackwell.

Taylor, P., C. Funk, and A. Clark. 2007. *From 1997 to 2007, Fewer Mothers Prefer Full-time Work.* Pew Research Center.

Taylor, Yvette. 2007. "Sexualities and Consumption." Pp. 4256–60 in *The Blackwell Encyclopedia of Sociology,* edited by George Ritzer. Malden, MA: Blackwell.

Teivainen, Teivo. 2007. "World Social Forum." Pp. 1302–04 in *Encyclopedia of Globalization,* edited by Jan Aart Scholte and Roland Robertson. New York: MTM Publishing.

Telegraph. 2010, April 26. "Louisiana Oil Rig Explosion: Underwater Machines Attempt to Plug Leak." Retrieved March 31, 2012 (http://www.telegraph.co.uk/finance/newsbysector/energy/oilandgas/7633286/Louisiana-oil-rig-explosion-Underwater-machines-attempt-to-plug-leak.html).

Tepperman, Lorne. 2010. *Deviance, Crime, and Control Beyond the Straight and Narrow.* 2nd ed. Toronto, ON: Oxford University Press.

Tewksbury, Richard. 2007. "Sexual Deviance." Pp. 4230–32 in *The Blackwell Encyclopedia of Sociology,* edited by George Ritzer. Malden, MA: Blackwell.

"That Pesky Glass Ceiling." 2011. *Diverse: Issues in Higher Education* 27:7.

The Tobacco Public Policy Center at Capital University Law School. 2006. "Ohio's Tobacco Law Resource." Retrieved May 23, 2011 (http://www.law.capital.edu/tobacco/federal_laws.asp).

Thoits, Peggy A. 1985. "Self-labeling Processes in Mental Illness: The Role of Emotional Deviance." *American Journal of Sociology* 91(2):221–49.

Thoits, Peggy. 2011. "Perceived Social Support and the Voluntary, Mixed, or Pressured Use of Mental Health Services." *Society and Mental Health* 1:4–19.

Thomas, George. 2012. "Christianity." Pp. 179–87 in *The Wiley-Blackwell Encyclopedia of Globalization,* edited by George Ritzer. Malden, MA: Wiley-Blackwell.

Thomas, Landon, Jr. 2011. "Pondering a Day: Leaving the Euro." *The New York Times,* December 13, pp. B1, B8.

Thomas, Samuel S. 2009. "Early Modern Midwifery: Splitting the Profession, Connecting the History." *Journal of Social History* 43:115–38.

Thomas, William I., and Dorothy S. Thomas. 1928. *The Child in America: Behavior Problems and Programs.* New York: Knopf.

Thompson, Ginger. 2008. "Fewer People Are Entering US Illegally, Report Says." *The New York Times,* October 3.

Thompson, G., and M. Lacey. 2010. "U.S. and Mexico Revise Joint Antidrug Strategy." *The New York Times,* March 23. Retrieved March 31, 2012 (http://www.nytimes.com/2010/03/24/world/americas/24mexico.html).

Thorn, Elizabeth. 2007. "Gender, Work, and Family." Pp. 1880–85 in *The Blackwell Encyclopedia of Sociology,* edited by George Ritzer. Malden, MA: Blackwell.

Thorne, Barrie. 1993. *Gender Play: Girls and Boys in School.* Rutgers University Press.

Thornton, Arland, William Axinn, and Y. Xie. 2007. *Marriage and Cohabitation.* Chicago: University of Chicago Press.

Thornton, A., and K. McAuliffe. 2006. "Teaching in Wild Meerkats." *Science* 313:227–29.

Thornton, S. 1995. *Club Culture: Music, Media and Subcultural Capital.* Cambridge, UK: Polity Press.

Thrane, Lisa E., and Xiaojin Chen. 2010. "Impact of Running Away on Girls' Sexual Onset." *Journal of Adolescent Health* 46(1):32–36.

Tibi, Bassam. 2002. *The Challenge of Fundamentalism: Political Islam and the New World Order.* Berkeley: University of California Press.

Tibi, Bassam. 2007. *Political Islam, World Politics and Europe.* London: Routledge.

Tiffani, C., and M. Phillips. 2004. "Social Reproduction and Child-rearing Practices: Social Class, Children's Agency, and the Summer Activity Gap." *Sociology of Education* 77:185–210.

Timasheff, N. S. 1965. *War and Revolution.* New York: Sheed and Ward.

Timberlake, Michael, and Xiulian Ma. 2007. "Cities and Globalization." Pp. 254–71 in *The Blackwell Companion to Globalization,* edited by George Ritzer. Malden, MA: Blackwell.

Timmermans, Stefan and Hyeyoung Oh. 2010. "The Continued Social Transformation of the Medical Profession." *Journal of Health and Social Behavior* 51:S94–S106.

Timms, Jill. 2012. "Labor Movements." Pp. 1259–61 in *The Encyclopedia of Globalization,* edited by George Ritzer. Malden, MA: Wiley-Blackwell.

Tocqueville, Alex de. [1835–1840] 1969. *Democracy in America.* Garden City, NY: Doubleday.

Toennies, Ferdinand. [1887] 1957. *Community and Society.* New York: Harper Torchbooks.

Tomlinson, John. 1999. *Globalization and Culture.* Chicago: University of Chicago Press.

Tomlinson, John. 2000. "Globalization and Cultural Identity." Pp. 269–77 in *The Global Transformations Reader,* edited by David Held and Anthony McGrew. Cambridge, UK: Polity.

Tomlinson, John. 2012. "Cultural Imperialism." Pp. 371–74 in *The Wiley-Blackwell Encyclopedia of Globalization,* edited by George Ritzer. Malden, MA: Wiley-Blackwell.

Tong, Rosemarie. 2009. *Feminist Thought: A More Comprehensive Introduction.* 3rd ed. Boulder, CO: Westview Press.

Tönnies, F. [1887] 1963. *Community and Society.* New York: Harper & Row.

Toobin, Jeffrey. 2009. "The Celebrity Defense." *The New Yorker,* December 14:50.

"Top Sites in China." 2011. Alexa. Retrieved June 20, 2011 (http://www.alexa.com/topsites/countries/CN).

Torpey, John C. 2000. *The Invention of the Passport: Citizenship, Surveillance, and the State.* New York: Cambridge University Press.

Torpey, John. 2012. "Passports." Pp. 1644–47 in *The Wiley-Blackwell Encyclopedia of Globalization,* edited by George Ritzer. Malden, MA: Wiley-Blackwell.

Townsend, Peter. 2010. "The Meaning of Poverty." *British Journal of Sociology* 61:85–102.

Trask, Bahira Sherif. 2010. *Globalization and Families: Accelerated Systemic Social Change.* New York: Springer.

Troeltsch, Ernst. 1932. *The Social Teaching of the Christian Churches,* translated by Olive Wyon. New York: Macmillan.

Tsutsui, Kiyoteru, and Christine Min Wotipka. 2004. "Global Civil Society and the International Human Rights Movement: Citizen Participation in Human Rights International Nongovernmental Organizations." *Social Forces* 83(2):587–620.

Tuchman, Gaye. 1972. "Objectivity as Strategic Ritual: An Examination of Newsmen's Notions of Objectivity." *American Journal of Sociology* 77(4):660–79.

Tufekci, Zeynep. 2010. "Internet Use and Social Ties of Americans: An Analysis of General Social Survey Data." Paper presented at Meetings of the American Sociological Association, Atlanta, Georgia.

Tugend, Alina. 2010. "Spending Less in a Recession, and Talking about It, Too." *The New York Times,* February 13.

Tumber, Howard, and Frank Webster. 2006. *Journalists under Fire: Information War and Journalistic Practices.* London: Sage.

Tumin, Melvin E. 1953. "Some Principles of Stratification: A Critical Analysis." *American Sociological Review* 18:387–94.

Tunnell, Kenneth D. 2007. "Crime, Political." Pp. 835–36 in *The Blackwell Encyclopedia of Sociology,* edited by George Ritzer. Malden, MA: Blackwell.

Turcotte, Martin. 2011. "Intergenerational Education Mobility: University Completion in Relation to Parents' Education Level." *Canadian Social Trends* August, Cat. #11-008-X.

Turkle, Sherry. 1995. *Life on Screen: Identity in the Age of the Internet.* New York: Simon & Schuster.

Turkle, Sherry. 1997. *Life on Screen: Identity in the Age of the Internet.* New York: Touchstone.

Turkle, Sherry. 2011. *Alone Together: Why We Expect More from Technology and Less from Each Other.* New York: Basic Books.

Turner, Bryan S. 2007a. "Body and Cultural Sociology." Pp. 324–28 in *The Blackwell Encyclopedia of Sociology,* edited by George Ritzer. Malden, MA: Blackwell.

Turner, Bryan S. 2007b. "Body and Society." Pp. 335–38 in *The Blackwell Encyclopedia of Sociology,* edited by George Ritzer. Malden, MA: Blackwell.

Turner, Bryan. 2008. *The Body and Society: Explorations in Social Theory.* London: Sage.

Turner, Bryan S. 2010. "McCitizens: Risk, Coolness, and Irony in Contemporary Politics." Pp. 229–32 in *McDonaldization: The Reader,* edited by George Ritzer. Thousand Oaks, CA: Pine Forge Press.

Turner, Bryan S. 2011. *Religion and Modern Society: Citizenship, Secularisation and the State.* Cambridge, UK: Cambridge University Press.

Turner, Jonathan. 2005. "A New Approach for Theoretically Integrating Micro and Macro Analysis." Pp. 403–22 in *The Sage Handbook of Sociology,* edited by Craig Calhoun, Chris Rojek, and Bryan Turner. London: Sage.

Turner, Jonathan. 2009. "A New Approach for Theoretically Integrating Micro and Macro Analysis." Pp. 403–22 in *The Sage Handbook of Sociology,* edited by Craig Calhoun, Chris Rojek, and Bryan Turner. London: Sage.

Turner, Jonathan H. 2010. "The Micro Basis of the Meso and Macro Social Realms." *Theoretical Principles of Sociology* 2:271–301.

Turner, Jonathan, and Barry Markovsky. 2007. "Micro-macro Links." Pp. 2997–3004 in *The Blackwell Encyclopedia of Sociology*, edited by George Ritzer. Malden, MA: Blackwell.

Turner, Leigh. 2007. "'First World Health Care at Third World Prices': Globalization, Bioethics and Medical Tourism." *BioSocieties* 2:303–25.

Turner, Ralph H., and Lewis M. Killian. 1987. *Collective Behavior.* 3rd ed. Englewood Cliffs, NJ: Prentice-Hall.

Turner, Victor. 1967. *The Forest of Symbols: Aspects of Ndembu Ritual.* Ithaca, NY: Cornell University Press.

Twaddle, Andrew C. 2007. "Sick Role." Pp. 4317–20 in *The Blackwell Encyclopedia of Sociology,* edited by George Ritzer. Malden, MA: Blackwell.

Tyerman, Andrew, and Christopher Spencer. 1983. "A Critical Test of the Sherifs' Robber's Cave Experiments." *Small Group Research* 14(4):515–31.

Tyrell, Hartmann. 2010. "History and Sociology—The First Century: From Ranke to Weber." *InterDisciplines: Journal of History and Sociology* 1(1):94–111.

Uchitelle, Louis. 2010. "Another Shifting Industry." *The New York Times,* January 19, pp. B1, B5.

Ultee, Wout. 2007a. "Mobility, Horizontal and Vertical." Pp. 3060–61 in *The Blackwell Encyclopedia of Sociology,* edited by George Ritzer. Malden, MA: Blackwell.

Ultee, Wout. 2007b. "Mobility, Intergenerational and Intragenerational." Pp. 3061–62 in *The Blackwell Encyclopedia of Sociology,* edited by George Ritzer. Malden, MA: Blackwell.

UNAIDS. 2010. "Report on the Global AIDS Epidemic." Geneva: Author.

UNAIDS. 2012. "Report on the Global AIDS Epidemic." Retrieved May 14, 2013 (http://www.unaids.org/en/media/unaids/contentassets/documents/epidemiology/2012/gr2012/2012 1120_UNAIDS_Global_Report_2012_en.pdf).

UNICEF. 2012. "Measuring Child Poverty: New League Tables for Child Poverty in the World's Rich Countries." Innocenti Research Centre, Florence Italy.

Ungar, Sheldon. 2012. "Ozone Depletion." Pp. 1630–34 in *The Wiley-Blackwell Encyclopedia of Globalization,* edited by George Ritzer. Malden, MA: Wiley-Blackwell.

United Nations. 2006. "Ending Violence against Women: From Words to Action Study of the Secretary-General, Fact Sheet." Retrieved March 31, 2012 (http://www.un.org/womenwatch/daw/vaw/launch/english/v.a.w-exeE-use.pdf).

United Nations Global Initiative to Fight Human Trafficking. 2007. "Human Trafficking: The Facts." Retrieved March 31, 2012 (http://www.unglobalcompact.org/docs/issues_doc/labour/Forced_labour/HUMAN_TRAFFICKING_-_THE_FACTS_-_final.pdf).

United Nations Office on Drugs and Crime. 2012. "World Drug Report." Retrieved May 3, 2013 (http://www.unodc.org/unodc/en/data-and-analysis/WDR-2012.html).

Uriely, Natan, and Yaniv Belhassen. 2005. "Drugs and Tourists' Experiences." *Journal of Travel Research* February 43(3):238–46.

Urry, John. 2007. *Mobilities.* Cambridge: Polity.

U.S. Bureau of Justice Statistics. 2008. "Identity Theft." Retrieved November 6, 2011 (http://www.bjs.gov/index.cfm?ty=tp&tid=42).

U.S. Bureau of Justice Statistics. 2009. "Sourcebook of Criminal Justice Statistics" (Section 6: Persons Under Criminal Supervision). Retrieved December 21, 2011 (http://www.albany.edu/sourcebook/tost_6.html#6_e).

U.S. Bureau of Labor Statistics. 2008. "Chart Book: Occupational Employment and Wages." Retrieved January 31, 2010 (http://bls.gov/oes/2008/may/chartbook.htm).

U.S. Census Bureau. 2004. *American Community Survey: Selected Population Profiles,* S0201.

U.S. Census Bureau. 2009. "Statistical Abstracts of the United States, 2009." Retrieved March 31, 2012 (http://www.census.gov/compendia/statab).

U.S. Census Bureau. 2011c. "Statistical Abstract of the United States 2011" (Tables 225 and 226). Retrieved March 31, 2012 (http://www.census.gov/compendia/statab/2011/tables/11s0225.pdf).

U.S. Census Bureau. 2011d. "Statistical Abstract of the United States 2011" (Tables 227 and 228). Retrieved March 31, 2012 (http://www.census.gov/compendia/statab/2011/tables/11s0228.pdf).

U.S. Census Bureau. 2012a. "Population." The 2011 Statistical Abstract. Retrieved March 31, 2012 (http://www.census.gov/compendia/statab/cats/population.html).

U.S. Census Bureau. 2012b. "Trade in Goods with China." Retrieved March 31, 2012 (http://www.census.gov/foreign-trade/balance/c5700.html).

U.S. Census Bureau International Programs. 2012. "International Data Base." U.S. Census Bureau. Retrieved February 28, 2012 (http://www.census.gov/population/international/data/idb/country.php).

U.S. Commission on Civil Rights. 2000. "Voting Irregularities in Florida During the 2000 Presidential Election." Retrieved March 31, 2012 (http://www.usccr.gov/pubs/vote2000/report/exesum.htm).

U.S. Department of Commerce Economics and Statistics Administration, Executive Office of the President Office of Management and Budget, and White House Council on Women and Girls. 2011. "Women in America: Indicators of Economic and Social Well-being." Retrieved May 25, 2011 (http://www.whitehouse.gov/sites/default/files/rss_viewer/Women_in_America.pdf).

U.S. Department of Justice. 2012. "Family Violence Initiative." Retrieved December 21, 2012 (http://www.justice.gc.ca/eng/pi/fv-vf/about-aprop/).

U.S. Department of Justice—Federal Bureau of Investigation. 2010. "Crime in the United States, 2009." Retrieved December 21, 2011 (http://www2.fbi.gov/ucr/cius2009/data/table_29.html).

U.S. Department of Justice Office of Justice Programs. 2007. "Black Victims of Violent Crime." Washington, DC: U.S. Department of Justice.

U.S. Department of Labor, U.S. Bureau of Labor Statistics. 2009. "Ranks of Discouraged Workers and Others Marginally Attached to the Labor Force Rise During Recession." *Issues in Labor Statistics* April.

U.S. State Department. 2010. "Trafficking in Persons Report." Retrieved March 31, 2012 (www.state.gov/documents/organization/142980.pdf).

Useem, Elizabeth L. 1992. "Middle Schools and Math Groups: Parents' Involvement in Children's Placement." *Sociology of Education* 65:263–79.

Vago, Steven. 2004. *Social Change.* Upper Saddle River, NJ: Prentice Hall.

Vaidhyanathan, Siva. 2011. *The Googlization of Everything (and Why We Should Worry).* Berkeley: University of California Press.

Vail, D. Angus. 1999. "Tattoos Are Like Potato Chips . . . You Can't Have Just One: The Process of Becoming and Being a Collector." *Deviant Behavior* 20:253–73.

Vail, D. Angus. 2007. "Body Modification." Pp. 328–30 in *The Blackwell Encyclopedia of Sociology,* edited by George Ritzer. Malden, MA: Blackwell.

Vallone, Robert, Lee Ross, and Mark Lepper. 1985. "The Hostile Media Phenomenon: Biased Perception and Perceptions of Media Bias in Coverage of the Beirut Massacre." *Journal of Personality and Social Psychology* 49(3):577–85.

Valocchi, Stephen. 2007. "Gay and Lesbian Movement." Pp. 1833–38 in *The Blackwell Encyclopedia of Sociology,* edited by George Ritzer. Malden, MA: Blackwell.

Van De Belt, Thomas H., et al. 2010. "Definition of Heath 2.0 and Medicine 2.0: A Systematic Review." *Journal of Medical Internet Research* 12, April–June. Retrieved March 31, 2012 (http://www.jmir.org/2010/2/e18/).

Van de Poel, Ellen, Ahmad Reza Hosseinpoor, Niko Speybroeck, Tom Van Ourti, and Jeanette Vega. 2008. "Socioeconomic Inequality in Malnutrition in Developing Countries." *Bulletin of the World Health Organization* 86(4):282–291.

Van de Werfhorst, Herman G., and Jonathan J. B. Mij. 2010. "Achievement Inequality and the Institutional Structure of Educational Systems: A Comparative Perspective." *Annual Review of Sociology* 36:407–28.

Van den Berg, Alex, Claus-H von Restorff, Daniel Parent, and Anthony Masi. 2008. "From Unemployment to Employment Insurance: Towards Transitional Labour Markets in Canada." Pp. 308–35 in *Flexibility and Employment Security in Europe: Labour Markets in Transition,* edited by Rudd J. Muffels. Cheltenham, UK: Edward Elgar.

Van den Berghe, Pierre L. 2007. "Race (Racism)." Pp. 3749–51 in *The Blackwell Encyclopedia of Sociology,* edited by George Ritzer. Malden, MA: Blackwell.

Van Gennep, Arnold. [1908] 1960. *The Rites of Passage.* London: Routledge and Kegan Paul.

van Leeuwen, Marco H. D., and Ineke Maas. 2010. "Historical Studies of Social Mobility and Stratification." *Annual Review of Sociology* 36:429–51.

Van Maanen, J. 1983. "The Moral Fix: On the Ethics of Field Work." In *Contemporary Field Research: Perspectives and Formulations,* 1st ed., edited by R. M. Emerson. Longrove, IL: Waveland Press.

Van Valen, L. 1974. "Brain Size and Intelligence in Man." *American Journal of Physical Anthropology* 40:417–23.

Varcoe, Ian. 2007. "Historical and Comparative Methods." Pp. 2133–36 in *The Blackwell Encyclopedia of Sociology,* edited by George Ritzer. Malden, MA: Blackwell.

Vaughan, Diane. 1996. *The Challenger Launch Decision: Risky Technology, Culture, and Deviance at NASA.* Chicago: University of Chicago Press.

Veblen, Thorstein. [1899] 1994. *The Theory of the Leisure Class.* New York: Penguin Books.

Veenstra, Gerry. 2009. "Social Inequality and Health." In *Social Inequality in Canada,* edited by Edward Grabb and Neil Guppy. Toronto, ON: Pearson, Prentice-Hall.

Veldhuis, Niels, Amela Karabegovic, and Milagros Palacios. 2012. "BC Welfare Levels Are Adequate." *Fraser Forum* March/April 7–9.

Venkatesh, Alladi. 2007. "Postmodern Consumption." Pp. 3552–56 in *The Blackwell Encyclopedia of Sociology,* edited by George Ritzer. Malden, MA: Blackwell.

Venkatesh, Sudhir. 1994. "Learnin' the Trade: Conversations with a Gangsta." *Public Culture* 6:319–41.

Venkatesh, Sudhir. 2002. "'Doin' the Hustle': Constructing the Ethnographer in the American Ghetto." *Ethnography* 3:91–111.

Venkatesh, Sudhir. 2008. *Gang Leader for a Day: A Rogue Sociologist Takes to the Streets.* New York: Penguin.

Venturi, Robert, Denise Scott Brown, and Steven Izenour. 1972. *Learning from Las Vegas: The Forgotten Symbolism of Architectural Form.* Cambridge, MA: MIT Press.

Vidal, John. 1997. *McLibel: Burger Culture on Trial.* New York: New Press.

Villareal, Andres, and Wei-hsin Yu. 2007. "Economic Globalization and Women's Employment: The Case of Manufacturing in Mexico." *American Sociological Review* 72(3):365–89.

Vobejda, B. 1996. "Clinton Signs Welfare Bill Amid Division." *The Washington Post.* Retrieved June 29, 2011 (http://www.washingtonpost.com/wp-srv/politics/special/welfare/stories/wf 082396.htm).

Vogel, Ezra F. 2011. *Deng Xiaoping and the Transformation of China.* Belknap Press of Harvard University Press.

vom Lehn, Dirk. 2007. "Interaction." Pp. 2361–65 in *The Blackwell Encyclopedia of Sociology,* edited by George Ritzer. Malden, MA: Blackwell.

Waddington, Ivan. 2007. "Health and Sport." Pp. 2091–95 in *The Blackwell Encyclopedia of Sociology,* edited by George Ritzer. Malden, MA: Blackwell.

Wafi. 2009. "Wafi." Retrieved May 19, 2011 (www.wafi.com/page.aspx?id=3417&TID=216).

Wajcman, Judy. 2010. "Feminist Theories of Technology." *Cambridge Journal of Economics* 34:143–52.

Wakefield, Sara, and Christopher Uggen. 2010. "Incarceration and Stratification." *Annual Review of Sociology* 36:387–406.

Walder, Andrew. 2009. "Political Sociology and Social Movements." *Annual Review of Sociology* 35:393–412.

Waldmeir, Patti. [1997] 2001. *Anatomy of a Miracle: The End of Apartheid and the Birth of a New South Africa.* New Brunswick, NJ: Rutgers University Press.

Walker, Henry A., and Willer David. 2007. "Experimental Methods." Pp. 1537–41 in *The Blackwell Encyclopedia of Sociology,* edited by George Ritzer. Malden, MA: Blackwell.

Walker, Janet. 2007. "Child Custody and Child Support." Pp. 451–55 in *The Blackwell Encyclopedia of Sociology,* edited by George Ritzer. Malden, MA: Blackwell.

Walker, Samuel, Cassia Spohn, and Miriam DeLone. 2000. *The Color of Justice: Race, Ethnicity and Crime in America.* 2nd ed. Belmont, CA: Wadsworth Thomson.

Walks, Alan, and Richard Maaranen. 2008. *The Timing, Patterning, and Forms of Community Gentrification and Neighbourhood Change in Montreal, Toronto, and Vancouver, 1961 to 2001.* Research paper 211. Toronto, ON: Centre for Urban and Community Studies, University of Toronto.

Wallerstein, Immanuel. 1974. *The Modern World-system.* New York: Academic Press.

Wallerstein, James S., and Clement J. Wyle. 1947. "Our Law-abiding Law-breakers." *Federal Probation* 25:107–12.

Walsh, Anthony. 1990. "Twice Labeled: The Effect of Psychiatric Labeling on the Sentencing of Sex Offenders." *Social Problems* 37:375–89.

Walters, G. D. 2003. "Changes in Criminal Thinking and Identity in Novice and Experienced Inmates: Prisonization Revisited." *Criminal Justice and Behavior* 30(4):399–421.

Wanner, Richard. 2009. "Social Mobility in Canada: Concepts, Patterns, and Trends." Pp. 116–32 in *Social Inequality in Canada: Patterns, Problems, and Policies,* edited by Edward Grabb and Neil Guppy. Toronto, ON: Prentice Hall.

Ward, Kathryn. 1990. "Introduction and Overview." Pp. 1–24 in *Women Workers and Global Restructuring,* edited by Kathryn Ward. Ithaca, NY: ILR Press.

Warner, R. Steven. 1993. "Work in Progress toward a New Paradigm for the Sociological Study of Religion in the United States." *American Journal of Sociology* 98:1044–93.

Warren, John Robert, and Elaine M. Hernandez. 2007. "Did Socioeconomic Inequalities in Morbidity and Mortality Change in the United States over the Course of the Twentieth Century?" *Journal of Health and Social Behavior* 48:335–51.

Wasserman, J., M. A. Flannery, and J. M. Clair. 2007. "Raising the Ivory Tower: The Production of Knowledge and Distrust of Medicine among African Americans." *Journal of Medical Ethics* 33(3):177–80.

Wasson, Leslie. 2007. "Identity Politics/Relational Politics." Pp. 2214–15 in *The Blackwell Encyclopedia of Sociology,* edited by George Ritzer. Malden, MA: Blackwell.

Watkins, S. Craig. 2009. *The Young and the Digital: What the Migration to Social Network Sites, Games, and Anytime, Anywhere Media Means for Our Future.* Boston: Beacon Press.

Wattenberg, M. P. 2002. *Where Have All the Voters Gone?* Cambridge, MA: Harvard University Press.

Watts, Jonathan. 2006. "Internet Censorship." *The Guardian,* January 25.

Wax, Emily. 2007. "An Ancient Indian Craft Left in Tatters." *The Washington Post,* June 6.

Way, Sandra. 2007. "School Discipline." Pp. 4019–23 in *The Blackwell Encyclopedia of Sociology,* edited by George Ritzer. Malden, MA: Blackwell.

Wayne, Leslie. 2009. "Dubious Claims for H1N1 Cures Are Rife Online." *The New York Times,* November 6.

Weber, Max. [1921] 1968. *Economy and Society: An Outline of Interpretative Sociology,* edited by Guenther Roth and Claus Wittich. Totowa, NJ: Bedminster Press.

Weber, Max. 1963. *The Sociology of Religion,* translated by E. Fischoff. Boston: Beacon Press.

Weber, Max. [1904–1905] 1958. *The Protestant Ethic and the Spirit of Capitalism.* New York: Scribner.

Webster, Murray, and Jane Sell. 2012. "Groups and Institutions, Structures and Processes." Pp. 139–63 in *The Wiley-Blackwell Companion to Sociology,* edited by George Ritzer. Malden, MA: Wiley-Blackwell.

Weeks, John R. 2007. "Demographic Transition Theory." Pp. 1033–38 in *The Blackwell Encyclopedia of Sociology,* edited by George Ritzer. Malden, MA: Blackwell.

Weeks, John R. 2011. *Population: An Introduction to Concepts and Issues.* 11th ed. Belmont, CA: Wadsworth.

Wegener, B. 1991. "Job Mobility and Social Ties: Social Resources, Prior Job, and Status Attainment." *American Sociological Review* 56:60–71.

Weiler, Bernd. 2007. "Cultural Relativism." Pp. 908–10 in *The Blackwell Encyclopedia of Sociology,* edited by George Ritzer. Malden, MA: Blackwell.

Weininger, F., and A. Lareau. 2009. "Paradoxical Pathways: An Ethnographic Extension of Kohn's Findings on Class and Childrearing." *Journal of Marriage and the Family* 71:680–95.

Weinrath, Michael. 2007. "Sentencing Disparity: Aboriginal Canadians, Drunk Driving, and Age." *Western Criminology Review* 8(2):16–28.

Weinstein, Jay. 2010. *Social Change.* 3rd ed. Lanham, MD: Rowman and Littlefield.

Weisman, Steven R. 2008. "U.S. Security Concerns Block China's 3Com Deal." *The New York Times,* February 21.

Weiss, Gregory L., and Lonnquist, Lynne E. 2009. *Sociology of Health, Healing, and Illness.* Upper Saddle River, NJ: Pearson/Prentice Hall.

Weitz, Rose. 2010. *The Sociology of Health, Illness, and Health Care: A Critical Approach.* 5th ed. Boston: Wadsworth Cengage.

Weitzer, Ronald. 2009. "Sociology of Sex Work." *Annual Review of Sociology* 35:213–34.

Weitzman, Lenore J., Deborah Eifler, Elizabeth Hokada, and Catherine Ross. 1972.

"Sex-role Socialization in Picture Books for Preschool Children." *The American Journal of Sociology* 77:1125–50.

"Welcome to Our Shrinking Jungle." 2008. *The Economist,* June 5. Retrieved March 9, 2012 (http://www.economist.com/node/11496950).

Wellard, Ian. 2012. "Body-reflexive Pleasures: Exploring Bodily Experiences within the Context of Sport and Physical Activity." *Sport, Education and Society* 17:21–33.

Wellford, Charles. 2012. "Criminology." Pp. 229–42 in *The Wiley-Blackwell Companion to Sociology,* edited by George Ritzer. Malden, MA: Wiley-Blackwell.

Wellings, Kaye, Martine Collumbien, Emma Slaymaker, Susheela Singh, Zoe Hodges, Dhavai Patel, and Nathalie Bajos. 2009. "Sexual Behavior in Context: A Global Perspective." *The Lancet* 368:349–58.

Wellman, Elizabeth. 2004. *The Road to Seneca Falls: Elizabeth Cady Stanton and the First Woman's Rights Convention.* Champaign: University of Illinois Press.

Welter, Barbara. 1966. "The Cult of True Womanhood: 1820–1860." *American Quarterly* 18(2,1):151–74.

Welzel, Christian, and Ronald Inglehart. 2009. "Mass Beliefs and Democratization." Chapter 9 in *Democratization,* edited by Christian W. Haerpfer, Patrick Bernhagen, Ronald F. Inglehart, and Christian Welzel. Oxford.

Wenman, Wanda, Michel R. Joffres, Ivanna V. Tataryn, and the Edmonton Perinatal Infections Group. 2004. "A Prospective Cohort Study of Pregnancy Risk Factors and Birth Outcomes in Aboriginal Women." *Canadian Medical Association Journal* 171(6):235–42.

Wentland, Jocelyn, and Elke Reissing. 2011. "Taking Casual Sex Not Too Casually: Exploring Definitions of Casual Sexual Relationships." *Canadian Journal of Human Sexuality* 20(3):75–91.

Wentzel, Kathryn, and Lisa Looney. 2007. "Socialization in School Settings." In *Handbook of Socialization: Theory and Research,* edited by Joan E. Grusec and Paul David Hastings. New York: Guilford Press.

Wernick, Andrew. 2006. "University." *Theory, Culture and Society* 23:557–63.

West, Candace, and Don Zimmerman. 1987. "Doing Gender." *Gender & Society* 1:125–51.

Weyler, Rex. 2004. *Greenpeace: How a Group of Ecologists, Journalists, and Visionaries Changed the World.* Vancouver, BC: Raincoast Books.

Wharton, A. S., and M. Blair-Loy. 2006. "Long Work Hours and Family Life: A Cross-national Study of Employees' Concerns." *Family Issues* 27(3):415–36.

White, Michael J., and Ann H. Kim. 2007. "Urban Ecology." Pp. 5109–12 in *The Blackwell Encyclopedia of Sociology,* edited by George Ritzer. Malden, MA: Blackwell.

White, Phillip, Kevin Young, and William G. McTeer. 1995. "Sport, Masculinity, and the Injured Body." Pp. 158–82 in *Men's Health and Illness,* edited by Don Sabo and Frederick Gordon. Thousand Oaks, CA: Sage.

Whitehead, John T. 2007. "Crime." Pp. 818–22 in *The Blackwell Encyclopedia of Sociology,* edited by George Ritzer. Malden, MA: Blackwell.

Whiteside, Alan. 2008. *A Very Short Introduction to HIV/AIDS.* Oxford: Oxford University Press.

Whiteside, Alan. 2012. "AIDS." Pp. 45–49 in *The Wiley-Blackwell Encyclopedia of Globalization,* edited by George Ritzer. Malden, MA: Wiley-Blackwell.

Whyte, William Foote. 1943. *Street Corner Society: The Social Structure of an Italian Slum.* Chicago: University of Chicago.

Wight, Vanessa R. 2007. "Demography." Pp. 1038–45 in *The Blackwell Encyclopedia of Sociology,* edited by George Ritzer. Malden, MA: Blackwell.

"WikiLeaks." 2010. Retrieved December 12, 2010 (http://213.251.145.96/about.html).

Wiklund, Maria, Carita Bengs, Eva-Britt Malmgren-Olsson, and Ann Öhman. 2010. "Young Women Facing Multiple and Intersecting Stressors of Modernity, Gender Orders and Youth." *Social Science Medicine* 71(9):1567–75.

Wilk, Kenneth Aarskaug, Eva Bernhardt, and Turid Noack. 2010. "Love or Money? Marriage Intentions among Young Cohabitors in Norway and Sweden." *Acta Sociologica* 53:269–87.

Wilk, Richard. 2006a. "Bottled Water: The Pure Commodity in the Age of Branding." *Journal of Consumer Culture* 6(3):303–25.

Wilk, Richard. 2006b. "Consumer Culture and Extractive Industry on the Margins of the World System." Pp. 123–44 in *Consuming Cultures, Global Perspectives: Historical Trajectories, Transnational Exchanges,* edited by John Brewer and Frank Trentmann. Oxford, UK: Berg.

Wilkes, Rima, Catherine Corrigall-Brown, and Daniel Myers. 2010. "Packaging Protest: Media Coverage of Indigenous People's Collective Action." *Canadian Review of Sociology* 47:327–57.

Wilkes, Rima, Neil Guppy, and Lily Farris. 2008. "'No Thanks, We're Full': Individual Characteristics, National Context, and Changing Attitudes towards Immigration." *International Migration Review,* 42(2):302–332.

Wilkinson, Gary. 2006. "McSchools for McWorld? Mediating Global Pressures with a McDonaldizing Education Policy Response." *Cambridge Journal of Education* 36(March): 81–98.

Wilkinson, Michael. 2009. *Canadian Pentecostalism: Transition and Transformation.* Montreal, QC: McGill-Queen's University Press.

Williams, Christine. 1995. *Still a Man's World.* Berkeley: University of California Press.

Williams, Christine. 2006. *Inside Toyland: Working, Shopping, and Social Inequality.* Berkeley: University of California Press.

Williams, Christine, and Laura Sauceda. 2007. "Gender, Consumption and." Pp. 1848–52 in *The Blackwell Encyclopedia of Sociology,* edited by George Ritzer. Malden, MA: Blackwell.

Williams, David R. 1999. "Race, Socioeconomic Status and Health: The Added Effects of Racism and Discrimination." *Annals of the New York Academy of Sciences* 896:173–88.

Williams, Erica. 2012. Sex Work." Pp. 1856–58 in *The Wiley-Blackwell Encyclopedia of Globalization,* edited by George Ritzer. Malden, MA: Wiley Blackwell.

Williams, Frank P., and Marilyn D. McShane. 2007. "Lombroso, Cesare (1835–1909)." Pp. 2662–63 in *The Blackwell Encyclopedia of Sociology,* Vol. 6, edited by George Ritzer. Malden, MA: Blackwell.

Williams, Patrick, and Laura Chrisman, eds. 1994a. *Colonial Discourse and Post-colonial Theory: A Reader.* New York: Columbia University Press.

Williams, Patrick, and Laura Chrisman, eds. 1994b. "Introduction." *Colonial Discourse and Post-colonial Theory: A Reader.* New York: Columbia University Press.

Williams, Rosalind. [1982] 1991. *Dream Worlds: Mass Consumption In Late Nineteenth-century France.* Berkeley: University of California Press.

Williams, Tanis MacBeth. 1986. *The Impact of Television: A Natural Experiment in Three Communities.* Orlando, FL: Academic Press.

Williamson, O. E. 1975. *Markets and Hierarchies: Analysis and Antitrust Implications.* New York: Free Press.

Williamson, O. E. 1985. *The Economic Institutions of Capitalism.* New York: Free Press.

Williamson, Vanessa, Theda Skocpol, and John Coggin. 2011. "The Tea Party and the Remaking of Republican Conservativism." *Perspectives on Politics* 9:25–43.

Willis, Leigh A. 2007. "Health and Race." Pp. 2078–81 in *The Blackwell Encyclopedia of Sociology,* edited by George Ritzer. Malden, MA: Blackwell.

Willis, P. 1977. *Learning to Labor: How Working Class Kids Get Working Class Jobs.* New York: Teachers College Press.

Wilper, Andrew P., Steffie Woolhandler, Karen E. Lasser, Danny McCormick, David H. Bor, and David U. Himmelstein. 2009. "Health Insurance and Mortality in US Adults." Retrieved April 1, 2012 (http://pnhp .org/excessdeaths/health-insurance-and-mortality-in-US-adults.pdf).

Wilson, Brian. (2002). "The Canadian Rave Scene and Five Theses on Youth Resistance." *Canadian Journal of Sociology* 27:373–412.

Wilson, Daniel, and David McDonald. 2010. *The Income Gap between Aboriginal Peoples and the Rest of Canada.* Ottawa, ON: Canadian Centre for Policy Alternatives.

Wilson, S. R. 1984. *Sociological Analysis* 45(4):301–14.

Wilson, William Julius. 1978. *The Declining Significance of Race: Blacks and Changing American Institutions.* Chicago: University of Chicago Press.

Wilson, William Julius. 1987. *The Truly Disadvantaged: The Inner City, the Underclass, and Public Policy.* Chicago: University of Chicago Press.

Wilson, William Julius. 1997. *When Work Disappears: The World of the New Urban Poor.* New York: Vintage.

Wilson, William Julius. 2009. *More than Just Race: Being Black and Poor in the Inner City.* New York: Norton.

Wilterdink, Nico. 2007. "Inequality, Wealth." Pp. 2310–13 in *The Blackwell Encyclopedia of Sociology,* edited by George Ritzer. Malden, MA: Blackwell.

Winant, Howard. 2001. *The World Is a Ghetto: Race and Democracy Since World War II.* New York: Basic Books.

Wines, Michael. 2010. "China Keeps 7 Million Tireless Eyes on Its People." *The New York Times,* August 3, pp. A1, A7.

Wines, Michael. 2011. "Picking Brand Names in China Is a Business Itself." *The New York Times,* November 11. Retrieved April 1, 2012 (http://www.nytimes.com/2011/11/12/world/asia/picking-brand-names-in-china-is-a-business-itself.html).

Wing, B. 2001. "White Power in Election 2000." Retrieved April 1, 2012 (http://www .colorlines.com/archives/2001/03/white_power_in_election_2000.html).

Winlow, Simon, Dick Hobbs, Stuart Lister, and Philip Hadfield. 2001. "Get Ready to Duck: Bouncers and the Realities of Ethnographic Research on Violent Groups." *British Journal of Criminology* 41:536–48.

Winks, Robin. n.d. "Slavery." *The Canadian Encyclopedia.* Retrieved October 22, 2012 (http://www.thecanadianencyclopedia .com/articles/slavery).

Wirth, Louis. [1928] 1997. *The Ghetto.* Transaction Books.

Wirth, Louis. 1938. "Urbanism as a Way of Life." *American Journal of Sociology* 44(1).

Wise, Tim. 2010. *Colorblind: The Rise of Post-racial Politics and the Retreat from Racial Equity.* San Francisco: City Lights.

Wister, Andrew. 2011. "Population Pressures, System-level Inertia and Healthy Aging Policy Revisited." *HealthcarePapers* 11(1):41–45.

Witz, Ann. 1992. *Professions and Patriarchy.* London: Routledge.

Wolf, Diane L., ed. 1996. *Feminist Dilemmas in Fieldwork.* Boulder, CO: Westview Press.

Wolf, Naomi. [1991] 2002. *The Beauty Myth: How Images of Beauty Are Used against Women.* New York: Anchor Books.

Wolff, Kristina. 2007. "Content Analysis." Pp. 776–79 in *The Blackwell Encyclopedia of Sociology,* edited by George Ritzer. Malden, MA: Blackwell.

Wolfson, Andrew. 2005. "A Hoax Most Cruel." *The Courier-Journal,* October 9.

Wong, Edward. 2010. "18 Orgies Later, China Swinger Gets Prison Bed." *The New York Times,* May 21, pp. A1, A8.

Wong, William C. W., Eleanor Holroyd, and Amie Bingham. 2011. "Stigma and Sex Work from the Perspective of Female Sex Workers in Hong Kong." *Sociology of Health & Illness* 33:50–65.

Woodruff, G., and David Premack. 1979. "Intentional Communication in the Chimpanzee: The Development of Deception." *Cognition* 7:333–62.

Woods, Andrew. 2011. "These Revolutions Are Not All Twitter." *The New York Times,* February 1.

Woodward, Bob. 2010. *Obama's Wars.* New York: Simon & Schuster.

Wooffitt, Robin. 2006. *The Language of Mediums and Psychics: The Social Organization of Everyday Miracles.* Aldershot, UK: Ashgate.

Worldatlas. 2010. "Largest Cities of the World." Retrieved February 28, 2012 (http://www .worldatlas.com/citypops.htm).

World Bank. 2011. "GNI per Capita, PPP (Current International $)." Retrieved June 5, 2011 (http://data.worldbank.org/indicator/NY.GNP.PCAP.PP.CD?cid=GPD_8).

World Health Organization. 2000. "World Health Report: Health Systems: Improving Performance." Retrieved March 16, 2012 (http://www.who.int/whr/2000/en/).

World Health Organization. 2008. "Eliminating Female Genital Mutilation." Retrieved May 16, 2013 (http://web.unfpa.org/upload/lib_pub_file/756_filename_fgm.pdf).

World Health Organization. 2009. "Women and Health: Today's Evidence, Tomorrow's Agenda." Geneva: Author. Retrieved May 11, 2013 (http://whqlibdoc.who.int/publications/2009/9789241563857_eng.pdf).

World Health Organization. 2010a. "Tobacco Free Initiative: China Releases Its Global Adult Tobacco Survey Data." Retrieved April 1, 2012 (http://www.who.int/tobacco/surveillance/gats_china/en/index.html).

World Health Organization. 2010b. "World Health Report: Health Systems Financing: The Path to Universal Coverage." Geneva: Author. Retrieved April 1, 2012 (http://whqlibdoc.who.int/whr/2010/9789241564021_eng.pdf).

World Health Organization. 2011. "Tobacco." Retrieved April 1, 2012 (http://www.who.int/mediacentre/factsheets/fs339/en/).

"The World Is Not Flat: Putting Globalization in Its Place." 2008. *Cambridge Journal of Regions, Economic and Society* 1(3):Chapter 6.

World Scripture. n.d. "Chapter 19: Live for Others—Love Your Enemy." Retrieved March 28, 2012 (www.origin.org/ucs/ws/theme144.cfm).

World Values Survey. n.d. "Values Change the World." Retrieved April 1, 2012 (http://www.worldvaluessurvey.org/wvs/articles/folder_published/article_base_110/files/WVSbrochure5-2008_11.pdf).

Worth, Robert. 2009. "Laid-off Foreigners Flee as Dubai Spirals Down." *The New York Times,* February 11.

Wortham, Jenna. 2010. "Chatroulette Gives Rise to a Genre." *The New York Times,* November 22, pp. B1, B2.

Wortley, Scot, and Julian Tanner. 2003. "Data, Denials and Confusion: The Racial Profiling Debate in Toronto." *Canadian Journal of Criminology and Criminal Justice* 45(3): 367–89.

Wortmann, Susan L. 2007. "Sex Tourism." Pp. 4200–203 in *The Blackwell Encyclopedia of Sociology,* edited by George Ritzer. Malden, MA: Blackwell.

Wotherspoon, Terry. 2009. *The Sociology of Education in Canada: Critical Perspectives.* 3rd ed. Toronto, ON: Oxford University Press.

Wright, Will. 2001. *The Wild West: The Mythical Cowboy and Social Theory.* London: Sage.

Wu, Bin, and Jackie Sheehan. 2011. "Globalization and Vulnerability of Chinese Migrant Workers in Italy: Empirical Evidence on Working Conditions and Their Consequences." *Journal of Contemporary China* 20(68):135–52.

Wunder, Delores F. 2007. "Agents, Socialization of." Pp. 4566–68 in *The Blackwell Encyclopedia of Sociology,* edited by George Ritzer. Malden, MA: Blackwell.

Wylie, Lana. 2010. *Perceptions of Cuba: Canadian and American Policies in Comparative Perspective.* Toronto, ON: University of Toronto Press.

Wysocki, Diane Kholos, and Cheryl D. Childers. 2011. "'Let My Fingers Do the Talking': Sexting and Infidelity in Cyberspace." *Sexuality & Culture* 15:217–39.

Yach, Derek, and Farnoosh Yashemian. 2007. "Public Health in a Globalizing World." Pp. 516–38 in *The Blackwell Companion to Globalization,* edited by George Ritzer. Malden, MA: Blackwell.

Yalnizyan, Armine. 2010. *The Rise of Canada's Richest One Percent.* Ottawa, ON: Centre for Policy Alternatives.

Yamamoto, Ryoko. 2012. "Undocumented Immigrants." Pp. 1005–1008 in *The Wiley-Blackwell Encyclopedia of Globalization,* edited by George Ritzer. Malden, MA: Wiley-Blackwell.

Yamane, David. 2007. "Civil Religion." Pp. 506–507 in *The Blackwell Encyclopedia of Sociology,* edited by George Ritzer. Malden, MA: Blackwell.

Yancy, George. 2008. *Black Bodies, White Gazes: The Continuing Significance of Race.* Lanham, MD: Rowman & Littlefield.

Yang, Lian, Hai-Yen Sung, Zhengzhong Mao, Teh-wei Hu, and Keqin Rao. 2011. "Economic Costs Attributable to Smoking in China: Update and an 8-year Comparison, 2000–2008." *Tobacco Control* 20:266–72.

Yardley, Jim. 2010. "Soaring above India's Poverty, a 27-story Single-family Home." *The New York Times,* October 29, pp. A1, A9.

Ye, Juliet. 2008. "In China, Internet Users Prefer to Say It by 'IM.'" *The Wall Street Journal,* May 22. Retrieved May 23, 2011 (http://online.wsj.com/article/SB121139669127611315.html).

Yearley, Steve. 2007. "Globalization and the Environment." Pp. 239–53 in *The Blackwell Companion to Globalization,* edited by George Ritzer. Malden, MA: Blackwell.

Yeates, Nicola. 2009. *Globalizing Care Economies and Migrant Workers: Explorations in Global Care Chains.* New York: Palgrave Macmillan.

Yeates, Nicola. 2012. "Care Chain." Pp. 161–64 in *The Wiley-Blackwell Encyclopedia of Globalization,* edited by George Ritzer. Malden, MA: Wiley-Blackwell.

Yetman, Norman R., ed. 1991. *Majority and Minority: The Dynamics of Race and Ethnicity in American Life.* 5th ed. Boston: Allyn & Bacon.

Yetman, Norman, ed. 1999. *Life Voices from Slavery: 100 Authentic Slave Narratives.* Dover.

Yeung, Wei-Jun J., and Kathryn M. Pfeiffer. 2009. "The Black–White Test Score Gap and Early Home Environment." *Social Science Research* 38:412–37.

Yew, Lee Kuan. 2000. *From Third World to First: The Singapore Story: 1965–2000.* New York: Harper.

York, Richard, and Riley E. Dunlap. 2012. "Environmental Sociology." Pp. 504–521 in *The Wiley-Blackwell Companion to Sociology,* edited by George Ritzer. Malden, MA: Wiley-Blackwell.

York, Richard, and Eugene A. Rosa. 2007. "Environment and Urbanization." Pp. 1423–26 in *The Blackwell Encyclopedia of Sociology,* edited by George Ritzer. Malden, MA: Blackwell.

Young, Marisa, and Jean Wallace. 2009. "Family Responsibilities, Productivity, and Earnings: A Study of Gender Differences among Canadian Lawyers." *Journal of Family and Economic Issues* 30(3):305–29.

Young, Nathan, and Eric Dugas. 2012. "Comparing Climate Change Coverage in Canadian English and French-Language Print Media: Environmental Values, Media Cultures, and the Narration of Global Warming." *Canadian Journal of Sociology* 37(1):25–54.

Young, Nathan and Ralph Matthews. 2010. *The Aquaculture Controversy in Canada: Activism, Policy, and Contested Science.* Vancouver: University of British Columbia Press.

Yunus, Mohammed. 2003. *Banker to the Poor: Micro-lending and the Battle against World Poverty.* Public Affairs.

Yuval-Davis, Nira. 2006. "Human/Women's Rights and Feminist Transversal Politics." In *Global Feminism: Transnational Women's Activism, Organizing, and Human Rights,* edited by Myra Marx Ferree and Aili Mari Tripp. New York: New York University Press.

Zeiler, Kristin, and Annette Wickstrom. 2009. "Why Do 'We' Perform Surgery on Newborn Intersexed Children? The Phenomenology of the Parental Experience of Having a Child with Intersex Anatomies." *Feminist Theory* 10:359–77.

Zelizer, Viviana. 1997. *Social Meaning of Money.* Princeton, NJ: Princeton University Press.

Zellner, William W. 1995. *Counterculture: A Sociological Analysis.* New York: St. Martin's Press.

Zeni, Jane. 2007. "Ethics, Fieldwork." Pp. 1442–47 in *The Blackwell Encyclopedia of Sociology,* edited by George Ritzer. Malden, MA: Blackwell.

Zepp, Ira G., Jr. 1997. *The New Religious Image of Urban America: The Shopping Mall as Ceremonial Center.* 2nd ed. Niwot: University Press of Colorado.

Zerelli, Sal. 2007. "Socialization." Pp. 4558–63 in *The Blackwell Encyclopedia of Sociology,* edited by George Ritzer. Malden, MA: Blackwell.

Zhang, Lena. 2006. "Behind the 'Great Firewall': Decoding China's Internet Media Policies from the Inside." *Convergence* 12:271–91.

Zhong-Cheng Lou, Sacha Senecal, Fabienne Simonet, Eric Guimond, Christopher Penney, and Russell Wilkins. 2010. "Birth Outcomes in the Inuit-inhabited Areas of Canada." *Canadian Medical Association Journal* 182(3):235–42.

Zhou, Min. 2009. *Contemporary Chinese America: Immigration, Ethnicity, and Community Transformation.* Philadelphia: Temple University Press.

Zilberfarb, Ben-Zion. 2005. "From Socialism to Free Market: The Israeli Economy, 1948–2003." *Israel Affairs* 11:12–22.

Zimbardo, Philip. 1973. "On the Ethics of Intervention in Human Psychological Research: With Special Reference to the Stanford Prison Experiment." *Cognition* 2:243–56.

Zimmerman, Don. 1988. "The Conversation: The Conversation Analytic Perspective." *Communication Yearbook* 11:406–32.

Zippel, Kathrin. 2007. "Sexual Harassment." Pp. 4233–34 in *The Blackwell Encyclopedia of Sociology,* edited by George Ritzer. Malden, MA: Blackwell.

Zlatunich, Nichole. 2009. "Prom Dreams and Prom Reality: Girls Negotiating 'Perfection' at the High School Prom." *Sociological Inquiry* 79(3):351–75.

Zola, Irving Kenneth. 1963. "Observations on Gambling in a Lower-class Setting." *Social Problems* 10(4):353–61.

Zukin, Sharon. 1969. *Loft Living: Culture and Capital in Urban Change.* Rutgers University Press.

Zukin, Sharon. 2005. *Point of Purchase: How Shopping Changed American Culture.* New York: Routledge.

Zukin, Sharon. 2009. *Naked City: The Death and Life of Authentic Urban Places.* Oxford, UK: Oxford University Press.

Zureik, Elia. 2011. "Colonialism, Surveillance and Population Control: Israel/Palestine." Pp. 3–46 in *Surveillance and Control in Israel/Palestine,* edited by Elia Zuriek, David Lyon, and Yasmeen Abu-Laban. New York: Routledge.

PHOTO CREDITS

Bourke-White// Time Life Pictures/Getty Images; Photo 6.5, page 201. ©1995 Jim Graham/GSI. Courtesy of Harriet Zuckerman; Photo 6.6, page 204. GABRIEL BOUYS/AFP/ Getty Images ; Photo 6.7, page 206. U.S. Coast Guard Photo/U.S. Department of Homeland Security; Photo 6.8, page 206. AP Photo/Allan Tannenbaum/Mary Altaffer; Photo 6.9, page 208. MOHAMMED ABED/AFP/Getty Images; Photo 6.10, page 209. Bloomberg via Getty Images; Photo 6.11, page 210. Imagebroker/ Alamy; Photo 6.12, page 213. Photo by Jelena Maksimovic; Photo 6.13, page 217. Thinkstock/ Getty Images; Photo 6.14, page 218. Oleg Babich/ iStockphoto; Photo 6.15, page 219. Magnolia Pictures/Everett Collection; Photo 6.16, page 220. TheSilentPhotographer; Photo 6.17, page 221. Alex Craig/Getty Images; Photo 6.18, page 222. Charles Haynes; Photo 6.19, page 223. Rex Features via AP Images; Photo 6.20, page 224. facebook.com/yalaYL; Photo 6.21, page 225. AP Photo/Harry Hamburg; Photo 6.22, page 226. Mark Spowart/Alamy

Chapter 7: CO Photo, page 230. AP Photo/ Mustafa Quraishi; Photo 7.1, page 233. Tim Sloan/AFP/Getty Images; Photo 7.2, page 234. AP Photo/Dima Gavrysh; Photo 7.3, page 235. Alamy; Photo 7.4, page 238. Iain Masterton/ Alamy; Photo 7.5, page 242. © SHAUN BEST/ Reuters/Corbis; Photo 7.6, page 243. Photo 7.6, page 243. Press Association via AP Images; Photo 7.7, page 244. China Photos/Getty Images; Photo 7.8, page 247. © Charles Rex Arbogast/ /AP/Corbis; Photo 7.9, page 249. Jonathan Newton/The Washington Post via Getty Images; Photo 7.10, page 249. Vetta/ Getty Images; Photo 7.11, page 251. Alamy; Photo 7.12, page 252. AP Photo/Themba Hadebe; Photo 7.13, page 253. American Sociological Association; Photo 7.14, page 256. MCT via Getty Images; Photo 7.15, page 258. AP Photo/ Geoff Howe; Photo 7.16, page 260. Scott Houston/Alamy; Photo 7.17, page 262. Magictorch / Alamy; Photo 7.18, page 264. AP Photo/Allan Bovill; Photo 7.19, page 265. PORNCHAI KITTIWONGSAKUL/AFP/Getty Images; Photo 7.20, page 269. Friedrich Stark/ Alamy; Photo 7.21, page 269. Planetpix/Alamy

Chapter 8: CO Photo, page 274. © iStockphoto. com/Nikada; Photo 8.1, page 278. AP Photo/ Andrew Burton; Photo 8.2, page 280. Terry Smith/Time Life Pictures/Getty Images; Photo 8.3, page 281. Ulf Andersen/ Getty Images Entertainment/Getty Images; Photo 8.4, page 285. Dalton Conley; Photo 8.5, page 286. James Devaney/WireImage/ Getty Images; Photo 8.6, page 287. Marco Cristofori/Alamy; Photo 8.7, page 290. JACQUES BOISSINOT/ASSOCIATED PRESS; Photo 8.8, page 290. AFP/Getty Images; Photo 8.9, page 294. ©iStockphoto.com/narvikk/; Photo 8.10, page 295. Dorris Whitteker; Photo 8.11, page 296. Stringer/AFP/Getty Images;

Photo 8.12, page 297. africa924/iStockphoto; Photo 8.13, page 299. Richard Smith/Alamy; Photo 8.14, page 301. ©iStockphoto.com/ VikramRaghuvanshi; Photo 8.15, page 303. Library of Congress; Photo 8.16, page 304. Majdi Mohammed/AP/Corbis; Photo 8.17, page 304. Alexei Kouprianov; Photo 8.18, page 305. Jupiterimages/Thinkstock; Photo 8.19, page 308. Gianni Muratore/Alamy; Photo 8.20, page 310. Imagestate Media Partners Limited—Impact Photos/Alamy; Photo 8.21, page 311. Urbanmyth/Alamy

Chapter 9: CO Photo 9, page 318. AP Photo/Juan Karita; Photo 9.1, page 322. © iStockphoto.com/ez_thug; Photo 9.2, page 324. Alex Wong/Getty Images; Photo 9.3, page 327. AP Photo/Katsumi Kasahara Ho; Photo 9.4, page 331. Toronto Star via Getty Images; Photo 9.5, page 334. © Lynne Sladky/AP/Corbis; Photo 9.6, page 335. © MAXPPP/IVES SALVAT/epa/Corbis; Photo 9.7, page 335. Ryan McVay/Getty Images/ Thinkstock; Photo 9.8, page 337. AP Photo/ Kamran Jebreili; Photo 9.9, page 337. © Shawn Baldwin/Corbis; Photo 9.10, page 338. Photo courtesy of Patricia Hill Collins; Photo 9.11, page 339. Sherab / Alamy; Photo 9.12, page 342. © Bill Bachmann / Alamy; Photo 9.13, page 342. Discovernikkei.org; Photo 9.14, page 343. Raymond Breton; Photo 9.15, page 344. © Karen Kasmauski/ Corbis; Photo 9.16, page 345. Sean Kilpatrick/ Associated Press; Photo 9.18, page 349. AP Photo/Greg English; Photo 9.19, page 349. © Dai Kurokawa/epa/Corbis; Photo 9.20, page 350. © Robert Harding Picture Library Ltd/Alamy; Photo 9.21, page 352. Philippe Merle/AFP/Getty Images; Photo 9.22, page 354. Philippe Merle/ AFP/Getty Images; Photo 9.23, page 355. © United Artists/courtesy Everett Collection

Chapter 10: CO Photo, page 360. © Steve Raymer/ Corbis; Photo 10.1, page 363. Steve Granitz/ WireImage/Getty Images; Photo 10.2, page 364. AP Photo/Greg Baker; Photo 10.3, page 366. Edmonton Journal; Photo 10.4, page 367. Jupiterimages/ Polka Dot/Thinkstock; Photo 10.5, page 368. AP Photo/Mike Wintroath; Photo 10.6, page 370. Photo courtesy of Ken Plummer; Photo 10.7, page 371. © iStockphoto/ Rubberball; Photo 10.8, page 372. Sergei Supinsky/AFP/Getty Images; Photo 10.9, page 374. Photodisc/Ableimages/Thinkstock; Photo 10.10, page 375. Photo by Dianne Reggett; Photo 10.11, page 379. © Gideon Mendel/In Pictures/Corbis; Photo 10.12, page 383. Brand X Pictures/ Jupiterimages/Thinkstock; Photo 10.13, page 383. Jamie Roach/Demotix/Corbis; Photo 10.14, page 386. © Peter Dench/In Pictures/ Corbis; Photo 10.15, page 387. © Peter Dench/ In Pictures/Corbis; Photo 10.16, page 388. Arlie Hochschild; Photo 10.17, page 389. © Andrew Lichtenstein/Corbis; Photo 10.18, page 391.

Bllomberg/Getty Images; Photo 10.19, page 393. © Rebecca Blackwell/AP/Corbis

Chapter 11: CO Photo, page 398. © BETH HALL/ AP/Corbis; Photo 11.1, page 401. Jeff Randall/ Digital Vision/Thinkstock; Photo 11.2, page 401. © TravelStockCollection— Homer Sykes/ Alamy; Photo 11.3, page 402. © PhotoAlto sas/ Alamy; Photo 11.4, page 403. © AF archive/ Alamy; Photo 11.5, page 405. © Hugh Threlfall/ Alamy; Photo 11.6, page 407. Valentine's Day mass marriage in Calcutta; Photo 11.7, page 409. Gary S. Chapman/ The Image Bank/Getty Images; Photo 11.8, page 413. © Joe Stevens./Retna Ltd./ Corbis; Photo 11.9, page 414. Didier Robcis/ Stone/ Getty Images; Photo 11.10, page 416. © amana images inc./Alamy; Photo 11.11, page 417. AP Photo/Gemma La Mana; Photo 11.12, page 418. Michael Hall/Taxi/Getty images; Photo 11.13, page 421. Photomondo/Photodisc/Getty Images; Photo 11.14, page 422. © Nathan Benn/ Alamy; Photo 11.15, page 423. © iStockphoto/ danilovi; Photo 11.16, page 424. Peter Cade/ Iconica/Getty Images; Photo 11.17, page 425. Shah Marai/AFP/ Getty Images; Photo 11.18, page 427. AP Photo/ Chris Young; Photo 11.19, page 429. Toronto Star via Getty Images; Photo 11.20, page 430. Bloomberg via Getty Images; Photo 11.21, page 430. Christian Science Monitor/Getty Images; Photo 11.22, page 431. © Alexandra Boulat/VII/ Corbis; Photo 11.23, page 431. Anne Martin Matthews; Photo 11.24, page 434. Toronto Star via Getty Images; Photo 11.25, page 436. © John Henshall/Alamy; Photo 11.26, page 438. © Martin Thomas Photography/Alamy

Chapter 12: CO Photo, page 442. AP Photo/ M. Spencer Green; Photo 12.1, page 445. AP Photo/International News; Photo 12.2, page 446. Photo by Kate Weiman; Photo 12.3, page 448. ©TriStar Pictures/Everett Collection; Photo 12.4, page 451. Ap Photo/International News; Photo 12.5, page 453. PETER JONES/ Reuters/Corbis; Photo 12.6, page 455. AP Photo/The Canadian Press, Paul Chiasson; Photo 12.7, page 457. AP Photo/Sang Tan; Photo 12.8, page 460. Bush Library; Photo 12.9, 461. AP Photo/Gervasio Sanchez; Photo 12.10, page 464. NICHOLAS KAMM/AFP/ Getty Images; Photo 12.11, page 467. Lewis Wickes Hine/National Archives; Photo 12.12, page 470. AP Photo; Photo 12.13, page 472. © Colin McPherson/ Colin McPherson/Corbis; Photo 12.14, page 473. AP Photo/Thanassis Stavrakis; Photo 12.15, page 475. Bill Pugliano/ Getty Images; Photo 12.16, page 476. AP Photo/DAN LASSITER; Photo 12.17, page 479. ©iStockphoto/lisafx; Photo 12.18, page 481. AP Photo/Dong Jinlin; Photo 12.19, page 481. Jeff Greenberg / Alamy;

INDEX

⑤SAGE researchmethods

The essential online tool for researchers from the world's leading methods publisher

Find exactly what you are looking for, from basic explanations to advanced discussion

More content and new features added this year!

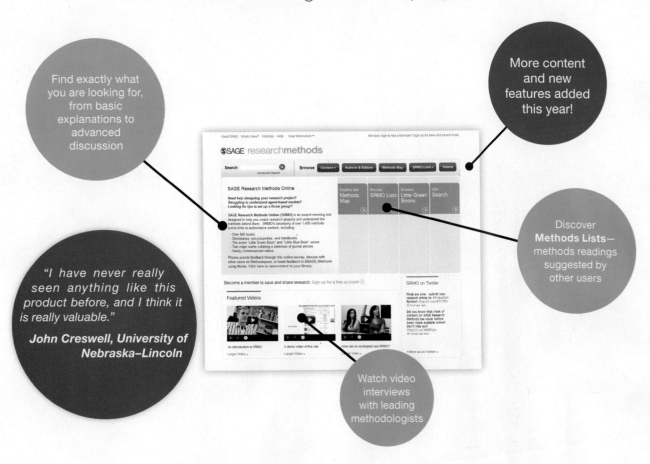

"I have never really seen anything like this product before, and I think it is really valuable."

John Creswell, University of Nebraska–Lincoln

Discover **Methods Lists**—methods readings suggested by other users

Watch video interviews with leading methodologists

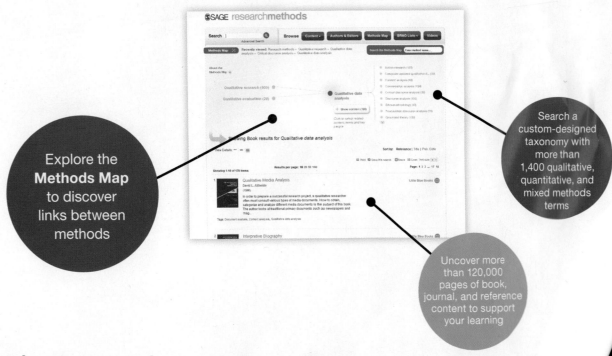

Explore the **Methods Map** to discover links between methods

Search a custom-designed taxonomy with more than 1,400 qualitative, quantitative, and mixed methods terms

Uncover more than 120,000 pages of book, journal, and reference content to support your learning

Find out more at
www.sageresearchmethods.com